Lecture Notes in Computer Science 13747

More information about this series at https://link.springer.com/bookseries/558

Eike Kiltz · Vinod Vaikuntanathan (Eds.)

Theory of Cryptography

20th International Conference, TCC 2022
Chicago, IL, USA, November 7–10, 2022
Proceedings, Part I

 Springer

Editors
Eike Kiltz 🆔
Ruhr University Bochum
Bochum, Germany

Vinod Vaikuntanathan 🆔
Massachusetts Institute of Technology
Cambridge, MA, USA

ISSN 0302-9743   ISSN 1611-3349 (electronic)
Lecture Notes in Computer Science
ISBN 978-3-031-22317-4   ISBN 978-3-031-22318-1 (eBook)
https://doi.org/10.1007/978-3-031-22318-1

This Springer imprint is published by the registered company Springer Nature Switzerland AG
The registered company address is: Gewerbestrasse 11, 6330 Cham, Switzerland

Preface

The 20th Theory of Cryptography Conference (TCC 2022) was held during November 7–10, 2022, at the University of Chicago, USA. It was sponsored by the International Association for Cryptologic Research (IACR). The general chair of the conference was David Cash.

The conference received 139 submissions, of which the Program Committee (PC) selected 60 for presentation giving an acceptance rate of 43%. Each submission was reviewed by at least three PC members in a single-blind process. The 44 PC members (including PC chairs), all top researchers in our field, were helped by 116 external reviewers, who were consulted when appropriate. These proceedings consist of the revised version of the 60 accepted papers. The revisions were not reviewed, and the authors bear full responsibility for the content of their papers.

We are extremely grateful to Kevin McCurley for providing fast and reliable technical support for the HotCRP review software whenever we had any questions. We made extensive use of the interaction feature supported by the review software, where PC members could anonymously interact with authors. This was used to ask specific technical questions, such as those about suspected bugs or unclear connections to prior work. We believe this approach improved our understanding of the papers and the quality of the review process. We also thank Kay McKelly for her fast and meticulous help with the conference website.

This was the eighth year that TCC presented the Test of Time Award to an outstanding paper that was published at TCC at least eight years ago, making a significant contribution to the theory of cryptography, preferably with influence also in other areas of cryptography, theory, and beyond. This year, the Test of Time Award Committee selected the following paper, published at TCC 2011: "Perfectly secure oblivious RAM without random oracles" by Ivan Damgård, Sigurd Meldgaard, and Jesper Buus Nielsen. The award committee recognized this paper for "the first perfectly secure unconditional Oblivious RAM scheme and for setting the stage for future Oblivious RAM and PRAM schemes". The authors were invited to deliver a talk at TCC 2022. The conference also featured two other invited talks, by Rahul Santhanam and by Eran Tromer.

This year, TCC awarded a Best Young Researcher Award for the best paper authored solely by young researchers. The award was given to the paper "A Tight Computational Indistinguishability Bound of Product Distributions" by Nathan Geier.

We are greatly indebted to the many people who were involved in making TCC 2022 a success. A big thanks to the authors who submitted their papers and to the PC members and external reviewers for their hard work, dedication, and diligence in reviewing the papers, verifying their correctness, and discussing the papers in depth. We thank the University of Chicago Computer Science department, Google Research, Algorand Foundation, NTT Research, and Duality Technologies for their generous sponsorship of the conference. A special thanks goes to the general chair David Cash, and to Brian LaMacchia, Kevin McCurley, Kay McKelly, Sandry Quarles, Douglas Stebila, and the

TCC Steering Committee. Finally, we are thankful to the thriving and vibrant community of theoretical cryptographers. Long Live TCC!

September 2022   Eike Kiltz
                                                         Vinod Vaikuntanathan

Organization

General Chair

David Cash   University of Chicago, USA

Program Committee Chairs

Eike Kiltz   Ruhr-Universität Bochum, Germany
Vinod Vaikuntanathan   MIT, USA

Steering Committee

Jesper Buus Nielsen	Aarhus University, Denmark
Krzysztof Pietrzak	Institute of Science and Technology, Austria
Huijia (Rachel) Lin	UCSB, USA
Yuval Ishai	Technion, Israel
Tal Malkin	Columbia University, USA
Manoj M. Prabhakaran	IIT Bombay, India
Salil Vadhan	Harvard University, USA

Program Committee

Gilad Asharov	Bar-Ilan University, Israel
Marshall Ball	New York University, USA
Amos Beimel	Ben Gurion University, Israel
Fabrice Benhamouda	Algorand Foundation, USA
Nir Bitansky	Tel Aviv University, Israel
Zvika Brakerski	Weizmann Institute of Science, Israel
Anne Broadbent	University of Ottawa, Canada
Yilei Chen	Tsinghua University, China
Ran Cohen	Reichman University, Israel
Geoffroy Couteau	CNRS, IRIF, Université Paris Cité, France
Nils Fleischhacker	Ruhr University Bochum, Germany
Rishab Goyal	University of Wisconsin-Madison, USA
Siyao Guo	NYU Shanghai, China
Dennis Hofheinz	ETH Zurich, Switzerland
Gabe Kaptchuk	Boston University, USA
Jonathan Katz	University of Maryland, USA

Dakshita Khurana	UIUC, USA
Susumu Kiyoshima	NTT Research, USA
Karen Klein	ETH Zurich, Switzerland
Venkata Koppula	Indian Institute of Technology Delhi, India
Eyal Kushilevitz	Technion, Israel
Alex Lombardi	University of California, Berkeley, USA
Julian Loss	CISPA Helmholtz Center for Information Security, Germany
Fermi Ma	Simons Institute and UC Berkeley, USA
Mohammad Mahmoody	University of Virginia, USA
Ryo Nishimaki	NTT Corporation, Japan
Adam O'Neill	University of Massachusetts Amherst, USA
Emmanuela Orsini	KU Leuven, Belgium
Omer Paneth	Tel Aviv University, Israel
Alon Rosen	Bocconi University, Italy
Lior Rotem	The Hebrew University, Israel
Ron Rothblum	Technion, Israel
Peter Scholl	Aarhus University, Denmark
Sruthi Sekar	UC Berkeley, USA
Katerina Sotiraki	UC Berkeley, USA
Nicholas Spooner	University of Warwick, UK
Noah Stephens-Davidowitz	Cornell University, USA
Stefano Tessaro	University of Washington, USA
Prashant Vasudevan	National University of Singapore, Singapore
David Wu	University of Texas at Austin, USA
Yu Yu	Shanghai Jiao Tong University, China
Mark Zhandry	NTT Research and Princeton University, USA

Additional Reviewers

Damiano Abram	Rohit Chatterjee	Ben Fisch
Amit Agarwal	Arka Rai Choudhuri	Danilo Francati
Shweta Agrawal	Kelong Cong	Tore Frederiksen
Nicolas Alhaddad	Hongrui Cui	Cody Freitag
Benedikt Auerbach	Eric Culf	Rachit Garg
Renas Bacho	Dana Dachman-Soled	Romain Gay
Christian Badertscher	Pratish Datta	Nicholas Genise
Saikrishna Badrinarayanan	Lalita Devadas	Suparno Ghoshal
James Bartusek	Nico Döttling	Aarushi Goel
Gabrielle Beck	Thomas Espitau	Eli Goldin
Alexander Bienstock	Jaiden Fairoze	Shai Halevi
Dung Bui	Oriol Farràs	Mathias Hall-Andersen
Suvradip Chakraborty	Weiqi Feng	Dominik Hartmann

Contents – Part I

Identity-Based Encryption and Functional Encryption

Attribute-Based Encryption and Functional Encryption

Contents – Part II

Theory I: Sampling and Friends

Multi-party Computation II

Lattices

Anonymity, Verifiability and Robustness

Contents – Part III

Post-quantum Cryptography

Post-quantum Insecurity from LWE

Alex Lombardi[1], Ethan Mook[2], Willy Quach[2(✉)], and Daniel Wichs[2,3]

[1] MIT, Cambridge, USA
alexjl@mit.edu
[2] Northeastern, Boston, USA
{mook.e,quach.w}@northeastern.edu, wichs@ccs.neu.edu
[3] NTT Research, Palo Alto, USA

Abstract. We show that for many fundamental cryptographic primitives, proving classical security under the learning-with-errors (LWE) assumption, does *not* imply post-quantum security. This is despite the fact that LWE is widely believed to be post-quantum secure, and our work does not give any evidence otherwise. Instead, it shows that post-quantum insecurity can arise inside cryptographic constructions, even if the assumptions are post-quantum secure.

Concretely, our work provides (contrived) constructions of pseudorandom functions, CPA-secure symmetric-key encryption, message-authentication codes, signatures, and CCA-secure public-key encryption schemes, all of which are proven to be classically secure under LWE via black-box reductions, but demonstrably fail to be post-quantum secure. All of these cryptosystems are stateless and non-interactive, but their security is defined via an interactive game that allows the attacker to make oracle queries to the cryptosystem. The polynomial-time quantum attacker can break these schemes by only making a few *classical* queries to the cryptosystem, and in some cases, a single query suffices.

Previously, we only had examples of post-quantum insecurity under post-quantum assumptions for stateful/interactive protocols. Moreover, there appears to be a folklore intuition that for stateless/non-interactive cryptosystems with black-box proofs of security, a quantum attack against the scheme should translate into a quantum attack on the assumption. This work shows otherwise. Our main technique is to carefully embed interactive protocols inside the interactive security games of the above primitives.

As a result of independent interest, we also show a 3-round *quantum disclosure of secrets (QDS)* protocol between a classical sender and a receiver, where a quantum receiver learns a secret message in the third round but, assuming LWE, a classical receiver does not.

The full version of this paper is available online [33].
A. Lombardi—Supported in part by DARPA under Agreement No. HR00112020023, a grant from MIT-IBM Watson AI, a grant from Analog Devices, a Microsoft Trustworthy AI grant, the Thornton Family Faculty Research Innovation Fellowship and a Charles M. Vest fellowship. Any opinions, findings and conclusions or recommendations expressed in this material are those of the author(s) and do not necessarily reflect the views of the United States Government or DARPA.
D. Wichs—Research supported by NSF grant CNS-1750795, CNS-2055510 and the Alfred P. Sloan Research Fellowship.

E. Kiltz and V. Vaikuntanathan (Eds.): TCC 2022, LNCS 13747, pp. 3–32, 2022.
https://doi.org/10.1007/978-3-031-22318-1_1

1   Introduction

Recent years have seen tremendous investment and progress in quantum computing (e.g., [3]), raising our hopes and fears that quantum computing may one day become a reality. The fear is due to the fact that the public-key cryptosystems in use today, based on the hardness of factoring and discrete-logarithms, are known to be efficiently breakable by quantum computers. This brought about the search for *post-quantum secure* cryptosystems that would remain unbreakable even by quantum computers, and there is an ongoing NIST competition to standardize such cryptosystems [35]. While there are several candidates, arguably the most appealing ones are based on the *learning with errors (LWE)* assumption [36], which is widely believed to be post-quantum secure. The LWE assumption is also extremely versatile and enables us to construct many types of advanced cryptosystems, such as fully homomorphic encryption [14,22], attribute-based encryption [25], and more.

Post-quantum Security of Cryptosystems? While the post-quantum security of LWE itself has been well studied, the post-quantum security of the various cryptosystems based on LWE has been given considerably less scrutiny. In general, one can ask:

> When does classical security under a post-quantum assumption imply
> post-quantum security?

For example, is it the case that cryptosystems (encryption, signatures, PRFs, etc.) with classical black-box proofs of security under LWE[1] are also guaranteed to be post-quantum[2] secure? At first glance, it may seem that this should generally hold, based on the following reasoning: black-box reductions should be oblivious to the computational model and should therefore work equally well for classical attackers and quantum attackers. In particular, a black-box reduction should convert any attack on the cryptosystem, whether classical or quantum, into an equivalent attack on the underlying assumption.

Post-Quantum Insecurity for Protocols. Unfortunately, the above intuition is not rigorous and fails on closer inspection. The most glaring reason for this is due to *rewinding* in the context of interactive protocols.

---

[1] The same question could also be asked for cryptosystems based on any of the other candidate post-quantum assumptions such as isogenies or even post-quantum secure one-way functions or collision-resistant hashing. We frame our discussion in terms of LWE for concreteness and because our eventual results specifically rely on LWE.

[2] We focus on "post-quantum security", where only the adversary is quantum, but all interaction with the cryptosystem is classical. We distinguish this from what is sometimes called "quantum security" [45], where the cryptosystem needs to also accept quantum inputs. For the latter, it is already known that, e.g., allowing an adversary quantum query access to a PRF may compromise security. We discuss this in detail in Sect. 1.2.

A classical black-box security reduction for interactive protocols can (and typically does) rewind the adversary and restore its state to some earlier point in the execution. While this is a valid form of analysis for classical adversaries, we cannot always rewind and restore the state of a quantum adversary. In particular, if the adversary performs some measurements on its internal quantum state during the protocol execution, then this can destroy the state in a way that makes it impossible to restore.

The issue of rewinding has been known for some time in the context of establishing zero knowledge [27,41] and computational soundness [1,39,40] for interactive proofs/arguments. For example, it was recognized that classical black-box security proofs of zero-knowledge do not appear to generically translate to the post-quantum setting; instead, there has been much recent work trying to understand and prove the security of specific interactive protocols [9,16,17,32, 41] by relying on substantially more complex techniques.

We highlight that this issue is not merely a limitation of our security analysis; we can also provide explicit examples of interactive protocols that are classically secure under LWE, but are demonstrably not post-quantum secure. One way to see this is by considering "interactive proofs of quantumness" (IPQs) [13]. An IPQ is an interactive protocol consisting of classical communication between a (potentially quantum) prover and a classical verifier, such that there is an efficient *quantum prover* that causes the verifier to accept at the end of the protocol, but no efficient *classical prover* should be able to do so with better than negligible probability. In other words, an IPQ is precisely an example of an interactive protocol that is classically computationally sound but quantumly unsound. We have constructions of IPQs from LWE with 4 rounds of interaction [13,30], where classical soundness is proved via a black-box reduction from LWE using rewinding. It is easy to embed such IPQs inside other interactive cryptosystems, such as zero-knowledge proofs or multi-party computation protocols, to get constructions that are classically secure under LWE, but are demonstrably post-quantum insecure.

What About Non-interactive Cryptography? So far, we have seen that rewinding poses a problem for post-quantum security of interactive protocols. However, it may appear that such examples of post-quantum insecurity under post-quantum assumptions are limited to the interactive setting. Can this phenomenon also occur in non-interactive cryptographic primitives such as pseudorandom functions, encryption, signatures etc.? One might expect that this should not be possible. After all, the only reason we have seen primitives fail to inherit post-quantum security is due to rewinding, and rewinding does not appear to come up for non-interactive primitives.

1.1   Our Results

In this work, we show that the above intuition is wrong! We provide explicit (contrived) examples of many of the most fundamental cryptographic primitives, including pseudorandom functions (PRFs), CPA-secure symmetric-key encryption, message-authentication codes (MACs), signatures, and CCA-secure public-key encryption schemes, all of which are proven to be classically secure under LWE via a black-box reduction, but demonstrably fail to be post-quantum secure.

These primitives are qualitatively different from interactive protocols such as zero-knowledge proof systems. First of all, the primitives are stateless – they maintain a secret key, but do not keep any other state between operations. Second of all, the basic operations (e.g., PRF evaluation, encryption, decryption, signing, verifying) are non-interactive. However, the security of these primitives is defined via an interactive game that allows the attacker to make oracle queries to the cryptosystem (e.g., PRF queries, encryption queries, decryption queries, signing queries). The quantum attacker can keep internal quantum state, but can only query the cryptosystem on classical inputs. We show that even these cryptosystems may be insecure against quantum attacks, despite having provable classical security under LWE.

Concretely, we give the following constructions under the LWE assumption:

- A PRF scheme that is classically secure in the standard sense, but broken by a quantum adversary making 3 classical PRF queries. If we consider a PRF with *public parameters* (e.g., the adversary gets some public parameters that depend on the secret key at the beginning of the game) then we get a scheme that can be quantumly broken with only 2 queries.[3]
- A symmetric-key encryption scheme that is classically CPA-secure in the standard sense, but broken by a quantum adversary making 2 encryption queries before seeing the challenge ciphertext. If we consider symmetric-key encryption with public parameters, then we get a scheme that is broken by a quantum adversary making just 1 encryption query before seeing the challenge ciphertext.
- A MAC that is classically secure in the standard sense, but broken by a quantum adversary making 2 authentication queries. If we consider a MAC with public parameters, then we get a scheme that is quantumly broken with just 1 authentication query.
- A signature scheme that is classically secure in the standard sense, but broken by a quantum adversary making 2 signing queries.
- A public-key encryption scheme that is classically CCA-2 secure in the standard sense, but is broken by a quantum adversary making 2 decryption queries before seeing the challenge ciphertext.

Additional Counterexamples for One-Time *Cryptography.* Using a modified technique, we construct further examples of schemes that are quantumly broken using even *a single classical query*, but are also only classically secure for a single query:

- A PRF scheme with public parameters that is classically but not post-quantum secure against an adversary making a single query.

---

[3] Note that PRFs (and other symmetric-key primitives) with public parameters are natural to consider; for instance, the group-based PRFs (e.g., [34]) would naturally have public parameters that include a description of the group.

- A one-time symmetric-key encryption scheme (i.e., the adversary only gets a single challenge ciphertext) with public parameters that is classically but not post-quantum secure.
- A one-time signature scheme that is classically but not post-quantum secure.
- A bounded-CCA public-key encryption scheme that is classically but not post-quantum secure against an adversary making a single decryption query.

These examples are incomparable to the previous ones, since they give a more dramatic demonstration of post-quantum insecurity with minimal interaction, but they also only satisfy a limited form of classical security against a bounded number of queries. We view these examples as particularly surprising: a one-time signature scheme seems *very* non-interactive, so how can we distinguish between classical and quantum attacks?

Our Techniques. All of our examples are constructed by carefully embedding instances of interactive quantum advantage—either an IPQ or a new protocol that we call "quantum disclosure of secrets" (QDS)—into stateless/non-interactive cryptographic primitives. The key conceptual insight is that although the primitives we consider are non-interactive, the corresponding security games are interactive, allowing us to use a quantum attacker that wins an IPQ to also win in the security game of the given primitive. The classical security of our constructions follows via a black-box reduction that rewinds the adversary, which is the underlying reason that it fails to translate into the quantum setting.

Towards showing the above results, we also develop new ways of demonstrating quantumness that may be of independent interest. Firstly, we observe that the known 4-round IPQs also satisfy *resettable soundness* against classical provers that can arbitrarily rewind the verifier to earlier points in the execution. Using this observation, we construct a stateless/deterministic *quantum advantage function* F_{sk} keyed by some secret key sk that is generated together with some public parameters pp: an efficient classical attacker given pp and oracle access to F_{sk} cannot cause it to ever output a special "accept" symbol (in fact, cannot even distinguish it from a random function), while a quantum attacker can do so by only making 2 classical queries.

Secondly, we construct a 3-round *quantum disclosure of secrets (QDS)* protocol between a classical sender that has some message m and a receiver, where a classical receiver does not learn anything about m during the protocol (assuming LWE), while a quantum receiver learns m at the end of the protocol. This gives a kind of interactive quantum advantage *in three rounds*, despite the fact that interactive proofs of quantumness in three rounds are not known under post-quantum assumptions (e.g., LWE) in the plain model. This primitive is used to prove our second slate of results. Our QDS protocol makes essential use of the recent quantum advantage technique of [30].

We give a more detailed description of our techniques in Sect. 2.

Conclusion: Counterexamples in Cryptography. This paper provides counterexamples to the folklore belief that classical proofs of security under post-quantum assumptions (e.g., LWE) imply post-quantum security for basic cryptographic primitives, including PRFs, symmetric/public-key encryption, and signatures. To do so, we construct schemes that are classically secure under LWE but demonstrably fail to be post-quantum secure. Why are we putting effort into constructing schemes that *fail* to be post-quantum secure? This result fits into a broader and important area of cryptography that provides demonstrable counterexamples to intuitive but incorrect beliefs that certain forms of security should generically hold. Other examples of such results include counterexamples for the random-oracle heuristics [5,15,24], circular security [26,31,37,42], selective-opening attacks [21,28], hardness amplification [4,6,20], security composition [21,23], etc. Such counterexamples are extremely important and serve as a warning that can hopefully prevent us from making such mistakes in the future. Having a demonstrable counterexample is much more convincing than just pointing out that our intuition for why security should hold is flawed. Counterexamples also point to specific pitfalls that need to be avoided if we want to prove security. They enhance our understanding of otherwise elusive topics. Lastly, they often lead to new techniques that tend to find positive applications down the line.

1.2   Related Work

One of the primary goals of the study of quantum computation is to understand which tasks can be solved efficiently by quantum computers but not by classical ones. This is informally referred to as a *quantum advantage*. Many instances of quantum advantage have implications for the security of classical cryptography; the implications will typically hold in the particular computational model specified by the kind of quantum advantage obtained. We list a few examples below.

Shor's Algorithm. [38] gives a quantum polynomial-time algorithm for factoring integers and computing discrete logarithms in finite cyclic groups with computationally efficient group operations. This renders typical cryptosystems based on discrete logarithms, factoring, or RSA-type assumptions broken in quantum polynomial time.

Interactive Proofs of Quantumness. As discussed above, [13,29,30] give surprising examples of interactive quantum advantage under LWE, *despite* the fact that LWE is believed to be hard for efficient quantum algorithms. They construct interactive protocols where an honest quantum prover causes the verifier to accept, but any efficient classical prover cannot cause the verifier to accept assuming the hardness of LWE. This immediately implies that certain interactive protocols can be classically secure under LWE but quantumly insecure.

Counterexamples in the Random Oracle Model. Many cryptosystems are built using a generic "unstructured" hash function H; security is argued in the *random oracle model* [7], a model in which the adversary can make only polynomially many *queries* to H (and H is treated as a uniformly random function).

For these schemes, the random oracle model serves as a heuristic indicating that the scheme *might* be secure when instantiated with a good concrete hash function. However, when quantum attacks on the scheme are considered, a serious problem arises [10]: given a concrete hash function H, a quantum algorithm can query H *in superposition* (that is, compute the unitary map $|x\rangle|y\rangle \mapsto |x\rangle|y \oplus H(x)\rangle$ on an arbitrary input state). Thus, to heuristically capture security of these schemes against quantum attacks, one should prove security in the *quantum random oracle model* (QROM), in which the adversary can make polynomially many superposition queries (rather than classical queries).

Prior work [10,43,44,47] has constructed examples of cryptosystems, defined relative to an arbitrary hash function H, that are secure in the classical random oracle model (possibly under an additional computational assumption) but insecure in the QROM. For example, [43] construct encryption and signature schemes that are secure in the ROM but not the QROM, while [44] even constructs such examples for one-way functions!

We note that counterexamples for ROM cryptosystems are fundamentally different from what we are asking in this work. ROM vs. QROM separations highlight the insufficiency of the classical ROM for accurately describing the security of hash function-based cryptosystems against quantum attacks. And at the technical level, the ROM "has room" for counterexamples by embedding an *oracle separation* between classical and quantum computation, which may even be unconditional. Of course, ROM based examples also translate into plain model examples that are quantum insecure and heuristically classically secure when instantiated with a good hash function. For example, [44] gives a construction of a one-way function with this property. However, the classical security of the resulting one-way function is only heuristic and does not appear to be provable under any standard post-quantum assumption such as LWE. Indeed, since one-wayness is defined via a completely non-interactive security game with no room for rewinding, if one had a black-box reduction showing one-wayness under LWE, then it would also imply the post-quantum insecurity of LWE (at least in the uniform setting without [quantum] auxiliary input, see discussion on [8] below). In contrast, our work shows quantum insecurity for primitives whose classical security is proved under LWE using a black-box reduction.

Quantum Oracle Queries in the Security Game. When the security game underlying a cryptographic primitive involves giving an adversary *oracle access* to some functionality (such as a PRF), the natural definition of post-quantum security is to consider a quantum attacker breaking a cryptosystem used by classical honest users who perform operations on classical inputs. Modeling this corresponds to a security game where the attacker is restricted to querying the oracle on classical inputs. However, one could imagine a stronger notion of "quantum security" [45], where even the honest users want to perform cryptographic operations on quantum inputs, in which case we need to give the adversary quantum oracle access.

In these situations, classical security proofs do not generically carry over to the quantum query setting, and there often exist counterexample protocols that are secure against adversaries that make classical queries but *insecure* in the presence of quantum queries [11,12,45,46].

On the other hand, in this work we are interested in understanding whether there are quantum attacks on *classical* cryptosystems that only operate on classical inputs, and therefore the above counterexamples do not apply.

Quantum Auxiliary Input. The recent work of [8] noticed that rewinding may be an issue even for completely non-interactive security games (e.g., one-way functions or pseudorandom generators), if one considers a setting where a non-uniform adversary may have quantum auxiliary input. They provide techniques for showing that certain (but not all) forms of classical rewinding-based reductions do in fact carry over to the quantum setting. While they provide some examples were their techniques fail, it does not translate into an overall example showing insecurity. It would be extremely interesting to see if one can come up with examples of (e.g.,) one-way functions that are proven secure classically via a black-box reduction under a post-quantum assumption, but are not secure in the quantum setting with quantum auxiliary input.

2   Technical Overview

Our main technique in constructing cryptographic primitives that are classically secure but post-quantum insecure is to embed interactive proofs of quantumness (IPQs) [13,29,30] based on LWE inside these primitives. Such IPQs consist of 4-message interactive protocols, where the verifier sends the first message and the prover sends the last message. The main difficulty is that IPQs are stateful/interactive protocols, while the primitives we consider are stateless/non-interactive.

For concreteness, let's start with *signature schemes* as an illustrative example, but we will later explain how to extend the ideas all the other primitives as well.

Stateful Signatures. As a start, let's relax the standard notion of signatures to allow the signing algorithm to be stateful. Then we can take any standard signature scheme (under LWE) and easily augment it to incorporate an IPQ as follows. In addition to signing the messages with the standard signature scheme, our augmented signing algorithm also runs the verifier of an IPQ on the side. It interprets any messages to be signed as prover message in an IPQ and appends the appropriate verifier responses to the signatures (the verification algorithm of the augmented signature scheme simply ignores these appended values). Since the IPQ verifier is stateful, this also requires the signing algorithm to be stateful. If at any point in time the IPQ verifier accepts, then the signing algorithm simply appends the secret key of the signature scheme to the signature.

It is easy to see that the above augmented signature scheme is classically secure under LWE, since a classical adversary making signing queries will be unable to get the IPQ verifier to accept. It is also easy to see that the scheme is insecure against a quantum attacker who acts as the quantum prover in an IPQ, causes it to accept, and recovers the secret key of the signing algorithm, which it then uses to construct its forgery. If we use a 4-message IPQ and append the initial verifier message to the verification key of the signature, then the above attack corresponds to making 2 signing queries.

Stateless Signatures. Unfortunately, the above idea seems to crucially rely on having a stateful signing algorithm, and our goal is to extend it to the stateless setting. To do so, we essentially construct an IPQ with a stateless verifier and resettable security: even if the classical prover can reset the verifier and run it many times with different prover messages, it cannot cause the verifier to accept.

We rely on the fact that the 4-message IPQs of [13,30] have special structure. The first round is secret-coin and the verifier generates an initial message v_1 together with some secret state st and sends v_1. The prover responds with p_1. The verifier then uses public-coins to send a uniformly random message v_2 and the prover responds with p_2. At the end of the 4th round, the verifier uses the secret state st to decide if the transcript (v_1, p_1, v_2, p_2) is accepting or rejecting. We observe that we can convert the verifier of such an IPQ (as long as it has negligible soundness error) into a deterministic/stateless IPQ verifier V_{sk} that just maintains a secret key $sk = (v_1, st, k)$ consisting of the first round verifier message v_1 of the original IPQ, the secret st, and a key k for a PRF f_k. We define the function V_{sk} as follows:

– On input the empty string, output v_1.
– On input p_1, output $v_2 = f_k(p_1)$.
– On input p_1, p_2, compute $v_2 = f_k(p_1)$ and use st to check if (v_1, p_1, v_2, p_2) is an accepting transcript: if so accept, else reject.

An efficient quantum prover with oracle access to V_{sk} can cause it to accept, using the same strategy as in the original IPQ.[4] However, an efficient classical prover with oracle access to V_{sk} cannot cause it to accept, even if it can make arbitrarily many queries on arbitrary inputs, effectively being able to run many executions of the original interactive protocol with rewinding. We show this via a simple reduction where we convert any adversary that causes the stateless IPQ verifier V_{sk} to accept into an adversary on the original stateful IPQ.

We use the above stateless IPQ to derive our counterexample for stateless signatures. We start with any standard signature scheme (secure under LWE) and augment it by incorporating the stateless IPQ as follows. Firstly, we generate the secret key sk of the stateless IPQ verifier V_{sk} as above, and append sk to the original signature secret key sk_{Sig}. We also append v_1 to the original verification

---

[4] Technically, it may be possible that the completeness error of the IPQ increases non-negligibly if the PRF is only classically secure but not post-quantum secure. But it is easy to solve this by relying on a PRF that is one-wise independent.

key. We then modify the signing algorithm: we append the output of $V_{sk}(m)$ to any signature of m, and, if at any point $V_{sk}(m)$ accepts, then we append the original signature signing key sk_{Sig} to the signature. The verification algorithm ignores these appended components.

We have an efficient quantum adversary on this signature scheme by running the quantum prover of the IPQ: the adversary gets v_1 from the verification key and queries the signing algorithm twice, once on p_1 to get v_2 and once on p_1, p_2 to cause the IPQ verifier to accept and recover sk_{Sig}. At this point, the adversary can forge a signature on any message of its choosing. On the other hand, an efficient classical adversary cannot cause V_{sk} to accept and hence does not learn any additional information about sk_{Sig} beyond what it would get in the original signature game. Therefore the above signature scheme is classically secure under LWE, but quantumly broken with just 2 signing queries.

Generalizing: Quantum Advantage Function. We abstract out the above idea of stateless IPQs via a *quantum advantage function* (QAF). A QAF is a deterministic/stateless function F_{sk}, indexed by a secret key sk. A classical polynomial-time adversary with oracle access to F_{sk} can never cause it to output a special accept value (except with negligible probability), while a quantum polynomial-time adversary can cause it to do so by only making 3 classical oracle queries. We can set the QAF $F_{sk} = V_{sk}$ to be the stateless IPQ verifier defined above.

Alternatively, we can define a QAF with public parameters pp that depend on sk: even given pp a classical polynomial-time adversary with oracle access to F_{sk} can never cause it to output accept, while a quantum polynomial-time adversary given pp can do so by only making 2 classical oracle queries. We can construct such a QAF by setting the public parameters $pp = v_1$ to be the first verifier message and setting $F_{sk} = V_{sk}$ to be the stateless IPQ verifier above.[5]

We can embed our QAF inside various stateless/non-interactive cryptosystems to get our remaining counterexamples:

- Symmetric-key message authentication codes (MAC): Take any existing secure MAC and augment it by running a QAF on the side. The QAF outputs are appended to the tags of the original scheme, and the verification procedure is augmented to automatically accept any message on which the QAF accepts. This gives a classically secure MAC that can be quantumly broken using 2 authentication queries, or alternately, even just 1 authentication query in the setting with public parameters.[6] In particular, the quantum attacker uses the k queries needed to get the QAF to accept ($k = 3$ or $k = 2$ depending on public parameter) as $k - 1$ authentication queries and a forgery.
- CCA-2 secure public-key encryption: Take any existing secure scheme and augment it with a QAF with public parameters as follows. Append the public

---

[5] In this case, we can remove the instruction that V_{sk} outputs v_1 on the empty string, since we already give out v_1 in the public parameters.

[6] For symmetric-key primitives in the public-parameter setting, the secret key of the primitive is generated together with some public parameters that are given to the adversary, but are not otherwise needed for correctness.

parameters to the public key of the scheme. Modify encryption to ensure that all valid ciphertexts start with a 0 bit. Modify the decryption procedure so that, it decrypts valid ciphertexts correctly, but if it gets as an invalid ciphertext it evaluates the QAF on it instead of decrpyting. If the QAF ever accepts, the decryption procedure outputs the secret key of the encryption scheme. The scheme remains correct and classically secure, but can be quantumly broken using just 2 decryption queries (made before receiving the challenge ciphertext) to recover the secret key.

- Pseudorandom functions (PRF): We notice that the outputs our QAF can be either: (i) v_1 which is pseudorandom for known IPQs, (ii) $v_2 = F_k(p_1)$ which is pseudorandom, or (iii) accept/reject. We can modify the QAF so that instead of rejecting it applies an independent PRF. With this modification, a classical attacker cannot distinguish it from a random function, since it cannot cause the original QAF to ever accept. On the other hand, a quantum attacker can easily distinguish, by causing the original QAF to accept, using just 3 queries, or even 2 queries in the setting with public parameters.

- Symmetric-key encryption: Take any existing secure scheme and augment it with a pseudorandom QAF (as constructed in the previous bullet) as follows. When encrypting a message m, choose some fresh randomness r and append r together with the output of the QAF applied on $m\|r$ to the ciphertext. If the QAF accepts, also append the secret key of the original symmetric-key encryption to the ciphertext. The decryption algorithm ignores the appended values.

  For classical adversaries, we can rely on the fact that the QAF is pseudorandom (and cannot be caused to accept) to argue that this modification does not break CPA security. For quantum adversaries, we show that it is possible to cause the QAF to accept using 3 CPA queries, or even just 2 CPA queries in the setting with public parameters. There is a minor difficulty that the quantum adversary only gets to pick the left half m of the QAF inputs, while the right half r is chosen randomly. Nevertheless, by starting with an IPQ protocol where we expand prover messages to contain a dummy "right half" that the verifier ignores, we get a QAF that can be efficiently quantumly attacked even if the right half of the inputs is chosen randomly.

One-Time Security and Quantum Disclosure of Secrets. We also give alternate examples of cryptosystems that are classically "one-time" secure, but are not post-quantum one-time secure. As an example, let's consider one-time signatures. The security game for one-time signatures consists of 4 rounds: the challenger sends a verification key, the attacker chooses a message, the challenger sends a signature and the attacker produces a forgery. Therefore, there is hope that we can embed a 4-message IPQ into the 4-message security game of one-time signatures. However, we notice that the one-time signature game has an additional feature that we call *public verifiablity*: just by looking at the transcript of the game, an external observer can tell whether the verifier accepted or rejected. On the other hand, the known 4-message IPQs from LWE do not have public verifiability. Therefore, to give a counterexample for signatures, we at the very least need to construct a 4-message *publicly verifiable* IPQ.[7] Alternately, let's consider one-time symmetric-key encryption with public parameters. There, the security game consists of only 3 rounds: the challenger chooses the secret key with public parameters and sends the latter to the attacker, the attacker chooses two messages m_0, m_1 and gets an encryption of m_b. At the end of the 3 rounds the adversary has to distinguish between $b = 0$ and $b = 1$. Therefore, we would need some sort of a 3 round game with *quantum advantage*, where a quantum adversary can distinguish between two possibilities, but a classical one cannot. Current IPQs from LWE all require 4 rounds.

We solve both of the above issues by constructing a new type of 3-message protocol with quantum advantage under LWE, which we refer to as a *quantum disclosure of secrets* (QDS). A QDS is an interactive protocol between a classical *sender* who has some message m and a (potentially quantum) *receiver*. No efficient classical receiver can distinguish between any two possible sender messages m_0, m_1 at the end of the protocol, while a quantum receiver can fully recover m. We construct a 3-message QDS under LWE and we give an overview of this construction further below.[8] For now, let us assume we have such a 3-message QDS, whose execution consists of three messages s_1, r_1, s_2, where s_i denotes sender messages and r_i the receiver message. We use it to get various counterexamples to post-quantum security of one-time primitives under LWE. For simplicity, we just discuss one-time signatures and one-time symmetric-key encryption (with public parameters), but the other counterexamples are all similar:

- One-time Signatures: Take any secure one-time signature scheme and augment it by running a QDS on the side, where the sender's message is set to be the signing key of the original scheme. Append the first message s_1 of the QDS to the verification key and st to the signing key. To sign some message, sign it under the original signature scheme, but also interpret the message as the receiver's message r_1 in the QDS protocol and run the QDS on it to produce the response s_2 (using st), and append s_2 to the signature. The verification algorithm ignores the appended components.

  A classical attacker cannot break one-time security since it does not learn anything about the signing key from the QDS when making one signing query. However, a quantum attacker can break security by recovering the original signing key from the QDS using one signing query, and then can forge the signature of an arbitrary new message.

- One-time Symmetric-Key Encryption (with public parameters): Take any secure one-time encryption (e.g., one-time pad) and augment it with a QDS,

---

[7] It is easy to make an IPQ publicly verifiable simply by adding an additional round where the verifier publicly declares whether it accepted or rejected, but this would require 5 rounds and we need 4.

[8] A 3-message QDS also implies a 4-message publicly verifiable IPQ. This is shown implicitly by our one-time signature counterexample below, but can be done more directly as follows. Use a QDS to send a random message x and append a one-way function $f(x)$ to the 3rd round; then accept in the 4th round if the prover replies a valid preimage x' for $f(x)$.

where the sender's message is set to be the secret key of the original encryption scheme. Set the public parameters to consist of the first round QDS message s_1 and append st to the secret key. To encrypt a message, use the original one-time encryption scheme, but also interpret the message as the receiver's message r_1 in the QDS protocol and run the QDS on it to produce the response s_2 (using st), and append s_2 to the ciphertext.

To argue (computational) classical security, we rely on the fact that, for a classical receiver in the QDS, not only is the sender's message hidden but entire sender response s_2 sent in the third round looks pseudorandom. On the other hand, a quantum adversary can recover the key of the original encryption scheme and decrypt.

We note that the 3-message QDS scheme that we construct is *not* resettably secure: if a classical receiver can rewind the sender with many different values of r_1 and get the corresponding values s_2 then it can learn the sender's message. This is the reason that our results above are incomparable to the previous ones and only achieve one-time classical security. If we were able to construct a resettably secure QDS, we would get the best of both worlds and construct schemes that are fully secure in the standard sense against classical adversaries, but not even one-time secure against quantum adversaries.

Quantum Disclosure of Secrets from LWE. We now give an overview of our construction of 3-message QDS from LWE. Our main idea is to start with a special 4-message IPQ from LWE that has a *unique final answer*: given (v_1, p_1, v_2) and st, the verifier can efficiently compute a unique prover answer p_2 that would cause it to accept. We can convert such a 4-message IPQ into a 3-message QDS. We keep the first two messages of the IPQ and QDS the same with $s_1 = v_1, r_1 = p_1$. Then, in the beginning of the third round, we have the sender choose a random v_2 as the IPQ verifier would, compute the unique correct p_2^* that would make the IPQ verifier accept, take a Goldreich-Levin hardcore bit $GL(p_2^*)$ and use it to one-time pad the sender-message m by setting $s_2 = (v_2, GL(p_2^*) \oplus m)$.[9] By relying on Goldreich-Levin decoding, we can translate any classical attack on the 3-message QDS into a classical attack on the original 4-message IPQ. On the other hand, we can use a quantum attack on the 4-message IPQ to easily recover the message m in the 3-message QDS by computing the correct p_2 from v_2 and then using the hardcore bit of p_2 to un-blind the message.

Therefore, to construct a 3-message QDS, we need to construct a 4-message IPQ with a unique final answer. Unfortunately, the IPQ schemes of [13] do not have this property (either directly or with any simple modification). On the other hand, the work of [30] gives a general template for constructing 4-message IPQ schemes. We review this template and show that there is a careful instantiation of it that does have a unique final answer.

The template of [30] construct a (4-message) IPQ from any 2-prover nonlocal game. A 2-prover non-local game consists of 2 provers who cannot communicate and are given two questions (q_1, q_2 respectively) sampled from some joint

---

[9] This allows us to encrypt a single bit, but we can repeat this in parallel to encrypt a multi-bit message one bit at a time. Security follows via a simple hybrid argument.

distribution. Their goal is to reply with answers a_1, a_2 respectively, and they win if some relation $R(q_1, q_2, a_1, a_2)$ holds. Such a game has quantum advantage if quantum provers who share entangled quantum state at the beginning of the game can have a noticeably larger winning probability than classical provers who only share classical shared randomness. For example, the CHSH game [18] sets q_1, q_2, a_1, a_2 to be bits, samples (q_1, q_2) uniformly and independently, and defines $R(q_1, q_2, a_1, a_2)$ to hold if $a_1 \oplus a_2 = q_1 \wedge q_2$. Classical provers can only win with probability .75, but quantum provers can win with probability $\cos^2(\pi/8) > .85$.

The work of [30] compiles any such game into a 4-message IPQ with a single prover by using quantum fully homomorphic encryption. The verifier sends $v_1 = \mathsf{Enc}(q_1)$ the prover responds with $p_1 = \mathsf{Enc}(a_1)$, the verifier sends q_2 and the prover responds with a_2: the verifier accepts if $R(q_1, q_2, a_1, a_2)$ holds. The good news is that, if we instantiate this template with the CHSH game, then there is a unique final answer $a_2 = (q_1 \wedge q_2) \oplus a_1$. However, the resulting IPQ only has a noticeable gap between the success of a classical prover and a quantum one (.75 vs .85), but we want an IPQ where the classical prover only has a negligible success probability while the quantum one can win with all but negligible probability. We can achieve this by using parallel repetition of many copies of the CHSH game and accepting if the prover wins in $> .8$ fraction of them. But now there is no longer a unique final answer that wins the IPQ, since the prover can win any .8 fraction of the games to get the verifier to accept (and even a quantum prover won't be able to win significantly more that .85 fraction)! Instead, we start with a different non-local game, which is a variant of the *magic square game* [2,19].[10] In this game, there is a unique final answer a_2 determined by q_1, q_2, a_1, and there is a pair of entangled quantum provers that can win with probability 1, while classical provers only win with probability at most 17/18. By taking a sufficiently large parallel repetition and accepting if *all* copies accept, we can drive down the winning probability of classical provers to negligible, while allowing quantum provers to win with probability 1 and preserving a unique final answer a_2 determined by q_1, q_2, a_1. Therefore, if we apply the [30] framework with the parallel-repeated variant of Magic Square as above, we get a 4-message IPQ with a unique final answer as desired.[11]

---

[10] We think of a 3×3 square of bits. The challenge q_1 corresponds to a random row or column (6 possibilities) and q_2 corresponds to a random location inside that row/column. The provers are supposed to answer with a_1 being the 3 bits in the given row/column specified by q_1 and a_2 being the bit in the position specified by q_2. They win if the answers are consistent and if the bits of a_1 have parity 0 when q_1 is a row or parity 1 when q_1 is a column.

[11] Unfortunately, if we use this 2-prover non-local game, then the resulting 4-message IPQ cannot be made resettably sound. This is because the challenge q_2 gives information about q_1. By rewinding the verifier and seeing many values of q_2, a classical adversary can learn q_1 and win the game. (Even if the 4-message IPQ was resettably sound, it wouldn't guarantee that the 3-message QDS would be, because it reveals various GL bits in the 3rd round.) In contrast, in the original instantiation of the [30] framework with the CHSH game and threshold parallel repetition, the resulting 4-message IPQ does not have unique final answers, but can be given resettable security using a PRF to generate q_2, because q_2 is random and independent of q_1.

3   Open Problems

We mention several fascinating open problems left by our work.

- Can we construct a CPA-secure public-key encryption scheme which is classically secure under LWE but post-quantum insecure? The CPA security game for public-key encryption consists of 3 rounds, so it may seem like we should be able to embed a QDS scheme inside it. But the 3rd round of the CPA security game must be publicly computable from the first 2 rounds, while our QDS requires secret state to compute the 3rd round.
- Can we construct a 3-message stateless/resettable QDS under LWE? This would allow us to construct cryptosystems that are classically secure in the standard sense under LWE, but fail to be even one-time post-quantum secure.
- Can we construct IPQs and classically secure/quantum-insecure cryptosystems under other plausibly post-quantum assumptions beyond LWE? Ideally we would even be able to do so under generic assumptions, such as one-way functions.
- Can we construct 3-message (resettably secure) IPQs from LWE? This would allow us to get rid of the public parameters in our symmetric-key examples.
- Inspired by [8], can we construct one-way functions under post-quantum assumptions (e.g., LWE), where the one-way function is classically secure, but post-quantum insecure given quantum auxiliary input? As noted in [8], this may be possible even if classical security is proven via a black-box reduction.
- Can we construct one-way functions under a post-quantum assumptions (e.g., LWE), where the one-way function is classically secure but post-quantum insecure, even without quantum auxiliary input? Since the security game of one-way function is non-interactive, there is no possibility of rewinding distinguishing between classical and quantum adversaries. Therefore, the classical security of such one-way functions could not be proven via a black-box reduction. Could we perhaps have such an example nevertheless by using a non-black-box reduction?

4   Preliminaries

We use QPT to denote quantum polynomial time and PPT to denote classical probabilistic polynomial time. We say that a function $f(n)$ is *negligible* if for all constants $c > 0$, $f(n) < n^{-c}$ for all but finitely many n.

4.1   Interactive Proofs of Quantumness

For concreteness and simplicity of notation, we will focus throughout this work on interactive proofs of quantumness with 4 messages in total. Note that this corresponds to the best round complexity known for interactive proofs of quantumness in the plain model.

Definition 1. *An* interactive proof of quantumness *is an interactive protocol Π between a prover $\mathcal{P}$ and a verifier $\mathcal{V}$, with the following properties:*

- *Quantum completeness: there exists a efficient quantum prover $\mathcal{P}$ such that:*

$$\Pr\left[(\mathcal{P},\mathcal{V})(1^{\lambda}) = 1\right] \geq 1 - \mathrm{negl}(\lambda).$$

- *Classical soundness: for any efficient classical prover $\mathcal{P}^*$:*

$$\Pr\left[(\mathcal{P}^*,\mathcal{V})(1^{\lambda}) = 1\right] \leq \mathrm{negl}(\lambda).$$

Let v_1, v_2 (resp. p_1, p_2) denote the messages sent by the verifier (resp. the prover) during the execution of an interactive proof of quantumness Π.

An interactive proof of quantumness can furthermore satisfy the following optional properties:

1. Public-coin second verifier message: the second verifier message v_2 consists of uniformly and independently sampled random coins.
2. (Classically) Pseudorandom verifier messages: for any efficient classical prover $\mathcal{P}^*$, the messages (v_1, v_2), output by the verifier in a protocol execution with $\mathcal{P}^*$, are computationally indistinguishable from uniformly random strings, even if $\mathcal{P}^*$ learns the outcome of the execution.[12]
3. Unique final answer: given any partial transcript $\tau = (v_1, p_1, v_2)$ and any verifier state st, there exists an efficient algorithm $\mathsf{UniqueAnswer}(v_1, p_1, v_2, \mathsf{st}) \rightarrow p_2^* \in \{0,1\}^{\ell}$ which outputs the unique final prover message that can make the verifier accept (namely, output 1) if such a final prover message exists.

We will make use of constructions of two different interactive proofs of quantumness in this paper:

Lemma 1. *Under the LWE assumption, there exists a 4-message interactive proof of quantumness satisfying properties 1 (public-coin second verifier messages) and 2 (classically pseudorandom verifier messages) (Definition 1).*

Lemma 1 is obtained by combining ([30], Theorem 3.7) using a λ-wise parallel repetition of the independent question magic square game [2,19]. We refer to the full version of the paper [33] for more details.

We will also use a proof of quantumness with unique answers (while still requiring completeness $1 - \mathrm{negl}(\lambda)$ and negligible soundness). While we are not aware of any explicit constructions satisfying this property in the literature, we observe that instantiating [30] with an appropriate non-local game gives such a proof of quantumness.

---

[12] Allowing $\mathcal{P}^*$ to learn the outcome of the protocol execution is without loss of generality by negligible classical soundness: all executions of the protocol with $\mathcal{P}^*$ will be rejected with overwhelming probability.

Lemma 2. *Under the LWE assumption, there exists a 4-message interactive proof of quantumness satisfying properties 2 (classically pseudorandom verifier messages) and 3. (unique final answers) (Definition 1).*

Lemma 2 also follows from combining [30], with now a unique answer version of the magic square game [2,19]. We refer to the full version of the paper [33] for more details.

5   Deterministic Oracles with Quantum Advantage

5.1   Quantum Advantage for Unbounded-Classical Query Algorithms

We introduce quantum advantage functions, which are by default stateless and deterministic functions that demonstrate a quantum advantage given only classical query access. In its stronger form, such a function acts as a pseudorandom function against classical adversaries.

Definition 2 (Quantum Advantage Functions). *A quantum advantage function family is a pair of efficient algorithms* (Setup, $F_{\sf sk}$) *with the following syntax:*

- Setup(1^λ): *sample some public parameters* pp, *a secret key* sk *and outputs* (pp, sk). *Without loss of generality, we will consider throughout the paper that* sk *includes the public parameters* pp.
- $F_{\sf sk}(\cdot)$: *on input a message* x, *either output a message* y, *or a special "accept" symbol denoted* accept, *or a special "reject" symbol denoted* reject. *We require by default that* $F_{\sf sk}$ *is stateless and deterministic.*

We additionally require the following properties:

1. *(k-Quantum easiness) There exists a QPT oracle algorithm* $\mathcal{A}^{F(\cdot)}(\sf pp)$ *such that:*
$$\Pr\left[\mathcal{A}^{F_{\sf sk}(\cdot)}({\sf pp}) = x^* \wedge F_{\sf sk}(x^*) = {\sf accept}\right] = 1 - {\rm negl}(\lambda),$$

    where $\mathcal{A}^{F_{\sf sk}(\cdot)}(\sf pp)$ *makes* k *classical oracle queries in total to* $F_{\sf sk}(\cdot)$ *before outputting* x^*, *and where the probability is over* (pp, sk) $\leftarrow$ Setup(1^λ). *We simply say that* (Setup, $F_{\sf sk}$) *satisfies quantum easiness if it satisfies 1-quantum easiness.*
2. *(Classical hardness) For all PPT oracle algorithms* $\mathcal{A}^{\mathcal{O}(\cdot)}(\sf pp)$:

$$\Pr\left[\mathcal{A}^{F_{\sf sk}(\cdot)}({\sf pp}) = x^* \wedge F_{\sf sk}(x^*) = {\sf accept}\right] = {\rm negl}(\lambda).$$

    over (pp, sk) $\leftarrow$ Setup(1^λ).
    We optionally require the following stronger notion of classical hardness:

3. *((Classical) Pseudorandomness of outputs and public parameters) For all PPT distinguishers $\mathcal{A}$:*

$$\left| \Pr\left[\mathcal{A}^{F_{\sf sk}(\cdot)}({\sf pp}) = 1 \right] - \Pr\left[\mathcal{A}^{R}(\widetilde{\sf pp}) = 1 \right] \right| \leq {\rm negl}(\lambda).$$

over $({\sf pp}, {\sf sk}) \leftarrow {\sf Setup}(1^\lambda)$, *and where R is a uniformly random function, and $\widetilde{\sf pp}$ is uniformly random.*

Theorem 1. *Let Π be a 4-message interactive proof of quantumness satisfying the properties specified in Lemma 1: (Item 1) the second verifier message is public-coin and (Item 2) verifier messages are pseudorandom (Definition 1). Then additionally assuming one-way functions, there exists a quantum advantage function with pseudorandom outputs satisfying quantum easiness (Definition 2).*

Combined with Lemma 1, we obtain the following:

Corollary 1. *Assuming the (classical) hardness of LWE, there exists a quantum advantage function with pseudorandom outputs satisfying quantum easiness (Definition 2).*

Construction. Let Π be a 4-message interactive proof of quantumness. Let $({\sf PRF.KeyGen}, {\sf PRF})$ be a one-wise independent PRF (see [33] for a definition).

We define our quantum advantage function $({\sf Setup}, F_{\sf sk})$ as follows:

- ${\sf Setup}(1^\lambda)$: Sample $K \leftarrow {\sf PRF.KeyGen}(1^\lambda)$. Compute a first verifier message v_1 for Π, using some fresh randomness ρ. Set ${\sf pp} = v_1$, ${\sf sk} = ({\sf pp}, K, \rho)$, and output $({\sf pp}, {\sf sk})$.
- $F_{\sf sk}$: on input x, we consider two distinguished cases:[13]
  - If x is of the form p_1: Compute the public-coin verifier message $v_2 = {\sf PRF}_K(p_1)$, which we interpret as a second verifier message with partial transcript (v_1, p_1) (where $v_1 = {\sf pp}$). Output $y = v_2$.
  - If x is of the form (p_1, p_2): Compute $v_2 = {\sf PRF}_K(p_1)$. If the verifier for Π accepts the transcript (v_1, p_1, v_2, p_2) with secret state ρ, output ${\sf accept}$, otherwise output ${\sf reject}$.
  - Otherwise output ${\sf reject}$.

Lemma 3 (Quantum easiness). *Suppose Π satisfies quantum completeness (Definition 1), and $({\sf PRF.KeyGen}, {\sf PRF})$ is one-wise independent (see [33] for a definition). Then $({\sf Setup}, F_{\sf sk})$ satisfies quantum easiness.*

Proof. Let $\mathcal{P}$ denote the efficient quantum prover for Π such that

$$\Pr\left[(\mathcal{P}, \mathcal{V})(1^\lambda) = 1 \right] \geq 1 - {\rm negl}(\lambda).$$

Define the following QPT algorithm $\mathcal{A}({\sf pp})$:

---

[13] Technically, to have $F_{\sf sk}$ be defined over a fixed input domain, we actually distinguish the cases $x = (0\|p_1\|*)$ and $x = (1\|p_1, p_2)$ where $*$ denotes a 0 padding of appropriate length, and where $F_{\sf sk}$ outputs ${\sf reject}$ on inputs not of this form. We keep the notation of the construction above for clarity of exposition.

- On input pp, parse pp $= v_1$ as a first verifier message in Π, and compute a first prover message p_1 according to $\mathcal{P}$. Query F_{sk} on input p_1, and receive v_2.
- Given (v_1, p_1, v_2), compute the second prover message p_2 according to $\mathcal{P}$. Output $x^* = (p_1, p_2)$.

By construction, (v_1, p_1, v_2, p_2) denotes a transcript generated by $\mathcal{P}, \mathcal{V}$, where $\mathcal{V}$ uses randomness ρ and $\rho_2 = \mathsf{PRF}_K(p_1)$ to generate its messages v_1 and v_2 respectively. Since PRF is one-wise independent, $\mathcal{A}$ perfectly simulates the view of $\mathcal{P}$ in an interaction with $\mathcal{V}$. Thus $F_{\mathsf{sk}}(x^*)$ outputs accept with probability $1 - \mathsf{negl}(\lambda)$. $\qquad\square$

Lemma 4 (Classical hardness). *Suppose Π is sound against classical provers and has public-coin intermediate verifier messages (Definition 1, Property 1) and that $(\mathsf{PRF.KeyGen}, \mathsf{PRF})$ is a (classically secure) PRF. Then $(\mathsf{Setup}, F_{\mathsf{sk}})$ satisfies classical hardness.*

Proof. Let $\mathcal{A}(\mathsf{pp})$ denote a PPT adversary with oracle access to F_{sk}. Without loss of generality, we assume that $\mathcal{A}$ queries its output x^* to F_{sk} before halting, and that $\mathcal{A}$ outputs the first x^* it queries such that $F_{\mathsf{sk}}(x^*) = \mathsf{accept}$, if such a query exists. Let Q denote the number of oracle queries $\mathcal{A}$ makes. We define a sequence of hybrid experiments, where we change the input-output behaviour of F_{sk}, as follows:

- **Hybrid 0:** This is the classical hardness experiment (Definition 2, Property 2) where $\mathcal{A}$ has oracle access to $\mathcal{O}_{\mathsf{sk}}^0 := F_{\mathsf{sk}}$, where $(\mathsf{pp}, \mathsf{sk}) \leftarrow \mathsf{Setup}(1^\lambda)$. We say that the adversary *wins* the experiment if he outputs x^* such that $\mathcal{O}_{\mathsf{sk}}^0(x^*) = \mathsf{accept}$.
- **Hybrid 1:** We change how the oracle queries are handled, and define $\mathcal{O}_{\mathsf{sk}}^1$ as follows. The (now stateful) oracle computes v_2 using a lazily-sampled random function R instead of a PRF. Specifically, on queries of the form $x = p_1$ if $R(x)$ is not yet defined, sample v_2 uniformly and set $R(x) = v_2$, then output v_2.
- **Hybrid 2:** We do not change the behavior of the oracle ($\mathcal{O}_{\mathsf{sk}}^2 = \mathcal{O}_{\mathsf{sk}}^1$), but we change the win condition of the experiment. We now guess two uniformly random indices $j_1, j_2 \leftarrow [Q]$, where Q denotes the number of oracle queries made by $\mathcal{A}$. We now say that $\mathcal{A}$ wins if and only if the following conditions hold:
  (1) the j_2th oracle query from $\mathcal{A}$, on input x_{j_2}, is of the form $x_{j_2} = (p_1^*, p_2^*)$,
  (2) $\mathcal{O}_{\mathsf{sk}}^2(x_{j_2}) = \mathsf{accept}$, and, for all prior oracle queries x, $\mathcal{O}_{\mathsf{sk}}^2(x) \neq \mathsf{accept}$,
  (3) the j_1th oracle query from $\mathcal{A}$, on input x_{j_1} has p_1^* as a prefix (i.e. either $x_{j_1} = p_1^*$ or $x_{j_1} = (p_1^*, p_2)$ for some p_2), and, for all prior oracle queries x, the prefix of x with appropriate length is not equal to p_1^*.
- **Hybrid 3:** We change how oracle queries are handled and define $\mathcal{O}_{\mathsf{sk}}^3$ as follows. On any query $j \neq j_2$ of the form $x_j = (p_1, p_2)$, $\mathcal{O}_{\mathsf{sk}}^3$ rejects.

We refer to the full version [33] for an analysis of these consecutive hybrid games, which shows that the success probability of $\mathcal{A}$ in hybrid 0 is negligible. $\square$

Last, we show that we can obtain pseudorandomness of F_{sk} with a simple modification.

Lemma 5 (Pseudorandomness). *Under the same hypotheses as Lemmas 3 and 4 there exists a quantum advantage function $\widetilde{F}_{sk}$ satisfying pseudorandomness.*

Proof. Let (Setup, F_{sk}) denote the previous construction. We define $\widetilde{F}_{sk}$ as follows: on input x, compute $F_{sk}(x)$. If $F_{sk}(x) = \mathsf{reject}$, output $\mathsf{PRF}_K(x)$; otherwise output $F_{sk}(x)$. Pseudorandomness of non-special outputs of F_{sk} (that is, accept or reject) follows by the public-coin property of second verifier messages of Π (Definition 1, Property 1). Furthermore, it is classically hard to find inputs x such that $F_{sk}(x) = \mathsf{accept}$ by classical hardness of F_{sk}, and inputs x such that $F_{sk}(x) = \mathsf{reject}$ are mapped by $\widetilde{F}_{sk}$ to pseudorandom outputs by PRF security. The proofs of quantum easiness and classical hardness for $\widetilde{F}_{sk}$ follow almost identically to the ones for F_{sk}. □

Remark 1 (Generalizing to constant-round proofs of quantumness). Our definitions, construction and proofs can readily be extended to work starting with any constant-round interactive proof of quantumness, assuming all intermediate verifier messages are public-coin (that is, not counting the first verifier message if the verifier produces the first message of the protocol). Starting with a $2k$-message protocol, this gives a quantum advantage function with $(k-1)$-quantum easiness (and where classical hardness and pseudorandomness hold as in Definition 2).

Removing Public Parameters. We observe that any quantum advantage function with public parameters induces one without public parameters. Let $(\overline{\mathsf{Setup}}, \overline{F}_{\overline{sk}})$ be a quantum advantage function. Consider the following algorithms (Setup, F_{sk}):

- $\mathsf{Setup}(1^\lambda)$: run $(\overline{\mathsf{pp}}, \overline{sk}) \leftarrow \overline{\mathsf{Setup}}(1^\lambda)$ and output $sk = (\overline{\mathsf{pp}}, \overline{sk})$.
- F_{sk}: on input x, if $x = \mathsf{init}$ where init is a special input symbol, output $\overline{\mathsf{pp}}$. Otherwise output $\overline{F}_{\overline{sk}}(x)$.[14]

Claim 1. *Assume that $(\overline{\mathsf{Setup}}, \overline{F}_{\overline{sk}})$ is a quantum advantage function. Then (Setup, F_{sk}) satisfies 2-quantum easiness, and classical hardness (Definition 2). Furthermore, assuming that $(\overline{\mathsf{Setup}}, \overline{F}_{\overline{sk}})$ has pseudorandom outputs and public parameters (Definition 2), then (Setup, F_{sk}) also has pseudorandom outputs (against classical distinguishers).*

Corollary 2. *Assuming the (classical) hardness of LWE, there exists a quantum advantage function without public parameters, that satisfies 2-quantum easiness, and have pseudorandom outputs (against classical distinguishers).*

---

[14] Technically, we pad the shorter of $\overline{\mathsf{pp}}$ and $\overline{F}_{\overline{sk}}(x)$ to obtain outputs with fixed length. We define the padding as an independent PRF of the input to conserve pseudorandomness of outputs.

Randomized Quantum Advantage Functions. It will also be useful to us in some cases to consider *randomized* quantum advantage functions, for which we can consider the following stronger notion of pseudorandomness:

3' (Strong pseudorandomness of outputs and public parameters) For all PPT distinguishers $\mathcal{A}$:

$$\left| \Pr\left[\mathcal{A}^{F_{\mathsf{sk}}(\cdot)}(\mathsf{pp}) = 1 \right] - \Pr\left[\mathcal{A}^{U}(\widetilde{\mathsf{pp}}) = 1 \right] \right| \leq \mathrm{negl}(\lambda).$$

over $(\mathsf{pp}, \mathsf{sk}) \leftarrow \mathsf{Setup}(1^{\lambda})$, and where U is defined as sampling and outputting *fresh* independent randomness at every call, and where $\widetilde{\mathsf{pp}}$ is uniformly random.

We observe that our previous construction of (deterministic) quantum advantage function can be extended to satisfy the stronger property above. We refer to the full version [33] for details.

5.2 Quantum Disclosure of Secrets

Definition 3 (Quantum Disclosure of Secrets). *Let Π_{QDS} denote an interactive protocol between a sender and receiver. The sender S has as input a message m, while the receiver R has no input.*

We say that Π_{QDS} is a quantum disclosure of secrets *if there is the following quantum-classical gap:*

1. *(Quantum correctness) There is an efficient quantum receiver R^* such that, if R^* interacts with the honest sender S, R^* outputs the sender's message m with probability $1 - \mathrm{negl}(\lambda)$.*
2. *(Classical privacy) For any efficient classical receiver R, if R interacts with the honest sender S, for any pair of messages m_0, m_1, the view of R when interacting with $S(m_0)$ is computationally indistinguishable from the view of R when interacting with $S(m_1)$.*

Theorem 2. *Let Π be a 4-message interactive proof of quantumness with unique final answer (Definition 1, Property 3.). Then there exists a 3-message quantum disclosure of secrets protocol. Furthermore, if Π has pseudorandom verifier messages (Definition 1, Property 2), then the sender messages in Π_{QDS} are jointly classically indistinguishable from uniformly random.*

Combined with Lemma 2, we obtain the following:

Corollary 3. *Assuming the classical hardness of LWE, there exists a 3-message quantum disclosure of secrets protocol, such that sender messages are jointly classically indistinguishable from uniformly random.*

Construction. We focus on one-bit messages. Extending it to arbitrary length messages is then done by executing independent copies of the protocol in parallel for each bit of the message; security follows by a hybrid argument.

Let Π be a 4-round interactive proof of quantumness with unique final answer (Lemma 2). We define our 3-message quantum disclosure of secrets protocol Π_{QDS} as follows:

- The sender $\mathcal{S}$ generates a first verifier message v_1 for the interactive proof of quantumness and internal state st. The sender sends a first message $s_1 = v_1$ to the receiver.
- The receiver $\mathcal{R}$ responds with a prover message $r_1 = p_1$ for the interactive proof of quantumness.
- The sender $\mathcal{S}$ computes a third message v_2 for the interactive proof of quantumness as well as $p_2^* = \textsf{UniqueAnswer}(v_1, p_1, v_2, \textsf{st})$. The sender sends its second message $s_2 = (v_2, r, y = \langle r, p_2^* \rangle \oplus m)$ for uniformly random $r \leftarrow \{0,1\}^\ell$ where $\ell = |p_2^*|$.

We now state correctness, privacy and pseudorandomness of our construction. We refer to the full version [33] for proofs.

Lemma 6 (Quantum correctness). *Suppose Π is a 4-message interactive proof of quantumness with unique final answer (Definition 1). Then Π_{QDS} satisfies quantum correctness.*

Lemma 7 (Classical privacy). *Suppose Π is a 4-round interactive proof of quantumness with unique final answer (Definition 1). Then Π_{QDS} satisfies classical privacy.*

Lemma 8 (Pseudorandomness of verifier messages). *Suppose that Π has pseudorandom verifier messages (Definition 1, Property 2). Then the sender messages in Π_{QDS} are jointly classically indistinguishable from uniformly random.*

Quantum Disclosure of Secrets Function. Let Π_{QDS} be a quantum disclosure of secrets. We define, for all messages m, the following *quantum disclosure of secrets function* (Setup, $F_{\textsf{sk},m}$):

- $\textsf{Setup}(1^\lambda)$:[15] Sample the first sender message s_1 in Π_{QDS}, along with an internal state st and some (potentially correlated) randomness for the second sender message ρ_2, and output $(\textsf{pp} = s_1, \textsf{sk} = (s_1, \textsf{st}, \rho_2))$.
- $F_{\textsf{sk},m}$: On input x, parse x as a receiver message r_1 in Π_{QDS}, and compute a second sender message s_2 given $(s_1, r_1, \textsf{st}, m)$ using randomness ρ_2.

---

[15] In general, the first sender message in the QDS s_1 depends on the message m, and so in general Setup would take m as input. For simplicity of notation, we note that our construction of QDS above is delayed-input, in the sense that s_1 is computed independently of m, which allows Setup to be independent of m. Our counterexamples in Sect. 6 would work even if the QDS was not delayed input.

We note that $F_{\mathsf{sk},m}$ is stateless and deterministic. The properties of Π_{QDS} translate directly to properties of $(\mathsf{Setup}, F_{\mathsf{sk},m})$:

- Quantum easiness: there exists a QPT algorithm $\mathcal{A}$ such that

$$\Pr\left[\mathcal{A}^{F_{\mathsf{sk},m}}(\mathsf{pp}) = m\right] = 1 - \mathrm{negl}(\lambda),$$

  where $(\mathsf{pp}, \mathsf{sk}) \leftarrow \mathsf{Setup}(1^\lambda)$, and where $\mathcal{A}$ makes one classical query to $F_{\mathsf{sk},m}$;
- Weak pseudorandomness: for all PPT algorithms $\mathcal{A}$ *that make at most one oracle query*:

$$\left|\Pr\left[\mathcal{A}^{F_{\mathsf{sk},m}(\cdot)}(\mathsf{pp}) = 1\right] - \Pr\left[\mathcal{A}^R(\widetilde{\mathsf{pp}}) = 1\right]\right| \le \mathrm{negl}(\lambda),$$

  where $(\mathsf{pp}, \mathsf{sk}) \leftarrow \mathsf{Setup}(1^\lambda)$, R denotes a random function and $\widetilde{\mathsf{pp}}$ is uniformly sampled.

Removing Public Parameters from the QDS Function. We observe that any QDS function with public parameters induces a QDS function without public parameters as follows. Let $(\overline{\mathsf{Setup}}, \overline{F}_{\overline{\mathsf{sk}},m})$ be a QDS function, and $\mathcal{H}$ be a family of pairwise independent hash functions with uniformly random description.[16] Consider the following algorithms $(\mathsf{Setup}, F_{\mathsf{sk},m})$:

- $\mathsf{Setup}(1^\lambda)$: Sample $(\overline{\mathsf{pp}}, \overline{\mathsf{sk}}) \leftarrow \overline{\mathsf{Setup}}(1^\lambda)$, and sample a pairwise independent hash function $h \leftarrow \mathcal{H}$. Output $\mathsf{sk} = (\overline{\mathsf{pp}}, \overline{\mathsf{sk}}, h)$.
- $F_{\mathsf{sk},m}$: on input x, if $x = \mathsf{init}$ where init is a special input symbol, output $y = (h, \overline{\mathsf{pp}})$. Otherwise output $y = \overline{F}_{\overline{\mathsf{sk}},m}(x) \oplus h(x)$.

The resulting QDS function $(\mathsf{Setup}, F_{\mathsf{sk},m})$ has the following properties:

- 2-Quantum easiness: there exists a QPT algorithm $\mathcal{A}$ that outputs m using two classical queries to $F_{\mathsf{sk},m}$. This follows by calling $F_{\mathsf{sk},m}$ on input $\underline{\mathsf{init}}$, receiving $(\overline{\mathsf{pp}}, h)$, and then calling the quantum easiness algorithm for $(\overline{\mathsf{Setup}}, \overline{F}_{\overline{\mathsf{sk}},m})$ to (1) obtain an input query x, and (2) recover m from the output from $(\overline{\mathsf{Setup}}, \overline{F}_{\overline{\mathsf{sk}},m})$ (which can be recovered by computing $h(x)$ given h and unmasking the output of $F_{\mathsf{sk},m}$).
- 2-Query weak pseudorandomness: for any PPT algorithm $\mathcal{A}$ making at most 2 oracle queries, $F_{\mathsf{sk},m}$ is computationally indistinguishable from a random function. This follows by considering the following cases. If none of the two queries are made on input $x = \mathsf{init}$, pseudorandomness follows by pairwise independence of h. Otherwise at most one query is made on an input $x \ne \mathsf{init}$, and weak pseudorandomness follows by 1-query weak pseudorandomness of $(\overline{\mathsf{Setup}}, \overline{F}_{\overline{\mathsf{sk}},m})$.

---

[16] Uniform description follows by considering for instance random affine functions over the field $\{0, 1\}^n$ where n denotes the input size, so that hash functions have descriptions $h = (a, b) \leftarrow \{0, 1\}^n \times \{0, 1\}^n$.

6   Counterexamples for Post-quantum Security

In this section we use our functions from Sect. 5 to give examples of classically secure primitives that are quantum insecure.

6.1   Counterexamples for Standard Cryptographic Primitives

We first focus on cryptographic primitives with usual security notions. We refer to the full version [33] for formal definitions of the cryptographic primitives we consider. Note that that the precise formulations of the security experiments do influence the exact query complexity in the theorem below.

Theorem 3. *Assuming the existence of a quantum advantage function with pseudorandom outputs (Definition 2), there exists:*

- *A signature scheme that is secure against classical adversaries, but insecure against quantum adversaries making two classical queries to the signing oracle.*
- *Additionally assuming the existence of CCA-1 (resp. CCA-2)-secure public-key encryption, there exists a CCA-1 (resp. CCA-2)-secure public-key encryption scheme that is secure against classical adversaries, but insecure against quantum adversaries making two classical queries to the decryption oracle before making its challenge query.[17]*
- *A PRF with public parameters that is secure against classical adversaries, but insecure against quantum adversaries making two classical queries to the PRF.*
- *A CPA-secure symmetric-key encryption scheme with public parameters that is secure against classical adversaries, but insecure against quantum adversaries making one query to the encryption oracle before making its challenge query (see [33] for a definition).*
- *A MAC with public parameters that is secure against classical adversaries, but insecure against quantum adversaries making one query to the authentication oracle.*

Furthermore there exists a PRF, MAC and CPA-secure symmetric encryption scheme each without public parameters and with the same classical security, but insecurity against quantum adversaries making one additional query to the respective oracles than listed above.

Combined with Corollary 1, such constructions exist assuming the (classical) hardness of LWE.

Counterexample for Signatures. Let $(\mathsf{Setup}, F_{\mathsf{sk}})$ be a quantum advantage function (Definition 2). Let $(\overline{\mathsf{KeyGen}}, \overline{\mathsf{Sign}}, \overline{\mathsf{Verify}})$ be a (classically) secure signature scheme. We define the following signature scheme $(\mathsf{KeyGen}, \mathsf{Sign}, \mathsf{Verify})$:

---

[17] In other words, the quantum attack is a CCA-1 attack.

- $\mathsf{KeyGen}(1^\lambda)$: Sample $(\overline{\mathsf{Sig}.\mathsf{vk}}, \overline{\mathsf{Sig}.\mathsf{sk}}) \leftarrow \overline{\mathsf{KeyGen}}(1^\lambda)$ and $(\mathsf{pp}, \mathsf{sk}) \leftarrow \mathsf{Setup}(1^\lambda)$. Output $(\mathsf{Sig}.\mathsf{vk} = (\overline{\mathsf{Sig}.\mathsf{vk}}, \mathsf{pp}), \mathsf{Sig}.\mathsf{sk} = (\overline{\mathsf{Sig}.\mathsf{sk}}, \mathsf{sk}))$.
- $\mathsf{Sign}(\mathsf{Sig}.\mathsf{sk}, m)$: Compute $\overline{\sigma} \leftarrow \overline{\mathsf{Sign}}(\overline{\mathsf{Sig}.\mathsf{sk}}, m)$ and $y = F_{\mathsf{sk}}(m)$. If $y = \mathsf{accept}$, output $\sigma = (\overline{\sigma}, \overline{\mathsf{Sig}.\mathsf{sk}})$. Otherwise, output $\sigma = (\overline{\sigma}, y)$.
- $\mathsf{Verify}(\overline{\mathsf{Sig}.\mathsf{vk}}, m, \sigma)$: Output $\overline{\mathsf{Verify}}(\overline{\mathsf{Sig}.\mathsf{vk}}, m, \overline{\sigma})$.

Correctness of $(\mathsf{KeyGen}, \mathsf{Sign}, \mathsf{Verify})$ follows directly from correctness of the scheme $(\overline{\mathsf{KeyGen}}, \overline{\mathsf{Sign}}, \overline{\mathsf{Verify}})$.

Claim 2. *Suppose that* $(\mathsf{Setup}, F_{\mathsf{sk}})$ *satisfies quantum easiness (Definition 2), and that* $(\overline{\mathsf{KeyGen}}, \overline{\mathsf{Sign}}, \overline{\mathsf{Verify}})$ *is correct. Then there exists a QPT adversary* $\mathcal{F}$ *that breaks unforgeability of* $(\mathsf{KeyGen}, \mathsf{Sign}, \mathsf{Verify})$ *using two (classical) signing queries.*

Proof. Let $\mathcal{A}$ be the QPT algorithm associated to the quantum easiness of $(\mathsf{Setup}, F_{\mathsf{sk}})$ (Definition 2). Define $\mathcal{F}$ as follows. Run $\mathcal{A}$ to obtain $x_1 \leftarrow \mathcal{A}(\mathsf{pp})$, and send a signing query with message x_1. Upon receiving $\sigma_1 = (\overline{\sigma}_1, y_1)$, continue the execution of $\mathcal{A}$, setting the oracle response as y_1, so that $\mathcal{A}$ produces $x_2 = x^*$ as a candidate accepting input for F_{sk}. $\mathcal{F}$ submit x_2 as the second query. $\mathcal{F}$ receives as response σ_2 which it parses as $\sigma_2 = (\overline{\sigma}_2, y_2)$. It picks an arbitrary $m \neq q_1, q_2$ and outputs as its forgery $\sigma^* = \overline{\mathsf{Sign}}(y_2, m)$.

By quantum easiness of $(\mathsf{Setup}, F_{\mathsf{sk}})$, we have with overwhelming probability $F_{\mathsf{sk}}(x_2) = \mathsf{accept}$, so that $y_2 = \overline{\mathsf{Sig}.\mathsf{sk}}$. Thus $\mathcal{F}$ produces a valid forgery with overwhelming probability by correctness of $(\overline{\mathsf{KeyGen}}, \overline{\mathsf{Sign}}, \overline{\mathsf{Verify}})$. □

Claim 3. *Suppose* $(\mathsf{Setup}, F_{\mathsf{sk}})$ *satisfies classical hardness (Definition 2), and that* $(\overline{\mathsf{KeyGen}}, \overline{\mathsf{Sign}}, \overline{\mathsf{Verify}})$ *is unforgeable (against classical adversaries). Then* $(\mathsf{KeyGen}, \mathsf{Sign}, \mathsf{Verify})$ *is unforgeable against classical adversaries.*

Proof. We define the following hybrid experiment:

- **Hybrid 1:** We modify the behavior of the signing oracle. Compute $\overline{\sigma} \leftarrow \overline{\mathsf{Sign}}(\overline{\mathsf{Sig}.\mathsf{sk}}, m)$ and $y = F_{\mathsf{sk}}(m)$ as normal. If $y = \mathsf{accept}$, abort. Otherwise, output $\sigma = (\overline{\sigma}, y)$.

For any PPT adversary $\mathcal{F}$, the probability of $\mathcal{F}$ making a signing query with some input m that makes the signing oracle abort in hybrid 1 is negligible by classical hardness of $(\mathsf{Setup}, F_{\mathsf{sk}})$ (Theorem 1). Therefore the output of the unforgeability experiment for $(\mathsf{KeyGen}, \mathsf{Sign}, \mathsf{Verify})$ is indistinguishable from its output in hybrid 1.

Now unforgeability in hybrid 1 follows directly from (classical) unforgeability of $(\overline{\mathsf{KeyGen}}, \overline{\mathsf{Sign}}, \overline{\mathsf{Verify}})$, where the reduction samples $(\mathsf{pp}, \mathsf{sk}) \leftarrow \mathsf{Setup}(1^\lambda)$ and computes $y = F_{\mathsf{sk}}(m)$ on its own upon receiving a signing query with message m. □

The counterexamples for CCA-secure encryption, PRFs, symmetric-key encryption and MACS, along with the claimed classical security and quantum insecurity, follow in an almost identical manner. We refer to the full version [33] for the constructions.

Removing Public Parameters in Secret-Key Primitives. Using a (deterministic) quantum advantage function without public parameters (Claim 1 and Corollary 2), we obtain a PRF (respectively, a MAC) without public parameters, that is quantum insecure using three classical PRF queries (resp. two MAC queries).

To remove public parameters from the secret-key encryption counterexample, we simply modify the scheme to append the public parameters pp of the randomized quantum advantage function to all ciphertexts (and new ciphertexts therefore have the form $(\mathsf{pp}, \overline{\mathsf{ct}}, y)$, where either $y = F_{\mathsf{sk}}(m')$ for some m' or $y = \mathsf{Enc.sk}$). The new scheme is still quantumly broken using 2 (classical) queries, where the additional query (on a dummy input) is used to obtain pp. Classical security is maintained given that classical security for the original counterexample held given pp.

6.2   Counterexamples for One-Time Primitives

We now study one-time counterparts of the primitives considered in the previous section. Using the results from Sect. 5.2 we obtain constructions of "one-time" analogs of counterexamples in Sect. 6.1, that are only secure against classical attackers that are allowed to make only a limited number of queries to their respective oracles. However they are broken by quantum attackers that make one fewer query than their counterparts for the constructions from the previous section. We refer again to the full version [33] for formal definitions (again, note that the precise formulations of the security experiments do influence the exact query complexity in the theorem below).

Theorem 4. *Assuming the existence of a quantum disclosure of secrets function (see Sect. 5.2), there exists:*

- *A one-time signature scheme that is secure against classical adversaries making one query to the signing oracle, but insecure against quantum adversaries making one classical query.*
- *Additionally assuming the existence of single-decryption CCA-1 (resp. CCA-2)-secure public-key encryption, there exists a single-decryption CCA-1 (resp. CCA-2)-secure public-key encryption scheme that is secure against classical adversaries making one query to the decryption oracle, but insecure against quantum adversaries making one classical query.*
- *A one-query PRF with public parameters that is secure against classical adversaries making one query to the PRF, but insecure against quantum adversaries making one classical query. Furthermore, there exists a PRF (without public parameters) that is secure against classical adversaries making two queries to the PRF but insecure against quantum adversaries making two classical queries.*
- *A one-time symmetric-key encryption scheme with public parameters that is secure against classical adversaries (making one challenge query and no encryption queries), but insecure against quantum adversaries. Furthermore, there exists a symmetric-key encryption scheme (without public parameters)*

that is secure against classical adversaries making one encryption query and one challenge query but insecure against quantum adversaries making one classical encryption query and one challenge query.

Combined with Corollary 3, such constructions exist assuming the (classical) hardness of LWE.

Counterexample for One-Time Signatures. Let $(\mathsf{Setup}, F_{\mathsf{sk},\cdot})$ be a quantum disclosure of secrets function (see Sect. 5.2). Let $(\overline{\mathsf{KeyGen}}, \overline{\mathsf{Sign}}, \overline{\mathsf{Verify}})$ be a (classically) secure one-time signature scheme (see [33] for a definition).

We define the following one-time signature scheme $(\mathsf{KeyGen}, \mathsf{Sign}, \mathsf{Verify})$:

- $\mathsf{KeyGen}(1^\lambda)$: Sample $(\overline{\mathsf{Sig.vk}}, \overline{\mathsf{Sig.sk}}) \leftarrow \overline{\mathsf{KeyGen}}(1^\lambda)$ and $(\mathsf{pp}, \mathsf{sk}) \leftarrow \mathsf{Setup}(1^\lambda)$.
  Output $(\mathsf{Sig.vk} = (\overline{\mathsf{Sig.vk}}, \mathsf{pp}), \mathsf{Sig.sk} = (\overline{\mathsf{Sig.sk}}, \mathsf{sk}))$.
- $\mathsf{Sign}(\mathsf{Sig.sk}, m)$: Compute $\overline{\sigma} \leftarrow \overline{\mathsf{Sign}}(\overline{\mathsf{Sig.sk}}, m)$ and compute the quantum disclosure of secrets function with message $\overline{\mathsf{Sig.sk}}$: $y = F_{\mathsf{sk}, \overline{\mathsf{Sig.sk}}}(m)$. Output $\sigma = (\overline{\sigma}, y)$.
- $\mathsf{Verify}(\mathsf{Sig.vk}, m, \sigma)$: Parse $\sigma = (\overline{\sigma}, y)$. Output $\overline{\mathsf{Verify}}(\overline{\mathsf{Sig.vk}}, m, \overline{\sigma})$

Claim 4. *Assume* $(\mathsf{Setup}, F_{\mathsf{sk},\cdot})$ *satisfies quantum easiness (see Sect. 5.2), and* $(\overline{\mathsf{KeyGen}}, \overline{\mathsf{Sign}}, \overline{\mathsf{Verify}})$ *is correct. Then there exists a QPT adversary $\mathcal{F}$ that breaks unforgeability of* $(\mathsf{KeyGen}, \mathsf{Sign}, \mathsf{Verify})$ *using one (classical) signing query.*

Proof. By the quantum easiness property of $(\mathsf{Setup}, F_{\mathsf{sk}, \overline{\mathsf{Sig.sk}}})$, $\mathcal{F}$ can recover $\overline{\mathsf{Sig.sk}}$ with overwhelming probability by making only one (classical) query to the signing oracle. Then $\mathcal{F}$ can produce a forgery by running $\overline{\mathsf{Sign}}(\overline{\mathsf{Sig.sk}}, m)$ for an arbitrary message m (different from the one used in the query).   □

Claim 5. *Assume* $(\mathsf{Setup}, F_{\mathsf{sk},\cdot})$ *satisfies weak pseudorandomness (see Sect. 5.2), and* $(\overline{\mathsf{KeyGen}}, \overline{\mathsf{Sign}}, \overline{\mathsf{Verify}})$ *is one-time unforgeable. Then* $(\mathsf{KeyGen}, \mathsf{Sign}, \mathsf{Verify})$ *is one-time unforgeable against classical adversaries (see [33] for a definition).*

Proof. We define the following hybrid experiment:

- **Hybrid 1**: We modify the behavior of the signing oracle. Instead of computing $y = F_{\mathsf{sk}, \overline{\mathsf{Sig.sk}}}(m)$, sample y uniformly at random.

Given that forgers in the one-time experiment are only allowed to make a single signing query, the output of the experiment defined by hybrid 1 is indistinguishable from that of the one-time unforgeability experiment for $(\mathsf{KeyGen}, \mathsf{Sign}, \mathsf{Verify})$, by weak pseudorandomness of $(\mathsf{Setup}, F_{\mathsf{sk}, \overline{\mathsf{Sig.sk}}})$. (One-time) unforgeability in hybrid 1 follows directly from (one-time) unforgeability of $(\overline{\mathsf{KeyGen}}, \overline{\mathsf{Sign}}, \overline{\mathsf{Verify}})$.   □

The counterexamples for single-decryption CCA-secure public-key encryption, one-query PRFs and one-time secure symmetric-key encryption are constructed in a nearly identical manner to the corresponding ones from Sect. 6.1, with similar modifications as in the above construction for one-time signatures.

We refer to the full version [33] for the constructions, where we also discuss how to remove public parameters for secret-key primitives.

References

1. Ambainis, A., Rosmanis, A., Unruh, D.: Quantum attacks on classical proof systems: the hardness of quantum rewinding. In: 55th FOCS, pp. 474–483. IEEE Computer Society Press, October 2014.https://doi.org/10.1109/FOCS.2014.57
2. Aravind, P.: The magic squares and Bell's theorem. Technical report (2002)
3. Arute, F., Arya, K., Babbush, R., et al.: Quantum supremacy using a programmable superconducting processor. Nature **574**(7779), 505–510 (2019)
4. Badrinarayanan, S., Ishai, Y., Khurana, D., Sahai, A., Wichs, D.: Refuting the dream XOR lemma via ideal obfuscation and resettable MPC. ITC (2022). https://eprint.iacr.org/2022/681
5. Barak, B.: How to go beyond the black-box simulation barrier. In: 42nd FOCS, pp. 106–115. IEEE Computer Society Press, October 2001. https://doi.org/10.1109/SFCS.2001.959885
6. Bellare, M., Impagliazzo, R., Naor, M.: Does parallel repetition lower the error in computationally sound protocols? In: 38th FOCS, pp. 374–383. IEEE Computer Society Press, October 1997. https://doi.org/10.1109/SFCS.1997.646126
7. Bellare, M., Rogaway, P.: Entity authentication and key distribution. In: Stinson, D.R. (ed.) CRYPTO 1993. LNCS, vol. 773, pp. 232–249. Springer, Heidelberg (1994). https://doi.org/10.1007/3-540-48329-2_21
8. Bitansky, N., Brakerski, Z., Kalai, Y.T.: Constructive post-quantum reductions. Cryptology ePrint Archive (2022)
9. Bitansky, N., Shmueli, O.: Post-quantum zero knowledge in constant rounds. In: Makarychev, K., Makarychev, Y., Tulsiani, M., Kamath, G., Chuzhoy, J. (eds.) 52nd ACM STOC, pp. 269–279. ACM Press, June 2020. https://doi.org/10.1145/3357713.3384324
10. Boneh, D., Dagdelen, Ö., Fischlin, M., Lehmann, A., Schaffner, C., Zhandry, M.: Random oracles in a quantum world. In: Lee, D.H., Wang, X. (eds.) ASIACRYPT 2011. LNCS, vol. 7073, pp. 41–69. Springer, Heidelberg (2011). https://doi.org/10.1007/978-3-642-25385-0_3
11. Boneh, D., Zhandry, M.: Quantum-secure message authentication codes. In: Johansson, T., Nguyen, P.Q. (eds.) EUROCRYPT 2013. LNCS, vol. 7881, pp. 592–608. Springer, Heidelberg (2013). https://doi.org/10.1007/978-3-642-38348-9_35
12. Boneh, D., Zhandry, M.: Secure signatures and chosen ciphertext security in a quantum computing world. In: Canetti, R., Garay, J.A. (eds.) CRYPTO 2013. LNCS, vol. 8043, pp. 361–379. Springer, Heidelberg (2013). https://doi.org/10.1007/978-3-642-40084-1_21
13. Brakerski, Z., Christiano, P., Mahadev, U., Vazirani, U.V., Vidick, T.: A cryptographic test of quantumness and certifiable randomness from a single quantum device. In: Thorup, M. (ed.) 59th FOCS, pp. 320–331. IEEE Computer Society Press, October 2018. https://doi.org/10.1109/FOCS.2018.00038
14. Brakerski, Z., Vaikuntanathan, V.: Efficient fully homomorphic encryption from (standard) LWE. In: Ostrovsky, R. (ed.) 52nd FOCS, pp. 97–106. IEEE Computer Society Press, October 2011. https://doi.org/10.1109/FOCS.2011.12
15. Canetti, R., Goldreich, O., Halevi, S.: The random oracle methodology, revisited (preliminary version). In: 30th ACM STOC, pp. 209–218. ACM Press, May 1998. https://doi.org/10.1145/276698.276741

16. Chia, N.-H., Chung, K.-M., Yamakawa, T.: A black-box approach to post-quantum zero-knowledge in constant rounds. In: Malkin, T., Peikert, C. (eds.) CRYPTO 2021. LNCS, vol. 12825, pp. 315–345. Springer, Cham (2021). https://doi.org/10.1007/978-3-030-84242-0_12

17. Chiesa, A., Ma, F., Spooner, N., Zhandry, M.: Post-quantum succinct arguments: breaking the quantum rewinding barrier. In: 2021 IEEE 62nd Annual Symposium on Foundations of Computer Science (FOCS), pp. 49–58. IEEE (2021)

18. Clauser, J.F., Horne, M.A., Shimony, A., Holt, R.A.: Proposed experiment to test local hidden-variable theories. Phys. Rev. Lett. **23**, 880–884 (1969)

19. Cleve, R., Hoyer, P., Toner, B., Watrous, J.: Consequences and limits of nonlocal strategies. In: Proceedings. 19th IEEE Annual Conference on Computational Complexity, pp. 236–249. IEEE (2004)

20. Dodis, Y., Jain, A., Moran, T., Wichs, D.: Counterexamples to hardness amplification beyond negligible. In: Cramer, R. (ed.) TCC 2012. LNCS, vol. 7194, pp. 476–493. Springer, Heidelberg (2012). https://doi.org/10.1007/978-3-642-28914-9_27

21. Dwork, C., Naor, M., Reingold, O., Stockmeyer, L.J.: Magic functions. In: 40th FOCS, pp. 523–534. IEEE Computer Society Press, October 1999. https://doi.org/10.1109/SFFCS.1999.814626

22. Gentry, C.: Fully homomorphic encryption using ideal lattices. In: Mitzenmacher, M. (ed.) 41st ACM STOC, pp. 169–178. ACM Press, May/June 2009. https://doi.org/10.1145/1536414.1536440

23. Goldreich, O., Krawczyk, H.: On the composition of zero-knowledge proof systems. SIAM J. Comput. **25**(1), 169–192 (1996)

24. Goldwasser, S., Kalai, Y.T.: On the (in)security of the Fiat-Shamir paradigm. In: 44th FOCS, pp. 102–115. IEEE Computer Society Press, October 2003. https://doi.org/10.1109/SFCS.2003.1238185

25. Gorbunov, S., Vaikuntanathan, V., Wee, H.: Attribute-based encryption for circuits. In: Boneh, D., Roughgarden, T., Feigenbaum, J. (eds.) 45th ACM STOC, pp. 545–554. ACM Press, June 2013. https://doi.org/10.1145/2488608.2488677

26. Goyal, R., Koppula, V., Waters, B.: Lockable obfuscation. In: Umans, C. (ed.) 58th FOCS, pp. 612–621. IEEE Computer Society Press, October 2017. https://doi.org/10.1109/FOCS.2017.62

27. van de Graaf, J.: Towards a formal definition of security for quantum protocols. Ph.D. thesis, University of Montreal (1997)

28. Hofheinz, D., Rao, V., Wichs, D.: Standard security does not imply indistinguishability under selective opening. In: Hirt, M., Smith, A. (eds.) TCC 2016, Part II. LNCS, vol. 9986, pp. 121–145. Springer, Heidelberg (2016). https://doi.org/10.1007/978-3-662-53644-5_5

29. Kahanamoku-Meyer, G.D., Choi, S., Vazirani, U.V., Yao, N.Y.: Classically-verifiable quantum advantage from a computational bell test. arXiv preprint arXiv:2104.00687 (2021)

30. Kalai, Y.T., Lombardi, A., Vaikuntanathan, V., Yang, L.: Quantum advantage from any non-local game. Cryptology ePrint Archive, Report 2022/400 (2022). https://ia.cr/2022/400

31. Koppula, V., Ramchen, K., Waters, B.: Separations in circular security for arbitrary length key cycles. In: Dodis, Y., Nielsen, J.B. (eds.) TCC 2015. LNCS, vol. 9015, pp. 378–400. Springer, Heidelberg (2015). https://doi.org/10.1007/978-3-662-46497-7_15

32. Lombardi, A., Ma, F., Spooner, N.: Post-quantum zero knowledge, revisited (or: how to do quantum rewinding undetectably). Cryptology ePrint Archive, Report 2021/1543 (2021). https://eprint.iacr.org/2021/1543
33. Lombardi, A., Mook, E., Quach, W., Wichs, D.: Post-quantum insecurity from LWE. Cryptology ePrint Archive, Paper 2022/869 (2022). https://eprint.iacr.org/2022/869,
34. Naor, M., Reingold, O.: Number-theoretic constructions of efficient pseudo-random functions. In: 38th FOCS, pp. 458–467. IEEE Computer Society Press, October 1997. https://doi.org/10.1109/SFCS.1997.646134
35. NIST CSRC: Post-quantum cryptography. https://csrc.nist.gov/Projects/Post-Quantum-Cryptography
36. Regev, O.: On lattices, learning with errors, random linear codes, and cryptography. In: Gabow, H.N., Fagin, R. (eds.) 37th ACM STOC, pp. 84–93. ACM Press, May 2005. https://doi.org/10.1145/1060590.1060603
37. Rothblum, R.D.: On the circular security of bit-encryption. In: Sahai, A. (ed.) TCC 2013. LNCS, vol. 7785, pp. 579–598. Springer, Heidelberg (2013). https://doi.org/10.1007/978-3-642-36594-2_32
38. Shor, P.W.: Algorithms for quantum computation: discrete logarithms and factoring. In: 35th FOCS, pp. 124–134. IEEE Computer Society Press, November 1994. https://doi.org/10.1109/SFCS.1994.365700
39. Unruh, D.: Quantum proofs of knowledge. In: Pointcheval, D., Johansson, T. (eds.) EUROCRYPT 2012. LNCS, vol. 7237, pp. 135–152. Springer, Heidelberg (2012). https://doi.org/10.1007/978-3-642-29011-4_10
40. Unruh, D.: Computationally binding quantum commitments. In: Fischlin, M., Coron, J.-S. (eds.) EUROCRYPT 2016. LNCS, vol. 9666, pp. 497–527. Springer, Heidelberg (2016). https://doi.org/10.1007/978-3-662-49896-5_18
41. Watrous, J.: Zero-knowledge against quantum attacks. In: Kleinberg, J.M. (ed.) 38th ACM STOC, pp. 296–305. ACM Press, May 2006. https://doi.org/10.1145/1132516.1132560
42. Wichs, D., Zirdelis, G.: Obfuscating compute-and-compare programs under LWE. In: Umans, C. (ed.) 58th FOCS, pp. 600–611. IEEE Computer Society Press, October 2017. https://doi.org/10.1109/FOCS.2017.61
43. Yamakawa, T., Zhandry, M.: Classical vs quantum random oracles. In: Canteaut, A., Standaert, F.-X. (eds.) EUROCRYPT 2021. LNCS, vol. 12697, pp. 568–597. Springer, Cham (2021). https://doi.org/10.1007/978-3-030-77886-6_20
44. Yamakawa, T., Zhandry, M.: Verifiable quantum advantage without structure. arXiv preprint arXiv:2204.02063 (2022)
45. Zhandry, M.: How to construct quantum random functions. In: 53rd FOCS, pp. 679–687. IEEE Computer Society Press, October 2012. https://doi.org/10.1109/FOCS.2012.37
46. Zhandry, M.: Secure identity-based encryption in the quantum random oracle model. In: Safavi-Naini, R., Canetti, R. (eds.) CRYPTO 2012. LNCS, vol. 7417, pp. 758–775. Springer, Heidelberg (2012). https://doi.org/10.1007/978-3-642-32009-5_44
47. Zhang, J., Yu, Y., Feng, D., Fan, S., Zhang, Z., Yang, K.: Interactive proofs for quantum black-box computations. Cryptology ePrint Archive (2020)

Adaptive Versus Static Multi-oracle Algorithms, and Quantum Security of a Split-Key PRF

Jelle Don[1], Serge Fehr[1,2], and Yu-Hsuan Huang[1(✉)]

[1] Centrum Wiskunde & Informatica (CWI), Amsterdam, The Netherlands
{jelle.don,serge.fehr,yhh}@cwi.nl
[2] Mathematical Institute, Leiden University, Leiden, The Netherlands

Abstract. In the first part of the paper, we show a generic compiler that transforms any oracle algorithm that can query multiple oracles *adaptively*, i.e., can decide on *which* oracle to query at what point dependent on previous oracle responses, into a *static* algorithm that fixes these choices at the beginning of the execution. Compared to naive ways of achieving this, our compiler controls the blow-up in query complexity for each oracle *individually*, and causes a very mild blow-up only.

In the second part of the paper, we use our compiler to show the security of the very efficient hash-based *split-key PRF* proposed by Giacon, Heuer and Poettering (PKC 2018), in the *quantum* random-oracle model. Using a split-key PRF as the key-derivation function gives rise to a secure KEM combiner. Thus, our result shows that the hash-based construction of Giacon *et al.* can be safely used in the context of quantum attacks, for instance to combine a well-established but only classically-secure KEM with a candidate KEM that is believed to be quantum-secure.

Our security proof for the split-key PRF crucially relies on our adaptive-to-static compiler, but we expect our compiler to be useful beyond this particular application. Indeed, we discuss a couple of other, known results from the literature that would have profitted from our compiler, in that these works had to go though serious complications in order to deal with adaptivity.

1 Introduction

This paper offers two main contributions. In a first part, we show a generic reduction from adaptive to static multi-oracle algorithms, with a mild increase of the query complexity *for each oracle individually*, and in the second part, exploiting the reduction from the first part, we prove quantum security of the hash–based split-key pseudorandom function (skPRF) proposed in [6]. We now discuss these two contributions in more detail.

Adaptive Versus Static Multi-oracle Algorithms. In certain cryptographic security games, the attacker $\mathcal{A}$ is an *oracle* algorithm that is given query

© The Author(s), under exclusive license to Springer Nature Switzerland AG 2022
E. Kiltz and V. Vaikuntanathan (Eds.): TCC 2022, LNCS 13747, pp. 33–51, 2022.
https://doi.org/10.1007/978-3-031-22318-1_2

access to *multiple* oracles. This is in particular the case when considering the design of a cryptographic scheme in an idealized setting. Consider for instance the security definitions of public-key encryption and signature schemes in the (quantum) random-oracle model, where the attacker is given oracle access to both: the random-oracle and to a decryption/signing oracle.

By default, such an attacker $\mathcal{A}$ can then choose *adaptively*, i.e., depending on answers to previous queries, at what point to query *which oracle*. This is in contrast to a *static* $\mathcal{A}$ that has a predefined order of when it queries which oracle.[1] In certain cases, proving security for a static attacker is easier than proving security for a full fledged adaptive attacker, or taking care of adaptivity (naively) results in an unnecessary blow-up in the error term (see later).

In this light, it seems to be desirable to have a generic compiler that transforms any adaptive attacker $\mathcal{A}$ into a static attacker $\bar{\mathcal{A}}$ that is equally successful in the attack. And there is actually a simple, naive solution for that. Indeed, let $\mathcal{A}$ be an arbitrary oracle algorithm that makes adaptive queries to n oracles $\mathcal{O}_1, \ldots, \mathcal{O}_n$, and consider the static oracle algorithm $\bar{\mathcal{A}}$ defined as follows: $\bar{\mathcal{A}}$ simply runs $\mathcal{A}$, and at every point in time when $\mathcal{A}$ makes a query to one of $\mathcal{O}_1, \ldots, \mathcal{O}_n$ (but due to the adaptivity it will only become clear at the time of the query *which* $\mathcal{O}_i$ is to be queried then), the algorithm $\bar{\mathcal{A}}$ makes n queries, one to every $\mathcal{O}_i$, and it relays $\mathcal{A}$'s query to the right oracle, while making dummy queries to the other oracles.

At first glance, this simple solution is not too bad. It certainly transforms any adaptive $\mathcal{A}$ into a static $\bar{\mathcal{A}}$ that will be equally successful, and the blow-up in the total query complexity is a factor n only, which is mild given that the typical case is $n = 2$. However, it turns out that in many situations, considering the blow-up in the total query complexity is not good enough.

For example, consider again the case of an attacker against a public-key encryption scheme in the random-oracle model. In this example, it is typically assumed that $\mathcal{A}$ may make many more queries to the random-oracle than to the decryption oracle, i.e., $q_H \gg q_D$. But then, applying the above simple compiler, $\bar{\mathcal{A}}$ makes the same number of queries to the random-oracle and to the decryption oracle; namely $\bar{q}_H = \bar{q}_D = q_H + q_D$. Furthermore, the actual figure of merit, namely the advantage of an attacker $\bar{\mathcal{A}}$, is typically not (bounded by) a function of the total query complexity, but a function of the two respective query complexities q_H and q_D *individually*. For example, if one can show that the advantage of any *static* attacker $\bar{\mathcal{A}}$ with respective query complexities $\bar{q}_H$ and $\bar{q}_D$ is bounded by, say, $\bar{q}_H \bar{q}_D^2$, then the above compiler gives a bound on the advantage of any *adaptive* attacker $\mathcal{A}$ with respective query complexities q_H and q_D of $q_H^3 + 2q_H^2 q_D + q_H q_D^2$. If $q_H \gg q_D$ then this is significantly worse than $\approx q_H q_D^2$, which one might hope for given the bound for static $\bar{\mathcal{A}}$.

Our first result is a compiler that transforms any *adaptive* oracle algorithm $\mathcal{A}$ that makes at most q_i queries to oracle $\mathcal{O}_i$ for $i = 1, \ldots, n$ into a *static* oracle algorithm $\bar{\mathcal{A}}$ that makes at most $\bar{q}_i = nq_i$ queries to oracle $\mathcal{O}_i$ for $i = 1, \ldots, n$.

---

[1] In either case, we allow $\mathcal{A}$ to decide adaptively *what input* to query, when having decided (adaptively or statically) on which oracle to query.

Thus, rather than controlling the blow-up in the total number of queries, we can control the blow-up in the number of queries for each oracle *individually*, yet still with the same factor n. Our result applies for *any* vector $\mathbf{q} = (q_1, \ldots, q_n) \in \mathbb{N}^n$ and contains no hidden constants. Our compiler naturally depends on $\mathbf{q}$ (or, alternatively, needs $\mathbf{q}$ as input) but otherwise only requires straight-line black-box access to $\mathcal{A}$, and it preserves efficiency: the run time of $\bar{\mathcal{A}}$ is polynomial in $Q = q_1 + \cdots + q_n$, plus the time needed to run $\mathcal{A}$. Furthermore, the compiler is applicable to any classical or quantum oracle algorithm $\mathcal{A}$, where in the latter case the queries to the oracles $\mathcal{O}_1, \ldots, \mathcal{O}_n$ may be classical or quantum as well; however, the *choice* of the oracle for each query is assumed to be classical (so that individual query complexities are well defined).

In the above made-up example of a public-key encryption scheme with advantage bounded by $\bar{q}_H \bar{q}_D^2$ for any static $\bar{\mathcal{A}}$ with respective query complexities $\bar{q}_H$ and $\bar{q}_D$, we now get the bound $8q_H q_D^2$ for any adaptive $\mathcal{A}$ with respective query complexities q_H and q_D.

We show the usefulness of our adaptive-to-static compiler by discussing two example results from the literature. One is the security proof by Alkim *et al.* [3] of the qTESLA signature scheme [2] in the quantum random-oracle model; the other is the recent work by Alagic, Bai, Katz and Majenz [1] on the quantum security of the famous Even-Mansour cipher. In both these works, the adaptivity of the attacker was a serious obstacle and caused a significant overhead and additional complications in the proof. With our results, these complications could have been avoided without sacrificing much in the security loss (as would be the case with using a naive compiler). We also exploit our adaptive-to-static compiler in our second main contribution, discussed below.

Interestingly, all three example applications are in the realm of quantum security (of a classical scheme). This seems to suggest that the kind of adaptivity we consider here is not so much of a hurdle in the case of classical queries. Indeed, in that case, a typical argument works by inspecting the entire query transcript and identifying an event with the property that conditioned on this event, whatever needs to be shown holds *with certainty*, and then it remains to show that this event is very likely to occur. In the case of quantum queries, this kind of reasoning does not apply since one cannot "inspect" the query transcript anymore; instead, one then typically resorts to some sort of hybrid argument where queries are replaced one-by-one, and then adaptivity of the queries may — and sometimes does, as we discuss — form a serious obstacle.

Quantum-Security of a Split-Key PRF. In the upcoming transition to post-quantum secure cryptographic standards, *combiners* may play an important role. A combiner can be used compile several cryptographic schemes into a new, "combined" scheme, which offers the same (or a similar) functionality, and so that the new scheme is secure as long as *at least one* of the original schemes is secure. For example, combining a well-established but quantum-insecure scheme with a believed-to-be quantum-secure (but less well studied) scheme then offers the best of both worlds: it offers security against quantum attacks, should there really be a quantum computer in the future, but it also offers some protection in case the latter scheme turns out to be insecure (or less secure than expected) even against classical attacks. In other words, using a combiner in this context ensures that we are not making things less secure by trying to aim for quantum security.

In [6], Giacon, Heuer and Poettering showed that any *split-key PRF* (skPRF) gives rise to a secure KEM combiner. In more detail, they show that if a skPRF is used in the (rather) obvious way as a key-derivation function in a KEM combiner, then the resulting combined KEM is IND-CCA secure if at least one of the component KEMs is IND-CCA secure. They also suggest a few candidates for skPRFs. The most efficient of the proposed constructions is a hash-based skPRF, which is proven secure in [6] in the random-oracle model. However, in the context of a quantum attack, which is in particular relevant in the above example application of a combiner, it is crucial to prove security in the *quantum* random-oracle model [4]. Here, we close this gap by proving security of the hash-based skPRF construction proposed by Giacon *et al.* in the quantum random-oracle model.

Our security proof crucially exploits our adaptive-to-static compiler to reduce a general, adaptive attacker/distinguisher to a static one. Namely, in spirit, our security proof is a typical hybrid proof, where we replace, one by one, the queries to the (sk)PRF by queries to a truly random function; however, the crux is that for each hybrid, corresponding to a particular function query that is to be replaced, the closeness of the current to the previous hybrid depends on the number of hash queries *between the current and the previously replaced function query*. In case of an adaptive $\mathcal{A}$, *each* such "window" of hash queries between two function queries could be as large as the total number of hash queries in the worst case, giving rise to a huge multiplicative blow-up when using this naive bound. Instead, for a static $\mathcal{A}$, each such window is bounded by a fixed number, with the sum of these numbers being the total number of hash queries.

By means of our compiler, we can turn the possibly adaptive $\mathcal{A}$ into a static one (almost) for free, and this way avoid an unnecessary blow-up, respectively bypass additional complications that arise by trying to avoid this blow-up by other means.

2   Preliminaries

We consider oracle algorithms $\mathcal{A}^{\mathcal{O}_1,\ldots,\mathcal{O}_n}$ that make queries to (possibly unspecified) oracles $\mathcal{O}_1,\ldots,\mathcal{O}_n$, see Fig. 1 (left). Sometimes, and in particular when the oracles are not specified, we just write $\mathcal{A}$ and leave it implicit that $\mathcal{A}$ makes oracle calls. We allow $\mathcal{A}$ to be classical or quantum, and in the latter case we may also allow the queries (to some of the oracles) to be quantum; however, the choice of *which* oracle is queried is always classical. For the purpose of our work, we may assume $\mathcal{A}$ to have no input; any potential input could be hardwired into $\mathcal{A}$. For a vector $\mathbf{q} = (q_1,\ldots,q_n) \in \mathbb{N}^n$, we say that $\mathcal{A}$ is a $\mathbf{q}$-*query* oracle algorithm if it makes at most q_i queries to the oracle $\mathcal{O}_i$.

In general, such an oracle algorithm $\mathcal{A}$ may decide *adaptively* which oracle to query at what step, dependent on previous oracle responses. In contrast to this, a *static* oracle algorithm has an arbitrary but pre-defined order in querying the oracles.

Our goal will be to transform any *adaptive* oracle algorithm $\mathcal{A}$ into a *static* oracle algorithm $\bar{\mathcal{A}}$ that is functionally equivalent, while keeping the blow-up in query complexity for each individual oracle, i.e., the blow-up for each individual q_i, small. By *functionally equivalent* (for certain oracle instantiations) we mean the respective executions of $\mathcal{A}^{O_1,\dots,O_n}$ and $\bar{\mathcal{A}}^{O_1,\dots,O_n}$ give rise to the same output distribution *for all* (the considered) instantiations $O_1,\dots,O_n$ of the oracles $\mathcal{O}_1,\dots,\mathcal{O}_n$. In case of *quantum* oracle algorithms, we require the output state to be the same.

For this purpose, we declare that an *interactive oracle algorithm* $\mathcal{B}$ is an interactive algorithm with two distinct interaction interfaces, one for the interaction with $\mathcal{A}$ (we call this the *simulation interface*), and one for the oracle queries (we call this the *oracle interface*), see Fig. 1 (middle). For any oracle algorithm $\mathcal{A}$, we then denote by $\mathcal{B}[\mathcal{A}]$ the oracle algorithm that is obtained by composing $\mathcal{A}$ and $\mathcal{B}$ in the obvious way. In other words, $\mathcal{B}[\mathcal{A}]$ runs $\mathcal{A}$ and answers all of $\mathcal{A}$'s oracle queries using its simulation interface; furthermore, $\mathcal{B}[\mathcal{A}]$ outputs whatever $\mathcal{A}$ outputs at the end of this run of $\mathcal{A}$, see Fig. 1 (right).[2]

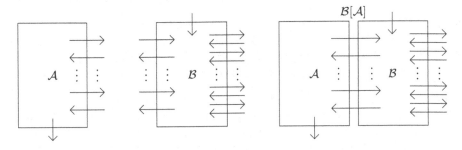

Fig. 1. An oracle algorithm $\mathcal{A}$ (left), an interactive oracle algorithm $\mathcal{B}$ (middle), and the oracle algorithm $\mathcal{B}[\mathcal{A}]$ obtained by composing $\mathcal{A}$ and $\mathcal{B}$ (right).

In contrast to $\mathcal{A}$ (where, for our purpose, any input could be hardwired), we explicitly allow an interactive oracle algorithm $\mathcal{B}$ to obtain an input. Indeed, our transformation, which turns any adaptive oracle algorithm $\mathcal{A}$ into a static oracle algorithm $\bar{\mathcal{A}}$, needs to "know" $\mathbf{q}$, i.e., the number of queries $\mathcal{A}$ makes to the different oracles. Thus, this will be provided in the form of an input to $\mathcal{B}$; for reasons to be clear, it be provided in unary, i.e., as $1^{\mathbf{q}} := (1^{q_1},\dots,1^{q_n})$.

We stress that we do not put any computational restriction on the oracle algorithms $\mathcal{A}$ (beyond bounding the queries to the individual oracles); however,

---

[2] Note, we silently assume consistency between $\mathcal{A}$ and $\mathcal{B}$, i.e. $\mathcal{A}$ should send a message when $\mathcal{B}$ expects one and the format of these messages should match the format of the messages that $\mathcal{B}$ expects (and vice versa), so that the above composition makes sense. Should $\mathcal{B}$ encounter some inconsistency, it will abort.

we do want our transformation to preserve efficiency. Therefore, we say that an interactive oracle algorithm $\mathcal{B}$ is *polynomial-time* if the number of local computation steps it performs is bounded to be polynomial in its input size, and where we declare that copying an *incoming* message on the simulation interface to an *outgoing* message on the oracle interface, and vice versa, is unit cost (irrespectively of the size of the message). By providing $\mathbf{q}$ in unary, we thus ensure that $\mathcal{B}$ is polynomial-time in $q_1 + \cdots + q_n$.

3   A General Adaptive-to-Static Reduction for Multi-oracle Algorithms

3.1   Our Result

Let $n \in \mathbb{N}$ be an arbitrary positive integer. We present here a generic adaptiv-to-static compiler $\mathcal{B}$ that, on input a vector $\mathbf{q} \in \mathbb{N}^n$, turns any *adaptive* $\mathbf{q}$-query oracle algorithm $\mathcal{A}^{\mathcal{O}_1,\ldots,\mathcal{O}_n}$ into a *static* $n\mathbf{q}$-query algorithm.

Theorem 1. *There exists a polynomial-time interactive oracle algorithm $\mathcal{B}$, such that for any $\mathbf{q} \in \mathbb{N}^n$ and any adaptive $\mathbf{q}$-query oracle algorithm $\mathcal{A}^{\mathcal{O}_1,\ldots,\mathcal{O}_n}$, the oracle algorithm $\mathcal{B}[\mathcal{A}](1^{\mathbf{q}})$ is a static $n\mathbf{q}$-query oracle algorithm that is functionally equivalent to $\mathcal{A}$ for all stateless instantiations of the oracles $\mathcal{O}_1,\ldots,\mathcal{O}_n$.*

Remark 1. As phrased, Theorem 1 applies to oracle algorithms $\mathcal{A}$ that have no input. This is merely for simplicity. In case of an oracle algorithm $\mathcal{A}$ that takes an input, we can simply apply the statement to the algorithm $\mathcal{A}(x)$ that has the input x hardwired, and so argue that Theorem 1 also applies in that case.

Remark 2. $\mathcal{B}[\mathcal{A}]$ is guaranteed to behave the same way as $\mathcal{A}$ for *stateless* (instantiations of the) oracles only. This is become most of the queries that $\mathcal{B}[\mathcal{A}]$ makes are actually dummy queries (i.e., queries on a default input and with the response ignored), which have no effect in case of stateless oracles, but may mess up things in case of stateful oracles. Theorem 1 extends to arbitrary stateful oracles if we allow $\mathcal{B}[\mathcal{A}]$ to *skip* queries instead of making dummy queries (but the skipped queries would still count towards the query complexity).

Given the vector $\mathbf{q} = (q_1,\ldots,q_n) \in \mathbb{N}^n$, the core of the problem is to find a *fixed* sequence of $\mathcal{O}_i$'s in which each individual $\mathcal{O}_i$ occurs at most nq_i times, and so that *every* sequence of $\mathcal{O}_i$'s that contains each individual $\mathcal{O}_i$ at most q_i times can be embedded into the former. We consider and solve this abstract problem in the following section, and then we wrap up the proof of Theorem 1 in Sect. 3.3.

3.2   The Technical Core

Let Σ be an non-empty finite set of cardinality n. We refer to Σ as the *alphabet*. As is common, Σ^* denotes the set of finite strings over the alphabet Σ. In other words, the elements of Σ^* are the strings/sequences $s = (s_1, \ldots, s_\ell) \in \Sigma^\ell$ with arbitrary $\ell \in \mathbb{N}$ (including $\ell = 0$).

Following standard terminology, for $s = (s_1, \ldots, s_\ell)$ and $s' = (s_1', \ldots, s_m')$ in Σ^*, the *concatenation* of s and s' is the string $s\|s' = (s_1, \ldots, s_\ell, s_1', \ldots, s_m')$, and s' is a *subsequence* of s, denoted $s' \sqsubseteq s$ if there exist integers $1 \le j_1 < \cdots < j_m \le \ell$ with $(s_{j_1}, \ldots, s_{j_m}) = (s_1', \ldots, s_m')$. Such an integer sequence $(j_1, \ldots, j_m)$ is then called an *embedding* of s' into s. [3]

Finally, for a function $q : \Sigma \to \mathbb{N}, \sigma \mapsto q_\sigma$, we say that $s = (s_1, \ldots, s_\ell) \in \Sigma^*$ has *characteristic* (at most) q if $\#\{i \mid s_i = \sigma\} = q_\sigma \; (\le q_\sigma)$ for any $\sigma \in \Sigma$.

Lemma 1 (Embedding Lemma). *Let Σ be an alphabet of size n, and let $q : \Sigma \to \mathbb{N}, \sigma \mapsto q_\sigma$. Then, there exists a string $s \in \Sigma^*$ with characteristic $n \cdot q : \sigma \mapsto n \cdot q_\sigma$ such that any string $s' \in \Sigma^*$ with characteristic at most q is a subsequence of s, i.e., $s' \sqsubseteq s$.*

The idea of the construction of the sequence s is quite simple: First, we evenly distribute $n \cdot q_\sigma$ copies of σ within the interval $(0, n]$ by "attaching" one copy of σ to every point in $(0, n]$ that is an integer multiple of $1/q_\sigma$ (see Fig. 2). Note that it may happen that different symbols are "attached" to the same point. Then, we walk along the interval from 0 and n, and one by one, collect the symbols we encounter in order to build up s' from left to right; in case we encounter a point with multiple symbols "attached" to it, we collect them in an arbitrary order.

Fig. 2. Constructing the string s by distributing the different symbols evenly within the interval $(0, n]$ (here with $3/q_{\sigma_1} = 2/q_{\sigma_2}$), and then collecting them from left to right.

It is then not too hard to convince yourself that this s indeed satisfies the claim. Namely, for any $s' = (s_1', \ldots, s_m')$ as considered, we can again walk along the interval from 0 and n, and we will then encounter all the symbols of s', one by one: we will encounter the symbol s_1' within the walk from 0 to $1/q_{s_1'}$, the symbol s_2' then within the walk from $1/q_{s_1'}$ to $1/q_{s_1'} + 1/q_{s_2'}$, etc.

Putting this idea into a formal proof is somewhat tedious, but in the end not too difficult. In order to formalize things properly, we generalize the standard notion of a sequence $s \in \Sigma^*$ in a way that allows us to talk about "attaching" a symbol to a point on $\mathbb{R}$, etc., in a rigorous way. Formally, we define a *line sequence* to be an arbitrary finite (possibly empty) subset $S \subseteq \mathbb{R} \times \Sigma$, i.e.,

$$S = \{(t_1, s_1), \ldots, (t_\ell, s_\ell)\} \in \mathcal{P}_{<\infty}(\mathbb{R} \times \Sigma),$$

---

[3] We use *string* and *sequence* interchangeably; however, following standard terminology, there is a difference between a *substring* and *subsequence*: namely, a substring is a subsequence that admits an embedding with $j_{i+1} = j_i + 1$.

where w.l.o.g. we will always assume that $t_1 \leq \ldots \leq t_\ell$. We may think of the symbol s_i to "occur at the time" t_i.[4] For a subset $T \subset \mathbb{R}$, the set $\mathcal{P}_{<\infty}(T \times \Sigma)$ then obviously denotes the set of line sequences with $t_1, \ldots, t_\ell \in T$.

Assuming that the alphabet Σ is equipped with a total order $\leq$, any line sequence $S = \{(t_1, s_1), \ldots, (t_\ell, s_\ell)\}$ is naturally associated with the ordinary sequence

$$\pi(S) := (s_1, \ldots, s_\ell) \in \Sigma^*,$$

which is uniquely determined by the convention $t_1 \leq \ldots \leq t_\ell$ and insisting on $s_i \leq s_j$ whenever $t_i = t_j$ for $i < j$.

This *projection* $\pi : \mathcal{P}_{<\infty}(\mathbb{R} \times \Sigma) \to \Sigma^*$ preserves the characteristic of the sequence, i.e., if $s = (s_1, \ldots, s_\ell) = \pi(S)$ then

$$\#\{t \mid (t, \sigma) \in S\} = \#\{i \mid s_i = \sigma\} \tag{1}$$

for any $\sigma \in \Sigma$. Furthermore, for $T, T' \subset \mathbb{R}$ with $T < T'$ point-wise, and for $S \in \mathcal{P}_{<\infty}(T \times \Sigma)$ and $S' \in \mathcal{P}_{<\infty}(T' \times \Sigma)$, it is easy to see that $\pi(S \cup S') = \pi(S) \| \pi(S')$, from which it then follows that for ordinary sequences $s, s' \in \Sigma^*$

$$s \sqsubseteq \pi(S) \wedge s' \sqsubseteq \pi(S') \implies s \| s' \sqsubseteq \pi(S) \| \pi(S') = \pi(S \cup S'). \tag{2}$$

A final, simple observation, which follows directly from the definitions, is that for $\sigma \in \Sigma$, i.e. a sequence of length $m = 1$, $\sigma \sqsubseteq \pi(S)$ holds if and only if there exists a time $t \in \mathbb{R}$ such that $(t, \sigma) \in S$.

Proof of Lemma 1. For any symbol $\sigma \in \Sigma$ let S_σ be a line sequence

$$S_\sigma := \left\{ \tfrac{1}{q_\sigma}, \ldots, \tfrac{nq_\sigma}{q_\sigma} \right\} \times \{\sigma\} \in \mathcal{P}_{<\infty}((0, n] \times \Sigma),$$

and set $S := \bigcup_{\sigma \in \Sigma} S_\sigma$. We will show that $s := \pi(S)$ is as claimed.

The claim on the characteristic of s follows from the preservation of the characteristic under π, i.e. (1), and from $\#\{t \mid (t, \sigma) \in S\} = \#S_\sigma = n \cdot q_\sigma$, which holds by construction of S.

Let $s' = (s'_1, \ldots, s'_m) \in \Sigma^*$ be arbitrary with characteristic bounded by q. We consider the times $\tau_j := 1/q_{s'_1} + \cdots + 1/q_{s'_j}$ for $j \in \{1, \ldots, m\}$, and we let T_j be the interval

$$T_j := (\tau_{j-1}, \tau_j] = (\tau_{j-1}, \tau_{j-1} + \tfrac{1}{q'_j}] \subset \mathbb{R},$$

and decompose $S = S_1 \cup \ldots \cup S_m$ with $S_j := S \cap (T_j \times \Sigma) \in \mathcal{P}_{<\infty}(T_j \times \Sigma)$. Here, we exploit that

$$\tau_m = \sum_{\sigma \in \Sigma} \frac{\#\{i \mid s'_i = \sigma\}}{q_\sigma} \leq \sum_{\sigma \in \Sigma} \frac{q_\sigma}{q_\sigma} = n,$$

and so the S_j's indeed cover all of $S \in \mathcal{P}_{<\infty}((0, n] \times \Sigma)$. Given that the interval $T_j \subset (0, n]$ has size $1/q_{s'_j}$, there exists a time $t_j \in T_j \cap \{\frac{1}{q_\sigma}, \ldots, \frac{nq_\sigma}{q_\sigma}\}$. But then,

---

[4] Note that we allow $t_i = t_j$ for $i \neq j$ while the definition prohibits $(t_i, s_i) = (t_j, s_j)$. If desired, one could allow the latter by letting S be a multi-set, but this is not necessary for us.

$(t_j, s'_j) \in S_j$ by construction of S, and therefore $s'_j \sqsubseteq \pi(S_j)$. Finally, since $T_{j-1} < T_j$, property (2) implies that

$$s' = s'_1 \| \cdots \| s'_m \sqsubseteq \pi(S_1 \cup \ldots \cup S_m) = s$$

which was to be shown.

While Lemma 1 above settles the existence question, the following two observations settle the corresponding efficiency questions. For concreteness, we assume $\Sigma = \{1, \ldots, n\}$ below, and thus can identify the function $q : \Sigma \to \mathbb{N}$, $\sigma \mapsto q_\sigma$ with the vector $\mathbf{q} = (q_1, \ldots, q_n)$.

First, we observe that the line sequence S defined in the proof above, as well as its projection $s = \pi(S)$, can be computed in polynomial time in $q_1 + \cdots + q_n$; thus, we have the following.

Lemma 2. *There exists a polynomial-time algorithm that, on input $1^\mathbf{q}$, computes a string $s \in \Sigma^*$ as specified in the proof of Lemma 1.*

Furthermore, for any $s' \in \Sigma^*$ with characteristic at most q, for which we then know by Lemma 1 that s' can be embedded into s, the following ensures that this embedding can be computed efficiently and *on the fly*.

Lemma 3. *There exists a polynomial-time algorithm $\mathcal{E}$ such that for every string $s \in \Sigma^*$ and every subsequence $s' = (s'_1, \ldots, s'_m) \sqsubseteq s$, the following holds. Computing inductively $j_i \leftarrow \mathcal{E}(s, s'_i, j_{i-1})$ for every $i \in [m]$, where $j_0 := 0$, results in an increasing sequence $j_1 < \cdots < j_m$ with*

$$s' = (s_{j_1}, \ldots, s_{j_m}) .$$

The algorithm $\mathcal{E}$ simply follows the obvious greedy strategy: for each s'_i it looks for the next j_i for which $s'_i = s_{j_i}$. More formally:

Proof. The algorithm $\mathcal{E}(s, s'_i, j_{i-1})$ computes

$$j_i := \min \{k \in \mathbb{N} \mid j_{i-1} < k \leq m, s_k = s'_i\} . \tag{3}$$

It can be easily shown that the minimum is well-defined, i.e. taken over a non-empty set for each i by the assumption that s' is a subsequence of s, and thus by construction, every j_i is such that $s'_i = s_{j_i}$ while keeping $j_1 < \cdots < j_n$ increasing. This concludes the proof. $\square$

3.3 Wrapping up the Proof of Theorem 1

The claimed interactive oracle algorithm $\mathcal{B}$ now works in the obvious way. On input $\mathbf{q}$ (provided in unary) and for any $\mathcal{A}$, $\mathcal{B}[\mathcal{A}]$ will make static oracle queries to $\mathcal{O}_{s_1}, \mathcal{O}_{s_2}, \ldots, \mathcal{O}_{s_{nQ}}$, where $s = (s_1, \ldots, s_{nQ}) \in \{1, \ldots, n\}^*$ is the string promised to exist by Lemma 1, with $Q = q_1 + \cdots + q_n$. In more detail, it first computes s using the algorithm from Lemma 2. Then, for the i-th oracle query that $\mathcal{B}$

receives from $\mathcal{A}$ (starting with $i = 1$), and which consists of the identifier $s_i' \in \{1, \ldots, n\}$ of which oracle to query now and of the actual input to the oracle $\mathcal{O}_{s_i'}$, the algorithm $\mathcal{B}$ does the following: it computes $j_i \leftarrow \mathcal{E}(s, s_i', j_{i-1})$ using the algorithm from Lemma 3, makes dummy queries to $\mathcal{O}_{s_{j_{i-1}+1}}, \ldots, \mathcal{O}_{s_{j_i - 1}}$, and forwards $\mathcal{A}$'s query input to $\mathcal{O}_{s_{j_i}} = \mathcal{O}_{s_i'}$. The fact that $(j_1, \ldots, j_Q)$ computed this way forms an embedding of $s' = (s_1', \ldots, s_Q')$ into s ensures that $\mathcal{B}$ is able to forward all the queries that $\mathcal{A}$ makes to the right oracle, and so $\mathcal{A}$ will produce its output as in an ordinary run with direct adaptive access to the oracles.

3.4 Applications

To demonstrate the usefulness of our adaptive-to-static compiler, we briefly discuss three results from the literature. For two of them, the adaptivity of the attacker was explicitly declared as an obstacle in the security proof, and dealing with it complicated the proof substantially. These complications could be avoided/removed by means of our adaptive-to-static compiler. For the third one, we can immediately strengthen one of the results, which is restricted to hold for static multi-oracle adversaries, by dropping this restriction via our compiler.

Quantum Security of qTESLA. Our first application is in the context of qTESLA [2], which is a signature scheme that made it into the second round of the NIST post-quantum competition. Its security is based on the Ring-LWE problem, to which the authors of [3] give a reduction in the quantum random-oracle model (QROM).[5] In the reduction, which starts from the security notion of *Unforgeability under Chosen Message Attack* (UF-CMA), the adversary can query a random-oracle H as well as a signing oracle, where the order of oracle queries may be adaptive.

The reduction strategy of [3] applies only to a static adversary, with a fixed query pattern. Thus, the authors first compile the adaptive into a naive static attacker by letting it do q_H (the number of H-queries of the original adaptive adversary) H-queries between any two signing queries. Leaving it with this would blow up the number of H-queries to $q_S q_H$. In order to avoid that, they give the attacker a "*live-switch*", meaning that each query to H may be in superposition of making the query and not making the query, and the total "*query magnitude*" on actual H-queries is still restricted to q_H. Not so surprising, adding even more "quantumness" to the problem in this way, makes the analysis more complicated (compared to using standard "all-or-nothing" static queries and a standard classical bound on the query complexity), but it allows the authors to avoid the above blow-up in the (classical) query complexity to transpire into the security loss. The overall loss they obtain in the end is $O((q_S q_H^2 + q_S^3 + q_S^2 q_H) \cdot \epsilon)$ for small ϵ determined by the parameters of the scheme.

---

[5] We note that some versions of qTESLA have been broken [8], but the attack only applies to an optimized variant that was developed for the NIST-competition, and does not apply to the scheme in [3] that we discuss here.

Since the security reduction in [3] intertwines the adaptive to static hurdle with other aspects of the proof, we cannot simply insert our Theorem 1 and then continue the proof as is. Still, by applying our result, we could obtain a static adversary with almost no cost in the number of H-queries, avoiding the need for the rather complicated "live-switch superposition" attacker, thus simplifying the overall proof significantly. Furthermore, looking ahead at Sect. 4, our result allows us to obtain the much better $O(\sqrt{q_O q_H^2 \epsilon} + \sqrt{q_O^2 q_H \epsilon})$ loss in a similar context — similar in the sense that it also involves two oracles where one reprograms the other at some high-entropy input. The adaptive to static reduction there allows us to apply some additional QROM tools that could potentially also be applied in the setting of qTESLA to improve the bound. However, actually doing this would require us to rewrite the entire proof of [3], which we consider outside the scope of this work.

Quantum Security of the Function FX. Our second application is to [7], where the post-quantum security of the FX key-length extension is studied (which is a generalization of the Even-Mansour cipher). In a first part, post-quantum security of FX is shown under the restriction that the inputs to the queries are fixed in advance. In a second part, towards avoiding this restriction, the authors consider a variation of the FX construction, which they call FFX (for "function FX"), and they show in their Theorem 3 post-quantum security of FFX under the restriction that the attacker is *"order consistent"*, as they call it in [7], which is precisely our notion of a *static* multi-oracle algorithm. Thus, by a direct application of our Theorem 1, this restriction can be dropped (almost) for free, i.e., with a small constant blow-up on the attackers advantage.

Quantum Security of the Even-Mansour Cipher. The recent work [1] shows full post-quantum security of the (unmodified) Even-Mansour cipher. Is in the case of qTESLA, the fact that the attacker can choose adaptively whether to query the public permutation of the cipher complicates the proof. Indeed, as is explained on page 3 in [1], this adaptivity issue forces the authors to extend the blinding lemma of Alagic et al. to a variant that gives a bound in terms of the *expected* number of queries. While the authors succeed in providing such an extended version of the blinding lemma (Lemma 3 in [1]), it further increases the complexity of an already involved proof. [6]

Thus, again, our Theorem 1 could be used to simplify the given proof by bypassing the complications that arise due to the attacker choosing adaptively which oracle to query at what point.

---

[6] To be fully precise, Lemma 3 in [1] also generalizes the original blinding lemma in a different direction by allowing to reprogram to an arbitrary value instead of a uniformly random one; however, this generalization comes for free in that the original proof still applies up to obvious changes, while allowing an expected number of queries, which is needed to deal with the adaptivity issue, requires a new proof.

4   Quantum Security of a Split-Key PRF

4.1   Hybrid Security and skPRFs

A *split-key pseudorandom function* (skPRF), as introduced in [6], is a polynomial-time computable function $F : \mathcal{K}_1 \times \cdots \times \mathcal{K}_n \times \mathcal{X} \rightarrow \mathcal{Y}$ that is a pseudorandom function (PRF) in the standard sense *for every $i \in [n]$* when considered as a keyed function with key space $\mathcal{K}_i$ and message space $\mathcal{K}_1 \times \cdots \times \mathcal{K}_{i-1} \times \mathcal{K}_{i+1} \times \cdots \times \mathcal{K}_n \times \mathcal{X}$, with the additional restriction that the distinguisher $\mathcal{A}$ (in the standard PRF security definition) must use a fresh $x \in \mathcal{X}$ in every query $(k_1, \ldots, k_{i-1}, k_{i+1}, \ldots, k_n, x)$.

This restriction on the PRF distinguisher may look artificial, but is motivated by this definition of a skPRF being good enough for the intended purpose of a skPRF, namely to give rise to a *secure KEM combiner*. Indeed, [6] shows that the naturally combined KEM, obtained by concatenating the individual ciphertexts to $C = (c_1, \ldots, c_n)$, and combining the individual session keys $k_1, \ldots, k_n$ using the above mentioned skPRF as

$$K = F(k_1, \ldots, k_n, C) \,,$$

is IND-CCA secure if at least one of the individual KEM's is IND-CCA secure.

The paper [6] also proposes a particularly efficient hash-based construction, given by

$$F(k_1, \ldots, k_n, x) := H(g(k_1, \ldots, k_n), x) \tag{4}$$

where $g : \mathcal{K}_1 \times \cdots \times \mathcal{K}_n \rightarrow \mathcal{W}$ is a polynomial-time mapping with the property that, for some small ϵ,

$$\Pr_{k_i \leftarrow \mathcal{K}_i} [g(k_1, \ldots, k_n) = w] \leq \epsilon \,, \tag{5}$$

for every $i \in [n]$ and for every $k_1, \ldots, k_{i-1}, k_{i+1}, \ldots, k_n$ and every w; furthermore, $H : \mathcal{W} \rightarrow \mathcal{Y}$ is a cryptographic hash function. Simple choices for the function g are $g(k_1, \ldots, k_n) = (k_1, \ldots, k_n)$ and $g(k_1, \ldots, k_n) = k_1 + \cdots + k_n$.

It is shown in [6] that this construction is a skPRF when H is modelled as a random-oracle; indeed, it is shown that the distinguishing advantage is upper-bounded by $q_H \epsilon$, where q_H is the number of queries to the random-oracle H.

Given the natural use of combiners in the context of the upcoming transition to post-quantum cryptography, it is natural — and well-motivated — to ask whether F can be proven to be a skPRF in the presence of a *quantum attacker*, i.e., when H is modeled as a *quantum* random-oracle. Below, we answer this in the affirmative.

4.2   Quantum-Security of the skPRF

The goal of this section is to show the security of the skPRF (4) in the quantum random-oracle model. In essence, this requires proving that F is a PRF (in the quantum random-oracle model) with respect to *any* of the k_i's being the key, subject to the restriction of asking a fresh x in each query.

To simplify the notation, we fix the index $i \in [n]$ and simply write k for k_i and x for $(k_1, \ldots, k_{i-1}, k_{i+1}, \ldots, k_n, x)$, and we abstract away the properties of the function g as follows. We let

$$F(k, x) := H(h(k, x)),$$

where $h : \mathcal{K} \times \mathcal{X} \to \mathcal{W}$ is an arbitrary function with the property that, for some parameter $\epsilon > 0$,

$$\Pr_{k \leftarrow \mathcal{K}} [h(k, x) = w] \leq \epsilon \qquad (6)$$

for all $w \in \mathcal{W}$ and $x \in \mathcal{X}$. Furthermore, in the PRF security game, we restrict the attacker/distinguisher $\mathcal{A}$ to queries x with a fresh value of $h(k, x)$, no matter what k is.

More formally, let $\mathcal{A}^{\mathcal{H}, \mathcal{O}}$ be an arbitrary quantum oracle algorithm, making quantum superposition queries to an oracle $\mathcal{H}$ and classical queries to another oracle $\mathcal{O}$, with the restriction that for every query x to $\mathcal{O}$ it holds that

$$h(\kappa, x) \neq h(\kappa, x'), \qquad (7)$$

for any prior query x' to $\mathcal{O}$ and all $\kappa \in \mathcal{K}$. For any such oracle algorithm $\mathcal{A}^{\mathcal{H}, \mathcal{O}}$, we consider the standard PRF security games

$$\mathsf{PR}^1 := \mathcal{A}^{H, F} \qquad \text{and} \qquad \mathsf{PR}^0 := \mathcal{A}^{H, R},$$

obtained by instantiating $\mathcal{H}$ with a random function H (the random-oracle) in both games, and in one game we instantiate $\mathcal{O}$ with the pseudorandom function F, which we understand to return $F(k, x)$ on query x for a random $k \leftarrow \mathcal{K}$, chosen once and for all queries, and in the other we instantiate $\mathcal{O}$ with a truly random function R instead.

We show that the distinguishing advantage for these two games is bounded as follows.

Theorem 2. *Let $\mathcal{A}^{\mathcal{H}, \mathcal{O}}$ be a $(q_{\mathcal{H}}, q_{\mathcal{O}})$-query oracle algorithm satisfying (7). Then*

$$\left| \Pr \left[1 \leftarrow \mathsf{PR}^1 \right] - \Pr \left[1 \leftarrow \mathsf{PR}^0 \right] \right| \leq 4\sqrt{2q_{\mathcal{O}}^2 q_{\mathcal{H}} \epsilon} + 4\sqrt{2q_{\mathcal{H}}^2 q_{\mathcal{O}} \epsilon}.$$

We can now apply Theorem 2 to the function $h(k, x) := (g(k_1, \ldots, k_n), \tilde{x})$, where $k := k_i$ and $x := (k_1, \ldots, k_{i-1}, k_{i+1}, \ldots, k_n, \tilde{x})$. Indeed, the condition (5) on g implies the corresponding condition (7) on h, and the restriction on $\tilde{x}$ being fresh in the original skPRF definition implies the above restriction on $h(k, x)$ being fresh no matter what k is, i.e., 6). Thus, we obtain the following.

Corollary 1. *For any function g satisfying (5) for a given $\epsilon > 0$, the function $F(k_1, \ldots, k_n, x) := H(g(k_1, \ldots, k_n), x)$ is a skPRF in the quantum random-oracle model with distinguishing advantage at most $4\sqrt{2q_{\mathcal{O}}^2 q_{\mathcal{H}} \epsilon} + 4\sqrt{2q_{\mathcal{H}}^2 q_{\mathcal{O}} \epsilon}$.*

4.3   Proof of Theorem 2

Proof (of Theorem 2). Let $\mathcal{A}^{\mathcal{H},\mathcal{O}}$ be an oracle algorithm as considered in the previous subsection. Thanks to Theorem 1, taking a factor-2 blow-up in the query complexity into account, we may assume $\mathcal{A}$ to be a *static* $(q_{\mathcal{H}}, q_{\mathcal{O}})$-query oracle algorithm. It will be convenient to write such a static algorithm as

$$\mathcal{A}^{[\mathcal{H}_0 \mathcal{O} \mathcal{H}_1 \mathcal{O} \mathcal{H}_2 ... \mathcal{O} \mathcal{H}_{q_{\mathcal{O}}}]},$$

where each block $\mathcal{H}_i = \mathcal{H} \cdots \mathcal{H}$ consists of a (possibly empty) sequence of symbols $\mathcal{H}$ of length $q_i^{\mathcal{H}} = |\mathcal{H}_i|$, and with the understanding that $\mathcal{A}$ first makes $q_0^{\mathcal{H}}$ queries to $\mathcal{H}$, then a query to $\mathcal{O}$, then $q_1^{\mathcal{H}}$ queries to $\mathcal{H}$, etc., where, obviously, $q_0^{\mathcal{H}} + \cdots + q_{q_{\mathcal{O}}}^{\mathcal{H}} = q_{\mathcal{H}}$ then. Instantiating $\mathcal{H}$ with H, and $\mathcal{O}$ with F and R, respectively, we can then write

$$\mathsf{PR}^0 = \mathcal{A}^{[\mathbf{H}_0 R \mathbf{H}_1 ... R \mathbf{H}_{q_{\mathcal{O}}}]} \quad \text{and} \quad \mathsf{PR}^1 = \mathcal{A}^{[\mathbf{H}_0 F \mathbf{H}_1 ... F \mathbf{H}_{q_{\mathcal{O}}}]}.$$

For the proof, we introduce certain hybrid games. For this purpose, we introduce the following alternative (*stateful* and *R-dependent*) instantiation H' of $\mathcal{H}$. To start with, H' is set to be equal to H, but whenever R is queried on some input x, H' is *reprogrammed* at the point $h(k, x)$ to the value $H'(h(k, x)) := R(x)$. For any i, we now define the two hybrid games

$$\mathsf{PR}_i^2 := \mathcal{A}^{[\mathbf{H}_0 R ... R \mathbf{H}_i F \mathbf{H}'_{i+1} F ... F \mathbf{H}'_{q_{\mathcal{O}}}]}$$

$$\widetilde{\mathsf{PR}}_i^2 := \mathcal{A}^{[\mathbf{H}_0 R ... R \mathbf{H}_i R \mathbf{H}'_{i+1} F ... F \mathbf{H}'_{q_{\mathcal{O}}}]}$$

and also spell out

$$\mathsf{PR}_{i+1}^2 = \mathcal{A}^{[\mathbf{H}_0 R ... R \mathbf{H}_i R \mathbf{H}_{i+1} F ... F \mathbf{H}'_{q_{\mathcal{O}}}]}$$

to emphasize its relation to $\widetilde{\mathsf{PR}}_i^2$. We note that in all of the above, the first occurrences of $\mathcal{H}$ and $\mathcal{O}$ are instantiated with R and H, respectively, but at some point we switch to R and H' instead.

The extreme cases match up the games we are interested in. Indeed,

$$\mathsf{PR}_0^2 = \mathcal{A}^{[\mathbf{H}_0 F \mathbf{H}'_1 ... F \mathbf{H}'_{q_{\mathcal{O}}}]} = \mathcal{A}^{[\mathbf{H}_0 F \mathbf{H}_1 ... F \mathbf{H}_{q_{\mathcal{O}}}]} = \mathsf{PR}^1,$$

where we exploit that there are no queries to R and thus H' remains equal to H, and, by definition,

$$\mathsf{PR}_{q_{\mathcal{O}}}^2 = \mathcal{A}^{[\mathbf{H}_0 R \mathbf{H}_1 ... R \mathbf{H}_{q_{\mathcal{O}}}]} = \mathsf{PR}^0.$$

Our goal is to prove the closeness of the following games

$$\mathsf{PR}^1 = \mathsf{PR}_0^2 \approx \widetilde{\mathsf{PR}}_0^2 \approx \mathsf{PR}_1^2 \cdots \approx \mathsf{PR}_{q_{\mathcal{O}}-1}^2 \approx \widetilde{\mathsf{PR}}_{q_{\mathcal{O}}-1}^2 \approx \mathsf{PR}_{q_{\mathcal{O}}}^2 = \mathsf{PR}^0.$$

We do this by means of applying Lemma 4 and 5, which we state here and prove further down.

Lemma 4. *For each* $0 \leq i < q_{\mathcal{O}}$,

$$\left| \Pr\left[1 \leftarrow \mathsf{PR}_i^2\right] - \Pr\left[1 \leftarrow \widetilde{\mathsf{PR}}_i^2\right] \right| \leq 2\sqrt{\sum_{1 \leq j \leq i} q_j^{\mathcal{H}}\epsilon}\,.$$

Lemma 5. *For each* $0 \leq i < q_{\mathcal{O}}$,

$$\left| \Pr\left[1 \leftarrow \widetilde{\mathsf{PR}}_i^2\right] - \Pr\left[1 \leftarrow \mathsf{PR}_{i+1}^2\right] \right| \leq 2q_{i+1}^{\mathcal{H}}\sqrt{q_{\mathcal{O}}\epsilon}\,.$$

Indeed, by repeated applications of these lemmas, and additionally using that $q_0^{\mathcal{H}} + \cdots + q_i^{\mathcal{H}} \leq q_{\mathcal{H}}$ for all $0 \leq i \leq q_{\mathcal{O}}$, we obtain

$$\left| \Pr\left[1 \leftarrow \mathsf{PR}^1\right] - \Pr\left[1 \leftarrow \mathsf{PR}^0\right] \right| \leq 2\sum_{i=0}^{q_{\mathcal{O}}} \sqrt{\sum_{1 \leq j \leq i} q_j^{\mathcal{H}}\epsilon} + 2\sum_{i=0}^{q_{\mathcal{O}}} q_{i+1}^{\mathcal{H}}\sqrt{q_{\mathcal{O}}\epsilon}$$

$$\leq 2\sqrt{q_{\mathcal{O}}^2 q_{\mathcal{H}}\epsilon} + 2\sqrt{q_{\mathcal{H}}^2 q_{\mathcal{O}}\epsilon}$$

which concludes the claim of Theorem 2 when incorporating the factor-2 increase in $q_{\mathcal{H}}$ and $q_{\mathcal{O}}$ due to switching to a static $\mathcal{A}$. $\square$

It remains to prove Lemma 4 and 5, which we do below. In both proofs, we use the *gentle measurement lemma* [9, Lemma 9.4.1], which states that if a projective measurement has a very likely outcome then the measurement causes only little disturbance on the state. More formally, for any density operator ρ and any projector P, where $p := \mathsf{tr}(P\rho P)$ then is the probability to observe the outcome associated with P when measured using the measurement $\{P, \mathbb{I} - P\}$, the trace distance between the original state ρ and the post-measurement state $\rho' := P\rho P/p$ is bounded by $\sqrt{1-p}$. This in turn implies that ρ and ρ' can be distinguished with an advantage $\sqrt{1-p}$ only.

The proof of Lemma 4 additionally makes use of Zhandry's compressed oracle technique [10]. It is out of scope of this work to give a self-contained description of this technique; we refer to the original work [10] instead, or to [5], which offers an alternative concise description. At the core is the observation that one can *purify* the random choice of the function H and then, by switching to the Fourier basis and doing a suitable measurement, one can check whether a certain input x has been "recorded" in the database (mind though that such a measurement disturbs the state). If the outcome is negative then the oracle is still in a uniform superposition over all possible hash values for x, and as a consequence, when removing the purification by doing a full measurement of H (in the computational basis), $H(x)$ is ensured to be a "fresh" uniformly random value, with no information on $H(x)$ having been leaked in prior queries.

In the proof of Lemma 4, we use this technique to check whether *prior* to the crucial query, which is to F in one and to R in the other game, there was a query to H that would reveal the difference, and we use (6) to argue that it is unlikely that such a query occurred. Since this measurement has a likely outcome, it is also ensured by the gentle measurement lemma that this measurement causes little disturbance.

Proof (of Lemma 4). For convenience, we refer to the *crucial query* as the respective query to F and R that differs between

$$\mathsf{PR}_i^2 = \mathcal{A}^{[\mathbf{H}_0 R...R\mathbf{H}_i F\mathbf{H}'_{i+1}F...F\mathbf{H}'_{q_O}]} \quad \text{and} \quad \widetilde{\mathsf{PR}}_i^2 = \mathcal{A}^{[\mathbf{H}_0 R...R\mathbf{H}_i R\mathbf{H}'_{i+1}F...F\mathbf{H}'_{q_O}]}.$$

Furthermore, we let x be the input to that query, and we set $w := h(k, x)$, with k being the key chosen and used by F. Note that up to this very query, the two games are identical. Also, by (7) it is ensured that for any prior query x' to R it holds that $h(k, x') \neq w$.

First, we consider the games $\mathbf{G}^1$ and $\widetilde{\mathbf{G}}^1$ that work exactly as PR_i^2 and $\widetilde{\mathsf{PR}}_i^2$, respectively, except that, at the beginning of the games we set up the compressed oracle and answer all queries made to H prior to the crucial query using the compressed oracle. Then, once x is received during the crucial query, we do a full measurement of the purified (i.e. uncompressed) oracle in order to obtain the function H, which is then to be used in the remainder of the games. We note that setting up the function H' is then necessarily also deferred to after this measurement, where H' is then set to be equal to H, except that for any prior query x' to R it is reprogrammed to $H'(h(k, x')) := R(x')$. Only once H has been measured and H' set up as above, is the crucial query then actually answered.

It follows from basic properties of the compressed oracle that the respective output distributions of $\mathbf{G}^1$ and $\widetilde{\mathbf{G}}^1$ match with those of PR_i^2 and $\widetilde{\mathsf{PR}}_i^2$.

Then, we define $\mathbf{G}^2$ and $\widetilde{\mathbf{G}}^2$ from $\mathbf{G}^1$ and $\widetilde{\mathbf{G}}^1$, respectively, by introducing one more measurement. Namely, right after x is sent by $\mathcal{A}$ and before H is measured, we measure in the compressed oracle whether the input $w = h(k, x)$ has been recorded in the database, and in case of a positive outcome, the game aborts. By the gentle measurement lemma (and basic properties of the trace distance),

$$\left| \Pr\left[1 \leftarrow \mathbf{G}^1\right] - \Pr\left[1 \leftarrow \mathbf{G}^2\right] \right| \leq \sqrt{\Pr\left[\mathbf{G}^2 \text{ aborts}\right]}$$

and similarly for $\widetilde{\mathbf{G}}^1$ and $\widetilde{\mathbf{G}}^2$, where $\widetilde{\mathbf{G}}^2$ aborts with the same probability as $\mathbf{G}^2$.

By basic properties, after $t := q_0^{\mathcal{H}} + \cdots + q_i^{\mathcal{H}}$ queries to the compressed oracle, no more than t values have been recorded. I.e., if we were to measure, for the sake of the argument, the entire compressed oracle to obtain the full database D, it would hold that $\mathrm{supp}(D) := \{u \mid D(u) \neq \bot\}$ has cardinality at most t. Since k has not been used yet and so is still freshly random (i.e., independent of x and D), the high-entropy condition (6) then ensures that

$$\Pr\left[\widetilde{\mathbf{G}}^2 \text{ abort}\right] = \Pr\left[\mathbf{G}^2 \text{ abort}\right] = \Pr\left[w \in \mathrm{supp}(D)\right] \leq \sum_{j<i} q_j^{\mathcal{H}} \epsilon.$$

It remains to show that $\mathbf{G}^2$ and $\widetilde{\mathbf{G}}^2$ behave identically conditioned on not aborting. The only difference between the two games is that in $\mathbf{G}^2$ the crucial query is answered with $y := H(h(k, x)) = H(w)$ and H' is *not* reprogrammed at the point w, while in $\widetilde{\mathbf{G}}^2$ the crucial query is answered with $y := R(x)$ and H' *is* reprogrammed at the point w to $H'(w) := R(x)$. We argue that this difference is not noticable by $\mathcal{A}$.

First, we note that y is a fresh random value in both games. In the former game it is because, conditioned on not aborting, the compressed oracle at the register $h(k,x)$ is $\perp$, and so when uncompressing and measuring to obtain H, the hash value $H(w)$ will be a fresh random value. In the latter game it is because $R(x)$ is a truly random function and, due to (7), x has not been queried to R before.

Second, we observe that $y = H'(w)$ in both games. Indeed, in $\widetilde{\mathbf{G}}^2$ this holds by definition; in $\mathbf{G}^2$ it holds because $H'(w) = H(w)$, which follows from the fact that H' is reprogrammed only at points $w' = h(k,x')$ with x' being a prior query to R, but then (7) ensures that $w' \neq w$.

Thus, in both games, from $\mathcal{A}$'s perspective, the tuple $(k, y, H', H\backslash w)$ of random variables has the same distribution, where $H\backslash w$ refers to the function (table of) H but with the value at the point w removed. The only difference is that in one game $H'(w) = H(w)$ and in the other not (necessarily). However, the future behavior of $\mathcal{A}$ in both games only depends on $(k, y, H', H\backslash w)$, and thus $\mathcal{A}$ behaves the same way in both games. Here we are exploiting that the future hash queries by $\mathcal{A}$ are to H' (and not to H anymore), and, once more, we are using the restriction (7), here to ensure that for any future F-query x' by $\mathcal{A}$, it holds that $h(k, x') \neq w$, and thus the response does not depend on $H(w)$. Thus, $H(w)$ does indeed not affect $\mathcal{A}$'s behavior after the crucial query.

Exploiting that $\mathsf{PR}_i^2 = \mathbf{G}^1 \approx \mathbf{G}^2 = \widetilde{\mathbf{G}}^2 \approx \widetilde{\mathbf{G}}^1 = \widetilde{\mathsf{PR}}_i^2$, with the approximations bounded as discussed further up, we obtain the claimed closeness claim. This concludes the proof. $\qquad\square$

Proof of Lemma 5. In order to show the closeness between $\widetilde{\mathsf{PR}}_i^2$ and PR_{i+1}^2, we define the intermediate games

$$\mathbf{G}_{i,j} := \mathcal{A}^{[\mathbf{H}_0 R \ldots \mathbf{H}_i R \mathbf{H}'_{i,j} \mathbf{H}_{i,j} F \ldots F \mathbf{H}'_{q_\mathcal{O}}]}$$

for $0 \leq j \leq m := q_{i+1}^{\mathcal{H}}$, where $\mathbf{H}'_{i,j}$ and $\mathbf{H}_{i,j}$ consists of j and $m - j$ copies of H' and H respectively. Note that for the extreme cases we have

$$\mathbf{G}_{i,0} = \widetilde{\mathsf{PR}}_i^2 \qquad \text{and} \qquad \mathbf{G}_{i,m} = \mathsf{PR}_{i+1}^2.$$

Thus, it suffices to show closeness between $\mathbf{G}_{i,j}$ and $\mathbf{G}_{i,j+1}$ for any $0 \leq j < m$. Note that they only differ at one query, which is either to H' or to H, which we will refer to as the *crucial query* for convenience. In the remainder, i and j are arbitrary (in the considered ranges) but fixed.

Define the games $\widetilde{\mathbf{G}}^1$ and $\mathbf{G}^1$ from $\mathbf{G}_{i,j}$ and $\mathbf{G}_{i,j+1}$ respectively as follows. Let X be the set of queries x made to R prior to the crucial query, and set $S := \{h(k,x) \,|\, x \in X\}$. We then measure the crucial query, which may be in a superposition, with the binary measurement that checks whether the crucial query is an element of S, and we abort if this is the case.

In case of a negative outcome, i.e., the crucial query is *not* in S, there is no difference between the reply provided by H and by H', and thus there is no difference between the two games — and in case of a positive outcome, they both abort. In order to argue that this measurement causes little disturbance, we again use the gentle measurement lemma to argue that

$$\left| \Pr \left[1 \leftarrow \mathbf{G}^1 \right] - \Pr \left[1 \leftarrow \mathbf{G}_{i,j+1} \right] \right| \leq \sqrt{\Pr \left[\mathbf{G}^1 \text{ abort} \right]},$$

and correspondingly for $\mathbf{G}_{i,j}$ and $\widetilde{\mathbf{G}}^1$. So it remains to bound the abort probability. For the purpose of the argument, let us do a full measurement of the query, and let w be the outcome. We note that k has not been used yet, and thus remains a fresh random key, independent of w and X. Thus, using (6),

$$\Pr \left[\mathbf{G}^1 \text{ abort} \right] = \Pr \left[\widetilde{\mathbf{G}}^1 \text{ abort} \right] = \Pr \left[w \in S \right] \leq \sum_{x \in X} \Pr \left[w = h(k,x) \right] \leq q_{\mathcal{O}} \epsilon .$$

Adding up this error term over the sequence $\mathbf{G}_{i,0} \approx \cdots \approx \mathbf{G}_{i,m}$ of approximations, the proof is concluded.   □

Acknowledgments.

JD was funded by the ERC-ADG project ALGSTRONGCRYPTO (project number 740972). YHH was funded by the Dutch Research Agenda (NWA) project HAPKIDO (project number NWA.1215.18.002), which is financed by the Dutch Research Council (NWO).

References

1. Alagic, G., Bai, C., Katz, J., Majenz, C.: Post-quantum security of the Even-Mansour cipher. Cryptology ePrint Archive, Report 2021/1601 (2021). https://ia.cr/2021/1601
2. Alkim, E., Barreto, P.S.L.M., Bindel, N., Krämer, J., Longa, P., Ricardini, J.E.: The lattice-based digital signature scheme qTESLA. In: Conti, M., Zhou, J., Casalicchio, E., Spognardi, A. (eds.) ACNS 2020. LNCS, vol. 12146, pp. 441–460. Springer, Cham (2020). https://doi.org/10.1007/978-3-030-57808-4_22
3. Alkim, E., et al.: Revisiting TESLA in the quantum random oracle model. In: Lange, T., Takagi, T. (eds.) PQCrypto 2017. LNCS, vol. 10346, pp. 143–162. Springer, Cham (2017). https://doi.org/10.1007/978-3-319-59879-6_9
4. Boneh, D., Dagdelen, Ö., Fischlin, M., Lehmann, A., Schaffner, C., Zhandry, M.: Random oracles in a quantum world. In: Lee, D.H., Wang, X. (eds.) ASIACRYPT 2011. LNCS, vol. 7073, pp. 41–69. Springer, Heidelberg (2011). https://doi.org/10.1007/978-3-642-25385-0_3
5. Chung, K.-M., Fehr, S., Huang, Y.-H., Liao, T.-N.: On the compressed-oracle technique, and post-quantum security of proofs of sequential work. In: Canteaut, A., Standaert, F.-X. (eds.) EUROCRYPT 2021. LNCS, vol. 12697, pp. 598–629. Springer, Cham (2021). https://doi.org/10.1007/978-3-030-77886-6_21
6. Giacon, F., Heuer, F., Poettering, B.: KEM combiners. In: Abdalla, M., Dahab, R. (eds.) PKC 2018. LNCS, vol. 10769, pp. 190–218. Springer, Cham (2018). https://doi.org/10.1007/978-3-319-76578-5_7
7. Jaeger, J., Song, F., Tessaro, S.: Quantum key-length extension. In: Nissim, K., Waters, B. (eds.) TCC 2021. LNCS, vol. 13042, pp. 209–239. Springer, Cham (2021). https://doi.org/10.1007/978-3-030-90459-3_8

8. Lyubashevsky, V., Schwabe, P.: Round 2 official comment: qTESLA. https://csrc. nist.gov/CSRC/media/Projects/Post-Quantum-Cryptography/documents/ round-2/official-comments/qTESLA-round2-official-comment.pdf   (2019). Accessed 18 May 2022

9. Wilde, M.M.: From classical to quantum Shannon theory. arXiv preprint arXiv:1106.1445 (2011)

10. Zhandry, M.: How to record quantum queries, and applications to quantum indifferentiability. In: Boldyreva, A., Micciancio, D. (eds.) CRYPTO 2019. LNCS, vol. 11693, pp. 239–268. Springer, Cham (2019). https://doi.org/10.1007/978-3-030-26951-7_9

The Parallel Reversible Pebbling Game: Analyzing the Post-quantum Security of iMHFs

Jeremiah Blocki[iD], Blake Holman[iD], and Seunghoon Lee[(✉)][iD]

Purdue University, West Lafayette, IN 47906, USA
{jblocki,holman14,lee2856}@purdue.edu

Abstract. The classical (parallel) black pebbling game is a useful abstraction which allows us to analyze the resources (space, space-time, cumulative space) necessary to evaluate a function f with a static data-dependency graph G. Of particular interest in the field of cryptography are data-independent memory-hard functions $f_{G,H}$ which are defined by a directed acyclic graph (DAG) G and a cryptographic hash function H. The pebbling complexity of the graph G characterizes the amortized cost of evaluating $f_{G,H}$ multiple times as well as the total cost to run a brute-force preimage attack over a fixed domain $\mathcal{X}$, i.e., given $y \in \{0,1\}^*$ find $x \in \mathcal{X}$ such that $f_{G,H}(x) = y$. While a classical attacker will need to evaluate the function $f_{G,H}$ at least $m = |\mathcal{X}|$ times a quantum attacker running Grover's algorithm only requires $\mathcal{O}\left(\sqrt{m}\right)$ blackbox calls to a quantum circuit $C_{G,H}$ evaluating the function $f_{G,H}$. Thus, to analyze the cost of a quantum attack it is crucial to understand the space-time cost (equivalently width times depth) of the quantum circuit $C_{G,H}$. We first observe that a legal black pebbling strategy for the graph G does not necessarily imply the existence of a quantum circuit with comparable complexity—in contrast to the classical setting where any efficient pebbling strategy for G corresponds to an algorithm with comparable complexity for evaluating $f_{G,H}$. Motivated by this observation we introduce a new parallel reversible pebbling game which captures additional restrictions imposed by the No-Deletion Theorem in Quantum Computing. We apply our new reversible pebbling game to analyze the reversible space-time complexity of several important graphs: Line Graphs, Argon2i-A, Argon2i-B, and DRSample. Specifically, (1) we show that a line graph of size N has reversible space-time complexity at most $\mathcal{O}\left(N^{1+\frac{2}{\sqrt{\log N}}}\right)$. (2) We show that any (e, d)-reducible DAG has reversible space-time complexity at most $\mathcal{O}\left(Ne + dN2^d\right)$. In particular, this implies that the reversible space-time complexity of Argon2i-A and Argon2i-B are at most $\mathcal{O}\left(N^2 \log \log N/\sqrt{\log N}\right)$ and $\mathcal{O}\left(N^2/\sqrt[3]{\log N}\right)$, respectively. (3) We show that the reversible space-time complexity of DRSample is at most $\mathcal{O}\left(N^2 \log \log N/\log N\right)$. We also study the cumulative pebbling cost of reversible pebblings extending a (non-reversible) pebbling attack of Alwen and Blocki on depth-reducible graphs.

E. Kiltz and V. Vaikuntanathan (Eds.): TCC 2022, LNCS 13747, pp. 52–79, 2022.
https://doi.org/10.1007/978-3-031-22318-1_3

Keywords: Parallel reversible pebbling · Argon2i · DRSample · Data-independent memory-hard function

1   Introduction

The (parallel) black pebbling game [PH70, Coo73] is a powerful abstraction which can be used to analyze the resources (space, space-time, amortized space-time) necessary to evaluate any function f_G with a static data-dependency graph G. In the black pebbling game we are given a directed acyclic graph (DAG) $G = (V, E)$ where nodes intuitively represent intermediate data values and edges represent dependencies between these values, e.g., if $z = x \times y$ then we would add directed edges from nodes x and y to node z to indicate that x and y are required to compute z. However, while the parallel black pebbling game is a useful abstraction for classical computation it is not a suitable model for reversible computation as in quantum computation. In this paper, we introduce a parallel reversible pebbling game as an abstraction which can be used to analyze the resources required to build a reversible quantum circuit evaluating our function f_G. We use the parallel reversible pebbling game to analyze the space-time cost of several important graphs (the line graph, Argon2i-A, Argon2i-B, DRSample) associated with prominent data-independent memory-hard functions (iMHFs)—used in cryptography to design egalitarian proof of work puzzles and to protect low-entropy secrets (e.g., passwords) against brute-force attacks.

Review: Parallel Black Pebbling. The classical parallel black pebbling game begins with no pebbles on the graph ($P_0 = \{\}$), and during each round of the pebbling game, we may only place a new pebble on a node v if all of v's parents were pebbled in the previous round. Intuitively, if the data value X_v corresponding to node v is computed as $X_v := H(X_u, X_{v-1})$ then G would include directed edges (u, v) and $(v - 1, v)$ indicating that we cannot compute value X_v (resp. place a pebble on node v) unless X_u and X_{v-1} are already available in memory (resp. we already have pebbles on nodes u and $v - 1$). More formally, if $P_i \subseteq V$ denotes the set of pebbled nodes during round i, then we require that $\mathsf{parents}(P_{i+1} \setminus P_i, G) \subseteq P_i$ where $\mathsf{parents}(S, G) = \bigcup_{v \in S} \{u : (u, v) \in E\}$. In the black pebbling game we are given a subset $T \subseteq V$ of target nodes (corresponding to output data values) and the goal of the black pebbling game is to eventually place a pebble on each node in T. A pebbling $P = (P_0, P_1, \ldots, P_t)$ is legal if $P_0 = \{\}$ and $\mathsf{parents}(P_{i+1} \setminus P_i, G) \subseteq P_i$ for each $i < t$. Intuitively, the requirement that $\mathsf{parents}(P_{i+1} \setminus P_i, G) \subseteq P_i$ enforces the natural constraint that we cannot compute a new data value before all dependent data values are available in memory. In the sequential pebbling game, we additionally require that $|P_{i+1} \setminus P_i| \leq 1$ so that only one new pebble can be placed on the graph in each round while the parallel pebbling game has no such restriction. Thus, a legal parallel (resp. sequential) pebbling of a data-dependency graph G naturally corresponds to a parallel (resp. sequential) algorithm to compute f_G and the number of pebbles $|P_i|$ on the graph in each round i corresponds to memory usage during each round of computation.

The sequential black pebbling game has been used to analyze space complexity [HPV77, PTC76] and to examine space-time tradeoffs [Cob66, Coo73, Pau75, PV76, Tom81]. In the field of cryptography, the parallel black pebbling game has been used to analyze the security of data-independent memory-hard functions (iMHFs). An iMHF $f_{G,H}$ is defined using a cryptographic hash function H and a data-dependency graph G [AS15, AB16, ABP17, BZ17]. The output of $f_{G,H}(x)$ is defined to be the label X_N of the final sink node N in G where the label $X_1 = H(X)$ of the first (source) node is obtained by hashing the input and the label of each internal node v is obtained by hashing the labels of all of v's parents, e.g., if $\mathsf{parents}(v, G) = \{u, v - 1\}$ then we would set $X_v = H(X_u, x_{v-1})$. In many cryptographic applications (e.g., password hashing), we want to ensure that it is moderately expensive to evaluate $f_{G,H}$ to ensure that a brute-force pre-image attack (given y find some x such that $f_{G,H}(x) = y$) is prohibitively expensive even when the domain $\mathcal{X}$ of inputs is smaller (e.g., low entropy passwords). When modeling the cryptographic hash function H as a random oracle, one can prove that the cost to evaluate $f_{G,H}$ in the parallel random oracle model is exactly captured by the pebbling cost of G [AS15, AT17, ABP18]. Thus, we would like to pick a graph G with high pebbling costs and/or understand the pebbling costs associated with candidate iMHFs. Prior work demonstrated that the amortized space-time complexity of prominent iMHF candidates, including Password Hashing Competition winner Argon2i, was lower than previously hoped [AB16, ABP17, AB17, BZ17]. On the positive side, recent work has shown how to use depth-robust graphs [EGS75] to construct iMHFs with (essentially) optimum amortized space-time complexity [ABP17, ABH17, BHK+19]. However, it is important to note that the classical black pebbling game does not include any rules constraining our ability to remove pebbles. We are allowed to remove pebbles from the graph at any point in time which corresponds to freeing memory and can be done to reduce the space usage. While the classical pebbling game allows us to discard pebbles at any point in time to free memory, this action is often not possible in a quantum circuit due to the No-Deletion Theorem [KPB00]. In this sense, the black pebbling game cannot be used to model reversible computation as in a quantum circuit and an efficient parallel black pebbling for a graph G does not necessarily imply the existence of a quantum circuit $C_{G,H}$ with comparable cost.

Review: Measuring Pebbling Costs. There are several natural ways to measure the cost of a pebbling. The space cost of a pebbling $P = (P_0, \ldots, P_t)$ measures the maximum number of pebbles on the graph during any round, i.e., $\max_i |P_i|$ and the space complexity of a graph measures the minimum space cost over all legal pebblings of G. Similarly, the space-time cost of a pebbling $P = (P_0, \ldots, P_t)$ measures the product $t \times \max_i |P_i|$ and the cumulative pebbling cost is $\sum_i |P_i|$. Intuitively, space complexity measures the amount of memory (e.g., RAM) required for a computation and space-time cost measures the full cost of the computation by telling how long the memory will be locked up during computation. Cumulative pebbling cost gives the amortized space-time complexity of pebbling multiple copies of the graph G, i.e., when we are evaluating our function f_G on multiple different inputs in parallel [AS15].

(Quantum) Pre-image Attacks. Understanding the amortized space-time complexity of a graph G is important to estimate the cost of a classical brute-force pre-image attack over a domain $\mathcal{X}$ of size m. In particular, suppose we are given a target output y (e.g., $y = f_{G,H}(x')$ for a secret input $x \in \mathcal{X}$) and we wish to find some input $x' \in \mathcal{X}$ such that $y = f_{G,H}(x')$. Classically, the space-time cost of a black-box pre-image attack would require us to evaluate the function $f_{G,H}$ on $\Omega(m)$ inputs. If the cumulative pebbling cost of G is given by $\sum_i |P_i|$ then the total space-time cost of the pre-image attack would scale proportionally to $m \sum_i |P_i|$, i.e., m times the amortized space-time complexity. Thus, a more efficient black pebbling strategy for G yields a lower-cost pre-image attack.

In the context of quantum computing, Grover's algorithm [Gro96] substantially reduces the cost of a brute-force pre-image attack over a domain $\mathcal{X}$ of size m. In particular, Grover's algorithm only requires $O(\sqrt{m})$ black-box queries to the function $f_{G,H}$ evaluating the function $f_{G,H}$ and this is optimal—any quantum algorithm using $f_{G,H}$ as a black box must make at least $\Omega(\sqrt{m})$ queries [BBBV97]. If we instantiate $f_{G,H}$ with a quantum circuit of width w and depth d then full Grover circuit would have width $W = O(w)$ and depth $D = d \times O(\sqrt{m})$. In particular, the total space-time (equivalently width-depth) cost of the attack would be $wd \times O(\sqrt{m})$. Thus, to analyze the cost of a quantum pre-image attack it is crucial to understand the space-time (or width-depth) cost of a quantum circuit $C_{G,H}$ computing $f_{G,H}$. Our goal will be to treat H as a black box and use graph pebbling to characterize the space-time cost. A natural first attempt would be to use the classical black pebbling game to analyze the parallel pebbling cost of G as above. If this approach worked we could simply leverage prior (parallel) black pebbling analysis of prominent iMHF candidates [AB16, ABP17, AB17, BZ17] to analyze the cost of a quantum pre-image attack. Unfortunately, this approach breaks down because a legal black pebbling strategy *does not* necessarily correspond to a valid quantum circuit $C_{G,H}$ with comparable cost. Thus, we will require a different pebbling game to analyze the width-depth cost of the quantum circuit $C_{G,H}$.

Notation. We use the notation $[N]$ (resp. $[a,b]$) to denote the set $\{1,\ldots,N\}$ (resp. $\{a, a+1, \ldots, b\}$) for a positive integer N (resp. $a \leq b$). The notation $\xleftarrow{\$}$ denotes a uniformly random sampling, e.g., we say $x \xleftarrow{\$} [N]$ when x is a uniformly sampled integer from 1 to N. For simplicity, we let $\log(\cdot)$ be a log base 2, i.e., $\log x := \log_2 x$.

Let $G = (V, E)$ be a directed acyclic graph (DAG) where we denote N to be the number of nodes in $V = [N]$. Given a node $v \in V$, we define $\mathsf{parents}(v, G)$ to be the *immediate parents* of node v in G, and we extend this definition to a subset of nodes as well; for a set $W \subseteq V$, we define $\mathsf{parents}(W, G) := \bigcup_{w \in W} \{u : (u, w) \in E\}$. We let $\mathsf{ancestors}(v, G)$ be the set of all ancestors of v in G, i.e., $\mathsf{ancestors}(v, G) := \bigcup_{i \geq 1} \mathsf{parents}^i(v, G)$, where $\mathsf{parents}^1(v, G) = \mathsf{parents}(v, G)$ and $\mathsf{parents}^i(v, G) = \mathsf{parents}(\mathsf{parents}^{i-1}(v, G), G)$.

Similarly, for a set $W \subseteq V$, we define $\mathsf{ancestors}(W, G) := \bigcup_{i \geq 1} \mathsf{parents}^i(W, G)$, where $\mathsf{parents}^1(W, G) = \mathsf{parents}(W, G)$ and recursively define $\mathsf{parents}^i(W, G) = \mathsf{parents}(\mathsf{parents}^{i-1}(W, G), G)$.

We denote the set of all sink nodes of G with $\mathsf{sinks}(G) := \{v \in V : \nexists(v, u) \in E\}$ – note that $\mathsf{ancestors}(\mathsf{sinks}(G), G) = V$. We define $\mathsf{depth}(v, G)$ to refer to the number of the longest directed path in G ending at node v and we define $\mathsf{depth}(G) = \max_{v \in V} \mathsf{depth}(v, G)$ to refer to the number of nodes in the longest directed path in G. Given a node $v \in V$, we define $\mathsf{indeg}(v) := |\mathsf{parents}(v, G)|$ to denote the number of incoming edges into v, and we also define $\mathsf{indeg}(G) := \max_{v \in V} \mathsf{indeg}(v)$. Given a set $S \subseteq V$ of nodes, we use $G - S$ to refer to the subgraph of G obtained by deleting all the nodes in S and all edges that are incident to S. We also use the notation $S_{\leq k} := S \cap [k]$ denotes the subset of S that only intersects with $[k]$. We say that a DAG $G = (V, E)$ is (e, d)-depth robust if for any subset $S \subseteq V$ such that $|S| \leq e$ we have $\mathsf{depth}(G - S) \geq d$. Otherwise, we say that G is (e, d)-reducible and call the subset S a depth-reducing set (which is of size at most e and yields $\mathsf{depth}(G - S) < d$).

We denote with $\mathcal{P}_{G,T}$ and $\mathcal{P}^{\parallel}_{G,T}$ the set of all legal sequential and parallel classical pebblings of G with target set T, respectively. In the case where $T = \mathsf{sinks}(G)$, we simply write $\mathcal{P}_G$ and $\mathcal{P}^{\parallel}_G$, respectively.

1.1   Our Results

We introduce the parallel reversible pebbling game as a tool to analyze the (amortized) space-time cost of a quantum circuit evaluating a function f with a static data-dependency graph G. Prior work [Ben89, Krá01, MSR+19] introduced a sequential reversible pebbling game. As we discuss, there are several key subtleties that arise when extending the sequential reversible pebbling game to the parallel setting. We argue that any parallel quantum pebbling $P = (P_0, \ldots, P_t)$ of the graph G corresponds to a quantum circuit C_P evaluating f with comparable costs, e.g., the depth of the quantum circuit C_P corresponds to the number of pebbling rounds t and the width of the circuit corresponds to the space complexity of the pebbling, i.e., $\max_i |P_i|$. Thus, any reversible pebbling attack will yield a more efficient quantum pre-image attack[1].

As an application, we use the parallel reversible pebbling game to analyze the space-time cost of several important password hashing functions $f_{G,H}$ including PBKDF2, BCRYPT, Argon2i, and DRSample.

Reversible Pebbling Attacks on Line Graphs. We first focus on analyzing the reversible pebbling cost of a line graph L_N with N nodes $\{1, \ldots, N\}$ and edges

---

[1] While one could use the parallel reversible pebbling game as a heuristic to *lower bound* the cost of a quantum pre-image attack we stress that, at this time, there is no pebbling reduction which provably lower bounds the cost of a quantum pre-image attack on $f_{G,H}$ using reversible pebbling cost of the underlying DAG G. We do have pebbling reductions for classical (non-reversible) pebblings in the parallel random oracle model [AS15], but there are several technical barriers which make it difficult to extend this reduction to the quantum random oracle model.

$(i, i+1)$ for each $1 \leq i < N$. Classically, there is a trivial black pebbling strategy for the line graph with simply walks a single pebble from node 1 to node N over N pebbling rounds, i.e., in each round i we place a new pebble on node i and then delete the pebble on node $i - 1$. This pebbling strategy is clearly optimal as the maximum space usage is just 1 and the space-time cost is just $N \times 1 = N$. However, this simple pebbling strategy is no longer legal in the reversible pebbling game and it is a bit tricky just to find a reversible pebbling strategy whose space-time cost is significantly lower than $\mathcal{O}\left(N^2\right)$—the space-time cost of the naïve pebbling strategy which avoids removing pebbles. In Theorem 1 we show that the (sequential) reversible space-time complexity of a line graph is $\mathcal{O}\left(N^{1 + \frac{2}{\sqrt{\log N}}}\right)$. A similar argument seems to be implicitly assumed by Bennett [Ben89] though the argument was never explicitly formalized as a reversible pebbling strategy. The result improves upon a result of Li and Vitányi [LV96] who showed that the space-time complexity is at most $\mathcal{O}\left(N^{\log 3} \log N\right)^2$.

Because the space-time complexity of the line graph $G = L_N$ is so low, it is a poor choice for an iMHF $f_{G,H}$ or for password hashing [BHZ18]. However, the line graph L_N naturally corresponds to widely deployed password hashing algorithms like BCRYPT [PM99] and PBKDF2 [Kal00] which use hash iteration to increase costs where the parameter N controls the number of hash iterations. Thus, to understand the cost of a (quantum) brute-force password cracking attack it is useful to analyze the (reversible) pebbling cost of L_N.

Reversible Pebbling Attack for Depth-Reducible DAGs. In Theorem 2 we give a generic parallel reversible pebbling attack on any (e, d)-reducible DAG G with space-time cost $\mathcal{O}\left(Ne + dN2^d\right)$ which corresponds to a meaningful attack whenever $e = o(N)$ and $d2^d = o(N)$. A DAG G is said to be (e, d)-reducible if there is a subset $S \subseteq V$ of at most e nodes such that any length d path P in G contains at least one node in S. As we show this leads to meaningful reversible pebbling attacks on Argon2i, the winner of the Password Hashing Competition. Specifically, we demonstrate how to construct depth-reducing sets for Argon2i-A (an older version of Argon2i) and Argon2i-B (the current version of Argon2i) with $e = o(N)$ and $d2^d = o(N)$. This leads to reversible pebbling attacks with space-time complexity $\mathcal{O}\left(N^2 \log \log N / \sqrt{\log N}\right)$ and $\mathcal{O}\left(N^2 / \sqrt[3]{\log N}\right)$ against Argon2i-A and Argon2i-B, respectively—see Corollary 1.

In the classical pebbling setting, Alwen and Blocki [AB16] previously gave a generic pebbling attack on (e, d)-reducible DAGs with amortized space-time cost $\mathcal{O}\left(Ne + N^2 d/e\right)$. However, this pebbling attack is not legal in the reversible setting, and without amortization, the space-time cost is still N^2—the average number of pebbles on the graph per round is just $e + Nd/e$ but at the peak, the pebbling strategy still requires $\Omega(N)$ pebbles. In our pebbling strategy, the maximum space usage is $\mathcal{O}\left(e + d2^d\right)$.

---

[2] The pebbling of Li and Vitányi [LV96] runs in time $\mathcal{O}\left(N^{\log 3}\right)$ while using at most $\mathcal{O}(\log N)$ pebbles. Our pebbling strategy uses more pebbles to reduce the overall space-time cost by improving the pebbling time.

Reversible Pebbling Attack Against DRSample. Finally, we use the parallel reversible pebbling game to analyze DRSample [ABH17]—a proposal to update the edge distribution in Argon2i with a depth-robust graph. With high probability, a randomly sampled DRSample DAG G will not be (e, d)-reducible for parameters e, d as large as $e = \Omega(N/\log N)$ and $d = \Omega(N)$. Thus, the generic reversible pebbling attack on (e, d)-reducible graphs does not seem to apply. We give an alternate pebbling strategy by partitioning the nodes of G into $\lceil N/b \rceil$ consecutive blocks of size b and converting a parallel reversible pebbling of the line graph $L_{\lceil N/b \rceil}$ into a legal reversible pebbling of G. The reversible pebbling strategy will be cost-effective as long as we have an efficient pebbling strategy for $L_{\lceil N/b \rceil}$ and the graph G does not contain too many "long" edges (u, v) with $|v - u| \geq b$ — we show that DRSample does not contain too many long edges when $b = N/\log^2 N$. Combined with our parallel reversible pebbling strategies for the line graph, this leads to an attack on DRSample with space-time cost at most $\mathcal{O}\left(N^2 \log \log N/\log N\right)$—see Corollary 2.

More generally, in Theorem 3 we give an efficient reversible pebbling algorithm which transforms a legal reversible pebbling $P' = (P'_1, \ldots, P'_{t'})$ of the line graph $L_{\lceil N/b \rceil}$ into a legal reversible pebbling $P = (P_1, \ldots, P_t)$ of a DAG $G = (V, E)$. The reversible pebbling requires $t = \mathcal{O}(bt')$ rounds and space $bs' + (\#skip)$ where $\#skip$ is upper bounded by the number of long edges $(u, v) \in E$ with $|v - u| \geq b$ and $s' = \max_i |P'_i|$ upper bounds the space usage of the pebbling P'. Thus, the total space-time complexity will be $\mathcal{O}\left(b^2 s' t' + N \#skip\right)$ and we will be able to obtain an efficient reversible pebbling attack as long as $b = o(N)$ and $(\#skip) = o(N)$—we show that this is the case for DRSample.

Cumulative Pebbling Cost and Parallel Reversible Pebbling. Alwen and Blocki [AB16] gave a general parallel black pebbling attack on any (e, d)-reducible graph. This general pebbling attack was used to upper bound the cumulative cost of many prominent iMHFs including Argon2i-A [AB16] and Argon2i-B [AB17]. More generally the attack shows that *any* constant indegree DAG G has cumulative pebbling cost at most $\mathcal{O}\left(N^2 \log \log N/\log N\right)$. We show how the pebbling attack of Alwen and Blocki [AB16] can be extended to the parallel reversible pebbling game[3]. In particular, we can show that the cumulative reversible pebbling costs of an (e, d)-reducible DAG with maximum indegree δ is upper bounded by $\mathcal{O}\left(eN + g\delta N + \frac{N^2 d}{g}\right)$ for any parameter $g \geq d$ matching the non-reversible pebbling attacks of Alwen and Blocki [AB16]—see Theorem 4. More specifically, since any DAG G with constant indegree $\delta = O(1)$ is (e, d)-reducible with $d = N/\log^2 N$ and $e = \mathcal{O}(N \log \log N/\log N)$ [AB16] we can plug

---

[3] Alwen, Blocki and Pietrzak [ABP17] later provided a recursive version of the pebbling attacks of Alwen and Blocki [AB16] which can further reduces the cumulative pebbling cost of a DAG which is (e_i, d_i)-reducible at a sequence of points (e_i, d_i) with $d_i < d_{i-1}$ and $e_i \geq d_{i-1}$. The recursive pebbling attack yields tighter asymptotic upper bounds for some iMHF candidates [BZ17, ABP17]. We conjecture that these recursive pebbling attacks can also be generalized to the reversible pebbling setting though we leave this as an open problem.

in $g = e$ to obtain a reversible pebbling strategy with cumulative cost at most $\mathcal{O}\left(N^2 \log \log N / \log N\right)$—see Corollary 3. We can also upper bound the cumulative reversible pebbling costs of Argon2i-A and Argon2i-B as $\mathcal{O}\left(N^{1.75} \log N\right)$ and $\mathcal{O}\left(N^{1.8}\right)$ respectively—see the full version for the details.

1.2   Technical Overview

Defining the Parallel Reversible Pebbling Game. We begin by defining and motivating the parallel reversible pebbling game. We want to ensure that any legal (parallel) reversible pebbling strategy for G corresponds to a quantum circuit $C_{G,H}$ evaluating $f_{G,H}$ that could be used as part of a pre-image attack using Grover's algorithm.

We first consider the parallel quantum random oracle model [BDF+11] where the random oracle is a function $H : \{0,1\}^{\leq 2\lambda} \to \{0,1\}^{\lambda}$. In the parallel quantum random oracle model we are given access to a quantum oracle maps basis states of the form $|x_1, y_1, \ldots, x_k, y_k, z\rangle$ to the new state $|x_1, y_1 \oplus H(x_1), \ldots, x_k, y_k \oplus H(x_k), z\rangle$. Here, $x_1, \ldots, x_k$ denote the queries, $y_1, \ldots, y_k$ denote the output registers and z denotes any auxiliary data. Notice that if $y_i = 0^{\lambda}$ then the ith output register will just be $H(x_i)$ after the query is submitted.

Now consider the function $f(x) = H^N(x)$ where $H^1(x) = H(x)$ and $H^{i+1}(x) = H(H^i(x))$. The data-dependency graph for f is simply the line graph $G = L_N$. In our reversible pebbling game, we want to ensure that each pebbling transition corresponds to a legal state transition in the quantum random oracle model. If $N = 5$, then the pebbling configuration $P_i = \{2, 3, 4\}$ intuitively corresponds to a quantum state containing the labels $X_2 = H^2(x)$, $X_3 = H^3(x)$ and $X_4 = H^4(x)$. From this state, we could use X_4 and an input register and submit the query $|X_4, 0^{\lambda}\rangle$ to the random oracle to obtain $X_5 = H(X_4)$ from the resulting state $|X_4, H(X_4)\rangle$. Similarly, while we cannot simply delete X_3 we could uncompute this value by using X_3 as an output register and submitting the random oracle query $|X_2, X_3\rangle$ to obtain the new state $|X_2, H(X_2) \oplus X_3\rangle = |X_2, 0^{\lambda}\rangle$ in which the label X_3 has been removed. However, without the label X_1 there is no way to uncompute X_2 without first recomputing X_1.

The above example suggests that we extend the parallel pebbling game by adding the rule that $\mathsf{parents}(P_i \setminus P_{i+1}, G) \subseteq P_i$, i.e., a pebble can only be deleted if all of its parents were pebbled at the end of the previous pebbling round. While this rule is necessary, it is not yet sufficient to prevent impossible quantum state transitions. In particular, the rule would not rule out the pebbling transition from $P_i = \{1, 2, \ldots, i\}$ to the new configuration $P_{i+1} = \{\}$ where all labels have been removed from memory. This pebbling transition would correspond to a quantum transition from a state in which labels $X_1, \ldots, X_i$ are stored in memory to a new state where all of these labels have been uncomputed after just one (parallel) query to the random oracle. Because quantum computation is reversible this would also imply that we could directly transition from the original state (no labels computed) to a state in which all of the labels $X_1, \ldots, X_i$ are available after just one (parallel) query to the quantum random oracle. However, it is known that computing $X_i = H^i(x)$ requires at least i rounds of computation even in the parallel quantum random oracle model [BLZ21]. Thus, the pebbling transition from $P_i = \{1, 2, \ldots, i\}$ to $P_{i+1} = \{\}$ must be disallowed by our reversible pebbling rules as the corresponding quantum state transition is impossible.

We address this last issue by adding another pebbling rule: if $v \in$ parents$(P_i \setminus P_{i-1}, G) \cup$ parents$(P_{i-1} \setminus P_i, G)$, then $v \in P_i$. Intuitively, the rule ensures that if the label X_v appeared in an input register to either compute or uncompute some other data label then we cannot also uncompute X_v in this round, i.e., we must keep a pebble at node v.

We make several observations about the reversible pebbling game. First, any legal reversible pebbling of a DAG G is also a legal (classical) parallel black pebbling of G since we only added additional pebbling restrictions. More formally, if $\mathcal{P}_G^{\parallel}$ (resp. $\mathcal{P}_G$) denotes the set of all legal parallel (resp. sequential) black pebblings of G and $\mathcal{P}_G^{\leftrightarrow,\parallel}$ (resp. $\mathcal{P}_G^{\leftrightarrow}$) denotes the set of all legal parallel (resp. sequential) reversible pebblings of G then we have $\mathcal{P}_G^{\leftrightarrow,\parallel} \subseteq \mathcal{P}_G^{\parallel}$ and $\mathcal{P}_G^{\leftrightarrow} \subseteq \mathcal{P}_G$. Thus, any lower bounds on the classical parallel pebbling cost of G will immediately carry over to the reversible setting. However, upper bounds will not necessarily carry over since classical pebbling attacks may not be legal in the reversible pebbling game. Second, we observe that the following sequential reversible pebbling strategy works for any DAG $G = (V = [N], E)$. In the first N rounds, pebble all nodes in topological order without deleting any pebbles. In the next $N - 1$ rounds remove pebbles from all nodes (excluding sinks(G)) in reverse topological order. More formally, assuming that $1, \ldots, N$ is a topological order and that node N is the only sink node we have $P_i = [i]$ for each $i \leq N$ and $P_{N+j} = [N] \setminus [N - j, N - 1]$ for each $j \leq N - 1$. The pebbling requires N pebbles and finishes in $t = 2N - 1$ rounds so the space-time cost is $2N^2 - N$. We refer to the above sequential strategy as the naïve reversible pebbling for a graph G.

Reversible Pebbling Attack on Line Graphs. We give a reversible pebbling attack on a line graph L_N of size N with the space-time cost $\mathcal{O}\left(N^{1+\frac{2}{\sqrt{\log N}}}\right)$. This can be achieved by generalizing Li and Vitányi's work [LV96]. Li and Vitányi [LV96] gave a reversible pebbling strategy on a line graph of size N with space-time cost $\mathcal{O}\left(N^{\log 3} \log N\right)$ by translating ideas of Bennett [Ben89] into a reversible pebbling argument. Intuitively, if we define $N(k)$ using the recurrence relationship $N(k) = k + \sum_{j=0}^{k-1} N(j)$, solving to $N(k) = 2^k - 1$, then they show that the line graph with $N(k)$ nodes can be pebbled using space $S(k) = S(k-1) + 1 = k$ and time $T(k) = 3T(k-1) + 1 = \mathcal{O}\left(3^k\right)$ for a total space-time cost of $\mathcal{O}\left(k3^k\right) = \mathcal{O}\left((N(k))^{\log 3} \log N(k)\right)$. Their pebbling strategy works as follows: (1) recursively apply the pebbling strategy to place a pebble on node $N(k-1)$ using space at most $S(k-1)$ and time at most $T(k-1)$, (2) place a pebble on node $v_1 = N(k-1) + 1$, (3) recursively apply the strategy (in reverse) to clear any leftover pebbles from nodes 1 to $N(k-1)$ in time $T(k-1)$ and (additional) space at most $S(k-1)$. We are left with $(k-1) + \sum_{j=1}^{k-2} N(j) = N(k-1)$ remaining nodes which will be handled recursively using time $T(k-1)$ and (additional) space $S(k-1)$.

We observe that by increasing the space usage slightly we can decrease the pebbling time to obtain a superior space-time cost. We note that Bennett [Ben89] mentions a similar idea in his paper, but that this idea was not formalized as a reversible pebbling strategy either by Bennett [Ben89] or by Li and Vitányi [LV96]. The key modification is as follows: we redefine $N(k) = ck + \sum_{j=0}^{k-1} cN(j)$ solving to $N(k) = \Theta\left((c+1)^k\right)$. We can now recursively pebble a line graph with $N(k)$ nodes in sequential time $T(k) = (2c+2)T(k-1) + c = \mathcal{O}\left((2c+2)^k\right)$ and space $S(k) = c + S(k-1) = ck$. Intuitively, the recursive pebbling strategy will begin by dropping pebbles on each of the nodes $N(k-1) + 1, 2N(k-1) + 2, ..., cN(k-1) + c$ using space at most $S(k-1) + c$ and time $2c \cdot T(k-1)$. We are left with $c(k-1) + \sum_{j=0}^{k-2} cN(j) = N(k-1)$ remaining nodes which can then be handled recursively. Setting $c = 2^k$, we have $k = \Theta(\sqrt{\log N(k)})$ yielding an upper bound of $\mathcal{O}\left(N(k)^{1+(2+o(1))\frac{1}{\sqrt{\log N(k)}}}\right)$ on the sequential space-time cost.

We can obtain a minor improvement by exploiting parallelism to save time while increasing space usage slightly. In particular, our parallel strategy uses space $\mathcal{O}\left(c2^k\right)$ and time $\mathcal{O}\left((c+2)^k\right)$ with total space-time cost $\mathcal{O}\left(c(2c+4)^k\right)$. Setting $c+1 = 2^k$ we have a slightly better upper bound $\mathcal{O}\left(N(k)^{1+\frac{2}{\sqrt{\log N(k)}}}\right)$ on the space-time cost. Further details can be found in the full version.

Generic Reversible Pebbling Attack on Depth-Reducible Graphs. We give a generic reversible pebbling attack on any (e, d)-reducible DAG $G = (V = [N], E)$ with maximum indegree 2. The space-time cost of our reversible pebbling attack is at most $\mathcal{O}\left(Ne + Nd2^d\right)$. Thus, the attack will be superior to the naïve reversible pebbling strategy as long as $e = o(N)$ and $d2^d = o(N)$. We begin with a depth-reducing set $S \subseteq V$ of size $|S| \leq e$. Our reversible pebbling strategy will never remove pebbles from the set S until all of the sink nodes in G are pebbled and we are ready to remove pebbles from the remaining nodes. On each round $i \leq N$ we will place a new pebble on node $\{i\}$. To ensure that this step is legal, we consider the subgraph formed by all of node i's ancestors in $G - S$. Since $G - S$ does not contain a directed path of length d and each node has at most 2 parents there are at most 2^d ancestors of node i in $G - S$. Once again applying the observation that the depth of $G - S$ is at most d we can start to repebble i's ancestors in round $i - d - 1$ to ensure that i's immediate parents are pebbled by round $i - 1$. After we place a pebble on node i we can remove pebbles from i's ancestors in $G - S$ over the next d rounds. Since we only keep pebbles on the set S and the ancestors of *up to* $2d$ nodes in $G - S$, the maximum space usage of this reversible pebbling strategy will be $\mathcal{O}\left(e + d2^d\right)$.

We apply the generic attack to Argon2i-A and Argon2i-B. In particular, we apply ideas from the previous work [AB17, BZ17] to show that Argon2i-A (resp. Argon2i-B) graphs are (e, d)-reducible with $e = \mathcal{O}\left(N \log\log N/\sqrt{\log N}\right)$ and $d = \log N/\log\log N$ (resp. $e = \mathcal{O}\left(N/\sqrt[3]{\log N}\right)$ and $d = (\log N)/2$). This leads to reversible pebbling attacks with cost $\mathcal{O}\left(N^2 \log\log N/\sqrt{\log N}\right)$ and $\mathcal{O}\left(N^2/\sqrt[3]{\log N}\right)$ for Argon2i-A and Argon2i-B, respectively. An intriguing open question is whether or not these are the best reversible pebbling attacks for Argon2i-A and Argon2i-B?

Reversible Pebbling Attack on DRSample. We provide a general reversible pebbling attack on any DAG G with the property that G contains few *skip nodes* (defined below). Intuitively, given a DAG $G = (V, E)$ with $|V| = N$ and a parameter $b \geq 1$, we can imagine partitioning the nodes of V into consecutive blocks $B_1 = \{v_1, \ldots, v_b\}, B_2 = \{v_{b+1}, \ldots, v_{2b}\}, \ldots, B_{\lceil N/b \rceil} = \{v_{(\lceil N/b \rceil - 1)b+1}, \ldots, v_N\}$ such that we have $\lceil N/b \rceil$ blocks in total and each block contains exactly b nodes (with the possible exception of the last block if N/b is not an integer). We call a node u in block B_i a *skip node* if G contains a directed edge (u, v) from u to some node $v \in B_j$ with $j > i+1$ and we call the edge (u, v) a *skip edge*, i.e., the edge (u, v) skips over the block B_{i+1} entirely.

We first observe that if the graph G contained no skip edges then it would be trivial to transform a (parallel) reversible pebbling P' of the line graph $L_{\lceil N/b \rceil} = (V', E')$ with space-time cost $\Pi_{st}^{\leftrightarrow,\|}(P')$ into a (parallel) reversible pebbling P of G with space-time cost $\mathcal{O}\left(b^2 \Pi_{st}^{\leftrightarrow,\|}(P')\right)$ (see Definition 2 for the definition of $\Pi_{st}^{\leftrightarrow,\|}(\cdot)$). In particular, placing a pebbling on node $v' \in V'$ of the line graph corresponds to b rounds in which we pebble all nodes in block $B_{v'}$. Thus, the pebbling time increases by a factor of $\mathcal{O}(b)$, and the total space usage also increases by a factor b. Unfortunately, this strategy may result in an illegal reversible pebbling when G contains skip edges. However, we can modify the above strategy to avoid removing pebbles on skip nodes which intuitively increases our space usage by s—the total number of skip nodes in the graph G. The procedure $P = \mathsf{Trans}(G, P', b)$ and an example for the reversible pebbling strategy are formally described in the full version. As long as s is sufficiently small, we obtain an efficient parallel reversible pebbling attack on G. In particular, given a reversible pebbling P' of the line graph $L_{\lceil N/b \rceil} = (V', E')$ with space-time cost $\Pi_{st}^{\leftrightarrow,\|}(P')$ we can find a reversible pebbling P of G with space-time cost $\mathcal{O}\left(sN + b^2 \Pi_{st}^{\leftrightarrow,\|}(P')\right)$. Combining this observation with our efficient reversible pebbling attacks on the line graph we can see that the space-time costs will be at most $\mathcal{O}\left(sN + b^2(N/b)^{1+\epsilon}\right)$ for any constant $\epsilon > 0$. For graphs like DRSample [ABH17], we can show that (whp) the number of skip nodes is at most $s = \mathcal{O}\left(\frac{N \log\log N}{\log N}\right)$ when we set the block size $b = \mathcal{O}\left(\frac{N}{\log^2 N}\right)$ leading to a reversible pebbling attack with space-time cost $\mathcal{O}\left(\frac{N^2 \log\log N}{\log N}\right)$.

Cumulative Cost for Reversible Pebblings: Depth-Reducing Reversible Pebbling Attacks. Alwen and Blocki [AB16] gave a non-reversible pebbling attack with reduced cumulative pebbling cost for any (e, d)-reducible DAG G. While their pebbling attack is non-reversible, we observe that almost all pebbling rounds respect the constraints of reversible pebbling. We then identify the few non-reversible rounds and how these steps can be patched to respect the additional constraints of reversible pebbling. See details in Sect. 4.

1.3 Related Work

Related Pebbling Games. Prior work [Ben89, Krá01, MSR+19] introduced a reversible pebbling game to capture restrictions imposed by the Quantum No-Deletion Theorem and analyze space-time tradeoffs in quantum computing. However, the pebbling game considered in these works is sequential and only allows for the addition/removal of one pebble in each round. Thus, the sequential reversible pebbling game is not suitable for analyzing the space-time cost of a quantum circuit evaluating $f_{G,H}$ since the circuit can evaluate H multiple times in parallel. We note that there are several important subtleties that must be considered when extending the game to the parallel setting.

More recently, Kornerup et al. [KSS21] introduced a new (sequential) pebbling game called the *spooky pebble game* to model measurement-based deletion in quantum computation. Intuitively, measurement-based deletion allows for the conversion of some qubits into (cheaper) classical bits which can later be used to restore the quantum state. The spooky pebble game only allows for sequential computation and the cost model ignores classical storage. One disadvantage of instantiating a spooky pebbling attack as part of a quantum pre-image attack is that the final attack requires many intermediate measurements which introduces additional technical challenges, i.e., we need to ensure that *each and every* intermediate measurement does not disturb the state of the nearby qubits or the rest of the quantum computer [Div00]. By contrast, a pebbling attack in our parallel reversible pebbling game naturally corresponds to a quantum circuit which does not require any intermediate measurements and our cost model accounts for the total storage cost (classical + quantum). While Kornerup et al. [KSS21] introduced a spooky pebbling attack on the line graph, we note this spooky pebbling strategy does not yield an efficient reversible pebbling attack in our model as their pebbling attack inherently relies on frequent intermediate measurements to reduce the number of qubits.

Remark 1. One could always try to eliminate the intermediate measurements by applying the "principle of deferred measurement" [NC02]. However, "deferred measurement" increases the space and/or depth of a quantum circuit. For example, if the quantum circuit C acts on s qubits and performs m intermediate measurements then we can obtain an equivalent quantum circuit C' with no intermediate measurements with the caveat that C' operates on $s' = s + \mathsf{poly}(m)$ qubits. The space blowup is especially high if C makes many intermediate measurements, e.g., $s = \mathcal{O}(\log m)$. Fefferman and Remscrim [FR21] gave a space-efficient version of the transform, but their transform yields a large penalty in running time cost, i.e., the transform incurs a multiplicative $\mathsf{poly}(t2^s)$ overhead in the total running time t.

If we apply spooky pebbling in the context of Grover's search then the total number of intermediate measurements m would be exponential, i.e., even if we have a quantum circuit C_f evaluating a function $f : \{0,1\}^k \rightarrow \{0,1\}^k$ with just a single intermediate measurement, performing the full Grover's search to find a pre-image of f would involve $m = \mathcal{O}\left(2^{k/2}\right)$ intermediate measurements and applying "deferred measurement" to the full Grover circuit would incur a massive time (or space) penalty. Thus, finding a quantum circuit C_f which has reduced space-time cost and does not require any intermediate measurements would yield a more compelling quantum pre-image attack.

2 Parallel Reversible Pebbling Games

The biggest difference between the classical and reversible pebbling games occurs when removing pebbles from a pebbling configuration. In a classical setting, we can always delete any pebbles in any point in time when they are no longer needed. On the other hand, in a reversible setting, this is not feasible by quantum no-cloning theorem. Since we can only free a pebble by querying a random oracle at the same input, we can observe that a pebble can be deleted only if we know all of its parents, i.e., all of its parents were previously pebbled. The following definition captures this property:

Definition 1 (Parallel/Sequential Reversible Graph Pebbling). *Let $G = (V, E)$ be a DAG and let $T \subseteq V$ be a target set of nodes to be pebbled. A pebbling configuration (of G) at round i is a subset $P_i \subseteq V$. Let $P = (P_0, \dots, P_t)$ be a sequence of pebbling configurations. Below are the following properties which define various aspects of reversible pebblings.*

(1) The pebbling should start with no pebbles ($P_0 = \emptyset$) and end with pebbles on all of the target nodes i.e., $T \subseteq P_t$.

(2) A pebble can be added only if all of its parents were pebbled at the end of the previous pebbling round, i.e., $\forall i \in [t] : x \in (P_i \setminus P_{i-1}) \Rightarrow \mathsf{parents}(x, G) \subseteq P_{i-1}$.

(3) (Quantum No-Deletion Property) A pebble can be deleted only if all of its parents were pebbled at the end of the previous pebbling round, i.e., $\forall i \in [t] : x \in (P_{i-1} \setminus P_i) \Rightarrow \mathsf{parents}(x, G) \subseteq P_{i-1}$.

(4) (Quantum Reversibility) If a pebble was required to generate new pebbles (or remove pebbles), then we must keep the corresponding pebble around, i.e., $\forall i \in [t] : x \in \mathsf{parents}(P_i \setminus P_{i-1}, G) \cup \mathsf{parents}(P_{i-1} \setminus P_i, G) \Rightarrow x \in P_i$.

(5) (Remove Excess Pebbles) We also consider an optional constraint that $P_t = T$. If a pebbling does not satisfy this optional constraint we call it a relaxed pebbling.

(6) (Sequential pebbling only) At most one pebble is added or removed in each round, i.e., $\forall i \in [t] : |(P_i \cup P_{i-1}) \setminus (P_i \cap P_{i-1})| \leq 1$.

Now we give pebbling definitions with respect to the above properties.

– *A legal parallel reversible pebbling of T is a sequence $P = (P_0, \dots, P_t)$ of pebbling configurations of G where $P_0 = \emptyset$ and which satisfies conditions (1), (2), (3), (4) and (5) above. If our pebbling additionally satisfies condition (6)* *then we say that it is a sequential pebbling. Similarly, if our pebbling does not satisfy condition (5) then we call our pebbling strategy a relaxed pebbling.*

- *A legal reversible pebbling sequence is a sequence of pebbling configurations $(P_0, \ldots, P_t)$ which satisfies properties (2) and (3) and (4) without requiring $P_0 = \{\}$.*
- *A legal (non-reversible) pebbling sequence is a sequence of pebbling configurations $(P_0, \ldots, P_t)$ satisfying condition (2).*

We denote with $\mathcal{P}_{G,T}^{\leftrightarrow}$ and $\mathcal{P}_{G,T}^{\leftrightarrow,\|}$ the set of all legal sequential and parallel reversible pebblings of G with a target set T, respectively. We denote with $\widetilde{\mathcal{P}}_{G,T}^{\leftrightarrow}$ and $\widetilde{\mathcal{P}}_{G,T}^{\leftrightarrow,\|}$ the set of all legal relaxed sequential and parallel reversible pebblings of G with target set T, respectively. Note that we have $\mathcal{P}_{G,T}^{\leftrightarrow} \subseteq \mathcal{P}_{G,T}^{\leftrightarrow,\|}$ and $\widetilde{\mathcal{P}}_{G,T}^{\leftrightarrow} \subseteq \widetilde{\mathcal{P}}_{G,T}^{\leftrightarrow,\|}$. We will mostly be interested in the case where $T = \mathsf{sinks}(G)$ in which case we simply write $\mathcal{P}_G^{\leftrightarrow}$ and $\mathcal{P}_G^{\leftrightarrow,\|}$ or $\widetilde{\mathcal{P}}_G^{\leftrightarrow}$ and $\widetilde{\mathcal{P}}_G^{\leftrightarrow,\|}$, respectively.

Remark 2. We first note that from any parallel relaxed reversible pebbling of G we can obtain a quantum circuit $C_{G,H}$ which computes $f_{G,H}$. If our pebbling is not relaxed then the circuit $C_{G,H}$ will map the basis state $|x, y, z\rangle$ to the new state $|x, y \oplus f_{G,H}(x), z\rangle$ with no ancilla bits although this property is not necessary for Grover's search. Including the requirement that a reversible pebbling eliminates excess pebbles makes it easier to apply the pebbling attack as a recursive subroutine. Thus, in this paper, we will focus on finding non-relaxed reversible pebbling attacks. We also note that the space-time cost of a relaxed/non-relaxed reversible pebbling is not fundamentally different. In particular, if $(P_1, \ldots, P_t)$ is a relaxed pebbling where $P_t = T$ contains the final sink node N, then $(P_1, \ldots, P_t, P_{t-1} \cup T, \ldots, P_1 \cup T, T)$ is a legal and complete (non-relaxed) reversible pebbling of G. The running time increases by a multiplicative factor of 2 and the space increases by an additive factor of $|T| \leq |P_t|$ where T is the target set. In particular, the overall space-time costs increase by a multiplicative factor of 4 *at most.* In the remainder of the paper, when we write "legal reversible pebbling" we assume that the pebbling is parallel and non-relaxed by default.

Definition 2 (Reversible Pebbling Complexity). *Given a DAG $G = (V, E)$, we essentially use the same definitions for the reversible pebbling complexity as defined in the previous literature [AS15, ABP17, ABP18]. That is, the standard notion of time, space, space-time and cumulative pebbling complexity (CC) of a reversible pebbling $P = \{P_0, \ldots, P_t\} \in \mathcal{P}_G^{\leftrightarrow,\|}$ are also defined to be:*

- *(time complexity) $\Pi_t^{\leftrightarrow,\|}(P) = t$,*
- *(space complexity) $\Pi_s^{\leftrightarrow,\|}(P) = \max_{i \in [t]} |P_i|$,*
- *(space-time complexity) $\Pi_{st}^{\leftrightarrow,\|}(P) = \Pi_t^{\leftrightarrow,\|}(P) \cdot \Pi_s^{\leftrightarrow,\|}(P)$, and*
- *(cumulative pebbling complexity) $\Pi_{cc}^{\leftrightarrow,\|}(P) = \sum_{i \in [t]} |P_i|$.*

For $\alpha \in \{s, t, st, cc\}$ and a target set $T \subseteq V$, the parallel reversible pebbling complexities of G are defined as

$$\Pi_\alpha^{\leftrightarrow,\|}(G, T) = \min_{P \in \mathcal{P}_{G,T}^{\leftrightarrow,\|}} \Pi_\alpha^{\leftrightarrow,\|}(P).$$

When $T = \mathsf{sinks}(G)$ we simplify notation and write $\Pi_\alpha^{\leftrightarrow,\|}(G)$.

We define the time, space, space-time and cumulative pebbling complexity of a sequential reversible pebbling $P = \{P_0, \ldots, P_t\} \in \mathcal{P}_G^{\leftrightarrow}$ in a similar manner: $\Pi_t^{\leftrightarrow}(P) = t$, $\Pi_s^{\leftrightarrow}(P) = \max_{i \in [t]} |P_i|$, $\Pi_{st}^{\leftrightarrow}(P) = \Pi_t^{\leftrightarrow}(P) \cdot \Pi_s^{\leftrightarrow}(P)$, and $\Pi_{cc}^{\leftrightarrow}(P) = \sum_{i \in [t]} |P_i|$. Similarly, for $\alpha \in \{s, t, st, cc\}$ and a target set $T \subseteq V$, the sequential reversible pebbling complexities of G are defined as $\Pi_\alpha^{\leftrightarrow}(G, T) = \min_{P \in \mathcal{P}_{G,T}^{\leftrightarrow}} \Pi_\alpha^{\leftrightarrow}(P)$. When $T = \mathsf{sinks}(G)$ we simplify notation as well and write $\Pi_\alpha^{\leftrightarrow}(G)$.

When compared to the definition of a *classical* pebbling, we can observe that a reversible pebbling has more restrictions, i.e., it only allows us to have pebbles exactly on the target nodes at the end of the pebbling steps, and it further requires quantum no-deletion property and quantum reversibility. This implies that any legal reversible pebblings are also legal classical pebblings, i.e., $\mathcal{P}_{G,T}^{\|} \subseteq \mathcal{P}_{G,T}^{\leftrightarrow,\|}$ (resp. $\mathcal{P}_{G,T} \subseteq \mathcal{P}_{G,T}^{\leftrightarrow}$). This implies that for any graph G, target set T and cost metric $\alpha \in \{s, t, st, cc\}$, we have $\Pi_\alpha^{\|}(G, T) \leq \Pi_\alpha^{\leftrightarrow,\|}(G, T)$ (resp. $\Pi_\alpha(G, T) \leq \Pi_\alpha^{\leftrightarrow}(G, T)$) for a DAG $G = (V, E)$ and a target set $T \subseteq V$, where $\Pi_\alpha^{\|}(G, T)$ (resp. $\Pi_\alpha(G, T)$) denotes the parallel (resp. sequential) classical pebbling complexities which are defined essentially the same as in Definition 2 with a *classical* pebbling $P = \{P_0, \ldots, P_t\} \in \mathcal{P}_G^{\|}$ (resp. $\mathcal{P}_G$). This means that any lower bound on the classical pebbling complexity of a graph G immediately carries over to the reversible setting and an upper bound (attack) on the reversible pebbling cost immediately carries over to the setting classical pebbling.

In the context of quantum pre-image attacks, parallel space-time costs are arguably the most relevant metric. In particular, the depth of the full Grover circuit scales with the number of queries to our quantum circuit $C_{G,H}$ for $f_{G,H}$ multiplied by the number of pebbling rounds for G. Similarly, the width of the full Grover circuit will essentially be given by the space usage of our pebbling. Thus, the space-time of Grover's algorithm will scale directly with $\Pi_s^{\leftrightarrow,\|}(P)$. The cumulative pebbling complexity would still be relevant in settings where we are running multiple instances of Grover's algorithm in parallel and can amortize space usage over multiple inputs. In this paper, we primarily focus on analyzing reversible space-time costs, as this would likely be the most relevant metric in practice. However, cumulative pebbling complexity still can be worthwhile to study and we provide some initial results in this direction.

3   Reversible Pebbling Attacks and Applications on iMHFs

3.1   Warmup: Parallel Reversible Pebbling Attack on a Line Graph

We first consider two widely deployed hash functions, PBKDF2 [Kal00] and BCRYPT [PM99], as motivating examples for analyzing a line graph. Basically, they are constructed by hash iterations so they can be modeled as a line graph when simplified. Hence, the pebbling analysis of a line graph tells us about the costs of PBKDF2 and BCRYPT. Although there has been some effort to replace such password-hash functions with memory-hard functions such as Argon2 or SCRYPT [BHZ18], PBKDF2 and BCRYPT are still commonly used by a number of organizations. Thus, it is still important to understand the costs of an offline brute-force attack on passwords protected by functions like PBKDF2 and BCRYPT. In fact, NIST recommends using memory-hard functions for password hashing [GNP+17] but they still allow PBKDF2 and BCRYPT when used with long enough hash iterations. Hence, there is still value to analyze the quantum resistance of these functions. Our reversible pebbling attack on DRSample relies on efficient pebbling strategies for line graphs as a subroutine providing further motivation to understand the reversible pebbling costs of a line graph.

As we illustrated in Sect. 1.2, we give a (sequential/parallel) reversible pebbling strategy for a line graph L_N using recursion. It can be done by recursively define the sequence of consecutive locations $I(k)$ as $I(k) = I(k-1)' \circ I(k-2)' \circ \ldots \circ I(0)'$ for $k > 0$ and $I(0) = \{\}$, where for $0 \leq j < k$, $I(j)'$ is defined to be a concatenation of c copies of $I(j)$ and i_j (which is an incident node to $I(j)$), i.e., $I(j)' := I(j)^{(1)} \circ i_j^{(1)} \circ I(j)^{(2)} \circ i_j^{(2)} \circ \ldots \circ I(j)^{(c)} \circ i_j^{(c)}$, where $A^{(\ell)}$ denotes the ℓth copy of A. Intuitively, we can sequentially pebble $I(k)$ by pebbling $I(k-1)', I(k-2)', \ldots, I(0)'$. Here, pebbling $I(j)'$ means that we pebble $I(j)^{(\ell)}$, $i_j^{(\ell)}$, and unpebble $I(j)^{(\ell)}$, and we move on to the next copy to pebble $I(j)^{(\ell+1)}$. We can parallelize this strategy by removing and adding pebbles on the consecutive copies at the same time, which requires more space usage but saves time. Here, we only state the space-time cost of our reversible pebbling strategy on a line graph in Theorem 1. Details of our pebbling strategy can be found in the full version.

Theorem 1. Let L_N be a line graph of size N. Then we have $\Pi_{st}^{\leftrightarrow}(L_N) = \mathcal{O}\left(N^{1+(2+o(1))\frac{1}{\sqrt{\log N}}}\right)$ and $\Pi_{st}^{\leftrightarrow,\|}(L_N) = \mathcal{O}\left(N^{1+\frac{2}{\sqrt{\log N}}}\right)$.

The proof of Theorem 1 can be found in the full version.

3.2   Reversible Pebbling Attacks on (e, d)-Reducible DAGs

In this section, we introduce another type of reversible pebbling attack on (e, d)-reducible DAGs with depth-reducing sets with d very small. In this paper, we only consider DAGs with constant indegree, and especially the current state-of-the-art constructions of iMHFs have indegree 2. Therefore, we will assume that $\mathsf{indeg}(G) = 2$ for the DAGs that we consider.

Since the graph has indegree 2, if we find a depth-reducing set S such that $G - S$ has depth d, then we observe that $|\mathsf{ancestors}(v, G - S)| \le 2^d$ for any node v in $G - S$. If d is small, i.e., $d \ll \log N$, then $2^d \ll N$ and we can expect that the space-time cost for pebbling such (e, d)-reducible DAG becomes $o(N^2)$. More precisely, we start with giving a regular pebbling strategy (without quantum restrictions) for such DAGs.

Classical Black Pebbling Strategy. We begin by giving a classical pebbling strategy with small space-time complexity. Note that prior pebbling strategies focused exclusively on minimizing cumulative pebbling cost, but the pebbling attacks of Alwen and Blocki [AB16][4] for (e, d)-reducible graphs still have the space-time cost $\Omega(N^2)$.

We first introduce the following helpful notation. For nodes x and y in a DAG $G = (V, E)$, let $\mathsf{LongestPath}_G(x, y)$ denote the number of nodes in the longest path from x to y in G. Then for a node $w \in V$, a depth-reducing set $S \subseteq V$, and a positive integer $i \in \mathbb{Z}_{>0}$, we first define a set $A_{w,S,i}$ which consists of the nodes v where the longest directed path from v to w in $G - S_{\le w-1}$ has length i, i.e., it contains exactly i nodes.

$$A_{w,S,i} := \left\{ v : \mathsf{LongestPath}_{G-S_{\le w-1}}(v, w) = i \right\}.$$

It is trivial by definition that for any $v \in V$, $A_{v,S,1} = \{v\}$.

Let $G = (V = [N], E)$ be an (e, d)-reducible DAG. We observe that $\mathsf{depth}(G_{\le k} - S_{\le k}) \le d$ is still true for any $k \le N$. At round k, we have always ensured that we have pebbles on the set $S_{\le k}$ and on $\{k\}$ itself. Further, at round k, we can look d steps into the future so that at round $k + d$ we can pebble node $k + d$ without delay. Hence, we start to repebble $\mathsf{ancestors}(k + d, G - S)$ in this round and because $\mathsf{depth}(G_{\le k} - S_{\le k}) \le d$ we are guaranteed to finish within d rounds—just in time to pebble node $k + d$. Taken together, in round k, we have pebbles on $\{k\}$, $S_{\le k}$, and $\mathsf{ancestors}(k + i, G - S)$ for all $i \le d$. More precisely, for $v \in V$, let $P_v = S_{\le v} \cup \left(\bigcup_{j=1}^{d} \bigcup_{i=j}^{d} A_{v-1+j,S,i} \right)$. Since each ancestor graph has size at most 2^d and there are at most d of them, we observe that the total number of pebbles in each round is at most $1 + |S_{\le k}| + \sum_{i=1}^{d} |\mathsf{ancestors}(k + i, G - S)| \le 1 + e + d2^d$. Hence, we have that $\Pi_{st}^{\|}(G) \le N(1 + e + d2^d)$.

Reversible Pebbling Strategy. While the above strategy works in the classical setting it will need to be tweaked to obtain a legal reversible pebbling. In particular, after node $k + d$ is pebbled we cannot immediately remove pebbles from

---

[4] If G is (e, d)-reducible then Alwen and Blocki [AB16] showed that $\Pi_{cc}^{\|}(G) \le \min_{g \ge d} \left(eN + gN \cdot \mathsf{indeg}(G) + \frac{N^2 d}{g} \right) = o(N^2)$.

all nodes in $\mathsf{ancestors}(k + d, G - S)$ because this would violate our quantum reversibility property. Instead, we can reverse the process and unpebble nodes in $\mathsf{ancestors}(k+d, G - S)$ over the next $G - S$ rounds—with the possible exception of nodes $v \in \mathsf{ancestors}(k+d, G - S)$ which are part of $\mathsf{ancestors}(k+d+j, G - S)$ and are still required for some future node $k + d + j$. Thus, if a DAG G is (e, d)-reducible we can establish the following result.

Theorem 2. *Let* $G = (V = [N], E)$ *be an* (e, d)-reducible DAG. Then $\Pi_{st}^{\leftrightarrow, \|}(G) = \mathcal{O}\left(Ne + Nd2^d\right)$.

We will give the proof of Theorem 2 later in the subsection. To prove Theorem 2, we first would need to give a legal reversible pebbling for an (e, d)-reducible DAG G. Lemma 1 provides the desired reversible pebbling for G. The proof of Lemma 1 can be found in the full version.

Lemma 1. *Let* $G = (V = [N], E)$ *be an* (e, d)-reducible DAG and let $S \subseteq V$ be a depth-reducing set. Define

$$B_v := \bigcup_{j=1}^{d+1} \bigcup_{i=j}^{d+1} \left(A_{v+1-j,S,i} \cup A_{v-1+j,S,i}\right),$$

for $v \in V$. Then $P = (P_0, P_1, \ldots, P_{2N})$, where each pebbling configuration is defined by

- $P_0 = \varnothing$,
- *for* $v \in [N]$, $P_v := S_{\leq v} \cup B_v$, *and*
- *for* $N < v \leq 2N$, $P_v := P_{2N-v} \cup \{N\}$,

is a legal parallel reversible pebbling for G.

Now we are ready to prove Theorem 2.

Proof of Theorem 2: Let $P = \{P_0, P_1, \ldots, P_{2N}\}$ as defined in Lemma 1, in which we showed that it is a legal quantum pebbling. Clearly, $\Pi_t^{\leftrightarrow, \|}(P) = 2N$. Further, we observe that $\Pi_s^{\leftrightarrow, \|}(P) \leq \max_{v \in V}\{|S_{\leq v}| + |B_v| + 1\}$. Since we assume that $\mathsf{indeg}(G) = 2$, we have

$$|B_v| = \left| \bigcup_{j=1}^{d+1} \bigcup_{i=j}^{d+1} \left(A_{v+1-j,S,i} \cup A_{v-1+j,S,i}\right) \right|$$

$$\leq \sum_{j=1}^{d+1} \sum_{i=j}^{d+1} |A_{v+1-j,S,i}| + |A_{v-1+j,S,i}|$$

$$\leq \sum_{j=1}^{d+1} \sum_{i=j}^{d+1} 2^{i+1} = 8d2^d + 2.$$

Taken together, $\Pi_{st}^{\leftrightarrow, \|}(P) \leq 2N(e + 8d2^d + 3) = \mathcal{O}\left(Ne + Nd2^d\right)$. Hence, $\Pi_{st}^{\leftrightarrow, \|}(G) = \min_{P \in \mathcal{P}_{G,\{N\}}^{\leftrightarrow, \|}} \Pi_{st}^{\leftrightarrow, \|}(P) = \mathcal{O}\left(Ne + Nd2^d\right)$. $\qquad \square$

Analysis of Argon2i. There are a number of variants for the Argon2i graphs. We will focus on Argon2i-A [BCS16] and Argon2i-B[5] [BDKJ16] here. Recall that Argon2i-A is a graph $G = (V = [N], E)$, where $E = \{(i, i+1) : i \in [N-1]\} \cup \{(r(i), i)\}$, where $r(i)$ is a random value that is picked uniformly at random from $[i-2]$. Argon2i-B has the same structure, except that $r(i)$ is not picked uniformly at random but has a distribution as follows:

$$\Pr[r(i) = j] = \Pr_{x \in [N]}\left[i\left(1 - \frac{x^2}{N^2}\right) \in (j-1, j]\right].$$

Lemma 2. *Let $G_{\text{Arg-A}} = (V_A = [N], E_A)$ and $G_{\text{Arg-B}} = (V_B = [N], E_B)$ be randomly sampled graphs according to the Argon2i-A and Argon2i-B edge distributions, respectively. Then with high probability, the following holds:*

(1) $G_{\text{Arg-A}}$ is (e_1, d_1)-reducible for $e_1 = \frac{N}{d'} + \frac{N \ln \lambda}{\lambda}$ and $d_1 = d'\lambda$, for any $0 < \lambda < N$ and $0 < d' < \frac{N}{\lambda}$.

(2) $G_{\text{Arg-B}}$ is (e_2, d_2)-reducible for $e_2 = \frac{N}{d'} + \frac{2N}{\sqrt{\lambda}}$ and $d_2 = d'\lambda$, for any $0 < \lambda < N$ and $0 < d' < \frac{N}{\lambda}$.

Alwen and Blocki [AB16, AB17] established similar bounds to Lemma 2, but focused on parameter settings where the depth d is large. By contrast, we will need to pick a depth-reducing set with a smaller depth parameter $d \ll \log N$ to minimize the $d2^d$ cost term in our pebbling attack. The full proof of Lemma 2 can be found in the full version. Here, we only give a brief intuition of the proof. To reduce the depth of a graph, we follow the approach of Alwen and Blocki [AB16, AB17] and divide N nodes into λ layers of size N/λ and then reduce the depth of each layer to d' so that the final depth becomes $d = d'\lambda$. To do so, we delete all nodes with parents in the same layer, and then delete one out of d' nodes in each layer. And then we count the number of nodes to be deleted in both steps for each graph.

Applying the result from Lemma 2 to Theorem 2, we have the following space-time cost of reversible pebbling for Argon2i-A and Argon2i-B. Intuitively, we obtain Corollary 1 by setting $\lambda = \sqrt{\log N}$ and $d' = \lambda/\ln \lambda \approx 2\sqrt{\log N}/\log \log N$ (resp. $\lambda = \sqrt[3]{\log^2 N}$ and $d' = \sqrt[3]{\log N}/2$) in Lemma 2 for Argon2i-A (resp. Argon2i-B). The full proof of Corollary 1 can be found in the full version.

Corollary 1. *Let $G_{\text{Arg-A}} = (V_A = [N], E_A)$ and $G_{\text{Arg-B}} = (V_B = [N], E_B)$ be randomly sampled graphs according to the Argon2i-A and Argon2i-B edge distributions, respectively. Then with high probability, $\Pi_{st}^{\overleftrightarrow{},\|}(G_{\text{Arg-A}}) = \mathcal{O}\left(\frac{N^2 \log \log N}{\sqrt{\log N}}\right)$, and $\Pi_{st}^{\overleftrightarrow{},\|}(G_{\text{Arg-B}}) = \mathcal{O}\left(\frac{N^2}{\sqrt[3]{\log N}}\right)$.*

3.3   Reversible Pebbling Attacks Using an Induced Line Graph

In this section, we give another general strategy to pebble DAGs by "reducing" the DAG G to a line graph, as shown in Fig. 1. Intuitively, given a DAG

---

[5] We will follow the naming convention of Alwen and Blocki [AB17] throughout the paper and use Argon2i-A to refer to Argon2i-A v1.1 and Argon2i-B to refer to v1.2+.

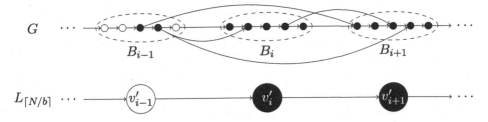

Fig. 1. A line graph $L_{\lceil N/b \rceil}$ induced from a DAG G. Note that each block in an original graph corresponds to a node in the corresponding line graph, e.g., a block B_i in G that consists of five nodes correspond to the node v_i' in $L_{\lceil N/b \rceil}$.

$G = (V, E)$ with $|V| = N$ and an integer parameter $b \geq 1$, we can partition V into consecutive blocks $B_1, \ldots, B_{\lceil N/b \rceil}$ such that each block contains exactly b nodes, while for the last block we can have less than b nodes if N/b is not an integer.

Notation. Now we consider a reversible pebbling P' of the line graph $L_{\lceil N/b \rceil} = (V' = [\lceil N/b \rceil], E')$. Intuitively, each node in $L_{\lceil N/b \rceil}$ corresponds to each block in G. To transform P' into a pebbling P of G, it will be useful to introduce some notation. Given a node $v' \in V'$ and the pebbling P' of $L_{\lceil N/b \rceil}$, we define $\mathsf{LastDelete}(P', v') := \max\{i : v' \in P_i'\}$ to denote the unique index i such that node $v' \in P_i'$, but $v' \notin P_j'$ for all rounds $j > i$, i.e., the pebble on node v' was removed for the final time in round $i + 1$. Similarly, it will be convenient to define $\mathsf{LastAdd}(P') := \max\{i : \lceil N/b \rceil \notin P_{i-1}'\}$ to be the unique round where a pebble was placed on the last node $v = \lceil N/b \rceil$ for the final time (Note: it is possible that a legal pebbling P' places/removes a pebble on node $v = \lceil N/b \rceil$ several times). We make a couple of basic observations. First, we note that if $u' < v'$ then $\mathsf{LastDelete}(P', u') > \mathsf{LastDelete}(P', v')$ since we need node $v' - 1$ on the graph to remove a pebble from node v'. Similarly, we note that for any node $v' < \lceil N/b \rceil$ that $\mathsf{LastDelete}(P', v') > \mathsf{LastAdd}(P')$ since we need node $\lceil N/b \rceil - 1$ to be pebbled before we can place a pebble on the final node. Given our graph $G = (V, E)$, a parameter b, and a partition $B_1, \ldots, B_{\lceil N/b \rceil}$ of V into consecutive blocks of size b, we define $\mathsf{Skip}(B_i, G)$, for each i, to be the set of all skip nodes in block B_i, i.e., the set of nodes with an outgoing edge that skips over block B_{i+1}:

$$\mathsf{Skip}(B_i, G) := \{v \in B_i : \exists j > i + 1 \text{ such that } v \in \mathsf{parents}(B_j, G)\}. \qquad (1)$$

We further define $\mathsf{NumSkip}(G, b)$ as the total number of skip nodes in $G = (V, E)$ after partitioning the set of nodes V into consecutive blocks of size b, i.e., $\mathsf{NumSkip}(G, b) := \sum_{i=1}^{\lceil N/b \rceil} |\mathsf{Skip}(B_i, G)|$, where B_i's are defined as before.

Pebbling Attempt 1. Our first approach to convert $P' \in \mathcal{P}_{L_{\lceil N/b \rceil}}^{\overleftrightarrow{\rightarrow}, \|}$ to a legal reversible pebbling P of G is as follows. Since each node in $L_{\lceil N/b \rceil}$ corresponds to a block (of size at most b) in G, we can transform placing a pebble on a node in $L_{\lceil N/b \rceil}$ to pebbling all nodes in the corresponding block in G in at most b steps. Similarly, we can convert removing a pebble on a node in $L_{\lceil N/b \rceil}$ to removing pebbles from all nodes in the corresponding block in G in at most b steps. It gives us $\Pi_s^{\leftrightarrow,\|}(P) \leq b\Pi_s^{\leftrightarrow,\|}(P')$ since each node is transformed to a block of size at most b, and $\Pi_t^{\leftrightarrow,\|}(P) \leq b\Pi_t^{\leftrightarrow,\|}(P')$ since one pebbling/removing step in $L_{\lceil N/b \rceil}$ is transformed to at most b pebbling/removing steps in G.

However, this transformation does *not* yield a legal reversible pebbling of G due to the skip nodes. In particular, given a reversible pebbling configuration $P'_k = \{v'\}$ of $L_{\lceil N/b \rceil}$, it is legal to proceed as $P'_{k+1} = \{v', v'+1\}$. However, when converting it to a reversible pebbling of G, one would need to place pebbles on block $B_{v'+1}$ while only having pebbles on block $B_{v'}$. This could be illegal if there is a node $v \in V$ such that $v \in B_i$ for $i < v'$ and $v \in \mathsf{parents}(B_{v'+1}, G)$, i.e., v is a skip node in B_i, because v must be previously pebbled to place pebbles on block $B_{v'+1}$.

Reversible Pebbling Strategy. To overcome this barrier, when we convert $P' \in \mathcal{P}_{L_{\lceil N/b \rceil}}^{\leftrightarrow,\|}$ to a legal reversible pebbling P of G, we define a transformation $P = \mathsf{Trans}(G, P', b)$ which convert placing/removing a pebble on/from a node v' in $L_{\lceil N/b \rceil}$ to placing/removing pebbles on/from all nodes in the corresponding block $B_{v'}$ in G in at most b steps as our first attempt, but when we remove pebbles from $B_{v'}$ in G, we keep skip nodes for the block in the transformation until we delete pebbles from the block for the last time, i.e., after round $\mathsf{LastDelete}(P', v')$, since these skip nodes will no longer needed to pebble nodes in other blocks in the future.

Furthermore, for the last block (in G), when a pebble is placed on the last node (in $L_{\lceil N/b \rceil}$) for the final time, i.e., in round $\mathsf{LastAdd}(P')$, we indeed want to only pebble the last node (sink node) in the block but not the entire block. Hence, we need additional (at most $b-1$) steps to remove pebbles from all nodes except for the last node in the block.

We can argue the legality of the converted pebbling of G because pebbling steps in each block is legal and keeping skip nodes during the transformation does not affect the legality of pebbling. Intuitively, whenever we pebble a new node v in $L_{\lceil N/b \rceil}$ the node $v-1$ must have been pebbled in the previous round. Thus, in G we will have pebbles on all nodes in the block B_{v-1}. Now for every node $w \in B_v$ and every edge of the form (u, w) we either have (1) $u \in B_{v-1}$, (2) $u \in B_v$ or (3) $u \in B_j$ with $j < v-1$. In the third case, u is a skip node and will already be pebbled allowing us to legally place a pebble on node w. Similarly, in the first case, we are guaranteed that u is already pebbled before we begin pebbling nodes in block B_v since every node in B_{v-1} is pebbled, and in the second case, u will be (re)pebbled before node w. A similar argument shows that all deletions are legal as well. The full proof of Lemma 3 can be found in the full version.

Lemma 3. *Let $G = (V = [N], E)$ and $b \in [N]$ be a parameter. If $P' \in \mathcal{P}^{\rightleftharpoons,\|}_{L_{\lceil N/b \rceil}}$, then $P = \mathsf{Trans}(G, P', b) \in \mathcal{P}^{\rightleftharpoons,\|}_G$.*

The formal definition of the procedure $\mathsf{Trans}(G, P', b)$ and an example for the reversible pebbling strategy can be found in the full version. Now we observe the following theorem describing the space-time cost of the converted pebbling in terms of the cost of the reduced pebbling of the line graph. We defer the proof of Theorem 3 to the full version.

Theorem 3. *Given a DAG $G = (V, E)$ with $|V| = N$ nodes, a reduced line graph $L_{\lceil N/b \rceil} = (V', E')$ with $|V'| = \lceil N/b \rceil$ nodes (where b is a positive integer), and a legal reversible pebbling $P' \in \mathcal{P}^{\rightleftharpoons,\|}_{L_{\lceil N/b \rceil}}$, there exists a legal reversible pebbling $P = \mathsf{Trans}(G, P', b) \in \mathcal{P}^{\rightleftharpoons,\|}_G$ such that*

$$\Pi^{\rightleftharpoons,\|}_{st}(P) \leq 2b^2 \Pi^{\rightleftharpoons,\|}_{st}(P') + 2b\Pi^{\rightleftharpoons,\|}_t(P') \cdot \mathsf{NumSkip}(G, b).$$

Analysis on DRSample. DRSample [ABH17] is the first practical construction of an iMHF which modified the edge distribution of Argon2i. Consider a DAG $G = (V = [N], E)$. Intuitively, similar to Argon2i, each node $v \in V \setminus \{1\}$ has at most two parents, i.e., there is a directed edge $(v - 1, v) \in E$ and a directed edge from a random predecessor $r(v)$. While Argon2i-A picks $r(v)$ uniformly at random from $[v - 2]$, DRSample picks $r(v)$ according to the following random process: (1) We randomly select a bucket index $i \leq \log v$, (2) We randomly sample $r(v)$ from the bucket $B_i(v) = \{u : 2^{i-1} < v - u \leq 2^i\}$. We can upper bound the number of skip nodes when we sample G according to this distribution. In particular, we observe that $\mathsf{NumSkip}\left(G_{\mathsf{DRS}}, \left\lceil \frac{N}{\log^2 N} \right\rceil\right) = \mathcal{O}\left(\frac{N \log \log N}{\log N}\right)$ where G_{DRS} is a randomly sampled graph according to the DRSample edge distribution. Intuitively, to count the number of skip nodes, we need to find edges with length $> b$ so that the edge skips over a block. There are at most $\log v - \log b$ (out of $\log v$) buckets which potentially could result in a skip node, which implies that the probability that the edge $(r(v), v)$ is longer than b is at most $1 - \log b / \log v \leq 1 - \log b / \log N = \log(N/b) / \log N$. Thus, the expected number of skip nodes in DRSample is at most $N \log(N/b) / \log N$ and standard concentration bounds imply that the number of skip nodes will be upper bounded by $\mathcal{O}(N \log(N/b) / \log N)$ with high probability. Setting $b = \lceil N / \log^2 N \rceil$ we can conclude that the expected number of skip nodes in DRSample is at most $\mathcal{O}(N \log \log N / \log N)$ with high probability. Further details can be found in the full version. Applying this result to Theorem 3, we have the following space-time cost of reversible pebbling for DRSample.

Corollary 2. *Let $G_{\mathsf{DRS}} = (V_{\mathsf{DRS}} = [N], E_{\mathsf{DRS}})$ be a randomly sampled graph according to the DRSample edge distribution. Then with high probability, $\Pi^{\rightleftharpoons,\|}_{st}(G_{\mathsf{DRS}}) = \mathcal{O}\left(\frac{N^2 \log \log N}{\log N}\right)$.*

The proof of Corollary 2 is deferred to the full version and we only give a brief intuition here. Basically, we can reduce G_{DRS} to the induced line graph $L_{\lceil \log^2 N \rceil}$

of size $\lceil \log^2 N \rceil$. Then by plugging in the reversible time and space-time cost of $L_{\lceil \log^2 N \rceil}$ and the number of skip nodes of G_{DRS} in Theorem 3 with setting $b = \lceil N/ \log^2 N \rceil$, we can conclude that $\Pi_{st}^{\leftrightarrow,\|}(G_{\mathsf{DRS}}) = \mathcal{O}\left(\frac{N^2 \log \log N}{\log N}\right)$.

4 Reversible Pebbling Attacks for Minimizing Cumulative Complexity

In this section, we adapt the depth-reducing pebbling attack GenPeb from Alwen and Blocki [AB16] to a reversible pebbling attack with the same asymptotic CC. The pebbling attack of Alwen and Blocki [AB16] applies to any (e, d)-reducible DAG G with $e = o(N)$ and $d = o(N)$. We first provide an overview of their pebbling strategy before describing how we extend the attack to obtain a reversible pebbling.

Overview of the Attack [AB16]. Suppose that we are given a DAG $G = (V = [N], E)$ with constant indegree δ along with a depth-reducing set S of size $|S| \leq e$. Intuitively, the pebbling attack of Alwen and Blocki [AB16] can be divided into a series of alternating "light phases" and "balloon phases." It is also helpful to imagine partitioning the nodes $[N]$ into intervals $I_i = [(i-1)g + 1, ig]$ of g consecutive nodes.

- *Light Phases:* During the ith light phase our goal will be to pebble all of the nodes in I_i over the next g consecutive pebbling rounds. The pre-condition for the ith light phase is that we start off with pebbles on all of the nodes $(\mathsf{parents}(I_i) \cup S) \cap [(i-1)g]$ where $\mathsf{parents}(I_i) = \{u : \exists v \in I_i \text{ s.t. } (u, v) \in E\}$ denotes the set of parents of nodes in I_i. Similarly, the post-condition for the ith light phase is that we have pebbles on all of the nodes $(\mathsf{parents}(I_i) \cup S) \cap [(i-1)g] \cup I_i$. If $P_j = (\mathsf{parents}(I_i) \cup S) \cap [(i-1)g]$ denotes the initial pebbling configuration at the start of the light phase then we can set $P_{j+x} = P_j \cup [(i-1)g, (i-1)g + x]$ so that P_{j+g} gives us our post-condition. During each light phase we keep *at most* $|(\mathsf{parents}(I_i) \cup S) \cap [(i-1)g] \cup I_i| \leq e + \delta g + g$ pebbles on the graph. Thus, the total cost incurred during each light phase is at most $(e + \delta g + g)g$ and the total cost incurred over all $\frac{N}{g}$ light phases is at most $N(e + \delta g + g)$.
- *Balloon Phases:* The ith balloon phase takes place immediately after the ith light phase with the goal of quickly recovering previously discarded pebbles to satisfy the pre-condition for the next $((i+1)^{st})$ light phase. In particular, the post-condition for the ith balloon phase should match the pre-condition for the $(i+1)^{st}$ light phase. The pre-condition for the ith balloon phase is that our starting configuration contains pebbles on all of the nodes $S \cap [ig]$. During a balloon phase, we are not worried about space so we can recover pebbles on the entire set $[ig]$ within d rounds by exploiting the fact that $G - S$ contains no directed path of length d. Once we have recovered pebbles on the entire set $[ig]$ we can then discard all of the pebbles that are not needed for the next light phase. Thus, the total cost incurred by each individual balloon phase is

at most dN and the total cost incurred over all $\frac{N}{g}$ balloon phases is at most $\frac{N^2 d}{g}$.

4.1   A Reversible Pebbling Attack

We first note that the pebbling attack above [AB16] is not reversible. In particular, at the end of each balloon phase we immediately transition from the pebbling configuration with pebbles on all of the nodes $[ig]$ to the pebbling configuration with pebbles only on the nodes $(\mathsf{parents}(I_{i+1}) \cup S) \cap [ig]$. The purpose of this pebbling transition is to save space during the next light phase by discarding unnecessary pebbles. Unfortunately, the rules of the reversible pebbling game would prevent us from discarding all of these pebbles.

To address this challenge we define a reversible balloon phase which reaches the desired target pebbling configuration $(\mathsf{parents}(I_{i+1}) \cup S) \cap [ig]$ in at most $2d$ pebbling rounds. Intuitively, our reversible balloon phase is based on several observations: (1) any legal monotonic black pebbling sequence $P_j \subseteq P_{j+1} \subseteq \ldots \subseteq P_{j+k}$ is also a legal reversible pebbling sequence the reversible pebbling game only places additional restrictions on which pebbles can be removed, (2) if $(S \cap [ig]) \subseteq P_j$ then there is a monotonic black pebbling sequence $P_j \subseteq P_{j+1} \subseteq \ldots \subseteq P_{j+d}$ with $P_{j+d} = [ig]$, (3) if $P_j, \ldots, P_{j+d}$ and $P'_j, \ldots, P'_{j+d}$ are both legal reversible pebbling sequences and $P_{j+d} = P'_{j+d}$ then the sequence $P_j, \ldots, P_{j+d}, P'_{j+d-1}, \ldots, P'_j$ is also a legal reversible pebbling sequence taking us from initial configuration P_j to final configuration P'_j—we defer the formal proof to the full version of this paper, (4) setting $P_j = ((\mathsf{parents}(I_i) \cup S) \cap [(i-1)g]) \cup [(i-1)g+1, ig]$ (the configuration from the post-condition at the end of the ith light phase) and $P'_j = (\mathsf{parents}(I_{i+1}) \cup S) \cap [ig]$ (the configuration from the precondition at the beginning of the $(i+1)^{st}$ light phase) we observe that $S \cap [ig] \subseteq P_j \cap P'_j$. Thus, we can exploit the above observation to obtain reversible pebbling sequences $P_j, \ldots, P_{j+d}$ and $P'_j, \ldots, P'_{j+d}$ with $P_{j+d} = [ig] = P'_{j+d}$ allowing us to transition from P_j to P'_j in time $2d$. Using the modified reversible balloon phase (above) we obtain our main result Theorem 4. In particular, given a (e, d) depth-reducible DAG we obtain a reversible pebbling strategy with cumulative pebbling cost $Ne + N(\delta+1)g + \frac{2N^2 d}{g}$. This result is asymptotically equivalent to the non-reversible pebbling attacks of Alwen and Blocki [AB16] so we can apply it to analyze the reversible CC of any iMHF. The detailed pebbling attack and legality proofs are deferred to the full version.

The proof of Lemma 4 can be found in the full version.

Lemma 4. *Let $\langle P_1, \ldots, P_t \rangle$ and $\langle P'_1, \ldots, P'_{t'} \rangle$ be two legal reversible pebbling sequences for some graph G such that $P_t = P'_{t'}$. Then for any $T \subseteq P_t$,*

$$\langle P_1, \ldots, P_t, P'_{t'-1} \cup T, P'_{t'-2} \cup T, \ldots, P'_1 \cup T \rangle$$

is also a legal reversible pebbling sequence for G.

Each balloon phase from [AB16] is monotonic because it simply pebbles all possible nodes each round. To extend the non-reversible balloon phase of [AB16], observe that the final pebbling configuration is $[ig]$ for some $i \geq 1$, i.e., we end with pebbles on all of the nodes $1, 2, \ldots, ig$. While the final target configuration (after the balloon phase completes) discards many pebbles from the graph we note that it still includes pebbles on *all* nodes in $S \cap [ig]$. Thus, there is also a monotonic pebbling from this target configuration to the configuration with pebbles on $[ig]$. Lemma 4 shows that we can combine these halves to form a reversible balloon phase.

This gives an upper bound on the reversible CC of pebbling graphs. The proof of Theorem 4 can be found in the full version of this paper.

Theorem 4. *For any (e, d)-reducible graph G on N nodes and any $g \in [d, N]$,*

$$\Pi_{cc}^{\leftrightarrow, \|}(G) \leq 2N \left(\frac{2Nd}{g} + e + (\delta + 1)g \right) + N + \frac{2N^2 d}{g}.$$

For any iMHF corresponding to a DAG G the reversible cumulative pebbling complexity obtained from our attack is identical to the attack from Alwen and Blocki [AB16]. In particular, for Argon2i-A and Argon2i-B we have $\Pi_{cc}^{\leftrightarrow, \|}(G_{\mathsf{Arg\text{-}A}}) = \mathcal{O}\left(N^{1.75} \log N\right)$ and $\Pi_{cc}^{\leftrightarrow, \|}(G_{\mathsf{Arg\text{-}B}}) = \mathcal{O}\left(N^{1.8}\right)$.

Alwen and Blocki [AB16] showed that any constant indegree DAG is (e, d)-reducible with $e = \mathcal{O}\left(N \log \log N / \log N\right)$ and $d = N / \log^2 N$. Applying Theorem 4 we obtain the following upper bound for any DAG G with constant indegree.

Corollary 3. *For any DAG $G = (V = [N], E)$ with constant indegree $\delta = \mathcal{O}(1)$ the reversible cumulative pebbling cost is at most $\Pi_{cc}^{\leftrightarrow, \|}(G) = \mathcal{O}\left(\frac{N^2 \log \log N}{\log N}\right)$.*

Acknowledgements. Jeremiah Blocki was supported in part by the National Science Foundation under NSF CAREER Award CNS-2047272 and NSF Award CCF-1910659. Seunghoon Lee was supported in part by the Center for Science of Information (NSF CCF-0939370). Blake Holman was supported in part by a Ross Fellowship at Purdue University and by a Ford Foundation Fellowship. We would like to thank anonymous reviewers for helpful feedback which improved this paper.

References

[AB16] Alwen, J., Blocki, J.: Efficiently computing data-independent memory-hard functions. In: Robshaw, M., Katz, J. (eds.) CRYPTO 2016. Part II. LNCS, vol. 9815, pp. 241–271. Springer, Heidelberg (2016). https://doi.org/10.1007/978-3-662-53008-5_9

[AB17] Alwen, J., Blocki, J.: Towards practical attacks on argon2i and balloon hashing. In: 2017 IEEE European Symposium on Security and Privacy (EuroS&P), pp. 142–157. IEEE (2017)

[ABH17] Alwen, J., Blocki, J., Harsha, B.: Practical graphs for optimal side-channel resistant memory-hard functions. In: Thuraisingham, B.M., Evans, D., Malkin, T., Xu, D. (eds.) ACM CCS 2017, pp. 1001–1017. ACM Press, October/November 2017

[ABP17] Alwen, J., Blocki, J., Pietrzak, K.: Depth-robust graphs and their cumulative memory complexity. In: Coron, J.-S., Nielsen, J.B. (eds.) EUROCRYPT 2017. Part III. LNCS, vol. 10212, pp. 3–32. Springer, Cham (2017). https://doi.org/10.1007/978-3-319-56617-7_1

[ABP18] Alwen, J., Blocki, J., Pietrzak, K.: Sustained space complexity. In: Nielsen, J.B., Rijmen, V. (eds.) EUROCRYPT 2018, Part II. LNCS, vol. 10821, pp. 99–130. Springer, Cham (2018). https://doi.org/10.1007/978-3-319-78375-8_4

[AS15] Alwen, J., Serbinenko, V.: High parallel complexity graphs and memory-hard functions. In: Servedio, R.A., Rubinfeld, R. (eds.) 47th ACM STOC, pp. 595–603. ACM Press, June 2015

[AT17] Alwen, J., Tackmann, B.: Moderately hard functions: definition, instantiations, and applications. In: Kalai, Y., Reyzin, L. (eds.) TCC 2017. Part I. LNCS, vol. 10677, pp. 493–526. Springer, Cham (2017). https://doi.org/10.1007/978-3-319-70500-2_17

[BBBV97] Bennett, C.H., Bernstein, E., Brassard, G., Vazirani, U.V.: Strengths and weaknesses of quantum computing. SIAM J. Comput. **26**(5), 1510–1523 (1997)

[BCS16] Boneh, D., Corrigan-Gibbs, H., Schechter, S.: Balloon hashing: a memory-hard function providing provable protection against sequential attacks. In: Cheon, J.H., Takagi, T. (eds.) ASIACRYPT 2016. Part I. LNCS, vol. 10031, pp. 220–248. Springer, Heidelberg (2016). https://doi.org/10.1007/978-3-662-53887-6_8

[BDF+11] Boneh, D., Dagdelen, Ö., Fischlin, M., Lehmann, A., Schaffner, C., Zhandry, M.: Random oracles in a quantum world. In: Lee, D.H., Wang, X. (eds.) ASIACRYPT 2011. LNCS, vol. 7073, pp. 41–69. Springer, Heidelberg (2011). https://doi.org/10.1007/978-3-642-25385-0_3

[BDKJ16] Biryukov, A., Dinu, D., Khovratovich, D., Josefsson, S.: The memory-hard argon2 password hash and proof-of-work function. In: Internet-Draft draft-irtf-cfrg-argon2-00, Internet Engineering Task Force (2016)

[Ben89] Bennett, C.H.: Time/space trade-offs for reversible computation. SIAM J. Comput. **18**(4), 766–776 (1989)

[BHK+19] Blocki, J., Harsha, B., Kang, S., Lee, S., Xing, L., Zhou, S.: Data-independent memory hard functions: new attacks and stronger constructions. In: Boldyreva, A., Micciancio, D. (eds.) CRYPTO 2019. Part II. LNCS, vol. 11693, pp. 573–607. Springer, Cham (2019). https://doi.org/10.1007/978-3-030-26951-7_20

[BHZ18] Blocki, J., Harsha, B., Zhou, S.: On the economics of offline password cracking. In: 2018 IEEE Symposium on Security and Privacy, pp. 853–871. IEEE Computer Society Press, May 2018

[BLZ21] Blocki, J., Lee, S., Zhou, S.: On the security of proofs of sequential work in a post-quantum world. In: Tessaro, S. (ed.) 2nd Conference on Information-Theoretic Cryptography (ITC 2021). Leibniz International Proceedings in Informatics (LIPIcs), vol. 199, pp. 22:1–22:27, Dagstuhl, Germany. Schloss Dagstuhl - Leibniz-Zentrum für Informatik (2021)

[BZ17] Blocki, J., Zhou, S.: On the depth-robustness and cumulative pebbling cost of Argon2i. In: Kalai, Y., Reyzin, L. (eds.) TCC 2017. Part I. LNCS, vol. 10677, pp. 445–465. Springer, Cham (2017). https://doi.org/10.1007/978-3-319-70500-2_15

[Cob66] Cobham, A.: The recognition problem for the set of perfect squares. In: 7th Annual Symposium on Switching and Automata Theory (swat 1966), pp. 78–87 (1966)

[Coo73] Cook, S.A.: An observation on time-storage trade off. In: Proceedings of the Fifth Annual ACM Symposium on Theory of Computing, STOC 1973, pp. 29–33. Association for Computing Machinery, New York (1973)

[Div00] Divincenzo, D.P.: The physical implementation of quantum computation. Fortschr. Phys. **48**, 2000 (2000)

[EGS75] Erdös, P., Graham, R.L., Szemerédi, E.: On sparse graphs with dense long paths. Comput. Math. Appl. **1**(3), 365–369 (1975)

[FR21] Fefferman, B., Remscrim, Z.: Eliminating intermediate measurements in space-bounded quantum computation. In Proceedings of the 53rd Annual ACM SIGACT Symposium on Theory of Computing, STOC 2021, pp. 1343–1356. Association for Computing Machinery, New York (2021)

[GNP+17] Grassi, P., et al.: Digital identity guidelines: authentication and lifecycle management, 2017-06-22 (2017)

[Gro96] Grover, L.K.: A fast quantum mechanical algorithm for database search. In: 28th ACM STOC, pp. 212–219. ACM Press, May 1996

[HPV77] Hopcroft, J., Paul, W., Valiant, L.: On time versus space. J. ACM **24**(2), 332–337 (1977)

[Kal00] Kaliski, B.: PKCS #5: Password-Based Cryptography Specification Version 2.0. RFC 2898, RSA Laboratories, September 2000

[KPB00] Pati, A.K., Braunstein, S.: Impossibility of deleting an unknown quantum state. Nature **404**, 164–165 (2000)

[Krá01] Král'ovič, R.: Time and space complexity of reversible pebbling. In: Pacholski, L., Ružička, P. (eds.) SOFSEM 2001. LNCS, vol. 2234, pp. 292–303. Springer, Heidelberg (2001). https://doi.org/10.1007/3-540-45627-9_26

[KSS21] Kornerup, N., Sadun, J., Soloveichik, D.: The spooky pebble game (2021)

[LV96] Li, M., Vitányi, P.: Reversibility and adiabatic computation: trading time and space for energy. Proc. Roy. Soc. Lond. Ser. A: Math. Phys. Eng. Sci. **452**(1947), 769–789 (1996)

[MSR+19] Meuli, G., Soeken, M., Roetteler, M., Bjorner, N., De Micheli, G.: Reversible pebbling game for quantum memory management. In: 2019 Design, Automation Test in Europe Conference Exhibition (DATE), pp. 288–291 (2019)

[NC02] Nielsen, M.A., Chuang, I.: Quantum computation and quantum information (2002)

[Pau75] Paul, W.J., A 2.5 n-lower bound on the combinational complexity of Boolean functions. In: Proceedings of the Seventh Annual ACM Symposium on Theory of Computing, STOC 1975, pp. 27–36. Association for Computing Machinery, New York (1975)

[PH70] Paterson, M.S., Hewitt, C.E.: Comparative Schematology, pp. 119–127. Association for Computing Machinery, New York (1970)

[PM99] Provos, N., Mazières, D.: A future-adaptive password scheme. In: Proceedings of the Annual Conference on USENIX Annual Technical Conference, ATEC 1999, p. 32. USENIX Association, USA (1999)

[PTC76] Paul, W.J., Tarjan, R.E., Celoni, J.R.: Space bounds for a game on graphs. In: Proceedings of the Eighth Annual ACM Symposium on Theory of Computing, STOC 1976, pp. 149–160. Association for Computing Machinery, New York (1976)

[PV76] Pippenger, N., Valiant, L.G.: Shifting graphs and their applications. J. ACM **23**(3), 423–432 (1976)

[Tom81] Tompa, M.: Corrigendum: time-space tradeoffs for computing functions, using connectivity properties of their circuits. J. Comput. Syst. Sci. **23**(1), 106 (1981)

Quantum Rewinding for Many-Round Protocols

Russell W. F. Lai[1], Giulio Malavolta[2]([✉]), and Nicholas Spooner[3]

[1] Aalto University, Espoo, Finland
russell.lai@aalto.fi
[2] Max Planck Institute for Security and Privacy, Bochum, Germany
giulio.malavolta@hotmail.it
[3] University of Warwick, Coventry, UK
nicholas.spooner@warwick.ac.uk

Abstract. We investigate the security of succinct arguments against quantum adversaries. Our main result is a proof of knowledge-soundness in the post-quantum setting for a class of multi-round interactive protocols, including those based on the recursive folding technique of Bulletproofs. To prove this result, we devise a new quantum rewinding strategy, the first that allows for rewinding across many rounds. This technique applies to any protocol satisfying natural multi-round generalizations of special soundness and collapsing. For our main result, we show that recent Bulletproofs-like protocols based on lattices satisfy these properties, and are hence sound against quantum adversaries.

Keywords: Succinct arguments · lattice · Bulletproofs · Quantum · Knowledge-soundness

1 Introduction

Succinct arguments [13,20] allow a prover to convince a verifier that a statement x belongs to a language $\mathcal{L}$, with communication shorter than the witness length for the corresponding relation. Succinct arguments have become a cornerstone of modern cryptography and fueled the development of many real-world applications, such as verifiable computation and anonymous cryptocurrencies. Recent years have seen an explosion of new constructions of succinct arguments, based on a variety of cryptographic assumptions.

However, the advent of quantum computation poses a significant threat to these advancements. On the one hand, Shor's algorithm [22] forces us to transition to cryptographic systems based on *post-quantum* assumptions, such as the hardness of the learning with errors (LWE) problem [21]. On the other hand, some known techniques to prove security of cryptographic protocols no longer apply in the post-quantum regime, due to the fundamentally different nature of quantum information. Most notable are *rewinding* techniques, which are ubiquitous in security proofs for succinct arguments.

E. Kiltz and V. Vaikuntanathan (Eds.): TCC 2022, LNCS 13747, pp. 80–109, 2022.
https://doi.org/10.1007/978-3-031-22318-1_4

In a rewinding proof, it is argued that an adversary that succeeds on a single random challenge with high enough probability must succeed on multiple challenges. This classically intuitive idea fails in the quantum setting, because measuring the adversary's response to one challenge causes an irreversible loss of information which may render it useless for answering other challenges.

An important family of succinct arguments are interactive protocols based on the recursive folding technique of [7,10], also known in the literature as *Bulletproofs*. Leveraging algebraic properties of cryptographic schemes, Bulletproofs-like protocols can achieve much smaller proof sizes than PCP- and IOP-based succinct arguments [6,13] while retaining the benefit of a public-coin setup. Unlike PCP- and IOP-based arguments, however, the original Bulletproofs constructions are not post-quantum secure, being based on the hardness of the discrete logarithm problem. This has motivated a line of work that aims to design "post-quantum Bulletproofs" [2,4,8,9]. While these works do not rely on cryptographic assumptions which are quantum-insecure, their analysis of post-quantum security is only *heuristic*, in the sense that soundness is only shown against a *classical* adversary. Motivated by this state of affairs, we ask the following question:

Can we prove post-quantum security for Bulletproofs-like protocols?

Known techniques for rewinding quantum adversaries [11,24] do not appear to generalize to multi-round challenge-response protocols, let alone to logarithmic-round protocols like Bulletproofs. Thus, answering the above question requires us to develop new quantum rewinding techniques.

1.1 Our Results

In this work, we show that a class of "recursive" many-round interactive protocols is knowledge-sound against quantum adversaries. As a special case, we establish that lattice-based Bulletproofs protocols are post-quantum secure, assuming the quantum hardness of LWE. Loosely speaking, our main result can be restated as follows.

Theorem 1 (Informal). *Assuming the quantum hardness of the (Ring-)LWE problem, lattice-based Bulletproofs protocols are knowledge-sound against quantum algorithms.*

Our main result is obtained by developing two technical contributions of independent interest:

Fold-Collapsing Hash: We show that the lattice-based hash function $\mathsf{Hash}_\mathbf{A}(\mathbf{x}) = \mathbf{A}\mathbf{x} \bmod q$, where $\mathbf{A}$ is sampled uniformly at random and $\mathbf{x}$ is a "short" vector, satisfies a strong *collapsing* property[1]. Intuitively, we show

---

[1] Collapsing can be thought of as the quantum analogue of collision-resistance, and loosely speaking it requires that it is hard to determine whether a register containing valid pre-images of a given $\mathbf{y}$ was measured or not.

that Hash$_A$ remains collapsing even when the key $\mathbf{A}$ is compressed via linear combinations of its columns with coefficients being short units in the base ring. This *fold-collapsing* property can be based on a variety of computational assumptions, including the (Ring-)LWE assumption.

Quantum Tree Rewinding: We develop a new quantum rewinding technique that allows us to extract from multi-round interactive protocols with certain collapsing and "recursive special soundness" properties. Our method combines the state-repair procedure of [11] with a probability estimation step that determines the success probability of the adversary on a given sub-tree. Combined with the collapsing property above and the recursive special soundness of Bulletproofs-like arguments, this establishes the post-quantum security of these protocols.

1.2   Related Work

The witness folding technique for constructing succinct arguments was first introduced by Bootle et al. [7] and later optimized by Bünz et al. [10], who called their protocols Bulletproofs. The term "Bulletproofs" is now used to refer to a family of succinct arguments with a certain recursive structure. The early Bulletproofs protocols [7,10] prove quadratic relations of exponents of elements in prime-order cyclic groups, and their soundness relies on the discrete logarithm assumption over these groups. Lai, Malavolta, and Ronge [14] generalized the folding technique to prove quadratic relations over bilinear pairing groups under a variant of the discrete logarithm assumption defined over these groups. As the discrete logarithm problems can be solved by Shor's algorithm [22] in quantum polynomial time, none of these protocols are post-quantum sound.

While it is necessary to consider non-linear relations to obtain an argument for NP, Attema and Cramer [3] showed how to linearize the non-linear relations using secret-sharing techniques, and apply the folding technique to compress the argument for the linearized relations. Although their protocols for proving linear relations over groups are in fact *unconditionally* sound, they are trivial in the quantum setting because the relations that they prove are in BQP.

Bootle et al. [9] adapted the Bulletproofs folding technique to the lattice setting, giving a succinct argument for proving knowledge of the witness of a short integer solution (SIS) instance, i.e. a short vector $\mathbf{x}$ satisfying $\mathbf{A}\mathbf{x} = \mathbf{y}$ mod q, over the m-th cyclotomic ring with m being a power of 2. The protocol, however, has large "slack": the knowledge extractor is only able to extract a short vector $\mathbf{x}'$ satisfying $\mathbf{A}\mathbf{x}' = 8^t \cdot \mathbf{y}$ mod q, where $\ell = 2^t$ is the dimension of the witness $\mathbf{x}$. Albrecht and Lai [2] revisited this protocol and reduced the slack from 8^t to 2^t with a careful choice of the challenge set R. They further eliminated the slack in the case of prime-power cyclotomic rings, i.e. when m is a power of a polynomially-large prime. Attema, Cramer, and Kohl [4] improved the soundness analysis of [2,9], reducing the knowledge error from $O(\log \ell / |R|)$ to $2 \log \ell / |R|$, which is tight. Bootle, Chiesa, and Sotiraki [8] proposed the abstract framework of sumcheck arguments which captures all Bulletproofs-like protocols, particularly lattice-based ones, mentioned above. Although lattice-based Bulletproofs for proving SIS relations are shown to be unconditionally sound against classical provers, the security proofs implicitly assume that the success probability of a prover remains unchanged after rewinding, which is generally false in the quantum setting.

1.3 Organization

In Sect. 2 we give an overview of our technical results. In Sect. 3 we recall standard preliminaries. In Sect. 4 we recall the notion of public-coin interactive arguments and introduce the notions of recursive special soundness and last-round collapsing. In Sect. 5 we show that protocols satisfying these properties are also knowledge-sound, even against quantum provers. In Sect. 6 we study the collapsing properties of hash function families implicit in lattice-based Bulletproof protocols. In the full version we build upon the results of Sect. 6 to show that lattice-based Bulletproof protocols are recursive special sound and last-round collapsing, and hence knowledge-sound, even against quantum provers.

2 Technical Overview

We give a brief overview of the main technical steps of our work. Before delving into the details of our analysis, we summarize the main conceptual steps of our proof:

Step I: We formalize a family of public-coin protocols Σ that satisfy two main properties of interest, namely recursive special soundness and last-round collapsing.

Step II: We describe a new quantum rewinding strategy that allows us to extract a witness from any recursive special sound and last-round collapsing protocol of the above defined family.

Step III: We show that the lattice-based hash function $\mathsf{Hash}_{\mathbf{A}}(\mathbf{x}) = \mathbf{Ax}$ is fold-collapsing, assuming that the (Ring-)LWE problem is intractable for quantum algorithms.

Step IV: Using the result from the previous step, we show that lattice-based Bulletproofs protocols are recursive special sound and last-round collapsing.

The remainder of the technical overview will be split into two parts, detailing Step I–II and Step III–IV respectively.

2.1 Quantum Rewinding

We first establish some context. Consider a $(2t + 1)$-message public-coin interactive argument Σ where both the prover and the verifier input a statement x and the prover additionally inputs a witness w. The first $2t$ rounds of the protocol consists of the prover sending a "commitment" z_i and the verifier sending a challenge r_i for $i \in [t]$. The protocol ends with the prover sending a response w_{t+1} and the verifier outputting a single bit. The protocol Σ is k-tree-special sound, or $(k, \ldots, k)$-special sound, for a relation $\mathfrak{R}$ if the following holds: There exists an efficient extractor E which, given a statement x and complete k-ary tree of (edge-)depth t where the nodes and edges in each root-to-leaf path are labelled by a transcript $(z_1, r_1, \ldots, z_t, r_t, w_{t+1})$ of Σ which is accepting, extracts a witness w satisfying $\mathfrak{R}(x, w) = 1$.

In the following, we first review how tree-special soundness classically implies knowledge-soundness, and discuss where the classical reduction fails in the quantum setting. We then overview how post-quantum knowledge-soundness can be proven for protocols which satisfy a strengthening of tree special soundness along with a natural "collapsing" property.

Classical Tree Rewinding. To prove that a tree-special sound argument is knowledge-sound, the classical extraction proof (e.g. given in [9]) is based on the tree extraction technique of [7]. This technique obtains a k-ary tree of transcripts using a simple recursive strategy. This tree can then be provided to E in order to obtain the witness. For $i \in [t]$, [7] define subtree extractors T_i which, given a transcript prefix, obtain a k-ary subtree rooted at that prefix:

$\underline{T_i(r_1, \ldots, r_{i-1})}$:

1. Let τ be a graph containing a single (root) node v.
2. Query the adversary at $(r_1, \ldots, r_{i-1})$ to obtain the i-th round commitment z_i. Label v with z_i.
3. Repeat until v has k children: Choose $r_i \leftarrow R_i$ uniformly at random, and run $\tau' \leftarrow T_{i+1}(r_1, \ldots, r_i)$. If T_{i+1} does not abort, attach τ' to v via an edge labelled with r_i.
   If T_{i+1} aborts, and this is the first loop iteration, then abort.
4. Return τ.

The base case $T_{t+1}(r_1, \ldots, r_t)$ queries the adversary at $(r_1, \ldots, r_t)$ to obtain a full protocol transcript $(z_1, \ldots, z_{t+1})$ and returns z_{t+1} if that transcript is accepting (and otherwise aborts). The italicized condition above ensures that the procedure runs in expected polynomial time. Concretely, let ε denote the probability for r_i chosen uniformly at random that $T_{i+1}(r_1, \ldots, r_i)$ does not abort. The number of calls that T_i makes to T_{i+1} is then 1 with probability $1 - \varepsilon$ (due to the italicized condition) and $1 + (k-1)/\varepsilon$ (in expectation) with probability ε. Hence the overall expected number of calls is k, and by induction T_i runs in expected time $O(k^{t-i} \cdot t_A)$, where t_A is the running time of the adversary.

Quantum Tree Rewinding. Moving now to the quantum setting, the immediate problem is that Step 3 is a rewinding step: The above argument implicitly uses the fact that a classical adversary can be rewound to ensure that the success probability of T_{i+1} in each iteration is always ε. For quantum adversaries, the situation is more complicated, since measurements are in general irreversible operations. Known techniques [11,24] allow one to recover this type of rewinding in the quantum setting, provided the protocol satisfies a special "collapsing" condition.

Roughly speaking, this condition says the measurement performed by the reduction in the rewinding loop to obtain the response (in this case τ) is indistinguishable (to the adversary) from a binary measurement of whether the obtained response is valid or not (in this case, whether T_{i+1} aborts). Unfortunately, for the extractor above for general tree-special sound protocols we do not have this guarantee. The issue is that τ contains information about the set of challenges *to which the adversary produces an accepting response*. Measuring this information can cause the adversary's state to be disturbed in a detectable way. As a result, we do not know how to achieve general tree extraction in the quantum setting.

Instead, we observe that Bulletproofs-like protocols satisfy additional structural properties such that extracting the full tree is not necessary. Specifically, we can identify a family of protocols $(\Sigma_i)_{i=0}^{t}$ associated to Σ, where Σ_i has $2i+1$ messages, $\Sigma_t = \Sigma$ and Σ_0 is a noninteractive protocol where the prover sends w and the verifier checks $\mathfrak{R}(x, w)$.

This family has the property that, given a k-ary tree of accepting transcripts for Σ_i, we can obtain a k-ary tree of accepting transcripts for Σ_{i-1} by applying only "local" operations at the i-th layer: specifically, we compute a new label for each node v_i at depth i by applying a function E_i to the labels of its children. With this structural property, we can modify T_i (for all i) to directly output a witness (label) w_i instead of a tree τ. As a result, T_0 will directly output a witness w for x.

Moreover, we identify that if each Σ_i satisfies another property called *last-round collapsing* and, crucially, T_{i+1} is executed *projectively* by T_i, then measuring the output of T_{i+1} is in fact indistinguishable from a binary measurement. It turns out that the key technical challenge here is the *projectivity* of T_{i+1}.

The Extractor. A general quantum measurement given by a circuit can be implemented projectively in a standard way using the principle of deferred measurement. Specifically, a circuit C has a corresponding unitary dilation U (given by replacing measurement gates with controlled-NOTs); the projective implementation is obtained by applying U, measuring the output register, and then applying $U^\dagger$.

Unfortunately, this method only applies to circuits, whereas in the above template, T_{i+1} is an algorithm with variable (expected polynomial) runtime. The unitary dilation of an expected (quantum) polynomial time (EQPT) algorithm is not generally efficiently implementable[2]. To avoid this problem, we design an extractor where the recursive call is to a *strict* polynomial-time algorithm. To give a sense of our construction, we will (for now) return to the classical setting. A natural first attempt is to simply *truncate* T_{i+1} to some strict number of repetitions N; applying this to all layers of the tree yields an extractor that

---

[2] [16] proposes an extended computational model (in the context of zero knowledge simulation) which does permit this. However, this is not sufficient for our setting: While the model supports black-box access to unitary dilations of EQPT algorithms, here we would require a unitary dilation of an EQPT algorithm which itself calls the unitary dilation of an EQPT algorithm, etc.

makes N^t calls to the adversary. How large does N need to be? By Markov's inequality, the error incurred by truncation is $O(k/N)$; hence to achieve any guarantee, we require that $N = \Omega(k/\varepsilon)$. As a result, N^t is superpolynomial (since ε is an arbitrary inverse polynomial).

The key to overcoming this issue is to ensure that, no matter how many repetitions of Step 3 we execute, we only make k recursive calls. In particular, we must guarantee that whenever we make a call to T_{i+1}, it succeeds with high probability. To do this in the classical setting, we can modify the extractor as follows.

$\underline{T_{i,\varepsilon}(r_1, \ldots, r_{i-1})} :$

1. Repeat at most N times until $|W| = k$:
   (a) Choose $r_i \leftarrow R_i$ uniformly at random.
   (b) Estimate $\varepsilon' \leftarrow \Pr_{r_{i+1}, \ldots, r_t} [A(r_1, \ldots, r_t) \text{ convinces } V]$.
   (c) If $\varepsilon' \geq \varepsilon - \beta$, compute $w_i \leftarrow T_{i+1, \varepsilon - \beta}(r_1, \ldots, r_i)$. Add (r_i, w_{i+1}) to W.
2. Return $w_i \leftarrow E_i(W)$.

Note that we explicitly provide T with a lower bound ε on the success probability of A. We choose $\beta = 1/\text{poly}(\lambda)$ to be small enough so that the adversary still has high enough success probability at the base of the recursion. The estimation step must be accurate to within an additive $o(\beta) = 1/\text{poly}(\lambda)$ factor, which can be achieved using polynomially many calls to A. By Markov's inequality, the probability that $\varepsilon' \geq \varepsilon - \beta$ is at least β, and so by setting $N = O(\lambda/\beta) = \text{poly}(\lambda)$ we see k successful iterations with probability $2^{-\lambda}$. The running time of $T_{i,\varepsilon}$ is then $k \cdot |T_{i+1, \varepsilon - \beta}| + N \cdot \text{poly}(\lambda) = O(k^{t-i} \cdot \text{poly}(\lambda))$.

Instantiating the above template in the quantum setting requires some care. The estimation step is achieved using e.g. the Marriott-Watrous algorithm [19] as described in [11]. We facilitate the main rewinding loop using the state repair technique of [11]. The state repair technique recovers the success probability of a state after it is disturbed by a (binary) projective measurement. In our setting, this measurement is "does the estimation step output $\varepsilon' \geq \varepsilon - \beta$?" All of these procedures have associated error; this error must be managed to ensure that it does not increase too much throughout the recursion. For more details, we refer the reader to Sect. 5.

2.2   Lattice-Based Bulletproofs

In the above, we established that if a $(2t + 1)$-message public-coin argument Σ induces a family $(\Sigma_i)_{i=0}^t$ which is *recursive special sound*, and each Σ_i is *last-round collapsing*, then Σ has post-quantum knowledge-soundness. In the following, we consider the case where Σ is a lattice-based Bulletproofs protocol, describe what it means for $(\Sigma_i)_{i=0}^t$ to be *recursive special sound* and Σ_i to be *last-round collapsing*, and outline how the properties can be achieved.

We recall the lattice-based Bulletproofs protocols from [2,4,9]. In such protocols, both the prover and the verifier receive as input a SIS instance $(\mathbf{A}, \mathbf{y})$

defined over a ring $\mathcal{R}^3$, and the prover additionally receives a short vector $\mathbf{x}$ satisfying $\mathbf{A}\mathbf{x} = \mathbf{y} \bmod q^4$. The interactive protocol consists of a recursive application of a subroutine that allows the prover and the verifier to cut the size of the relation in half at each iteration: On input a hash key $\mathbf{A} = \mathbf{A}_0 \| \mathbf{A}_1$ and an image $\mathbf{y}$, the verifier samples a random (short) ring element r from a challenge set $R \subseteq \mathcal{R}$. The hash key is then "folded" by taking the appropriate linear combination of the columns $\mathbf{A}' = r \cdot \mathbf{A}_0 + \mathbf{A}_1$. Next, the prover updates the witness $\mathbf{x} = \mathbf{x}_0 \| \mathbf{x}_1$ to $\mathbf{x}' = \mathbf{x}_0 + r \cdot \mathbf{x}_1$, thus defining a new SIS instance $(\mathbf{A}', \mathbf{y}')$ satisfying

$$
\begin{aligned}
\mathbf{A}'\mathbf{x}' &= (r \cdot \mathbf{A}_0 + \mathbf{A}_1)(\mathbf{x}_0 + r \cdot \mathbf{x}_1) \\
&= \mathbf{A}_1\mathbf{x}_0 + r \cdot (\mathbf{A}_0\mathbf{x}_0 + \mathbf{A}_1\mathbf{x}_1) + r^2 \cdot \mathbf{A}_0\mathbf{x}_1 \\
&= \underbrace{\mathbf{A}_1\mathbf{x}_0}_{\mathbf{l}} + r \cdot \mathbf{y} + r^2 \cdot \underbrace{\mathbf{A}_0\mathbf{x}_1}_{\mathbf{r}} = \mathbf{y}'
\end{aligned}
$$

where the terms $(\mathbf{l}, \mathbf{r})$ are sent by the prover to help the verifier compute the new image $\mathbf{y}'$. This effectively reduces the dimension of the statement by half. Repeating this procedure t-times, where $\ell = 2^t$ is the dimension of the witness $\mathbf{x}$, brings the dimension down to 1, at which point the prover can simply send the witness in the plain to the verifier.

Recursive Special Soundness. To define recursive special soundness, we first specify the family of protocols $(\Sigma_i)_{i=0}^t$ induced by a lattice-based Bulletproofs protocol Σ. For each i, the $(2i + 1)$-message protocol Σ_i applies the folding technique recursively on the input statement $(\mathbf{A}, \mathbf{y})$ for i times, each taking 2 messages, and the final message is simply the witness $\mathbf{x}_i$ of the i-th folded statement $(\mathbf{A}_i, \mathbf{y}_i)$. Note that Σ_0 is the trivial 1-message protocol where the prover simply sends the witness $\mathbf{x}$ of $(\mathbf{A}, \mathbf{y})$, while $\Sigma_t = \Sigma$. Recursive special soundness requires that, for each $i \in [t]$, given k accepting transcripts (for Bulletproofs $k = 3$) for Σ_i that differ only in the last challenge-response rounds (i.e. messages $2i$ and $2i + 1$), it is possible to efficiently recover a valid last-round (i.e. $(2i - 1)^{\text{th}}$) message for the protocol Σ_{i-1}. From this definition, we can see that given a complete k-ary tree of accepting transcripts for Σ_t, it is possible to recursively recover a valid prover message $\mathbf{x}$ for the trivial protocol Σ_0.

With its close connection to the standard special soundness property, it is natural that the recursive special soundness of $(\Sigma_i)_{i=0}^t$ can be proven similarly: Given an accepting transcript of Σ_i of the form

$$
(\mathbf{A}, \mathbf{y}, (\mathbf{l}_1, \mathbf{r}_1), r_1, \ldots, (\mathbf{l}_{i-1}, \mathbf{r}_{i-1}), r_{i-1}, (\mathbf{l}_i, \mathbf{r}_i), (r_i^{(j)}, \mathbf{x}_i^{(j)})_{j \in [k]})
$$

---

[3] Rigorously, the matrix $\mathbf{A}$ is sampled uniformly at random by a setup algorithm, and is taken as input by the prover and the verifier as a public parameter.

[4] We focus only on the component of lattice-based Bulletproofs protocols where the witness folding technique is applied, since this is the technically challenging component in the quantum setting.

the extractor E_i first derives $(\mathbf{A}_i, \mathbf{y}_i^{(j)})_{j \in [k]}$ satisfying

$$\mathbf{A}_i \left(\mathbf{x}_i^{(1)}\, \mathbf{x}_i^{(2)}\, \mathbf{x}_i^{(3)} \right) = \mathbf{y}_i \bmod q,$$

then extracts $\mathbf{x}_{i-1}$ satisfying $\mathbf{A}_{i-1}\mathbf{x}_{i-1} = \mathbf{y}_{i-1} \bmod q$, provided that the challenges $(r_i^{(j)})_{j \in [k]}$ are chosen from a subtractive set [2][5]. The tuple

$$(\mathbf{A}, \mathbf{y}, (\mathbf{l}_1, \mathbf{r}_1), r_1, \ldots, (\mathbf{l}_{i-1}, \mathbf{r}_{i-1}), r_{i-1}, \mathbf{x}_{i-1})$$

is then an accepting transcript of Σ_{i-1}. As usual, two subtleties in the lattice setting are that the norm of the witness is slightly increased with each extraction step, and that the extracted witness may only be a preimage of $s \cdot \mathbf{y}_{i-1}$ for some short slack element $s \in \mathcal{R}$. These soundness gap issues can be handled by making an appropriate choice of (extraction relation) $\mathfrak{R}$, and choosing the challenge set and other parameters carefully.

Fold-Collapsing. Finally, we describe what it means for Σ_i to be last-round collapsing and how it is achieved. Last-round collapsing requires that, provided an *accepting* transcript of Σ_i where all messages but the last one are measured, it is computationally hard to tell whether the last message was also measured or not. In the procotol Σ_i induced above, the last message consists of a witness $\mathbf{x}_i$ of the statement $(\mathbf{A}_i, \mathbf{y}_i)$ defined by the previous rounds of interaction. Importantly, $(\mathbf{A}_i, \mathbf{y}_i)$ is fixed by the first $2i$ messages of the protocol. Thus, proving the above property is equivalent to establishing that the hash function

$$\mathsf{Hash}_{\mathbf{A}_i}(\mathbf{x}_i) = \mathbf{A}_i \mathbf{x}_i \bmod q$$

is *collapsing* for all $i \in \{0, \ldots, t\}$. It is known that such function satisfies the collapsing property, if the key $\mathbf{A}$ is uniformly chosen [1,15]. However, recall that $\mathbf{A}_i$ is obtained by progressively folding the original key $\mathbf{A}$, so we need to show that the function remains collapsing even after we perform such operations over the hash key. We refer to this notion as *fold-collapsing*.

Our strategy to prove that the function is fold-collapsing proceeds in three steps: First, we appeal to the well-known fact that collapsing is implied by the stronger notion of somewhere statistically binding (SSB). Loosely speaking, SSB requires that the hash function has an alternative key generation mode, which is (i) computationally indistinguishable from the original mode, and that (ii) makes the hash statistically binding for a chosen position (say the j-th one) of the pre-image. Second, we show that the function $\mathsf{Hash}_{\mathbf{A}}$ is SSB. This is done by embedding ciphertexts of a linearly homomorphic encryption (with the appropriate ciphertext space) as the columns of the key $\mathbf{A}$. In the alternative mode, the key $\tilde{\mathbf{A}}_j$ consists of

$$\tilde{\mathbf{A}}_j = \left(\mathsf{Enc}(0) \ldots \mathsf{Enc}(0) \underbrace{\mathsf{Enc}(1)}_{j\text{-th position}} \mathsf{Enc}(0) \ldots \mathsf{Enc}(0) \right).$$

---

[5] A subtractive set, also known as an exceptional sequence, is a set of ring elements such that the difference between any distinct members is invertible over the ring.

Since $\mathsf{Hash}_{\tilde{\mathbf{A}}_j}$ is a linear function, by the linearly-homomorphic property of the encryption scheme, we have $\tilde{\mathbf{A}}_j\mathbf{x} = \mathsf{Enc}(x_j) \bmod q$. Then, by the correctness of the encryption scheme, the hash function statistically binds the j-th coordinate of $\mathbf{x}$, as desired. Finally, to show that the folded key is still SSB, it suffices to observe that if the challenge set R consists of only units, i.e. $R \subseteq \mathcal{R}^\times$, then $r\mathbf{A}_0 + \mathbf{A}_1$ still preserves the invariant that exactly one ciphertext is not an encryption of 0 for any $r \in R$, again invoking the linear homomorphism of the encryption scheme. Thus, the folded key is still statistically binding on exactly one position of the input vector. Repeating this process recursively yields the desired statement.

Conveniently, for each of the subtractive sets R' suggested in [2] to be used as a challenge set, all but one element (i.e. 0) in R' are units in $\mathcal{R}$. Instantiating R with $R' \setminus \{0\}$ therefore meets all our requirements.

Remark 1. We stress that all of our results concern the protocol in the interactive setting. In particular, it should be noted that all lattice-based Bulletproofs protocols have at most inverse polynomial soundness, due to the fact that the challenge space is only polynomial size. While one can always reduce this to negligible by sequentially repeating the protocol, parallel repetition for superconstant round arguments is much less well-understood. In the classical setting, this was recently solved for tree special sound protocols in [5]; we leave open the problem of extending this to the quantum setting. Note that this required to establish that existing lattice-based Bulletproofs protocols can be made non-interactive in the QROM via Fiat-Shamir; importantly, sequential repetition does not suffice.

3   Preliminaries

Let $\lambda \in \mathbb{N}$ be the security parameter. We write $[n] := \{1, 2, \ldots, n\}$ and $\mathbb{Z}_n := \{0, 1, \ldots, n-1\}$ for $n \in \mathbb{N}$. We write $\varphi(n)$ for the Euler totient function, i.e. the number of positive integers at most and coprime with n. If a is a ring element, we write $\langle a \rangle$ for the ideal generated by a.

We make use of the following simple fact, a consequence of Markov's inequality.

Proposition 1. *Let X be a random variable supported on $[0, 1]$. Then for all $\alpha \geq 0$, $\Pr[X \geq \alpha] \geq E[X] - \alpha$.*

3.1   Lattices

For $m \in \mathbb{N}$, let $\zeta = \zeta_m \in \mathbb{C}$ be any fixed primitive m-th root of unity. We write $\mathbb{K} = \mathbb{Q}(\zeta)$ for the cyclotomic field of order $m \geq 2$ and degree $\varphi(m)$, and $\mathcal{R} = \mathbb{Z}[\zeta]$ for its ring of integers, called a cyclotomic ring for short. It is well-known that $\mathcal{R} \cong \mathbb{Z}[x]/\langle \Phi_m(x) \rangle$, where $\Phi_m(x)$ is the m-th cyclotomic polynomial. For $q \in \mathbb{N}$, write $\mathcal{R}_q := \mathcal{R}/q \cdot \mathcal{R}$.

For elements $x \in \mathcal{R}$ we denote the infinity norm of its coefficient vector (with the powerful basis $\{1, \zeta, \ldots, \zeta^{\varphi(m)-1}\}$) as $\|x\|$. If $\mathbf{x} \in \mathcal{R}^k$ we write $\|\mathbf{x}\|$ for the infinity norm of $\mathbf{x}$.

The ring expansion factor of $\mathcal{R}$ is defined as $\gamma_{\mathcal{R}} := \max_{a,b \in \mathcal{R}} \frac{\|a \cdot b\|}{\|a\| \cdot \|b\|}$. By definition, we have for any $x, y \in \mathcal{R}$ that $\|x \cdot y\| \leq \gamma_{\mathcal{R}} \cdot \|x\| \cdot \|y\|$.

For any ordered set $T = (r_i)_{i \in \mathbb{Z}_t} \subseteq \mathcal{R}$, we write

$$\mathbf{V}_T := \begin{pmatrix} 1 & 1 & \cdots & 1 \\ r_0 & r_1 & \cdots & r_{t-1} \\ \vdots & \vdots & \ddots & \vdots \\ r_0^{t-1} & r_1^{t-1} & \cdots & r_{t-1}^{t-1} \end{pmatrix}$$

for the (column-style) Vandermonde matrix induced by T.

Definition 1 ((s,t)-Subtractive Sets [2]). *Let $s \in \mathcal{R}$ and $t \in [n]$. A set $R \subseteq \mathcal{R}$ is said to be (s,t)-subtractive if for any t-subset $T = \{r_i\}_{i \in \mathbb{Z}_t} \subseteq R$, it holds that $s \in \langle \det(\mathbf{V}_T) \rangle$. If R is $(1,2)$-subtractive, we simply say that R is subtractive.*

Proposition 2 ([2]). *If m is a power of a prime p and $\mathcal{R}$ is the m-th order cyclotomic ring, then the set $R := \left\{ 1, 1 + \zeta, \ldots, \sum_{i \in \mathbb{Z}_{p-1}} \zeta^i \right\} \subseteq_{p-1} \mathcal{R}$ is subtractive. Furthermore, for any ordered set $T = (r_0, r_1, r_2) \subseteq R$ and any $x_0, x_1, x_2 \in \mathcal{R}$ with $\|x_j\| \leq \beta$,*

$$\left\| \begin{pmatrix} r_0 \cdot x_0 & r_1 \cdot x_1 & r_2 \cdot x_2 \\ x_0 & x_1 & x_2 \end{pmatrix} \cdot \mathbf{V}_T^{-1} \cdot \begin{pmatrix} 0 \\ 1 \\ 0 \end{pmatrix} \right\| \leq 24 \cdot \varphi(m) \cdot \gamma_{\mathcal{R}} \cdot \beta.$$

If m is a power of 2 and $\mathcal{R}$ is the m-th order cyclotomic ring, then the set $R := \{1, \zeta, \ldots, \zeta^{\varphi(m)-1}\} \subseteq_{\varphi(m)} \mathcal{R}$ is $(2,3)$-subtractive. Furthermore, for any ordered set $T = (r_0, r_1, r_2) \subseteq R$ and any $x_0, x_1, x_2 \in \mathcal{R}$ with $\|x_j\| \leq \beta$,

$$\left\| \begin{pmatrix} r_0 \cdot x_0 & r_1 \cdot x_1 & r_2 \cdot x_2 \\ x_0 & x_1 & x_2 \end{pmatrix} \cdot s \cdot \mathbf{V}_T^{-1} \cdot \begin{pmatrix} 0 \\ 1 \\ 0 \end{pmatrix} \right\| \leq 3 \cdot \varphi(m) \cdot \gamma_{\mathcal{R}} \cdot \beta.$$

3.2   Quantum Information

We recall the basics of quantum information. Most of the following is taken almost in verbatim from [11]. A (pure) *quantum state* is a vector $|\psi\rangle$ in a complex Hilbert space $\mathcal{H}$ with $\||\psi\rangle\| = 1$; in this work, $\mathcal{H}$ is finite-dimensional. We denote by $\mathbf{S}(\mathcal{H})$ the space of Hermitian operators on $\mathcal{H}$. A *density matrix* is a positive semi-definite operator $\rho \in \mathbf{S}(\mathcal{H})$ with $\mathrm{Tr}(\rho) = 1$. A density matrix represents a probabilistic mixture of pure states (a mixed state); the density matrix corresponding to the pure state $|\psi\rangle$ is $|\psi\rangle\langle\psi|$. Typically we divide a Hilbert space into *registers*, e.g. $\mathcal{H} = \mathcal{H}_1 \otimes \mathcal{H}_2$. We sometimes write, e.g., $\rho^{\mathcal{H}_1}$ to specify that $\rho \in \mathbf{S}(\mathcal{H}_1)$.

A unitary operation is a complex square matrix U such that $UU^\dagger = \mathbf{I}$. The operation U transforms the pure state $|\psi\rangle$ to the pure state $U|\psi\rangle$, and the density matrix ρ to the density matrix $U\rho U^\dagger$. We write $U(\mathcal{H})$ for the set of unitary operators on $\mathcal{H}$.

A *projector* Π is a Hermitian operator ($\Pi^\dagger = \Pi$) such that $\Pi^2 = \Pi$. A *projective measurement* is a collection of projectors $\mathsf{P} = (\Pi_i)_{i \in S}$ such that $\sum_{i \in S} \Pi_i = \mathbf{I}$. This implies that $\Pi_i \Pi_j = 0$ for distinct i and j in S. The application of P to a pure state $|\psi\rangle$ yields outcome $i \in S$ with probability $p_i = \| \Pi_i |\psi\rangle \|^2$; in this case the post-measurement state is $|\psi_i\rangle = \Pi_i |\psi\rangle / \sqrt{p_i}$. We refer to the post-measurement state $\Pi_i |\psi\rangle / \sqrt{p_i}$ as the result of applying P to $|\psi\rangle$ and *post-selecting* (conditioning) on outcome i. A state $|\psi\rangle$ is an *eigenstate* of P if it is an eigenstate of every Π_i. A two-outcome projective measurement is called a *binary projective measurement*, and is written as $\mathsf{P} = (\Pi, \mathbf{I} - \Pi)$, where Π is associated with the outcome 1, and $\mathbf{I} - \Pi$ with the outcome 0.

General (non-unitary) evolution of a quantum state can be represented via a *completely-positive trace-preserving (CPTP)* map $T: \mathbf{S}(\mathcal{H}) \to \mathbf{S}(\mathcal{H}')$. We omit the precise definition of these maps in this work; we only use the facts that they are trace-preserving (for every $\rho \in \mathbf{S}(\mathcal{H})$ it holds that $\mathrm{Tr}(T(\rho)) = \mathrm{Tr}(\rho)$) and linear. For every CPTP map $T: \mathbf{S}(\mathcal{H}) \to \mathbf{S}(\mathcal{H})$ there exists a *unitary dilation* U that operates on an expanded Hilbert space $\mathcal{H} \otimes \mathcal{K}$, so that $T(\rho) = \mathrm{Tr}_{\mathcal{K}}(U(\rho \otimes |0\rangle\langle0|^{\mathcal{K}})U^\dagger)$. This is not necessarily unique; however, if T is described as a circuit then there is a dilation U_T represented by a circuit of size $O(|T|)$.

For Hilbert spaces $\mathcal{A}, \mathcal{B}$ the *partial trace* over $\mathcal{B}$ is the unique CPTP map $\mathrm{Tr}_{\mathcal{B}}: \mathbf{S}(\mathcal{A} \otimes \mathcal{B}) \to \mathbf{S}(\mathcal{A})$ such that $\mathrm{Tr}_{\mathcal{B}}(\rho_A \otimes \rho_B) = \mathrm{Tr}(\rho_B)\rho_A$ for every $\rho_A \in \mathbf{S}(\mathcal{A})$ and $\rho_B \in \mathbf{S}(\mathcal{B})$.

A *general measurement* is a CPTP map $\mathsf{M}: \mathbf{S}(\mathcal{H}) \to \mathbf{S}(\mathcal{H} \otimes \mathcal{O})$, where $\mathcal{O}$ is an ancilla register holding a classical outcome. Specifically, given measurement operators $\{M_i\}_{i=1}^N$ such that $\sum_{i=1}^N M_i M_i^\dagger = \mathbf{I}$ and a basis $\{|i\rangle\}_{i=1}^N$ for $\mathcal{O}$, $\mathsf{M}(\rho) = \sum_{i=1}^N (M_i \rho M_i^\dagger \otimes |i\rangle\langle i|^{\mathcal{O}})$. We sometimes implicitly discard the outcome register. A projective measurement is a general measurement where the M_i are projectors. A measurement induces a probability distribution over its outcomes given by $\Pr[i] = \mathrm{Tr}(|i\rangle\langle i|^{\mathcal{O}} \mathsf{M}(\rho))$; we denote sampling from this distribution by $i \leftarrow \mathsf{M}(\rho)$. The *trace distance* between states ρ, σ, denoted $d(\rho, \sigma)$, is defined as

$$d(\rho, \sigma) = \frac{1}{2} \mathrm{Tr}\left(\sqrt{(\rho - \sigma)^2} \right).$$

The trace distance is contractive under CPTP maps (for any CPTP map T, $d(T(\rho), T(\sigma)) \leq d(\rho, \sigma)$). It follows that for any measurement M, the statistical distance between the distributions $\mathsf{M}(\rho)$ and $\mathsf{M}(\sigma)$ is bounded by $d(\rho, \sigma)$.

We also define a notion of quantum *computational* distinguishability. Specifically, for states ρ, σ,

$$d_{\mathsf{comp}}(\rho, \sigma)_N := \max_{D, |D| \leq N} |\Pr[D(\rho) \to 1] - \Pr[D(\sigma) \to 1]|,$$

where D is a quantum circuit. For sequences of states $(\rho_\lambda)_\lambda, (\sigma_\lambda)_\lambda$ we say that $d_{\mathsf{comp}}(\rho_\lambda, \sigma_\lambda) \leq \varepsilon + \mathsf{negl}\,(\lambda)$ if for all polynomials p, $d_{\mathsf{comp}}(\rho_\lambda, \sigma_\lambda)_{p(\lambda)} \leq \varepsilon + \mathsf{negl}\,(\lambda)$.

Clearly d_{comp} satisfies the triangle inequality and for all $\lambda \in \mathbb{N}$, $d_{\mathsf{comp}}(\rho, \sigma)(\lambda) \leq d(\rho, \sigma)$. For bipartite states on $\mathcal{A} \otimes \mathcal{B}$ we affix a superscript $\mathcal{A}$ to d and d_{comp} to indicate that the distance is with respect to $\mathcal{A}$ only, i.e.

$$d^{\mathcal{A}}(\rho, \sigma) = d(\mathrm{Tr}_{\mathcal{B}}(\rho), \mathrm{Tr}_{\mathcal{B}}(\sigma)) \ .$$

Gentle Measurement. We have the following *gentle measurement lemma*, which bounds how much a state is disturbed by applying a measurement whose outcome is almost certain.

Lemma 1 (Gentle Measurement [26]). *Let $\rho \in \mathbf{S}(\mathcal{H})$ and $\mathsf{P} = (\Pi, \mathbf{I} - \Pi)$ be a binary projective measurement on $\mathcal{H}$ such that $\mathrm{Tr}(\Pi\rho) \geq 1 - \delta$. Let*

$$\rho' = \frac{\Pi\rho\Pi}{\mathrm{Tr}(\Pi\rho)} \quad and \quad \rho'' = \Pi\rho\Pi + (I - \Pi)\rho(I - \Pi).$$

Then

$$d(\rho, \rho') \leq 2\sqrt{\delta} \quad and \quad d(\rho, \rho'') \leq 2\sqrt{\delta}.$$

Quantum Algorithms. In this work, a *quantum adversary* is a family of quantum circuits $\{A_\lambda\}_{\lambda \in \mathbb{N}}$ represented classically using some standard universal gate set. A quantum adversary is *polynomial-size* if there exists a polynomial p and $\lambda_0 \in \mathbb{N}$ such that for all $\lambda > \lambda_0$ it holds that $|A_\lambda| \leq p(\lambda)$ (i.e., quantum adversaries have classical non-uniform advice).

A circuit C with *black-box* access to a unitary U, denoted C^U, is a standard quantum circuit with special gates that act as U and $U^\dagger$. We also use C^T to denote black-box access to a map T, which we interpret as C^{U_T} for a unitary dilation U_T of T; all of our results are independent of the choice of dilation. This allows, for example, the "partial application" of a projective measurement, and the implementation of a general measurement via a projective measurement on a larger space.

Interactive Quantum Circuits. We introduce the definition for interactive quantum circuits.

Definition 2. *A t-round interactive quantum circuit A is a sequence of maps $(U_1, \ldots, U_t)$ where $U_i : R_i \to U(\mathcal{I} \otimes \mathcal{Z}_i)$. We also denote by U_i the unitary $\sum_{r_i \in R_i} |r_i\rangle\langle r_i| \otimes U_i(r_i)$. The size of an interactive quantum circuit is the sum of the sizes of the circuits implementing the unitaries $U_1, \ldots, U_t$.*

Let $P^* = (U_1, \ldots, U_t, |\psi\rangle)$; then E^{P^*} is a quantum circuit with special gates corresponding to the unitaries U_i and $(U_i)^\dagger$ for $i \in [t]$. The requirement that the U_i be unitary is without loss of generality, in the sense that any interactive quantum adversary not of this form can be "purified" into a circuit of this form that is only a constant factor larger with the same observable behavior. Using this formulation, we can sample the random variable $\langle P^*(|\psi\rangle), V \rangle$ equivalently as:

1. Initialize the register $\mathcal{I}$ to $|\psi\rangle$, and $\tau = ()$.
2. For $i = 1 \ldots t$:
   (a) Sample $r_i \leftarrow R_i$.
   (b) Apply unitary $U_i(r_i)$ to $\mathcal{I} \otimes \mathcal{Z}_i$.
   (c) Measure $\mathcal{Z}_i$ in the computational basis to obtain response z_i. Append (r_i, z_i) to τ.
3. Return the output of $V(\tau)$.

In particular, the interaction is *public coin*. Note again that we restrict the operation of P^* in each round to be unitary except for the measurement of $\mathcal{Z}_i$ in the computational basis.

4 Recursive Special Sound and Last-Round Collapsing Arguments

We recall the definitions of interactive arguments and their knowledge soundness. We then define the new notions of recursive special soundness and last-round collapsing.

Definition 3 (Arguments). *Let $i \geq 0$ be an integer. A $(2i+1)$-message public-coin argument system $\Pi = (\mathsf{Setup}, \Sigma = (P, V))$ consists of a PPT algorithm Setup and a $(2i + 1)$-message protocol $\Sigma = (P, V)$ between an interactive PPT prover P and an interactive PPT verifier V, is associated to a tuple of spaces $(X, W, (Z_j, R_j)_{j \in [i]}, W_{i+1})$, and has the following structural properties:*

- *The Setup algorithm takes as input the security parameter 1^λ and outputs some public parameters pp.*
- *Both P and V receive as input the public parameters pp and a statement $x \in X$. The prover P additionally receives a witness $w \in W$.*
- *The public parameters, the statement x, and the $2i + 1$ messages sent by P and V in the protocol Σ, called collectively a transcript, is labelled by $(\mathsf{pp}, x, z_1, r_1, \ldots, z_i, r_i, w_{i+1})$, where $z_j \in Z_j$ sent by P are called commitments, $r_j \in R_j$ sent by V are called challenges, and $w_{i+1} \in W_{i+1}$ sent by P is called a response.*
- *The challenges r_j are sampled by V uniformly randomly from R_j[6].*

---

[6] In general, r_j could be sampled from a public distribution over R_j.

A transcript $(\mathsf{pp}, x, z_1, r_1, \ldots, z_i, r_i, w_{i+1})$ is said to be accepting for Σ if it holds that $V(\mathsf{pp}, x, z_1, r_1, \ldots, z_i, r_i, w_{i+1}) = 1$. A k-branch of transcripts of Σ is a tuple consisting of some public parameters, a statement, and a prefix of messages

$$(\mathsf{pp}, x, z_1, r_1, \ldots, z_{i-1}, r_{i-1}, z_i)$$

along with k distinct i-th round challenges $(r_i^{(j)})_{j \in [k]}$, and k responses $(w_{i+1}^{(j)})_{j \in [k]}$. A k-branch of transcripts is said to be accepting for Σ if

$$(\mathsf{pp}, x, z_1, r_1, \ldots, z_{i-1}, r_{i-1}, z_i, r_i^{(j)}, w_{i+1}^{(j)})$$

is accepting for Σ for all $j \in [k]$.

Note that if $i = 0$ then the protocol is non-interactive: the transcript consists only of (pp, x, w_1).

For the protocols we consider, the statement to be proved depends on the public parameters pp. As such, we will define proofs of knowledge with respect to relations on triples (pp, x, w). Observe, in particular, that when $i = 0$ in Definition 3 the verifier itself defines such a relation. Our proof of knowledge definition is somewhat weaker than standard definitions of proof of knowledge in that the extractor is permitted a given additive inverse polynomial loss.

Definition 4 (Proof of knowledge). *We say that an argument system $\Pi = (\mathsf{Setup}, \Sigma = (P, V))$ is a (post-quantum) proof of knowledge with knowledge error κ for a relation $\mathfrak{R}$ if there exists a (quantum) polynomial-time extractor E and such that for any inverse polynomial ν and any (quantum) polynomial-size adversary P^*,*

$$\Pr\left[\mathfrak{R}(\mathsf{pp}, x, w) \,\middle|\, \begin{array}{l} \mathsf{pp} \leftarrow \mathsf{Setup}(1^\lambda) \\ w \leftarrow \mathsf{Extract}^{P^*}(\mathsf{pp}, x, 1^{1/\nu}) \end{array}\right] \geq \Pr\left[\langle P^*, V\rangle = 1\right] - \kappa(\lambda) - \nu(\lambda) .$$

Definition 5 (Recursive k-Special Soundness). *For $i \in \mathbb{Z}_{t+1}$, let $\Pi_i = (\mathsf{Setup}, \Sigma_i = (P_i, V_i))$ be a $(2i + 1)$-message public-coin argument system with a common Setup algorithm associated to the spaces $(X, W, (Z_j, R_j)_{j \in [i]}, W_{i+1})$. The family $(\Pi_i)_{i=0}^t$ is said to be recursive k-special sound if for each $i \in [t]$ there exists an efficient extractor E_i satisfying the following properties:*

- *The extractor E_i takes as input $(r_i^{(j)}, w_{i+1}^{(j)})_{j \in [k]} \in (R_i \times W_{i+1})^k$ and outputs $w_i \in W_i$.*
- *If*

$$(\mathsf{pp}, x, z_1, r_1, \ldots, z_{i-1}, r_{i-1}, z_i, (r_i^{(j)}, w_i^{(j)})_{j \in [k]})$$

is an accepting k-branch of transcripts for Σ_i, and $w_i = E_i((r_i^{(j)}, w_{i+1}^{(j)})_{j \in [k]})$, then

$$(\mathsf{pp}, x, z_1, r_1, \ldots, z_{i-1}, r_{i-1}, w_i)$$

is an accepting transcript for Σ_{i-1}.

Definition 6 (Last-Round Collapsing). *Let Π be a $(2i+1)$-message public-coin argument system associated to the spaces $(X, W, (Z_j, R_j)_{j \in [i]}, W_{i+1})$. We say that Π is last round collapsing if for any efficient (quantum) adversary A*

$$\left| \Pr\left[\mathsf{LastRoundCollapsing}^0_{\Pi,A}(1^\lambda) = 1\right] - \Pr\left[\mathsf{LastRoundCollapsing}^1_{\Pi,A}(1^\lambda) = 1\right] \right|$$
$$\leq \mathsf{negl}(\lambda),$$

where the experiment $\mathsf{LastRoundCollapsing}^b_{\Pi,A}$ is defined as follows:

$\underline{\mathsf{LastRoundCollapsing}^b_{\Pi,A}(1^\lambda)}$:

1. *The challenger generates* $\mathsf{pp} \leftarrow \mathsf{Setup}(1^\lambda)$.
2. *The challenger runs* $x \leftarrow A(\mathsf{pp})$.
3. *The challenger executes the interaction* $(A, V(\mathsf{pp}, x))$ *up until measuring the last message of the adversary. Let* $\tau = (\mathsf{pp}, x, z_1, r_1, \ldots, z_t, r_t)$ *be the protocol transcript thus far (excluding the last message) and let* W *be the register that contains the state corresponding to the last message of the adversary.*
4. *Let* V_τ *be the unitary that acts on* W *and a fresh ancilla, and CNOTs into the fresh ancilla the bit that determines whether the transcript is valid. Apply* V_τ, *measure the ancilla, and apply* $V_\tau^\dagger$.
5. *If the output of the measurement is* 0, *then abort the experiment. Else proceed.*
6. *If* $b = 0$ *do nothing.*
7. *If* $b = 1$ *measure the register* W *in the computational basis, discard the result.*
8. *Return to* A *all registers and output whichever bit* A *outputs.*

5   Quantum Tree-Extraction

In this section we give an algorithm for extracting a witness from a recursively k-special sound, last-round collapsing protocol. We prove the following general theorem.

Theorem 2. *Let* $(\Pi_i = (\mathsf{Setup}, \Sigma_i = (P_i, V_i)))_{i=0}^t$ *be a recursively k-special sound family where Π_i is last-round collapsing for all i. Then Π_t is a post-quantum proof of knowledge for (the relation induced by) V_0 with knowledge error*

$$\sum_{i=1}^t \frac{k-1}{|R_i|}.$$

In Sect. 5.1 we give some notation which will be used in this section, and specify the quantum algorithms we require. We also prove a new result about the Repair algorithm of [11], which gives a better characterization of the distribution of outcomes from repeated applications of the repair experiment; this is necessary for our main result. In Sect. 5.2 we specify our extractor and show that it runs in polynomial time. In Sect. 5.3 we prove that the extractor is correct.

5.1   Notation and Quantum Algorithms

For a classical predicate $f: R \times Z \to \{0,1\}$, let $\Pi_{f(r,\cdot)} := \sum_{z \in Z, f(r,z)=1} |z\rangle\langle z|_Z$. Given also a mapping $U: r \to U(\mathcal{A}, \mathcal{Z})$, we define the Hermitian matrix $E_{U,f} := \frac{1}{|R|} \sum_{r \in R} U(r)^\dagger \Pi_{f(r,\cdot)} U(r)$. Let $\mathsf{T}^{U,f}_{\geq p} := (\Pi^{U,f}_{\geq p}, I - \Pi^{U,f}_{\geq p})$, where

$$\Pi^{U,f}_{\geq p} := \sum_{j, p_j \geq p} |j\rangle\langle j| ,$$

for $\sum_j p_j |j\rangle\langle j|$ the spectral decomposition of $E_{U,f}$. Note that $0 \leq p_j \leq 1$ for all j.

Lemma 2 ([11,27]).   *For every $\varepsilon, \delta > 0$ there is a quantum algorithm* $\mathsf{Estimate}_{\varepsilon,\delta}$ *with the following guarantees. For any classical predicate $f: R \times Z \to \{0,1\}$, mapping $U: r \to U(\mathcal{A}, \mathcal{Z})$ and state $\rho \in \mathcal{A} \otimes \mathcal{Z}$:*

- $\mathbb{E}[p \mid (p, \rho') \leftarrow \mathsf{Estimate}^{U,f}_{\varepsilon,\delta}(\rho)] = \mathrm{Tr}(E_{U,f}\rho) = \frac{1}{|R|} \sum_{r \in R} \mathrm{Tr}\big(\Pi_{f(r,\cdot)} U_r \rho U_r^\dagger\big)$;
- $\mathsf{Estimate}^{U,f}_{\varepsilon,\delta}$ *is (ε, δ)-almost projective; and*
- *For any $q \in [0,1]$,*

$$\Pr\left[p \geq q \wedge b = 0 \,\middle|\, \begin{array}{l} (p, \rho') \leftarrow \mathsf{Estimate}^{U,f}_{\varepsilon,\delta}(\rho) \\ b \leftarrow \mathsf{T}^{U,f}_{\geq q-\varepsilon}(\rho') \end{array}\right] \leq \delta .$$

$\mathsf{Estimate}^{U,f}_{\varepsilon,\delta}$ *has quantum circuit complexity $O(|f| \cdot \frac{1}{\varepsilon} \log \frac{1}{\delta})$ given oracle access to* $U := \sum_{r \in R} |r\rangle\langle r| \otimes U(r)$.

We denote by $\mathsf{Threshold}_{\gamma,\varepsilon,\delta}$ the quantum algorithm which runs $\mathsf{Estimate}$ and outputs 1 if its output is at least γ, and 0 otherwise.

$\mathsf{RepExpt}^{M,P}_T$:
1. (Estimate) Apply the (ε, δ)-almost-projective measurement M, obtaining outcome p;
2. (Disturb) Apply the projective measurement P, obtaining outcome $k \in [N]$;
3. (Repair) Run $\mathsf{Repair}_T[M, P](k, p)$.
4. (Re-estimate) Apply M again, obtaining outcome p'.
5. Output (p, p').

$\mathsf{MultiExpt}^{(D_s)_{s=1}^N, (M_i)_{i \in \mathbb{N}}}_T$:
1. Apply $\mathsf{Estimate}$, obtaining outcome p_0.
2. For $s = 1, \ldots, N$:
   (a) Apply $\mathsf{Estimate}$, obtaining outcome p_s.
   (b) Sample $i_s \leftarrow D_s(i_1, b_1, \ldots, i_{s-1}, b_{s-1})$, and measure $b_s \leftarrow M_{i_s}$.
   (c) Run $\mathsf{Repair}_T[\mathsf{Estimate}, M_{i_s}](b_s, p_s)$.
3. Output $\sum_{s=1}^N b_s$.

Fig. 1. Experiments involving the Repair algorithm.

We recall the state repair theorem of [11].

Theorem 3 (State repair, [11]). *Let* M *be an* (ε, δ)*-almost projective measurement on* $\mathcal{H}$*, let* P *be an* n*-outcome projective measurement on* $\mathcal{H}$*, and let* T *be any positive integer. There is quantum procedure* Repair *such that* $\mathsf{RepExpt}_T^{M,P}$ *(see Fig. 1) satisfies the following guarantee. For any state* ρ *on* $\mathcal{H}$ *and* $(p, p') \leftarrow \mathsf{RepExpt}_T^{M,P}(\rho)$:

$$\Pr\left[|p' - p| > 2\varepsilon\right] \leq n(\delta + 1/T) + 4\sqrt{\delta}.$$

Moreover, Repair *has quantum circuit complexity* $O(T)$ *given oracle access to* P *and* $\overline{M}$.

Fix M to be the procedure $\mathsf{Estimate}_{\varepsilon, \delta}^{U,f}$ from Lemma 2, and for $r \in R$, denote by P_r the binary measurement $(U_r^{\dagger} \Pi_{f(r,\cdot)} U_r, I - U_r^{\dagger} \Pi_{f(r,\cdot)} U_r)$. In [11] it is observed that Theorem 3 directly implies the following. If we choose a uniformly random sequence $(r_1, \ldots, r_N) \in R^N$ and apply $\mathsf{RepExpt}_T^{M,P_{r_1}}, \ldots, \mathsf{RepExpt}_T^{M,P_{r_N}}$ sequentially, the expected number of 1-outcomes for the P_{r_i} is at least $p - O(\varepsilon N)$, where p is the prover's success probability in the protocol.

For our application we will need to strengthen this result in two ways. First, we allow the sequence to be drawn from a more general distribution, even depending on prior measurement outcomes. Second, we require a strong concentration guarantee, which we obtain by showing that the number of successes dominates a binomial distribution of the appropriate parameters. The relevant experiment is given as MultiExpt in Fig. 1. Note that the setting in [11] is obtained by choosing D_s as the uniform distribution over R for all s.

Lemma 3. *For each* $s = 1, \ldots, N$*, let* D_s *be a randomized function that takes an element of* $(\mathbb{N} \times \{0, 1\})^{s-1}$ *and outputs* $i_s \in \mathbb{N}$*. Let* $(M_i)_{i \in \mathbb{N}}$ *be a list of measurements.*

For any state $\rho \in \mathbf{S}(\mathcal{A} \otimes \mathcal{Z})$*, the following holds:*

$$\Pr_{S \leftarrow \mathsf{MultiExpt}(\rho)}[S < k] \leq \Pr\left[\sum_{i=1}^{N} Y_s < k\right] + N/T + O(\sqrt{\delta} + (N/T)^2),$$

where the $(Y_s)_{s=1}^N$ *are distributed as follows:*

1. *Apply* $\mathsf{Estimate}_{\varepsilon, \delta}^{U,f}$ *to* ρ*, obtaining outcome* p_0*. Let* $\alpha := p_0 - 2\varepsilon N$.
2. *For each* $s \in [N]$*, sample* Y_s *from a Bernoulli distribution with parameter*

$$\zeta := \min_{|v\rangle \in \mathrm{im}(\Pi_{\geq \alpha}^{U,f})} \min_{\substack{i \in \mathbb{N}^{s-1} \\ \mathbf{b} \in \{0,1\}^{s-1}}} \mathbb{E}_{i_s \leftarrow D_s(\mathbf{i}, \mathbf{b})} \Pr\left[M_{i_s}(|v\rangle\langle v|) \to 1\right].$$

Proof. By Theorem 3, for each $s \in [N]$ it holds that

$$\Pr\left[p_s < p_{s-1} - 2\varepsilon\right] \leq 2/T + O(\sqrt{\delta}).$$

Denote by E the event that, for any $s \in [N]$, $p_s < p_{s-1} - 2\varepsilon$. By a union bound,

$$\Pr[E] \leq 2N/T + O(N\sqrt{\delta} + (N/T)^2) .$$

Now consider the following hybrid experiment:

$\mathsf{Hyb}^{\mathsf{P}}_T$:
1. Apply Estimate, obtaining outcome p_0.
2. For $s = 1, \ldots, N$:
   (a) Apply Estimate, obtaining outcome p_s.
   (b) Apply $\mathsf{T}^{U,f}_{\geq p_s - \varepsilon}$, and $postselect$ on obtaining outcome 1.
   (c) Sample $(i_s, \mathsf{M}) \leftarrow D_s(i_1, b_1, \ldots, i_{s-1}, b_{s-1})$, and measure $b_s \leftarrow \mathsf{M}$.
   (d) Run $\mathsf{Repair}_T[\mathsf{Estimate}, \mathsf{M}_i](b_s, p_s)$.

By Lemma 2, in each iteration s, $\mathsf{T}^{U,f}_{\geq p_s - \varepsilon}$ yields outcome 1 with probability at least $1 - \delta$. Hence by gentle measurement, $d(\mathsf{MultiExpt}, \mathsf{Hyb}) = O(N\sqrt{\delta})$. Switching to Hyb, it holds by definition of ζ that

$$\Pr_{\mathsf{Hyb}}[b_s = 1 \mid \neg E, i_1, b_1, \ldots, i_{s-1}, b_{s-1}] \geq \zeta .$$

Therefore the distribution of $(\sum_{s=1}^{N} b_s \mid \neg E)$ induced by Hyb stochastically dominates $\sum_{s=1}^{N} Y_s$; that is, for all k,

$$\Pr_{\mathsf{Hyb}}\left[\sum_{s=1}^{N} b_s < k \,\middle|\, \neg E\right] \leq \Pr\left[\sum_{s=1}^{N} Y_s < k\right] .$$

Since $\Pr[A] \leq \Pr[A|B]\Pr[B]$, we have that

$$\Pr_{\mathsf{Hyb}}\left[\sum_{s=1}^{N} b_s < k\right] \leq \frac{\Pr\left[\sum_{s=1}^{N} Y_s < k\right]}{\Pr_{\mathsf{Hyb}}[E]}$$

$$\leq \Pr\left[\sum_{s=1}^{N} Y_s < k\right] + 2N/T + O(N\sqrt{\delta} + (N/T)^2) .$$

The lemma then follows by trace distance.   □

5.2   Description of the Extractor

For a measurement channel $\mathsf{M} \colon \mathbf{S}(\mathcal{A}) \to \mathbf{S}(\mathcal{A} \otimes \mathcal{O})$, we denote by $\overline{\mathsf{M}} \in U(\mathcal{A} \otimes \mathcal{O} \otimes \mathcal{B})$ some unitary dilation of M. We denote by $\underline{\mathsf{M}} \colon \mathbf{S}(\mathcal{A} \otimes \mathcal{B}) \to \mathbf{S}(\mathcal{A} \otimes \mathcal{O} \otimes \mathcal{B})$ a $projective$ dilation of M, given by

$$\underline{\mathsf{M}}(\rho) := \sum_i \overline{\mathsf{M}}^{\dagger} |i\rangle\langle i|_{\mathcal{O}} \overline{\mathsf{M}} \rho \overline{\mathsf{M}}^{\dagger} |i\rangle\langle i|_{\mathcal{O}} \overline{\mathsf{M}}$$

where $\{|i\rangle\}_i$ is a basis for $\mathcal{O}$. All of our procedures and correctness analyses are independent of the choice of dilation, and we assume that the circuit complexity of $\overline{\mathsf{M}}, \underline{\mathsf{M}}$ is linear in the circuit complexity of M.

We now describe the extractor, which is a measurement channel $\text{Extract}_{i,\nu} \colon \mathbf{S}(\mathcal{A} \otimes \mathcal{Z}) \to \mathbf{S}(\mathcal{A} \otimes \mathcal{Z} \otimes \mathcal{O})$, where $\mathcal{Z} = (\mathcal{Z}_1, \ldots, \mathcal{Z}_t, \mathcal{W}_{t+1})$ are the prover's output registers. Recall that we model the prover as a sequence of unitaries $U_1, \ldots, U_t$.

For $i \in [t]$, denote by $U^{(i)} \colon R_i \times \cdots \times R_t \to U(\mathcal{A} \otimes \mathcal{Z}_{i+1} \otimes \cdots \otimes \mathcal{Z}_t \otimes \mathcal{W}_{t+1})$ the map

$$U^{(i)}(r_i, \ldots, r_t) = U_t(r_t) \cdots U_i(r_i) .$$

For $i \in [t], \mathbf{r} = (r_1, \ldots, r_{i-1}) \in R_1 \times \cdots \times R_{i-1}$, let $f_{(\mathbf{r})}^{(i)} \colon (R_i \times \cdots \times R_t) \times (\mathcal{Z}_1 \times \cdots \times \mathcal{Z}_t \times \mathcal{W}_{t+1}) \to \{0,1\}$ denote the function $f_{(\mathbf{r})}^{(i)}(r_i, \ldots, r_t, z_1, \ldots, z_t, w_{t+1}) := V(z_1, r_1, \ldots, z_t, r_t, w_{t+1})$.

$\text{Extract}_{i,\nu}(r_1, \ldots, r_{i-1})$:

1. Set $N := \lceil 2t \ln(1/\delta)/\nu^2 \rceil$, $\varepsilon := \nu/4kNt$, $\beta := \nu/2k^t$.

2. Compute $p_0 \leftarrow \text{Estimate}_{\varepsilon,\delta}^{U^{(i)}, f_{\mathbf{r}}^{(i)}}$. If $p_0 < \gamma := \sum_{j=i}^{t} \frac{k-1}{R_i} + \nu$, stop and output $\bot$.

3. For $j = 1, \ldots, k$:

   (a) Set $b := 0$.

   (b) For $s = 1, \ldots, N$, apply the following steps:

   i. Compute $p_s \leftarrow \text{Estimate}_{\varepsilon,\delta}^{U^{(i)}, f_{\mathbf{r}}^{(i)}}$.

   ii. Choose $r_i \leftarrow R_i \setminus \text{Supp} W$ uniformly at random and apply $U_i(r_i)$.

   iii. Initialize ancilla register $\mathcal{B}$ (for $\underline{\text{Threshold}}$) to $|0\rangle$.

   iv. Measure $b \leftarrow \underline{\text{Threshold}}_{\gamma',\varepsilon,\delta}^{U^{(i+1)}, f^{(i+1)}}$, where $\gamma' := \sum_{j=i+1}^{t} \frac{k-1}{R_i} + \nu \cdot \frac{t-i-1}{t-i} + \varepsilon$. If $b = 1$, go to Step 3c.

   v. Apply $U_i(r_i)^\dagger$.

   vi. Run $\text{Repair}_{kN/2\beta^2}[\text{Estimate}_{\varepsilon,\delta}^{U^{(i)}, f_{\mathbf{r}}^{(i)}}, (U_i(r_i))^\dagger \cdot \underline{\text{Threshold}}_{\gamma',\varepsilon,\delta}^{U^{(i+1)}, f^{(i+1)}} \cdot U_i(r_i)]$.

   (c) Apply $\overline{\text{Threshold}}_{\gamma',\varepsilon,\delta}^{U^{(i+1)}, f^{(i+1)}}$.

   (d) Compute $\mathcal{W}_{i+1} \leftarrow \overline{\text{Extract}}_{i+1,\nu'}(r_1, \ldots, r_i)$ coherently, for $\nu' := \nu \cdot \frac{t-i-1}{t-i}$.

   (e) If $b = 1$, measure $b' \leftarrow V_i(\mathcal{Z}_1, r_1, \ldots, \mathcal{Z}_i, r_i, \mathcal{W}_i)$.

   (f) If $b = b' = 1$, measure $w_{i+1} \leftarrow \mathcal{W}_{i+1}$ and add $(r_i \mapsto w_i)$ to W.

   (g) Apply $\overline{\text{Extract}}_{i+1,\nu'}(r_1, \ldots, r_i)^\dagger$.

   (h) Apply $(\overline{\text{Threshold}}_{\gamma',\varepsilon,\delta}^{U^{(i+1)}, f^{(i+1)}})^\dagger$, then $U_i(r_i)^\dagger$.

   (i) Run $\text{Repair}_{kN/2\beta^2}[\text{Estimate}_{\varepsilon,\delta}^{U^{(i)}, f_{\mathbf{r}}^{(i)}}, (U_i(r_i))^\dagger \cdot \underline{\text{Threshold}}_{\gamma',\varepsilon,\delta}^{U^{(i+1)}, f^{(i+1)}} \cdot U_i(r_i)]$.

4. Output $w_i \leftarrow E_i(W)$.

$\text{Extract}_{t,\nu}(r_1, \ldots, r_{t-1})$ is simply the [11] extractor, modified to sample r_t without replacement:

$\text{Extract}_{t,\nu}(r_1, \ldots, r_{t-1})$:

1. Compute $p_0 \leftarrow \text{Estimate}_{\varepsilon,\delta}^{U^{(i)}, f_{\mathbf{r}}^{(i)}}$. If $p_0 < \gamma := \frac{k-1}{R_t} + \nu$, stop and output 0.

2. For $j = 1, \ldots, k$:

   (a) Set $b := 0$.

   (b) For $s = 1, \ldots, N$, and while $b = 0$, apply each of the following steps:

       i. Compute $p_s \leftarrow \text{Estimate}_{\varepsilon,\delta}^{U_t, f_{\mathbf{r}}^{(t)}}$.

       ii. Choose $r_t \leftarrow R_t \setminus \text{Supp} W$ uniformly at random and apply $U_t(r_t)$.

       iii. Measure $b \leftarrow V_t(\mathcal{Z}_1, r_1, \ldots, \mathcal{Z}_t, r_t, \mathcal{W}_{t+1})$.

       iv. If $b = 1$, measure $w_{t+1} \leftarrow \mathcal{W}_{t+1}$ and add $(r_t \mapsto w_{t+1})$ to W.

       v. Apply $U_t(r_t)^\dagger$.

       vi. Run $\text{Repair}_{kN/2\beta^2}[\text{Estimate}_{\varepsilon,\delta}^{U_t, f_{\mathbf{r}}^{(t)}}, (U_t(r_t))^\dagger \cdot \Pi_{V_t(\mathbf{r}, \cdot)} \cdot U_i(r_i)]$.

3. Output $E_t(W)$.

Lemma 4. $\text{Extract}_{i,\nu}$ *is a circuit of size* $P(t, k, \log(1/\delta), 1/\nu) \cdot (ck)^{t-i}$ *for some polynomial P and constant c. In particular, if* $k = O(1)$, $t = O(\log n)$, $\delta = 2^{-\lambda}$ *and* $\nu = 1/\text{poly}(\lambda)$ *then* $\text{Extract}_\nu = \text{Extract}_{1,\nu}$ *is a polynomial-size quantum circuit.*

Proof. Let P be a polynomial (with positive coefficients) such that for any i,

$$|\text{Extract}_{i,\nu}| \leq P(t, k, \log(1/\delta), 1/\beta, 1/\nu) + k \cdot 2|\text{Extract}_{i+1,\nu'}| \,.$$

Such a polynomial exists by Lemma 2 and Theorem 3. Let c be a constant such that $P(1, 1, 1, 1, 2) \leq c \cdot P(1, 1, 1, 1, 1)$. The circuit size of $\text{Extract}_{i,\nu}$ is then bounded by

$$
\begin{aligned}
&P(t, k, \log(1/\delta), 1/\beta, 1/\nu) + k \cdot 2|\text{Extract}_{i+1,\nu'}| \\
&\leq P(t, k, \log(1/\delta), 1/\beta, 1/\nu) + 2c^{t-i-1}k^{t-i} \cdot P(t, k, \log(1/\delta), 1/\beta, \frac{1}{\nu} \cdot \frac{t-i}{t-i-1}) \\
&\leq (ck)^{t-i} P(t, k, \log(1/\delta), 1/\beta, 1/\nu) \,,
\end{aligned}
$$

since $\frac{t-i}{t-i-1} \leq 2$ for all $i \in \{1, \ldots, t-1\}$. $\qquad\square$

5.3 Correctness

The key lemma which establishes the correctness of the extractor is the following.

Lemma 5. *Let* $\text{Extract}'$ *be as* Extract*, except that its output is 0 if* Extract *outputs* $\perp$ *and*

$$V_{i-1}(z_1, r_1, \ldots, z_{i-1}, r_{i-1}, w_{i-1})$$

otherwise. Then for $\gamma := \sum_{j=i}^{t} \frac{k-1}{R_i} + \nu$ *and all* $\mathbf{r} = (r_1, \ldots, r_{i-1})$,

$$d_{\text{comp}}^{\mathcal{A},\mathcal{Z},\mathcal{O}}(\underline{\text{Extract}}'_{i,\nu}(\mathbf{r};\rho), \underline{\text{Threshold}}_{\gamma,\varepsilon,\delta}^{U^{(i)},f_{\mathbf{r}}^{(i)}}(\rho))$$

$$\leq k^{t-i} \cdot (\beta + O(\beta^2) + \text{poly}(\lambda) \cdot \sqrt[4]{\delta}) + \text{negl}(\lambda) .$$

Before proving the lemma, we discuss the intuition behind it and then show how to use it to prove Theorem 2. $\underline{\text{Extract}}'_{i,\nu}$ measures whether the extractor succeeds at the i-th level. $\underline{\text{Threshold}}_{\gamma,\varepsilon,\delta}^{U^{(i)},f_{\mathbf{r}}^{(i)}}$ measures whether the prover's success probability in the i-th round is at least γ. The lemma bounds the computational distinguishability of these measurements; in particular, it implies that if we first measure $\underline{\text{Threshold}}_{\gamma,\varepsilon,\delta}^{U^{(i)},f_{\mathbf{r}}^{(i)}}$ and obtain an outcome $b \in \{0,1\}$, then the outcome of applying $\underline{\text{Extract}}'_{i,\nu}$ to the post-measurement state is also b with all but inverse polynomial probability. Hence to determine whether $\underline{\text{Extract}}'_{i,\nu}$ will succeed it suffices to measure $\underline{\text{Threshold}}_{\gamma,\varepsilon,\delta}^{U^{(i)},f_{\mathbf{r}}^{(i)}}$; the complexity of the latter does not grow with decreasing i.

We note that it is crucial that Lemma 5 bounds the distinguishability of these measurements and not simply the probability that they produce different outcomes when applied in sequence. While gentle measurement allows one to move from the latter property to the former, this incurs a square-root loss in the bound. Compounding this loss over $\log n$ rounds would make the bound trivial.

Proof (Theorem 2). Let $P^* = (U_1, \ldots, U_t, \rho)$ be an adversary for Π_t. By Lemma 2, $\mathbb{E}[\text{Estimate}_{\varepsilon,\delta}^{U^{(1)},f^{(1)}}(\rho)] = \Pr[\langle P^*, V_t \rangle \to 1]$. Hence by Proposition 1,

$$\Pr\left[\text{Threshold}_{\gamma,\varepsilon,\delta}^{U^{(1)},f^{(1)}}(\rho) \to 1\right] \geq \Pr[\langle P^*, V_t \rangle \to 1] - \gamma.$$

It follows by Lemma 5 that

$$\Pr\left[\text{Extract}'_{1,\nu/2} \to 1\right] \geq \Pr[\langle P^*, V_t \rangle \to 1] - \kappa - \nu$$

for $\kappa := \sum_{i=1}^{t} \frac{k-1}{|R_i|}$ and since $\beta = \nu/2k^t$. The theorem follows by noting that, by definition, the probability that Extract succeeds is equal to the probability that $\text{Extract}'$ outputs 1. □

Proof. We argue the inductive step. The base case follows by a similar (simpler) argument.

Consider a hybrid extractor Hyb_1 in which we replace Steps 3f and 4 with

3f'. If $b' = 1$, add $(r_i \mapsto \bot)$ to W.
4'. Output 1 if $|W| = k$, else 0.

By last-round collapsing, $d_{\text{comp}}^{\mathcal{A},\mathcal{Z},\mathcal{O}}(\text{Extract}'_{i,\gamma,\varepsilon}, \text{Hyb}_1) = \text{negl}(\lambda)$.

Observe that after removing the measurement of $\mathcal{W}_i$ in $\text{Extract}'$, Steps 3d,3e and 3g are equivalent to an invocation of $\underline{\text{Extract}}'_{i+1,\nu'}$. We can now invoke the inductive hypothesis. Specifically, we consider another hybrid extractor Hyb_2, in which we replace Steps 3d to 3g with the following:

– If $b = 1$, measure $b' \leftarrow \underline{\text{Threshold}}^{U_{\mathsf{r}},f_{\mathsf{r}}}_{\gamma'-\varepsilon,\varepsilon,\delta}$. If $b' = 1$, add $(r_i \to \bot)$ to W.

By induction and the triangle inequality, $d(\mathsf{Hyb}_1, \mathsf{Hyb}_2) \leq k^{t-i} \cdot (\varepsilon + O(\varepsilon^2) +$ poly $(\lambda) \cdot \sqrt[4]{\delta} + \mathsf{negl}(\lambda))$.

Hyb_3 is obtained from Hyb_2 by replacing Step 5.3 with

5.3' If $b = 1$, add $(r_i \to \bot)$ to W.

If $b = 1$, then by Lemma 2, $\Pr[b' = 1] \geq 1 - \delta$. Hence by gentle measurement, $d^{\mathcal{A},\mathcal{Z},\mathcal{O}}(\mathsf{Hyb}_2, \mathsf{Hyb}_3) = O(k\sqrt{\delta})$. We write out Hyb_3 in full, simplifying where possible.

Hyb_3:

1. Compute $p_0 \leftarrow \mathsf{Estimate}^{U^{(i)},f^{(i)}_{\mathsf{r}}}_{\varepsilon,\delta}$. If $p_0 < \gamma$, stop and output 0.
2. For $j = 1, \ldots, k$:
   (a) Set $b := 0$.
   (b) For $s = 1, \ldots, N$, and while $b = 0$, apply each of the following steps:
      i. Compute $p_s \leftarrow \mathsf{Estimate}^{U^{(i)},f^{(i)}_{\mathsf{r}}}_{\varepsilon,\delta}$.
      ii. Choose $r_i \leftarrow R_i \backslash \mathsf{Supp}W$ uniformly at random and apply $U_i(r_i)$.
      iii. Initialize ancilla register $\mathcal{B}$ to $|0\rangle$.
      iv. Measure $b \leftarrow \underline{\text{Threshold}}^{U^{(i+1)},f^{(i+1)}}_{\gamma',\varepsilon,\delta}$, where $\gamma' := \sum_{j=i+1}^{t} \frac{k-1}{R_i} + \nu \cdot \frac{t-i-1}{t-i} + \varepsilon$.
      v. If $b = 1$, add $(r_i \mapsto \bot)$ to W.
      vi. Apply $U_i(r_i)^\dagger$.
      vii. Run $\mathsf{Repair}_{kN/2\beta^2}[\mathsf{Estimate}^{U^{(i)},f^{(i)}_{\mathsf{r}}}_{\varepsilon,\delta}, (U_i(r_i))^\dagger$. $\underline{\text{Threshold}}^{U^{(i+1)},f^{(i+1)}}_{\gamma',\varepsilon,\delta} \cdot U_i(r_i)]$.
3. Output 1 if $|W| = k$, else 0.

Consider now the j-th iteration of the outer loop. We compute the quantity ζ from Lemma 3. Let $|v\rangle \in \mathrm{im}(\Pi^{U^{(i)},f^{(i)}_{\mathsf{r}}}_{\geq \alpha})$. Then

$$\mathbb{E}_{r_i \leftarrow R_i \backslash \mathsf{Supp}W}[\mathsf{Estimate}^{U^{(i+1)},f^{(i+1)}}_{\varepsilon,\delta}(U_i(r_i)|v\rangle)]$$
$$\geq \langle v|\, \mathbb{E}_{U^{(i)},f^{(i)}_{\mathsf{r}}}\,|v\rangle - \frac{j-1}{|R_i|} \geq \alpha - \frac{k-1}{|R_i|}\,.$$

So by Proposition 1,

$$\Pr_{r_i \leftarrow R_i \backslash \mathsf{Supp}W}\left[\underline{\text{Threshold}}^{U^{(i+1)},f^{(i+1)}}_{\gamma',\varepsilon,\delta}(U_i(r_i)|v\rangle) \to 1\right] \geq \alpha - \frac{k-1}{|R_i|} - \gamma'.$$

Since we abort if $p_0 < \gamma$, by our choice of ε we have that $\alpha - \frac{k-1}{|R_i|} \geq \gamma' + \frac{\nu}{2t}$. Hence $\zeta \geq \nu/2t$.

Then by Lemma 3, the probability that b is never set to 1 is at most

$$(1 - \nu/2t)^N + O(N(1/T + \sqrt{\delta})) \leq \beta^2/2k + O(N\sqrt{\delta} + \beta^4/k^2)$$

given our choice of N. Hence the probability that $p_0 \geq \gamma$ and Hyb_3 outputs 0 is at most $\beta^2/2 + O(kN\sqrt{\delta} + \beta^4)$. By gentle measurement,

$$d^{\mathcal{A},\mathcal{Z},\mathcal{O}}(\underline{\mathsf{Hyb}_3}, \underline{\mathsf{Threshold}}_{\gamma,\varepsilon,\delta}^{U^{(i)},f_r^{(i)}}) \leq \beta + O(\sqrt{kN}\sqrt[4]{\delta} + \beta^2).$$

The lemma then follows by the triangle inequality. $\square$

6   Collapsing Hash Function Families

In the following, we show that the hash functions $\mathsf{Hash}_{\mathbf{A}}(\mathbf{x}) = \mathbf{A} \cdot \mathbf{x} \bmod q$, indexed by the matrix $\mathbf{A}$, are collapsing and even when $\mathbf{A}$ is "folded" with coefficients being small units in the base ring.

6.1   Definitions

We recall the definition of a hash function family and the desired properties.

Definition 7 (Hash Function Family). *Let $\ell, k \in \mathsf{poly}(\lambda)$. A hash function family $\mathsf{Hash} = (\mathsf{Setup}, \mathsf{H})$ from $\mathcal{X}^\ell$ to $\mathcal{Y}^h$ consists of a PPT Setup algorithm and a deterministic polynomial-time H algorithm. The Setup algorithm inputs a security parameter 1^λ and outputs the public parameters pp. The H algorithm inputs pp and a preimage $\mathbf{x} \in \mathcal{X}^\ell$. It outputs an image $\mathbf{y} \in \mathcal{Y}^h$. When it is clear from the context, we omit the input pp and write $\mathbf{y} = \mathsf{H}(\mathbf{x})$.*

We define below the notion of collapsing for hash functions [25].

Definition 8 (Collapsing). *Let $\ell, k \in \mathsf{poly}(\lambda)$ and $\mathcal{W} \subseteq \mathcal{X}$. Let $\mathsf{Hash} = (\mathsf{Setup}, \mathsf{H})$ be a hash function from $\mathcal{X}^\ell$ to $\mathcal{Y}^h$. We say that Hash is collapsing over $\mathcal{W}^\ell$ if for any efficient (quantum) adversary A*

$$\left| \Pr\left[\mathsf{Collapsing}_A^0(1^\lambda) = 1\right] - \Pr\left[\mathsf{Collapsing}_A^1(1^\lambda) = 1\right] \right| \leq \mathsf{negl}(\lambda),$$

where the experiment $\mathsf{Collapsing}_A^b$ is defined as follows:

$\underline{\mathsf{Collapsing}_A^b(1^\lambda)}$:

1. *Sample pp using the $\mathsf{Setup}(1^\lambda)$ algorithm and send it over to A.*
2. *A replies with a classical bitstring y and a quantum state on a register $\mathcal{X}$.*
3. *Let $U_{\mathsf{H},y}$ be the unitary that acts on $\mathcal{X}$ and a fresh ancilla, and CNOTs into the fresh ancilla the bit that determines whether the output of $\mathsf{H}(\cdot)$ equals y and the input belongs to $\mathcal{W}^\ell$. Apply $U_{\mathsf{pp},y}$, measure the ancilla, and apply $U_{\mathsf{pp},y}^\dagger$.*
4. *If the output of the measurement is 0, then abort the experiment. Else proceed.*
5. *If $b = 0$ do nothing.*

6. *If $b = 1$ measure the register X in the computational basis, discard the result.*
7. *Return to A all registers and output whichever bit A outputs.*

Note that the security experiment $\mathsf{Collapsing}_A^b$ in the definition of collapsing is a quantum algorithm. It is often easier to work with the classical security notion of somewhere-statistically binding (SSB), defined below, which is known to imply collapsing.

Definition 9 (Somewhere-Statistically Binding). *Let $h, \ell \in \mathsf{poly}(\lambda)$ and $\mathcal{W} \subseteq \mathcal{X}$. A hash function family $\mathsf{Hash} = (\mathsf{Setup}, \mathsf{H})$ from $\mathcal{X}^\ell$ to $\mathcal{Y}^h$ is said to be somewhere-statistically binding (SSB) over $\mathcal{W}^\ell$ if there exists a PPT BSetup algorithm such that the following hold:*

- *The BSetup algorithm inputs a security parameter 1^λ and an index $i \in \mathbb{Z}_\ell$. It outputs the public parameters pp.*
- *For all $i \in \mathbb{Z}_\ell$, the distributions $\mathsf{Setup}(1^\lambda)$ and $\mathsf{BSetup}(1^\lambda, i)$ are computationally indistinguishable.*
- *For all $i \in \mathbb{Z}_\ell$,*

$$\Pr\left[\exists\, \mathbf{x}_0, \mathbf{x}_1 \in \mathcal{W}^\ell : x_{0,i} \neq x_{1,i} \wedge \mathsf{H}(\mathsf{pp}, \mathbf{x}_0) = \mathsf{H}(\mathsf{pp}, \mathbf{x}_1) \mid \mathsf{pp} \leftarrow \mathsf{BSetup}(1^\lambda, i)\right]$$
$$\leq \mathsf{negl}(\lambda).$$

Lemma 6 ([1,18]). *Let $\mathsf{Hash} = (\mathsf{Setup}, \mathsf{H})$ be a hash function family from $\mathcal{X}^\ell$ to $\mathcal{Y}^h$ and $\mathcal{W} \subseteq \mathcal{X}$. If Hash is SSB over $\mathcal{W}^\ell$, then Hash is collapsing over $\mathcal{W}^\ell$.*

6.2 Bounded Homomorphic Public-Key Encryption

We recall the notion of public-key encryption. Note that we define a variant of public-key encryption with perfect correctness.

Definition 10 (Public-Key Encryption). *A public-key encryption $(\mathsf{Gen}, \mathsf{Enc}, \mathsf{Dec})$ consists of a key generation algorithm Gen that takes as input the security parameter 1^λ and returns a key pair $(\mathsf{pk}, \mathsf{sk})$. The encryption algorithm Enc takes as input pk and a message m an produces a ciphertext c. We require that for all $\lambda \in \mathbb{N}$, all $(\mathsf{pk}, \mathsf{sk})$ in the support of $\mathsf{Gen}(1^\lambda)$ and all messages m, it holds that $\mathsf{Dec}(\mathsf{sk}, \mathsf{Enc}(\mathsf{pk}, m)) = m$.*

To prove the security of the hash function family $f_{\mathbf{A}}$ we assume the existence of a bounded linearly homomorphic encryption scheme, that we define in the following.

Definition 11 ((ℓ, β)-Bounded Linearly Homomorphic Encryption over $\mathcal{R}_q^h$). *Let $h, q \in \mathbb{N}$. An encryption scheme $(\mathsf{Gen}, \mathsf{Enc}, \mathsf{Dec})$ is (ℓ, β)-bounded linearly homomorphic over $\mathcal{R}_q^h$ if the following hold:*

- *(Ciphertext Indistinguishability) For a uniformly sampled key pair $(\mathsf{pk}, \mathsf{sk}) \leftarrow \mathsf{Gen}(1^\lambda)$, and for all bits $b \in \{0, 1\}$ it holds that the following distributions are computationally indistinguishable:*

$$\mathbf{c} \leftarrow_\$ \mathsf{Enc}(\mathsf{pk}, b) \approx \mathbf{u} \leftarrow_\$ \mathcal{R}_q^h.$$

– *(Bounded Homomorphism)* For all key pairs $(\mathsf{pk}, \mathsf{sk})$ in the support of $\mathsf{Gen}(1^\lambda)$, all bits $(b_1, \ldots, b_\ell) \in \{0, 1\}^\ell$, all ciphertexts $(\mathbf{c}_1, \ldots, \mathbf{c}_\ell) \in \mathcal{R}_q^{h \times \ell}$ in the support of $(\mathsf{Enc}(\mathsf{pk}, b_1), \ldots, \mathsf{Enc}(\mathsf{pk}, b_\ell))$, and all vectors $\mathbf{x} \in \mathcal{R}^\ell$ where $\|\mathbf{x}\| \leq \beta$, it holds that:

$$\mathsf{Dec}(\mathsf{sk}, (\mathbf{c}_1, \ldots, \mathbf{c}_\ell) \cdot \mathbf{x} \bmod q) = \sum_{i=1}^{\ell} b_i \cdot \mathbf{x}_i.$$

Examples of encryption schemes that satisfy the above property are NTRU [12, 23] (for $h = 1$) and Regev encryption based on (Ring)-LWE [17,21] (for $h > 1$).

6.3   A Fold-Collapsing Hash Function

Let $h, t \in \mathbb{N}$, $\ell = 2^t$, $i \in \{0, 1, \ldots, t\}$, and $(r_j)_{j \in [i]} \in \mathcal{R}^i$. Define $\ell_i := \ell/2^i = 2^{t-i}$. For any matrix $\mathbf{A}_i \in \mathcal{R}_q^{h \times \ell_i}$, we denote by $(\mathbf{A}_{i,0}, \mathbf{A}_{i,1}) \in (\mathcal{R}_q^{h \times \ell_{i+1}})^2$ an arbitrary fixed partitioning of the columns of $\mathbf{A}$ into two disjoint sets of columns of identical cardinality. Similarly, for any vector $\mathbf{x}_i \in \mathcal{R}^{\ell_i}$, we denote by $(\mathbf{x}_{i,0}, \mathbf{x}_{i,1}) \in (\mathcal{R}_q^{\ell_{i+1}})^2$ the partitioning of $\mathbf{x}$ induced by that of $\mathbf{A}$. In Fig. 2 we define a hash function family $\mathsf{Hash}_i := \mathsf{Hash}[h, \ell, (r_j)_{j \in [i]}]$ from $\mathcal{X}^{\ell_i}$ to $\mathcal{Y}^h$.

$\mathsf{Hash}_i.\mathsf{Setup}(1^\lambda)$	$\mathsf{Hash}_i.\mathsf{H}(\mathbf{x}_i)$
if $i = 0$ **then return** $\mathbf{A}_0 \leftarrow_\$ \mathcal{R}_q^{h \times \ell}$	**return** $\mathbf{y} := \mathbf{A}_i \cdot \mathbf{x}_i \bmod q$
else $\mathbf{A}_{i-1} \leftarrow \mathsf{Hash}_{i-1}.\mathsf{Setup}(1^\lambda)$	
$\mathbf{A}_i := r_i \cdot \mathbf{A}_{i-1,0} + \mathbf{A}_{i-1,1} \bmod q$	
return $\mathsf{pp} := \mathbf{A}_i$	

Fig. 2. Construction of hash function families Hash_i from $\mathcal{X}^{\ell_i}$ to $\mathcal{Y}^h$, where $\ell_i := \ell/2^i = 2^{t-i}$. For $i = 0$, we denote the family by $\mathsf{Hash}_0 = \mathsf{Hash}[h, \ell]$.

We are now ready to show that the hash function as defined above is SSB, generalizing a Theorem from [1]. As an immediate corollary, we obtain that the hash function is also collapsing.

Lemma 7 (Collapsing). *Let $\beta_0 \in \mathbb{R}$. Let $\mathcal{W}_0 := \{x \in \mathcal{R} : \|x\| \leq \beta_0\}$. If there exists an (ℓ, β_0)-bounded linearly homomorphic encryption over $\mathcal{R}_q^h$, then $\mathsf{Hash}[h, \ell]$ is SSB over $\mathcal{W}_0$.*

Proof. Let $(\mathsf{Gen}, \mathsf{Enc}, \mathsf{Dec})$ be an (ℓ, β_0)-bounded linearly homomorphic encryption over $\mathcal{R}_q^h$. Let $\mathbf{A}$ be a uniformly sampled hash key. We define ℓ hybrid distributions where we gradually substitute the columns of $\mathbf{A}$ with encryptions of 0. That is, in the i-th hybrid, the key of the hash function consists of

$$(\mathbf{c}_1, \ldots, \mathbf{c}_i, \mathbf{B}_i)$$

where $(\mathbf{c}_i \dots \mathbf{c}_i) \leftarrow_\$ \mathsf{Enc}(\mathsf{pk}, 0)$ and $\mathbf{B}_i \leftarrow_\$ \mathcal{R}_q^{h \times (\ell - i)}$. It is easy to show that the hybrids of each neighbouring pair are computationally indistinguishable by the ciphertext indistinguishability of the encryption scheme. Note that, in the ℓ-th hybrid, the hash key consists of a concatenation of encryption of 0.

We will now show that the hash function defined in the ℓ-th hybrid is SSB, and the lemma statement will follow. We define $\mathsf{BSetup}(1^\lambda, i)$ to be identical to the distribution above, except that we substitute the i-th column of the key with $\mathbf{c}_i \leftarrow_\$ \mathsf{Enc}(\mathsf{pk}, 1)$. The two distributions are computationally indistinguishable by another application of ciphertext indistinguishability. We now show that there does not exist a pair $(\mathbf{x}_0, \mathbf{x}_1) \in \mathcal{W}_0^{2\ell}$ such that $\mathsf{H}(\mathbf{x}_0) = \mathsf{H}(\mathbf{x}_1)$ and $x_{0,i} \neq x_{1,i}$. Assume towards contradiction that it exists, then we have that

$$\tilde{c} = (\mathbf{c}_1, \dots, \mathbf{c}_\ell) \cdot \mathbf{x}_0 = (\mathbf{c}_1, \dots, \mathbf{c}_\ell) \cdot \mathbf{x}_1 \bmod q.$$

By the (ℓ, β_0)-bounded linear homomorphism of the encryption scheme, it holds that $\tilde{c}$ decrypts to two different $x_{0,i}$ and $x_{1,i}$. This contradicts the correctness of the scheme.   □

Next we show that the function remains collapsing even if we fold the hashing key by linear combinations with short units. We refer to this property as *fold-collapsing*.

Lemma 8 (Fold-Collapsing). *Let* $\beta_i \in \mathbb{R}$, $i \in \mathbb{Z}_t$, $r_{i+1} \in \mathcal{R}^\times$ *be a unit with* $\|r_{i+1}\| = 1$, $\mathcal{W}_i := \{x \in \mathcal{R} : \|x\| \leq \beta_i\}$, $\mathcal{W}_{i+1} := \{x \in \mathcal{R} : \|x\| \leq \gamma_\mathcal{R}^{-1} \cdot \beta_i\}$, $\mathsf{Hash}_i := \mathsf{Hash}[h, \ell, (r_j)_{j \in [i]}] = (\mathsf{Setup}_i, \mathsf{H}_i)$, *and* $\mathsf{Hash}_{i+1} := \mathsf{Hash}[h, \ell, (r_j)_{j \in [i+1]}] = (\mathsf{Setup}_{i+1}, \mathsf{H}_{i+1})$. *If* Hash_i *is SSB over* $\mathcal{W}_i^{\ell_i}$, *then* Hash_{i+1} *is SSB over* $\mathcal{W}_{i+1}^{\ell_{i+1}}$.

Proof. Since Hash_i is SSB over $\mathcal{W}_i^{\ell_i}$, there exists a PPT algorithm BSetup_i such that

1. BSetup_i inputs 1^λ and $j \in \mathbb{Z}_{\ell_i}$ and outputs pp.
2. For any $j \in \mathbb{Z}_{\ell_i}$, $\mathsf{Setup}_i(1^\lambda)$ and $\mathsf{BSetup}_i(1^\lambda, j)$ are computationally indistinguishable.
3. For any $j \in \mathbb{Z}_{\ell_i}$,

$$\Pr\left[\mathsf{BAD}(i, j) \mid \mathbf{A}_i \leftarrow \mathsf{BSetup}_i(1^\lambda, j)\right] \leq \mathsf{negl}(\lambda)$$

where $\mathsf{BAD}(\mathsf{i}, \mathsf{j})$ is defined as the following event:

$$\left\{\exists \, \mathbf{x}_{i,0}, \mathbf{x}_{i,1} \in \mathcal{W}_i^{\ell_i} : x_{i,0,j} \neq x_{i,1,j} \wedge \mathbf{A}_i \cdot \mathbf{x}_{i,0} = \mathbf{A}_i \cdot \mathbf{x}_{i,1} \bmod q\right\}.$$

We construct a PPT algorithm BSetup_{i+1} which, on input $j' \in \mathbb{Z}_{\ell_{i+1}}$, samples $b \in \{0, 1\}$, runs BSetup_i on $j = j' + b \cdot \ell_{i+1}$ to obtain $\mathbf{A}_i$, and returns $\mathbf{A}_{i+1} := r_{i+1} \cdot \mathbf{A}_{i,0} + \mathbf{A}_{i,1} \bmod q$. By Property 2 above, we clearly have that $\mathsf{Setup}_{i+1}(1^\lambda)$ and $\mathsf{BSetup}_{i+1}(1^\lambda, j')$ are computationally indistinguishable for all $j' \in \mathbb{Z}_{\ell_{i+1}}$.

Fix any $j \in \mathbb{Z}_{\ell_i}$ and $j' \in \mathbb{Z}_{\ell_{i+1}}$ satisfying $j = j' \bmod \ell_{i+1}$, any $\mathbf{A}_i \in \mathsf{BSetup}_i(1^\lambda, j)$, any $\mathbf{A}_{i+1} = r_{i+1} \cdot \mathbf{A}_{i,0} + \mathbf{A}_{i,1} \bmod q \in \mathsf{BSetup}_{i+1}(1^\lambda, j')$, and any $\mathbf{x}_{i+1,0}, \mathbf{x}_{i+1,1} \in \mathcal{W}_{i+1}^{\ell_{i+1}}$ satisfying $\mathbf{A}_{i+1} \cdot \mathbf{x}_{i+1,0} = \mathbf{A}_{i+1} \cdot \mathbf{x}_{i+1,1} \bmod q$. Define $\mathbf{x}_{i,0} := (r_{i+1} \cdot \mathbf{x}_{i+1,0}, \mathbf{x}_{i+1,0})$ and $\mathbf{x}_{i,1} = (r_{i+1} \cdot \mathbf{x}_{i+1,1}, \mathbf{x}_{i+1,1})$.

Note that $\|\mathbf{x}_{i+1,0}\| \leq \gamma_{\mathcal{R}}^{-1} \cdot \beta_i$ and $\|\mathbf{x}_{i+1,1}\| \leq \gamma_{\mathcal{R}}^{-1} \cdot \beta_i$. Clearly $\|\mathbf{x}_{i,0}\| \leq \beta_i$ and $\|\mathbf{x}_{i,1}\| \leq \beta_i$. In other words, we have $\mathbf{x}_{i,0}, \mathbf{x}_{i,1} \in \mathcal{W}_i^{\ell_i}$.

Since $\mathbf{A}_{i+1} \cdot \mathbf{x}_{i+1,0} = \mathbf{A}_{i+1} \cdot \mathbf{x}_{i+1,1} \bmod q$, we have

$$\mathbf{A}_{i+1} \cdot \mathbf{x}_{i+1,0} = \mathbf{A}_{i+1} \cdot \mathbf{x}_{i+1,1} \bmod q,$$
$$(r_{i+1} \cdot \mathbf{A}_{i,0} + \mathbf{A}_{i,1}) \cdot \mathbf{x}_{i+1,0} = (r_{i+1} \cdot \mathbf{A}_{i,0} + \mathbf{A}_{i,1}) \cdot \mathbf{x}_{i+1,1} \bmod q,$$
$$\mathbf{A}_i \cdot (r_{i+1} \cdot \mathbf{x}_{i+1,0}, \mathbf{x}_{i+1,0}) = \mathbf{A}_i \cdot (r_{i+1} \cdot \mathbf{x}_{i+1,1}, \mathbf{x}_{i+1,1}) \bmod q,$$
$$\mathbf{A}_i \cdot \mathbf{x}_{i,0} = \mathbf{A}_i \cdot \mathbf{x}_{i,1} \bmod q.$$

Furthermore, if $x_{i+1,0,j'} \neq x_{i+1,1,j'}$, we have $x_{i,0,j'} \neq x_{i,1,j}$ and $x_{i,0,j'+\ell_{i+1}} \neq x_{i,1,j'+\ell_{i+1}}$ since $r_{i+1} \in \mathcal{R}^{\times}$ is a unit in $\mathcal{R}$.

Suppose Hash_{i+1} is not SSB over $\mathcal{W}_{i+1}^{\ell_{i+1}}$, then there exists $j' \in \mathbb{Z}_{\ell_{i+1}}$ such that

$$\Pr\left[\mathsf{BAD}(i+1, j') \mid \mathbf{A}_{i+1} \leftarrow \mathsf{BSetup}_{i+1}(1^{\lambda}, j')\right]$$

is non-negligible. Consequently, by the above derivation, the average

$$\frac{1}{2} \cdot \Pr\left[\mathsf{BAD}(i, j') \mid \mathbf{A}_i \leftarrow \mathsf{BSetup}_i(1^{\lambda}, j')\right]$$
$$+ \frac{1}{2} \cdot \Pr\left[\mathsf{BAD}(i, j' + \ell_{i+1}) \mid \mathbf{A}_i \leftarrow \mathsf{BSetup}_i(1^{\lambda}, j' + \ell_{i+1})\right]$$

is non-negligible. We conclude that there exists $j \in \{j', j' + \ell_{i+1}\} \subseteq \mathbb{Z}_{\ell_i}$ such that

$$\Pr\left[\mathsf{BAD}(i, j) \mid \mathbf{A}_i \leftarrow \mathsf{BSetup}_i(1^{\lambda}, j)\right]$$

is non-negligible, contradicting Property 3 above. $\square$

Note that the elements r_j of the sets R defined in Proposition 2 satisfy the requirements in Lemma 8.

Acknowledgments. The authors thank Fermi Ma for many helpful discussions throughout the development of this work.

G.M. is partially supported by the German Federal Ministry of Education and Research BMBF (grant 16K15K042, project 6GEM) and funded by the Deutsche Forschungsgemeinschaft (DFG, German Research Foundation) under Germany's Excellence Strategy - EXC 2092 CASA - 390781972.

References

1. Albrecht, M.R., Cini, V., Lai, R.W.F., Malavolta, G., Thyagarajan, S.A.K.: Lattice-based snarks: publicly verifiable, preprocessing, and recursively composable. In: Dodis, Y., Shrimpton, T. (eds.) Advances in Cryptology–CRYPTO 2022. Lecture Notes in Computer Science, vol. 13508, pp. 102–132. Springer, Cham (2022). https://doi.org/10.1007/978-3-031-15979-4_4

2. Albrecht, M.R., Lai, R.W.F.: Subtractive sets over cyclotomic rings. In: Malkin, T., Peikert, C. (eds.) CRYPTO 2021. LNCS, vol. 12826, pp. 519–548. Springer, Cham (2021). https://doi.org/10.1007/978-3-030-84245-1_18

3. Attema, T., Cramer, R.: Compressed Σ-protocol theory and practical application to plug & play secure algorithmics. In: Micciancio, Daniele, Ristenpart, Thomas (eds.) CRYPTO 2020. LNCS, vol. 12172, pp. 513–543. Springer, Cham (2020). https://doi.org/10.1007/978-3-030-56877-1_18

4. Attema, T., Cramer, R., Kohl, L.: A compressed Σ-protocol theory for lattices. In: Malkin, T., Peikert, C. (eds.) CRYPTO 2021, Part II. LNCS, vol. 12826, pp. 549–579. Springer, Heidelberg, Virtual Event (Aug 2021). https://doi.org/10.1007/978-3-030-84245-1_19

5. Attema, T., Fehr, S.: Parallel repetition of $(k_1, \ldots, k_\mu)$-special-sound multi-round interactive proofs. Cryptology ePrint Archive, Report 2021/1259 (2021). https://ia.cr/2021/1259

6. Ben-Sasson, E., Chiesa, A., Spooner, N.: Interactive oracle proofs. In: Hirt, M., Smith, A. (eds.) TCC 2016. LNCS, vol. 9986, pp. 31–60. Springer, Heidelberg (2016). https://doi.org/10.1007/978-3-662-53644-5_2

7. Bootle, J., Cerulli, A., Chaidos, P., Groth, J., Petit, C.: Efficient zero-knowledge arguments for arithmetic circuits in the discrete log setting. In: Fischlin, M., Coron, J.-S. (eds.) EUROCRYPT 2016. LNCS, vol. 9666, pp. 327–357. Springer, Heidelberg (2016). https://doi.org/10.1007/978-3-662-49896-5_12

8. Bootle, J., Chiesa, A., Sotiraki, K.: Sumcheck arguments and their applications. In: Malkin, T., Peikert, C. (eds.) CRYPTO 2021. LNCS, vol. 12825, pp. 742–773. Springer, Cham (2021). https://doi.org/10.1007/978-3-030-84242-0_26

9. Bootle, J., Lyubashevsky, V., Nguyen, N.K., Seiler, G.: A non-PCP approach to succinct quantum-safe zero-knowledge. In: Micciancio, D., Ristenpart, T. (eds.) CRYPTO 2020. LNCS, vol. 12171, pp. 441–469. Springer, Cham (2020). https://doi.org/10.1007/978-3-030-56880-1_16

10. Bünz, B., Bootle, J., Boneh, D., Poelstra, A., Wuille, P., Maxwell, G.: Bulletproofs: short proofs for confidential transactions and more. In: 2018 IEEE Symposium on Security and Privacy, pp. 315–334. IEEE (2018). https://doi.org/10.1109/SP.2018.00020

11. Chiesa, A., Ma, F., Spooner, N., Zhandry, M.: Post-quantum succinct arguments: Breaking the quantum rewinding barrier. In: FOCS, pp. 49–58. IEEE (2021)

12. Hoffstein, J., Pipher, J., Silverman, J.H.: NTRU: a ring-based public key cryptosystem. In: Buhler, J.P. (ed.) ANTS 1998. LNCS, vol. 1423, pp. 267–288. Springer, Heidelberg (1998). https://doi.org/10.1007/BFb0054868

13. Kilian, J.: A note on efficient zero-knowledge proofs and arguments (extended abstract). In: 24th ACM STOC, pp. 723–732. ACM Press (1992). https://doi.org/10.1145/129712.129782

14. Lai, R.W.F., Malavolta, G., Ronge, V.: Succinct arguments for bilinear group arithmetic: practical structure-preserving cryptography. In: Cavallaro, L., Kinder, J., Wang, X., Katz, J. (eds.) ACM CCS 2019, pp. 2057–2074. ACM Press (2019). https://doi.org/10.1145/3319535.3354262

15. Liu, Q., Zhandry, M.: Revisiting post-quantum fiat-Shamir. In: Boldyreva, A., Micciancio, D. (eds.) CRYPTO 2019. LNCS, vol. 11693, pp. 326–355. Springer, Cham (2019). https://doi.org/10.1007/978-3-030-26951-7_12

16. Lombardi, A., Ma, F., Spooner, N.: Post-quantum zero knowledge, revisited (or: How to do quantum rewinding undetectably). CoRR abs/2111.12257 (2021)

17. Lyubashevsky, V., Peikert, C., Regev, O.: On ideal lattices and learning with errors over rings. In: Gilbert, H. (ed.) EUROCRYPT 2010. LNCS, vol. 6110, pp. 1–23. Springer, Heidelberg (2010). https://doi.org/10.1007/978-3-642-13190-5_1
18. Ma, F.: Quantum-secure commitments and collapsing hash functions. https://www.cs.princeton.edu/fermim/talks/collapse-binding.pdf (2020)
19. Marriott, C., Watrous, J.: Quantum arthur-merlin games. In: Computational Complexity Conference, pp. 275–285. IEEE (2004)
20. Micali, S.: CS proofs (extended abstracts). In: 35th FOCS, pp. 436–453. IEEE (1994). https://doi.org/10.1109/SFCS.1994.365746
21. Regev, O.: On lattices, learning with errors, random linear codes, and cryptography. In: Gabow, H.N., Fagin, R. (eds.) 37th ACM STOC, pp. 84–93. ACM Press (2005). https://doi.org/10.1145/1060590.1060603
22. Shor, P.W.: Algorithms for quantum computation: discrete logarithms and factoring. In: 35th FOCS, pp. 124–134. IEEE (1994). https://doi.org/10.1109/SFCS.1994.365700
23. Stehlé, D., Steinfeld, R.: Making NTRU as secure as worst-case problems over ideal lattices. In: Paterson, K.G. (ed.) EUROCRYPT 2011. LNCS, vol. 6632, pp. 27–47. Springer, Heidelberg (2011). https://doi.org/10.1007/978-3-642-20465-4_4
24. Unruh, D.: Quantum proofs of knowledge. In: Pointcheval, D., Johansson, T. (eds.) EUROCRYPT 2012. LNCS, vol. 7237, pp. 135–152. Springer, Heidelberg (2012). https://doi.org/10.1007/978-3-642-29011-4_10
25. Unruh, D.: Computationally binding quantum commitments. In: Fischlin, M., Coron, J.-S. (eds.) EUROCRYPT 2016. LNCS, vol. 9666, pp. 497–527. Springer, Heidelberg (2016). https://doi.org/10.1007/978-3-662-49896-5_18
26. Winter, A.: Coding theorem and strong converse for quantum channels. IEEE Trans. Inf. Theory 45(7), 2481–2485 (1999). https://doi.org/10.1109/18.796385, https://doi.org/10.1109
27. Zhandry, M.: Schrödinger's pirate: how to trace a quantum decoder. In: Pass, R., Pietrzak, K. (eds.) TCC 2020. LNCS, vol. 12552, pp. 61–91. Springer, Cham (2020). https://doi.org/10.1007/978-3-030-64381-2_3

Interactive Proofs

Fiat-Shamir Transformation
of Multi-round Interactive Proofs

Thomas Attema[1,3,4($\boxtimes$)], Serge Fehr[1,3], and Michael Klooß[2]

[1] CWI, Cryptology Group, Amsterdam, The Netherlands
serge.fehr@cwi.nl
[2] Karlsruhe Institute of Technology, KASTEL, Karlsruhe, Germany
michael.klooss@kit.edu
[3] Leiden University, Mathematical Institute, Leiden, The Netherlands
[4] TNO, Cyber Security and Robustness, The Hague, The Netherlands
thomas.attema@tno.nl

Abstract. The celebrated Fiat-Shamir transformation turns any public-coin interactive proof into a non-interactive one, which inherits the main security properties (in the random oracle model) of the interactive version. While originally considered in the context of 3-move public-coin interactive proofs, i.e., so-called Σ-protocols, it is now applied to multi-round protocols as well. Unfortunately, the security loss for a $(2\mu + 1)$-move protocol is, in general, approximately Q^μ, where Q is the number of oracle queries performed by the attacker. In general, this is the best one can hope for, as it is easy to see that this loss applies to the μ-fold sequential repetition of Σ-protocols, but it raises the question whether certain (natural) classes of interactive proofs feature a milder security loss.

In this work, we give positive and negative results on this question. On the positive side, we show that for $(k_1, \ldots, k_\mu)$-special-sound protocols (which cover a broad class of use cases), the knowledge error degrades linearly in Q, instead of Q^μ. On the negative side, we show that for t-fold *parallel repetitions* of typical $(k_1, \ldots, k_\mu)$-special-sound protocols with $t \geq \mu$ (and assuming for simplicity that t and Q are integer multiples of μ), there is an attack that results in a security loss of approximately $\frac{1}{2}Q^\mu/\mu^{\mu+t}$.

1 Introduction

1.1 Background and State of the Art

The celebrated and broadly used Fiat-Shamir transformation turns any public-coin interactive proof into a *non-interactive* proof, which inherits the main security properties (in the random oracle model) of the interactive version. The rough idea is to replace the random challenges, which are provided by the verifier in the interactive version, by the hash of the current message (concatenated with the messages from previous rounds). By a small adjustment, where also the to-be-signed message is included in the hashes, the transformation turns any public-coin interactive proof into a signature scheme. Indeed, the latter is a commonly used design principle for constructing very efficient signature schemes.

While originally considered in the context of 3-move public-coin interactive proofs, i.e., so-called Σ-protocols, the Fiat-Shamir transformation also applies to *multi-round* protocols. However, a major drawback in the case of multi-round protocols is that, in general, the security loss obtained by applying the Fiat-Shamir transformation grows exponentially with the number of rounds. Concretely, for any $(2\mu + 1)$-move interactive proof Π (where we may assume that the prover speaks first and last, so that the number of communication rounds is indeed odd) that admits a cheating probability of at most ϵ, captured by the knowledge or soundness error, the Fiat-Shamir-transformed protocol FS$[\Pi]$ admits a cheating probability of (approximately) at most $Q^{\mu} \cdot \epsilon$, where Q denotes the number of random-oracle queries admitted to the dishonest prover. A tight reduction is due to [11] with a security loss $\binom{Q}{\mu} \approx \frac{Q^{\mu}}{\mu^{\mu}}$, where the approximation holds whenever μ is much smaller than Q, which is the typical case. More concretely, [11] introduces the notions of *state-restoration soundness (SRS)* and *state-restoration knowledge (SRK)*, and it shows that any (knowledge) sound protocol Π satisfies these notions with the claimed security loss. [1] The security of FS$[\Pi]$ (with the same loss) then follows from the fact that these soundness notions imply the security of the Fiat-Shamir transformation.

Furthermore, there are (contrived) examples of multi-round protocols Π for which this Q^{μ} security loss is almost tight. For instance, the μ-fold sequential repetition Π of a special-sound Σ-protocol with challenge space $\mathcal{C}$ is ϵ-sound with $\epsilon = \frac{1}{|\mathcal{C}|^{\mu}}$, while it is easy to see that, by attacking the sequential repetitions round by round, investing Q/μ queries per round to try to find a "good" challenge, and assuming $|\mathcal{C}|$ to be much larger than Q, its Fiat-Shamir transformation FS$[\Pi]$ can be broken with probability approximately $\left(\frac{Q}{\mu} \frac{1}{|\mathcal{C}|}\right)^{\mu} = \frac{Q^{\mu}}{\mu^{\mu}} \cdot \epsilon$.[2]

For μ beyond 1 or 2, let alone for non-constant μ (e.g., for IOP-based protocols [3,10,11] and also Bulletproofs-like protocols [13,15]), this is a very unfortunate situation when it comes to choosing concrete security parameters. If one wants to rely on the proven security reduction, one needs to choose a large security parameter for Π, in order to compensate for the order Q^{μ} security loss, effecting its efficiency; alternatively, one has to give up on proven security and simply *assume* that the security loss is much milder than what the general bound suggests. Often, the security loss is simply ignored.

This situation gives rise to the following question: *Do there exist natural classes of multi-round public-coin interactive proofs for which the security loss behaves more benign than what the general reduction suggests?* Ideally, the general Q^{μ} loss appears for contrived examples *only*.

---

[1] As a matter of fact, [11] considers arbitrary *interactive oracle proofs (IOPs)*, but these notions are well-defined for ordinary interactive proofs too.

[2] This is clearly a contrived example since the natural construction would be to apply the Fiat-Shamir transformation to the *parallel* repetition of the original Σ-protocol, where no such huge security loss would then occur.

So far, the only positive results, establishing a security loss linear in Q, were established in the context of *straight-line/online* extractors that do not require rewinding. These extractors either rely on the algebraic group model (AGM) [22], or are restricted to protocols using hash-based commitment schemes in the random oracle model [11]. To analyze the properties of straight-line extractors, new auxiliary soundness notions were introduced: *round-by-round (RBR) soundness* [17] and *RBR knowledge* [18]. However, it is unclear if and how these notions can be used in scenarios where straight-line extraction does not apply.

In this work, we address the above question (in the plain random-oracle model, and without restricting to schemes that involve hash-based commitments), and give both positive and negative answers, as explained in more detail below.

1.2 Our Results

Positive Result. We show that the Fiat-Shamir transformation of any $(k_1, \ldots, k_\mu)$-special-sound interactive proof has a security loss of at most $Q + 1$. More concretely, we consider the *knowledge error* κ as the figure of merit, i.e., informally, the maximal probability of the verifier accepting the proof when the prover does not have a witness for the claimed statement, and we prove the following result, also formalized in the theorem below. For any $(k_1, \ldots, k_\mu)$-special-sound $(2\mu + 1)$-move interactive proof Π with knowledge error κ (which is a known function of $(k_1, \ldots, k_\mu)$), the Fiat-Shamir transformed protocol $\mathsf{FS}[\Pi]$ has a knowledge error at most $(Q + 1) \cdot \kappa$. This result is directly applicable to a long list of recent zero-knowledge proof systems, e.g., [4,6,12,13,15,16,21,26,29]. While all these works consider the Fiat-Shamir transformation of special-sound protocols, most of them ignore the associated security loss.

Main Theorem (Theorem 2). *Let Π be a $(k_1, \ldots, k_\mu)$-out-of-$(N_1, \ldots, N_\mu)$ special-sound interactive proof with knowledge error κ. Then the Fiat-Shamir transformation $\mathsf{FS}[\Pi]$ of Π is knowledge sound with knowledge error*

$$\kappa_{\mathsf{fs}}(Q) = (Q + 1) \cdot \kappa.$$

Since in the Fiat-Shamir transformation of any $(2\mu + 1)$-move protocol Π, a dishonest prover can simulate any attack against Π, and can try Q/μ times when allowed to do Q queries in total, our new upper bound $(Q + 1) \cdot \kappa$ is close to the trivial lower bound $1 - (1 - \kappa)^{Q/\mu} \approx Q\kappa/\mu$. Another, less explicit, security measure in the context of knowledge soundness is the run time of the knowledge extractor. Our bound on the knowledge error holds by means of a knowledge extractor that makes an expected number of $K + Q \cdot (K - 1)$ queries, where $K = k_1 \cdots k_\mu$. This is a natural bound: K is the number of necessary distinct "good" transcripts (which form a certain tree-like structure). The loss of $Q \cdot (K - 1)$ captures the fact that a prover may finish different proofs, depending on the random oracle answers, and only one out of Q proofs may be useful for extraction, as explained below.

Our result on the *knowledge* soundness of FS[Π] for special-sound protocols Π immediately carries over to *ordinary* soundness of FS[Π], with the same security loss $Q + 1$. However, proving knowledge soundness is more intricate; showing a linear-in-Q loss for ordinary soundness can be obtained via simpler arguments (e.g., there is no need to argue efficiency of the extractor).

The construction of our knowledge extractor is motivated by the extractor from [5] in the interactive case, but the analysis here in the context of a non-interactive proof is much more involved. We analyze the extractor in an inductive manner, and capture the induction step (and the base case) by means of an abstract experiment. The crucial idea for the analysis (and extractor) is how to deal with accepting transcripts which are not useful.

To see the core problem, consider a Σ-protocol, i.e., a 3-move k-special-sound interactive proof, and a semi-honest prover that knows a witness and behaves as follows. It prepares, independently, Q first messages $a^1, \ldots, a^Q$ and asks for all hashes $c^i = \mathsf{RO}(a^i)$, and then decides "randomly" (e.g., using a hash over all random oracle answers) which thread to complete, i.e., for which i^* to compute the response z and then output the valid proof (a^{i^*}, z). When the extractor then reprograms the random oracle at the point a^{i^*} to try to obtain another valid response but now for a different challenge, this affects i^*, and most likely the prover will then use a different thread j^* and output the proof (a^{j^*}, z') with $a^{j^*} \neq a^{i^*}$. More precisely, $\Pr(j^* = i^*) = 1/Q$. Hence, an overhead of Q appears in the run-time.

In case of an *arbitrary* dishonest prover with an unknown strategy for computing the a^i's above, and with an arbitrary (unknown) success probability ϵ, the intuition remains: after reprogramming, we still expect $\Pr(j^* = i^*) \geq 1/Q$ and thus a linear-in-Q overhead in the run-time of the extractor. However, providing a rigorous proof is complicated by the fact that the event $j^* = i^*$ is not necessarily independent of the prover producing a *valid* proof (again) after the reprogramming. Furthermore, conditioned on the prover having been successful in the first run and conditioned on the corresponding i^*, the success probability of the prover after the reprogramming may be skewed, i.e., may not be ϵ anymore. As a warm-up for our general multi-round result, we first give a rigorous analysis of the above case of a Σ-protocol. For that purpose, we introduce an abstract sampling game that mimics the behavior of the extractor in finding two valid proofs with $j^* = i^*$, and we bound the success probability and the "cost" (i.e., the number of samples needed) of the game, which directly translate to the success probability and the run-time of the extractor.

Perhaps surprisingly, when moving to *multi-round* protocols, dealing with the knowledge error is relatively simple by recursively composing the extractor for the Σ-protocol. However, controlling the run-time is intricate. If the extractor is recursively composed, i.e., it makes calls to a sub-extractor to obtain a sub-tree, then a naive construction and analysis gives a blow-up of Q^μ in the run-time. Intuitively, because only $1/Q$ of the sub-extractor runs produce useful sub-trees, i.e., sub-trees which extend the current a^{i^*}. The other trees belong to some a^{j^*}

with $j^* \neq i^*$ and are thus useless. This overhead of Q then accumulates per round.

The crucial observation that we exploit in order to overcome the above issue is that the very first (accepting) transcript sampled by a sub-extractor already determines whether a sub-tree will be (potentially) useful, or not. Thus, if this very first transcript already shows that the sub-tree will not be useful, there is no need to run the full-fledged sub-tree extractor, saving precious time.

To illustrate this more, we again consider the simple case of a dishonest prover that succeeds with certainty. Then, after the first run of the sub-extractor to produce the first sub-tree (which requires expected time linear in Q) and having reprogrammed the random oracle with the goal to find another sub-tree that extends the current a^{i^*}, it is cheaper to first do a single run of the prover to learn j^* and only run the full fledged sub-extractor if $j^* = i^*$, and otherwise reprogram and re-try again. With this strategy, we expect Q tries, followed by the run of the sub-extractor, to find a second fitting sub-tree. Altogether, this amounts to linear-in-Q runs of the prover, compared to the Q^2 using the naive approach.

Again, what complicates the rigorous analysis is that the prover may succeed with bounded probability ϵ only, and the event $j^* = i^*$ may depend on the prover/sub-extractor being successful (again) after the reprogramming. Furthermore, as an additional complication, conditioned on the sub-extractor having been successful in the first run and conditioned on the corresponding i^*, *both* the success probability of the prover *and* the run-time of the sub-extractor after the reprogramming may be skewed now. Again, we deal with this by considering an abstract sampling game that mimics the behavior of the extractor, but where the cost function is now more fine-grained in order to distinguish between a single run of the prover and a run of the sub-extractor. Because of this more fine-grained way of defining the "cost", the analysis of the game also becomes substantially more intricate.

Negative Result. We also show that the general exponential security loss of the Fiat-Shamir transformation, when applied to a multi-round protocol, is *not* an artefact of contrived examples, but there exist *natural* protocols that indeed have such an exponential loss. For instance, our negative result applies to the lattice-based protocols in [5,14]. Concretely, we show that the t-fold parallel repetition Π^t of a typical $(k_1, \ldots, k_\mu)$-special-sound $(2\mu + 1)$-move interactive proof Π features this behavior when $t \geq \mu$. For simplicity, let us assume that t and Q are multiples of μ. Then, in more detail, we show that for any typical $(k_1, \ldots, k_\mu)$-special-sound protocol Π there exists a poly-time Q-query prover $\mathcal{P}^*$ against $\mathsf{FS}[\Pi^t]$ that succeeds in making the verifier accept with probability $\approx \frac{1}{2} Q^\mu \kappa^t / \mu^{\mu+t}$ for *any* statement x, where κ is the knowledge error (as well as the soundness error) of Π. Thus, with the claimed probability, $\mathcal{P}^*$ succeeds in making the verifier accept for statements x that are not in the language and/or for which $\mathcal{P}^*$ does not know a witness. Given that κ^t is the soundness error of Π^t (i.e., the soundness error of Π^t as an interactive proof), this shows that the *soundness error* of Π^t grows proportionally with Q^μ when applying the Fiat-Shamir transformation. Recent work on the knowledge error of the parallel repetition of special-sound multi-round interactive proofs [7] shows that κ^t is also the knowledge error of Π^t, and so the above shows that the same exponential loss holds in the *knowledge error* of the Fiat-Shamir transformation of a parallel repetition.

1.3   Related Work

Independent Concurrent Work. In independent and to a large extent concurrent work,[3] Wikström [31] achieves a similar positive result on the Fiat-Shamir transformation, using a different approach and different techniques: [31] reduces non-interactive extraction to a form of interactive extraction and then applies a generalized version of [30], while our construction adapts the interactive extractor from [5] and offers a direct analysis. One small difference in the results, which is mainly of theoretical interest, is that our result holds and is meaningful for *any* $Q < |\mathcal{C}|$, whereas [31] requires the challenge set $\mathcal{C}$ to be large.

The Forking Lemma. Security of the Fiat–Shamir transformation of k-special-sound 3-move protocols is widely used for construction of signatures. There, unforgeability is typically proven via a forking lemma [9,28], which extracts, with probability roughly ϵ^k/Q, a witness from a signature-forging adversary with success probability ϵ, where Q is the number of queries to the random oracle. The loss ϵ^k is due to *strict* polynomial time extraction (and can be decreased, but in general not down to ϵ). Such a k-th power loss in the success probability for a constant k is fine in certain settings, e.g., for proving the security of signature schemes; however, not for proofs of knowledge (which, on the other hand, consider *expected* polynomial time extraction [8]).

A previous version of [20] generalizes the original forking lemma [9,28] to accommodate Fiat-Shamir transformations of a larger class of (multi-round) interactive proofs. However, their forking lemma only targets a subclass of the $(k_1, \ldots, k_\mu)$-special-sound interactive proofs considered in this work. Moreover, in terms of (expected) runtime and success probability, our techniques significantly outperform their generalized forking lemma. For this reason, the latest version of [20] is based on our extraction techniques instead.

A forking lemma for *interactive* multi-round proofs was presented in [13] and its analysis was improved in a line of follow-up works [2,24,25,27,30]. This forking lemma shows that multi-round special-sound interactive proofs satisfy a notion of knowledge soundness called *witness extended emulation*. Eventually, it was shown that $(k_1, \ldots, k_\mu)$-special-soundness tightly implies knowledge soundness [5].

The aforementioned techniques for interactive proofs are not directly applicable to the Fiat-Shamir mode. First, incorporating the query complexity Q of

---

[3] When finalizing our write-up, we were informed by Wikström that he derived similar results a few months earlier, subsequently made available online [31].

a dishonest prover $\mathcal{P}^*$ attacking the non-interactive Fiat–Shamir transformation complicates the analysis. Second, a naive adaptation of the forking lemmas for interactive proofs gives a blow-up of Q^μ in the run-time.

1.4 Structure of the Paper

Section 2 recalls essential preliminaries. In Sect. 3, the abstract sampling game is defined and analyzed. It is used in Sect. 4 to handle the Fiat–Shamir transformation of Σ-protocols. Building on the intuition, Sect. 5 introduces the *refined game*, and Sect. 6 uses it to handle multi-round protocols. Lastly, our negative result on parallel repetitions is presented in Sect. 7.

2 Preliminaries

2.1 (Non-)Interactive Proofs

We assume the reader to be familiar with the basic concepts related to interactive proofs, and to non-interactive proofs in the random oracle model. We briefly recall here the notions that are important for us and fix the notation that we will be using. For formal definitions and more details, we refer to the full version [1].

Special-Sound Protocols. We consider a public-coin interactive proof Π for an NP relation R. If Π consists of 3 moves, it is called a Σ-protocol, and we then typically write a for the first message, c for the challenge, and z for the response. A Σ-protocol Π is called k-*special-sound* if there exists a polynomial-time algorithm that computes a witness w for the statement x from any k accepting transcripts $(a, c_1, z_1), \ldots, (a, c_k, z_k)$ for x with the same fist message a and pairwise distinct challenges $c_i \neq c_j$. We refer to Π as being k-*out-of-N special-sound* to emphasize that the challenge space $\mathcal{C}$ has cardinality N.

More generally, we consider $(2\mu + 1)$-move public-coin interactive proofs.[4] The communication transcript is then written as $(a_1, c_1, \ldots, a_\mu, c_\mu, a_{\mu+1})$ by default. Such a protocol is called $(k_1, \ldots, k_\mu)$-*special-sound*, or $(k_1, \ldots, k_\mu)$-*out-of-$(N_1, \ldots, N_\mu)$ special-sound* when we want to be explicit about the sizes of the challenge sets, if there exists a polynomial-time algorithm that computes a witness w for the statement x from any accepting $(k_1, \ldots, k_\mu)$-*tree of transcripts* for x, defined in Definition 1 and illustrated in Fig. 1.

Definition 1 (Tree of Transcripts). *Let $k_1, \ldots, k_\mu \in \mathbb{N}$. A $(k_1, \ldots, k_\mu)$-tree of transcripts for a $(2\mu+1)$-move public-coin interactive proof $\Pi = (\mathcal{P}, \mathcal{V})$ is a set of $K = \prod_{i=1}^{\mu} k_i$ transcripts arranged in the following tree structure. The nodes in this tree correspond to the prover's messages and the edges to the verifier's challenges. Every node at depth i has precisely k_i children corresponding to k_i pairwise distinct challenges. Every transcript corresponds to exactly one path from the root node to a leaf node. See Fig. 1 for a graphical illustration. We refer to the corresponding tree of challenges as a $(k_1, \ldots, k_\mu)$-tree of challenges.*

---

[4] We always assume that the prover sends the first and the last message.

A $(k_1, \ldots, k_\mu)$-out-of-$(N_1, \ldots, N_\mu)$ special-sound protocol is known to be (knowledge) sound with knowledge/soundness error

$$\mathrm{Er}(k_1, \ldots, k_\mu; N_1, \ldots, N_\mu) = 1 - \prod_{i=1}^{\mu} \frac{N_i - k_i + 1}{N_i} = 1 - \prod_{i=1}^{\mu} \left(1 - \frac{k_i - 1}{N_i}\right), \quad (1)$$

which is tight in general [5]. Note that $\mathrm{Er}(k; N) = (k-1)/N$ and, for all $1 \leq m \leq \mu$,

$$\begin{aligned}
&\mathrm{Er}(k_m, \ldots, k_\mu; N_m, \ldots, N_\mu) \\
&\qquad = 1 - \frac{N_m - k_m + 1}{N_m} \left(1 - \mathrm{Er}(k_{m+1}, \ldots, k_\mu; N_{m+1}, \ldots, N_\mu)\right),
\end{aligned} \quad (2)$$

where we define $\mathrm{Er}(\emptyset; \emptyset) = 1$. If $N_1 = \cdots = N_\mu = N$, we simply write $\mathrm{Er}(k_1, \ldots, k_\mu; N)$, or $\mathrm{Er}(\mathbf{k}; N)$ for $\mathbf{k} = (k_1, \ldots, k_\mu)$.

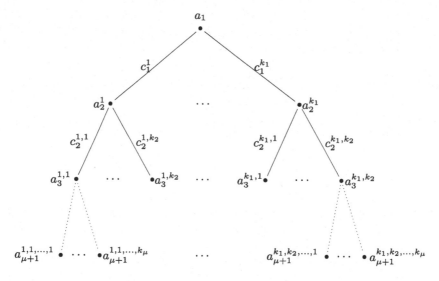

Fig. 1. $(k_1, \ldots, k_\mu)$-tree of transcripts of a $(2\mu + 1)$-move interactive proof [5].

The Fiat-Shamir Transformation and NIROPs. By applying the Fiat-Shamir transformation [19] to a public-coin interactive proof, one obtains a *non-interactive* proof in the *random oracle model*, i.e., a so-called *non-interactive random oracle proof (NIROP)*. In the case of a Σ-protocol, the Fiat-Shamir transformation replaces the random choice of the challenge c by setting $c = \mathsf{RO}(a)$ (or $c = \mathsf{RO}(x, a)$ in case of adaptive security), where RO is a random oracle. In case of multi-round protocols, the idea is the same, but one has to be careful with "chaining" the challenges properly. For concreteness, we specify that the i-th challenge is set to be

$$c_i = \mathsf{RO}_i(a_1, \ldots, a_{i-1}, a_i).$$

Note that, for simplicity, we assume μ different random oracles RO_i then. Furthermore, we assume the range of RO_i to be the corresponding challenge set $\mathcal{C}_i$, and the domain to be $\{0,1\}^{\leq u}$ for large enough u.

The notion of knowledge soundness that we consider for NIROPs, and in particular for the Fiat-Shamir transformation of special-sound protocols, is the natural modification of the knowledge soundness definition of interactive proofs as introduced by Goldreich [23], to the setting of non-interactive proofs in the random oracle model. In more detail, a NIROP is *knowledge sound* with *knowledge error* $\kappa : \mathbb{N} \times \mathbb{N} \to [0,1]$, if there exists an expected polynomial time *knowledge extractor* $\mathcal{E}$ and a polynomial q such that for every Q-query dishonest prover $\mathcal{P}^*$ that succeeds to convince the verifier about a statement x with probability $\epsilon(\mathcal{P}^*, x)$, when $\mathcal{E}$ is given black-box access to $\mathcal{P}^*$ it holds that

$$\Pr\big((x; w) \in R : w \leftarrow \mathcal{E}^{\mathcal{P}^*}(x)\big) \geq \frac{\epsilon(\mathcal{P}^*, x) - \kappa(|x|, Q)}{q(|x|)},$$

i.e., $\mathcal{E}$ succeeds to extract a witness w for x with the above probability. It is not too hard to see that it is sufficient to consider *deterministic* provers $\mathcal{P}^*$.

2.2 Negative Hypergeometric Distribution

An important tool in our analysis is the negative hypergeometric distribution. Consider a bucket containing ℓ green balls and $N - \ell$ red balls, i.e., a total of N balls. In the negative hypergeometric experiment, balls are drawn uniformly at random from this bucket, without replacement, until k green balls have been found or until the bucket is empty. The number of red balls X drawn in this experiment is said to have a *negative hypergeometric distribution* with parameters N, ℓ, k, which is denoted by $X \sim \mathsf{NHG}(N, \ell, k)$.

Lemma 1 (Negative Hypergeometric Distribution). *Let $N, \ell, k \in \mathbb{N}$ with $\ell, k \leq N$, and let $X \sim \mathsf{NHG}(N, \ell, k)$. Then $\mathbb{E}[X] \leq k\frac{N-\ell}{\ell+1}$.*

Remark 1. Typically, negative hypergeometric experiments are restricted to the non-trivial case $\ell \geq k$. For reasons to become clear later, we also allow parameter choices with $\ell < k$ resulting in a trivial negative hypergeometric experiment in which all balls are always drawn.

Remark 2. The above has a straightforward generalization to buckets with balls of more than 2 colors: say ℓ green balls and m_i balls of color i for $1 \leq i \leq M$. The experiment proceeds as before, i.e., drawing until either k green balls have been found or the bucket is empty. Let X_i be the number of balls of color i that are drawn in this experiment. Then $X_i \sim \mathsf{NHG}(\ell + m_i, \ell, k)$ for all i. To see this, simply run the generalized negative hypergeometric experiment without counting the balls that are neither green nor of color i.

3 An Abstract Sampling Game

Towards the goal of constructing and analyzing a knowledge extractor for the Fiat-Shamir transformation $FS[\Pi]$ of special-sound interactive proofs Π, we define and analyze an abstract sampling game. Given access to a deterministic Q-query prover $\mathcal{P}^*$, attacking the non-interactive random oracle proof $FS[\Pi]$, our extractor will essentially play this abstract game in the case Π is a Σ-protocol, and it will play this game recursively in the general case of a multi-round protocol. The abstraction allows us to focus on the crucial properties of the extraction algorithm, without unnecessarily complicating the notation.

The game considers an arbitrary but fixed U-dimensional array M, where, for all $1 \leq j_1, \ldots, j_U \leq N$, the entry $M(j_1, \ldots, j_U) = (v, i)$ contains a bit $v \in \{0, 1\}$ and an index $i \in \{1, \ldots, U\}$. Think of the bit v indicating whether this entry is "good" or "bad", and the index i points to one of the U dimensions. The goal will be to find k "good" entries with the same index i, and with all of them lying in the 1-dimensional array $M(j_1, \ldots, j_{i-1}, \cdot, j_{i+1}, \ldots, j_U)$ for some $1 \leq j_1, \ldots, j_{i-1}, j_{i+1}, \ldots, j_U \leq N$.

Looking ahead, considering the case of a Σ-protocol first, this game captures the task of our extractor to find k proofs that are valid and feature the same first message but have different hash values assigned to the first message. Thus, in our application, the sequence $j_1, \ldots, j_U$ specifies the function table of the random oracle $RO: \{1, \ldots, U\} \rightarrow \{1, \ldots, N\}, i \mapsto j_i$, while the entry $M(j_1, \ldots, j_U) = (v, i)$ captures the relevant properties of the proof produced by the considered prover when interacting with that particular specification of the random oracle. Concretely, the bit v indicates whether the proof is valid, and the index i is the first message a of the proof. Replacing j_i by j_i' then means to reprogram the random oracle at the point $i = a$. Note that after the reprogramming, we want to obtain another valid proof with the *same* first message, i.e., with the same index i (but now a different challenge, due to the reprogramming).

The game is formally defined in Fig. 2 and its core properties are summarized in Lemma 2 below. Looking ahead, we note that for efficiency reasons, the extractor will not sample the entire sequence $j_1, \ldots, j_U$ (i.e., function table), but will sample its components on the fly using lazy sampling.

It will be useful to define, for all $1 \leq i \leq U$, the function

$$a_i: \{1, \ldots, N\}^U \rightarrow \mathbb{N}_{\geq 0},$$

$$(j_1, \ldots, j_U) \mapsto \left| \{j : M(j_1, \ldots, j_{i-1}, j, j_{i+1}, \ldots, j_U) = (1, i)\} \right|. \tag{3}$$

The value $a_i(j_1, \ldots, j_U)$ counts the number of entries that are "good" and have index i in the 1-dimensional array $M(j_1, \ldots, j_{i-1}, \cdot, j_{i+1}, \ldots, j_U)$. Note that a_i does not depend on the i-th entry of the input vector $(j_1, \ldots, j_U)$, and so, by a slight abuse of notation, we sometimes also write $a_i(j_1, \ldots, j_{i-1}, j_{i+1}, \ldots, j_U)$.

Lemma 2 (Abstract Sampling Game). *Consider the game in Fig. 2. Let $J = (J_1, \ldots, J_U)$ be uniformly distributed in $\{1, \ldots, N\}^U$, indicating the first entry sampled, and let $(V, I) = M(J_1, \ldots, J_U)$. Further, for all $1 \leq i \leq U$, let*

Parameters: $k, N, U \in \mathbb{N}$, and M a U-dimensional array with entries in $M(j_1, \ldots, j_U) \in \{0, 1\} \times \{1, \ldots, U\}$ for all $1 \leq j_1, \ldots, j_U \leq N$.

- Sample $(j_1, \ldots, j_U) \in \{1, \ldots, N\}^U$ at random and set $(v, i) = M(j_1, \ldots, j_U)$.
- If $v = 0$, abort.
- Else, repeat
  - sample $j' \in \{1, \ldots, N\} \setminus \{j_i\}$ (without replacement),
  - compute $(v', i') = M(j_1, \ldots, j_{i-1}, j', j_{i+1}, \ldots, j_U)$,

  until either $k - 1$ additional entries equal to $(1, i)$ have been found or until all indices j' have been tried.

Fig. 2. Abstract sampling game.

$A_i = a_i(J)$. Moreover, let X be the number of entries of the form $(1, i)$ with $i = I$ sampled (including the first one), and let Λ be the total number of entries sampled in this game. Then

$$\mathbb{E}[\Lambda] \leq 1 + (k-1)P \quad and$$

$$\Pr(X = k) \geq \frac{N}{N - k + 1} \left(\Pr(V = 1) - P \cdot \frac{k-1}{N} \right),$$

where $P = \sum_{i=1}^{U} \Pr(A_i > 0)$.

Remark 3. Note the abstractly defined parameter P. In our application, where the index i of $(v, i) = M(j_1, \ldots, j_U)$ is determined by the output of a prover making no more than Q queries to the random oracle with function table $j_1, \ldots, j_U$, the parameter P will be bounded by $Q + 1$. We show this formally (yet again somewhat abstractly) in Lemma 3. Intuitively, the reason is that the events $A_i > 0$ are *disjoint* for all but Q indices i (those that the considered prover does *not* query), and so their probabilities add up to at most 1. Indeed, if $a_i(j_1, \ldots, j_U) > 0$ for an index i that the algorithm did *not* query then $M(j_1, \ldots, j_U) \in \{(0, i), (1, i)\}$; namely, since i has not been queried, the index i output by the algorithm is oblivious to the value of j_i. Therefore, given $j_1, \ldots, j_U$, there is at most one *unqueried* index i with $a_i(j_1, \ldots, j_U) > 0$.

Proof (of Lemma 2). **Expected Number of Samples.** Let us first derive an upper bound on the expected value of Λ. To this end, let X' denote the number of sampled entries of the form $(1, i)$ with $i = I$, but, in contrast to X, *without* counting the first one. Similarly, let Y' denote the number of sampled entries of the form (v, i) with $v = 0$ or $i \neq I$, again without counting the first one. Then $\Lambda = 1 + X' + Y'$ and

$$\Pr(X' = 0 \mid V = 0) = \Pr(Y' = 0 \mid V = 0) = 1.$$

Hence, $\mathbb{E}[X' \mid V = 0] = \mathbb{E}[Y' \mid V = 0] = 0$.

Let us now consider the expected value $\mathbb{E}[Y' \mid V = 1]$. To this end, we observe that, conditioned on the event $V = 1 \wedge I = i \wedge A_i = a$ with $a > 0$, Y' follows a negative hypergeometric distribution with parameters $N - 1$, $a - 1$ and $k - 1$. Hence, by Lemma 1,

$$\mathbb{E}[Y' \mid V = 1 \wedge I = i \wedge A_i = a] \leq (k - 1)\frac{N - a}{a} ,$$

and thus, using that $\Pr(X' \leq k - 1 \mid V = 1) = 1$,

$$\mathbb{E}[X' + Y' \mid V = 1 \wedge I = i \wedge A_i = a] \leq (k - 1) + (k - 1)\frac{N - a}{a} = (k - 1)\frac{N}{a} .$$

On the other hand

$$\Pr(V = 1 \wedge I = i \mid A_i = a) = \frac{a}{N}$$

and thus

$$\Pr(V = 1 \wedge I = i \wedge A_i = a) = \Pr(A_i = a)\frac{a}{N} . \tag{4}$$

Therefore, and since $\Pr(V = 1 \wedge I = i \wedge A_i = 0) = 0$,

$$\begin{aligned}
\Pr(V = 1) \cdot \mathbb{E}[X' + Y' \mid V = 1] &= \sum_{i=1}^{U} \sum_{a=1}^{N} \Pr(V = 1 \wedge I = i \wedge A_i = a) \\
&\qquad \cdot \mathbb{E}[X' + Y' \mid V = 1 \wedge I = i \wedge A_i = a] \\
&\leq \sum_{i=1}^{U} \sum_{a=1}^{N} \Pr(A_i = a)(k - 1) \\
&= (k - 1) \sum_{i=1}^{U} \Pr(A_i > 0) \\
&= (k - 1)P ,
\end{aligned}$$

where $P = \sum_{i=1}^{U} \Pr(A_i > 0)$. Hence,

$$\begin{aligned}
\mathbb{E}[\Lambda] &= \mathbb{E}[1 + X' + Y'] \\
&= 1 + \Pr(V = 0) \cdot \mathbb{E}[X' + Y' \mid V = 0] + \Pr(V = 1) \cdot \mathbb{E}[X' + Y' \mid V = 1] \\
&\leq 1 + (k - 1)P ,
\end{aligned}$$

which proves the claimed upper bound on $\mathbb{E}[\Lambda]$.

Success Probability. Let us now find a lower bound for the "success probability" $\Pr(X = k)$ of this game. Using (4) again, we can write

$$\Pr(X = k) = \sum_{i=1}^{U} \Pr(V = 1 \wedge I = i \wedge A_i \geq k) = \sum_{i=1}^{U} \sum_{a=k}^{N} \Pr(A_i = a)\frac{a}{N} .$$

Now, using $a \leq N$, note that

$$\frac{a}{N} = 1 - \left(1 - \frac{a}{N}\right) \geq 1 - \frac{N}{N-k+1}\left(1 - \frac{a}{N}\right)$$

$$= \frac{N}{N-k+1}\left(\frac{N-k+1}{N} - 1 + \frac{a}{N}\right) = \frac{N}{N-k+1}\left(\frac{a}{N} - \frac{k-1}{N}\right).$$

Therefore, combining the two, and using that the summand becomes negative for $a < k$ to argue the second inequality, and using (4) once more, we obtain

$$\Pr(X = k) \geq \sum_{i=1}^{U}\sum_{a=k}^{N} \Pr(A_i = a)\frac{N}{N-k+1}\left(\frac{a}{N} - \frac{k-1}{N}\right)$$

$$\geq \sum_{i=1}^{U}\sum_{a=1}^{N} \Pr(A_i = a)\frac{N}{N-k+1}\left(\frac{a}{N} - \frac{k-1}{N}\right)$$

$$= \frac{N}{N-k+1}\sum_{i=1}^{U}\sum_{a=1}^{N}\left(\Pr(V = 1 \wedge I = i \wedge A_i = a) - \Pr(A_i = a)\cdot\frac{k-1}{N}\right)$$

$$= \frac{N}{N-k+1}\left(\Pr(V = 1) - \frac{k-1}{N}\sum_{i=1}^{U}\Pr(A_i > 0)\right)$$

$$= \frac{N}{N-k+1}\left(\Pr(V = 1) - P\cdot\frac{k-1}{N}\right),$$

where, as before, we have used that $\Pr(V = 1 \wedge I = i \wedge A_i = 0) = 0$ for all $1 \leq i \leq U$ to conclude the second equality, and finally that $P = \sum_{i=1}^{U} \Pr(A_i > 0)$. This completes the proof of the lemma.   □

Our knowledge extractor will instantiate the abstract sampling game via a deterministic Q-query prover $\mathcal{P}^*$ attacking the Fiat-Shamir transformation $\mathsf{FS}[\Pi]$. The index i of $M(v, i) = (j_1, \ldots, j_U)$ is then determined by the output of $\mathcal{P}^*$, with the random oracle being given by the function table $j_1, \ldots, j_U$. Since the index i is thus determined by Q queries to the random oracle, the following shows that the parameter P will in this case be bounded by $Q + 1$.

Lemma 3. *Consider the game in Fig. 2. Let v and idx be functions such that $M(j) = (v(j), \mathsf{idx}(j))$ for all $j \in \{1, \ldots, N\}^U$. Furthermore, let $J = (J_1, \ldots, J_U)$ be uniformly distributed in $\{1, \ldots, N\}^U$, and set $A_i = a_i(J)$ for all $1 \leq i \leq U$. Let us additionally assume that for all $j \in \{1, \ldots, N\}^U$ there exists a subset $S(j) \subseteq \{1, \ldots, U\}$ of cardinality at most Q such that $\mathsf{idx}(j) = \mathsf{idx}(j')$ for all j' with $j'_\ell = j_\ell$ for all $\ell \in S(j)$. Then*

$$P = \sum_{i=1}^{U} \Pr(A_i > 0) \leq Q + 1.$$

Proof. By basic probability theory, it follows that[5]

$$P = \sum_{i=1}^{U} \Pr(A_i > 0) = \sum_{j \in \{1,\ldots,N\}^U} \Pr(J = j) \sum_{i=1}^{U} \Pr(A_i > 0 \mid J = j)$$

$$= \sum_{j} \Pr(J = j) \Bigg(\sum_{i \in S(j)} \Pr(A_i > 0 \mid J = j) + \sum_{i \notin S(j)} \Pr(A_i > 0 \mid J = j) \Bigg)$$

Since $|S(j)| \leq Q$ for all j, it follows that

$$P \leq \sum_{j} \Pr(J = j) \Bigg(Q + \sum_{i \notin S(j)} \Pr(A_i > 0 \mid J = j) \Bigg)$$

$$\leq Q + \sum_{j} \Pr(J = j) \sum_{i \notin S(j)} \Pr(A_i > 0 \mid J = j)$$

Now note that, by definition of the sets $S(j)$, for all $j \in \{1, \ldots, N\}^U$, $i \notin S(j)$ and $j^* \in \{1, \ldots, N\}$, it holds that

$$\Pr\big(\mathsf{idx}(J_1, \ldots, J_{I-1}, j^*, J_{i+1}, \ldots, J_U) = \mathsf{idx}(j) \mid J = j\big) = 1.$$

Therefore, for all $i \notin S(j) \cup \{\mathsf{idx}(j)\}$,

$$\Pr(A_i > 0 \mid J = j) = 0.$$

Hence,

$$\sum_{i \notin S(j)} \Pr(A_i > 0 \mid J = j) \leq \Pr(A_{\mathsf{idx}(j)} > 0 \mid J = j) \leq 1.$$

Altogether, it follows that

$$P \leq Q + \sum_{j} \Pr(J = j) = Q + 1,$$

which completes the proof. □

4   Fiat-Shamir Transformation of Σ-Protocols

Let us first consider the Fiat-Shamir transformation of a k-special-sound Σ-protocol Π, i.e., a 3-move interactive proof, with challenge set $\mathcal{C}$; subsequently, in Sect. 6, we move to general *multi-round* interactive proofs.

Let $\mathcal{P}^*$ be a deterministic dishonest Q-query random-oracle prover, attacking the Fiat-Shamir transformation $\mathsf{FS}[\Pi]$ of Π on input x. Given a statement x as input, after making Q queries to the random oracle $\mathsf{RO}: \{0,1\}^{\leq u} \to \mathcal{C}$, $\mathcal{P}^*$

---

[5] The probabilities $\Pr(A_i > 0 \mid J = j)$ are all 0 or 1; however, it's still convenient to use probability notation here.

outputs a proof $\pi = (a, z)$. For reasons to become clear later, we re-format (and partly rename) the output and consider $I := a$ and π as $\mathcal{P}^*$'s output. We refer to the output I as the *index*. Furthermore, we extend $\mathcal{P}^*$ to an algorithm $\mathcal{A}$ that additionally checks the correctness of the proof π. Formally, $\mathcal{A}$ runs $\mathcal{P}^*$ to obtain I and π, queries RO to obtain $c := \mathsf{RO}(I)$, and then outputs

$$I = a, \quad y := (a, c, z) \quad \text{and} \quad v := V(y),$$

where $V(y) = 1$ if y is an accepting transcript for the interactive proof Π on input x and $V(y) = 0$ otherwise. Hence, $\mathcal{A}$ is a random-oracle algorithm making at most $Q + 1$ queries; indeed, it relays the oracle queries done by $\mathcal{P}^*$ and makes the one needed to do the verification. We may write $\mathcal{A}^{\mathsf{RO}}$ to make the dependency of $\mathcal{A}$'s output on the choice of the random oracle RO explicit. $\mathcal{A}$ has a naturally defined success probability

$$\epsilon(\mathcal{A}) := \Pr\big(v = 1 : (I, y, v) \leftarrow \mathcal{A}^{\mathsf{RO}}\big),$$

where $\mathsf{RO} \colon \{0,1\}^{\leq u} \to \mathcal{C}$ is chosen uniformly at random. The probability $\epsilon(\mathcal{A})$ equals the success probability $\epsilon(\mathcal{P}^*, x)$ of the random-oracle prover $\mathcal{P}^*$ on input x.

Our goal is now to construct an extraction algorithm that, when given black-box access to $\mathcal{A}$, aims to output k accepting transcripts $y_1, \ldots, y_k$ with common first message a and distinct challenges. By the k-special-soundness property of Π, a witness for statement x can be computed efficiently from these transcripts.

The extractor $\mathcal{E}$ is defined in Fig. 3. We note that, after a successful first run of $\mathcal{A}$, having produced a first accepting transcript (a, c, z), we rerun $\mathcal{A}$ from the very beginning and answer all oracle queries consistently, except the query to a; i.e., we *only* reprogram the oracle at the point $I = a$. Note that since $\mathcal{P}^*$ and thus $\mathcal{A}$ is deterministic, and we only reprogram the oracle at the point $I = a$, in each iteration of the repeat loop $\mathcal{A}$ is ensured to make the query to I again.[6]

A crucial observation is the following. Within a run of $\mathcal{E}$, all the queries that are made by the different invocations of $\mathcal{A}$ are answered *consistently* using lazy sampling, except for the queries to the index I, where different responses $c, c', \ldots$ are given. This is indistinguishable from having them answered by a full-fledged random oracle, i.e., by means of a pre-chosen function $\mathsf{RO} \colon \{0,1\}^{\leq u} \to \mathcal{C}$, but then replacing the output $\mathsf{RO}(I)$ at I by fresh challenges c' for the runs of $\mathcal{A}$ in the repeat loop. By enumerating the elements in the domain and codomain of RO, it is easily seen that the extractor is actually running the abstract game from Fig. 2. Thus, bounds on the success probability and the expected run time (in terms of queries to $\mathcal{A}$) follow from Lemma 2 and Lemma 3. Altogether we obtain the following result.

Lemma 4 (Extractor). *The extractor $\mathcal{E}$ of Fig. 3 makes an expected number of at most $k + Q \cdot (k - 1)$ queries to $\mathcal{A}$ and succeeds in outputting k transcripts*

---

[6] Of course, it would be sufficient to rewind $\mathcal{A}$ to the point where it makes the (first) query to a, but this would make the description more clumsy.

Parameters: $k, Q \in \mathbb{N}$
Black-box access to: $\mathcal{A}$ as above

- Run $\mathcal{A}$ as follows to obtain (I, y_1, v): answer all (distinct) oracle queries with uniformly random values in $\mathcal{C}$. Let c be the response to query I.
- If $v = 0$, abort.
- Else, repeat
  - sample $c' \in \mathcal{C} \setminus \{c\}$ (without replacement);
  - run $\mathcal{A}$ as follows to obtain (I', y', v'): answer the query to I with c', while answering all other queries consistently if the query was performed by $\mathcal{A}$ already on a previous run and with a fresh random value in $\mathcal{C}$ otherwise; until either $k - 1$ additional challenges c' with $v' = 1$ and $I' = I$ have been found or until all challenges $c' \in \mathcal{C} \setminus \{c\}$ have been tried.
- In the former case, output the k accepting transcripts $y_1, \ldots, y_k$.

Fig. 3. Extractor $\mathcal{E}$.

$y_1, \ldots, y_k$ *with common first message a and distinct challenges with probability at least*

$$\frac{N}{N - k + 1} \left(\epsilon(\mathcal{A}) - (Q + 1) \cdot \frac{k - 1}{N} \right).$$

Proof. By enumerating all the elements in the domain and codomain of the random oracle RO, we may assume that $\mathsf{RO} \colon \{1, \ldots, U\} \to \{1, \ldots, N\}$, and thus RO can be represented by the function table $(j_1, \ldots, j_U) \in \{1, \ldots, N\}^U$ for which $\mathsf{RO}(i) = j_i$. Further, since $\mathcal{P}^*$ is deterministic, the outputs I, y and v of the algorithm $\mathcal{A}$ can be viewed as functions taking as input the function table $(j_1, \ldots, j_U) \in \{1, \ldots, N\}^U$ of RO, and so we can consider the array $M(j_1, \ldots, j_U) = \big(I(j_1, \ldots, j_U), v(j_1, \ldots, j_U)\big)$.

Then, a run of the extractor perfectly matches up with the abstract sampling game of Fig. 2 instantiated with array M. The only difference is that, in this sampling game, we consider full-fledged random oracles encoded by vectors $(j_1, \ldots, j_U) \in \{1, \ldots, N\}^U$, while the actual extractor implements these random oracles by lazy sampling. Thus, we can apply Lemma 2 to obtain bounds on the success probability and the expected run time. However, in order to control the parameter P, which occurs in the bound of Lemma 2, we make the following observation, so that we can apply Lemma 3 to bound $P \leq Q + 1$.

For every $(j_1, \ldots, j_U)$, let $S(j_1, \ldots, j_U) \subseteq \{1, \ldots, U\}$ be the set of points that $\mathcal{P}^*$ queries to the random oracle when $(j_1, \ldots, j_U)$ corresponds to the entire function table of the random oracle. Then, $\mathcal{P}^*$ will produce the same output when the random oracle is reprogrammed at an index $i \notin S(j_1, \ldots, j_U)$. In particular, $I(j_1, \ldots, j_{i-1}, j, j_{i+1}, \ldots, j_U) = I(j_1, \ldots, j_{i-1}, j', j_{i+1}, \ldots, j_U)$ for all j, j' and for all $i \notin S(j_1, \ldots, j_U)$. Furthermore, $|S(j_1, \ldots, j_U)| \leq Q$. Hence, the conditions of Lemma 3 are satisfied and $P \leq Q + 1$. The bounds on the success probability and the expected run time now follow, completing the proof. $\square$

The existence of the above extractor, combined with the k-special-soundness property, implies the following theorem.

Theorem 1 (Fiat-Shamir Transformation of a Σ-Protocol). *The Fiat-Shamir transformation $\mathsf{FS}[\Pi]$ of a k-out-of-N special-sound Σ-protocol Π is knowledge sound with knowledge error*

$$\kappa_{\mathsf{fs}}(Q) = (Q+1) \cdot \kappa,$$

where $\kappa := \mathrm{Er}(k; N) = (k-1)/N$ is the knowledge error of Π.

5   Refined Analysis of the Abstract Sampling Game

Before we prove knowledge soundness of the Fiat-Shamir transformation of *multi-round* interactive protocols, we reconsider the abstract game of Sect. 3, and consider a refined analysis of the cost of playing the game. The multi-round knowledge extractor will essentially play a recursive composition of this game; however, the analysis of Sect. 3 is insufficient for our purposes (resulting in a super-polynomial bound on the run-time of the knowledge extractor). Fortunately, it turns out that a refinement allows us to prove the required (polynomial) upper bound.

In Sect. 3, the considered cost measure is the number of entries visited during the game. For Σ-protocols, every entry corresponds to a single invocation of the dishonest prover $\mathcal{P}^*$. For multi-round protocols, every entry will correspond to a single invocation of a *sub-tree extractor*. The key observation is that some invocations of the sub-tree extractor are *expensive* while others are *cheap*. For this reason, we introduce a cost function Γ and a constant cost γ to our abstract game, allowing us to differentiate between these two cases. Γ and γ assign a cost to every entry of the array M; Γ corresponds to the cost of an expensive invocation of the sub-tree extractor and γ corresponds to the cost of a cheap invocation. While this refinement presents a natural generalization of the abstract game of Sect. 3, its analysis becomes significantly more involved.

The following lemma provides an upper bound for the total cost of playing the abstract game in terms of these two cost functions.

Lemma 5 (Abstract Sampling Game - Weighted Version). *Consider again the game of Fig. 2, as well a cost function $\Gamma: \{1, \ldots, N\}^U \to \mathbb{R}_{\geq 0}$ and a constant cost $\gamma \in \mathbb{R}_{\geq 0}$. Let $J = (J_1, \ldots, J_U)$ be uniformly distributed in $\{1, \ldots, N\}^U$, indicating the first entry sampled, and let $(V, I) = M(J_1, \ldots, J_U)$. Further, for all $1 \leq i \leq U$, let $A_i = a_i(J)$, where the function a_i is as defined in Eq. 3.*

We define the cost of sampling an entry $M(j_1, \ldots, j_U) = (v, i)$ with index $i = I$ to be $\Gamma(j_1, \ldots, j_U)$ and the cost of sampling an entry $M(j_1, \ldots, j_U) = (v, i)$ with index $i \neq I$ to be γ. Let Δ be the total cost of playing this game. Then

$$\mathbb{E}[\Delta] \leq k \cdot \mathbb{E}[\Gamma(J)] + (k-1) \cdot T \cdot \gamma$$

where $T = \sum_{i=1}^{U} \Pr(I \neq i \wedge A_i > 0) \leq P$.

Remark 4. Note that the parameter T in the statement here differs slightly from its counterpart $P = \sum_i \Pr(A_i > 0)$ in Lemma 2. Recall the informal discussion of P in the context of our application (Remark 3), where the array M is instantiated via a Q-query prover $\mathcal{P}^*$ attacking the Fiat-Shamir transformation of an interactive proof. We immediately see that now the defining events $I \neq i \wedge A_i > 0$ are *empty* for all $U - Q$ indices that the prover does not query, giving the bound $T \leq Q$ here, compared to the bound $P \leq Q + 1$ on P. The formal (and more abstract) statement and proof is given in Lemma 6.

Proof. Let us split up Δ into the cost measures Δ_1, Δ_2 and Δ_3, defined as follows. Δ_1 denotes the total costs of the elements $M(j_1, \ldots, j_U) = (1, i)$ with $i = I$ sampled in the game, i.e., the elements with bit $v = 1$ and index $i = I$; correspondingly, X denotes the number of entries of the form $(1, i)$ with $i = I$ sampled (including the first one if $V = 1$). Second, Δ_2 denotes the total costs of the elements $M(j_1, \ldots, j_U) = (0, i)$ with $i = I$ sampled, i.e., the elements with bit $v = 0$ and index $i = I$; correspondingly, Y denotes the number of entries of the form $(0, i)$ with $i = I$ sampled (including the first one if $V = 0$). Finally, Δ_3 denotes the total costs of the elements $M(j_1, \ldots, j_U) = (v, i)$ with $i \neq I$ sampled; correspondingly, Z denotes the number of entries of this form sampled.

Clearly $\Delta = \Delta_1 + \Delta_2 + \Delta_3$. Moreover, since the cost γ is constant, it follows that $\mathbb{E}[\Delta_3] = \gamma \cdot \mathbb{E}[Z]$. In a similar manner, we now aim to relate $\mathbb{E}[\Delta_1]$ and $\mathbb{E}[\Delta_2]$ to $\mathbb{E}[Y]$ and $\mathbb{E}[Z]$, respectively. However, since the cost function $\Gamma \colon \{1, \ldots, N\}^U \to \mathbb{R}_{\geq 0}$ is not necessarily constant, this is more involved.

For $1 \leq i \leq U$ let us write $J_i^* = (J_1, \ldots, J_{i-1}, J_{i+1}, \ldots, J_U)$, which is uniformly random with support $\{1, \ldots, N\}^{U-1}$. Moreover, for all $1 \leq i \leq U$ and $j^* = (j_1^*, \ldots, j_{i-1}^*, j_{i+1}^*, \cdots, j_U) \in \{1, \ldots, N\}^{U-1}$, let $\Lambda(i, j^*)$ denote the event

$$\Lambda(i, j^*) = [I = i \wedge J_i^* = j^*].$$

We note that conditioned on the event $\Lambda(i, j^*)$, all samples are picked from the subarray $M(j_1^*, \ldots, j_{i-1}^*, \cdot, j_{i+1}^*, \cdots, j_U^*)$; the first one uniformly at random subject to the index I being i, and the remaining ones (if $V = 1$) uniformly at random (without replacement).

We first analyze and bound $\mathbb{E}[\Delta_1 \mid \Lambda(i, j^*)]$. We observe that, for all i and j^* with $\Pr(\Lambda(i, j^*)) > 0$,

$$\mathbb{E}[\Delta_1 \mid \Lambda(i, j^*)] = \sum_{\ell=0}^{N} \Pr(X = \ell \mid \Lambda(i, j^*)) \cdot \mathbb{E}[\Delta_1 \mid \Lambda(i, j^*) \wedge X = \ell].$$

Since, conditioned on $\Lambda(i, j^*) \wedge X = \ell$ for $\ell \in \{0, \ldots, N\}$, any size-$\ell$ subset of elements with $v = 1$ and index i is equally likely to be sampled, it follows that

$$\mathbb{E}[\Delta_1 \mid \Lambda(i, j^*) \wedge X = \ell] = \mathbb{E}[\Gamma(J) \mid V = 1 \wedge \Lambda(i, j^*)] \cdot \ell.$$

Hence,

$$\mathbb{E}[\Delta_1 \mid \Lambda(i, j^*)] = \mathbb{E}[\Gamma(J) \mid V = 1 \wedge \Lambda(i, j^*)] \cdot \sum_{\ell} \Pr(X = \ell \mid \Lambda(i, j^*)) \cdot \ell$$

$$= \mathbb{E}[\Gamma(J) \mid V = 1 \wedge \Lambda(i, j^*)] \cdot \mathbb{E}[X \mid \Lambda(i, j^*)].$$

Similarly,

$$\mathbb{E}[\Delta_2 \mid \Lambda(i,j^*)] = \mathbb{E}[\Gamma(J) \mid V = 0 \wedge \Lambda(i,j^*)] \cdot \mathbb{E}[Y \mid \Lambda(i,j^*)].$$

Next, we bound the expected values of X and Y conditioned on $\Lambda(i,j^*)$. The analysis is a more fine-grained version of the proof of Lemma 2. Bounding $\mathbb{E}[X \mid \Lambda(i,j^*)]$ is quite easy: since $V = 0$ implies $X = 0$ and $V = 1$ implies $X \le k$, it immediately follows that

$$\mathbb{E}[X \mid \Lambda(i,j^*)] = \Pr(V = 0 \mid \Lambda(i,j^*)) \cdot \mathbb{E}[X \mid V = 0 \wedge \Lambda(i,j^*)]$$
$$+ \Pr(V = 1 \mid \Lambda(i,j^*)) \cdot \mathbb{E}[X \mid V = 1 \wedge \Lambda(i,j^*)]$$
$$\le \Pr(V = 1 \mid \Lambda(i,j^*)) \cdot k.$$

Hence,

$$\mathbb{E}[\Delta_1 \mid \Lambda(i,j^*)] \le k \cdot \Pr(V = 1 \mid \Lambda(i,j^*)) \cdot \mathbb{E}[\Gamma(J) \mid V = 1 \wedge \Lambda(i,j^*)]. \tag{5}$$

Suitably bounding the expectation $\mathbb{E}[Y \mid \Lambda(i,j^*)]$, and thus $\mathbb{E}[\Delta_2 \mid \Lambda(i,j^*)]$, is more involved. For that purpose, we introduce the following parameters. For the considered fixed choice of the index $1 \le i \le U$ and of $j^* = (j_1^*, \dots, j_{i-1}^*, j_{i+1}^*, \cdots, j_U^*)$, we let[7]

$$a := a_i(j^*) = \left| \{ j : (v_j, i_j) = M(j_1^*, \dots, j_{i-1}^*, j, j_{i+1}^*, \dots, j_U^*) = (1, i) \} \right| \quad \text{and}$$

$$b := b_i(j^*) := \left| \{ j : (v_j, i_j) = M(j_1^*, \dots, j_{i-1}^*, j, j_{i+1}^*, \dots, j_U^*) = (0, i) \} \right|.$$

Let us first note that

$$\Pr(V = 1 \mid \Lambda(i,j^*)) = \frac{a}{a+b} \quad \text{and} \quad \Pr(V = 0 \mid \Lambda(i,j^*)) = \frac{b}{a+b}$$

for all i and j^* with $\Pr(\Lambda(i,j^*)) > 0$. Therefore, if we condition on the event $V = 1 \wedge \Lambda(i,j^*)$ we implicitly assume that i and j^* are so that a is positive. Now, towards bounding $\mathbb{E}[Y \mid \Lambda(i,j^*)]$, we observe that conditioned on the event $V = 1 \wedge \Lambda(i,j^*)$, the random variable Y follows a negative hypergeometric distribution with parameters $a + b - 1$, $a - 1$ and $k - 1$. Hence, by Lemma 1,

$$\mathbb{E}[Y \mid V = 1 \wedge \Lambda(i,j^*)] \le (k-1)\frac{b}{a},$$

and thus

$$\mathbb{E}[Y \mid \Lambda(i,j^*)] = \Pr(V = 0 \mid \Lambda(i,j^*)) \cdot \mathbb{E}[Y \mid V = 0 \wedge \Lambda(i,j^*)]$$
$$+ \Pr(V = 1 \mid \Lambda(i,j^*)) \cdot \mathbb{E}[Y \mid V = 1 \wedge \Lambda(i,j^*)]$$
$$\le \Pr(V = 0 \mid \Lambda(i,j^*)) + \Pr(V = 1 \mid \Lambda(i,j^*)) \cdot (k-1)\frac{b}{a}$$
$$= \frac{b}{a+b} + \frac{a}{a+b} \cdot (k-1)\frac{b}{a} = k\frac{b}{a+b}$$
$$= k \cdot \Pr(V = 0 \mid \Lambda(i,j^*)),$$

---

[7] Recall that we use $a_i(j_1, \dots, j_U)$ and $a_i(j_1, \dots, j_{i-1}, j_{i+1}, \dots, j_U)$ interchangeably, exploiting that $a_i(j_1, \dots, j_U)$ does not depend on the i-th input j_i.

where we use that $\mathbb{E}[Y \mid V = 0 \wedge \Lambda(i, j^*)] = 1$. Hence,

$$\mathbb{E}[\Delta_2 \mid \Lambda(i, j^*)] \leq k \cdot \Pr(V = 0 \mid \Lambda(i, j^*)) \cdot \mathbb{E}[\Gamma(J) \mid V = 0 \wedge \Lambda(i, j^*)],$$

and thus, combined with Eq. 5,

$$\mathbb{E}[\Delta_1 + \Delta_2 \mid \Lambda(i, j^*)] \leq k \cdot \mathbb{E}[\Gamma(J) \mid \Lambda(i, j^*)].$$

Since this inequality holds for all i and j^* with $\Pr(\Lambda(i, j^*)) > 0$, it follows that

$$\mathbb{E}[\Delta_1 + \Delta_2] \leq k \cdot \mathbb{E}[\Gamma(J)].$$

What remains is to show that $\mathbb{E}[Z] \leq (k-1)T$. The slightly weaker bound $\mathbb{E}[Z] \leq (k-1)P$ follows immediately from observing that $Z \leq Y'$ for Y' as in the proof of Lemma 2 (the number of entries counted by Z is a subset of those counted by Y'), and using that $\mathbb{E}[Y'] \leq \mathbb{E}[X' + Y'] \leq (k-1)P$ as derived in the proof of Lemma 2. This then implies $\mathbb{E}[\Delta_3] \leq (k-1) \cdot P \cdot \gamma$, and so, altogether, we obtain the weaker version of the claimed bound:

$$\mathbb{E}[\Delta] = \mathbb{E}[\Delta_1 + \Delta_2 + \Delta_3] \leq k \cdot \mathbb{E}[\Gamma(J)] + (k-1) \cdot P \cdot \gamma.$$

For the stronger version in terms of T, we refer to the full version [1].   □

Lemma 6. *Consider the game in Fig. 2. Let v and* idx *be functions such that $M(j) = (v(j), \mathsf{idx}(j))$ for all $j \in \{1, \ldots, N\}^U$. Furthermore, let $J = (J_1, \ldots, J_U)$ be uniformly distributed in $\{1, \ldots, N\}^U$ and set $A_i = a_i(J)$ for all $1 \leq i \leq U$ as in Eq. 3. Let us additionally assume that for all $j \in \{1, \ldots, N\}^U$ there exists a subset $S(j) \subseteq \{1, \ldots, U\}$ of cardinality at most Q such that $\mathsf{idx}(j) = \mathsf{idx}(j')$ for all j, j' with $j_\ell = j'_\ell$ for all $\ell \in S(j)$. Then*

$$T = \sum_{i=1}^{U} \Pr(\mathsf{idx}(J) \neq i \wedge A_i > 0) \leq Q.$$

See the full version [1] for a proof of lemma 6.

6   Fiat-Shamir Transformation of Multi-round Protocols

Let us now move to multi-round interactive proofs. More precisely, we consider the Fiat-Shamir transformation $\mathsf{FS}[\Pi]$ of a $\mathbf{k}$-special-sound $(2\mu + 1)$-move interactive proof Π, with $\mathbf{k} = (k_1, \ldots, k_\mu)$. While the multi-round extractor has a natural recursive construction, it requires a more fine-grained analysis to show that it indeed implies knowledge soundness.

To avoid a cumbersome notation, below we first handle $(2\mu + 1)$-move interactive proofs in which the verifier samples all μ challenges uniformly at random from the *same* set $\mathcal{C}$. In the full version [1], we consider a generalization for varying challenges sets and extend our results to *adaptive* security.

Consider a deterministic dishonest Q-query random-oracle prover $\mathcal{P}^*$, attacking the Fiat-Shamir transformation $\mathsf{FS}[\Pi]$ of a $\mathbf{k}$-special-sound interactive proof Π on input x. We assume all challenges to be elements in the same set $\mathcal{C}$. After making at most Q queries to the random oracle, $\mathcal{P}^*$ outputs a proof $\pi = (a_1, \ldots, a_{\mu+1})$. We re-format the output and consider

$$I_1 := a_1, \ I_2 := (a_1, a_2), \ldots, \ I_\mu := (a_1, \ldots, a_\mu) \quad \text{and} \quad \pi$$

as $\mathcal{P}^*$'s output. Sometimes it will be convenient to also consider $I_{\mu+1} := (a_1, \ldots, a_{\mu+1})$. Furthermore, we extend $\mathcal{P}^*$ to a random-oracle algorithm $\mathcal{A}$ that additionally checks the correctness of the proof π. Formally, relaying all the random oracle queries that $\mathcal{P}^*$ is making, $\mathcal{A}$ runs $\mathcal{P}^*$ to obtain $\mathbf{I} = (I_1, \ldots, I_\mu)$ and π, additionally queries the random oracle to obtain $c_1 := \mathsf{RO}(I_1), \ldots, c_\mu := \mathsf{RO}(I_\mu)$, and then outputs

$$\mathbf{I}, \quad y := (a_1, c_1, \ldots, a_\mu, c_\mu, a_{\mu+1}) \quad \text{and} \quad v := V(x, y),$$

where $V(x, y) = 1$ if y is an accepting transcript for the interactive proof Π on input x and $V(x, y) = 0$ otherwise. Hence, $\mathcal{A}$ makes at most $Q + \mu$ queries (the queries done by $\mathcal{P}^*$, and the queries to $I_1, \ldots, I_\mu$). Moreover, $\mathcal{A}$ has a naturally defined success probability

$$\epsilon(\mathcal{A}) := \Pr\big(v = 1 : (I, y, v) \leftarrow \mathcal{A}^{\mathsf{RO}}\big),$$

where $\mathsf{RO} \colon \{0, 1\}^{\leq u} \to \mathcal{C}$ is distributed uniformly. As before, $\epsilon(\mathcal{A}) = \epsilon(\mathcal{P}^*, x)$.

Our goal is now to construct an extraction algorithm that, when given black-box access to $\mathcal{A}$, and thus to $\mathcal{P}^*$, aims to output a $\mathbf{k}$-tree of accepting transcripts. By the $\mathbf{k}$-special-soundness property of Π, a witness for statement x can then be computed efficiently from these transcripts.

To this end, we recursively introduce a sequence of "sub-extractors" $\mathcal{E}_1, \ldots, \mathcal{E}_\mu$, where $\mathcal{E}_m$ aims to find a $(1, \ldots, 1, k_m, \ldots, k_\mu)$-tree of accepting transcripts. The main idea behind this recursion is that such a $(1, \ldots, 1, k_m, \ldots, k_\mu)$-tree of accepting transcripts is the composition of k_m appropriate $(1, \ldots, 1, k_{m+1}, \ldots, k_\mu)$-trees.

For technical reasons, we define the sub-extractors $\mathcal{E}_m$ as *random-oracle* algorithms, each one making $Q + \mu$ queries to a random oracle. As we will see, the recursive definition of $\mathcal{E}_m$ is very much like the extractor from the 3-move case, but with $\mathcal{A}$ replaced by the sub-extractor $\mathcal{E}_{m+1}$; however, for this to work we need the sub-extractor to be the same kind of object as $\mathcal{A}$, thus a random-oracle algorithm making the same number of queries. As base for the recursion, we consider the algorithm $\mathcal{A}$ (which outputs a single transcript, i.e., a $(1, \ldots, 1)$-tree); thus, the sub-extractor $\mathcal{E}_\mu$ (which outputs a $(1, \ldots, 1, k_\mu)$-tree) is essentially the extractor of the 3-move case, but with $\mathcal{A}$ now outputting an index *vector* $\mathbf{I} = (I_1, \ldots, I_\mu)$, and with $\mathcal{E}_\mu$ being a *random-oracle* algorithm, so that we can recursively replace the random-oracle algorithm $\mathcal{A}$ by $\mathcal{E}_\mu$ to obtain $\mathcal{E}_{\mu-1}$, etc.

Formally, the recursive definition of $\mathcal{E}_m$ from $\mathcal{E}_{m+1}$ is given in Fig. 4, where $\mathcal{E}_{\mu+1}$ (the base case) is set to $\mathcal{E}_{\mu+1} := \mathcal{A}$, and where $\mathcal{E}_m$ exploits the following *early abort* feature of $\mathcal{E}_{m+1}$: like $\mathcal{A}$, the sub-extractor $\mathcal{E}_{m+1}$ computes the index vector it eventually outputs by running $\mathcal{P}^*$ *as its first step* (see Lemma 7 below). This allows the executions of $\mathcal{E}_{m+1}$ in the repeat loop in Fig. 4 to abort after a single run of $\mathcal{P}^*$ if the requirement $I'_m = I_m$ on its index vector $\mathbf{I}$ is not satisfied, without proceeding to produce the remaining parts y', v' of the output (which would invoke more calls to $\mathcal{P}^*$).

The actual extractor $\mathcal{E}$ is then given by a run of $\mathcal{E}_1$, with the $Q + \mu$ random-oracle queries made by $\mathcal{E}_1$ being answered using lazy-sampling.

Parameters: $k_m, Q \in \mathbb{N}$
Black-box access to: $\mathcal{E}_{m+1}$
Random oracle queries: $Q + \mu$

- Run $\mathcal{E}_{m+1}$ as follows to obtain $(\mathbf{I}, y_1, v)$: relay the $Q+\mu$ queries to the random oracle and record all query-response pairs. Let c be the response to query I_m.
- If $v = 0$, abort with output $v = 0$.
- Else, repeat
  - sample $c' \in \mathcal{C} \setminus \{c\}$ (without replacement);
  - run $\mathcal{E}_{m+1}$ as follows to obtain $(\mathbf{I}', y', v')$, aborting right after the initial run of $\mathcal{P}^*$ if $I'_m \neq I_m$: answer the query to I_m with c', while answering all other queries consistently if the query was performed by $\mathcal{E}_{m+1}$ already on a previous run and with a fresh random value in $\mathcal{C}$ otherwise;
  - until either $k_m - 1$ additional challenges c' with $v' = 1$ and $I'_m = I_m$ have been found or until all challenges $c' \in \mathcal{C} \setminus \{c\}$ have been tried.
- In the former case, output $\mathbf{I}$, the k_m accepting $(1, \ldots, 1, k_{m+1}, \ldots, k_\mu)$-trees $y_1, \ldots, y_{k_m}$, and $v := 1$; in the latter case, output $v := 0$.

Fig. 4. Sub-extractor $\mathcal{E}_m$, as a $(Q + \mu)$-query random-oracle algorithm.

Remark 5. Let us emphasize that within *one* run of $\mathcal{E}_m$, except for the query to I_m for which the response is "reprogrammed", all the queries made by the multiple runs of the sub-extractor $\mathcal{E}_{m+1}$ in the repeat loop are answered *consistently*, both with the run of $\mathcal{E}_{m+1}$ in the first step and among the runs in the repeat loop. This means, a query to a value ξ that has been answered by η in a previous run on $\mathcal{E}_{m+1}$ (within the considered run of $\mathcal{E}_m$) is again answered by η, and a query to a value ξ' that has not been queried yet in a previous run on $\mathcal{E}_{m+1}$ (within the considered run of $\mathcal{E}_m$) is answered with a freshly chosen uniformly random $\eta' \in \mathcal{C}$. In *multiple* runs of $\mathcal{E}_m$, very naturally the random tape of $\mathcal{E}_m$ will be refreshed, and thus there is no guaranteed consistency among the answers to the query calls of $\mathcal{E}_{m+1}$ across multiple runs of $\mathcal{E}_m$.

The following lemma captures some technical property of the sub-extractors $\mathcal{E}_m$. Subsequently, Proposition 1 shows that $\mathcal{E}_m$, if successful, indeed outputs a $(1, \ldots, 1, k_m \ldots, k_\mu)$-tree of accepting transcripts. Proposition 2 bounds the success probability and expected run time of $\mathcal{E}_m$. All statements are understood to hold for any statement x and any $m \in \{1, \ldots, \mu + 1\}$.

Lemma 7 (Consistency of $\mathcal{P}^*$ and $\mathcal{E}_m$). *$\mathcal{E}_m$ obtains the index vector $\mathbf{I}$, which it eventually outputs, by running $(\mathbf{I}, \pi) \leftarrow \mathcal{P}^*$ as its first step. In particular, for any fixed choice of the random oracle RO, the index vector $\mathbf{I}$ output by $\mathcal{E}_m^{\mathsf{RO}}$ matches the one output by $\mathcal{P}^{*,\mathsf{RO}}$.*

Proof. The first claim holds for $\mathcal{E}_{\mu+1} = \mathcal{A}$ by definition of $\mathcal{A}$, and it holds for $\mathcal{E}_m$ with $m \leq \mu$ by induction, given that $\mathcal{E}_m$ runs $\mathcal{E}_{m+1}$ as a first step. The claim on the matching index vectors then follows trivially. $\square$

Proposition 1 (Correctness). *For any fixed choice of the random oracle let $(\mathbf{I}, y_1, \ldots, y_{k_m}, v) \leftarrow \mathcal{E}_m^{\mathsf{RO}}(x)$. If $v = 1$ then $(y_1, \ldots, y_{k_m})$ forms a $(1, \ldots, 1, k_m, \ldots, k_\mu)$-tree of accepting transcripts.*

Proof. All $k_{m+1} \cdots k_\mu$ transcripts in a $(1, \ldots, 1, k_{m+1}, \ldots, k_\mu)$-tree contain the same partial transcript $(a_1, c_1, \ldots, c_m, a_{m+1})$, i.e., the first $2m - 1$ messages in all these transcripts coincide. Hence, any $(1, \ldots, 1, k_{m+1}, \ldots, k_\mu)$-tree of transcripts has a well-defined *trunk* $(a_1, c_1, \ldots, c_m, a_{m+1})$.

By induction on m, we will prove that if $v = 1$ then $(y_1, \ldots, y_{k_m})$ forms a $(1, \ldots, 1, k_m, \ldots, k_\mu)$-tree of accepting transcripts with trunk $(a_1, \mathsf{RO}(I_1), \ldots, \mathsf{RO}(I_{m-1}), a_m)$, where $I_{m+1} = (a_1, \ldots, a_{m+1})$. This obviously implies the correctness claim.

For the base case $m = \mu + 1$, recall that $\mathcal{E}_{\mu+1} = \mathcal{A}$, and that by definition of $\mathcal{A}$ and its output $(\mathbf{I}, y, v)$, if $v = 1$ then y is an accepting transcript, and thus a $(1, \ldots, 1)$-tree of accepting transcripts with $(a_1, \mathsf{RO}(I_1), \ldots, \mathsf{RO}(I_\mu), a_{\mu+1})$ as trunk where $I_{\mu+1} = (a_1, \ldots, a_{\mu+1})$, by definition of $\mathbf{I} = (I_1, \ldots, I_\mu)$.

For the induction step, by the induction hypothesis on $\mathcal{E}_{m+1}$ and its output $(\mathbf{I}, y, v)$, if $v = 1$ then y is a $(1, \ldots, 1, k_{m+1}, \ldots, k_\mu)$-tree of accepting transcripts with trunk $(a_1, \mathsf{RO}(I_1), \ldots, a_m, \mathsf{RO}(I_m), a_{m+1})$, where $I_{m+1} = (a_1, \ldots, a_{m+1})$. This holds for $(\mathbf{I}, y_1, v)$ output by $\mathcal{E}_{m+1}$ in the first step of $\mathcal{E}_m$, but also for any invocation of $\mathcal{E}_{m+1}$ in the repeat loop with output $(\mathbf{I}', y', v')$, here with trunk $(a_1', \mathsf{RO}'(I_1'), \ldots, a_m', \mathsf{RO}'(I_m'), a_{m+1}')$, where $I_{m+1}' = (a_1', \ldots, a_{m+1}')$ and RO' is such that $\mathsf{RO}'(I_j) = \mathsf{RO}(I_j)$ for all $j \neq m$, while $\mathsf{RO}(I_m) = c_i$ and $\mathsf{RO}'(I_m) = c_i'$. By definition of the output of $\mathcal{E}_m$, for y_1 and y' occurring in the output of $\mathcal{E}_m$, it is ensured that $I_m = I_m'$.

Now note that, by Lemma 7, for the purpose of the argument, $\mathcal{E}_m$ could have run $\mathcal{P}^*$ instead of $\mathcal{E}_{m+1}$ to obtain $\mathbf{I}$ and $\mathbf{I}'$. Therefore, by definition of the index vectors output by $\mathcal{P}^*$, which is such that I_j is a (fixed-size) prefix of I_m for $j < m$, it follows that also $I_j = I_j'$ for all $j < m$.

Therefore, the output $y_1, \ldots, y_{k_m}$ of $\mathcal{E}_m$ forms a $(1, \ldots, 1, k_m, \ldots, k_\mu)$-tree of accepting transcripts with trunk $(a_1, \mathsf{RO}(I_1), \ldots, a_{m-1}, \mathsf{RO}(I_{m-1}), a_m)$, where $I_m = (a_1, \ldots, a_m)$. This completes the proof. $\square$

Proposition 2 (Run Time and Success Probability).   *Let $K_m = k_m \cdots k_\mu$. The extractor $\mathcal{E}_m$ makes an expected number of at most $K_m + Q \cdot$*

$(K_m - 1)$ *queries to* $\mathcal{A}$ *(and thus to* $\mathcal{P}^*$*) and successfully outputs* $v = 1$ *with probability at least*

$$\frac{\epsilon(\mathcal{A}) - (Q + 1) \cdot \kappa_m}{1 - \kappa_m}$$

where $\kappa_m := \mathrm{Er}(k_m, \ldots, k_\mu; N)$ *is as defined in Eq. 1.*

Proof. The proof goes by induction on m. The base case $m = \mu+1$ holds trivially, understanding that $K_{\mu+1} = 1$ and $\mathrm{Er}(\emptyset, N) = 0$. Indeed, $\mathcal{E}_{\mu+1}$ makes 1 call to $\mathcal{A}$ and outputs $v = 1$ with probability $\epsilon(\mathcal{A})$. Alternatively, we can take $m = \mu$ as base case, which follows immediately from Lemma 4.

For the induction step, we assume now that the lemma is true for $m' = m+1$ and consider the extractor $\mathcal{E}_m$. As in the 3-move case, we observe that, within a run of $\mathcal{E}_m$, all the queries that are made by the different invocations of $\mathcal{E}_{m+1}$ are answered *consistently* using lazy sampling, except for the queries to the index I_m, which is answered with different responses c'. This is indistinguishable from having them answered by a full-fledged random oracle $\mathsf{RO} \colon \{1, \ldots, U\} \to \{1, \ldots, N\}$, where we have enumerated the domain and codomain of RO as before. This enumeration allows RO to be identified with its function table $(j_1, \ldots, j_U) \in \{1, \ldots, N\}^U$. Thus, the extractor is actually running the abstract sampling game from Fig. 2.

However, in contrast to the instantiation of Sect. 4, the entries of the array M are now *probabilistic*. Namely, while $\mathcal{A}$ is deterministic, the extractor $\mathcal{E}_{m+1}$ is a probabilistic algorithm. Fortunately, this does not influence the key properties of the abstract sampling game. For the purpose of the analysis we may namely fix the randomness of the extractor $\mathcal{E}_{m+1}$. By linearity of the success probability and the expected run time, the bounds that hold for any fixed choice of randomness also hold when averaged over the randomness. Thus, we can apply Lemma 2 and Lemma 5 to bound the success probability and the expected run time.[8]

To control the parameters P and T, which occur in the bounds of these lemmas, we make the following observation. A similar observation was required in the proof of Lemma 4.

First, by Lemma 7, the index vector $\mathbf{I}$ output by $\mathcal{E}_{m+1}$ matches the index vector output by $\mathcal{P}^*$, when given the same random oracle RO. Second, since $\mathcal{P}^*$ is deterministic, its output can only change when the random oracle is reprogrammed at one of the indices $i \in \{1, \ldots, U\}$ queried by $\mathcal{P}^*$. Therefore, for every $(j_1, \ldots, j_U)$, let $S(j_1, \ldots, j_U) \subseteq \{1, \ldots, U\}$ be the set of points that $\mathcal{P}^*$ queries to the random oracle when $(j_1, \ldots, j_U)$ corresponds to the entire function table of the random oracle. Then, $\mathcal{P}^*$ will produce the same output when the random oracle is reprogrammed at an index $i \notin S(j_1, \ldots, j_U)$. In particular, $\mathbf{I}(j_1, \ldots, j_{i-1}, j, j_{i+1}, \ldots, j_U) = \mathbf{I}(j_1, \ldots, j_{i-1}, j', j_{i+1}, \ldots, j_U)$ for all j, j' and

---

[8] To be more precise, to allow for fresh randomness in the different runs of $\mathcal{E}_{m+1}$ within $\mathcal{E}_m$, we first replace the randomness of $\mathcal{E}_{m+1}$ by $F(j_1, \ldots, j_U)$ for a random function F, where $(j_1, \ldots, j_U)$ is the function table of the random oracle providing the answers to $\mathcal{E}_{m+1}$'s queries, and then we fix the choice of F and average over F after having applied Lemma 2 and Lemma 5.

for all $i \notin S(j_1, \ldots, j_U)$. Furthermore, $|S(j_1, \ldots, j_U)| \leq Q$. Hence, the conditions of Lemma 3 and Lemma 6 are satisfied, and it follows that $P \leq Q + 1$ and $T \leq Q$. We are now ready to analyze the success probability and the expected number of $\mathcal{A}$ queries of $\mathcal{E}_m$.

Success Probability. By the induction hypothesis, the success probability p_{m+1} of $\mathcal{E}_{m+1}$ is bounded by

$$p_{m+1} \geq \frac{\epsilon(\mathcal{A}) - (Q + 1) \cdot \kappa_{m+1}}{1 - \kappa_{m+1}}.$$

Then, by Lemma 2 and Lemma 3, the success probability of $\mathcal{E}_m$ is bounded by

$$\frac{N}{N - k_m + 1} \left(p_{m+1} - (Q + 1) \frac{k_m - 1}{N} \right)$$

$$\geq \frac{N}{N - k_m + 1} \left(\frac{\epsilon(\mathcal{A}) - (Q + 1) \cdot \kappa_{m+1}}{1 - \kappa_{m+1}} - (Q + 1) \frac{k_m - 1}{N} \right).$$

By the recursive property (2) of $\kappa_m = \mathrm{Er}(k_m, \ldots, k_\mu; N, \ldots, N)$, it follows that

$$\frac{N - k_m + 1}{N} (1 - \kappa_{m+1}) = 1 - \kappa_m.$$

Hence,

$$p_m \geq \frac{\epsilon(\mathcal{A}) - (Q + 1) \cdot \kappa_{m+1}}{1 - \kappa_m} - (Q + 1) \frac{k_m - 1}{N - k_m + 1}$$

$$= \frac{1}{1 - \kappa_m} \left(\epsilon(\mathcal{A}) - (Q + 1) \cdot \left(\kappa_{m+1} + (1 - \kappa_m) \frac{k_m - 1}{N - k_m + 1} \right) \right)$$

$$= \frac{1}{1 - \kappa_m} \left(\epsilon(\mathcal{A}) - (Q + 1) \cdot \left(1 - (1 - \kappa_m) \cdot \right. \right.$$

$$\left. \left. \frac{N}{N - k_m + 1} + (1 - \kappa_m) \frac{k_m - 1}{N - k_m + 1} \right) \right)$$

$$= \frac{\epsilon(\mathcal{A}) - (Q + 1) \cdot \kappa_m}{1 - \kappa_m},$$

which proves the claimed success probability.

Expected Number of $\mathcal{A}$-Queries. Let the random variable T_m denote the number of $\mathcal{A}$-queries made by extractor $\mathcal{E}_m$. By the induction hypothesis,

$$\mathbb{E}[T_{m+1}] \leq K_{m+1} + Q \cdot (K_{m+1} - 1).$$

We make one crucial observation, allowing us to achieve the claimed query complexity, linear in Q. Namely, we can view the run of a (sub)extractor as a *two-stage* algorithm that allows an *early abort*. By Lemma 7, after only one $\mathcal{A}$-query $\mathcal{E}_{m+1}$ already returns the index I_m. At this stage, $\mathcal{E}_m$ can decide whether to continue the execution of $\mathcal{E}_{m+1}$ or to *early abort* this execution. If the index is incorrect, i.e., it does not match the one obtained in the first invocation of $\mathcal{E}_{m+1}$, then $\mathcal{E}_m$ early aborts the execution of $\mathcal{E}_{m+1}$. Only if the index is correct, the $\mathcal{E}_{m+1}$ execution has to be finished.

For this reason, we define the function $(j_1, \ldots, j_U) \mapsto \Gamma(j_1, \ldots, j_U)$, where $\Gamma(j_1, \ldots, j_U)$ is the (expected) costs of running $\mathcal{E}_{m+1}$ (completely) with random oracle $(j_1, \ldots, j_U)$. Moreover, we set $\gamma = 1$ indicating the cost of an early abort invocation of $\mathcal{E}_{m+1}$. These cost functions measure the expected number of calls to $\mathcal{A}$.

Hence, by Lemma 5 and Lemma 6, the expected cost of running $\mathcal{E}_m$ is

$$\mathbb{E}[T_m] \leq k_m \cdot \mathbb{E}[\Gamma(C)] + \gamma \cdot Q \cdot (k_m - 1) = k_m \cdot \mathbb{E}[T_{m+1}] + Q \cdot (k_m - 1)$$
$$\leq K_m + Q \cdot (K_m - k_m) + Q \cdot (k_m - 1) = K_m + Q \cdot (K_m - 1),$$

where C is distributed uniformly at random in $\mathcal{C}^U$. This completes the proof. $\square$

The existence of extractor $\mathcal{E}_1$, combined with the **k**-special-soundness property, implies the following. This theorem shows that the Fiat-Shamir security loss for **k**-out-of-**N** special-sound $(2\mu + 1)$-round interactive proofs is $Q + 1$, i.e., the security loss is linear in the query complexity Q of provers $\mathcal{P}^*$ attacking the considered non-interactive random oracle proof $\mathsf{FS}[\Pi]$. In particular, the Fiat-Shamir security loss is independent of the number of rounds $(2\mu + 1)$ of Π.

Theorem 2 (FS Transformation of a $(k_1, \ldots, k_\mu)$-Special-Sound Protocol). *The Fiat-Shamir transformation $\mathsf{FS}[\Pi]$ of a $\mathbf{k} = (k_1, \ldots, k_\mu)$-special-sound interactive proof Π, in which all challenges are sampled from a set $\mathcal{C}$ of size N, is knowledge sound with knowledge error*

$$\kappa_{\mathrm{fs}}(Q) = (Q + 1)\kappa,$$

where $\kappa := \mathrm{Er}(\mathbf{k}; N)$ is the knowledge error of the interactive proof Π.

7   The Fiat-Shamir Transformation of Parallel Repetitions

In the previous sections we have established a positive result; for a broad class of interactive proofs the Fiat-Shamir security loss is only linear in the query complexity Q and independent of the number of rounds. One might therefore wonder whether the generic $(Q + 1)^\mu$ security loss, for $(2\mu + 1)$-move protocols, is only tight for contrived examples. In this section, we show that this is *not* the case. We demonstrate a non-trivial attack on the Fiat–Shamir transformation of the *parallel repetition* of **k**-special-sound protocols.

Let $\Pi = (\mathcal{P}, \mathcal{V})$ be a $(2\mu+1)$-move **k**-special-sound interactive proof. We write $\Pi^t = (\mathcal{P}^t, \mathcal{V}^t)$ for its t-fold parallel repetition. That is, the prover $\mathcal{P}^t(x; w)$ runs t instances of $\mathcal{P}(x; w)$, i.e., each message is a tuple $(a^1, \ldots, a^t)$ of messages, one for each parallel thread of execution. Likewise, the verifier $\mathcal{V}^t(x)$ runs t instances of $\mathcal{V}(x)$ in parallel, i.e., each challenge is a tuple $(c^1, \ldots, c^t)$ of challenges, one for each parallel thread of the execution. Finally, the verifier accepts if all parallel instances are accepting.

Assuming certain natural properties on Π, which are satisfied by typical examples, and assuming again for simplicity that the challenge spaces $\mathcal{C}_i$ all have the same cardinality N, we show that, when $t \geq \mu$, there exists a malicious Q-query prover $\mathcal{P}^*$, attacking $\mathsf{FS}[\Pi^t]$, that, for any statement x, succeeds in convincing the verifier with probability at least

$$\frac{1}{2} \frac{Q^\mu}{\mu^{t+\mu}} \, \mathrm{Er}(\mathbf{k}; N)^t \,,$$

assuming some mild conditions on the parameters. Given that $\mathrm{Er}(\mathbf{k}; N)^t$ equals the soundness as well as the knowledge error of Π^t,[9] our attack shows that the security loss of the Fiat-Shamir transformation, when applied to the t-fold parallel repetition of Π, is at least $\frac{1}{2}Q^\mu/\mu^{t+\mu}$. This stands in stark contrast to a single execution of a $\mathbf{k}$-special-sound protocol, where the loss is linear in Q and independent of μ.

We go on to discuss the kind of $\mathbf{k}$-special-sound protocols Π for which our attack applies. For simplicity, we restrict our attention here to $\mathbf{k} = (k, \ldots, k)$ and assume t and Q to be multiples of μ. In the full version [7], we consider the case of arbitrary $\mathbf{k}$, and the restrictions on t and Q can be easily avoided with some adjustments to the bound and the reasoning. Let $\boldsymbol{\ell} = (\ell, \ldots, \ell)$ where $\ell \leq k - 1$. The attack on $\mathsf{FS}[\Pi^t]$ uses a property most $\mathbf{k}$-special-sound protocols Π satisfy, namely that there exists an efficient attack strategy $\mathcal{A}$ against Π which tries to guess challenges up front so that:

1. In any round, $\mathcal{A}$ can prepare and send a message so that if he is lucky and the next challenge falls in a certain set Γ of cardinality ℓ, $\mathcal{A}$ will be able to complete the protocol and have the verifier accept (no matter what challenges $\mathcal{A}$ encounters in the remaining rounds), and
2. until $\mathcal{A}$ is lucky in the above sense, in any round $\mathcal{A}$ can actually prepare B distinct messages as above, for a given parameter B.

We call protocols which admit such an attack strategy $\boldsymbol{\ell}$-*special-unsound with B potential responses per round* (see the full version [7] for a formal definition). The first point in particular implies an attack strategy for the interactive proof Π that succeeds with probability $\mathrm{Er}(\boldsymbol{\ell} + 1, N)$. Since many $\mathbf{k}$-special-sound interactive proofs Π are $\boldsymbol{\ell}$-special-unsound with $\boldsymbol{\ell} = \mathbf{k} - 1$, this confirms the tightness of the knowledge error $\mathrm{Er}(\mathbf{k}, N)$. The second point implies that in the context of the Fiat-Shamir transformation, an attacker can produce and try multiple message-challenge pairs in any round.

---

[9] The soundness and knowledge error of a single invocation of Π are both equal to $\mathrm{Er}(\mathbf{k}; N)$. Therefore, it immediately follows that the soundness error of the parallel repetition Π^t is $\mathrm{Er}(\mathbf{k}; N)^t$. The fact that the knowledge error of Π^t also equals $\mathrm{Er}(\mathbf{k}; N)^t$ follows from the recent work [7].

These requirements are very common (for non-trivial ℓ and large B). For example, the folding technique of [13], when used to fold two parts into one, satisfies $(3, \ldots, 3)$-special-soundness and $(2, \ldots, 2)$-special-unsoundness with an exponential parameter B. Note that, while the *honest* prover is *deterministic*, a dishonest prover can produce different messages (and hope to be lucky with one of the corresponding challenges).

The following theorem gives a lower bound for the success probability of our attack on the Fiat-Shamir transformation $\mathsf{FS}[\Pi^t]$ of the t-fold parallel repetition Π^t of an interactive proof Π with certain common soundness and unsoundness properties.

Theorem 3. *Let Π be a $(2\mu + 1)$-move $(k, \ldots, k)$-out-of-$(N, \ldots, N)$ special-sound interactive proof that is $(\ell, \ldots, \ell)$-special-unsound with B responses per round for $\ell = k - 1$. Furthermore, let $t, Q \in \mathbb{N}$ be integer multiples of μ such that $Q \cdot \left(\frac{\ell}{N}\right)^{t/\mu} \leq 1/4$ and $B \geq Q$. Then there exists a Q-query dishonest prover $\mathcal{P}^*$ against $(\mathcal{P}, \mathcal{V}) = \mathsf{FS}[\Pi^t]$ such that, for any statement $x \in \{0, 1\}^*$,*

$$\epsilon(\mathcal{P}^*, x) = \Pr\left(\mathcal{V}^{\mathsf{RO}}(x, \mathcal{P}^{*, \mathsf{RO}}) = 1\right) \geq \frac{1}{2} \frac{Q^\mu}{\mu^{t+\mu}} \, \mathrm{Er}(\mathbf{k}; N)^t \, .$$

The run-time of $\mathcal{P}^*$ is at most tQ times the run-time of attack strategy $\mathcal{A}$.

Proof. The basic idea of the attack is that (groups of) parallel threads can be attacked individually and independently from each other over the different rounds of the protocol. Concretely, the attack is given by the adversary $\mathcal{P}^*$ against $\mathsf{FS}[\Pi^t]$, which makes up to $Q = \mu \cdot Q'$ queries, defined as follows: $\mathcal{P}^*$ runs attack strategy $\mathcal{A}$ in parallel against all $t = \mu \cdot t'$ threads. Let us call a thread *green* if strategy $\mathcal{A}$ succeeds in guessing the challenge for that thread (and hence, $\mathcal{V}$ will eventually accept for that thread). Otherwise, a thread is *red*. All threads start out red, and the goal of $\mathcal{P}^*$ is to turn all threads green. To do so, in every round $\mathcal{P}^*$ tries to turn at least $t' = t/\mu$ red threads into green threads (or all red threads into green threads if fewer than t/μ remain). For this, $\mathcal{P}^*$ uses $\mathcal{A}$ to get the messages which it feeds to the random oracle. If $\mathcal{P}^*$ was lucky with the received challenges for at least $t' = t/\mu$ threads, then enough red threads turn green. Else, $\mathcal{P}^*$ tries the considered round again, exploiting that $\mathcal{A}$ can produce up to B distinct messages that give him a chance, each one giving a fresh challenge from the random oracle. The dishonest prover $\mathcal{P}^*$ tries up to $Q' = Q/\mu$ times per round until it gives up (and fails).

The number of queries $\mathcal{P}^*$ makes to the random oracle is at most Q, hence $\mathcal{P}^*$ is a Q-query adversary. The probability that $\mathcal{P}^*$ succeeds for any try in any round to turn at least $t' = t/\mu$ red threads into green threads is at least $\left(\frac{\ell}{N}\right)^{t'} = \lambda^{t'}$, where we introduce $\lambda = \frac{\ell}{N}$ to simplify the upcoming expressions. Therefore, since $\mathcal{P}^*$ makes at most $Q' = Q/\mu$ queries in every round, the success probability for any fixed round is at least

$$1 - \left(1 - \lambda^{t'}\right)^{Q'} \geq Q'\lambda^{t'} - 2Q'^2\lambda^{2t'} = Q'\lambda^{t'}\left(1 - 2Q'\lambda^{t'}\right). \tag{6}$$

where the inequality follows from the fact that $1 - (1 - x)^n \geq nx - 2n^2x^2$, which can be shown to hold when $nx \leq 1/2$, which is (more than) satisfied for $x = \lambda^{t'}$ and $n = Q'$ by assumption. Hence, $\mathcal{P}^*$ succeeds (in all μ rounds) with probability at least

$$Q'^{\mu}\lambda^t(1 - 2Q'\lambda^{t'})^{\mu} \geq Q'^{\mu}\lambda^t(1 - 2Q\lambda^{t'}) \geq \frac{1}{2}Q'^{\mu}\lambda^t,$$

where we use that $(1 - z)^n \geq 1 - nz$ for $n \in \mathbb{N}$ and $z \in [0, 1]$ to argue the first inequality, and $Q \cdot \left(\frac{\ell}{N}\right)^{t'} \leq 1/4$ for the second. To complete the analysis of $\mathcal{P}^*$'s success probability, we observe that

$$\mathrm{Er}(\mathbf{k}; N) = 1 - \left(1 - \frac{k-1}{N}\right)^{\mu} \leq \mu \cdot \frac{k-1}{N} = \mu \cdot \frac{\ell}{N} = \mu \cdot \lambda.$$

Hence, the success probability of $\mathcal{P}^*$ is at least $\frac{1}{2}Q'^{\mu}\left(\frac{\mathrm{Er}(\mathbf{k};N)}{\mu}\right)^t$, as claimed. □

Acknowledgments. The first author was supported by EU H2020 project No. 780701 (PROMETHEUS) and the Vraaggestuurd Programma Cyber Security & Resilience, part of the Dutch Top Sector High Tech Systems and Materials program. The third author was supported by the topic Engineering Secure Systems (46.23.01) of the Helmholtz Association (HGF) and by KASTEL Security Research Labs.

References

1. Full version of this paper. IACR ePrint 2021/1377
2. Albrecht, M.R., Lai, R.W.F.: Subtractive sets over cyclotomic rings - limits of schnorr-like arguments over lattices. In: CRYPTO, pp. 519–548 (2021)
3. Ames, S., Hazay, C., Ishai, Y., Venkitasubramaniam, M.: Ligero: lightweight sublinear arguments without a trusted setup. In: CCS, pp. 2087–2104. ACM (2017)
4. Attema, T., Cramer, R.: Compressed Σ-protocol theory and practical application to plug & play secure algorithmics. In: CRYPTO, pp. 513–543 (2020)
5. Attema, T., Cramer, R., Kohl, L.: A compressed Σ-protocol theory for lattices. In: CRYPTO, pp. 549–579 (2021)
6. Attema, T., Cramer, R., Rambaud, M.: Compressed Σ-protocols for bilinear group arithmetic circuits and application to logarithmic transparent threshold signatures. In: ASIACRYPT, pp. 526–556 (2021)
7. Attema, T., Fehr, S.: Parallel repetition of $(k_1, \ldots, k_{\mu})$-special-sound multi-round interactive proofs. In: CRYPTO (2022)
8. Barak, B., Lindell, Y.: Strict polynomial-time in simulation and extraction. In: STOC, pp. 484–493 (2002)
9. Bellare, M., Neven, G.: Multi-signatures in the plain public-key model and a general forking lemma. In: CCS, pp. 390–399 (2006)
10. Ben-Sasson, E., Chiesa, A., Riabzev, M., Spooner, N., Virza, M., Ward, N.P.: Aurora: transparent succinct arguments for R1CS. In: EUROCRYPT, pp. 103–128 (2019)
11. Ben-Sasson, E., Chiesa, A., Spooner, N.: Interactive oracle proofs. In: TCC, pp. 31–60 (2016)
12. Block, A.R., Holmgren, J., Rosen, A., Rothblum, R.D., Soni, P.: Time- and space-efficient arguments from groups of unknown order. In: CRYPTO, pp. 123–152 (2021)

13. Bootle, J., Cerulli, A., Chaidos, P., Groth, J., Petit, C.: Efficient zero-knowledge arguments for arithmetic circuits in the discrete log setting. In: EUROCRYPT, pp. 327–357 (2016)
14. Bootle, J., Lyubashevsky, V., Nguyen, N.K., Seiler, G.: A non-PCP approach to succinct quantum-safe zero-knowledge. In: CRYPTO, pp. 441–469 (2020)
15. Bünz, B., Bootle, J., Boneh, D., Poelstra, A., Wuille, P., Maxwell, G.: Bulletproofs: short proofs for confidential transactions and more. In: S&P, pp. 315–334 (2018)
16. Bünz, B., Fisch, B., Szepieniec, A.: Transparent SNARKs from DARK compilers. In: EUROCRYPT, pp. 677–706 (2020)
17. Canetti, R., Chen, Y., Holmgren, J., Lombardi, A., Rothblum, G.N., Rothblum, R.D., Wichs, D.: Fiat-Shamir: from practice to theory. In: STOC, pp. 1082–1090. ACM (2019)
18. Chiesa, A., Manohar, P., Spooner, N.: Succinct arguments in the quantum random oracle model. In: TCC, pp. 1–29 (2019)
19. Fiat, A., Shamir, A.: How to prove yourself: Practical solutions to identification and signature problems. In: CRYPTO, pp. 186–194 (1986)
20. Ganesh, C., Khoshakhlagh, H., Kohlweiss, M., Nitulescu, A., Zajac, M.: What makes Fiat-Shamir zkSNARKs (updatable SRS) simulation extractable? In: SCN, pp. 735–760 (2022)
21. Gentry, C., Halevi, S., Lyubashevsky, V.: Practical non-interactive publicly verifiable secret sharing with thousands of parties. In: EUROCRYPT, pp. 458–487 (2022)
22. Ghoshal, A., Tessaro, S.: Tight state-restoration soundness in the algebraic group model. In: CRYPTO, pp. 64–93 (2021)
23. Goldreich, O.: The Foundations of Cryptography. Basic Applications, Vol. 2. Cambridge University Press (2004)
24. Hoffmann, M., Klooß, M., Rupp, A.: Efficient zero-knowledge arguments in the discrete log setting, revisited. In: CCS, pp. 2093–2110 (2019)
25. Jaeger, J., Tessaro, S.: Expected-time cryptography: generic techniques and applications to concrete soundness. In: TCC, pp. 414–443 (2020)
26. Maller, M., Bowe, S., Kohlweiss, M., Meiklejohn, S.: Sonic: zero-knowledge SNARKs from linear-size universal and updatable structured reference strings. In: CCS, pp. 2111–2128 (2019)
27. del Pino, R., Lyubashevsky, V., Seiler, G.: Short discrete log proofs for FHE and ring-LWE ciphertexts. In: PKC, pp. 344–373 (2019)
28. Pointcheval, D., Stern, J.: Security proofs for signature schemes. In: EUROCRYPT, pp. 387–398 (1996)
29. Wahby, R.S., Tzialla, I., Shelat, A., Thaler, J., Walfish, M.: Doubly-efficient zkSNARKs without trusted setup. In: S&P, pp. 926–943 (2018)
30. Wikström, D.: Special soundness revisited. IACR ePrint 2018/1157 (2018)
31. Wikström, D.: Special soundness in the random oracle model. IACR ePrint 2021/1264 (2021)

Steganography-Free Zero-Knowledge

Behzad Abdolmaleki[1(✉)], Nils Fleischhacker[2], Vipul Goyal[3,4], Abhishek Jain[5], and Giulio Malavolta[1]

[1] Max Planck Institute for Security and Privacy, Bochum, Germany
{behzad.abdolmaleki,giulio.malavolta}@mpi-sp.org
[2] Ruhr University Bochum, Bochum, Germany
mail@nilsfleischhacker.de
[3] NTT Research, Palo Alto, USA
[4] Carnegie Mellon University, Pittsburgh, USA
vipul@cmu.edu
[5] Johns Hopkins University, Baltimore, USA
abhishek@cs.jhu.edu

Abstract. We revisit the well-studied problem of preventing steganographic communication in multi-party communications. While this is known to be a provably impossible task, we propose a new model that allows circumventing this impossibility. In our model, the parties first publish a single message during an honest *non-interactive* pre-processing phase and then later interact in an execution phase. We show that in this model, it is indeed possible to prevent any steganographic communication in zero-knowledge protocols. Our solutions rely on standard cryptographic assumptions.

1 Introduction

Consider the following scenario: a computer at a government agency storing highly classified data has been infected with a stealthy malware. The malware's main purpose is to communicate the classified data to an attacker on the Internet. To minimize the possibility of being detected and quarantined, the malware has been designed to stealthily "encode" the secret data in ordinary communication between the infected computer and the outside world. This may include communication with "honest" entities on the Internet or potentially even the attacker (disguised as an honest user). An intriguing question, which forms the basis of the present work, is whether it is possible to detect such communication?

The above scenario is representative of a broader theme concerning *steganographic communication*, where a party A wants to transmit a secret message to another party B by communicating over a public broadcast channel without being detected by an external *observer* who is listening on the channel. Since the use of an encrypted channel can be easy to detect, A may instead try to embed its message in an innocuous-looking conversation. For example, [34], it may send a photograph of a person to securely transmit bit 0 if the 30th hair from the left is white, and 1 otherwise.

© The Author(s), under exclusive license to Springer Nature Switzerland AG 2022
E. Kiltz and V. Vaikuntanathan (Eds.): TCC 2022, LNCS 13747, pp. 143–172, 2022.
https://doi.org/10.1007/978-3-031-22318-1_6

A sequence of works [3,14,29,31] have established that such steganographic communication is always possible in any system with some entropy, and is provably *impossible* to detect. As such, it may seem that the answer to the aforementioned question is negative.

A New Model for Preventing Steganography. In this work, we propose a new model for circumventing the aforementioned impossibility result. In our model, any communication (via an interactive protocol) proceeds in two phases: a *non-interactive pre-processing* phase and an *execution* phase. Each party publishes a single message during the pre-processing phase, while the execution phase corresponds to the actual protocol execution. We assume that the parties are honest during the pre-processing phase, but may be completely malicious during the execution phase. *Our main goal is to ensure that any attempts at steganographic communication during the execution phase will be detected by the external observer.*

We, in fact, consider a stronger model where *only one of the parties is required to be honest* during the pre-processing phase. In this case, the malicious parties may be able to subliminally embed information in their pre-processing messages. However, we require that such subliminal communication is limited to the (non-interactive) pre-processing and that no steganographic communication can be performed during the execution phase. Our model is meaningful in our motivating example: if the pre-processing step is executed before the computer is infected, then it ensures that no information can be later leaked by the malware without being detected.

Let us now explain why the pre-processing model can help in preventing steganography. As observed in many prior works, the key source of the problem is that the parties' algorithms may be *randomized*, which opens an avenue for subliminal communication. Removing the use of randomness altogether does not yield a solution since randomness is necessary for most of cryptography [21]. The pre-processing model helps resolve this dilemma. The main insight is that the pre-processing step can be used to "fix" the randomness of the parties, thereby forcing them to become *deterministic* during the execution phase. If the parties deviate from the prescribed strategy, they can be detected by the observer.

A common method to detect deviation from prescribed strategy in any protocol is to use zero-knowledge (ZK) proofs [27], à la Goldreich, Micali, Wigderson (GMW) compiler [26]. However, ZK proofs themselves require randomness [21]. As such, a priori, it might not be clear how to implement the above idea.

1.1   Our Contribution

We present a general method for preventing steganographic communication in interactive protocols.

Defining Steganography Freeness. We start by defining *steganography freeness* for generic interactive protocols (S, R) in the non-interactive pre-processing model. Intuitively, our notion requires that no adversarial sender S can steganographically communicate even a single bit of information to the receiver R during the execution phase as long as at least one of them was honest during the pre-processing phase. We formalize this via a game-based definition (Sect. 3) where at the start of the execution phase, the adversarial sender is given a randomly chosen bit b. We require that at the end of the execution phase, the probability that the receiver correctly guesses b and the execution transcript is accepted by the observer is only negligibly more than one half.

Steganography-Free Zero-Knowledge. Our main tool for achieving steganography freeness in a generic interactive protocol is a new notion of *steganography-free zero-knowledge* (SF-ZK). An SF-ZK argument proceeds in two phases: first, the prover and the verifier participate in a non-interactive pre-processing step where they send a single message to each other. This step is executed *before* the prover receives the statement and the witness. Next, the prover and the verifier participate in the execution phase where the prover proves the validity of the statement.

An SF-ZK argument system must satisfy the standard completeness, soundness, and ZK properties. In particular, soundness (resp. ZK) must hold even if the prover (resp. verifier) is malicious both during the pre-processing as well as the execution phase. Further, SF-ZK must satisfy two new security properties:

- *Observer Soundness:* This property states that for any *false* statement, no coalition of prover and verifier can produce a transcript that will be accepted by the external observer as long as either the prover or the verifier was honest during the pre-processing phase.
- *Computationally Unique Transcripts (CUT):* We define this property w.r.t. languages $\mathcal{L}$ with unique witnesses; however, it can be naturally extended to the multiple witnesses case. Intuitively, it states that once the pre-processing phase has been executed (where either the prover or the verifier was honest), then for any statement $x \in \mathcal{L}$, two different sets of efficient prover and verifier strategies cannot produce two different transcripts of the execution phase that will both be accepted by the observer.

We show that the CUT property implies steganography freeness. Further, we note that the observer soundness property is crucial in natural applications of SF-ZK. Indeed, if we use SF-ZK to implement a GMW-style compiler for constructing steganography-free protocols, then observer soundness would be necessary to ensure that an adversarial party cannot deviate from a prescribed strategy in the underlying protocol and therefore cannot use the execution tran-script to perform steganographic communication.

We refer the reader to Sect. 3.1 for a formal definition of SF-ZK.

Positive Results. We construct an SF-ZK argument system with black-box simulation for all languages in NP. We, in fact, provide two constructions: first, assuming sub-exponentially hard injective one-way functions, we devise a solution in the *single-execution* setting, where the pre-processing phase can only be used once. Then, assuming the existence of fully homomorphic encryption [24], we present a solution in the *multi-execution* setting, where the pre-processing can be refreshed to allow for an unbounded number of execution phases.

Our construction of SF-ZK directly works for circuit satisfiability and avoids any use of expensive NP reductions. In Sect. 4, we provide a construction of SF-ZK in the single-execution setting. While this protocol follows a conceptually clean approach, it involves a computationally expensive sub-protocol where the prover is required to give a "proof of proof," namely, proof of honest behavior in the execution of another proof. To obtain a more efficient solution, we also present another construction that follows the same key ideas as in our first construction but avoids the expensive sub-protocol by instead using *cut-and-choose* techniques [37].

In the full version of the paper, we extend our construction of SF-ZK to the multi-execution setting.

Optimality of our Model. In the full version, we show that our adversarial model is "tight". Specifically, we show that when *both* the prover and the verifier are malicious during the pre-processing, SF-ZK is *impossible*, except for languages in BPP.

1.2   Applications

In the following we highlight a few interesting applications of SF-ZK.

Online Games. Imagine a group of players that want to engage in a game of poker without a trusted dealer. The standard solution for this is to use a multi-party computation (MPC) protocol to simulate a dealer by combining the randomness of all players. MPC is however an inherently randomized machinery and the same randomness could be used by colluding players to communicate information (say, about their hands) in an undetectable way. This problem was considered in [34], where the authors proposed a solution based on generic MPC together with unique ZK proof.[1] Their solution relies on players physically exchanging sealed envelopes prior to the execution of the protocol and hence cannot be used over the internet (see Sect. 1.4 for a more detailed comparison).

In contrast, using SF-ZK allows us to bypass any physical interaction among participants at the cost of a non-interactive pre-processing phase. The resulting protocol is sanitized from any covert communication, since transmitting information covertly via SF-ZK is computationally hard.

Private Classifier. Consider the scenario where a server holds a trained classifier and wants to give clients oracle access to the prediction without revealing the logic implemented by the predictor. At the same time, the client wants to be assured that the answers of the server are consistent and indeed correspond to the output of the classifier. An obvious solution to this problem is to augment the client-server interaction with a standard ZK proof of correctness.

Consider the event the server gets infected by a virus. The malicious program might instruct the machine to simply output the full description of the classifier. However, such behavior is easy to detect for anyone observing the network traffic.

---

[1] In unique ZK only a single valid proof exists for a given statement-witness pair.

What if the virus implements a more clever strategy: use the ZK proof as a vector to slowly exfiltrate secret information? Since ZK proofs must be randomized, there is plenty of room to transmit information in an undetectable manner.

One solution is to use SF-ZK instead: the (computational) uniqueness of the transcripts ensures that the virus cannot embed information in the randomness of the protocol and observer soundness forces the server to behave correctly. That is, whatever the client can learn from an infected machine he can also learn by honest queries to the non-corrupted server. Note that in this scenario we can assume that the server is not infected during the training of the model, which can be paired with the computation of the honest prover pre-processing.

A similar argument applies to any interaction in the client-server setting where the server holds some amount of secret data (e.g., a password file, or, classified emails) and might get infected with a virus.

1.3   Our Techniques

In this section, we provide an overview of the main ideas underlying our constructions of SF-ZK, both in the single-execution and multi-execution settings.

How to Simulate? We start by describing a key conceptual challenge in constructing SF-ZK. Recall that a black-box simulator works by rewinding the adversarial verifier potentially multiple times. This involves creating multiple protocol transcripts which are necessarily different (for the rewinding to be "successful"). This seems to be at odds with the computationally unique transcripts (CUT) property of SF-ZK; indeed, since the simulator is also an efficient algorithm, intuitively, it should also not be able to produce multiple transcripts of the execution phase. This presents a catch-22: how can we achieve ZK property without violating the CUT property (or vice-versa)?

Towards resolving this conundrum, recall that the CUT property is required to hold against two *different* pairs of prover and verifier strategies (P_1, V_1) and (P_2, V_2), who cannot communicate with each other. This rules out *oblivious* black-box simulation strategies that involve running multiple execution threads (with a common prefix) in parallel since such a strategy implies multiple transcript choices during an honest execution. However, it does *not* rule out *non-oblivious* black-box simulation strategies. In particular, *a non-oblivious simulator can potentially create a transcript, and then use information learned from that transcript to create another one.* This does not violate the CUT property but opens up an avenue for black-box simulation.

Starting Approach. To explain our approach, let us first recall the notion of *delayed-input* witness indistinguishable (WI) proofs, where the statement and the witness is only required for computing the last prover message. Such proofs are known in three rounds with a public-coin verifier based on one-way functions [33]. In particular, a recent work of [28] constructed such proofs for circuit satisfiability[2] based on garbled circuits.

Now consider the following template for SF-ZK: during the pre-processing phase, the prover publishes the first message α of the delayed-input WI and additionally commits to some randomness (say) r. The verifier commits in advance to the second (public-coin) message β of the WI and additionally publishes a "trapdoor" statement with a (verifiably) unique witness. Both the prover and verifier use a non-interactive commitment scheme with unique decommitment[3] to compute their respective commitments.

At the start of the execution phase, both the prover and the verifier receive the statement x and the prover additionally receives a (unique) witness w. The execution phase proceeds as follows:

- The prover first simply sends a commitment c to 0 using randomness r.
- Next, the verifier decommits to the second message of WI and additionally reveals the (unique) witness for the trapdoor statement.
- Finally, the prover sends the third message γ of the WI proof to prove the statement: "either x is true or I committed to the trapdoor witness in c using randomness r that was committed in the pre-processing".

Let us now see why the above template enables black-box simulation. A simulator can first produce a partial transcript of the execution phase by simply committing to 0 in c and then learn the witness for the trapdoor statement. Now, the simulator can rewind the verifier to the start of the execution phase and generate a new transcript where it commits to the trapdoor witness. It then continues the computation of the second transcript and produces the WI proof using the second branch of the statement. Note that the simulator can use the second branch in the WI because it is now true.

Challenges with CUT. In order to achieve the CUT property, we require the delayed-input WI proof to have a *unique* accepting third message γ for a fixed partial transcript (α, β) and a fixed statement and witness. Towards this, let us briefly recall the construction of [28]. Below, we describe the basic version which achieves soundness one half; the full protocol with negligible soundness error is achieved by parallel repetition of the basic protocol.

- First, the prover computes and sends a garbled circuit for the NP verification circuit. Additionally, it commits to all the wire labels of the garbled circuit.
- Next, the verifier sends a random challenge bit.
- If the challenge bit is 0, the prover "opens" everything by revealing its random tape, otherwise, it decommits to wire labels corresponding to the statement and the witness. In the latter case, the verifier simply evaluates the garbled circuit to check if its output is accepting.

---

[2] The choice of circuit satisfiability as the language is not arbitrary. We use it to avoid the potential issue of using NP reductions that do not preserve the number of witnesses, which can open up an avenue for subliminal communication.

[3] Such schemes are known based on injective one-way functions.

At a first glance, it may seem that the above construction satisfies the unique third message property if the witness is unique. A closer inspection, however, reveals a subtle problem when we use the above WI in our template for SF-ZK. The issue is that a cheating prover can simply guess in advance, e.g., the first index (among all the parallel repetitions) where the challenge bit is 1. In that repetition, he can choose to garble a trivial circuit that outputs 1 on every input. Clearly, in this case, there are exponentially many accepting third messages. As such, the adversarial prover can violate the CUT property with non-negligible probability.

Towards addressing the above problem, our first observation is that the above protocol can be transformed into one that satisfies the unique third message property *at the cost of losing the delayed input property*. The transformation is simple: for every repetition, the prover pre-commits to both of its possible third messages (one for every challenge bit) in the first round. Now, in the last round, it simply decommits to the appropriate response. Clearly, this protocol satisfies the unique third message property but is no longer delayed input since the prover must know the statement and the witness in order to compute the first message. The latter means that we can not directly use it in our template for SF-ZK.

Nevertheless, as we now describe, the above observation can be used to construct a delayed-input WI with the required property. Our main observation is as follows: the aforementioned attack required the prover to deviate from the honest strategy, namely, sending a garbling of a circuit different from the NP verification circuit (i.e., the circuit which outputs 1 on every input). If we could ensure that the prover garbled the "correct" circuit, then the protocol would indeed satisfy the aforementioned uniqueness property.

Towards this end, we modify the protocol template and now require the prover to additionally prove via a separate three-round proof system that it computed the garbling in the first round message of delayed-input WI "honestly". Crucially, *a non-delayed-input proof with unique third message suffices for this task* since the statement and the witness is known in advance. The first and second messages of this proof are fixed in the pre-processing (in a manner as discussed before in the template); the prover only sends the third message of the proof in the execution phase. The uniqueness of this message ensures that it cannot be used for subliminal communication. More importantly, the soundness of this proof ensures that the prover's first message in the delayed-input WI is well-formed, and therefore, the last message is unique.[4]

Challenges in ZK. The above idea resolves the main challenge in achieving CUT property, but creates a new challenge in achieving the ZK property. Specifically, the main issue is that in order to perform simulation, it seems that we

---

[4] We remark that our actual protocol slightly differs from the above description in that instead of using delayed-input WI, we introduce and use the notion of (computationally) unique non-interactive WI with honest prover pre-processing. This approach yields a more simplified construction. In this Section, however, we ignore this distinction.

need the non-delayed-input proof to itself be a (steganography-free) ZK proof. However, this is very close to the goal we started with in the first place.

To resolve this seeming circularity, we observe that the non-delayed-input proof does *not* always need to be simulated. In particular, this proof would only need to be simulated when we invoke the WI property of the delayed-input WI inside the hybrids for proving the ZK property of our main SF-ZK construction. Therefore, we do not need this proof to satisfy the standard notion of ZK with polynomial-time simulation, and instead, it suffices to use ZK with *super-polynomial-time* simulation. Indeed, the super-polynomial-time simulator would only be invoked in the "intermediate" hybrids, but not the final one; therefore, the running time of our final simulator for SF-ZK is *unaffected*. Fortunately, the three-round proof system we described earlier indeed satisfies the super-polynomial-time simulation property.

Observer Soundness. While the above solution template resolves the main challenges in achieving ZK and CUT properties, it does not achieve observer soundness property of SF-ZK. Indeed, consider the scenario where the verifier is malicious during the pre-processing phase and uses some a priori fixed randomness (e.g., all 0's). Now, in the execution phase, a malicious prover can use the trapdoor witness (i.e., the witness of the second branch) in the WI proof in the last round.

To address this challenge, we observe that if the verifier is dishonest during pre-processing, then by our assumption that at least one of the parties be honest, we have that the prover must be honest during pre-processing. We use this observation to create an "asymmetry" between a malicious prover and the simulator. Specifically, we require the prover to commit to bit 0 in the pre-processing phase. We also modify the second branch of the WI in the execution phase. Specifically, the second branch will now additionally require the prover to prove that it committed to 1 in the pre-processing phase. Note that since the prover was honest in the pre-processing, it can never execute the second branch since it is always false. However, a simulator can choose to commit to 1 in the pre-processing phase and therefore still use the second branch of the WI.

Other Details. The above discussion is oversimplified and ignores several additional technical issues that we need to address to obtain a secure construction of SF-ZK. For example, we must deal with aborting verifiers who may choose to abort on one of the branches of WI with a high probability to skew the distribution of transcripts generated by the simulator. We also need to enable some mechanism for proving soundness as well as the CUT property via *extraction*, even when the verifier's randomness is fixed during the pre-processing. We resolve these issues by using techniques from [25], and by relying on complexity leveraging in some of our proofs. We refer the reader to the technical Sections for more details.

Multi-execution SF-ZK. The pre-processing phase of the above construction is *non-reusable*, i.e., it can only be used for a single execution phase. We now describe a strategy to *refresh* the pre-processing phase. Our starting idea is simple: During the i-th execution phase, the prover and the verifier simply generate new pre-processing messages using pre-committed randomness and give a new SF-ZK proof to establish that the new message was computed honestly. Note, however, that in regular ZK proofs, the size of the prover's message grows with the size of the relation circuit. This means that the size of the i-th pre-processing messages must be larger than the size of the $(i+1)$-th pre-processing messages, at least by a multiplicative overhead of the security parameter. This means that this approach becomes infeasible after a constant number of refreshes.

A plausible approach to allow unlimited refreshing is to use an SF-ZK where the communication complexity does not grow with the size of the relation circuit. Four round ZK arguments (without SF property) that satisfy such a succinctness property are known for all of NP based on collision-resistant hash functions [32]. Unfortunately, it is not clear how to use such argument systems in our setting: first, we need the argument system to be *delayed-input*, namely, where the first message of the prover is independent of the statement. Further, it is unclear how to force uniqueness of last prover message while only relying on *non-interactive* pre-processing.

We instead use a different solution based on (leveled) fully-homomorphic encryption. The main idea is that instead of having the prover perform an "expensive" computation and prove its validity to the verifier, we instead require both the prover and the verifier to perform the expensive computation "locally" on their own. Since the computation involves the private state of the prover, we use FHE to send it to the verifier, who can use the homomorphism property to perform the computation. Now, the prover only needs to prove a simple statement that the resulting encryption (after homomorphic evaluation) decrypts to the "correct" value. The size of this statement (and the corresponding relation circuit) is fixed, and does not cause a blowup as before. Also observe that the maximum size of the circuit to be computed homomorphically is a priori fixed, therefore leveled FHE suffices. We note that this idea has been previously used (see, e.g., [30]) to construct "short" non-interactive zero-knowledge proofs.

1.4   Related Work

Preventing steganographic communication has been the subject of a large body of literature addressing the problem in variety models. We provide a short summary of other directions that address the challenge of protecting cryptosystems against different forms of subversion in below (also refer the reader to [38] for an excellent comprehensive survey).

Collusion-Free Protocols. Our work is closely related to prior work on collusion-free protocols [34] (see also [35]). Roughly speaking, a collusion-free multiparty protocol prevents a group of adversarial parties from colluding with each other to gain an unfair advantage over honest participants, e.g., in a game of poker. As Lepinski *et al.* explain in their work, a key challenge in designing such protocols is preventing steganographic communication between the adversarial parties. They use *physical assumptions*, namely, simultaneous exchange of sealed envelopes, and an *interactive* pre-processing model to construct collusion-free protocols. While their overall goal is very similar to ours, we note that their constructions require strong physical assumptions (e.g., sealed envelopes) to ensure verifiable determinism.

We further note that our notion of steganography-free ZK is similar in spirit to the notion of "unique ZK" [35], which is used by [34] in their constructions. In particular, unique ZK requires a one-to-one mapping between a proof transcript and the witness used to compute the transcript, which is similar to the CUT property of steganography-free ZK. However, while our notion of steganography-free ZK is a *strengthening* of zero-knowledge, the notion of unique ZK is not. Unique ZK requires a common reference string as well as a pre-processing step where the prover must necessarily be honest. This means that if the prover was dishonest from the beginning, the soundness no longer holds (even if the verifier continues to be honest from the beginning). Unique ZK also does not require the observer soundness property, which makes it harder to use in our applications.

Preventing Steganography via Sanitization. Multiple lines of works have used the approach of using "sanitization" to prevent steganographic communication. The work of Alwen *et al.* [1] considered a mediator model for collusion-free protocols to avoid the use of pre-processing and physical channels. This active mediator has the ability to modify the messages of the protocol participants. This approach is similar in spirit to prior work on subliminal-free ZK and divertible ZK protocols [9,11–13,18,39] who also use an active "warden" to modify the messages of the prover and the verifier. More recently, Mironov and Stephens-Davidowitz [38] (see also [20]) initiated the study of "reverse firewalls" to prevent steganographic communication in general two-party communication. Roughly speaking, a reverse firewall for a party P is an external entity that sits between P and the outside world and whose scope is to sanitize P's incoming and outgoing messages in the face of subversion of their computer. Later, there has been more efforts on secure computation protocols in this model [15,16,23].

Comparison to Our Model. In the sanitization-based model there is an entity (namely, the reverse firewall) that sits on the network of each participant and has the ability to re-randomize the messages sent by the parties. We note that all of these works differ fundamentally from ours in that they rely on an *active* mediator (or warden, or reverse firewall) who can sanitize the messages of the parties, whereas we consider the classical steganographic communication setting, where there is a *passive* observer who can look at the messages of the parties (but not modify them). This allows one to *detect* steganography by just looking at the communication transcript.

Kleptography and Algorithmic-Substitution Attacks. A sequence of works starting from [44,45], and more recently followed by a series of papers [2,5,7,8,41,42], consider the problem of designing cryptographic primitives which retain meaningful security even against adversaries who can tamper with the implementation of the cryptographic algorithm. In particular, these works consider "functionality-preserving" tampering where the adversary does not break the functionality of the cryptographic algorithm to avoid detection. However, this still leaves open the possibility of the tampered implementation leaking any secret information used by the cryptographic algorithm (e.g., a secret-key for encryption, or a signing key for signature schemes) to the adversary by misusing the randomness. For this reason, these works either avoid the use of randomness altogether (whenever possible), or rely on external sanitizers (such as random oracles) or consider split-state tampering.

There has been another the line of work for protection mechanisms by Dodis *et al.* [19] that studies backdoored pseudorandom generators (BPRGs). In their setting, public parameters are secretly generated together with secret backdoors by a subversive that allows to bypass security, while for any adversary that does not know the backdoor it remains secure.[5] They showed that BPRGs can be immunized by applying a non-trivial function (e.g., a PRF or a seeded extractor) to the outputs of a possibly backdoored pseudorandom generator.

Comparison to Our Model . Our setting (involving ZK proofs and multi-party computation) necessarily relies on the use of randomness. As such, the solutions we achieve in our model restrict the use of randomness to the pre-processing step, without relying on external sanitizers, or other such means.

Trusted Initialization Phase. Assuming the trust initialization phase setting, Fischlin and Mazaheri [22] proposed an alternative defense mechanism, so-called self-guarding that contrary to the aforementioned approaches that rely on external sanitizers, does not depend on external parties. The security definitions in this model rely on the assumption of having a "secure initialization phase". This assumption makes our problem substantially easier: The NIZK by Sahai and Waters [43] has a deterministic prover and it trivially yields a construction of steganography-free ZK in the common reference string (CRS) model.

Comparison to Our Model. Self-guarding requires one to rely on a trusted initialization phase where the cryptosystem is unsubverted. In our model, each party runs a local pre-processing, and security is guaranteed if *either of the parties* is honest during the pre-processing phase.

2   Preliminaries

We denote by $n \in \mathbb{N}$ the security parameter that is implicitly given as input to all algorithms in unary representation 1^n. We denote by $\{0,1\}^\ell$ the set of all bit-strings of length ℓ. For a finite set S, we denote the action of sampling x uniformly at random from S by $x \leftarrow_\$ S$, and we denote the cardinality of S by $|S|$. An algorithm is efficient or PPT if it runs in time polynomial in the security parameter. If $\mathcal{A}$ is randomized then by $y := \mathcal{A}(x; r)$ we denote that $\mathcal{A}$ is run on

---

[5] Parameter subversion has been considered for several primitives, including pseudorandom generators [17,19], non-interactive zero knowledge [4], and public-key encryption [2].

input x and with random coins r and produces output y. If no randomness is specified, then it is assumed that $\mathcal{A}$ is run with freshly sampled uniform random coins, and we write this as $y \leftarrow \mathcal{A}(x)$. A function $\mathsf{negl}(n)$ is negligible if for all positive polynomial $\mathsf{poly}(n)$, there exists an $N \in \mathbb{N}$, such that for all $n > N$, $\mathsf{negl}(n) \leq 1/\mathsf{poly}(n)$.

We recall the notions of projective garbling schemes [6], homomorphic encryption [24], zero-knowledge arguments with super-polynomial simulation (SPS-ZK) [40], and non-Interactive witness indistinguishable arguments with honest pre-processing (HPP-NIWI) [10] in the full version of this paper.

3   Defining Steganography-Freeness

In this section, we introduce the definitions of steganography-free zero-knowledge interactive arguments and steganography-free multi-party computation. Steganography-freeness is generally impossible for regular protocols because without being constrained, a malicious party could always try to correlate its randomness with the secrets it wishes to subliminally communicate. We prevent such attacks by utilizing a non-interactive pre-processing phase. Specifically, we consider protocols that proceed in two phases: A non-interactive pre-processing phase, and an interactive execution phase. As we will see below, our definitions guarantee that no steganographic communication can be performed in the execution phase, once the pre-processing was completed.

We begin by defining steganography-freeness for generic interactive protocols (with pre-processing), which closely matches the intuition behind this notion. Roughly speaking, our notion steganography-free says that no machines can communicate through a protocol execution without being detected. This is captured as a game between a sender and a receiver, where the sender is given a random bit b and interacts with the receiver. In order to win the game the receiver must output b, without raising the suspicion of an external observer. The formal definition is given in the following.

Definition 1 (Steganography-Freeness). *A protocol* $\Pi = (\mathsf{S}^1, \mathsf{R}^1, \mathsf{S}^2, \mathsf{R}^2)$ *is steganography-free relative to a* PPT *observer* Θ *if for all admissible pairs* $(\tilde{\mathsf{S}}^1, \tilde{\mathsf{R}}^1)$, *and for all* PPT *algorithms* $(\mathsf{S}^*, \mathsf{R}^*)$ *it holds that*

$$\Pr\left[\begin{matrix}(s_1, p_1) \leftarrow \tilde{\mathsf{S}}^1(1^\lambda), (s_2, p_2) \leftarrow \tilde{\mathsf{R}}^1(1^\lambda), & \Theta(p_1, p_2, \mathcal{T}) = 1 \wedge \\ b \leftarrow_\$ \{0,1\}, \mathcal{T} := \langle \mathsf{S}^*(s_1, p_2, b), \mathsf{R}^*(s_2, p_1) \rangle & \mathsf{R}^*(s_2, p_1, \mathcal{T}) = b\end{matrix}\right] \leq \frac{1}{2} + \mathsf{negl}(n)$$

where $(\mathsf{S}^*, \mathsf{R}^*)$ *are the (possibly) corrupted versions of* $(\mathsf{S}^2, \mathsf{R}^2)$. *Both parties* $(\mathsf{S}^1$ *and* $\mathsf{R}^1)$ *individually compute pre-processing information comprising of a public output and a secret state in the pre-processing stage. In the execution phase, both parties* $(\mathsf{S}^2$ *and* $\mathsf{R}^2)$ *receive as input their respective secret states as well as the other party's public output from the pre-processing phase.*

Note that the definition is *relative* to some observer Θ. Generally, any protocol is steganography-free relative to *some* observer, e.g., the trivial Θ that does not accept *any* transcript. However, this is of course not a useful property. The challenge, therefore, is to achieve steganography-freeness relative to a meaningful observer that accepts honest communication.

It is also important to observe that the definition is conditioned on some admissibility criterion on the behavior of the players in the pre-processing. In this work we are interested in what we call a *partial-honest* pre-processing, i.e., a pair $(\tilde{S}^1, \tilde{R}^1)$ is considered admissible if both algorithms are PPT and at least one of them is honest. Note that for this case we consider *rushing* adversaries that sample their pre-processing after the honest one is fixed. We mention that the definition can be extended to capture a bounded amount of covert communication by sampling multiple bits.

3.1   Steganography-Free Zero-Knowledge

Towards defining steganography-free zero-knowledge, we extend the standard definitions in a natural way to accommodate an input-independent pre-processing phase. In the pre-processing stage, both parties (P^1 and V^1) individually compute pre-processing information comprising of a public output and a secret state. In the execution phase, both parties (P^2 and V^2) receive as input their respective secret states as well as the other party's public output from the pre-processing phase, together with the statement x. The prover additionally receives a witness w. At the end of this phase, the honest verifier outputs either 0 or 1. In addition to the standard properties for a zero-knowledge protocol, a steganography-free zero-knowledge protocol must additionally satisfy the following new properties:

1. *Observer Completeness:* There exists an efficient algorithm Θ, that takes as input the protocol transcript and accepts if both parties are honest.
2. *Observer Soundness:* The (possibly colluding) prover and verifier cannot convince the observer to accept a transcript for any $x \notin \mathcal{L}$, as long as either the prover or the verifier executes the pre-processing phase honestly.
3. *Computationally Unique Transcripts:* Given a language with unique witnesses, no two independent coalitions of prover and verifier can produce two different transcripts that are both accepted by the observer. This is again conditioned on the fact that at least one of the parties was honest during the pre-processing.

This set of properties will guarantee that the protocol execution cannot be used as a covert channel. Later we will show that these conditions are indeed sufficient to achieve steganography-freeness. The formal definition is given in the following.

Definition 2 (Steganography-Free Zero-Knowledge Arguments). *Let $\mathcal{L}$ be a language in NP with corresponding relation $\mathcal{R}$. A steganography-free interactive argument system $\Pi = (P, V)$ for language $\mathcal{L}$ in the non-interactive pre-processing model with observer Θ must satisfy the following properties:*

Completeness. For all $(x, w) \in \mathcal{R}$ it holds that

$$\Pr \left[\begin{array}{l} (s_1, p_1) \leftarrow \mathsf{P}^1(1^n), \\ (s_2, p_2) \leftarrow \mathsf{V}^1(1^n) \end{array} : 1 \leftarrow \langle \mathsf{P}^2(x, w, s_1, p_2), \mathsf{V}^2(x, s_2, p_1) \rangle \right] \geq 1 - \mathsf{negl}(n).$$

Computational Non-adaptive Soundness. For all $x \notin \mathcal{L}$ and all malicious PPT provers P^* it holds that

$$\Pr \left[\begin{array}{l} (s_1, p_1) \leftarrow \mathsf{P}^*(x), \\ (s_2, p_2) \leftarrow \mathsf{V}^1(1^n) \end{array} : 1 \leftarrow \langle \mathsf{P}^*(x, s_1, p_2), \mathsf{V}^2(x, s_2, p_1) \rangle \right] \leq \mathsf{negl}(n).$$

Computational Soundness. For all malicious PPT provers P^* it holds that

$$\Pr \left[\begin{array}{l} (s_1, p_1) \leftarrow \mathsf{P}^*(1^n), \\ (s_2, p_2) \leftarrow \mathsf{V}^1(1^n), \\ x \leftarrow \mathsf{P}^*(s_1, p_2) \end{array} : 1 \leftarrow \langle \mathsf{P}^*(x, s_1, p_2), \mathsf{V}^2(x, s_2, p_1) \rangle \wedge x \notin \mathcal{L} \right] \leq \mathsf{negl}(n).$$

Here, we use the terms computational soundness and adaptive computational soundness interchangeably.

Zero-Knowledge. For all malicious PPT verifiers V^* there exists an expected polynomial time simulator Sim, such that for all PPT distinguishers $\mathcal{D}$, it holds that for all tuples $(x, w) \in \mathcal{R}$

$$\left| \begin{array}{l} \Pr \left[\begin{array}{l} (s_1, p_1) \leftarrow \mathsf{P}^1(1^n), \\ (s_2, p_2) \leftarrow \mathsf{V}^*(x) \end{array} : \mathcal{D}(\langle \mathsf{P}^2(x, w, s_1, p_2), \mathsf{V}^*(x, s_2, p_1) \rangle) = 1 \right] \\ - \Pr \left[\begin{array}{l} (s_1, p_1) \leftarrow \mathsf{Sim}(1^n), \\ (s_2, p_2) \leftarrow \mathsf{V}^*(x) \end{array} : \mathcal{D}(\langle \mathsf{Sim}(x, s_1, p_2), \mathsf{V}^*(x, s_2, p_1) \rangle) = 1 \right] \end{array} \right| \leq \mathsf{negl}(n).$$

Observer Completeness. For all $(x, w) \in \mathcal{R}$ it holds that

$$\Pr \left[\begin{array}{l} (s_1, p_1) \leftarrow \mathsf{P}^1(1^n), (s_2, p_2) \leftarrow \mathsf{V}^1(1^n), \\ \mathcal{T} := \langle \mathsf{P}^2(s_1, p_2, x, w), \mathsf{V}^2(s_2, p_1, x) \rangle \end{array} : \Theta(p_1, p_2, \mathcal{T}, x) = 1 \right] \geq 1 - \mathsf{negl}(n).$$

Non-Adaptive Observer Soundness. For all $x \notin \mathcal{L}$, for all admissible pairs $(\tilde{\mathsf{P}}^1, \tilde{\mathsf{V}}^1)$, for all PPT algorithms P^* and V^* it holds that

$$\Pr \left[\begin{array}{l} (s_1, p_1) \leftarrow \tilde{\mathsf{P}}^1(x), (s_2, p_2) \leftarrow \tilde{\mathsf{V}}^1(x), \\ \mathcal{T} := \langle \mathsf{P}^*(s_1, p_2, x), \mathsf{V}^*(s_2, p_1, x) \rangle \end{array} : \Theta(p_1, p_2, \mathcal{T}, x) = 1 \right] \leq \mathsf{negl}(n)$$

Observer Soundness. For all admissible pairs $(\tilde{\mathsf{P}}^1, \tilde{\mathsf{V}}^1)$, for all PPT algorithms P^* and V^* it holds that

$$\Pr \left[\begin{array}{l} (s_1, p_1) \leftarrow \tilde{\mathsf{P}}^1(1^n), (s_2, p_2) \leftarrow \tilde{\mathsf{V}}^1(1^n), \\ x \leftarrow \mathsf{P}^*(s_1, p_2); \mathcal{T} := \langle \mathsf{P}^*(s_1, p_2, x), \mathsf{V}^*(s_2, p_1, x) \rangle \end{array} : \begin{array}{l} \Theta(p_1, p_2, \mathcal{T}, x) = 1 \\ \wedge\ x \notin \mathcal{L} \end{array} \right] \leq \mathsf{negl}(n)$$

where a pair $(\tilde{\mathsf{P}}^1, \tilde{\mathsf{V}}^1)$ is considered admissible if both algorithms are PPT *and it holds that* $\tilde{\mathsf{P}}^1(w, x) = \mathsf{P}^1(1^n)$ *or* $\tilde{\mathsf{V}}^1(x) = \mathsf{V}^1(1^n)$. *Notice that, we use the terms observer soundness and adaptive observer soundness interchangeably.*

Computationally Unique Transcripts. *For all* $x \in \mathcal{L}$ *such that there exists a unique* w *such that* $\mathcal{R}(x, w) = 1$, *for all admissible pairs* $(\tilde{\mathsf{P}}^1, \tilde{\mathsf{V}}^1)$, *for all* PPT *algorithms* $(\mathsf{P}^*, \mathsf{V}^*, \hat{\mathsf{P}}^*, \hat{\mathsf{V}}^*)$ *it holds that*

$$\Pr\left[\begin{array}{c} (s_1, p_1) \leftarrow \tilde{\mathsf{P}}^1(w, x), (s_2, p_2) \leftarrow \tilde{\mathsf{V}}^1(x), \quad \Theta(p_1, p_2, \mathcal{T}_1, x) = 1 \wedge \\ \mathcal{T}_1 := \langle \mathsf{P}^*(s_1, p_2, x, w), \mathsf{V}^*(s_2, p_1, x) \rangle, \; : \; \Theta(p_1, p_2, \mathcal{T}_2, x) = 1 \wedge \\ \mathcal{T}_2 := \left\langle \hat{\mathsf{P}}^*(s_1, p_2, x, w), \hat{\mathsf{V}}^*(s_2, p_1, x) \right\rangle \qquad \mathcal{T}_1 \neq \mathcal{T}_2 \end{array} \right] \leq \mathsf{negl}(n)$$

where a pair $(\tilde{\mathsf{P}}^1, \tilde{\mathsf{V}}^1)$ *is considered admissible if both algorithms are* PPT *and it holds that* $\tilde{\mathsf{P}}^1(w, x) = \mathsf{P}^1(1^n)$ *or* $\tilde{\mathsf{V}}^1(x) = \mathsf{V}^1(1^n)$.

Observe that, although the honest pre-processing algorithms do not require the statement or the witness as input, we still provide the (possibly) malicious machines with x (and w if the prover is malicious). This guarantees that the properties are preserved even if the algorithm has partial knowledge of the statement (and possibly the witness) ahead of time.

We further remark that our definition of computationally unique transcripts is going to be useful only for languages with unique witnesses, since the prover might be able to produce two accepting transcripts by simply executing the protocol with two different witnesses. While this suffices for our applications, the definition can be naturally extended to the k-witnesses case by requiring the coalitions to output $k + 1$ distinct valid transcripts.

Steganography-Freeness. In the following, we argue that our conditions defined above suffice to show that the protocol satisfies steganography-freeness.

Theorem 1 (Steganography-Freeness). *Let* $\mathcal{L}$ *be a language with unique witnesses and let* (P, V) *be an observer sound zero-knowledge protocol for* $\mathcal{L}$ *with computationally unique transcripts. Then* (P, V) *is steganography-free relative to the observer with partially honest pre-processing.*

We defer the proof to the full version.

Multi-execution SF-ZK. The above definition refers to *single-execution* SF-ZK where all of the properties are required to hold for a single execution phase, after the pre-processing is fixed. In the full version of the paper, we extend the notion of SF-ZK to the *multi-execution* setting.

4   A Steganography-Free ZK Protocol

Let $\tilde{\mathcal{L}}$ be any average-case hard language with unique witnesses and let $f : \{0,1\}^{n_{\mathsf{OWF}}} \rightarrow \{0,1\}^{m_{\mathsf{OWF}}}$ be a one-way function with an efficiently checkable range. Let (WI-P, WI-V) be an HPP-NIWI with unique proofs for the following language: $\mathcal{L}_{\mathsf{NIWI}} =$

$$
\left\{
\begin{pmatrix} x, y, \tilde{w}, \\ c_0, \bar{c}, \tilde{c} \end{pmatrix}
\;\middle|\;
\begin{array}{l}
\exists (w, s, \tilde{r}) : ((x, w) \in \mathcal{R} \wedge \mathsf{Com}(\tilde{r}; s) = \bar{c} \wedge \mathsf{Com}(0^n; \tilde{r}) = \tilde{c}) \\
[-1ex] \vee \; \exists (r, \tilde{r}) : (\mathsf{Com}(1; r) = c_0 \wedge \mathsf{Com}(\tilde{w}; \tilde{r}) = \tilde{c}) \\
[-1ex] \vee \; \exists (w, r, z) : ((x, w) \in \mathcal{R} \wedge \mathsf{Com}(1; r) = c_0 \wedge f(z) = y)
\end{array}
\right\}
$$

where the first branch (1) is going to be used by the prover and the second branch (2) will allow one to simulate without knowing the witness. Interestingly the third branch (3) is used neither by the honest prover nor by the simulator, but it is only instrumental to prove the indistinguishability of the two. Finally, we let (SPS-P, SPS-V) be a three-round SPS-ZK argument system with unique last messages for the following language:

$$
\mathcal{L}_{\mathsf{SPSZK}} = \{ \tau \mid \exists u : \mathsf{WI}\text{-}\mathsf{P}_1(u) = \tau \}.
$$

Prover $\mathsf{P}^1(1^n)$ — Pre-Processing — **Verifier $\mathsf{V}^1(1^n)$**

Prover $\mathsf{P}^1(1^n)$

Sample $(r, \tilde{r}, s) \leftarrow\!\!\$\; \{0,1\}^{3n_{\mathsf{COM}}}$

$\quad u \leftarrow\!\!\$\; \{0,1\}^{n_{\mathsf{NIWI}}}$

$\quad v \leftarrow\!\!\$\; \{0,1\}^{n_{\mathsf{SPSZK}}}$

Commit to $c_0 \leftarrow \mathsf{Com}(0; r)$

$\quad \bar{c} \leftarrow \mathsf{Com}(\tilde{r}; s)$

Compute $\tau \leftarrow \mathsf{WI}\text{-}\mathsf{P}_1(1^{n_{\mathsf{NIWI}}}; u)$

$\quad \alpha \leftarrow \mathsf{SPS}\text{-}\mathsf{P}_1(\tau, u; v)$

Define $s_1 := (r, \tilde{r}, s, u, v)$

$\quad p_1 := (\tau, \alpha, c_0, \bar{c})$

Return (s_1, p_1)

Verifier $\mathsf{V}^1(1^n)$

Sample $(\tilde{x}, \tilde{w}) \leftarrow\!\!\$\; \tilde{\mathcal{R}}$

$\quad t \leftarrow\!\!\$\; \{0,1\}^{n_{\mathsf{COM}}}$

$\quad z \leftarrow\!\!\$\; \{0,1\}^{n_{\mathsf{OWF}}}$

Compute $y \leftarrow f(z)$

$\quad \beta \leftarrow \mathsf{SPS}\text{-}\mathsf{V}_1(1^{n_{\mathsf{SPSZK}}})$

$\quad c \leftarrow \mathsf{Com}(\beta; t)$

Define $s_2 := (\beta, y, t, \tilde{w})$

$\quad p_2 := (c, \tilde{x}, y)$

Return (s_2, p_2)

- -

Prover $\mathsf{P}^2(s_1, p_2, x, w)$ — Execution — **Verifier $\mathsf{V}^2(s_2, p_1, x)$**

Prover $\mathsf{P}^2(s_1, p_2, x, w)$

Parse $s_1 := (r, \tilde{r}, s, u, v)$

$\quad p_2 := (c, \tilde{x}, y)$

Compute $\tilde{c} \leftarrow \mathsf{Com}(0^n; \tilde{r})$

$\xrightarrow{\;\tilde{c}\;}$

$\xleftarrow{\;(\tilde{w}, \beta, t)\;}$

If $(\tilde{x}, \tilde{w}) \notin \tilde{\mathcal{R}}$ **or** $\mathsf{Com}(\beta; t) \neq c$ **abort**

Compute $\gamma \leftarrow \mathsf{SPS}\text{-}\mathsf{P}_2(\tau, u, \beta; v)$

$\quad \pi \leftarrow \mathsf{WI}\text{-}\mathsf{P}_2((x, y, \tilde{w}, c_0, \bar{c}, \tilde{c}), (w, s, \tilde{r}); u)$

$\xrightarrow{\;(\gamma, \pi)\;}$

Verifier $\mathsf{V}^2(s_2, p_1, x)$

Parse $s_2 := (\beta, y, t, \tilde{w})$

$\quad p_1 := (\tau, \alpha, c_0, \bar{c})$

If $\mathsf{SPS}\text{-}\mathsf{V}_2(\tau, \alpha, \beta, \gamma) \neq 1$ **or** $\mathsf{WI}\text{-}\mathsf{V}((x, y, \tilde{w}, c_0, \bar{c}, \tilde{c}), \tau, \pi) \neq 1$ **return** 0

Else return 1

Fig. 1. Our SF-ZK protocol.

4.1   Our Protocol

Our protocol SF-ZK is formally described in Fig. 1. We describe extensions to the multi-execution setting in the full version.

Pre-processing. In the pre-processing phase, the honest prover computes a commitment to 0 and to some random coins $\tilde{r}$. The former guarantees that, if the prover's pre-processing is honest, then it is hard to cheat in the execution phase, whereas the latter fixes the random coins used later in the execution phase. The prover also initializes the pre-processing τ of an HPP-NIWI proof and computes the first message α of an SPS-ZK proof that asserts that τ is well-formed. The public output of the prover's pre-processing consists of the commitments together with the messages (τ, α). The secret state consists of the random coins used in the pre-processing.

On the other hand, the verifier samples a random image y from the domain of the one-way function f and computes a commitment c to a randomly sampled second message β of the SPS-ZK proof. Furthermore, it samples a random instance $\tilde{x}$ of an average-case hard language with unique witnesses. The public output of the verifier's pre-processing consists of $(c, \tilde{x}, y)$, and the secret state consists of the random coins used in the pre-processing.

Execution. The execution phase is started by the prover, who sends a commitment $\tilde{c}$ to 0^n, using the random coins $\tilde{r}$ fixed in the pre-processing. Then the verifier replies with the decommitment (β, t) to c and reveals the unique witness $\tilde{w}$. The prover checks that (β, t) is a valid decommitment for c and computes the last message γ of the SPS-ZK protocol that certifies that τ is well-formed. Finally, it computes the proof π using the first branch (1) thereby proving that $\tilde{c}$ was correctly formed using the random coins committed in the pre-processing and that x is indeed an accepting instance of $\mathcal{L}$. The verifier simply checks whether the transcript (α, β, γ) and the proof π verify correctly.

While $\tilde{c}$ might seem purposeless, it is going to be useful in the simulation: The simulator will spawn a lookahead thread to learn $\tilde{w}$, which will allow it to rewind the execution to compute $\tilde{c}$ as a commitment to $\tilde{w}$. This in turn allows it to compute the proof π using the second branch (2), which does not require knowledge of the witness for x. This is however not a feasible strategy for any malicious prover (which cannot rewind the execution of the protocol), since it requires to know $\tilde{w}$ ahead of time.

4.2 Analysis

Parameters. Let n be the security parameter of our scheme, we consider the following parameters that are (implicitly) given as input to each algorithm of our building blocks:

- n_{SPSZK} : The security parameter for the SPS-ZK argument (SPS-P, SPS-V).
- n_{NIWI} : The security parameter for the non-interactive witness indistinguishable argument (WI-P, WI-V).
- n_{COM} : The security parameter for the perfectly binding commitment scheme Com with unique openings.
- n_{L} : The security parameter for the average-case hard language with unique witnesses $\tilde{\mathcal{L}}$.
- n_{OWF} : The security parameter for the one-way function f.

We require that the parameters satisfy the following relation

$$2^{n_{\mathsf{SPSZK}}} \ll 2^{n_{\mathsf{OWF}}} \ll 2^{n_{\mathsf{COM}}} \ll 2^{n_{\mathsf{NIWI}}} = 2^{n_{\mathsf{L}}},$$

where $a \ll b$ means that for all polynomial functions $a \cdot \mathsf{poly}(n) < b$. In particular we require the SPS-ZK argument to be sound against an adversary that runs in time $\mathsf{poly}(n_{\mathsf{SPSZK}})$ and to be simulatable in time $O(2^{n_{\mathsf{SPSZK}}})$. By setting the security parameter of the underlying perfectly binding commitment scheme to be also n_{SPSZK}, then one can find the committed message in time $O(2^{n_{\mathsf{SPSZK}}})$ by exhaustive search.[6] We require the one-way function to be hard to invert in time $O(2^{n_{\mathsf{SPSZK}}})$ but easy to invert in time $O(2^{n_{\mathsf{OWF}}})$, similarly the commitment scheme is hiding against $O(2^{n_{\mathsf{OWF}}})$ bounded machines but extractable in time $O(2^{n_{\mathsf{COM}}})$. Finally, the HPP-NIWI and the average-case hard language shall be hard even for adversaries running in time $O(2^{n_{\mathsf{COM}}}) \gg O(2^{n_{\mathsf{OWF}}}) \gg O(2^{n_{\mathsf{SPSZK}}})$.

Security Proof. In the following, we state our main theorems:

Theorem 2 (Soundness). *If* $(\mathsf{WI\text{-}P}, \mathsf{WI\text{-}V})$ *is an HPP-NIWIs with unique proofs,* $\tilde{\mathcal{L}}$ *is an average-case hard language with unique witnesses,* $(\mathsf{SPS\text{-}P}, \mathsf{SPS\text{-}V})$ *is an SPS-ZK argument, and the commitment scheme* Com *is perfectly binding, then the argument system SF-ZK in Fig. 1 is computationally sound.*

Proof. The proof consists of two steps. In the first step, we prove that it in present of non-adaptive (selective) security notation in a way that the adversary is not allow to adaptively choose the statement. In the second step, we invoke complexity leveraging to lift the reduction to the adaptive settings.

Non-adaptive Soundness. Assume that there exists an $x^* \notin \mathcal{L}$ and a malicious PPT prover P^* such that the verifier on input x^* and interaction with P^* will accept with probability ϵ. Let $x_{\mathsf{NIWI}} := (x, y, \tilde{w}, c_0, \bar{c}, \tilde{c})$ We can split this probability into two parts: Either P^* cheats in such away that $x_{\mathsf{NIWI}} \notin \mathcal{L}_{\mathsf{NIWI}}$ (in which case we will be able to use the soundness of the HPP-NIWI to show that P^* would not be successful) or P^* cheats in such away that $x_{\mathsf{NIWI}} \in \mathcal{L}_{\mathsf{NIWI}}$. In this case, we show that this event can only occur with negligible probability due to the average-case hardness of $\tilde{\mathcal{L}}$. Let cheat be the event that a malicious prover causes the honest verifier to accept x^*.

$$
\begin{aligned}
\epsilon &= \Pr[\mathsf{cheat}] \\
&= \underbrace{\Pr[\mathsf{cheat}|x_{\mathsf{NIWI}} \notin \mathcal{L}_{\mathsf{NIWI}}] \cdot \Pr[x_{\mathsf{NIWI}} \notin \mathcal{L}_{\mathsf{NIWI}}]}_{\epsilon'} \\
&\quad + \underbrace{\Pr[\mathsf{cheat}|x_{\mathsf{NIWI}} \in \mathcal{L}_{\mathsf{NIWI}}] \cdot \Pr[x_{\mathsf{NIWI}} \in \mathcal{L}_{\mathsf{NIWI}}]}_{\epsilon''}
\end{aligned}
$$

---

[6] This instantiation of the perfectly binding commitment scheme used inside the SPS-ZK protocol is different from the perfectly binding commitment scheme Com used in our protocol. In particular, we use different security levels for these schemes.

Bounding ϵ'. We will first bound ϵ' using the soundness of the HPP-NIWI and the super-polynomial extractability of the SPS-ZK. Assume towards contradiction, that $\epsilon' \geq 1/\text{poly}(n)$. We then construct a malicious WI-P^* as follows: WI-P^* engages with P^* in a protocol execution where it impersonates the verifier and computes all of the messages honestly. Let (α, β, γ) be the variables determined by the transcript of the execution. Then WI-P^* checks that $\mathsf{SPS\text{-}V}(\tau, \alpha, \beta, \gamma) = 1$ and extracts the witness u from (α, β, γ) in time $O(2^{n_{\mathsf{SPSZK}}})$ (recall the choice of parameters from Sect. 4.2) if this is the case. If the extraction fails or the transcript does not verify, then WI-P^* aborts. Finally, WI-P^* outputs $(x_{\mathsf{NIWI}}, \tau, \pi, u)$.

It is easy to see that WI-P^* perfectly simulates the verifier's preprocessing as well as the execution phase for P^*. WI-P^* successfully cheats, if (τ, π) verifies, extraction is successful, and $x_{\mathsf{NIWI}} \notin \mathcal{L}_{\mathsf{NIWI}}$.

Note that $1 \leftarrow \langle \mathsf{P}^*(x^*, s_1, p_2), \mathsf{V}^1(x^*, s_2, p_1) \rangle$ implies that both (α, β, γ) as well as (τ, π) verify correctly. Assume for the moment that the extraction from (α, β, γ) is successful with probability $1 - \text{negl}(n)$. Then it holds that

$$\Pr\left[(x_{\mathsf{NIWI}}, \tau, \pi, u) \leftarrow \mathsf{WI\text{-}P}^*(1^n) : \begin{array}{c} x_{\mathsf{NIWI}} \notin \mathcal{L}_{\mathsf{NIWI}} \wedge \mathsf{WI\text{-}P}_1(u) = \tau \\ \wedge\ \mathsf{WI\text{-}V}(x_{\mathsf{NIWI}}, \tau, \pi) = 1 \end{array}\right]$$

$$\geq \Pr[\text{cheat}|x_{\mathsf{NIWI}} \notin \mathcal{L}_{\mathsf{NIWI}}] \cdot \Pr[x_{\mathsf{NIWI}} \notin \mathcal{L}_{\mathsf{NIWI}}] \cdot (1 - \text{negl}(n))$$

$$= \epsilon' - \text{negl}(n) = 1/\text{poly}(n) - \text{negl}(n).$$

Since WI-P^* runs in time $O(2^{n_{\mathsf{SPSZK}}}) + \text{poly}(n)$ this would contradict the soundness of the HPP-NIWI. What is left to be shown is that the probability that the extraction from (α, β, γ) is not successful is bounded by a negligible function. If this was not the case, then α and the randomness used to compute it would uniquely determine β (recall the properties of SPS-ZK from Sect. 2). Therefore we could find the randomness in time $O(2^{n_{\mathsf{SPSZK}}}) + \text{poly}(n)$ and use it together with α, to break the hiding property of $c = \mathsf{Com}(\beta)$. It follows that the extraction must succeed with all but negligible probability. We can conclude that $\epsilon' \leq \text{negl}(n)$.

Bounding ϵ''. Assume towards contradiction that $\epsilon'' \geq 1/\text{poly}(n)$. Since $x^* \notin \mathcal{L}$, the definition of $\mathcal{L}_{\mathsf{NIWI}}$ implies that for an $x_{\mathsf{NIWI}} \in \mathcal{L}_{\mathsf{NIWI}}$ there exists an $(r, \tilde{r})$ such that $\mathsf{Com}(1; r) = c_0$ and $\mathsf{Com}(\tilde{w}; \tilde{r}) = \tilde{c}$. However, we can show that this would allow us to decide $\tilde{\mathcal{L}}$ in the average case as follows.

Given a random instance $\tilde{x}$, compute a verifier preprocessing honestly using $\tilde{x}$ as the random instance of the average-case hard language. The prover P^* returns its pre-processing and the commitment $\tilde{c}$. Then extract the content of $\tilde{c}$ in time $O(2^{n_{\mathsf{COM}}})$. If it contains a valid witness for $\tilde{x}$ return 1, else return a random bit. Note that if $\tilde{x} \notin \tilde{\mathcal{L}}$ then $\tilde{w}$ does not exist and therefore the algorithm described above will always output a random bit. On the other hand, if $\tilde{x} \in \tilde{\mathcal{L}}$ then we can lower bound the probability of the algorithm outputting 1 by $1/2 + \epsilon'' = 1/2 + 1/\text{poly}(n)$. Since the described algorithm runs in time $O(2^{n_{\mathsf{COM}}}) + \text{poly}(n)$ this clearly contradicts the average case hardness of $\tilde{\mathcal{L}}$ as specified in Sect. 4.2. We have thus established that $\epsilon = \epsilon' + \epsilon'' \leq \text{negl}(n)$ and SF-ZK is therefore computationally sound.

From Selective to Adaptive. For the second step of the proof, we rely on complexity leveraging. Let l_x be the domain size of the statement $l_x = |x|$. Let $\mathcal{B}$ against the adaptive security. We set l_x to be

$$2^{l_x} \ll 2^{n_{\mathsf{SPSZK}}} \ll 2^{n_{\mathsf{OWF}}} \ll 2^{n_{\mathsf{COM}}} \ll 2^{n_{\mathsf{NIWI}}} = 2^{n_L}.$$

We construct a reduction which behaves identically as the non-adaptive case, except that it guesses a statement x and aborts if $x \neq x^*$. The analysis is identical to what described above, except that the advantage drops by a factor at most $1/2^{l_x}$.

Theorem 3 (Observer Soundness). *If* $(\mathsf{WI\text{-}P}, \mathsf{WI\text{-}V})$ *is an HPP-NIWI with unique proofs,* $\tilde{\mathcal{L}}$ *is an average-case hard language with unique witnesses,* Com *is a perfectly binding commitment scheme with unique openings, and* $(\mathsf{SPS\text{-}P}, \mathsf{SPS\text{-}V})$ *is an SPS-ZK argument, then the argument system SF-ZK in Fig. 1 is observer sound.*

$\Theta(p_1, p_2, \mathcal{T}, x)$

---

1 :   **if** $\mathsf{Com}(\beta; t) \neq c$ **or** $(\tilde{x}, \tilde{w}) \notin \tilde{\mathcal{R}}$

2 :   **return** 0

3 :   **elseif** $\mathsf{SPS\text{-}V}(\tau, \alpha, \beta, \gamma) = 0$ **or** $\mathsf{WI\text{-}V}((x, y, \tilde{w}, c_0, \bar{c}, \tilde{c}), \tau, \pi) = 0$

4 :   **return** 0

5 :   **else return** 1

Fig. 2. The observer algorithm Θ

Proof. We describe the observer algorithm in Fig. 2. Recall that the observer soundness definition considers two cases. In one case the prover acts honestly during the pre-processing phase ($\tilde{\mathsf{P}} = \mathsf{P}^1$), in the other case the verifier does ($\tilde{\mathsf{V}} = \mathsf{V}^1$). We analyze the two cases separately.

Honest P^1. Assume towards contradiction, that there exists an $x^* \notin \mathcal{L}$, a malicious prover P^*, and a malicious verifier V^* such that

$$\frac{1}{\mathsf{poly}(n)} \leq \Pr\left[\begin{array}{l} (s_1, p_1) \leftarrow \mathsf{P}^1(1^n), (s_2, p_2) \leftarrow \mathsf{V}^*(x^*), \\ \mathcal{T} := \langle \mathsf{P}^*(x^*, s_1, p_2), \mathsf{V}^*(x^*, s_2, p_1) \rangle \end{array} : \Theta(p_1, p_2, \mathcal{T}, x) = 1 \right].$$

From this it follows that

$$\frac{1}{\mathsf{poly}(n)} \leq \Pr\left[\begin{array}{l} (r, \tau) \leftarrow \mathsf{P}^1(1^n), \\ \pi \in \mathcal{T} \end{array} : \mathsf{WI\text{-}V}((x, y, \tilde{w}, c_0, \bar{c}, \tilde{c}), \tau, \pi) = 1 \right]. \quad (1)$$

where Eq. 1 stems from the fact that the prover's pre-processing is honest and the observer always verifies the proof π. Recall that the statement $(x, y, \tilde{w}, c_0, \bar{c}, \tilde{c}) \in \mathcal{L}_{\mathsf{NIWI}}$ if and only if

$$\exists(s,\tilde{r}) : (\underline{x^* \in \mathcal{L}} \wedge \mathsf{Com}(\tilde{r};s) = \bar{c} \wedge \mathsf{Com}(0^n,\tilde{r}) = \tilde{c})$$
$$\vee\ \exists(r,\tilde{r}) : (\underline{\mathsf{Com}(1;r) = c_0} \wedge \mathsf{Com}(\tilde{w},\tilde{r}) = \tilde{c}) \tag{2}$$
$$\vee\ \exists(r,z) : (\underline{x^* \in \mathcal{L}} \wedge \underline{\mathsf{Com}(1;r) = c_0} \wedge f(z) = y)$$

By assumption, $x^* \notin \mathcal{L}$ and $\mathsf{Com}(0;r) = c_0$, since the prover's pre-processing is generated honestly and the commitment scheme is perfectly binding. Therefore each of the parts underlined in Eq. 2 is false. By extensions, this makes the conjunction in each of the three branches false. It follows then that π is a proof for a false statement given an honestly generated τ, which contradicts the soundness of the HPP-NIWI.

Honest V^1. For this case we can bootstrap the verifier's honest preprocessing into a fully honest verifier execution and then simply reduce observer soundness to regular soundness.

Assume towards contradiction that there exists an $x^* \notin \mathcal{L}$, a malicious prover P^*, and a malicious verifier V^* such that

$$\frac{1}{\mathsf{poly}(n)} \le \Pr\left[\begin{array}{l}(s_1,p_1) \leftarrow \mathsf{P}^*(x^*), (s_2,p_2) \leftarrow \mathsf{V}^1(1^n), \\ \mathcal{T} := \langle \mathsf{P}^*(x^*,s_1,p_2), \mathsf{V}^*(x^*,s_2,p_1)\rangle\end{array} : \Theta(p_1,p_2,\mathcal{T},x) = 1\right].$$

From this it follows that

$$\frac{1}{\mathsf{poly}(n)} \le \Pr\left[\begin{array}{l}(s_1,p_1) \leftarrow \mathsf{P}^*(x^*), \\ (s_2,p_2) \leftarrow \mathsf{V}^1(1^n), \\ \mathcal{T} := \langle \mathsf{P}^*(x^*,s_1,p_2), \mathsf{V}^2(x^*,s_2,p_1)\rangle\end{array} : \Theta(p_1,p_2,\mathcal{T},x) = 1\right] \tag{3}$$

$$= \Pr\left[\begin{array}{l}(s_1,p_1) \leftarrow \mathsf{P}^*(x^*), \\ (s_2,p_2) \leftarrow \mathsf{V}^1(1^n)\end{array} : 1 \leftarrow \langle \mathsf{P}^*(x^*,s_1,p_2), \mathsf{V}^2(x^*,s_2,p_1)\rangle\right] \tag{4}$$

To see why Eq. 3 holds, first note that the commitment scheme is perfectly binding and the language $\tilde{\mathcal{L}}$ has unique witnesses. Since Θ verifies in line 1 that (β,t) is a valid decommitment of c and that $\tilde{w}$ is indeed a witness of $\tilde{x}$, it follows that given the verifier's honest pre-processing there exists only a unique verifier message that does *not* cause the observer to output 0. For every possible transcript of the interaction between P^* and V^* consider the following two possibilities. Either the message sent by V^* is exactly that unique message or it sends any other message. In the first case, the malicious verifier behaves identically to the honest verifier and replacing V^* by V^2 does not change the resulting transcript or the output of Θ at all. In the latter case, Θ already outputs 0 for this transcript anyway and the only change could be that Θ now outputs 1. Thus we can conclude that the probability of Θ outputting 1 can only increase. Thus Eq. 3 must hold.

To see that Eq. 4 must hold we simply need to consider the checks performed by Θ in line 3. It's easy to see that $\Theta(p_1,p_2,\mathcal{T},x) = 1$ implies that $\mathsf{SPS\text{-}V}(\tau,\alpha,\beta,\gamma) = 1$ and $\mathsf{WI\text{-}V}((x,y,\tilde{w},c_0,\bar{c},\tilde{c}),\tau,\pi) = 1$, since the protocols are public-coin (and therefore publicly verifiable). However, these coincide with all checks performed by the honest verifier. Therefore, in an execution between the malicious prover and the honest verifier, the honest verifier accepts if and only if the transcript is accepted by the observer. Equation 4 therefore holds. We've thus shown that

$$\frac{1}{\mathsf{poly}(n)} \leq \Pr \left[\begin{array}{c} (s_1, p_1) \leftarrow \mathsf{P}^*(x^*), \\ (s_2, p_2) \leftarrow \mathsf{V}^1(1^n) \end{array} : 1 \leftarrow \langle \mathsf{P}^*(x^*, s_1, p_2), \mathsf{V}^2(x^*, s_2, p_1) \rangle \right]$$

which would contradict the soundness of SF-ZK. Therefore, an x^* and P^* as assumed above cannot exist and SF-ZK must also be (selective) observer sound. The proof for the adaptive observer sound is the same as above.

Theorem 4 (Zero Knowledge).   *If* (WI-P, WI-V) *is an HPP-NIWIs with unique proofs,* (SPS-P, SPS-V) *is an SPS-ZK argument with unique last message, f is a one-way function with efficiently checkable range, and* Com *is a perfectly binding and computationally hiding commitment scheme, then the argument system SF-ZK in Fig. 1 is computationally zero knowledge.*

Proof. We specify the zero-knowledge simulator Sim in the following. The simulator keeps a record of its running time and aborts if the number of steps exceeds 2^n.

1. During the preprocessing phase the simulator acts exactly like the honest prover, except that it commits to 1 in $c_0 \leftarrow \mathsf{Com}(1, r)$.
2. In the execution phase, it initializes a counter $i = 0$ and runs the following lookahead thread.
   (a) Commit to 0^n in $\tilde{c}$ using fresh randomness and send $\tilde{c}$.
   (b) As a response V^* either aborts or sends a response $(\tilde{w}, \beta, t)$.
   (c) If $i = 0$ check whether the verifier aborts or $(\tilde{x}, \tilde{w}) \notin \tilde{\mathcal{R}}$ and abort the whole simulation if any of these conditions are met, outputting whatever V^* outputs. Otherwise set $i := 1$ and return to step 2a.
   (d) If $i \neq 0$ check whether the verifier aborts or $(\tilde{x}, \tilde{w}) \notin \tilde{\mathcal{R}}$ and return to step 2a if this is the case. Otherwise set $i := i + 1$; if $i = 12n$ exit the loop, otherwise return to step 2a.
3. Let T be the number of iterations of the previous loop. Let $\tilde{p} := 12n/T$. Then the simulator enters in the following loop up to $(n^2/\tilde{p})$-many times.
   (a) Use the alternative witness $\tilde{w}$ to compute $\tilde{c} := \mathsf{Com}(\tilde{w}; r^*)$, using fresh random coins r^*, and send $\tilde{c}$ to the verifier.
   (b) As a response V^* either aborts or sends a second message $(\tilde{w}, \beta, t)$.
   (c) If the verifier aborts or the second message is invalid, return to step 3a, else exit the loop.
4. If $n^2/\tilde{p}$ iterations were reached without a valid $\tilde{w}$ being output by the verifier, output fail. Else use the alternative witness (r, r^*) to compute π using the second branch (2) of the HPP-NIWI proof and compute γ honestly. Send (γ, π) to the verifier.
5. The simulator outputs whatever V^* outputs.

We first bound the running time of the simulator and the probability of the simulator outputting fail.

Lemma 1. Sim *runs in expected polynomial time in* n.

Proof. Let $p(n)$ be the probability that V^* outputs a well-formed response given $\tilde{c}$ computed as in step 2a. Observe that the work of the simulator is strictly polynomial time except for the number of rewindings, therefore it is sufficient to bound the number of iterations. Note that from [36] the expected number of iterations of the first loop is exactly $\frac{12n}{p(n)}$. With this observation in mind, we distinguish between two cases

1. $\frac{p(n)}{\tilde{p}} \neq O(1)$. In this case, we use the trivial bound 2^n. However, this case can be shown to happen with negligible probability by the Chernoff bound.
2. $\frac{p(n)}{\tilde{p}} = O(1)$. In this case we can bound the running time by

$$\mathsf{poly}\,(n) \cdot p(n) \cdot \left(\frac{12n}{p(n)} + \frac{n^2}{\tilde{p}} \right) = \mathsf{poly}\,(n) \cdot \frac{p(n)}{\tilde{p}} = \mathsf{poly}\,(n)$$

which concludes our analysis.

Next we bound the probability that the simulator outputs fail.

Claim. The probability that Sim outputs fail is negligible in n.

Let $q(n)$ be the probability that V^* outputs a well-formed response given $\tilde{c}$ (computed as in step 3). We state and prove the following helping lemma.

Lemma 2. *There exists a negligible function such that* $q(n) \geq p(n) - \mathsf{negl}\,(n)$.

Proof. If $p(n)$ is negligible than it is trivial. Else it can be easily shown via a two-step argument. Let us define $\mathsf{q}(n)$ as $q(n)$ except that in the simulation the commitment $\tilde{c}$ is computed as the commitment to a random string. Note that in the real protocol the corresponding opening s is used only after the last message of V^* and therefore $q(n) = \mathsf{q}(n) - \mathsf{negl}\,(n)$ by the hiding of the commitment scheme.

Recall that $p(n)$ is defined as the probability of V^* to abort given $\tilde{c} = \mathsf{Com}(0)$ using fresh randomness and $\mathsf{q}(n)$ is defined as the probability of V^* to abort given $\tilde{c} = \mathsf{Com}(\tilde{w})$ using fresh randomness. Thus we can use V^* as a distinguisher for the commitment scheme and it will succeed with probability $p(n) - \mathsf{q}(n)$. Since this value can be bound by a negligible function by the computational hiding of Com, we have that

$$p(n) - (q(n) + \mathsf{negl}\,(n)) = p(n) - \mathsf{q}(n) \leq \mathsf{negl}\,(n)$$

which implies that $q(n) \geq p(n) - \mathsf{negl}\,(n)$ and concludes our proof.

We are now in the position of proving our claim.

Proof. Recall that the simulator outputs fail if all $\frac{n^2}{\tilde{p}}$ iterations in step 3 are not successful. We consider two cases.

1. $p(n) \leq 2 \cdot \mathsf{negl}(n)$. In this case the simulator reaches step 3 with negligible probability and therefore fail happens with the same probability.
2. $p(n) > 2 \cdot \mathsf{negl}(n)$. For conceptual simplicity we split the loop in step 3 to n independent rewinds, each upper-bounded by $\frac{n}{\tilde{p}}$ steps. Then fail happens if all of the rewinds as not successful. By a routine calculation we obtain that the expected number of iterations of each rewinding until a successful instance is found is

$$\frac{1}{q(n)} \leq \frac{1}{p(n) - \mathsf{negl}(n)} < \frac{2}{p(n)} = O\left(\frac{1}{\tilde{p}}\right),$$

where the first inequality is by Lemma 2 and last equality is discussed above. By Markov's inequality the probability that the simulator tries more than $\frac{n}{\tilde{p}}$ iterations is at most $O(1/n)$. Since we consider n independent instances, the total probability is bounded by $O(1/n)^n$.

Finally, we show that the distribution induced by the output of the simulator is computationally indistinguishable from the honest one. Consider the following sequence of hybrids.

Hybrid H_1: The first hybrid is the interaction between the simulator Sim and the malicious verifier V^*.

Hybrid H_2: The last message γ of the SPS-ZK is simulated in time $O(2^{n_{\mathsf{SPSZK}}})$.

Hybrid H_3: The simulator inverts the one-way function to obtain $\tilde{z}$ such that $f(\tilde{z}) = y$ and uses it, together with the original witness w and the randomness r, to compute π by satisfying the third branch (3).

Hybrid H_4: The simulator computes $\tilde{c}$ as $\mathsf{Com}(0^n)$ using fresh random coins.

Hybrid H_5: The simulator no longer rewinds the verifier and simply executes the protocol in a single thread.

Hybrid H_6: The commitment $\tilde{c}$ is computed using the committed randomness $\tilde{r}$, instead of a fresh r^*.

Hybrid H_7: The simulator computes π using the original witness $(w, s, \tilde{r})$, without inverting f.

Hybrid H_8: The SPS-ZK is no longer simulated and instead computed honestly.

Hybrid H_9: The simulator now commits to 0 in $c_0 = \mathsf{Com}(0; r)$.

It is easy to see that the last hybrid exactly matches the honest execution. We will show that each δ_i defined as

$$\delta_i := |\Pr[\mathcal{D}(\langle \mathsf{H}_i(x, w), \mathsf{V}^*(x)\rangle) = 1] - \Pr[\mathcal{D}(\langle \mathsf{H}_{i+1}(x, w), \mathsf{V}^*(x)\rangle) = 1]|$$

is negligible in n. Note that the simulator Sim runs in expected (super) polynomial-time, whereas all of the following reductions must terminate in strict (super) polynomial-time. This issue can be dealt with by truncating Sim to twice its expected running time. By Markov's inequality, this reduces its success probability by at most $1/2$.

Observe that the difference in the first hybrid is that the SPS-ZK protocol is simulated in super-polynomial time. The simulator simply guesses the challenge of the verifier ahead of time and restarts the whole execution if the guess was not correct. The expected number of attempts is in the order of $O(2^{n_{\text{SPSZK}}})$, however, when the simulator is successful, the transcript of the execution is statistically close to the transcript of an honest run. This bounds the value of δ_1 (and analogously of δ_7) to a negligible function.

The differences δ_2 and δ_6 can be shown to be negligible with a reduction to the witness indistinguishability of the HPP-NIWI arguments: The reduction simply sets π to be the challenge proof and returns the output of the distinguisher. Note that the random coins of the setup are not required for the simulation. The reduction runs in time $O(2^{n_{\text{OWF}}}) + O(2^{n_{\text{SPSZK}}}) + \text{poly}(n)$ and therefore the differences among these hybrids can be bound by a negligible function (recall the parameter setup from Sect. 4.2).

Note that the fifth hybrid differs from the fourth only in case fail happens, however by Lemma 4.2 this happens with negligible probability and the bound on δ_4 follows. δ_3 and δ_5 can be shown to be negligible with a trivial reduction to the hiding property of the commitment scheme. Note that the reduction runs in time $O(2^{n_{\text{OWF}}}) + O(2^{n_{\text{SPSZK}}}) + \text{poly}(n)$, however the commitment scheme is assumed to be hiding for machines bounded by such a runtime. The bound on δ_8 uses an identical argument except that now the reduction runs in (strict) polynomial time. We can conclude that

$$|\Pr[\mathcal{D}(\langle \mathsf{P}(x,w), \mathsf{V}^*(x)\rangle) = 1] - \Pr[\mathcal{D}(\mathsf{Sim}(x)) = 1]| \leq \sum_{i=1}^{9} \delta_i \leq \mathsf{negl}(n).$$

Theorem 5 (Computationally Unique Transcripts). *If* (WI-P, WI-V) *is an HPP-NIWI with unique proofs,* $\tilde{\mathcal{L}}$ *is an average-case hard language with unique witnesses,* f *is a one-way function,* (SPS-P, SPS-V) *is an SPS-ZK argument with unique last messages, and the commitment scheme* Com *is perfectly binding and has unique openings, then the argument system SF-ZK in Fig. 1 has computationally unique transcripts.*

Proof. Recall that a pair of machines $(\tilde{\mathsf{P}}^1, \tilde{\mathsf{V}}^1)$ is admissible if at least one of the two is identical to an honest generation algorithm. We treat the two cases separately.

Honest P^1. First observe that the verifier only sends the decommitment (β, t) and the witness $\tilde{w}$. Since the commitment scheme is perfectly binding and has unique decommitments and Θ verifies that the decommitment is correct, then (β, t) is uniquely determined by the preprocessing. Further, $\tilde{\mathcal{L}}$ has unique witnesses, therefore $\tilde{w}$ is also fixed by the preprocessing, for any choice of $\tilde{x}$.

On the prover's side the tuple $(\tilde{c}, \gamma, \pi)$ collects all messages sent in the execution. Since the prover's preprocessing phase is honest, c_0 is a commitment to 0. Since the commitment scheme is perfectly binding and has unique decommitments, then $\bar{c}$ from the pre-processing fixes both $(s, \tilde{r})$. If we assume towards contradiction that there exists two different accepting $\tilde{c}$ and $\hat{c}$, by the soundness of π we have that $\tilde{c} = \mathsf{Com}(0^n, \tilde{r})$ and $\hat{c} = \mathsf{Com}(0^n, \hat{r})$, where $\bar{c} = \mathsf{Com}(\tilde{r}, s)$ and $\bar{c} = \mathsf{Com}(\hat{r}, s)$. However this is a contradiction since the commitment has unique openings. It follows that $\tilde{r} = \hat{r}$ and therefore $\tilde{c}$ is unique. Recall that both the HPP-NIWI and the SPS-ZK have unique last messages, and therefore (γ, π) are uniquely determined by the pre-processing.

Honest V^1. Given an honest verifier pre-processing p_2 and a (possibly malicious) prover pre-processing p_1 for a certain statement x with unique witnesses, let $\mathcal{T}_1 := (\tilde{c}, \beta, t, \tilde{w}, \pi, \gamma)$ and $\mathcal{T}_2 := (\hat{c}, \hat{\beta}, \hat{t}, \hat{w}, \hat{\pi}, \hat{\gamma})$ be the two transcripts such that $\Theta(p_1, p_2, \mathcal{T}_1, x) = \Theta(p_1, p_2, \mathcal{T}_2, x) = 1$. We shall prove that $\mathcal{T}_1 = \mathcal{T}_2$ with all but negligible probability.

$\underline{(\beta, t) = (\hat{\beta}, \hat{t})}$: Since the commitment scheme is perfectly binding and has unique openings and $c = \mathsf{Com}(\beta; t)$ is fixed in the pre-processing, this equality must hold.

$\underline{\tilde{w} = \hat{w}}$: The witness is uniquely determined by the statement $\tilde{x}$, since $\tilde{\mathcal{L}}$ has unique witnesses.

$\underline{\gamma = \hat{\gamma}}$: Fix τ and (α, β), which are all part of the pre-processing, then γ is unique since the SPS-ZK has unique last messages.

$\underline{\pi = \hat{\pi}}$: First note that there must exist some u such that $\mathsf{WI}\text{-}\mathsf{P}_1(u) = \tau$. To see why this is the case, recall either the transcript of the SPS-ZK proof uniquely determines the witness or α (together with the randomness used to compute it) uniquely determines the challenge β. If a valid u does not exist, then we are left with the latter case, which implies that we can guess the content of c running in time $O(2^{n_{\mathsf{SPSZK}}})$. This contradicts the hiding property of Com (refer to Sect. 2 for further discussion). It follows that τ is well-formed except with negligible probability.

Therefore both π and $\hat{\pi}$ are generated using the witness for one of the following branches:

$$\exists (s, \tilde{r}) : (x^* \in \mathcal{L} \wedge \mathsf{Com}(\tilde{r}; s) = \bar{c} \wedge \mathsf{Com}(0^n, \tilde{r}) = \tilde{c})$$
$$\vee \; \exists (r, \tilde{r}) : (\mathsf{Com}(1; r) = c_0 \wedge \mathsf{Com}(\tilde{w}, \tilde{r}) = \tilde{c})$$
$$\vee \; \exists (r, z) : (x^* \in \mathcal{L} \wedge \mathsf{Com}(1; r) = c_0 \wedge f(z) = y)$$

We bound the probability that π or $\hat{\pi}$ is a valid proof for the second branch (2) in the following. Assume without loss of generality that such proof is π. Since the commitment scheme is perfectly binding we can extract $\tilde{w}$ from $\tilde{c}$ (by exhaustive search) in time $O(2^{n_{\mathsf{COM}}})$. Note that the extraction is successful with probability 1 since $\tilde{c}$ is perfectly binding. Recall that $\tilde{V}^1$ is honest by assumption and therefore we can plug in a hard instance $\tilde{x}$ and break the average-case hardness of $\tilde{\mathcal{L}}$ from the first message of the prover.

On the other hand, if the third branch (3) is proven with non-negligible probability then we can invert y in time $O(2^{n_{\mathsf{SPSZK}}}) + \mathsf{poly}(n)$ by extracting u from (α, β, γ) and running the polynomial-time extractor of the HPP-NIWI proof. It follows that both proofs are for the first branch (1), which implies that they are identical.

$\tilde{c} = \hat{c}$: As we argued above, π must be a proof for the first branch. Since $(s, \tilde{r})$ are fixed in the pre-processing by $\bar{c}$, then $\tilde{c}$ is also uniquely determined, unless π is a proof for a false statement. This happens only with negligible probability. $\square$

Acknowledgements. Behzad Abdolmaleki and Giulio Malavolta were supported by the German Federal Ministry of Education and Research BMBF (grant 16K15K042, project 6GEM). Nils Fleischhacker and Giulio Malavolta were supported by the Deutsche Forschungsgemeinschaft (DFG, German Research Foundation) under Germany's Excellence Strategy - EXC 2092 CASA - 390781972. Vipul Goyal was supported by the NSF award 1916939, DARPA SIEVE program under Agreement No. HR00112020025, a gift from Ripple, a DoE NETL award, a JP Morgan Faculty Fellowship, a PNC center for financial services innovation award, and a Cylab seed funding award. Abhishek Jain was supported in part by NSF CNS-1814919, NSF CAREER 1942789, Johns Hopkins University Catalyst award, AFOSR Award FA9550-19-1-0200 and the Office of Naval Research Grant N00014-19-1-2294.

References

1. Alwen, J., Shelat, A., Visconti, I.: Collusion-free protocols in the mediated model. In: Wagner, D. (ed.) CRYPTO 2008. LNCS, vol. 5157, pp. 497–514. Springer, Heidelberg (2008). https://doi.org/10.1007/978-3-540-85174-5_28
2. Auerbach, B., Bellare, M., Kiltz, E.: Public-key encryption resistant to parameter subversion and its realization from efficiently-embeddable groups. In: Abdalla, M., Dahab, R. (eds.) PKC 2018. LNCS, vol. 10769, pp. 348–377. Springer, Cham (2018). https://doi.org/10.1007/978-3-319-76578-5_12
3. Backes, M., Cachin, C.: Public-key steganography with active attacks. In: Kilian, J. (ed.) TCC 2005. LNCS, vol. 3378, pp. 210–226. Springer, Heidelberg (2005). https://doi.org/10.1007/978-3-540-30576-7_12
4. Bellare, M., Fuchsbauer, G., Scafuro, A.: NIZKs with an untrusted CRS: security in the face of parameter subversion. In: Cheon, J.H., Takagi, T. (eds.) ASIACRYPT 2016. LNCS, vol. 10032, pp. 777–804. Springer, Heidelberg (2016). https://doi.org/10.1007/978-3-662-53890-6_26
5. Bellare, M., Hoang, V.T.: Resisting randomness subversion: fast deterministic and hedged public-key encryption in the standard model. In: Oswald, E., Fischlin, M. (eds.) EUROCRYPT 2015. LNCS, vol. 9057, pp. 627–656. Springer, Heidelberg (2015). https://doi.org/10.1007/978-3-662-46803-6_21
6. Bellare, M., Hoang, V.T., Rogaway, P.: Foundations of garbled circuits. In: Yu, T., Danezis, G., Gligor, V.D. (eds.) ACM CCS 2012: 19th Conference on Computer and Communications Security, pp. 784–796. ACM Press, Raleigh, 16–18 October 2012
7. Bellare, M., Jaeger, J., Kane, D.: Mass-surveillance without the state: strongly undetectable algorithm-substitution attacks. In: Ray, I., Li, N., Kruegel, C. (eds.) ACM CCS 2015: 22nd Conference on Computer and Communications Security, pp. 1431–1440. ACM Press, Denver, 12–16 October 2015
8. Bellare, M., Paterson, K.G., Rogaway, P.: Security of symmetric encryption against mass surveillance. In: Garay, J.A., Gennaro, R. (eds.) CRYPTO 2014. LNCS, vol. 8616, pp. 1–19. Springer, Heidelberg (2014). https://doi.org/10.1007/978-3-662-44371-2_1

9. Blaze, M., Bleumer, G., Strauss, M.: Divertible protocols and atomic proxy cryptography. In: Nyberg, K. (ed.) EUROCRYPT 1998. LNCS, vol. 1403, pp. 127–144. Springer, Heidelberg (1998). https://doi.org/10.1007/BFb0054122

10. Brakerski, Z., Garg, S., Tsabary, R.: FHE-based bootstrapping of designated-prover NIZK. In: Pass, R., Pietrzak, K. (eds.) TCC 2020. LNCS, vol. 12550, pp. 657–683. Springer, Cham (2020). https://doi.org/10.1007/978-3-030-64375-1_23

11. Burmester, M., Desmedt, Y.: Broadcast interactive proofs. In: Davies, D.W. (ed.) EUROCRYPT 1991. LNCS, vol. 547, pp. 81–95. Springer, Heidelberg (1991). https://doi.org/10.1007/3-540-46416-6_7

12. Burmester, M., Desmedt, Y., Itoh, T., Sakurai, K., Shizuya, H.: Divertible and subliminal-free zero-knowledge proofs for languages. J. Cryptol. **12**(3), 197–223 (1999)

13. Burmester, M., Desmedt, Y.G., Itoh, T., Sakurai, K., Shizuya, H., Yung, M.: A progress report on subliminal-free channels. In: Anderson, R. (ed.) IH 1996. LNCS, vol. 1174, pp. 157–168. Springer, Heidelberg (1996). https://doi.org/10.1007/3-540-61996-8_39

14. Cachin, C.: An information-theoretic model for steganography. Inf. Comput. **192**(1), 41–56 (2004)

15. Chakraborty, S., Dziembowski, S., Nielsen, J.B.: Reverse firewalls for actively secure MPCs. In: Micciancio, D., Ristenpart, T. (eds.) CRYPTO 2020. LNCS, vol. 12171, pp. 732–762. Springer, Cham (2020). https://doi.org/10.1007/978-3-030-56880-1_26

16. Chakraborty, S., Ganesh, C., Pancholi, M., Sarkar, P.: Reverse firewalls for adaptively secure MPC without setup. In: Tibouchi, M., Wang, H. (eds.) ASIACRYPT 2021. LNCS, vol. 13091, pp. 335–364. Springer, Cham (2021). https://doi.org/10.1007/978-3-030-92075-3_12

17. Degabriele, J.P., Paterson, K.G., Schuldt, J.C.N., Woodage, J.: Backdoors in pseudorandom number generators: possibility and impossibility results. In: Robshaw, M., Katz, J. (eds.) CRYPTO 2016. LNCS, vol. 9814, pp. 403–432. Springer, Heidelberg (2016). https://doi.org/10.1007/978-3-662-53018-4_15

18. Desmedt, Y.: Abuses in cryptography and how to fight them. In: Goldwasser, S. (ed.) CRYPTO 1988. LNCS, vol. 403, pp. 375–389. Springer, New York (1990). https://doi.org/10.1007/0-387-34799-2_29

19. Dodis, Y., Ganesh, C., Golovnev, A., Juels, A., Ristenpart, T.: A formal treatment of backdoored pseudorandom generators. In: Oswald, E., Fischlin, M. (eds.) EUROCRYPT 2015. LNCS, vol. 9056, pp. 101–126. Springer, Heidelberg (2015). https://doi.org/10.1007/978-3-662-46800-5_5

20. Dodis, Y., Mironov, I., Stephens-Davidowitz, N.: Message transmission with reverse firewalls—secure communication on corrupted machines. In: Robshaw, M., Katz, J. (eds.) CRYPTO 2016. LNCS, vol. 9814, pp. 341–372. Springer, Heidelberg (2016). https://doi.org/10.1007/978-3-662-53018-4_13

21. Dodis, Y., Ong, S.J., Prabhakaran, M., Sahai, A.: On the (im)possibility of cryptography with imperfect randomness. In: 45th Annual Symposium on Foundations of Computer Science, pp. 196–205. IEEE Computer Society Press, Rome, 17–19 October 2004

22. Fischlin, M., Mazaheri, S.: Self-guarding cryptographic protocols against algorithm substitution attacks. In: IEEE 31st Computer Security Foundations Symposium (CSF) (2018)

23. Ganesh, C., Magri, B., Venturi, D.: Cryptographic reverse firewalls for interactive proof systems. Cryptology ePrint Archive, Report 2020/204 (2020)

24. Gentry, C.: Fully homomorphic encryption using ideal lattices. In: Mitzenmacher, M. (ed.) 41st Annual ACM Symposium on Theory of Computing, pp. 169–178. ACM Press, Bethesda, 31 May–2 June 2009

25. Goldreich, O., Kahan, A.: How to construct constant-round zero-knowledge proof systems for NP. J. Cryptol. 9(3), 167–190 (1996)

26. Goldreich, O., Micali, S., Wigderson, A.: How to play any mental game or A completeness theorem for protocols with honest majority. In: Aho, A. (ed.) 19th Annual ACM Symposium on Theory of Computing, pp. 218–229. ACM Press, New York City, 25–27 May 1987

27. Goldwasser, S., Micali, S., Rackoff, C.: The knowledge complexity of interactive proof-systems (extended abstract). In: 17th Annual ACM Symposium on Theory of Computing, pp. 291–304. ACM Press, Providence, 6–8 May 1985

28. Hazay, C., Venkitasubramaniam, M.: On the power of secure two-party computation. In: Robshaw, M., Katz, J. (eds.) CRYPTO 2016. LNCS, vol. 9815, pp. 397–429. Springer, Heidelberg (2016). https://doi.org/10.1007/978-3-662-53008-5_14

29. Hopper, N.J., Langford, J., von Ahn, L.: Provably secure steganography. In: Yung, M. (ed.) CRYPTO 2002. LNCS, vol. 2442, pp. 77–92. Springer, Heidelberg (2002). https://doi.org/10.1007/3-540-45708-9_6

30. Kalai, Y.T., Kanukurthi, B., Sahai, A.: Cryptography with tamperable and leaky memory. In: Rogaway, P. (ed.) CRYPTO 2011. LNCS, vol. 6841, pp. 373–390. Springer, Heidelberg (2011). https://doi.org/10.1007/978-3-642-22792-9_21

31. Katzenbeisser, S., Petitcolas, F.A.P.: Defining security in steganographic systems (2002)

32. Kilian, J.: A note on efficient zero-knowledge proofs and arguments (extended abstract). In: 24th Annual ACM Symposium on Theory of Computing, pp. 723–732. ACM Press, Victoria, 4–6 May 1992

33. Lapidot, D., Shamir, A.: Publicly verifiable non-interactive zero-knowledge proofs. In: Menezes, A.J., Vanstone, S.A. (eds.) CRYPTO 1990. LNCS, vol. 537, pp. 353–365. Springer, Heidelberg (1991). https://doi.org/10.1007/3-540-38424-3_26

34. Lepinski, M., Micali, S., Shelat, A.: Collusion-free protocols. In: Gabow, H.N., Fagin, R. (eds.) 37th Annual ACM Symposium on Theory of Computing, pp. 543–552. ACM Press, Baltimore, 22–24 May 2005

35. Lepinski, M., Micali, S., Shelat, A.: Fair-zero knowledge. In: Kilian, J. (ed.) TCC 2005. LNCS, vol. 3378, pp. 245–263. Springer, Heidelberg (2005). https://doi.org/10.1007/978-3-540-30576-7_14

36. Lindell, Y.: How to simulate it - a tutorial on the simulation proof technique. Cryptology ePrint Archive, Report 2016/046, (2016). https://ia.cr/2016/046

37. Lindell, Y., Pinkas, B.: An Efficient Protocol for Secure Two-Party Computation in the Presence of Malicious Adversaries. In: Naor, M. (ed.) EUROCRYPT 2007. LNCS, vol. 4515, pp. 52–78. Springer, Heidelberg (2007). https://doi.org/10.1007/978-3-540-72540-4_4

38. Mironov, I., Stephens-Davidowitz, N.: Cryptographic reverse firewalls. In: Oswald, E., Fischlin, M. (eds.) EUROCRYPT 2015. LNCS, vol. 9057, pp. 657–686. Springer, Heidelberg (2015). https://doi.org/10.1007/978-3-662-46803-6_22

39. Okamoto, T., Ohta, K.: How to utilize the randomness of zero-knowledge proofs. In: Menezes, A.J., Vanstone, S.A. (eds.) CRYPTO 1990. LNCS, vol. 537, pp. 456–475. Springer, Heidelberg (1991). https://doi.org/10.1007/3-540-38424-3_33

40. Pass, R.: Simulation in quasi-polynomial time, and its application to protocol composition. In: Biham, E. (ed.) EUROCRYPT 2003. LNCS, vol. 2656, pp. 160–176. Springer, Heidelberg (2003). https://doi.org/10.1007/3-540-39200-9_10

41. Russell, A., Tang, Q., Yung, M., Zhou, H.-S.: Cliptography: clipping the power of kleptographic attacks. In: Cheon, J.H., Takagi, T. (eds.) ASIACRYPT 2016. LNCS, vol. 10032, pp. 34–64. Springer, Heidelberg (2016). https://doi.org/10.1007/978-3-662-53890-6_2

42. Russell, A., Tang, Q., Yung, M., Zhou, H.-S.: Generic semantic security against a kleptographic adversary. In: Thuraisingham, B.M., Evans, D., Malkin, T., Xu, D. (eds.) ACM CCS 2017: 24th Conference on Computer and Communications Security, pp. 907–922. ACM Press, Dallas, 31 October–2 November 2017

43. Sahai, A., Waters, B.: How to use indistinguishability obfuscation: deniable encryption, and more. In: Shmoys, D.B. (ed.) 46th Annual ACM Symposium on Theory of Computing, pp. 475–484. ACM Press, New York, 31 May–3 June 2014

44. Young, A., Yung, M.: Kleptography: using cryptography against cryptography. In: Fumy, W. (ed.) EUROCRYPT 1997. LNCS, vol. 1233, pp. 62–74. Springer, Heidelberg (1997). https://doi.org/10.1007/3-540-69053-0_6

45. Young, A., Yung, M.: The prevalence of kleptographic attacks on discrete-log based cryptosystems. In: Kaliski, B.S. (ed.) CRYPTO 1997. LNCS, vol. 1294, pp. 264–276. Springer, Heidelberg (1997). https://doi.org/10.1007/BFb0052241

Vector Commitments over Rings and Compressed Σ-Protocols

Thomas Attema[1,2,3], Ignacio Cascudo[4], Ronald Cramer[1,2], Ivan Damgård[5], and Daniel Escudero[6(✉)]

[1] CWI, Amsterdam, The Netherlands
[2] Leiden University, Leiden, The Netherlands
[3] TNO, The Hague, The Netherlands
[4] IMDEA Software Institute, Madrid, Spain
[5] Aarhus University, Aarhus, Denmark
[6] J.P. Morgan AI Research, New York, USA
daniel.escudero@protonmail.com

Abstract. Compressed Σ-Protocol Theory (CRYPTO 2020) presents an "alternative" to Bulletproofs that achieves the same communication complexity while adhering more elegantly to existing Σ-protocol theory, which enables their techniques to be directly applicable to other widely used settings in the context of "plug & play" algorithmics. Unfortunately, their techniques are restricted to arithmetic circuits over *prime* fields, which rules out the possibility of using more machine-friendly moduli such as powers of 2, which have proven to improve efficiency in applications. In this work we show that such techniques can be generalized to the case of arithmetic circuits modulo *any* number. This enables the use of powers of 2, which can prove to be beneficial for efficiency, but it also facilitates the use of other moduli that might prove useful in different applications.

In order to achieve this, we first present an instantiation of the main building block of the theory of compressed Σ-protocols, namely compact vector commitments. Our construction, which may be of independent interest, is homomorphic modulo *any* positive integer m, a result that was not known in the literature before. Second, we generalize Compressed Σ-Protocol Theory from finite fields to $\mathbb{Z}_m$. The main challenge here is ensuring that there are large enough challenge sets as to fulfill the necessary soundness requirements, which is achieved by considering certain ring extensions. Our techniques have direct application for example to verifiable computation on homomorphically encrypted data.

1 Introduction

Zero knowledge proofs, introduced in [36], constitute an important tool used all across cryptography to build several other powerful constructions, and they also find applications outside cryptography thanks to their considerable flexibility

D. Escudero—Work partially done while Daniel Escudero was at Aarhus University.

E. Kiltz and V. Vaikuntanathan (Eds.): TCC 2022, LNCS 13747, pp. 173–202, 2022.
https://doi.org/10.1007/978-3-031-22318-1_7

and high potential. In a nutshell, a zero knowledge proof enables a *prover* to convince a *verifier* that a given statement belongs to certain language, without revealing anything else beyond this fact. In addition, in a zero knowledge *proof of knowledge* the verifier gets convinced that the prover actually knows certain information, without leaking the information itself.

Zero knowledge proofs are used thoroughly in several cryptographic constructions such as secure multiparty computation and other distributed protocols to prove, without leaking sensitive information, that certain messages are "well formed" (e.g. [10, 34]). In many cases this turns out to be essential to be able to support "active adversaries", which model real-world attackers who can deviate from the specification of the cryptographic construction at hand. Furthermore, thanks to a rich and fruitful series of works [2, 9, 14, 15, 19, 32, 37, 43, 44], several zero knowledge protocols with a wide range of desirable properties and trade-offs exist today.

Typically, zero knowledge techniques operate by somehow translating general statements to *arithmetic* statements, ultimately dealing with additions and multiplications over some algebraic structure. Traditionally, this arithmetic happens over what is known as a *finite field*, such as $\mathbb{Z}_p$, the set of integers modulo p, for prime p. The tendency to use this type of structures is also present in other areas such as secure multiparty computation [1, 17, 23, 25] and, in essence, this is due to the fact that these structures possess very nice properties that make them "easy" to work with.

Finite fields, on top of being simple and well-structured algebraic constructions, can be used in a wide range of applications. For instance, the set $\{0, 1\}$ with the XOR and AND operations is a finite field ($\mathbb{Z}_2$, integers modulo 2), so any binary circuit as traditionally known from electrical engineering can be expressed in terms of arithmetic over the field $\mathbb{Z}_2$. Additionally, by choosing p to be large enough so that wrap-around modulo p does not occur, $\mathbb{Z}_p$ can be used to emulate integer arithmetic, which facilitates numerical applications. However, from a mere use-case standpoint, the choice of arithmetic modulo a prime number may seem a bit arbitrary; after all, what is so special about prime numbers?[1]

Depending on the context, other moduli may be considered equally or perhaps even more important. A natural example is the case of arithmetic modulo powers of two like 2^{64} or 2^{128}, since this corresponds to the type of basic arithmetic performed by arithmetic logic units and is expected to lead to improvements in efficiency, as is the case for secure multiparty computation [23, 25], or certain zero-knowledge protocols [6]. Some other examples may include moduli structured in specific ways, such as RSA integers $N = p \cdot q$ for large prime numbers p and q, and variants of this, which could benefit applications making use of these constructions. Finally, we observe that, in mathematics, it is customary and quite enlightening to gradually reduce/abstract the required properties of a given construction to see, in essence, what are the features or patterns that

---

[1] Of course, within mathematics, prime numbers hold a special throne, but from an application point of view modular arithmetic is essentially the same regardless of the chosen modulus.

enable certain propositions or constructions to hold. It is in this direction that it becomes natural to wonder if nice and well-behaved algebraic structures such as finite fields are really "necessary" within the context of zero knowledge proofs, or if they are simply more "convenient" to deal with.

Compressed Σ-Protocols. Of particular importance among existing zero knowledge proof techniques is the concept of Σ-protocols [21]. These tools constitute *honest verifier zero knowledge proofs of knowledge*, meaning that they enable a verifier to be convinced that a prover knows certain secret data, and this data is not leaked assuming that the verifier behaves honestly. Σ-protocols have proven to be an essential tool for building more complex protocols, like actual malicious verifier zero knowledge proofs, but also more elaborate systems such as proofs of disjunctions and proofs of some-out-of-many statements [24], identification schemes [42], among many others. They have also been used in contexts such as maliciously secure multiparty computation with a dishonest majority (e.g. [10]).

In [3], the authors presented a series of techniques for *compressing Σ-*protocols, in a way that adheres to the existing theory of Σ-protocols and therefore inherits all the results and applications from the field. Other works such as [15] achieved similar results in terms of communication efficiency, but were presented as a replacement for standard Σ-protocol theory and, as a result, do not serve as a building block for constructions making use of Σ-protocols, or at least not without any (typically non-trivial) adaptation.

The results in [3] shed an important light on the expressibility and efficiency of the Σ-protocol framework. However, as is the case with most of the literature on interactive proofs and zero knowledge proofs, their techniques are restricted to finite fields, which is made evident from the fact that they use several tools restricted to finite fields such as polynomial interpolation or Pedersen commitments, among others. Given the importance of this general theory, a worthy goal is then to extend the results in [3] to the setting in which the algebraic structure under consideration is not necessarily a finite field $\mathbb{Z}_p$. This would enable the use of these tools in a much wider range of applications and scenarios, and it could also potentially boost its efficiency by considering rings of the form $\mathbb{Z}_{2^k}$, as seen in works such as [6]. In addition, as discussed earlier, such study would make more clear what is the inherent reach and limitation of the theory on compressed Σ-protocols, in terms of the underlying algebraic structure.

1.1   Our Contribution

In this work we explore an extension of the compressed Σ-protocol framework from [3], from the case in which the algebraic structure is a field of the form $\mathbb{Z}_p$, to the more general setting of $\mathbb{Z}_m$, for an *arbitrary* positive integer m. Our results show that compressed Σ-protocols for partial openings over $\mathbb{Z}_m$, where a prover shows that it knows how to open a commitment to a vector that maps to a given value under certain $\mathbb{Z}_m$-linear map, are possible in a direct and efficient manner, without the need to "emulate" arithmetic using existing field-based techniques.

Our techniques inherit all the "plug & play" applications of [3], and in particular, they can be used in a wide range of settings in which Σ-protocols prove useful, without the restriction of having a prime modulus. As an example of this, we show in Sect. 6 an application to the domain of efficient verifiable computation schemes on encrypted data, where [13] offered a framework that can deal efficiently with the general case in which the ciphertext space of the homomorphic encryption scheme is a polynomial ring with coefficients in a ring $\mathbb{Z}_m$. Some of their constructions require commit-and-prove arguments for certain statements (mainly linear) defined over $\mathbb{Z}_m$ and over extension Galois rings. They leave open the existence of succinct arguments that work directly over such rings. Our results are well suited for this application and can be directly plugged in that framework.

At a high level, our results are obtained as a combination of the following two main contributions.

Compact Vector Commitments over $\mathbb{Z}_m$. One of the core ingredients in the context of zero-knowledge proofs, and in particular [3], are *(vector) commitment schemes* allowing a prover to commit to long vectors of (secret) information.[2] These must be homomorphic over the given algebraic domain, which is $\mathbb{Z}_m$ for an arbitrary integer m in our setting. In [3] different instantiations of this construction are considered, namely Pedersen commitments and also RSA-based commitments. However, these constructions are restricted to m being a prime, and, besides a few exceptions that will be discussed in Sect. 1.2 below, no construction of a compact vector commitment scheme with homomorphism over $\mathbb{Z}_m$ for an arbitrary m is known. To tackle this issue we present in Sect. 4, as a contribution of potential independent interest, an efficient construction of said commitment schemes. This is achieved by first abstracting and generalizing a template present in several previous schemes like Pedersen's to obtain a compact vector commitment scheme from a single-value construction, and then focusing on instantiating the latter type of commitments. Simply using homomorphic commitments over the integers, such as the one by Damgård and Fujisaki [26], does not achieve the properties needed for their application in the context of Σ-protocols: we need to guarantee that opening a commitment to a linear combination *modulo m* of committed messages does not reveal any additional information about the initial messages. Integer commitments would reveal too much, namely the same linear combination over $\mathbb{Z}$. Instead, we show a construction where, depending on the parity of m, we either rely on the hardness of finding roots over RSA groups, or factoring.

Compressing Mechanism over $\mathbb{Z}_m$. In order to compress a basic three-move Σ-protocol, the work of [3] resorts to using an efficient proof of knowledge to handle the last message in such a protocol, which constitutes the prover's response to the verifier's challenge. In [3], the proof of knowledge used is an adaptation of Bulletproof's folding technique [14,15]. This is not restricted to finite fields per

---

[2] We note that [18] additionally requires a vector commitment scheme to admit a protocol for opening individual coordinates of the committed vector. We do not impose this requirement and refer to a *vector* commitment scheme simply as a scheme for committing to vectors.

se, but it does require large enough *exceptional sets*, also known as *challenge sets*, for it to obtain reasonably small soundness error. If m is prime, and in general, if m does not have small prime factors, then such sets over $\mathbb{Z}_m$ exist, but if m is divisible by a small prime then this does not hold. To address this issue, we resort to considering ring extensions of the form $\mathbb{Z}_m[X]/(f(X))$ for a polynomial $f(X)$, which increases the sizes of the required exceptional sets. We show in Sect. 5 that our commitment construction is compatible with this type of arithmetic, and that this leads to a natural adaptation of the results from [3] from the field setting to $\mathbb{Z}_m$, for an arbitrary m.

1.2 Related Work

Compressed Σ-protocol theory [3] presents a Σ-protocol for proving knowledge that a vector underlying a given commitment satisfies certain linear relation. The linear communication complexity of this initial Σ-protocol is then compressed down to logarithmic by adapting the techniques from [14,15]. Additionally, in [3] it is shown how to linearize non-linear relations, showing that arbitrary NP statements can be proven with logarithmic communication complexity by using compressed Σ-protocols. As we have already mentioned, the techniques in the references cited above are mostly suitable when the computation domain is a finite field $\mathbb{Z}_q$.

An instantiation of compressed Σ-protocol theory in the context of lattices is presented in [4]. Lattice-based (compressed) Σ-protocols allow provers to prove knowledge of a *short* homomorphism preimage, i.e., a preimage of bounded norm. However, these protocols have the additional complication that the norm bound β of the secret witness, known by an honest prover, differs from the norm bound $\tau \cdot \beta$ that the prover ends up proving. The factor τ is referred to as the *soundness slack*. In most practical scenarios, this relaxed functionality is sufficient. However, due to the soundness slack, lattice-based compressed Σ-protocols have polylogarithmic, instead of logarithmic, communication complexity. More precisely, lattice-based compressed Σ-protocols require the prover to send logarithmically many messages to the verifier, but due to the soundness slack, which grows with the size of the witness, larger protocol parameters are warranted. For this reason, the size of individual messages grows (logarithmically) with the size of the witness. These complications would be attenuated by using ring extensions as we do here, so their techniques do not directly fit our purpose.

Further, [16] presents an adaptation of Bulletproofs defined over the integers $\mathbb{Z}$. Their techniques allow a prover to prove knowledge of a vector of *bounded* integers satisfying arbitrary constraints captured by a circuit over $\mathbb{Z}$. However, Block et al. [12] recently found a gap in the analysis of [16]. A non-trivial adaptation, increasing the communication complexity from logarithmic to polylogarithmic, was required to overcome this issue [12].

By appropriately encoding vectors $\mathbf{x} \in \mathbb{Z}_m^n$ as (bounded) integers, we thus obtain a zero-knowledge proof system for relations defined over the ring $\mathbb{Z}_m$ for an arbitrary $m \in \mathbb{N}$. However, this indirect approach results in polylogarithmic communication complexity, while our construction works directly over $\mathbb{Z}_m$

and achieves $\mathcal{O}(\log n \log \log n)$ communication complexity. Moreover, it cannot harness the efficiency improvements foreseen when the arithmetic takes place in rings $\mathbb{Z}_m$, with $m = 2^{64}$ or $m = 2^{128}$, corresponding to machine computations. These efficiency improvements have already been demonstrated in multiparty computation applications [23,25], and in zero-knowledge proof systems [6].

Zero knowledge for more general rings has not been studied in great detail, to the best of our knowledge. The only works we are aware of are Rinocchio [30], which presents a succinct non-interactive arguments of knowledge (SNARK) protocol for statements represented as circuits over general commutative rings having large enough exceptional sets, and the "Appenzeller to Brie" zero-knowledge protocol from [7]. None of these works are based on Σ-protocols.

Finally, in terms of homomorphic and compact vector commitments, to the best of our knowledge, no previous work has tackled the case in which the underlying algebraic structure is $\mathbb{Z}_m$, for an arbitrary m. Most existing constructions only work for m a prime, as is the case with Pedersen commitments [41] and also constructions based on homomorphic encryption such as ElGamal [27]. Furthermore, schemes such as Paillier [40] or Okamoto-Uchiyama [39] operate over non-prime modulus, but these are still very structured (e.g., $N = PQ$ or $N = P^2Q$). Even many lattice-based homomorphic commitments such as [8,11] require a prime modulus so that their associated algebraic structure factors nicely. Homomorphic commitments over $\mathbb{Z}_{2^k}$ exist, such as the Joye-Libert construction [38], but it is not clear how to generalize this approach to other m and moreover it requires RSA moduli whose bitlength is linear on k, while in our instantiation we use standard RSA moduli of length independent of k.

2   Technical Overview

As a starting point, we begin with the theory of compressed Σ-protocols presented in [3], and analyze in detail which parts are inherently dependent on the underlying algebraic structure being $\mathbb{Z}_p$ for a prime number p. Let us begin with a short overview of the techniques in [3], which will be followed by the aforementioned analysis.

Overview of the Techniques in [3]. The basic "pivot" presented in [3], from which most of their results are derived, is a Σ-protocol that enables a prover to convince a verifier that, given a commitment and certain value, he knows how to open that commitment to a vector that maps, under a some public linear mapping, to the given value. More precisely, let $\mathbb{G}$ be a finite abelian group of prime order q. Let P be a *Pedersen commitment* $P = h^\gamma \prod_{i=1}^n g_i^{x_i}$ to a vector $\mathbf{x} = (x_1, \ldots, x_n) \in \mathbb{Z}_q^n$, where the $g_1, \ldots, g_n, h$ are uniformly random elements from $\mathbb{G}$ sampled in a setup phase. Also, let $L : \mathbb{Z}_q^n \to \mathbb{Z}_q$ be a linear form, and let $y \in \mathbb{Z}_q$ be a given value. The authors of [3] devise a communication efficient Σ-protocol that enables a prover to prove knowledge of $\mathbf{x}$, the vector underlying the commitment P, while proving that this vector satisfies $L(\mathbf{x}) = y$. At a high level, such protocol is achieved by first considering a basic and natural three-move Σ-protocol for this relation, which would involve the prover sending a long response to the challenge provided by the verifier, and then optimizing this last step by making use of a more efficient proof of knowledge of this response, which is derived from the techniques in Bulletproofs [14,15].

The basic three-move Σ-protocol looks as follows:

1. The prover samples $\mathbf{r} \leftarrow \mathbb{Z}_q^n$ and $\rho \leftarrow \mathbb{Z}_q$, and sends $t = L(\mathbf{r})$ and $A = h^\rho \prod_{i=1}^n g_i^{r_i}$ to the verifier;
2. The verifier samples a challenge $c \leftarrow \mathbb{Z}_q$ to the prover;
3. The prover responds with $\mathbf{z} = c\mathbf{x} + \mathbf{r}$ and $\phi = c\gamma + \rho$, and the verifier checks that $h^\phi \prod_{i=1}^n g_i^{z_i} = AP^c$ and $L(\mathbf{z}) = cy + t$.

In the second part, instead of the prover sending $\mathbf{z}$ and ϕ as the last step of the protocol above, the prover uses a more efficient proof of knowledge to prove to the verifier that he knows $\mathbf{z}$ and ϕ satisfying $h^\phi \prod_{i=1}^n g_i^{z_i} = AP^c$ and $L(\mathbf{z}) = cy + t$. This proof has logarithmic (in n) communication complexity, and it is based on the core pivot of the Bulletproof protocol [14,15]. It is quite difficult to provide a general intuition on these techniques in a few paragraphs but, in a nutshell, they consist of splitting the data into two halves, and combining them via a new challenge that makes it hard for the prover to cheat. This can be recursed to obtain logarithmic communication.

Dependencies on $\mathbb{Z}_q$ for a Prime q. At this point, we can identify two main locations in the protocol from [3] that seem to depend heavily on the algebraic structure being $\mathbb{Z}_q$ for a prime q.

- *Challenges and soundness.* To ensure low cheating probability, challenges are sampled by the verifier to somehow "randomize" the response the prover needs to provide. Ultimately, to show special soundness, one must show that successfully replying to multiple challenges enables us to extract a witness. This is typically done by solving a linear equation, or more generally, a set of linear equations. Such approach proves difficult when not operating over a field given the lack of invertible elements.
- *Homomorphic commitments.* The techniques from [3] depend on a commitment scheme that is homomorphic over the desired algebraic structure. We considered above Pedersen commitments, but the results from [3] include other constructions whose security depends on different assumptions such as Strong RSA and Knowledge-of-Exponent, and Lattices were considered in [4]. All of these techniques, however, require a specific type of modulus. For instance, Pedersen commitments are defined over cyclic groups, and the construction from [3] based on the Strong RSA assumption only allows for RSA moduli.

Our Approach to Extend to $\mathbb{Z}_m$ for Any m

- *Challenges and soundness.* Fortunately, we can address the issue of soundness and non-invertibility by sampling challenges from an *exceptional set*, which consists of elements whose non-zero pairwise differences are invertible. This approach has been used in quite a few works in the context of secure multiparty computation [1], but also recently in zero-knowledge proofs [30]. For some choices of m, $\mathbb{Z}_m$ may not admit large enough exceptional sets, but this can be fixed by considering a ring extension of $\mathbb{Z}_m$ of large enough degree.

– *Homomorphic commitments.* Arguably, the biggest difficulty in extending the techniques in [3] to any ring of the form $\mathbb{Z}_m$ lies in efficiently and securely instantiating the homomorphic commitment scheme used to hide/bind the vectors on which statements are proved. Traditionally, most commitment schemes that support any notion of homomorphism, do so modulo very structured integers. For example, constructions based on discrete-log-type assumptions typically work modulo a prime, since operations are carried out over a cyclic group. Alternatively, systems based on RSA-type assumptions tend to operate either modulo a prime, or modulo products of two primes.

To address this difficulty we present, as a contribution of potential independent interest, a novel construction of a vector commitment scheme that is homomorphic modulo m, for an *arbitrary* integer m. Our construction follows a two-step approach. First, we show how to derive a compact vector commitment scheme from any single-value commitment scheme. This consists, in a nutshell, of committing using the single-value scheme to a uniformly random linear combination of the coordinates of the desired vector, making sure to randomize the commitment with a commitment to zero. This approach is already present in other compact commitment schemes such as Pedersen's, and in this work we present an abstraction of this "compactification" technique, together with a generalization to the setting in which the modulus is any integer m.

Second, we provide an instantiation for the homomorphic single-value commitment scheme. We provide two constructions depending on the parity of m. For odd m we propose a generic template based on what we call *commitment-friendly groups*, which are essentially groups where exponentiating to all primes dividing m leads to a collision-resistant function. These groups can be used to obtain a single-value commitment scheme defined as $\mathrm{COM}_{\mathsf{pk}=a}(x, r) = (a^m)^x r^m$. This is clearly hiding, and it can be proven to be binding under the assumption that p-th roots are hard to find, for any prime p dividing m. Furthermore, we instantiate commitment-friendly groups with an RSA group $\mathbb{Z}_N^*$.

The template above does not directly work for m even given that the resulting group cannot be commitment-friendly: raising to a square power clearly leads to collisions since $x^2 = (-x)^2$. To address this complication, we instead work on a subgroup of $\mathbb{Z}_N^*$, containing all elements in $\mathbb{Z}_N^*$ having Jacobi symbol 1. This way, even though it still holds that $x^2 = (-x)^2$ in this group, we can carefully choose N in such a way that this does not play any effect into the binding property.

3   Preliminaries

Some General Notation. Let m be a positive integer. The ring of integers modulo m is denoted by $\mathbb{Z}_m$. Vectors are denoted by bold letters, like $\mathbf{x}$ and $\mathbf{y}$, and their coordinates will be denoted by the same letter with normal font, e.g. x_i and y_i.

The notation $\mathbf{x} + \mathbf{y} \bmod m$ represents addition modulo m coordinate-wise. We will omit the "mod m" when it is clear from context. Given a finite set A, $a \leftarrow A$ denotes sampling a uniformly random value a from A.

3.1   Vector Commitments

At a high level, a vector commitment over $\mathbb{Z}_m^n$ enables a party to compute some data from an n-dimensional vector over $\mathbb{Z}_m$ in such a way that (1) the derived data does not reveal anything about the original vector and (2) if the party decides to "open" the vector (e.g. announce it to other parties) at a later point, then the additional computed data ensures he cannot "change his mind" by announcing a different vector.

Definition 1 (Vector commitments). *A homomorphic vector commitment scheme for $\mathbb{Z}_m^n$ is a tuple $(\mathcal{G}, \mathrm{COM}, R)$, where $\mathcal{G}$ is a probabilistic polynomial time algorithm, called the key generation algorithm, and COM, R are polynomial time computable functions, satisfying the following syntax.*

- $\mathcal{G}(m, n, \kappa)$ *outputs a public key* pk.
- COM_{pk} *takes as input the public key* pk, *a vector* $\mathbf{x} \in \mathbb{Z}_m^n$ *and a uniformly random r sampled from $\mathcal{R}$, and produces a string c. We assume that the image. of COM_{pk} is a finite group, and that the group operation (for which we use multiplication notation) can be computed efficiently given* pk.
- R_{pk} *takes as input the public key* pk *and produces as output an element of $\mathcal{R}$. It receives different possible inputs which will be clarified below. We abbreviate by R when clear from the context.*

Let pk $\leftarrow \mathcal{G}(m, n, \kappa)$. *We require the following properties.*

- **Perfect Hiding.** *For any $\mathbf{x}, \mathbf{x}' \in \mathbb{Z}_m^n$, the distributions of $\mathrm{COM}_{pk}(\mathbf{x}, r)$ and $\mathrm{COM}_{pk}(\mathbf{x}', r')$ for uniformly random $r, r' \in \mathcal{R}$ are identical.*
- **Computational Binding.** *For any PPT A, consider the following experiment: Send* pk *to A, who wins the game if it outputs $(\mathbf{x}, r, \mathbf{x}', r')$ such that $\mathbf{x} \neq \mathbf{x}'$ and $\mathrm{COM}_{pk}(\mathbf{x}, r) = \mathrm{COM}_{pk}(\mathbf{x}', r')$. Then A wins with negligible probability (over the choice of* pk *and the random coins of A).*
- **Homomorphic property.** *It holds that[3] $\mathrm{COM}_{pk}(\mathbf{x}, r) \cdot \mathrm{COM}_{pk}(\mathbf{x}', r') = \mathrm{COM}_{pk}(\mathbf{x} + \mathbf{x}', R(\mathbf{x}, \mathbf{x}', r, r'))$, and $\mathrm{COM}_{pk}(\mathbf{x}, r)^{-1} = \mathrm{COM}_{pk}(-\mathbf{x}, R(\mathbf{x}, -1, r))$.*
- **Randomized property.** *For any $\mathbf{x}', \mathbf{x} \in \mathbb{Z}_m^n$, if at least one of r or r' is chosen uniformly at random in $\mathcal{R}$, then $R(\mathbf{x}, \mathbf{x}', r, r')$ is uniform in $\mathcal{R}$.*

Note that the homomorphic property implies that for commitment $c = \mathrm{COM}_{pk}(\mathbf{x}, r)$ and integer a, c^a can be opened as $a \cdot \mathbf{x}$ (modulo m). We write the associated randomness as $R(\mathbf{x}, a, r)$, i.e., $\mathrm{COM}_{pk}(\mathbf{x}, r)^a = \mathrm{COM}_{pk}(a \cdot \mathbf{x}, R(\mathbf{x}, a, r))$. On the other hand, the randomization property will enable us to randomize commitments by multiplying by a random commitment: if one opens a product commitment $\mathrm{COM}_{pk}(\mathbf{x} + \mathbf{x}', R(\mathbf{x}, \mathbf{x}', r, r'))$, then, as long as one of r, r' is uniform,

---

[3] Note that we allow the R-function to take both 1 (zero-openings), 3 and 4 arguments.

the only information this reveals on $\mathbf{x}, \mathbf{x}'$ is $\mathbf{x} + \mathbf{x}' \bmod m$. The combination of these two facts will be essential in the Sigma-protocols where, given a commitment to secret $\mathbf{x}$, the prover first commits to random $\mathbf{x}'$ and then opens $\mathbf{x} + a \cdot \mathbf{x}'$ for challenge a. This should not give information about $\mathbf{x}$. We remark that using an *integer* commitment such as the one in [26] falls short in our scenario for a similar reason: given commitments to $\mathbf{x}, \mathbf{x}'$ opening their sum over $\mathbb{Z}$, $\mathbf{x} + \mathbf{x}'$, reveals more information about $\mathbf{x}, \mathbf{x}'$ than opening $\mathbf{x} + \mathbf{x}' \bmod m$.

Single-Value Commitment. We consider the notion of single-value commitment scheme. A single-value commitment scheme is a vector commitment scheme that only allows $n = 1$. However, for our needs, we impose the following additional condition on single-value commitment schemes.

Definition 2. *A single-value homomorphic commitment scheme for $\mathbb{Z}_m$ is a homomorphic vector commitment scheme for $\mathbb{Z}_m^n$ that only allows $n = 1$, and has the following additional property.*

- **Zero-commitment opening.** *For any single-value commitment c, the commitment c^m can be opened as zero. More specifically, we have that[4] $c^m = \mathrm{COM}_{\mathsf{pk}}(0, R(c))$.*

This property implies that c^m can be opened by a party who possibly did not create c. The fact that c^m is a commitment to 0 is already implied by the homomorphic property implies given that, if $c = \mathrm{COM}_{\mathsf{pk}}(\mathbf{x}, r)$, then $c^m = \mathrm{COM}_{\mathsf{pk}}(m \cdot \mathbf{x}, R(\mathbf{x}, m, r)) = \mathrm{COM}_{\mathsf{pk}}(\mathbf{0}, R(\mathbf{x}, m, r))$; but the above property further ensures that the corresponding randomness can be derived from c alone. Intuitively, the reason why this property is needed is the following. The commitment schemes we consider in this work are homomorphic modulo m, i.e. their message space forms a module over $\mathbb{Z}_m$, and (linear) operations over commitments should correspond to the analogue operations over the message space. Nevertheless, we are only assuming that the set in which the commitments live is a finite group, and we do not assume anything about its order. The zero-commitment property ensures that, even though this group's exponent may not be a divisor of m (so c^m may not equal the identity of the group), raising to m still leads to commitments that can be easily dealt with. We use this property, for example, in Theorem 2 when we prove the homomorphic property of our vector commitment scheme.

3.2 Interactive Proofs

In this work we consider interactive proofs that, given an NP-relation R, enable a prover to prove, to a verifier, knowledge of a witness w with respect to a given statement x, i.e., $(x; w) \in R$. In this work we consider *public coin* interactive proofs in which the messages sampled by the verifier are uniformly random.

---

[4] Here we, once again, abuse notation and let R take a commitment as input.

An interactive proof is (perfectly) *complete* (or satisfies *completeness*) if for all inputs $(x; w)$, if $(x; w) \in R$, then the verifier outputs accept with probability 1. Further, informally, an interactive proof is said to be knowledge sound with knowledge error κ if a dishonest prover without knowledge of a witness can not succeed is convincing the verifier with probability larger than κ. For a formal definition we refer to [33].

We also consider the notion of $(k_1, \dots, k_\mu)$-special-soundness or more precisely $(k_1, \dots, k_\mu)$-out-of-$(N_1, \dots, N_\mu)$ special-soundness. We follow the notation of [4]. To this end, let $(\mathcal{P}, \mathcal{V})$ be a $(2\mu + 1)$-move public-coin interactive proof. Moreover, we assume the verifier to sample its i-th challenge from a challenge set $\mathcal{C}_i$ of cardinality N_i. The following defines a $(k_1, \dots, k_\mu)$-tree of transcripts for $(\mathcal{P}, \mathcal{V})$ to be a set of $K = k_1 \cdots k_\mu$ protocol transcripts of the form $(a_1, c_1, a_2, \dots, c_\mu, a_{\mu+1})$ that are in a certain tree structure. For a graphical representation see [4].

Definition 3 (Tree of Transcripts). *Let $k_1, \dots, k_\mu \in \mathbb{N}$. A $(k_1, \dots, k_\mu)$-tree of transcripts for a $(2\mu + 1)$-move public-coin protocol $(\mathcal{P}, \mathcal{V})$ is a set of $K = \prod_{i=1}^\mu k_i$ transcripts arranged in the following tree structure. The nodes in this tree correspond to the prover's messages and the edges to the verifier's challenges. Every node at depth i has precisely k_i children corresponding to k_i pairwise distinct challenges. Every transcript corresponds to exactly one path from the root node to a leaf node.*

Definition 4 ($(k_1, \dots, k_\mu)$-out-of-$(N_1, \dots, N_\mu)$ Special-Soundness). *A $(2\mu + 1)$-move public-coin protocol $(\mathcal{P}, \mathcal{V})$ for relation R, where $\mathcal{V}$ samples the i-th challenge from a set of cardinality $N_i \geq k_i$ for $1 \leq i \leq \mu$, is $(k_1, \dots, k_\mu)$-out-of-$(N_1, \dots, N_\mu)$ special-sound if there exists a polynomial time algorithm that, on input a statement x and a $(k_1, \dots, k_\mu)$-tree of accepting transcripts outputs a witness w such that $(x; w) \in R$. We also say $(\mathcal{P}, \mathcal{V})$ is $(k_1, \dots, k_\mu)$-special-sound.*

It is well known that, for 3-move protocols, k-special-soundness implies knowledge soundness, but only recently it was shown that more generally, for public-coin $(2\mu + 1)$-move protocols, $(k_1, \dots, k_\mu)$-special-soundness tightly implies knowledge soundness [4].

Theorem 1 [4]. *A $(k_1, \dots, k_\mu)$-out-of-$(N_1, \dots, N_\mu)$ special-sound interactive proof is knowledge sound with knowledge error*

$$\kappa = 1 - \prod_{i=1}^{\mu}\left(1 - \frac{k_i - 1}{N_i}\right).$$

With regards to zero-knowledge, as typical with Σ-protocols, we restrict our attention to *special honest-verifier zero-knowledge* (SHVZK), which requires that, given a statement x and a set of uniformly random verifier messages, it is possible to produce (without knowing any witness) an accepting transcript that follows the same distribution as an honest interaction between the prover and the verifier.

4   Vector Commitments over $\mathbb{Z}_m$

In this section we present one of our main contributions, namely the construction of a compact modulo-m homomorphic vector commitment scheme. In Sect. 4.1 we show a generic method to obtain a compact vector commitment scheme from *any* single-value commitment scheme. In Sect. 4.2, we present a construction of a single-value commitment scheme based on what we call commitment friendly groups. We also present an instantiation of commitment friendly groups that, unfortunately, is restricted to odd values of m, since a similar instantiation for even m would require an expensive set-up. To address this issue, we present in Sect. 4.3 a construction of single-value commitment schemes for the case in which m is even.

4.1   Vector Commitments from Single-Value Commitments

Let $(\mathcal{G}', \text{COM}', R')$ be a single-value commitment scheme for $\mathbb{Z}_m$. The goal of this section is to derive from this scheme, for any integer $n > 0$, a compact vector commitment scheme $(\mathcal{G}, \text{COM}, R)$. At a high level, our construction generalizes the approach followed in Pedersen's construction to obtain compact commitments to long vectors, by taking a "random linear combination in the exponent".

$\mathsf{VC}_{m,n}$: Vector Commitment Scheme for $\mathbb{Z}_m^n$

$(\mathcal{G}', \text{COM}', R')$ is a single-value commitment scheme for elements over $\mathbb{Z}_m$

- $\mathcal{G}$, on input n, m, κ, proceeds as follows.
  1. Run $\mathsf{pk}' = \mathcal{G}'(m, \kappa)$.
  2. For $i = 1, \ldots, n$, sample $a_i \leftarrow \mathbb{Z}_m$ and $r_i \leftarrow R$. Set $g_i = \text{COM}'_{\mathsf{pk}'}(a_i, r_i)$
  3. Output $\mathsf{pk} = (\mathsf{pk}', g_1, \ldots, g_n)$.
- Given $\mathbf{x} = (x_1, \ldots, x_n)$ and $r \in R$ as input, COM_{pk} outputs $\text{COM}'_{\mathsf{pk}'}(0, r) \cdot \prod_{i=1}^n g_i^{x_i}$.

We remark that in some cases, including our instantiations, the g_i's can be sampled obliviously (without knowing a_i) and hence without a trusted set-up. As we shall see in a moment, there is a very efficient reduction that shows that the binding property holds in $\mathsf{VC}_{m,n}$, assuming that it holds on the underlying single-value commitment scheme, with only a $1/2$ factor loss (which is independent of n) in terms of the success probability of the adversary attacking the binding property, i.e., the adversary trying to output two different openings for the same commitment. In addition, observe that the vector commitment scheme $\mathsf{VC}_{m,n}$ is compact, given that a commitment is made of a homomorphic combination of single-value commitments.

Theorem 2. *When based on a single-value homomorphic commitment scheme for $\mathbb{Z}_m$ satisfying Definition 2, $\mathsf{VC}_{m,n}$ is a homomorphic vector commitment scheme for $\mathbb{Z}_m^n$, according to Definition 1.*

Proof. To see that the perfect hiding property holds, begin by observing that, by construction of the g_i's and the homomorphic property of the single value scheme, we have $\mathrm{COM}_{\mathsf{pk}}(\mathbf{x}, r) = \mathrm{COM}'_{\mathsf{pk}'}\left(\sum_{i=1}^{n} a_i x_i, s\right) \cdot \mathrm{COM}'_{\mathsf{pk}'}(0, r)$, for some s that can be computed by applying the R-function of the single value scheme several times on inputs $\mathbf{x}$ and $r_1, \ldots, r_n$. Perfect hiding now follows immediately from the perfect hiding property of the underlying single-value scheme, together with its randomization property, which ensures that the randomness appearing in the overall commitment above is uniformly random.

For the the binding property, assume the existence of an adversary A that wins the binding experiment for $\mathsf{VC}_{m,n}$ with probability ϵ. We will show that such an adversary can be used to build an adversary B that breaks binding experiment of the original single-value scheme with probability at least $\epsilon/2$. Since ϵ is negligible, given that the underlying single-value scheme satisfies the binding property, we obtain that $\mathsf{VC}_{m,n}$ satisfies the property as well.

We define the algorithm B as follows. B gets a public key pk' as input, and then expands this to a public key $\mathsf{pk} = (\mathsf{pk}', g_1, \ldots, g_n)$ following the definition of $\mathcal{G}$. Then B runs A on input pk. Now, assume that A wins, which means that A outputs $(\mathbf{x}, r, \mathbf{x}', r')$ with $\mathbf{x} \neq \mathbf{x}'$ and $\mathrm{COM}_{\mathsf{pk}}(\mathbf{x}, r) = \mathrm{COM}_{\mathsf{pk}}(\mathbf{x}', r')$. As we did with the hiding property, we can write both sides of the expression above in terms of single-value commitments, as follows: the left-hand side equals

$$\mathrm{COM}'_{\mathsf{pk}'}\left(\sum_{i=1}^{n} a_i x_i, s\right) \cdot \mathrm{COM}'_{\mathsf{pk}'}(0, r),$$

while the right-hand side is

$$\mathrm{COM}'_{\mathsf{pk}'}\left(\sum_{i=1}^{n} a_i x_i', s'\right) \cdot \mathrm{COM}'_{\mathsf{pk}'}(0, r')$$

for values s, s' that can be efficiently computed. Using the homomorphic property of the original scheme once more, we get

$$\mathrm{COM}'_{\mathsf{pk}'}\left(\sum_{i=1}^{n} a_i x_i, R'\left(\sum_{i=1}^{n} a_i x_i, 0, s, r\right)\right) = \mathrm{COM}'_{\mathsf{pk}'}\left(\sum_{i=1}^{n} a_i x_i', R'\left(\sum_{i=1}^{n} a_i x_i', 0, s', r'\right)\right).$$

If $\sum_i a_i x_i \neq \sum_i a_i x_i' \bmod m$, this clearly means that B can break binding of the original scheme by outputting these values together with the corresponding randomness used for the commitments above. To finish the proof of our main claim, it suffices then to show that $\sum_i a_i x_i \neq \sum_i a_i x'_i \bmod m$ happens with probability at least $1/2$.

To see this, assume that $\sum_i a_i(x_i - x'_i) = 0 \bmod m$. Since we are assuming that A wins, we have $x_{i_0} - x'_{i_0} \neq 0 \bmod m$ for some i_0. From this, it must be the case that $x_{i_0} - x'_{i_0} \neq 0 \bmod p$ for at least one prime factor p in m. Additionally, notice that $\sum_{i=1}^{n} a_i(x_i - x'_i) = 0 \bmod p$, given that the corresponding congruence holds modulo m, so we can rewrite $a_{i_0} = -(x_{i_0} - x'_{i_0})^{-1} \cdot \sum_{i \neq i_0} a_i(x_i - x'_i) \bmod p$. Now, notice that by the hiding property of the single-value scheme, the g_i's included in the public key of $VC_{m,n}$ follow a distribution that is independent of the a_i's, so, in particular, the $x_i - x'_i$ values produced by A are independent of these a_i's. From this, we see that the right-hand side of the previous expression is independent of the left-hand side, which is uniformly random, so the probability of this equation being satisfied is at most $1/p$, or, in other words, B wins the binding experiment with probability $1 - 1/p \geq 1 - 1/2 = 1/2$. This implies that B succeeds with an overall probability of at least $\epsilon/2$, which proves the binding property of the vector commitment scheme.

To establish the homomorphic property, consider commitments

$$\text{COM}_{\text{pk}}(\mathbf{x}, r) = \text{COM}'_{\text{pk}'}(0, r) \cdot \prod_{i=1}^{n} g_i^{x_i}$$

and

$$\text{COM}_{\text{pk}}(\mathbf{x}', r') = \text{COM}'_{\text{pk}'}(0, r') \cdot \prod_{i=1}^{n} g_i^{x'_i}.$$

Using the homomorphic property of the single-value scheme, we can write

$$\text{COM}_{\text{pk}}(\mathbf{x}, r) \cdot \text{COM}_{\text{pk}}(\mathbf{x}', r') = \prod_{i=1}^{n} g_i^{x_i + x'_i} \cdot \text{COM}'_{\text{pk}'}(0, r) \cdot \text{COM}'_{\text{pk}'}(0, r')$$

$$= \prod_{i=1}^{n} g_i^{x_i + x'_i} \cdot \text{COM}'_{\text{pk}'}(0, R'(0, 0, r, r'))$$

$$= \prod_{i=1}^{n} g_i^{x_i + x'_i \bmod m} g_i^{\ell_i m} \cdot \text{COM}'_{\text{pk}'}(0, R'(0, 0, r, r')),$$

where ℓ_i is defined by $x_i + x'_i = ((x_i + x'_i) \bmod m) + \ell_i m$. Now, recall that the zero-commitment opening property from Definition 2 of the single-value commitment scheme enables, for any commitment c, to open c^m to zero. Since $g_i^{\ell_i}$ is a valid commitment (to $\ell_i \cdot a_i \bmod m$, but this is irrelevant), we have that $(g_i^{\ell_i})^m = \text{COM}'_{\text{pk}'}(0, R'(g_i^{\ell_i}))$. Inserting this in the above is easily seen to imply that

$$\text{COM}_{\text{pk}}(\mathbf{x}, r) \cdot \text{COM}_{\text{pk}}(\mathbf{x}', r')$$

$$= \prod_{i=1}^{n} g_i^{x_i + x_i' \bmod m} \text{COM}_{\text{pk}'}'(0, R'(g_i^{\ell_i})) \cdot \text{COM}_{\text{pk}'}'(0, R'(0, 0, r, r'))$$

$$= \prod_{i=1}^{n} g_i^{x_i + x_i' \bmod m} \text{COM}_{\text{pk}'}'(0, s) = \text{COM}_{\text{pk}}(\mathbf{x} + \mathbf{x}', s),$$

for some $s \in \mathcal{R}$ that can be computed by applying the randomness function R' of the single value scheme several times on inputs $\mathbf{x}, \mathbf{x}', r, r', g_1, \ldots, g_n$. This (implicitly) defines the randomness function R of the vector scheme. In a very similar way, one proves that $\text{COM}_{\text{pk}}(\mathbf{x}, r)^{-1}$ can be opened as $-\mathbf{x} \bmod m$. Namely, if we insert the expression for $\text{COM}_{\text{pk}}(\mathbf{x}, r)$, we get $-x_i$'s appearing in the exponent, but these are equal to $-x_i \bmod m$ except for a multiple of m which can "absorbed" into the randomness factor in the commitment using the zero-commitment opening property.

The randomization property follows immediately from the randomization property of the original scheme. $\square$

4.2   Single-Value Commitments via Commitment Friendly Groups

Commitment Friendly Groups. We will assume we have a PPT algorithm $\mathcal{GG}$ which, on input m and security parameter κ, outputs a finite Abelian group G, whose order does not have to be related to m. For a prime p dividing m, consider the function $\phi_p \colon G \mapsto G$ given by $\phi_p(g) = g^p$, where p is a prime factor in m.

Definition 5 (Commitment friendly groups). *We say that $\mathcal{GG}$ is commitment friendly if for all primes $p \mid m$, the following holds:*

1. *ϕ_p is collision intractable, i.e., it is hard to find $g \neq g'$ such that $\phi_p(g) = \phi_p(g')$. More formally, for any PPT algorithm A, the experiment where $\mathcal{GG}$ is run on input (m, κ) to get G, and then A is run on input G will result in a collision with negligible probability.*
2. *Let $G^m = \{a^m \mid a \in G\}$, which is a subgroup of G. For uniformly random $g \in G^m$, it is hard to find $h \in G$ with $\phi_p(h) = g$. More formally, for any PPT A, the experiment where $\mathcal{GG}$ is run on input (m, κ) to get G, g is sampled at random in G^m, and A is run on input (G, g), will result in a p'th root of g only with negligible probability.*

G can reasonably be conjectured to be commitment friendly if computing the order of G is hard, which can be the case if G is a class group or an RSA group, as we discuss in more detail later. Indeed, if $\phi_p(g) = \phi_p(g')$ and $g \neq g'$, then the order of $g'g^{-1}$ is p, and finding such an element can be conjectured hard if the order of G is not known. More precisely, finding an element of known order p immediately reveals that p is a divisor of the group order. This contradicts the assumption that the order of the group is unknown. Moreover, notice that ϕ_p is collision intractable if $\gcd(p, |G|) = 1$, since in this case ϕ_p is injective.

Commitments from Commitment Friendly Groups. We now construct a single value commitment scheme for $\mathbb{Z}_m$, assuming a generator algorithm $\mathcal{GG}$ for commitment friendly groups.

SV_m: Single-Value Commitment Scheme over $\mathbb{Z}_m$

- *Key generation.* Run $\mathcal{GG}$ on input m and κ to get G. Let $g = a^m$ for a uniformly random $a \in G$. Return $\mathsf{pk} = (G, g)$.
- *Commitment.* Set $\mathcal{R} = G$ and compute $\mathrm{COM}_{\mathsf{pk}}(x, r) = g^x r^m$.

Intuitively, the commitment is hiding because r^m is uniformly random in G^m, the group where the commitments takes values, and it is binding because of the required properties on ϕ_p for all $p|m$: in a nutshell, for any $x \neq x' \bmod m$ there is some prime power p^ℓ dividing m and not (the integer) $x - x'$. In these conditions, we show in the proof of Theorem 3 below that given openings to both x and x', and if ϕ_p is collision intractable, then one can extract s with $\phi_p(s) = g$, contradicting the second property, since g is uniform in G^m.

Theorem 3. SV_m *is a single-value commitment scheme over $\mathbb{Z}_m$.*

Proof. First, observe that the perfect hiding and randomization properties follow immediately from the fact that a commitment to any value is a uniformly random element in G^m.

The homomorphic property follows from

$$\mathrm{COM}_{\mathsf{pk}}(x, r)\mathrm{COM}_{\mathsf{pk}}(x', r') = g^{x+x'}(rr')^m = g^{x+x' \bmod m}(g^t rr')^m =$$
$$\mathrm{COM}_{\mathsf{pk}}(x + x' \bmod m, g^t rr'),$$

where t is defined by $x + x' = ((x + x') \bmod m) + tm$. So we can set $R(x, x', r, r') = g^t rr'$.

Likewise, we have that $\mathrm{COM}_{\mathsf{pk}}(x, r)^{-1} = g^{-x}(r^{-1})^m$, which in turn equals $g^{-x \bmod m}(g^\ell r^{-1})^m$, where ℓ is defined by $-x = (-x \bmod m) + \ell m$, so we set $R(x, -1, r) = g^\ell r^{-1}$. Also, the zero-opening property follows trivially since $\mathrm{COM}_{\mathsf{pk}}(x, r)^m = \mathrm{COM}_{\mathsf{pk}}(0, \mathrm{COM}_{\mathsf{pk}}(x, r))$.

Finally to argue binding, assume an adversary is able to produce $x \neq x'$, r, r' such that $g^x r^m = g^{x'} r'^m$. Setting $s = r'r^{-1}$ we get $g^{x-x'} = s^m$. Since $x - x' \neq 0 \bmod m$, there must be a prime factor p dividing m such that, if p^t is the maximal p-power dividing $x - x'$ and p^k is the maximal power dividing m, we have $p^t < p^k$. The equation above can be written as $(g^{(x-x')/p^t})^{p^t} = (s^{m/p^t})^{p^t}$. Since ϕ_p is assumed collision intractable, we conclude[5] that $g^{(x-x')/p^t} = s^{m/p^t}$. Now, because $p^t < p^k$, we can define $a = s^{m/p^{t+1}}$, and inserting in the equation gives $g^{(x-x')/p^t} = a^p$.

---

[5] We use that if ϕ_p is collision intractable, then it is hard to find $a \neq b$ with $a^{p^t} = b^{p^t}$. Indeed, given such a and b, there must exist $0 \leq i < t$ such that $a^{p^i} \neq b^{p^i}$ but $a^{p^{i+1}} = b^{p^{i+1}}$ which yields the collision (a^{p^i}, b^{p^i}) for ϕ_p.

Observe that $\gcd(p, (x - x')/p^t) = 1$ and hence we can compute α, β such that $\alpha p + \beta(x - x')/p^t = 1$. Now set $h = g^\alpha a^\beta$, and observe that

$$h^p = g^{\alpha p}(a^p)^\beta = g^{\alpha p}(g^{(x-x')/p^t})^\beta = g^{\alpha p + \beta(x-x')/p^t} = g.$$

Hence, we have found a p'th root of g. This contradicts the assumption that G is commitment friendly, and so the binding property of the commitment scheme holds. $\square$

Examples of Commitment Friendly Groups for Odd m. We now discuss instantiations of commitment friendly groups. A first natural example is to choose an RSA modulus N and set $G = \mathbb{Z}_N^*$. If m is odd, we can choose N such that m is relatively prime to $\varphi(N)$. As discussed above, the collision intractability of $\phi_p(g) = g^p$ is then trivially satisfied for all $p \mid m$. Furthermore, the assumption about p-th roots being hard to compute is essentially the RSA assumption. In more detail, even if m is exponentially large, it can only have a polynomial number of different prime factors, so in contrast to the strong RSA assumption the adversary cannot choose the "public exponent" freely in the p-th root finding experiment, which makes this assumption weaker with respect to the strong RSA assumption. But of course in applications where the adversary can choose the modulus m, security directly reduces to the strong RSA assumption.

4.3   Single-Value Commitment Schemes for Even m

If m is even, collision intractability is violated for $p = 2$ because we have $x^2 = (-x)^2 \bmod N$. As a result, we cannot use the template presented before with $G = \mathbb{Z}_N^*$ in a direct manner.

If $N = PQ$ with $P, Q \equiv 3 \bmod 4$, then we could use the template by setting G to be directly $\mathsf{QR}(N)$, the group of quadratic residues modulo N, because its order is odd and $\mathsf{QR}(N)$ satisfies the properties of a commitment-friendly group. However, this construction has the practical drawback that it requires an expensive set-up to establish g, because membership in $\mathsf{QR}(N)$ cannot be efficiently decided (so rejection sampling on random elements in $\mathbb{Z}_N^*$ does not work), and the alternative of sampling an element in $\mathbb{Z}_N^*$ and squaring it would require a protocol that keeps the initial value hidden for everybody, only revealing the squared value, which is possible, but expensive.

Instead, we will describe a slight variant of the single-value commitment construction from Sect. 4.2 that solves this problem. We will use $G = \mathsf{J}^+(N)$, the subgroup of numbers with Jacobi symbol 1 modulo N. This has the advantage that one can compute the Jacobi symbol efficiently given only N, so membership in $\mathsf{J}^+(N)$ can be verified efficiently. Moreover, we use $N = PQ$ such that both P and Q are congruent to 3 modulo 4. With this setup, G has even order $(P - 1)(Q - 1)/2$, and also $-1 \in G$; so it is unfortunately still the case that, for $x \in G$, $-x$ is also in G and $x^2 = (-x)^2 \bmod N$. In fact, squaring maps $\mathsf{J}^+(N)$ into $\mathsf{QR}(N) \le \mathsf{J}^+(N)$, a proper subgroup (where $|\mathsf{J}^+(N)| = 2|\mathsf{QR}(N)|$).

To address this issue, we modify the construction as shown below. Note that now we sample g directly in $G = \mathsf{J}^+(N)$ (which can be done by rejection sampling), rather than as a^m. The choice of N ensures that the subgroup of quadratic residues $\mathsf{QR}(N)$ has odd order (more precisely, $|\mathsf{QR}(N)| = (P-1)(Q-1)/4$). Therefore we can choose N in such a way that $\gcd(|\mathsf{QR}(N)|, m) = 1$. This also implies that $-1 \in \mathsf{J}^+(N) \setminus \mathsf{QR}(N)$. These facts ensure not only that $(-1)^b r^m$ is uniform in $\mathsf{J}^+(N)$, guaranteeing perfect hiding, but still allow us to guarantee the binding property. For more information, see the proof of Theorem 4 below.

SV_m: Single-Value Commitment Scheme over $\mathbb{Z}_m$, for even m

- *Key generation.* Return $\mathsf{pk} = (G, g)$, where $G = \mathsf{J}^+(N)$ and N is chosen as above, and $g \leftarrow G$.
- *Commitment.* Set $\mathcal{R} = \{0,1\} \times G$. Given $x \in \mathbb{Z}_m$, choose $(b, r) \in \mathcal{R}$, and output $\mathrm{COM}_{\mathsf{pk}}(x, (b, r)) = g^x (-1)^b r^m \bmod N$.

Theorem 4. *Under the assumption that factoring N is hard, the construction SV_m from above constitutes a single-value commitment scheme over $\mathbb{Z}_m$.*

Proof. Perfect hiding follows because r^m is uniform in $\mathsf{QR}(N)$ and therefore $(-1)^b r^m$ is uniform in $\mathsf{J}^+(N)$. The homomorphic and randomization properties are easy to verify in much the same way as in Theorem 3.

For binding, we proceed in a similar way as the aforementioned theorem. If an adversary breaks the binding property this means it would be able to find x, x', r, r', b, b' such that $g^x (-1)^b r^m = g^{x'} (-1)^{b'} r'^m \bmod N$. There must be a prime factor p in m such that the maximal p-power p^t dividing $x - x'$ is smaller than the maximal p-power p^k dividing m. If p is odd, we can proceed in exactly the same way as in Theorem 3, except that in our current case the powers of -1 may lead to the equations being satisfied up to a ± 1 factor. We therefore end up concluding that we can compute h such that $h^p = \pm g \bmod N$. If we have $h^p = -g \bmod N$, then since p is odd, this implies that $(-h)^p = g \bmod N$, so we get a p'th root of g in any case.

The more challenging case is when $p = 2$. In this case, the same arguments will lead to the equation $\left(g^{(x-x')/2^t}\right)^{2^t} = \pm \left(s^{m/2^t}\right)^{2^t} \bmod N$.

First, since both sides are squares and -1 is not a square modulo N, it must be the case that $\left(g^{(x-x')/2^t}\right)^{2^t} = \left(s^{m/2^t}\right)^{2^t} \bmod N$. Unfortunately, since G has even order, we cannot conclude that $g^{(x-x')/2^t} = s^{m/2^t}$. However, we can instead say that $g^{(x-x')/2^t} = s^{m/2^t} \alpha \bmod N$, where $\alpha^{2^t} \bmod N = 1$. In particular, α has order a 2-power, and by construction of N, the only possible orders of α would be 1 or 2.

Given the above, one possibility is that α is a non-trivial square root of 1. In this case, we can use α to factor N easily since $(\alpha - 1)(\alpha + 1) = 0 \bmod N$ implies that $\gcd(\alpha - 1, N)$ is either P or Q, which breaks the assumption. Otherwise, α is plus or minus 1. We can now continue the reasoning in the same way as in the original proof, and find that we can compute h such that $h^2 \bmod N = \pm g$. Computing such a square-root easily implies you can factor N and break the computational assumption.   □

Remark 1 (Using class groups). Alternatively, we can take G to be a class group. Such a group is constructed from a discriminant Δ, and it is a standard assumption that for large enough Δ, the order of the corresponding class group is hard to compute. If Δ is a prime, then the order of the group is odd, but otherwise we do not know any way to efficiently compute information on prime factors in the order. However, as we have already mentioned, if one finds a collision for ϕ_p as defined above, one can find an element of order p, and for odd p one can reasonably conjecture that this is a hard problem in class groups. The assumption on p'th roots is motivated by the fact that the group order is hard to compute, in a similar way as for RSA.

The case of $p = 2$ requires special care. The issue is that if the prime factors of Δ are known, one can compute square roots efficiently in the class group. Therefore, for even m, we need that Δ is hard to factor. One can of course use an RSA modulus as discriminant, but this provides little advantage as then it would be more efficient to do the RSA based solution directly. For an alternative, see the discussion below on trusted set-up.

Remark 2 (On trusted setup). It can be an advantage in practice if the public key of the commitment scheme can be chosen in such a way that no one knows any side information that would allow breaking the scheme. Delegating key generation to a trusted party will work, but one would clearly prefer a solution where no trusted party is needed.

For the RSA-based schemes, this cannot be completely satisfied since the factors of the modulus must be unknown to the committer, and we cannot generate a correctly formed modulus without access to the prime factors, or using a less efficient solution based on multiparty computation. However, observe that once the modulus N is generated, the rest of the public key, namely g, can be chosen "in public", since it is in fact just a random group element (either in $\mathbb{Z}_N^*$ for odd m, or in $\mathsf{J}^+(N)$ for even m). The vector commitment scheme we derived in Sect. 4.1 inherits this property since the n commitments in the public key are also random group elements. This can be useful, e.g., in case we have an RSA-based PKI. In such a setting we must assume to begin with that the factorization of the CA's modulus N is safe, and we can then leverage this modulus to generate the rest of the public key without trusted setup.

For class groups, one can generate the group G without trusted setup since the discriminant is public in a first place. In this case, however, it is not possible to determine whether $G^m = G$ or not, as the order of G cannot be computed efficiently. Yet, precisely because of this, it seems reasonable to conjecture that, for odd m, elements in G^m are indistinguishable from random elements in G. Under this assumption we can choose g randomly in G and get a scheme that requires no trusted setup at all and still is computationally hiding since a random g cannot be distinguished from an m'th power.

For even m we need in addition, as mentioned above, that the discriminant is hard to factor. We can get such a scheme with no trusted setup by using a random discriminant large enough that it cannot be factored completely. This results in a scheme that is not very efficient in practice, but is still interesting from a theoretical point of view since no trusted setup is required.

Remark 3 (On q-one-way homomorphisms). In [22], the notion of q-one-way homomorphisms for a prime q is introduced. Informally, this is a homomorphism $f\colon G \mapsto H$ between two finite groups G and H such that (1) f is hard to invert and yet, (2) for any $y \in H$ it is easy to compute a preimage of y^q. A commitment is constructed based on this notion: the public key is $y \in \mathsf{Im}(f)$, and a commitment to $x \in \mathbb{Z}_q$ is of the form $y^x f(r)$, where $r \in G$ is uniformly random. It is very easy to see that this scheme satisfies our definition of a single-value commitment scheme, where $m = q$, and therefore implies a vector commitment scheme based on Theorem 2.

One example of a q-one-way homomorphism is $f(x) = g^x \bmod p$, where p is prime and $g \in \mathbb{Z}_p^*$ has order q. In this case, we recover the well-known Pedersen commitment scheme and its vector commitment variant (which in particular shows that our efficient reduction for proving binding applies to Pedersen vector commitments). Another example is $f(x) = x^q \bmod N$ for an RSA modulus N. Unfortunately, these constructions only work when q is prime, so they are not suitable for our needs, where we require a single-value commitment scheme over $\mathbb{Z}_m$, for *any* positive integer m.

5   Compressed Σ-Protocol

Let $(\mathcal{G}, \mathrm{COM}, R)$ be a vector commitment scheme as defined in Sect. 4.1, allowing a prover to commit to vectors $\mathbf{x} \in \mathbb{Z}_m^n$. In this section, we consider the problem of proving knowledge of an opening $(\mathbf{x}, \gamma)$ of a commitment $P = \mathrm{COM}_{pk}(\mathbf{x}, \gamma)$ satisfying a *linear* constraint $L(\mathbf{x}) = y$ captured by a linear form $L\colon \mathbb{Z}_m^n \to \mathbb{Z}_m$. We construct a *compressed Σ-protocol* [3] for this problem.

In contrast to the compressed Σ-protocols of [3], our protocols are not defined over a finite field $\mathbb{F}$ but over the ring $\mathbb{Z}_m$. Because non-zero challenge differences are required to be invertible, a challenge set $\mathcal{C} \subseteq \mathbb{Z}_m$ has to be *exceptional*. Recall that a subset $\mathcal{C}$ of a ring is said to be exceptional if $c - c'$ is invertible for all distinct $c, c' \in \mathcal{C}$. The largest exceptional subset of $\mathbb{Z}_m$ has cardinality p, where p is the smallest prime divisor of m. Therefore, a straightforward application of [3] can result in (much) smaller challenges sets and therefore larger knowledge errors. In many scenarios, this can be overcome by a t-fold parallel repetition reducing the knowledge error from κ down to κ^t [5]. However, this parallel repetition approach is sub-optimal and in some cases even insufficient. Namely, since the compression mechanism is 3-special sound, the challenge set is required to have cardinality at least 3. This is impossible when $2 \mid m$. For this reason, we adapt the compressed Σ-protocols of [3] to allow for challenges sampled from an appropriate extension of the ring $\mathbb{Z}_m$.

In Sect. 5.1, we extend our $\mathbb{Z}_m$-vector commitment scheme to a commitment scheme or vectors defined over an extension $\mathcal{S}$ of the ring $\mathbb{Z}_m$. In Sect. 5.2, we describe a standard Σ-protocol for proving that a committed vector $\mathbf{x} \in \mathcal{S}^n$ satisfies a linear constraint, whose communication complexity is linear in n. Subsequently, we describe a compression mechanism (Sect. 5.3) and, as a recursive composition of the basic Σ-protocol and this compression mechanism, we obtain the final compressed Σ-protocol (Sect. 5.4) with logarithmic communication complexity for a fixed ring extension $\mathcal{S}$.

5.1   Vector Commitments over Ring Extensions

Let $f(X) \in \mathbb{Z}_m[X]$ be a monic polynomial of degree d and let $\mathcal{S} = \mathbb{Z}_m[X]/(f(X))$ be a degree d ring extension of $\mathbb{Z}_m$. Then the commitment scheme $(\mathcal{G}, \mathrm{COM}, R)$ for $\mathbb{Z}_m$-vectors has an extension to a scheme $(\mathcal{G}, \mathrm{COM}', R')$ for $\mathcal{S}$-vectors[6] where vectors are committed *coefficient-wise*, i.e.,

$$\mathrm{COM}'_{pk}\left(\begin{pmatrix} \sum_{i=1}^d a_{1,i}X^{i-1} \\ \vdots \\ \sum_{i=1}^d a_{n,i}X^{i-1} \end{pmatrix}, \begin{pmatrix} \gamma_1 \\ \vdots \\ \gamma_d \end{pmatrix}\right) \mapsto \begin{pmatrix} \mathrm{COM}_{pk}\big((a_{1,1}, \ldots, a_{n,1}), \gamma_1\big) \\ \vdots \\ \mathrm{COM}_{pk}\big((a_{1,d}, \ldots, a_{n,d}), \gamma_d\big) \end{pmatrix}.$$

Hence, COM'_{pk} commits to an n-dimensional $\mathcal{S}$-vector $\mathbf{x} \in \mathcal{S}^n$ by committing to the d coefficient vectors of $\mathbf{x}$ (which are vectors in $\mathbb{Z}_m^n$) using d invocations of the $\mathbb{Z}_m$-vector commitment scheme COM_{pk}.

This commitment scheme inherits the *homomorphic, randomization* and *zero-opening* properties of $(\mathcal{G}, \mathrm{COM}, R)$. Additionally, committed vectors can be multiplied by ring elements $a \in \mathcal{S}$, i.e., for $c = \mathrm{COM}'_{pk}(\mathbf{x}, \gamma)$ and $a \in \mathcal{S}$, the commitment c^a is well-defined and can be opened to $a \cdot \mathbf{x} \in \mathcal{S}^n$. To see this note that any $a \in \mathcal{S}$ corresponds to a matrix $\mathcal{M}(a) \in \mathbb{Z}_m^{d \times d}$, such that for all $b \in \mathcal{S}$, $a \cdot \sum_{i=1}^d b_i X^{i-1} = \sum_{i=1}^d c_i X^{i-1} \in \mathcal{S}$ iff $\mathcal{M}(a) \cdot (b_1, \ldots, b_d)^\mathsf{T} = (c_1, \ldots, c_d)^\mathsf{T} \in \mathbb{Z}_m^d$.

By lifting this matrix to $\mathbb{Z}^{d \times d}$,[7] it follows that the homomorphic operation c^a can be expressed in terms of the standard homomorphic properties of the $\mathbb{Z}_m$-commitment scheme $(\mathcal{G}, \mathrm{COM}, R)$. As before, we write $R'(\mathbf{x}, a, \gamma)$ for the randomness required to open c^a to $a \cdot \mathbf{x} \in \mathcal{S}^n$. We say that this commitment scheme is $\mathcal{S}$-homomorphic. Finally, a $\mathbb{Z}_m$-vector commitment P can also be viewed as a $\mathcal{S}$-vector commitment $(P, 1, \ldots, 1)$, now with $\mathcal{S}$-homomorphic properties.

Notice that, in contrast, committing by concatenating all coefficients over $\mathbb{Z}_m$ would only be $\mathbb{Z}_m$-homomorphic and not $\mathcal{S}$-homomorphic.

5.2   Standard Σ-Protocol

The reason for considering vectors defined over $\mathcal{S} = \mathbb{Z}_m[X]/(f(X))$ is that when this extension is appropriately chosen it contains larger *exceptional subsets* than

---

[6] Note that in Sect. 3.1 we only defined commitments for vectors over $\mathbb{Z}_m$, while here we need commitments for vectors over $\mathcal{S}$, which are homomorphic as a $\mathcal{S}$-module. This notion is defined in a similar manner as the one in Sect. 3.1.

[7] We lift to $\mathbb{Z}^{d \times d}$ because the homomorphic properties are defined over $\mathbb{Z}$.

the ring $\mathbb{Z}_m$. Namely, if $f(X)$ is irreducible modulo all prime divisors of m, then $\mathcal{S}$ contains an exceptional subset of cardinality p^d where p is the smallest prime dividing m. This allows us to design (compressed) Σ-protocols with larger challenge sets and therefore smaller knowledge errors. We will assume $f(X)$ to be of this form and $\mathcal{C} \subseteq \mathcal{S}$ to be an exceptional subset of cardinality p^d.

Protocol 1, denoted by Π_1, is a standard Σ-protocol, with challenge set $\mathcal{C}$, for proving knowledge of a commitment opening satisfying a linear constraint, i.e., it is a Σ-protocol for relation $\mathcal{X}^d$ given by $\{(P, y; \mathbf{x}, \gamma) : \text{COM}'_{pk}(\mathbf{x}, \gamma) = P, L(\mathbf{x}) = y\}$, where $\mathbf{x} \in \mathcal{S}^n$ and $L : \mathcal{S}^n \to \mathcal{S}$ is a linear form. The properties of Π_1 are summarized in Theorem 5.

Protocol 1. Standard Σ-Protocol Π_1 for relation $\mathcal{X}^d$.

$$\text{INPUT}(P, y; \mathbf{x}, \gamma),$$
$$P = \text{COM}'_{pk}(\mathbf{x}, \gamma), \quad y = L(\mathbf{x})$$

Prover		Verifier
$\mathbf{r} \leftarrow_R \mathcal{S}^n, \quad \rho \leftarrow_R \mathcal{R}^d$		
$A = \text{COM}'_{pk}(\mathbf{r}, \rho), \quad t = L(\mathbf{r})$	$\xrightarrow{\quad A, t \quad}$	
		$c \leftarrow_R \mathcal{C} \subseteq \mathcal{S}$
	$\xleftarrow{\quad c \quad}$	
$\mathbf{z} = \mathbf{r} + c\mathbf{x}$		
$\psi = R'(\mathbf{r}, c\mathbf{x}, \rho, R'(\mathbf{x}, c, \gamma))$	$\xrightarrow{\quad \mathbf{z}, \psi \quad}$	
		$\text{COM}'_{pk}(\mathbf{z}, \psi) \overset{?}{=} A \cdot P^c$
		$L(\mathbf{z}) \overset{?}{=} t + cy$

Theorem 5 (Standard Σ-Protocol). *Protocol Π_1 is a Σ-protocol for $\mathcal{X}^d$. More precisely, it is a 3-round protocol that is perfectly complete, special honest-verifier zero-knowledge and unconditionally knowledge sound with knowledge error $1/p^d$, where p is the smallest prime dividing m.*

Proof. **Completeness** follows directly by the homomorphic properties of $\text{COM}_{pk}(\cdot)$ and the linearity of L.

SHVZK: We simulate a transcript as follows. Given a challenge c, sample $(\mathbf{z}, \psi) \leftarrow_R \mathcal{S}^n \times \mathcal{R}^d$ uniformly at random and let $A = \text{COM}'_{pk}(\mathbf{z}, \psi) \cdot P^{-c}$ and $t = L(\mathbf{z}) - cy$. By the randomization property of COM'_{pk} it follows that the simulated transcripts $(A, t, c, \mathbf{z}, \psi)$ have exactly the same distribution as honestly generated transcripts.

Knowledge Soundness: We show that Π_1 is special-sound. Knowledge soundness is then implied. Let $(A, t, c, \mathbf{z}, \psi)$, $(A, t, c', \mathbf{z}', \psi')$ be two accepting transcripts with $c \neq c' \in \mathcal{C}$, and let $\tilde{c} = (c - c')^{-1}$. Then define $\tilde{\mathbf{z}} := \tilde{c}(\mathbf{z} - \mathbf{z}')$ and $\tilde{\psi} := R'(\tilde{c}\mathbf{z}, -\tilde{c}\mathbf{z}', R'(\mathbf{z}, \tilde{c}, \psi), R'(\mathbf{z}', -\tilde{c}, \psi'))$. By the homomorphic properties of $\text{COM}'_{pk}(\cdot)$ and since the transcripts are accepting, it follows that $\text{COM}'_{pk}(\tilde{\mathbf{z}}, \tilde{\psi}) = P^{\tilde{c}(c-c')} = P \cdot P^{\ell m}$ for some $\ell \in \mathbb{Z}$. Hence, by the zero-opening property of $\text{COM}'_{pk}(\cdot)$, $(\tilde{\mathbf{z}}, \tilde{\psi})$ is an opening of commitment P, where $\tilde{\psi} = R'(\tilde{\mathbf{z}}, 0, \tilde{\psi}, R'(P^{-\ell}))$. By the linearity of L, it additionally follows that $L(\tilde{\mathbf{z}}) = y$, i.e., $(\tilde{\mathbf{z}}, \tilde{\psi})$ is a witness for statement $(P, y) \in L_{\mathcal{X}^d}$.

$\square$

Remark 4 (Proving openings of d $\mathbb{Z}_m$-commitments). Protocol Π_1 can be used to prove knowledge of the openings of d different $\mathbb{Z}_m$-commitments $P_1, \ldots, P_d$, all satisfying a constraint captured by the same linear form L, by defining $P = (P_1, \ldots, P_d)$, i.e., a protocol for proving knowledge of d witnesses for relation $\mathcal{X}^1$. This compares positively to the alternatives: instantiating d different Σ-protocols defined directly over $\mathbb{Z}_m$ would result in a larger knowledge error; while applying standard amortization techniques to prove knowledge of d witnesses with the same communication costs as proving knowledge of only 1 witness (see e.g. [3]) would reduce communication costs by a factor d but again increase the knowledge error. See Table 1.

Table 1. Properties of different Σ-protocols for proving knowledge of d witnesses for relation $\mathcal{X}^1$. Columns 2–4 contain communication costs, while the last column contains knowledge error.

Protocol	# $\mathbb{Z}_m$-elements	# $\mathcal{R}$-elements	# $\mathbb{Z}_m^n$-Commitments	K. error
d Separate Σ-Protocols	$d(n+1)$	d	d	$1/p$
Amortized Σ-Protocol	$n+1$	1	1	d/p
Our Σ-Protocol Π_1	$d(n+1)$	d	d	$1/p^d$

5.3 Compression Mechanism

The communication complexity of the standard Σ-protocol Π_1 is linear in the dimension n of vector $\mathbf{x} \in \mathcal{S}^n$. The compression mechanism for Σ-protocols of [3], based on Bulletproof's folding technique [14,15], allows the communication complexity to be reduced from linear down to logarithmic. A key observation of this compression mechanism is that the final message of protocol Π_1 is a witness for relation $\mathcal{X}^d$, i.e., the final message is a trivial proof-of-knowledge (PoK) for this relation. Therefore, this message can also be replaced by another PoK for relation $\mathcal{X}^d$ with a smaller communication complexity. This is the case of compression mechanism Π_2, described in Protocol 2. Protocol 2 is identical to the compression mechanism of [3], although here we use the notation introduced in the previous sections. Bulletproof's folding technique takes an n-dimensional witness $\mathbf{x} = (\mathbf{x}_L, \mathbf{x}_R) \in \mathcal{S}^n$ and, given a challenge $c \in \mathcal{C}$, it folds the left and right halves $\mathbf{x}_L, \mathbf{x}_R \in \mathcal{S}^{n/2}$ onto each other obtaining a new message $\mathbf{z} = \mathbf{x}_L + c\mathbf{x}_R$ of dimension $n/2$. This technique reduces the communication complexity by roughly a factor 2. The properties of this protocol are summarized in Theorem 6. For more details we refer to [3].

Theorem 6 (Compression Mechanism) *Let n be even. Protocol Π_2 (as defined in Protocol 2) is a 3-round protocol for relation $\mathcal{X}^d$. It is perfectly complete and unconditionally knowledge sound with knowledge error $2/p^d$, where p is the smallest prime diving m. Its communication costs from Prover to Verifier are 2 $\mathcal{S}$-commitments, $n/2 + 2$ elements in $\mathcal{S}$ and 1 elements in $\mathcal{R}^d$, and from Verifier to Prover are 1 challenge in $\mathcal{C} \subseteq \mathcal{S}$.*

Protocol 2. Compression Mechanism Π_2 for Relation $\mathcal{X}^d$ [3].

$$\text{INPUT}(P, y; \mathbf{x}, \gamma)$$
$$P = \text{COM}'_{pk}(\mathbf{x}, \gamma), y = L(\mathbf{x})$$

Prover		Verifier
$\rho \leftarrow_R \mathcal{R}^d$		
$A = \text{COM}'_{pk}((\mathbf{0}, \mathbf{x}_L), \rho), \quad a = L(\mathbf{0}, \mathbf{x}_L)$		
$B = \text{COM}'_{pk}((\mathbf{x}_R, \mathbf{0}), \rho), \quad b = L(\mathbf{x}_R, \mathbf{0})$		

$$\xrightarrow{\quad A, B, a, b \quad}$$

$$c \leftarrow_R \mathcal{C} \subseteq \mathcal{S}$$

$$\xleftarrow{\quad c \quad}$$

$$\mathbf{z} = \mathbf{x}_L + c\mathbf{x}_R$$
$$\psi_1 = R'\left((\mathbf{0}, \mathbf{x}_L), c\mathbf{x}, \rho, R'(\mathbf{x}, c, \gamma)\right)$$
$$\psi_2 = R'\left((\mathbf{x}_R, \mathbf{0}), c^2, \rho\right)$$
$$\psi = R'\left((\mathbf{0}, \mathbf{x}_L) + c\mathbf{x}, c^2(\mathbf{x}_R, \mathbf{0}), \psi_1, \psi_2\right)$$

$$\xrightarrow{\quad \mathbf{z}, \psi \quad}$$

$$\text{COM}'_{pk}\left((c\mathbf{z}, \mathbf{z}), \psi\right) \overset{?}{=}$$
$$A \cdot P^c \cdot B^{c^2}$$
$$L(c\mathbf{z}, \mathbf{z}) \overset{?}{=} a + cy + c^2 b$$

Proof. **Completeness**: Observe that $(c\mathbf{z}, \mathbf{z}) = (\mathbf{0}, \mathbf{x}_L) + c\mathbf{x} + c^2(\mathbf{x}_R, \mathbf{0})$. Completeness now follows from the homomorphic properties of $\text{COM}'_{pk}(\cdot)$ and the linearity of L.

3-Special Soundness: Let $(A, B, a, b, c_1, \mathbf{z}_1, \psi_1)$, $(A, B, a, b, c_2, \mathbf{z}_2, \psi_2)$ and $(A, B, a, b, c_3, \mathbf{z}_3, \psi_3)$ be three accepting transcripts for pairwise distinct challenges $c_1, c_2, c_3 \in \mathcal{C} \subset \mathcal{R}$. Let $(a_1, a_2, a_3) \in \mathcal{S}^3$ be such that

$$\begin{pmatrix} 1 & 1 & 1 \\ c_1 & c_2 & c_3 \\ c_1^2 & c_2^2 & c_3^2 \end{pmatrix} \begin{pmatrix} a_1 \\ a_2 \\ a_3 \end{pmatrix} = \begin{pmatrix} 0 \\ 1 \\ 0 \end{pmatrix}.$$

Note that such a vector (a_1, a_2, a_3) exists because the Vandermonde matrix has determinant $(c_2 - c_1)(c_3 - c_1)(c_3 - c_2)$ and challenge differences are invertible modulo in $\mathcal{S}$.

Let $\tilde{\mathbf{z}} := \sum_{i=1}^{3} a_i(c_i \mathbf{z}_i, \mathbf{z}_i)$. Then, for some $\ell \in \mathbb{Z}$, $\text{COM}'_{pk}(\tilde{\mathbf{z}}, \tilde{\phi}) = P \cdot P^{\ell m}$, where $\tilde{\phi}$ can be computed by a recursive application of the randomness function R'.

Hence, by the zero-opening property, $(\tilde{\mathbf{z}}, \tilde{\phi})$ is an opening of commitment $(P, y) \in \mathcal{L}_R$, where $\tilde{\phi} = R'\left(\tilde{\mathbf{z}}, 0, \tilde{\psi}, R'(P^{-\ell})\right)$. By the linearity of L, it additionally follows that $L(\tilde{\mathbf{z}}) = y$, i.e., $(\tilde{\mathbf{z}}, \tilde{\psi})$ is a witness for statement $(P, y) \in \mathcal{L}_{\mathcal{X}^d}$, which completes the proof. $\square$

5.4   Compressed Σ-Protocol

To reduce the communication costs of the Σ-protocol Π_1 down to logarithmic the compression mechanism is applied recursively, i.e., instead of sending the final message of protocol Π_2 the protocol is applied again until the dimension of the final message equals 4. Note that the compression mechanism could be applied even further, reducing the dimension of the final message to 2 or 1. However, since the prover has to send 4 elements in every compression, this would result in a sub-optimal communication costs. This recursive composition is referred to as *Compressed Σ-Protocol*, it is denoted by $\Pi_c = \Pi_2 \diamond \cdots \diamond \Pi_2 \diamond \Pi_1$ (composition of Π_2 happens $\lceil \log_2(n) \rceil - 2$ times) and its properties are summarized in the following theorem. In particular the protocol is $(2, 3, \ldots, 3)$-special-sound, which has recently been shown to tightly imply knowledge soundness [4].

Theorem 7 (Compressed Σ-Protocol). *Let $n = 2^\mu \geq 4$. Then, Protocol Π_c is a $(2\mu - 1)$-round protocol for relation $\mathcal{X}^d$. It is perfectly complete, special honest-verifier zero-knowledge. Moreover, it is unconditionally $(2, 3, \ldots, 3)$-special-sound and therefore knowledge sound with knowledge error $\leq (2\mu - 3)/p^d$, where p is the smallest prime dividing m. In terms of communication costs, from* **Prover** *to* **Verifier** *there are $2\mu - 3$ S-commitments, $2\mu + 1$ elements in S and 1 element in $\mathcal{R}^d$, while from* **Verifier** *to* **Prover** *there are $\mu - 1$ challenges in $\mathcal{C} \subseteq S$.*

In practical applications, Π_c should be instantiated with knowledge error at most $2^{-\lambda}$, where λ denotes the security parameter. To this end, we choose a ring extension S of degree $d \geq (1 + \lambda + \log \log n)/\log p = \mathcal{O}(\lambda + \log \log n)$. Hence, to obtain a knowledge error negligible in the security parameter, the degree must depend on the input dimension n. However, thus far we have only considered the communication complexity for *fixed* ring extensions S of degree d and thus with *fixed*, not necessarily negligible, knowledge error. In fact, the communication complexity of Π_c is only logarithmic in n for fixed S and d. For $d = \mathcal{O}(\lambda + \log \log n)$, the communication complexity is actually $\mathcal{O}(\lambda \log n + \log n \log \log n)$, i.e., it is not logarithmic in n. However, this is still an improvement over the polylogarithmic communication complexity achieved by the naive approach using integer commitment schemes.

Further, the knowledge error of Π_c shows that we must choose the degree d of the ring extension such that $p^d > 2$. In particular, if $p = 2$ the compression mechanism can not be defined directly over $\mathbb{Z}_m$. If $p > 2$, then the compressed Σ-protocol could have been defined over $\mathbb{Z}_m$ directly. However, this would result in a larger knowledge error. Reducing this knowledge error by a d-fold parallel composition would result in exactly the same communication costs as the protocol defined over the ring extension S. However, this parallel composition approach results in a knowledge error that can be bounded by $(2\mu - 3)^d/p^d$, which is larger than the the knowledge error of our protocol. Hence, even for the case $p > 2$, it is beneficial to define the protocols over the ring extension S. Moreover, this approach allows a prover to prove d $\mathbb{Z}_m$-statements simultaneously (coordinate-wise) with exactly the same costs as proving only 1 statement.

Remark 5. The communication complexity of protocol Π_c can be further reduced with roughly factor $1/2$, by incorporating the linear form evaluation $L(\mathbf{x})$ into the commitment. More precisely, before evaluating the Compressed Σ-Protocol, the verifier sends a random challenge $c \in \mathcal{C} \subseteq S$ to the prover, and relation $\mathcal{X}$ is transformed into relation $\mathcal{X}_c^d$ given by $\{(P, y; \mathbf{x}, \gamma) : \text{COM}'_{pk}(\mathbf{x}, c \cdot L(\mathbf{x}), \gamma) = P\}$. After this transformation the prover does not have to send the linear form evaluations a, b in compression mechanism Π_2 to the verifier. For more details see [3].

Remark 6. With small adaptations to existing work, we can use our Σ-protocols to prove non-linear constraints. Namely, following [3], we can "linearize" this type of constraints by an arithmetic secret sharing based technique, after which the protocols described in previous sections can be used in a black-box manner. In the lattice-based compressed Σ-protocols of [4] it was already shown how to adapt this techniques to the ring scenario.[8] For a general arithmetic circuit C over $\mathcal{S}$ we can then construct a protocol that can prove the relation $\{(P, y; \mathbf{x}, \gamma) : \mathrm{COM}'_{pk}(\mathbf{x}, \gamma) = P, \; C(\mathbf{x}) = y\}$, with communication complexity logarithmic in the dimension n of $\mathbf{x} \in \mathcal{S}^n$ and the number of multiplication gates m in the circuit C.

Finally, our protocols are also compatible with the Fiat-Shamir heuristic, which is discussed in the full version.

6   An Application: Verifiable Computation on Encrypted Data with Context-Hiding

In this section, we argue that our commitments and compressed Σ-protocols over rings are useful in the context of proofs of correct computation on homomorphically encrypted data. We illustrate this concretely by considering the problem of verifiable computation on encrypted data supporting non-deterministic computations and context hiding from the recent work [13].

In verifiable computation [31], a client wants to delegate a (typically expensive) computation $\mathbf{y} = g(\mathbf{x})$ to a server, which must later prove that the computation has been carried out correctly. When the client does not want the server to learn information about the actual inputs $\mathbf{x}$ of the computation, we speak of private verifiable computation. To address this privacy consideration, several works [13,28,29] have proposed to combine verifiable computation and homomorphic encryption: the client encrypts the input data with a fully homomorphic scheme and sends the ciphertexts $\mathrm{ct}_{x_1}, \mathrm{ct}_{x_2}, \ldots$ to the server, which carries out the corresponding computation $\hat{g}(\mathrm{ct}_{x_1}, \mathrm{ct}_{x_2}, \ldots)$ on the encrypted data and proves its correctness via a verifiable computation scheme.

[13] introduced a scheme that provides flexibility in this combination, where the idea is that the proof of correctness of the computation is done on a "homomorphic hash" version of it into a smaller algebraic domain, more specifically a Galois ring $\mathbb{Z}_q[X]/(h)$. For this, one can use as succinct argument a version of the GKR protocol [35] adapted for Galois rings, presented in [20].

However, an additional challenge appears if the privacy of the input data needs to be preserved with respect to a (public) verifier too. In this case, we speak of verifiable computation with context-hiding, as introduced in [29], and [13] proposes to use a commit-and-proof strategy where the client and server additionally commit publicly to the input and output ciphertexts respectively

---

[8] On the other hand, since they only considered rings with large enough exceptional sets, their protocol for proving linear statements could be defined over the base ring and therefore the adaptations of the previous sections were not required in [4].

(plus some additional blinding encryptions of 0 in the case of the server) and the server uses a commit-and-proof argument to show that the computation is done correctly on the hashed values (which, for adequate parameters, can be made public with no harm to privacy). This strategy even extends to non-deterministic computations $\mathbf{y} = g(\mathbf{x}; \mathbf{w})$ which may depend on private randomness $\mathbf{w}$ chosen by the server.

While [13] propose these generic solutions, they leave as an open question the existence of succinct commit-and-proof arguments that directly handle statements over (Galois) rings, so that there is no need to emulate the ring arithmetic with an argument over a finite field, which causes considerable overhead in this application.

Given the type of statements required in this application, our homomorphic commitments and compressed Sigma-protocols provide a simple and efficient way of instantiating the type of commit-and-proof arguments needed in this context; indeed, the statements are of two types: knowledge of ct_x with $H(\mathsf{ct}_x) = y$, where $H : \mathbb{Z}_m^\ell \to \mathbb{Z}_m[X]/(h)$ is a $\mathbb{Z}_m$-linear map, y is public and ct_x has been committed to, which is precisely the situation we have considered in Sect. 5 (and further, since H is always the same map, we can efficiently batch several proofs together, as per Remark 4); and statements consisting on proving that a given commitment hides a correct encryption, which can be reduced to a number of range proofs and addressed by adapting the efficient protocols for range proofs described in [3] to a large enough extension ring of $\mathbb{Z}_m$.

Acknowledgments. This research has been partially supported by EU H2020 project PROMETHEUS (No. 780701), the Spanish Governement under project SecuRing (ref. PID2019-110873RJ-I00/MCIN/AEI/10.13039/501100011033), by a grant from the Tezos Foundation and by Madrid regional government as part of the program S2018/TCS-4339 (BLOQUES-CM) co-funded by EIE Funds of the European Union.

References

1. Abspoel, M., Cramer, R., Damgård, I., Escudero, D., Yuan, C.: Efficient information-theoretic secure multiparty computation over $\mathbb{Z}/p^k\mathbb{Z}$ via galois rings. In: Hofheinz, D., Rosen, A. (eds.) TCC 2019. LNCS, vol. 11891, pp. 471–501. Springer, Cham (2019). https://doi.org/10.1007/978-3-030-36030-6_19

2. Ames, S., Hazay, C., Ishai, Y., Venkitasubramaniam, M.: Ligero: lightweight sublinear arguments without a trusted setup. In: Thuraisingham, B.M., Evans, D., Malkin, T., Xu, D. (eds.) ACM CCS 2017, pp. 2087–2104. ACM Press, October 2017

3. Attema, T., Cramer, R.: Compressed Σ-protocol theory and practical application to plug & play secure algorithmics. In: Micciancio, D., Ristenpart, T. (eds.) CRYPTO 2020. Part III. LNCS, vol. 12172, pp. 513–543. Springer, Cham (2020). https://doi.org/10.1007/978-3-030-56877-1_18

4. Attema, T., Cramer, R., Kohl, L.: A compressed Σ-protocol theory for lattices. In: Malkin, T., Peikert, C. (eds.) CRYPTO 2021, Part II. LNCS, vol. 12826, pp. 549–579. Springer, Cham (2021). https://doi.org/10.1007/978-3-030-84245-1_19

5. Attema, T., Fehr, S.: Parallel repetition of $(k_1, \ldots, k_\mu)$-special-sound multi-round interactive proofs. In: Dodis, Y., Shrimpton, T. (eds.) CRYPTO 2022. LNCS, vol. 13507, pp. 415–443. Springer, Cham (2022). https://doi.org/10.1007/978-3-031-15802-5_15

6. Baum, C., Braun, L., Munch-Hansen, A., Razet, B., Scholl, P.: Appenzeller to brie: efficient zero-knowledge proofs for mixed-mode arithmetic and Z2k. In: Vigna, G., Shi, E. (eds.) ACM CCS 2021, pp. 192–211. ACM Press, November 2021

7. Baum, C., Braun, L., Munch-Hansen, A., Scholl, P.: Appenzeller to brie: efficient zero-knowledge proofs for mixed-mode arithmetic and z2k (2021)

8. Baum, C., Damgård, I., Lyubashevsky, V., Oechsner, S., Peikert, C.: More efficient commitments from structured lattice assumptions. In: Catalano, D., De Prisco, R. (eds.) SCN 2018. LNCS, vol. 11035, pp. 368–385. Springer, Cham (2018). https://doi.org/10.1007/978-3-319-98113-0_20

9. Ben-Sasson, E., Chiesa, A., Riabzev, M., Spooner, N., Virza, M., Ward, N.P.: Aurora: transparent succinct arguments for R1CS. In: Ishai, Y., Rijmen, V. (eds.) EUROCRYPT 2019. LNCS, vol. 11476, pp. 103–128. Springer, Cham (2019). https://doi.org/10.1007/978-3-030-17653-2_4

10. Bendlin, R., Damgård, I., Orlandi, C., Zakarias, S.: Semi-homomorphic encryption and multiparty computation. In: Paterson, K.G. (ed.) EUROCRYPT 2011. LNCS, vol. 6632, pp. 169–188. Springer, Heidelberg (2011). https://doi.org/10.1007/978-3-642-20465-4_11

11. Benhamouda, F., Krenn, S., Lyubashevsky, V., Pietrzak, K.: Efficient zero-knowledge proofs for commitments from learning with errors over rings. In: Pernul, G., Ryan, P.Y.A., Weippl, E. (eds.) ESORICS 2015. LNCS, vol. 9326, pp. 305–325. Springer, Cham (2015). https://doi.org/10.1007/978-3-319-24174-6_16

12. Block, A.R., Holmgren, J., Rosen, A., Rothblum, R.D., Soni, P.: Time- and space-efficient arguments from groups of unknown order. In: Malkin, T., Peikert, C. (eds.) CRYPTO 2021. LNCS, vol. 12828, pp. 123–152. Springer, Cham (2021). https://doi.org/10.1007/978-3-030-84259-8_5

13. Bois, A., Cascudo, I., Fiore, D., Kim, D.: Flexible and efficient verifiable computation on encrypted data. In: Garay, J.A. (ed.) PKC 2021. LNCS, vol. 12711, pp. 528–558. Springer, Cham (2021). https://doi.org/10.1007/978-3-030-75248-4_19

14. Bootle, J., Cerulli, A., Chaidos, P., Groth, J., Petit, C.: Efficient zero-knowledge arguments for arithmetic circuits in the discrete log setting. In: Fischlin, M., Coron, J.-S. (eds.) EUROCRYPT 2016. LNCS, vol. 9666, pp. 327–357. Springer, Heidelberg (2016). https://doi.org/10.1007/978-3-662-49896-5_12

15. Bünz, B., Bootle, J., Boneh, D., Poelstra, A., Wuille, P., Maxwell, G.: Bulletproofs: short proofs for confidential transactions and more. In: 2018 IEEE Symposium on Security and Privacy, pp. 315–334. IEEE Computer Society Press, May 2018

16. Bünz, B., Fisch, B., Szepieniec, A.: Transparent SNARKs from DARK compilers. In: Canteaut, A., Ishai, Y. (eds.) EUROCRYPT 2020. LNCS, vol. 12105, pp. 677–706. Springer, Cham (2020). https://doi.org/10.1007/978-3-030-45721-1_24

17. Catalano, D., Di Raimondo, M., Fiore, D., Giacomelli, I.: MonZ$_{2^k}$a: fast maliciously secure two party computation on Z$_{2^k}$. In: Kiayias, A., Kohlweiss, M., Wallden, P., Zikas, V. (eds.) PKC 2020. LNCS, vol. 12111, pp. 357–386. Springer, Cham (2020). https://doi.org/10.1007/978-3-030-45388-6_13

18. Catalano, D., Fiore, D.: Vector commitments and their applications. In: Kurosawa, K., Hanaoka, G. (eds.) PKC 2013. LNCS, vol. 7778, pp. 55–72. Springer, Heidelberg (2013). https://doi.org/10.1007/978-3-642-36362-7_5

19. Chase, M., et al.: Post-quantum zero-knowledge and signatures from symmetric-key primitives. In: Thuraisingham, B.M., Evans, D., Malkin, T., Xu, D. (eds.) ACM CCS 2017, pp. 1825–1842. ACM Press, October 2017

20. Chen, S., Cheon, J.H., Kim, D., Park, D.: Verifiable computing for approximate computation. Cryptology ePrint Archive, Report 2019/762 (2019). https://eprint.iacr.org/2019/762

21. Cramer, R.: Modular design of secure yet practical cryptographic protocols. Ph.D. thesis, CWI and University of Amsterdam (1996)

22. Cramer, R., Damgård, I.: Zero-knowledge proofs for finite field arithmetic, or: Can zero-knowledge be for free? In: Krawczyk, H. (ed.) CRYPTO 1998. LNCS, vol. 1462, pp. 424–441. Springer, Heidelberg (1998). https://doi.org/10.1007/BFb0055745

23. Cramer, R., Damgård, I., Escudero, D., Scholl, P., Xing, C.: SPDZ$_{2^k}$: efficient MPC mod 2^k for dishonest majority. In: Shacham, H., Boldyreva, A. (eds.) CRYPTO 2018. LNCS, vol. 10992, pp. 769–798. Springer, Cham (2018). https://doi.org/10.1007/978-3-319-96881-0_26

24. Cramer, R., Damgård, I., Schoenmakers, B.: Proofs of Partial Knowledge and Simplified Design of Witness Hiding Protocols. In: Desmedt, Y.G. (ed.) CRYPTO 1994. LNCS, vol. 839, pp. 174–187. Springer, Heidelberg (1994). https://doi.org/10.1007/3-540-48658-5_19

25. Damgård, I., Escudero, D., Frederiksen, T.K., Keller, M., Scholl, P., Volgushev, N.: New primitives for actively-secure MPC over rings with applications to private machine learning. In: 2019 IEEE Symposium on Security and Privacy, pp. 1102–1120. IEEE Computer Society Press, May 2019

26. Damgård, I., Fujisaki, E.: A statistically-hiding integer commitment scheme based on groups with hidden order. In: Zheng, Y. (ed.) ASIACRYPT 2002. LNCS, vol. 2501, pp. 125–142. Springer, Heidelberg (2002). https://doi.org/10.1007/3-540-36178-2_8

27. ElGamal, T.: A public key cryptosystem and a signature scheme based on discrete logarithms. IEEE Trans. Inf. Theory 31, 469–472 (1985)

28. Fiore, D., Gennaro, R., Pastro, V.: Efficiently verifiable computation on encrypted data. In: Ahn, G.-J., Yung, M., Li, N. (eds.) ACM CCS 2014, pp. 844–855. ACM Press, November 2014

29. Fiore, D., Nitulescu, A., Pointcheval, D.: Boosting verifiable computation on encrypted data. In: Kiayias, A., Kohlweiss, M., Wallden, P., Zikas, V. (eds.) PKC 2020. LNCS, vol. 12111, pp. 124–154. Springer, Cham (2020). https://doi.org/10.1007/978-3-030-45388-6_5

30. Ganesh, C., Nitulescu, A., Soria-Vazquez, E.: Rinocchio: snarks for ring arithmetic. IACR Cryptology ePrint Archive 2021:322 (2021)

31. Gennaro, R., Gentry, C., Parno, B.: Non-interactive verifiable computing: outsourcing computation to untrusted workers. In: Rabin, T. (ed.) CRYPTO 2010. LNCS, vol. 6223, pp. 465–482. Springer, Heidelberg (2010). https://doi.org/10.1007/978-3-642-14623-7_25

32. Giacomelli, I., Madsen, J., Orlandi, C.: ZKBoo: faster zero-knowledge for Boolean circuits. In: Holz, T., Savage, S. (eds.) USENIX Security 2016, pp. 1069–1083. USENIX Association, August 2016

33. Goldreich, O.: Foundations of Cryptography: Basic Applications, vol. 2. Cambridge University Press, Cambridge (2004)

34. Goldreich, O., Micali, S., Wigderson, A.: How to play any mental game or A completeness theorem for protocols with honest majority. In: Aho, A. (ed.) 19th ACM STOC, pp. 218–229. ACM Press, May 1987

35. Goldwasser, S., Kalai, Y.T., Rothblum, G.N.: Delegating computation: interactive proofs for muggles. In: Ladner, R.E., Dwork, C. (eds.) 40th ACM STOC, pp. 113–122. ACM Press, May 2008

36. Goldwasser, S., Micali, S., Rackoff, C.: The knowledge complexity of interactive proof-systems (extended abstract). In: 17th ACM STOC, pp. 291–304. ACM Press, May 1985

37. Groth, J.: On the size of pairing-based non-interactive arguments. In: Fischlin, M., Coron, J.-S. (eds.) EUROCRYPT 2016. LNCS, vol. 9666, pp. 305–326. Springer, Heidelberg (2016). https://doi.org/10.1007/978-3-662-49896-5_11

38. Joye, M., Libert, B.: Efficient cryptosystems from 2^k. In: Johansson, T., Nguyen, P.Q. (eds.) EUROCRYPT 2013. LNCS, vol. 7881, pp. 76–92. Springer, Heidelberg (2013). https://doi.org/10.1007/978-3-642-38348-9_5

39. Okamoto, T., Uchiyama, S.: A new public-key cryptosystem as secure as factoring. In: Nyberg, K. (ed.) EUROCRYPT 1998. LNCS, vol. 1403, pp. 308–318. Springer, Heidelberg (1998). https://doi.org/10.1007/BFb0054135

40. Paillier, P.: Public-key cryptosystems based on composite degree residuosity classes. In: Stern, J. (ed.) EUROCRYPT 1999. LNCS, vol. 1592, pp. 223–238. Springer, Heidelberg (1999). https://doi.org/10.1007/3-540-48910-X_16

41. Pedersen, T.P.: Non-interactive and information-theoretic secure verifiable secret sharing. In: Feigenbaum, J. (ed.) CRYPTO 1991. LNCS, vol. 576, pp. 129–140. Springer, Heidelberg (1992). https://doi.org/10.1007/3-540-46766-1_9

42. Schnorr, C.P.: Efficient identification and signatures for smart cards. In: Brassard, G. (ed.) CRYPTO 1989. LNCS, vol. 435, pp. 239–252. Springer, New York (1990). https://doi.org/10.1007/0-387-34805-0_22

43. Wahby, R.S., Tzialla, I., shelat, A., Thaler, J., Walfish, M.: Doubly-efficient zkSNARKs without trusted setup. In: 2018 IEEE Symposium on Security and Privacy, pp. 926–943. IEEE Computer Society Press, May 2018

44. Xie, T., Zhang, J., Zhang, Y., Papamanthou, C., Song, D.: Libra: succinct zero-knowledge proofs with optimal prover computation. In: Boldyreva, A., Micciancio, D. (eds.) CRYPTO 2019. LNCS, vol. 11694, pp. 733–764. Springer, Cham (2019). https://doi.org/10.1007/978-3-030-26954-8_24

Universally Composable Σ-protocols in the Global Random-Oracle Model

Anna Lysyanskaya[iD] and Leah Namisa Rosenbloom[(✉)][iD]

Brown University, Providence, RI 02906, USA
{anna_lysyanskaya,leah_rosenbloom}@brown.edu

Abstract. Numerous cryptographic applications require efficient non-interactive zero-knowledge proofs of knowledge (NIZKPoK) as a building block. Typically they rely on the Fiat-Shamir heuristic to do so, as security in the random-oracle model is considered good enough in practice. However, there is a troubling disconnect between the stand-alone security of such a protocol and its security as part of a larger, more complex system where several protocols may be running at the same time. Provable security in the general universal composition model (GUC model) of Canetti et al. is the best guarantee that nothing will go wrong when a system is part of a larger whole, even when all parties share a common random oracle. In this paper, we prove the minimal necessary properties of generally universally composable (GUC) NIZKPoK in any global random-oracle model, and show how to achieve efficient and GUC NIZKPoK in both the restricted programmable and restricted observable (non-programmable) global random-oracle models.

1 Introduction

Non-interactive zero-knowledge proofs of knowledge (NIZKPoK) [5,28,42] form the basis of many cryptographic protocols that are on the cusp of widespread adoption in practice. For example, the Helios voting system [1] and other efficient systems employing cryptographic shuffles [46] use zero-knowledge proofs of knowledge to ensure that each participant in the system correctly followed the protocol and shuffled or decrypted its inputs correctly. Anonymous e-cash [12] and e-token [11] systems use them to compute proofs of validity of an e-coin or e-token. In group signatures [2,18] they are used to ensure that the signer is in possession of a group signing key. In anonymous credential constructions [13,14], they are used to ensure that the user identified by a given pseudonym is in possession of a credential issued by a particular organization.

The non-interactive aspect of NIZKPoK is especially important to most of these applications—it enables a prover to form a proof of some attribute for a *general* verifier rather than forcing the prover to talk to each verifier individually, which is inefficient in most cases and infeasible for some applications. It is also extremely important that the NIZKPoK be efficient. Thus, the constructions cited above use efficient Σ-protocols [26] made non-interactive via the Fiat-Shamir heuristic [29] to instantiate the NIZKPoK in the random-oracle model

E. Kiltz and V. Vaikuntanathan (Eds.): TCC 2022, LNCS 13747, pp. 203–233, 2022.
https://doi.org/10.1007/978-3-031-22318-1_8

(ROM) [3]. Recall that a Σ-protocol for a relation R is, in a nutshell, a $(1 - \mathsf{negl})$-sound honest-verifier three-move proof system in which the single message from the verifier to the prover is a random ℓ-bit string. The Fiat-Shamir transform makes the proof system non-interactive by replacing the message from the verifier with the output of a random oracle (RO).

Recently, a better understanding of how badly such NIZKPoK fare in the *concurrent* setting emerged [4, 27, 39, 44]. Allowing for secure concurrent executions is of vital importance for the real-world application of any of the cryptographic protocols mentioned above, and especially for distributed protocols. But Drijvers et al. [27] demonstrated subtleties in the proofs of security for concurrent protocol executions that often go undetected, leaving building-block cryptographic protocols vulnerable to attacks like Wagner [44] and Benhamouda et al.'s exploitation of the ROS problem [4].

One way to circumvent the unique subtleties of composing cryptographic primitives is to prove that each primitive is *universally composable* using Canetti's universal composition (UC) framework [19]. In the UC framework, the security of a particular session of a protocol is analyzed with respect to an environment, which represents an arbitrary set of concurrent protocols. The environment in the UC framework can talk to and collude with the traditional "adversary" in cryptographic protocols, directing it to interfere with the protocol. However, the original UC framework did not provide a mechanism for parties in different settings to use a shared global functionality, for instance a shared RO or common reference string (CRS). In real-world applications, it is virtually guaranteed that parties will share setup and state between sessions.

To address the issue of shared state and concurrency in the UC framework, Canetti, Dodis, Pass, and Walfish developed the *general* UC (GUC) framework, which considers "global" functionalities $\mathcal{G}$ that can be queried by any party in any session at any time, including the environment [20]. Canetti, Jain, and Scafuro later showed several practical applications of the GUC framework with a restricted observable global RO $\mathcal{G}_{\mathrm{roRO}}$ as the only trusted setup. They include commitment, oblivious transfer, and secure function evaluation protocols, all GUC in the $\mathcal{G}_{\mathrm{roRO}}$-hybrid model [22]. Building on Canetti et al.'s framework, Camenisch, Drijvers, Gagliardoni, Lehmann, and Neven developed a restricted *programmable* observable global RO, denoted $\mathcal{G}_{\mathrm{rpoRO}}$, that allows for more efficient GUC commitments in the $\mathcal{G}_{\mathrm{rpoRO}}$-hybrid model [10].

Thus, the $\mathcal{G}_{\mathrm{roRO}}$- and $\mathcal{G}_{\mathrm{rpoRO}}$-hybrid models are attractive ones for constructing and analyzing practical and composable non-interactive zero-knowledge proofs. Obtaining an efficient NIZKPoK (for a relation R) in either global ROM from an efficient Σ-protocol (for the same relation) is a natural goal. We begin by showing that any protocol that can be considered a GUC NIZKPoK in *any* global ROM must satisfy particular flavors of completeness, zero-knowledge, and soundness (formalized in Definitions 3, 4, and 5, respectively)—i.e., that these flavors are necessary to achieve security in the global RO model.

Theorem 1 (Informal). *If a protocol is a GUC NIZKPoK in any global ROM, then it satisfies Definitions 3, 4, and 5.*

Next, we obtain GUC NIZKPoK in the (programmable) $\mathcal{G}_{\mathrm{rpoRO}}$-hybrid model by using a straight-line compiler on *any* Σ-protocol. A straight-line compiler [30] transforms a Σ-protocol into a non-interactive zero-knowledge proof system in which the knowledge extractor uses the proof itself as well as the adversary's random-oracle query history in order to compute an adversarial prover's witness. (More formally, the resulting protocol satisfies our Definitions 3–5.)

Theorem 2 (Informal). *The non-interactive proof system obtained by running any Σ-protocol for relation R through any straight-line compiler is a GUC NIZKPoK for relation R in the $\mathcal{G}_{\mathrm{rpoRO}}$-hybrid model.*

While the programming property of $\mathcal{G}_{\mathrm{rpoRO}}$ is helpful in proving security, it also localizes aspects of the global RO by providing a programming verification interface that concurrent protocols cannot access. It is unclear how localized interfaces that are vital to the security of component protocols might impact the security analysis of composed protocols.

Therefore, we also consider NIZKPoK in the less restrictive (non-programmable) $\mathcal{G}_{\mathrm{roRO}}$-hybrid model, where $\mathcal{G}_{\mathrm{roRO}}$'s interfaces are completely public. Unfortunately, Pass [40] and Canetti et al. [22] point out that it is not possible to construct NIZKPoK using *only* a global functionality, because there is no way for the simulator in the security experiment to exercise control over it. We introduce a new model called the $\mathcal{G}_{\mathrm{roRO}}$-$\mathcal{F}_{\mathrm{CRS}}$-hybrid model, in which protocol participants have access to a trusted common reference string (CRS) functionality. Participants can compute this CRS for a one-time cost at the beginning of the session using only $\mathcal{G}_{\mathrm{roRO}}$ and Canetti et al.'s GUC non-interactive secure computation (NISC) protocol [22]. We prove that any straight-line compiler in conjunction with our new construction, which uses a special type of Σ-protocol called an OR-protocol [24,26], is sufficient to transform any Σ-protocol into a GUC NIZKPoK in the $\mathcal{G}_{\mathrm{roRO}}$-$\mathcal{F}_{\mathrm{CRS}}$-hybrid model.

Theorem 3 (Informal). *The non-interactive proof system obtained by composing any Σ-protocol for relation R with a local CRS relation S and running the combined OR-protocol through any straight-line compiler is a GUC NIZKPoK for relation $R \vee S$ in the $\mathcal{G}_{\mathrm{roRO}}$-$\mathcal{F}_{\mathrm{CRS}}$-hybrid model.*

The straight-line compiler we use ensures that the protocols we obtain satisfy the flavors of completeness, zero-knowledge, and soundness from Definitions 3, 4, and 5. Combined with Theorem 1, this demonstrates that these flavors are both necessary and sufficient.

Finally, we realize our GUC transforms for Σ-protocols using Kondi and shelat's randomized version of the Fischlin transform [30,35], demonstrating that it is possible to construct *efficient* GUC NIZKPoK from a broad class of Σ-protocols in both the $\mathcal{G}_{\mathrm{rpoRO}}$ and $\mathcal{G}_{\mathrm{roRO}}$-$\mathcal{F}_{\mathrm{CRS}}$-hybrid models.

Along the way, we uncover theoretical observations that may be of independent interest. First, that straight-line compilers afford strong security guarantees: because they work exclusively using information the adversary already knows, we can compose them with other building blocks such as zero-knowledge simulators without compromising the security of the overall system. This "decoupling" property [30], and security properties of non-rewinding extractors in general, are of interest in the quantum random-oracle model (QROM), where rewinding is tricky because of the no-cloning theorem [34,43,45]. It is the subject of future work to explore whether other mechanisms of straight-line extraction (for example, ones that do not rely on the adversary's query history) [17,34,40,43] are sufficient to bootstrap Σ-protocols into GUC NIZKPoK in the $\mathcal{G}_{\mathrm{rpoRO}}$- or $\mathcal{G}_{\mathrm{roRO}}$-$\mathcal{F}_{\mathrm{CRS}}$-hybrid models, a different global ROM, or the QROM.

Organization. In the remainder of the introduction, we provide general background information on Σ-protocols, the GUC model, the global ROM(s), and straight-line extraction. In Sect. 2, we give formal definitions of Σ-protocols and straight-line compilers. Section 3 contains definitions of GUC-security in various global ROMs and a proof of Theorem 1 (that any GUC NIZKPoK must have the security properties afforded by straight-line compilers). In Sect. 4, we prove Theorem 2 (that any straight-line compiler is sufficient to transform any Σ-protocol into a GUC NIZKPoK in the $\mathcal{G}_{\mathrm{rpoRO}}$-hybrid model), and in Sect. 5 we prove Theorem 3 (that any straight-line compiler in conjunction with our OR-protocol construction is sufficient to complete the transform in the $\mathcal{G}_{\mathrm{roRO}}$-$\mathcal{F}_{\mathrm{CRS}}$-hybrid model). Finally in Sect. 6, we leverage the randomized Fischlin transform to efficiently realize our constructions in both global ROMs.

Σ-Protocols. A Σ-protocol for a binary $\mathcal{NP}$ relation R is a three-round, public-coin proof system. On input x and w such that $(x, w) \in R$, the prover generates its first message com (in the literature on Σ protocols, this first message is often referred to as a "commitment"). In response, the honest verifier sends a unique ℓ-length *random* "challenge" chl to the prover. Finally, the prover "responds" with a value res. The resulting transcript (com, chl, res) is then fed to a verification algorithm that determines whether the verifier accepts or rejects.

Σ-protocols must additionally satisfy three properties. First, they must satisfy *completeness*: if the prover has a valid witness and both parties engage in the protocol honestly, the verifier always accepts. Next, they must be *special honest-verifier zero-knowledge*: there must exist a simulator algorithm that on input x and chl $\in \{0,1\}^\ell$ outputs an accepting transcript (com, chl, res) for x such that, if chl was chosen uniformly at random, (com, chl, res) is indistinguishable from that output by an honest prover on input x. Finally, they must have *special soundness*: if there are two accepting transcripts for any statement with the same commitment com but different challenges chl $\neq$ chl$'$, there exists an extractor algorithm that can produce a valid witness from the transcripts. The stronger version of soundness, special *simulation* soundness, says that special soundness must still hold even if an adversary has oracle access to the simulator.

The Σ-protocol format captures many practical zero-knowledge proof systems. For example, Wikström [46] shows Σ-protocols for proving a rich set of relations between ElGamal ciphertexts, which in turn allow proving that a set of ciphertexts was shuffled correctly; similar protocols exist for Paillier ciphertexts [17,23]. A robust body of literature exists giving Σ-protocols for proving that values committed using Pedersen [41] and Fujisaki-Okamoto [32] commitments satisfy general algebraic and Boolean circuits [8,15,16] and lie in certain integer ranges [6,36]. For all the Σ-protocols listed above, the size and complexity of the proof system is a $O(1)$ factor of the complexity of verifying the underlying relation $R(x, w)$, making Σ-protocols extremely desirable in practice.

Σ-protocols are also the most efficient technique to achieve zero-knowledge proofs of knowledge of a commitment opening in the lattice setting [25,38], where the complexity grows by a factor of $O(k)$ in order to achieve soundness $(1 - 2^{-k})$. Thus, for all the relations R cited above, our results immediately yield the most efficient known GUC NIZKPoK in the global ROM.

The General Universal Composability (GUC) Model. Our security experiment is that of the GUC model of Canetti et al. [20], which enables the UC-security analysis of protocols with global functionalities.

Briefly, the UC and GUC modeling of the world envisions an adversarial environment $\mathcal{Z}$, which provides inputs to honest participants, observes their outputs, and (at a high level) directs the order in which messages are passed between different system components. Additionally, the world includes honest participants (that receive inputs from $\mathcal{Z}$ and let $\mathcal{Z}$ observe their outputs) and adversarial participants controlled by the adversary $\mathcal{A}$ (whose behavior is also directed and observed by $\mathcal{Z}$).

The ideal world additionally contains an ideal functionality $\mathcal{F}$ and an ideal adversary $\mathcal{S}$, also called the simulator. In the ideal world, the honest participants pass their inputs directly to $\mathcal{F}$ and receive output from it. The real world does not contain such a functionality; instead, the honest participants run a cryptographic protocol. The corrupted participants in the ideal world always communicate through $\mathcal{S}$, who simulates their view and may pass their inputs to $\mathcal{F}$ through a private channel. There are also worlds in between these two: in a $\mathcal{G}$-hybrid world, the honest participants run a protocol that can make calls to an ideal functionality $\mathcal{G}$. In the GUC model, $\mathcal{G}$ is accessible not only to the honest participants, but also to $\mathcal{Z}$. A cryptographic protocol is said to be (G)UC with respect to a functionality $\mathcal{F}$ (in other words, the protocol (G)UC-realizes $\mathcal{F}$) if for any real-world adversary $\mathcal{A}$, there exists an "ideal" adversary (simulator) $\mathcal{S}$ which creates a view for the environment (in the ideal world) that is indistinguishable from its view of the cryptographic protocol.

In our case, the ideal functionality is the NIZKPoK ideal functionality, or $\mathcal{F}_{\text{NIZK}}$, which works as follows. An honest participant in a protocol session s can compute a proof π of knowledge of w such that $(x, w) \in R$ by querying $\mathcal{F}_{\text{NIZK}}$'s **Prove** interface and giving it (s, x, w). The string π itself is computed according to the algorithm SimProve provided by the ideal adversary $\mathcal{S}$. The functionality guarantees the zero-knowledge property because SimProve is independent of w. An honest participant can also verify a supposed proof π for x by querying $\mathcal{F}_{\texttt{NIZK}}$'s **Verify** interface on input (x, π). $\mathcal{F}_{\texttt{NIZK}}$ ensures the soundness of the proof system as follows: if the proof π was *not* issued by $\mathcal{F}_{\texttt{NIZK}}$, then it runs an extractor algorithm Extract provided by $\mathcal{S}$ to try to compute a witness w from the proof π. The Extract algorithm may also require additional inputs from $\mathcal{S}$.

The Global Random-Oracle Models (Global ROMs). The traditional random oracle (RO) $H : \{0,1\}^* \to \{0,1\}^\ell$ is a function that takes any string as input and returns a uniformly random ℓ-bit string as output [3]. The global random-oracle model (global ROM) allows us to capture the realistic scenario in which the same RO is reused by many parties over many (potentially concurrent) executions of numerous distinct protocols. As envisioned by Canetti et al. [22] and formalized by Camenisch et al. [10], the "strict" global RO functionality $\mathcal{G}_{\texttt{sRO}}$ is a public, universally-accessible RO that can be queried by any party in any protocol execution, including by the arbitrary concurrent protocols modeled by the environment in the UC framework [20].

Pass [40], Canetti and Fischlin [21], Canetti et al. [20,22], and Camenisch et al. [10] have all discussed the limitations of $\mathcal{G}_{\texttt{sRO}}$. In particular, Canetti and Fischlin [21] demonstrated that it is impossible to achieve UC commitments with *only* a global setup, and Canetti et al. extended this argument to commitments and zero knowledge in the GUC framework [20] and the $\mathcal{G}_{\texttt{roRO}}$-hybrid model [22]. The limitation stems from the fact that in a "strict" setup, the simulator does not have any special advantage over a regular protocol participant. In our setting, $\mathcal{F}_{\texttt{NIZK}}$ needs to *observe* the adversary's RO queries in order to extract witnesses and ensure the special soundness property. Most zero-knowledge simulators also rely on the extra ability to *program* the RO at selected points in order to simulate proofs of statements without witnesses.

Canetti et al. first introduced a global RO $\mathcal{G}_{\texttt{roRO}}$ with a restricted "observability" property [22]. The ideal adversary (simulator) $\mathcal{S}$ in the security proof of a protocol Π emulating an ideal functionality $\mathcal{F}$ in the $\mathcal{G}_{\texttt{roRO}}$-hybrid model is able to observe all adversarial queries to $\mathcal{G}_{\texttt{roRO}}$ as follows. First, $\mathcal{S}$ can observe the corrupted parties' queries to $\mathcal{G}_{\texttt{roRO}}$ by directly monitoring their input and output wires (recall that in the ideal world, corrupted parties communicate through $\mathcal{S}$). The *environment's* queries to $\mathcal{G}_{\texttt{roRO}}$, on the other hand, are not directly monitored by $\mathcal{S}$. Since $\mathcal{G}_{\texttt{roRO}}$ is completely public, the environment is free to query it anytime; however, the environment is not free to query it with the same session identifier (SID) as the participants in Π or $\mathcal{F}$, because it is external to legitimate sessions of Π by definition. In order to ensure the environment's queries are still available to the simulator, $\mathcal{G}_{\texttt{roRO}}$ checks whether the SID for a query matches the SID of the querent. In the event that it does not, this query is labelled "illegitimate," creating the restriction. $\mathcal{G}_{\texttt{roRO}}$ makes a record of all illegitimate queries available to an ideal functionality $\mathcal{F}$ with the correct SID, if it exists. We will see that for our construction of GUC NIZKPoK in the $\mathcal{G}_{\texttt{rpoRO}}$- and $\mathcal{G}_{\texttt{roRO}}$-$\mathcal{F}_{\texttt{CRS}}$-

hybrid models, $\mathcal{F}_{\text{NIZK}}$ can leverage these queries to extract witnesses from the environment's proofs.

Camenisch et al.'s restricted *programmable* observable global RO $\mathcal{G}_{\text{rpoRO}}$ [10] builds on the functionality of $\mathcal{G}_{\text{roRO}}$ as follows. In order to ensure that programming is restricted to the simulator, $\mathcal{G}_{\text{rpoRO}}$ has an IsProgrammed interface that allows participants with a particular SID to check whether the output of $\mathcal{G}_{\text{rpoRO}}$ was programmed on some input pertaining to the *same session*. Honest parties in the challenge session can therefore check whether the adversary has programmed $\mathcal{G}_{\text{rpoRO}}$, and can refuse to continue the protocol if so. In the real world, no programming occurs; in the ideal world, the simulator, who controls the corrupted parties' views of the experiment, can program $\mathcal{G}_{\text{rpoRO}}$ and then pretend it did not program anything by returning "false" to all of the corrupted parties' IsProgrammed queries. Since only parties running a legitimate protocol session s are allowed to use the IsProgrammed interface for s, the environment cannot make IsProgrammed queries for s—if it could, it would easily be able to distinguish between the real and ideal experiments by checking whether honest parties' responses were programmed.

We show how to construct efficient, GUC NIZKPoK in the $\mathcal{G}_{\text{rpoRO}}$-hybrid model. However, we believe there may be downsides to programmable global ROs like $\mathcal{G}_{\text{rpoRO}}$: it is not clear how compromising the fully-public aspect of the global RO with a locally-restricted interface might impact the overall composability of protocols proven secure in the $\mathcal{G}_{\text{rpoRO}}$-hybrid model.[1] In order to achieve efficient GUC NIZKPoK *without* this localized interface, we build a new hybrid model called the $\mathcal{G}_{\text{roRO}}$-$\mathcal{F}_{\text{CRS}}$-hybrid model. The $\mathcal{G}_{\text{roRO}}$-$\mathcal{F}_{\text{CRS}}$-hybrid model shifts the localized interface from inside of the global RO to *inside of the protocol*. For a one-time cost at the beginning of the protocol execution, participants can compute this CRS securely and realize $\mathcal{F}_{\text{NIZK}}$ *using only the observable global RO* $\mathcal{G}_{\text{roRO}}$ by leveraging Canetti et al.'s GUC NISC protocol [22]. Similar mechanisms are used in practice to obtain practical NIZKPoK in other ROMs [7].

In the real world, our ideal CRS functionality $\mathcal{F}_{\text{CRS}}$ returns a random string CRS (the CRS our real-world participants might compute using the NISC protocol). In the ideal world, the simulator generates CRS itself, along with a trapdoor trap that only it knows. The proof-generation process in our construction of GUC NIZKPoK in the $\mathcal{G}_{\text{roRO}}$-$\mathcal{F}_{\text{CRS}}$-hybrid model is to show that the prover either knows a "real" witness w for a statement x such that $(x, w) \in R$, *or* it knows the trapdoor to the CRS. The Prove and SimProve algorithms differ only in the witness used: a real prover must use a real witness, while the simulator can use trap in a way that we will show is imperceptible to the environment. We formalize this intuition using an OR-protocol [24,26] over the original relation R and what we call a samplable-hard relation for the CRS.

Straight-Line Extraction and the Fischlin Transform. The original Fischlin transform [30] is a non-interactive transform for Σ-protocols in the

---

[1] For a full discussion of the subtle differences between observation and programming privileges in the global ROM(s), see Appendix A.2 in the full version [37].

standard ROM that allows for *straight-line* (or *online*) extraction. Straight-line extraction is a process by which the extractor can produce a witness straight from a valid proof without any further interaction with the prover. (In order to do so, it will need additional, auxiliary information available to the extractor algorithm only.) This is in contrast to extraction in the "rewinding" model, in which the extractor resets the prover to a previous state and hopes for a certain pattern of interaction before it can obtain a witness. Straight-line extraction is necessary in the (G)UC model, which does not allow the simulator to rewind the environment [20]. Furthermore, straight-line extraction produces a tight reduction, which avoids security nuances surrounding the forking lemma [33].

In order to create a straight-line extractable proof system from a Σ-protocol, the Fischlin transform essentially forces the prover to rewind itself, requiring multiple proofs on repeated commitments until the probability that the prover has generated at least two responses to different challenges on the same commitment is overwhelming. Kondi and shelat recently showed that because the Fischlin prover is deterministic—that is, because it tests challenges by iterating from zero to some fixed constant—the original transform is open to a "replay" attack that breaks the the witness indistinguishability property of OR-protocols [35]. To avoid the attack, Fischlin's original construction requires the underlying Σ-protocols to have a property called *quasi-unique responses*, which Kondi and shelat demonstrate precludes the transformation of OR-protocols. Kondi and shelat show how this property can be omitted (and most OR-protocols transformed) by randomizing the challenge selection process and replacing the quasi-unique responses property with a (more general) property called *strong special soundness*. We review the details of the resulting "randomized" Fischlin transform [31,35] in Appendix A.12 of the full version of the paper [37].

2 Preliminaries

We use standard notation, available in Appendix A.1 of the full version [37].

2.1 Σ-protocols, Revisited

Let R be any efficiently computable binary relation. For pairs $(x, w) \in R$, or equivalently such that $R(x, w) = 1$, we call x a statement in the language of R, denoted L_R, and say w is a witness to $x \in L_R$. We consider Σ-protocols over a relation R between a prover P and a verifier V that have the general commit-challenge-respond format discussed in Sect. 1, which Damgård formalizes as a protocol template [26]. Since we will later introduce compilers for Σ-protocols—first to make them non-interactive and straight-line extractable and then to make them GUC—it will be helpful to define Σ-protocol interfaces with precise inputs and outputs. We begin by formalizing an algorithmic version of the protocol template τ as a tuple of algorithms (Setup, Commit, Challenge, Respond, Decision), the details of which are provided alongside Damgård's original version in Appendix A.3 [37].

Σ-protocols must also satisfy the properties of completeness, special honest-verifier zero-knowledge (SHVZK), and special soundness (SS). The SHVZK property requires the existence of a simulator algorithm SimProve for simulating proofs, and the SS property requires an extractor algorithm Extract for extracting witnesses. Therefore, our algorithmic specification of a Σ-protocol includes three additional algorithms: SimSetup, SimProve, and Extract.

In order to more easily translate our definition of Σ-protocols into the non-interactive setting, we combine the Commit, Challenge, and Respond algorithms of the protocol template into a Prove interface. For now we are still dealing with the interactive version, and the specification of Prove below is a two-party protocol where the first input to the algorithm is the prover's input, and the second input is the verifier's. After running Prove, both parties obtain the same copy of the proof transcript $\pi = (\text{com}, \text{chl}, \text{res})$. In the next section, we will introduce a straight-line compiler that makes the Prove interface a non-interactive algorithm in the random-oracle model (ROM). The non-interactive, straight-line extractable (NISLE) proof system resulting from the transformation will have different versions of the SHVZK and SS properties; because we will work almost exclusively with these versions, we defer formal definitions and discussions of the original formulations [26] to Appendix A.5 of the full version of the paper [37].

Definition 1 (Σ-protocol). *A Σ-protocol for a relation R based on a protocol template τ (Definition 15 in [37]) is a tuple of efficient procedures $\Sigma_{R,\tau} = $ (Setup, Prove, Verify, SimSetup, SimProve, Extract), defined as follows.*

- ppm $\leftarrow$ Setup(1^λ): *Given a security parameter 1^λ, invoke τ.Setup(1^λ) to obtain the public parameters* ppm.

- π $\leftarrow$ Prove((ppm, x, w), (ppm, x)): *Let the first (resp. second) argument to Prove be the input of the prover (resp. verifier), where both parties get* ppm *and the statement x, but only the prover gets w. P and V run τ.Commit, τ.Challenge, and τ.Respond. Output $\pi = (\text{com}, \text{chl}, \text{res})$.*

- $\{0,1\}$ $\leftarrow$ Verify(ppm, x, π): *Given a proof π for statemenet x, parse π as (com, chl, res) and output the result of running τ.Decision on input $(x, \text{com}, \text{chl}, \text{res})$. Verify must satisfy the completeness property from Definition 18 in Appendix A.5 of the full version of the paper [37].*

- (ppm, z) $\leftarrow$ SimSetup(1^λ): *Generate* ppm *and the simulation trapdoor z. Together, SimSetup and SimProve must satisfy the special honest-verifier zero-knowledge property from Definition 19 in Appendix A.5.*

- π $\leftarrow$ SimProve(ppm, z, x, chl) : *Given public parameters* ppm, *trapdoor z, statement x, and a challenge chl, produce a proof $\pi = (\text{com}, \text{chl}, \text{res})$.*

- w $\leftarrow$ Extract(ppm, x, π, π') : *Given two proofs $\pi = (\text{com}, \text{chl}, \text{res})$ and $\pi' = (\text{com}, \text{chl}', \text{res}')$ for a statement x such that τ.Decision(x, π) $= \tau$.Decision(x, π') $= 1$ and chl $\neq$ chl', output a witness w. Extract must satisfy the special soundness property from Definition 20 in Appendix A.5.*

For convenience and when the meaning is clear, we use Σ_R to represent $\Sigma_{R,\tau}$ and omit ppm *from the input of the algorithms.*

2.2   Straight-Line Compilers

Inspired by the straight-line transform due to Fischlin [30,31] described in Sect. 1, our formalization of a straight-line compiler (SLC) for Σ-protocols in the random-oracle model (ROM) takes any interactive Σ-protocol Σ_R for relation R and creates a non-interactive, straight-line extractable (NISLE) proof system Π_R^{SLC} for the same relation. Both the proof simulation and witness extraction procedures in a NISLE proof system are non-interactive *algorithms* in the ROM—the challenger in the security experiment may not rely on rewinding the prover, but is permitted to use the adversary's previous queries to the RO.

The non-interactive equivalent of the special honest-verifier zero-knowledge (SHVZK) game must reflect the fact that the zero-knowledge simulator might be programming the RO. The SHVZK property must continue to hold even as the RO is updated, meaning that if the simulator changes the RO at all, it must be done in a way that is imperceptible to to the adversary $\mathcal{A}$. Note that the definition does not imply that the simulator *has* to program the RO—just that if it does, it must do so imperceptibly. This nuance is important because we will later give a construction in Sect. 5.3 for GUC NIZKPoK in the (non-programmable) $\mathcal{G}_{\mathrm{roRO}}$-$\mathcal{F}_{\mathrm{CRS}}$-hybrid model—this construction should not (and does not) contradict our result from Theorem 1, which says that any GUC NIZKPoK must meet the requirements of non-interactive (multiple) SHVZK.

In the non-interactive version of the special soundness (SS) game in Fischlin's construction, the Extract algorithm works on input $(x, \pi, \mathcal{Q}_{\mathcal{A}})$, where $\mathcal{Q}_{\mathcal{A}}$ are $\mathcal{A}$'s queries to the RO. Fischlin's approach is not the only one for achieving straight-line extraction. Verifiable encryption [9,17] provides a different mechanism: the parameters ppm contain a public key, and the proof π contains an encryption of the witness under this key. The extractor's trapdoor is the decryption key. The latter approach requires additional machinery: it needs a proof system for proving that a plaintext of a particular ciphertext is a witness w, and thus cannot be constructed directly from Σ_R. It is the subject of future work to determine how such a "key-based" extractor would fare; for now, we assume the extractor works on the adversary's queries to the RO.

Finally, Fischlin proposes an optional (negligible) weakening of the completeness property, which we call overwhelming completeness, that allows protocol designers to optimize other parameters for efficiency reasons. Certainly any SLC that satisfies the regular notion of completeness will also satisfy the weaker notion, so we recall the weaker property below and demonstrate in Sect. 3.5 that it is sufficient for GUC NIZKPoK.

Definition 2 (Straight-Line Compiler). *An algorithm SLC is a straight-line compiler (SLC) in the random-oracle model if given any Σ-protocol Σ_R for relation R (Definition 1) as input, it outputs a tuple of algorithms $\Pi_R^{\mathrm{SLC}} = (\mathrm{Setup}^H, \mathrm{Prove}^H, \mathrm{Verify}^H, \mathrm{SimSetup}, \mathrm{SimProve}, \mathrm{Extract})$ with access to random oracle H that satisfy the following properties: overwhelming completeness (Definition 3), non-interactive multiple special honest-verifier zero-knowledge (Definition 4), and non-interactive special simulation-soundness (Definition 5).*

We refer to $\Pi_R^{\text{SLC}} \leftarrow \text{SLC}(\Sigma_R)$ as a non-interactive, straight-line extractable (NISLE) proof system for R, and proofs generated by Π_R^{SLC} as non-interactive, straight-line extractable zero-knowledge proofs of knowledge (NISLE ZKPoK).

Definition 3 (Overwhelming Completeness). *A NISLE proof system* $\Pi_R^{\text{SLC}} = (\text{Setup}^H, \text{Prove}^H, \text{Verify}^H, \text{SimSetup}, \text{SimProve}, \text{Extract})$ *for relation R in the random-oracle model has the* overwhelming completeness *property if for any security parameter λ, any random oracle H, any $(x, w) \in R$, and any proof $\pi \leftarrow \Pi_R^{\text{SLC}}.\text{Prove}^H(x, w)$,*

$$\Pr[\Pi_R^{\text{SLC}}.\text{Verify}^H(x, \pi) = 1] \geq 1 - \text{negl}(\lambda).$$

Recall from the introduction of this section that the simulator in the non-interactive version of the SHVZK experiment is allowed to program the RO. In order to precisely describe this programming, we differentiate in Fig. 1 the traditional RO H_f, which is parameterized by a function $f \leftarrow_\$ F$ selected from random function family F, from the programmable RO H_L, which is parameterized by a *list* L that can be added to (but not edited by) the simulator. We call this type of oracle a "Random List Oracle," and provide the simulator algorithms in the non-interactive SHVZK game oracle access to an interface Prog_L, which allows the caller to map any (previously unmapped) input x to an output v of its choice. The adversary's inability to distinguish between the real-world oracle H_f that is simply a random function and the ideal-world oracle H_L that is a list managed by the simulator is an essential part of the non-interactive SHVZK experiment—it ensures that the introduction of the non-interactivity property (via queries to a programmable RO) does not compromise the SHVZK property.

RO $H_f(x)$	Random List Oracle $H_L(x)$	Interface $\text{Prog}_L(x, v)$
1: **return** $f(x)$	1: **if** $\exists v$ **s.t.** $(x, v) \in L$:	1: **if** $\nexists v'$ **s.t.** $(x, v') \in L$:
	2: **return** v	2: $L.\textbf{append}(x, v)$
	3: **else** :	
	4: $v \leftarrow \{0, 1\}^\ell$	
	5: $L.\textbf{append}(x, v)$	
	6: **return** v	

Fig. 1. Random oracle functionalities for NIM-SHVZK and NI-SSS games.

In the standard definition of SHVZK, $\mathscr{A}$ is only permitted to issue *one* Prove query. In the GUC security experiment (and in most natural applications of Σ-protocols), the environment is allowed to issue polynomially-many Prove queries, and we will still need the SHVZK property to hold. Therefore, we present a version of non-interactive *multiple* SHVZK (NIM-SHVZK) [30].

Definition 4 (Non-interactive Multiple SHVZK). *A NISLE proof system* $\Pi_R^{\mathrm{SLC}} = (\mathrm{Setup}^H, \mathrm{Prove}^H, \mathrm{Verify}^H, \mathrm{SimSetup}, \mathrm{SimProve}, \mathrm{Extract})$ *for relation* R *in the random-oracle model has the* non-interactive multiple special honest-verifier zero-knowledge *(NIM-SHVZK) property if for any security parameter* λ, *any random oracle* H, *any* PPT *adversary* $\mathscr{A}$, *and a bit* $b \leftarrow_\$ \{0, 1\}$, *there exists some negligible function* negl *such that* $\Pr[b' = b] \leq \frac{1}{2} + \mathrm{negl}(\lambda)$, *where* b' *is the result of running the game* $\mathrm{NIM\text{--}SHVZK}_{\mathscr{A}, \Pi_R^{\mathrm{SLC}}}^{H*,*}(1^\lambda, b)$ *from Fig. 2. We say* $\mathscr{A}$ *wins the* NIM–SHVZK *game if* $\Pr[b' = b] > \frac{1}{2} + \mathrm{negl}(\lambda)$.

$\mathrm{NIM\text{--}SHVZK}_{\mathscr{A}, \Pi_R^{\mathrm{SLC}}}^{H*, F}(1^\lambda, 0) : \mathrm{REAL}$		$\mathrm{NIM\text{--}SHVZK}_{\mathscr{A}, \Pi_R^{\mathrm{SLC}}}^{H*, \mathrm{Prog}}(1^\lambda, 1) : \mathrm{IDEAL}$	
1 :	$f \leftarrow_\$ F$	1 :	$L \leftarrow \perp$
2 :	$\mathrm{ppm} \leftarrow \Pi_R^{\mathrm{SLC}}.\mathrm{Setup}^{H_f}(1^\lambda)$	2 :	$\mathrm{ppm}, z \leftarrow \Pi_R^{\mathrm{SLC}}.\mathrm{SimSetup}^{\mathrm{Prog}_L}(1^\lambda)$
3 :	$\mathrm{st} \leftarrow \mathscr{A}^{H_f}(1^\lambda, \mathrm{ppm})$	3 :	$\mathrm{st} \leftarrow \mathscr{A}^{H_L}(1^\lambda, \mathrm{ppm})$
4 :	$\mathbf{while}\ \mathrm{st} \notin \{0, 1\}$:	4 :	$\mathbf{while}\ \mathrm{st} \notin \{0, 1\}$:
5 :	$(\mathrm{Prove}, x, w, \mathrm{st}) \leftarrow \mathscr{A}^{H_f}(\mathrm{st})$	5 :	$(\mathrm{Prove}, x, w, \mathrm{st}) \leftarrow \mathscr{A}^{H_L}(\mathrm{st})$
6 :	$\mathbf{if}\ R(x, w) = 1$:	6 :	$\mathbf{if}\ R(x, w) = 1$:
7 :	$\pi \leftarrow \Pi_R^{\mathrm{SLC}}.\mathrm{Prove}^{H_f}(x, w)$	7 :	$\pi \leftarrow \Pi_R^{\mathrm{SLC}}.\mathrm{SimProve}^{\mathrm{Prog}_L}(z, x)$
8 :	$\mathbf{else}$:	8 :	$\mathbf{else}$:
9 :	$\pi \leftarrow \perp$	9 :	$\pi \leftarrow \perp$
10 :	$\mathrm{st} \leftarrow \mathscr{A}^{H_f}(\mathrm{st}, \pi)$	10 :	$\mathrm{st} \leftarrow \mathscr{A}^{H_L}(\mathrm{st}, \pi)$
11 :	$\mathbf{return}\ \mathrm{st}$	11 :	$\mathbf{return}\ \mathrm{st}$

Fig. 2. Non-interactive multiple SHVZK (NIM-SHVZK) game.

Similarly, the environment in the ideal-world GUC experiment will have access to polynomially-many proofs generated by the SimProve algorithm, which $\mathcal{F}_{\mathrm{NIZK}}$ will use to simulate proofs. We therefore define our straight-line compilers to have the NI special *simulation* soundness property (NI-SSS), which says that special soundness must still hold even after an adversary has seen polynomially-many proofs from the simulator. Fischlin's original construction is both NIM-SHVZK and NI-SSS [30]. We will use his results in Sect. 6.1 to prove that the randomized Fischlin transform [30,35] is also NIM-SHVZK and NI-SSS.

Definition 5 (Non-interactive Special Simulation-Soundness). *A NISLE proof system* $\Pi_R^{\mathrm{SLC}} = (\mathrm{Setup}^H, \mathrm{Prove}^H, \mathrm{Verify}^H, \mathrm{SimSetup}, \mathrm{SimProve}, \mathrm{Extract})$ *for relation* R *in the random-oracle model has the* non-interactive special simulation-soundness *property if for any security parameter* λ, *any random oracle* H, *and any* PPT *adversary* $\mathscr{A}$, *there exists some negligible function* negl *such that*

$$\Pr[\mathbf{Fail} \leftarrow \mathrm{NI\text{--}SSS}_{\mathscr{A}, \Pi_R^{\mathrm{SLC}}}^{H*, \mathrm{Prog}}(1^\lambda)] \leq \mathrm{negl}(\lambda),$$

where NI–SSS *is the game described in Fig. 3. We say* $\mathscr{A}$ *wins if* $\Pr[\mathtt{Fail} \leftarrow$ NI-$\mathrm{SSS}^{H_*,\mathtt{Prog}}_{\mathscr{A},\Pi^{\mathrm{SLC}}_R}(1^\lambda)] > \mathsf{negl}(\lambda)$.

$$\mathrm{NI\text{–}SSS}^{H_*,\mathtt{Prog}}_{\mathscr{A},\Pi^{\mathrm{SLC}}_R}(1^\lambda)$$

1:   $L \leftarrow \bot$

2:   $\mathbf{ppm}, z \leftarrow \Pi^{\mathrm{SLC}}_R.\mathsf{SimSetup}^{\mathtt{Prog}_L}(1^\lambda)$

3:   $\mathbf{st} \leftarrow \mathscr{A}^{H_L}(1^\lambda, \mathbf{ppm})$

4:   $\mathbf{pflist}, \mathtt{Response} \leftarrow \bot$

5:   **while** $\mathbf{st} \neq \bot$:

6:    $(\mathtt{Query}, \mathcal{Q}_{\mathscr{A}}, \mathbf{st}) \leftarrow \mathscr{A}^{H_L}(\mathbf{st})$

7:    **if** $\mathtt{Query} = (\mathtt{Prove}, x, w)$:

8:     **if** $R(x, w) = 1$:

9:      $\pi \leftarrow \Pi^{\mathrm{SLC}}_R.\mathsf{SimProve}^{\mathtt{Prog}_L}(z, x)$

10:      $\mathbf{pflist}.\mathbf{append}(x, \pi)$

11:      $\mathtt{Response} \leftarrow (x, \pi)$

12:    **elseif** $\mathtt{Query} = (\mathtt{Challenge}, x, \pi)$:

13:     **if** $\Pi^{\mathrm{SLC}}_R.\mathsf{Verify}^{H_L}(x, \pi) = 1 \wedge (x, \pi) \notin \mathbf{pflist}$:

14:      $w \leftarrow \Pi^{\mathrm{SLC}}_R.\mathsf{Extract}(x, \pi, \mathcal{Q}_{\mathscr{A}})$

15:      **if** $R(x, w) = 0$:

16:       **return** $\mathtt{Fail}$

17:    $\mathbf{st} \leftarrow \mathscr{A}^{H_L}(\mathbf{st}, \mathtt{Response})$

18: **return** $\mathtt{Success}$

Fig. 3. Non-interactive special simulation-soundness (NI-SSS) game.

Σ-protocols that maintain the SHVZK property under any non-interactive transform in the ROM must additionally have com messages with entropy that is superlogarithmic in the security parameter [31], such that the adversary cannot exhaustively query commitments to the RO and check whether the challenge supplied by the prover matches what it receives. We recall and discuss Fischlin's *superlogarithmic commitment entropy* property further in Appendix A.7 [37].

2.3   OR-Protocols

Rather than producing a proof corresponding to a single statement x in a language L_R, the prover in an OR-protocol proves that it knows a witness for *either* a statement x_0 in L_{R_0} *or* another statement x_1 in L_{R_1}. At a high level, the prover does this by simulating the proof of the statement for which it does not have a witness, while computing the proof of the statement for which it *does* have a witness honestly.

Our definition is adapted directly from Damgård's [26], with a few minor tweaks to make it more general. Since we will use the OR-protocol functionality as a black box in our construction, it suffices for the purpose of understanding our results to treat the OR-protocol as a Σ-protocol (according to Definition 1) with *compound inputs*. For example, we represent the compound statement $x_0 \vee x_1$ with the upper-case variable $X = (x_0, x_1)$. The witness $W = (w, b)$ includes a witness along with a bit b such that $(x_b, w) \in R_b$. We provide the detailed version of our definition alongside Damgård's, as well as a discussion of the minor differences between them, in Appendix A.8 of the full version [37].

3   Properties of GUC NIZKPoK

In this section we formalize the definitions of the programmable global RO $\mathcal{G}_{\text{rpoRO}}$ and the observable global RO $\mathcal{G}_{\text{roRO}}$, the ideal NIZKPoK functionality $\mathcal{F}_{\text{NIZK}}$, the CRS ideal functionality $\mathcal{F}_{\text{CRS}}$, and the security requirements for protocols that GUC-realize $\mathcal{F}_{\text{NIZK}}$ in the $\mathcal{G}_{\text{rpoRO}}$- and $\mathcal{G}_{\text{roRO}}$-$\mathcal{F}_{\text{CRS}}$-hybrid models. We then show that the non-interactive multi-SHVZK and non-interactive special simulation-soundness properties are *strictly necessary* to obtain GUC NIZKPoK in any global ROM.

3.1 $\mathcal{G}_{\text{roRO}}$ and $\mathcal{G}_{\text{rpoRO}}$, Revisited

Building on the overview of the global ROM(s) given in Sect. 1, we now formalize Canetti et al.'s restricted observable global RO $\mathcal{G}_{\text{roRO}}$ [22] and Camenisch et al.'s restricted programmable observable global RO $\mathcal{G}_{\text{rpoRO}}$. As with traditional ROs, both oracles act as functions that respond to each input string $x_i \in \{0,1\}^*$ with a uniformly random ℓ-bit string $v_i \in \{0,1\}^\ell$. We call this original algorithm Query. Since $\mathcal{G}_{\text{rpoRO}}$ builds on the interfaces of $\mathcal{G}_{\text{roRO}}$, we will start with the specification of $\mathcal{G}_{\text{roRO}}$ and follow with the extra interfaces of $\mathcal{G}_{\text{rpoRO}}$.

The first thing $\mathcal{G}_{\text{roRO}}$ does when it receives a query is to check whether the querent's SID sid matches the session s for which it has requested randomness. If $\text{sid} \neq s$, $\mathcal{G}_{\text{roRO}}$ assumes this is an "illegitimate" query made by the environment, and records the query in its special list of illegitimate queries for s, denoted $\mathcal{Q}_s$. In the original version of the definition [22], only the ideal functionality $\mathcal{F}^s$ for session s can query $\mathcal{G}_{\text{roRO}}$ using the Observe interface to get the list of illegitimate queries for s. However, note that no honest provers' queries will ever be recorded in this list, as they will only ever be querying $\mathcal{G}_{\text{roRO}}$ for randomness sessions in which they are participating legitimately. Therefore, we follow Camenisch et al.'s version of the restricted observability property [10] and simply release the list $\mathcal{Q}_s$ to anyone who wants it.

Definition 6 (Observable Global RO $\mathcal{G}_{\text{roRO}}$). *[10, 22] The observable global RO $\mathcal{G}_{\text{roRO}}$ is a tuple of algorithms (Query, Observe) defined over an output length ℓ and an initially empty list of queries $\mathcal{Q}$:*

- $v \leftarrow$ Query(x) : *Parse x as (s, x') where s is an SID. If a list $\mathcal{Q}_s$ of illegitimiate queries for s does not yet exist, set $\mathcal{Q}_s = \perp$. If the caller's SID $\neq s$, add (x, v) to $\mathcal{Q}_s$. If there already exists a pair (x, v) in the query list $\mathcal{Q}$, return v. Otherwise, choose v uniformly at random from $\{0,1\}^\ell$, store the pair (x, v) in $\mathcal{Q}$, and return v.*

- $\mathcal{Q}_s \leftarrow$ Observe(s) : *If a list $\mathcal{Q}_s$ of illegitimate queries for s does not yet exist, set $\mathcal{Q}_s = \perp$. Return $\mathcal{Q}_s$.*

In addition to the Query and Observe interfaces, Camenisch et al.'s restricted *programmable* observable global RO $\mathcal{G}_{\mathrm{rpoRO}}$ has two extra interfaces, Program and IsProgrammed. $\mathcal{G}_{\mathrm{rpoRO}}$ keeps track of which queries have been programmed using the set prog. Note that since privileged (simulator-only) programming is not allowed in the GUC model, anyone can program $\mathcal{G}_{\mathrm{rpoRO}}$. In order to functionally restrict this privilege to the simulator, Camenisch et al. introduces the IsProgrammed interface, which reveals whether or not $\mathcal{G}_{\mathrm{rpoRO}}$ was programmed on an index $x = (s, x')$, but only to a calling party with sid $= s$. Notably, this interface directly restricts the environment from ever seeing whether or not the oracle was programmed (since the environment is by definition not part of any legitimate protocol session), and indirectly restricts the adversary from ever seeing whether or not the oracle was programmed (since the simulator is in charge of its view in the ideal-world experiment in which programming is employed.)

Definition 7 (Restricted Programmable Observable Global RO $\mathcal{G}_{\mathrm{rpoRO}}$).
[10] The restricted programmable observable global random oracle $\mathcal{G}_{\mathrm{rpoRO}}$ is a tuple of algorithms (Query, Observe, Program, IsProgrammed) defined over an output length ℓ and initially empty lists $\mathcal{Q}$ (queries) and prog (programmed queries):

- $v \leftarrow$ Query(x) : *Same as Definition 6 above.*
- $\mathcal{Q}_s \leftarrow$ Observe(s) : *Same as Definition 6 above.*
- $\{0,1\} \leftarrow$ Program(x, v) : *If $\exists v' \in \{0,1\}^\ell$ such that $(x, v') \in \mathcal{Q}$ and $v \neq v'$, output 0. Otherwise, add (x, v) to $\mathcal{Q}$ and prog and output 1.*
- $\{0,1\} \leftarrow$ IsProgrammed(x) : *Parse x as (s, x'). If the caller's SID $\neq s$, output $\perp$. Otherwise if $x \in$ prog, output 1. Otherwise, output 0.*

3.2 The NIZKPoK Ideal Functionality

We now formalize the NIZKPoK ideal functionality $\mathcal{F}_{\mathrm{NIZK}}$. Recall from Sect. 1 that in the "ideal" world, the honest parties who would execute protocol Π are actually dummy parties who do not perform any computations of their own. Instead, they pass all of their inputs to an ideal functionality $\mathcal{F}_{\mathrm{NIZK}}$, who instructs them on how to respond. As is standard in the (G)UC framework [19,20,22], there is one ideal functionality for each SID s. A dummy party with SID s can only send input and receive output from the $\mathcal{F}_{\mathrm{NIZK}}$ with the same SID, denoted $\mathcal{F}_{\mathrm{NIZK}}^s$.

Each $\mathcal{F}_{\mathrm{NIZK}}^s$ will need to run some kind of setup, then process proofs and verifications on behalf of the honest parties in its session. Recall that in order to be NIZKPoK, the proofs must be *non-interactive, zero-knowledge* (satisfying the SHVZK property), and *proofs of knowledge* (satisfying the SS property). These properties imply the existence of SHVZK simulator algorithms SimSetup and SimProve that do not take the prover's witness as input, as well as of the SS algorithm Extract that can compute witnesses from adversarially-created proofs. During $\mathcal{F}_{\texttt{NIZK}}$'s **Setup** procedure, $\mathcal{F}_{\texttt{NIZK}}$ requests the specifications of these algorithms from the ideal adversary (simulator) $\mathcal{S}$.

Note that there are two conditions in which $\mathcal{F}_{\texttt{NIZK}}$ can output Fail. The first is a completeness error, where $\mathcal{F}_{\texttt{NIZK}}$'s execution of the SimProve algorithm on input $(x, w) \in R$ fails to produce a proof π such that $\texttt{Verify}(x, \pi) = 1$. The second is an extraction error, where $\mathcal{F}_{\texttt{NIZK}}$'s execution of the Extract algorithm on input a valid, non-simulated proof tuple (x, π) fails to produce a witness w such that $R(x, w) = 1$. In the proof of Theorem 1 in Sect. 3.5, we will draw a direct correspondence between these failures and the functionality of a Σ-protocol.

Definition 8 (NIZKPoK Ideal Functionality). *The ideal functionality $\mathcal{F}_{\texttt{NIZK}}$ of a non-interactive zero-knowledge proof of knowledge (NIZKPoK) is defined as follows.*

Setup: *Upon receiving the request* (Setup, s) *from a party* $P = (\texttt{pid}, \texttt{sid})$, *first check whether* $\texttt{sid} = s$. *If it doesn't, output* $\bot$. *Otherwise, if this is the first time that* (Setup, s) *was received, pass* (Setup, s) *to the ideal adversary* $\mathcal{S}$, *who returns the tuple* (Algorithms, s, Setup, Prove, Verify, SimSetup, SimProve, Extract) *with definitions for the algorithms* $\mathcal{F}_{\texttt{NIZK}}$ *will use.* $\mathcal{F}_{\texttt{NIZK}}$ *stores the tuple.*

Prove: *Upon receiving a request* (Prove, s, x, w) *from a party* $P = (\texttt{pid}, \texttt{sid})$, *first check that* $\texttt{sid} = s$ *and* $R(x, w) = 1$. *If not, output* $\bot$. *Otherwise, compute* π *according to the* SimSetup *and* SimProve *algorithms and check that* $\texttt{Verify}(x, \pi) = 1$. *If it doesn't, output* Fail. *Otherwise, record then output the message* (Proof, s, x, π).

Verify: *Upon receiving a request* (Verify, s, x, π) *from a party* $P = (\texttt{pid}, \texttt{sid})$, *first check that* $\texttt{sid} = s$. *If it doesn't, output* $\bot$. *Otherwise if* $\texttt{Verify}(x, \pi) = 0$, *output* (Verification, s, x, π, 0). *Otherwise if* (Proof, s, x, π) *is already stored, output* (Verification, s, x, π, 1). *Otherwise, compute* w *according to the* Extract *algorithm. If* $R(x, w) = 1$, *output* (Verification, s, x, π, 1) *for a successful extraction. Else if* $R(x, w) = 0$, *output* Fail.

3.3 The CRS Ideal Functionality

Below is the ideal common reference string (CRS) functionality, which relies on a generic "GenCRS" algorithm. In Sect. 5.1, we will articulate the properties that GenCRS must have for the purposes of our construction.

Definition 9 (CRS Ideal Functionality). *The ideal functionality $\mathcal{F}_{\texttt{CRS}}$ of a common reference string (CRS) for a particular CRS generation mechanism* GenCRS *is defined as follows.*

Query: *Upon receiving a request* (Query, s) *from a party* $P = (\text{pid}, \text{sid})$, *first check whether* $\text{sid} = s$. *If it doesn't, output* $\bot$. *Otherwise, if this is the first time that* (Query, s) *was received, compute* x *according to the algorithm* GenCRS *and store the tuple* (CRS, s, x). *Return* (CRS, s, x).

3.4 GUC Security Definitions

We are now ready to formalize what it means for a protocol Π to be a GUC NIZKPoK in the $\mathcal{G}_{\text{rpoRO}}$- and $\mathcal{G}_{\text{roRO}}$-$\mathcal{F}_{\text{CRS}}$-hybrid models. We review the standard GUC model real- and ideal-world experiments given by Canetti et al. [20] in Appendix A.9 of the full version of the paper [37], noting that we are working in the *passive corruption model*—i.e. $\mathcal{Z}$ must decide at the time of a party's invocation whether or not they are corrupt.

Definition 10 (GUC NIZKPoK in the $\mathcal{G}_{\text{rpoRO}}$-hybrid Model). *A protocol* $\Pi = (\text{Setup}, \text{Prove}, \text{Verify}, \text{SimSetup}, \text{SimProve}, \text{Extract})$ *with security parameter* λ *GUC-realizes the NIZKPoK ideal functionality* $\mathcal{F}_{\text{NIZK}}$ *in the* $\mathcal{G}_{\text{rpoRO}}$-*hybrid model if for all efficient* $\mathcal{A}$, *there exists an ideal adversary* $\mathcal{S}$ *efficient in expectation such that for all efficient environments* $\mathcal{Z}$,

$$\text{IDEAL}^{\mathcal{G}_{\text{rpoRO}}}_{\mathcal{F}_{\text{NIZK}}, \mathcal{S}, \mathcal{Z}}(1^\lambda, \text{aux}) \approx_c \text{REAL}^{\mathcal{G}_{\text{rpoRO}}}_{\Pi, \mathcal{A}, \mathcal{Z}}(1^\lambda, \text{aux}),$$

where $\mathcal{G}_{\text{rpoRO}}$ *is the restricted programmable observable global RO (Definition 7) and* aux *is any auxiliary information provided to the environment.*

Definition 11 (GUC NIZKPoK in the $\mathcal{G}_{\text{roRO}}$-$\mathcal{F}_{\text{CRS}}$-hybrid Model). *A protocol* $\Pi = (\text{Setup}, \text{Prove}, \text{Verify}, \text{SimSetup}, \text{SimProve}, \text{Extract})$ *with security parameter* λ *GUC-realizes the NIZKPoK ideal functionality* $\mathcal{F}_{\text{NIZK}}$ *in the* $\mathcal{G}_{\text{roRO}}$-$\mathcal{F}_{\text{CRS}}$ *hybrid model if for all efficient* $\mathcal{A}$, *there exists an ideal adversary* $\mathcal{S}$ *efficient in expectation such that for all efficient environments* $\mathcal{Z}$,

$$\text{IDEAL}^{\mathcal{G}_{\text{roRO}}}_{\mathcal{F}_{\text{NIZK}}, \mathcal{S}, \mathcal{Z}}(1^\lambda, \text{aux}) \approx_c \text{REAL}^{\mathcal{G}_{\text{roRO}}, \mathcal{F}_{\text{CRS}}}_{\Pi, \mathcal{A}, \mathcal{Z}}(1^\lambda, \text{aux}),$$

where $\mathcal{G}_{\text{roRO}}$ *is the restricted observable global RO (Definition 6),* $\mathcal{F}_{\text{CRS}}$ *is the ideal CRS functionality (Definition 9), and* aux *is any auxiliary information provided to the environment.*

3.5 GUC NIZKPoK are Complete, NIM-SHVZK, and NI-SSS

We prove in this section that any protocol $\Pi = (\text{Setup}, \text{Prove}, \text{Verify}, \text{SimSetup}, \text{SimProve}, \text{Extract})$ that GUC-realizes $\mathcal{F}_{\text{NIZK}}$ in *any* global ROM must be overwhelmingly complete, non-interactive multiple special honest-verifier zero-knowledge (NIM-SHVZK) and non-interactive special simulation simulation-sound (NI-SSS) according to the definitions in Sect. 2.2. In other words, the NIM-SHVZK and NI-SSS properties guaranteed by a straight-line compiler (SLC) are *strictly necessary* to create GUC NIZKPoK in the global ROM.

As we show briefly in Appendix B.1 [37], any ordinary Σ-protocol that is regular SHVZK is also multi-SHVZK. The more interesting result is the necessity of special simulation-soundness, since that is not a property guaranteed by all Σ-protocols—it will be up to the SLC to create a special simulation-sound NISLE proof system even when the underlying Σ-protocol is only regular special-sound. In the proof of Theorem 3 in the full version of his paper [30], Fischlin shows that the NISLE proof systems resulting from his transform satisfy both NIM-SHVZK and NI-SSS. A key element in Fischlin's proof that will surface again in the proof of Theorem 1 below, as well as in the proofs of Theorems 3 and 4, is the observation that an `Extract` algorithm based on the adversary's query history functionally decouples the extraction process from the rest of the experiment—interacting with the extractor does not influence the adversary's view in any way. Intuitively, this is because `Extract` works solely using inputs that the adversary already knows.

Since the following result is independent of the choice of global RO, we recall the strict global RO $\mathcal{G}_{sRO}$ outlined by Canetti et al. [22] and formalized by Camenisch et al. [10] described in the introduction. $\mathcal{G}_{sRO}$ has the same parameters as $\mathcal{G}_{rpoRO}$ and $\mathcal{G}_{roRO}$ but only one interface, `Query`, which acts as globally accessible random function. The functionality of $\mathcal{G}_{sRO}$ is the minimal-most assumption of an RO in the GUC model, creating a direct correspondence to the standard RO H in the NIM-SHVZK and NI-SSS experiments. Because the point of using $\mathcal{G}_{sRO}$ here is to convey the *minimal* assumption needed (and not to prove the result *only* for $\mathcal{G}_{sRO}$), we use the generic notation $\mathcal{G}_{RO}$, which represents any global RO with a minimum of $\mathcal{G}_{sRO}$'s `Query` interface. The GUC security definition in the $\mathcal{G}_{RO}$-hybrid model is the same as in Definition 10, except that $\mathcal{G}_{rpoRO}$ is replaced with $\mathcal{G}_{RO}$ in the notation.

Theorem 1. *Let Π be a protocol that GUC-realizes $\mathcal{F}_{NIZK}$ in the $\mathcal{G}_{RO}$-hybrid model (Definition 10 where $\mathcal{G}_{rpoRO}$ is replaced with $\mathcal{G}_{RO}$). Then Π must be overwhelmingly complete (Definition 3), NIM-SHVZK (Definition 4) and NI-SSS (Definition 5).*

Proof Sketch. We proceed by cases and show that if Π is not overwhelmingly complete and NIM-SHVZK then it does not GUC-realize $\mathcal{F}_{NIZK}$, and similarly that if Π is not NI-SSS then it does not GUC-realize $\mathcal{F}_{NIZK}$. The full proof is available in Appendix B.2 of the full version of the paper [37].

In the first half of the proof, we construct a reduction that uses an adversary $\mathcal{A}$ that can win the NIM-SHVZK experiment from Fig. 2 with non-negligible advantage to determine whether it is living in the real- or ideal-world GUC experiment. The reduction forwards $\mathcal{A}$'s oracle queries to and from $\mathcal{G}_{RO}$ and `Prove` queries to the GUC challenger, returning the proofs it receives back to $\mathcal{A}$. We note that since the reduction has no control over $\mathcal{G}_{RO}$, its view of $\mathcal{G}_{RO}$ is exactly the same as $\mathcal{A}$'s, so anything $\mathcal{A}$ can learn about the proofs from interacting with $\mathcal{G}_{RO}$, the reduction can also learn. Furthermore if the GUC challenger is running the ideal-world experiment and $\mathcal{F}_{NIZK}$ outputs `Fail` (indicating that `Simulate` failed to compute a valid proof for a statement-witness pair $(x, w) \in R$), the reduction can immediately tell it is living in the ideal world. As long as $\mathcal{F}_{\text{NIZK}}$ does not produce Fail, the reduction simulates $\mathcal{A}$'s exact view of the challenger in the NIM-SHVZK game and succeeds in distinguishing the real- from ideal-world GUC experiments with the same probability as $\mathcal{A}$.

The second reduction uses an $\mathcal{A}$ that can win the NI-SSS game from Fig. 3 with non-negligible advantage in order to distinguish between the GUC experiments. This reduction proceeds similarly to the last, forwarding all of $\mathcal{A}$'s queries to the relevant parties. The argument regarding the reduction's view of $\mathcal{G}_{\text{RO}}$ is identical to the argument above. In this case, however, there is a nuance to $\mathcal{A}$'s view: the regular NI–SSS challenger always produces *simulated* proofs, while the reduction will only produce simulated proofs if the GUC challenger is running the ideal-world experiment. We argue that in the case that the GUC challenger is running the real-world experiment, $\mathcal{A}$'s view from the reduction reduces to the regular non-interactive special soundness property given in Appendix A.6 [37], in which $\mathcal{A}$ can only run the regular Prove algorithm itself (and does not have oracle access to the simulator). The reduction therefore runs two copies of $\mathcal{A}$, returning proofs from the GUC challenger to the first copy $\mathcal{A}$ and generating proofs for the second copy $\mathcal{A}'$ itself using Π.Prove. If the GUC challenger is running the ideal-world experiment, the reduction is able to simulate $\mathcal{A}$'s exact view of the NI-SSS game, and the reduction will be able to determine that it is living in the ideal-world experiment with the same probability that $\mathcal{A}$ is able to output a proof that causes $\mathcal{F}_{\text{NIZK}}$'s Extract algorithm to output Fail. If the GUC challenger is running the real-world experiment and $\mathcal{A}'$ can output a valid proof such that Π.Extract fails but the GUC challenger does not fail, the reduction knows it is playing against the real-world GUC challenger, and can therefore distinguish the experiments with the same probability that $\mathcal{A}'$ succeeds in winning the NI-SS game.

Note that in order to check the result of Π.Extract against the GUC challenger's verification, the reduction must be able to be able to compute Π.Extract itself, which it can only do because it operates using $\mathcal{Q}_{\mathcal{A},\mathcal{A}'}$. It is the subject of future work to attempt the reduction in the case that the Extract algorithm requires a secret decryption key, as discussed in Sect. 2.2. Finally, note the reduction would not work if Π were *only* SS, since the adversary in the NI-SS game does not have well-defined behavior with respect to simulated proofs.   □

4   GUC NIZKPoK in the Programmable Global ROM

We will now prove that any straight-line compiler (SLC) is sufficient to transform any Σ-protocol into a GUC NIZKPoK in the the $\mathcal{G}_{\text{rpoRO}}$-hybrid model.

Theorem 2. *Let Σ_R be any Σ-protocol for relation R (Definition 1), $\mathcal{G}_{\text{rpoRO}}$ be the restricted programmable observable global random oracle (Definition 6), and SLC be any straight-line compiler (Definition 2). Then the NISLE proof system $\Pi_R^{\text{SLC}} \leftarrow \text{SLC}(\Sigma_R)$ GUC-realizes $\mathcal{F}_{\text{NIZK}}$ in the $\mathcal{G}_{\text{rpoRO}}$-hybrid model (Definition 10).*

Proof Sketch. In the ideal-world experiment, our simulator $\mathcal{S}$ hands the ideal functionality $\mathcal{F}_{\text{NIZK}}$ the tuple of algorithms Π_R^{SLC}, returns false to the corrupted parties' `IsProgrammed` queries, and otherwise functions as a dummy adversary, forwarding communications between the environment and the protocol.

We proceed by creating a hybrid reduction starting in the real-world experiment that replaces each piece of the real-world protocol Π_R^{SLC} with the functionality of $\mathcal{F}_{\text{NIZK}}$. First, we replace all of the environment's and adversary's connections to the real-world protocol participants with the "challenger" of our reduction, $\mathcal{C}$. This difference is syntactic, so the first two hybrids are identical.

In the next hybrid, we replace $\mathcal{C}$'s `Prove` functionality with the **Prove** interface of $\mathcal{F}_{\text{NIZK}}$, and show the environment's views are indistinguishable between these experiments as long as Π_R^{SLC} has the non-interactive multiple special honest-verifier zero-knowledge (NIM-SHVZK) property. The reduction proceeds as follows. First, $\mathcal{C}$ always returns `false` to any of the adversary's `IsProgrammed` queries. As long as 1) Π_R^{SLC}.SimProve produces valid proofs for statements $x \in L_R$ with overwhelming probability (which follows from overwhelming completeness), and 2) the environment's view of $\mathcal{G}_{\text{rpoRO}}$ remains statistically indistinguishable between the hybrids (which follows from the NIM-SHVZK property and the restriction of the `IsProgrammed` interface), it remains to show that the outputs of Π_R^{SLC}.Prove and Π_R^{SLC}.SimProve are similarly indistinguishable. If the outputs are *statistically* indistinguishable—i.e. if Σ_R is statistical SHVZK and SLC preserves this property such that Π_R^{SLC} is statistical NIM-SHVZK—we are done. In the event that Π_R^{SLC} is only *computationally* NIM-SHVZK, we construct a (tight) reduction that uses an environment that can distinguish the two hybrids to win the NIM-SHVZK game from Fig. 2. The reduction simply proceeds by forwarding all of the environment's RO queries to $\mathcal{G}_{\text{rpoRO}}$, all **Prove** queries to the NIM-SHVZK challenger, and answering **Verify** queries itself by running Π_R^{SLC}.Verify. If the NIM-SHVZK challenger is playing with bit $b = 0$ and the proofs are according to Π_R^{SLC}.Prove, the reduction produces the environment's exact view of the first hybrid; otherwise if $b = 1$ and the proofs are according to Π_R^{SLC}.SimProve, it produces a view of the second hybrid. Therefore, our reduction succeeds with the same probability as the hybrid-distinguisher environment, contradicting the NIM-SHVZK property of Π_R^{SLC}.

In the penultimate hybrid, we replace $\mathcal{C}$'s **Verify** functionality with the **Verify** interface of $\mathcal{F}_{\text{NIZK}}$, and show the environment's views are computationally indistinguishable between these hybrids as long as Π_R^{SLC} has the non-interactive special simulation-soundness (NI-SSS) property. Recall that the **Verify** functionality of $\mathcal{F}_{\text{NIZK}}$ uses the Π_R^{SLC}.Extract algorithm, and fails whenever the witness extracted from a valid (non-simulated) proof is such that $R(x, w) = 0$. Our reduction uses an environment that can distinguish the simulate-only hybrid from the simulate-and-extract hybrid as a black-box to produce a proof that wins the NI-SSS game from Fig. 3 as follows.

For **Prove** queries, the reduction simulates proofs according to either hybrid (both use Π_R^{SLC}.SimProve). Any time the environment wants to verify a proof that the reduction did not create itself, it gathers the environment's queries (which are freely available—recall that all of the environment's wires pass through $\mathcal{C}$) and sends the proof along with the environment's queries to the

NI-SSS challenger. Note that since the only difference between the hybrids is that the second hybrid can output `Fail` while the first never does, the only way for the environment to distinguish between them is to produce such a failure by outputting a valid (non-simulated) proof that causes Π_R^{SLC}.`Extract` to fail. Since the challenger in the NI-SSS game also uses the Π_R^{SLC}.`Extract` algorithm, the reduction succeeds with the same probability as the environment, contradicting the NI-SSS property and proving that the hybrids must be computationally indistinguishable.

The final step is to replace $\mathcal{C}$ with $\mathcal{F}_{\text{NIZK}}$ and $\mathcal{S}$. Note that since $\mathcal{C}$ already runs the algorithms of $\mathcal{F}_{\text{NIZK}}$ and returns `false` to corrupted parties' `IsProgrammed` queries, this is again only a syntactic difference, and the last two hybrids are identical. The full proof is available in Appendix B.3 of the full version of the paper [37]. □

5   GUC NIZKPoK in the Observable Global ROM

Recall from Sect. 1 that in order to avoid the session-localized `IsProgrammed` interface, we pursue GUC NIZKPoK in the $\mathcal{G}_{\text{roRO}}$-$\mathcal{F}_{\text{CRS}}$-hybrid model, where $\mathcal{F}_{\text{CRS}}$ is the ideal CRS functionality from Sect. 3.3. We begin by discussing the specific properties of $\mathcal{F}_{\text{CRS}}$'s CRS generation mechanism `GenCRS`, then introduce a compiler that creates GUC NIZKPoK from any Σ-protocol and any SLC in the $\mathcal{G}_{\text{roRO}}$-$\mathcal{F}_{\text{CRS}}$-hybrid model.

5.1   Generating a CRS that Plays Nice with Σ-protocols

In our construction, the prover convinces the verifier that either it knows a "real" witness, or else it knows the trapdoor to the CRS. In the real world, nobody knows the trapdoor (as long as the CRS is generated securely, for instance using Canetti et al.'s NISC protocol and only $\mathcal{G}_{\text{roRO}}$ [22]). Therefore, all proofs executed by the regular `Prove` algorithm will be using real witnesses. In the ideal world, the simulator gets to generate the CRS for each session s with a trapdoor as part of the `SimProve` algorithm. `SimProve` is otherwise the same as `Prove`, except the witness is always the trapdoor for the CRS.

In order for this OR-proof to work, `Prove` and `SimProve` must be able to interpret the CRS as a statement $x = \text{CRS}_s$ with a corresponding trapdoor witness $w = \text{trap}_s$, such that the pair $(\text{CRS}_s, \text{trap}_s)$ satisfies some binary $\mathcal{NP}$ relation S. For efficiency purposes (since the simulator must run in polynomial-time) the CRS must be efficiently computable, and for security purposes, the trapdoor must be difficult to compute from the CRS. We call a relation that satisfies the efficiency property *samplable* and a relation that satisfies the security property *hard*. The intuition is similar to that of Fischlin's one-way instance generator [31].

Definition 12 (Samplable-Hard Relation). *A binary $\mathcal{NP}$ relation S is samplable-hard with respect to a security parameter λ if it has the following properties.*

1. **Sampling a statement-witness pair is easy.** *There exists a sampling algorithm κ_S that on input 1^λ outputs (x, w) such that $S(x, w) = 1$ and $|x| = \mathsf{poly}(\lambda)$.*
2. **Computing a witness from a statement is hard.** *For a randomly sampled statement-witness pair $(x, w) \leftarrow \kappa_S(1^\lambda)$ the probability that an efficient adversary $\mathscr{A}$ can find a valid witness given only the statement is negligible. Formally, for all PPT $\mathscr{A}$,*

$$\Pr[(x, w) \leftarrow \kappa_S(1^\lambda), w' \leftarrow \mathscr{A}(1^\lambda, x, \kappa_S) : (x, w') \in R] \leq \mathsf{negl}(\lambda).$$

Finally, we require that the relation S underlying the CRS has an efficient corresponding Σ-protocol Σ_S. Our construction will instantiate an OR-protocol Σ_{RVS} based on Σ_R and Σ_S for the relation $R \vee S$.

Putting the pieces together, the CRS generation mechanism $\mathtt{GenCRS}$ for $\mathcal{F}_{\mathsf{CRS}}$ in our construction fixes S as a samplable-hard relation with corresponding efficient Σ-protocol Σ_S, and consists of running $(\mathsf{CRS}_s, \mathsf{trap}_s) \leftarrow \kappa_S(1^\lambda)$. We combine this $\mathcal{F}_{\mathsf{CRS}}$ with the restricted observable global RO $\mathcal{G}_{\mathsf{roRO}}$ to instantiate the $\mathcal{G}_{\mathsf{roRO}}$-$\mathcal{F}_{\mathsf{CRS}}$-hybrid model, and are now ready to introduce our GUC compiler.

5.2   GUC Compiler

We propose a compiler that uses any SLC in conjunction with the OR-protocol discussed in Sects. 2.3 and 5.1 to transform any Σ-protocol into a GUC NIZKPoK in the $\mathcal{G}_{\mathsf{roRO}}$-$\mathcal{F}_{\mathsf{CRS}}$-hybrid model. The compiler works as follows.

First, $\mathcal{F}_{\mathsf{CRS}}$ is fixed as described in Sect. 5.1. The real-world $\mathtt{Setup}$ functionality runs the OR-protocol Σ_{RVS} for relation $R \vee S$ through any SLC to obtain $\Pi_{\mathsf{RVS}}^{\mathsf{SLC}}$, and returns the same setup parameters as $\Pi_{\mathsf{RVS}}^{\mathsf{SLC}}$.

For each session s, provers in the real world query the CRS ideal functionality $\mathcal{F}_{\mathsf{CRS}}^s$ to obtain CRS_s. Each time a real prover with SID s needs to create a proof of a statement x using witness w, it obtains CRS_s and sets the compound statement $X = (x, \mathsf{CRS}_s)$. It then generates a proof Π using $\Pi_{\mathsf{RVS}}^{\mathsf{SLC}}.\mathtt{Prove}(X, W)$, where $W = (w, 0)$ to indicate it knows a witness for the first statement x. In order to verify the proof, a verifier first obtains CRS_s from $\mathcal{F}_{\mathsf{CRS}}^s$, then checks whether it is the correct CRS for session s. If it is, it the verifier outputs the result of running $\Pi_{\mathsf{RVS}}^{\mathsf{SLC}}.\mathtt{Verify}(X, \Pi)$.

In the ideal world, the $\mathtt{SimSetup}$ algorithm begins by generating an empty list in which to store the simulated CRS for each session, denoted $\mathtt{simcrs}$. When it is time to prove a statement on behalf of an honest (dummy) party in session s, the compiler's $\mathtt{SimProve}$ algorithm generates $(\mathsf{CRS}_s, \mathsf{trap}_s) \leftarrow \kappa_S(1^\lambda)$ (if one has not been generated already), and computes the proof using $\Pi_{\mathsf{RVS}}^{\mathsf{SLC}}.\mathtt{Prove}$, this time using trap_s as the witness.

Given a *non-simulated* proof and a list $\mathcal{Q}_{P^*}^s$ of adversarial provers' queries for session s, the compiler's $\mathtt{Extract}$ algorithm runs $\Pi_{\mathsf{RVS}}^{\mathsf{SLC}}.\mathtt{Extract}$ using $\mathcal{Q}_{P^*}^s$ and tests the compound witness $W = (w_0, w_1)$. If $R_{\mathsf{RVS}}(X, W) = 1$ but $R(x_0, w_0) = 0$, $\mathtt{Extract}$ outputs $\mathtt{Fail}$. Otherwise, it outputs W.

Note that this formulation diverges from the general intuition of an OR-protocol extractor (see Appendix A.8 of the full version of the paper [37]) in that we require any valid witness W to imply that $R(x_0, w_0) = 1$, not that *either $R(x_0, w_0) = 1$ or $S(x_1, w_1) = 1$*. This is because we need to account for the fact that $\mathcal{F}_{\text{NIZK}}$ will never invoke the Extract algorithm on proofs it has generated using SimProve, and nobody else should ever have access to the CRS trapdoor. If $\mathcal{F}_{\text{NIZK}}$ gets a proof that verifies because $S(\text{CRS}_s, w_1) = 1$, it must be the case that an adversarial prover has acquired the trapdoor, and Extract forms its output in such a way that $\mathcal{F}_{\text{NIZK}}$ will output Fail. In our proof of security, we will bound the probability of this failure by constructing a reduction to the hardness property of S.

We give a formal construction of the candidate compiler below, and prove in Sect. 5.3 that it creates GUC NIZKPoK in the $\mathcal{G}_{\text{roRO}}$-$\mathcal{F}_{\text{CRS}}$-hybrid model.

Definition 13 (Candidate Compiler). *Let Σ_R be any Σ-protocol for relation R (Definition 1), $\mathcal{G}_{\text{roRO}}$ be the restricted observable global random oracle (Definition 6), Σ_S be an efficient Σ-protocol for samplable-hard relation S (Definition 12), $\mathcal{F}_{\text{CRS}}$ be the ideal CRS functionality (Definition 9) where GenCRS $:= \kappa_S$, and SLC be any straight-line compiler (Definition 2). Then our candidate compiler guc is an algorithm that, on input Σ_R and SLC, produces a tuple of algorithms $\Pi_{\text{RVS}}^{\text{guc}} = (\text{Setup}^{\mathcal{G}_{\text{roRO}}}, \text{Prove}^{\mathcal{G}_{\text{roRO}}, \mathcal{F}_{\text{CRS}}}, \text{Verify}^{\mathcal{G}_{\text{roRO}}, \mathcal{F}_{\text{CRS}}}, \text{SimSetup}, \text{SimProve}, \text{Extract})$, defined in Fig. 4.*

5.3   Realizing $\mathcal{F}_{\text{NIZK}}$ in the $\mathcal{G}_{\text{RO}}$-$\mathcal{F}_{\text{CRS}}$-hybrid Model

We now prove that the algorithm guc from Definition 13 compiles any Σ-protocol into a GUC NIZKPoK in the $\mathcal{G}_{\text{RO}}$-$\mathcal{F}_{\text{CRS}}$-hybrid model.

Theorem 3. *Let Σ_R be any Σ-protocol for relation R (Definition 1), $\mathcal{G}_{\text{roRO}}$ be the restricted observable global random oracle (Definition 6), Σ_S be an efficient Σ-protocol for samplable-hard relation S (Definition 12), $\mathcal{F}_{\text{CRS}}$ be the ideal CRS functionality (Definition 9) where GenCRS $:= \kappa_S$, SLC be any straight-line compiler (Definition 2), and guc be our candidate compiler (Definition 13). Then $\Pi_{\text{RVS}}^{\text{guc}} \leftarrow \text{guc}(\Sigma_R, \text{SLC})$ GUC-realizes $\mathcal{F}_{\text{NIZK}}$ in the $\mathcal{G}_{\text{roRO}}$-$\mathcal{F}_{\text{CRS}}$-hybrid model (Definition 11).*

Proof Sketch. The proof proceeds similarly to that of Theorem 2 in Sect. 4, where we construct a sequence of hybrids that transition between the real- and ideal-world GUC experiments. In the ideal-world experiment, our simulator $\mathcal{S}$ hands the ideal functionality $\mathcal{F}_{\text{NIZK}}$ the tuple of algorithms $\Pi_{\text{RVS}}^{\text{guc}}$ and otherwise functions as a dummy adversary, forwarding communications between the environment and the protocol. Throughout the proof when we say an argument is identical to an argument from the proof of Theorem 2, we mean identical up to the handling of the IsProgrammed interface, which does not exist in the $\mathcal{G}_{\text{roRO}}$-$\mathcal{F}_{\text{CRS}}$-hybrid model.

The first hybrid is identical to the first hybrid in the proof of Theorem 2: we replace all of the real-world protocol participants, $\mathcal{G}_{\text{roRO}}$, and now $\mathcal{F}_{\text{CRS}}$ with a

---

guc Compiler Parameters

$1^\lambda, R, \Sigma_R, S, \Sigma_S, \text{SLC}, \mathcal{G}_{\text{roRO}}, \mathcal{F}_{\text{CRS}}$ with $\text{GenCRS} := (x, w) \leftarrow \kappa_S(1^\lambda)$

$\Pi_{\text{RVS}}^{\text{guc}}.\text{Setup}^{\mathcal{G}_{\text{RO}}}(1^\lambda)$

1 : **ppm** $\leftarrow \Pi_{\text{RVS}}^{\text{SLC}}.\text{Setup}^{\mathcal{G}_{\text{RO}}}(1^\lambda)$

2 : **return ppm**

$\Pi_{\text{RVS}}^{\text{guc}}.\text{SimSetup}(1^\lambda)$

1 : **ppm** $\leftarrow \Pi_{\text{RVS}}^{\text{SLC}}.\text{SimSetup}(1^\lambda)$

2 : **simcrs** $\leftarrow \perp$

3 : **return (ppm, simcrs)**

$\Pi_{\text{RVS}}^{\text{guc}}.\text{Prove}^{\mathcal{G}_{\text{RO}}, \mathcal{F}_{\text{CRS}}}(s, x, w)$

1 : **if** $R(x, w) \neq 1$:

2 :   **return** $\perp$

3 : $\text{CRS}_s \leftarrow \mathcal{F}_{\text{CRS}}^s.\text{Query}(s)$

4 : $X \leftarrow (x, \text{CRS}_s)$

5 : $W \leftarrow (w, 0)$

6 : $\Phi \leftarrow \Pi_{\text{RVS}}^{\text{SLC}}.\text{Prove}^{\mathcal{G}_{\text{RO}}}(X, W)$

7 : **return** (s, X, Φ)

$\Pi_{\text{RVS}}^{\text{guc}}.\text{SimProve}(\text{simcrs}, s, x, w)$

1 : **if** $R(x, w) \neq 1$:

2 :   **return** $\perp$

3 : **if** $\nexists(\text{CRS}_s, \text{trap}_s)$ s.t.

4 : $(s, \text{CRS}_s, \text{trap}_s) \in \text{simcrs}$:

5 : $(\text{CRS}_s, \text{trap}_s) \leftarrow \kappa_S(1^\lambda)$

6 : $\text{simcrs.append}(s, \text{CRS}_s, \text{trap}_s)$

7 : $X \leftarrow (x, \text{CRS}_s)$

8 : $W \leftarrow (\text{trap}_s, 1)$

9 : $\Phi \leftarrow \Pi_{\text{RVS}}^{\text{SLC}}.\text{Prove}^{\mathcal{G}_{\text{RO}}}(X, W)$

10 : **return** $(s, X, \Phi, \text{simcrs})$

$\Pi_{\text{RVS}}^{\text{guc}}.\text{Verify}^{\mathcal{G}_{\text{RO}}, \mathcal{F}_{\text{CRS}}}(s, X, \Phi)$

1 : **parse** $X = (x, \text{CRS}_s)$

2 : $\text{CRS}_s' \leftarrow \mathcal{F}_{\text{CRS}}.\text{Query}(s)$

3 : **if** $\text{CRS}_s = \text{CRS}_s' \wedge$

4 : $\Pi_{\text{RVS}}^{\text{SLC}}.\text{Verify}^{\mathcal{G}_{\text{RO}}}(X, \Phi) = 1$:

5 :   **return** 1

6 : **else** :

7 :   **return** 0

$\Pi_{\text{RVS}}^{\text{guc}}.\text{Extract}(X, \Phi, \mathcal{Q}_{P*})$

1 : $W \leftarrow \Pi_{\text{RVS}}^{\text{SLC}}.\text{Extract}(X, \Phi, \mathcal{Q}_{P*})$

2 : **parse** $X = (x, \text{CRS})$

3 : **parse** $W = (w, \text{trap})$

4 : **if** $R_{\text{RVS}}(X, W) = 1 \wedge R(x, w) = 0$:

5 :   **return Fail**

6 : **else** :

7 :   **return** W

Fig. 4. Compiler $\Pi_{\text{RVS}}^{\text{guc}} \leftarrow \text{guc}(\Sigma_R, \text{SLC})$ for Σ_R in the $\mathcal{G}_{\text{roRO}}$-$\mathcal{F}_{\text{CRS}}$-hybrid Model

challenger $\mathcal{C}$ who controls all of the wires in and out of the environment and the adversary, noting this step permits $\mathcal{C}$ to program $\mathcal{G}_{\text{roRO}}$.[2] The second hybrid is also identical to the one in the proof of Theorem 2 above, except instead of jumping straight to replacing $\mathcal{C}$'s real-world Prove algorithm with the **Prove** interface of the ideal functionality, which will use $\Pi_{\text{RVS}}^{\text{guc}}$.SimSetup and $\Pi_{\text{RVS}}^{\text{guc}}$.SimProve, we instead replace Prove with $\Pi_{\text{RVS}}^{\text{SLC}}$.SimSetup and $\Pi_{\text{RVS}}^{\text{SLC}}$.SimProve. This step allows us to postpone giving the reduction access to the CRS trapdoors, since we will need to ensure that any adversarially-created proofs in the next hybrid will only avoid extraction if the adversary is somehow able to generate the trapdoor itself. By the arguments used in the proof of Theorem 2, we can reduce the indistinguishability of the first two hybrids to the NIM-SHVZK property of $\Pi_{\text{RVS}}^{\text{SLC}}$.

The third hybrid is identical to the third hybrid in the proof of Theorem 2 in that we replace $\mathcal{C}$'s Verify procedure with $\mathcal{F}_{\text{NIZK}}$'s **Verify** interface, which uses $\Pi_{\text{RVS}}^{\text{guc}}$.Extract. The proof of indistinguishability of the second and third hybrids will differ slightly due to the new failure condition in the $\Pi_{\text{RVS}}^{\text{guc}}$.Extract algorithm: namely, the clause that says if the overall witness $W = (w, \text{trap}_s)$ is a valid witness for the statement $X = (x, \text{CRS}_s)$ but w is not a valid witness for x, output Fail. We can limit the probability of this failure by constructing a reduction to the hardness property of the samplable-hard relation: if the environment is able to produce a proof that meets the failure condition, the reduction can produce a tuple $(\text{CRS}_s, \text{trap}_s)$ given only $\text{CRS}_s \leftarrow \kappa_S(1^\lambda)$. Since the probability of generating such a tuple is negligible by the hardness property of S, the probability of such a failure is similarly negligible. The only other way for the environment to distinguish the hybrids is to produce a valid, non-extractable proof of a statement X—i.e. such that $R_{\text{RVS}}(X, W) = 0$ for $W \leftarrow \Pi_{\text{RVS}}^{\text{SLC}}$.Extract$(X, W)$. In this case, $\mathcal{C}$ can use this proof to contradict the NI-SSS (or NI-SS) property of $\Pi_{\text{RVS}}^{\text{SLC}}$ in the exact same way as the parallel reduction in the proof of Theorem 2.

Finally, the penultimate hybrid replaces $\Pi_{\text{RVS}}^{\text{SLC}}$.SimSetup and $\Pi_{\text{RVS}}^{\text{SLC}}$.SimProve with the candidate compiler's algorithms $\Pi_{\text{RVS}}^{\text{guc}}$.SimSetup and $\Pi_{\text{RVS}}^{\text{guc}}$.SimProve. This step effectively reverts the proofs back to the real-world Prove mechanism, except $\mathcal{C}$ is using trapdoors rather than real witnesses. If $\Pi_{\text{RVS}}^{\text{SLC}}$ is statistical NIM-SHVZK, then there is automatically negligible difference in view between the third and penultimate hybrids. If, however, there is computational wiggle room between the proofs in the two experiments, *and* the distinguisher environment now has access to the extractor, we must ensure that the *only* way the environment can distinguish the hybrids is by the contents of the proofs (as opposed to somehow using its view of the new proofs, which use the CRS trapdoor, to cause the extractor to fail). We argue here that because the straight-line extractor works exclusively based on statements, proofs, and oracle queries that the environment made itself, anything the environment can learn from the extractor it could have learned on its own. Therefore, it cannot have possibly

---

[2] As discussed by Camenish et al. [10], the challenger in such a hybrid experiment can make use of techniques like programming and rewinding that are otherwise "illegal" for the simulator to employ in the GUC model.

learned anything new about the hybrids from the extractor, and the reduction to computational NIM-SHVZK proceeds the same as before.

The last hybrid replaces $\mathcal{C}$ with $\mathcal{F}_{\text{NIZK}}$ and $\mathcal{S}$—this is again a syntactic rearrangement, and is functionally identical to the ideal-world experiment. The full version of this proof is available in Appendix B.4 of the full version [37].   □

6   Constructions via the Randomized Fischlin Transform

We demonstrated in the last two sections that any straight-line compiler (SLC) that satisfies Definition 2 is sufficient to transform any Σ-protocol Σ_R into a GUC NIZKPoK in the $\mathcal{G}_{\text{rpoRO}}$-hybrid model, and sufficient in conjunction with our OR-protocol compiler to complete the transformation in the $\mathcal{G}_{\text{roRO}}$-$\mathcal{F}_{\text{CRS}}$-hybrid model. In this section, we will show that the randomized Fischlin transform [31,35] meets our definition of an SLC for a broad class of Σ-protocols, and therefore enables us to practically instantiate both sets of GUC NIZKPoK. The efficiency of the resulting proof systems reduce to the efficiency of the randomized Fischlin transform, which requires only a linear increase in the size of the proofs for small multiplicative and additive constants.

In this section, we review the randomized Fischlin transform rFis and show that it meets our definition of an SLC. We then apply rFis to efficiently realize GUC NIZKPoK in the $\mathcal{G}_{\text{rpoRO}}$- and $\mathcal{G}_{\text{roRO}}$-$\mathcal{F}_{\text{CRS}}$-hybrid models, respectively.

6.1   The Randomized Fischlin Transform, Revisited

Recall from Sect. 1 that the randomized Fischlin transform due to Kondi and shelat [35] is a version of the Fischlin transform [30,31] in which the challenges are selected uniformly at random from the challenge space. In Fischlin's original construction, the Σ-protocols under transformation need a property called *quasi-unique responses*, which Kondi and shelat demonstrate precludes the transformation of OR-protocols. In order to use the randomized Fischlin transform on our OR-protocol construction in a way that preserves security, the OR-protocol must have the (more general) *strong* special soundness property. We consolidate the two properties below, and a brief discussion of the necessity of strong special soundness in Appendix A.10 of the full version of the paper [37].

Definition 14 (Required Properties for rFis). *A Σ-protocol Σ_R for relation R (Definition 1) has* required properties for the randomized Fischlin transform rFis *if it has the* quasi-unique responses property *(Definition 25 in Appendix A.10 [37]) or the* strong special soundness property *(Definition 26 in Appendix A.10 [37]).*

In the full version of his paper, Fischlin proves that his transform over Σ-protocols with quasi-unique responses creates a protocol that is both NIM-SHVZK and NI-SSS in the standard ROM [30]. Kondi and shelat show that the randomized Fischlin transform over a Σ-protocol with the more general strong special soundness property creates a protocol that is standard (non-multi) NI-SHVZK and standard (non-simulation) strong NI-SS [35]. Therefore, it remains to show that the NI *multi*-SHVZK and strong special *simulation* soundness properties are similarly preserved under the randomized transform for strong special-sound Σ-protocols. Our proof of the theorem below draws heavily on arguments from Fischlin [30] and Kondi and shelat [35]; the only novelty is in the (nearly verbatim) application of Fischlin's arguments for NIM-SHVZK and NI-SSS to the randomized transform. We therefore defer the technical details of the randomized Fischlin transform to Definition 29 in Appendix A.12, and the full proof to Appendix B.5 of the full version of the paper [37].

Theorem 4. *Let Σ_R be any Σ-protocol for relation R (Definition 1) with the required properties for rFis (Definition 14). Then the randomized Fischlin transform rFis (Definition 29 in Appendix A.12 [37]) is a straight-line compiler for Σ_R (Definition 2).*

Proof sketch. Recall that a straight-line compiler according to our definition must create protocols that are NIM-SHVZK and NIM-SSS. Kondi and shelat prove in Theorem 6.4 [35] that the tuple of algorithms Π_R^{rFis} (denoted $\pi_{\text{NIZK}}^{F-\text{rand}}$ in their paper) produced by running the randomized Fischlin transform on any strong special sound Σ-protocol Σ_R for relation R is a NISLE ZKPoK for L_R in the standard random-oracle model. Since Kondi and shelat use the standard definitions of SHVZK and strong special soundness (Definitions 19 and 14 in the full version, respectively [37]), it remains to show that Π_R^{rFis} satisfies NIM-SHVZK and NIM-SSS.

Fischlin shows in the proof of Theorem 3 [30] that his original transform satisfies the NIM-SHVZK and NI-SSS properties. Since the strong special soundness property replaces the quasi-unique responses property and the challenges in the randomized version are identically distributed to those in the original version, the proof of NIM-SHVZK and NI-SSS for the randomized Fischlin transform is almost identical to Fischlin's proof of Theorem 3. We discuss the minor differences in the full proof (Appendix B.5 [37]). □

6.2   Efficient, GUC NIZKPoK in the $\mathcal{G}_{\text{rpoRO}}$-hybrid Model

We demonstrated in Sect. 4 that any SLC is sufficient to compile any Σ-protocol into a GUC NIZKPoK in the $\mathcal{G}_{\text{rpoRO}}$-hybrid model, and argued in Sect. 6.1 above that the transform rFis is an SLC. Therefore, given any Σ-protocol Σ_R that meets the requirements for rFis, $\Pi_R^{\text{rFis}} \leftarrow$ rFis(Σ_R) is sufficient to create GUC NIZKPoK in the $\mathcal{G}_{\text{rpoRO}}$-hybrid model.

Corollary 1. *Let Σ_R be any Σ-protocol for a relation R (Definition 1) with the required properties for rFis (Definition 14) and rFis be the randomized Fischlin transform (Definition 29 in Appendix A.12 [37]). Then $\Pi_R^{\text{SLC}} \leftarrow$ rFis(Σ_R) GUC-realizes $\mathcal{F}_{\text{NIZK}}$ in the $\mathcal{G}_{\text{rpoRO}}$-hybrid model (Definition 10).*

Proof. The corollary follows directly from Theorems 2 and 4. □

6.3 Efficient, GUC NIZKPoK in the $\mathcal{G}_{\text{roRO}}$-$\mathcal{F}_{\text{CRS}}$-hybrid Model

Our construction for the $\mathcal{G}_{\text{roRO}}$-$\mathcal{F}_{\text{CRS}}$-hybrid model requires two layered compilers: any SLC, and our OR-protocol compiler guc from Definition 13. We proved in Theorem 3 that $\Pi_{\text{RVS}}^{\text{guc}} \leftarrow \text{guc}(\Sigma_R, \text{SLC})$ GUC-realizes $\mathcal{F}_{\text{NIZK}}$ for any Σ-protocol Σ_R, and again in Sect. 6.1 that rFis is an SLC. Therefore, $\Pi_{\text{RVS}}^{\text{guc}} \leftarrow \text{guc}(\Sigma_R, \text{rFis})$ creates GUC NIZKPoK in the $\mathcal{G}_{\text{roRO}}$-$\mathcal{F}_{\text{CRS}}$-hybrid model.

Corollary 2. *Let Σ_R be any Σ-protocol for a relation R (Definitions 1) with the required properties for rFis (Definition 14), rFis be the randomized Fischlin transform (Definition 29 in Appendix A.12 [37]), and guc be the candidate compiler from Definition 13. Then $\Pi_{\text{RVS}}^{\text{guc}} \leftarrow \text{guc}(\Sigma_R, \text{rFis})$ GUC-realizes $\mathcal{F}_{\text{NIZK}}$ in the $\mathcal{G}_{\text{roRO}}$-$\mathcal{F}_{\text{CRS}}$-hybrid model (Definition 11).*

Proof. The corollary follows directly from Theorems 3 and 4. □

Acknowledgements. Many thanks to Yashvanth Kondi and abhi shelat for crucial security analysis of our original OR-protocol construction, and to Jack Doerner for insightful discussions about $\mathcal{F}_{\text{NIZK}}$ that inspired our results in Sect. 3.5. This research was supported by NSF grant 2154170, and by grants from Meta.

References

1. Adida, B.: Helios: web-based open-audit voting. In: Paul, C.. van Oorschot (eds.) Proceedings of the 17th USENIX Security Symposium, pp. 335–348 (2008)
2. Ateniese, G., Camenisch, J., Joye, M., Tsudik, G.: A practical and provably secure coalition-resistant group signature scheme. In: Bellare, M. (ed.) CRYPTO 2000. LNCS, vol. 1880, pp. 255–270. Springer, Heidelberg (2000). https://doi.org/10.1007/3-540-44598-6_16
3. Bellare, M., Rogaway, P.: Random oracles are practical: a paradigm for designing efficient protocols. In: Proceedings of the 1st ACM Conference on Computer and Communications Security, pp. 62–73 (1993)
4. Benhamouda, F., Lepoint, T., Loss, J., Orru, M., Raykova, M.: On the (in) security of ROS. In: Annual International Conference on the Theory and Applications of Cryptographic Techniques, pp. 33–53. Springer (2021)
5. Blum, M., De Santis, A., Micali, S., Persiano, G.: Non-interactive zero-knowledge. SIAM J. Comput. **20**(6), 1084–1118 (1991)
6. Boudot, F.: Efficient proofs that a committed number lies in an interval. In: Preneel, B. (ed.) EUROCRYPT 2000. LNCS, vol. 1807, pp. 431–444. Springer, Heidelberg (2000). https://doi.org/10.1007/3-540-45539-6_31
7. Bowe, S., Gabizon, A., Miers, I.: Scalable multi-party computation for ZK-snark parameters in the random beacon model. ePrint Archive (2017)
8. Brands, S.: Rethinking Public Key Infrastructure and Digital Certificates– Building in Privacy. PhD thesis, Eindhoven Inst. of Tech., The Netherlands (1999)
9. Camenisch, J., Damgård, I.: Verifiable encryption, group encryption, and their applications to separable group signatures and signature sharing schemes. In: Okamoto, T. (ed.) ASIACRYPT 2000. LNCS, vol. 1976, pp. 331–345. Springer, Heidelberg (2000). https://doi.org/10.1007/3-540-44448-3_25

10. Camenisch, J., Drijvers, M., Gagliardoni, T., Lehmann, A., Neven, G.: The wonderful world of global random oracles. In: Nielsen, J.B., Rijmen, V. (eds.) EUROCRYPT 2018. LNCS, vol. 10820, pp. 280–312. Springer, Cham (2018). https://doi.org/10.1007/978-3-319-78381-9_11

11. Camenisch, J., Hohenberger, S., Kohlweiss, M., Lysyanskaya, A., Meyerovich, M.: How to win the clonewars: efficient periodic n-times anonymous authentication. In: Proceedings of the 13th ACM Conference on Computer and Communications Security, pp. 201–210. ACM (2006)

12. Camenisch, J., Hohenberger, S., Lysyanskaya, A.: Compact E-cash. In: Cramer, R. (ed.) EUROCRYPT 2005. LNCS, vol. 3494, pp. 302–321. Springer, Heidelberg (2005). https://doi.org/10.1007/11426639_18

13. Camenisch, J., Lysyanskaya, A.: An efficient system for non-transferable anonymous credentials with optional anonymity revocation. In: Pfitzmann, B. (ed.) EUROCRYPT 2001. LNCS, vol. 2045, pp. 93–118. Springer, Heidelberg (2001). https://doi.org/10.1007/3-540-44987-6_7

14. Camenisch, J., Lysyanskaya, A.: A signature scheme with efficient protocols. In: Cimato, S., Persiano, G., Galdi, C. (eds.) SCN 2002. LNCS, vol. 2576, pp. 268–289. Springer, Heidelberg (2003). https://doi.org/10.1007/3-540-36413-7_20

15. Camenisch, J., Michels, M.: Proving in zero-knowledge that a number is the product of two safe primes. In: Stern, J. (ed.) EUROCRYPT 1999. LNCS, vol. 1592, pp. 107–122. Springer, Heidelberg (1999). https://doi.org/10.1007/3-540-48910-X_8

16. Camenisch, J., Michels, M.: Separability and efficiency for generic group signature schemes. In: Wiener, M. (ed.) CRYPTO 1999. LNCS, vol. 1666, pp. 413–430. Springer, Heidelberg (1999). https://doi.org/10.1007/3-540-48405-1_27

17. Camenisch, J., Shoup, V.: Practical verifiable encryption and decryption of discrete logarithms. In: Boneh, D. (ed.) CRYPTO 2003. LNCS, vol. 2729, pp. 126–144. Springer, Heidelberg (2003). https://doi.org/10.1007/978-3-540-45146-4_8

18. Camenisch, J., Stadler, M.: Efficient group signature schemes for large groups. In: Kaliski, B.S. (ed.) CRYPTO 1997. LNCS, vol. 1294, pp. 410–424. Springer, Heidelberg (1997). https://doi.org/10.1007/BFb0052252

19. Canetti, R.: Universally composable security: a new paradigm for cryptographic protocols. In: Proceedings 42nd IEEE Symposium on Foundations of Computer Science, pp. 136–145. IEEE (2001)

20. Canetti, R., Dodis, Y., Pass, R., Walfish, S.: Universally composable security with global setup. In: Vadhan, S.P. (ed.) TCC 2007. LNCS, vol. 4392, pp. 61–85. Springer, Heidelberg (2007). https://doi.org/10.1007/978-3-540-70936-7_4

21. Canetti, R., Fischlin, M.: Universally composable commitments. In: Kilian, J. (ed.) CRYPTO 2001. LNCS, vol. 2139, pp. 19–40. Springer, Heidelberg (2001). https://doi.org/10.1007/3-540-44647-8_2

22. Canetti, R., Jain, A., Scafuro, A.: Practical UC security with a global random oracle. In: Proceedings of the 2014 ACM SIGSAC Conference on Computer and Communications Security, pp. 597–608 (2014)

23. Cramer, R., Damgård, I., Nielsen, J.B.: Multiparty computation from threshold homomorphic encryption. In: Pfitzmann, B. (ed.) EUROCRYPT 2001. LNCS, vol. 2045, pp. 280–300. Springer, Heidelberg (2001). https://doi.org/10.1007/3-540-44987-6_18

24. Cramer, R., Damgård, I., Schoenmakers, B.: Proofs of partial knowledge and simplified design of witness hiding protocols. In: Desmedt, Y.G. (ed.) CRYPTO 1994. LNCS, vol. 839, pp. 174–187. Springer, Heidelberg (1994). https://doi.org/10.1007/3-540-48658-5_19

25. Cramer, R., Damgård, I., Xing, C., Yuan, C.: Amortized complexity of zero-knowledge proofs revisited: achieving linear soundness slack. In: Coron, J.-S., Nielsen, J.B. (eds.) EUROCRYPT 2017. LNCS, vol. 10210, pp. 479–500. Springer, Cham (2017). https://doi.org/10.1007/978-3-319-56620-7_17

26. Damgård, I.: On σ-protocols. University of Aarhus, Department of Computer Science (2002)

27. Drijvers, M., et al.: On the security of two-round multi-signatures. In: 2019 IEEE Symposium on Security and Privacy, pp. 1084–1101. IEEE (2019)

28. Feige, U., Lapidot, D., Shamir, A.: Multiple noninteractive zero knowledge proofs under general assumptions. SIAM J. Comput. **29**(1), 1–28 (1999)

29. Fiat, A., Shamir, A.: How to prove yourself: practical solutions to identification and signature problems. In: Odlyzko, A.M. (ed.) CRYPTO 1986. LNCS, vol. 263, pp. 186–194. Springer, Heidelberg (1987). https://doi.org/10.1007/3-540-47721-7_12

30. Fischlin, M.: Communication-efficient non-interactive proofs of knowledge with online extractors (2005). Manuscript. http://www.cryptoplexity.informatik.tu-darmstadt.de/media/crypt/publications_1/fischlinonline-extractor2005.pdf

31. Fischlin, M.: Communication-efficient non-interactive proofs of knowledge with online extractors. In: Shoup, V. (ed.) CRYPTO 2005. LNCS, vol. 3621, pp. 152–168. Springer, Heidelberg (2005). https://doi.org/10.1007/11535218_10

32. Fujisaki, E., Okamoto, T.: Statistical zero knowledge protocols to prove modular polynomial relations. In: Kaliski, B.S. (ed.) CRYPTO 1997. LNCS, vol. 1294, pp. 16–30. Springer, Heidelberg (1997). https://doi.org/10.1007/BFb0052225

33. Goh, E.-J., Jarecki, S.: A signature scheme as secure as the Diffie-Hellman problem. In: Biham, E. (ed.) EUROCRYPT 2003. LNCS, vol. 2656, pp. 401–415. Springer, Heidelberg (2003). https://doi.org/10.1007/3-540-39200-9_25

34. Katsumata, S.: A new simple technique to bootstrap various lattice zero-knowledge proofs to QROM secure NIZKs. In: Malkin, T., Peikert, C. (eds.) CRYPTO 2021. LNCS, vol. 12826, pp. 580–610. Springer, Cham (2021). https://doi.org/10.1007/978-3-030-84245-1_20

35. Kondi, Y., Shelat, A.: Improved straight-line extraction in the random oracle model with applications to signature aggregation. Cryptology ePrint Archive (2022)

36. Lipmaa, H.: Statistical zero-knowledge proofs from diophantine equations (2001). http://eprint.iacr.org/2001/086

37. Lysyanskaya, A., Rosenbloom, L.N.: Universally composable sigma-protocols in the global random-oracle model. Cryptology ePrint Archive (2022)

38. Lyubashevsky, V.: Lattice signatures without trapdoors. In: Pointcheval, D., Johansson, T. (eds.) EUROCRYPT 2012. LNCS, vol. 7237, pp. 738–755. Springer, Heidelberg (2012). https://doi.org/10.1007/978-3-642-29011-4_43

39. Nick, J., Ruffing, T., Seurin, Y.: MuSig2: simple two-round schnorr multi-signatures. In: Malkin, T., Peikert, C. (eds.) CRYPTO 2021. LNCS, vol. 12825, pp. 189–221. Springer, Cham (2021). https://doi.org/10.1007/978-3-030-84242-0_8

40. Pass, R.: On deniability in the common reference string and random oracle model. In: Boneh, D. (ed.) CRYPTO 2003. LNCS, vol. 2729, pp. 316–337. Springer, Heidelberg (2003). https://doi.org/10.1007/978-3-540-45146-4_19

41. Pedersen, T.P.: Non-interactive and information-theoretic secure verifiable secret sharing. In: Feigenbaum, J. (ed.) CRYPTO 1991. LNCS, vol. 576, pp. 129–140. Springer, Heidelberg (1992). https://doi.org/10.1007/3-540-46766-1_9

42. De Santis, A., Di Crescenzo, G., Ostrovsky, R., Persiano, G., Sahai, A.: Robust non-interactive zero knowledge. In: Kilian, J. (ed.) CRYPTO 2001. LNCS, vol. 2139, pp. 566–598. Springer, Heidelberg (2001). https://doi.org/10.1007/3-540-44647-8_33

43. Unruh, D.: Non-interactive zero-knowledge proofs in the quantum random oracle model. In: Oswald, E., Fischlin, M. (eds.) EUROCRYPT 2015. LNCS, vol. 9057, pp. 755–784. Springer, Heidelberg (2015). https://doi.org/10.1007/978-3-662-46803-6_25
44. Wagner, D.: A generalized birthday problem. In: Yung, M. (ed.) CRYPTO 2002. LNCS, vol. 2442, pp. 288–304. Springer, Heidelberg (2002). https://doi.org/10.1007/3-540-45708-9_19
45. Watrous, J.: Zero-knowledge against quantum attacks. SIAM J. Comput. **39**(1), 25–58 (2009)
46. Wikström, D.: A commitment-consistent proof of a shuffle. In: Boyd, C., ález Nieto, J.M.G., (eds.), ACISP, pp. 407–421. Springer (2009)

Quantum Cryptography

Pseudorandom (Function-Like) Quantum State Generators: New Definitions and Applications

Prabhanjan Ananth[1], Aditya Gulati[1(✉)], Luowen Qian[2], and Henry Yuen[3]

[1] University of California, Santa Barbara, USA
`prabhanjan@cs.ucsb.edu`, `adityagulati@ucsb.edu`
[2] Boston University, Boston , USA
`luowenq@bu.edu`
[3] Columbia University, Columbia, USA
`hyuen@cs.columbia.edu`

Abstract. Pseudorandom quantum states (PRS) are efficiently constructible states that are computationally indistinguishable from being Haar-random, and have recently found cryptographic applications. We explore new definitions, new properties and applications of pseudorandom states, and present the following contributions:

1. **New Definitions:** We study variants of pseudorandom *function-like* state (PRFS) generators, introduced by Ananth, Qian, and Yuen (CRYPTO'22), where the pseudorandomness property holds even when the generator can be queried adaptively or in superposition. We show feasibility of these variants assuming the existence of post-quantum one-way functions.
2. **Classical Communication:** We show that PRS generators with logarithmic output length imply commitment and encryption schemes with *classical communication*. Previous constructions of such schemes from PRS generators required quantum communication.
3. **Simplified Proof:** We give a simpler proof of the Brakerski–Shmueli (TCC'19) result that polynomially-many copies of uniform superposition states with random binary phases are indistinguishable from Haar-random states.
4. **Necessity of Computational Assumptions:** We also show that a secure PRS with output length logarithmic, or larger, in the key length necessarily requires computational assumptions.

1 Introduction

The study of pseudorandom objects is central to the foundations of cryptography. After many decades, cryptographers have developed a deep understanding

L. Qian: Supported by DARPA under Agreement No. HR00112020023.
H. Yuen: Supported by AFOSR award FA9550-21-1-0040 and NSF CAREER award CCF-2144219.

E. Kiltz and V. Vaikuntanathan (Eds.): TCC 2022, LNCS 13747, pp. 237–265, 2022.
https://doi.org/10.1007/978-3-031-22318-1_9

of the zoo of pseudorandom primitives such as one-way functions (OWF), pseudorandom generators (PRG), and pseudorandom functions (PRF) [8,9].

The study of pseudorandomness in the quantum setting, on the other hand, is just getting started. Objects such as state and unitary k-designs have been studied extensively, but these are best thought of as quantum analogues of k-wise independent hash functions [1,6]. There are unconditional constructions of state and unitary designs and they do not imply any computational assumptions [1, 18].

Quantum pseudorandomness requiring computational assumptions, in contrast, has been studied much less. Ji, Liu, and Song introduced the notion of *pseudorandom quantum states (PRS)* and *pseudorandom quantum unitaries (PRU)* [11]. At a high level, these are efficiently sampleable distributions over states/unitaries that are computationally indistinguishable from being sampled from the Haar distribution (i.e., the uniform measure over the space of states/ unitaries). Ji, Liu, and Song as well as Brakerski and Shmueli have presented constructions of PRS that are based on quantum-secure OWFs [3,4,11]. Kretschmer showed, however, that PRS do not necessarily imply OWFs; there are oracles relative to which PRS exist but OWFs don't [12]. This was followed by recent works that demonstrated the cryptographic utility of PRS: basic cryptographic tasks such as bit commitment, symmetric-key encryption, and secure multiparty computation can be accomplished using only PRS as a primitive [2,16]. It is an intriguing research direction to find more cryptographic applications of PRS and PRU.

The key idea in [2] that unlocked the aforementioned applications was the notion of a *pseudorandom function-like state (PRFS) generator*. To explain this we first review the definition of PRS generators. A quantum polynomial-time (QPT) algorithm G is a PRS generator if for a uniformly random key $k \in \{0,1\}^{\lambda}$ (with λ being the security parameter), polynomially-many copies of the state $|\psi_k\rangle = G(k)$ is indistinguishable from polynomially-many copies of a state $|\vartheta\rangle$ sampled from the Haar measure by all QPT algorithms. One can view this as a quantum analogue of classical PRGs. Alternately, one could consider a version of PRS where the adversary only gets one copy of the state. However, as we will see later, the multi-copy security of PRS will play a crucial role in our applications.

The notion of PRFS generator introduced by [2] is a quantum analogue of PRF (hence the name *function-like*): in addition to taking in a key k, the generator G also takes an *input* x (just like a PRF takes a key k and an input x). Let $|\psi_{k,x}\rangle = G(k,x)$. The pseudorandomness property of G is that for all sequences of inputs $(x_1, \ldots, x_s)$ for polynomially large s, averaged over the key k, the collection of states $|\psi_{k,x_1}\rangle^{\otimes t}, \ldots, |\psi_{k,x_s}\rangle^{\otimes t}$ for polynomially large t is computationally indistinguishable from $|\vartheta_1\rangle^{\otimes t}, \ldots, |\vartheta_s\rangle^{\otimes t}$ where the $|\vartheta_i\rangle$'s are sampled independently from the Haar measure. In other words, while PRS generators look like (to a computationally bounded distinguisher) they are sampling a *single* state from the Haar measure, PRFS generators look like they are sampling *many* (as compared to the key length) states from the Haar measure. Importantly, this still holds true even when the distinguisher is given the inputs $x_1, \ldots, x_s$.

As mentioned, this (seemingly) stronger notion of quantum pseudorandomness provided a useful conceptual tool to perform cryptographic tasks (encryption, commitments, secure computation, etc.) using pseudorandom states alone. Furthermore, [2] showed that for a number of applications, PRFS generators with logarithmic input length suffices and furthermore such objects can be constructed in a black-box way from PRS generators.[1]

Despite exciting progress in this area in the last few years, there is still much to understand about the properties, relationships, and applications of pseudorandom states. In this paper we explore a number of natural questions about pseudorandom states:

- *Feasibility of Stronger Definitions of PRFS*: In the PRFS definition of [2], it was assumed that the set of inputs on which the adversary obtains the outputs are determined ahead of time. Moreover, the adversary could obtain the output of PRFS on only classical inputs. This is often referred to as *selective security* in the cryptography literature. For many interesting applications, this definition is insufficient[2]. This leads us to ask: *is it feasible to obtain strengthened versions of PRFS that maintain security in the presence of adaptive and superposition queries?*
- *Necessity of Assumptions*: In the classical setting, essentially all cryptographic primitives require computational assumptions, at the very least $P \neq NP$. What computational assumptions are required by pseudorandom quantum states? The answer appears to depend on the output length of the PRS generator. Brakerski and Shmueli [4] constructed PRS generators with output length $c \log \lambda$ for some $c > 0$ satisfying statistical security (in other words, the outputs are statistically close to being Haar-random). On the other hand, Kretschmer showed that the existence of PRS generators with output length λ implies that $BQP \neq PP$ [12]. This leads to an intriguing question: *is it possible to unconditionally show the existence of $n(\lambda)$-length output PRS, for some $n(\lambda) \geq \log(\lambda)$?*
- *Necessity of Quantum Communication*: A common theme in all the different PRS-based cryptographic constructions of [2,16] is that the parties involved in the system perform quantum communication. Looking forward, it is conceivable that quantum communication will be a much more expensive resource than having access to a quantum computer. Achieving quantum cryptography with classical communication has been an important direction, dating back to Gavinsky [7]. We ask the following question: *is quantum communication inherent in the cryptographic constructions based on PRS?*

---

[1] However, unlike the equivalence between PRG and PRF in the classical setting [8], it is not known whether *every* PRFS generator can be constructed from PRS generators in a black-box way.

[2] For example, the application of private-key encryption from PRFS as described in [2] is only selectively secure. This is due to the fact that the underlying PRFS is selectively secure.

1.1 Our Results

We explore the aforementioned questions. Our results include the following.

Adaptive-Secure and Quantum-Accessible PRFS. As mentioned earlier, the notion of PRFS given by [2] has *selective security*, meaning that the inputs $x_1, \ldots, x_s$ are fixed ahead of time. Another way of putting it is, the adversary can only make non-adaptive, classical queries to the PRFS generator (where by query we mean, submit an input x to the generator and receive $|\psi_{k,x}\rangle = G(k, x)$ where k is the hidden, secret key).

We study the notion of *adaptively secure PRFS*, in which the security holds with respect to adversaries that can make queries to the generator adaptively. We consider two variants of this: one where the adversary is restricted to making classical queries to the generator (we call this a *classically-accessible adaptively secure PRFS*), and one where there are no restrictions at all; the adversary can even query the generator on a *quantum superposition of inputs* (we call this a *quantum-accessible adaptively secure PRFS*). These definitions can be found in Sect. 3.

We then show feasibility of these definitions by constructing classically- and quantum-accessible adaptively secure PRFS generators from the existence of post-quantum one-way functions. These constructions are given in the full version of the paper.

A Sharp Threshold for Computational Assumptions. In Sect. 4 we show that there is a sharp threshold between when computational assumptions are required for the existence of PRS generators: we give a simple argument that demonstrates that PRS generators with $\log \lambda$-length outputs require computational assumptions on the adversary[3]. This complements the aforementioned result of Brakerski and Shmueli [4] that shows $c \log \lambda$-length PRS for some $c > 0$ do not require computational assumptions. We also note that the calculations of [12] can be refined to show that the existence of $(1 + \epsilon) \log \lambda$-length PRS for all $\epsilon > 0$ implies that $\mathsf{BQP} \neq \mathsf{PP}$.

PRS-Based Constructions with Classical Communication. We show that bit commitments and pseudo one-time pad schemes can be achieved using only classical communication based on the existence of PRS with λ-bit keys and $O(\log(\lambda))$-output length. This improves upon the previous result of [2] who achieved bit commitments and pseudo one-time pad schemes from PRS using quantum communication. However, we note that [2] worked with a wider range

---

[3] We also note that there is a much more roundabout argument for a quantitatively weaker result: [2] constructed bit commitment schemes from $O(\log \lambda)$-length PRS. If such PRS were possible to construct unconditionally, this would imply information-theoretically secure bit commitment schemes in the quantum setting. However, this contradicts the famous results of [13,15], which rules out this possibility. Our calculation, on the other hand, directly shows that $\log \lambda$ (without any constants in front) is a sharp threshold.

of parameters while our constructions are based on PRS with $O(\log(\lambda))$-output length.

En route, we use quantum state tomography (or tomography for short), a well studied concept in quantum information. Roughly speaking, tomography, allows for obtaining a classical string u that captures some properties of an unknown quantum state ρ, given many copies of this state.

We develop a new notion called *verifiable tomography* that might particularly be useful in cryptographic settings. Verifiable tomography allows for verifying whether a given string u is consistent (according to some prescribed verification procedure) with a quantum state ρ. We present the definition and instantiations of verifiable tomography in Sect. 5. In Sect. 6, we use verifiable tomography to achieve the aforementioned applications. At a high level, our constructions are similar to the ones in [2], except that verifiable tomography is additionally used to make the communication classical.

A Simpler Analysis of Binary-Phase PRS. Consider the following construction of PRS. Let $\{F_k : \{0,1\}^n \to \{0,1\}\}_{k \in \{0,1\}^\lambda}$ denote a (quantum-secure) pseudorandom function family. Then $\{|\psi_k\rangle\}_k$ forms a PRS, where $|\psi_k\rangle$ is defined as

$$|\psi_k\rangle = 2^{-n/2} \sum_{x \in \{0,1\}^n} (-1)^{F_k(x)} |x\rangle \ . \tag{1}$$

In other words, the pseudorandom states are *binary phase states* where the phases are given by a pseudorandom function. This is a simpler construction of PRS than the one originally given by [11], where the phases are pseudorandomly chosen N-th roots of unity with $N = 2^n$. Ji, Liu, and Song conjectured that the binary phase construction should also be pseudorandom, and this was confirmed by Brakerski and Shmueli [3].

We give a simpler proof of this in the full version, which may be of independent interest.

1.2   Threshold for Computational Assumptions

We show that PRS generators with λ-bit keys and $\log \lambda$-length outputs cannot be statistically secure. To show this we construct an inefficient adversary, given polynomially many copies of a state, can distinguish whether the state was sampled from the output distribution of a $\log \lambda$-length PRS generator or sampled from the Haar distribution on $\log \lambda$-qubit states with constant probability.

Simple Case: PRS output is always pure. Let us start with a simple case when the PRS generator is such that each possible PRS state is pure. Consider the subspace spanned by all possible PRS outputs. The dimension of the subspace spanned by these states is almost 2^λ: the reason being that there are at most 2^λ keys. Now, consider the subspace spanned by t-copies of PRS states. The dimension of this subspace is still at most 2^λ and in particular, independent of t. Define $P^{(t)}$ to be a projector (which could have an inefficient implementation) onto this subspace. By definition, the measurement of t copies of the output of a PRS generator with respect to $P^{(t)}$ always succeeds.

Recall that the subspace spanned by t-copies of states sampled from the Haar distribution (of length $\log \lambda$) is a symmetric subspace of dimension $\binom{2^\lambda+t-1}{t}$. By choosing t as an appropriate polynomial (in particular, set $t \gg \lambda$), we can make $\binom{2^\lambda+t-1}{t} \gg 2^\lambda$, such that a measurement with $P^{(t)}$ on t copies of states sampled from the Haar distribution fails with constant probability. Hence, an adversary, who just runs P, can successfully distinguish between t copies of the output of a $\log \lambda$-length PRS generator and t copies of a sample from a Haar distribution with constant probability.

General Case. Now let us focus on the case when the PRS generator can also output mixed states. Then we have 2 cases:

- *The majority of outputs of the PRS generator are negligibly close to a pure state:* In this case, we show that the previous approach still works. We replace the projector $P^{(t)}$ with a projection onto the space spanned by states closest to the output states of the PRS generator and we can show that modified projector still succeeds with constant probability.
- *The majority of outputs of the PRS generator are not negligibly close to a pure state:* In this case, most PRS outputs have purity[4] non-negligibly away from 1. Thus, we can violate the security of PRS as follows: run polynomially (in λ) many SWAP tests to check if the state is mixed or not. When the input state is from a Haar distribution, the test will always determine the input state to be pure. On the other hand, if the input state is the output of a PRS generator, the test will determine the input to be pure with probability that is non-negligibly bounded away from 1. Thus, this case cannot happen if the PRS generator is secure.

Details can be found in Sect. 4.

1.3 Cryptographic Applications with Classical Communication

We show how to construct bit commitments and pseudo one-time encryption schemes from $O(\log(\lambda))$-output PRS with classical communication. Previously, [2] achieved the same result for a wider range of parameters. In this overview, we mainly focus on bit commitments since the main techniques used in constructing commitments will be re-purposed for designing pseudo one-time encryption schemes.

We use the construction of bit commitments from [2] as a starting point. Let $d = O(\log \lambda)$, $n = O(\log \lambda)$ and G is a (d, n)-PRFS generator[5]. The commitment scheme from [2] is as follows:

---

[4] A density matrix ρ has purity p if $\text{Tr}(\rho^2) = p$.

[5] This in turn can be built from $O(\log(\lambda))$-output PRS as shown in [2].

- In the commit phase, the receiver sends a random $2^d n$-qubit Pauli $P = P_1 \otimes P_2 \otimes \cdots \otimes P_{2^d-1}$ to the sender, where each P_i is an n-qubit Pauli. The sender on input bit b, samples a key k uniformly at random from $\{0,1\}^\lambda$. The sender then sends the state $\rho = \bigotimes_{x \in [2^d]} P_x^b \sigma_{k,x} P_x^b$, where $\sigma_{k,x} = G(k,x)$ to the receiver.
- In the reveal phase, the sender sends (k,b) to the receiver. The receiver accepts if $P^b \rho P^b$ is a tensor product of the PRFS evaluations of (k,x), for all $x = 0, \ldots, 2^d - 1$.

To convert this scheme into one that only has classical comunication, we need a mechanism to generate classical information c from ρ, where ρ is generated from (k,b) as above, that have the following properties:

1. *Classical Description*: c can be computed efficiently and does not leak any information about b.
2. *Correctness*: (k,b) is accepted as a valid opening for c,
3. *Binding*: (k',b'), for $b \neq b'$, is rejected as an opening for c

State Tomography. To design such a mechanism, we turn to quantum state tomography. Quantum state tomography is a process that takes as input multiple copies of a quantum state σ and outputs a string u that is close (according to some distance metric) to a classical description of the state σ. In general, tomography procedures require exponential in d number of copies of a state and also run in time exponential in d, where d is the dimension of the state. Since the states in question are $O(\log(\lambda))$-output length PRFS states, all the algorithms in the commitment scheme would still be efficient.

Since performing tomography on a PRFS state does not violate its pseudorandomness property, the hiding property is unaffected. For achieving correctness and binding properties, we need to also equip the tomography process with a verification algorithm, denoted by Verify. A natural verification algorithm that can be associated with the tomography procedure is the following: to check if u is a valid classical description of a state σ, simply run the above tomography procedure on many copies of σ and check if the output density matrix is close to u.

More formally, we introduce a new tomography called verifiable tomography and we present a generic transformation that converts a specific tomography procedure into one that is also verifiable. We will see how verifiable tomography helps us achieve both correctness and binding. Before we dive into the new notion and understand its properties, we will first discuss the specific tomography procedure that we consider.

Instantiation. We develop a tomography procedure based on [14] that outputs a denisity matrix close (constant distance away) to the input with $1 - \mathsf{negl}(\lambda)$ probability. This is an upgrade to the tomography procedure in [14], the expected distance of whose output was a constant. To achieve this, we make use of the fact that if we repeat [14]'s tomography procedure polynomially many times, most output states cluster around the input at a constant distance with $1 - \mathsf{negl}(\lambda)$

probability. We believe this procedure might be of independent interest. Details about this procedure can be found in Sect. 5.2.

Verifiable Tomography. Verifiable tomography is a pair of efficient algorithms (Tomography, Verify) associated with a family of channels Φ_λ such that the following holds:

- *Same-input correctness:* Let $u_1 = \mathsf{Tomography}(\Phi_\lambda(x))$ and $u_2 = \mathsf{Tomography}(\Phi_\lambda(x))$, then $\mathsf{Verify}(u_1, u_2)$ accepts with high probability.
- *Different-input correctness:* Let $u_1 = \mathsf{Tomography}(\Phi_\lambda(x_1))$ and $u_2 = \mathsf{Tomography}(\Phi_\lambda(x_2))$, and $x_1 \neq x_2$, then $\mathsf{Verify}(u_1, u_2)$ rejects with high probability.

The family of channels we consider corresponds to the PRFS state generation. That is, $\Phi_\lambda(x = (k, i))$ outputs $G(k, i)$. As mentioned earlier, we can generically convert the above instantiation into a verifiable tomography procedure. Let us see how the generic transformation works.

For simplicity, consider the case when the underlying PRFS has perfect state generation, i.e., the output of PRFS is always a pure state. In this case, the verification algorithm is the canonical one that we described earlier: on input u and PRFS key k, input i, it first performs tomography on many copies of $G(k, i)$ to recover u' and then checks if u is close to u' or not. The same-input correctness follows from the tomography guarantee of the instantiation. To prove the different-input correctness, we use the fact that PRFS outputs are close to uniformly distributed and the following fact [2, Fact 6.9]: for two arbitrary n-qubit states $|\psi\rangle$ and $|\phi\rangle$,

$$\underset{P \xleftarrow{\$} \mathcal{P}_n}{\mathbb{E}} \left[|\langle \psi | P | \phi \rangle|^2 \right] = 2^{-n}.$$

Thus, if $x_1 \neq x_2$ then u_1 and u_2 are most likely going to be far and thus, differing-input correctness property is satisfied as well.

The proofs get more involved when the underlying PRFS does not satisfy perfect state generation. We consider PRFS generators that satisfy recognisable abort; we note that this notion of PRFS can be instantiated from PRS, also with $O(\log(\lambda))$ outpout length, using [2]. A $(d(\lambda), n(\lambda))$-PRFS generator G has the *strongly recognizable abort property* if its output can be written as follows: $G_\lambda(k, x) = Tr_\mathcal{A} (\eta |0\rangle\langle 0| \otimes |\psi\rangle\langle\psi| + (1 - \eta) |\bot\rangle\langle\bot|)$, where $\mathcal{A}$ is the register with the first qubit. Moreover, $|\bot\rangle$ is of the form $|1\rangle |\widehat{\bot}\rangle$ for some $n(\lambda)$-qubit state state $|\widehat{\bot}\rangle$ so that, $(\langle 0| \otimes \langle\psi|)(|\bot\rangle) = 0$. The same-input correctness essentially follows as before; however arguing differing-input correctness property seems more challenging.

Arguing different-input correctness is more tricky. Consider the following degenerate case: suppose k be a key and x_1, x_2 be two inputs such that PRFS on input (k, x_1) and PRFS on (k, x_2) abort with very high probability (say, close to 1). Note that the recognizable abort property does not rule out this degenerate case. Then, it holds that the outputs $u_1 = \mathsf{Tomography}(\Phi_\lambda(x_1))$

and $u_2 = \mathsf{Tomography}(\Phi_\lambda(x_2))$ are close. $\mathsf{Verify}(u_1, u_2)$ accepts and thus, the different-input correctness is not satisfied. To handle such degenerate cases, we incorporate the following into the verification procedure: on input (u_1, u_2), reject if either u_1 or u_2 is close to an abort state. Checking whether a classical description of a state is close to an abort state can be done efficiently.

From Verifiable Tomography to Commitments. Incorporating verifiable tomography into the commitment scheme, we have the following:

- The correctness follows from the same-input correctness of the tomography procedure.
- The binding property follows from the different-input correctness of the tomography procedure.
- The hiding property follows from the fact that the output of a PRFS generator is indistinguishable from Haar random, even given polynomially many copies of the state.

2   Preliminaries

We present the preliminaries in this section. We use λ to denote the security parameter. We use the notation $\mathsf{negl}(\cdot)$ to denote a negligible function.

We refer the reader to [17] for a comprehensive reference on the basics of quantum information and quantum computation. We use I to denote the identity operator. We use $\mathcal{D}(\mathcal{H})$ to denote the set of density matrices on a Hilbert space $\mathcal{H}$.

Haar Measure. The Haar measure over $\mathbb{C}^d$, denoted by $\mathscr{H}(\mathbb{C}^d)$ is the uniform measure over all d-dimensional unit vectors. One useful property of the Haar measure is that for all d-dimensional unitary matrices U, if a random vector $|\psi\rangle$ is distributed according to the Haar measure $\mathscr{H}(\mathbb{C}^d)$, then the state $U |\psi\rangle$ is also distributed according to the Haar measure. For notational convenience we write $\mathscr{H}_m$ to denote the Haar measure over m-qubit space, or $\mathscr{H}((\mathbb{C}^2)^{\otimes m})$.

Fact 1. *We have*

$$\underset{|\psi\rangle \leftarrow \mathscr{H}(\mathbb{C}^d)}{\mathbb{E}} |\psi\rangle\langle\psi| = \frac{I}{d} .$$

2.1   Distance Metrics and Matrix Norms

Trace Distance. Let $\rho, \sigma \in \mathcal{D}(\mathcal{H})$ be density matrices. We write $\mathrm{TD}(\rho, \sigma)$ to denote the trace distance between them, i.e.,

$$\mathrm{TD}(\rho, \sigma) = \frac{1}{2}\|\rho - \sigma\|_1$$

where $\|X\|_1 = \mathrm{Tr}(\sqrt{X^\dagger X})$ denotes the trace norm.

We denote $\|X\| := \sup_{|\psi\rangle}\{\langle\psi|X|\psi\rangle\}$ to be the operator norm where the supremum is taken over all unit vectors. For a vector x, we denote its Euclidean norm to be $\|x\|_2$.

Frobenius Norm. The Frobenius norm of a matrix M is

$$\|M\|_F = \sqrt{\sum_{i,j} |M_{i,j}|^2} = \sqrt{\mathrm{Tr}\,(MM^\dagger)},$$

where $M_{i,j}$ denotes the $(i,j)^{th}$ entry of M.

We state some useful facts about Frobenius norm below.

Fact 2. *For all matrices A, B we have $\|A - B\|_F^2 = \|A\|_F^2 + \|B\|_F^2 - 2\mathrm{Tr}(A^\dagger B)$.*

Fact 3. *Let M_0, M_1 be density matricies and $|\psi\rangle$ be a pure state such that $\langle\psi| M_0 |\psi\rangle \leq \alpha$ and $\|M_0 - M_1\|_F^2 \leq \beta$, where $\beta + 2\alpha < 1$ then*

$$\langle\psi| M_1 |\psi\rangle \leq \alpha + \sqrt{\beta} + \sqrt{(2 - 2\alpha)\,\beta}.$$

Proof. From fact 2, we have the following:

$$\|M_0 - |\psi\rangle\langle\psi| \,\|_F = \sqrt{\|M_0\|_F^2 + \| \,|\psi\rangle\langle\psi| \,\|_F^2 - 2\mathrm{Tr}(M_0^\dagger \,|\psi\rangle\langle\psi|)}$$

$$= \sqrt{\|M_0\|_F^2 + 1 - 2 \langle\psi| M_0 |\psi\rangle}$$

$$\geq \sqrt{\|M_0\|_F^2 + 1 - 2\alpha}.$$

By triangle inequality, we know

$$\|M_1\|_F \leq \|M_0\|_F + \|M_0 - M_1\|_F \leq \|M_0\|_F + \sqrt{\beta}.$$

Similarly by fact 2,

$$\|M_1 - |\psi\rangle\langle\psi| \,\|_F = \sqrt{1 + \|M_1\|_F^2 - 2 \langle\psi| M_1 |\psi\rangle}$$

$$\leq \sqrt{1 + \left(\|M_0\|_F + \sqrt{\beta}\right)^2 - 2 \langle\psi| M_1 |\psi\rangle}.$$

By triangle inequality, we know $\|M_0 - |\psi\rangle\langle\psi| \,\|_F \leq \|M_1 - |\psi\rangle\langle\psi| \,\|_F + \|M_0 - M_1\|_F$. Hence,

$$\sqrt{1 + \|M_0\|_F^2 - 2\alpha} \leq \sqrt{1 + \left(\|M_0\|_F + \sqrt{\beta}\right)^2 - 2 \langle\psi| M_1 |\psi\rangle} + \sqrt{\beta}.$$

By some easy manipulation, we get

$$\langle\psi| M_1 |\psi\rangle \leq \alpha + \|M_0\|_F^2 \sqrt{\beta} + \sqrt{(1 + \|M_0\|_F^2 - 2\alpha)\,\beta} \leq \alpha + \sqrt{\beta} + \sqrt{(2 - 2\alpha)\,\beta}.$$

$\square$

Fact 4. *For any $0 \leq \varepsilon \leq 1$,*

$$\mathrm{Pr}_{|\psi_1\rangle,|\psi_2\rangle \leftarrow \mathscr{H}_n} \left[\| \,|\psi_1\rangle\langle\psi_1| - |\psi_2\rangle\langle\psi_2| \,\|_F^2 \leq \varepsilon\right] \leq \frac{1}{e^{2^n \left(1 - \frac{\varepsilon}{2}\right)}}.$$

Proof. From fact 2,

$$\| \, |\psi_1\rangle\langle\psi_1| - |\psi_2\rangle\langle\psi_2| \, \|_F^2 = \| \, |\psi_1\rangle\langle\psi_1| \, \|_F^2 + \| \, |\psi_2\rangle\langle\psi_2| \, \|_F^2 - 2\mathrm{Tr}\left(|\psi_1\rangle\langle\psi_1| \, |\psi_2\rangle\langle\psi_2|\right)$$
$$= 2 - 2|\langle\psi_1|\psi_2\rangle|^2$$

Thus, we have the following:

$$\Pr\nolimits_{|\psi_1\rangle,|\psi_2\rangle \leftarrow \mathscr{H}_n}\left[\| \, |\psi_1\rangle\langle\psi_1| - |\psi_2\rangle\langle\psi_2| \, \|_F^2 \leq \varepsilon\right] = \Pr\nolimits_{|\psi_1\rangle,|\psi_2\rangle \leftarrow \mathscr{H}_n}\left[|\langle\psi_1|\psi_2\rangle|^2 \geq 1 - \frac{\varepsilon}{2}\right]$$
$$\leq \frac{1}{e^{2^n(1-\frac{\varepsilon}{2})}},$$

where the last inequality was shown in [5] (Eq. 14).   □

2.2   Quantum Algorithms

A quantum algorithm A is a family of generalized quantum circuits $\{A_\lambda\}_{\lambda \in \mathbb{N}}$ over a discrete universal gate set (such as $\{CNOT, H, T\}$). By generalized, we mean that such circuits can have a subset of input qubits that are designated to be initialized in the zero state, and a subset of output qubits that are designated to be traced out at the end of the computation. Thus a generalized quantum circuit A_λ corresponds to a *quantum channel*, which is a is a completely positive trace-preserving (CPTP) map. When we write $A_\lambda(\rho)$ for some density matrix ρ, we mean the output of the generalized circuit A_λ on input ρ. If we only take the quantum gates of A_λ and ignore the subset of input/output qubits that are initialized to zeroes/traced out, then we get the *unitary part* of A_λ, which corresponds to a unitary operator which we denote by $\hat{A}_\lambda$. The *size* of a generalized quantum circuit is the number of gates in it, plus the number of input and output qubits.

We say that $A = \{A_\lambda\}_\lambda$ is a *quantum polynomial-time (QPT) algorithm* if there exists a polynomial p such that the size of each circuit A_λ is at most $p(\lambda)$. Furthermore we say that A is *uniform* if there exists a deterministic polynomial-time Turing machine M that on input 1^n outputs the description of A_λ.

We also define the notion of a *non-uniform* QPT algorithm A that consists of a family $\{(A_\lambda, \rho_\lambda)\}_\lambda$ where $\{A_\lambda\}_\lambda$ is a polynomial-size family of circuits (not necessarily uniformly generated), and for each λ there is additionally a subset of input qubits of A_λ that are designated to be initialized with the density matrix ρ_λ of polynomial length. This is intended to model non-uniform quantum adversaries who may receive quantum states as advice. Nevertheless, the reductions we show in this work are all uniform.

The notation we use to describe the inputs/outputs of quantum algorithms will largely mimic what is used in the classical cryptography literature. For example, for a state generator algorithm G, we write $G_\lambda(k)$ to denote running the generalized quantum circuit G_λ on input $|k\rangle\langle k|$, which outputs a state ρ_k.

Ultimately, all inputs to a quantum circuit are density matrices. However, we mix-and-match between classical, pure state, and density matrix notation; for example, we may write $A_\lambda(k, |\theta\rangle, \rho)$ to denote running the circuit A_λ on input

$|k\rangle\langle k| \otimes |\theta\rangle\langle\theta| \otimes \rho$. In general, we will not explain all the input and output sizes of every quantum circuit in excruciating detail; we will implicitly assume that a quantum circuit in question has the appropriate number of input and output qubits as required by context.

2.3   Pseudorandomness Notions

Next, we recall the different notions of pseudorandomness. First, in Sect. 2.3, we recall (classical) pseudorandom functions (prfs) and consider two notions of security associated with it. Then in Sect. 2.3, we define pseudorandom quantum state (PRS) generators, which are a quantum analogue of pseudorandom generators (PRGs). Finally in Sect. 2.3, we define pseudorandom function-like quantum state (PRFS) generators, which are a quantum analogue of pseudorandom functions. To make it less confusing to the reader, we use the abbreviation "prfs" (small letters) for classical pseudorandom functions and "PRFS" (all caps) for pseudorandom function-like states.

Pseudorandom Functions. We present two security notions of pseudorandom functions. First, we consider the notion of post-quantum security, defined below.

Definition 1 (Post-Quantum Pseudorandom Functions). *We say that a deterministic polynomial-time algorithm $F : \{0,1\}^\lambda \times \{0,1\}^{d(\lambda)} \to \{0,1\}^{n(\lambda)}$ is a post-quantum secure pseudorandom function (pq-prf) if for all QPT (non-uniform) distinguishers $A = (A_\lambda, \rho_\lambda)$ there exists a negligible function $\varepsilon(\cdot)$ such that the following holds:*

$$\left| \Pr_{k \leftarrow \{0,1\}^\lambda} \left[A_\lambda^{\mathcal{O}_{\mathsf{prf}}(k,\cdot)}(\rho_\lambda) = 1 \right] - \Pr_{\mathcal{O}_{\mathsf{Rand}}} \left[A_\lambda^{\mathcal{O}_{\mathsf{Rand}}(\cdot)}(\rho_\lambda) = 1 \right] \right| \leq \varepsilon(\lambda),$$

where:

- *$\mathcal{O}_{\mathsf{prf}}(k,\cdot)$, modeled as a classical algorithm, on input $x \in \{0,1\}^{d(\lambda)}$, outputs $F(k,x)$.*
- *$\mathcal{O}_{\mathsf{Rand}}(\cdot)$, modeled as a classical algorithm, on input $x \in \{0,1\}^{d(\lambda)}$, outputs y_x, where $y_x \leftarrow \{0,1\}^{n(\lambda)}$.*

Moreover, the adversary A_λ only has classical access to $\mathcal{O}_{\mathsf{prf}}(k,\cdot)$ and $\mathcal{O}_{\mathsf{Rand}}(\cdot)$. That is, any query made to the oracle is measured in the computational basis.

We also say that F is a $(d(\lambda), n(\lambda))$-pq-prf to succinctly indicate that its input length is $d(\lambda)$ and its output length is $n(\lambda)$.

Next, we consider the quantum-query security, as considered by Zhandry [19]. In this security notion, the adversary has superposition access to either $\mathcal{O}_{\mathsf{prf}}$ or $\mathcal{O}_{\mathsf{Rand}}$. By definition, quantum-query security implies post-quantum security.

Unlike all the other pseudorandom notions considered in this section, we are going to use a different convention and allow the key length to be a polynomial in λ, instead of it being just λ. We also parameterize the advantage of the adversary.

Definition 2 (Quantum-Query Secure Pseudorandom Functions). *We say that a deterministic polynomial-time algorithm* $F : \{0,1\}^{\ell(\lambda)} \times \{0,1\}^{d(\lambda)} \rightarrow \{0,1\}^{n(\lambda)}$ *is a* quantum-query ε-secure pseudorandom function (qprf) *if for all QPT (non-uniform) distinguishers* $A = (A_\lambda, \rho_\lambda)$ *there exists a function* $\varepsilon(\cdot)$ *such that the following holds:*

$$\left| \Pr_{k \leftarrow \{0,1\}^{\ell(\lambda)}} \left[A_\lambda^{|\mathcal{O}_{\mathsf{prf}}(k,\cdot)\rangle}(\rho_\lambda) = 1 \right] - \Pr_{\mathcal{O}_{\mathsf{Rand}}} \left[A_\lambda^{|\mathcal{O}_{\mathsf{Rand}}(\cdot)\rangle}(\rho_\lambda) = 1 \right] \right| \leq \varepsilon(\lambda),$$

where:

- $\mathcal{O}_{\mathsf{prf}}(k, \cdot)$ *on input a* $(d + n)$-*qubit state on registers* **X** *(first d qubits) and* **Y***, applies an* $(n + d)$-*qubit unitary* U *described as follows:* $U |x\rangle |a\rangle = |x\rangle |a \oplus F(k,x)\rangle$. *It sends back the registers* **X** *and* **Y***.*
- $\mathcal{O}_{\mathsf{Rand}}(\cdot)$ *on input a* $(d + n)$-*qubit state on registers* **X** *(first d qubits) and* **Y***, applies an* $(n+d)$-*qubit unitary* R *described as follows:* $R |x\rangle |a\rangle = |x\rangle |a \oplus y_x\rangle$, *where* $y_x \leftarrow \{0,1\}^{n(\lambda)}$. *It sends back the registers* **X** *and* **Y***.*

Moreover, A_λ *has superposition access to* $\mathcal{O}_{\mathsf{prf}}(k, \cdot)$ *and* $\mathcal{O}_{\mathsf{Rand}}(\cdot)$. *We denote the fact that* A_λ *has quantum access to an oracle* $\mathcal{O}$ *by* $A_\lambda^{|\mathcal{O}\rangle}$.

We also say that F *is a* $(\ell(\lambda), d(\lambda), n(\lambda), \varepsilon)$-*qprf to succinctly indicate that its input length is* $d(\lambda)$ *and its output length is* $n(\lambda)$. *When* $\ell(\lambda) = \lambda$, *we drop* $\ell(\lambda)$ *from the notation. Similarly, when* $\varepsilon(\lambda)$ *can be any negligible function, we drop* $\varepsilon(\lambda)$ *from the notation.*

Zhandry [19] presented a construction of quantum-query secure pseudorandom functions from one-way functions.

Lemma 1 (Zhandry [19]). *Assuming post-quantum one-way functions, there exists quantum-query secure pseudorandom functions.*

Useful Lemma. We will use the following lemma due to Zhandry [20]. The lemma states that any q-query algorithm cannot distinguish (quantum) oracle access to a random function versus a $2q$-wise independent hash function. We restate the lemma using our notation.

Lemma 2 ([20, Theorem 3.1]). *Let A be a q-query algorithm. Then, for any* $d, n \in \mathbb{N}$, *every* $2q$-*wise independent hash function* $H : \{0,1\}^{\ell(q)} \times \{0,1\}^d \rightarrow \{0,1\}^n$ *satisfies the following:*

$$\left| \Pr_{k \leftarrow \{0,1\}^{\ell(q)}} \left[A_\lambda^{|\mathcal{O}_{\mathsf{H}}(k,\cdot)\rangle}(\rho_\lambda) = 1 \right] - \Pr_{\mathcal{O}_{\mathsf{Rand}}} \left[A_\lambda^{|\mathcal{O}_{\mathsf{Rand}}(\cdot)\rangle}(\rho_\lambda) = 1 \right] \right| = 0,$$

where $\mathcal{O}_{\mathsf{Rand}}$ *is as defined in Definition 2 and* $\mathcal{O}_{\mathsf{H}}$ *is defined similarly to* $\mathcal{O}_{\mathsf{prf}}$ *except that the unitary* U *uses* H *instead of* F.

Pseudorandom Quantum State Generators. We move onto the pseudo-random notions in the quantum world. The notion of pseudorandom states were first introduced by Ji, Liu, and Song in [11]. We reproduce their definition here:

Definition 3 (PRS Generator [11]). *We say that a QPT algorithm G is a pseudorandom state (PRS) generator if the following holds.*

1. **State Generation.** *For all λ and for all $k \in \{0,1\}^\lambda$, the algorithm G behaves as*

$$G_\lambda(k) = |\psi_k\rangle\langle\psi_k| .$$

for some $n(\lambda)$-qubit pure state $|\psi_k\rangle$.

2. **Pseudorandomness.** *For all polynomials $t(\cdot)$ and QPT (nonuniform) distinguisher A there exists a negligible function $\varepsilon(\cdot)$ such that for all λ, we have*

$$\left| \Pr_{k \leftarrow \{0,1\}^\lambda} \left[A_\lambda(G_\lambda(k)^{\otimes t(\lambda)}) = 1 \right] - \Pr_{|\vartheta\rangle \leftarrow \mathscr{H}_{n(\lambda)}} \left[A_\lambda(|\vartheta\rangle^{\otimes t(\lambda)}) = 1 \right] \right| \leq \varepsilon(\lambda) .$$

We also say that G is a $n(\lambda)$-PRS generator to succinctly indicate that the output length of G is $n(\lambda)$.

Ji, Liu, and Song showed that post-quantum one-way functions can be used to construct PRS generators.

Theorem 5 ([4, 11]). *If post-quantum one-way functions exist, then there exist PRS generators for all polynomial output lengths.*

Pseudorandom Function-Like State (PRFS) Generators. In this section, we recall the definition of pseudorandom function-like state (PRFS) generators by Ananth, Qian and Yuen [2]. PRFS generators generalize PRS generators in two ways: first, in addition to the secret key k, the PRFS generator additionally takes a (classical) input x. The second way in which this definition generalizes the definition of PRS generators is that the output of the generator need not be a pure state.

However, they considered the weaker selective security definition where the adversary needs to choose all the inputs to be queried to the PRFS ahead of time. Later we will introduce the stronger and the more useful definition of adaptive security.

Definition 4 (Selectively Secure PRFS Generator). *We say that a QPT algorithm G is a (selectively secure) pseudorandom function-like state (PRFS) generator if for all polynomials $s(\cdot), t(\cdot)$, QPT (nonuniform) distinguishers A and a family of indices $\left(\{x_1, \ldots, x_{s(\lambda)}\} \subseteq \{0,1\}^{d(\lambda)}\right)_\lambda$, there exists a negligible function $\varepsilon(\cdot)$ such that for all λ,*

$$\left| \Pr_{k \leftarrow \{0,1\}^\lambda} \left[A_\lambda(x_1, \ldots, x_{s(\lambda)}, G_\lambda(k, x_1)^{\otimes t(\lambda)}, \ldots, G_\lambda(k, x_{s(\lambda)})^{\otimes t(\lambda)}) = 1 \right] \right.$$
$$\left. - \Pr_{|\vartheta_1\rangle, \ldots, |\vartheta_{s(\lambda)}\rangle \leftarrow \mathscr{H}_{n(\lambda)}} \left[A_\lambda(x_1, \ldots, x_{s(\lambda)}, |\vartheta_1\rangle^{\otimes t(\lambda)}, \ldots, |\vartheta_{s(\lambda)}\rangle^{\otimes t(\lambda)}) = 1 \right] \right| \leq \varepsilon(\lambda) .$$

We say that G is a $(d(\lambda), n(\lambda))$-PRFS generator to succinctly indicate that its input length is $d(\lambda)$ and its output length is $n(\lambda)$.

Our notion of security here can be seen as a version of *(classical) selective security*, where the queries to the PRFS generator are fixed before the key is sampled.

State Generation Guarantees. Towards capturing a natural class of PRFS generators, [2] introduced the concept of *recognizable abort*. At a high level, recognizable abort is the property that the output of PRFS can be written as a convex combination of a pure state and a known abort state, denoted by $|\perp\rangle$. In more detail, the PRFS generator works in two stages. In the first stage it either generates a valid PRFS state $|\psi\rangle$ or it aborts. If it outputs a valid PRFS state then the first qubit is set to $|0\rangle$ and if it aborts, the entire state is set to $|\perp\rangle$. We have the guarantee that $|0\rangle |\psi\rangle$ is orthogonal to $|\perp\rangle$. In the next stage, the PRFS generator traces out the first qubit and outputs the resulting state. Our definition could be useful to capture many generators that don't always succeed in generating the pseudorandom state; for example, Brakerski and Shmueli [4] design generators that doesn't always succeed in generating the state.

We formally define the notion of recognizable abort[6] below.

Definition 5 (Recognizable Abort). *A $(d(\lambda), n(\lambda))$-PRFS generator G has the strongly recognizable abort property if there exists an algorithm $\widehat{G}$ and a special $(n(\lambda) + 1)$-qubit state $|\perp\rangle$ such that $G_\lambda(k, x)$ has the following form: it takes as input $k \in \{0,1\}^\lambda$, $x \in \{0,1\}^{d(\lambda)}$ and does the following,*

- *Compute $\widehat{G}_\lambda(k, x)$ to obtain an output of the form $\eta |0\rangle\langle 0| \otimes |\psi\rangle\langle\psi| + (1 - \eta) |\perp\rangle\langle\perp|$ and moreover, $|\perp\rangle$ is of the form $|1\rangle |\widehat{\perp}\rangle$ for some $n(\lambda)$-qubit state state $|\widehat{\perp}\rangle$. As a consequence, $(\langle 0| \otimes \langle\psi|)(|\perp\rangle) = 0$.*
- *Trace out the first bit of $\widehat{G}_\lambda(k, x)$ and output the resulting state.*

As observed by [2], the definition alone does not have any constraint on η being close to 1. The security guarantee of a PRFS generator implies that η will be negligibly close to 1 with overwhelming probability over the choice of k [2, Lemma 3.6].

3 Adaptive Security

The previous work by [2] only considers PRFS that is selectively secure. That is, the adversary needs to declare the input queries ahead of time. For many applications, selective security is insufficient. For example, in the application of PRFS to secret-key encryption (satisfying multi-message security), the resulting scheme was also only proven to be selectively secure, whereas one could ask for security against adversaries that can make *adaptive* queries to the PRFS generator. Another drawback of the notion considered by [2] is the assumption

---

[6] We note that [2] define a slightly weaker definition of recognizable abort. However, the definitions and results considered in [2] also work with our (stronger) definition of recognizable abort.

that the adversary can make classical queries to the challenger who either returns PRFS states or independent Haar random states, whereas one would ideally prefer security against adversaries that can make *quantum superposition* queries.

In this work, we consider stronger notions of security for PRFS. We strengthen the definitions of [2] in two ways. First, we allow the the adversary to make adaptive queries to the PRFS oracle, and second, we allow the adversary to make *quantum* queries to the oracle. The oracle model we consider here is slightly different from the usual quantum query model. In the usual model, there is an underlying function f and the oracle is modelled as a unitary acting on two registers, a *query* register $\mathbf{X}$ and an *answer* register $\mathbf{Y}$ mapping basis states $|x\rangle_{\mathbf{X}} \otimes |y\rangle_{\mathbf{Y}}$ to $|x\rangle_{\mathbf{X}} \otimes |y \oplus f(x)\rangle_{\mathbf{Y}}$ (in other words, the function output is XORed with answer register in the standard basis). The query algorithm also acts on the query and answer registers; indeed, it is often useful in quantum algorithms to initialize the answer register to something other than all zeroes.

In the PRS/PRFS setting, however, there is no underlying classical function: the output of the PRFS generator G could be an entangled pseudorandom state far from any standard basis state; it seems unnatural to XOR the pseudorandom the state with a standard basis state. Instead we consider a model where the query algorithm submits a query register $\mathbf{X}$ to the oracle, and the oracle returns the query register $\mathbf{X}$ as well as an answer register $\mathbf{Y}$. If the algorithm submits query $|x\rangle_{\mathbf{X}}$, then the joint state register $\mathbf{XY}$ after the query is $|x\rangle_{\mathbf{X}} \otimes |\psi_x\rangle_{\mathbf{Y}}$ for some pure state $|\psi_x\rangle$. Each time the algorithm makes a query, the oracle returns a fresh answer register. Thus, the number of qubits that the query algorithm acts on grows with the number of queries.[7]

How the oracle behaves when the query algorithm submits a superposition $\sum_x \alpha_x |x\rangle_{\mathbf{X}}$ in the query register is a further modeling choice. In the most general setting, the oracle behaves as a unitary on registers $\mathbf{XY}$,[8] and the resulting state of the query and answer registers is $\sum_x \alpha_x |x\rangle_{\mathbf{X}} \otimes |\psi_x\rangle_{\mathbf{Y}}$. That is, queries are answered in superposition. We call such an oracle *quantum-accessible*.

We also consider the case where the queries are forced to be *classical*, which may already be useful for some applications. Here, the oracle is modeled as a channel (instead of a unitary) that first measures the query register in the standard basis before returning the corresponding state $|\psi_x\rangle$. In other words, if the query is $\sum_x \alpha_x |x\rangle_{\mathbf{X}}$, then the resulting state becomes the mixed state $\sum_x |\alpha_x|^2 |x\rangle\langle x|_{\mathbf{X}} \otimes |\psi_x\rangle\langle\psi_x|_{\mathbf{Y}}$. This way, the algorithm cannot take advantage of quantum queries – but it can still make queries adaptively. We call such an oracle *classically-accessible*.

To distinguish between classical and quantum access to oracles, we write $A^{\mathcal{O}}$ to denote a quantum algorithm that has classical access to the oracle $\mathcal{O}$, and $A^{|\mathcal{O}\rangle}$ to denote a quantum algorithm that has quantum access to the oracle $\mathcal{O}$.

---

[7] Alternatively, one can think of answer registers $\mathbf{Y}_1, \mathbf{Y}_2, \ldots$ as being initialized in the zeroes state at the beginning, and the query algorithm is only allowed to act nontrivially on $\mathbf{Y}_i$ after the i'th query.

[8] Alternatively, one can think of the oracle as an *isometry* mapping register $\mathbf{X}$ to registers $\mathbf{XY}$.

3.1 Classical Access

We define adaptively secure PRFS, where the adversary is given *classical access* to the PRFS/Haar-random oracle.

Definition 6 (Adaptively-Secure PRFS). *We say that a QPT algorithm G is an* adaptively secure pseudorandom function-like state (APRFS) *generator if for all QPT (non-uniform) distinguishers A, there exists a negligible function ε, such that for all λ, the following holds:*

$$\left| \Pr_{k \leftarrow \{0,1\}^\lambda} \left[A_\lambda^{\mathcal{O}_{\mathsf{PRFS}}(k,\cdot)}(\rho_\lambda) = 1 \right] - \Pr_{\mathcal{O}_{\mathsf{Haar}}} \left[A_\lambda^{\mathcal{O}_{\mathsf{Haar}}(\cdot)}(\rho_\lambda) = 1 \right] \right| \le \varepsilon(\lambda),$$

where:

- $\mathcal{O}_{\mathsf{PRFS}}(k, \cdot)$, *on input $x \in \{0,1\}^{d(\lambda)}$, outputs $G_\lambda(k, x)$.*
- $\mathcal{O}_{\mathsf{Haar}}(\cdot)$, *on input $x \in \{0,1\}^{d(\lambda)}$, outputs $|\vartheta_x\rangle$, where, for every $y \in \{0,1\}^{d(\lambda)}$, $|\vartheta_y\rangle \leftarrow \mathscr{H}_{n(\lambda)}$.*

Moreover, the adversary A_λ has classical access to $\mathcal{O}_{\mathsf{PRFS}}(k, \cdot)$ and $\mathcal{O}_{\mathsf{Haar}}(\cdot)$. That is, we can assume without loss of generality that any query made to either oracle is measured in the computational basis.

We say that G is a $(d(\lambda), n(\lambda))$-APRFS generator to succinctly indicate that its input length is $d(\lambda)$ and its output length is $n(\lambda)$.

Some remarks are in order.

Instantiation. For the case when $d(\lambda) = O(\log(\lambda))$, selectively secure PRFS is equivalent to adaptively secure PRFS. The reason being that we can assume without loss of generality, the selective adversary can query on all possible inputs (there are only polynomially many) and use the outputs to simulate the adaptive adversary. As a consequence of the result that log-input selectively-secure PRFS can be built from PRS [2], we obtain the following.

Lemma 3. *For $d = O(\log(\lambda))$ and $n = d + \omega(\log \log \lambda)$, assuming the existence of $(d+n)$-PRS, there exists a (d, n)-APRFS.*

In the case when $d(\lambda)$ is an arbitrary polynomial in λ, we present a construction of APRFS from post-quantum one-way functions in the full version of the paper.

Test Procedure. It was shown by [2] that a PRFS admits a Test procedure (See Sect. 3.3 in [2]). The goal of a Test procedure is to determine whether the given state is a valid PRFS state or not. Having a Test procedure is useful in applications. For example, [2] used a Test procedure in the construction of a bit commitment scheme. We note that the same Test procedure also works for adaptively secure PRFS.

Multiple Copies. In the definition of PRS (Definition 3) and selectively-secure PRFS (Definition 4), the adversary is allowed to obtain multiple copies of the same pseudorandom (or haar random) quantum state. While we do not explicitly state it, even in Definition 6, the adversary can indeed obtain multiple copies of a (pseudorandom or haar random) quantum state. To obtain t copies of the output of $G_\lambda(k, x)$ (or $|\vartheta_x\rangle$), the adversary can query the same input x, t times, to the oracle $\mathcal{O}_{\mathsf{PRFS}}(k, \cdot)$ (or $\mathcal{O}_{\mathsf{Haar}}(\cdot)$).

3.2   Quantum Access

We further strengthen our notion of adaptively secure PRFS by allowing the adversary to make superposition queries to either $\mathcal{O}_{\mathsf{PRFS}}(k, \cdot)$ or $\mathcal{O}_{\mathsf{Haar}}(\cdot)$. Providing superposition access to the adversary not only makes the definition stronger[9] than Definition 6 but is also arguably more useful for a larger class of applications. To indicate quantum query access, we put the oracle inside the ket notation: $A^{|\mathcal{O}\rangle}$ (whereas for classical query access we write $A^{\mathcal{O}}$).

We provide the formal definition below.

Definition 7 (Quantum-Accessible Adaptively-Secure PRFS). *We say that a QPT algorithm G is a quantum-accessible adaptively secure pseudorandom function-like state (QAPRFS) generator if for all QPT (non-uniform) distinguishers A if there exists a negligible function ε, such that for all λ, the following holds:*

$$\left| \Pr_{k \leftarrow \{0,1\}^\lambda} \left[A_\lambda^{|\mathcal{O}_{\mathsf{PRFS}}(k, \cdot)\rangle}(\rho_\lambda) = 1 \right] - \Pr_{\mathcal{O}_{\mathsf{Haar}}} \left[A_\lambda^{|\mathcal{O}_{\mathsf{Haar}}(\cdot)\rangle}(\rho_\lambda) = 1 \right] \right| \leq \varepsilon(\lambda),$$

where:

- *$\mathcal{O}_{\mathsf{PRFS}}(k, \cdot)$, on input a d-qubit register $\mathbf{X}$, does the following: it applies a channel that controlled on the register $\mathbf{X}$ containing x, it creates and stores $G_\lambda(k, x)$ in a new register $\mathbf{Y}$. It outputs the state on the registers $\mathbf{X}$ and $\mathbf{Y}$.*
- *$\mathcal{O}_{\mathsf{Haar}}(\cdot)$, modeled as a channel, on input a d-qubit register $\mathbf{X}$, does the following: it applies a channel that controlled on the register $\mathbf{X}$ containing x, stores $|\vartheta_x\rangle\langle\vartheta_x|$ in a new register $\mathbf{Y}$, where $|\vartheta_x\rangle$ is sampled from the Haar distribution. It outputs the state on the registers $\mathbf{X}$ and $\mathbf{Y}$.*

Moreover, A_λ has superposition access to $\mathcal{O}_{\mathsf{PRFS}}(k, \cdot)$ and $\mathcal{O}_{\mathsf{Haar}}(\cdot)$.

We say that G is a $(d(\lambda), n(\lambda))$-QAPRFS generator to succinctly indicate that its input length is $d(\lambda)$ and its output length is $n(\lambda)$.

We present a construction satisfying the above definition in the full version of the paper.

Unlike Definition 6, it is not without loss of generality that A_λ can get multiple copies of a quantum state. To illustrate, consider an adversary that submits

---

[9] It is stronger in the sense that an algorithm that has quantum query access to the oracle can simulate an algorithm that only has classical query access.

a state of the form $\sum_x \alpha_x |x\rangle$ to the oracle. It then gets back $\sum_x \alpha_x |x\rangle |\psi_x\rangle$ (where $|\psi_x\rangle$ is either the output of PRFS[10] or it is Haar random) instead of $\sum_x \alpha_x |x\rangle |\psi_x\rangle^{\otimes t}$, for some polynomial t. On the other hand, if the adversary can create multiple copies of $\sum_x \alpha_x |x\rangle$, the above definition allows the adversary to obtain $(\sum_x \alpha_x |x\rangle |\psi_x\rangle)^{\otimes t}$ for any polynomial $t(\cdot)$ of its choice.

4 On the Necessity of Computational Assumptions

The following lemma shows that the security guarantee of a PRS generator (and thus of PRFS generators) can only hold with respect to computationally bounded distinguishers, provided that the output length is at least $\log \lambda$.

Lemma 4. *Let G be a PRS generator with output length $n(\lambda) \geq \log \lambda$. Then there exists a polynomial $t(\lambda)$ and a quantum algorithm A (not efficient in general) such that*

$$\left| \Pr_{k \leftarrow \{0,1\}^\lambda} \left[A_\lambda \left(G_\lambda(k)^{\otimes t(\lambda)} \right) = 1 \right] - \Pr_{|\vartheta\rangle \leftarrow \mathscr{H}_{n(\lambda)}} \left[A_\lambda \left(|\vartheta\rangle\langle\vartheta|^{\otimes t(\lambda)} \right) = 1 \right] \right| \geq \frac{1}{3}$$

for all sufficiently large λ.

Proof. For notational convenience we abbreviate $n = n(\lambda)$ and $t = t(\lambda)$. We split the proof into two cases.

Case 1: if there does not exist a negligible function $\nu(\cdot)$ such that

$$\Pr_k \left[\min_{|\theta\rangle} \mathrm{TD}(G_\lambda(k), |\theta\rangle\langle\theta|) \leq \nu(\lambda) \right] \geq \frac{1}{2}. \tag{2}$$

Then there exists some non-negligible function $\kappa(\cdot)$ such that with probability at least $\frac{1}{2}$ over the choice of k, $\min_{|\theta\rangle} \mathrm{TD}(G_\lambda(k), |\theta\rangle\langle\theta|) \geq \kappa(\lambda)$. Let $\nu_{k,1} \geq \ldots \geq \nu_{k,2^n}$ and $|\alpha_{k,1}\rangle, ..., |\alpha_{k,2^n}\rangle$ be eigenvalues and eigenvectors for $G_\lambda(k)$. Then $\kappa \leq \mathrm{TD}(G_\lambda(k), |\alpha_{k,1}\rangle\langle\alpha_{k,1}|) = \frac{1}{2}(1 - \nu_{k,1} + \nu_{k,2} + \cdots + \nu_{k,2^n}) = 1 - \nu_{k,1}$. Thus by Hölder's inequality, $\mathrm{Tr}(G_\lambda(k)^2) \leq 1 - \kappa$. Therefore, a purity test using $t = O(1/\kappa(\lambda))$ copies will correctly reject PRS states with probability at least $\frac{1}{3}$ but never incorrectly reject any Haar random state.

Case 2: if there exists a negligible function $\nu(\cdot)$ such that (2) holds. There exists a polynomial $t(\lambda)$ such that

$$2^\lambda \leq \frac{1}{6} \cdot \dim \Pi_{\mathsf{sym}}^{2^n, t} = \frac{1}{6} \cdot \binom{2^n + t - 1}{t}$$

for all sufficiently large λ. This is because by setting $t = \lambda + 1$, we can lower bound the dimension of $\Pi_{\mathsf{sym}}^{2^n, t}$ by $\binom{2\lambda}{\lambda+1}$ and

$$\binom{2\lambda}{\lambda} \geq \frac{\lambda}{\lambda + 1} \frac{4^\lambda}{\sqrt{\pi\lambda}} \left(1 - \frac{1}{8\lambda} \right)$$

---

[10] In this illustration, we are pretending that the PRFS satisfies perfect state generation property. That is, the output of PRFS is always a pure state.

which is much larger than $6 \cdot 2^\lambda$ for all sufficiently large λ.

Let $g \subseteq \{0,1\}^\lambda$ be the set of k's such that $\min_{|\theta\rangle} \mathrm{TD}(G_\lambda(k), |\theta\rangle\langle\theta|) \leq \nu(\lambda)$. Note that 2^λ is an upper bound on the rank of the density matrix

$$\mathop{\mathbb{E}}_{k \leftarrow g} |\psi_k\rangle\langle\psi_k|^{\otimes t}, \tag{3}$$

where $|\psi_k\rangle = \arg\min_{|\theta\rangle} \mathrm{TD}(G_\lambda(k), |\theta\rangle\langle\theta|)$. Note that the rank of the density matrix

$$\mathop{\mathbb{E}}_{|\vartheta\rangle \leftarrow \mathscr{H}_{n(\lambda)}} |\vartheta\rangle\langle\vartheta|^{\otimes t} = \frac{\Pi_{\mathsf{sym}}^{2^n,t}}{\dim \Pi_{\mathsf{sym}}^{2^n,t}} \tag{4}$$

is equal to $\dim \Pi_{\mathsf{sym}}^{2^n,t}$.

For all λ, define the quantum circuit A_λ that, given a state on tn qubits, performs the two-outcome measurement $\{P, I - P\}$ where P is the projector onto the support of $\mathbb{E}_{k \leftarrow g} |\psi_k\rangle\langle\psi_k|^{\otimes t}$, and accepts if the P outcome occurs.

By assumption of case 2, given the density matrix (3) the circuit A_λ will accept with probability at least $\frac{1}{2}$. On the other hand, given the density matrix (4) the circuit A_λ will accept with probability

$$\mathrm{Tr}\left(P \cdot \frac{\Pi_{\mathsf{sym}}^{2^n,t}}{\dim \Pi_{\mathsf{sym}}^{2^n,t}}\right) \leq \mathrm{Tr}\left(\frac{P}{\dim \Pi_{\mathsf{sym}}^{2^n,t}}\right) = \frac{\mathrm{rank}(P)}{\dim \Pi_{\mathsf{sym}}^{2^n,t}} \leq \frac{1}{6}.$$

Letting $A = \{A_\lambda\}_\lambda$ we obtained the desired Lemma statement.   □

We remark that the attack given in Lemma 4 cannot be used on smaller output length, up to additive factors of superpolynomially smaller order in the output length. Suppose $n = \log\lambda - \omega(\log\log\lambda)$ and for any $t = \lambda^{O(1)}$,

$$\log\binom{2^n + t - 1}{t} \leq 2^n \cdot \log \frac{e(2^n + t - 1)}{2^n - 1}$$

$$= \frac{\lambda}{\omega(\log\lambda)} \cdot O(\log\lambda).$$

This means that $\binom{2^n + t - 1}{t} = 2^{\lambda/\omega(\log\lambda)} \ll 2^\lambda$ and therefore the attack above does not necessarily apply. Indeed, Brakerski and Shmueli [4] have shown that PRS generators with output length $n(\lambda) \leq c\log\lambda$ for some $c > 0$ can be achieved with statistical security.

We conclude the section by remarking that the result of Kretschmer [12] can be easily generalized so that PRS generators with output length at least $\log\lambda + c$ (for some small constant $0 < c < 2$) imply $\mathsf{BQP} \neq \mathsf{PP}$ as well[11].

---

[11] For readers familiar with [12], it can be verified that a sufficient condition for that proof to go through is if $2^\lambda \cdot e^{-2^n/3}$ is negligible, which is satisfied if $n \geq \log\lambda + 2$.

5   Tomography with Verification

Quantum state tomography (or just *tomography* for short) is a process that takes as input multiple copies of a quantum state ρ and outputs a string u that is a classical description of the state ρ; for example, u can describe an approximation of the density matrix ρ, or it could be a a more succinct description such as a *classical shadow* in the sense of [10]. In this paper, we use tomography as a tool to construct protocols based on pseudorandom states with only *classical* communication.

For our applications, we require tomography procedures satisfying a useful property called verification. Suppose we execute a tomography algorithm on multiple copies of a state to obtain a classical string u. The verification algorithm, given u and the algorithm to create this state, checks if u is consistent with this state or not. Verification comes in handy when tomography is used in cryptographic settings, where we would like to make sure that the adversary has generated the classical description associated with a quantum state according to some prescribed condition (this will be implicitly incorporated in the verification algorithm).

Verifiable Tomography. Let $\mathcal{C} = \{\Phi_\lambda : \lambda \in \mathbb{N}\}$ be a family of channels where each channel Φ_λ takes as input $\ell(\lambda)$ qubits for some polynomial $\ell(\cdot)$. A *verifiable tomography scheme* associated with $\mathcal{C}$ is a pair (Tomography, Verify) of QPT algorithms, which have the following input/output behavior:

- Tomography: given as input a quantum state $\rho^{\otimes L}$ for some density matrix ρ and some number L, output a classical string u (called a *tomograph* of ρ).
- Verify: given as input a pair of classical strings $(\mathbf{x}, u)$ where $\mathbf{x}$ has length $\ell(\lambda)$, output Valid or Invalid.

We would like (Tomography, Verify) to satisfy correctness which we describe next.

5.1   Correctness Notions for Verifiable Tomography

We can consider two types of correctness. The first type of correctness, referred to as *same-input correctness*, states that Verify$(\mathbf{x}, u)$ outputs Valid if u is obtained by running the Tomography procedure on copies of the output of $\Phi_\lambda(\mathbf{x})$. The second type of correctness, referred to as *different-input correctness*, states that Verify$(\mathbf{x}', u)$ outputs Invalid if u is obtained by applying tomography to $\Phi_\lambda(\mathbf{x})$, where $(\mathbf{x}', \mathbf{x})$ do not satisfy a predicate Π.

Same-Input Correctness. Consider the following definition.

Definition 8 (Same-Input Correctness). *We say that* (Tomography, Verify) *satisfies L-same-input correctness, for some polynomial $L(\cdot)$, such that for every* $\mathbf{x} \in \{0,1\}^{\ell(\lambda)}$, *if the following holds:*

$$\Pr\left[\text{Valid} \leftarrow \text{Verify}\left(\mathbf{x}, \text{Tomography}\left((\Phi_\lambda(\mathbf{x}))^{\otimes L(\lambda)}\right)\right)\right] \geq 1 - \text{negl}(\lambda),$$

For some applications, it suffices to consider a weaker definition. Instead of requiring the correctness guarantee to hold for every input, we instead require that it holds over some input distribution.

Definition 9 (Distributional Same-Input Correctness). *We say that* (Tomography, Verify) *satisfies* $(L, \mathcal{D})$*-distributional same-input correctness, for some polynomial* $L(\cdot)$ *and distribution* $\mathcal{D}$ *on* $\ell(\lambda)$*-length strings, if the following holds:*

$$\Pr\left[\mathsf{Valid} \leftarrow \mathsf{Verify}\left(\mathbf{x}, \mathsf{Tomography}\left((\Phi_\lambda(\mathbf{x}))^{\otimes L(\lambda)}\right)\right) : \mathbf{x} \leftarrow \mathcal{D}\right] \geq 1 - \mathsf{negl}(\lambda)$$

Different-Input Correctness. Ideally, we would require that $\mathsf{Verify}(\mathbf{x}, u)$ outputs Invalid if u is produced by tomographing $\Phi_\lambda(\mathbf{x}')$, and $\mathbf{x}'$ is any string such that $\mathbf{x}' \neq \mathbf{x}$. However, for applications, we only require that this be the case when the pair $(\mathbf{x}, \mathbf{x}')$ satisfy a relation defined by a predicate Π. In other words, we require $\mathsf{Verify}(\mathbf{x}, u)$ outputs Invalid only when u is a tomograph of $\Phi_\lambda(\mathbf{x}')$ and $\Pi(\mathbf{x}', \mathbf{x}) = 0$.

We define this formally below.

Definition 10 (Different-Input Correctness). *We say that* (Tomography, Verify) *satisfies* (L, Π)*-different-input correctness, for some polynomial* $L(\cdot)$ *and predicate* $\Pi : \{0,1\}^{\ell(\lambda)} \times \{0,1\}^{\ell(\lambda)} \to \{0,1\}$*, such that for every* $\mathbf{x}, \mathbf{x}' \in \{0,1\}^{\ell(\lambda)}$ *satisfying* $\Pi(\mathbf{x}, \mathbf{x}') = 0$*, if the following holds:*

$$\Pr\left[\mathsf{Invalid} \leftarrow \mathsf{Verify}\left(\mathbf{x}', \mathsf{Tomography}\left((\Phi_\lambda(\mathbf{x}))^{\otimes L(\lambda)}\right)\right)\right] \geq 1 - \mathsf{negl}(\lambda)$$

Analogous to Definition 9, we correspondingly define below the notion of $(L, \mathcal{D}, \Pi)$-different-input correctness.

Definition 11 (Distributional Different-Input Correctness). *We say that* (Tomography, Verify) *satisfies* $(L, \Pi, \mathcal{D})$*-distributional different-input correctness, for some polynomial* $L(\cdot)$*, predicate* $\Pi : \{0,1\}^\lambda \times \{0,1\}^\lambda \to \{0,1\}$ *and distribution* $\mathcal{D}$ *supported on* $(\mathbf{x}, \mathbf{x}') \in \{0,1\}^{\ell(\lambda)} \times \{0,1\}^{\ell(\lambda)}$ *satisfying* $\Pi(\mathbf{x}, \mathbf{x}') = 0$*, if the following holds:*

$$\Pr_{(\mathbf{x}, \mathbf{x}') \leftarrow \mathcal{D}}\left[\mathsf{Invalid} \leftarrow \mathsf{Verify}\left(\mathbf{x}', \mathsf{Tomography}\left((\Phi_\lambda(\mathbf{x}))^{\otimes L(\lambda)}\right)\right)\right] \geq 1 - \mathsf{negl}(\lambda)$$

Sometimes we will use the more general $(\varepsilon, L, \Pi, \mathcal{D})$-*distributional different-input correctness* definition. In this case, the probability of Verify outputting Invalid is bounded below by $1 - \varepsilon$ instead of $1 - \mathsf{negl}(\lambda)$.

5.2 Verifiable Tomography Procedures

We will consider two different instantiations of (Tomography, Verify) where the first instantiation will be useful for bit commitments and the second instantiation will be useful for pseudo one-time pad schemes.

In both the instantiations, we use an existing tomography procedure stated in the lemma below.

Lemma 5 (Sect. 1.5.3, [14]). *There exists a tomography procedure $\mathcal{T}$ that given sN^2 copies of an N-dimensional density matrix ρ, outputs a matrix M such that $\mathbb{E}\|M - \rho\|_F^2 \leq \frac{N}{s}$ where the expectation is over the randomness of the tomography procedure. Moreover, the running time of $\mathcal{T}$ is polynomial in s and N.*

We state and prove a useful corollary of the above lemma.

Corollary 1. *There exists a tomography procedure $\mathcal{T}_{\mathsf{imp}}$ that given $4sN^2\lambda$ copies of an N-dimensional density matrix ρ, outputs a matrix M such that the following holds:*

$$\Pr\left[\|M - \rho\|_F^2 \leq \frac{9N}{s}\right] \geq 1 - \mathsf{negl}(\lambda)$$

Moreover, the running time of $\mathcal{T}_{\mathsf{imp}}$ is polynomial in s, N and λ.

The proof of this corollary can be found in the full version.

First Instantiation. We will work with a verifiable tomography procedure that will be closely associated with a PRFS. In particular, we will use a $(d(\lambda), n(\lambda))$-PRFS $\{G_\lambda(\cdot, \cdot)\}$ satisfying recognizable abort property (Definition 5). Let $\widehat{G}$ be the QPT algorithm associated with G according to Definition 5. Note that the output length of $\widehat{G}$ is $n + 1$. We set $d(\lambda) = \lceil \frac{\log(\lambda)}{\log(\log(\lambda))} \rceil$ and $n(\lambda) = \lceil 3 \log(\lambda) \rceil$.

We will describe the algorithms (Tomography, Verify) in Fig. 1. The set of channels $\mathcal{C} = \{\Phi_\lambda : \lambda \in \mathbb{N}\}$ is associated with (Tomography, Verify), where Φ_λ is defined as follows:

- Let the input be initialized on register **A**.
- Controlled on the first register containing the value (P_x, k, x, b), where P_x is an n-qubit Pauli, $k \in \{0,1\}^\lambda, b \in \{0,1\}$, do the following: compute $(I \otimes P_x^b)\,\widehat{G}_\lambda(k, x)\,(I \otimes P_x^b)$ and store it in the register **B**.
- Trace out **A** and output **B**.

The channel Φ_λ can be represented as a quantum circuit of size polynomial in λ as the PRFS generator $\widehat{G}$ runs in time polynomial in λ.

Distributional Same-Input Correctness. We prove below that (Tomography, Verify) satisfies distributional same-input correctness. For every $x \in \{0,1\}^{d(\lambda)}$, for every n-qubit Pauli P_x and $b \in \{0,1\}$, define the distribution $\mathcal{D}_{P_x, x, b}$ as follows: sample $k \xleftarrow{\$} \{0,1\}^\lambda$ and output $\mathbf{x} = (P_x, k, x, b)$.

Lemma 6. *Let $L = O(2^{3n}\lambda)$. The verifiable tomography scheme (Tomography, Verify) described in Fig. 1 satisfies $(L, \mathcal{D}_{P_x, x, b})$-distributional same-input correctness for all P_x, x, b.*

The proof of this lemma can be found in the full version.

Tomography($\rho^{\otimes L}$): On input L copies of an $2^{(n+1)}$-dimensional density matrix ρ, compute $\mathcal{T}_{\mathsf{imp}}(\rho^{\otimes L})$ to obtain M, where $\mathcal{T}_{\mathsf{imp}}$ is given in Corollary 1. Output M.

Verify($\mathbf{x}, M$):

1. Run $\rho^{\otimes L} \leftarrow (\Phi_\lambda(\mathbf{x}))^{\otimes L}$, where $L = 3^8 2^{3(n+1)+2}\lambda$.
2. Compute $\widehat{M} \leftarrow$ Tomography $(\rho^{\otimes L})$.
3. If $\langle \perp | M | \perp \rangle > \frac{1}{9}$ for any $x \in \{0,1\}^d$, output Invalid.
4. If $\|M - \widehat{M}\|_F^2 \leq \frac{4}{729}$ output Valid. Output Invalid otherwise.

Fig. 1. First instantiation of Tomography

Distributional Different-Input Correctness. We prove below that (Tomography, Verify) satisfies $(\varepsilon, L, \Pi, \mathcal{D}_x)$-different-input correctness, where Π and $\mathcal{D}_x$ are defined as follows:

$$\Pi\left((P_0, k_0, x_0, b_0), (P_1, k_1, x_1, b_1)\right) = \begin{cases} 0 & P_0 = P_1, x_0 = x_1 \text{ and } b_0 \neq b_1, \\ 1 & \text{otherwise.} \end{cases}$$

The sampler for $\mathcal{D}_x$ is defined as follows: sample $P_x \xleftarrow{\$} \mathcal{P}_n$, $k_0, k_1 \xleftarrow{\$} \{0,1\}^\lambda$ and output $((P_x, k_0, x, 0), ((P_x, k_1, x, 1))$. We first prove an intermediate lemma that will be useful for proving distributional different-input correctness. Later on, this lemma will also be useful in the application of bit commitments.

Lemma 7. *Let $P_x \in \mathcal{P}_n$ and there exists a density matrix M such that* Verify($P_x \| k_0 \| x \| 0, M$) = Valid *and* Verify($P_x \| k_1 \| x \| 1, M$) = Valid, *for some $k_0, k_1 \in \{0,1\}^\lambda$. Then*

$$\mathrm{Tr}\left(P_x | \psi_{k_1,x}\rangle\langle\psi_{k_1,x}| P_x | \psi_{k_0,x}\rangle\langle\psi_{k_0,x}|\right) \geq \frac{542}{729}.$$

The proof of this lemma can be found in the full version.

With the above lemma in mind, we can prove the different-input correctness.

Lemma 8. (Tomography, Verify) *in Fig. 1 satisfies $(O(2^{-n}), L, \Pi, \mathcal{D}_x)$-different-input correctness, where $L = O(2^{3n}\lambda)$.*

The proof of this lemma can be found in the full version. We give a second instantiation in the full version that is used to achieve a psuedo-random one time pad.

6   Applications

In this section, we show how to use PRFS to constrtuct a variety of applications:

1. Bit commitments with classical communication and,
2. Pseudo one-time pad schemes with classical communication.

To accomplish the above applications, we use verifiable tomography from Sect. 5. The construction and proofs of the pseudo one-time pad schemes can be found in the full version of the paper.

6.1   Commitment Scheme

We construct bit commitments with classical communication from pseudorandom function-like quantum states. We recall the definition by [2].

A (bit) commitment scheme is given by a pair of (uniform) QPT algorithms (C, R), where $C = \{C_\lambda\}_{\lambda \in \mathbb{N}}$ is called the *committer* and $R = \{R_\lambda\}_{\lambda \in \mathbb{N}}$ is called the *receiver*. There are two phases in a commitment scheme: a commit phase and a reveal phase.

- In the (possibly interactive) commit phase between C_λ and R_λ, the committer C_λ commits to a bit, say b. We denote the execution of the commit phase to be $\sigma_{CR} \leftarrow \mathsf{Commit}\langle C_\lambda(b), R_\lambda \rangle$, where σ_{CR} is a joint state of C_λ and R_λ after the commit phase.
- In the reveal phase C_λ interacts with R_λ and the output is a trit $\mu \in \{0, 1, \bot\}$ indicating the receiver's output bit or a rejection flag. We denote an execution of the reveal phase where the committer and receiver start with the joint state σ_{CR} by $\mu \leftarrow \mathsf{Reveal}\langle C_\lambda, R_\lambda, \sigma_{CR} \rangle$.

We require that the above commitment scheme satisfies the correctness, computational hiding, and statistical binding properties below.

Definition 12 (Correctness). *We say that a commitment scheme (C, R) satisfies correctness if*

$$\Pr\left[b^* = b \; : \; \begin{matrix} \sigma_{CR} \leftarrow \mathsf{Commit}\langle C_\lambda(b), R_\lambda \rangle, \\ b^* \leftarrow \mathsf{Reveal}\langle C_\lambda, R_\lambda, \sigma_{CR} \rangle \end{matrix} \right] \geq 1 - \nu(\lambda),$$

where $\nu(\cdot)$ is a negligible function.

Definition 13 (Computational Hiding). *We say that a commitment scheme (C, R) satisfies computationally hiding if for any malicious QPT receiver $\{R_\lambda^*\}_{\lambda \in \mathbb{N}}$, for any QPT distinguisher $\{D_\lambda\}_{\lambda \in \mathbb{N}}$, the following holds:*

$$\Bigg| \Pr_{(\tau, \sigma_{CR^*}) \leftarrow \mathsf{Commit}\langle C_\lambda(0), R_\lambda^* \rangle} [D_\lambda(\sigma_{R^*}) = 1]$$
$$- \Pr_{(\tau, \sigma_{CR^*}) \leftarrow \mathsf{Commit}\langle C_\lambda(1), R_\lambda^* \rangle} [D_\lambda(\sigma_{R^*}) = 1] \Bigg| \leq \varepsilon(\lambda),$$

for some negligible $\varepsilon(\cdot)$.

Definition 14 (Statistical Binding). *We say that a commitment scheme* (C, R) *satisfies statistical binding if for every QPT sender* $\{C_\lambda^*\}_{\lambda \in \mathbb{N}}$, *there exists a (possibly inefficient) extractor* $\mathcal{E}$ *such that the following holds:*

$$\Pr\left[\mu \neq b^* \wedge \mu \neq \bot : \begin{array}{c} (\tau, \sigma_{C^*R}) \leftarrow \text{Commit}\langle C_\lambda^*, R_\lambda \rangle, \\ b^* \leftarrow \mathcal{E}(\tau), \\ \mu \leftarrow \text{Reveal}\langle C_\lambda^*, R_\lambda, \sigma_{C^*R} \rangle \end{array}\right] \leq \nu(\lambda),$$

where $\nu(\cdot)$ *is a negligible function and* τ *is the transcript of the* Commit *phase.*

Remark 1. (Comparison with [2]). In the binding definition of [2], given the fact that the sender's and the receiver's state could potentially be entangled with each other, care had to be taken to ensure that after the extractor was applied on the receiver's state, the sender's state along with the decision bit remains (indistinguishable) to the real world. In the above definition, however, since the communication is entirely classical, any operations performed on the receiver's end has no consequence to the sender's state. As a result, our definition is much simpler than [2].

Construction. Towards constructing a commitment scheme with classical communication, we use a verifiable tomography from Fig. 1.

Construction. We present the construction in Fig. 2. In the construction, we require $d(\lambda) = \lceil \log \frac{3\lambda}{n} \rceil \geq 1$.

Commit(b):

- The reciever R_λ samples an m-qubit Pauli $P = \bigotimes_{x \in \{0,1\}^d} P_x$ where $m = 2^d n$. It sends P to the commiter.
- The committer C_λ on intput $b \in \{0, 1\}$ does the following:
  - Sample $k \xleftarrow{\$} \{0, 1\}^\lambda$.
  - For all $x \in \{0, 1\}^d$
    * Generate $\sigma_x^{\otimes L} \leftarrow (\Phi_\lambda (P_x || k || x || b))^{\otimes L}$, where $L = 3^8 2^{3n+5} \lambda$.
    * $M_x \leftarrow \text{Tomography}(\sigma_x^{\otimes L})$.
  - Send $M = (M_x)_{x \in \{0,1\}^d}$ to the reciever.

Reveal:

- The commiter sends (k, b) as the decommitment. If $b \notin \{0, 1\}$, the reciever outputs $\bot$. Output b if for each $x \in \{0, 1\}^d$, $\text{Verify}(P_x || k || x || b, M) = \text{Valid}$, output $\bot$ otherwise.

Fig. 2. Commitment scheme

We prove that the construction in Fig. 2 satisfies correctness, computational hiding and statistical binding properties.

Lemma 9 (Correctness). *The commitment scheme in Fig. 2 satisfies correctness.*

Proof. This follows from Lemma 6. □

Lemma 10 (Computational Hiding). *The commitment scheme in Fig. 2 satisfies computational hiding.*

Proof. We prove the security via a hybrid argument. Fix $\lambda \in \mathbb{N}$. Consider a QPT adversary R_λ^*.

Hybrid $H_{1,b}$, for all $b \in \{0,1\}$. This corresponds to C commiting to the bit b.

Hybrid $H_{2,b}$, for all $b \in \{0,1\}$. This hybrid is the same as before except that for all $x \in \{0,1\}^d$, $\Phi_\lambda(P||k||x||b)$ replaced with $\left(|0\rangle\langle 0| \otimes \left(P_x^b\right)(|\vartheta_x\rangle\langle\vartheta_x|)\left(P_x^b\right)\right)$ where $|\vartheta_1\rangle, ..., |\vartheta_{2^d}\rangle \leftarrow \mathscr{H}_n$.

The hybrids $H_{1,b}$ and $H_{2,b}$ are computationally indistinguishable because of the security of $PRFS$. $H_{2,0}$ and $H_{2,1}$ are identical by the unitary invariance property of Haar distribution. Hence, $H_{1,0}$ and $H_{1,1}$ are computationally indistinguishable. □

Lemma 11 (Statistical Binding). *The commitment scheme in Fig. 2 satisfies $O(2^{-0.5\lambda})$-statistical binding.*

Proof. of Lemma 11. Let $C^* = \{C_\lambda^*\}_{\lambda \in \mathbb{N}}$ be a malicious committer. Execute the commit phase between C_λ^* and R_λ. Let τ be the classical transcript and let σ_{C^*R} be the joint state of C^*R. We first provide the description of an extractor.

Description of $\mathcal{E}$. On the input $\tau = (P, M)$, the extractor does the following:

1. For all $k'||b' \in \{0,1\}^\lambda \times \{0,1\}$, run for all $x \in \{0,1\}^d$, $\mathsf{Verify}(P_x||k'||x||b', M)$.
2. If for all $x \in \{0,1\}^d$, $\mathsf{Verify}(P||k'||x||b', M) = \mathsf{Valid}$, output b'.
3. Else output $\perp$.

□

Fact 6. *Let $\mathcal{P}_m$ be the m-qubit Pauli group. Then,*

$$\Pr_{P \xleftarrow{\$} \mathcal{P}_m}\left[\exists k_0, k_1 : \forall x \in \{0,1\}^d, |\langle\psi_{k_0,x}| P_x |\psi_{k_1,x}\rangle|^2 \geq \delta\right] \leq \delta^{-2^d} 2^{2\lambda - m}.$$

Proof. We use the following fact [2, Fact 6.9]: Let $|\psi\rangle$ and $|\phi\rangle$ be two arbitrary n-qubit states. Then,

$$\mathbb{E}_{P_x \xleftarrow{\$} \mathcal{P}_n}\left[|\langle\psi| P_x |\phi\rangle|^2\right] = 2^{-n}.$$

For any k_0, k_1, x by the above fact, $\mathbb{E}_{P_x \xleftarrow{\$} \mathcal{P}_n}\left[|\langle\psi_{k_0,x}| P_x |\psi_{k_1,x}\rangle|^2\right] = 2^{-n}$. Using Markov's inequality we get that for all $\delta > 0$,

$$\Pr_{P_x \xleftarrow{\$} \mathcal{P}_n}\left[|\langle\psi_{k_0,x}| P_x |\psi_{k_1,x}\rangle|^2 \geq \delta\right] \leq \delta^{-1} 2^{-n}.$$

Since, all P_x's are independent,

$$\Pr_{P \xleftarrow{\$} \mathcal{P}_m} \left[\forall x \in \{0,1\}^d, |\langle \psi_{k_0,x}| P_x |\psi_{k_1,x}\rangle|^2 \geq \delta \right] \leq \left(\delta^{-1} 2^{-n} \right)^{2^d}.$$

Using a union bound over all k_0, k_1,

$$\Pr_{P \xleftarrow{\$} \mathcal{P}_m} \left[\exists k_0, k_1 : \forall x \in \{0,1\}^d, |\langle \psi_{k_0,x}| P_x |\psi_{k_1,x}\rangle|^2 \geq \delta \right] \leq \delta^{-2^d} 2^{2\lambda - m}.$$

$\square$

Let the transcript be (P, M) where P is chosen uniformly at random. Let

$$p = \Pr \left[\mu \neq b^* \wedge \mu \neq \perp : \begin{array}{c} (\tau, \sigma_{C^*R}) \leftarrow \mathsf{Commit}\langle C^*_\lambda, R_\lambda \rangle, \\ b^* \leftarrow \mathcal{E}(\tau), \\ \mu \leftarrow \mathsf{Reveal}\langle \tau, \sigma_{C^*R} \rangle \end{array} \right]$$

Then

$$p = \Pr_{P \xleftarrow{\$} \mathcal{P}_m} \left[\exists k_0, k_1, b_0, b_1 : \forall x \in \{0,1\}^d \begin{array}{c} \mathsf{Verify}(P_x||k_0||x||b_0, M_x)=\mathsf{Valid}, \\ \mathsf{Verify}(P_x||k_1||x||b_1, M_x)=\mathsf{Valid}, \\ b_0 \neq b_1 \end{array} \right].$$

Without loss of generality we can assume $b_0 = 0$ and $b_1 = 1$,

$$p = \Pr_{P \xleftarrow{\$} \mathcal{P}_m} \left[\exists k_0, k_1 : \forall x \in \{0,1\}^d \begin{array}{c} \mathsf{Verify}(P_x||k_0||x||0, M_x)=\mathsf{Valid}, \\ \mathsf{Verify}(P_x||k_1||x||1, M_x)=\mathsf{Valid} \end{array} \right].$$

By Lemma 7,

$$p \leq \Pr_{P \xleftarrow{\$} \mathcal{P}_m} \left[\exists k_0, k_1 : \forall x \in \{0,1\}^d, \right.$$

$$\left. Tr(P_x |\psi_{k_1,x}\rangle\langle\psi_{k_1,x}| P_x |\psi_{k_0,x}\rangle\langle\psi_{k_0,x}|) \geq 542/729 \right]$$

By Fact 6,

$$p \leq \frac{729}{542}^{2^d} \left(2^{2\lambda - m} \right).$$

For $m \geq 3\lambda$, the protocol satisfies $O(2^{-0.5\lambda})$-statistical binding. $\square$

Acknowledgements. The authors would like to thank the anonymous TCC 2022 reviewers for their helpful comments. The authors would also like to thank Fermi Ma for his suggestions that improved the bounds and the analysis in the proof of binary phase PRS.

References

1. Ambainis, A., Emerson, J.: Quantum t-designs: t-wise independence in the quantum world. In: 22nd Annual IEEE Conference on Computational Complexity (CCC 2007), 13–16 June 2007, San Diego, California, USA, pp. 129–140. IEEE Computer Society (2007)

2. Ananth, P., Qian, L., Yuen, H.: Cryptography from pseudorandom quantum states. In: Annual International Cryptology Conference 2022, pp. 208–236. Springer, Cham (2022)
3. Brakerski, Z., Shmueli, O.: (Pseudo) random quantum states with binary phase. In: Hofheinz, D., Rosen, A. (eds.) TCC 2019. LNCS, vol. 11891, pp. 229–250. Springer, Cham (2019). https://doi.org/10.1007/978-3-030-36030-6_10
4. Brakerski, Z., Shmueli, O.: Scalable pseudorandom quantum states. In: Micciancio, D., Ristenpart, T., (eds.), Advances in Cryptology - CRYPTO 2020–40th Annual International Cryptology Conference, CRYPTO 2020, Santa Barbara, CA, USA, August 17–21, 2020, Proceedings, Part II LNCS, vol. 12171, pp. 417–440. Springer (2020)
5. Brandão, F.G.S.L., Harrow, A.W., Horodecki, M.: Local random quantum circuits are approximate polynomial-designs. Commun. Math. Phys. **346**(2), 397–434 (2016). https://doi.org/10.1007/s00220-016-2706-8
6. Dankert, C., Cleve, R., Emerson, J., Livine, E.: Exact and approximate unitary 2-designs and their application to fidelity estimation. Phys. Rev. **80**, 012304 (2009)
7. Gavinsky, D.: Quantum money with classical verification. In: Proceedings of the 27th Conference on Computational Complexity, CCC 2012, Porto, Portugal, June 26–29, 2012, pp. 42–52. IEEE Computer Society (2012)
8. Goldreich, O., Goldwasser, S., Micali, S.: How to construct random functions. J. ACM **33**(4), 792–807 (1986)
9. Håstad, J., Impagliazzo, R., Levin, L.A., Luby, M.: A pseudorandom generator from any one-way function. SIAM J. Comput. **28**(4), 1364–1396 (1999)
10. Huang, H.Y., Kueng, R., Preskill, J.: Predicting many properties of a quantum system from very few measurements. Nat. Phys. **16**(10), 1050–1057 (2020)
11. Ji, Z., Liu, Y.-K., Song, F.: Pseudorandom quantum states. In: Shacham, H., Boldyreva, A. (eds.) CRYPTO 2018. LNCS, vol. 10993, pp. 126–152. Springer, Cham (2018). https://doi.org/10.1007/978-3-319-96878-0_5
12. Kretschmer, W.: Quantum pseudorandomness and classical complexity. In Hsieh, M.H., (ed.) 16th Conference on the Theory of Quantum Computation, Communication and Cryptography, TQC 2021, July 5–8, 2021, Virtual Conference, vol. 197 of LIPIcs, pp. 2:1–2:20. Schloss Dagstuhl - Leibniz-Zentrum für Informatik (2021)
13. Lo, H.K., Chau, H.F.: Is quantum bit commitment really possible? Phys. Rev. Lett. **78**, 3410–3413 (1997)
14. Lowe, A.: Learning quantum states without entangled measurements. Master's thesis (2021)
15. Mayers, D.: Unconditionally secure quantum bit commitment is impossible. Phys. Rev. Lett. **78**, 3414–3417 (1997)
16. Morimae, T., Yamakawa, T.: Quantum commitments and signatures without one-way functions. In: CRYPTO (2022)
17. Nielsen, M.A., Chuang, I.L.: Quantum Computation and Quantum Information: 10th Anniversary Edition. Cambridge University Press (2010)
18. Roy, A., Scott, A.J.: Unitary designs and codes. Des. Codes Cryptography, **53**(1), 13–31 (2009)
19. Zhandry, M.: How to construct quantum random functions. In: 53rd Annual IEEE Symposium on Foundations of Computer Science, FOCS 2012, New Brunswick, NJ, USA, October 20–23, 2012, pp. 679–687. IEEE Computer Society (2012)
20. Zhandry, M.: Secure identity-based encryption in the quantum random oracle model. In: Reihaneh, S.-N., Canetti, R., (eds.), Advances in Cryptology - CRYPTO 2012–32nd Annual Cryptology Conference, Santa Barbara, CA, USA, 19–23 August 2012. Proceedings, LNCS, vol. 7417, pp. 758–775. Springer (2012)

Candidate Trapdoor Claw-Free Functions from Group Actions with Applications to Quantum Protocols

Navid Alamati[1], Giulio Malavolta[2], and Ahmadreza Rahimi[2(✉)]

[1] VISA Research, Palo Alto, CA, USA
nalamati@visa.com
[2] Max Planck Institute for Security and Privacy, Bochum, Germany
{giulio.malavolta,ahmadreza.rahimi}@mpi-sp.org

Abstract. Trapdoor Claw-free Functions (TCFs) are two-to-one trapdoor functions where it is computationally hard to find a claw, i.e., a colliding pair of inputs. TCFs have recently seen a surge of renewed interest due to new applications to quantum cryptography: as an example, TCFs enable a classical machine to verify that some quantum computation has been performed correctly. In this work, we propose a new family of (almost two-to-one) TCFs based on conjectured hard problems on isogeny-based group actions. This is the first candidate construction that is not based on lattice-related problems and the first scheme (from any plausible post-quantum assumption) with a *deterministic* evaluation algorithm. To demonstrate the usefulness of our construction, we show that our TCF family can be used to devise a *computational* test of a qubit, which is the basic building block used in the general verification of quantum computations.

Keywords: Trapdoor claw-free · Quantum protocols · Isogeny

1 Introduction

Trapdoor claw-free functions (TCFs) consist of pairs of functions $(f_0, f_1) : X \rightarrow Y$ that are easy to evaluate in the forward direction, but the knowledge of a trapdoor is required in order to efficiently invert such functions. Furthermore, for any y in the image of these two functions, there are exactly two pre-images (x_0, x_1) such that $f_0(x_0) = f_1(x_1) = y$ and the pair (x_0, x_1) is referred to as a *claw*. Claws are guaranteed to exist, though they are computationally hard to find, without the knowledge of the trapdoor. TCFs have been a central object in the theory of cryptography, and they have recently seen a surge of interest with a newly established connection with quantum cryptography. TCFs are the

G. Malavolta—Research partially supported by the German Federal Ministry of Education and Research BMBF (grant 16K15K042, project 6GEM) and partially funded by the Deutsche Forschungsgemeinschaft (DFG, German Research Foundation) under Germany's Excellence Strategy - EXC 2092 CASA - 390781972.

E. Kiltz and V. Vaikuntanathan (Eds.): TCC 2022, LNCS 13747, pp. 266–293, 2022.
https://doi.org/10.1007/978-3-031-22318-1_10

main cryptographic building block that enabled a series of recent breakthroughs in the area of quantum computation. To mention a few applications: the first protocol for testing the randomness of a single quantum device [BCM+18], classical verification of quantum computation [Mah18b], quantum fully homomorphic encryption [Mah18a], verifiable test of quantumness [BKVV20], remote state preparation [GV19], and deniable encryption [CGV22].

At present, there is a *single* family of (noisy) TCFs [BCM+18] known to satisfy all of the properties needed for the above applications, whose security is based on the (quantum) hardness of the learning with errors (LWE) problem. While we have no reasons to cast doubts on the validity of this assumption, we believe that this situation is unsatisfactory and reflects our lack of understanding of cryptographic primitives useful for constructing protocols in the quantum regime.

This work aims to progress on this point and to place the security of the above protocols on broader cryptographic foundations. Towards this end, we turn our attention to alternative proposals for quantum-safe cryptographic schemes: Alongside lattices, another notable class of assumptions that enable advanced cryptographic applications (such as key exchange) is isogeny-based assumptions, including recent proposals based on group actions [CLM+18, BKV19]. Thus, we ask the following question:

Can we construct TCFs (or relaxations thereof) from isogeny-based group actions?

1.1   Our Results

We propose the first candidate construction of an "almost" TCF family from a class of isogeny-based assumptions, where by almost we mean that for all but an inverse polynomial fraction of inputs $x \in X$, there is an $x' \in X$ such that $f_0(x) = f_1(x')$. We later formalize this notion as a *weak TCF* (wTCF) family.

We show the security of our construction assuming an extended version of the linear hidden shift (LHS) problem (which plausibly holds over the isogeny-based group action of [BKV19]), introduced in [ADMP20]. A noteworthy aspect of our scheme is that the evaluation of the function is *deterministic*, which is in contrast with LWE-based schemes, where the function maps to a probability distribution. Thus, strictly speaking, our scheme is the first example of a wTCF *function* with plausible post-quantum security.

Our construction also satisfies a weaker variant of the *adaptive hardcore bit* property [BCM+18]: loosely speaking, it guarantees that one cannot simultaneously solve the adaptive hardcore bit problem for n independent instances, except with probability negligible in n. Interestingly, our proof strategy is completely different from that of [BCM+18], and does not rely on any leakage-resilience property. To obtain the stronger variant of the adaptive hardcore bit property (as formulated in [BCM+18]) we conjecture that computing the XOR of adaptive hardcore bits amplifies the security to negligibly close to $1/2$. In the context of one-wayness, it is known that direct-product hardness implies the XOR lemma [GNW11, GSV18], and we leave open the problem of proving a similar statement for the adaptive hardcore bit property.

To substantiate the usefulness of our construction, we show that our wTCF family can be used to devise a *computational* test of qubit [BCM+18, Vid20], which is the basic building block used in the general verification of quantum computations.

1.2   Technical Overview

We now provide a simplified overview of how we construct a wTCF family from an assumption that plausibly holds over isogeny-based group actions. We present our overview entirely in terms of group actions (based on the framework of [ADMP20]), and thus we do not assume any familiarity with CSIDH and its variants [CLM+18, BKV19]. The starting point for our construction is a recently introduced assumption in [ADMP20], called the linear hidden shift (LHS) assumption. In a nutshell, LHS assumption over a regular and abelian group action $\star : \mathbb{G} \times \mathbb{X} \to \mathbb{X}$ states that for any $\ell = \text{poly}(\lambda)$, if $\mathbf{M} \leftarrow \mathbb{G}^{\ell \times n}$, $\mathbf{v} \leftarrow \{0,1\}^n$, and $\mathbf{x} \leftarrow \mathbb{X}^\ell$ (for some sufficiently large n) then

$$(\mathbf{x}, \mathbf{M}, \mathbf{Mv} \star \mathbf{x}) \stackrel{c}{\approx} (\mathbf{x}, \mathbf{M}, \mathbf{u}),$$

where $\mathbf{u} \leftarrow \mathbb{X}^\ell$ is sampled uniformly and $\star$ is applied component-wise. Given this assumption, we rely on an observation by [KCVY21] to construct a function family that is (almost) 2-to-1. It can be verified by inspection that if $B = \text{poly}(\lambda)$ is a large enough integer, then for any injective function $\bar{f}$ whose domain is a superset of $[B+1]^n$, the function f with domain $\{0,1\} \times [B]^n$ defined by $f(b \in \{0,1\}, \mathbf{s} \in [B]^n) = \bar{f}(\mathbf{s} + b \cdot \mathbf{v})$ is an "almost" 2-to-1 function. Based on this simple observation, an initial attempt to define a claw-free "almost" 2-to-1 function (from LHS) would be

$$f_{\mathsf{pp}}(b, \mathbf{s}) = \mathbf{M}(\mathbf{s} + b \cdot \mathbf{v}) \star \mathbf{x}, \quad \mathsf{pp} = (\mathbf{M} \leftarrow \mathbb{G}^{n \times n}, \mathbf{Mv} \star \mathbf{x}, \mathbf{x} \leftarrow \mathbb{X}^n), \qquad (*)$$

where $\mathbf{v} \leftarrow \{0,1\}^n$. As a sanity check, any claw-pair $((0, \mathbf{s}_0), (1, \mathbf{s}_1))$ can be used to break the LHS assumption by simply computing $\mathbf{v} = \mathbf{s}_0 - \mathbf{s}_1$. There are two major issues with the initial attempt above: (1) unlike the DDH-based construction of [KCVY21], a cryptographic group action does not seem to be amenable for a "DDH-style" trapdoor [FGK+10] (in fact, any such technique would immediately break the post-quantum security of LHS assumption), and (2) it is not clear how to translate the LWE-based proof of adaptive hardcore bit property from [BCM+18] to the group action setting. Indeed, the latter seems to be a major bottleneck, because [BCM+18] relies on the lossy mode of LWE to prove the adaptive hardcore bit property via a lossiness argument, a technique that seems to be out of reach based on our current understanding of cryptographic group actions. At a high level, any change in the structure of matrix $\mathbf{M}$ (say using a "rank" 1 matrix) can be easily detected by a quantum adversary. Thus, we opt for an entirely *computational* approach to prove the adaptive hardcore bit property. We first describe our approach for showing adaptive hardcore bit property, and later we explain how to add input recoverability based on a related computational assumption.

From a Claw-Based Inner Product to a Shift-Based Equation. Note that for the function (family) f_{pp} above $(*)$, the adaptive hardcore bit property means that no QPT adversary can simultaneously hold a preimage $(b, \mathbf{s}_b)$ and a pair $(\mathbf{d}, c \in \{0,1\})$ such that $c = \langle \mathbf{d}, \mathbf{s}_0 \oplus \mathbf{s}_1 \rangle$, where $\mathbf{s}_{1-b}$ is the preimage of $f_{\mathsf{pp}}(b, \mathbf{s}_b)$ such that $\mathbf{s}_{1-b} \neq \mathbf{s}_b$ and the inner product is computed over $\mathbb{F}_2$. To simplify the proof, an observation by [BCM+18] showed that any such tuple $(b, \mathbf{s}_b, \mathbf{d}, c)$ can be transformed into a binary equation in terms of the *shift vector* $\mathbf{v}$, i.e., there is an efficient transformation T that given $(b, \mathbf{s}_b, \mathbf{d}, c)$ outputs a binary vector $\mathbf{d}'$ and $c' \in \{0,1\}$ such that $c' = \langle \mathbf{d}', \mathbf{v} \rangle$, and that for a uniformly chosen $\mathbf{d}$ the resulting $\mathbf{d}'$ is non-zero with overwhelming probability. Thus, the adaptive hardcore bit property can be rephrased as the infeasibility of computing *any* non-trivial parity of the shift vector $\mathbf{v}$ with a probability noticeably more than $1/2$. Although our final construction will be quite different from the simple one outlined above $(*)$, it would still be amenable to a transformation from a claw-based inner product into a shift-based equation. Therefore, we focus on the latter in the remaining part of this overview. Looking ahead, in our final construction the shift vector $\mathbf{v}$ will consist of n binary vectors $\mathbf{v}_i$ (for $i \in [n]$). In the next step, we describe a generic approach to prove that no attacker can succeed in outputting n non-zero vectors $\mathbf{d}'_i$ and n bits c_i $(i \in [n])$ such that $c_i = \langle \mathbf{d}'_i, \mathbf{v}_i \rangle$ for all $i \in [n]$.

Direct-Product Adaptive Hardcore Bit. Let $F_{\mathsf{pp}} : \{0,1\}^n \to Y$ be a function (family) such that pp is generated via a randomized algorithm Gen. In addition, assume that F satisfies *correlated pseudorandomness*, i.e., for uniformly sampled $\mathbf{w} \leftarrow \{0,1\}^n$ and n independently sampled $(\mathsf{pp}_i)_{i \in [n]}$ (via Gen) we have

$$(\mathsf{pp}_1, \ldots, \mathsf{pp}_n, F_{\mathsf{pp}_1}(\mathbf{w}), \ldots, F_{\mathsf{pp}_n}(\mathbf{w})) \stackrel{c}{\approx} (\mathsf{pp}_1, \ldots, \mathsf{pp}_n, u_1, \ldots, u_n),$$

where $u_i \leftarrow Y$ for $i \in [n]$. Suppose that there is a procedure $\mathcal{P}$ that given $(\mathsf{pp}_i, F_{\mathsf{pp}_i}(\mathbf{w}))_{i \in [n]}$ (where pp_i is generated independently for $i \in [n]$) and n (random) binary vectors $(\mathbf{r}_i)_{i \in [n]}$, it outputs

$$(\mathsf{pp}'_i, F_{\mathsf{pp}'_i}(\mathbf{w} \oplus \mathbf{r}_i))_{i \in [n]}$$

such that

$$(\mathsf{pp}'_i, F_{\mathsf{pp}'_i}(\mathbf{w} \oplus \mathbf{r}_i))_{i \in [n]} \stackrel{s}{\approx} (\overline{\mathsf{pp}}_i, F_{\overline{\mathsf{pp}}_i}(\mathbf{v}_i))_{i \in [n]}, \qquad (**)$$

where $\mathbf{v}_i \leftarrow \{0,1\}^n$ for $i \in [n]$ and each $\overline{\mathsf{pp}}_i$ is generated independently. Moreover, the procedure $\mathcal{P}$ should map a random tuple $(\mathsf{pp}_i, u_i)_{i \in [n]}$ (where $u_i \leftarrow Y$) to a random tuple.

Given such a function family with corresponding procedure $\mathcal{P}$, below we briefly outline a reduction that shows for any QPT[1] adversary $\mathcal{A}$, given $(\mathsf{pp}_i, F_{\mathsf{pp}_i}(\mathbf{v}_i))_{i \in [n]}$ where pp_i and $\mathbf{v}_i$ are sampled independently for $i \in [n]$, it is

---

[1] The reduction is entirely classical, so if correlated pseudorandomness holds with respect to all classical PPT adversaries, then the proposition holds for the same class of adversaries as well.

infeasible to produce n non-zero vectors $\mathbf{d}'_i$ and n bits c_i (for $i \in [n]$) such that $c_i = \langle \mathbf{d}'_i, \mathbf{v}_i \rangle$ for all $i \in [n]$, where the inner product is computed over $\mathbb{F}_2$. We informally refer to this property as *direct-product* adaptive hardcore bit property.

Let $H = (\mathsf{pp}_1, \ldots, \mathsf{pp}_n, y_1, \ldots, y_n)$ be a correlated pseudorandomness challenge. The reduction samples $\mathbf{r}_i$ for $i \in [n]$ and it runs $\mathcal{P}$ on $(H, \mathbf{r}_1, \ldots, \mathbf{r}_n)$. Let $(\mathbf{d}'_i, \beta_i)$ for $i \in [n]$ be the output of $\mathcal{A}$. Observe that if the advantage of $\mathcal{A}$ is non-negligible and H is pseudorandom, i.e., $y_i = F_{\mathsf{pp}_i}(\mathbf{w})$ for all $i \in [n]$, the reduction can use $(\mathbf{d}'_i, \beta_i)$ and $\mathbf{r}_i$ to compute $c_i = \langle \mathbf{d}'_i, \mathbf{w} \rangle$ for $i \in [n]$. If there exists an index n' such that $\mathbf{d}'_{n'}$ lies in the span of $(\mathbf{d}'_1, \ldots, \mathbf{d}'_{n'-1})$, i.e.,

$$\mathbf{d}'_{n'} = \sum_{i=1}^{n'-1} \alpha_i \mathbf{d}'_i, \quad (\alpha_1, \ldots, \alpha_{n'-1}) \in \{0,1\}^{n'-1},$$

the reduction can simply check $c_{n'} \stackrel{?}{=} \sum_{i=1}^{n'-1} \alpha_i c_i$. If the equality holds the reduction outputs 0, otherwise it outputs a random bit. On the other hand, a routine information-theoretic argument shows that if H is a truly random tuple then the check above passes with a probability close to $1/2$, because $\mathbf{r}_i$ (for any $i \in [n]$) is statistically hidden from the view of $\mathcal{A}$, allowing us to deduce the direct-product adaptive hardcore bit property (a slight modification of the argument also works in case all $\mathbf{d}'_i$ for $i \in [n]$ are linearly independent).

So far, we argued that if $F_{\mathsf{pp}} : \{0,1\}^n \to Y$ is a function family with correlated pseudorandomness and a corresponding procedure $\mathcal{P}$, it also satisfies the direct-product adaptive hardcore bit property. In the next step, we rely on a conjecture to deduce the (plain) adaptive hardcore bit property (defined below), which will allow us to deduce the adaptive hardcore bit property (for an almost 2-to-1 function) in our final construction. A non-adaptive version of the following conjecture has already been proved via a transformation from direct-product hardness to (Yao's) XOR lemma [GNW11].

Conjecture 1 (Informal). If $F_{\mathsf{pp}} : \{0,1\}^n \to Y$ is a function family (with the properties described above) that satisfies the direct-product adaptive hardcore bit property, it also satisfies the following adaptive hardcore bit property defined as:

$$\Pr\left[\mathcal{A}(\{\mathsf{pp}_i\}_{i \in [n]}, \{F_{\mathsf{pp}_i}(\mathbf{v}_i)\}_{i \in [n]}) \to \left(\{\mathbf{d}'_i \neq 0^n\}_{i \in [n]}, \bigoplus_{i=1}^{n} \langle \mathbf{d}'_i, \mathbf{v}_i \rangle \right) \right] \leq 1/2 + \mathsf{negl}.$$

Remark 1. While the adaptive hardcore bit property in the conjecture above is different from the adaptive hardcore bit property in the case of the (2-to-1) TCF family, they can be related via the transformation that has been described before, namely the transformation from a claw-based inner product to a shift-based equation.

Realizing (Direct-Product) Adaptive Hardcore Bit.

It remains to show how we can realize the abstraction above using LHS or a related assumption. First, observe that correlated pseudorandomness can be easily handled since for n randomly generated pp_i of the following form, it follows immediately by the

LHS assumption that for $i \in [n]$:

$$(\mathbf{x}_i, \mathbf{M}_i, \mathbf{M}_i \mathbf{w} \star \mathbf{x}_i)_{i \in [n]} \stackrel{c}{\approx} (\mathbf{x}_i, \mathbf{M}_i, \mathbf{u}_i)_{i \in [n]} \quad \mathsf{pp}_i = (\mathbf{M}_i \leftarrow \mathbb{G}^{n \times n}, \mathbf{x}_i \leftarrow \mathbb{X}^n)$$

where $\mathbf{w} \leftarrow \{0, 1\}^n$ and $\mathbf{u}_i \leftarrow \mathbb{X}^n$ for $i \in [n]$. However, it is unclear how to find a corresponding efficiently computable procedure $\mathcal{P}$ (defined in the previous part). To get around this issue, we work with a slightly different form of the LHS assumption. Specifically, we can work with the following form of the LHS assumption (which is implied by the original LHS assumption via a simple reduction):

$$\mathsf{pp}_i = (\mathbf{M}_i^{(0)} \leftarrow \mathbb{G}^{n \times n}, \mathbf{M}_i^{(1)} \leftarrow \mathbb{G}^{n \times n}, \mathbf{x}_i \leftarrow \mathbb{X}^n), \quad i \in [n],$$

$$\left(\mathbf{x}_i, \mathbf{M}_i^{(0)}, \mathbf{M}_i^{(1)}, \left[\mathbf{M}_i^{(0)}(\mathbf{1} - \mathbf{w}) + \mathbf{M}_i^{(1)}\mathbf{w}\right] \star \mathbf{x}_i\right)_{i \in [n]} \stackrel{c}{\approx} \left(\mathbf{x}_i, \mathbf{M}_i^{(0)}, \mathbf{M}_i^{(1)}, \mathbf{u}_i\right)_{i \in [n]},$$

where $\mathbf{1}$ is an all-one vector. It is not hard to see that based on the new form of the assumption, given $(\mathsf{pp}_i, F_{\mathsf{pp}_i}(\mathbf{w}))$ and binary vectors $\mathbf{r}_i$ for $i \in [n]$, one can efficiently produce

$$(\mathsf{pp}_i', F_{\mathsf{pp}_i'}(\mathbf{w} \oplus \mathbf{r}_i)), \quad i \in [n],$$

where $F_{\mathsf{pp}_i'}(\mathbf{w} \oplus \mathbf{r}_i) = F_{\mathsf{pp}_i}(\mathbf{w})$, and pp_i' is simply obtained by swapping the jth column of $\mathbf{M}_i^{(0)}$ and $\mathbf{M}_i^{(1)}$ for all positions j such that the jth bit of $\mathbf{r}_i$ is 1. One can also verify that the aforementioned procedure also satisfies the indistinguishability $(**)$.

Input Recoverability and Extended LHS Assumption. To add input recoverability, we informally define one-matrix version of an extended form of the LHS assumption, which asserts that

$$\left(\mathbf{M}, \mathbf{m}, \mathbf{x}^{(\beta)}, \mathbf{y}^{(\beta)}\right)_{\beta \in \{0,1\}} \stackrel{c}{\approx} \left(\mathbf{M}, \mathbf{m}, \mathbf{u}^{(\beta)}, \mathbf{u}'^{(\beta)}\right)_{\beta \in \{0,1\}},$$

where each of the terms above is distributed as

$$\mathbf{w} \leftarrow \{0,1\}^n, \quad \mathbf{M} \leftarrow \mathbb{G}^{n \times n}, \quad \mathbf{m} \leftarrow \mathbb{G}^n, \quad \mathbf{x}^{(0)} \leftarrow \mathbb{X}^n,$$

$$\mathbf{t} \leftarrow \mathbb{G}^n, \quad \mathbf{u}^{(\beta)} \leftarrow \mathbb{X}^n, \quad \mathbf{u}'^{(\beta)} \leftarrow \mathbb{X}^n, \quad (\beta \in \{0,1\})$$

$$\mathbf{x}^{(1)} := [\mathbf{M}\mathbf{w}] \star \mathbf{x}^{(0)}, \quad \mathbf{y}^{(0)} := \mathbf{t} \star \mathbf{x}^{(0)},$$

$$\mathbf{y}^{(1)} := [\mathbf{M}\mathbf{w} + \mathbf{m} \odot \mathbf{w}] \star \mathbf{y}^{(0)},$$

and $\odot$ denotes the component-wise product of an integer and a group element (defined in a natural way). Note that for the left-hand side of the assumption above, knowing (a trapdoor) $\mathbf{t}$ is enough to recover $\mathbf{w}$,[2] since

$$-\mathbf{t} \star \mathbf{y}^{(1)} = (\mathbf{m} \odot \mathbf{w}) \star \mathbf{x}^{(1)}.$$

---

[2] Note that knowledge of $\mathbf{t}$ is enough to recover $\mathbf{w}$ even if $\mathbf{w}$ is non-binary but with short entries, i.e., if each entry of $\mathbf{w}$ is polynomially bounded.

Final Construction. Now we provide the final construction of our wTCF family. To generate a key-trapdoor pair, for each $i \in [n]$ and $\beta \in \{0,1\}$ sample

$$\mathbf{v}_i \leftarrow \{0,1\}^n, \quad \mathbf{M}_i^{(\beta)} \leftarrow \mathbb{G}^{n \times n}, \quad \mathbf{m}_i^{(\beta)} \leftarrow \mathbb{G}^n, \quad \mathbf{x}_i^{(0)} \leftarrow \mathbb{X}^n, \quad \mathbf{t}_i \leftarrow \mathbb{G}^n,$$

and set

$$\mathbf{x}_i^{(1)} := \left[\mathbf{M}_i^{(0)}(1 - \mathbf{v}_i) + \mathbf{M}_i^{(1)}\mathbf{v}_i\right] \star \mathbf{x}_i^{(0)}, \quad \mathbf{y}_i^{(0)} := \mathbf{t}_i \star \mathbf{x}_i^{(0)},$$

$$\mathbf{y}_i^{(1)} := \left[\mathbf{M}_i^{(0)}(1 - \mathbf{v}_i) + \mathbf{M}_i^{(1)}\mathbf{v}_i + \mathbf{m}_i^{(0)} \odot (1 - \mathbf{v}_i) + \mathbf{m}_i^{(1)} \odot \mathbf{v}_i\right] \star \mathbf{y}_i^{(0)},$$

where $\odot$ denotes component-wise product. Output $(\mathsf{ek}, \mathsf{td})$ where

$$\mathsf{td} = \left(\mathbf{v}_i, \mathbf{t}_i\right)_{i \in [n]}, \quad \mathsf{ek} = \left(\mathbf{M}_i^{(\beta)}, \mathbf{m}_i^{(\beta)}, \mathbf{x}_i^{(\beta)}, \mathbf{y}_i^{(\beta)}\right)_{i \in [n], \beta \in \{0,1\}}.$$

To evaluate the function $f_{\mathsf{ek}, b}$ on input $(\mathbf{s}_i)_{i \in [n]} \in ([B]^n)^n$, output $(\bar{\mathbf{z}}_i, \mathbf{z}_i)$ for $i \in [n]$ where

$$\bar{\mathbf{z}}_i = \left[(1 - b) \cdot \mathbf{M}_i^{(0)}\mathbf{1} + (\mathbf{M}_i^{(1)} - \mathbf{M}_i^{(0)})\mathbf{s}_i\right] \star \mathbf{x}_i^{(b)},$$

$$\mathbf{z}_i = \left[(1 - b) \cdot \mathbf{M}_i^{(0)}\mathbf{1} + (\mathbf{M}_i^{(1)} - \mathbf{M}_i^{(0)})\mathbf{s}_i + (1 - b) \cdot \mathbf{m}_i^{(0)} + (\mathbf{m}_i^{(1)} - \mathbf{m}_i^{(0)}) \odot \mathbf{s}_i\right] \star \mathbf{y}_i^{(b)}.$$

Observe that if $f_{\mathsf{ek}, b}((\mathbf{s}_i)_{i \in [n]}) = (\bar{\mathbf{z}}_i, \mathbf{z}_i)_{i \in [n]}$ then the following relation holds for any $i \in [n]$:

$$(-\mathbf{t}_i - \mathbf{m}_i^{(0)}) \star \mathbf{z}_i = \left[(\mathbf{m}_i^{(1)} - \mathbf{m}_i^{(0)}) \odot (\mathbf{s}_i + b \cdot \mathbf{v}_i)\right] \star \bar{\mathbf{z}}_i.$$

Because the action is applied component-wise and each entry of $\mathbf{s}_i$ lies in $[B]$, one can recover each entry of $\mathbf{s}_i$ efficiently by a simple brute force, since both $\mathbf{v}_i$ and $\mathbf{t}_i$ are included in the trapdoor.

Computational Qubit Test. To exemplify the usefulness of our wTCF family, we show how it can be used as the cryptographic building block in the computational qubit test described by Vidick [Vid20]. Such a test allows a quantum prover to certify the possession of a qubit in its internal state. Importantly, the verifier and the communication are entirely classical. The protocol that we present is largely unchanged from [Vid20], except for a few syntactical modifications due to the presence of non-perfect matchings in the input domain of our wTCFs. For more details, we refer the reader to Sect. 5. We view this protocol as a promising first step towards the usage of our isogeny-based wTCF in more complex protocols for the verification of more involved quantum tasks.

2 Preliminaries

We denote by $\lambda \in \mathbb{N}$ the security parameter. A function negl is negligible if it vanishes faster than any polynomial. We denote by $[n]$ the set $\{1, \ldots, n\}$.

2.1   Quantum Information

We recall a few facts about quantum information to establish some notation and we refer the reader to [NC02] for a more comprehensive overview. A (pure) quantum state $|\psi\rangle$ is a unit vector in a separable Hilbert space $\mathcal{H}$. Throughout this work, we will only consider finite-dimensional Hilbert spaces and so we will always assume that $\mathcal{H} \simeq \mathbb{C}^d$, for some integer $d \geq 1$. A Projector-Valued Measure (PVM) consists of a set of projectors $\{\Pi_i\}$ that sum up to identity, and if Π_i are not required to be projectors, it is called a Positive Operator-Valued Measure (POVM). Given a POVM $\{\Pi_i\}$, the *Born rule* establishes that measuring a state $|\psi\rangle$ will yield outcome i with probability $\langle\psi|\Pi_i|\psi\rangle$.

An *observable* O is a Hermitian operator on $\mathcal{H}$. Let $O = \sum_i \lambda_i \Pi_i$ be the spectral decomposition of O, then we call an *eigenstate* of O a pure state $|\psi\rangle$ such that $\Pi_i|\psi\rangle$ will deterministically yield outcome λ_i, when measured according to O. Throughout this work, we will only consider *binary observables* O such that $O^2 = \mathsf{Id}$, and that $O = \Pi_0 - \Pi_1$. I.e., they are the sum of two projectors and have eigenvalues $\lambda_i \in \{-1, +1\}$. It is convenient to define the *expected outcome* of an observable O on a state $|\psi\rangle$ as

$$\sum_i \lambda_i \langle\psi|\Pi_i|\psi\rangle = \langle\psi|O|\psi\rangle.$$

2.2   Cryptographic Group Actions and Extended LHS Assumption

In this part we recall some definitions related to cryptographic group actions from [ADMP20], which provided a framework to capture certain isogeny-based assumptions (e.g., variants of CSIDH [CLM+18,BKV19]). We refer to [ADMP20] for a detailed explanation of these definitions. Towards the end of the section, we provide a definition of extended linear hidden shift assumption, from which we later show the construction of wTCF family. We present our results entirely in terms of group actions with certain hardness properties (based on the framework of [ADMP20]), and thus we do not assume familiarity with CSIDH and its variants [CLM+18,BKV19]. We refer to [Pei20,BS20] for an overview of quantum attacks against CSIDH for certain choices of parameters.

Throughout the paper, we use the abbreviated notation $(\mathbb{G}, \mathbb{X}, \star)$ to denote a group action $\star : \mathbb{G} \times \mathbb{X} \to \mathbb{X}$. Moreover, we are going to assume that group actions are abelian and *regular*, i.e., both free and transitive (which is the case for all isogeny-based group actions). For such group actions, we have $|\mathbb{G}| = |\mathbb{X}|$. Note that if a group action is regular, then for any $x \in \mathbb{X}$, the map $f_x : g \mapsto g \star x$ defines a bijection between $\mathbb{G}$ and $\mathbb{X}$.

We recall the definition of an effective group action (EGA) from [ADMP20]. In a nutshell, an effective group action allows us to efficiently perform certain tasks over $\mathbb{G}$ (e.g., group operation, inversion, and sampling uniformly) efficiently, along with an efficient procedure to compute the action of any group element on any set element. As a concrete example, a variant of CSIDH [BKV19] (called "CSI-FiSh") can be modeled as an effective group action, for which the group $\mathbb{G}$ is isomorphic to $(\mathbb{Z}_N, +)$.[3]

Definition 1 (Effective Group Action (EGA)). *A group action* $(\mathbb{G}, \mathbb{X}, \star)$ *is effective if it satisfies the following properties:*

1. *The group* $\mathbb{G}$ *is finite and there exist efficient (PPT) algorithms for:*
   (a) *Membership testing (deciding whether a binary string represents a group element).*
   (b) *Equality testing and sampling uniformly in* $\mathbb{G}$.
   (c) *Group operation and computing inverse of any element.*
2. *The set* $\mathbb{X}$ *is finite and there exist efficient algorithms for:*
   (a) *Membership testing (to check if a string represents a valid set element),*
   (b) *Unique representation.*
3. *There exists a distinguished element* $x_0 \in \mathbb{X}$ *with known representation.*
4. *There exists an efficient algorithm that given any* $g \in \mathbb{G}$ *and any* $x \in \mathbb{X}$, *outputs* $g \star x$.

Notation. For a group action $\star : \mathbb{G} \times \mathbb{X} \to \mathbb{X}$, we always use the additive notation $+$ to denote the group operation in $\mathbb{G}$. Since $\mathbb{G}$ is abelian, it can be viewed as a $\mathbb{Z}$-module, and hence for any $z \in \mathbb{Z}$ and $g \in \mathbb{G}$ the term zg is well-defined. This property naturally extends to vectors and matrices as well, so if $\mathbf{g} \in G^n$ and $\mathbf{z} \in \mathbb{Z}^n$ for some $n \in \mathbb{N}$, then we use $\langle \mathbf{g}, \mathbf{z} \rangle$ to denote $\sum_{i=1}^n z_i g_i$. Thus, for any matrix $\mathbf{M} \in \mathbb{G}^{m \times n}$ and any vector $\mathbf{z} \in \mathbb{Z}^n$, the term $\mathbf{Mz}$ is also well-defined.

For any two vectors $\mathbf{z} \in \mathbb{Z}^n$ and $\mathbf{g} \in G^n$ we use the notation $\mathbf{z} \odot \mathbf{g}$ to denote a vector whose ith component is $z_i g_i$ (component-wise/Hadamard product). The group action also extends to the direct product group $\mathbb{G}^n$ for any positive integer n. If $\mathbf{g} \in \mathbb{G}^n$ and $\mathbf{x} \in X^n$, we use $\mathbf{g} \star \mathbf{x}$ to denote a vector of set elements whose ith component is $g_i \star x_i$.

Definition 2 (Weak Pseudorandom EGA). *An (effective) group action* $(\mathbb{G}, \mathbb{X}, \star)$ *is said to be a weak pseudorandom EGA if it holds that*

$$(x, y, t \star x, t \star y) \overset{c}{\approx} (x, y, u, u'),$$

where $x \leftarrow \mathbb{X}$, $y \leftarrow \mathbb{X}$, $t \leftarrow \mathbb{G}$, $u \leftarrow \mathbb{X}$, *and* $u' \leftarrow \mathbb{X}$.

Definition 3 (Linear Hidden Shift (LHS) assumption [ADMP20]). *Let* $(\mathbb{G}, \mathbb{X}, \star)$ *be an effective group action (EGA), and let* $n > \log |\mathbb{G}| + \omega(\log \lambda)$ *be a positive integer. We say that liner hidden shift (LHS) assumption holds over* $(\mathbb{G}, \mathbb{X}, \star)$ *if for any* $\ell = \mathrm{poly}(\lambda)$ *the following holds:*

$$(\mathbf{x}, \mathbf{M}, \mathbf{Mw} \star \mathbf{x}) \overset{c}{\approx} (\mathbf{x}, \mathbf{M}, \mathbf{u}),$$

---

[3] Although we present our results in terms of EGA, one can also obtain the same results from a *restricted* EGA assuming a one-time quantum preprocessing, since EGA and restricted EGA are quantumly equivalent [ADMP20].

where each of the terms above is distributed as

$$\mathbf{x} \leftarrow \mathbb{X}^{\ell}, \quad \mathbf{M} \leftarrow \mathbb{G}^{\ell \times n}, \quad \mathbf{w} \leftarrow \{0,1\}^n, \quad \mathbf{u} \leftarrow \mathbb{X}^{\ell}.$$

Definition 4 (Extended LHS assumption). *Let $(\mathbb{G}, \mathbb{X}, \star)$ be an effective group action (EGA), and let $n > \log |\mathbb{G}| + \omega(\log \lambda)$ be a positive integer. We say that extended LHS assumption holds over $(\mathbb{G}, \mathbb{X}, \star)$ if for any $\ell = \mathrm{poly}(\lambda)$ the following holds:*

$$\left(\mathbf{M}_i, \mathbf{m}_i, \mathbf{x}_i^{(\beta)}, \mathbf{y}_i^{(\beta)}\right)_{i \in [\ell], \beta \in \{0,1\}} \stackrel{c}{\approx} \left(\mathbf{M}_i, \mathbf{m}_i, \mathbf{u}_i^{(\beta)}, {\mathbf{u}'}_i^{(\beta)}\right)_{i \in [\ell], \beta \in \{0,1\}},$$

where each of the terms above is distributed as

$$\mathbf{w} \leftarrow \{0,1\}^n, \quad \mathbf{M}_i \leftarrow \mathbb{G}^{n \times n}, \quad \mathbf{m}_i \leftarrow \mathbb{G}^n, \quad \mathbf{x}_i^{(0)} \leftarrow \mathbb{X}^n,$$

$$\mathbf{t}_i \leftarrow \mathbb{G}^n, \quad \mathbf{u}_i^{(\beta)} \leftarrow \mathbb{X}^n, \quad {\mathbf{u}'}_i^{(\beta)} \leftarrow \mathbb{X}^n,$$

$$\mathbf{x}_i^{(1)} := \left[\mathbf{M}_i \mathbf{w}\right] \star \mathbf{x}_i^{(0)}, \quad \mathbf{y}_i^{(0)} := \mathbf{t}_i \star \mathbf{x}_i^{(0)},$$

$$\mathbf{y}_i^{(1)} := \left[\mathbf{M}_i \mathbf{w} + \mathbf{m}_i \odot \mathbf{w}\right] \star \mathbf{y}_i^{(0)}.$$

Remark 2. Note that in the assumption above if $\mathbf{y}_i^{(1)}$ were distributed as $\mathbf{y}_i^{(1)} = \left[\mathbf{M}_i \mathbf{w}\right] \star \mathbf{y}_i^{(0)}$, then the extended LHS assumption would be implied by any weak pseudorandom EGA over which LHS assumption holds. In other words, the presence of the term $\mathbf{m}_i \odot \mathbf{w}$ makes the extended LHS assumption seemingly stronger than the plain LHS assumption.

3 Weak Trapdoor Claw-Free Functions

We define the notion of a weak trapdoor claw-free function (wTCF) family. We adopt a slightly simplified syntax compared to [BCM+18] as each function in our definition of wTCF family will be a deterministic function rather than mapping to a probability distribution.

Definition 5 (wTCF). *Let $n = n(\lambda)$ be an integer such that $n = \mathrm{poly}(\lambda)$. Let $\mathcal{F}$ be a family of functions*

$$\mathcal{F} = \{f_{\mathsf{ek},b} : X^n \to Y\}_{(\mathsf{ek},b) \in K \times \{0,1\}},$$

where X, Y, and K are finite sets indexed by λ, and K denotes the the key space. We say that $\mathcal{F}$ is a weak trapdoor claw-free (wTCF) function family if it satisfies the following properties:

1. *There exists a PPT algorithm Gen which generates an evaluation key ek along with a trapdoor td as $(\mathsf{ek}, \mathsf{td}) \leftarrow \mathsf{Gen}(1^{\lambda})$.*
2. *For all but a negligible fraction of key-trapdoor pairs $(\mathsf{ek}, \mathsf{td}) \in supp(\mathsf{Gen}(1^{\lambda}))$, the following properties hold.*

(a) *There exists an efficient algorithm* Invert *that for any* $b \in \{0,1\}$ *and any* $\mathbf{x} \in X^n$, *it holds that*

$$\mathsf{Invert}(\mathsf{td}, b, f_{\mathsf{ek},b}(\mathbf{x})) = \mathbf{x}.$$

(b) *There exists two* dense *subsets* $\mathbf{X}_0 \subseteq X^n$ *and* $\mathbf{X}_1 \subseteq X^n$ *and a perfect matching* $R_{\mathsf{ek}} \subseteq \mathbf{X}_0 \times \mathbf{X}_1$ *such that for any* $(\mathbf{x}_0, \mathbf{x}_1) \in \mathbf{X}_0 \times \mathbf{X}_1$ *it holds that* $f_{\mathsf{ek},0}(\mathbf{x}_0) = f_{\mathsf{ek},1}(\mathbf{x}_1)$ *iff* $(\mathbf{x}_0, \mathbf{x}_1) \in R_{\mathsf{ek}}$, *where a dense subset* $\mathbf{X} \subseteq X^n$ *is defined as a subset that satisfies*

$$\Pr_{\mathbf{x} \leftarrow X^n}[\mathbf{x} \in \mathbf{X}] \geq 1 - n^{-c},$$

for some constant $c \geq 1$. *For any* $\mathbf{x} \in X^n$, *membership in* $\mathbf{X}_0$ *or* $\mathbf{X}_1$ *can be checked efficiently given the trapdoor* td. *In addition, there exists a dense subset* $\bar{\mathbf{X}} \subseteq \mathbf{X}_0 \cap \mathbf{X}_1 \subseteq X^n$ *such that membership in* $\bar{\mathbf{X}}$ *can be checked without* td.

Informally, this property means that a randomly sampled $\mathbf{x} \leftarrow X^n$ *lies in* $\bar{\mathbf{X}} \subseteq \mathbf{X}_0 \cap \mathbf{X}_1$ *with "good" probability. Moreover, for any* $\mathbf{x} \in \mathbf{X}_0 \cap \mathbf{X}_1$ *and any* $b \in \{0,1\}$, *the image* $y = f_{\mathsf{ek},b}(\mathbf{x})$ *has exactly one preimage* $\mathbf{x}_0 \in \mathbf{X}_0$ *under* $f_{\mathsf{ek},0}$ *and one preimage* $\mathbf{x}_1 \in \mathbf{X}_1$ *under* $f_{\mathsf{ek},1}$.

3. (a) *There exists an efficiently computable "binary encoding" function* $\mathsf{B} : X^n \rightarrow \{0,1\}^{n\ell}$ *such that* B^{-1} *is also efficiently computable on the range of* B.

(b) *For any* $b \in \{0,1\}$ *and any* $\mathbf{x} \in X^n$, *there exists a set* $\mathbb{Y}_{b,\mathbf{x}} \subseteq \{0,1\}^{n\ell}$ *such that*

$$\Pr_{\mathbf{d} \leftarrow \{0,1\}^{n\ell}}[\mathbf{d} \notin \mathbb{Y}_{b,\mathbf{x}}] \leq \mathsf{negl},$$

and membership in $\mathbb{Y}_{b,\mathbf{x}}$ *can be checked efficiently given* b *and* $\mathbf{x}$.

(c) *Let* W_{ek} *be a (key-dependent) set of tuples defined as*

$$W_{\mathsf{ek}} = \left\{ \left(b, \mathbf{x}_b, \mathbf{d}, (\langle \mathbf{d}_i, \mathsf{B}_i(\mathbf{x}_0) \oplus \mathsf{B}_i(\mathbf{x}_1) \rangle)_{i \in [n]} \right) \middle| \begin{array}{l} b \in \{0,1\}, (\mathbf{x}_0, \mathbf{x}_1) \in R_{\mathsf{ek}}, \\ \mathbf{d} \in \mathbb{Y}_{0,\mathbf{x}_0} \cap \mathbb{Y}_{1,\mathbf{x}_1} \end{array} \right\},$$

where $\mathbf{d}_i$ *and* $\mathsf{B}_i(\cdot)$ *denote the* ith ℓ-bit chunk of $\mathbf{d}$ and $\mathsf{B}(\cdot)$, respectively (the inner product is computed over* $\mathbb{F}_2$). *We require that for any QPT adversary* $\mathcal{A}$, *if* $(\mathsf{ek}, \mathsf{td}) \leftarrow \mathsf{Gen}(1^\lambda)$ *then*

$$\Pr[\mathcal{A}(\mathsf{ek}) \in W_{\mathsf{ek}}] \leq \mathsf{negl},$$

where the probability is taken over all randomness in the experiment.

3.1   XOR Lemmas for Adaptive Hardcore Bits

The weak version (direct-product) of the adaptive hardcore bit property (property 3c) will not be sufficient for our protocol. In the following, we define a stronger version of the property that we will need in our analysis. Note that the only difference with respect to property 3c is that the adversary is required to output a single bit h, which is the XOR of the n bits required before.

Definition 6 (Adaptive Hardcore Bit). *Let $\mathcal{F}$ be a wTCF, and let W_{ek} be a (key-dependent) set of tuples defined as*

$$W_{ek} = \left\{ \left(b, \mathbf{x}_b, \mathbf{d}, h \right) \middle| \begin{array}{l} b \in \{0, 1\}, (\mathbf{x}_0, \mathbf{x}_1) \in R_{ek}, \mathbf{d} \in \mathbb{Y}_{0,\mathbf{x}_0} \cap \mathbb{Y}_{1,\mathbf{x}_1}, \\ h = \bigoplus_{i=1}^{n} \langle \mathbf{d}_i, B_i(\mathbf{x}_0) \oplus B_i(\mathbf{x}_1) \rangle \end{array} \right\},$$

where $\mathbf{d}_i$ and $B_i(\cdot)$ denote the ith ℓ-bit chunk of $\mathbf{d}$ and $B(\cdot)$, respectively. We require that for any QPT adversary $\mathcal{A}$, if $(ek, td) \leftarrow Gen(1^\lambda)$ then

$$\Pr[\mathcal{A}(ek) \in W_{ek}] \leq 1/2 + \text{negl},$$

where the probability is taken over all randomness in the experiment.

We define the following property for a wTCF family, which requires that any key/input/output can be viewed as n independent instances. Our construction of wTCF will satisfy this property.

Definition 7. *Let $\mathcal{F}$ be a wTCF family of functions with domain X^n and range $Y = \bar{Y}^n$. Let Gen, Eval, and Invert be the associated algorithms. We say that $\mathcal{F}$ is a wTCF family with independent evaluations (wTCF-IE) if there exists algorithms $\overline{Gen}$, $\overline{Eval}$, and $\overline{Invert}$ such that*

- Gen *is identically distributed to the concatenation of n independent runs of $\overline{Gen}$.*
- *For each $(ek, td) = \{(ek_i, td_i)\}_{i \in [n]}$ in the support of $Gen \equiv (\overline{Gen})^n$, the output of any function $f_{ek,b} \in \mathcal{F}$ on any $\mathbf{x} \in X^n$ is identical to the concatenation of $\overline{Eval}_{ek_i,b}$ on x_i for $i \in [n]$.*
- *For each $(ek, td) = \{(ek_i, td_i)\}_{i \in [n]}$ in the support of $Gen \equiv (\overline{Gen})^n$, the output of $Invert_{td,b}$ on any $\mathbf{y} \in \bar{Y}^n$ is identical to the concatenation of $\overline{Invert}_{td_i,b}$ on y_i for $i \in [n]$.*

Next we state our conjecture, namely that any wTCF-IE that satisfies direct-product adaptive hardcore bit property (3c), also satisfies the adaptive hardcore bit property.

Conjecture 2. If $\mathcal{F}$ is a wTCF-IE family that satisfies the direct-product adaptive hardcore bit property 3c, then $\mathcal{F}$ satisfies the property in Definition 6.

Remark 3. Note that for our construction, the conjecture above is implied by the (informal) Conjecture 1 via a transformation (from claw-based inner product to shift-based equation) that we will see later. We omit the formal details as it is going to be similar to the proof of Lemma 7.

Random Subset Adaptive Hardcore Bit. To gain confidence in our conjecture, we show that a weaker variant of it is implied by property 3c. Roughly speaking, this notion says that it is hard to predict the XOR of a random subset of the adaptive n hardcore bits. However, note that the predictor is not given the subset ahead of time.

Definition 8 (Random Subset Adaptive Hardcore Bit). *Let $\mathcal{F}$ be a wTCF. For any QPT adversary $\mathcal{A}$, the success probability in the following experiment is negligibly close to $1/2$.*

- *The challenger samples $(\mathsf{ek}, \mathsf{td}) \leftarrow \mathsf{Gen}(1^\lambda)$ and sends ek to $\mathcal{A}$.*
- *$\mathcal{A}$ sends a tuple $(b, \mathbf{x}_b, \mathbf{d})$.*
- *The challenger samples a subset $\mathbf{r} \leftarrow \{0,1\}^n$ and sends $\mathbf{r}$ to $\mathcal{A}$.*
- *$\mathcal{A}$ returns a bit $h \in \{0,1\}$ and succeeds if the following conditions are satisfied:*
  - *$(\mathbf{x}_0, \mathbf{x}_1) \in R_{\mathsf{ek}}$*
  - *$\mathbf{d} \in \mathbb{Y}_{0,\mathbf{x}_0} \cap \mathbb{Y}_{1,\mathbf{x}_1}$*
  - *$h = \bigoplus_{i=1}^n r_i \cdot \langle \mathbf{d}_i, \mathsf{B}_i(\mathbf{x}_0) \oplus \mathsf{B}_i(\mathbf{x}_1) \rangle$*

  where $\mathbf{d}_i$ and $\mathsf{B}_i(\cdot)$ denote the ith ℓ-bit chunk of $\mathbf{d}$ and $\mathsf{B}(\cdot)$, respectively.

Next we show that this new variant is directly implied by Definition 5. This is an almost immediate application of a theorem from [AC02].

Lemma 1. *Let $\mathcal{F}$ be a wTCF, then $\mathcal{F}$ satisfies Definition 8.*

Proof. The proof consists of a reduction to the direct-product adaptive hardcore bit property of the wTCF (property 3c). Let $\mathcal{A}$ be a QPT algorithm that succeeds in the above game with probability greater than $1/2 + \varepsilon$, for some inverse-polynomial ε. Let $|\psi\rangle$ denote the internal state of the adversary after the second step of the protocol, and in particular after the tuple $(b, \mathbf{x}_b, \mathbf{d})$ has been sent to the challenger. Let G_{ek} be a set defined as follows:

$$G_{\mathsf{ek}} = \left\{ (b, \mathbf{x}_b, \mathbf{d}, |\psi\rangle) : \Pr\left[\mathcal{A}(\mathbf{r}; |\psi\rangle) = \bigoplus_{i=1}^n r_i \cdot \langle \mathbf{d}_i, \mathsf{B}_i(\mathbf{x}_0) \oplus \mathsf{B}_i(\mathbf{x}_1) \rangle \right] \geq 1/2 + \varepsilon/2 \right\}$$

where the probability is taken over the random choice of $\mathbf{r}$ and over the internal coins of $\mathcal{A}$. We use the abbreviation $\mathcal{A}(\mathbf{r}; |\psi\rangle)$ to denote the output of the adversary $\mathcal{A}$ run on state $|\psi\rangle$ and on input $\mathbf{r}$. Observe that the above set is well-defined, since $\mathbf{x}_b$ uniquely determines the claw $(\mathbf{x}_0, \mathbf{x}_1)$, provided that $(\mathbf{x}_0, \mathbf{x}_1) \in R_{\mathsf{ek}}$.

We argue that $\Pr[(b, \mathbf{x}_b, \mathbf{d}, |\psi\rangle) \in G_{\mathsf{ek}}] \geq \varepsilon/2$, where the probability is over the random choice of ek and the random coins of $\mathcal{A}$. For notational convenience, we relabel $h_i = \mathbf{d}_i \cdot \left[\mathsf{B}_i(\mathbf{x}_0) \oplus \mathsf{B}_i(\mathbf{x}_1)\right]$.

Assume towards contradiction that $\Pr[(b, \mathbf{x}_b, \mathbf{d}, |\psi\rangle) \in G_{\mathsf{ek}}] < \varepsilon/2$. We can then rewrite:

$$
\begin{aligned}
\Pr\left[\mathcal{A} \text{ succeeds}\right] &= \Pr\left[\mathcal{A}(\mathbf{r}; |\psi\rangle) = \bigoplus_{i=1}^n r_i \cdot h_i\right] \\
&= \Pr\left[\mathcal{A}(\mathbf{r}; |\psi\rangle) = \bigoplus_{i=1}^n r_i \cdot h_i \middle| (b, \mathbf{x}_b, \mathbf{d}, |\psi\rangle) \in G_{\mathsf{ek}}\right] \Pr\left[(b, \mathbf{x}_b, \mathbf{d}, |\psi\rangle) \in G_{\mathsf{ek}}\right] \\
&\quad + \Pr\left[\mathcal{A}(\mathbf{r}; |\psi\rangle) = \bigoplus_{i=1}^n r_i \cdot h_i \middle| (b, \mathbf{x}_b, \mathbf{d}, |\psi\rangle) \notin G_{\mathsf{ek}}\right] \Pr\left[(b, \mathbf{x}_b, \mathbf{d}, |\psi\rangle) \notin G_{\mathsf{ek}}\right] \\
&< \varepsilon/2 + (1/2 + \varepsilon/2) \\
&= 1/2 + \varepsilon
\end{aligned}
$$

which contradicts our initial hypothesis. Conditioned on $(b, \mathbf{x}_b, \mathbf{d}, |\psi\rangle) \in G_{\mathsf{ek}}$, we then consider the algorithm $\mathcal{A}(\cdot; |\psi\rangle)$. Such an algorithm runs in polynomial time and, on input $\mathbf{r}$, it returns

$$h = \bigoplus_{i=1}^{n} r_i \cdot h_i = \bigoplus_{i=1}^{n} r_i \cdot \langle \mathbf{d}_i, \mathsf{B}_i(\mathbf{x}_0) \oplus \mathsf{B}_i(\mathbf{x}_1) \rangle$$

with probability at least $\varepsilon/2$ (over the random choice of $\mathbf{r}$ and the internal coins of $\mathcal{A}$). By the Adcock-Cleve theorem [AC02], it follows that there exists an efficient algorithm that, with a *single query* to $\mathcal{A}(\cdot; |\psi\rangle)$, returns $(h_1, \ldots, h_n)$ with inverse polynomial probability. This violates the direct-product adaptive hardcore bit property of $\mathcal{F}$.

4   wTCF from Extended LHS Assumption

Here we show how to construct a wTCF family from extended LHS assumption (Definition 4) over a group action $(\mathbb{G}, \mathbb{X}, \star)$.

Construction. Let n be the secret dimension of underlying extended LHS assumption, and let $B > 2n^3$ be an integer. We define a wTCF family as follows. Let $X = [B]^n$, and $Y = (\mathbb{X}^{2n})^n$. Note that $X^n = ([B]^n)^n$ and Y will be the input and output space of our wTCF family, respectively. To generate a key-trapdoor pair, for each $i \in [n]$ and $\beta \in \{0, 1\}$ sample

$$\mathbf{v}_i \leftarrow \{0,1\}^n, \quad \mathbf{M}_i^{(\beta)} \leftarrow \mathbb{G}^{n \times n}, \quad \mathbf{m}_i^{(\beta)} \leftarrow \mathbb{G}^n, \quad \mathbf{x}_i^{(0)} \leftarrow \mathbb{X}^n, \quad \mathbf{t}_i \leftarrow \mathbb{G}^n,$$

and set

$$\mathbf{x}_i^{(1)} := \left[\mathbf{M}_i^{(0)}(\mathbf{1} - \mathbf{v}_i) + \mathbf{M}_i^{(1)} \mathbf{v}_i \right] \star \mathbf{x}_i^{(0)}, \quad \mathbf{y}_i^{(0)} := \mathbf{t}_i \star \mathbf{x}_i^{(0)},$$

$$\mathbf{y}_i^{(1)} := \left[\mathbf{M}_i^{(0)}(\mathbf{1} - \mathbf{v}_i) + \mathbf{M}_i^{(1)} \mathbf{v}_i + \mathbf{m}_i^{(0)} \odot (\mathbf{1} - \mathbf{v}_i) + \mathbf{m}_i^{(1)} \odot \mathbf{v}_i \right] \star \mathbf{y}_i^{(0)},$$

where $\odot$ denotes component-wise product. Output $(\mathsf{ek}, \mathsf{td})$ where

$$\mathsf{td} = \left(\mathbf{v}_i, \mathbf{t}_i \right)_{i \in [n]}, \quad \mathsf{ek} = \left(\mathbf{M}_i^{(\beta)}, \mathbf{m}_i^{(\beta)}, \mathbf{x}_i^{(\beta)}, \mathbf{y}_i^{(\beta)} \right)_{i \in [n], \beta \in \{0,1\}}.$$

To evaluate the function $f_{\mathsf{ek}, b}$ on input $(\mathbf{s}_i)_{i \in [n]} \in ([B]^n)^n$, output $(\bar{\mathbf{z}}_i, \mathbf{z}_i)$ for $i \in [n]$ where

$$\bar{\mathbf{z}}_i = \left[(1 - b) \cdot \mathbf{M}_i^{(0)} \mathbf{1} + (\mathbf{M}_i^{(1)} - \mathbf{M}_i^{(0)}) \mathbf{s}_i \right] \star \mathbf{x}_i^{(b)},$$

$$\mathbf{z}_i = \left[(1 - b) \cdot \mathbf{M}_i^{(0)} \mathbf{1} + (\mathbf{M}_i^{(1)} - \mathbf{M}_i^{(0)}) \mathbf{s}_i + (1 - b) \cdot \mathbf{m}_i^{(0)} + (\mathbf{m}_i^{(1)} - \mathbf{m}_i^{(0)}) \odot \mathbf{s}_i \right] \star \mathbf{y}_i^{(b)}.$$

To invert the function $f_{\mathsf{ek}, b}$ on some value $(\bar{\mathbf{z}}_i, \mathbf{z}_i)_{i \in [n]}$, we recover each $\mathbf{s}_i$ (for $i \in [n]$) as follows. Observe that if $f_{\mathsf{ek}, b}((\mathbf{s}_i)_{i \in [n]}) = (\bar{\mathbf{z}}_i, \mathbf{z}_i)_{i \in [n]}$ then the following relation holds for any $i \in [n]$:

$$(-\mathbf{t}_i - \mathbf{m}_i^{(0)}) \star \mathbf{z}_i = \left[(\mathbf{m}_i^{(1)} - \mathbf{m}_i^{(0)}) \odot (\mathbf{s}_i + b \cdot \mathbf{v}_i) \right] \star \bar{\mathbf{z}}_i.$$

Because the action is applied component-wise and each entry of $\mathbf{s}_i$ lies in $[B]$, one can recover each entry of $\mathbf{s}_i$ efficiently by a simple brute force, since both $\mathbf{v}_i$ and $\mathbf{t}_i$ are included in the trapdoor.

We have already shown the construction above satisfies the properties (1) and (2a) of a wTCF family, thus proving the following lemma.

Lemma 2. *Let $\mathcal{F}$ be the function family (with associated algorithms) as described in the construction, then $\mathcal{F}$ satisfies the properties 1 and 2a.*

Next, we show the construction above satisfies the remaining properties of a wTCF family (Definition 5) via the following lemmata.

Lemma 3. *Let $\mathcal{F}$ be the function family (with associated algorithms) as described in the construction, then $\mathcal{F}$ satisfies the property 2b.*

Proof. It is easy to see that for all but a negligible fraction of key-trapdoor pairs $(\mathsf{ek}, \mathsf{td}) \in \mathrm{supp}(\mathsf{Gen}(1^\lambda))$

– Any evaluation key ek uniquely determines $\mathbf{v}_i$ for $i \in [n]$.[4]
– $f_{\mathsf{ek},b}$ is an injective function.

For a given evaluation key ek, consider the following two subsets:

$$\mathbf{X}_0 = \left\{ (\mathbf{s}_i)_{i \in [n]} \mid \forall i \in [n] : \mathbf{s}_i \in [B]^n \wedge \mathbf{s}_i - \mathbf{v}_i \in [B]^n \right\},$$
$$\mathbf{X}_1 = \left\{ (\mathbf{s}_i)_{i \in [n]} \mid \forall i \in [n] : \mathbf{s}_i \in [B]^n \wedge \mathbf{s}_i + \mathbf{v}_i \in [B]^n \right\}.$$

Let $R_{\mathsf{ek}} \subseteq \mathbf{X}_0 \times \mathbf{X}_1$ be the relation defined as

$$R_{\mathsf{ek}} = \left\{ \left((\mathbf{s}_i^{(0)})_{i \in [n]}, (\mathbf{s}_i^{(1)})_{i \in [n]} \right) \in \mathbf{X}_0 \times \mathbf{X}_1 \mid \forall i \in [n] : \mathbf{s}_i^{(0)} = \mathbf{s}_i^{(1)} + \mathbf{v}_i \right\}.$$

One can immediately verify that R_{ek} is a perfect matching. Because $f_{\mathsf{ek},b}$ is injective, it holds that

$$\forall \left((\mathbf{s}_i^{(0)})_{i \in [n]}, (\mathbf{s}_i^{(1)})_{i \in [n]} \right) \in \mathbf{X}_0 \times \mathbf{X}_1 :$$
$$f_{\mathsf{ek},0}\left((\mathbf{s}_i^{(0)})_{i \in [n]} \right) = f_{\mathsf{ek},1}\left((\mathbf{s}_i^{(1)})_{i \in [n]} \right) \qquad \Longleftrightarrow$$
$$(\mathbf{s}_i^{(0)})_{i \in [n]} = (\mathbf{s}_i^{(1)} + \mathbf{v}_i)_{i \in [n]} \qquad \Longleftrightarrow$$
$$\left((\mathbf{s}_i^{(0)})_{i \in [n]}, (\mathbf{s}_i^{(1)})_{i \in [n]} \right) \in R_{\mathsf{ek}}.$$

Since each $\mathbf{v}_i$ is a binary vector, it follows that for any $b \in \{0, 1\}$

$$\Pr_{(\mathbf{s}_i)_{i \in [n]} \leftarrow ([B]^n)^n} \left[(\mathbf{s}_i)_{i \in [n]} \in \mathbf{X}_b \right] \geq 1 - n^2 (B - 1)^{-1} \geq 1 - n^{-1}.$$

---

[4] Recall that $\mathbb{G}$ is a superpolynomially (and possibly exponentially) large group. For example, in case of the variant from [BKV19] the group is cyclic, and hence a randomly chosen evaluation key uniquely determines $\mathbf{v}_i$ with overwhelming probability [BM87].

For any $b \in \{0, 1\}$, given any tuple $(\mathbf{s}_i)_{i \in [n]}$ membership in $\mathbf{X}_b$ can be checked efficiently using the trapdoor, simply by testing whether $\mathbf{s}_i - (-1)^b \mathbf{v}_i \in [B^n]$ for all $i \in [n]$.

Finally, define the set $\bar{\mathbf{X}}$ as

$$\bar{\mathbf{X}} = \left\{ (\mathbf{s}_i)_{i \in [n]} \mid \forall i \in [n] : \mathbf{s}_i \in \{2, \dots, B - 1\}^n \right\}.$$

Membership in $\bar{\mathbf{X}}$ can be checked efficiently without a trapdoor. Moreover, by a simple argument, we have

$$\Pr_{(\mathbf{s}_i)_{i \in [n]} \leftarrow ([B]^n)^n} \left[(\mathbf{s}_i)_{i \in [n]} \in \bar{\mathbf{X}} \right] \geq 1 - 2n^2 (B - 1)^{-1} \geq 1 - n^{-1},$$

and hence $\bar{\mathbf{X}}$ is a dense subset of the input space $([B]^n)^n$.

Lemma 4. *Let $\mathcal{F}$ be the function family (with associated algorithms) as described in the construction, then $\mathcal{F}$ satisfies the properties 3a and 3b.*

Proof. Consider the binary encoding function $\mathsf{B} : (([B])^n)^n \to \{0, 1\}^{n\ell}$ where $\ell = n\lceil \log B \rceil$. Specifically, $\mathsf{B}((\mathbf{s}_i)_{i \in [n]})$ outputs the binary representation of $(\mathbf{s}_i)_{i \in [n]}$, where each component of $\mathbf{s}_i$ is represented using a chunk of $\lceil \log B \rceil$-bit string. It is immediate to see that B is injective and it is also efficiently invertible on its range, and hence $\mathcal{F}$ satisfies the property 3a.

To avoid abusing the notation, we also define a simple function $\bar{\mathsf{B}} : [B] \to \{0, 1\}^{\lceil \log B \rceil}$, which outputs the binary representation of any $s \in [B]$. For a tuple $(b, \mathbf{s}, \mathbf{d}) \in \{0, 1\} \times [B]^n \times \{0, 1\}^\ell$, let $\mathsf{T}_{b,\mathbf{d}} : [B]^n \to \{0, 1\}^n$ be a function that maps $\mathbf{s} = (s_1, \dots, s_n)$ to $\mathbf{d}' = (d_1', \dots, d_n')$ where

$$d_j' = \langle \mathbf{d}^{(j)}, \bar{\mathsf{B}}(s_j) \oplus \bar{\mathsf{B}}(s_j - (-1)^b) \rangle, \quad j \in [n],$$

and $\mathbf{d}^{(j)}$ denotes the jth $\lceil \log B \rceil$-bit chunk of $\mathbf{d}$. Note that the inner product is computed over $\mathbb{F}_2$, while the operation $-$ is performed over $\mathbb{Z}$. As we will see later, the motivation for defining the transformation $\mathsf{T}_{b,\mathbf{d}}$ stems from the following observation [BCM+18] that given $(\mathbf{s}, \mathbf{d}, \langle \mathbf{d}, (\mathbf{s} + \mathbf{v}) \rangle) \in [B]^n \times \{0, 1\}^\ell \times \{0, 1\}$ for some binary $\mathbf{v} \in \{0, 1\}^n$, where the inner product is computed over $\mathbb{F}_2$ and the addition $+$ is over integers, one can use $\mathsf{T}_{b,\mathbf{d}}$ to obtain a pair of the form $(\mathbf{d}', \langle \mathbf{d}', \mathbf{v} \rangle) \in \{0, 1\}^n \times \{0, 1\}$. This transformation will be useful in proving the weak adaptive hardcore bit property 3c.

For any $\mathbf{s} \in [B]^n$, since $\bar{\mathsf{B}}$ is an injective function it follows that the term $\bar{\mathsf{B}}(s_j) \oplus \bar{\mathsf{B}}(s_j - (-1)^b)$ is non-zero for any $j \in [n]$. Therefore, if $\mathbf{d}^{(j)} \leftarrow \{0, 1\}^{\lceil \log B \rceil}$ then d_j' will be 0 with probability $1/2$. It follows that for any $\mathbf{s} \in [B]^n$ and any $b \in \{0, 1\}$, if $\mathbf{d} \leftarrow \{0, 1\}^\ell$ then

$$\Pr[\mathsf{T}_{b,\mathbf{d}}(\mathbf{s}) = 0^n] \leq \mathsf{negl}.$$

For any $b \in \{0,1\}$ and any $(\mathbf{s}_i)_{i\in[n]} \in ([B]^n)^n$, consider the following set

$$\mathbb{Y}_{b,(\mathbf{s}_i)_{i\in[n]}} = \left\{ (\mathbf{d}_i)_{i\in[n]} \in \{0,1\}^{n\ell} \middle| \forall i \in [n] : \mathsf{T}_{b,\mathbf{s}_i}(\mathbf{d}_i) \neq 0^n \right\}.$$

By a simple union bound it follows that for any $b \in \{0,1\}$ and $(\mathbf{s}_i)_{i\in[n]} \in ([B]^n)^n$ we have

$$\Pr_{(\mathbf{d}_i)_{i\in[n]}\leftarrow\{0,1\}^{n\ell}} \left[(\mathbf{d}_i)_{i\in[n]} \in \mathbb{Y}_{b,(\mathbf{s}_i)_{i\in[n]}} \right] \leq \mathsf{negl},$$

where we used the fact that for each $i \in [n]$ it holds that $\Pr_{\mathbf{d}_i}[\mathsf{T}_{b,\mathbf{d}_i}(\mathbf{s}_i) = 0^n] \leq$ negl. Clearly, $\mathsf{T}_{b,\mathbf{d}}$ is efficiently computable, and hence membership in $\mathbb{Y}_{b,(\mathbf{s}_i)_{i\in[n]}}$ is efficiently checkable given b and $(\mathbf{s}_i)_{i\in[n]}$, establishing the property 3b.

Lemma 5. *Let $\mathcal{F}$ be the function family (with associated algorithms) as described in the construction, then $\mathcal{F}$ satisfies the property 3c based on the extended LHS assumption.*

Proof. The lemma follows from putting together Lemma 6 (proving hardness of an alternative formulation of the extended LHS assumption), Lemma 7 (which shows a transformation relating claw-based equations to linear equations in $\mathbf{v}_i$), and Lemma 8 (showing hardness of predicting concatenation of any non-trivial parity of $\mathbf{v}_i$ for $i \in [n]$ based on the extended LHS assumption), all of which will be proved subsequently.

Theorem 1. *Let $\mathcal{F}$ be the function family (with associated algorithms) as described in the construction, then $\mathcal{F}$ is a wTCF-IE family based on the extended LHS assumption.*

Proof. We have already established that $\mathcal{F}$ is a wTCF family by putting together Lemma 2, 3, 4, and 5. It follows by inspection that $\mathcal{F}$ also satisfies the independent evaluation property in Definition 7, and hence $\mathcal{F}$ is a wTCF-IE family.

The following lemma establishes the hardness of a different formulation of the extended LHS assumption.

Lemma 6. *If H_0 and H_1 be two distributions defined as follows then $H_0 \overset{c}{\approx} H_1$ based on the extended LHS assumption.*

$$\mathbf{w} \leftarrow \{0,1\}^n, \quad \mathbf{M}_i^{(\beta)} \leftarrow \mathbb{G}^{n\times n}, \quad \mathbf{m}_i^{(\beta)} \leftarrow \mathbb{G}^n,$$
$$\mathbf{x}_i^{(0)} \leftarrow \mathbb{X}^n, \quad \mathbf{t}_i \leftarrow \mathbb{G}^n, \quad \mathbf{u}_i^{(\beta)} \leftarrow \mathbb{X}^n, \quad \mathbf{u'}_i^{(\beta)} \leftarrow \mathbb{X}^n,$$

$$\mathbf{x}_i^{(1)} := \big[\mathbf{M}_i^{(0)}(1 - \mathbf{w}) + \mathbf{M}_i^{(1)}\mathbf{w}\big] \star \mathbf{x}_i^{(0)}, \quad \mathbf{y}_i^{(0)} := \mathbf{t}_i \star \mathbf{x}_i^{(0)},$$

$$\mathbf{y}_i^{(1)} := \big[\mathbf{M}_i^{(0)}(1 - \mathbf{w}) + \mathbf{M}_i^{(1)}\mathbf{w} + \mathbf{m}_i^{(0)} \odot (1 - \mathbf{w}) + \mathbf{m}_i^{(1)} \odot \mathbf{w}\big] \star \mathbf{y}_i^{(0)},$$

$$H_0 := \big(\mathbf{M}_i^{(\beta)}, \mathbf{m}_i^{(\beta)}, \mathbf{x}_i^{(\beta)}, \mathbf{y}_i^{(\beta)}\big)_{i \in [n], \beta \in \{0,1\}}, \quad H_1 := \big(\mathbf{M}_i^{(\beta)}, \mathbf{m}_i^{(\beta)}, \mathbf{u}_i^{(\beta)}, \mathbf{u'}_i^{(\beta)}\big)_{i \in [n], \beta \in \{0,1\}},$$

Proof. Given a challenge of the form

$$H' = \big(\mathbf{M}_i, \mathbf{m}_i, \mathbf{x}_i^{(\beta)}, \mathbf{y}_i^{(\beta)}\big)_{i \in [n], \beta \in \{0,1\}},$$

the reduction samples two matrices $\mathbf{M}_i^{(0)}$ and $\mathbf{M}_i^{(1)}$ and two vectors $\mathbf{m}_i^{(0)}$ and $\mathbf{m}_i^{(1)}$ uniformly *conditioned* on

$$\mathbf{M}_i = \mathbf{M}_i^{(1)} - \mathbf{M}_i^{(0)}, \quad \mathbf{m}_i = \mathbf{m}_i^{(1)} - \mathbf{m}_i^{(0)}.$$

It then sets

$$\bar{\mathbf{x}}_i^{(0)} := \mathbf{x}_i^{(0)}, \qquad\qquad \bar{\mathbf{y}}_i^{(0)} := \mathbf{y}_i^{(0)},$$

$$\bar{\mathbf{x}}_i^{(1)} := \mathbf{M}_i^{(0)}\mathbf{1} \star \mathbf{x}_i^{(0)}, \qquad\qquad \bar{\mathbf{y}}_i^{(1)} := \big[\mathbf{M}_i^{(0)}\mathbf{1} + \mathbf{m}_i^{(0)} \odot \mathbf{1}\big] \star \mathbf{y}_i^{(0)},$$

and outputs the following tuple

$$\big(\mathbf{M}_i^{(\beta)}, \mathbf{m}_i^{(\beta)}, \bar{\mathbf{x}}_i^{(\beta)}, \bar{\mathbf{y}}_i^{(\beta)}\big)_{i \in [n], \beta \in \{0,1\}}.$$

Observe that in the tuple above $\mathbf{M}_i^{(\beta)}, \mathbf{m}_i^{(\beta)}$ are distributed uniformly for $i \in [n]$ and $\beta \in \{0,1\}$. If H' corresponds to extended LHS samples, a routine calculation shows that the tuple above is distributed as H_0. On the other hand, if H' corresponds to truly random samples then the tuple above would be distributed as H_1. Therefore, based on the extended LHS assumption it follows that H_0 is indistinguishable from H_1.

Lemma 7. *Let* $\mathsf{ek} = \big(\mathbf{M}_i^{(\beta)}, \mathbf{m}_i^{(\beta)}, \mathbf{x}_i^{(\beta)}, \mathbf{y}_i^{(\beta)}\big)_{i \in [n], \beta \in \{0,1\}}$ *be a tuple distributed as in the construction, i.e.,*

$$\mathbf{v}_i \leftarrow \{0,1\}^n, \quad \mathbf{M}_i^{(\beta)} \leftarrow \mathbb{G}^{n \times n}, \quad \mathbf{m}_i^{(\beta)} \leftarrow \mathbb{G}^n, \quad \mathbf{x}_i^{(0)} \leftarrow \mathbb{X}^n, \quad \mathbf{t}_i \leftarrow \mathbb{G}^n,$$

$$\mathbf{x}_i^{(1)} := \big[\mathbf{M}_i^{(0)}(1 - \mathbf{v}_i) + \mathbf{M}_i^{(1)}\mathbf{v}_i\big] \star \mathbf{x}_i^{(0)}, \quad \mathbf{y}_i^{(0)} := \mathbf{t}_i \star \mathbf{x}_i^{(0)},$$

$$\mathbf{y}_i^{(1)} := \big[\mathbf{M}_i^{(0)}(1 - \mathbf{v}_i) + \mathbf{M}_i^{(1)}\mathbf{v}_i + \mathbf{m}_i^{(0)} \odot (1 - \mathbf{v}_i) + \mathbf{m}_i^{(1)} \odot \mathbf{v}_i\big] \star \mathbf{y}_i^{(0)},$$

and let W_{ek} *be the set defined in the property 3c with respect to the construction of wTCF family, i.e.,*

$$W_{\mathsf{ek}} = \Big\{ \big(b, (\mathbf{s}_i^{(b)})_{i \in [n]}, \mathbf{d}, (\langle \mathbf{d}_i, \mathsf{B}_i((\mathbf{s}_i^{(0)})_{i \in [n]}) \rangle \oplus \mathsf{B}_i((\mathbf{s}_i^{(1)})_{i \in [n]}) \rangle)_{i \in [n]} \big) \Big|$$

$$b \in \{0,1\}, \big((\mathbf{s}_i^{(0)})_{i \in [n]}, (\mathbf{s}_i^{(1)})_{i \in [n]}\big) \in R_{\mathsf{ek}}, \mathbf{d} \in \mathbb{Y}_{0,(\mathbf{s}_i^{(0)})_{i \in [n]}} \cap \mathbb{Y}_{1,(\mathbf{s}_i^{(1)})_{i \in [n]}} \Big\},$$

where B, R_{ek}, *and* $\mathbb{Y}_{b,(\mathbf{s}_i)_{i\in[n]}}$ *are defined in the proof of Lemma 4. If there is an attacker* $\mathcal{A}$ *such that*

$$\Pr[\mathcal{A}(\mathsf{ek}) \in W_{\mathsf{ek}}] = \varepsilon,$$

then there is an attacker $\mathcal{A}'$ *such that*

$$\Pr\left[\mathcal{A}'(\mathsf{ek}) \to (\mathbf{d}'_i \neq 0^n, \langle \mathbf{d}'_i, \mathbf{v}_i \rangle)_{i\in[n]}\right] \geq \varepsilon.$$

Proof. Let the following tuple

$$\gamma := \left(b, \left(\mathbf{s}_i^{(b)}\right)_{i\in[n]}, \mathbf{d}, (c_i)_{i\in[n]}\right),$$

be the output $\mathcal{A}$ on ek. We are going to argue that if $\gamma \in W_{\mathsf{ek}}$ and $\mathbf{d}'_i$ is computed as $\mathbf{d}'_i = \mathsf{T}_{b,\mathbf{s}_i^{(b)}}(\mathbf{d}_i)$ for $i \in [n]$, then $c_i = \langle \mathbf{d}'_i, \mathbf{v}_i \rangle$ for all $i \in [n]$, where T is the transformation defined in the proof of Lemma 4. Observe that since

$$\mathbf{d} \in \mathbb{Y}_{0,(\mathbf{s}_i^{(0)})_{i\in[n]}} \cap \mathbb{Y}_{1,(\mathbf{s}_i^{(1)})_{i\in[n]}} \subseteq \mathbb{Y}_{b,(\mathbf{s}_i^{(b)})_{i\in[n]}},$$

it follows from the definition of these sets (in the proof of Lemma 4) that for each $i \in [n]$ we have $\mathbf{d}'_i \neq 0^n$. Furthermore, relying again on the proof of Lemma 4 we have

$$\left((\mathbf{s}_i^{(0)})_{i\in[n]}, (\mathbf{s}_i^{(1)})_{i\in[n]}\right) \in R_{\mathsf{ek}} \implies (\mathbf{s}_i^{(0)})_{i\in[n]} = (\mathbf{s}_i^{(1)} + \mathbf{v}_i)_{i\in[n]} \implies$$

$$\mathsf{B}\left((\mathbf{s}_i^{(0)})_{i\in[n]}\right) \oplus \mathsf{B}\left((\mathbf{s}_i^{(1)})_{i\in[n]}\right) = \mathsf{B}\left((\mathbf{s}_i^{(b)})_{i\in[n]}\right) \oplus \mathsf{B}\left((\mathbf{s}_i^{(1-b)} - (-1)^b \mathbf{v}_i)_{i\in[n]}\right).$$

Let $d'_{i,j}$, $s_{i,j}^{(b)}$, and $v_{i,j}$ be the jth component of $\mathbf{d}'_i$, $\mathbf{s}_i^{(b)}$, and $\mathbf{v}_i$, respectively. Let $\mathbf{d}_{i,j} \in \{0,1\}^{\lceil \log B \rceil}$ be the jth $\lceil \log B \rceil$-bit chunk of $\mathbf{d}_i$. By definition of T and $\bar{\mathsf{B}}$ from the proof of Lemma 4, it follows that for any $i \in [n]$ we have

$$
\begin{aligned}
c_i &= \sum_{j=1}^{n} \langle \mathbf{d}_{i,j}, (\bar{\mathsf{B}}(s_{i,j}^{(b)}) \oplus \bar{\mathsf{B}}(s_{i,j}^{(b)} - (-1)^b v_{i,j})) \rangle \\
&= \sum_{j=1}^{n} v_{i,j} \langle \mathbf{d}_{i,j}, (\bar{\mathsf{B}}(s_{i,j}^{(b)}) \oplus \bar{\mathsf{B}}(s_{i,j}^{(b)} - (-1)^b)) \rangle \\
&= \sum_{j=1}^{n} v_{i,j} d'_j = \langle \mathbf{d}'_i, \mathbf{v}_i \rangle,
\end{aligned}
$$

where the second line follows from the fact that $v_{i,j} \in \{0,1\}$ and the last line follows from the definition of T. Note that any computation inside $\bar{\mathsf{B}}$ is done over $\mathbb{Z}$, while any other computation (including the overall summation) is performed over $\mathbb{F}_2$.

Viewing any evaluation key ek as a (one-way) function of $(\mathbf{v}_i)_{i\in[n]}$ in the construction, the following lemma establishes that any QPT adversary cannot predict a string obtained by concatenating *any* non-trivial parity of $\mathbf{v}_i$ for $i \in [n]$.

Lemma 8. *If* ek $= \left(\mathbf{M}_i^{(\beta)}, \mathbf{m}_i^{(\beta)}, \mathbf{x}_i^{(\beta)}, \mathbf{y}_i^{(\beta)}\right)_{i \in [n], \beta \in \{0,1\}}$ *be a tuple distributed as in the construction, i.e.,*

$$\mathbf{v}_i \leftarrow \{0,1\}^n, \quad \mathbf{M}_i^{(\beta)} \leftarrow \mathbb{G}^{n \times n}, \quad \mathbf{m}_i^{(\beta)} \leftarrow \mathbb{G}^n, \quad \mathbf{x}_i^{(0)} \leftarrow \mathbb{X}^n, \quad \mathbf{t}_i \leftarrow \mathbb{G}^n,$$

$$\mathbf{x}_i^{(1)} := \left[\mathbf{M}_i^{(0)}(1 - \mathbf{v}_i) + \mathbf{M}_i^{(1)}\mathbf{v}_i\right] \star \mathbf{x}_i^{(0)}, \quad \mathbf{y}_i^{(0)} := \mathbf{t}_i \star \mathbf{x}_i^{(0)},$$
$$\mathbf{y}_i^{(1)} := \left[\mathbf{M}_i^{(0)}(1 - \mathbf{v}_i) + \mathbf{M}_i^{(1)}\mathbf{v}_i + \mathbf{m}_i^{(0)} \odot (1 - \mathbf{v}_i) + \mathbf{m}_i^{(1)} \odot \mathbf{v}_i\right] \star \mathbf{y}_i^{(0)},$$

then for any QPT adversary $\mathcal{A}$ we have

$$\Pr\left[\mathcal{A}(\text{ek}) \to (\mathbf{d}_i' \neq 0^n, \langle \mathbf{d}_i', \mathbf{v}_i \rangle)_{i \in [n]}\right] \leq \text{negl},$$

where the probability is taken over randomness of ek *and $\mathcal{A}$, and the inner product is computed over $\mathbb{F}_2$.*

Proof. Consider the following two hybrids H_0 and H_1 defined as

$$\mathbf{w} \leftarrow \{0,1\}^n, \quad \mathbf{M}_i^{(\beta)} \leftarrow \mathbb{G}^{n \times n}, \quad \mathbf{m}_i^{(\beta)} \leftarrow \mathbb{G}^n, \quad \mathbf{x}_i^{(0)} \leftarrow \mathbb{X}^n, \quad \mathbf{t}_i \leftarrow \mathbb{G}^n,$$

$$\mathbf{x}_i^{(1)} := \left[\mathbf{M}_i^{(0)}(1 - \mathbf{w}) + \mathbf{M}_i^{(1)}\mathbf{w}\right] \star \mathbf{x}_i^{(0)}, \quad \mathbf{y}_i^{(0)} := \mathbf{t}_i \star \mathbf{x}_i^{(0)},$$
$$\mathbf{y}_i^{(1)} := \left[\mathbf{M}_i^{(0)}(1 - \mathbf{w}) + \mathbf{M}_i^{(1)}\mathbf{w} + \mathbf{m}_i^{(0)} \odot (1 - \mathbf{w}) + \mathbf{m}_i^{(1)} \odot \mathbf{w}\right] \star \mathbf{y}_i^{(0)},$$

$$H_0 := (\mathbf{M}_i^{(\beta)}, \mathbf{m}_i^{(\beta)}, \mathbf{x}_i^{(\beta)}, \mathbf{y}_i^{(\beta)})_{i \in [n], \beta \in \{0,1\}}, \quad H_1 := (\mathbf{M}_i^{(\beta)}, \mathbf{m}_i^{(\beta)}, \mathbf{u}_i^{(\beta)}, \mathbf{u'}_i^{(\beta)})_{i \in [n], \beta \in \{0,1\}},$$

where $\mathbf{u}_i^{(\beta)} \leftarrow \mathbb{X}^n$ and $\mathbf{u'}_i^{(\beta)} \leftarrow \mathbb{X}^n$ for $i \in [n]$ and $\beta \in \{0,1\}$. Note that H_0 does *not* correspond to the distribution of a "real" evaluation key, as H_0 incorporates a *single* vector $\mathbf{w} \in \{0,1\}^n$ across different samples. We show that given any adversary with a non-negligible advantage in outputting concatenation of adaptive hardcore bits, one construct another adversary that can distinguish between H_0 and H_1 with a non-negligible advantage. By Lemma 6, we know that H_0 is computationally distinguishable from H_1 and hence the statement of the lemma follows.

For any vector $\mathbf{r} \in \{0,1\}^n$, let $\pi_\mathbf{r}$ be a simple mapping that takes two n by n matrices $\mathbf{M}^{(0)}$ and $\mathbf{M}^{(1)}$, and for each $i \in [n]$ it *swaps* the ith column of $\mathbf{M}^{(0)}$ and $\mathbf{M}^{(1)}$ if $r_i = 1$. As two simple examples, we have

$$\pi_{0^n}\left(\mathbf{M}^{(0)}, \mathbf{M}^{(1)}\right) = \left(\mathbf{M}^{(0)}, \mathbf{M}^{(1)}\right), \quad \pi_{1^n}\left(\mathbf{M}^{(0)}, \mathbf{M}^{(1)}\right) = \left(\mathbf{M}^{(1)}, \mathbf{M}^{(0)}\right).$$

As a simple special case, we also use the notation $\pi_\mathbf{r}(\mathbf{m}^{(0)}, \mathbf{m}^{(1)})$ to denote swapping components of two vectors $\mathbf{m}^{(0)}$ and $\mathbf{m}^{(1)}$ with respect to $\mathbf{r}$. Let the following

$$\left(\mathbf{M}_i^{(0)}, \mathbf{M}_i^{(1)}, \mathbf{m}_i^{(0)}, \mathbf{m}_i^{(1)}, \mathbf{x}_i^{(\beta)}, \mathbf{y}_i^{(\beta)}\right)_{i \in [n], \beta \in \{0,1\}}$$

be a tuple that is distributed as H_0 (with a slight reformatting). For any n binary vectors $\mathbf{r}_i \in \{0,1\}^n$, set

$$\left(\mathbf{M'}_i^{(0)}, \mathbf{M'}_i^{(1)}\right) := \pi_{\mathbf{r}_i}\left(\mathbf{M}_i^{(0)}, \mathbf{M}_i^{(1)}\right), \qquad \left(\mathbf{m'}_i^{(0)}, \mathbf{m'}_i^{(1)}\right) := \pi_{\mathbf{r}_i}\left(\mathbf{m}_i^{(0)}, \mathbf{m}_i^{(1)}\right),$$

and observe that the tuple

$$H_0' := \left(\mathbf{M'}_i^{(0)}, \mathbf{M'}_i^{(1)}, \mathbf{m'}_i^{(0)}, \mathbf{m'}_i^{(1)}, \mathbf{x}_i^{(\beta)}, \mathbf{y}_i^{(\beta)}\right)_{i \in [n], \beta \in \{0,1\}}$$

is distributed as follows:

$$\mathbf{x}_i^{(1)} := \left[\mathbf{M'}_i^{(0)}(1 - (\mathbf{w} \oplus \mathbf{r}_i)) + \mathbf{M'}_i^{(1)}(\mathbf{w} \oplus \mathbf{r}_i)\right] \star \mathbf{x}_i^{(0)},$$

$$\mathbf{y}_i^{(1)} := \left[\mathbf{M'}_i^{(0)}(1 - (\mathbf{w} \oplus \mathbf{r}_i)) + \mathbf{M'}_i^{(1)}(\mathbf{w} \oplus \mathbf{r}_i) + \mathbf{m'}_i^{(0)} \odot (1 - (\mathbf{w} \oplus \mathbf{r}_i)) + \mathbf{m'}_i^{(1)} \odot (\mathbf{w} \oplus \mathbf{r}_i)\right] \star \mathbf{y}_i^{(0)}.$$

Now if we sample each $\mathbf{r}_i$ randomly, it is not hard to see that H_0' is *statistically* indistinguishable from an honestly generated evaluation ek as defined in the lemma. Thus, there is an efficient randomized procedure $\mathcal{P}$ that maps an instance of H_0 to an honestly generated ek. Furthermore, applying the same procedure $\mathcal{P}$ would still map an instance of H_1 to an instance of H_1.

Let H_b (for some challenge $b \in \{0,1\}$) be a challenge tuple of the form

$$\left(\mathbf{M}_i^{(0)}, \mathbf{M}_i^{(1)}, \mathbf{m}_i^{(0)}, \mathbf{m}_i^{(1)}, \mathbf{x}_i^{(\beta)}, \mathbf{y}_i^{(\beta)}\right)_{i \in [n], \beta \in \{0,1\}},$$

and let $\mathcal{A}$ be an attacker that outputs concatenation of adaptive hardcore bits. We construct an adversary $\mathcal{A}'$ that distinguishes H_0 and H_1. First, $\mathcal{A}'$ samples n random vector $\mathbf{r}_i \leftarrow \{0,1\}^n$ and sets

$$\left(\mathbf{M'}_i^{(0)}, \mathbf{M'}_i^{(1)}\right) := \pi_{\mathbf{r}_i}\left(\mathbf{M}_i^{(0)}, \mathbf{M}_i^{(1)}\right), \qquad \left(\mathbf{m'}_i^{(0)}, \mathbf{m'}_i^{(1)}\right) := \pi_{\mathbf{r}_i}\left(\mathbf{m}_i^{(0)}, \mathbf{m}_i^{(1)}\right).$$

It then runs $\mathcal{A}$ on $\bar{\text{ek}}$ where

$$\bar{\text{ek}} = \left(\mathbf{M'}_i^{(0)}, \mathbf{M'}_i^{(1)}, \mathbf{m'}_i^{(0)}, \mathbf{m'}_i^{(1)}, \mathbf{x}_i^{(\beta)}, \mathbf{y}_i^{(\beta)}\right)_{i \in [n], \beta \in \{0,1\}}.$$

Let $(\mathbf{d}_i', c_i)_{i \in [n]}$ be the output of $\mathcal{A}(\bar{\text{ek}})$. In the next step $\mathcal{A}'$ proceeds as follows:

$\mathcal{A}'$ computes $c_i' = \langle \mathbf{d}_i', \mathbf{r}_i \rangle \oplus c_i$ for $i \in [n]$. Let $\mathbf{D}' \in \{0,1\}^{n \times n}$ be a matrix whose rows are $\mathbf{d}_i'$.

- <u>Case 1:</u> If $(\mathbf{d}_i')_{i \in [n]}$ are linearly independent vectors, $\mathcal{A}'$ computes $\mathbf{w}' = \mathbf{D'}^{-1}\mathbf{c}'$, where operations are performed over $\mathbb{F}_2$. If the following holds, $\mathcal{A}'$ outputs 0. Otherwise it outputs a random bit b'.

$$\mathbf{x}_1^{(1)} = \left[\mathbf{M}_1^{(0)}(1 - \mathbf{w}') + \mathbf{M}_1^{(1)}\mathbf{w}'\right] \star \mathbf{x}_1^{(0)}.$$

- <u>Case 2:</u> There is a minimal index $n' > 1$ and $n' - 1$ bits $(\alpha_1, \ldots, \alpha_{n'-1})$ such that $\mathbf{d}_{n'}' = \sum_{i=1}^{n'-1} \alpha_i \mathbf{d}_i'$. If the following holds, $\mathcal{A}'$ outputs 0. Otherwise, it outputs a random bit b'.

$$c_{n'}' = \sum_{i=1}^{n'-1} \alpha_i c_i'.$$

We now analyze the advantage of $\mathcal{A}'$ in distinguishing H_0 and H_1.

- H_b is distributed as H_0: Since $\mathcal{A}'$ maps an instance of H_0 to a tuple that is statistically indistinguishable from an honestly generated evaluation key, it follows that if ε be the advantage of $\mathcal{A}$, then

$$\Pr\left[\mathcal{A}(\bar{\mathrm{ek}}) \to \left(\mathbf{d}_i' \neq 0^n, \langle \mathbf{d}_i', \mathbf{w} \oplus \mathbf{r}_i \rangle\right)_{i \in [n]}\right] = \varepsilon,$$

and hence with probability ε we have

$$c_i' = \langle \mathbf{d}_i', \mathbf{r}_i \rangle \oplus c_i = \langle \mathbf{d}_i', \mathbf{r}_i \rangle \oplus \langle \mathbf{d}_i', \mathbf{w} \oplus \mathbf{r}_i \rangle = \langle \mathbf{d}_i', \mathbf{w} \rangle, \quad \forall i \in [n].$$

Furthermore, it is easy to see that conditioned on the event that $\mathcal{A}$ succeeds, $\mathcal{A}'$ outputs 0. This follows immediately by observing that in case 1, $\mathcal{A}'$ recovers $\mathbf{w}$, and in case 2

$$c_{n'}' = \langle \mathbf{d}_{n'}', \mathbf{w} \rangle = \langle \sum_{i=1}^{n'-1} \alpha_i \mathbf{d}_i', \mathbf{w} \rangle = \sum_{i=1}^{n'-1} \alpha_i \langle \mathbf{d}_i', \mathbf{w} \rangle = \sum_{i=1}^{n'-1} \alpha_i c_i'.$$

Therefore, it holds that

$$\Pr[\mathcal{A}'(H_0) = 0] \geq \varepsilon + (1 - \varepsilon) \cdot \Pr[b' = 0] = (1 + \varepsilon)/2.$$

- H_b is distributed as H_1: Although $\mathcal{A}'$ maps a truly random instance (i.e., H_1) to a truly random instance, we can still argue that $\mathcal{A}'$ outputs 0 with probability negligibly close to $1/2$. First, observe that the vectors $(\mathbf{r}_i)_{i \in [n]}$ are information-theoretically hidden from the view of $\mathcal{A}$. Thus, conditioned on the event that case 2 happens we have

$$\Pr\left[c_{n'}' = \sum_{i=1}^{n'-1} \alpha_i c_i'\right] = \Pr\left[\underbrace{\langle \mathbf{d}_{n'}', \mathbf{r}_{n'} \rangle \oplus c_{n'}}_{\sigma_L} = \underbrace{\sum_{i=1}^{n'-1} \alpha_i \cdot \left(\langle \mathbf{d}_i', \mathbf{r}_i \rangle \oplus c_i\right)}_{\sigma_R}\right].$$

Because $\mathbf{d}_i' \neq 0^n$ (for all $i \in [n]$) and there exists at least one index i^* such that $\alpha_{i^*} \neq 0$, it follows that the left-hand side (σ_L) and the right-hand side (σ_R) are distributed independently from each other, and hence we have

$$\Pr\left[c_{n'}' = \sum_{i=1}^{n'-1} \alpha_i c_i'\right] = 1/2.$$

A similar argument implies that conditioned on the event that case 1 happens, $\mathcal{A}'$ outputs 0 with probability $1/2 + \mathrm{negl}$. Therefore, it holds that

$$\Pr[\mathcal{A}'(H_0) = 0] \leq 1/2 + \mathrm{negl},$$

and hence the advantage of $\mathcal{A}'$ in distinguishing H_0 and H_1 is at least $\varepsilon/2 - \mathrm{negl}$, as required.

5   Computational Test of Qubit

We show that our wTCF can be used to devise a computational test that the prover has a qubit. The protocol closely follows the outline of [Vid20], with a few syntactical modifications, due to the usage of wTCFs.

5.1   Definition

We start by recalling the definition of a qubit. We denote $\{A, B\} \equiv AB + BA$ as the *anti-commuter* of two operators A and B, and we say A *anti-commutes* B if $\{A, B\} = 0$.

Definition 9 (Qubit). *A* qubit *is a triple* $(|\psi\rangle, X, Z)$ *such that* $|\psi\rangle$ *is a unit vector on* $\mathcal{H}$ *and* X, Z *are binary observables on* $\mathcal{H}$, *such that*

$$\{X, Z\} |\psi\rangle = 0.$$

As usual in the computational settings, we will be interested in a slightly weaker guarantee, where the above quantity is bounded by a negligible function negl, in which case we say that the tuple $(|\psi\rangle, X, Z)$ is computationally close to a qubit. The following lemma justifies the definition of a qubit, and its proof can be found in [Vid20].

Lemma 9 ([Vid20]). *Let* $(|\psi\rangle, X, Z)$ *be a qubit on* $\mathcal{H}$. *Then there exists a Hilbert space* $\mathcal{H}'$ *and an isometry* $V : \mathcal{H} \to \mathbb{C}^2 \otimes \mathcal{H}'$ *such that:*

$$VX |\psi\rangle = (\sigma_X \otimes \mathsf{Id})V |\psi\rangle \qquad and \qquad VZ = (\sigma_Z \otimes \mathsf{Id})V |\psi\rangle$$

where

$$\sigma_X = \begin{pmatrix} 0 & 1 \\ 1 & 0 \end{pmatrix} \qquad and \qquad \sigma_Z = \begin{pmatrix} 1 & 0 \\ 0 & -1 \end{pmatrix}$$

are the Pauli observables.

5.2   Protocol

Let $\mathcal{F}$ be a wTCF function family. The protocol for a computational test of a qubit is described below.

1. The verifier samples $(\mathsf{ek}, \mathsf{td}) \leftarrow \mathsf{Gen}(1^\lambda)$ and sends ek to the prover.
2. The prover prepares the state

$$\frac{1}{\sqrt{2 \cdot |X^n|}} \sum_{b \in \{0,1\}} \sum_{\mathbf{x}_b \in X^n} |b\rangle |\mathbf{x}_b\rangle |f_{\mathsf{ek},b}(\mathbf{x}_b)\rangle$$

which is efficiently computable since $f_{\mathsf{ek},b}$ is efficiently computable. Then it uncomputes the first register and traces it out to obtain

$$\frac{1}{\sqrt{2 \cdot |X^n|}} \sum_{b \in \{0,1\}} \sum_{\mathbf{x}_b \in X^n} |\mathbf{x}_b\rangle |f_{\mathsf{ek},b}(\mathbf{x}_b)\rangle.$$

Note that this mapping is efficiently computable since, given $\mathbf{x}_b$ and $f_{ek,b}(\mathbf{x}_b)$, the bit b is efficiently computable. The prover then measures the last register in the computational basis to obtain some $y \in Y$. The prover returns y to the verifier.

3. The verifier computes

$$\mathsf{Invert}(\mathsf{td}, 0, y) = \mathbf{x}_0 \quad \text{and} \quad \mathsf{Invert}(\mathsf{td}, 1, y) = \mathbf{x}_1$$

and aborts if $\mathbf{x}_0 \notin \bar{\mathbf{X}}$ and $\mathbf{x}_1 \notin \bar{\mathbf{X}}$. The verifier then selects a uniformly random challenge $c \leftarrow \{0,1\}$ and sends c to the prover.

4. (a) (Preimage test) If $c = 0$, the prover measures the first register in the computational basis to obtain an $\mathbf{x}$, which is sent to the verifier. The verifier accepts if there exists a $b \in \{0,1\}$ such that $f_{ek,b}(\mathbf{x}) = y$.
   (b) (Equation test) If $c = 1$, the prover measures the first register in the Hadamard basis to obtain some $\mathbf{d} = (\mathbf{d}_1, \ldots, \mathbf{d}_n) \in \{0,1\}^{n\ell}$, which is sent to the verifier. Let $(\mathbf{x}_0, \mathbf{x}_1)$ be the vectors defined in the previous step, and B is defined in Definition 5. The verifier accepts if

$$\mathbf{d} \in \mathbb{Y}_{0,\mathbf{x}_0} \cap \mathbb{Y}_{1,\mathbf{x}_1} \qquad \text{and} \qquad \bigoplus_{i=1}^{n} \langle \mathbf{d}_i, \mathsf{B}_i(\mathbf{x}_0) \oplus \mathsf{B}_i(\mathbf{x}_1) \rangle = 0.$$

5.3   Analysis

First, we argue that the protocol is correct, i.e., the honest prover passes the tests with probability $1 - n^{-c}$, for some constant c. Observe that the verifier accepts at step 3 if $\mathbf{x}_0 \in \bar{\mathbf{X}}$ or $\mathbf{x}_1 \in \bar{\mathbf{X}}$. Since $\bar{\mathbf{X}}$ is a dense subset of X^n, it follows that:

- $\mathbf{x}_0 \in \bar{\mathbf{X}}$ or $\mathbf{x}_1 \in \bar{\mathbf{X}}$, and
- $(\mathbf{x}_0, \mathbf{x}_1) \in R_{ek}$

except with inverse polynomial probability. Thus, the verifier rejects y with probability at most inverse polynomial. Conditioning on the verifier accepting in step 3, we have that the state of the prover equals

$$\frac{1}{\sqrt{2}} \left(|\mathbf{x}_0\rangle + |\mathbf{x}_1\rangle \right) |y\rangle$$

where $(\mathbf{x}_0, \mathbf{x}_1)$ are the pre-images of y under $f_{ek,0}$ and $f_{ek,1}$, respectively. On the one hand, measuring the first register in the computational basis returns a random pre-image of y, which allows the prover to pass the pre-image test with probability one, on the other hand, measuring the register in the Hadamard basis, returns a random vector orthogonal to $\mathsf{B}(\mathbf{x}_0) \oplus \mathsf{B}(\mathbf{x}_1)$, where B is the bit-decomposition operator. By definition, we have that

$$\langle \mathbf{d}, \mathsf{B}(\mathbf{x}_0) \oplus \mathsf{B}(\mathbf{x}_1) \rangle = \bigoplus_{i=1}^{n} \langle \mathbf{d}_i, \mathsf{B}_i(\mathbf{x}_0) \oplus \mathsf{B}_i(\mathbf{x}_1) \rangle = 0.$$

Furthermore, $\mathbf{d}$ belongs to the set $\mathbb{Y}_{0,\mathbf{x}_0} \cap \mathbb{Y}_{1,\mathbf{x}_1}$ with overwhelming probability. Thus the prover passes the equation test with probability negligibly close to one.

Next, we argue that the prover's state contains a qubit assuming that $\mathcal{F}$ is a wTCF family satisfying the adaptive hardcore bit property. The argument is essentially identical to the one shown in [Vid20] with minor syntactical modifications and we report it here only for completeness.

Theorem 2. *Let $\mathcal{F}$ be a wTCF family that satisfies the adaptive hardcore bit property. Let $|\psi\rangle$ be the state of a prover (after step 2) that succeeds with probability negligibly close to one. Then there exist two binary observables X and Z, such that $(|\psi\rangle, X, Z)$ is computationally close to a qubit. In particular, assuming the Conjecture 2, the protocol can be instantiated based on the extended LHS assumption.*

Proof. Let $|\psi\rangle$ be the state of the prover after sending the y to the verifier. We assume without loss of generality that $|\psi\rangle$ is a pure bipartite state on $\mathcal{H}_\mathsf{P} \otimes \mathcal{H}_\mathsf{M}$, where the register P keeps the internal state of the prover. We also assume without loss of generality that the answer for $c = 0$ is obtained by measuring M on the computational basis. On the other hand, we also assume that the answer for $c = 1$ is obtained by computing $U|\psi\rangle$, for some unitary U, and measuring the resulting register M in the Hadamard basis. Next, we define the observables X and Z as

$$Z = \sum_{\mathbf{x} \in X^n} (-1)^{z_{\mathsf{ek},y}(\mathbf{x})} |\mathbf{x}\rangle\langle\mathbf{x}| \otimes \mathsf{Id}_\mathsf{P}$$

and

$$X = \sum_{\mathbf{d} \in \mathbb{Y}_{0,\mathbf{x}_0} \cap \mathbb{Y}_{1,\mathbf{x}_1}} (-1)^{x_{\mathsf{ek},y}(\mathbf{d})} U^\dagger (H_\mathsf{M}^{\otimes n\ell} \otimes \mathsf{Id}_\mathsf{P})^\dagger (|\mathbf{d}\rangle\langle\mathbf{d}|_\mathsf{M} \otimes \mathsf{Id}_\mathsf{P})(H_\mathsf{M}^{\otimes n\ell} \otimes \mathsf{Id}_\mathsf{P})U$$

where the predicate $z_{\mathsf{ek},y}(\mathbf{x})$ labels as 0 the pre-image of y under $f_{\mathsf{ek},0}$ and as 1 the pre-image of y under $f_{\mathsf{ek},1}$ (other vectors are labeled arbitrarily). On the other hand, the predicate $x_{\mathsf{ek},y}(\mathbf{d})$ labels as 0 the $\mathbf{d}$ such that $\langle \mathbf{d}, \mathsf{B}(\mathbf{x}_0) \oplus \mathsf{B}(\mathbf{x}_1) \rangle = 0$ and as 1 all other vectors. We are now ready to show that $(|\psi\rangle, X, Z)$ is computationally close to a qubit. Let us rewrite

$$\frac{1}{4}\|\{X, Z\}|\psi\rangle\|^2$$

$$= \frac{1}{4}\|(XZ + ZX)|\psi\rangle\|^2$$

$$= \frac{1}{4}\langle\psi|(XZ + ZX)^\dagger(XZ + ZX)|\psi\rangle$$

$$= \frac{1}{4}\langle\psi|(XZ + ZX)^2|\psi\rangle$$

$$= \frac{1}{2}(\langle\psi|(XZ_0XZ_0)|\psi\rangle + \langle\psi|(XZ_1XZ_1)|\psi\rangle + \langle\psi|(Z_0XZ_0X)|\psi\rangle + \langle\psi|(Z_1XZ_1X)|\psi\rangle)$$

$$= \langle\psi|(Z_0XZ_0)|\psi\rangle + \langle\psi|(Z_1XZ_1)|\psi\rangle + \mathrm{negl}$$

where the third equality uses that $(XZ + ZX)$ is Hermitian, the fourth equality follows from Lemma 10, and the last equality follows since we assume the prover to succeed with probability close to 1 and this $|\psi\rangle$ is negligibly close to an eigenstate of X with eigenvalue $+1$.

To complete the proof, we, therefore, need to show that the quantities $\langle\psi|\,(Z_0 X Z_0)\,|\psi\rangle$ and $\langle\psi|\,(Z_1 X Z_1)\,|\psi\rangle$ are negligible. We show this for the first term and the second case follows by symmetry. The proof consists of a reduction against the adaptive hardcore bit of property of $\mathcal{F}$: The reduction receives the key ek for the challenger and internally runs the prover to obtain the state $|\psi\rangle$ then it measures the register M in the computational basis to obtain some $\mathbf{x}$. If $\mathbf{x}$ is a pre-image of 1, then the reduction returns a $(\mathbf{x}, \mathbf{d})$, for a randomly sampled $\mathbf{d}$. Else, it applies the unitary U to $|\psi\rangle$ and measures the register M in the Hadamard basis to obtain $\mathbf{d}$. It returns $(\mathbf{x}, \mathbf{d})$.

In the former case ($\mathbf{x}$ being a pre-image of 1), we can lower bound the success probability of the reduction to be negligibly close to $1/2 \langle\psi|\, Z_1\,|\psi\rangle$, since the prover is assumed to succeed with probability close to 1 and thus the post-measurement state is close to $Z_1 |\psi\rangle$. Analogously, in the latter case ($\mathbf{x}$ being a pre-image of 0), the success probability of the reduction is negligibly close to

$$\langle\psi|\, Z_0 X_0 Z_0\,|\psi\rangle = 1/2(\langle\psi|\, Z_0\,|\psi\rangle + \langle\psi|\, Z_0 X Z_0\,|\psi\rangle).$$

Overall, the success probability of the reduction is $1/2 + 1/2 \langle\psi|\, Z_0 X Z_0\,|\psi\rangle$. We can conclude that the second summand is negligible unless the reduction can break the adaptive hardcore bit property with a non-negligible probability. "In particular" part of theorem follows from Theorem 1.

To complete the proof, we need the following Lemma, which follows in verbatim from [Vid20].

Lemma 10. *Let X and Z be binary observables, then*

$$\frac{1}{2}(XZ + ZX)^2 = X Z_0 X Z_0 + X Z_1 X Z_1 + Z_0 X Z_0 X + Z_1 X Z_1 X.$$

Proof. Since X and Z are Hermitian and square to identity, we can rewrite

$$(XZ + ZX)^2 = 2\mathsf{Id} + XZXZ + ZXZX.$$

Recall that $Z = Z_0 - Z_1$, and thus we can expand

$$ZXZ = (Z_0 - Z_1)X(Z_0 - Z_1) = Z_0 X Z_0 + Z_1 X Z_1 - Z_0 X Z_1 - Z_1 X Z_0.$$

Using that $Z_0 + Z_1 = \mathsf{Id}$ we have

$$X = \mathsf{Id} X \mathsf{Id} = (Z_0 + Z_1)X(Z_0 + Z_1) = Z_0 X Z_0 + Z_1 X Z_1 + Z_0 X Z_1 + Z_1 X Z_0.$$

Combining the two equations above we obtain that $ZXZ = 2(Z_0 X Z_0 + Z_1 X Z_1) - X$. Plugging this into our first equation we obtain

$$
\begin{aligned}
(XZ + ZX)^2 &= 2\mathsf{Id} + XZXZ + ZXZX \\
&= 2\mathsf{Id} + X(2(Z_0 X Z_0 + Z_1 X Z_1) - X) + (2(Z_0 X Z_0 + Z_1 X Z_1) - X)X \\
&= 2\mathsf{Id} + 2X Z_0 X Z_0 + 2X Z_1 X Z_1 + 2Z_0 X Z_0 X + 2Z_1 X Z_1 X - 2X^2 \\
&= 2(X Z_0 X Z_0 + X Z_1 X Z_1 + Z_0 X Z_0 X + Z_1 X Z_1 X).
\end{aligned}
$$

Proof of Quantumness. We mention that our wTCF can be plugged into the work of [BKVV20][5] to obtain a classically verifiable proof of quantumness (PoQ). While PoQ is a *strictly weaker* goal than the qubit test that we described above, we explicitly mention this application since PoQ only requires the claw-freeness property. In particular, this means that we obtain a protocol for PoQ without the need to invoke Conjecture 2 by relying only on the extended LHS assumption.

References

[AC02] Adcock, M., Cleve, R.: A quantum Goldreich-Levin theorem with cryptographic applications. In: Alt, H., Ferreira, A. (eds.) STACS 2002. LNCS, vol. 2285, pp. 323–334. Springer, Heidelberg (2002). https://doi.org/10.1007/3-540-45841-7_26

[ADMP20] Alamati, N., De Feo, L., Montgomery, H., Patranabis, S.: Cryptographic group actions and applications. In: Moriai, S., Wang, H. (eds.) ASIACRYPT 2020, Part II. LNCS, vol. 12492, pp. 411–439. Springer, Cham (2020). https://doi.org/10.1007/978-3-030-64834-3_14

[BCM+18] Brakerski, Z., Christiano, P., Mahadev, U., Vazirani, U.V., Vidick, T.: A cryptographic test of quantumness and certifiable randomness from a single quantum device. In: Thorup, M. (ed.) 59th FOCS, pp. 320–331. IEEE Computer Society Press, October 2018

[BKV19] Beullens, W., Kleinjung, T., Vercauteren, F.: CSI-FiSh: efficient isogeny based signatures through class group computations. In: Galbraith, S.D., Moriai, S. (eds.) ASIACRYPT 2019, Part I. LNCS, vol. 11921, pp. 227–247. Springer, Cham (2019). https://doi.org/10.1007/978-3-030-34578-5_9

[BKVV20] Brakerski, Z., Koppula, V., Vazirani, U.V., Vidick, T.: Simpler proofs of quantumness. In: Flammia, S.T. (ed.) 15th Conference on the Theory of Quantum Computation, Communication and Cryptography, TQC 2020, Riga, Latvia, 9–12 June 2020. LIPIcs, vol. 158, pp. 8:1–8:14. Schloss Dagstuhl - Leibniz-Zentrum für Informatik (2020)

[BM87] Brent, R.P., McKay, B.D.: Determinants and ranks of random matrices over Z_m. Discret. Math. **66**(1–2), 35–49 (1987)

[BS20] Bonnetain, X., Schrottenloher, A.: Quantum security analysis of CSIDH. In: Canteaut, A., Ishai, Y. (eds.) EUROCRYPT 2020, Part II. LNCS, vol. 12106, pp. 493–522. Springer, Cham (2020). https://doi.org/10.1007/978-3-030-45724-2_17

[CGV22] Coladangelo, A., Goldwasser, S., Vazirani, U.V.: Deniable encryption in a quantum world. In: STOC 2022 (2022, to appear)

[CLM+18] Castryck, W., Lange, T., Martindale, C., Panny, L., Renes, J.: CSIDH: an efficient post-quantum commutative group action. In: Peyrin, T., Galbraith, S. (eds.) ASIACRYPT 2018, Part III. LNCS, vol. 11274, pp. 395–427. Springer, Cham (2018). https://doi.org/10.1007/978-3-030-03332-3_15

---

[5] Note that one needs to explicitly check for the domain membership of the preimages, similar to what is done for the qubit test protocol.

[FGK+10] Freeman, D.M., Goldreich, O., Kiltz, E., Rosen, A., Segev, G.: More constructions of lossy and correlation-secure trapdoor functions. In: Nguyen, P.Q., Pointcheval, D. (eds.) PKC 2010. LNCS, vol. 6056, pp. 279–295. Springer, Heidelberg (2010). https://doi.org/10.1007/978-3-642-13013-7_17

[GNW11] Goldreich, O., Nisan, N., Wigderson, A.: On Yao's XOR-Lemma. In: Goldreich, O. (ed.) Studies in Complexity and Cryptography. Miscellanea on the Interplay between Randomness and Computation. LNCS, vol. 6650, pp. 273–301. Springer, Heidelberg (2011). https://doi.org/10.1007/978-3-642-22670-0_23

[GSV18] Grinberg, A., Shaltiel, R., Viola, E.: Indistinguishability by adaptive procedures with advice, and lower bounds on hardness amplification proofs. In: Thorup, M. (ed.) 59th FOCS, pp. 956–966. IEEE Computer Society Press, October 2018

[GV19] Gheorghiu, A., Vidick, T.: Computationally-secure and composable remote state preparation. In: Zuckerman, D. (ed.) 60th FOCS, pp. 1024–1033. IEEE Computer Society Press, November 2019

[KCVY21] Kahanamoku-Meyer, G.D., Choi, S., Vazirani, U.V., Yao, N.Y.: Classically-verifiable quantum advantage from a computational bell test (2021)

[Mah18a] Mahadev, U.: Classical homomorphic encryption for quantum circuits. In: Thorup, M. (ed.) 59th FOCS, pp. 332–338. IEEE Computer Society Press, October 2018

[Mah18b] Mahadev, U.: Classical verification of quantum computations. In: Thorup, M. (ed.) 59th FOCS, pp. 259–267. IEEE Computer Society Press, October 2018

[NC02] Nielsen, M.A., Chuang, I.: Quantum computation and quantum information (2002)

[Pei20] Peikert, C.: He gives C-Sieves on the CSIDH. In: Canteaut, A., Ishai, Y. (eds.) EUROCRYPT 2020, Part II. LNCS, vol. 12106, pp. 463–492. Springer, Cham (2020). https://doi.org/10.1007/978-3-030-45724-2_16

[Vid20] Vidick, T.: Course FSMP, Fall'20: interactions with quantum devices (2020). http://users.cms.caltech.edu/~vidick/teaching/fsmp/fsmp.pdf

Collusion Resistant Copy-Protection for Watermarkable Functionalities

Jiahui Liu[1], Qipeng Liu[2(✉)], Luowen Qian[3], and Mark Zhandry[4]

[1] University of Texas at Austin, Austin, USA
jiahui@cs.utexas.edu
[2] Simons Institute for the Theory of Computing, Berkeley, USA
qipengliu0@gmail.com
[3] Boston University, Boston, USA
luowenq@bu.edu
[4] Princeton University and NTT Research, Princeton, USA

Abstract. Copy-protection is the task of encoding a program into a quantum state to prevent illegal duplications. A line of recent works studied copy-protection schemes under "1 → 2 attacks": the adversary receiving one program copy can not produce two valid copies. However, under most circumstances, vendors need to sell more than one copy of a program and still ensure that no duplicates can be generated. In this work, we initiate the study of collusion resistant copy-protection in the plain model. Our results are twofold:

- The feasibility of copy-protecting all watermarkable functionalities is an open question raised by Aaronson et al. (CRYPTO' 21). In the literature, watermarking decryption, digital signature schemes and PRFs have been extensively studied.
  For the first time, we show that digital signature schemes can be copy-protected. Together with the previous work on copy-protection of decryption and PRFs by Coladangelo et al. (CRYPTO' 21), it suggests that many watermarkable functionalities can be copy-protected, partially answering the above open question by Aaronson et al.
- We make all the above schemes (copy-protection of decryption, digital signatures and PRFs) k bounded collusion resistant for any polynomial k, giving the first bounded collusion resistant copy-protection for various functionalities in the plain model.

1 Introduction

The idea of exploiting the quantum no-cloning principle for building cryptography was pioneered by Wiesner. In his seminal work [27], he proposed the notion of quantum banknotes that cannot be counterfeited due to the unclonability of quantum information. This idea has profoundly influenced quantum cryptography, for example, inspiring the famous work on secure quantum key

© The Author(s), under exclusive license to Springer Nature Switzerland AG 2022
E. Kiltz and V. Vaikuntanathan (Eds.): TCC 2022, LNCS 13747, pp. 294–323, 2022.
https://doi.org/10.1007/978-3-031-22318-1_11

exchange [10]. Since all classical information is inherently clonable, unclonable cryptography is only achievable through the power of quantum information.

Aaronson [2] further leveraged the capability of no-cloning to achieve copy-protection. The idea of copy-protection is the following. A software vendor wants to sell a piece of software, abstracted as a classical function f. It prepares a quantum state ρ_f so that anyone with a copy of ρ_f can evaluate f on a polynomial number of inputs. However, no efficient pirate receiving a single copy of ρ_f, could produce two programs that compute f correctly.

The notion above intuitively captures the security of a copy-protection scheme under what we call an "$1 \to 2$ attack": the adversary receives 1 program copy, and attempts to produce 2 copies with the correct functionality. A recent line of works [4,6,13,14] achieve secure copy-protection for various functionalities under $1 \to 2$ attacks.

However, such a security notion is extremely limiting: in most circumstances, we cannot expect the software vendor to issue only one copy of the program. When the vendor gives out multiple copies, all users can collude and generate pirate copies together. Therefore, a useful copy-protection scheme should be secure against any "$k \to k + 1$ attack" for any polynomial k. Such security is usually referred to as collusion resistance in the literature.

Prior Works on Copy-Protection. We first recall on a high level how most existing copy-protection schemes work: a copy-protection program consists of a quantum state as an "unclonable token", and a classical part containing an obfuscated program (either as an oracle or the output coming out of some obfuscation functionality). The obfuscated program takes in a token and an input one requests to evaluate on; it verifies the validity of the token and if the verification passes, it outputs the evaluation on the requested input.[1]

Until now, collusion resistant copy-protection has essentially been wide open. The only work that considers issuing more than a single program is Aaronson's original work [2], which is proven to be secure in the $k \to k + r$ setting for $r \geq k$ in some structured quantum oracle model. This is undesirable in two ways: (a) it is unclear whether the scheme allows an adversary to double the copies of programs (Aaronson leaves improving r as a challenging open question), which is not a complete break but still potentially devastating to applications; but more importantly, (b) unlike a classical oracle which could be heuristically instantiated using indistinguishability obfuscation, we do not even know how to heuristically instantiate a quantum oracle. Moreover, we believe that any extension of Aaronson's scheme would very likely still require some obfuscation of quantum circuits, since we have evidence that Haar random states, which is the core of Aaronson's scheme, lack the structure that can be verified by a classical circuit [22].

---

[1] The *general functionality* copy protection schemes in [2,4] and the schemes in [7,13] all satisfy this format. The copy-protection schemes for *point/compute-and-compare functions* in [2,6,11,14] are not necessarily of such a format.

If we turn to the other works constructing copy-protection without using quantum oracles, one naïve idea is to take any such scheme that is $1 \to 2$ secure, and simply generate and hand out multiple copies of ρ_f. It turns out that while this satisfies correctness, they are all trivially broken once two copies are given. This is because they are all based on quantum states that are unclonable for one copy, but trivially clonable as soon as two copies are given.

To get around this issue, another idea is to instead employ a quantum state that already bears a "$(k \to k+1)$-unclonable" property. However, the only known such states are Haar random states and its computationally (or statistically) close neighbors, such as pseudorandom states (or t-designs), which leads us back to the verification issue without a quantum oracle from before.

Therefore, we raise the natural question: *Is collusion resistant copy-protection feasible, either resisting $k \to k+1$ attacks, or without using a quantum oracle? (Ideally both?)*

Copy-Protection in the Plain Model. In this work, we restrict our attention to investigate the question above in the plain model, i.e. we want provably secure protocols without any oracle or heuristics. Unfortunately, it has been known that copy-protection in the plain model even for unlearnable functions is impossible in general [7], and thus we have to further restrict ourselves to construct copy-protection for specific classes of functions that evade the impossibility.

Secure software leasing (SSL) [7] is a weakened notion for copy-protection: in (infinite-term) SSL, the malicious pirate may attempt to make pirate copies as it wants. However, the freeloaders are restricted to running a fixed public quantum circuit on some quantum state produced by the pirate. On the other hand, in copy-protection, the freeloaders are free to execute any quantum circuit that the pirate asks them to. Despite facing the same impossibility as copy-protection, secure software leasing has also been built for various functionalities [4,7,11,14,21].[2]

Especially, [4,21] showed that secure software leasing for watermarkable functions could be obtained from watermarking and public key quantum money in a black-box way. Watermarking [8] is a primitive that embeds a watermark into a program so that any attempt to remove the watermark would destroy the program's functionality. Observing this, Aaronson et al. [4] raised the following open question: *Can all watermarkable functions also be copy-protected in the plain model?*

In this work, we will use the word "major watermarkable functions" to denote (decrypting) public key encryption, (signing) signatures, and (evaluating) PRFs and only focus on copy-protecting those functionalities. Starting from the work by Cohen et al. [12], a line of works [18–20,28,29] focuses on watermarking these three functionalities. Copy-protecting these cryptographic functionalities also has a natural and strong motivation: the ability to evaluate these functions is supposedly private in many circumstances. If owners of a decryption key, signing key, or PRF

---

[2] The formal security definitions for SSL in [4,7,11,14,21] vary slightly from one to another. We will discuss them in Sect. 1.2.

key can share their key with others, it will trigger severe security concerns. Furthermore, copy-protecting a cryptographic function can lead to copy-protecting a software entity of which this cryptographic function is a component.

We observe that collusion resistant secure software leasing for watermarkable functions can be achieved as long as the underlying watermarking scheme and quantum money scheme are both collusion resistant, by looking into the construction in [4,21]. (Bounded) collusion resistant watermarking for PRFs, public-key encryptions, etc. are constructed in the plain model [18,28,29, ...] and quantum money can be made collusion resistant with a digital signature on its serial number [3]. This observation seems to suggest that collusion resistant copy-protection could be a much more challenging goal.

1.1 Our Results

In this work, we (partially) answer all of the questions above. In particular, we show how, in the plain model, to construct collusion resistant copy-protection for (decrypting) public-key encryption, (signing) signatures, and (evaluating) PRFs. Our results, together with the prior work on copy-protection of decryption and PRFs (Coladangelo et al. [13]), show that major watermarkable cryptographic functionalities can be copy-protected against even colluding adversaries, in the plain model. We now explain this in more detail.

Collusion Resistant Unclonable Decryption. Our first result is collusion resistant copy-protection for decryption keys in a public-key encryption scheme. We refer to such copy-protection scheme as *unclonable decryption* by convention, as first proposed by Georgiou and Zhandry [17].

Theorem 1. *Assuming post-quantum subexponentially secure indistinguishability obfuscation and subexponentially secure LWE, there exists k-bounded collusion resistant unclonable decryption for any polynomial k.*

Our collusion resistant unclonable decryption scheme is based on the construction from the prior work of Coladangelo et al. [13] that achieves the same except with only $1 \to 2$ security. Note that while we require subexponential security, these assumptions match those already required in the prior work. In particular, here, we invoke subexponential security only for a compute-and-compare obfuscation scheme with certain properties as our building block. All the reductions in this work are polynomial.

While we do achieve $k \to k+1$ security, a caveat is that we only achieve "k-bounded collusion resistance", by which we mean that we need a preset number of users k to generate the public key. Still, we consider *all* users as potentially malicious and colluding. We note that this is similar to watermarking decryption circuits of public-key encryption schemes, where to the best of our knowledge, unbounded collusion resistance is also unknown [18,28]. Furthermore, it is foreseeable that bounded collusion resistance suffices in certain enterprise use cases where the number of (partially) authorized parties is a priori known and fixed; furthermore, such tokens can be transferred to a new employee irrevocably.

The main challenges are in the anti-piracy security proof. The prior proof idea for $1 \to 2$ anti-piracy does not translate to the $k \to k+1$ setting. We present a new view on security reductions to handle a polynomial number of possibly entangled quantum adversaries, which we will elaborate in the technical overview.

Copy-Protecting Watermarkable Functionalities. We complement the previous theorem regarding public-key encryption, with the following result on collusion resistant copy-protection for signatures and PRFs:

Theorem 2. *Assuming post-quantum subexponentially secure indistinguishability obfuscation and subexponentially secure LWE, there exists k-bounded collusion resistant copy-protection for digital signatures and PRFs, for any polynomial k.*

We base our construction on the signature token scheme and unclonable PRF in the plain model built in [13] (with $1 \to 2$ anti-piracy). However, our signature scheme is significantly different in two aspects: (a) the signing key in [13] will be consumed after one use whereas our scheme is reusable, and (b) unforgeability breaks down when multiple signature queries can be issued, whereas ours satisfies standard existential unforgeability.

1.2 Related Works

[2] first built copy-protection for all unlearnable functions based on a quantum oracle, with weak collusion resistance. Besides [13] which we have discussed, [4] showed a construction for all unlearnable functions based on a classical oracle. [6,14] constructed copy-protection for point functions and compute-and-compare functions in QROM, the latter improving the security of the former.[3]

Regarding the negative results: [7] demonstrated that it is impossible to have a copy-protection scheme for all unlearnable circuits in the plain model, assuming LWE and quantum FHE. [5] extended this impossibility result to the setting where we allow approximate correctness of the copy-protection program and working in the classical-accessible random oracle model.

[7] put forward secure software leasing (SSL). In the finite-term case, a software vendor would lease a quantum state as the software to a user; later, the user needs to return a part of a bipartite state to the vendor, and the vendor will use its own secret key to verify if this returned state is the one issued in the authentic program. The security guarantees that while passing the above verification, the user should not be able to evaluate the functionality correctly using the other part of its bipartite state executed under a public, fixed quantum circuit eval (specified by the vendor). In the infinite-term case, the user does not need to return the state to the vendor; the security guarantees that it should not produce two states that can both evaluate the function correctly when executed

---

[3] All constructions discussed in this section are not proved under collusion resistant security unless otherwise specified.

under eval. [7] also built an (infinite-term) SSL scheme for searchable compute-and-compare circuits under iO and LWE.

[4] observed that under a definition essentially equivalent to infinite-term SSL, namely copy-detection, one could obtain a black-box construction for infinite-term SSL from watermarking and public-key quantum money. [21] constructed finite-term SSL for PRFs and compute-and-compare functions from (subexponential) LWE, with similar observations.

[11,14] constructed secure software leasing for point functions and compute-and-compare functions; [11] is information-theoretically secure and [14] is secure under QROM. They both used a stronger version of finite-term SSL security: while the vendor will honestly check the returned state from the adversary, the adversary can execute the leftover half of its bipartite state maliciously, i.e., not following the instructions in eval. SSL security of this stronger finite-term variant is only known for point/compute-and-compare functions up till now.

1.3 Technical Overview

We start by showing how to overcome the aforementioned barriers and construct Collusion Resistant Unclonable Decryption (CRUD). As briefly discussed in the introduction, there are challenges to constructing collusion resistant copy-protection based on the so-called "$k \rightarrow (k+1)$ no-cloning theorem". Instead, we take a different approach by constructing collusion resistant unclonable decryption CRUD from unclonable decryption UD whose security only holds for "$1 \rightarrow 2$ attacks". The construction uses UD in a black-box manner:

- For every $i \in [k]$, sample $(|\mathsf{sk}_i\rangle, \mathsf{pk}_i) \leftarrow \mathsf{UD.KeyGen}$; $|\mathsf{sk}_i\rangle$ will be the i-th copy of the quantum unclonable decryption key; the public key will be $\mathsf{pk} = (\mathsf{pk}_1, \cdots, \mathsf{pk}_k)$.
- The encryption algorithm takes a single bit message m and outputs a classical ciphertext ct that consists of k copies of ciphertext, among which the i-th copy ct_i is the ciphertext of m under pk_i.
- To decrypt $\mathsf{ct} = (\mathsf{ct}_1, \cdots, \mathsf{ct}_k)$ with $|\mathsf{sk}_i\rangle$, one can decrypt the i-th ciphertext ct_i.

Intuitively in the above encryption scheme, one can decrypt only if it knows the decryption key for at least one of the public keys. Note that our k decryption keys are sampled independently at random and each state satisfies $1 \rightarrow 2$ unclonability. To establish anti-piracy, we want to prove a security reduction from a $k \rightarrow k+1$ quantum pirate decryptors to the $1 \rightarrow 2$ unclonability of one of the decryption keys.

Unfortunately, we do not know how to prove the security of this scheme generically. As we will elaborate in Sect. 1.4, we need to open up the construction of the underlying unclonable encryption in order to establish the security.

More importantly, in the following section, we demonstrate that even if we open up the construction and the proof, the proof technique in [13] seems not sufficient for CRUD and we thereby work on a new technique that subsumes that in [13] to complete the proof. We start by recalling the definition of regular UD and the proof in [13].

Regular Unclonable Decryption. Let UD be a regular $(1 \to 2)$ unclonable decryption scheme. For the sake of convenience, we assume the message space is $\{0,1\}$. A pair of a classical public key pk and a quantum unclonable secret key $|\text{sk}\rangle$ is generated by KeyGen.

The anti-piracy security guarantees that no efficient adversary with $|\text{sk}\rangle$ can produce two "working" keys by a CPA indistinguishability standard: if one estimates the success probabilities of both decryption keys on distinguishing a ciphertext of 0 from a ciphertext of 1, their success probabilities cannot be *simultaneously* significantly greater than $1/2$, except with negligible probability. This security notion has been previously studied by Aaronson et al. [4] and Coladangelo et al. [13]

Before we delve into the security proof, it is enlightening to see how this security guarantee is efficiently "falsifiable". Estimating the success probability of a *classical* decryptor is easy. One can generate a ciphertext for a random message using the public key and check whether the classical decryptor is correct on that ciphertext; then, a simple counting estimates its success probability within any inverse polynomial error. Unfortunately, this method does not naturally work in the quantum setting since a single execution of the decryption key (produced by the adversary) may disturb the state and prevent further execution of the same key.

Nevertheless, Zhandry [30] shows that such estimation can be done analogous to the classical setting, inspired by the famous work of Marriott and Watrous [23] for witness-preserving error reduction for quantum Arthur–Merlin game. Informally, the work of Zhandry utilizes a measurement procedure called "projective implementation" (abbreviated as PI)[4] to estimate the success probability of a quantum adversary (see Fig. 1).

1. Let $\mathcal{D}$ be a ciphertext distribution we define the procedure with respect to.
2. For any quantum decryptor σ with success probability p over $\mathcal{D}$, running $\text{PI}_{\mathcal{D}}$ on the decryptor produces a probability p' and σ collapses to σ';
3. σ' as a decryptor, has success probability p' over $\mathcal{D}$;
4. Applying $\text{PI}_{\mathcal{D}}$ on σ' always produces p' and σ' remains intact;
5. The expectation of p' is p.

$$(\sigma,p) \longrightarrow \boxed{\text{PI}_{\mathcal{D}}} \longrightarrow (\sigma',p') \longrightarrow \boxed{\text{PI}_{\mathcal{D}}} \longrightarrow (\sigma',p')$$

$$\mathbb{E}[p'] = p$$

Fig. 1. PI: measure success probability of a decryptor.

---

[4] For simplicity, we only use the inefficient estimation procedure. The same argument in the technical overview holds using an efficient and approximated version. Similarly for TI.

Put shortly, this measurement procedure will output an estimation of the success probability p' for a quantum decryptor σ. After the measurement, the decryptor collapsed to another decryptor σ', whose success probability is still p'. We will intuitively call PI as "probability estimation' instead of its original name in the scope of the overview.

In the anti-piracy security definition, we care about whether both decryptors have the success probability significantly greater than $1/2$. [13] defines the following "threshold measurement" or "goodness measurement" $\mathsf{TI}_{\mathcal{D},\epsilon}$ for deciding if a quantum decryptor σ is good, for some inverse-polynomial ϵ:

1. Let $\mathcal{D}$ be a ciphertext distribution we define the procedure with respect to.
2. Run $\mathsf{PI}_{\mathcal{D}}$ coherently on σ and measure if the outcome register (containing the resulting probability p') is greater than $1/2 + \epsilon$, which produces a single bit outcome b. The quantum decryptor collapses to σ'.
3. If $b = 1$, σ' lies in the span of good decryptors, whose success probability is at least $1/2+\epsilon$; otherwise, σ' is in the subspace with the basis being quantum decryptors whose winning probability is strictly less than $1/2 + \epsilon$.

$$\sigma \longrightarrow \boxed{\mathsf{TI}_{\mathcal{D},\epsilon}} \longrightarrow (\sigma', b)$$

Fig. 2. TI: measure goodness of a decryptor.

We note that $\mathsf{TI}_{\mathcal{D},\epsilon}$ is a projection, which says if σ' is the collapsed decryptor for outcome b, applying $\mathsf{TI}_{\mathcal{D},\epsilon}$ will always produce b and σ' does not change.

We are now ready to formally define the anti-piracy security in [13]. Let $\mathcal{D}$ be the ciphertext distribution for honestly generated ciphertext, which encodes a uniformly random message. No efficient adversary can turn $|\mathsf{sk}\rangle$ into a possibly entangled decryptors σ over two registers, such that applying the threshold measurement $\mathsf{TI}_{\mathcal{D},\epsilon}$ on both decryptors $\sigma[1], \sigma[2]$ will produce two outcomes 1s with non-negligible probability. To put it another way, no efficient adversary can produce two decryptors such that they jointly have non-negligible weight on good decryptors.

Security Proof for "1 → 2 Attacks". Before scoping the proof of our collusion resistant unclonable decryption, we recall the security proof in [13] for "1 → 2 unclonability". In this following section, we will highlight the difficulties of applying the same ideas to CRUD and introduce a new approach to resolve this issue.

The proof works as follows:

– A reduction applies $\mathsf{TI}_{\mathcal{D},\epsilon}$ on both decryptors $\sigma[1], \sigma[2]$. With some non-negligible probability, it will produce two outcomes 1s and the two decryptors become $\sigma'[1], \sigma'[2]$.

- **Extraction on the First Register.** Let $\mathcal{D}'$ be the ciphertext distribution for "junk" ciphertext which only encrypts an empty symbol $\perp$. Applying $\mathsf{TI}_{\mathcal{D}',\epsilon}$ on $\sigma'[1]$ always result in outcome 0, whereas the outcome of applying $\mathsf{TI}_{\mathcal{D},\epsilon}$ on $\sigma'[1]$ is always 1.
  We can thereby conclude that $\sigma'[1]$ must contain some secret information about the secret key $|\mathsf{sk}\rangle$. In fact, we can use an extraction algorithm to extract the classical information about the secret key. Note that the algorithm may be destructive that, for example, may measure $\sigma'[1]$ completely.
- **Extraction on the Second Register.** Conditioned on the successful extraction on $\sigma'[1]$, we want to argue that a similar extraction on the second register works. If so, we can *simultaneously* extract secret information about $|\mathsf{sk}\rangle$ from two non-communicating parties. This will violate the underlying quantum information guarantee[5].

The remaining is to show such an extraction is feasible on the second decryptor, even conditioned on the successful extraction on $\sigma'[1]$. This is because $\mathsf{TI}_{\mathcal{D},\epsilon}$ is a projection, conditioned on the outcome being 1, $\sigma'[2]$ will be in the span of good decryptors (see bullet (3) of the description of TI). Regardless of what event is conditioned on $\sigma'[1]$, the second decryptor is still in the span of good decryptors. Thus, an extraction algorithm would extract the classical information about the secret key from $\sigma'[2]$ with non-negligible probability. This concludes the proof idea in [13].

To conclude, the core idea in the proof is that, a "$1 \to 2$ attack" produces two quantum registers that

1. they have a non-negligible probability $w_1 = \gamma$ on both registers being good decryptors on $\mathcal{D}$ (with success probabilities at least $1/2 + \epsilon$);
2. they have a negligible probability w_2 on both being good decryptors on $\mathcal{D}'$.

If both 1 and 2 are satisfied, a simultaneous extraction succeeds with a non-negligible probability.

In the next few paragraphs, we still denote w_1 as the joint probability of both decryptors being good on distribution $\mathcal{D}$; w_2 as the joint probability of both decryptors being good on distribution $\mathcal{D}'$.

In the above proof for $1 \to 2$ attack, we crucially require w_1 is non-negligible and w_2 is negligible or zero, in order to argue that extraction would succeed even after conditioned on successful extraction on one side.

We can also observe that for the $1 \to 2$ proof, w_2 is automatically zero. As $\mathcal{D}'$ does not encode a real message, no quantum decryptor can achieve any advantage over random guessing. But this is *not* always the case when it turns to our CRUD security proof: for which, $\mathcal{D} = (\mathsf{ct}_\perp, \cdots, \mathsf{ct}_j, \mathsf{ct}_{j+1}, \cdots)$ has the first $(j-1)$ ciphertexts being junk and the rest being real; whereas $\mathcal{D}' = (\mathsf{ct}_\perp, \cdots, \mathsf{ct}_\perp, \mathsf{ct}_{j+1}, \cdots)$ has the first j ciphertexts being junk.

---

[5] In the actual proof, two non-communicating parties will extract two vectors, one in the primal coset and the other in the dual coset of a coset state. This will violate the strong computational monogamy-of-entanglement property of coset states.

As we will see in the following section, for CRUD, the condition "$w_1 - w_2$ is non-negligible" is the best we can hope for. Therefore, we attempted to see if a proof similar to the above exists, when we can only condition on "$w_1 - w_2$ is non-negligible". Unfortunately, the answer to this attempt is negative, as we will provide some intuition in the immediate next paragraph. We thereby conclude that the proof technique in [13] cannot extend to collusion resistant anti-piracy security proof in a generic way.

To see why the condition "$w_1 - w_2$ is non-negligible" does not necessarily give a simultaneous extraction, we consider the time when a successful extraction has already been done on the first decryptor $\sigma'[1]$. If w_2 is negligible, the leftover state of the second decryptor $\sigma'[2]$ has at most w_2/ζ weight lying in the span of bad decryptors. Here ζ is the probability of a successful extraction on the first decryptor and conditioned on this extraction, the weight w_2 will be amplied by at most $1/\zeta$. Since w_2/ζ is still negligible, this allows an extraction from $\sigma'[2]$ happens with a non-negligible chance. However, if w_2 is not negligible but only satisfies $w_1 - w_2$ is non-negligible, $\sigma'[2]$ can lie in the span of bad decryptors: the extreme case will be the event of successful extraction on $\sigma'[1]$ has "positive correlation" with $\sigma'[2]$ being bad; in this case, the weight can be as large as $w_2/\zeta \approx 1$.

Obstacles for Extraction from Quantum Decryptors. The high-level intuition for why such a construction would satisfy $k \to k+1$ is comprehensible. Assume an adversary uses $|\mathsf{sk}_1\rangle, \cdots, |\mathsf{sk}_k\rangle$ to produce $(k+1)$ (possibly entangled) malicious decryptors σ. Let $\sigma[i]$ denote the i-th pirate decryptor. Since each $\sigma[i]$ is a "working" pirate decryptor, it should at least decrypt one of $\mathsf{ct}_1, \cdots, \mathsf{ct}_k$ (say ct_j). Applying pigeonhole principle, there are two decryptors that decrypts the same ciphertext slot, which would violate $1 \to 2$ unclonability. However, such an intuition is nontrivial to formalize since a quantum adversary could distribute these secret keys in multiple ways in superposition.

A straightforward idea is to extract secret information for the j-th private key $|\mathsf{sk}_j\rangle$ from $\sigma[i]$. Let $\mathcal{D}'$ be the ciphertext distribution $(\mathsf{ct}_\perp, \mathsf{ct}_\perp, \cdots, \mathsf{ct}_\perp)$ containing all junk ciphertext. Clearly, if we apply $\mathsf{TI}_{\mathcal{D}',\epsilon}$ on any quantum decryptor, the result is always 0 (meaning "bad"). If we can find an index j such that $\mathcal{D}_j$ is the distribution $(\mathsf{ct}_\perp, \mathsf{ct}_\perp, \cdots, \mathsf{ct}_j, \cdots, \mathsf{ct}_\perp)$ and applying $\mathsf{TI}_{\mathcal{D}_j,\epsilon}$ on $\sigma[i]$ gives 1 with non-negligible chance, we can extract secrets for $|\mathsf{sk}_j\rangle$ from $\sigma[i]$. If one can extract from every $\sigma[i]$, by the pigeonhole principle, it breaks the underlying quantum information guarantee for one of the unclonable decryption keys. Unfortunately, this idea does not go through, considering the following bad situation.

Even if $\sigma[i]$ has success probability 1, such j may not exist. Consider a quantum program that knows all the decryption keys $|\mathsf{sk}_1\rangle, \cdots, |\mathsf{sk}_k\rangle$ but only decrypts ct if and only if every $|\mathsf{sk}_j\rangle$ can successfully decrypt ct_j; if any decryption fails to decrypt, it outputs a random guess. Feeding $(\cdots, \mathsf{ct}_\perp, \mathsf{ct}_j, \mathsf{ct}_\perp, \cdots,)$ to the decryptor will always result in a random guessing.

Note that this is not only an issue for quantum decryptors but also presents if decryptors are classical.

A natural fix of the above idea is to consider the following hybrid distributions. We define $\mathcal{D}_j$ for every $j \in \{0, 1, \cdots, k\}$:

- $\mathcal{D}_j := (\mathsf{ct}_\perp, \cdots, \mathsf{ct}_\perp, \mathsf{ct}_j, \mathsf{ct}_{j+1} \cdots)$. In other words, only the last $k - j$ ciphertexts encode the same random message $m \in \{0, 1\}$, the first j ciphertexts are junk ciphertexts .
- $\mathsf{TI}_j := \mathsf{TI}_{\mathcal{D}_j, \epsilon}$: the goodness estimation with respect to the ciphertext distribution $\mathcal{D}_j$ and threshold $1/2 + \epsilon$.

That is, each $\mathcal{D}_j$ will replace the first non-junk ciphertext from $\mathcal{D}_{j-1}$ with a junk ciphertext. Note that $\mathcal{D} := \mathcal{D}_0$. By the definition of $\sigma[i]$ is a working decryptor, applying TI_0 on $\sigma[i]$ will produce 1 with a non-negligible probability. On the flip side, applying TI_k on $\sigma[i]$ will always produce 0.

We denote w_j as the probability of applying $\mathsf{TI}_{\mathcal{D}_j, \epsilon}$ on the decryptor $\sigma[i]$ and getting outcome 1. By a standard hybrid argument, we can conclude that there must exist an index $j \in [k]$ such that,

$$w_{j-1} - w_j \text{ is non-negligible.}$$

The gap allows extraction on $\sigma[i]$. However, as we discussed in the last section, it does not satisfy the condition "w_{j-1} is non-negligible and w_j is negligible", which can not guarantee a simultaneous extraction when we consider two decryptors.

A bad example looks like the following: $w_0 = \gamma$ for some inverse polynomial γ and $w_j = \gamma/2^j$ for all $j \neq k$ and $w_k = 0$. There does not exists a j such that w_{j-1} is non-negligible but w_j is negligible.

We now elaborate on our approaches to resolve these obstacles. Our approach directly takes advantage of the probability measure PI instead of TI. This also gives an alternative security proof for the construction in [13].

Extract a Single Decryption Key: Detect a Large Jump in Success Probability. Let us start with attempts to extract from a single "working" decryptor σ, using the probability estimation PI. Recall that by the definition of "working", we mean applying $\mathsf{PI}_\mathcal{D}$ on σ yields some probability p significantly larger than the trivial guessing probability $1/2$.

We first recall the following ciphertext distributions $\mathcal{D}_j$ and define probability estimation procedure PI_j for every $j \in \{0, 1, \cdots, k\}$:

- $\mathcal{D}_j := (\mathsf{ct}_\perp, \cdots, \mathsf{ct}_\perp, \mathsf{ct}_j, \mathsf{ct}_{j+1} \cdots)$.
- $\mathsf{PI}_j := \mathsf{PI}_{\mathcal{D}_j}$: the probability estimation with respect to the ciphertext distribution $\mathcal{D}_j$.

Now we give the following attempted extraction, which almost works but has one caveat. We call this extraction procedure a "repeated probability estimation/measurement":

1. We first apply PI_0 to σ and obtain p_0 and a collapsed decryption key σ_0.
2. We then apply PI_1 to the collapsed σ_0 to obtain p_1 and σ_1.

   Now if $p_1 - p_0$ is at least $\frac{p_0 - \frac{1}{2}}{k}$, we perform an extraction procedure to extract secrets for $|\mathsf{sk}_1\rangle$ from σ_0. Intuitively, since we observe a noticeable probability decrease when ct_1 is replaced with junk ciphertext, there must be some part of $\sigma[i]$ that uses ct_1 to recover the original plaintext. We then abort the procedure.
3. Otherwise, p_0 and p_1 should be negligibly close. We again apply PI_2 on σ_1 and obtain p_2, σ_2. If $p_2 - p_1$ is at least $\frac{p_0 - \frac{1}{2}}{k}$, we perform extraction on σ_1 and abort.
4. We continue this process for all $j = 3, ..., k$.

We claim that the above repeated measurement procedure will always terminate at some $j \in [k]$. To see this, think of $p_1, ..., p_k$ as a sequence of random variables, whose values are only observed when the corresponding measurement is applied. Note that $p_k = 1/2$ always, because the underlying ciphertext distribution $\mathcal{D}_k$ encodes all junk ciphertexts, so no adversary can achieve better advantage than guessing. Therefore, the claim follows from triangle inequality.

$$(\sigma_0, p_0) \xrightarrow{\mathsf{PI}_1} (\sigma_1, p_1) \xrightarrow{\mathsf{PI}_2} (\sigma_2, p_2) \xrightarrow{\mathsf{PI}_3} \cdots \xrightarrow{\mathsf{PI}_{k-1}} (\sigma_k, p_k)$$

The above extraction procedure almost works. But it is actually not physically executable: we need σ_{j-1} in order to perform extraction as that is the state with a "working" component for ciphertext ct_j, but by the time that we decide to extract, we already get to state σ_j because we have to obtain measurement outcome p_j to claim a jump in probability happens. It is generally infeasible to rewind a quantum state, in this case from σ_j to σ_{j-1}.[6]

Fortunately, it is plausible for a single decryptor: we guess j (denoting the first index having a probability jump) and stop the procedure when we have done $\mathsf{PI}_0, \cdots, \mathsf{PI}_{j-1}$. With probability at least $1/k$, we can extract for $|\mathsf{sk}_j\rangle$ from the current decryptor σ_{j-1}. We will get to why this procedure avoids the rewinding issue and preserves our success probability, when it comes to the $(k+1)$ decryptors case in the next paragraph.

Extending to $(k + 1)$ decryptors. Finally, we show how to generalize the above extraction strategy to extracting secrets from the same key $|\mathsf{sk}_j\rangle$.

We apply the repeated measurement individually to every decryptor: that is, for the i-th decryptor, we apply $\mathsf{PI}_0, \mathsf{PI}_1, \cdots, \mathsf{PI}_k$, one upon another. The procedure will yield $p_{i,0}, p_{i,1}, \cdots, p_{i,k}$. Since $p_{i,0}$ is always greater than $1/2 + \gamma$ and $p_{i,k} = 1/2$, there must exist a large probability gap between p_{i,j_i-1} and p_{i,j_i} for some $j_i \in [k]$. By the pigeonhole principle, for some $x \neq y$, $j := j_x = j_y$. We hope to stop at the x-th and y-th decryptors before applying PI_j and simultaneously turn them into two keys for ct_j.

---

[6] The probability estimation PI_j will preserve the success probability of the state but nothing else. Applying PI_j will likely change σ_{j-1}.

Since there will always be two decryptors having large probability gaps for the same index, the chance of having such gaps for randomly guessed x, y and j is at least $\frac{1}{\binom{k+1}{2}k} \geq 1/k^3$. But the success probability of this guess is not immediately guaranteed, because we need to stop before the j-th probability estimation for states $\sigma[x], \sigma[y]$ otherwise we can't rewind to this state needed for extraction. We are still two unpredictable measurements away from the event we guess for. Fortunately, guessing and stopping before the j-th PI will indeed work with probability at least $1/(2k^3)$, through a trick for randomized algorithms.

Now we can apply repeated measurement and stop before applying PI_j on any of these two decryptors. Let the leftover decryptors be $\sigma^*[x, y]$ and the last probability outcomes be $p_{x,j-1}$ and $p_{y,j-1}$. With probability at least $1/(2k^3)$, $(\sigma^*[x, y], p_{x,j-1}, p_{y,j-1})$ satisfy the following conditions (*) and (**):

(*) Applying PI_{j-1} on both $\sigma^*[x]$ and $\sigma^*[y]$ always produces $p_{x,j-1}$ and $p_{y,j-1}$.

(**) Applying PI_j on both $\sigma^*[x]$ and $\sigma^*[y]$, with probability at least $1/(2k^3)$, produces large probabilities gaps for both $p_{x,j-1}$ and $p_{y,j-1}$.

It seems that we have come to the right "spot" for extraction. However, we still face a challenge. How do we guarantee that we can simultaneously extract from two possibly entangled states? A possible malicious behavior is that measuring one decryptor's key will collapse the other decryptor to a "not working" state.

We can clearly extract secrets for $|sk_j\rangle$ from either $\sigma^*[x]$ or $\sigma^*[y]$: since there is a probability gap, it must mean $\sigma^*[x]$ (or $\sigma^*[y]$) use ct_j for decryption at some point. From the probability point of view, we then argue why simultaneous extraction is feasible.

Define $\mathbf{E}_x$ ($\mathbf{E}_y$, here $\mathbf{E}$ stands for "(E)xtraction") be the event of a successful extraction on the x-th decryptor (or on the y-th decryptor respectively). Define $\mathbf{G}_x$ ($\mathbf{G}_y$, here $\mathbf{G}$ stands for "(G)ap") be the event that applying PI_j on the x-th decryptor (or on the y-th decryptor respectively) yields a large probability gap. We will prove $\Pr[\mathbf{E}_x \wedge \mathbf{E}_y]$ is non-negligible by contradiction.

It is clear that $\Pr[\mathbf{E}_x]$ is non-negligible. To show $\Pr[\mathbf{E}_y|\mathbf{E}_x]$ is non-negligible, it is sufficient to show that $\Pr[\mathbf{G}_y|\mathbf{E}_x]$ is non-negligible, since a large gap implies a large chance of extraction.

We can intuitively think of $\Pr[\mathbf{E}_x] = 0.1 \Pr[\mathbf{G}_x]$ and $\Pr[\mathbf{E}_y] = 0.1 \Pr[\mathbf{G}_y]$[7]. We may expect that $\Pr[\mathbf{E}_x \wedge \mathbf{E}_y] = 0.1 \Pr[\mathbf{G}_x \wedge \mathbf{G}_y]$, which would conclude the proof. However, this does not follow immediately from above as it could be the case that $\mathbf{G}_x \wedge \mathbf{G}_y$ occurs with non-negligible probability, but $\mathbf{E}_x \wedge \mathbf{E}_y$ never occurs. The main insight here is that we can instead show that $\Pr[\mathbf{E}_x|\mathbf{G}_y] = 0.1 \Pr[\mathbf{G}_x|\mathbf{G}_y]$, as finding the gap for y does not impact the extraction for x. Invoking Bayes' rule, this shows that $\Pr[\mathbf{G}_y|\mathbf{E}_x] = \Pr[\mathbf{E}_x|\mathbf{G}_y] \Pr[\mathbf{G}_y]/\Pr[\mathbf{E}_x]$ is non-negligible as well. As a consequence, $\Pr[\mathbf{E}_y|\mathbf{E}_x]$ and thus $\Pr[\mathbf{E}_x \wedge \mathbf{E}_y]$ (simultaneous extraction) are both large.

---

[7] The choice of 0.1 is arbitrary here. Indeed, they are polynomially related. For the sake of simplicity, we assume they are linearly related.

Collusion Resistant Copy-Protection for Signatures and PRFs. Now with the building block of collusion resistant unclonable decryption, we come to copy-protect more cryptographic functions.

As briefly discussed in the introduction, even though [13] presented the first unclonable signature scheme without oracles, its scheme is a signature token that will be consumed after one use. One-time signature is a security notion interesting under many circumstances [9,17], but it's crucial that we investigate the possibility of copy-protecting a standard digital signature. Moreover, once achieved, this construction helps us get closer to the goal of copy-protecting all watermarkable functionalities.

The [13] signature token is one-time because when signing a message, the signer simply measures the quantum key and the measurement outcome is a signature. It is not existentially unforgeable for the same reason: if an adversary gets a few random measurement results of quantum keys, he is granted the power to sign, without the need of an intact quantum key.

To resolve the problem, we resort to the classic picture of generic copy-protection: the signing program first verifies if a quantum key is a valid "token" and then outputs a signature (computed independently of the quantum key) as well as the almost unharmed key. In particular, we observe that the unclonable decryption scheme in [13] will pave the way for such a construction. Their scheme can be extended to a copy-protection for evaluating puncturable PRFs with the "hidden trigger" technique from [25]. Meanwhile, such PRF evaluation functionality can be used as a signing program after obfuscation.

We thereby give a copy-protection for existentially unforgeable, publicly-verifiable signature scheme, based on the above ideas. Along the way, we deal with a few subtleties that emerge because we need public verification and generalization to collusion resistance. More specifically, we present a k-party version of the [25] hidden trigger technique to obtain both collusion resistant copy-protection for signatures and for PRFs.

1.4   Discussions and Open Problems

Comparisons to [13]. An informed reader may claim that one main obstacle (namely simultaneous extraction) for proving anti-piracy security in this paper resembles the obstacle in the $1 \to 2$ anti-piracy schemes of [4,13]. We emphasize that while this issue may be bumped into in all quantum copy-protection proofs, our approach of resolving the issue is different from previous works, especially to identify gaps in a repeated probability estimation procedure (see more details in the technical overview). In particular, our approach can be used to prove security for the schemes in [4,13], but as we have discussed in the technical overview, their techniques will *not* work for the $k \to k + 1$ setting[8]

---

[8] The approach for simultaneous extraction when showing $1 \to 2$ anti-piracy in [4] bears a high-level similarity with [13]. We have discussed [13] in the overview since we focus on unclonable decryption.

On Non-Black-Box Reduction. In the technical overview, we describe a black-box way of reducing "$k \to (k+1)$ security" to "$1 \to 2$ security". As mentioned earlier, we cheat in the technical overview and the approach is not entirely black-box.

A high-level summary for the reason is: a black-box reduction algorithm (i.e. an adversary for a $1 \to 2$ unclonable decryption scheme) is not able to generate the correct distribution for the ciphertext to feed to the k collusion resistant adversary. Elaborated as follows:

First, recall that in a k collusion resistant scheme, an encryption for a message m is an ensemble of ciphertexts $\mathsf{ct} = (\mathsf{ct}_1, ..., \mathsf{ct}_k)$ where $\mathsf{ct}_i = \mathsf{Enc}(\mathsf{pk}_i, m)$ for all $i \in [k]$.

In the reduction, we want to apply $\mathsf{PI}_{\mathcal{D}_j}$ on a malicious decryptor to extract secrets from $|\mathsf{sk}_j\rangle$ for some $j \in [k]$:

> $\mathcal{D}_j$: the first j ciphertexts (that is, $\mathsf{ct}_1, \cdots$ up to ct_j) are simulated ciphertexts, the rest of them encrypt the same message.

The problem is the following: the reduction only gets a single ciphertext ct_{j+1}, whereas the malicious decryptor takes input of the form in $\mathcal{D}_j$. The reduction needs to generate other ciphertext on its own: including those simulated and those encrypting the same message as c_{j+1}. Since the reduction does not know which message is encrypted in ct_{j+1} (otherwise, the reduction itself already breaks the security of the underlying $1 \to 2$ unclonable decryption), it cannot generate a valid ciphertext $\mathsf{ct} = (\mathsf{ct}_1, \cdots, \mathsf{ct}_k)$ from the distribution $\mathcal{D}_j$.

Therefore, we need to open this proof up in a non-black-box way: it's based on the security of coset states. When we break the security of coset states, the message (encrypted in ct_{j+1}) is known by the reduction. In fact, it is even sampled by the reduction R.

Open Problems. The main limitation of our constructions is that the number of collisions is bounded to a polynomial specified during setup, and the parameters grow with the collusion bound. Because of this collusion bound, our results are technically incomparable to [2], which, despite having a much weaker copy-protection guarantee and using a strong oracle, required no prefixed user number. We leave achieving unbounded $k \to k + 1$ collusion resistance as an interesting open question.

1.5   Organization

The rest of the paper is organized as follows. In Sect. 2, we recall the definitions and properties of coset states and how to measure success probabilities of quantum adversaries. In Sect. 3, we present the definition, construction, and security proof of collusion resistant unclonable decryption. Our constructions and security proofs for (collusion resistant) copy-protection for signature schemes and PRFs are covered in the full version.

2   Preliminaries

In this paper, λ denotes the security parameter. $\mathsf{poly}(\cdot)$ denotes a polynomial function. We say a function $f(\cdot) : \mathbb{N} \to \mathbb{R}^{\geq 0}$ is negligible if for all constant $c > 0$, $f(n) \leq \frac{1}{n^c}$ for all sufficiently large n. $\mathsf{negl}(\cdot)$ denotes a negligible function. Similarly, we say a function $f(\cdot) : \mathbb{N} \to \mathbb{R}^{\geq 0}$ is sub-exponential if there exists a constant $c < 1$, such that $f(n) \leq 2^{n^c}$ for all sufficiently large n. $\mathsf{subexp}(\cdot)$ denotes a sub-exponential function. For an integer k, We denote $\{1, 2, \cdots, k\}$ by $[k]$. We denote $\mathbb{F}_2$ to be the binary field.

We refer the reader to [24] for a reference of basic quantum information and computation concepts. We also leave the definition for indistinguishability obfuscation in the full version. Readers can also find the definition in [8, 16].

2.1   Coset States

We recall the notion of coset states, introduced by [26] and later studied by [13] in the setting of quantum copy-protection. We then present a property of coset states: a strong computational monogamy-of-entanglement (MOE) property. This property is used to obtain an unclonable decryption scheme and other copy-protection of watermarkable cryptographic primitives in this work. Some part of this section is taken verbatim from [13].

Definitions. For any subspace A, its complement is $A^\perp = \{b \in \mathbb{F}_2^n \mid \langle a, b \rangle = 0, \forall a \in A\}$. It satisfies $\dim(A) + \dim(A^\perp) = n$. We also let $|A| = 2^{\dim(A)}$ denote the number of elements in the subspace A.

Definition 1 (Coset States). *For any subspace $A \subseteq \mathbb{F}_2^n$ and vectors $s, s' \in \mathbb{F}_2^n$, the coset state $|A_{s,s'}\rangle$ is defined as:*

$$|A_{s,s'}\rangle = \frac{1}{\sqrt{|A|}} \sum_{a \in A} (-1)^{\langle s', a \rangle} |a + s\rangle.$$

By applying $H^{\otimes n}$ (Hadamard on every qubit) on the state $|A_{s,s'}\rangle$, one obtains exactly $|A_{s',s}^\perp\rangle$. Given A, s and s', there is an efficient quantum algorithm that generates $|A_{s,s'}\rangle$, by [13].

For a subspace A and vectors s, s', we define cosets $A + s = \{v + s : v \in A\}$, and $A^\perp + s' = \{v + s' : v \in A^\perp\}$. It is also convenient for later sections to define a canonical representative, with respect to subspace A, of the coset $A + s$.

Definition 2 (Canonical Representative of a Coset). *For a subspace A, we define the function $\mathsf{Can}_A(\cdot)$ such that $\mathsf{Can}_A(s)$ is the lexicographically smallest vector contained in $A + s$ (we call this the canonical representative of coset $A + s$).*

[13] showed that, Can_A and $\mathsf{Can}_{A^\perp}$ are efficiently computable given the classical description of A.

When it is clear from the context, we will write $A + s$ to denote the *program* that checks membership in $A + s$. The following equivalences, which follow straightforwardly from the security of iO, will be useful in our security proofs later on.

Proposition 1. *For any subspace* $A \subseteq \mathbb{F}_2^n$, $iO(A+s) \approx_c iO(CC[Can_A, Can_A(s)])$. *Recall that* $CC[Can_A, Can_A(s)]$ *refers to the compute-and-compare program which on input x outputs 1 if and only if $Can_A(x) = Can_A(s)$.*

This is due to the fact that $A+s$ has the same functionality as $CC[Can_A, Can_A(s)]$. The lemma then follows the security of iO.

Strong Monogamy-of-Entanglement Property. Consider a game between a challenger and an adversary $(\mathcal{A}_0, \mathcal{A}_1, \mathcal{A}_2)$:

- The challenger picks a uniformly random subspace $A \subseteq \mathbb{F}_2^n$ of dimension $\frac{n}{2}$, and two uniformly random elements $s, s' \in \mathbb{F}_2^n$. It sends $|A_{s,s'}\rangle$, $iO(A + s)$, and $iO(A^{\perp} + s')$ to $\mathcal{A}_0$.
- $\mathcal{A}_0$ creates a bipartite state on registers B and C. Then, $\mathcal{A}_0$ sends register B to $\mathcal{A}_1$, and C to $\mathcal{A}_2$.
- The classical description of A is then sent to both $\mathcal{A}_1, \mathcal{A}_2$.
- $\mathcal{A}_1$ and $\mathcal{A}_2$ return respectively s_1 and s_2.

$(\mathcal{A}_0, \mathcal{A}_1, \mathcal{A}_2)$ wins if and only if $s_1 \in A + s$ and $s_2 \in A^{\perp} + s'$.

Let $\mathsf{CompStrongMonogamy}((\mathcal{A}_0, \mathcal{A}_1, \mathcal{A}_2), n)$ be a random variable which takes the value 1 if the game above is won by adversary $(\mathcal{A}_0, \mathcal{A}_1, \mathcal{A}_2)$, and takes the value 0 otherwise.

Theorem 3. *Assuming the existence of sub-exponentially secure post-quantum iO and one-way functions, then for any QPT adversary $(\mathcal{A}_0, \mathcal{A}_1, \mathcal{A}_2)$,*

$$\Pr[\mathsf{CompStrongMonogamy}((\mathcal{A}_0, \mathcal{A}_1, \mathcal{A}_2), n) = 1] \leq 1/\mathsf{subexp}(n).$$

[15] proved an information-theoretic version of the strong monogamy property (without giving out the iO programs to the adversary). [13] showed that one can obtain the computational statement by lifting the information-theoretic statement.

2.2 Measure Success Probabilities of Quantum Adversaries: Projective/Threshold Implementation

In this section, we include several definitions and results about estimating success probabilities or estimating whether the probability is above a threshold. Part of this section is taken verbatim from [4,13]. In this section, we will mainly talk about how to measure probability in an inefficient way. The proofs in the main body of the proof use this inefficient measuring procedure as subroutines. All these proofs can be translated easily using the efficient version of such measuring procedures. We will cover those in the full version.

Estimating success probabilities of adversaries is essential in many settings, especially for a reduction to know whether the adversary is good or if an extraction on the adversary can succeed with high probability. Classically it is easy. Let $\mathcal{D}$ be a testing input distribution and C be a classical program for which we want to estimate probability. We can keep running C on uniformly fresh inputs sampled from $\mathcal{D}$ to estimate the probability up to any inverse polynomial error. Such procedure is infeasible for quantum adversaries, since a single execution of a quantum program may completely collapse the program, leading to failure for future executions.

Projective Implementation. Zhandry [30] formalizes the following probability measurement procedure for a quantum program ρ under some test distribution $\mathcal{D}$.

Consider the following procedure as a binary POVM $\mathcal{P}_{\mathcal{D}} = (P_{\mathcal{D}}, Q_{\mathcal{D}})$ acting on a quantum program ρ (whose success probability is equal to p): sample an input x from $\mathcal{D}$, evaluates the quantum program ρ on x, and checks if the output is correct. Let $P_{\mathcal{D}}$ denote the operator for output being correct and $Q_{\mathcal{D}}$ be the quantum operator for the output being incorrect.

Zhandry proposed a procedure that applies an appropriate projective measurement which *measures* the success probability of ρ on input $x \leftarrow \mathcal{D}$, and outputs the probability p'. Conditioned on the outcome is some probability p', the quantum program collapsed to ρ' whose success probability is exactly p'. Furthermore, the expectation of p' equals to p.

Theorem 4 (Projective Implementation). *Let $\mathcal{D}$ be a distribution of inputs. Let $\mathcal{P}_{\mathcal{D}} = (P_{\mathcal{D}}, Q_{\mathcal{D}})$ be a binary outcome POVM described above with respect to the distribution $\mathcal{D}$. There exists a projective measurement $\mathsf{PI}(\mathcal{P}_{\mathcal{D}})$ such that for any quantum program ρ with success probability p on $\mathcal{D}$:*

(i) Applying $\mathsf{PI}(\mathcal{P}_{\mathcal{D}})$ on ρ yields ρ', p'.
(ii) ρ' has success probability p' with respect to $\mathcal{D}$. Furthermore, applying $\mathsf{PI}(\mathcal{P}_{\mathcal{D}})$ on ρ' always produces p'.
(iii) The expectation of p' equals to p.

We say the above measurement procedure is a projective implementation of $\mathcal{P}_{\mathcal{D}}$. When the distribution is clear from the context, we sometimes ignore the subscript $\mathcal{D}$ in both $\mathcal{P}_{\mathcal{D}}$ and $\mathsf{PI}(\mathcal{P}_{\mathcal{D}})$.

Threshold Implementation. The concept of threshold implementation [4] is similar to projective implementation, except it now outputs a binary outcome indicating whether the probability is above or below some threshold.

Theorem 5 (Threshold Implementation). *Let $\mathcal{D}$ be a distribution of inputs. Let $\mathcal{P}_{\mathcal{D}} = (P_{\mathcal{D}}, Q_{\mathcal{D}})$ be a binary outcome POVM described above with respect to the distribution $\mathcal{D}$. For any $0 \leq \gamma \leq 1$, there exists a projective measurement $\mathsf{TI}_\gamma(\mathcal{P}_{\mathcal{D}})$ such that for any quantum program ρ:*

(i) Applying $\mathsf{TI}_\gamma(\mathcal{P}_{\mathcal{D}})$ on ρ yields a binary outcome b' and a collapsed program ρ'.

(ii) If $b' = 1$, ρ' has success probability at least γ with respect to $\mathcal{D}$. Furthermore, applying $\mathsf{TI}_\gamma(\mathcal{P}_\mathcal{D})$ on ρ' always produces 1.

(iii) If $b' = 0$, ρ' has success probability less than γ with respect to $\mathcal{D}$. Furthermore, applying $\mathsf{TI}_\gamma(\mathcal{P}_\mathcal{D})$ on ρ' always produces 0.

We say the above measurement procedure is a threshold implementation of $\mathcal{P}_\mathcal{D}$ with threshold γ. When the distribution is clear from the context, we sometimes ignore the subscript $\mathcal{D}$ in $\mathsf{TI}(\mathcal{P}_\mathcal{D})$.

Moreover, $\mathsf{TI}(\mathcal{P}_\mathcal{D})$ can be implemented by first applying $\mathsf{PI}(\mathcal{P}_\mathcal{D})$ to get a outcome p and outputting 1 if $p \geq \gamma$ or 0 otherwise.

For simplicity, we denote by $\mathrm{Tr}[\mathsf{TI}_\gamma(\mathcal{P}_\mathcal{D})\,\rho]$ the probability that the threshold implementation applied to ρ **outputs 1**. Thus, whenever $\mathsf{TI}_\gamma(\mathcal{P}_\mathcal{D})$ appears inside a trace Tr, we treat $\mathsf{TI}_\gamma(\mathcal{P}_\mathcal{D})$ as a projection onto the 1 outcome.

The approximate and efficient versions of both PI and TI will be covered in the full version

3 Collusion Resistant Unclonable Decryption

In this section, we give the formal definition of collusion resistant unclonable decryption. We will then show the construction for achieving bounded collusion resistance for any k — polynomial number of parties. Finally, we prove the construction satisfies correctness, semantic security and anti-piracy against colluding adversaries. Our scheme has security against bounded number of parties. It requires to know the parameter k in the setup phase and only k copies of keys can be generated later. Furthermore, the public key, secret key and ciphertext have length linear in the number of parties k. Note that our scheme is secure even if an adversary takes control of all copies of decryption keys; the adversary still can not produce any additional functioning key.

3.1 Definitions

Definition 3 (Bounded Collusion Resistant Unclonable Decryption Scheme). *A bounded collusion resistant unclonable decryption scheme CRUD for a message space $\mathcal{M}$ consists of the following efficient algorithms:*

- $\mathsf{Setup}(1^\lambda, k) \to (\mathsf{sk}, \mathsf{pk})$: *a (classical) probabilistic polynomial-time (in λ, k) algorithm that takes as input an upper bound k on the number of users and a security parameter λ and outputs a classical secret key sk and a classical public key pk.*
- $\mathsf{QKeyGen}(\mathsf{sk}) \to \rho_{\mathsf{sk},1} \otimes \rho_{\mathsf{sk},2} \otimes \cdots \otimes \rho_{\mathsf{sk},k}$: *a quantum algorithm that takes as input a secret key sk and outputs k copies of quantum secret keys.*
- $\mathsf{Enc}(\mathsf{pk}, m) \to \mathsf{ct}$: *a (classical) probabilistic algorithm that takes as input a public key pk, a message m and outputs a classical ciphertext ct.*
- $\mathsf{Dec}(\rho_{\mathsf{sk}}, \mathsf{ct}) \to m/\bot$: *a quantum algorithm that takes as input a quantum secret key ρ_{sk} and a classical ciphertext ct, and outputs a message m or a decryption failure symbol $\bot$.*

Here 'bounded' refers to the restriction that the Setup procedure requires to know the maximal number of keys distributed in the QKeyGen.

A bounded collusion resistant unclonable decryption scheme should satisfy the following:

Correctness: For every polynomial $k(\cdot)$, there exists a negligible function $\mathsf{negl}(\cdot)$, for all $\lambda \in \mathbb{N}$, let $k := k(\lambda)$, for all $m \in \mathcal{M}$, all $i \in [k]$,

$$
\Pr\left[\mathsf{Dec}(\rho_{\mathsf{sk},i}, \mathsf{ct}) = m \,\middle|\,
\begin{array}{c}
(\mathsf{sk}, \mathsf{pk}) \leftarrow \mathsf{Setup}(1^\lambda, k), \\
\rho_{\mathsf{sk},1} \otimes \cdots \otimes \rho_{\mathsf{sk},k} \leftarrow \mathsf{QKeyGen}(\mathsf{sk}), \\
\mathsf{ct} \leftarrow \mathsf{Enc}(\mathsf{pk}, m)
\end{array}
\right] \geq 1 - \mathsf{negl}(\lambda)
$$

In other words, correctness says the i-th quantum decryption key will always decrypt correctly (except with negligible probability). By the gentle measurement lemma [1], each decryption key can function correctly polynomially many times for honestly generated encryptions.

CPA Security: This is the regular semantic security for an encryption scheme. An adversary without getting any decryption key (neither sk nor these quantum keys) can not distinguish ciphertexts of chosen plaintexts.

Formally, for every (stateful) QPT adversary $\mathcal{A}$, for every polynomial $k(\cdot)$, there exists a negligible function $\mathsf{negl}(\cdot)$ such that for all $\lambda \in \mathbb{N}$, the following holds:

$$
\Pr\left[\mathcal{A}(\mathsf{ct}) = b :
\begin{array}{c}
(\mathsf{sk}, \mathsf{pk}) \leftarrow \mathsf{Setup}(1^\lambda, k) \\
((m_0, m_1) \in \mathcal{M}^2) \leftarrow \mathcal{A}(1^\lambda, \mathsf{pk}) \\
b \leftarrow \{0,1\}; \mathsf{ct} \leftarrow \mathsf{Enc}(\mathsf{pk}, m_b)
\end{array}
\right] \leq \frac{1}{2} + \mathsf{negl}(\lambda),
$$

Anti-Piracy Security. Finally, we define anti-piracy against colluding adversaries. Anti-piracy intuitively says there is no adversary who gets all copies of the decryption keys can successfully produce one additional "working" key.

We will follow the two different definitions of "working" proposed in [13] and give two definitions for anti-piracy. The first definition allows a pirate to announce two messages (m_0, m_1), much like the semantic security. A decryption key is good if an adversary can distinguish encryptions of m_0 and m_1 by using the decryption key. The second definition of a "working" decryption key is basing on whether it decrypts correctly with high probability on uniformly random inputs.

Before describing the security games, we first recall the concept of a quantum decryptor (or a quantum decryption key) [13] with respect to a collusion resistant unclonable decryption scheme.

Definition 4 (Quantum Decryptor). *A quantum decryptor ρ for ciphertexts of length m, is an ℓ-qubit state for some polynomial ℓ. For a ciphertext c of length m, we say that we run the quantum decryptor ρ on ciphertext c to mean that we execute a universal quantum circuit U on inputs $|c\rangle$ and ρ, and measure the output registers.*

We are now ready to describe the CPA-style anti-piracy game as well as the random challenge anti-piracy game. We first introduce the notion of good decryptors with respect to two messages (m_0, m_1).

Definition 5 (($\frac{1}{2}+\gamma$)-**good Test with respect to** (m_0, m_1)). *Let* $\gamma \in [0, 1/2]$. *Let* pk *be a public key, and* (m_0, m_1) *be a pair of messages. We refer to the following procedure as a test for a γ-good quantum decryptor with respect to* pk *and* (m_0, m_1):

- *The procedure takes as input a quantum decryptor ρ.*
- *Let* $\mathcal{P} = (P, I - P)$ *be the following POVM acting on some quantum state ρ':*
  - *Sample a uniform $b \leftarrow \{0, 1\}$ and random coins r. Compute $c \leftarrow$* Enc(pk, $m_b; r$).
  - *Run the quantum decryptor on input c. Check whether the outcome is m_b. If so, output 1; otherwise output 0.*
- *Let* $(\mathsf{TI}_{1/2+\gamma}, I - \mathsf{TI}_{1/2+\gamma})$ *be the threshold implementation of $\mathcal{P}$ with threshold value $\frac{1}{2} + \gamma$, as defined in Theorem 5. Run the threshold implementation on ρ, and output the outcome. If the output is 1, we say that the test passed, otherwise the test failed.*

Definition 6 (*k-Strong-Anti-Piracy Game, CPA-style*). *Let* $\lambda, k \in \mathbb{N}^+$. *The CPA-style strong anti-piracy game for a collusion resistant unclonable decryption scheme is the following game between a challenger and an adversary $\mathcal{A}$.*

1. **Setup Phase:** *The challenger samples keys* (sk, pk) $\leftarrow$ Setup($1^\lambda, k$).
2. **Quantum Key Generation Phase:** *The challenger sends $\mathcal{A}$ the classical public key* pk *and all k copies of quantum decryption keys $\rho = \rho_{\mathsf{sk},1} \otimes \cdots \rho_{\mathsf{sk},k} \leftarrow$* KeyGen(sk).
3. **Output Phase:** *$\mathcal{A}$ outputs a pair of distinct messages (m_0, m_1). It also outputs a (possibly mixed and entangled) state σ over $k + 1$ registers $R_1, R_2, \cdots, R_{k+1}$. We interpret σ as $k + 1$ (possibly entangled) quantum decryptors $\sigma[R_1], \cdots, \sigma[R_{k+1}]$.*
4. **Challenge Phase:** *Let* $\mathsf{TI}_{1/2+\gamma}$ *be the $(\frac{1}{2} + \gamma)$-good test with respect to (m_0, m_1). The challenger applies* $\mathsf{TI}_{1/2+\gamma}$ *to each of these decryptors. The challenger outputs 1 if and only if all the measurements output 1.*

We denote by StrongAntiPiracyCPA($1^\lambda, 1/2 + \gamma, k, \mathcal{A}$) *a random variable for the output of the game.*

Definition 7 (**Strong Anti-Piracy-Security**). *Let* $\gamma : \mathbb{N}^+ \rightarrow [0, 1]$. *An unclonable decryption scheme satisfies strong γ-anti-piracy security, if for any polynomial $k(\cdot)$, for any QPT adversary $\mathcal{A}$, there exists a negligible function* negl($\cdot$) *such that the following holds for all $\lambda \in \mathbb{N}$:*

$$\Pr\left[b = 1, b \leftarrow \mathsf{StrongAntiPiracyCPA}(1^\lambda, 1/2 + \gamma(\lambda), k(\lambda), \mathcal{A})\right] \leq \mathsf{negl}(\lambda) \quad (1)$$

Note that the above strong anti-piracy security is defined by the threshold implementation TI. By [13], this definition implies a weaker notion called *regular CPA-style anti-piracy security*, which says the probability of all $k + 1$ malicious parties simultaneously distinguish encryptions of m_0 or m_1 (m_0 and m_1 are chosen independently for each malicious parties) is at most negligibly greater than $1/2$.

We can similarly define *regular anti-piracy security with random message challenges*: the probability of all $k + 1$ malicious parties simultaneously recover ciphertext of independent random messages is at most negligibly greater than $1/2^n$, where n is the message length.

3.2   Construction

We now give the construction of our collusion resistant unclonable decryption. Let UD be the unclonable decryption scheme based on coset states [13]. Our CRUD takes k as input and outputs k pairs of freshly generated keys for UD. A message is encrypted under each public key. Decryption works if a decryptor can decrypt any ciphertext. The construction of CRUD follows from the construction of UD. The security of our CRUD requires a non-black-box analysis for the last step.

CRUD.Setup($1^\lambda, k$) :
  - For $i \in [k]$, $(\mathsf{sk}_i, \mathsf{pk}_i) \leftarrow$ UD.Setup(1^λ).
  - Let $\mathsf{sk} = (\mathsf{sk}_1, \cdots, \mathsf{sk}_k)$ and $\mathsf{pk} = (\mathsf{pk}_1, \cdots, \mathsf{pk}_k)$. Output $(\mathsf{sk}, \mathsf{pk})$.
CRUD.QKeyGen(sk) :
  - Parse $\mathsf{sk} = (\mathsf{sk}_1, \cdots, \mathsf{sk}_k)$. Let $\rho_i \leftarrow$ UD.QKeyGen(sk_i).
  - Let $\rho_{\mathsf{sk},i}$ be ρ_i padded with a classical index i, i.e., $\rho_{\mathsf{sk},i} = \rho_i \otimes |i\rangle \langle i|$.
  - Output $\rho_{\mathsf{sk},1} \otimes \cdots \otimes \rho_{\mathsf{sk},k}$.
CRUD.Enc(pk, m) :
  - Parse $\mathsf{pk} = (\mathsf{pk}_1, \cdots, \mathsf{pk}_k)$. Let $\mathsf{ct}_i \leftarrow$ UD.Enc(pk_i, m).
  - Output $\mathsf{ct}_1, \cdots, \mathsf{ct}_k$.
CRUD.Dec($\rho_{\mathsf{sk}}, \mathsf{ct}$) :
  - Parse $\mathsf{ct} = (\mathsf{ct}_1, \cdots, \mathsf{ct}_k)$. Parse ρ_{sk} as ρ and i.
  - Output UD.Dec(ρ, ct_i).

Fig. 3. Collusion resistant unclonable decryption.

We recall the unclonable decrytion scheme in [13] (see Fig. 4).

There is one additional function Sim which takes a parameter n (message length) and outputs a junk ciphertext, which will be crucial for our anti-piracy proof. Intuitively, if one can distinguish from a honestly generated ciphertext with a simulated ciphertext, they can extract secrets for the underlying coset states.

The efficiency, correctness and CPA security of our CRUD scheme follows easily from those of UD. We are focusing on the proof of its anti-piracy in the next section.

UD.Setup(1^λ) → (sk, pk) :
- Sample ℓ random ($\lambda/2$)-dimensional subspaces $A_i \subseteq \mathbb{F}_2^\lambda$ for $i = 1, 2, \cdots, \ell$, where $\ell := \ell(\lambda)$ is a polynomial in λ.
- For each $i \in [\ell]$, choose two uniformly random vectors $s_i, s_i' \in \mathbb{F}_2^n$.
- Prepare the programs iO($A_i + s_i$) and iO($A_i^\perp + s_i'$) (where we assume that the programs $A_i + s_i$ and $A_i^\perp + s_i'$ are padded to some appropriate length).
- Output sk = $\{A_i, s_i, s_i'\}_{i\in[\ell]}$, pk = $\{$iO($A_i + s_i$), iO($A_i^\perp + s_i'$)$\}_{i\in[\ell]}$.

UD.KeyGen(sk) → ρ_{sk} : on input sk = $\{A_i, s_i, s_i'\}_{i\in[\ell]}$, output the "quantum secret key" $\rho_{sk} = \{|A_{i,s_i,s_i'}\rangle\}_{i\in[\ell]}$.

UD.Enc(pk, m) → ct : on input a public key pk = $\{$iO($A_i + s_i$), iO($A_i^\perp + s_i'$)$\}_{i\in[\ell]}$ and message m:
- Sample a uniformly random string $r \leftarrow \{0,1\}^\ell$.
- Let r_i be the i-th bit of r. Define $R_i^0 =$ iO($A_i + s_i$) and $R_i^1 =$ iO($A_i^\perp + s_i'$). Let $\mathsf{P}_{m,r}$ be the following program Figure 5.
- Let $\hat{\mathsf{P}}_{m,r} =$ iO($\mathsf{P}_{m,r}$). Output ciphertext ct = $(\hat{\mathsf{P}}_{m,r}, r)$.

UD.Dec(ρ_{sk}, ct) → $m/\perp$: on input $\rho_{sk} = \{|A_{i,s_i,s_i'}\rangle\}_{i\in[\ell]}$ and ct = $(\hat{\mathsf{P}}_{m,r}, r)$:
- For each $i \in [\ell]$, if $r_i = 1$, apply $H^{\otimes n}$ to the i-th state $|A_{i,s_i,s_i'}\rangle$; if $r_i = 0$, leave the i-th state $|A_{i,s_i,s_i'}\rangle$ unchanged. Denote the resulting state by ρ_{sk}^*.
- Evaluate the program $\hat{\mathsf{P}}_{m,r}$ on input ρ_{sk}^* in superposition; measure the evaluation register and denote the outcome by m'. Output m'.
- Rewind by applying the operations in the first step again.

UD.Sim(n) → ct : on input a message length n, ct ← iO(Sim(1^λ, P.param)) where Sim denotes the simulator for compute-and-compare obfuscator, P.param consists of all program parameters in $\mathsf{P}_{m,r}$ as in UD.Enc for any m of length n.

Fig. 4. Unclonable decryption in [13].

3.3   Proof of Anti-Piracy

In this section, we prove that our construction satisfies anti-piracy. Although the proof requires to open up the structure of UD, this only happens for the last step: for arguing we can extract secrets for the underlying coset states using the properties of compute-and-compare obfuscation. Therefore, we will present the main idea of the proof here, leaving the proof of successful extraction (see Claim 5) in the full version.

Theorem 6. *The construction in Sect. 3.2 has strong γ-anti-piracy for any inverse polynomial γ (as defined in Definition 7).*

Proof. We prove by contradiction. There exist inverse polynomials $\gamma(\cdot), \nu(\cdot), k(\cdot)$ and an adversary $\mathcal{A}$ such that for infinitely many $\lambda \in \mathbb{N}^+$, $\mathcal{A}$ outputs a pair of

On input $u = u_1 \| u_2 \| \cdots \| u_\ell$ (where each $u_i \in \mathbb{F}_2^n$):

1. If for all $i \in [\ell]$, $R_i^{r_i}(u_i) = 1$:
   Output m
2. Else:
   Output $\perp$

Fig. 5. Program $\mathcal{P}_{m,r}$

distinct messages (m_0, m_1) and a state σ over $k + 1$ registers (which are $k + 1$ decryptors) such that

$$\mathrm{Tr}\left[\left(\mathsf{TI}_{1/2+\gamma} \otimes \mathsf{TI}_{1/2+\gamma} \otimes \cdots \otimes \mathsf{TI}_{1/2+\gamma}\right) \sigma\right] \geq \nu. \tag{2}$$

Let σ^* be the leftover state (over the $k + 1$ registers), conditioned on all $\mathsf{TI}_{1/2+\gamma}$ outputting 1. With Equation (2), we can get to σ^* with probability at least ν.

Next we will prove the theorem assuming we have perfect projective implementation (see below). Therefore, the resulting reduction is inefficient. At the end of the section, we will show the proof translates easily when we replace every projective implementation with its approximated and efficient version. This replacement will give us an efficient reduction and only incur a small loss.

Defining Probability Measurement PI. We start by defining the following measurements PI_i for each $i \in [k]$. PI_i stands for the projective implementation where the underlying ciphertext distribution is: the first i ciphertexts are "fake", without encoding any information about the plaintext; the rest are generated honestly. pk are $(\mathsf{pk}_1, \cdots, \mathsf{pk}_k)$ as defined in our construction Sect. 3.2; similarly for sk_i.

- Let $\mathcal{P}_i = (P_i, I - P_i)$ be the following POVM acting on a quantum decryptor:
  - Sample a uniform $b \leftarrow \{0, 1\}$ and random coins (which will be used to generated ciphertexts $\mathsf{ct}_1, \cdots, \mathsf{ct}_k$).
  - For each $j \in \{1, \cdots, i - 1\}$, compute $\mathsf{ct}_j \leftarrow \mathsf{UD.Sim}(n)$ where n is the length of m_0 and m_1.
  - For each $j \in \{i, \cdots, k\}$, compute $\mathsf{ct}_j \leftarrow \mathsf{UD.Enc}(\mathsf{pk}_j, m_b)$.
  - Let $\mathsf{ct} = (\mathsf{ct}_1, \cdots, \mathsf{ct}_k)$.
  - Run the quantum decryptor on input ct. Check whether the outcome is m_b. If so, output 1; otherwise, output 0.
- Let PI_i be the projective implementation of $\mathcal{P}_i$.

It is easy to see that when a quantum decryptor is in the subspace defined by $\mathsf{TI}_{1/2+\gamma}$, applying PI_0 on the state will always produce a real number $\beta \geq 1/2 + \gamma$. This is a simple observation following Theorem 5: $\mathsf{TI}_{1/2+\gamma}$ is implemented by first applying PI_0 and comparing the outcome with $1/2 + \gamma$.

Let the outcome of applying PI_0 on the i-th quantum decryptor of σ^* be a random variable $b_{i,0}$. We have:

$$\Pr\left[\forall i \in [k+1], b_{i,0} \geq \frac{1}{2} + \gamma\right] = 1. \tag{3}$$

Repeated Probability Measure and Its Properties. We then define repeated projective implementation. For the first quantum decryptor $\sigma^*[1]$, we apply PI_0 to obtain a outcome $b_{1,0}$. Then we apply the next projective implementation PI_1 on the leftover state to obtain a outcome $b_{1,1}$. So on and so forth, until we stop after applying PI_k. The outcomes of all measurements are denoted by random variables $b_{1,0}, \cdots, b_{1,k}$.

Claim 1. There always exists $j \in [k]$ such that $b_{1,j-1} - b_{1,j} \geq \gamma/k$.

Proof. For any quantum decryptor, if we apply PI_k on it, the outcome will always be $1/2$. This is because the ciphertext in PI_k is always generated without any information about m_0 or m_1. Therefore, every decryptor's behavior is random guessing: $b_{1,k}$ is always $1/2$.

From Eq. (3), we know that $b_{1,0} \geq 1/2 + \gamma$. By triangle inequality, the claim holds.   □

We use a random variable j_1 for the first index such that $b_{1,j_1-1} - b_{1,j_1} \geq \gamma/k$.

We similarly define the above repeated projective implementation for every quantum decryptor $\sigma^*[i]$. Since the repeated measurement on the i-th decryptor commutes with the repeated measurement on the i'-th ($i' \neq i$) decryptor, we can safely assume they are done in any order. Let $(b_{i,0}, \cdots, b_{i,j}, \cdots, b_{i,k})$ be the outcome of the repeated projective implementation the i-th decryptor. Similarly, Claim 1 holds for every decryptor:

Claim 2. For every $i \in [k+1]$, there always exists $j \in [k]$ such that $b_{i,j-1} - b_{i,j} \geq \gamma/k$.

Let j_i be the first index such that $b_{i,j_i-1} - b_{i,j_i} \geq \gamma/k$. We next show that there always exist $x \neq y$ such that $j_x = j_y$.

Claim 3. $\Pr[\exists x \neq y, j_x = j_y] = 1$.

Proof. This is simply because for every $i \in [k+1]$, $j_i \in [k]$. The claim follows from the pigeonhole principle.

□

Guessing x, y and j_x. We describe the first half of our reduction algorithm. The algorithm takes as input σ^* (postselecting on all $\mathsf{TI}_{1/2+\gamma}$ output 1, and aborting if it fails).

In the second part of the reduction algorithm, it will extract a pair of secrets for the same coset states from $\sigma^{**}[x, y]$.

We prove the following claim for the above algorithm.

On input the $k+1$ quantum decryptors σ^*:

1. Randomly sample $1 \leq x < y \leq k+1$ and $j \in [k]$;
2. Apply repeated projective measurement PI_0 to PI_{j-1} to $\sigma^*[x]$. Let $b_{x,j-1}$ be the last outcome.
3. Apply repeated projective measurement PI_0 to PI_{j-1} to $\sigma^*[y]$. Let $b_{y,j-1}$ be the last outcome.
4. Output $(x, y, j, b_{x,j-1}, b_{y,j-1})$ and both the x-th and y-th decryptors, denoted by $\sigma^{**}[x, y]$.

Fig. 6. Reduction Algorithm Part 1

Claim 4. With probability at least $1/(2k^3)$, the above procedure produces $(x, y, j, b_{x,j-1}, b_{y,j-1})$ and $\sigma^{**}[x, y]$ satisfy:

1. Applying $\mathsf{PI}_{j-1}^{\otimes 2}$ jointly on $\sigma^*[x, y]$ produces $b_{x,j-1}, b_{y,j-1}$ with probability 1.
2. Applying $\mathsf{PI}_j^{\otimes 2}$ jointly on $\sigma^*[x, y]$ produces $b_{x,j}, b_{y,j}$, such that:

$$\Pr \left[b_{x,j-1} - b_{x,j} \geq \frac{\gamma}{k} \wedge b_{y,j-1} - b_{y,j} \geq \frac{\gamma}{k} \right] \geq \frac{1}{2k^3}.$$

Proof (Proof for Claim 4). By Claim 2, there is always a pair of indices $x < y$ and an integer $j \in [k]$ such that $b_{x,j-1} - b_{x,j} \geq \frac{\gamma}{k}$ and $b_{y,j-1} - b_{y,j} \geq \frac{\gamma}{k}$ simultaneously. As a consequence, suppose that we guess x, y and j uniformly at random *after* applying the repeated projective implementation $\mathsf{PI}_0, \cdots, \mathsf{PI}_k$ on every quantum decryptor, then

$$\Pr \left[b_{x,j-1} - b_{x,j} \geq \frac{\gamma}{k} \wedge b_{y,j-1} - b_{y,j} \geq \frac{\gamma}{k} \right] \geq \frac{1}{\binom{k+1}{2} \cdot k} \geq \frac{1}{k^3}, \qquad (4)$$

where the last inequality follows by $k \geq 1$.

Since the repeated projective implementations on disjoint quantum decryptors commute , the same probability can be achieved if we *only* apply the repeated measurements on the x-th and y-th decryptors, skipping the other $(k-1)$ ones (see Fig. 7).

We have

$$\Pr_{\mathsf{RandomMeasure}(\sigma^*)} \left[b_{x,j-1} - b_{x,j} \geq \frac{\gamma}{k} \wedge b_{y,j-1} - b_{y,j} \geq \frac{\gamma}{k} \right] \geq \frac{1}{k^3}. \qquad (5)$$

Eqs. (4) and (5) differ on how $b_{x,j-1}, b_{x,j}, b_{y,j-1}, b_{y,j}$ is sampled.

We can view our reduction algorithm (Fig. 6) as the first step of RandomMeasure (Fig. 7). More formally, RandomMeasure first runs the reduction algorithm to get $(x, y, j, b_{x,j-1}, b_{y,j-1})$ and $\sigma^{**}[x, y]$; it then applies PI_j on both registers to obtain $b_{x,j}$ and $b_{y,j}$.

If the claim we want to prove does not hold, then with probability $< 1/(2k^3)$, the outcome $(x, y, j, b_{x,j-1}, b_{y,j-1})$ and $\sigma^{**}[x, y]$ satisfy condition (2) in Claim 4.

On input the $k + 1$ quantum decryptors σ^*:
1. Randomly sample $1 \leq x < y \leq k + 1$ and $j \in [k]$;
2. Apply repeated projective measurement PI_0 to PI_j to $\sigma^*[x]$. Let $b_{x,j-1}, b_{x,j}$ be the last two outcomes.
3. Apply repeated projective measurement PI_0 to PI_j to $\sigma^*[y]$. Let $b_{y,j-1}, b_{y,j}$ be the last two outcomes.
4. Output $(x, y, j, b_{x,j-1}, b_{x,j}, b_{y,j-1}, b_{y,j})$.

Fig. 7. Algorithm RandomMeasure(σ^*)

Therefore, the probability in Eq. (5) is strictly smaller than $1/(2k^3) + 1/(2k^3)$. This is a contradiction .

$\square$

Extracting Secrets from $\sigma^{**}[x, y]$. We describe the second half of our reduction algorithm. Given $(x, y, j, b_{x,j-1}, b_{y,j-1})$ and $\sigma^{**}[x, y]$ that satisfy both conditions in Claim 4, we can extract secrets for both coset states. This violates the strong computational monogamy-of-entanglement property of coset states, thus finishes the proof.

Recall the underlying ciphertext distribution of PI_{j-1} and PI_j:

1. The first $j - 1$ ciphertexts $\mathsf{ct}_1, \cdots, \mathsf{ct}_{j-1}$ are generated by $\mathsf{Sim}(n)$.
2. The last $k - j$ ciphertexts $\mathsf{ct}_{j+1}, \cdots, \mathsf{ct}_k$ are generated honestly, using their corresponding public key.
3. The j-th ciphertext is either generated honestly using the j-th public key pk_j (in PI_{j-1}), or by $\mathsf{Sim}(n)$ (in PI_j). $\mathsf{pk}_j, \mathsf{sk}_j$ is generated by $\mathsf{UD.Setup}$ in Fig. 4. Let the underlying cosets be $\{A_l + s_l, A_l^\perp + s_l'\}_{l=1}^\ell$:

$$\mathsf{pk}_j = \{\mathsf{iO}(A_l + s_l), \mathsf{iO}(A_l^\perp + s_l')\}_{l \in [\ell]},$$
$$\mathsf{sk}_j = \{A_l, s_l, s_l'\}_{l \in [\ell]}.$$

The following claim says that if applying P_{j-1} or P_j on a quantum decryptor produce different values (with difference more than γ/k), then we can extract ℓ vectors $v_1, \cdots, v_\ell$: each v_l is uniformly in either $A_l + s_l$ or $A_l^\perp + s_l'$.

Claim 5. For any $k = \mathsf{poly}(\lambda)$, let $(\mathsf{sk}, \mathsf{pk}) \leftarrow \mathsf{CRUD.Setup}(1^\lambda, k)$ where $\mathsf{sk} = (\mathsf{sk}_1, \cdots, \mathsf{sk}_k)$ and $\mathsf{pk} = (\mathsf{pk}_1, \cdots, \mathsf{pk}_k)$. Let ρ_{sk} be the unclonable decryption key. For any $j \in [k]$, let PI_{j-1} and PI_j be defined at the beginning of the proof. Let $\mathsf{pk}_j = \{\mathsf{iO}(A_l + s_l), \mathsf{iO}(A_l^\perp + s_l')\}_{l \in [\ell]}, \mathsf{sk}_j = \{A_l, s_l, s_l'\}_{l \in [\ell]}$.

If there exist inverse polynomials $\alpha_1(\cdot), \alpha_2(\cdot)$ and an quantum algorithm $\mathcal{B}$ that takes $(\rho_{\mathsf{sk}}, \mathsf{pk})$ outputs ρ such that with probability at least α_1, ρ satisfies the following:

1. There exists $b_{j-1} \in (0, 1]$, applying PI_{j-1} on ρ always produces b_{j-1}.
2. Let the outcome of applying PI_j on ρ be b_j. Then $\Pr[b_{j-1} - b_j > \gamma/k] > \alpha_2$.

Then there exists another inverse polynomial $\beta(\cdot)$ and an efficient quantum algorithm $\mathcal{C}$ that takes all the descriptions of $\{A_l\}_{l=1}^{\ell}$ (denoted by $\mathbf{A}$), ρ and ℓ random coins $r_1, \cdots, r_\ell \in \{0, 1\}$ such that:

$$\Pr_{\substack{\mathsf{sk},\mathsf{pk},\rho_{\mathsf{sk}},r \\ \rho \leftarrow \mathcal{B}(\rho_{\mathsf{sk}},\mathsf{pk})}} \left[\forall l \in [\ell], v_l \in \begin{cases} A_l + s_l & \text{if } r_l = 0 \\ A_l^{\perp} + s_l' & \text{if } r_l = 1 \end{cases}, (v_1, \cdots, v_\ell) \leftarrow \mathcal{C}(\mathbf{A}, \rho, r) \right] \geq \beta.$$

The proof of this is similar to the extraction technique in [13] using compute-and-compare obfuscation. We refer interested readers to the full version.

By setting $\alpha_1 = \alpha_2 := 1/(2k^3)$, $\mathcal{B}$ be the reduction algorithm in Fig. 6 and $\rho := \sigma^{**}[x]$, we conclude that there exists another algorithm that takes $\sigma^{**}[x]$, random coins $r_1, \cdots, r_\ell$ and outputs $(v_1, \cdots, v_\ell)$ in the corresponding cosets (depending on each r_l).

Next, we show that after a successful extraction on the $\sigma^{**}[x]$, the other decryptor still satisfy the conditions (1) (2) for Claim 5. Therefore, we can extract another random set of vectors from the other decryptor, with non-negligible probability, even conditioned on a successful extraction on $\sigma^{**}[x]$.

Assume conditioned on a successful extraction on the $\sigma^{**}[x]$, the other decryptor becomes $\sigma'[y]$ and it does not satisfy the conditions in Claim 5.

First, applying PI_{j-1} on $\sigma'[y]$ always produces $b_{y,j-1}$. This is because the extraction on the $\sigma^{**}[x]$ register does not change the support of $\sigma'[y]$. Thus, condition (2) in Claim 5 can not hold. Let $\mathbf{E}_1$ denote a successful (E)xtraction on $\sigma^{**}[x]$ and $\mathbf{G}_2$ be a indicator that applying PI_j on $\sigma^{**}[y]$ to get $b_{y,j}$ and $b_{y,j} < b_{y,j-1} - \frac{\gamma}{k^3}$ (a big (G)ap). We know that in this case, $\Pr[\mathbf{E}_1 \wedge \mathbf{G}_2]$ is negligibly small.

However, this can not be true. We can imagine PI_j is implemented first. We know that $\Pr[\mathbf{G}_2]$ is non-negligible by the condition (2) in Claim 4. Conditioned on $\mathbf{G}_2$, let the x-th decryptor become $\sigma'[x]$. We know that $\sigma'[x]$ must satisfy both conditions in Claim 5. Otherwise, condition (2) in Claim 4 can not hold. Thus, $\Pr[\mathbf{G}_2|\mathbf{E}_1]$ must be non-negligible. This contradicts with the assumption that $\Pr[\mathbf{E}_1 \wedge \mathbf{G}_2]$ is negligibly small.

Thus, the reduction algorithm, with non-negligible probability, can extract $(v_1, \cdots, v_\ell)$ and $(v_1', \cdots, v_\ell')$ with respect to random $r_1, \cdots, r_\ell$ and $r_1', \cdots, r_\ell'$. With probability at least $1 - 2^{-\ell}$, there exist $l \in [\ell]$ such that $r_l \neq r_l'$. Thus, v_l and v_l' will be two vectors in each of the cosets $A_l + s_l$ and $A_l' + s_l'$. By guessing this l, this breaks the computational strong monogamy-of-entanglement game (Theorem 3). □

References

1. Aaronson, S.: Limitations of quantum advice and one-way communication. Theory Comput. 1(1), 1–28 (2005). https://doi.org/10.4086/toc.2005.v001a001
2. Aaronson, S.: Quantum copy-protection and quantum money. In: Proceedings of the 24th Annual IEEE Conference on Computational Complexity, CCC 2009, Paris, France, 15–18 July 2009, pp. 229–242. IEEE Computer Society (2009). https://doi.org/10.1109/CCC.2009.42

3. Aaronson, S., Christiano, P.: Quantum money from hidden subspaces. Theory Comput. **9**(9), 349–401 (2013). https://doi.org/10.4086/toc.2013.v009a009

4. Aaronson, S., Liu, J., Liu, Q., Zhandry, M., Zhang, R.: New approaches for quantum copy-protection. In: Malkin, T., Peikert, C. (eds.) CRYPTO 2021. LNCS, vol. 12825, pp. 526–555. Springer, Cham (2021). https://doi.org/10.1007/978-3-030-84242-0_19

5. Ananth, P., Kaleoglu, F.: A note on copy-protection from random oracles (2022). https://doi.org/10.48550/ARXIV.2208.12884. https://arxiv.org/abs/2208.12884

6. Ananth, P., Kaleoglu, F., Li, X., Liu, Q., Zhandry, M.: On the feasibility of unclonable encryption, and more. In: Dodis, Y., Shrimpton, T. (eds.) Advances in Cryptology - CRYPTO 2022. Lecture Notes in Computer Science, vol. 13507. Springer (2022). https://doi.org/10.1007/978-3-031-15979-4_8

7. Ananth, P., La Placa, R.L.: Secure software leasing. In: Canteaut, A., Standaert, F.-X. (eds.) EUROCRYPT 2021. LNCS, vol. 12697, pp. 501–530. Springer, Cham (2021). https://doi.org/10.1007/978-3-030-77886-6_17

8. Barak, B., et al.: On the (Im)possibility of obfuscating programs. In: Kilian, J. (ed.) CRYPTO 2001. LNCS, vol. 2139, pp. 1–18. Springer, Heidelberg (2001). https://doi.org/10.1007/3-540-44647-8_1

9. Ben-David, S., Sattath, O.: Quantum tokens for digital signatures (2016)

10. Bennett, C.H., Brassard, G.: Quantum cryptography: public key distribution and coin tossing. In: Proceedings of International Conference on Computers, Systems & Signal Processing, 9–12 Dec 1984, pp. 175–179. Bangalore, India (1984)

11. Broadbent, A., Jeffery, S., Lord, S., Podder, S., Sundaram, A.: Secure software leasing without assumptions. In: Nissim, K., Waters, B. (eds.) TCC 2021. LNCS, vol. 13042, pp. 90–120. Springer, Cham (2021). https://doi.org/10.1007/978-3-030-90459-3_4

12. Cohen, A., Holmgren, J., Nishimaki, R., Vaikuntanathan, V., Wichs, D.: Watermarking cryptographic capabilities. SIAM J. Comput. **47**(6), 2157–2202 (2018)

13. Coladangelo, A., Liu, J., Liu, Q., Zhandry, M.: Hidden cosets and applications to unclonable cryptography. In: Malkin, T., Peikert, C. (eds.) CRYPTO 2021. LNCS, vol. 12825, pp. 556–584. Springer, Cham (2021). https://doi.org/10.1007/978-3-030-84242-0_20

14. Coladangelo, A., Majenz, C., Poremba, A.: Quantum copy-protection of compute-and-compare programs in the quantum random oracle model (2020). https://arxiv.org/abs/2009.13865

15. Culf, E., Vidick, T.: A monogamy-of-entanglement game for subspace coset states (2021)

16. Garg, S., Gentry, C., Halevi, S., Raykova, M., Sahai, A., Waters, B.: Candidate indistinguishability obfuscation and functional encryption for all circuits. SIAM J. Comput. **45**(3), 882–929 (2016). https://doi.org/10.1137/14095772X

17. Georgiou, M., Zhandry, M.: Unclonable decryption keys (2020). https://eprint.iacr.org/2020/877

18. Goyal, R., Kim, S., Manohar, N., Waters, B., Wu, D.J.: Watermarking public-key cryptographic primitives. In: Boldyreva, A., Micciancio, D. (eds.) CRYPTO 2019. LNCS, vol. 11694, pp. 367–398. Springer, Cham (2019). https://doi.org/10.1007/978-3-030-26954-8_12

19. Kim, S., Wu, D.J.: Watermarking cryptographic functionalities from standard lattice assumptions. In: Katz, J., Shacham, H. (eds.) CRYPTO 2017. LNCS, vol. 10401, pp. 503–536. Springer, Cham (2017). https://doi.org/10.1007/978-3-319-63688-7_17

20. Kim, S., Wu, D.J.: Watermarking PRFs from lattices: stronger security via extractable PRFs. In: Boldyreva, A., Micciancio, D. (eds.) CRYPTO 2019. LNCS, vol. 11694, pp. 335–366. Springer, Cham (2019). https://doi.org/10.1007/978-3-030-26954-8_11

21. Kitagawa, F., Nishimaki, R., Yamakawa, T.: Secure software leasing from standard assumptions. In: Nissim, K., Waters, B. (eds.) TCC 2021. LNCS, vol. 13042, pp. 31–61. Springer, Cham (2021). https://doi.org/10.1007/978-3-030-90459-3_2

22. Kretschmer, W.: Quantum pseudorandomness and classical complexity. In: Hsieh, M. (ed.) 16th Conference on the Theory of Quantum Computation, Communication and Cryptography, TQC 2021, 5–8 July 2021, Virtual Conference. LIPIcs, vol. 197, pp. 1–20. Schloss Dagstuhl - Leibniz-Zentrum für Informatik (2021). https://doi.org/10.4230/LIPIcs.TQC.2021.2

23. Marriott, C., Watrous, J.: Quantum arthur-merlin games. computational complexity 14(2), 122–152 (2005). https://doi.org/10.1007/s00037-005-0194-x

24. Nielsen, M.A., Chuang, I.L.: Quantum computation and quantum information: 10th Anniversary Edition. Cambridge University Press (2010). https://doi.org/10.1017/CBO9780511976667

25. Sahai, A., Waters, B.: How to use indistinguishability obfuscation: Deniable encryption, and more. SIAM J. Comput. 50(3), 857–908 (2021). https://doi.org/10.1137/15M1030108

26. Vidick, T., Zhang, T.: Classical proofs of quantum knowledge. In: Canteaut, A., Standaert, F.-X. (eds.) EUROCRYPT 2021. LNCS, vol. 12697, pp. 630–660. Springer, Cham (2021). https://doi.org/10.1007/978-3-030-77886-6_22

27. Wiesner, S.: Conjugate coding. SIGACT News 15(1), 78–88 (1983). https://doi.org/10.1145/1008908.1008920

28. Yang, R., Au, M.H., Lai, J., Xu, Q., Yu, Z.: Collusion resistant watermarking schemes for cryptographic functionalities. In: Galbraith, S.D., Moriai, S. (eds.) ASIACRYPT 2019. LNCS, vol. 11921, pp. 371–398. Springer, Cham (2019). https://doi.org/10.1007/978-3-030-34578-5_14

29. Yang, R., Au, M.H., Yu, Z., Xu, Q.: Collusion resistant watermarkable PRFs from standard assumptions. In: Micciancio, D., Ristenpart, T. (eds.) CRYPTO 2020. LNCS, vol. 12170, pp. 590–620. Springer, Cham (2020). https://doi.org/10.1007/978-3-030-56784-2_20

30. Zhandry, M.: Schrödinger's pirate: how to trace a quantum decoder. In: Pass, R., Pietrzak, K. (eds.) TCC 2020. LNCS, vol. 12552, pp. 61–91. Springer, Cham (2020). https://doi.org/10.1007/978-3-030-64381-2_3

Secret-Sharing and Applications

On Secret Sharing, Randomness, and Random-less Reductions for Secret Sharing

Divesh Aggarwal[1], Eldon Chung[1]([✉]), Maciej Obremski[1], and João Ribeiro[2]

[1] National University of Singapore, Singapore, Singapore
dcsdiva@nus.edu.sg, eldon.chung@u.nus.edu
[2] Carnegie Mellon University, Pittsburgh, PA, USA
jlourenc@cs.cmu.edu

Abstract. Secret-sharing is one of the most fundamental primitives in cryptography, and has found several applications. All known constructions of secret sharing (with the exception of those with a pathological choice of parameters) require access to uniform randomness. However, in practice it is extremely challenging to generate a source of uniform randomness. This has led to a large body of research devoted to designing randomized algorithms and cryptographic primitives from imperfect sources of randomness. Motivated by this, Bosley and Dodis (TCC 2007) asked whether it is even possible to construct a 2-out-of-2 secret sharing scheme without access to uniform randomness.

In this work, we make significant progress towards answering this question. Namely, we resolve this question for secret sharing schemes with important additional properties: 1-bit leakage-resilience and non-malleability. We prove that, for not too small secrets, it is impossible to construct any 2-out-of-2 leakage-resilient or non-malleable secret sharing scheme without access to uniform randomness.

Given that the problem of whether 2-out-of-2 secret sharing requires uniform randomness has been open for more than a decade, it is reasonable to consider intermediate problems towards resolving the open question. In a spirit similar to NP-completeness, we also study how the existence of a t-out-of-n secret sharing without access to uniform randomness is related to the existence of a t'-out-of-n' secret sharing without access to uniform randomness for a different choice of the parameters t, n, t', n'.

1 Introduction

Secret sharing, introduced by Blakley [12] and Shamir [47], strikes a meaningful balance between availability and confidentiality of secret information. This fundamental cryptographic primitive has found a host of applications, most notably to threshold cryptography and multi-party computation (see [21] for an extensive discussion). In a secret sharing scheme for n parties, a dealer who holds a

E. Kiltz and V. Vaikuntanathan (Eds.): TCC 2022, LNCS 13747, pp. 327–354, 2022.
https://doi.org/10.1007/978-3-031-22318-1_12

secret s chosen from a domain $\mathcal{M}$ can compute a set of n *shares* by evaluating a randomized function on s which we write as $\textbf{Share}(s) = (\textsf{Sh}_1, \ldots, \textsf{Sh}_n)$. The notion of *threshold* secret sharing is particularly important: A t-out-of-n secret sharing scheme ensures that any t shares are sufficient to recover the secret s, but any $t - 1$ shares reveal no information about the secret s.

Motivated by practice, several variants of secret sharing have been suggested which guarantee security under stronger adversarial models. The notion of *leakage-resilient* secret sharing was put forth in order to model and handle side-channel attacks to secret shared data. In more detail, the adversary, who holds an unauthorized subset of shares, is furthermore allowed to specify a leakage function $\textsf{Leak}$ from a restricted family of functions and learn $\textsf{Leak}(\textsf{Sh}_1, \ldots, \textsf{Sh}_n)$. The goal is that this additional side information reveals almost no information about the secret. Typically one considers *local leakage*, where $\textsf{Leak}(\textsf{Sh}_1, \ldots, \textsf{Sh}_n) = (\textsf{Leak}_1(\textsf{Sh}_1), \ldots, \textsf{Leak}_n(\textsf{Sh}_n))$ for local leakage functions $\textsf{Leak}_i$ with bounded output length. This makes sense in a scenario where shares are stored in physically separated locations. The alternative setting where adversaries are allowed to *corrupt* all shares (e.g., by infecting storage devices with viruses) led to the introduction of *non-malleable* secret sharing. In this case, the adversary specifies tampering functions $f_1, f_2, \ldots, f_n$ which act on the shares, and then the reconstruction algorithm is applied to the tampered shares $f_1(\textsf{Sh}_1), \ldots, f_n(\textsf{Sh}_n)$. The requirement, roughly speaking, is that either the original secret is reconstructed or it is destroyed, i.e., the reconstruction result is unrelated to the original secret. Both leakage-resilient and non-malleable secret sharing have received significant attention in the past few years.

Cryptography with Weak Randomness. It is well-known that randomness plays a fundamental role in cryptography and other areas of computer science. In fact, most cryptographic goals cannot be achieved without access to a source of randomness. Almost all settings considered in the literature assume that this source of randomness is perfectly random: It outputs uniformly random and independent bits. However, in practice it is extremely hard to generate perfect randomness. The randomness needed for the task at hand is generated from some physical process, such as electromagnetic noise or user dependent behavior. While these sources have some inherent randomness, in the sense that they contain entropy, samples from such sources are not necessarily uniformly distributed. Additionally, the randomness generation procedure may be partially accessible to the adversary, in which case the quality of the randomness provided degrades even further. The difficulty in working with such imperfect randomness sources not only arises from the fact that they are not uniformly random, but also because the exact distribution of these sources is unknown. One can at best assume that they satisfy some minimal property, for example that none of the outcomes is highly likely as first considered by Chor and Goldreich [19].

The best one can hope for is to deterministically extract a nearly perfect random string for direct usage in the desired application. While there are source models which allow for deterministic randomness extraction, such as von Neumann sources [42], bit-fixing sources [20], affine sources [15], and other efficiently generated or recognizable sources [11,13,18,29,30,35,37,46,51], all these models make strong assumptions about the structure of the source. On the other hand, the most natural, flexible, and well-studied source model where we only assume a lower bound on the min-entropy of the source[1] does not allow deterministic extraction of even 1 almost uniformly random bit [19]. This holds even in the highly optimistic case where the source is supported on $\{0,1\}^d$ and has min-entropy $d - 1$. Nevertheless, it has been long known, for example, that min-entropy sources are sufficient for simulating certain randomized algorithms and interactive protocols [19].

This discussion naturally leads us to wonder whether perfect randomness is essential in different cryptographic primitives, in the sense that the underlying class of sources of randomness allows deterministic extraction of nearly uniformly random bits. We call such classes of sources *extractable*. More concretely, the following is our main question.

Question 1. Does secret sharing, or any of its useful variants such as leakage-resilient or non-malleable secret sharing, *require* access to *extractable* randomness?

This question was first asked by Bosley and Dodis [14] (for 2-out-of-2 secret sharing) and it remains open. Bosley and Dodis settled the analogous question for the case of information-theoretic private-key encryption, motivated by a series of (im)possibility results for such schemes in more specific source models [24,26,41]. More precisely, they showed that encryption schemes using d bits of randomness and encrypting messages of size $b > \log d$ require extractable randomness, while those encrypting messages of size $b < \log d - \log\log d - 1$ do not.

As noted in [14,25], private-key encryption schemes yield 2-out-of-2 secret sharing schemes by seeing the uniformly random key as the left share and the ciphertext as the right share. Therefore, we may interpret the main result of [14] as settling Question 1 for the artificial and highly restrictive class of secret sharing schemes where the left share is uniformly random and independent of the secret, and the right share is a deterministic function of the secret and the left share. No progress has been made on Question 1 since.

Random-Less Reductions for Secret Sharing. Given that the problem of whether 2-out-of-2 secret sharing requires extractable randomness has been open for 15 years, it is reasonable to consider intermediate problems towards resolving the open question. In a spirit similar to computational complexity, we consider how the question whether t out of n secret sharing requires extractable randomness is related to the same question for a different choice of the parameters t, n i.e.,

Question 2. Given t, n, t', n', does the fact that t-out-of-n secret sharing require extractable randomness imply that t'-out-of-n' secret sharing require extractable randomness?

---

[1] A source is said to have *min-entropy* k if the probability that it takes any fixed value is upper bounded by 2^{-k}.

A natural approach towards resolving this question is to try to construct a t-out-of-n secret sharing scheme from a t'-out-of-n' secret sharing scheme in a black-box manner without any additional randomness. Intuitively, since we don't have access to any additional randomness, it seems that the most obvious strategy to achieve such reductions is to choose n subsets of the set of n' shares in such a way that any t out of these n subsets contain at least t' out of the original n' shares and any $t-1$ subsets contain at most $t'-1$ of the original n' shares. In particular, there is a trivial reduction when $t = n = 2$ that chooses the first subset to contain the first of the n' shares, and the second subset to contain any $t'-1$ of the remaining shares. This shows the completeness of the extractability of 2-out-of-2 secret sharing with respect to these reductions. Such reductions can be formalized via distribution designs [49].

1.1   Our Results

In this work, we make progress on both Question 1 and Question 2. Before we proceed to discuss our results, we formalize the notions of an extractable class of randomness sources and threshold secret sharing.

Definition 1 (Extractable class of sources). *We say a class of randomness sources $\mathcal{Y}$ over $\{0,1\}^d$ is (δ, m)-extractable if there exists a deterministic function* $\mathsf{Ext} : \{0,1\}^d \to \{0,1\}^m$ *such that[2]* $\mathsf{Ext}(Y) \approx_\delta U_m$ *for every $Y \in \mathcal{Y}$, where U_m denotes the uniform distribution over $\{0,1\}^m$.*

Note that we may consider the support of all sources in $\mathcal{Y}$ to be contained in some set $\{0,1\}^d$ without loss of generality. Since we will be interested in studying the quality of randomness used by secret sharing schemes, we make the class of randomness sources allowed for a secret sharing scheme explicit in the definition of t-out-of-n threshold secret sharing below.

Definition 2 (Threshold secret sharing scheme). *A tuple $(\mathbf{Share}, \mathbf{Rec}, \mathcal{Y})$ with $\mathbf{Share} : \{0,1\}^b \times \{0,1\}^d \to \left(\{0,1\}^\ell\right)^n$ and $\mathbf{Rec} : \{0,1\}^* \to \{0,1\}^b$ deterministic algorithms and $\mathcal{Y}$ a class of randomness sources over $\{0,1\}^d$ is a (t, n, ε)-secret sharing scheme (for b-bit messages using d bits of randomness) if for every randomness source $Y \in \mathcal{Y}$ the following hold:*

1. *If $\mathcal{T} \subseteq [n]$ satisfies $|\mathcal{T}| \geq t$ (i.e., $\mathcal{T}$ is authorized), then*

$$\Pr_Y[\mathbf{Rec}(\mathbf{Share}(x,Y)_\mathcal{T}) = x] = 1$$

   for every $x \in \{0,1\}^b$;
2. *If $\mathcal{T} \subseteq [n]$ satisfies $|\mathcal{T}| < t$ (i.e., $\mathcal{T}$ is unauthorized), then for any $x, x' \in \{0,1\}^b$ we have*

$$\mathbf{Share}(x,Y)_\mathcal{T} \approx_\varepsilon \mathbf{Share}(x',Y)_\mathcal{T},$$

   where $\mathbf{Share}(x,Y)_\mathcal{T}$ denotes the shares of parties $i \in \mathcal{T}$.

---

[2] We use the notation $X \approx_\delta Y$ to denote the fact that $\Delta(X;Y) \leq \delta$, where $\Delta(\cdot;\cdot)$ corresponds to statistical distance (see Definition 8).

Leakage-Resilient 2-out-of-2 Secret Sharing Requires Extractable Randomness. As our first contribution, we settle Question 1 for the important sub-class of *leakage-resilient* 2-out-of-2 secret sharing. Intuitively, we consider 2-out-of-2 secret sharing schemes with the additional property that the adversary learns almost nothing about the message when they obtain bounded information from each share. More formally, we have the following definition.

Definition 3 (Leakage-resilient secret sharing scheme). *We say that a tuple* (**Share, Rec,** $\mathcal{Y}$) *with* **Share** : $\{0,1\}^b \times \{0,1\}^d \to (\{0,1\}^\ell)^2$ *and* **Rec** : $\{0,1\}^* \to \{0,1\}^b$ *deterministic algorithms and* $\mathcal{Y}$ *a class of randomness sources over* $\{0,1\}^d$ *is an* $(\varepsilon_1, \varepsilon_2)$-*leakage-resilient secret sharing scheme (for b-bit messages using d bits of randomness) if* (**Share, Rec,** $\mathcal{Y}$) *is a* $(t = 2, n = 2, \varepsilon_1)$-*secret sharing scheme and the following additional property is satisfied: For any two messages* $x, x' \in \{0,1\}^b$ *and randomness source* $Y \in \mathcal{Y}$, *let* $(\mathsf{Sh}_1, \mathsf{Sh}_2) = $ **Share**(x, Y) *and* $(\mathsf{Sh}_1', \mathsf{Sh}_2') = $ **Share**(x', Y). *Then, for any leakage functions* $f, g : \{0,1\}^\ell \to \{0,1\}$ *it holds that*

$$f(\mathsf{Sh}_1), g(\mathsf{Sh}_2) \approx_{\varepsilon_2} f(\mathsf{Sh}_1'), g(\mathsf{Sh}_2').$$

Leakage-resilient secret sharing has received significant attention recently, with several constructions and leakage models being analyzed [1,10,17,36,38, 39,48]. Comparatively, Definition 3 considers a significantly weaker notion of leakage-resilience than all works just mentioned. In particular, we do not require leakage-resilience to hold even when the adversary has full access to one of the shares on top of the leakage. This means that our results are widely applicable. Roughly speaking, we prove that every leakage-resilient secret sharing scheme for b-bit messages either requires a huge number of bits of randomness, or we can extract several bits of perfect randomness with low error from its underlying class of randomness sources. More formally, we prove the following.

Theorem 1. *Let* (**Share, Rec,** $\mathcal{Y}$) *be an* $(\varepsilon_1, \varepsilon_2)$-*leakage-resilient secret sharing scheme for b-bit messages. Then, either:*

1. *The scheme uses* $d \geq \min\left(2^{\Omega(b)}, (1/\varepsilon_2)^{\Omega(1)}\right)$ *bits of randomness, or;*

2. *The class of sources* $\mathcal{Y}$ *is* (δ, m)-*extractable with* $\delta \leq \max\left(2^{-\Omega(b)}, \varepsilon_2^{\Omega(1)}\right)$ *and* $m = \Omega(\min(b, \log(1/\varepsilon_2)))$. *Moreover, if* **Share** *is computable by a poly(b)-time algorithm, then* $\mathcal{Y}$ *is* (δ, m)-*extractable by a family of poly(b)-size circuits.*

An important corollary of Theorem 1 is that every efficient negligible-error leakage-resilient secret sharing scheme requires extractable randomness with negligible error.

Corollary 1. *If* (**Share, Rec,** $\mathcal{Y}$) *is an* $(\varepsilon_1, \varepsilon_2)$-*leakage-resilient secret sharing scheme for b-bit messages running in time poly(b) with* $\varepsilon_2 = \mathsf{negl}(b)$,[3] *it follows that* $\mathcal{Y}$ *is* (δ, m)-*extractable with* $\delta = \mathsf{negl}(b)$ *and* $m = \Omega(\min(b, \log(1/\varepsilon_2)))$.

---

[3] By $\varepsilon_2 = \mathsf{negl}(b)$, we mean that $\varepsilon_2 = o(1/b^c)$ for every constant $c > 0$ as $b \to \infty$.

Split-State Non-malleable Coding Requires Extractable Randomness. Non-malleable coding, introduced by Dziembowski, Pietrzak, and Wichs [31], is another recent notion which has attracted much attention, in particular regarding the *split-state* setting (see [3] and references therein). Informally, a split-state non-malleable code has the guarantee that if an adversary is allowed to split a codeword in half and tamper with each half arbitrarily but separately, then the tampered codeword either decodes to the same message, or the output of the decoder is nearly independent of the original message. More formally, we have the following definition.

Definition 4 (Split-state non-malleable code [31]**).** *A tuple* $(\mathbf{Enc}, \mathbf{Dec}, \mathcal{Y})$ *with* $\mathbf{Enc} : \{0,1\}^b \times \{0,1\}^d \to (\{0,1\}^\ell)^2$ *and* $\mathbf{Dec} : (\{0,1\}^\ell)^2 \to \{0,1\}^b \cup \{\bot\}$ *deterministic algorithms and* $\mathcal{Y}$ *a class of randomness sources is a* (split-state) ε-*non-malleable code if the following holds for every randomness source* $Y \in \mathcal{Y}$:

1. $\Pr[\mathbf{Dec}(\mathbf{Enc}(x, Y)) = x] = 1$ *for all* $x \in \{0,1\}^b$;
2. *For tampering functions* $f, g : \{0,1\}^\ell \to \{0,1\}^\ell$, *denote by* $\mathsf{Tamp}_x^{f,g}$ *the tampering random experiment which computes* $(L, R) = \mathbf{Enc}(x, Y)$ *and outputs* $\mathbf{Dec}(f(L), g(R))$. *Then, for any tampering functions* f *and* g *there exists a distribution* $D^{f,g}$ *over* $\{0,1\}^b \cup \{\bot, \mathsf{same}^*\}$ *such that*

$$\mathsf{Tamp}_x^{f,g} \approx_\varepsilon \mathsf{Sim}_x^{f,g}$$

for all $x \in \{0,1\}^b$, *where* $\mathsf{Sim}_x^{f,g}$ *denotes the random experiment which samples* z *according to* $D^{f,g}$ *and outputs* z *if* $z \neq \mathsf{same}^*$ *and* x *if* $z = \mathsf{same}^*$.

The notion of non-malleable code in the split-state model is equivalent to the notion of a **2-out-of-2 non-malleable secret sharing scheme** *[34].*

It is known by [2, Lemmas 3 and 4] that every ε-non-malleable coding scheme $(\mathbf{Enc}, \mathbf{Dec}, \mathcal{Y})$ for b-bit messages is also a $(2\varepsilon, \varepsilon)$-leakage-resilient secret sharing scheme, provided $b \geq 3$ and $\varepsilon < 1/20$. Combining this observation with Theorem 1 yields the following corollary, which states that every split-state non-malleable code either uses a huge number of bits of randomness, or requires extractable randomness with low error and large output length.

Corollary 2. *Let* $(\mathbf{Enc}, \mathbf{Dec}, \mathcal{Y})$ *be an* ε-*non-malleable code (i.e., 2-out-of-2* ε-*non-malleable secret sharing scheme) for* b-*bit messages with* $b \geq 3$ *and* $\varepsilon < 1/20$. *Then, either:*

1. *The scheme uses* $d \geq \min\left(2^{\Omega(b)}, (1/\varepsilon)^{\Omega(1)}\right)$ *bits of randomness, or;*
2. *The class of sources* $\mathcal{Y}$ *is* (δ, m)-*extractable with* $\delta \leq \max\left(2^{-\Omega(b)}, \varepsilon^{\Omega(1)}\right)$ *and* $m = \Omega(\min(b, \log(1/\varepsilon)))$. *Moreover, if* $\mathbf{Enc}$ *is computable by a* $\mathrm{poly}(b)$-*time algorithm, then* $\mathcal{Y}$ *is* (δ, m)-*extractable by a family of* $\mathrm{poly}(b)$-*size circuits.*

As a result, an analogous version of Corollary 1 also holds for split-state non-malleable coding. This resolves Question 1 for 2-out-of-2 non-malleable secret sharing.

Random-Less Reductions for Secret Sharing. In this section, we discuss our contribution towards resolving Question 2. We focus on the following complementary scenario: Suppose we have proved that all (t, n, ε)-secret sharing schemes for b-bit messages using d bits of randomness require a (δ, m)-extractable class of randomness sources. It is then natural to wonder whether such a result can be bootstrapped to conclude that all (t', n', ε)-secret sharing schemes for the same message length b and number of randomness bits d also require (δ, m)-extractable randomness, for different threshold t' and number of parties n'. A natural approach is to set up general *black-box reductions* between different types of secret sharing which, crucially, do not use extra randomness. In fact, if we can obtain from a (t', n', ε)-secret sharing scheme (**Share'**, **Rec'**, $\mathcal{Y}$) another (t, n, ε)-secret sharing scheme (**Share**, **Rec**, $\mathcal{Y}$) for b-bit messages which uses the same class of randomness sources $\mathcal{Y}$, then our initial assumption would allow us to conclude that $\mathcal{Y}$ is (δ, m)-extractable.

Remarkably, we are able to obtain the desired reductions for a broad range of parameters by exploiting a connection to the construction of combinatorial objects called *distribution designs*, a term coined by Stinson and Wei [49] for the old technique of devising a new secret sharing scheme by giving multiple shares of the original scheme to each party. Surprisingly, although these objects have roots going back to early work on secret sharing [9], they have not been the subject of a general study. In this work, we obtain general and simple constructions of, and bounds for, distribution designs, which are tight in certain parameter regimes. We give two examples of reductions we derive from these results.

Corollary 3 (Informal). *If every $(t = 2, n, \varepsilon)$-secret sharing scheme for b-bit messages using d bits of randomness requires a (δ, m)-extractable class of randomness sources, then so does every (t', n', ε)-secret sharing scheme for b-bit messages using d bits of randomness whenever $n \leq \binom{n'}{t'-1}$. Moreover, this is the best distribution-design-based reduction possible with $t = 2$.*

Corollary 4 (Informal). *If every (t, n, ε)-secret sharing scheme for b-bit messages using d bits of randomness requires a (δ, m)-extractable class of randomness sources, then so does every $(t' = n', n', \varepsilon)$-secret sharing scheme for b-bit messages using d bits of randomness whenever $n' \geq \binom{n}{t-1}$. Moreover, this is the best distribution-design-based reduction possible with $t' = n'$.*

1.2   Related Work

We begin by discussing the results on private-key encryption that led to the work of Bosley and Dodis [14] in more detail. Early work by McInnes and Pinkas [41] showed that min-entropy sources and Santha-Vazirani sources are insufficient for information-theoretic private-key encryption of even 1-bit messages. This negative result was later extended to *computationally* secure private-key encryption by Dodis, Ong, Prabhakaran, and Sahai [24], and was complemented by Dodis and Spencer [26], who showed that, in fact, non-extractable randomness *is* sufficient for information-theoretic private-key encryption of 1-bit messages. Later, the picture was completed by the aforementioned groundbreaking work of Bosley and Dodis [14].

Besides the results already discussed above for private-key encryption and secret sharing, the possibility of realizing other cryptographic primitives using certain classes of imperfect randomness sources has also been studied. Non-extractable randomness is known to be sufficient for message authentication [26,40], signature schemes [5,24], differential privacy [23,27,52], secret-key agreement [5], identification protocols [5], and interactive proofs [24]. On the other hand, Santha-Vazirani sources are insufficient for bit commitment, secret sharing, zero knowledge, and two-party computation [24], and in some cases this negative result even holds for Santha-Vazirani sources with efficient tampering procedures [5].

In other directions, the security loss incurred by replacing uniform randomness by imperfect randomness was studied in [6,8], and the scenario where a perfect common reference string is replaced by certain types of imperfect randomness has also been considered [4,16]. The security of keyed cryptographic primitives with non-uniformly random keys has also been studied [28].

1.3   Technical Overview

Leakage-Resilient Secret Sharing Requires Extractable Randomness. We present a high-level overview of our approach towards proving Theorem 1. Recall that our goal is to show that if $(\textbf{Share}, \textbf{Rec}, \mathcal{Y})$ is an $(\varepsilon_1, \varepsilon_2)$-leakage-resilient secret sharing for b-bit messages using d bits of randomness, then there exists a deterministic function $\textsf{Ext} : \{0,1\}^d \to \{0,1\}^m$ such that $\textsf{Ext}(Y) \approx_\delta U_m$ for all sources $Y \in \mathcal{Y}$, provided that the number of randomness bits d used is not huge.

Our candidate extractor $\textsf{Ext}$ works as follows on input some $y \in \{0,1\}^d$:

1. Compute $(\textsf{Sh}_1, \textsf{Sh}_2) = \textbf{Share}(0^b, y) \in \{0,1\}^\ell \times \{0,1\}^\ell$;
2. For appropriate leakage functions $f, g : \{0,1\}^\ell \to \{0,1\}^s$, compute the tuple $(f(\textsf{Sh}_1), g(\textsf{Sh}_2))$;
3. For an appropriate function $h : \{0,1\}^{2s} \to \{0,1\}^m$, output

$$\textsf{Ext}(y) = h(f(\textsf{Sh}_1), g(\textsf{Sh}_2)).$$

The proof of Theorem 1 follows from an analysis of this candidate construction, and we show the existence of appropriate functions f, g, and h via the probabilistic method. Note that the number of sources in $\mathcal{Y}$ may be extremely large. Consequently, our first step, which is similar in spirit to the first step of the related result for private-key encryption in [14], is to exploit the leakage-resilience of the scheme in question to show that it suffices to focus on a restricted family to prove the desired result. More precisely, it suffices to show the existence of functions f, g, and h as above satisfying

$$h(f(Z_1), g(Z_2)) \approx_{\delta'} U_m, \tag{1}$$

with δ' an appropriate error parameter, for all $(Z_1, Z_2) \in \mathcal{Z}$ defined as

$$\mathcal{Z} = \{\mathbf{Share}(U_b, y) : y \in \{0, 1\}^d\},$$

which contains at most 2^d distributions. Our analysis then proceeds in three steps:

1. We show that each $(Z_1, Z_2) \in \mathcal{Z}$ is close in statistical distance to a convex combination of joint distributions $(D_{1,i}, D_{2,i})$ with the property that $\mathbf{H}_\infty(D_{1,i}) + \mathbf{H}_\infty(D_{2,i})$ is sufficiently large for all i, where $\mathbf{H}_\infty(\cdot)$ denotes the min-entropy of a distribution;
2. Exploiting the previous step, we prove that if we pick f and g uniformly at random, then with high probability over this choice it holds that the joint distribution $(f(Z_1), g(Z_2))$ is close in statistical distance to a high min-entropy distribution;
3. A well known, standard application of the probabilistic method then shows that a uniformly random function h will extract many perfectly random bits from $(f(Z_1), g(Z_2))$ with high probability over the choice of h.

While this proves that there exist functions f, g, and h such that (1) holds for a given $(Z_1, Z_2) \in \mathcal{Z}$, we need (1) to be true simultaneously for all $(Z_1, Z_2) \in \mathcal{Z}$. We resolve this by employing a union bound over the at most 2^d distributions in $\mathcal{Z}$. Therefore, if d is not extremely large, we succeed in showing the existence of appropriate functions f, g, and h, and the desired result follows. More details can be found in Sect. 3.

Random-Less Reductions for Secret Sharing. In this section, we define distribution designs and briefly discuss how they can be used to provide the desired black-box reductions between different types of threshold secret sharing, in particular Corollaries 3 and 4. Intuitively, a (t, n, t', n')-distribution design distributes shares $(\mathsf{Sh}_1, \mathsf{Sh}_2, \ldots, \mathsf{Sh}_{n'})$ of some (t', n', ε)-secret sharing scheme into subsets of shares $\mathcal{S}_1, \ldots, \mathcal{S}_n$, with the property that $(\mathcal{S}_1, \ldots, \mathcal{S}_n)$ are now shares of a (t, n, ε)-secret sharing scheme. More formally, we have the following definition, which also appears in [49].

Definition 5 (Distribution design). *We say a family of sets $\mathcal{D}_1, \mathcal{D}_2, \ldots, \mathcal{D}_n \subseteq [n']$ is a (t, n, t', n')-distribution design if for every $\mathcal{T} \subseteq [n]$ it holds that*

$$\left| \bigcup_{i \in \mathcal{T}} \mathcal{D}_i \right| \geq t'$$

if and only if $|\mathcal{T}| \geq t$.

Given a (t, n, t', n')-distribution design $\mathcal{D}_1, \ldots, \mathcal{D}_n \subseteq [n']$, it is clear how to set up a black-box reduction without extra randomness from (t', n', ε)-secret sharing to (t, n, ε)-secret sharing: If $(\mathbf{Share'}, \mathbf{Rec'}, \mathcal{Y})$ is an arbitrary (t', n', ε)-secret sharing scheme for b-bit messages, we can obtain a (t, n, ε)-secret sharing scheme $(\mathbf{Share}, \mathbf{Rec}, \mathcal{Y})$ for b-bit messages by defining

$$\mathbf{Share}(x, y)_i = \mathbf{Share'}(x, y)_{\mathcal{D}_i}$$

for each $i \in [n]$, and

$$\mathbf{Rec}(\mathbf{Share}(x,y)_{\mathcal{T}}) = \mathbf{Rec}'\left(\mathbf{Share}'(x,y)_{\bigcup_{i \in \mathcal{T}} \mathcal{D}_i}\right)$$

for each $\mathcal{T} \subseteq [n]$. The following lemma is then straightforward from the definitions of threshold secret sharing and distribution designs, and this construction.

Lemma 1. *If every* (t,n,ε)*-secret sharing scheme for b-bit messages using d bits of randomness requires* (δ,m)*-extractable randomness and there exists a* (t,n,t',n')*-distribution design, then so does every* (t',n',ε)*-secret sharing scheme for b-bit messages using d bits of randomness.*

Details of our constructions of distribution designs and associated bounds can be found in Sect. 4. The black-box reductions then follow immediately by combining these constructions with Lemma 1.

1.4   Open Questions

We obtain distribution designs for a wide variety of parameters, but for some of these constructions we could not prove optimality or find a better construction. We leave this as an open question. A naturally related question is whether there is an alternative approach to obtain a random-less reduction for secret sharing that does not use distribution designs.

Finally, we hope this work further motivates research on the main open question of whether 2-out-of-2 secret sharing (or even t-out-of-n secret sharing for any t and n) requires extractable randomness.

2   Preliminaries

2.1   Notation

Random variables are denoted by uppercase letters such as X, Y, and Z, and we write U_m for the uniform distribution over $\{0,1\}^m$. We usually denote sets by uppercase calligraphic letters like $\mathcal{S}$ and $\mathcal{T}$, and write $[n]$ for the set $\{1,2,\ldots,n\}$. Given a vector $x \in \mathcal{S}^n$ and set $\mathcal{T} \subseteq [n]$, we define $x_{\mathcal{T}} = (x_i)_{i \in \mathcal{T}}$. We denote the $\mathbb{F}_2$-inner product between vectors $x,y \in \{0,1\}^n$ by $\langle x,y \rangle$. All logarithms in this paper are taken with respect to base 2.

2.2   Probability Theory

In this section, we introduce basic notions from probability theory that will be useful throughout this work.

Definition 6 (Min-entropy). *The* min-entropy *of a random variable* X *on a set* $\mathcal{X}$*, denoted by* $\mathbf{H}_\infty(X)$*, is defined as*

$$\mathbf{H}_\infty(X) = -\log \max_{x \in \mathcal{X}} \Pr[X = x].$$

Definition 7 ((n, k)-source). *We say a random variable X supported over $\{0, 1\}^n$ is an (n, k)-source if $\mathbf{H}_\infty(X) \geq k$. When the support of the random variable is clear from context we may instead say k-source. Moreover, we say X is flat if it is uniformly distributed over a subset of $\{0, 1\}^n$.*

Definition 8. *The* statistical distance *between random variables X and Y over a set $\mathcal{X}$, denoted by $\Delta(X, Y)$, is defined as*

$$\Delta(X, Y) = \max_{\mathcal{S} \subseteq \mathcal{X}} |\Pr[X \in \mathcal{S}] - \Pr[Y \in \mathcal{S}]| = \frac{1}{2} \sum_{x \in \mathcal{X}} |\Pr[X = x] - \Pr[Y = x]|.$$

Moreover, we say that X and Y are ε-close, denoted by $X \approx_\varepsilon Y$, if $\Delta(X, Y) \leq \varepsilon$, and ε-far if this does not hold.

The following lemma is a version of the well-known XOR lemma (see [33] for a detailed exposition of these types of results).

Lemma 2 (XOR Lemma). *If X and Y are distributions supported on $\{0, 1\}^t$ such that*

$$\langle a, X \rangle \approx_\varepsilon \langle a, Y \rangle$$

for all non-zero vectors $a \in \{0, 1\}^t$, then

$$X \approx_{\varepsilon'} Y$$

for $\varepsilon' = 2^{t/2} \varepsilon$.

We end this section with a standard lemma stemming from a straightforward application of the probabilistic method, which states that, with high probability, a random function extracts almost perfect randomness from a fixed source with sufficient min-entropy. By a union bound, this result also implies that a random function is a great extractor for all sufficiently small classes of flat sources (and convex combinations thereof), an observation we will exploit later on.

Lemma 3. *Fix an (n, k)-source X. Then, for every $\varepsilon > 0$ it holds that a uniformly random function $F : \{0, 1\}^n \to \{0, 1\}^m$ with $m \leq k - 2\log(1/\varepsilon)$ satisfies $F(X) \approx_\varepsilon U_m$ with probability at least $1 - 2e^{-\varepsilon^2 2^k}$ over the choice of F.*

Proof. See Appendix A. □

The following extension of Lemma 3, stating that a random function condenses weak sources with high probability, will also be useful.

Lemma 4. *Fix an (n, k)-source X. Then, for every $\varepsilon > 0$ it holds that a uniformly random function $F : \{0, 1\}^n \to \{0, 1\}^m$ satisfies $F(X) \approx_\varepsilon W$ for some W such that $\mathbf{H}_\infty(W) \geq \min(m, k - 2\log(1/\varepsilon))$ with probability at least $1 - 2e^{-\varepsilon^2 2^k}$ over the choice of F.*

Proof. For $m' = \min(m, k - 2\log(1/\varepsilon))$, let $F' : \{0, 1\}^n \to \{0, 1\}^{m'}$ be the restriction of F to its first m' bits. Then, Lemma 3 ensures that $F'(X) \approx_\varepsilon U_{m'}$ with probability at least $1 - 2e^{-\varepsilon^2 2^k}$ over the choice of F. Via a coupling argument, this implies that $F(X) \approx W$ for some W with $\mathbf{H}_\infty(W) \geq m'$. □

2.3 Amplifying Leakage-Resilience

Recall the definition of leakage-resilient secret sharing from Definition 3 already discussed in Sect. 1. The following lemma states that every secret sharing scheme withstanding 1 bit of leakage also withstands $t > 1$ bits of leakage from each share, at the cost of an increase in statistical error.

Lemma 5. *Let* $(\mathbf{Share}, \mathbf{Rec}, \mathcal{Y})$ *be an* $(\varepsilon_1, \varepsilon_2)$*-leakage-resilient secret sharing scheme. Then, for all secrets* $x, x' \in \{0,1\}^b$, *randomness source* $Y \in \mathcal{Y}$, *and functions* $f, g : \{0,1\}^\ell \to \{0,1\}^t$ *we have*

$$f(\mathsf{Sh}_1), g(\mathsf{Sh}_2) \approx_{\varepsilon'} f(\mathsf{Sh}'_1), g(\mathsf{Sh}'_2)$$

with $\varepsilon' = 2^t \varepsilon_2$, *where* $(\mathsf{Sh}_1, \mathsf{Sh}_2) = \mathbf{Share}(x, Y)$ *and* $(\mathsf{Sh}'_1, \mathsf{Sh}'_2) = \mathbf{Share}(x', Y)$.

Proof. Fix arbitrary secrets $x, x' \in \{0,1\}^b$ and a randomness source $Y \in \mathcal{Y}$, and define $(\mathsf{Sh}_1, \mathsf{Sh}_2) = \mathbf{Share}(x, Y)$ and $(\mathsf{Sh}'_1, \mathsf{Sh}'_2) = \mathbf{Share}(x', Y)$. Suppose that there exist functions $f, g : \{0,1\}^\ell \to \{0,1\}^t$ such that the distributions $(f(\mathsf{Sh}_1), g(\mathsf{Sh}_2))$ and $(f(\mathsf{Sh}'_1), g(\mathsf{Sh}'_2))$ are $(\varepsilon' = 2^t \varepsilon_2)$-far. Then, the XOR lemma implies that there is a non-zero vector $a \in \{0,1\}^{2t}$, which we may write as $a = (a^{(1)}, a^{(2)})$ for $a^{(1)}, a^{(2)} \in \{0,1\}^t$, such that the distributions

$$\langle a, (f(\mathsf{Sh}_1), g(\mathsf{Sh}_2)) \rangle = \langle a^{(1)}, f(\mathsf{Sh}_1) \rangle + \langle a^{(2)}, g(\mathsf{Sh}_2) \rangle$$

and

$$\langle a, (f(\mathsf{Sh}'_1), g(\mathsf{Sh}'_2)) \rangle = \langle a^{(1)}, f(\mathsf{Sh}'_1) \rangle + \langle a^{(2)}, g(\mathsf{Sh}'_2) \rangle$$

are ε_2-far. Consequently, for $f', g' : \{0,1\}^\ell \to \{0,1\}$ defined as $f'(z) = \langle a^{(1)}, f(z) \rangle$ and $g'(z) = \langle a^{(2)}, g(z) \rangle$ it holds that

$$f'(\mathsf{Sh}_1), g'(\mathsf{Sh}_2) \not\approx_{\varepsilon_2} f'(\mathsf{Sh}'_1), g'(\mathsf{Sh}'_2),$$

contradicting the fact that $(\mathbf{Share}, \mathbf{Rec}, \mathcal{Y})$ is an $(\varepsilon_1, \varepsilon_2)$-leakage-resilient secret sharing scheme. $\qquad\square$

3 Randomness Extraction from Leakage-Resilient Secret Sharing Schemes

In this section, we show that all 2-out-of-2 secret sharing schemes satisfying the weak leakage-resilience requirement from Definition 2 require extractable randomness with good parameters.

Theorem 2. *Given any* $\gamma \in (0, 1)$, *there are absolute constants* $c_\gamma, c'_\gamma, c''_\gamma > 0$ *such that the following holds: Suppose* $(\mathbf{Share}, \mathbf{Rec}, \mathcal{Y})$ *is an* $(\varepsilon_1, \varepsilon_2)$*-leakage-resilient secret sharing scheme for b-bit messages using d bits of randomness. Then, if* $b \geq c_\gamma$ *and* $d \leq 2^{c'_\gamma b}$ *it holds that* $\mathcal{Y}$ *is* (δ, m)*-extractable with* $\delta \leq 2^b \varepsilon_2 + 2^{-c''_\gamma b}$ *and* $m \geq (1 - \gamma)b$.

We prove Theorem 2 via a sequence of lemmas by showing the existence of an extractor $\mathsf{Ext} : \{0,1\}^d \to \{0,1\}^m$ for the class $\mathcal{Y}$ with appropriate parameters. Our construction works as follows: On input $y \in \{0,1\}^d$, the extractor Ext computes $(L_y, R_y) = \mathbf{Share}(0^b, y)$, applies special leakage functions $f, g : \{0,1\}^\ell \to \{0,1\}^b$ to be determined in order to obtain local leakage $(f(L_y), g(R_y))$, and finally outputs $\mathsf{Ext}(y) = h(f(L_y), g(R_y))$ for an appropriate function $h : \{0,1\}^{2b} \to \{0,1\}^m$. Our goal is to show that

$$\mathsf{Ext}(Y) \approx_\delta U_m \tag{2}$$

for all sources $Y \in \mathcal{Y}$. Similarly in spirit to [14], our first lemma shows that in order to prove (2) we can instead focus on extracting randomness from the family of distributions

$$\mathcal{Z} = \{\mathbf{Share}(U_b, y) : y \in \{0,1\}^d\}.$$

Lemma 6. *Fix functions $f, g : \{0,1\}^\ell \to \{0,1\}^b$ and $h : \{0,1\}^{2b} \to \{0,1\}^m$, and suppose that*

$$\mathsf{Ext}'(Z) = h(f(Z_1), g(Z_2)) \approx_{\delta'} U_m \tag{3}$$

for all $Z = (Z_1, Z_2) \in \mathcal{Z}$. Then, it holds that Ext given by $\mathsf{Ext}(y) = h(f(L_y), g(R_y))$, where $(L_y, R_y) = \mathbf{Share}(0^b, y)$, satisfies

$$\mathsf{Ext}(Y) \approx_\delta U_m$$

for all $Y \in \mathcal{Y}$ with $\delta = 2^b \varepsilon_2 + \delta'$.

Proof. Lemma 5 implies that

$$f(L_Y), g(R_Y) \approx_{\varepsilon'} f(L_Y'), g(R_Y'),$$

where $(L_Y', R_Y') = \mathbf{Share}(U_b, Y)$ holds with $\varepsilon' = 2^b \varepsilon_2$ for all $Y \in \mathcal{Y}$, and so $\mathsf{Ext}(Y) \approx_{\varepsilon'} h(f(L_K'), g(R_K'))$. Since (3) holds for all $Z \in \mathcal{Z}$ and $\mathbf{Share}(U_b, Y)$ is a convex combination of distributions in $\mathcal{Z}$, it follows that $h(f(L_Y'), g(R_Y')) \approx_{\delta'} U_m$. The triangle inequality yields the desired result. $\qquad\square$

Given Lemma 6, we will focus on proving (3) for appropriate functions f, g, and h and error δ' in the remainder of this section. We show the following lemma, which implies Theorem 2 together with Lemma 6.

Lemma 7. *Given any $\gamma \in (0,1)$, there are absolute constants $c_\gamma, c_\gamma', c_\gamma'' > 0$ such that if $b \geq c_\gamma$ and $d \leq 2^{c_\gamma' b}$, then there exist functions $f, g : \{0,1\}^\ell \to \{0,1\}^b$ and $h : \{0,1\}^{2b} \to \{0,1\}^m$ such that*

$$\mathsf{Ext}'(Z) = h(f(Z_1), g(Z_2)) \approx_{\delta'} U_m$$

for all $Z = (Z_1, Z_2) \in \mathcal{Z}$ with $\delta' \leq 2^{-c_\gamma'' b}$ and $m \geq (1 - \gamma)b$.

The roadmap for the proof ahead is that we are first going to fix a $Z \in \mathcal{Z}$, and then do the following:

1. Justify that $Z = (Z_1, Z_2)$ is statistically close to an appropriate convex combination of distributions with linear min-entropy that suit our purposes. (Lemma 8)
2. Show that if we pick f and g uniformly at random, then with high probability over this choice it holds that $(f(Z_1), g(Z_2))$ is statistically close to a distribution with decent min-entropy. (Lemma 9)
3. Note that a random function h extracts uniformly random bits from the tuple $(f(Z_1), g(Z_2))$ with high probability, provided that this distribution contains enough min-entropy. A union bound over the 2^d distributions in $\mathcal{Z}$ concludes the argument.

Lemma 8. *Fix $\beta \in (0,1)$ and an integer $r > 0$. Then, for all $(Z_1, Z_2) \in \mathcal{Z}$ it holds that (Z_1, Z_2) is $\left(r \cdot 2^{-(1-\beta-1/r)b}\right)$-close to a distribution $D = \sum_{i \in \mathcal{I}} p_i \cdot (D_{1,i}, D_{2,i})$ where for each $i \in \mathcal{I} \subseteq [r]$ it holds that $D_{1,i}, D_{2,i} \in \{0,1\}^\ell$, and $\mathbf{H}_\infty(D_{1,i}) \geq \left(\beta - \left(\frac{i-1}{r}\right)\right)b$ and $\mathbf{H}_\infty(D_{2,i}|D_{1,i} = \mathsf{sh}_1) \geq \left(\frac{i-1}{r}\right)b$ for every $\mathsf{sh}_1 \in \mathsf{supp}(D_{1,i})$.*

Proof. Fix some $y \in \{0,1\}^d$ and set $(Z_1, Z_2) = \mathbf{Share}(U_b, y)$. It will be helpful for us to see $\mathbf{Share}(\cdot, y)$ as a bipartite graph G with left and right vertex sets $\{0,1\}^\ell$ and an edge between sh_1 and sh_2 if $(\mathsf{sh}_1, \mathsf{sh}_2) \in \mathsf{supp}(Z_1, Z_2)$. Then, (Z_1, Z_2) is the uniform distribution on the 2^b edges of G by the correctness of the scheme. For every left vertex $\mathsf{sh}_1 \in \{0,1\}^\ell$, we define its neighborhood

$$\mathcal{A}(\mathsf{sh}_1) = \{\mathsf{sh}_2 : (\mathsf{sh}_1, \mathsf{sh}_2) \in \mathsf{supp}(Z_1, Z_2)\}$$

and its degree

$$\deg(\mathsf{sh}_1) = |\mathcal{A}(\mathsf{sh}_1)|.$$

Note that $(Z_2|Z_1 = \mathsf{sh}_1)$ is uniformly distributed over $\mathcal{A}(\mathsf{sh}_1)$, and so

$$\mathbf{H}_\infty(Z_2|Z_1 = \mathsf{sh}_1) = \log \deg(\mathsf{sh}_1).$$

Partition $\mathsf{supp}(Z_1)$ into sets

$$\mathcal{S}_i = \left\{\mathsf{sh}_1 : 2^{\left(\frac{i-1}{r}\right)b} \leq \deg(\mathsf{sh}_1) < 2^{\left(\frac{i}{r}\right)b}\right\}$$

for $i \in [r]$. With this definition in mind, we can express (Z_1, Z_2) as

$$\sum_{i \in [r]} \Pr[Z_1 \in \mathcal{S}_i](Z_1, Z_2|Z_1 \in \mathcal{S}_i),$$

where $(Z_1, Z_2|Z_1 \in \mathcal{S}_i)$ denotes the distribution (Z_1, Z_2) conditioned on the event that $Z_1 \in \mathcal{S}_i$. Call a non-empty set $\mathcal{S}_i$ *good* if $\sum_{\mathsf{sh}_1 \in \mathcal{S}_i} \deg(\mathsf{sh}_1) \geq 2^{(\beta+1/r)b}$. Otherwise the set $\mathcal{S}_i$ is *bad*. Let $\mathcal{I}$ denote the set of indices $i \in [r]$ such that $\mathcal{S}_i$ is good. We proceed to show that we can take the target distribution D in the lemma statement to be $D = \sum_{i \in \mathcal{I}} p_i \cdot (D_{1,i}, D_{2,i})$ for

$$p_i = \frac{\Pr[Z_1 \in \mathcal{S}_i]}{\Pr[Z_1 \text{lands on good set}]}$$

with $(D_{1,i}, D_{2,i}) = (Z_1, Z_2 | Z_1 \in \mathcal{S}_i)$ when $i \in \mathcal{I}$.

To see this, consider the case where $\mathcal{S}_i$ is good, i.e., we have $\sum_{\mathsf{sh}_1 \in \mathcal{S}_i} \deg(\mathsf{sh}_1) \geq 2^{(\beta + 1/r)b}$. For each $\mathsf{sh}_1 \in \mathcal{S}_i$, we have

$$\Pr[Z_1 = \mathsf{sh}_1 | Z_1 \in \mathcal{S}_i] = \frac{\deg(\mathsf{sh}_1)}{\sum_{s \in \mathcal{S}_i} \deg(s)}$$
$$\leq \frac{2^{\frac{i}{r}b}}{2^{(\beta + 1/r)b}}$$
$$= 2^{-(\beta - (\frac{i-1}{r}))b}.$$

Furthermore, for any $\mathsf{sh}_1 \in \mathcal{S}_i$ and sh_2 we know that

$$\Pr[Z_2 = \mathsf{sh}_2 | Z_1 = \mathsf{sh}_1] \leq 2^{-(\frac{i-1}{r})b}.$$

Combining these two observations shows that in this case we have $\mathbf{H}_\infty(Z_1 | Z_1 \in \mathcal{S}_i) \geq (\beta - (\frac{i-1}{r}))b$ and $\mathbf{H}_\infty(Z_2 | Z_1 = \mathsf{sh}_1) \geq (\frac{i-1}{r})b$ for all valid fixings $\mathsf{sh}_1 \in \mathcal{S}_i$.

To conclude the proof, consider D as above, which we have shown satisfies the properties described in the lemma statement. Noting that D corresponds exactly to (Z_1, Z_2) conditioned on Z_1 landing on a good set, we have

$$\Delta((Z_1, Z_2); D) \leq \Pr[Z_1 \text{lands in a bad set}].$$

It remains to bound this probability on the right-hand side. Assuming the set $\mathcal{S}_i$ is bad, it holds that $\sum_{\mathsf{sh}_1 \in \mathcal{S}_i} \deg(\mathsf{sh}_1) < 2^{(\beta + 1/r)b}$. Therefore, since (Z_1, Z_2) takes on any edge with probability 2^{-b}, it holds that Z_1 lands in $\mathcal{S}_i$ with probability at most $2^{-b} \cdot 2^{(\beta + 1/r)b} = 2^{-(1 - \beta - 1/r)b}$. There are at most r bad sets, so by a union bound we have $\Pr[Z_1 \text{lands in a bad set}] \leq r \cdot 2^{-(1 - \beta - 1/r)b}$. $\square$

Lemma 9. *Fix $\alpha, \beta \in (0, 1)$ and an integer r. Then, with probability at least $1 - 3r \cdot e^{b - \alpha^2 2^{\min(b/r, (\beta - 1/r)b)}}$ over the choice of uniformly random functions $f, g : \{0, 1\}^\ell \to \{0, 1\}^b$ it holds that $(f(Z_1), g(Z_2))$ is $(2\alpha + r \cdot 2^{-(1 - \beta - 1/r)b})$-close to a $(2b, (\beta - 1/r)b - 4\log(1/\alpha))$-source.*

Proof. Suppose we pick functions $f, g : \{0, 1\}^\ell \to \{0, 1\}^b$ uniformly at random. We begin by expressing $(f(Z_1), g(Z_2))$ as

$$\sum_{i \in [r]} \Pr[Z_1 \in \mathcal{S}_i](f(Z_1), g(Z_2) | Z_1 \in \mathcal{S}_i),$$

which by Lemma 8 is $(r \cdot 2^{-(1 - \beta - 1/r)b})$-close to

$$\sum_{i \in \mathcal{I}} \Pr[Z_1 \in \mathcal{S}_i](f(D_{1,i}), g(D_{2,i})).$$

We proceed by cases:

1. $\frac{i-1}{r} \geq \beta - 1/r$: We know from Lemma 8 that $\mathbf{H}_\infty(D_{2,i}|D_{1,i} = \mathsf{sh}_1) \geq (\beta - 1/r)b$ for all $\mathsf{sh}_1 \in \mathsf{supp}(D_{1,i})$. By Lemma 4, we have

$$(g(D_{2,i})|D_{1,i} = \mathsf{sh}_1) \approx_\alpha V$$

for some V with $\mathbf{H}_\infty(V) \geq (\beta - 1/r)b - 2\log(1/\alpha)$ with probability at least $1 - 2e^{-\alpha^2 2^{(\beta - 1/r)b}}$ over the choice of g. Since this holds for any valid fixing $D_{1,i} = \mathsf{sh}_1$, we conclude via a union bound over the at most 2^b possible fixings that

$$f(D_{1,i}), g(D_{2,i}) \approx_\alpha W_i$$

for some W_i with $\mathbf{H}_\infty(W_i) \geq (\beta - 1/r)b - 2\log(1/\alpha)$ with probability at least $1 - 2e^{b - \alpha^2 2^{(\beta - 1/r)b}}$ over the choice of f and g.

2. $1/r \leq \frac{i-1}{r} < \beta - 1/r$: We know from Lemma 8 that $\mathbf{H}_\infty(D_{1,i}) \geq \left(\beta - \frac{i-1}{r}\right)b$ and $\mathbf{H}_\infty(D_{2,i}|D_{1,i} = \mathsf{sh}_1) \geq \left(\frac{i-1}{r}\right)b$ for all $\mathsf{sh}_1 \in \mathsf{supp}(D_{1,i})$. First, by Lemma 4 we conclude that with probability at least

$$1 - 2e^{-\alpha^2 2^{\left(\beta - \frac{i-1}{r}\right)b}} \geq 1 - 2e^{-\alpha^2 2^{b/r}}$$

over the choice of f it holds that

$$f(D_{1,i}) \approx_\alpha V_1 \tag{4}$$

for some V_1 with $\mathbf{H}_\infty(V_1) \geq (\beta - \frac{i-1}{r})b - 2\log(1/\alpha)$. Analogously, for every $\mathsf{sh}_1 \in \mathsf{supp}(D_{1,i})$, we can again invoke Lemma 4 to see that with probability at least

$$1 - 2e^{-\alpha^2 2^{\left(\frac{i-1}{r}\right)b}} \geq 1 - 2e^{-\alpha^2 2^{b/r}}$$

over the choice of g, for any $\mathsf{sh}_1 \in \mathsf{supp}(D_{1,i})$ it holds that

$$(g(D_{2,i})|D_{1,i} = \mathsf{sh}_1) \approx_\alpha V_{2,\mathsf{sh}_1} \tag{5}$$

for some V_{2,sh_1} with $\mathbf{H}_\infty(V_{2,\mathsf{sh}_1}) \geq \left(\frac{i-1}{r}\right)b - 2\log(1/\alpha)$. By a union bound over the at most 2^b possible fixings sh_1, we conclude that (5) holds simultaneously for all $\mathsf{sh}_1 \in \mathsf{supp}(D_{1,i})$ with probability at least $1 - 2e^{b - \alpha^2 2^{b/r}}$ over the choice of g. An additional union bound shows that this holds simultaneously along (4) with probability at least $1 - 3e^{b - \alpha^2 2^{b/r}}$ over the choice of f and g, which implies that

$$f(D_{1,i}), g(D_{2,i}) \approx_{2\alpha} W_i$$

for some W_i with

$$\mathbf{H}_\infty(W_i) \geq \left(\beta - \frac{i-1}{r}\right)b - 2\log(1/\alpha) + \left(\frac{i-1}{r}\right)b - 2\log(1/\alpha)$$

$$= \beta b - 4\log(1/\alpha).$$

3. $i = 1$: In this case, by Lemma 8 we know that $\mathbf{H}_\infty(D_{1,i}) \geq \beta b$. Therefore, Lemma 4 implies that $f(D_{1,i}) \approx_\alpha V_1$ for some V_1 such that $\mathbf{H}_\infty(V_1) \geq \beta b - 2\log(1/\alpha)$ with probability at least $1 - 2e^{-\alpha^2 2^{\beta b}} \geq 1 - 2e^{-\alpha^2 2^{b/r}}$. This implies that $f(D_{1,i}), g(D_{2,i}) \approx_\alpha W_i$ for some W_i with $\mathbf{H}_\infty(W_i) \geq \beta b - 2\log(1/\alpha)$.

Finally, a union bound over the at most r indices $i \in \mathcal{I}$ yields the desired statement. $\qquad\square$

We are now ready to prove Lemma 7 with the help of Lemma 9.

Proof (Proof of Lemma 7). Fix some $\gamma \in (0,1)$. Then, we set $\beta = 1 - \gamma/2 > 1 - \gamma$, $\alpha = 2^{-cb}$ for a sufficiently small constant $c > 0$, and $r > 0$ a sufficiently large integer so that

$$1 - \gamma \leq \beta - 1/r - 6c \tag{6}$$

and

$$1/r + 6c \leq \frac{\min(\beta, 1 - \beta)}{100}. \tag{7}$$

According to Lemma 9, we know that for any given $Z = (Z_1, Z_2) \in \mathcal{Z}$ it holds that $(f(Z_1), g(Z_2))$ is $(2\alpha + r \cdot 2^{-(1-\beta-1/r)b})$-close to some $(2b, (\beta - 1/r)b - 4\log(1/\alpha))$-source W with probability at least $1 - 3r \cdot e^{-\alpha^2 2^{\min(b/r, (\beta-1/r)b)}}$ over the choice of f and g.

Let $m = (1 - \gamma)b$ and pick a uniformly random function $h : \{0,1\}^{2b} \to \{0,1\}^m$. Then, since $m \leq \mathbf{H}_\infty(W) - 2\log(1/\alpha)$ by (6), Lemma 3 implies that $h(W) \approx_\alpha U_m$, and hence

$$h(f(Z_1), g(Z_2)) \approx_{3\alpha + r \cdot 2^{-(1-\beta-1/r)b}} U_m, \tag{8}$$

with probability at least

$$1 - 2e^{-\alpha^2 2^{(\beta-1/r)b - 4\log(1/\alpha)}} - 3r \cdot e^{-\alpha^2 2^{\min(b/r, (\beta-1/r)b)}}$$
$$\geq 1 - 5r \cdot e^{-\alpha^2 2^{\min(b/r, (\beta-1/r)b)} - 4\log(1/\alpha)}$$

over the choice of f, g, and h, via a union bound.

Now, observe that from (7), if $b \geq c_\gamma$ for a sufficiently large constant $c_\gamma > 0$, it follows that

$$5r \cdot e^{-\alpha^2 2^{\min(b/r, (\beta-1/r)b)} - 4\log(1/\alpha)} \leq 2^{-2^{2c'_\gamma b}}$$

for some constant $c'_\gamma > 0$. Moreover, under (7) we also have that

$$\delta' := 3\alpha + r \cdot 2^{-(1-\beta-1/r)b} \leq 2^{-c''_\gamma b}$$

for some constant $c''_\gamma > 0$. Finally, a union bound over the 2^d distributions in $\mathcal{Z}$ shows that (8) holds simultaneously for all $Z \in \mathcal{Z}$ with probability at least $1 - 2^{d - 2^{2c'_\gamma b}}$. Consequently, if $d \leq 2^{c'_\gamma b}$ it follows that there exist functions f, g, and h such that (8) holds for all $Z \in \mathcal{Z}$ with the appropriate error δ' and output length m. $\qquad\square$

3.1   The Main Result

We now use Theorem 2 to obtain the main result of this section.

Theorem 3 (First part of Theorem 1, restated). *Suppose* (**Share, Rec,** $\mathcal{Y}$)
is an $(\varepsilon_1, \varepsilon_2)$*-leakage-resilient secret sharing scheme for b-bit messages. Then,*
either:

- *The scheme uses* $d \geq \min\left(2^{\Omega(b)}, (1/\varepsilon_2)^{\Omega(1)}\right)$ *bits of randomness, or;*
- *The class of sources* $\mathcal{Y}$ *is* (δ, m)*-extractable with* $\delta \leq \max\left(2^{-\Omega(b)}, \varepsilon_2^{\Omega(1)}\right)$ *and*
  $m = \Omega(\min(b, \log(1/\varepsilon_2)))$.

Proof. Given the scheme (**Share, Rec,** $\mathcal{Y}$) from the theorem statement, let $b' = \min\left(b, \left\lceil \frac{\log(1/\varepsilon_2)}{100} \right\rceil\right)$ and consider the modified scheme (**Share', Rec',** $\mathcal{Y}$) for b'-
bit messages obtained by appending $0^{b-b'}$ to every b'-bit message and running
the original scheme (**Share, Rec,** $\mathcal{Y}$). Applying Theorem 2 to (**Share', Rec',** $\mathcal{Y}$)
we conclude that either **Share'**, and hence **Share**, uses at least

$$2^{\Omega(b')} = \min\left(2^{\Omega(b)}, (1/\varepsilon_2)^{\Omega(1)}\right)$$

bits of randomness, or $\mathcal{Y}$ is (δ, m)-extractable with

$$\delta \leq 2^{-\Omega(b')} = \max\left(2^{-\Omega(b)}, \varepsilon_2^{\Omega(1)}\right)$$

and $m = \Omega(b') = \Omega(\min(b, \log(1/\varepsilon_2)))$. $\square$

3.2   Efficient Leakage-Resilient Secret Sharing Requires Efficiently Extractable Randomness

In this section, we prove the remaining part of Theorem 1. We show that every
low-error leakage-resilient secret sharing scheme (**Share, Rec,** $\mathcal{Y}$) for b-bit messages where **Share** is computed by a poly(b)-time algorithm admits a low-error
extractor for $\mathcal{Y}$ computable by a family of poly(b)-size circuits. Similarly to [14,
Section 3.1], this is done by replacing the uniformly random functions f, g, and
h in the proof of Theorem 2 by *t-wise independent functions*, for an appropriate
parameter t.

   We say that a family of functions $\mathcal{F}_t$ from $\{0, 1\}^p$ to $\{0, 1\}^q$ is *t-wise indepen-*
dent if for F sampled uniformly at random from $\mathcal{F}_t$ it holds that the random variables $F(x_1), F(x_2), \ldots, F(x_t)$ are independent and uniformly distributed over
$\{0, 1\}^q$ for any distinct $x_1, \ldots, x_t \in \{0, 1\}^p$. There exist t-wise independent families of functions $\mathcal{F}_t$ such that every $f \in \mathcal{F}_t$ can be computed in time poly(b)
and can be described by poly(b) bits whenever p, q, and t are poly(b) [14,22,51].
Therefore, since **Share** admits a poly(b)-time algorithm, it suffices to show the
existence of functions f, g, and h belonging to appropriate poly(b)-wise independent families of functions such that $\mathsf{Ext}(Y) = h(f(\mathsf{Sh}_1), g(\mathsf{Sh}_2))$ is statistically
close to uniform, where $(\mathsf{Sh}_1, \mathsf{Sh}_2) = \mathbf{Share}(0^b, Y)$, for every source $Y \in \mathcal{Y}$ (the

advice required to compute Ext would be the description of f, g, and h). We accomplish this with the help of some auxiliary lemmas. The first lemma states a standard concentration bound for the sum of t-wise independent random variables.

Lemma 10 ([22, **Theorem 5**], see also [7, **Lemma 2.2**]). *Fix an even integer $t \geq 2$ and suppose that $X_1, \ldots, X_N$ are t-wise independent random variables in $[0,1]$. Let $X = \sum_{i=1}^{N} X_i$ and $\mu = \mathbb{E}[X]$. Then, it holds that*

$$\Pr[|X - \mu| \geq \varepsilon \cdot \mu] \leq 3 \left(\frac{t}{\varepsilon^2 \mu} \right)^{t/2}$$

for every $\varepsilon < 1$.

We can use Lemma 10 to derive analogues of Lemmas 3 and 4 for t-wise independent functions.

Lemma 11. *Suppose $f : \{0,1\}^p \to \{0,1\}^q$ is sampled uniformly at random from a 2t-wise independent family of functions with $q \leq k - \log t - 2 \log(1/\varepsilon) - 5$ and $t \geq q$, and let Y be a (p,k)-source. Then, it follows that*

$$f(Y) \approx_\varepsilon U_q$$

with probability at least $1 - 2^{-t}$ over the choice of f.

Proof. Fix a (p,k)-source Y and suppose $f : \{0,1\}^p \to \{0,1\}^q$ is sampled from a family of $2t$-wise independent functions. Note that

$$\Delta(f(Y); U_q) = \frac{1}{2} \sum_{z \in \{0,1\}^q} |\Pr[f(Y) = z] - 2^{-q}|.$$

For each $y \in \{0,1\}^p$ and $z \in \{0,1\}^q$, consider the random variable $W_{y,z} = \Pr[Y = y] \cdot \mathbb{1}_{\{f(y)=z\}}$. Then, we may write

$$\Delta(f(Y); U_q) = \frac{1}{2} \sum_{z \in \{0,1\}^q} \left| \sum_{y \in \{0,1\}^p} W_{y,z} - 2^{-q} \right|.$$

Note that the $W_{y,z}$'s are $2t$-wise independent, $\mathbb{E}[\sum_{y \in \{0,1\}^n} W_{y,z}] = 2^{-q}$, and that $2^k \cdot W_{y,z} \in [0,1]$. Therefore, an application of Lemma 10 with the random variables $(2^k \cdot W_{y,z})_{y \in \{0,1\}^p, z \in \{0,1\}^q}$ shows that

$$\Pr \left[\left| \sum_{y \in \{0,1\}^p} W_{y,z} - 2^{-q} \right| > 2\varepsilon \cdot 2^{-q} \right] \leq 3 \left(\frac{t \cdot 2^q}{2\varepsilon^2 2^k} \right)^t.$$

Therefore, a union bound over all $z \in \{0,1\}^q$ shows that $f(Y) \approx_\varepsilon U_q$ fails to hold with probability at most $3 \cdot 2^q \cdot 2^{-t} \left(\frac{t \cdot 2^q}{\varepsilon^2 \cdot 2^k} \right)^t \leq 2^{-t}$ over the choice of f, where the inequality follows by the upper bound on q. $\qquad\square$

The proof of the following lemma is analogous to the proof of Lemma 4, but using Lemma 11 instead of Lemma 3.

Lemma 12. *Suppose* $f : \{0,1\}^p \to \{0,1\}^q$ *is sampled uniformly at random from a 2t-wise independent family of functions with* $t \geq q$, *and let* Y *be a* (p, k)-*source. Then, it follows that* $f(Y) \approx_\varepsilon W$ *for some* W *such that* $\mathbf{H}_\infty(W) \geq \min(q, k - \log t - 2\log(1/\varepsilon) - 5)$ *with probability at least* $1 - 2^{-t}$ *over the choice of* f.

Following the reasoning used in the proof of Theorem 2 but sampling $f, g : \{0,1\}^\ell \to \{0,1\}^b$ and $h : \{0,1\}^b \to \{0,1\}^m$ from 2t-wise independent families of functions with $t = 100\max(b, d) = \text{poly}(b)$, and using Lemmas 11 and 12 in place of Lemmas 3 and 4, respectively, yields the following result analogous to Theorem 2. Informally, it states that efficient low-error leakage-resilient secret sharing schemes require low-complexity extractors for the associated class of randomness sources.

Theorem 4. *There exist absolute constants* $c, c' > 0$ *such that the following holds for b large enough: Suppose* $(\mathbf{Share}, \mathbf{Rec}, \mathcal{Y})$ *is an* $(\varepsilon_1, \varepsilon_2)$-*leakage-resilient secret sharing for b-bit messages using d bits of randomness such that* $\mathbf{Share}$ *is computable by a* $\text{poly}(b)$-*time algorithm. Then, there exists a deterministic extractor* $\mathsf{Ext} : \{0,1\}^d \to \{0,1\}^m$ *computable by a family of* $\text{poly}(b)$-*size circuits with output length* $m \geq c \cdot b$ *such that*

$$\mathsf{Ext}(Y) \approx_\delta U_m$$

with $\delta = 2^b\varepsilon_2 + 2^{-c' \cdot b}$ *for every* $Y \in \mathcal{Y}$.

Finally, replacing Theorem 2 by Theorem 4 in the reasoning from Sect. 3.1 yields the remaining part of Theorem 1.

3.3   An Extension to the Setting of Computational Security

In this work we focus on secret sharing schemes with information-theoretic security. However, it is also natural to wonder whether our result extends to secret sharing schemes satisfying a reasonable notion of computational security. Indeed, a slight modification to the argument used to prove Theorem 1 also shows that computationally-secure efficient leakage-resilient secret sharing schemes require randomness sources from which one can efficiently extract bits which are pseudorandom (i.e., computationally indistinguishable from the uniform distribution). We briefly discuss the required modifications in this section. For the sake of exposition, we refrain from presenting fully formal definitions and theorem statements.

First, we introduce a computational analogue of Definition 3. We say that $(\mathbf{Share}, \mathbf{Rec}, \mathcal{Y})$ is a *computationally secure leakage-resilient secret sharing scheme (for b-bit messages)* if the scheme satisfies Definition 3 except that the leakage-resilience property is replaced by the following computational analogue: "For any leakage functions $f, g : \{0,1\}^\ell \to \{0,1\}$ computed by $\text{poly}(b)$-sized circuits and any two secrets $x, x' \in \{0,1\}^b$, it holds that any adversary computable by poly(b)-sized circuits cannot distinguish between the distributions $(f(\mathsf{Sh}_1), g(\mathsf{Sh}_2))$ and $(f(\mathsf{Sh}_1'), g(\mathsf{Sh}_2'))$ with non-negligible advantage (in some security parameter λ), where $(\mathsf{Sh}_1, \mathsf{Sh}_2) = \mathbf{Share}(x)$ and $(\mathsf{Sh}_1', \mathsf{Sh}_2') = \mathbf{Share}(x')$."

Using this definition, the exact argument we used to prove Theorem 1 combined with a modified version of Lemma 6 then shows that we can extract bits which are *computationally indistinguishable* from the uniform distribution using the class of randomness sources used to implement such a computationally-secure leakage-resilient secret sharing scheme. In fact, the proof of Theorem 1 only uses the leakage-resilience property of the secret sharing scheme in the proof of Lemma 6. The remaining lemmas only make use of the correctness property of the scheme, which remains unchanged in the computational analogue of Definition 3. Crucially, as shown in Sect. 3.2, we can construct the functions f, g, and h so that they are computed by poly(b)-sized circuits assuming that the sharing procedure is itself computable by poly(b)-sized circuits. Therefore, the following computational analogue of Lemma 6, which suffices to conclude the proof of the computational analogue of Theorem 1, holds: "Suppose that there are functions $f, g : \{0,1\}^\ell \to \{0,1\}$ and a function $h : \{0,1\}^{2b} \to \{0,1\}^m$ computable by poly(b)-sized circuits such that

$$h(f(Z_1), g(Z_1)) \approx_\delta U_m$$

for $\delta = \mathsf{negl}(\lambda)$ and for all (Z_1, Z_2) in $\mathcal{Z}$. Then, it holds that no adversary computable by poly(b)-sized circuits can distinguish $\mathsf{Ext}(Y)$ from a uniformly random string with $Y \in \mathcal{Y}$, where $\mathsf{Ext}(Y) = h(f(L_Y), g(R_Y))$ and $(L_y, R_y) = \mathbf{Share}(0^b, Y)$."

4 Random-Less Reductions for Secret Sharing

In this section, we study black-box deterministic reductions between different types of threshold secret sharing. Such reductions from (t', n', ε)-secret sharing schemes to (t, n, ε)-secret sharing schemes (for the same message length b and number of randomness bits d) would allow us to conclude that if all these (t, n, ε)-secret sharing schemes require a (δ, m)-extractable class of randomness sources, then so do all (t', n', ε)-secret sharing schemes. We provide reductions which work over a large range of parameters and prove complementary results showcasing the limits of such reductions. As already discussed in Sect. 1, our starting point for devising black-box reductions is the notion of a *distribution design* as formalized by Stinson and Wei [49] (with roots going back to early work on secret sharing [9]), which we defined in Definition 5. As stated in Lemma 1, the existence of a (t, n, t', n')-distribution design yields the desired reduction from (t', n', ε)-secret sharing to (t, n, ε)-secret sharing. Therefore, we focus directly on the study of distribution designs in this section.

We begin with a naive construction.

Theorem 5. *There exists a (t, n, t', n')-distribution design whenever $t' \geq t$ and $n' \geq n + (t' - t)$. In particular, if every (t, n, ε)-secret sharing scheme for b-bit* *messages and using d bits of randomness requires a (δ, m)-extractable class of randomness sources, then so does every (t', n', ε)-secret sharing scheme for b-bit messages using d bits of randomness whenever $t' \geq t$ and $n' \geq n + (t' - t)$.*

Proof. Consider the (t, n, t', n')-distribution design $\mathcal{D}_1, \ldots, \mathcal{D}_n$ obtained by setting $\mathcal{D}_i = \{i\} \cup \{n' - (t' - t) + 1, n' - (t' - t) + 2, \ldots, n'\}$, which is valid exactly when the conditions of the theorem are satisfied. □

The following result shows the limits of distribution designs, and will be used to show the optimality of our constructions when $t = 2$ or $t' = n'$.

Theorem 6. *A (t, n, t', n')-distribution design exists only if $\binom{n'}{t'-1} \geq \binom{n}{t-1}$ and $t' \geq t$.*

Proof. Consider an arbitrary (t, n, t', n')-distribution design $\mathcal{D}_1, \mathcal{D}_2, \ldots, \mathcal{D}_n$. First, note that it must be the case that all the $\mathcal{D}_i$'s are non-empty. This implies that we must have $t' \geq t$. Second, to see that $\binom{n'}{t'-1} \geq \binom{n}{t-1}$, consider all $\binom{n}{t-1}$ distinct subsets $\mathcal{T} \subseteq [n]$ of size $t-1$, and denote $\mathcal{D}_\mathcal{T} = \bigcup_{i \in \mathcal{T}} \mathcal{D}_i$. By the definition of distribution design, it must hold that

$$|\mathcal{D}_\mathcal{T}| \leq t' - 1.$$

Consider now modified sets $\widehat{\mathcal{D}_\mathcal{T}}$ obtained by adding arbitrary elements to $\mathcal{D}_\mathcal{T}$ so that $|\widehat{\mathcal{D}_\mathcal{T}}| = t' - 1$. Then, from the definition of distribution design, for any two distinct subsets $\mathcal{T}, \mathcal{T}' \subseteq [n]$ of size $t - 1$ it must be the case that

$$\left|\widehat{\mathcal{D}_\mathcal{T}} \cup \widehat{\mathcal{D}_{\mathcal{T}'}}\right| \geq t'.$$

This implies that $\widehat{\mathcal{D}_\mathcal{T}} \neq \widehat{\mathcal{D}_{\mathcal{T}'}}$ for all distinct subsets $\mathcal{T}, \mathcal{T}' \subseteq [n]$ of size $t - 1$, which can only hold if $\binom{n'}{t'-1} \geq \binom{n}{t-1}$. □

We now show that Theorem 6 is tight for a broad range of parameters. In particular, when $t = 2$ or $t' = n'$ we are able to characterize exactly under which parameters a (t, n, t', n')-distribution design exists.

Theorem 7. *There exists a $(t = 2, n, t', n')$-distribution design if and only if $n \leq \binom{n'}{t'-1}$. In particular, if every $(t = 2, n, \varepsilon)$-secret sharing scheme for b-bit messages using d bits of randomness requires (δ, m)-extractable randomness, then so does every (t', n', ε)-secret sharing scheme for b-bit messages using d bits of randomness whenever $n \leq \binom{n'}{t'-1}$.*

Proof. Note that the condition $n \leq \binom{n'}{t'-1}$ implies that we can take $\mathcal{D}_1, \ldots, \mathcal{D}_n$ to be distinct subsets of $[n']$ of size $t' - 1$, and so $|\mathcal{D}_i \cup \mathcal{D}_j| \geq t'$ for any distinct indices i and j. The reverse implication follows from Theorem 6. □

Theorem 8. *There exists a $(t, n, t' = n', n')$-distribution design if and only if $n' \geq \binom{n}{t-1}$. In particular, if every (t, n, ε)-secret sharing scheme for b-bit messages using d bits of randomness requires (δ, m)-extractable randomness, then so does every (n', n', ε)-secret sharing scheme for b-bit messages using d bits of randomness whenever $n' \geq \binom{n}{t-1}$.*

Proof. We show that a (t, n, n', n')-distribution design exists whenever $n' = \binom{n}{t-1}$, which implies the desired result. Let $\mathcal{P}$ denote the family of all subsets of $[n]$ of size $t - 1$, and set $n' = |\mathcal{P}| = \binom{n}{t-1}$ (we may use any correspondence between elements of $\mathcal{P}$ and integers in $[n']$). Then, we define the set $\mathcal{D}_i \subseteq \mathcal{P}$ for $i \in [n]$ to contain all elements of $\mathcal{P}$ except the subsets of $[n]$ which contain i. We argue that $\mathcal{D}_1, \ldots, \mathcal{D}_n$ is a distribution design with the desired parameters. First, observe that for any distinct indices $i_1, i_2, \ldots, i_{t-1} \in [n]$ it holds that

$$\bigcup_{j=1}^{t-1} \mathcal{D}_{i_j} = \mathcal{P} \setminus \{\{i_1, i_2, \ldots, i_{t-1}\}\}.$$

On the other hand, since $\{i_1, \ldots, i_{t-1}\} \in \mathcal{D}_{i_t}$ for any index $i_t \neq i_1, \ldots, i_{t-1}$, it follows that $\bigcup_{j=1}^{t} \mathcal{D}_{i_j} = \mathcal{P}$, as desired.

The reverse implication follows from Theorem 6.   □

4.1   Distribution Designs from Partial Steiner Systems

In this section, we show that every partial Steiner system is also a distribution design which beats the naive construction from Theorem 5 for certain parameter regimes. Such set systems have been previously used in seminal constructions of pseudorandom generators and extractors [43,50], and are also called combinatorial designs.

Definition 9 (Partial Steiner system). *We say a family of sets $\mathcal{D}_1, \ldots, \mathcal{D}_n \subseteq [n']$ is an (n, n', ℓ, a)-partial Steiner system if it holds that $|\mathcal{D}_i| = \ell$ for every $i \in [n]$ and $|\mathcal{D}_i \cap \mathcal{D}_j| \leq a$ for all distinct $i, j \in [n]$.*

The conditions required for the existence of a partial Steiner system are well-understood, as showcased in the following result from [32,43,50], which is nearly optimal [44,45].

Lemma 13 ([32,43,50]). *Fix positive integers n, ℓ, and $a \leq \ell$. Then, there exists an (n, n', ℓ, a)-partial Steiner system for every integer $n' \geq e \cdot n^{1/a} \cdot \frac{\ell^2}{a}$.*

Noting that every partial Steiner system with appropriate parameters is also a distribution design, we obtain the following theorem.

Theorem 9. *Fix an integer $a \geq 1$. Then, there exists a (t, n, t', n')-distribution design whenever $t' \geq t^2 + \frac{at(t-1)^2}{2}$ and $n' \geq \frac{en^{1/a}}{a} \cdot \left(1 + \frac{t'}{t} + \frac{a(t-1)}{2}\right)^2$.*

Proof. Fix an integer $a \geq 1$ and an (n, n', ℓ, a)-partial Steiner system $\mathcal{D}_1, \ldots, \mathcal{D}_n \subseteq [n']$ with $\ell = \left\lceil \frac{t'}{t} + \frac{a(t-1)}{2} \right\rceil$. By Lemma 13 and the choice of ℓ, such a partial Steiner system is guaranteed to exist whenever n' satisfies the condition in the theorem statement. We proceed to argue that this partial Steiner system is also a (t, n, t', n')-distribution design. First, fix an arbitrary set $\mathcal{T} \subseteq [n]$ of size $t - 1$. Then, we have

$$|\mathcal{D}_{\mathcal{T}}| \leq \ell(t-1) \leq t' - 1,$$

where the rightmost inequality holds by our choice of ℓ and the condition on t' and t in the theorem statement. Second, fix an arbitrary set $\mathcal{T} \subseteq [n]$ of size t. Then, it holds that

$$|\mathcal{D}_{\mathcal{T}}| \geq \ell + (\ell - a) + (\ell - 2a) + \cdots + (\ell - a(t-1))$$
$$= \ell \cdot t - \frac{at(t-1)}{2}$$
$$\geq t',$$

where the last equality follows again from our choice of ℓ and the condition on t' and t in the theorem statement. □

When n is sufficiently larger than t and t' and t' is sufficiently larger than t, the parameters in Theorem 9 cannot be attained by the naive construction from Theorem 5, which always requires choosing $t' \geq t$ and $n' \geq n$. For example, if $t^3 \leq t' \leq Ct^3$ for some constant $C \geq 1$ then we can choose $a = 2$, in which case we have

$$t^2 + \frac{at(t-1)^2}{2} \leq t^3 \leq t'. \tag{9}$$

Moreover, it holds that

$$\frac{en^{1/a}}{a} \cdot \left(1 + \frac{t'}{t} + \frac{a(t-1)}{2}\right)^2 \leq \frac{e\sqrt{n}}{2} \cdot (Ct^2 + t)^2$$
$$\leq 2eC^2 \sqrt{n} t^4. \tag{10}$$

Combining (9) and (10) with Theorem 9, we obtain the following example result showing it is possible to improve on Theorem 5 in some parameter regimes.

Corollary 5. *Suppose $t^3 \leq t' \leq Ct^3$ for some constant $C \geq 1$. Then, there exists a (t, n, t', n')-distribution design for any $n' \geq 2eC^2 \sqrt{n} t^4$. In particular, if $t \leq n^{1/9}$ and n is large enough, we may choose n' significantly smaller than n.*

Acknowledgment. JR was supported in part by the NSF grants CCF-1814603 and CCF-2107347 and by the NSF award 1916939, DARPA SIEVE program, a gift from Ripple, a DoE NETL award, a JP Morgan Faculty Fellowship, a PNC center for financial services innovation award, and a Cylab seed funding award. The work in CQT was supported in part by the Singapore National Research Foundation through National Research Foundation Research Fellowship (NRF RF) under Award NRF-NRFF2013-13; and in part by the Ministry of Education, Singapore, through the Research Centres of Excellence Programme by the Tier-3 Grant "Random numbers from quantum processes" under Grant MOE2012-T3-1-009. The work of Maciej Obremski was supported by the Foundations of Quantum-Safe Cryptography under Grant MOE2019-T2-1-145. The authors would like to thank Daniele Venturi for insightful comments.

A   Proof of Lemma 3

Fix an (n, k)-source X and pick a function $F : \{0,1\}^n \to \{0,1\}^m$ with $m \leq k - 2\log(1/\varepsilon)$ uniformly at random. It suffices to bound the probability that

$$|\Pr[F(X) \in \mathcal{T}] - \mu(\mathcal{T})| \leq \varepsilon$$

holds for every set $\mathcal{T} \subseteq \{0,1\}^m$, where $\mu(\mathcal{T}) = |\mathcal{T}|/2^m$ denotes the density of $\mathcal{T}$. Fix such a set $\mathcal{T}$, and let $Z_x = \Pr[X = x] \cdot \mathbf{1}_{F(x) \in \mathcal{T}}$. Then, we have $\Pr[F(X) \in \mathcal{T}] = \sum_{x \in \{0,1\}^n} Z_x$ and $\mathbb{E}\left[\sum_{x \in \{0,1\}^n} Z_x\right] = \mu(\mathcal{T})$. As a result, since $Z_x \in [0, \Pr[X = x]]$ for all $x \in \{0,1\}^n$, Hoeffding's inequality[4] implies that

$$\Pr\left[\left|\sum_{x \in \{0,1\}^n} Z_x - \mu(\mathcal{T})\right| > \varepsilon\right] \leq 2 \cdot \exp\left(-\frac{2\varepsilon^2}{\sum_{x \in \{0,1\}^n} \Pr[X = x]^2}\right)$$

$$\leq 2 \cdot e^{-2\varepsilon^2 2^k}.$$

The last inequality follows from the fact that

$$\sum_{x \in \{0,1\}^n} \Pr[X = x]^2 \leq \max_{x \in \{0,1\}^n} \Pr[X = x] \leq 2^{-k},$$

since X is an (n, k)-source. Finally, a union bound over all 2^{2^m} sets $\mathcal{T} \subseteq \{0,1\}^m$ shows that the event in question holds with probability at least

$$1 - 2 \cdot 2^{2^m} \cdot e^{-2\varepsilon^2 2^k} \geq 1 - 2e^{-\varepsilon^2 2^k}$$

over the choice of F, given the upper bound on m.

References

1. Aggarwal, D., et al.: Stronger leakage-resilient and non-malleable secret sharing schemes for general access structures. In: Boldyreva, A., Micciancio, D. (eds.) CRYPTO 2019. LNCS, vol. 11693, pp. 510–539. Springer, Cham (2019). https://doi.org/10.1007/978-3-030-26951-7_18
2. Aggarwal, D., Kazana, T., Obremski, M.: Inception makes non-malleable codes stronger. In: Kalai, Y., Reyzin, L. (eds.) TCC 2017. LNCS, vol. 10678, pp. 319–343. Springer, Cham (2017). https://doi.org/10.1007/978-3-319-70503-3_10
3. Aggarwal, D., Obremski, M.: A constant rate non-malleable code in the split-state model. In: 2020 IEEE 61st Annual Symposium on Foundations of Computer Science (FOCS), pp. 1285–1294 (2020). https://doi.org/10.1109/FOCS46700.2020.00122
4. Aggarwal, D., Obremski, M., Ribeiro, J., Siniscalchi, L., Visconti, I.: How to extract useful randomness from unreliable sources. In: Canteaut, A., Ishai, Y. (eds.) EUROCRYPT 2020. LNCS, vol. 12105, pp. 343–372. Springer, Cham (2020). https://doi.org/10.1007/978-3-030-45721-1_13
5. Austrin, P., Chung, K.-M., Mahmoody, M., Pass, R., Seth, K.: On the impossibility of cryptography with tamperable randomness. In: Garay, J.A., Gennaro, R. (eds.) CRYPTO 2014. LNCS, vol. 8616, pp. 462–479. Springer, Heidelberg (2014). https://doi.org/10.1007/978-3-662-44371-2_26

---

[4] The version of Hoeffding's inequality we use here states that if $X_1, \ldots, X_N$ are independent random variables and $X_i \in [m_i, M_i]$ for each i, then

$$\Pr\left[\left|\sum_{i=1}^N X_i - \mu\right| > \varepsilon\right] \leq 2 \cdot \exp\left(-\frac{2\varepsilon^2}{\sum_{i=1}^N (M_i - m_i)^2}\right), \text{ where } \mu = \mathbb{E}\left[\sum_{i=1}^N X_i\right].$$

6. Backes, M., Kate, A., Meiser, S., Ruffing, T.: Secrecy without perfect randomness: cryptography with (bounded) weak sources. In: Malkin, T., Kolesnikov, V., Lewko, A.B., Polychronakis, M. (eds.) ACNS 2015. LNCS, vol. 9092, pp. 675–695. Springer, Cham (2015). https://doi.org/10.1007/978-3-319-28166-7_33
7. Bellare, M., Rompel, J.: Randomness-efficient oblivious sampling. In: Proceedings 35th Annual Symposium on Foundations of Computer Science, pp. 276–287 (1994). https://doi.org/10.1109/SFCS.1994.365687
8. Bellare, M., et al.: Hedged public-key encryption: how to protect against bad randomness. In: Matsui, M. (ed.) ASIACRYPT 2009. LNCS, vol. 5912, pp. 232–249. Springer, Heidelberg (2009). https://doi.org/10.1007/978-3-642-10366-7_14
9. Benaloh, J., Leichter, J.: Generalized secret sharing and monotone functions. In: Goldwasser, S. (ed.) CRYPTO 1988. LNCS, vol. 403, pp. 27–35. Springer, New York (1990). https://doi.org/10.1007/0-387-34799-2_3
10. Benhamouda, F., Degwekar, A., Ishai, Y., Rabin, T.: On the local leakage resilience of linear secret sharing schemes. J. Cryptol. **34**(2), 1–65 (2021). https://doi.org/10.1007/s00145-021-09375-2
11. Bhowmick, A., Gabizon, A., Lê, T.H., Zuckerman, D.: Deterministic extractors for additive sources: extended abstract. In: Roughgarden, T. (ed.) Proceedings of the 2015 Conference on Innovations in Theoretical Computer Science, ITCS 2015, Rehovot, Israel, 11–13 January 2015, pp. 277–286. ACM (2015). https://doi.org/10.1145/2688073.2688090
12. Blakley, G.R.: Safeguarding cryptographic keys. In: 1979 International Workshop on Managing Requirements Knowledge (MARK), pp. 313–318 (1979). https://doi.org/10.1109/MARK.1979.8817296
13. Blum, M.: Independent unbiased coin flips from a correlated biased source-a finite state Markov chain. Combinatorica **6**(2), 97–108 (1986)
14. Bosley, C., Dodis, Y.: Does privacy require true randomness? In: Vadhan, S.P. (ed.) TCC 2007. LNCS, vol. 4392, pp. 1–20. Springer, Heidelberg (2007). https://doi.org/10.1007/978-3-540-70936-7_1
15. Bourgain, J.: On the construction of affine extractors. GAFA Geom. Funct. Anal. **17**(1), 33–57 (2007)
16. Canetti, R., Pass, R., Shelat, A.: Cryptography from sunspots: how to use an imperfect reference string. In: 48th Annual IEEE Symposium on Foundations of Computer Science (FOCS 2007), pp. 249–259 (2007). https://doi.org/10.1109/FOCS.2007.70
17. Chattopadhyay, E., et al.: Extractors and secret sharing against bounded collusion protocols. In: 2020 IEEE 61st Annual Symposium on Foundations of Computer Science (FOCS), pp. 1226–1242 (2020). https://doi.org/10.1109/FOCS46700.2020.00117
18. Chattopadhyay, E., Li, X.: Extractors for sumset sources. In: Proceedings of the Forty-Eighth Annual ACM Symposium on Theory of Computing, pp. 299–311. ACM (2016)
19. Chor, B., Goldreich, O.: Unbiased bits from sources of weak randomness and probabilistic communication complexity. SIAM J. Comput. **17**(2), 230–261 (1988). https://doi.org/10.1137/0217015
20. Chor, B., Goldreich, O., Håstad, J., Friedman, J., Rudich, S., Smolensky, R.: The bit extraction problem or t-resilient functions. In: Proceedings of the 26th IEEE Symposium on Foundation of Computer Science, pp. 396–407 (1985)
21. Cramer, R., Damgård, I.B., Nielsen, J.B.: Secure Multiparty Computation and Secret Sharing. Cambridge University Press (2015). https://doi.org/10.1017/CBO9781107337756

22. Dodis, Y.: Exposure-resilient cryptography. Ph.D. thesis, Massachusetts Institute of Technology (2000)
23. Dodis, Y., López-Alt, A., Mironov, I., Vadhan, S.: Differential privacy with imperfect randomness. In: Safavi-Naini, R., Canetti, R. (eds.) CRYPTO 2012. LNCS, vol. 7417, pp. 497–516. Springer, Heidelberg (2012). https://doi.org/10.1007/978-3-642-32009-5_29
24. Dodis, Y., Ong, S.J., Prabhakaran, M., Sahai, A.: On the (im)possibility of cryptography with imperfect randomness. In: 45th Annual IEEE Symposium on Foundations of Computer Science, pp. 196–205 (2004). https://doi.org/10.1109/FOCS.2004.44
25. Dodis, Y., Pietrzak, K., Przydatek, B.: Separating sources for encryption and secret sharing. In: Halevi, S., Rabin, T. (eds.) TCC 2006. LNCS, vol. 3876, pp. 601–616. Springer, Heidelberg (2006). https://doi.org/10.1007/11681878_31
26. Dodis, Y., Spencer, J.: On the (non)universality of the one-time pad. In: 43rd Annual IEEE Symposium on Foundations of Computer Science, pp. 376–385 (2002). https://doi.org/10.1109/SFCS.2002.1181962
27. Dodis, Y., Yao, Y.: Privacy with imperfect randomness. In: Gennaro, R., Robshaw, M. (eds.) CRYPTO 2015. LNCS, vol. 9216, pp. 463–482. Springer, Heidelberg (2015). https://doi.org/10.1007/978-3-662-48000-7_23
28. Dodis, Y., Yu, Yu.: Overcoming weak expectations. In: Sahai, A. (ed.) TCC 2013. LNCS, vol. 7785, pp. 1–22. Springer, Heidelberg (2013). https://doi.org/10.1007/978-3-642-36594-2_1
29. Dvir, Z.: Extractors for varieties. Comput. Complex. 21(4), 515–572 (2012). https://doi.org/10.1007/s00037-011-0023-3
30. Dvir, Z., Gabizon, A., Wigderson, A.: Extractors and rank extractors for polynomial sources. Comput. Complex. 18(1), 1–58 (2009). https://doi.org/10.1007/s00037-009-0258-4
31. Dziembowski, S., Pietrzak, K., Wichs, D.: Non-malleable codes. J. ACM 65(4) (2018). https://doi.org/10.1145/3178432
32. Erdös, P., Frankl, P., Füredi, Z.: Families of finite sets in which no set is covered by the union of r others. Isr. J. Math. 51(1–2), 79–89 (1985)
33. Goldreich, O.: Three XOR-lemmas — an exposition. In: Goldreich, O. (ed.) Studies in Complexity and Cryptography. Miscellanea on the Interplay between Randomness and Computation. LNCS, vol. 6650, pp. 248–272. Springer, Heidelberg (2011). https://doi.org/10.1007/978-3-642-22670-0_22
34. Goyal, V., Kumar, A.: Non-malleable secret sharing. In: STOC 2018, pp. 685–698 (2018). https://doi.org/10.1145/3188745.3188872
35. Kamp, J., Rao, A., Vadhan, S.P., Zuckerman, D.: Deterministic extractors for small-space sources. J. Comput. Syst. Sci. 77(1), 191–220 (2011). https://doi.org/10.1016/j.jcss.2010.06.014
36. Kumar, A., Meka, R., Sahai, A.: Leakage-resilient secret sharing against colluding parties. In: 2019 IEEE 60th Annual Symposium on Foundations of Computer Science (FOCS), pp. 636–660 (2019). https://doi.org/10.1109/FOCS.2019.00045
37. Lichtenstein, D., Linial, N., Saks, M.: Some extremal problems arising from discrete control processes. Combinatorica 9(3), 269–287 (1989)
38. Lin, F., Cheraghchi, M., Guruswami, V., Safavi-Naini, R., Wang, H.: Leakage-resilient secret sharing in non-compartmentalized models. In: Kalai, Y.T., Smith, A.D., Wichs, D. (eds.) 1st Conference on Information-Theoretic Cryptography (ITC 2020). Leibniz International Proceedings in Informatics (LIPIcs), vol. 163, pp. 7:1–7:24. Schloss Dagstuhl-Leibniz-Zentrum für Informatik, Dagstuhl (2020). https://doi.org/10.4230/LIPIcs.ITC.2020.7

39. Maji, H., Paskin-Cherniavsky, A., Suad, T., Wang, M.: On leakage-resilient secret sharing. Cryptology ePrint Archive, Report 2020/1517 (2020). https://eprint.iacr.org/2020/1517
40. Maurer, U., Wolf, S.: Privacy amplification secure against active adversaries. In: Kaliski, B.S. (ed.) CRYPTO 1997. LNCS, vol. 1294, pp. 307–321. Springer, Heidelberg (1997). https://doi.org/10.1007/BFb0052244
41. McInnes, J.L., Pinkas, B.: On the impossibility of private key cryptography with weakly random keys. In: Menezes, A.J., Vanstone, S.A. (eds.) CRYPTO 1990. LNCS, vol. 537, pp. 421–435. Springer, Heidelberg (1991). https://doi.org/10.1007/3-540-38424-3_31
42. von Neumann, J.: Various techniques used in connection with random digits. Monte Carlo Method. U.S. Nat. Bur. Stand. Appl. Math. Ser. **12**, 36–38 (1951)
43. Nisan, N., Wigderson, A.: Hardness vs randomness. J. Comput. Syst. Sci. **49**(2), 149–167 (1994). https://doi.org/10.1016/S0022-0000(05)80043-1
44. Raz, R., Reingold, O., Vadhan, S.: Extracting all the randomness and reducing the error in Trevisan's extractors. J. Comput. Syst. Sci. **65**(1), 97–128 (2002). https://doi.org/10.1006/jcss.2002.1824
45. Rödl, V.: On a packing and covering problem. Eur. J. Comb. **6**(1), 69–78 (1985). https://doi.org/10.1016/S0195-6698(85)80023-8
46. Santha, M., Vazirani, U.V.: Generating quasi-random sequences from semi-random sources. J. Comput. Syst. Sci. **33**(1), 75–87 (1986). https://doi.org/10.1016/0022-0000(86)90044-9
47. Shamir, A.: How to share a secret. Commun. ACM **22**(11), 612–613 (1979). https://doi.org/10.1145/359168.359176
48. Srinivasan, A., Vasudevan, P.N.: Leakage resilient secret sharing and applications. In: Boldyreva, A., Micciancio, D. (eds.) CRYPTO 2019. LNCS, vol. 11693, pp. 480–509. Springer, Cham (2019). https://doi.org/10.1007/978-3-030-26951-7_17
49. Stinson, D.R., Wei, R.: Combinatorial repairability for threshold schemes. Des. Codes Crypt. **86**(1), 195–210 (2017). https://doi.org/10.1007/s10623-017-0336-6
50. Trevisan, L.: Extractors and pseudorandom generators. J. ACM **48**(4), 860–879 (2001). https://doi.org/10.1145/502090.502099
51. Trevisan, L., Vadhan, S.: Extracting randomness from samplable distributions. In: 41st Annual Symposium on Foundations of Computer Science, Redondo Beach, California, pp. 32–42. IEEE, November 2000
52. Yao, Y., Li, Z.: Differential privacy with bias-control limited sources. IEEE Trans. Inf. Forensics Secur. **13**(5), 1230–1241 (2018). https://doi.org/10.1109/TIFS.2017.2780802

Leakage-resilient Linear Secret-sharing Against Arbitrary Bounded-size Leakage Family

Hemanta K. Maji[1], Hai H. Nguyen[1(✉)], Anat Paskin-Cherniavsky[2],
Tom Suad[2], Mingyuan Wang[3], Xiuyu Ye[1], and Albert Yu[1]

[1] Department of Computer Science, Purdue University, West Lafayette, USA
{hmaji,nguye245,ye151,yu646}@purdue.edu, nhhai196@gmail.com
[2] Department of Computer Science, Ariel University, Ariel, Israel
anatpc@ariel.ac.il, tom.suad@msmail.ariel.ac.il
[3] Department of EECS, University of California Berkeley, Berkeley, USA
mingyuan@berkeley.edu

Abstract. Motivated by leakage-resilient secure computation of circuits with addition and multiplication gates, this work studies the leakage-resilience of linear secret-sharing schemes with a small reconstruction threshold against any *bounded-size* family of joint leakage attacks, i.e., the leakage function can leak *global* information from all secret shares.

We first prove that, with high probability, the Massey secret-sharing scheme corresponding to a random linear code over a finite field F is leakage-resilient against any ℓ-bit joint leakage family of size at most $|F|^{k-2.01}/8^\ell$, where k is the reconstruction threshold. Our result (1) bypasses the bottleneck due to the existing Fourier-analytic approach, (2) enables secure multiplication of secrets, and (3) is near-optimal. We use combinatorial and second-moment techniques to prove the result.

Next, we show that the Shamir secret-sharing scheme over a prime-order field F with randomly chosen evaluation places and with threshold k is leakage-resilient to any ℓ-bit joint leakage family of size at most $|F|^{2k-n-2.01}/(k! \cdot 8^\ell)$ with high probability. We prove this result by marrying our proof techniques for the first result with the existing Fourier

Hemanta K. Maji, Hai H. Nguyen, Mingyuan Wang, Xiuyu Ye, and Albert Yu are supported in part by an NSF CRII Award CNS–1566499, NSF SMALL Awards CNS–1618822 and CNS–2055605, the IARPA HECTOR project, MITRE Innovation Program Academic Cybersecurity Research Awards (2019–2020, 2020–2021), a Ross-Lynn Research Scholars Grant (2021–2022), a Purdue Research Foundation (PRF) Award (2017–2018), and The Center for Science of Information, an NSF Science and Technology Center, Cooperative Agreement CCF–0939370. Anat Paskin-Cherniavsky and Tom Suad are supported by the Ariel Cyber Innovation Center in conjunction with the Israel National Cyber directorate in the Prime Minister's Office. Mingyuan Wang is also supported in part by DARPA under Agreement No. HR00112020026, AFOSR Award FA9550-19-1-0200, NSF CNS Award 1936826, and research grants by the Sloan Foundation, and Visa Inc. Any opinions, findings and conclusions or recommendations expressed in this material are those of the author(s) and do not necessarily reflect the views of the United States Government or DARPA.

E. Kiltz and V. Vaikuntanathan (Eds.): TCC 2022, LNCS 13747, pp. 355–383, 2022.
https://doi.org/10.1007/978-3-031-22318-1_13

analytical approach. Moreover, it is unlikely that one can extend this result beyond $k/n \leqslant 0.5$ due to the technical hurdle for the Fourier-analytic approach.

1   Introduction

Traditionally, the security of cryptographic primitives assumes cryptosystems as impervious black-boxes, faithfully realizing the desired input-output behavior while providing no additional information. Real-world implementations, however, do not always maintain this idealized assumption. Innovative side-channel attacks starting with the seminal works of [20,21] have repetitively found success in obtaining partial information on the secret states. These diverse side-channel attacks pose significant threats to the security of underlying cryptographic primitives and all the cryptographic constructions that rely on them.

Towards resolving such concerns, one could develop ad hoc countermeasures for every existing side-channel attack. This approach, however, is unable to address the threat of unknown attacks. On the other hand, leakage-resilient cryptography aims to define potential avenues of information leakages formally and provide provable security guarantees against all such information leakages, even including the unforeseen ones. In the last few decades, a large body of influential works has studied the feasibility and efficiency of leakage-resilient cryptography against various models of potential leakages. We refer the readers to the excellent survey [19] for more details.

Secret-sharing schemes, a fundamental primitive in cryptography that is essential to all threshold cryptography constructions, are also threatened by such leakage attacks. The standard security of secret-sharing schemes guarantees that, given the (entire) secret shares of any unauthorized set of parties, one cannot learn any information about the secret. However, the security of the secret is not apparent if an adversary obtains (partial) information from every secret share. Such potential loss in security may percolate into cryptographic constructions built using these vulnerable secret-sharing schemes.

Application: Leakage-resilient Secure Computation. For example, secret-sharing schemes are commonplace in *secure multi-party computation* schemes that privately compute over private data using the GMW-technique [14]. Linear secret-sharing schemes naturally enable the secure addition of secrets. Secure multiplication of secrets typically uses multiplication-friendly secret-sharing schemes (for example, Shamir's secret-sharing scheme [34] and secret-sharing schemes based on other Goppa codes [12,13,15,30]) or, more generally, some restrictive versions of linear secret-sharing schemes. Multiplication-friendly secret-sharing schemes require the reconstruction threshold $k+1$ to be less than half the number of parties n to facilitate secure multiplication. More generally, linear secret-sharing schemes facilitate secure multiplication when $(k+1) \leqslant \sqrt{n}$. If the secret-sharing scheme used in the secure computation is leakage-resilient, then the resulting computation is itself leakage-resilient. Motivated by this application in leakage-resilient secure computation involving the addition and multiplication of secrets, our work studies the leakage-resilience of *linear secret-sharing schemes* with a *small reconstruction threshold*.

State-of-the-Art. Initiated by Benhamouda, Degwekar, Ishai, and Rabin [5], many recent works [1,25,28,31] study the leakage-resilience of linear secret-sharing schemes against *local leakage* attacks. In the local leakage model, the adversary picks an independent leakage function for each secret share. The final leakage is the union of the local leakages from every secret share. Even for this restrictive model, our understanding of the leakage-resilience of secret-sharing schemes is still far from complete.

Benhamouda, Degwekar, Ishai, and Rabin [6] proved that $(k + 1)$-out-of-n Shamir secret-sharing is locally 1-bit leakage-resilient when $k/n > 0.85$. Recently, Maji, Nguyen, Paskin-Cherniavsky, and Wang [27] improved this to $k/n > 0.78$. Maji, Paskin-Cherniavsky, Suad, and Wang [28] proved that the Massey secret-sharing scheme [30] corresponding to a random linear code of dimension-$(k + 1)$ is locally leakage-resilient with overwhelming probability when $k/n > 0.5$. Since these secret-sharing schemes require $k/n > 0.5$ to achieve leakage-resilience, they cannot facilitate the secure multiplication of secrets as motivated above. Furthermore, Maji et al. [28] pointed out an inherent barrier when $k/n < 0.5$ for existing works' Fourier-analytic technical approaches. In particular, they pinpoint a local leakage function that leaks the quadratic residuosity of every secret share, and existing Fourier-analytic approaches cannot prove leakage-resilience against this single function when $k/n \leqslant 0.5$.

Maji, Nguyen, Paskin-Cherniavsky, Suad, and Wang [25] consider the natural physical-bit leakage family in the small reconstruction threshold regime. In this model, the secret shares are stored in their natural binary representation, and the leakage function can learn physical bits stored at specified locations. [25] proved that Shamir secret-sharing with random evaluation places is leakage-resilient to the physical-bit leakage even for the most stringent reconstruction threshold $(k + 1) = 2$ (and polynomially large n). However, their approach still follows the Fourier-analytic approach. Consequently, one cannot hope to extend their result to any small family of leakage functions containing the quadratic residuosity leakage.

Summary of Our Results and Technical Contribution. This work studies the Monte-Carlo construction of leakage-resilience secret-sharing schemes. Our work studies the *general leakage-resilience* of (1) the Massey secret-sharing scheme corresponding to a random linear code, and (2) the Shamir secret-sharing scheme with random evaluation places. The leakage function can leak global information from all secret shares.

First, we show that the Massey secret-sharing scheme corresponding to a random linear code[1] with dimension $(k + 1) \geqslant 4$ is leakage-resilient to any

---

[1] This random linear code only needs to be chosen once. With only an exponentially small failure probability, the Massey secret-sharing scheme corresponding to this code shall be leakage-resilient. For instance, this random linear code can be specified by, for example, a common random string (CRS).

bounded-size family of (joint) leakage functions, except with an exponentially small probability. For example, one can consider the family of leakage functions containing all physical-bit leakages, NC^0 leakages, and circuits of bounded size. In the context of leakage-resilient secure computation, we also consider the collusion of adversarial parties who (in addition to their respective secret shares) obtain leakage on the honest parties' secret shares. Our result is near-optimal as evidenced by the leakage attack family presented in Remark 1. We also present a partial derandomization of this Monte-Carlo construction using a variant of the Wozencraft ensemble. Technically, we prove our results using a purely combinatorial argument and the second-moment technique. This argument is different from existing works [5,25,27,28] as all of them rely on a Fourier-analytic approach to prove the leakage-resilience. In particular, our technical approach bypasses the bottleneck result from the quadratic residuosity local leakage function, as indicated by [28].

Second, we show that a $(k + 1)$-out-of-n Shamir secret-sharing scheme with $k > n/2$ and random evaluation places is leakage-resilience to any bounded-size leakage family except with an exponentially small probability. This result is a partial derandomization of the leakage-resilience of the Massey secret-sharing scheme corresponding to a random linear code. We prove our result using the second-moment technique inspired by the first result and the Fourier-analytic approach together with Bézout's theorem inspired by [25]. Our result is near-optimal due to the inherent barrier when $k/n \leqslant 0.5$ for the Fourier-analytic approach pointed out in [28] (see Remark 2 for details).

1.1   Our Contribution

Table 1. Summary of relevant prior work (in chronological order) and our results, where λ is the security parameter.

Relevant work	Secret sharing scheme	Leakage family	Reconstruction threshold $(k + 1)$
BDIR'18 [5]	Shamir secret-sharing with any fixed evaluation places	arbitrary local	$k > 0.85 \cdot n$
MPSW'21 [28]	Massey secret-sharing of a random linear code	arbitrary local	$k > 0.5 \cdot n$
MNPSW'21 [25]	Shamir secret-sharing with random evaluation places	physical-bit	$k \geqslant 1$, $n = \mathsf{poly}(\lambda)$
MNPW'22 [27]	Shamir secret-sharing with any fixed evaluation places	arbitrary local	$k > 0.78 \cdot n$
Our work	Massey secret-sharing of a random linear code	arbitrary global of bounded size	$k \geqslant 3$, $n = \mathsf{poly}(\lambda)$
	Shamir secret-sharing with random evaluation places	arbitrary global of bounded size	$k > 0.5 \cdot n$, $n = \mathsf{poly}(\lambda)$

In this section, we present the main result of this paper. We refer the readers to Table 1 for a comparison between our results and the state-of-the-art results.

This section introduces some notations to facilitate the introduction of our results. Let λ denote the security parameter, the number of bits in the secret shares of every party. Let F be a finite field such that $2^{\lambda-1} \leqslant |F| < 2^{\lambda}$. Let n be the number of parties and $k+1$ be the reconstruction threshold.

Leakage-resilient Secret-sharing. Consider a secret-sharing scheme among n parties, where every secret share is an element in F. An *ℓ-bit leakage function* is any function $L: F^n \to \{0,1\}^{\ell}$. That is, L takes all the secret shares as input and outputs an ℓ-bit (joint) leakage. For any ℓ-bit leakage function L and any secret $s \in F$, we define $\mathbf{L}(s)$ as the distribution of the leakage when one applies L to the secret shares of s. A secret-sharing scheme is ε-leakage-resilient against L if for all secrets $s^{(0)}$ and $s^{(1)}$, the statistical distance between the leakage joint distributions $\mathbf{L}\left(s^{(0)}\right)$ and $\mathbf{L}\left(s^{(1)}\right)$ is (at most) ε. Finally, let $\mathcal{L}$ be a collection of some ℓ-bit leakage functions. A secret-sharing scheme is an *$(\mathcal{L}, \varepsilon)$-leakage-resilient secret-sharing scheme* if it is ε-leakage-resilient against every leakage function $L \in \mathcal{L}$.

Linear Code. A linear code $C \subseteq F^{(n+1)}$ is a linear subspace. Suppose the dimension of C is $k+1$. A matrix $G^+ \in F^{(k+1) \times (n+1)}$ is a *generator matrix* of C if the rows of G^+ span the subspace C. The generator matrix G^+ is in the *standard form* if $G^+ = [I_{k+1}|P]$. That is, the first $k+1$ columns of G^+ is the identity matrix. We refer to P as the *parity-check matrix*.

Massey Secret-Sharing Schemes [30]. Given a linear code $C \subseteq F^{(n+1)}$, the Massey secret-sharing scheme corresponding to a code C is defined as follows. For a secret $s \in F$, one samples a random codeword $(s_0, s_1, \ldots, s_n) \in C$ such that $s_0 = s$. For $i \in \{1, 2, \ldots, n\}$, the ith secret share is $s_i \in F$.

Shamir Secret-Sharing Schemes [34]. Let $s \in F$ be the secret and $\vec{X} = (X_1, X_2, \ldots, X_n) \in (F^*)^n$ be distinct evaluation places, i.e., $X_i \neq X_j$ for all $i \neq j$. The $[n, k+1, \vec{X}]_F$-Shamir secret-sharing scheme picks a random polynomial $P(X) \in F[X]/X^{k+1}$ conditioned on the fact that $P(0) = s$. The secret shares of parties $1, 2, \ldots, n$ are $s_1 = P(X_1), s_2 = P(X_2), \ldots, s_n = P(X_n)$, respectively.

Result I: Leakage-resilience of Random Linear Codes. We prove the following theorem regarding the leakage-resilience of a random linear code.

Theorem 1 (Technical Result). *Let $\mathcal{L}$ be a family of ℓ-bit (joint) leakage functions and F be a finite field (possibly, of composite order). Let $n, k \in \mathbb{N}$ be arbitrary parameters such that $k < n$. Define $\mathbf{G}^+ = [I_{k+1}|\mathbf{P}]$ as a random variable over the sample space $F^{(k+1) \times (n+1)}$, where every element of $\mathbf{P} \in F^{(k+1) \times (n-k)}$ is sampled independently and uniformly at random from the field F. The Massey secret-sharing scheme corresponding to $\mathbf{G}^+$ is $(\mathcal{L}, \varepsilon)$-leakage-resilient except with probability (at most)*

$$\frac{8^{\ell}}{\varepsilon^2} \cdot \frac{|\mathcal{L}|}{|F|^{k-2}}.$$

In particular, if $\varepsilon = \left(8^{\ell} \cdot |\mathcal{L}|/|F|^{k-2}\right)^{1/3}$, then this failure probability is also (at most) ε.

Observe that the randomness complexity of this Monte-Carlo construction for leakage-resilient secret-sharing scheme is $\mathcal{O}(k \cdot (n-k) \cdot \lg|F|)$ bits. Next, we interpret our technical result via a sequence of corollaries. We always consider a finite field F such that $2^{\lambda-1} \leqslant |F| < 2^{\lambda}$ and $n, k = \mathsf{poly}(\lambda)$ unless specified.

Corollary 1. *Let $c > 0$ be an arbitrary positive constant. Let $\mathcal{L}$ be an arbitrary ℓ-bit leakage family such that*

$$|\mathcal{L}| \leqslant |F|^{k-2-c}/8^{\ell}.$$

Then, the Massey secret-sharing scheme corresponding to $\mathbf{G}^+$ is $(\mathcal{L}, \exp(-\Omega(\lambda)))$-leakage-resilient except with probability $\exp(-\Omega(\lambda))$.

We remark that for a small leakage family $\mathcal{L}$, such as the physical-bit leakage family, any constant n and $k = 3$ suffices to ensure leakage-resilience. For the Massey secret-sharing scheme corresponding to an arbitrary linear code, having a small reconstruction threshold is desirable in the following two ways.

First, when $n > (k+1)^2$, parties can locally transform the secret shares of two secrets into the secret shares of their product. This enables secret-sharing-based multiparty computation protocols to perform secure multiplication.

Second, when we consider malicious parties who may not report their shares honestly, reconstructing the secret is significantly challenging. In fact, decoding erroneous random linear code is believed to be computationally hard [32,33]. However, if k is a constant, one can efficiently decode using (exhaustive search-based) majority voting techniques.

Remark 1. Our result is near-optimal as follows. Define $\mathcal{L}^*$ as the set of all leakage functions defined by $(S, \alpha_1, \alpha_2, \ldots, \alpha_{k+1})$, where $S = \{i_1, i_2, \ldots, i_{k+1}\} \subseteq \{1, 2, \ldots, n\}$, and $\alpha_1, \ldots \alpha_{k+1} \in F$. The $(\ell = 1)$-bit leakage function corresponding to $(S, \alpha_1, \ldots, \alpha_{k+1})$ indicates whether

$$\alpha_1 \cdot s_{i_1} + \alpha_2 \cdot s_{i_2} + \cdots + \alpha_{k+1} \cdot s_{i_{k+1}} = 0,$$

or not. Here $s_{i_1}, \ldots, s_{i_{k+1}}$ represents the i_1-th, $\ldots$, i_{k+1}-th secret share, respectively. The size of this leakage family is $\mathcal{O}(n^{k+1} \cdot |F|^{k+1})$.

For any Massey secret-sharing scheme corresponding to the linear code generated by $[I_{k+1}|P]$, there is a leakage function in the family $\mathcal{L}$ that can distinguish the secret $s^{(0)} = 0$ from the secret $s^{(1)} = 1$. Given the generator matrix $[I_{k+1}|P]$ there are (at most) $k+1$ columns $i_1, \ldots, i_{k+1}$ that span the generator matrix's 0-th column. Therefore, there exists a linear reconstruction $\alpha_1 \cdot s_{i_1} + \cdots + \alpha_{k+1} \cdot s_{i_{k+1}}$ for the secret. The leakage function corresponding to $(S = \{i_1, \ldots, i_{k+1}\}, \alpha_1, \ldots, \alpha_{k+1})$ distinguishes the secret $s^{(0)} = 0$ from any $s^{(1)} \in F^*$ (for example, $s^{(1)} = 1$).

In comparison, we show that G^+ is leakage-resilient to any family $\mathcal{L}$ if $|\mathcal{L}| \leqslant |F|^{k-2-c}$ for an arbitrary constant $c > 0$. The near optimality of our result follows from the fact that $n = \mathsf{poly}(\lambda)$ and $|F| \approx 2^{\lambda}$.

Next, we interpret our result in context of the motivating example of leakage-resilient secure computation. Suppose t parties participating in the secure computation protocol collude and obtain additional one-bit physical-bit local leakage on the secret shares of the remaining honest parties. The total number of bits leaked is

$$\ell = t \cdot \lambda + (n - t) \leqslant t\lambda + n.$$

The total number of leakage functions is

$$|\mathcal{L}| = \binom{n}{t} \cdot \lambda^{n-t} \leqslant 2^n \cdot \lambda^n.$$

Therefore, $k = \omega(n \log \lambda / \lambda)$ and $t \leqslant k/3 - c'$ ensures that $|\mathcal{L}| \leqslant |F|^{k-2-c}/8^{\ell}$, for any positive constant c'. The following corollary summarizes this result.

Corollary 2. *Let $\mathcal{L}$ be the leakage family that leaks t secret shares in the entirety and one physical bit from the remaining shares. Then, Massey secret-sharing scheme corresponding to $\mathbf{G}^+$ is $(\mathcal{L}, \exp(-\Omega(\lambda)))$-leakage-resilient except with $\exp(-\Omega(\lambda))$ probability if we have*

$$k = \omega(n \log \lambda / \lambda) \qquad and \qquad t \leqslant k/3 - c',$$

where c' is an arbitrary constant.

Next, we interpret our result in the context of more sophisticated local leakage attacks. We consider the local leakage attack where every local leakage function is a small circuit. These circuits take the λ-bit binary representation of F as input. We consider two natural families of circuits.

Local Leakage with Bounded-Depth Circuits. Let NC_d^0 be the set of circuits with depth at most d. The size of NC_d^0 is upper-bounded by $\binom{\lambda}{2^d} \cdot 2^{2^d}$. The size of the local leakage family where every local leakage function is NC_d^0 that leaks one bit is upper-bounded by $\left(\binom{\lambda}{2^d} \cdot 2^{2^d}\right)^n$. Consequently, the prerequisite of Corollary 1 holds (for all constant d) as long as $k = \omega(n \log \lambda / \lambda)$. Hence, we have the following corollary.

Corollary 3. *Let $\mathcal{L}$ be the local leakage family where every local leakage function is NC^0 that leaks one bit. Massey secret-sharing scheme corresponding to $\mathbf{G}^+$ is $(\mathcal{L}, \exp(-\Omega(\lambda)))$-leakage-resilient except with $\exp(-\Omega(\lambda))$ probability if we have*

$$k = \omega(n \log \lambda / \lambda).$$

In particular, for any constant n and $k = 3$, the corresponding Massey secret-sharing scheme is leakage-resilient.

We remark that the NC^0-local leakage family is a superset of the physical-bit local leakage family (for example, as considered in the recent work of [25]). [25] proved that the Shamir secret-sharing scheme with reconstruction threshold $k \geqslant 2$ and random evaluation places is leakage-resilient to physical-bit leakages, which is a significantly smaller subset of the NC_d^0 local leakage considered in our work.

Local Leakage with Bounded-Size Circuits. The number of circuits of size (at most) s is upper-bounded by $(10s) \cdot 2^s$ [3]. Hence, the size of the local leakage family where every local leakage function is a circuit of size (at most) s that leaks one bit is upper-bounded by $(10s \cdot 2^s)^n$. Consequently, the prerequisite of Corollary 1 holds as long as $k = \omega(n \cdot s/\lambda)$. Thus, we have the following corollary.

Corollary 4. *Let $\mathcal{L}$ be the local leakage family where every local leakage function is a circuit of size (at most) s that leaks one bit. Massey secret-sharing scheme corresponding to $\mathbf{G}^+$ is $(\mathcal{L}, \exp(-\Omega(\lambda)))$-leakage-resilient except with $\exp(-\Omega(\lambda))$ probability if we have*

$$k = \omega(n \cdot s/\lambda).$$

In particular, when $s = o(\lambda/\sqrt{n})$, one may pick $k \leqslant \sqrt{n}$.

For example, using a large-enough finite field F such that $\lambda = n^2$, the Massey secret-sharing scheme corresponding to random linear codes is leakage-resilient to size-$(s = n)$ local leakage circuits.

Leakage-resilience of Randomly Twisted Additive Secret-Sharing. Fix a finite field F. The *additive secret-sharing scheme* over F for n parties chooses random secret shares $s_1, s_2, \ldots, s_n \in F$ conditioned on $s_1 + s_2 + \cdots + s_n = s$, where $s \in F$ is the secret. For a (publicly-known) *twist* $(\alpha_1, \alpha_2, \ldots, \alpha_n) \in (F^*)^n$, the corresponding *twisted additive secret-sharing scheme* chooses random secret shares $s_1, s_2, \ldots, s_n \in F$ conditioned on $\sum_{i=1}^n \alpha_i \cdot s_i = s$. The *randomly twisted additive secret-sharing scheme* picks a uniformly random public twist $(\alpha_1, \ldots, \alpha_n) \in (F^*)^n$ and shares the secret using the corresponding twisted additive secret-sharing scheme.

When the reconstruction threshold is identical to the number of parties, our result also implies the leakage-resilience of randomly twisted additive secret-sharing.[2]

Corollary 5. *Let $c > 0$ be an arbitrary positive constant. Let $\mathcal{L}$ be an arbitrary ℓ-bit leakage family such that*

$$|\mathcal{L}| \leqslant |F|^{n-2-c}/8^\ell.$$

If $n = o(\lambda)$, the randomly twisted additive secret-sharing scheme is $(\mathcal{L}, \exp(-\Omega(\lambda)))$-leakage-resilient except with probability $\exp(-\Omega(\lambda))$.

Reverse Multiplication Friendly Embedding (RMFE). The *reverse multiplication friendly embedding (RMFE)* [7,8,10] is a *bilinear map* that embeds SIMD-style multiple instances of the multiplication over a small field (say F') into a single multiplication instance over an extension field F. Therefore, RMFE *modularly packs* multiple F' secrets into one F secret in a manner that is addition and multiplication friendly, making these mappings suitable for cryptographic applications.

---

[2] This observation is due to that a random *square matrix* over a large enough field F is full-rank with overwhelming probability.

The number of packed secrets is linear in the degree of the extension [8,10]. For example, one can pack $\Theta(\lambda)$ secrets in $F' = GF[2]$) (i.e., binary secrets) into one $F = GF[2^\lambda]$ secret. An *RMFE-based packed secret-sharing scheme* packs F' secrets into one F secret and secret shares this F secret.

Observe that our leakage-resilience result for the Massey secret-sharing schemes corresponding to random linear codes also holds for extension fields F with arbitrary small characteristics (e.g., characteristic-2). Consequently, the RMFE-based packed secret-sharing scheme over F' (as described above) is leakage-resilient because the secret-sharing over F is leakage-resilient. This consequence extends our technical results to construct leakage-resilient secret-sharing schemes for (multiple) constant-size secrets.

The Monte-Carlo construction presented above samples a fully random parity check matrix $P \in F^{(k+1)\times(n-k)}$, which requires $k(n-k)$ independent and uniformly random elements from the finite field F. We partially derandomize this result using (a variant of) the Wozencraft ensemble. In particular, we use two types of partially random matrices.

Wozencraft Ensemble **W**. Consider a finite field K, which is a degree k extension of F. The Wozencraft ensemble maps every element $\alpha \in K$ to a matrix $M(\alpha) \in F^{k\times k}$. To sample a $k \times (n-k)$ matrix, one picks $m = \lceil (n-k)/k \rceil$ random elements $\alpha^{(1)}, \ldots, \alpha^{(m)} \in K$. The sampled matrix **W** shall be the first $n-k$ columns of the matrix $\left[M\left(\alpha^{(1)}\right) | \cdots | M\left(\alpha^{(m)}\right) \right]$. We refer the readers to Definition 3 for more details.

t-Row Random Matrix $\mathbf{M}^{(t)}$. For this random matrix, the first t rows are sampled independently and uniformly at random. The remaining rows are fixed to be 0. Refer to Definition 2 for more details.

Using these two types of partially random matrices, we prove the following theorem. A proof is provided in Appendix 6.

Theorem 2. *Let $\mathcal{L}$ be an arbitrary family of ℓ-bit leakage functions and F be a finite field (possibly, of composite order). Let $n, k \in \mathbb{N}$ be arbitrary parameters such that $k < n$. Define $\mathbf{G}^+ = [I_{k+1}|\mathbf{P}]$ as a random variable over the sample space $F^{(k+1)\times(n+1)}$, where $\mathbf{P}$ is sampled as follows.*

- *Entries of the first row of $\mathbf{P}$ are sampled independently and uniformly at random from F.*
- *The submatrix consisting of the rest of the rows, refer to as $\mathbf{R}$, is sampled as $\mathbf{W} + \mathbf{M}^{(t)}$, where $\mathbf{W}$ and $\mathbf{M}^{(t)}$ are sampled independently.*

The Massey secret-sharing scheme corresponding to $\mathbf{G}^+$ is $(\mathcal{L}, \varepsilon)$-leakage-resilient except with probability (at most)

$$\frac{8^\ell}{\varepsilon^2} \cdot \frac{|\mathcal{L}|}{|F|^{t-2}}.$$

In particular, $\varepsilon = \left(8^\ell \cdot |\mathcal{L}|/|F|^{t-2} \right)^{1/3}$ ensures that the failure probability is at most ε. Furthermore, ε is exponentially decaying when $|\mathcal{L}| \leqslant |F|^{t-2-c}/8^\ell$, where

$c > 0$ *is a constant. The random F-elements required to sample* $\mathbf{G}^+$ *is* $(t+1)(n-k) + k \cdot \lceil \frac{n-k}{k} \rceil$.

Result II: Leakage resilience of Shamir's secret sharing schemes with random evaluation places. Our second result is the following.

Theorem 3. *Let F be a prime order field of size p. Let $\mathcal{L}$ be an arbitrary family of ℓ-bit joint leakage functions. Define $\vec{\mathbf{X}}$ be a random variable, where $\vec{\mathbf{X}}$ is chosen uniformly at random from the set $(F^*)^n$ such that $\mathbf{X}_i \neq \mathbf{X}_j$ for all $i \neq j$. The $[n, k+1, \vec{\mathbf{X}}]_F$-Shamir's secret-sharing scheme corresponding to randomly chosen evaluation places $\vec{\mathbf{X}}$ is $(\mathcal{L}, \varepsilon)$-leakage-resilient except with probability at most*

$$\frac{4 \cdot |\mathcal{L}| \cdot 8^\ell \cdot p^{n-k+1} \cdot k!}{\varepsilon^2 \cdot (p-n)^k}.$$

In particular, setting $\varepsilon = \left(4 \cdot |\mathcal{L}| \cdot 8^\ell \cdot p^{n-k+1} \cdot k!/(p-n)^k\right)^{1/3}$ ensures that the failure probability is at most ε.

Our proof of this theorem combines the combinatorial proof techniques used in our first result with the Fourier-analytic approach in the literature [5,25,27,28].

Observe that the randomness complexity of this construction is $\mathcal{O}(n \cdot \lg|F|)$ bits. Next, we interpret our technical result as follows. We omit the details for the leakage-resilience of Shamir secret-sharing schemes against local leakage with bounded-depth or bounded-size circuits.

Corollary 6. *Let c and δ be arbitrary positive constants. Let $\mathcal{L}$ be an arbitrary ℓ-bit leakage family such that*

$$|\mathcal{L}| \leqslant \frac{(p-n)^{k-c}}{4 \cdot 8^\ell \cdot p^{n-k+1} \cdot k!}.$$

Let F be a finite field such that $2^{\lambda-1} \leqslant |F| < 2^\lambda$, $k = (1/2+\delta)n$, and $n = \mathsf{poly}(\lambda)$. Then, the $[n, k+1, \vec{\mathbf{X}}]_F$-Shamir's secret-sharing scheme is $(\mathcal{L}, \exp(-\Omega(\lambda)))$-leakage-resilient except with probability $\exp(-\Omega(\lambda))$.

We note that any constant n and $k > (n+1)/2$ suffices to ensure leakage-resilience for any small enough leakage family, for example, the physical-bit leakage family.

Remark 2. The inherent barrier of the existing Fourier's analytic approach as pointed out in [28] tells us that k/n must be greater than $1/2$ to achieve leakage-resilient even against a leakage family of size one that contains only the quadratic residue leakage function. Our result shows that any $k > (n+1)/2$ suffices, and the larger value of k the bigger size of the leakage family. Let $\mathcal{L}^{**}$ be the set of all 1-bit leakage functions that indicate whether $\lambda_1 \cdot s_1 + \lambda_2 \cdot s_2 + \cdots + \lambda_{k+1} \cdot s_{k+1} = 0$, where $s_1, s_2, \ldots, s_{k+1}$ are the secret shares of parties $1, 2, \ldots, k+1$, respectively, and λ_j are the Lagrange coefficients defined as

$$\lambda_j := \prod_{i \in \{1,2,\cdots,k+1\} \setminus \{j\}} \left(\frac{X_i}{X_i - X_j} \right).$$

The size of $\mathcal{L}^{**}$ is equal to the number of tuples $(\lambda_1, \lambda_2, \cdots, \lambda_k)$, which is equal to $(p-1){\cdot}(p-2)\cdots(p-k-1)$. For any Shamir's secret-sharing scheme corresponding to the evaluation places $\vec{\mathbf{X}}$, there is a leakage function in the family $\mathcal{L}^{**}$ that can distinguish the secret $s^{(0)} = 0$ from any other secret. Observe that when k is close to n, our result is near-optimal.

1.2 Prior Relevant Works

Since the introduction of leakage-resilient secret-sharing [5,16], there are two main research directions. The first direction is to construct new secret-sharing schemes that are leakage-resilient against various models of leakages [2,4,9,11, 16,22,35]. The other direction is to investigate the leakage-resilience of prominent secret-sharing schemes against local leakages [1,5,23,25,28]. We shall focus our discussion on the second line of work.

Interestingly, the leakage-resilience of the Massey secret-sharing scheme is connected to the exciting problem of repairing a linear code in the distributed storage setting. For example, Guruswami and Wootters [17,18] presented a reconstruction algorithm that obtains one bit from every block of a Reed-Solomon code to repair any block when the field has characteristic two. Their results show that Shamir's secret-sharing schemes over characteristic two fields are utterly broken against general one-bit local leakages.

For the case of prime-order fields, [6,28] proved that Shamir secret-sharing scheme is robust to one-bit local leakage if the reconstruction threshold $k \geqslant 0.85n$. Very recently, [27] improved this threshold to $k \geqslant 0.78n$. Furthermore, [28] proved that when $k > 0.5n$, the Massey secret-sharing scheme corresponding to a random linear code is leakage-resilient even if a constant number of bits are leaked from every share. For restricted families of leakages, [25] studied the physical-bit leakage attacks on the Shamir secret-sharing scheme. They proved that the Shamir secret-sharing scheme with random evaluation places is leakage-resilient to this family when reconstruction threshold $k \geqslant 2$.

From the lower bound perspective, Nielsen and Simkin [31] proved that Shamir secret-sharing scheme is not locally leakage-resilient if $m \approx k \cdot \log|F|/n$ bits is leaked from every secret share. Finally, the recent work of [26] proved that the "parity-of-parity" attack [25] on the additive secret sharing scheme has the optimal distinguishing advantage of $2^{-\Theta(n)}$. Hence, if an additive secret sharing scheme is 1-bit locally leakage-resilient it must hold that $n = \omega(\log \lambda)$.

2 Technical Overview

Let λ represent the security parameter. Let F be a finite field (possibly, of composite order) such that $2^{\lambda-1} \leqslant |F| < 2^{\lambda}$. That is, every element of F has a λ-bit representation. Let n represent the number of secret shares and $k+1$ represent the reconstruction threshold of the secret-sharing scheme.

Overview of Result I. Consider a generator matrix $G^+ \in F^{(k+1)\times(n+1)}$ in the standard form, i.e., $G^+ = [I_{k+1}|P]$. The linear code generated by G^+ (i.e., the row span of G^+) is denoted by $\langle G^+ \rangle$. We shall index the rows of G^+ by $\{0, 1, \ldots, k\}$ and the columns of G^+ by $\{0, 1, \ldots, n\}$. We refer to the submatrix $G^+_{\{1,\ldots,k\},\{1,\ldots,n\}}$ as G. Consider the Massey secret-sharing scheme corresponding to the linear code $\langle G^+ \rangle$. Observe that the secret shares corresponding to the secret 0 are identical to the linear code $\langle G \rangle$. Furthermore, we refer to the row vector $G^+_{0,\{1,\ldots,n\}}$ as $\vec{v}$. This representation has the benefit of succinctly expressing the secret shares of s as the affine subspace $s \cdot \vec{v} + \langle G \rangle$. Refer to Fig. 1 for a pictorial summary of these notations.

For now, we shall consider a fully random $\mathbf{G}^+$ such that every element of the parity check matrix $\mathbf{P}$ is sampled independently and uniformly at random from the finite field F.

Reduction 1. Fix any ℓ-bit (joint) leakage family $\mathcal{L}$. Our objective is to prove that the Massey secret-sharing scheme corresponding to a random code $\mathbf{G}^+$ is $(\mathcal{L}, \varepsilon)$-leakage-resilient, with overwhelming probability. Observe that it is sufficient to consider an arbitrary function L and prove an upper bound on the probability that $\mathbf{G}^+$ is not ε-leakage-resilient against L. Once we have this upper bound, invoking a union bound over all leakage functions contained in the set $\mathcal{L}$ yields an upper bound on the probability that $\mathbf{G}^+$ is not $(\mathcal{L}, \varepsilon)$-leakage-resilient. Hence, in the rest of the discussion, we fix the leakage function L and consider the probability that $\mathbf{G}^+$ is *not* ε-leakage-resilient against a particular ℓ-bit leakage function L.

Reduction 2. By definition, if $\mathbf{G}^+$ is not ε-leakage-resilient against L, there exists two secrets $s^{(0)}$ and $s^{(1)}$ such that the statistical distance between $\mathbf{L}(s^{(0)})$ and $\mathbf{L}(s^{(1)})$ is $> \varepsilon$. However, note that it suffices to restrict $s^{(0)} = 0$. This restriction is justified because the triangle inequality ensures that there must be a secret $s \in F^*$ such that the statistical distance between the leakage joint distributions $\mathbf{L}(0)$ and $\mathbf{L}(s)$ must be at least $\varepsilon/2$. Henceforth, our objective is to consider a pair of secret 0 and $s \in F^*$ and estimate the probability that the statistical distance between the joint leakage distribution $\mathbf{L}(0)$ and $\mathbf{L}(s)$ is $> \varepsilon/2$.

Reduction 3. Observe that the statistical distance between $\mathbf{L}(0)$ and $\mathbf{L}(s)$ is

$$\frac{1}{2} \cdot \sum_{\vec{w} \in \{0,1\}^\ell} \frac{1}{|F|^k} \Big| |\langle \mathbf{G} \rangle \cap A_{\vec{w}}| - |(s \cdot \vec{v} + \langle \mathbf{G} \rangle) \cap A_{\vec{w}}| \Big|,$$

where $A_{\vec{w}} := L^{-1}(\vec{w})$ is the preimage of the observed leakage $\vec{w}$. For any $A \subseteq F^n$ and secret $s \in F$, we define the random variable

$$\mathbf{X}_{s,A} := \frac{1}{|F|^k} \Big| |\langle \mathbf{G} \rangle \cap A| - |(s \cdot \vec{v} + \langle \mathbf{G} \rangle) \cap A| \Big|.$$

Our objective can be further reduced to show that the random variable $\mathbf{X}_{s,A}$ is sufficiently small with overwhelming probability. This bound is sufficient because one may complete the proof by union bounding over all the choices of $s \in F^*$ and $A_{\vec{w}} \subseteq F^n$.

Upper Bounding the Second Moment. We proceed via a second-moment technique to prove that the random variable $\mathbf{X}_{s,A}$ is sufficiently small with overwhelming probability. An upper bound on the expectation of the second moment suffices for our proof because one can use the Chebyshev inequality to prove that $\mathbf{X}_{s,A}$ is sufficiently small with overwhelming probability. Indeed, we prove that, when $\mathbf{G}^+$ is fully random, the expectation of the second moment is small. Our results on the second moment of the random variable $\mathbf{X}_{s,A}$ are summarized as Lemma 2.

Partial Derandomization. Finally, we show that one may prove a similar bound on the second moment of $\mathbf{X}_{s,A}$ when $\mathbf{G}^+$ is only partially random. In particular, we consider the sampling part of the parity check matrix $\mathbf{P}$ as the sum of the Wozencraft ensemble and the set of matrices with few random rows. Appendix 6 provides additional details on this result.

On the Combinatorial Approach. Our combinatorial approach deviates from the Fourier-analytical approach of prior works and, hence, circumvents the roadblocks that are inherent to it. Surprisingly, this elementary approach already gives us near-optimal results in terms of the size of the leakage family. However, our approach does not extend to proving the leakage-resilience of Massey secret-sharing corresponding to a fixed linear code or Shamir secret-sharing with fixed evaluation places. It seems that our ideas does not extend to large leakage family, for example, the entire local leakage family.

Overview of Result II. We shall restrict the field F to be a prime order field of size p in the following discussion. Let $\vec{X}$ be distinct evaluation places in $(F^*)^n$. Consider the $[n, k+1, \vec{X}]_F$-Shamir's secret-sharing scheme. Observe that the secret shares corresponding to the secret 0 are identical to the linear code $C_{\vec{X}} = \langle G_{\vec{X}} \rangle$, where $G_{\vec{X}}$ is the following matrix.

$$G_{\vec{X}} = \begin{pmatrix} X_1 & X_2 & \cdots & X_n \\ X_1^2 & X_2^2 & \cdots & X_n^2 \\ \vdots & \vdots & \ddots & \vdots \\ X_1^k & X_2^k & \cdots & X_n^k \end{pmatrix}.$$

Observe also that the secret shares of a secret $s \in F$ is the affine subspace $s \cdot \vec{1} + \langle G_{\vec{X}} \rangle$, where $\vec{1}$ is the vector of length n whose every coordinate is one. We note that $C_{\vec{X}}$ is an $[n, k]_F$ maximum distance separable code.

We shall consider random distinct evaluation places $\vec{\mathbf{X}}$, and so the random matrix $\mathbf{G}_{\vec{\mathbf{X}}}$, which is a partial derandomization of the matrix $\mathbf{G}$ considered in the first result. Our objective is to prove that Shamir's secret-sharing scheme corresponding to $\mathbf{G}_{\vec{\mathbf{X}}}$ is $(\mathcal{L}, \varepsilon)$-leakage-resilient, with overwhelming probability.

Using a similar argument as in the case of random linear code, our objective is reduced to show that the random variable $\mathbf{Y}_{s,A}$ is sufficiently small with overwhelming probability, where

$$\mathbf{Y}_{s,A} := \frac{1}{p^k} \cdot \left(|\langle \mathbf{G}_{\vec{\mathbf{X}}} \rangle \cap A| - |(\langle \mathbf{G}_{\vec{\mathbf{X}}} \rangle + s \cdot \vec{1}) \cap A| \right).$$

We once again use the second-moment technique to prove that the random variable $\mathbf{Y}_{s,A}$ is sufficiently small with high probability (see Lemma 3). However, we use a Fourier-analytical approach instead of the combinatorial approach for the random linear code. The randomness in $\mathbf{G}_{\vec{\mathbf{X}}}$ is much less compared to the randomness in $\mathbf{G}$. Consequently, the combinatorial proof does not go through for $\mathbf{G}_{\vec{\mathbf{X}}}$. To circumvent this, we rely on the Fourier-analytical approach [5,25,28]. However, unlike prior works, our analysis can handle not only local leakage but also global leakage. In addition, our proof imports a result (Claim 3) from [25] that upper-bounds the probability that a codeword $\vec{\alpha}$ belongs to a random code $\langle \mathbf{G}_{\vec{\mathbf{X}}} \rangle^{\perp}$, which follows from a generalization of Bézout's theorem.

Comparison with [25]. In a recent work, Maji et al. [25] considered the leakage-resilience of Shamir secret-sharing against physical-bit leakage. They proved that the Shamir secret-sharing scheme with random evaluation places is leakage-resilient to the physical-bit leakage family for any reconstruction threshold $(k + 1) \geqslant 2$. The Shamir secret-sharing scheme is multiplication-friendly for any $k < n/2$.

In comparison to our result I, for the physical-bit leakage family, we prove that the Massey secret-sharing scheme corresponding to a random linear code is leakage-resilient for any reconstruction threshold $(k + 1) \geqslant 4$. The product of the Massey secret-sharing scheme corresponding to a general linear code is a ramp secret-sharing scheme (with k-privacy and $(k + 1)^2$-reconstruction threshold). Hence, Massey's secret-sharing scheme corresponding to a general linear code is multiplication-friendly when $n \geqslant (k + 1)^2$. However, our result is significantly more general as it applies to arbitrary small (potentially joint) leakage families. In contrast, the techniques of [25] follow the Fourier analytic approach and, hence, cannot be extended to arbitrary local leakage families (due to the bottleneck presented by [28]).

The result in [25] is incomparable to our result II. Their result is only for the physical-bit leakage family but works for any $(k + 1) \geqslant 2$, while our result works for any bounded-size joint leakage family but requires that the reconstruction threshold is $> (n + 1)/2$.

Comparison with [6,28]. Benhamouda et al. [6] proved that the Shamir secret-sharing scheme is leakage-resilient to all local leakage functions when $k > 0.85n$. Similarly, Maji et al. [28] proved that the Massey secret-sharing scheme corresponding to a random linear code is leakage-resilient to all local leakage functions when $k > 0.5n$.

Both results are incomparable to our result I as they require a significantly higher threshold k, but proved a stronger result, i.e., leakage-resilience against all local leakage functions. In particular, the parameter settings for k and n in their results are not multiplication-friendly.

Again both results are incomparable to our result II as the size of all the local leakage functions is significantly larger than the size of the bounded-size joint leakage family in ours. Theirs and ours require a high reconstruction threshold.

3   Preliminaries

Throughout this paper, we use F for a finite field. Our work uses the length of the binary representation of the order of the field F as the security parameter λ, i.e., $\lambda = \log_2 |F|$. The total number of parties $n = \mathsf{poly}(\lambda)$ and the reconstruction threshold $k = \mathsf{poly}(\lambda)$ as well. The objective of our arguments shall be to show the insecurity of the cryptographic constructions is $\varepsilon = \mathsf{negl}(\lambda)$, i.e., a function that decays faster than any inverse-polynomial of the λ. For any two distributions $\mathbf{A}$ and $\mathbf{B}$ over the same sample space (which is enumerable), the *statistical distance* between the two distributions, represented by $\mathsf{SD}(\mathbf{A}, \mathbf{B})$, is defined as $\frac{1}{2} \cdot \sum_x |\Pr[\mathbf{A} = x] - \Pr[\mathbf{B} = x]|$.

For any set A, we denote the indicator function of the set A as $\mathbb{1}_A$. That is, $\mathbb{1}_A(x) = 1$ if $x \in A$ and 0 otherwise. For an element x and a set S, we use $x + S$ to denote the set $\{x + s \colon s \in S\}$.

3.1   Matrices

A matrix $M \in F^{k \times n}$ has k-rows and n-columns, and each of its element is in F. Let $I \subseteq \{1, \ldots, k\}$ and $J \subseteq \{1, \ldots, n\}$ be a subset of row and column indices, respectively. The matrix M restricted to rows I and columns J is represented by $M_{I,J}$. If $I = \{i\}$ is a singleton set, then we represent $M_{i,J}$ for $M_{\{i\},J}$. The analogous notation also holds for singleton J. Furthermore, $G_{*,J}$ represents the columns of G indexed by J (all rows are included). Similarly, $G_{*,j}$ represents the j-th column of the matrix G. Analogously, one defines $G_{I,*}$ and $G_{i,*}$.

Some parts of the documents use $\{0, 1, \ldots, k\}$ as row indices and $\{0, 1, \ldots, n\}$ as column indices for a matrix $G^+ \in F^{(k+1) \times (n+1)}$.

3.2   Codes and Linear Secret-sharing Schemes

We use the following notations for error-correcting codes as consistent with [24].

A *linear code* C (over the finite field F) of *length* $(n+1)$ and *rank* $(k+1)$ is a $(k+1)$-dimension vector subspace of F^{n+1}, referred to as an $[n+1, k+1]_F$-code. The *generator matrix* $G \in F^{(k+1) \times (n+1)}$ of an $[n+1, k+1]_F$ linear code C ensures that every element in C can be expressed as $\vec{x} \cdot G$, for an appropriate $\vec{x} \in F^{k+1}$. Given a generator matrix G, the row-span of G, i.e., the code generated by G, is represented by $\langle G \rangle$. A generator matrix G is in the *standard form* if $G = [I_{k+1} | P]$, where $I_{k+1} \in F^{(k+1) \times (k+1)}$ is the identity matrix and $P \in F^{(k+1) \times (n-k)}$ is the parity check matrix. In this work, we always assume that the generator matrices are in their standard form.

Maximum Distance Separable Codes. The *distance* of a linear code is the minimum weight of a non-zero codeword. An $[n, k]_F$-code is *maximum distance separable* (MDS) if its distance is $(n - k + 1)$.

Massey Secret-Sharing Schemes. Let $C \subseteq F^{n+1}$ be a linear code. Let $s \in F$ be a secret. The Massey secret-sharing scheme corresponding to C picks a random element $(s, s_1, \ldots, s_n) \in C$ to share the secret s. The secret shares of parties $1, \ldots, n$ are $s_1, \ldots, s_n$, respectively.

Recall that the set of all codewords of the linear code generated by the generator matrix $G^+ \in F^{(k+1) \times (n+1)}$ is

$$\left\{ \vec{y} : \vec{x} \in F^{k+1}, \vec{x} \cdot G^+ =: \vec{y} \right\} \subseteq F^{n+1}.$$

For such a generator matrix, its rows are indexed by $\{0, 1, \ldots, k\}$ and its columns are indexed by $\{0, 1, \ldots, n\}$. Let $s \in F$ be the secret. The secret-sharing scheme picks independent and uniformly random $r_1, \ldots, r_k \in F$. Let

$$(y_0, y_1, \ldots, y_n) := (s, r_1, \ldots, r_k) \cdot G^+.$$

Observe that $y_0 = s$ because the generator matrix G^+ is in the standard form. The secret shares for the parties $1, \ldots, n$ are $s_1 = y_1, s_2 = y_2, \ldots, s_n = y_n$, respectively. Observe that every party's secret share is an element of the field F. Of particular interest will be the set of all secret shares of the secret $s = 0$. Observe that the secret shares form an $[n, k]_F$-code that is $\langle G \rangle$, where $G = G^+_{\{1,\ldots,k\} \times \{1,\ldots,n\}}$. Note that the matrix G is also in the standard form. The secret shares of $s \in F^*$ form the affine space $s \cdot \vec{v} + \langle G \rangle$, where $\vec{v} = G^+_{0,\{1,\ldots,n\}}$. Refer to Fig. 1 for a pictorial summary.

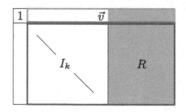

Fig. 1. A pictorial summary of the generator matrix $G^+ = [I_{k+1} | P]$, where P is the shaded matrix. The indices of rows and columns of G^+ are $\{0, 1, \ldots, k\}$ and $\{0, 1, \ldots, n\}$, respectively. The (blue) matrix $G = [I_k | R]$ is a submatrix of G^+. In particular, the secret shares of secret $s = 0$ form the code $\langle G \rangle$. The (red) vector is $\vec{v}$. In particular, for any secret s, the secret shares of s form the affine subspace $s \cdot \vec{v} + \langle G \rangle$. (Color figure online)

Suppose parties $i_1, \ldots, i_t \in \{1, \ldots, n\}$ come together to reconstruct the secret with their, respective, secret shares $s_{i_1}, \ldots, s_{i_t}$. Let $G^+_{*,i_1}, \ldots, G^+_{*,i_t} \in F^{(k+1) \times 1}$ represent the columns indexed by $i_1, \ldots, i_t \in \{1, \ldots, n\}$, respectively. If the column $G^+_{*,0} \in F^{(k+1) \times 1}$ lies in the span of $\{G^+_{*,i_1}, \ldots, G^+_{*,i_t}\}$ then these parties can reconstruct the secret s using a linear combination of their secret shares. If the column $G^+_{*,0}$ *does not* lie in the span of $\{G^+_{*,i_1}, \ldots, G^+_{*,i_t}\}$ then the secret remains *perfectly hidden* from these parties.

Shamir Secret-sharing Schemes. Let F be a prime field. Let $\vec{X} = (X_1, \ldots, X_n)$ be *evaluation places* satisfying (1) $X_i \in F^*$ for all $1 \leqslant i \leqslant n$, and (2) $X_i \neq X_j$ for all $1 \leqslant i < j \leqslant n$. The corresponding $[n, k, \vec{X}]_F$-Shamir secret-sharing is defined as follows.

- Given secret $s \in F$, $\mathsf{Share}^{\vec{X}}(s)$ independently samples a random $a_i \in F$, for all $1 \leqslant i < k$. The ith share of $\mathsf{Share}^{\vec{X}}(s)$ is

$$\mathsf{Share}^{\vec{X}}(s)_i := s + a_1 X_i + a_2 X_i^2 + \cdots + a_{k-1} X_i^{k-1}.$$

- Given shares $\left(\mathsf{Share}^{\vec{X}}(s)_{i_1}, \ldots, \mathsf{Share}^{\vec{X}}(s)_{i_t} \right)$, $\mathsf{Rec}^{\vec{X}}$ interpolates to obtain the unique polynomial $f \in F[X]/X^k$ such that $f(X_{i_j}) = \mathsf{Share}^{\vec{X}}(s)_{i_j}$ for all $1 \leqslant j \leqslant t$, and outputs $f(0)$ to be the reconstructed secret.

3.3   Joint Leakage-resilience of Secret-sharing Scheme

Consider an n-party secret-sharing scheme, where every party gets an element in F as their secret share. Let L be an ℓ-bit joint leakage function, i.e., $L : F^n \rightarrow \{0, 1\}^\ell$. Let $\mathbf{L}(s)$ be the distribution of the leakage defined by the experiment: (a) sample secret shares $(s_1, \ldots, s_n)$ for the secret s, and (b) output $L(s_1, \ldots, s_n)$.

Definition 1. *Let $\mathcal{L}$ be a family of ℓ-bit joint leakage functions. We say a secret-sharing scheme is ε-leakage-resilient against $\mathcal{L}$ if for all leakage functions $L \in \mathcal{L}$ and for all secrets $s^{(0)}$ and $s^{(1)}$, we have*

$$\mathsf{SD}\left(\mathbf{L}\left(s^{(0)}\right), \mathbf{L}\left(s^{(1)}\right) \right) \leqslant \varepsilon.$$

3.4   Fourier Analysis

Let F be a prime field of order p and let n be a positive integer. For any complex number $a \in \mathbb{C}$, let $\bar{a}$ represent its conjugate. For any two functions $f, g \colon F^n \rightarrow \mathbb{C}$, their *inner product* is

$$\langle f, g \rangle := \frac{1}{p^n} \cdot \sum_{\vec{x} \in F^n} f(\vec{x}) \cdot \overline{g(\vec{x})}.$$

Let $\omega = \exp(2\pi \imath / p)$ be the pth root of unity. For all $\vec{\alpha} \in F^n$, the function $\chi_{\vec{\alpha}} \colon F^n \rightarrow \mathbb{C}$ is defined to be

$$\chi_{\vec{\alpha}}(\vec{x}) := \omega^{\vec{\alpha} \cdot \vec{x}},$$

where $\vec{\alpha} \cdot \vec{x}$ is the inner product over F^n. The respective Fourier coefficient $\widehat{f}(\vec{\alpha})$ is defined as

$$\widehat{f}(\vec{\alpha}) := \langle f, \chi_{\vec{\alpha}} \rangle .$$

We have the following facts and lemma.

Fact 1 (Fourier Inversion Formula) $f(\vec{x}) = \sum_{\alpha \in F^n} \widehat{f}(\vec{\alpha}) \cdot \omega^{\vec{\alpha} \cdot \vec{x}}$.

Fact 2 (Parseval's Identity) $\frac{1}{p^n} \sum_{\vec{x} \in F^n} |f(\vec{x})|^2 = \sum_{\vec{\alpha} \in F^n} |\widehat{f}(\vec{\alpha})|^2$.

Lemma 1 (Poisson Summation Formula). *Let $C \subseteq F^n$ be a linear code with dual code $C^\perp$. Let $f \colon F^n \to \mathbb{C}$ be an arbitrary function. Then, the following identity holds.*

$$\operatorname*{E}_{\vec{x} \in C} [f(\vec{x})] = \sum_{\vec{\alpha} \in C^\perp} \widehat{f}(\vec{\alpha})$$

In particular, if $f(\vec{x}) = f_1(x_1) \cdot f_2(x_2) \cdots f_n(x_n)$, where $f_i \colon F \to \mathbb{C}$ for every $1 \leqslant i \leqslant n$, it holds that

$$\operatorname*{E}_{\vec{x} \leftarrow C} \left[\prod_{i=1}^{n} f_i(x_i) \right] = \sum_{\vec{y} \in C^\perp} \left(\prod_{i=1}^{n} \widehat{f_i}(y_i) \right) .$$

4   Leakage-resilience of Fully Random Code

In this section, we consider the fully random generator matrix $\mathbf{G}^+ = [I_{k+1} | \mathbf{P}]$. That is, every entry of the parity check matrix P is sampled as an independently uniformly random element from F. Fix any small leakage family $\mathcal{L}$. We shall show that the Massey secret-sharing scheme corresponding to $\mathbf{G}^+$ is leakage-resilient to $\mathcal{L}$ with overwhelming probability. In particular, we prove the following theorem.

Theorem 4. *Let $\mathcal{L}$ be an arbitrary family of ℓ-bit joint leakage functions. The Massey secret-sharing scheme corresponding to fully random $\mathbf{G}^+$ is ε-leakage-resilient against $\mathcal{L}$ except with probability*

$$\leqslant \frac{|\mathcal{L}| \cdot 8^\ell}{\varepsilon^2 \cdot |F|^{k-2}} .$$

In particular, letting $\varepsilon = \left(|\mathcal{L}| \cdot 8^\ell / |F|^{k-2} \right)^{1/3}$ ensures that the failure probability is at most ε. Furthermore, ε is exponentially decaying when $|\mathcal{L}| \leqslant |F|^{k-2-c}/8^\ell$, where $c > 0$ is an arbitrary constant.

Remark 3. We note that a fully random matrix over (exponentially large) F is *maximum distance separable* (MDS) with overwhelming probability when $2^n = o(|F|)$. Hence, the resulting Massey secret-sharing scheme is a $(k + 1)$-out-of-n threshold secret-sharing scheme with overwhelming probability. We refer the readers to Appendix B.1 of [28] for a proof.

We shall present a combinatorical proof of this theorem. First, it shall be convenient to define the following random variable. For any secret $s \in F$ and any subset $A \subseteq F^n$, define

$$\mathbf{X}_{s,A} := \frac{1}{|F|^k} \cdot \Big(|\langle \mathbf{G} \rangle \cap A| - |(\langle \mathbf{G} \rangle + s \cdot \mathbf{v}) \cap A| \Big).$$

Recall that $\langle G \rangle$ is the set of all the secret shares of secret 0. Furthermore, $\langle G \rangle + s \cdot \vec{v}$ is the set of all the secret shares of secret s. Hence, the random variable $\mathbf{X}_{s,A}$ represents the difference in the probability that the secret shares falls into the set A between secret being 0 and s. Our key technical lemma is the following.

Lemma 2 (Key Technical Lemma). *For any secret $s \in F$ and any subset $A \subseteq F^n$, it holds that*

$$\underset{\mathbf{G}^+}{\mathrm{E}} \left[(\mathbf{X}_{s,A})^2 \right] \leqslant \frac{1}{|F|^{k-1}}.$$

Let us first show why Lemma 2 is sufficient to prove Theorem 4.

Proof (Proof of Theorem 4 *using* Lemma 2*).* First, Lemma 2 implies that, for all $t > 0$, we have

$$\underset{\mathbf{G}^+}{\mathrm{Pr}} \left[|\mathbf{X}_{s,A}| \geqslant t \right] \leqslant \frac{1}{t^2 \cdot |F|^{k-1}} \tag{1}$$

since

$$\underset{\mathbf{G}^+}{\mathrm{Pr}} \left[|\mathbf{X}_{s,A}| \geqslant t \right] \leqslant \frac{\mathbb{E}[(\mathbf{X}_{s,A})^2]}{t^2} \qquad \text{(Markov's inequality)}$$

$$\leqslant \frac{1}{t^2 \cdot |F|^{k-1}}. \qquad \text{(Lemma 2)}$$

Given this, observe that

$$\underset{\mathbf{G}^+}{\mathrm{Pr}} \left[\mathbf{G}^+ \text{ is } not \text{ } \varepsilon\text{-leakage-resilient against } \mathcal{L} \right]$$

$$= \underset{\mathbf{G}^+}{\mathrm{Pr}} \left[\exists s^{(0)}, s^{(1)}, \ \exists L \in \mathcal{L}, \ \mathsf{SD} \left(\mathbf{L}\left(s^{(0)}\right), \mathbf{L}\left(s^{(1)}\right) \right) > \varepsilon \right]$$

$$\leqslant \underset{\mathbf{G}^+}{\mathrm{Pr}} \left[\exists s, \ \exists L \in \mathcal{L}, \ \mathsf{SD} \left(\mathbf{L}\left(0\right), \mathbf{L}\left(s\right) \right) > \varepsilon/2 \right]$$

$$\leqslant \sum_{L \in \mathcal{L}} \left(\underset{\mathbf{G}^+}{\mathrm{Pr}} \left[\exists s, \ \mathsf{SD} \left(\mathbf{L}\left(0\right), \mathbf{L}\left(s\right) \right) > \varepsilon/2 \right] \right). \qquad \text{(Union bound)}$$

Fix any $L \in \mathcal{L}$. For any leakage $\vec{w} \in \{0,1\}^\ell$, let $A_{\vec{w}} := L^{-1}(\vec{w})$. That is, $A_{\vec{w}}$ is the set of secret shares that would result in the leakage $\vec{w}$. It holds that

$$\underset{\mathbf{G}^+}{\mathrm{Pr}} \left[\exists s, \ \mathsf{SD} \left(\mathbf{L}\left(0\right), \mathbf{L}\left(s\right) \right) > \varepsilon/2 \right]$$

$$= \underset{\mathbf{G}^+}{\mathrm{Pr}} \left[\exists s, \ \frac{1}{2} \cdot \sum_{\vec{w} \in \{0,1\}^\ell} |\mathbf{X}_{s,A_{\vec{w}}}| > \varepsilon/2 \right] \qquad \text{(By definition of SD and } \mathbf{X}_{s,A_{\vec{w}}})$$

$$\leqslant \sum_{s\in F} \left(\Pr_{\mathbf{G}^+} \left[\sum_{\vec{w}\in\{0,1\}^\ell} |\mathbf{X}_{s,A_{\vec{w}}}| > \varepsilon \right] \right) \qquad \text{(Union bound)}$$

$$\leqslant \sum_{s\in F} \left(\Pr_{\mathbf{G}^+} \left[\exists \vec{w}\in\{0,1\}^\ell, \; |\mathbf{X}_{s,A_{\vec{w}}}| > \varepsilon/2^\ell \right] \right) \qquad \text{(Pigeon-hole principle)}$$

$$\leqslant \sum_{s\in F} \sum_{\vec{w}\in\{0,1\}^\ell} \left(\Pr_{\mathbf{G}^+} \left[|\mathbf{X}_{s,A_{\vec{w}}}| > \varepsilon/2^\ell \right] \right) \qquad \text{(Union bound)}$$

$$\leqslant |F|\cdot 2^\ell \cdot \frac{2^{2\ell}}{\varepsilon^2\cdot|F|^{k-1}} \qquad \text{(since Eq. 1 applies to arbitrary } A \text{ and } s)$$

$$= \frac{8^\ell}{\varepsilon^2\cdot|F|^{k-2}}.$$

Combining everything, we get

$$\Pr_{G,v}\left[G^+ \text{ is not } \varepsilon\text{-leakage-resilient} \right] \leqslant \frac{|\mathcal{L}|\cdot 8^\ell}{\varepsilon^2\cdot|F|^{k-2}}.$$

We complete the proof of Theorem 4 by proving our key technical lemma.

Proof (Proof of Lemma 2*)*. Recall that

$$\mathbf{X}_{s,A} = \frac{1}{|F|^k}\cdot\left(|\langle\mathbf{G}\rangle\cap A| - |(\langle\mathbf{G}\rangle + s\cdot\vec{v})\cap A| \right).$$

Hence, the second moment of $\mathbf{X}_{s,A}$ can be written as

$$(\mathbf{X}_{s,A})^2 = \frac{1}{|F|^{2k}}\cdot \sum_{\vec{x},\vec{y}\in F^k} \left(\mathbb{1}_A(\vec{x}\cdot\mathbf{G}) - \mathbb{1}_A(\vec{x}\cdot\mathbf{G}+s\cdot\vec{v}) \right)\cdot$$

$$\left(\mathbb{1}_A(\vec{y}\cdot\mathbf{G}) - \mathbb{1}_A(\vec{y}\cdot\mathbf{G}+s\cdot\vec{v}) \right).$$

For short, for all $\vec{x}$ and $\vec{y}$, let us define

$$\mathbf{T}_{\vec{x},\vec{y}} := \left(\mathbb{1}_A(\vec{x}\cdot\mathbf{G}) - \mathbb{1}_A(\vec{x}\cdot\mathbf{G}+s\cdot\vec{v}) \right)\left(\mathbb{1}_A(\vec{y}\cdot\mathbf{G}) - \mathbb{1}_A(\vec{y}\cdot\mathbf{G}+s\cdot\vec{v}) \right).$$

Recall that $\mathbf{G} = [I_k|\mathbf{R}]$ is in the standard form and the first k coordinates of $\vec{v}$ are 0 (refer to Fig. 1). Hence, one may write

$$\mathbf{T}_{\vec{x},\vec{y}} = \left(\mathbb{1}_{A(\vec{x})}(\vec{x}\cdot\mathbf{R}) - \mathbb{1}_{A(\vec{x})}(\vec{x}\cdot\mathbf{R}+s\cdot\vec{v}_{\{k+1,\dots,n\}}) \right)\cdot$$

$$\left(\mathbb{1}_{A(\vec{y})}(\vec{y}\cdot\mathbf{R}) - \mathbb{1}_{A(\vec{y})}(\vec{y}\cdot\mathbf{R}+s\cdot\vec{v}_{\{k+1,\dots,n\}}) \right)$$

where

$$A(\vec{x}) := A \cap \{x_1\}\times\cdots\times\{x_k\}\times \underbrace{F\times\cdots\times F}_{n-k \text{ times}}$$

and

$$A(\vec{y}) := A \bigcap \{y_1\} \times \cdots \times \{y_k\} \times \underbrace{F \times \cdots \times F}_{n-k \text{ times}}.$$

Clearly, $\vec{x} \cdot \mathbf{R}$ and $\vec{y} \cdot \mathbf{R}$ are both uniform over F^{n-k}. Moreover, observe that $\vec{x} \cdot \mathbf{R}$ and $\vec{y} \cdot \mathbf{R}$ are *independent* random variables when $\vec{x}$ and $\vec{y}$ are linearly independent. Therefore, fix any linearly independent $\vec{x}$ and $\vec{y}$, we have

$$\mathop{\mathrm{E}}_{\mathbf{G}^+} [\mathbf{T}_{\vec{x},\vec{y}}] = \mathop{\mathrm{E}}_{\vec{\mathbf{v}}} \left[\mathop{\mathrm{E}}_{\mathbf{R}} \left[\left(\mathbb{1}_{A(\vec{x})} (\vec{x} \cdot \mathbf{R}) - \mathbb{1}_{A(\vec{x})} (\vec{x} \cdot \mathbf{R} + s \cdot \vec{\mathbf{v}}_{\{k+1,\ldots,n\}}) \right) \right] \right.$$

$$\left. \cdot \mathop{\mathrm{E}}_{\mathbf{R}} \left[\left(\mathbb{1}_{A(\vec{y})} (\vec{y} \cdot \mathbf{R}) - \mathbb{1}_{A(\vec{y})} (\vec{y} \cdot \mathbf{R} + s \cdot \vec{\mathbf{v}}_{\{k+1,\ldots,n\}}) \right) \right] \right]$$

$$= \mathop{\mathrm{E}}_{\vec{\mathbf{v}}} \left[\left(\frac{|A(\vec{x})|}{|F|^{n-k}} - \frac{|A(\vec{x})|}{|F|^{n-k}} \right) \left(\frac{|A(\vec{x})|}{|F|^{n-k}} - \frac{|A(\vec{x})|}{|F|^{n-k}} \right) \right] = 0$$

Let us define the bad set as

$$\mathsf{Bad} := \{(\vec{x}, \vec{y}) : \vec{x} \text{ and } \vec{y} \text{ are linearly dependent}\}.$$

Hence, we have shown that

$$(\vec{x}, \vec{y}) \notin \mathsf{Bad} \implies \mathop{\mathrm{E}}_{\mathbf{G}^+} [\mathbf{T}_{\vec{x},\vec{y}}] = 0.$$

On the other hand, for all $\vec{x}$ and $\vec{y}$, it trivially holds that

$$\mathop{\mathrm{E}}_{\mathbf{G}^+} [\mathbf{T}_{\vec{x},\vec{y}}] \leqslant 1.$$

Therefore, this completes the proof as

$$\mathop{\mathrm{E}}_{\mathbf{G}^+} \left[(\mathbf{X}_{s,A})^2 \right] = \frac{1}{|F|^{2k}} \sum_{\vec{x},\vec{y} \in F^k} \mathop{\mathrm{E}}_{\mathbf{G}^+} [\mathbf{T}_{\vec{x},\vec{y}}] \qquad \text{(Linearity of expectation)}$$

$$\leqslant \frac{1}{|F|^{2k}} \left(\sum_{(\vec{x},\vec{y}) \notin \mathsf{Bad}} 0 + \sum_{(\vec{x},\vec{y}) \in \mathsf{Bad}} 1 \right) \leqslant \frac{1}{|F|^{k-1}}.$$

5   Leakage-resilience of Shamir Secret-sharing Schemes with Random Evaluation Places

This section considers Shamir secret-sharing over a prime order field and with randomly chosen evaluation places. Fix any small (joint) leakage family $\mathcal{L}$. We shall show that Shamir secret-sharing with distinct random evaluation places is leakage-resilient to $\mathcal{L}$.

In this section, we write $f(\lambda) \lesssim g(\lambda)$ for $f(\lambda) = (1 + o(1)) \cdot g(\lambda)$.

Theorem 5. *Let $\mathcal{L}$ be an arbitrary family of ℓ-bit joint leakage functions. The $[n, k+1, \vec{\mathbf{X}}]_F$-Shamir's secret-sharing scheme corresponding to randomly chosen evaluation places $\vec{\mathbf{X}}$ is ε-leakage-resilient against $\mathcal{L}$ except with probability at most*

$$\frac{4 \cdot |\mathcal{L}| \cdot 8^\ell \cdot p^{n-k+1} \cdot k!}{\varepsilon^2 \cdot (p-n)^k}.$$

In particular, letting $\varepsilon = \left(4 \cdot |\mathcal{L}| \cdot 8^\ell \cdot p^{n-k+1} \cdot k!/(p-n)^k\right)^{1/3}$ ensures that the failure probability δ is at most ε. Furthermore, ε is exponentially decaying when $|\mathcal{L}| \lesssim (p-n)^{k-c}/(4 \cdot 8^\ell \cdot p^{n-k+1} \cdot k!)$, where $c > 0$ is an arbitrary constant.

In contrast to the proof of Theorem 4, we rely on Fourier-analytical techniques to prove Theorem 5. In this section, we restrict to prime field F of order p. Consider an $[n, k+1, \vec{\mathbf{X}}]_F$-Shamir secret-sharing scheme with randomly chosen evaluation places $\vec{\mathbf{X}}$. Let $C_{\vec{\mathbf{X}}}$ be the set of all possible secret shares corresponding to the secret 0. Recall that $C_{\vec{\mathbf{X}}} = \langle G_{\vec{\mathbf{X}}} \rangle$, where the generator matrix of $G_{\vec{\mathbf{X}}}$ is the following matrix.

$$G_{\vec{\mathbf{X}}} = \begin{pmatrix} \mathbf{X}_1 & \mathbf{X}_2 & \cdots & \mathbf{X}_n \\ \mathbf{X}_1^2 & \mathbf{X}_2^2 & \cdots & \mathbf{X}_n^2 \\ \vdots & \vdots & \ddots & \vdots \\ \mathbf{X}_1^k & \mathbf{X}_2^k & \cdots & \mathbf{X}_n^k \end{pmatrix}.$$

Furthermore, $\langle G_{\vec{\mathbf{X}}} \rangle + s \cdot \vec{1}$ is the set of all the secret shares of secret s for any $s \in F$. For any secret $s \in F$ and any subset $A \subseteq F^n$, define

$$\mathbf{Y}_{s,A} := \frac{1}{p^k} \cdot \left(|\langle G_{\vec{\mathbf{X}}} \rangle \cap A| - |(\langle G_{\vec{\mathbf{X}}} \rangle + s \cdot \vec{1}) \cap A| \right)$$

$$= \operatorname*{E}_{\vec{x} \in C_{\vec{\mathbf{X}}}} [\mathbb{1}_A(\vec{x})] - \operatorname*{E}_{\vec{x} \in C_{\vec{\mathbf{X}}}} \left[\mathbb{1}_A(\vec{x} + s \cdot \vec{1}) \right]$$

Intuitively, the random variable $\mathbf{Y}_{s,A}$ represents the difference in the probability that the secrets shares falls into the set A between the secret being 0 and s. The following lemma is the main technical result of Theorem 5.

Lemma 3. *For any secret $s \in F$ and any subset $A \subseteq F^n$, it holds that*

$$\operatorname*{E}_{\vec{\mathbf{X}}} \left[(\mathbf{Y}_{s,A})^2 \right] \leqslant \frac{4 \cdot p^{n-k+1} \cdot k!}{(p-(n-k+1)) \cdots (p-n)} \lesssim \frac{4 \cdot p^{n-k+1} \cdot k!}{(p-n)^k}$$

Note that A need not be a product space. Now, we first prove Theorem 5 using Lemma 3.

Proof (Proof of Theorem 5). Using a similar argument as in the proof of Theorem 4, one can show that

$$\Pr_{\vec{\mathbf{X}}} \left[\mathbf{G}_{\vec{\mathbf{X}}} \text{ is } not \text{ } \varepsilon\text{-leakage-resilient against } \mathcal{L} \right]$$

$$\leqslant \sum_{L \in \mathcal{L}} \sum_{s \in F} \sum_{\vec{w} \in \{0,1\}^\ell} \left(\Pr_{\mathbf{G}_{\vec{\mathbf{x}}}} \left[|\mathbf{Y}_{s,A_{\vec{w}}}| \geqslant \varepsilon/2^\ell \right] \right) \qquad \text{(Union bound)}$$

$$\leqslant \sum_{L \in \mathcal{L}} \sum_{s \in F} \sum_{\vec{w} \in \{0,1\}^\ell} \frac{4 \cdot p^{n-k} \cdot k!}{(p - (n - k + 1)) \cdots (p - n)} \cdot \left(\frac{2^\ell}{\varepsilon} \right)^2$$

$$\text{(Lemma 3 and Markov's inequality)}$$

$$= |\mathcal{L}| \cdot p \cdot 2^\ell \cdot \frac{2^{2\ell} \cdot 4 \cdot p^{n-k} \cdot k!}{\varepsilon^2 \cdot (p - (n - k + 1)) \cdots (p - n)}$$

$$\lesssim \frac{4 \cdot |\mathcal{L}| \cdot 8^\ell \cdot p^{n-k+1} \cdot k!}{\varepsilon^2 \cdot (p - n)^k},$$

which completes the proof.

Next, we state all the claims that are needed for the proof of Lemma 3. Using the Poisson summation formula (Lemma 1), the variable $\mathbf{Y}_{s,A}$ can be rewritten as follow.

Claim 1. $\mathbf{Y}_{s,A} = \sum_{\vec{\alpha} \in C_{\vec{\mathbf{x}}}^{\perp} \setminus \{\vec{0}\}} \widehat{\mathbb{1} A}(\vec{\alpha}) \left(1 - \omega^{\langle \vec{\alpha}, s \cdot \vec{1} \rangle} \right).$

The next claim upper bounds the ℓ_2 norm of the Fourier weights corresponding to an indicator function of an arbitrary subset of F^n. This result follows from Parseval's identity directly.

Claim 2. For any subset $A \subseteq F^n$, it holds that

$$\sum_{\vec{\alpha} \in F^n \setminus \{\vec{0}\}} |\widehat{\mathbb{1} A}(\vec{\alpha})|^2 \leqslant 1.$$

Finally, the following claim upper bounds the probability of a non-zero vector that is in the dual space $C_{\vec{\mathbf{x}}}^{\perp}$, where the probability is taken over the randomness of the evaluation places $\vec{\mathbf{X}}$. This result was proven in [25] using a generalization of Bezout's theorem.

Claim 3 (Claim 4 of [25]). For any non-zero vector $\vec{\alpha} \in F^n$, the following bound holds.

$$\Pr_{\vec{\mathbf{X}}} \left[\vec{\alpha} \in C_{\vec{\mathbf{x}}}^{\perp} \right] \leqslant \frac{k!}{(p - (n - k + 1)) \cdots (p - n)}$$

Now, we are ready to prove Lemma 3.

Proof (Proof of Lemma 3). We have

$$\mathop{\mathrm{E}}_{\vec{\mathbf{X}}} \left[(\mathbf{Y}_{s,A})^2 \right] = \mathop{\mathrm{E}}_{\vec{\mathbf{X}}} \left[\left(\sum_{\vec{\alpha} \in C_{\vec{\mathbf{x}}}^{\perp} \setminus \{\vec{0}\}} \widehat{\mathbb{1}_A}(\vec{\alpha}) \left(1 - \omega^{\langle \vec{\alpha}, s \cdot \vec{1} \rangle} \right) \right)^2 \right] \qquad \text{(Claim 1)}$$

$$\leqslant \mathop{\mathrm{E}}_{\vec{\mathbf{x}}}\left[\left(\sum_{\vec{\alpha}\in C_{\vec{\mathbf{x}}}^{\perp}\setminus\{\vec{0}\}}|1-\omega^{\langle\vec{\alpha},s\cdot\vec{1}\rangle}|^2\right)\cdot\left(\sum_{\vec{\alpha}\in C_{\vec{\mathbf{x}}}^{\perp}\setminus\{\vec{0}\}}|\widehat{\mathbb{1}_A}(\vec{\alpha})|^2\right)\right]$$

(Cauchy-Schwarz)

$$\leqslant \mathop{\mathrm{E}}_{\vec{\mathbf{x}}}\left[\left(\sum_{\vec{\alpha}\in C_{\vec{\mathbf{x}}}^{\perp}\setminus\{\vec{0}\}}4\right)\cdot\left(\sum_{\vec{\alpha}\in C_{\vec{\mathbf{x}}}^{\perp}\setminus\{\vec{0}\}}|\widehat{\mathbb{1}_A}(\vec{\alpha})|^2\right)\right]$$

(Triangle inequality)

$$\leqslant 4\cdot p^{n-k+1}\cdot\mathop{\mathrm{E}}_{\vec{\mathbf{x}}}\left[\sum_{\vec{\alpha}\in C_{\vec{\mathbf{x}}}^{\perp}\setminus\{\vec{0}\}}|\widehat{\mathbb{1}_A}(\vec{\alpha})|^2\right]$$

$$= 4\cdot p^{n-k}\cdot\sum_{\vec{\alpha}\in F^n\setminus\{\vec{0}\}}|\widehat{\mathbb{1}_A}(\vec{\alpha})|^2\cdot\mathop{\mathrm{Pr}}_{\vec{\mathbf{x}}}\left[\vec{\alpha}\in C_{\vec{\mathbf{x}}}^{\perp}\right]$$

(Linearity of expectation)

$$\leqslant 4\cdot p^{n-k}\cdot\sum_{\vec{\alpha}\in F^n\setminus\{\vec{0}\}}|\widehat{\mathbb{1}_A}(\vec{\alpha})|^2\cdot\frac{k!}{(p-(n-k+1))\cdots(p-n)}$$

(Claim 3)

$$\leqslant \frac{4\cdot p^{n-k}\cdot k!}{(p-(n-k+1))\cdots(p-n)}$$

(Claim 2)

$$\lesssim \frac{4\cdot p^{n-k}\cdot k!}{(p-n)^k}.$$

This completes the proof.

6   Leakage-resilience of Partially Random Code

In this section, we show a natural trade off between the amount of randomness one uses and the size of the leakage family that the secret-sharing scheme is resilient against. Intuitively, we show that, for any constant $t\in\mathbb{N}$, one may employ $t\cdot(n-k)$ random elements from F to sample the random generator matrix such that the Massey secret-sharing scheme is resilient against any $\mathcal{L}$ of size (approximately) $|F|^t/8^\ell$. Let us start by defining some ways of sampling partially random matrices.

Definition 2 (t-row random matrix). *The t-row random matrix* $\mathbf{M}^{(t)}$ *is a matrix where elements* $\mathbf{M}_{i,j}^{(t)}$ *in the first t rows of the matrix are chosen independently uniformly random from F, and all the other elements are fixed to be zero.*

$$\mathbf{M}^{(t)} = \begin{pmatrix} \mathbf{M}_{1,1}^{(t)} & \mathbf{M}_{1,2}^{(t)} & \cdots & \mathbf{M}_{1,n-k}^{(t)} \\ \vdots & \vdots & & \vdots \\ \mathbf{M}_{t,1}^{(t)} & \mathbf{M}_{t,2}^{(t)} & \cdots & \mathbf{M}_{t,n-k}^{(t)} \\ 0 & 0 & \cdots & 0 \\ \vdots & \vdots & & \vdots \\ 0 & 0 & \cdots & 0 \end{pmatrix}$$

Clearly, one needs $t(n-k)$ random field elements to sample $\mathbf{M}^{(t)}$.

Next, we define Wozencraft ensemble, standard technique in derandomization.

Definition 3 (Wozencraft Ensemble [29].). *Let finite field K be a degree k extension of the finite field F. There is a bijection between elements of K and F^k. For every element $\vec{\alpha} \in F^k$, we shall represent the corresponding element in K to be $(\vec{\alpha})_K \in K$. Fix an element $(\vec{\beta})_K \in K$. There exists a (unique) matrix $M(\vec{\beta}) \in F^{k \times k}$ such that, for any $(\vec{x})_K \in K$, it ensures*

$$(\vec{x})_K \cdot (\vec{\beta})_K = \left(\vec{x} \cdot M(\vec{\beta}) \right)_K$$

That is, for all $\vec{x}$, the matrix product of $\vec{x}$ and $M(\vec{\beta})$ over F (which is a vector in F^k), corresponds to the product of $(\vec{x})_K$ and $(\vec{\beta})_K$ over K.

One may use the Wozencraft ensemble to sample a partially random matrix in $F^{k \times (n-k)}$ as follows. Let $m = \lceil (n-k)/k \rceil$ (i.e., $(m-1)k < (n-k) \leqslant mk$). One samples m random vectors $\vec{\alpha}^{(1)}, \vec{\alpha}^{(2)}, \ldots, \vec{\alpha}^{(m)}$ in F^k. One picks the first $(n-k)$ columns of the matrix

$$\left[M\left(\vec{\alpha}^{(1)} \right) \Big| M\left(\vec{\alpha}^{(2)} \right) \Big| \cdots \Big| M\left(\vec{\alpha}^{(m)} \right) \right]$$

as the sampled random matrix in $F^{k \times (n-k)}$. We shall use $\mathbf{W}$ as a partially random matrix sampled using Wozencraft ensemble. Clearly, one needs $\lceil \frac{n-k}{k} \rceil \cdot k \approx (n-k)$ random elements from F to sample $\mathbf{W}$.

We are now ready to state our theorem for this section.

Theorem 6. *Let $\mathcal{L}$ be an arbitrary collection of ℓ-bit joint leakage functions. Let $\mathbf{G}^+$ be the generator matrix (refer to Fig. 1) sampled as follows.*

1. *Entries of $\vec{\mathbf{v}}_{\{k+1,\ldots,n\}}$ are sampled independently uniformly random from F.*
2. *Matrix $\mathbf{R} \in F^{k \times (n-k)}$ is sampled as $\mathbf{M}^{(t)} + \mathbf{W}$, where $\mathbf{M}^{(t)}$ and $\mathbf{W}$ are sampled independently according to Definition 2 and Definition 3.*

The Massey secret-sharing scheme corresponding to $\mathbf{G}^+$ is ε-leakage-resilient to the leakage family $\mathcal{L}$ except with probability (at most)

$$\frac{|\mathcal{L}| \cdot 8^{\ell}}{\varepsilon^2 \cdot |F|^{t-2}}.$$

In particular, $\varepsilon = \left(|\mathcal{L}| \cdot 8^\ell / |F|^{t-2} \right)^{1/3}$ ensures that the failure probability is at most ε. Furthermore, ε is exponentially decaying when $|\mathcal{L}| \leqslant |F|^{t-2-\delta}/8^\ell$, where $\delta \in (0,1)$ is an appropriate constant. The random field elements required to sample $\mathbf{G}^+$ is (approximately) $(t+2)(n-k)$.

Intuitively, the Wozencraft ensemble ensures that G^+ is MDS with high probability and we rely on the t-row random matrix to prove our technical lemma below. The proof of this theorem follows analogously as the proof of Theorem 4. We present an outline of the proof below. First, we have our key technical lemma.

Lemma 4 (Key Technical Lemma). *For any secret $s \in F$ and any subset $A \subseteq F^n$, it holds that*

$$\mathop{\mathrm{E}}_{\mathbf{G}^+} \left[(\mathbf{X}_{s,A})^2 \right] \leqslant \frac{1}{|F|^{t-1}}.$$

The proof of Theorem 6 from Lemma 4 is identical to the previous section. Hence, we omit it. Before we present the proof of Lemma 4, we define the following notion of bad set.

Definition 4 (Bad Set). *A pair of vectors $\vec{x}, \vec{y} \in F^k$ is "bad" if the following $2(n-k)$ random variables are not independently uniform.*

$$\vec{x} \cdot \mathbf{R}_{*,j} \quad and \quad \vec{y} \cdot \mathbf{R}_{*,j} \qquad j \in \{1, 2, \ldots, n-k\}.$$

Succinctly, we use Bad $\subseteq F^k \times F^k$ *to denote the set of all "bad" $\vec{x}$ and $\vec{y}$. The density of badness of a (partially) random generator matrix is the density of the bad set, i.e., $|\mathsf{Bad}|/|F|^{2k}$.*

Let us assume that the density of badness is β. One may prove Lemma 4 in the exactly manner as in the previous section. That is,

$$\mathop{\mathrm{E}}_{\mathbf{G}^+} \left[(\mathbf{X}_{s,A})^2 \right] = \frac{1}{|F|^{2k}} \left(\sum_{(\vec{x},\vec{y}) \notin \mathsf{Bad}} \mathop{\mathrm{E}}_{\mathbf{G}^+} [\mathbf{T}_{\vec{x},\vec{y}}] + \sum_{(\vec{x},\vec{y}) \in \mathsf{Bad}} \mathop{\mathrm{E}}_{\mathbf{G}^+} [\mathbf{T}_{\vec{x},\vec{y}}] \right)$$

$$\leqslant \frac{1}{|F|^{2k}} \left(\sum_{(\vec{x},\vec{y}) \notin \mathsf{Bad}} 0 + \sum_{(\vec{x},\vec{y}) \in \mathsf{Bad}} 1 \right)$$

$$= \beta.$$

Now, we have reduced our problem to computing the density of badness. Note that, when $\mathbf{G}^+$ is the fully random matrix, the characterization of "bad" set is straightforward. "Bad" set is *exactly* those $\vec{x}$ and $\vec{y}$ that are linearly dependent.

However, for a partially random matrix such as the $\mathbf{G}^+$ that we consider in this section, the characterization of "bad" set might be highly non-trivial. Nevertheless, we note that an upper bound on the density of the badness suffices for this proof. And one may prove such upper bound by showing what $\vec{x}$ and $\vec{y}$ is *not* "bad". In particular, we note that

$$(x_1, \ldots, x_t) \text{ and } (y_1, \ldots, y_t) \text{ are linearly independent} \implies (\vec{x}, \vec{y}) \notin \mathsf{Bad}.$$

Clearly, when $(x_1, \ldots, x_t)$ and $(y_1, \ldots, y_t)$ are not linearly dependent, $\vec{x} \cdot \mathbf{M}^{(t)}$ and $\vec{y} \cdot \mathbf{M}^{(t)}$ are independently uniformly random. Since we sample $\mathbf{R}$ as $\mathbf{M}^{(t)} + \mathbf{W}$ where $\mathbf{W}$ is independent of $\mathbf{M}^{(t)}$, $\vec{x} \cdot \mathbf{R}$ and $\vec{y} \cdot \mathbf{R}$ are also independently uniformly random. Consequently, the density of badness is (at most) $1/|F|^{t-1}$, which completes the proof of Lemma 4 and, in turn, the proof of Theorem 6.

References

1. Adams, D. Q., et al.: Lower bounds for leakage-resilient secret sharing schemes against probing attacks. In: IEEE International Symposium on Information Theory ISIT 2021 (2021)
2. Aggarwal, D., et al.: Stronger leakage-resilient and non-malleable secret sharing schemes for general access structures. In: Boldyreva, A., Micciancio, D. (eds.) CRYPTO 2019. LNCS, vol. 11693, pp. 510–539. Springer, Cham (2019). https://doi.org/10.1007/978-3-030-26951-7_18
3. Arora, S., Barak, B.: Computational Complexity: A Modern Approach. Cambridge University Press, Cambridge (2009)
4. Badrinarayanan, S., Srinivasan, A.: Revisiting non-malleable secret sharing. In: Ishai, Y., Rijmen, V. (eds.) EUROCRYPT 2019. LNCS, vol. 11476, pp. 593–622. Springer, Cham (2019). https://doi.org/10.1007/978-3-030-17653-2_20
5. Benhamouda, F., Degwekar, A., Ishai, Y., Rabin, T.: On the local leakage resilience of linear secret sharing schemes. In: Shacham, H., Boldyreva, A. (eds.) CRYPTO 2018. LNCS, vol. 10991, pp. 531–561. Springer, Cham (2018). https://doi.org/10.1007/978-3-319-96884-1_18
6. Benhamouda, F., Degwekar, A., Ishai, Y., Rabin, T.: On the local leakage resilience of linear secret sharing schemes. J. Cryptol. **34**(2), 1–65 (2021). https://doi.org/10.1007/s00145-021-09375-2
7. Block, A.R., Maji, H.K., Nguyen, H.H.: Secure computation based on leaky correlations: high resilience setting. In: Katz, J., Shacham, H. (eds.) CRYPTO 2017. LNCS, vol. 10402, pp. 3–32. Springer, Cham (2017). https://doi.org/10.1007/978-3-319-63715-0_1
8. Block, A.R., Maji, H.K., Nguyen, H.H.: Secure computation with constant communication overhead using multiplication embeddings. In: Chakraborty, D., Iwata, T. (eds.) INDOCRYPT 2018. LNCS, vol. 11356, pp. 375–398. Springer, Cham (2018). https://doi.org/10.1007/978-3-030-05378-9_20
9. Bogdanov, A., Ishai, Y., Srinivasan, A.: Unconditionally secure computation against low-complexity leakage. In: Boldyreva, A., Micciancio, D. (eds.) CRYPTO 2019. LNCS, vol. 11693, pp. 387–416. Springer, Cham (2019). https://doi.org/10.1007/978-3-030-26951-7_14
10. Cascudo, I., Cramer, R., Xing, C., Yuan, C.: Amortized complexity of information-theoretically secure MPC revisited. In: Shacham, H., Boldyreva, A. (eds.) CRYPTO 2018. LNCS, vol. 10993, pp. 395–426. Springer, Cham (2018). https://doi.org/10.1007/978-3-319-96878-0_14

11. Chattopadhyay, E., et al.: Extractors and secret sharing against bounded collusion protocols. In: 61st Annual Symposium on Foundations of Computer Science, Durham, NC, USA, 16–19 November 2020, pp. 1226–1242. IEEE (2020). https://doi.org/10.1109/FOCS46700.2020.00117

12. Cramer, R.: The arithmetic codex: theory and applications. In: Paterson, K.G. (ed.) EUROCRYPT 2011. LNCS, vol. 6632, pp. 1–1. Springer, Heidelberg (2011). https://doi.org/10.1007/978-3-642-20465-4_1

13. Garcia, A., Stichtenoth, H.: A tower of Artin-Schreier extensions of function fields attaining the Drinfeld-Vladut bound. Inventiones Math. 121(1), 211–222 (1995)

14. Goldreich, O., Micali, S., Wigderson, A.: How to play any mental game or A completeness theorem for protocols with honest majority. In: Alfred A., ed., 19th Annual ACM Symposium on Theory of Computing, New York City, NY, USA, 25–27 May 1987, pp. 218–229. ACM Press (1987). https://doi.org/10.1145/28395.28420

15. Goppa, V.D.: A new class of linear correcting codes. Problemy Peredachi Informatsii 6(3), 24–30 (1970)

16. Goyal, V., Kumar, A.: Non-malleable secret sharing. In: Diakonikolas, I., Kempe, D., Henzinger, M., (eds.), 50th Annual ACM Symposium on Theory of Computing, Los Angeles, CA, USA, 25–29 June 2018, pp. 685–698. ACM Press (2018). https://doi.org/10.1145/3188745.3188872

17. Guruswami, V., Wootters, M.: Repairing reed-solomon codes. In: Wichs, D., Mansour, Y., (eds.), 48th Annual ACM Symposium on Theory of Computing, Cambridge, MA, USA, 18–21 June 2016, pp. 216–226. ACM Press (2018). https://doi.org/10.1145/2897518.2897525

18. Guruswami, V., Wootters, M.: Repairing reed-solomon codes. IEEE Trans. Inf. Theory 63(9), 5684–5698 (2017). https://doi.org/10.1109/TIT.2017.2702660

19. Kalai, Y.T., Reyzin, L.: A survey of leakage-resilient cryptography. Cryptology ePrint Archive, Report 2019/302 (2019). https://eprint.iacr.org/2019/302

20. Kocher, P.C.: Timing attacks on implementations of Diffie-Hellman, RSA, DSS, and other systems. In: Koblitz, N. (ed.) CRYPTO 1996. LNCS, vol. 1109, pp. 104–113. Springer, Heidelberg (1996). https://doi.org/10.1007/3-540-68697-5_9

21. Kocher, P., Jaffe, J., Jun, B.: Differential power analysis. In: Wiener, M. (ed.) CRYPTO 1999. LNCS, vol. 1666, pp. 388–397. Springer, Heidelberg (1999). https://doi.org/10.1007/3-540-48405-1_25

22. Kumar, A., Meka, R., Sahai, A.: Leakage-resilient secret sharing against colluding parties. In: Zuckerman, D., ed., 60th Annual Symposium on Foundations of Computer Science, Baltimore, MD, USA, 9–12 November 2019, pp. 636–660. IEEE Computer Society Press (2019). https://doi.org/10.1109/FOCS.2019.00045

23. Lin, F., Cheraghchi, M., Guruswami, V., Safavi-Naini, R., Wang, H.: Leakage-resilient secret sharing in non-compartmentalized models. In: Kalai, Y.T., Smith, A.D., Wichs, D., (eds.), ITC 2020: 1st Conference on Information-Theoretic Cryptography, Boston, MA, USA, 17–19 June 2020, pp. 7:1–7:24. Schloss Dagstuhl - Leibniz-Zentrum fuer Informatik. https://doi.org/10.4230/LIPIcs.ITC.2020.7

24. Florence Jessie MacWilliams and Neil James Alexander Sloane: The Theory of Error Correcting Codes, vol. 16. Elsevier, Amsterdam (1977)

25. Maji, H.K., Nguyen, H.H., Paskin-Cherniavsky, A., Suad, T., Wang, M.: Leakage-resilience of the Shamir secret-sharing scheme against physical-bit leakages. In: Canteaut, A., Standaert, F.-X. (eds.) EUROCRYPT 2021. LNCS, vol. 12697, pp. 344–374. Springer, Cham (2021). https://doi.org/10.1007/978-3-030-77886-6_12

26. Maji, H.K., et al.: Tight estimate of the local leakage resilience of the additive secret-sharing scheme & its consequences. In: Dachman-Soled, D., ed., 3rd Conference on Information-Theoretic Cryptography, ITC 2022, 5–7 July 2022, Cambridge, MA, USA, volume 230 of LIPIcs, pp. 16:1–16:19. Schloss Dagstuhl - Leibniz-Zentrum für Informatik (2022). https://doi.org/10.4230/LIPIcs.ITC.2022.16

27. Maji, H.K., Nguyen, H.H., Paskin-Cherniavsky, A., Wang, M.: Improved bound on the local leakage-resilience of Shamir's secret sharing. In IEEE International Symposium on Information Theory, ISIT 2022, Espoo, Finland, 26 June–1 July 2022, pp. 2678–2683. IEEE (2022). https://doi.org/10.1109/ISIT50566.2022.9834695

28. Maji, H.K., Paskin-Cherniavsky, A., Suad, T., Wang, M.: Constructing locally leakage-resilient linear secret-sharing schemes. In: Malkin, T., Peikert, C. (eds.) CRYPTO 2021. LNCS, vol. 12827, pp. 779–808. Springer, Cham (2021). https://doi.org/10.1007/978-3-030-84252-9_26

29. Massey, J.L.: Threshold decoding (1963)

30. Massey, J.L.: Some applications of coding theory in cryptography. Mat. Contemp. **21**(16), 187–209 (2001)

31. Nielsen, J.B., Simkin, M.: Lower bounds for leakage-resilient secret sharing. In: Canteaut, A., Ishai, Y. (eds.) EUROCRYPT 2020. LNCS, vol. 12105, pp. 556–577. Springer, Cham (2020). https://doi.org/10.1007/978-3-030-45721-1_20

32. Pietrzak, K.: Cryptography from learning parity with noise. In: Bieliková, M., Friedrich, G., Gottlob, G., Katzenbeisser, S., Turán, G. (eds.) SOFSEM 2012. LNCS, vol. 7147, pp. 99–114. Springer, Heidelberg (2012). https://doi.org/10.1007/978-3-642-27660-6_9

33. Regev, O.: The learning with errors problem. Invited Surv. CCC **7**(30), 11 (2010)

34. Shamir, A.: How to share a secret. Commun. Assoc. Comput. Mach. **22**(11), 612–613 (1979)

35. Srinivasan, A., Vasudevan, P.N.: Leakage resilient secret sharing and applications. In: Boldyreva, A., Micciancio, D. (eds.) CRYPTO 2019. LNCS, vol. 11693, pp. 480–509. Springer, Cham (2019). https://doi.org/10.1007/978-3-030-26951-7_17

Asymptotically Free Broadcast in Constant Expected Time via Packed VSS

Ittai Abraham[1], Gilad Asharov[2], Shravani Patil[3(✉)], and Arpita Patra[3]

[1] VMWare Research, Palo Alto, USA
iabraham@vmware.com
[2] Department of Computer Science, Bar-Ilan University, Ramat Gan, Israel
Gilad.Asharov@biu.ac.il
[3] Indian Institute of Science, Bangalore, India
{shravanip,arpita}@iisc.ac.in

Abstract. Broadcast is an essential primitive for secure computation. We focus in this paper on optimal resilience (i.e., when the number of corrupted parties t is less than a third of the computing parties n), and with no setup or cryptographic assumptions.

While broadcast with worst case t rounds is impossible, it has been shown [Feldman and Micali STOC'88, Katz and Koo CRYPTO'06] how to construct protocols with expected constant number of rounds in the private channel model. However, those constructions have large communication complexity, specifically $\mathcal{O}(n^2 L + n^6 \log n)$ expected number of bits transmitted for broadcasting a message of length L. This leads to a significant communication blowup in secure computation protocols in this setting.

In this paper, we substantially improve the communication complexity of broadcast in constant expected time. Specifically, the expected communication complexity of our protocol is $\mathcal{O}(nL + n^4 \log n)$. For messages of length $L = \Omega(n^3 \log n)$, our broadcast has no asymptotic overhead (up to expectation), as each party has to send or receive $\mathcal{O}(n^3 \log n)$ bits. We also consider parallel broadcast, where n parties wish to broadcast L bit messages in parallel. Our protocol has no asymptotic overhead for $L = \Omega(n^2 \log n)$, which is a common communication pattern in perfectly secure MPC protocols. For instance, it is common that all parties share their inputs simultaneously at the same round, and verifiable secret sharing protocols require the dealer to broadcast a total of $\mathcal{O}(n^2 \log n)$ bits.

As an independent interest, our broadcast is achieved by a *packed verifiable secret sharing*, a new notion that we introduce. We show a protocol that verifies $\mathcal{O}(n)$ secrets simultaneously with the same cost of verifying just a single secret. This improves by a factor of n the state-of-the-art.

Keywords: MPC · Byzantine agreement · Broadcast

© The Author(s), under exclusive license to Springer Nature Switzerland AG 2022
E. Kiltz and V. Vaikuntanathan (Eds.): TCC 2022, LNCS 13747, pp. 384–414, 2022.
https://doi.org/10.1007/978-3-031-22318-1_14

1   Introduction

A common practice in designing secure protocols is to describe the protocol in the broadcast-hybrid model, i.e., to assume the availability of a *broadcast channel*. Such a channel allows a distinguished party to send a message while guaranteeing that all parties receive and agree on the same message. Assuming the availability of a broadcast channel is reasonable only in a restricted setting, for instance, when the parties are geographically close and can use radio waves. In most settings, particularly when executing the protocol over the Internet, parties have to implement this broadcast channel over point-to-point channels.

The cost associated with the implementation of the broadcast channel is often neglected when designing secure protocols. In some settings, the implementation overhead is a real obstacle in practice. In this paper, we focus on the most demanding setting: **perfect security with optimal resilience**.

Perfect security means that the protocol cannot rely on any computational assumptions, and the error probability of the protocol is zero. Optimal resilience means that the number of parties that the adversary controls is bounded by $t < n/3$, where n is the total number of parties. This bound is known to be tight, as a perfectly-secure broadcast protocol tolerating $n/3$ corrupted parties or more is impossible to construct [44,48], even when a constant error probability is allowed [4].

Asymptotically-free broadcast. What is the best implementation of broadcast that we can hope for? For broadcasting an L bit message, consider the ideal trusted party that implements an "ideal broadcast". Since each party has to receive L bits, the total communication is $\mathcal{O}(nL)$. To avoid bottlenecks, we would also prefer *balanced* protocols where all parties have to communicate roughly the same number of bits, i.e., $\mathcal{O}(L)$, including the sender.

Regarding the number of rounds, it has been shown that for any broadcast protocol with perfect security there exists an execution that requires $t + 1$ rounds [32]. Therefore, a protocol that runs in strict constant number of rounds is impossible to achieve. The seminal works of Rabin and Ben-Or [10,49] demonstrated that those limitations can be overcome by using randomization. We define *asymptotically-free broadcast* as a balanced broadcast protocol that runs in *expected* constant number of rounds and with (expected) communication complexity of $\mathcal{O}(nL)$.

There are, in general, two approaches for implementing broadcast in our setting. These approaches provide an intriguing tradeoff between communication and round complexity:

- **Low communication complexity, high number of rounds:** For broadcasting a single bit, the first approach [13,22] requires $\mathcal{O}(n^2)$ bits of communication complexity, which is asymptotically optimal for any deterministic broadcast protocols [27], or in general, $\mathcal{O}(nL + n^2 \log n)$ bits for broadcasting a message of size L bits via a perfect broadcast extension protocol [20].[1] This comes at the expense of having $\Theta(n)$ rounds.

---

[1] Broadcast extension protocols handle long messages efficiently at the cost of a small number of single-bit broadcasts.

- **High communication complexity, constant expected number of rounds:** The second approach, originated by the seminal work of Feldman and Micali [29], followed by substantial improvements and simplifications by Katz and Koo [41], requires significant communication complexity of $\mathcal{O}(n^6 \log n)$ bits in expectation for broadcasting just a single bit, or $\mathcal{O}(n^2 L + n^6 \log n)$ bits for a message of L bits.[2] However, they work in *expected constant rounds*.

To get a sense of how the above translates to practice, consider a network with 200 ms delay per round-trip (such a delay is relatively high, but not unusual, see [1]), and $n = 300$. Using the first type of protocol, ≈ 300 rounds are translated to a delay of 1 min. Then, consider for instance computing the celebrated protocol of Ben-Or, Goldwasser and Wigderson [12] on an arithmetic circuit with depth 30. In each layer of the circuit the parties have to use broadcast, and thus the execution would take at least 30 min. The second type of protocols require at least $\Omega(n^6 \log n)$ bits of communication. The protocol is balanced and each party sends or receives $n^5 \log n$ bits ≈ 2.4 terabytes. Using 1Gbps channel, this is a delay of 5.4 h. Clearly, both approaches are not ideal.

This current state of the affairs calls for the design of faster broadcast protocols and in particular, understanding better the tradeoff between round complexity and communication complexity.

Why Perfect Security? Our main motivation for studying broadcast is for perfectly secure multiparty computation. Perfect security provides the strongest possible security guarantee. It does not rely on any intractable assumptions and provides unconditional, quantum, and everlasting security. Protocols with perfect security remain adaptively secure (with some caveats [6,18]) and secure under universal composition [43]. Perfect broadcast is an essential primitive in generic perfectly secure protocols.

Even if we relax our goals and aim for statistical security only, the situation is not much better. Specifically, the best upper bounds that we have are in fact already perfectly secure [13,20,22,41,46,47]. That is, current statistically secure results do not help in achieving a better communication complexity vs round complexity tradeoff relative to the current perfect security results. We remark that in the computational setting, in contrast, the situation is much better. Asymptotically-free broadcast with $f < n/2$ can be achieved assuming threshold signatures and setup assumption in constant expected rounds and with $\mathcal{O}(n^2 + nL)$ communication [3,41,50].

1.1 Our Results

We provide a significant improvement in the communication complexity of broadcast with perfect security and optimal resilience in the presence of a *static adversary*. Towards that end, we also improve a pivotal building block in secure computation, namely, verifiable secret sharing (VSS). Our new VSS has an $O(n)$

---

[2] Using broadcast extension of [46] we can bring the asymptotic cost to $\mathcal{O}(nL) + E(\mathcal{O}(n^7 \log n))$ bits. However, the minimum message size to achieve this $L = \Omega(n^6 \log n)$. This is prohibitively high even for $n = 100$.

complexity improvement that may be of independent interest. We present our results in a top-down fashion. Our main result is:

Theorem 1.1. *There exists a perfectly secure, balanced, broadcast protocol with optimal resilience, which allows a dealer to send L bits at the communication cost of $\mathcal{O}(nL)$ bits, plus $\mathcal{O}(n^4 \log n)$ expected bits. The protocol runs in constant expected number of rounds and assumes private channels.*

Previously, Katz and Koo [41] achieved $\mathcal{O}(n^2 L)$ bits plus $\mathcal{O}(n^6 \log n)$ expected number of bits. For messages of size $L = \Omega(n^3 \log n)$ bits, the total communication of our protocol is $\mathcal{O}(nL)$ bits. Thus, we say that our protocol is asymptotically free for messages of size $L = \Omega(n^3 \log n)$ bits. We recall that [41] together with [46] are also asymptotically free albeit only for prohibitively large value of L ($= \Omega(n^6 \log n)$). Table 1 compares our work to the state of the art in broadcast protocols.

To get a sense from a practical perspective, for broadcasting a single bit with $n = 300$, our protocol requires each party to send/receive roughly $n^3 \log n \approx 27$ MB (as opposed to ≈ 2.4 terabytes by [41]). Using a 1Gbps channel, this is 200ms. For broadcasting a message of size ≈ 27 MB, each party still has to send/receive roughly the same size of this message, and the broadcast is asymptotically free in that case.

Parallel Composition of Broadcast. In MPC, protocols often instruct the n parties to broadcast messages of the same length L in parallel at the same round. For instance, in the protocol of [12], all parties share their input at the same round, and for verifying the secret, each party needs to broadcast $L = \mathcal{O}(n^2 \log n)$ bits.[3] In fact, the notion of parallel-broadcast goes back to the work of Pease et al. [48]. We have the following extension to our main result:

Corollary 1.2. *There exists a perfectly-secure, balanced, parallel-broadcast protocol with optimal resilience, which allows n dealers to send messages of size L bits each, at the communication cost of $\mathcal{O}(n^2 L)$ bits, plus $\mathcal{O}(n^4 \log n)$ expected bits. The protocol runs in constant expected number of rounds.*

For message of size $L = \mathcal{O}(n^2 \log n)$ bits, which is common in MPC, our broadcast is asymptotically optimal. We obtain a cost of $\mathcal{O}(n^4 \log n)$ bits in expectation, with expected constant rounds. Note that each party receives $\mathcal{O}(nL)$ bits, and therefore $\mathcal{O}(n^2 L) = \mathcal{O}(n^4 \log n)$ bits is the best that one can hope for. Again, the protocol is balanced, which means that each party sends or receives only $\mathcal{O}(nL)$ bits.

For comparison, the other approach for broadcast based on [13,20,22] requires total $\mathcal{O}(n^4 \log n)$ bits for this task, but with $\Theta(n)$ rounds. We refer again to Table 1 for comparison.

---

[3] In fact, in each round of the protocol, each party performs $\mathcal{O}(n)$ verifiable secret sharings (VSSs), i.e., it has to broadcast $\mathcal{O}(n^3 \log n)$ bits. In [2] it has been shown how to reduce it to $\mathcal{O}(1)$ VSSs per party, i.e., each party might have to broadcast $\mathcal{O}(n^2 \log n)$.

Table 1. Comparison of communication complexity of our work with the state-of-the-art broadcast. $1 \times \mathcal{BC}(L)$ refers to the task of a single dealer broadcasting a L-element message. $n \times \mathcal{BC}(L)$ refers to the task of n dealers broadcasting a L-element message in parallel.

Task	Reference	Total P2P (in bits)	Rounds
$1 \times \mathcal{BC}(L)$	[13, 22]	$\mathcal{O}(n^2 L)$	$\mathcal{O}(n)$
	[13, 22] + [20]	$\mathcal{O}(nL + n^2 \log n)$	$\mathcal{O}(n)$
	[41]	$\mathcal{O}(n^2 L) + E(\mathcal{O}(n^6 \log n))$	$E(\mathcal{O}(1))$
	[41] + [46]*	$\mathcal{O}(nL) + E(\mathcal{O}(n^7 \log n))$	$E(\mathcal{O}(1))$
	Our work	$\mathbf{O(nL) + E(O(n^4 \log n))}$	$\mathbf{E(O(1))}$
$n \times \mathcal{BC}(L)$	[13, 22]	$\mathcal{O}(n^3 L)$	$\mathcal{O}(n)$
	[41]	$\mathcal{O}(n^3 L) + E(\mathcal{O}(n^6 \log n))$	$E(\mathcal{O}(1))$
	[41] + [46][a]	$\mathcal{O}(n^2 L) + E(\mathcal{O}(n^7 \log n))$	$E(\mathcal{O}(1))$
	Our work	$\mathbf{O(n^2 L) + E(O(n^4 \log n))}$	$\mathbf{E(O(1))}$

[a] Since the broadcast extension protocol of [20] requires $\mathcal{O}(n)$ rounds, combining [41] with [20] results in linear-round complexity and a worse communication complexity than what the second row ([13, 22] + [20]) provides.

To get a practical sense of those complexities, when $n = 300$ and parties have to broadcast simultaneously messages of size L, our protocol is asymptotically optimal for $L = n^2 \log n \approx 90\text{KB}$.

Packed Verifiable Secret Sharing. A pivotal building block in our construction, as well as perfectly secure multiparty protocols is *verifiable secret sharing* (VSS), originally introduced by Chor et al. [21]. It allows a dealer to distribute a secret to n parties such that no share reveal any information about the secret, and the parties can verify, already at the sharing phase, that the reconstruction phase would be successful.

To share a secret in the semi-honest setting, the dealer embeds its secret in a degree-t univariate polynomial, and it has to communicate $\mathcal{O}(n)$ field elements. In the malicious setting, the dealer embeds its secret in a bivariate polynomial of degree-t in both variables [12, 30]. The dealer then has to communicate $\mathcal{O}(n^2)$ field elements to share its secret. An intriguing question is whether this gap between the semi-honest (where the dealer has to encode its secret in a structure of size $\mathcal{O}(n)$) and the malicious setting (where the dealer has to encode its secret in a structure of size $\mathcal{O}(n^2)$) is necessary. While we do not answer this question, we show that the dealer can pack $\mathcal{O}(n)$ secrets, simultaneously in one bivariate polynomial. Then, it can share it at the same cost as sharing a single VSS, achieving an overhead of $\mathcal{O}(n)$ per secret. We show:

Theorem 1.3. *Given a synchronous network with pairwise private channels and a broadcast channel, there exists a perfectly secure packed VSS protocol with optimal resilience, which has a communication complexity of $\mathcal{O}(n^2 \log n)$ bits over point-to-point channels and $\mathcal{O}(n^2 \log n)$ bits broadcast for sharing $\mathcal{O}(n)$ secret field elements (i.e., $\mathcal{O}(n \log n)$ bits) in strict $\mathcal{O}(1)$ rounds. The optimistic case* *(where all the parties behave honestly) does not use the broadcast channel in the protocol.*

The best previous results achieve $\mathcal{O}(n^3 \log n)$ (point-to-point and broadcast) for sharing $\mathcal{O}(n)$ secret elements [5,12,30,42], this is an improvement by a factor of n in communication complexity.

Packing k secrets into one polynomial is a known technique, proposed by Franklin and Yung [34]. It was previously used in Shamir's secret sharing scheme. However, it comes with the following price: While Shamir's secret sharing allows protecting against even $n - 1$ corrupted parties, packing k secrets in one polynomial achieves privacy against only $n - k - 1$ parties. In the malicious case, VSS of a single secret is possible only when the number of corruption satisfies $t < n/3$. The idea of packing many secrets without trading off the allowed threshold of corruption has been explored by Damgård et al. [25]. However, this is achieved at the expense of having $\mathcal{O}(n)$ rounds. In contrast, our packed verifiable secret sharing enables packing $\mathcal{O}(n)$ secrets while keeping the threshold exactly the same and ensuring $\mathcal{O}(1)$ round complexity. Compared to a constant round VSS of a single secret, we obtain packed secret sharing completely for free (up to small hidden constants in the $\mathcal{O}$ notation of the above theorem).

Optimal Gradecast for $\Omega(n^2)$ Messages. Another building block that we improve along the way is gradecast. Gradecast is a relaxation of broadcast introduced by Feldman and Micali [29] ("graded-broadcast"). It allows a distinguished dealer to transmit a message, and each party outputs the message it receives together with a grade $g \in \{0, 1, 2\}$. If the dealer is honest, all honest parties receive the same message and grade 2. If the dealer is corrupted, but some honest party outputs grade 2, it is guaranteed that all honest parties output the same message (though some might have grade 1 only). We show that:

Theorem 1.4. *There exists a perfectly secure gradecast protocol with optimal resilience, which allows a party to send a message of size L bits with a communication cost of $\mathcal{O}(nL + n^3 \log n)$ bits and in $\mathcal{O}(1)$ rounds. The protocol is balanced.*

This result is optimal when $L = \Omega(n^2 \log n)$ bits as each party has to receive L bits even in an ideal implementation. Previously, the best gradecast protocol in the perfect security setting [29] required $\mathcal{O}(n^2 L)$ bits of communication.

1.2 Applications and Discussions

Applications: Perfect Secure Computation. We demonstrate the potential speed up of protocols in perfect secure computation using our broadcast. There are, in general, two lines of works in perfectly secure MPC, resulting again in an intriguing tradeoff between round complexity and communication complexity.

The line of work [2,8,12,19,24,37] achieves constant round per multiplication and round complexity of $\mathcal{O}(\mathsf{depth}(C))$, where C is the arithmetic circuit that the parties jointly compute. The communication complexity of those protocols results in $\mathcal{O}(n^3 |C| \log n)$ bits over point-to-point channels in the optimistic case, and an additional $\mathcal{O}(n^3|C|\log n)$ bits over the broadcast channel in the pessimistic case (recall that this means that each party has to send or receive a total of $\mathcal{O}(n^4|C|\log n)$ bits). In a nutshell, the protocol requires each party to perform $\mathcal{O}(1)$ VSSs in parallel for each multiplication gate in the circuit, and recall that in each VSS the dealer broadcasts $\mathcal{O}(n^2\log n)$ bits. This is exactly the setting in which our parallel broadcast gives asymptotically free broadcast (Corollary 1.2). Thus, we get a protocol with a total of $\mathcal{O}(n^4|C|\log n)$ bits (expected) and expected $\mathcal{O}(\text{depth}(C))$ rounds over point-to-point channels. Previously, using [41], this would have been resulted in expected $\mathcal{O}(n^6|C|\log n)$ communication complexity with $\mathcal{O}(\text{depth}(C))$ rounds.

Another line of work [9,39,40] in perfectly-secure MPC is based on the *player elimination* framework (introduced by Hirt and Maurer and Przydatek [40]). Those protocol identify parties that may misbehave and exclude them from the execution. Those protocols result in a total of $\mathcal{O}((n|C| + n^3)\log n)$ bits over point-to-point channels, and $\mathcal{O}(n\log n)$ bits over the broadcast channel. However, this comes at the expense of $\mathcal{O}(\text{depth}(C) + n)$ rounds. This can be compiled to $\mathcal{O}((n|C| + n^3)\log n)$ communication complexity with $\mathcal{O}(n^2 + \text{depth}(C))$ rounds using [13,22], or to $\mathcal{O}((n|C| + n^7)\log n)$ communication complexity with $\mathcal{O}(n + \text{depth}(C))$ rounds (expected) using [41]. Using our broadcast, the communication complexity is $\mathcal{O}((n|C| + n^5)\log n)$ with $\mathcal{O}(n + \text{depth}(C))$ rounds (expected). We remark that in many setting, a factor n in round complexity should not be treated the same as communication complexity. Roundtrips are slow (e.g., 200 ms delay for each roundtrip), whereas communication channels can send relatively large messages fast (1 or even 10 Gbps).

On Sequential and Parallel Composition of Our Broadcast. Like Feldman and Micali [29] and Katz and Koo [41] (and any $o(t)$-round expected broadcast protocol), our protocol cannot provide simultaneous termination. Sequentially composing such protocols is discussed in Lindell, Lysyanskaya and Rabin [45], Katz and Koo [41] and Cohen et al. [23]. Regarding parallel composition, unlike the black-box parallel composition of broadcasts studied by Ben-Or and El-Yaniv [11], we rely on the idea of Fitzi and Garay [33] that applies to OLE-based protocols. The idea is that multiple broadcast sub-routines are run in parallel when only a single election per iteration is required for all these subroutines. This reduces the overall cost and also guarantees that parallel broadcast is also constant expected number of rounds.

Modeling Broadcast Functionalities. We use standalone, simulation-based definition as in [16]. The standalone definition does not capture rounds in the ideal functionalities, or the fact that there is no simultaneous termination. The work of Cohen et al. [23] shows that one can simply treat the broadcast without simultaneous termination as an ideal broadcast as we provide (which, in particular, has simultaneous and deterministic termination). Moreover, it allows compiling a protocol using deterministic-termination hybrids (i.e., like our ideal functionalities) into a protocol that uses expected-constant-round protocols for emulating those hybrids (i.e.,. as our protocols) while preserving the expected round complexity of the protocol. We remark that in order to apply the compiler of [23], the functionalities need to follow a structure of (1) input from all parties; (2) leakage to the adversary; (3) output. For simplicity, we did not write our functionalities using this specific format, but it is clear that our functionalities can be written in this style.

Our Broadcast with Strict-Polynomial Run Time. Protocols in constant expected number of rounds might never terminate (although, with extremely small probability). Our protocols can be transformed into a protocol that runs in strict polynomial time using the approach of Goldreich and Petrank [38]: Specifically, after $\mathcal{O}(n)$ attempts to terminate, the parties can run the $\mathcal{O}(n)$ rounds protocol with guaranteed termination. See also [23].

1.3   Related Work

We review the related works below. Error-free byzantine agreement and broadcast are known to be possible only if $t < n/3$ holds [44,48]. Moreover, Fischer and Lynch [32] showed a lower bound of $t + 1$ rounds for any deterministic byzantine agreement protocol or broadcast protocol. Faced with this barrier, Rabin [49] and Ben-Or [10] independently studied the effect of randomization on round complexity, which eventually culminated into the work of Feldman and Micali [31] who gave an expected constant round protocol for byzantine agreement with optimal resilience. Improving over this work, the protocol of [41] requires a communication of $\mathcal{O}(n^2 L + n^6 \log n)$ for a message of size L bits, while achieving the advantage of expected constant rounds. In regards to the communication complexity, Dolev and Reischuk [28] established a lower bound of n^2 bits for deterministic broadcast or agreement on a single bit. With a round complexity of $\mathcal{O}(n)$, [13,22] achieve a broadcast protocol with a communication complexity of $\mathcal{O}(n^2)$ bits.

We quickly recall the state of the art perfectly-secure broadcast extension protocols. Recall that these protocols aim to achieve the optimal complexity of $\mathcal{O}(nL)$ bits for sufficiently large message size L and utilize a protocol for bit broadcast. The protocol of [35,47] communicates $\mathcal{O}(nL)$ bits over point-to-point channels and $\mathcal{O}(n^2)$ bits through a bit-broadcast protocol. The work of [46] improves the number of bits sent through a bit-broadcast protocol to $\mathcal{O}(n)$ bits. Both these extension protocols are constant round. The recent work of [20] presents a protocol that communicates $\mathcal{O}(nL + n^2 \log n)$ bits over point-to-point channels and a single bit through a bit-broadcast protocol. However, the round complexity of this protocol is $\mathcal{O}(n)$.

2   Technical Overview

We describe the high-level overview of our techniques. We start with our improved broadcast in Sect. 2.1, and then describe packed VSS in Sect. 2.2, followed by the gradecast protocol in Sect. 2.3. To aid readability, we summarize our different primitives and the relationship between them in Fig. 1. In each one of the those primitives we improve over the previous works.

Primitive	P2P	Broadcast	Reference	Remarks
Broadcast	$\mathcal{O}(nL) + E(\mathcal{O}(n^4 \log n))$	–	Section 8.2	L bit message
Byzantine Agreement	$\mathcal{O}(n^2) + E(\mathcal{O}(n^4 \log n))$	–	Section 8.1	–
Gradecast	$\mathcal{O}(nL + n^3 \log n)$	–	Section 5	L bit message
Oblivious Leader Election	$\mathcal{O}(n^4 \log n)$	–	Section 7	–
Multi-moderated VSS	$\mathcal{O}(n^4 \log n)$	–	Section 6	Sharing $\mathcal{O}(n)$ values
Packed VSS (w. Gradecast)	$\mathcal{O}(n^3 \log n)$	–	Section 4	Sharing $\mathcal{O}(n)$ values
Packed VSS (w. Broadcast)	$\mathcal{O}(n^2 \log n)$	$\mathcal{O}(n^2 \log n)$	Section 4	Sharing $\mathcal{O}(n)$ values

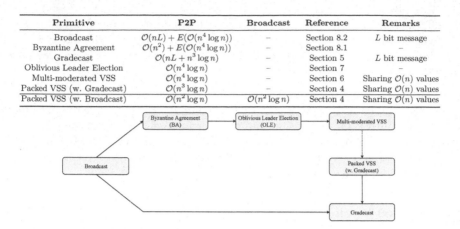

Fig. 1. Roadmap of our building blocks. All lines are compositions, except for the line from Multi-moderated VSS to Packed VSS, which is a white-box modification.

2.1   Improved Broadcast in Constant Expected Rounds

Our starting point is a high-level overview of the broadcast protocol of Katz and Koo [41], which simplifies and improves the construction of Feldman and Micali [29]. Following the approach of Turpin and Coan [51] for broadcast extension closely, broadcast can be reduced to two primitives: Gradecast and Byzantine agreement.

1. **Gradecast:** A gradecast is a relaxation of broadcast, where a distinguished dealer transmits a message, and parties output the message together with a grade. If the dealer is honest, all honest parties are guaranteed to output the dealer's message together with a grade 2. Moreover, if the dealer is corrupted and one honest party outputs grade 2, then it is guaranteed that all other honest parties also output the same message, though maybe with a grade 1. Looking ahead, we show how to improve gradecast of message of length L bits from $\mathcal{O}(n^2 L)$ bits to $\mathcal{O}(nL + n^3 \log n)$ bits, which is optimal for messages of $L = \Omega(n^2 \log n)$ bits. We overview our construction in Sect. 2.3.
2. **Byzantine agreement:** In Byzantine agreement all parties hold some bit as input, and all of them output a bit at the end of the protocol. If all honest parties hold the same value, then it is guaranteed that the output of all parties would be that value. Otherwise, it is guaranteed that the honest parties would agree and output the same (arbitrary) bit.

To implement broadcast, the dealer gradecasts its message M and then the parties run Byzantine agreement (BA) on the grade they received (using 1 as input when the grade of the gradecast is 2, and 0 otherwise). Then, if the output of the BA is 1, each party outputs the message it received from the gradecast, and otherwise it outputs $\perp$.

If the dealer is honest, then all honest parties receive grade 2 in the gradecast, and all would agree in the BA that the grade is 2. In that case, they all output M. If the dealer is corrupted, and all honest parties received grade 0 or 1 in the gradecast, they would all use 0 in the Byzantine agreement, and all would output $\perp$. The remaining case is when some honest parties receives grade 2 in the gradecast, and some receive 1. However, once there is a single honest party that received grade 2 in the gradecast, it is guaranteed that all honest parties hold the same message M. The Byzantine agreement can then go either way (causing all to output M or $\perp$), but agreement is guaranteed.

Oblivious Leader Election. It has been shown that to implement a Byzantine agreement (on a single bit), it suffices to obliviously elect a leader, i.e., a random party among the parties. In a nutshell, a Byzantine agreement proceeds in iterations, where parties exchange the bits they believe that the output should be and try to see if there is an agreement on the output. When there is no clear indication of which bit should be the output, the parties try to see if there is an agreement on the output bit suggested by the elected leader. A corrupted leader might send different bits to different parties. However, once an honest leader is elected, it must have sent the same bit to all parties. In that case the protocol guarantees that all honest parties will agree in the next iteration on the output bit suggested by the leader, and halt.

Oblivious leader election is a protocol where the parties have no input, and the goal is to agree on a random value in $\{1, \ldots, n\}$. It might have three different outcomes: (1) All parties agree on the same random index $j \in \{1, \ldots, n\}$, and it also holds that P_j is honest; this is the preferable outcome; (2) All parties agree on the same index $i \in \{1, \ldots, n\}$, but P_i is corrupted; (3) The parties do not agree on the index of the party elected. The goal is to achieve the outcome (1) with constant probability, say $\geq 1/2$. Recall that once outcome (1) occurs then the Byzantine agreement succeeds. Achieving outcome (1) with constant number of rounds and with constant probability implies Byzantine agreement with constant expected number of rounds.

The key idea to elect a leader is to randomly choose, for each party, some random value c_i. Then, the parties choose an index j of the party for which c_j is minimal. To do that, we cannot let each party P_j choose its random value c_j, as corrupted parties would always choose small numbers to be elected. Thus, all parties contribute to the random value associated with each party. That is, each party P_k chooses $c_{k \to j} \in \{1, \ldots, n^4\}$ and the parties define $c_j = \sum_{k=1}^{n} c_{k \to j} \mod n^4$ as the random value associated with P_j. This guarantees that each value c_j is uniform.

However, just as in coin-tossing protocols, a party cannot publicly announce its random choices, since then it would allow a rushing adversary to choose its random values as a function of the announced values. This is prevented by using *verifiable secret sharing*. Verifiable secret sharing provides *hiding* – given t shares, it is impossible to determine what is the secret, and *binding* – at the end of the sharing phase, the dealer cannot change the secret, and reconstruction is guaranteed. The parties verifiably share their random values $c_{k \to j}$ for every k, j.

After all parties share their values, it is safe to reconstruct the secret, reveal the random values, and elect the leader based on those values.

A Problem: VSS Uses a Broadcast Channel. A problem with the above solution is that protocols for VSS use a broadcast channel to reach an agreement on whether or not to accept the dealer's shares. Yet, the good news is that broadcast is used only during the sharing phase. Replacing each broadcast with a gradecast does not suffice since honest parties do not necessarily agree on the transmitted messages when corrupted senders gradecasts messages. This leads to the notion of "moderated VSS", where the idea is to have a party that is responsible for all broadcasted message. Specifically, now there are two distinguished parties: a dealer P_k and a moderator P_j. The parties run the VSS where P_k is the dealer; whenever a participant has to broadcast a message m, it first gradecasts it, and then the moderator P_j has to gradecast the message it received. Each party can then compare between the two gradecasted messages; however, the parties proceed the execution while using the message that the moderator had gradecasted as the message that was broadcasted. At the end of the execution, each party outputs together with the shares, a grade for the moderator in $\{0, 1\}$. For instance, if the moderator ever gradecasted some message and the message was received by some party P_i with grade ≤ 1, then the grade that P_i gives the moderator is 0 — P_i cannot know whether other parties received the same message at all. The idea is that honest parties might not necessarily output the same grade, but if there is one honest party that outputs grade 1, it is guaranteed that the VSS was successful, and we have binding. Moreover, if the moderator is honest, then all honest parties would give it grade 1.

Going back to leader election, the value $c_{k \to j}$ is distributed as follows: the parties run a VSS where P_k is the dealer and P_j is the moderator. After all values of all parties were shared (i.e., all parties committed to the values $c_{k \to j}$), each party defines for each moderator P_j the value $c_j = \sum_{k=1}^{n} c_{k \to j}$. If the grade of P_j was not 1 in all its executions as a moderator, then replace $c_j = \infty$. Each party elects the party P_ℓ for which c_ℓ is minimal.

If the moderator P_j is honest, then for both honest and corrupted dealer P_k, the VSS would end up with agreement, and all honest parties would give P_j grade 1 as a moderator. The value $c_j = \sum_{k=1}^{n} c_{k \to j} \mod n^4$ would be the same for all honest parties, and it must distribute uniformly as honest dealers contributed random values in this sum. Likewise, if a moderator P_j is corrupted but some honest party outputs grade 1 in all executions where P_j served as a moderator, then the value $c_j = \sum_{k=1}^{n} c_{k \to j} \mod n^4$ must be the same for all honest parties, and it also must be random, as honest dealers contributed random values. There might be no agreement if some honest parties gave grade 1 for that moderator, while others did not and defined $c_j = \infty$. In that case, we might not have an agreement on the elected leader. However, it is guaranteed that the value c_j is distributed uniformly. Thus, the inconsistency is bounded with constant probability (roughly $t/n \leq 1/3$).

Our Improvements. As noticed above, each party participates as the dealer in n executions, and as the role of the moderator in n executions. Thus, we have a total of n^2 executions of VSS. First, we show a new protocol that enables a dealer to pack $\mathcal{O}(n)$ secrets at the cost of just one VSS (assuming broadcast), called packed VSS (see an overview in Sect. 2.2). For leader election, we have to replace the broadcast in the packed VSS with a gradecast (with a moderator).

However, we cannot just pack all the $\mathcal{O}(n)$ values $c_{k \to j}$ where P_k is the dealer in one instance of a VSS with a moderator since each one of the secrets corresponds to a different moderator. We, therefore, introduce a new primitive which is called "Multi-moderated packed secret sharing": The dealer distributes $\mathcal{O}(n)$ values, where each corresponds to a different moderator, and have all parties serve as moderator in one shared execution of a VSS.

More precisely, the packed VSS uses several invocations of broadcasts in the sharing phase, just as a regular VSS. Until the very last round, the dealer also serves as the moderator within each of those broadcasts. In the last round, there is a vote among the parties whether accept or reject the dealer, where the vote is supposed to be performed over the broadcast channel. At this point, the execution is forked to $\mathcal{O}(n)$ executions. Each corresponds to a different moderator, where the moderator moderates just the last round's broadcasts. The idea is that the vast majority of the computation is shared between all $\mathcal{O}(n)$ executions, thus the additional cost introduced for each moderator is small. This allows us to replace all n executions where P_i serves as a dealer with just one execution where P_i is the dealer and other $\mathcal{O}(n)$ parties are moderators at the same time.

Another obstacle worth mentioning is that within multi-moderated packed VSS, the dealer broadcasts $\mathcal{O}(n^2 \log n)$ bits, whereas other participant broadcasts at most $\mathcal{O}(n \log n)$ bits. Our gradecast is not optimal for this message size, and thus when replacing those broadcasts with gradecasts, the overall cost would be $\mathcal{O}(n^5 \log n)$. We can do better by considering all the multi-moderated VSSs in parallel. Each party then participates in $\mathcal{O}(1)$ executions as a dealer and in $\mathcal{O}(n)$ executions as a participant. Therefore, each party has to broadcast $\mathcal{O}(n^2 \log n)$ bits in all invocations of multi-moderated packed VSS combined ($\mathcal{O}(n^2 \log n)$ bits when it serves as a dealer, and $(n-1) \times \mathcal{O}(n \log n)$ when it serves as a participant). For that size of messages, our gradecast is optimal.

To conclude, to obtain our broadcast, we build upon [29,41] and introduce: (1) an optimal gradecast protocol for $\Omega(n^2 \log n)$ messages which is used twice – for gradecasting the message before running the Byzantine agreement and within the Byzantine agreement as part of the VSSs; (2) a novel multi-moderated packed secret sharing, which is based on a novel packed VSS protocol; (3) carefully combine all the $\mathcal{O}(n)$ invocations of multi-moderated packed secret sharing to amortize the costs of the gradecasts.

When comparing to the starting point of $\mathcal{O}(n^2 L)$ plus $E(\mathcal{O}(n^6 \log n))$ of [41], the improved gradecast allows us to reduce the first term to $\mathcal{O}(nL)$, for large enough messages. Regarding the second term, packing $\mathcal{O}(n)$ values in the VSS reduces one n factor, and the improved gradecast within the VSS reduces another n factor. Overall this brings us to $\mathcal{O}(nL)$ plus $E(\mathcal{O}(n^4 \log n))$.

2.2 Packed Verifiable Secret Sharing

Our packed verifiable secret sharing protocol is the basis of the multi-moderated VSS. We believe that it will find applications in future constructions of MPC protocols, and is of independent interest. Communication cost wise, the best-known constant-round perfect VSS sharing one secret is $\mathcal{O}(n^2 \log n)$ bits over point-to-point channels in the optimistic case, and additional $\mathcal{O}(n^2 \log n)$ bits over the broadcast channel in the pessimistic case [7,12,36]. Here, we retain the same cost, yet "pack" $t+1$ secrets in one bivariate polynomial and generate $t+1$ independent Shamir-sharings at one go.

Sharing More Secrets at One Go. Our goal is to generate Shamir-sharing of $t+1$ secrets, $s_{-t}, \ldots, s_0$, at once. Denoting Shamir-sharing of a secret s by $[s]$, our goal is to produce $[s_{-t}], \ldots, [s_0]$ using a single instance of a VSS. For this, the dealer chooses a degree-$(2t, t)$ bivariate polynomial[4] $S(x, y)$ such that $S(l, 0) = s_l$ for each $l \in \{-t, \ldots, 0\}$. We set $f_i(x) = S(x, i)$ of degree $2t$ and $g_i(y) = S(i, y)$ of degree-t and observe that for every i, j it holds that $f_i(j) = S(j, i) = g_j(i)$. The goal of the verification part is that each P_i will hold $f_i(x)$ and $g_i(y)$ on the same bivariate polynomial $S(x, y)$. Then, each degree-t univariate polynomial $g_l(y)$ for $l \in \{-t, \ldots, 0\}$ is the standard Shamir-sharing of s_l amongst the parties. Once the shares of the parties are consistent, each party P_i can locally compute its share on $g_l(y)$ as $g_l(i) = f_i(l)$.

Our protocol is a strict improvement of [2]. Specifically, the work of [2] considers the VSS protocol of [12] when the dealer uses a $(2t, t)$-polynomial instead of a degree-(t, t) polynomial. It observes that by minor modifications, the protocol still provides weak verifiability even though the sharing is done on a higher degree polynomial. By "weak", we mean that the reconstruction phase of the polynomial might fail in the case of a corrupted dealer. Nevertheless, the guarantee is that the reconstruction phase would either end up successfully reconstructing $S(x, y)$, or $\perp$, and whether it would succeed or not depends on the adversary's behavior. In contrast, in a regular ("strong") VSS, reconstruction is always guaranteed.

The work of [2] utilizes this primitive to improve the efficiency of the degree-reduction step of the BGW protocol. However, this primitive is weak and does not suffice for most applications of VSS. For instance, it cannot be used as a part of our leader election protocol: The adversary can decide whether the polynomial would be reconstructed or not. Thus there is no "binding", and it can choose, adaptively and based on the revealed secrets of the honest parties, whether the reconstruction would be to the secret values or some default values. As such, it can increase its chance of being elected.

Our Work: Achieving Strong Binding. In our work, we show how to achieve strong binding. We omit the details in this high-level overview of achieving weak verifiability of [2] secret sharing while pointing out that the protocol is a variant of the VSS protocol of [12]. For our discussion, the protocol reaches the following

---

[4] We call a bivariate polynomial where the degree in x is $2t$ and in y is t, i.e., $S(x, y) = \sum_{i=0}^{2t} \sum_{j=0}^{t} a_{i,j} x^i y^j$ as a $(2t, t)$-bivariate polynomial.

stage: If the dealer is not discarded, then there is a CORE of $2t + 1$ parties that hold shares of a unique bivariate polynomial $S(x, y)$, and this set of parties is public and known to all (it is determined based on votes performed over the broadcast channel). Each party P_i in CORE holds two univariate shares $f_i(x) = S(x, i)$ of degree-$2t$ and $g_i(y) = S(i, y)$ of degree-t. Each party P_j for $j \notin$ CORE holds a polynomial $g_j(y) = S(j, y)$, where some of those polynomials are also public and were broadcasted by the dealer. In case the dealer is honest, then all honest parties are part of CORE, whereas if the dealer is corrupted, then it might be that only $t + 1$ honest parties are part of CORE. To achieve strong binding, the dealer has to provide shares for parties outside CORE, publicly, and in a constant number of rounds.

The first step is to make all the polynomials $g_j(y)$ for each $j \notin$ CORE public. This is easy, since each such polynomial is of degree t. The dealer can broadcast it, and the parties in CORE vote whether to accept. If there are no $2t + 1$ votes to accept, then the dealer is discarded. Since the shares of the honest parties in CORE are consistent and define a unique $(2t, t)$-bivariate polynomial $S(x, y)$, the dealer cannot publish any polynomial $g_j(y)$ which is not $S(j, y)$. Any polynomial $g'_j(y) \neq S(j, y)$ can agree with at most t points with $S(j, y)$ and thus it would receive at most t votes of honest parties in CORE, i.e., it cannot reach $2t + 1$ votes.

The next step is to make the dealer also publicize the shares $f_j(x)$ for each $j \notin$ CORE. This is more challenging since each $f_j(x)$ is of degree-$2t$, and therefore achieving $2t + 1$ votes is not enough, as t votes might be false. Therefore, the verification is more delicate:

1. First, the parties in CORE have to vote OK on the f-polynomials that the dealer publishes. If there are less than $2t + 1$ votes, the dealer is discarded.
2. Second, for each party P_j in CORE that did not vote OK, the dealer is required to publish its $g_j(y)$ polynomial. The parties in CORE then vote on the revealed polynomials as in the first step of boosting from weak to strong verification.

To see why this works, assume that the dealer tries to distribute a polynomial $f'_j(x) \neq S(x, j)$. Then, there must exist an honest party such that its share does not agree with $f'_j(x)$. If $f'_j(x)$ does not agree with shares that are public, then it would be immediately discarded. If $f'_j(x)$ does not agree with a share of an honest party P_k that is part of CORE, then $g_k(y)$ would become public in the next round, and the dealer would be publicly accused. The dealer cannot provide a share $g_k(y) \neq S(k, y)$ for the same reason as the first step of boosting from weak to strong VSS. At the end of this step we have that all honest parties are either part of CORE and their shares are private, or they are not in CORE and their shares are public. Overall, all honest parties hold shares on the bivariate polynomial $S(x, y)$. We refer to Sect. 4 for the formal protocol description.

2.3   Optimal Gradecast

A crucial building block in our construction is gradecast. We show how to implement gradecast of a message of length L bits using total communication of

$\mathcal{O}(n^3 \log n + nL)$ bits. For this overview, we just deal with the case where the dealer is honest and show that all honest parties output the message that the dealer gradecasted with grade 2. We leave the case of a corrupted dealer to the relevant section (Sect. 5).

Data Dissemination. Our construction is inspired in part by the data dissemination protocol of [26], while we focus here on the synchronous settings. In the task of data dissemination, $t + 1$ honest parties hold as input the same input M, while other honest parties hold the input $\bot$, and the goal is that all honest parties receive the same output M in the presence of t corrupted parties. In our protocol, assume for simplicity messages of size $(t + 1)^2$ field elements (i.e., a degree-(t, t) bivariate polynomial). Data dissemination can be achieved quite easily: (1) Each honest party sends to each party P_j the univariate polynomials $S(x, j), S(j, y)$. (2) Once a party receives $t + 1$ messages with the same pair of univariate polynomials, it forwards those polynomials to all others. An adversary might send different polynomials, but it can never reach plurality $t + 1$. (3) After all the honest parties forwarded their polynomials to the others, we are guaranteed that each party holds $2t + 1$ correct shares of S and at most t incorrect shares. Each party can reconstruct S efficiently using Reed Solomon decoding. Note that this procedure requires the transmission of $\mathcal{O}(n^3 \log n)$ bits overall. Therefore, our goal in the gradecast protocol is to reach a state where $t + 1$ honest parties hold shares of the same bivariate polynomial.

Gradecast. For the sake of exposition, we first describe a simpler protocol where the dealer is computationally unbounded, and then describe how to make the dealer efficient. Again, assume that the input message of the dealer is encoded as a bivariate polynomial $S(x, y)$. The dealer sends the entire bivariate polynomial to each party. Then, every pair P_i and P_j exchange the polynomials $S(x, i), S(i, y), S(x, j), S(j, y)$. The two parties check whether they agree on those polynomials or not. If P_i sees that the polynomials it received from P_j are the same as it received from the dealer, then it adds j to a set Agreed_i. The parties then send their sets Agreed_i to the dealer, who defines an undirected graph where the nodes are the set $\{1, \ldots, n\}$ and an edge $\{i, j\}$ exists if and only if $i \in \mathsf{Agreed}_j$ and $j \in \mathsf{Agreed}_i$. The dealer then (inefficiently) finds a maximal clique $K \subseteq \{1, \ldots, n\}$ of at least $2t + 1$ parties and gradecasts K to all parties using a naïve gradecast protocol of [29,41] (note that this is a gradecast of case $\mathcal{O}(n^2 L)$ with $L = \mathcal{O}(n \log n)$). A party P_i is happy if: (1) $i \in K$; (2) it received the gradecast message of the dealer with grade 2; and (3) $K \subseteq \mathsf{Agreed}_i$. The parties then proceed to data dissemination protocol.

The claim is that if the dealer is honest, then at least $t + 1$ honest parties are happy, and they all hold the same bivariate polynomial. This is because the set of honest parties defines a clique of size $2t + 1$, and any clique that the honest dealer finds of cardinality $2t + 1$ must include at least $t + 1$ honest parties. The result of the data dissemination protocol is that all honest parties output S. If the dealer is corrupted, we first claim that all honest parties that are happy must hold the same bivariate polynomial. Any two honest parties that are happy must be part of the same clique K that contains at least $t + 1$ honest parties, and all honest parties in that clique must agree with each other (all see the same clique K defined by the dealer, and verified that they agreed with each other). The univariate polynomials exchanged between those $t + 1$ honest parties define a unique bivariate polynomial. Again, data dissemination would guarantee that all honest parties would output that bivariate polynomial.

On Making the Dealer Efficient. To make the dealer efficient, we rely on a procedure that finds an approximation of a clique, known as the STAR technique, introduced by [14]. In the technical section, we show how we can use this approximation of a clique, initially introduced for the case of $t < n/4$, to the much more challenging scenario of $t < n/3$. We refer to Sect. 5 for the technical details.

3   Preliminaries

We consider a synchronous network model where the parties in $\mathcal{P} = \{P_1, \ldots, P_n\}$ are connected via pairwise private and authenticated channels. Additionally, for some of our protocols we assume the availability of a broadcast channel, which allows a party to send an identical message to all the parties. One of the goals of this paper is to implement such a broadcast channel over the pairwise private channels, and we mention explicitly for each protocol whether a broadcast channel is available or not. The distrust in the network is modelled as a *computationally unbounded* active adversary $\mathcal{A}$ which can maliciously corrupt up to t out of the n parties during the protocol execution and make them behave in an arbitrary manner. We prove security in the standard, stand-alone simulation-based model in the perfect setting [7,16] for a static adversary. Owing to the results of [18], this guarantees adaptive security with inefficient simulation. We derive universal composability [17] for free using [43]. We refer the readers to the full version for the security proofs and more details.

Our protocols are defined over a finite field $\mathbb{F}$ where $|\mathbb{F}| > n + t + 1$. We consider two sets of n and $t + 1$ distinct elements from $\mathbb{F}$ publicly known to all the parties, which we denote by $\{1, \ldots, n\}$ and $\{-t, \ldots, 0\}$ respectively. We use $[v]$ to denote the degree-t Shamir-sharing of a value v among parties in $\mathcal{P}$.

3.1   Bivariate Polynomials

A degree (l, m)-bivariate polynomial over $\mathbb{F}$ is of the form $S(x, y) = \sum_{i=0}^{l} \sum_{j=0}^{m} b_{ij} x^i y^j$ where $b_{ij} \in \mathbb{F}$. The polynomials $f_i(x) = S(x, i)$ and $g_i(y) = S(i, y)$ are called i^{th} f and g univariate polynomials of $S(x, y)$ respectively. In our protocol, we use $(2t, t)$-bivariate polynomials where the ith f and g univariate polynomials are associated with party P_i for every $P_i \in \mathcal{P}$.

3.2   Finding (n, t)-STAR

Definition 3.1. *Let G be a graph over the nodes $\{1, \ldots, n\}$. We say that a pair (C, D) of sets such that $C \subseteq D \subseteq \{1, \ldots, n\}$ is an (n, t)-star in G if the following* *hold: (a)* $|C| \geq n - 2t$; *(b)* $|D| \geq n - t$; *and (c) for every* $j \in C$ *and every* $k \in D$, *the edge* (j, k) *exists in* G.

Canetti [14,15] showed that if a graph has a clique of size $n - t$, then there exists an efficient algorithm which always finds an (n, t)-star. We refer the readers to the full version for details.

4 Packed Verifiable Secret Sharing

Here we present a packed VSS to generate Shamir sharing of $t + 1$ secrets at the cost of $\mathcal{O}(n^2 \log n)$ bits point-to-point and broadcast communication. The security proof appears in the full version of the paper.

The Functionality. On holding $t + 1$ secrets $s_{-t}, \ldots, s_0$, the dealer chooses a uniformly random $(2t, t)$-bivariate polynomial $S(x, y)$ such that $S(l, 0) = s_l$ for each $l \in \{-t, \ldots, 0\}$ and uses the polynomial as its input. Our functionality for VSS is as follows, followed by the VSS protocol.

Functionality 4.1: $\mathcal{F}_{\mathsf{VSS}}$ – **Packed VSS Functionality**

Input: The dealer holds a polynomial $S(x, y)$.

1. The dealer sends $S(x, y)$ to the functionality.
2. If $S(x, y)$ is of degree at most $2t$ in x and at most t in y, then the functionality sends to each party P_i the two univariate polynomials $S(x, i), S(i, y)$. Otherwise, the functionality sends $\perp$ to all parties.

Protocol 4.2: Π_{pVSS} – **Packed VSS Protocol**

Common input: The description of a field $\mathbb{F}$, two sets of distinct elements from it denoted as $\{1, \ldots, n\}$ and $\{-t, \ldots, 0\}$.
Input: The dealer holds a bivariate polynomial $S(x, y)$ of degree at most $2t$ in x and at most t in y. Each P_i initialises a happy bit $\mathsf{happy}_i = 1$[5].

1. **(Sharing)** The dealer sends $(f_i(x), g_i(y))$ to P_i where $f_i(x) = S(x, i)$, $g_i(y) = S(i, y)$.
2. **(Pairwise Consistency Checks)** Each P_i sends $(f_i(j), g_i(j))$ to every P_j. Let (f_{ji}, g_{ji}) be the values received by P_i from P_j. If $f_{ji} \neq g_i(j)$ or $g_{ji} \neq f_i(j)$, P_i broadcasts $\mathsf{complaint}(i, j, f_i(j), g_i(j))$.
3. **(Conflict Resolution)** For each $\mathsf{complaint}(i, j, u, v)$ such that $u \neq S(j, i)$ or $v \neq S(i, j)$, dealer broadcasts $g_i^D(y) = S(i, y)$. Let pubR be the set of parties for which the dealer broadcasts $g_i^D(y)$. Each $P_i \in \mathsf{pubR}$ sets $\mathsf{happy}_i = 0$. For two mutual complaints ($\mathsf{complaint}(i, j, u, v)$, $\mathsf{complaint}(j, i, u', v')$) with either $u \neq u'$ or $v \neq v'$, if the dealer does not broadcast anything, then discard the dealer.

---

[5] The happy bits will be used later for Multi-Moderated VSS in Sect. 6.

4. **(Identifying the CORE Set)** Each $P_i \notin$ pubR broadcasts OK if $f_i(k) = g_k^D(i)$ holds for every $k \in$ pubR. Otherwise, P_i sets happy$_i = 0$. Let CORE be the set of parties who broadcasted OK. If $|\text{CORE}| < 2t + 1$, then discard the dealer.

5. **(Revealing f-polynomials for non-CORE parties)** For each $P_k \notin$ CORE, the dealer broadcasts $f_k^D(x) = S(x, k)$. Discard the dealer if for any $P_j \in$ pubR and $P_k \notin$ CORE, $g_j^D(k) \neq f_k^D(j)$. Each $P_i \notin$ pubR broadcasts OK if $f_k^D(i) = g_i(k)$ holds for every broadcasted $f_k^D(x)$. Otherwise P_i sets happy$_i = 0$. Let $K = \{P_j | P_j \notin$ pubR and did not broadcast OK$\}$.

6. **(Opening g-polynomials for complaining parties)** For each $P_j \in K$, the dealer broadcasts $g_j^D(y) = S(j, y)$. Set pubR $=$ pubR $\cup K$. Discard the dealer if $f_k^D(j) \neq g_j^D(k)$ for any $P_k \notin$ CORE and $P_j \in K$. Each $P_i \in$ CORE with happy$_i = 1$ broadcasts OK if $f_i(j) = g_j^D(i)$ for every broadcasted $g_j^D(y)$. Otherwise, P_i sets happy$_i = 0$. If at least $2t + 1$ parties do not broadcast OK, then discard the dealer.

7. **(Output)** If the dealer is discarded, then each P_i outputs $\perp$. Otherwise, P_i outputs $(f_i(x), g_i(y))$, where $f_i(x) = f_i^D(x)$ if $P_i \notin$ CORE and $g_i(y) = g_i^D(y)$ if $P_i \in$ pubR.

Theorem 4.3. *Protocol Π_{pVSS} (Protocol 4.2) securely realizes $\mathcal{F}_{\text{VSS}}$ (Functionality 4.1) in the presence of a static malicious adversary controlling up to t parties with $t < n/3$.*

Lemma 4.4. *Protocol Π_{pVSS} has a communication complexity of $\mathcal{O}(n^2 \log n)$ bits over point-to-point channels and $\mathcal{O}(n^2 \log n)$ bits broadcast for sharing $\mathcal{O}(n)$ values (i.e., $\mathcal{O}(n \log n)$ bits) simultaneously in 9 rounds.*

5 Balanced Gradecast

In a Gradecast primitive, a dealer has an input and each party outputs a value and a grade $\{0, 1, 2\}$ such that the following properties are satisfied: **(Validity):** If the dealer is honest then all honest parties output the dealer's input and grade 2; **(Non-equivocation):** if two honest parties each output a grade ≥ 1 then they output the same value; and lastly **(Agreement):** if an honest party outputs grade 2 then all honest parties output the same output and with grade ≥ 1. We model this in terms of a functionality given in Functionality 5.1. The case of an honest dealer captures **validity**. Case 2a and Case 2b capture the **agreement** and **non-equivocation** respectively.

Functionality 5.1: $\mathcal{F}_{\text{Gradecast}}$

The functionality is parameterized by the set of corrupted parties, $I \subseteq \{1, \ldots, n\}$.

1. If the dealer is honest: the dealer sends m to the functionality, and all parties receive $(m, 2)$ as output.

2. If the dealer is corrupted then it sends some message M to the functionality.
   (a) If $M = (\mathsf{ExistsGrade2}, m, (g_j)_{j \notin I})$ for some $m \in \{0,1\}^*$ and each $g_j \in \{1,2\}$, then verify that each $g_j \geq 1$ and that at least one honest party receives grade 2. Send (m, g_j) to each party P_j.
   (b) If $M = (\mathsf{NoGrade2}, (m_j, g_j)_{j \notin I})$ where each $m_j \in \{0,1\}^*$ and $g_j \in \{0,1\}$, then verify that for every $j, k \notin I$ with $g_j = g_k = 1$ it holds that $m_j = m_k$. Then, send (m_j, g_j) to each party P_j.

In Sect. 5.1 we first describe a protocol that is not balanced, i.e., the total communication complexity is $\mathcal{O}(n^2 L)$ but in which the dealer sends $\mathcal{O}(n^2 L)$ and every other party sends $\mathcal{O}(nL)$. In Sect. 5.2 we show how to make the protocol balanced, in which each party (including the dealer) sends/receives $\mathcal{O}(nL)$ bits.

5.1 The Gradecast Protocol

We build our construction in Protocol 5.2 using the idea presented in Sect. 2.3. Recall that the gradecast used inside our protocol is the naïve gradecast with complexity $\mathcal{O}(n^2 L)$ bits for L-bit message, as in [29, 31]. The security of our protocol is stated in Theorem 5.3 and the proof appears in the full version.

Protocol 5.2: $\Pi_{\mathsf{Gradecast}}$

Input: The dealer $P \in \{P_1, \ldots, P_n\}$ holds $(t+1)^2$ field elements $(b_{i,j})_{i,j \in \{0,\ldots,t\}}$ where each $b_{i,j} \in \mathbb{F}$ that it wishes to distribute. All other parties have no input.

1. **(Dealer's polynomial distribution) The dealer:**
   (a) The dealer views its elements as a bivariate polynomial of degree at most t in both x and y, i.e., $S(x,y) = \sum_{i=0}^{t} \sum_{j=0}^{t} b_{i,j} x^i y^j$.
   (b) The dealer sends $S(x,y)$ to all parties.
2. **(Pair-wise Information Exchange) Each party P_i:**
   (a) Let $S_i(x,y)$ be the polynomial received from the dealer.
   (b) P_i sends to each party P_j the four polynomials $(S_i(x,j), S_i(j,y), S_i(x,i), S_i(i,y))$.
3. **(Informing dealer about consistency) Each party P_i:**
   (a) Initialize $\mathsf{Agreed}_i = \emptyset$. Let $(f_i^j(x), g_i^j(y), f_j^j(x), g_j^j(y))$ be the polynomials received from party P_j. If $f_i^j(x) = S_i(x,i)$, $g_i^j(y) = S_i(i,y)$, $f_j^j = S_i(x,j)$ and $g_j^j(y) = S_i(j,y)$ then add j to Agreed_i.
   (b) Send Agreed_i to the dealer.
4. **(Quorum forming by dealer) The dealer:**
   (a) Define an undirected graph G as follows: The nodes are $\{1, \ldots, n\}$ and an edge $\{i,j\} \in G$ if and only if $i \in \mathsf{Agreed}_j$ and $j \in \mathsf{Agreed}_i$. Use STAR algorithm (Algorithm ??) to find a set $(C, D) \in \{1, \ldots, n\}^2$ where $|C| \geq t+1$ and $|D| \geq 2t+1$, $C \subseteq D$, such that for every $c \in C$ and $d \in D$ it holds that $c \in \mathsf{Agreed}_d$ and $d \in \mathsf{Agreed}_c$.

(b) Let E be the set of parties that agree with at least $t + 1$ parties in C. That is, initialize $E = \emptyset$ and add i to E if $|\mathsf{Agreed}_i \cap C| \geq t + 1$.

(c) Let F be the set of parties that agree with at least $2t + 1$ parties in E. That is, initialize $F = \emptyset$ and add i to F if $|\mathsf{Agreed}_i \cap E| \geq 2t + 1$.

(d) If $|C| \geq t + 1$ and $|D|, |E|, |F| \geq 2t + 1$, then gradecast (C, D, E, F). Otherwise, gradecast $(\emptyset, \emptyset, \emptyset, \emptyset)$.

5. **(First reaffirmation) Each party P_i:**

   (a) Let (C_i, D_i, E_i, F_i, g) be the message that the dealer gradecasted and let g be the associated grade.

   (b) If (1) $g = 2$; (2) $i \in C_i$; (3) $|D_i| \geq 2t + 1$; and (4) $\mathsf{Agreed}_i \cap D_i = D_i$; then send OK_C to all parties. Otherwise, send nothing.

6. **(Second reaffirmation) Each party P_i:**

   (a) Let C_i' be the set of parties that sent OK_C in the previous round.

   (b) If $i \in E_i$ and $|\mathsf{Agreed}_i \cap C_i \cap C_i'| \geq t + 1$ then send OK_E to all parties.

7. **(Third reaffirmation and propagation) Each party P_i:**

   (a) Let E_i' be the set of parties that sent OK_E in the previous round.

   (b) If $i \in F_i$ and $|\mathsf{Agreed}_i \cap E_i \cap E_i'| \geq 2t + 1$ then send $(\mathsf{OK}_F, S_i(x, j), S_i(j, y))$ to each party P_j.

8. **(Final propagation) Each party P_i:** Among all messages that were received in the previous round, if there exist polynomials $f_i'(x), g_i'(y)$ that were received at least $t + 1$ times, then forward those polynomials to all. Otherwise, forward $\perp$.

9. **(Output) Each party P_i:** Let $((f_1'(x), g_1'(y)), \ldots, (f_n'(x), g_n'(y))$ be the messages received in the previous round. If received at least $2t + 1$ polynomials that are not $\perp$, then use robust interpolation to obtain a polynomial $S'(x, y)$. If there is no unique reconstruction or less than $2t + 1$ polynomials received, then output $(\perp, 0)$. Otherwise, if $S'(x, y)$ is unique, then:

   (a) If (1) P_i sent OK_F in Round 7; and (2) it received $2t + 1$ messages OK_F at the end of Round 7 from parties in F_i with the same polynomials $(f_i'(x), g_i'(y))$; then output $(S', 2)$.

   (b) Otherwise, output $(S', 1)$.

Theorem 5.3. *Let $t < n/3$. Protocol $\Pi_{\mathsf{Gradecast}}$ (Protocol 5.2) securely realizes Functionality $\mathcal{F}_{\mathsf{Gradecast}}$ (Functionality 5.1) in the presence of a malicious adversary controlling at most t parties. The parties send at most $\mathcal{O}(n^3 \log n)$ bits where $\mathcal{O}(n^2 \log n)$ is the number of bits of the dealer's input.*

5.2   Making the Protocol Balanced

To make the protocol balanced, note that each party sends or receives $\mathcal{O}(n^2 \log n)$ bits except for the dealer who sends $\mathcal{O}(n^3 \log n)$. We therefore change the first round of the protocol as follows:

1. **The dealer:**
   (a) The dealer views its elements as a bivariate polynomial of degree at most t in both x and y, i.e., $S(x, y) = \sum_{i=0}^{t} \sum_{j=0}^{t} b_{i,j} x^i y^j$.
   (b) The dealer sends $S(x, i)$ to each party P_i.
2. **Each party P_i:**
   (a) Forwards the message received from the dealer to every other party.
   (b) Given all univariate polynomials received, say $u(x, 1), \ldots, u(x, n)$, runs the Reed-Solomon decoding procedure to obtain the bivariate polynomial $S_i(x, y)$. If there is no unique decoding, then use $S_i(x, y) = \bot$.
3. Continue to run Protocol $\Pi_{\text{Gradecast}}$ (Protocol 5.2) from Step 2 to the end while interpreting $S_i(x, y)$ decoded from the prior round as the polynomial received from the dealer.

Theorem 5.4. *The modified protocol securely realizes Functionality $\mathcal{F}_{\text{Gradecast}}$ (Functionality 5.1) in the presence of a malicious adversary controlling at most t parties. Each party, including the dealer sends or receives $\mathcal{O}(n^2 \log n)$ bits (giving a total communication complexity of $\mathcal{O}(n^3 \log n)$).*

The following is a simple corollary, where for general message length of L bits the dealer simply breaks the message into $\ell = \lceil L/(t+1)^2 \log n \rceil$ blocks and runs ℓ parallel executions of gradecast. Each party outputs the concatenation of all executions, with the minimum grade obtained on all executions. The protocol is optimal for $L > n^2 \log n$. We thus obtain the following corollary.

Corollary 5.5. *Let $t < n/3$. There exists a gradecast protocol in the presence of a malicious adversary controlling at most t parties, where for transmitting L bits, the protocol requires the transmission of $\mathcal{O}(nL + n^3 \log n)$ bits, where each party sends or receives $\mathcal{O}(L + n^2 \log n)$ bits.*

6   Multi-moderated Packed Secret Sharing

At a high level multi-moderated packed secret sharing is a packed VSS moderated by a set $\mathcal{M}$ of $t + 1$ distinguished parties called moderators. The parties output a flag for every moderator in the end. We represent the flag for a moderator $M \in \mathcal{M}$ held by a party P_k as v_M^k. In addition, each party P_k holds a variable d_M^k taking values from $\{\text{accept}, \text{reject}\}$ for each $M \in \mathcal{M}$ which identifies whether the dealer is accepted or rejected when M assumes the role of the moderator.

If a moderator M is honest, then every honest party P_k will set $v_M^k = 1$ and the properties of VSS will be satisfied irrespective of whether the dealer is honest or corrupt. If the dealer is honest, every honest P_k will set $d_M^k = \text{accept}$. For a corrupt dealer, the bit can be 0 or 1 based on the dealer's behaviour, but all the honest parties will unanimously output the same outcome.

If a moderator M is corrupt, then it is guaranteed that: if some honest party P_k sets the flag $v_M^k = 1$, then the properties of VSS will be satisfied irrespective of whether the dealer is honest or corrupt. That is, if the dealer is honest every honest P_k outputs $d_M^k = \text{accept}$. For a corrupt dealer, it is guaranteed that all the honest parties unanimously output the same outcome for the dealer. We note that when no honest party sets its flag to 1 for a moderator M, then irrespective for whether the dealer is honest or corrupt, it is possible that the parties do not have agreement on their d_M^k. The functionality is defined as follows:

Functionality 6.1: $\mathcal{F}_{\mathsf{mm-pVSS}}$ – Multi-moderated Packed Secret Sharing

---

The functionality is parameterized by the set of corrupted parties $I \subseteq \{1, \ldots, n\}$, a set $\mathcal{M}$ of $t+1$ distinguished parties called as moderators.

1. The dealer sends polynomials $f_j(x), g_j(y)$ for every j. If the dealer is honest, then there exists a single $(2t, t)$ polynomial $S(x, y)$ that satisfies $f_j(x) = S(x, j)$ and $g_j(y) = S(j, y)$ for every $j \in \{1, \ldots, n\}$.
2. If the dealer is honest, then send $f_i(x), g_i(y)$ for every $i \in I$ to the adversary.
3. For each moderator $M_j \in \mathcal{M}$:
   (a) If the moderator M_j is honest, then set $v_{M_j}^k = 1$ for every $k \in \{1, \ldots, n\}$. Moreover:
      i. If the dealer is honest, then set $\mathsf{d}_{M_j}^k = \mathsf{accept}$ for every $k \in \{1, \ldots, n\}$.
      ii. If the dealer is corrupt, then receive a message m_j from the adversary. If $m_j = \mathsf{accept}$ then verify that the shares of the honest parties define a unique $(2t, t)$-polynomial. If so, set $\mathsf{d}_{M_j}^k = \mathsf{accept}$ for every $k \in \{1, \ldots, n\}$. In any other case, set $\mathsf{d}_{M_j}^k = \mathsf{reject}$ for every $k \in \{1, \ldots, n\}$.

   (b) If the moderator M_j is corrupt then receive m_j from the adversary.
      i. If $m_j = (\mathsf{Agreement}, (v_{M_j}^k)_{k \notin I}), \mathsf{d}_{M_j})$ where $\mathsf{d}_{M_j} \in \{\mathsf{accept}, \mathsf{reject}\}$, and for some $k \notin I$ it holds that $v_{M_j}^k = 1$. Set $(v_{M_j}^k)_{k \notin I}$ as received from the adversary. Verify that $S(x, y)$ is $(2t, t)$-polynomial. If not, set $\mathsf{d}_{M_j}^k = \mathsf{reject}$ for every $k \notin I$. Otherwise, set $\mathsf{d}_{M_j}^k = \mathsf{d}_{M_j}$ for every $k \notin I$.
      ii. If $m_j = (\mathsf{NoAgreement}, (\mathsf{d}_{M_j}^k)_{k \notin I})$ where each $\mathsf{d}_{M_j}^k \in \{\mathsf{accept}, \mathsf{reject}\}$, then set $v_{M_j}^k = 0$ for every $k \in \{1, \ldots, n\}$ and $\mathsf{d}_{M_j}^1, \ldots, \mathsf{d}_{M_j}^n$ as received from the adversary.
4. **Output:** Each honest party P_k $(k \notin I)$ receives as output $f_i(x), g_i(y)$, $(\mathsf{d}_M^k)_{M \in \mathcal{M}}$, and flags $(v_M^k)_{M \in \mathcal{M}}$.

To clarify, each party P_i receives global shares for all moderators, and an output d_M^i and flag v_M^i for each moderator $M \in \mathcal{M}$. If the dealer and the moderator are honest, then all the flags are 1 and the parties accept the shares. If the moderator M_j is corrupted, then as long as there is one honest party P_k with $v_{M_j}^k = 1$ there will be an agreement in the outputs $\mathsf{d}_{M_j}^1, \ldots, \mathsf{d}_{M_j}^n$ (either all the honest parties accept or all of them reject). When $v_{M_j}^k = 0$ for all the honest parties, we might have inconsistency in the outputs $\mathsf{d}_{M_j}^1, \ldots, \mathsf{d}_{M_j}^n$ with respect to that moderator.

The Protocol. We build on the discussion given in Sect. 2.1. We consider the protocol of VSS where the dealer inputs some bivariate polynomial $S(x, y)$ of degree at most $2t$ in x and degree at most t in y. For multi-moderated packed secret sharing, essentially, each broadcast from Π_{pVSS} is simulated with two sequential gradecasts. The first gradecast is performed by the party which intends to broadcast in the underlying packed VSS protocol, while the second is executed by a moderator. Note that these gradecasts are realized via the protocol $\Pi_{\mathsf{Gradecast}}$, presented in the Sect. 5, having the optimal communication complexity. Up to Step 6 of Π_{pVSS} (Protocol 4.2), the dealer is the moderator for each gradecast. At Step 6, we fork into $t + 1$ executions, with a unique party acting as the moderator in each execution. Since the protocol steps remain similar to Π_{pVSS}, we describe the multi-moderated packed secret sharing protocol below in terms of how the broadcast is simulated at each step and the required changes at Step 6 of the packed VSS protocol.

Protocol 6.2: $\Pi_{\mathsf{mm\text{-}pVSS}}$ – Multi-moderated Packed Secret Sharing

---

Simulating broadcast up to (including) Step 6 of Π_{pVSS}:

1. Simulating broadcast of a message by the dealer.
   (a) **The dealer:** When the dealer has to broadcast a message m it gradecasts it.
   (b) **Party P_i:** Let (m, g) be the message gradecasted by the dealer, where m is the message and g is the grade. Proceed with m as the message broadcasted by the dealer. If $g \neq 2$, then set $\mathsf{happy}_i = 0$ within the execution of Π_{pVSS}.
2. Simulating broadcast of a party P_j.
   (a) **Party P_j:** When P_j wishes to broadcast a message m, it first gradecasts it.
   (b) **The dealer:** Let (m, g) be the message and g its associated grade. The dealer gradecasts m.
   (c) **Each party P_i:** Let (m', g') be the messages gradecasted by the dealer. Use m' as the message broadcasted by P_j in the protocol. Moreover, if $g' \neq 2$; or if $g = 2$ but $m' \neq m$, then P_i sets $\mathsf{happy}_i = 0$ within the execution of Π_{pVSS}.

After Step 6 of Π_{pVSS}:

1. **Each party P_i:** Set $v_{M_j}^i = 1$, and let $f_i(x), g_i(y)$ be the pair of shares P_i is holding at end of Step 6. Gradecast accept if $\mathsf{happy}_i = 1$ and reject otherwise. At this point, we fork into $|\mathcal{M}|$ executions, one per moderator $M_j \in \mathcal{M}$ as follows:
   (a) **The moderator M_j:** Let $(a_1, \ldots, a_n)$ be the decisions of all parties as received from the gradecast. Gradecast $(a_1, \ldots, a_n)$.
   (b) **Each party P_i:** Let $(a_1, \ldots, a_n)$ be the decisions received directly from the parties, and let $(a_1', \ldots, a_n')$ be the message gradecasted from the moderator M_j with associated grade g'. Set $v_{M_j}^i = 0$ if $g' \neq 2$, or there exists a_k received from P_k with grade 2 but for which $a_k \neq a_k'$. Then:

     i. If there exists $2t+1$ accepts within $(a'_1, \ldots, a'_n)$, then set $\mathsf{d}^i_{M_j} = \mathsf{accept}$.

     ii. Otherwise, set $\mathsf{d}^i_{M_j} = \mathsf{reject}$.

2. **Output:** P_i outputs $(f_i(x), g_i(y)), (\mathsf{d}^i_{M_1}, \ldots, \mathsf{d}^i_{M_t})$ and $(v^i_{M_1}, \ldots, v^i_{M_t})$.

Theorem 6.3. *Protocol 6.2 computes $\mathcal{F}_{\mathsf{mm}\text{-}\mathsf{pVSS}}$ (Functionality 6.1) in the presence of a malicious adversary corrupting at most $t < n/3$ parties. The protocol requires the transmission of $\mathcal{O}(n^2 \log n)$ bits over point-to-point channels, the dealer gradecasts $\mathcal{O}(n^2 \log n)$ bits, and each party gradecasts at most $n \log n$ bits.*

6.1   Reconstruction

The reconstruction protocol ensures that even for a corrupt moderator, all the honest parties reconstruct the same value when its flag is set to 1 by some honest party. This aligns with the guarantees of the sharing phase, which ensures that the protocol achieves VSS corresponding to a moderator when there exists an honest party with its flag set to 1 at the end of the sharing phase.

Protocol 6.4: $\Pi^{\mathsf{Rec}}_{\mathsf{mm}\text{-}\mathsf{pVSS}}$ – Reconstruct of Multi-Moderated Packed Secret Sharing

---

The protocol is parameterized by the set of moderators $\mathcal{M}$ and a set B containing $|\mathcal{M}|$ distinct non-zero values in the field. To be specific B denotes the set $\{-t, \ldots, 0\}$ used in Π_{pVSS}. We assume a one-to-one mapping between $\mathcal{M}$ and $\{-t, \ldots, 0\}$.

Input: Each party P_i holds $(f_i(x), g_i(y)), (\mathsf{d}^i_M)_{M \in \mathcal{M}}$ and $(v^i_M)_{M \in \mathcal{M}}$.

1. Each party sends $f_i(x)$ to all. Let $(f_1(x)', \ldots, f_n(x)')$ be the polynomials received.
2. For each $M \in \mathcal{M}$ (let $\beta^* \in B$ be its associated value):
    (a) If $\mathsf{d}^i_M = \mathsf{accept}$, then use Reed Solomon decoding procedure to reconstruct the unique degree-t polynomial $g_{\beta^*}(y)$ that agrees with at least $2t + 1$ values $f_1(\beta^*), \ldots, f_n(\beta^*)$ and set $s^i_M = g_{\beta^*}(0)$. If there is not unique decoding, then set $s^i_M = 0$.
    (b) If $\mathsf{d}^i_M = \mathsf{reject}$, then set $s^i_M = 0$.
3. **Output:** Output $(s^i_M)_{M \in \mathcal{M}}$.

Theorem 6.5. *For each moderator $M \in \mathcal{M}$, if there exists an honest party with $v^k_M = 1$ then all honest parties hold the same $s^{k'}_M = s^k_M$.*

7   Oblivious Leader Election

We start with the functionality which captures OLE with fairness δ, where each party P_i outputs a value $\ell_i \in \{1, \ldots, n\}$ such that with probability at least δ there exists a value $\ell \in \{1, \ldots, n\}$ for which the following conditions hold: (a) each honest P_i outputs $\ell_i = \ell$, and (b) P_ℓ is an honest party. The functionality is parameterized by the set of corrupted parties I, a parameter $\delta > 0$ and a family of efficiently sampling distributions $\mathcal{D} = \{D\}$. Each $D \in \mathcal{D}$ is a distribution $D : \{0,1\}^{\mathsf{poly}(n)} \to \{1, \ldots, n\}^n$ satisfying: $\Pr_{r \leftarrow \{0,1\}^{\mathsf{poly}(n)}} [D(r) = (j, \ldots, j) \text{ s.t. } j \notin I] \geq \delta$.

Functionality 7.1: $\mathcal{F}_{\mathsf{OLE}}$ – **Oblivious Leader Election Functionality**

The functionality is parameterized by the set of corrupted parties $I \subset \{1, \ldots, n\}$ and the family $\mathcal{D}$.

1. The functionality receives from the adversary a sampler D and verifies that $D \in \mathcal{D}$. If not, then it takes some default sampler in $D \in \mathcal{D}$.
2. The functionality chooses a random $r \leftarrow \{0,1\}^{\mathsf{poly}(n)}$ and samples $(\ell_1, \ldots, \ell_n) = D(r)$.
3. It hands r to the adversary and it hands ℓ_i to every party P_i .

Looking ahead, our protocol will define a family $\mathcal{D}$ in which the functionality can efficiently determine whether a given sampler D is a member of $\mathcal{D}$. Specifically, we define the sampler as a parametrized algorithm with some specific values hardwired. Therefore, the ideal adversary can just send those parameters to the functionality to specify D in the family.

Protocol 7.2: Π_{OLE} – **Oblivious Leader Election Protocol**

---

1. **Choose and commit weights:** Each party $P_i \in \mathcal{P}$ acts as the dealer and chooses $c_{i \to j}$ as random values in $\{1, \ldots, n^4\}$, for every $j \in \{1, \ldots, n\}$. P_i then runs the following for $T := \lceil n/t + 1 \rceil$ times in parallel. That is, for $\ell \in [1, \ldots, T]$, each P_i acting as the dealer executes the following in parallel:
   (a) Let the set of moderators be $\mathcal{M}_\ell = (P_{(\ell-1) \cdot (t+1)+1}, \ldots, P_{\ell \cdot (t+1)})$.
   (b) The dealer P_i chooses a random $(2t, t)$-bivariate polynomial $S^{i,\ell}(x, y)$ while hiding the $t+1$ values $c_{i \to j}$ for every $j \in \{(\ell-1) \cdot (t+1)+1, \ldots, \ell \cdot (t+1)\}$, one corresponding to each moderator $P_j \in \mathcal{M}_\ell$. Specifically, P_i chooses $S^{i,\ell}(x, y)$ such that $S^{i,\ell}(0,0) = c_{i \to (\ell-1) \cdot (t+1)+1}$ and so on till $S^{i,\ell}(-t, 0) = c_{i \to \ell \cdot (t+1)}$. The parties invoke $\mathcal{F}_{\mathsf{mm-pVSS}}$ (Fig. 6.1) where P_i is the dealer, and the moderators are parties in $\mathcal{M}_\ell$.
   (c) Each party P_k gets as output a pair of shares $f_k^{i,\ell}(x), g_k^{i,\ell}(y)$, outputs $\mathsf{d}_{i,j}^k$ and a flag $v_{i,j}^k$ for each moderator $P_j \in \mathcal{M}_\ell$.

Note that the above is run for all dealers $P_1, \ldots, P_n$ in parallel, where each dealer has T parallel instances (in total $T \cdot n$ invocations).

Upon completion of the above, let $\mathsf{succeeded}_i$ be the set of moderators for which P_i holds a flag 1 in all executions, i.e., $\mathsf{succeeded}_i := \{j \mid v_{d,j}^i = 1$ for all dealers $P_d \in \mathcal{P}\}$.

2. **Reconstruct the weights and pick a leader:** The reconstruction phase, $\Pi_{\mathsf{mm\text{-}pVSS}}^{\mathsf{Rec}}$ (Fig. 6.4) of each of the above nT instances of multi-moderated packed secret sharing is run in parallel to reconstruct the secrets previously shared.

Let $c_{i \to j}^k$ denote P_k's view of the value $c_{i \to j}$ for every $i, j \in \{1, \ldots, n\}$, i.e., the reconstructed value for the instance where P_i is the dealer and P_j is the moderator.

Each party P_k sets $c_j^k = \sum_{i=1}^n c_{i \to j}^k \bmod n^4$ and outputs j that minimizes c_j^k among all $j \in \mathsf{succeeded}_k$ (break ties arbitrarily).

Theorem 7.3. *Protocol* Π_{OLE} *(Protocol 7.2) computes* $\mathcal{F}_{\mathsf{OLE}}$ *(Functionality 7.1) in the presence of a malicious adversary corrupting at most* $t < n/3$ *parties. The protocol requires a transmission of* $\mathcal{O}(n^4 \log n)$ *bits over point-to-point channels.*

8   Broadcast

8.1   Byzantine Agreement

In a Byzantine agreement, every party P_i holds initial input v_i and the following properties hold: **(Agreement):** All the honest parties output the same value; **(Validity):** If all the honest parties begin with the same input value v, then all the honest parties output v. We simply plug in our OLE in the Byzantine agreement of [41]. As described in Sect. 1.3, we present standalone functionalities for Byzantine agreement and broadcast, where the intricacies of sequential composition are tackled in [23]. The protocol for byzantine agreement (Π_{BA}) which follows from [41] and its proof of security appear in the full version of the paper.

Functionality 8.1: $\mathcal{F}_{\mathsf{BA}}$ – Byzantine Agreement

The functionality is parameterized by the set of corrupted parties I.

1. The functionality receives from each honest party P_j its input $b_j \in \{0, 1\}$. The functionality sends $(b_j)_{j \notin I}$ to the adversary.
2. The adversary sends a bit b.
3. If there exists a bit b such that $b_j = b$ for every $j \notin I$, then set $y = b$. Otherwise, set $y = \hat{b}$.
4. Send y to all parties.

Theorem 8.2. *Protocol* Π_{BA} *is a Byzantine agreement protocol tolerating* $t < n/3$ *malicious parties that works in constant expected rounds and requires the transmission of* $\mathcal{O}(n^2)$ *bits plus expected* $\mathcal{O}(n^4 \log n)$ *bits of communication.*

8.2   Broadcast and Parallel-broadcast

In a broadcast protocol, a distinguished dealer $P^* \in \mathcal{P}$ holds an initial input M and the following hold: **(Agreement):** All honest parties output the same value; **Validity:** If the dealer is honest, then all honest parties output M. We formalize it using the following functionality:

Functionality 8.3: $\mathcal{F}_{\mathsf{BC}}$

The functionality is parametrized with a parameter L.

1. The dealer (sender) P^* sends the functionality its message $M \in \{0,1\}^L$.
2. The functionality sends to all parties the message M.

To implement this functionality, the dealer just gradecasts its message M and then parties run Byzantine agreement on the grade they received, while parties use input 1 for the Byzantine agreement if and only if the grade of the gradecast is 2. If the output of the Byzantine agreement is 1, then they output the message they received in the gradecast, and otherwise, they output $\perp$. We simply plug in our gradecast and Byzantine agreement in the protocol below. Note that the communication complexity our protocol is asymptotically free (up to the expectation) for $L > n^3 \log n$.

Protocol 8.4: Π_{BC}– **Broadcast Protocol for a single dealer**

- **Input:** The dealer holds a message $M \in \{0,1\}^L$.
- **Common input:** A parameter L.
  1. **The dealer:** Gradecast M.
  2. **Each party P_i:** Let M' be the resultant message and let g be the associated grade. All parties run Byzantine agreement where the input of P_i is 1 if $g = 2$, and otherwise the input is 0.
- **Output:** If the output of the Byzantine agreement is 1 then output M'. Otherwise, output $\perp$.

Theorem 8.5. *Protocol 8.4 is a secure broadcast tolerating $t < n/3$ malicious parties. For an input message M of length L bits, the protocol requires $\mathcal{O}(nL)$ plus expected $\mathcal{O}(n^4 \log n)$ bits total communication, and constant expected rounds.*

Parallel Broadcast. Parallel broadcast relates to the case where n parties wish to broadcast a message of size L bits in parallel. In that case, we rely on an idea of Fitzi and Garay [33] that applies to OLE-based protocols. The idea is that the multiple broadcast sub-routines are run in parallel when only a single election per iteration is required for all these sub-routines. This results in the following corollary:

Corollary 8.6. *There exists a perfectly secure parallel-broadcast with optimal resilience, which allows n parties to broadcast messages of size L bits each, at the cost of $\mathcal{O}(n^2 L)$ bits communication, plus $\mathcal{O}(n^4 \log n)$ expected communicating bits. The protocols runs in constant expected number of rounds.*

For completeness, we provide the functionality for parallel broadcast below, and omit the proof since it follows from broadcast.

Functionality 8.7: $\mathcal{F}_{\mathsf{BC}}^{\mathsf{parallel}}$

The functionality is parametrized with a parameter L.

1. Each $P_i \in \mathcal{P}$ sends the functionality its message $M_i \in \{0,1\}^L$.
2. The functionality sends to all parties the message $\{M_i\}_{i \in \{1,\dots,n\}}$.

Efficiency. The protocol gradecasts n messages, each of which requires $O(nL)$ bits of communication and runs in constant rounds. In addition, we run Byzantine agreement where a single leader election per iteration is necessary across all the instances, which requires expected $O(n^4 \log n)$ bits of communication in expected constant rounds.

Acknowledgements. Gilad Asharov is sponsored by the Israel Science Foundation (grant No. 2439/20), by JPM Faculty Research Award, by the BIU Center for Research in Applied Cryptography and Cyber Security in conjunction with the Israel National Cyber Bureau in the Prime Minister's Office, and by the European Union's Horizon 2020 research and innovation programme under the Marie Skłodowska-Curie grant agreement No. 891234. Shravani Patil would like to acknowledge the support of DST National Mission on Interdisciplinary Cyber-Physical Systems (NM-ICPS) 2020-2025. Arpita Patra would like to acknowledge the support of DST National Mission on Interdisciplinary Cyber-Physical Systems (NM-ICPS) 2020-2025, Google India Faculty Award, and SERB MATRICS (Theoretical Sciences) Grant 2020-2023.

References

1. Aws latency monitoring. https://www.cloudping.co/grid. Accessed February 2022
2. Abraham, I., Asharov, G., Yanai, A.: Efficient perfectly secure computation with optimal resilience. In: Nissim, K., Waters, B. (eds.) TCC 2021. LNCS, vol. 13043, pp. 66–96. Springer, Cham (2021). https://doi.org/10.1007/978-3-030-90453-1_3
3. Abraham, I., Devadas, S., Dolev, D., Nayak, K., Ren, L.: Synchronous byzantine agreement with expected $O(1)$ rounds, expected $O(n^2)$ communication, and optimal resilience. In: Goldberg, I., Moore, T. (eds.) FC 2019. LNCS, vol. 11598, pp. 320–334. Springer, Cham (2019). https://doi.org/10.1007/978-3-030-32101-7_20
4. Abraham, I., Nayak, K.: Crusader agreement with $\leq 1/3$ error is impossible for $n \leq 3f$ if the adversary can simulate. Decentralized Thoughts, Blog Post (2021). https://tinyurl.com/decentralizedthougts. Accessed Sept 2021
5. Applebaum, B., Kachlon, E., Patra, A.: The round complexity of perfect MPC with active security and optimal resiliency. In: FOCS (2020)

6. Asharov, G., Cohen, R., Shochat, O.: Static vs. adaptive security in perfect MPC: a separation and the adaptive security of BGW. In: Conference on Information-Theoretic Cryptography - ITC 2022. (To Appear) (2022)

7. Asharov, G., Lindell, Y.: A full proof of the bgw protocol for perfectly secure multiparty computation. J. Cryptol. **30**(1), 58–151 (2017). https://doi.org/10.1007/s00145-015-9214-4

8. Asharov, G., Lindell, Y., Rabin, T.: Perfectly-secure multiplication for any t < n/3. In: Rogaway, P. (ed.) CRYPTO 2011. LNCS, vol. 6841, pp. 240–258. Springer, Berlin (2011). https://doi.org/10.1007/978-3-642-22792-9_14

9. Beerliová-Trubíniová, Z., Hirt, M.: Perfectly-secure MPC with linear communication complexity. In: Canetti, R. (ed.) TCC 2008. LNCS, vol. 4948, pp. 213–230. Springer, Heidelberg (2008). https://doi.org/10.1007/978-3-540-78524-8_13

10. Ben-Or, M.: Another advantage of free choice: completely asynchronous agreement protocols (extended abstract). In: PODC (1983)

11. Ben-Or, M., El-Yaniv, R.: Resilient-optimal interactive consistency in constant time. Distrib. Comput. **16**, 249–262 (2003). https://doi.org/10.1007/s00446-002-0083-3

12. Ben-Or, M., Goldwasser, S., Wigderson, A.: Completeness theorems for non-cryptographic fault-tolerant distributed computation (extended abstract). In: ACM Symposium on Theory of Computing (1988)

13. Berman, P., Garay, J.A., Perry, K.J.: Bit optimal distributed consensus. In: Baeza-Yates, R., Manber, U. (eds.) Computer Science. Springer, Boston (1992)

14. Canetti, R.: Asynchronous secure computation. Technion - Computer Science Department - Technical report (1993)

15. Canetti, R.: Studies in secure multiparty computation and applications. Ph.D. thesis, Citeseer (1996)

16. Canetti, R.: Security and composition of multiparty cryptographic protocols. J. Cryptology **13**(1), 143–202 (2000). https://doi.org/10.1007/s001459910006

17. Canetti, R.: Universally composable security: a new paradigm for cryptographic protocols. In: FOCS (2001)

18. Canetti, R., Damgaard, I., Dziembowski, S., Ishai, Y., Malkin, T.: On adaptive vs. non-adaptive security of multiparty protocols. In: Pfitzmann, B. (ed.) EUROCRYPT 2001. LNCS, vol. 2045, pp. 262–279. Springer, Heidelberg (2001). https://doi.org/10.1007/3-540-44987-6_17

19. Chaum, D., Crépeau, C., Damgård, I.: Multiparty unconditionally secure protocols (extended abstract). In: ACM Symposium on Theory of Computing (1988)

20. Chen, J.: Optimal error-free multi-valued byzantine agreement. In: DISC (2021)

21. Chor, B., Goldwasser, S., Micali, S., Awerbuch, B.: Verifiable secret sharing and achieving simultaneity in the presence of faults (extended abstract). In: 26th Annual Symposium on Foundations of Computer Science (1985)

22. Coan, B.A., Welch, J.L.: Modular construction of nearly optimal byzantine agreement protocols. In: ACM Symposium on Principles of Distributed Computing (1989)

23. Cohen, R., Coretti, S., Garay, J., Zikas, V.: Probabilistic termination and composability of cryptographic protocols. J. Cryptology **32**(3), 690–741 (2018). https://doi.org/10.1007/s00145-018-9279-y

24. Cramer, R., Damgård, I., Maurer, U.: General secure multi-party computation from any linear secret-sharing scheme. In: Preneel, B. (ed.) EUROCRYPT 2000. LNCS, vol. 1807, pp. 316–334. Springer, Heidelberg (2000). https://doi.org/10.1007/3-540-45539-6_22

25. Damgård, I., David, B., Giacomelli, I., Nielsen, J.B.: Compact VSS and efficient homomorphic UC commitments. In: Sarkar, P., Iwata, T. (eds.) ASIACRYPT 2014. LNCS, vol. 8874, pp. 213–232. Springer, Heidelberg (2014). https://doi.org/10.1007/978-3-662-45608-8_12

26. Das, S., Xiang, Z., Ren, L.: Asynchronous data dissemination and its applications. In: ACM CCS Conference on Computer and Communications Security (2021)

27. Dolev, D., Reischuk, R.: Bounds on information exchange for byzantine agreement. In: Symposium on Principles of Distributed Computing (1982)

28. Dolev, D., Reischuk, R.: Bounds on information exchange for byzantine agreement. J. ACM (JACM) **32**(1), 191–204 (1985)

29. Feldman, P., Micali, S.: Optimal algorithms for byzantine agreement. In: ACM Symposium on Theory of Computing (1988)

30. Feldman, P.N.: Optimal Algorithms for Byzantine Agreement. Ph.D. thesis, Massachusetts Institute of Technology (1988)

31. Feldman, P., Micali, S.: An optimal probabilistic protocol for synchronous byzantine agreement. SIAM J. Comput. **26**(4), 873–933 (1997)

32. Fischer, M.J., Lynch, N.A.: A lower bound for the time to assure interactive consistency. Information Processing Letters (1982)

33. Fitzi, M., Garay, J.A.: Efficient player-optimal protocols for strong and differential consensus. In: PODC (2003)

34. Franklin, M.K., Yung, M.: Communication complexity of secure computation (extended abstract). In: ACM Symposium on Theory of Computing (1992)

35. Ganesh, C., Patra, A.: Optimal extension protocols for byzantine broadcast and agreement. Distrib. Comput. **34**, 59–77 (2021). https://doi.org/10.1007/s00446-020-00384-1

36. Gennaro, R., Ishai, Y., Kushilevitz, E., Rabin, T.: The round complexity of verifiable secret sharing and secure multicast. In: STOC (2001)

37. Gennaro, R., Rabin, M.O., Rabin, T.: Simplified vss and fast-track multiparty computations with applications to threshold cryptography. In: PODC (1998)

38. Goldreich, O., Petrank, E.: The best of both worlds: guaranteeing termination in fast randomized byzantine agreement protocols. Inf. Process. Lett. **36**(1), 45–49 (1990)

39. Goyal, V., Liu, Y., Song, Y.: Communication-efficient unconditional mpc with guaranteed output delivery. In: Boldyreva, A., Micciancio, D. (eds.) CRYPTO 2019. LNCS, vol. 11693, pp. 85–114. Springer, Cham (2019). https://doi.org/10.1007/978-3-030-26951-7_4

40. Hirt, M., Maurer, U., Przydatek, B.: Efficient secure multi-party computation. In: Okamoto, T. (ed.) ASIACRYPT 2000. LNCS, vol. 1976, pp. 143–161. Springer, Heidelberg (2000). https://doi.org/10.1007/3-540-44448-3_12

41. Katz, J., Koo, C.-Y.: On expected constant-round protocols for byzantine agreement. In: Dwork, C. (ed.) CRYPTO 2006. LNCS, vol. 4117, pp. 445–462. Springer, Heidelberg (2006). https://doi.org/10.1007/11818175_27

42. Katz, J., Koo, C.-Y., Kumaresan, R.: Improving the round complexity of VSS in point-to-point networks. In: Aceto, L., Damgård, I., Goldberg, L.A., Halldórsson, M.M., Ingólfsdóttir, A., Walukiewicz, I. (eds.) ICALP 2008. LNCS, vol. 5126, pp. 499–510. Springer, Heidelberg (2008). https://doi.org/10.1007/978-3-540-70583-3_41

43. Kushilevitz, E., Lindell, Y., Rabin, T.: Information-theoretically secure protocols and security under composition. In: STOC (2006)

44. Lamport, L., Shostak, R., Pease, M.: The byzantine generals problem. ACM Trans. Program. Lang. Syst. **4**, 382–401 (1982)

45. Lindell, Y., Lysyanskaya, A., Rabin, T.: Sequential composition of protocols without simultaneous termination. In: PODC (2002)
46. Nayak, K., Ren, L., Shi, E., Vaidya, N.H., Xiang, Z.: Improved extension protocols for byzantine broadcast and agreement. arXiv preprint. arXiv:2002.11321 (2020)
47. Patra, A.: Error-free multi-valued broadcast and byzantine agreement with optimal communication complexity. In: Fernàndez Anta, A., Lipari, G., Roy, M. (eds.) OPODIS 2011. LNCS, vol. 7109, pp. 34–49. Springer, Heidelberg (2011). https://doi.org/10.1007/978-3-642-25873-2_4
48. Pease, M., Shostak, R., Lamport, L.: Reaching agreement in the presence of faults. J. ACM (JACM) **27**(2), 228–234 (1980)
49. Rabin, M.O.: Randomized byzantine generals. In: Symposium on Foundations of Computer Science (1983)
50. Shrestha, N., Bhat, A., Kate, A., Nayak, K.: Synchronous distributed key generation without broadcasts. IACR Cryptology ePrint Archive (2021)
51. Turpin, R., Coan, B.A.: Extending binary byzantine agreement to multivalued byzantine agreement. Inf. Process. Lett. **18**(2), 73–76 (1984)

Succinct Proofs

On Black-Box Constructions of Time and Space Efficient Sublinear Arguments from Symmetric-Key Primitives

Laasya Bangalore[1], Rishabh Bhadauria[2(✉)], Carmit Hazay[2],
and Muthuramakrishnan Venkitasubramaniam[1]

[1] Georgetown University, Washington, D.C., USA
laasyablr@gmail.com, vmuthu@gmail.com
[2] Bar-Ilan University, Ramat Gan, Israel
{rishabh.bhadauria,Carmit.Hazay}@biu.ac.il

Abstract. Zero-knowledge proofs allow a prover to convince a verifier of a statement without revealing anything besides its validity. A major bottleneck in scaling sub-linear zero-knowledge proofs is the high space requirement of the prover, even for NP relations that can be verified in a small space.

In this work, we ask whether there exist complexity-preserving (i.e. overhead w.r.t time and space are minimal) succinct zero-knowledge arguments of knowledge with minimal assumptions while making only black-box access to the underlying primitives. We design the first such zero-knowledge system with sublinear communication complexity (when the underlying NP relation uses non-trivial space) and provide evidence why existing techniques are unlikely to improve the communication complexity in this setting. Namely, for every NP relation that can be verified in time T and space S by a RAM program, we construct a public-coin zero-knowledge argument system that is black-box based on collision-resistant hash-functions (CRH) where the prover runs in time $\widetilde{O}(T)$ and space $\widetilde{O}(S)$, the verifier runs in time $\widetilde{O}(T/S + S)$ and space $\widetilde{O}(1)$ and the communication is $\widetilde{O}(T/S)$, where $\widetilde{O}()$ ignores polynomial factors in $\log T$ and κ is the security parameter. As our construction is public-coin, we can apply the Fiat-Shamir heuristic to make it non-interactive with sample communication/computation complexities. Furthermore, we give evidence that reducing the proof length below $\widetilde{O}(T/S)$ will be hard using existing symmetric-key based techniques by arguing the space-complexity of constant-distance error correcting codes.

1 Introduction

Zero-knowledge proofs, introduced by Goldwasser, Micali and Rackoff [20] are powerful cryptographic objects that allow a prover to convince a verifier of a statement while revealing nothing beyond the validity of the statement. Succinct non-interactive zero-knowledge arguments (ZK-SNARKs and ZK-SNARGs) are variants of zero-knowledge proof systems that offer very efficient verification,

© The Author(s), under exclusive license to Springer Nature Switzerland AG 2022
E. Kiltz and V. Vaikuntanathan (Eds.): TCC 2022, LNCS 13747, pp. 417–446, 2022.
https://doi.org/10.1007/978-3-031-22318-1_15

namely, proof lengths and verification times that are polylogarithmic in the size of the instance. ZK-SNARKs have been the focus of intense research from both theory and practice in the past few years as they are becoming an indispensable tool to bringing privacy and efficiency to blockchains (see [23,35] for two recent surveys).

While the initial constructions of concretely efficient ZK-SNARKs suffered from significantly high prover times, recent works have shown how to improve the computational complexity to essentially linear in the time taken compute the underlying relation (for an NP-language) [12,14,26,27,33,34,36,37]. However, these works come with a steep price in terms of *space*, namely, for computations that take time T and space S, the space complexity of the prover is $\Omega(T)$. Notably, only a few works provide time and space efficient constructions that we discuss next. This fact turns out to be a major bottleneck in scaling up zero-knowledge proofs to larger and larger computations.

To make the context precise, we focus on the task of proving that a non-deterministic RAM machine M accepts a particular instance x, i.e. uniform non-deterministic computations. The goal here is if M accepts/rejects x in time T and space S the resulting ZK proof system preserves these complexities on the prover's side and polylogarithmic in T (i.e. succinct) or even sublinear on the verifier's side.

When considering designated verifier ZK-SNARKs, complexity preserving solutions (i.e. poly-logarithmic overhead in space and time) have been constructed by Bitansky and Chiesa [8] and by Holmgren and Rothblum [22] in the non-interactive setting. The work of Ephraim et al. [18] show that assuming the existence of standard (circuit) SNARKs one can construct a non-interactive succinct argument of knowledge (i.e. SNARK) for parallel RAM computations where the complexities are preserved on the prover's side and the verifier requires polylogarithmic in T time and space based on collision-resistant hash functions (CRHF), where the underlying CRHF and SNARK is used in a non-black-box manner. Publicly-verifiable ZK-SNARKs with similar overheads can be accomplished via recursive composition [13,15,16]. However, these constructions have significant overheads as they typically rely on non-black-box usage of the underlying primitives. Imposing black-box access to the underlying primitives is an important step to obtain practically viable constructions [1,21,28].

More recently, two works by Block et al. [9,10], designed the first black-box construction of a ZK-SNARKs with polylogarithmic overhead in space and time based on "more standard" assumptions. The first work assumes hardness of discrete logarithm in prime-order groups and relies on the random oracle to construct a public-coin zero-knowledge argument where the proof length is $\mathsf{polylog}(T)$, the prover is complexity preserving and the verifier runtime is $T \cdot \mathsf{polylog}(T)$ while using $\mathsf{polylog}(T)$ space. The second work improves the verifier's runtime from $T \cdot \mathsf{polylog}(T)$ to $n \cdot \mathsf{polylog}(T)$, where n is the input length, under hardness assumptions on hidden order groups. We note that these works make extensive use of public-key operations - e.g., the prover needs to do $\Omega(T)$ exponentiations, and public-key operations are typically orders of magnitude more expensive than symmetric key operations.

Thus, the prior works leave the following question open:

Is it possible to design a complexity preserving (zero-knowledge) argument system based on minimal assumptions (e.g., symmetric-key primitives) with a succinct verifier where the underlying primitives are used in a black-box manner?

As noted above, the problem is solved if we are willing to assume (and extensively use) public-key primitives. We further highlight that the problem can be solved if we relax either the computation or the space requirements of the prover. The works of [5,7] demonstrate a ZK-SNARK with succinct proofs and verification (i.e. polylogarithmic in T), where the prover's running time and space are quasilinear in T. If we relax the time but restrict the space of the prover, it is easy to see how to extend the same constructions of [5,7] by observing that a Reed-Solomon encoding of streaming data of size T can be computed in time polynomial in T with space $\mathsf{polylog}(T)$. Finally, if we relax the black-box requirement, recursive composition can be used to construct (ZK-)SNARKS [13,15,16].

1.1 Our Results

Theorem 1. *Assume that collision-resistant hash functions exist. Then, every NP relation that can be verified by a time T and space S RAM machine has a public-coin zero-knowledge argument-system such that:*

1. *The prover runs in time $T \cdot \mathsf{poly}(\log(T), \lambda)$ and uses space $S \cdot \mathsf{poly}(\log(T), \lambda)$.*
2. *The verifier runs in time $(T/S + S) \cdot \mathsf{poly}(\log(T), \lambda)$ and uses space $\mathsf{poly}(\log(T), \lambda)$.*
3. *The communication complexity is $(T/S) \cdot \mathsf{poly}(\log(T), \lambda)$ and number of rounds is constant.*
4. *The protocol has perfect completeness and negligible soundness error.*

where λ is the computational security parameter. Moreover, applying the Fiat-Shamir heuristic results in a non-interactive sublinear zero-knoweldge argument of knowledge with the same asymptotic efficiencies.

We remark that our construction could lead to concretely efficient complexity preserving ZK-SNARKs that are possibly post-quantum secure since it is based on symmetric-key primitives and is black-box in the underlying primitives.

Next we complement our upper bound with a lower bound. We prove that any constant-distance code with an encoding algorithm that runs in time quasilinear in the input length n must require space at least $\tilde{\Omega}(n)$. More formally, we prove the following theorem.

Theorem 2 (Informal). *Suppose that a code over $\mathbb{F}$ with message length n, codeword length m and minimum relative distance δ (i.e. $[m, n, \delta m]$ code) can be encoded via a RAM machine with space S while making r passes over the input message, then $S \in \Omega(\delta n/r \cdot \log |\mathbb{F}|)$.*

Interpreting Theorem 2 in the context of proof systems, we note that most IOP/PCP constructions use constant-distance codes to encode the computation-transcript, which is of size $\widetilde{O}(T)$. Our lower bound implies that encoding an $\widetilde{O}(T)$ message with space S will have distance $\widetilde{O}(S/T)$ which implies a query complexity (and consequently proof length) of $\Omega(T/S)$ for the IOP/PCPs that encode the transcript and this matches our upper bound.

1.2   Technical Overview

The most common approach to design a ZK-SNARK black-box from symmetric-key primitives in a black-box way is to first design an interactive oracle proof (IOP) system [6,31], then compile it to an succinct interactive zero-knowledge proof system (honest-verifier) using collision-resistant hash functions and finally relying on the Fiat-Shamir heuristic [19] to make it non-interactive.

Interactive oracle proofs and probabilistically checkable proofs encode the computation in such a way that the verifier needs to query only few bits to verify its validity. These proofs typically involve encoding the computation transcript using some constant-rate constant-distance error-correcting codes. Computing these codes on a computational transcript of size T can be done efficiently, i.e. in time $\widetilde{O}(T)$ using FFTs. Unfortunately, all FFTs are believed to require a high space complexity. In fact, it was shown in a specific computational model that computing Fourier transforms on a domain of size n with time T and space S requires $T \cdot S \in \Omega(n^2)$ [32]. This means that if $S << T$, then the running time to compute Fourier transforms will no longer be quasi-linear in n. As mentioned above, we demonstrate that even designing codes with constant-distance requires significant space.

Our starting point for our upper bound is the Ligero ZK argument system [1] which is an instantiation of the IOP framework (based on the MPC-in-the-head paradigm [24]) but provides a trade-off between size of the Fourier transforms and proof length. Given a parameter β, for a computation of size T, the Ligero proof system provides a $O(T/\beta + \beta)$-sized proof and requires executing several $O(T/\beta)$ FFTs on size β. However, the proof system as we describe below still requires a space complexity of $O(T)$. Our main contribution is a new proof system that follows the blueprint of the Ligero proof system and preserves time and space efficiency.

We provide a high-level description of the Ligero proof system in the IOP model and identify the bottlenecks in making it time and space efficient. Given an arithmetic circuit C over a field $\mathbb{F}$, the Ligero system proves satisfiability of C as follows:

1. **Preparing the proof oracle:** In the first step in Ligero, the prover computes an "extended" witness (of size $O(|C|)$) that incorporates all intermediate computations (namely, output of each "gate") and encodes it using an Interleaved Reed-Solomon code. This code is set as the proof oracle.
2. **Testing the encoding:** Next, the verifier tests if the prover set the oracle with a valid encoding of some message. The Interleaved Reed-Solomon Code

can be interpreted as a matrix U where each row is a Reed-Solomon code of some message. The verifier challenges the prover with a set of random elements (one for each row of U) and the prover responds with a random linear combination of the rows based on the randomness provided by the prover. The verifier rejects if this combination is not a valid (Reed Solomon) code. The idea is that if each row of U is a valid Reed Solomon code, then by linearity the random linear combination provided by the prover must also be a valid Reed Solomon code.

3. **Testing linear constraints:** Linear constraints incorporate all the addition gates and circuit wiring in C. The verifier tests these constraints by providing randomness and obtaining an encoding of a random linear combination of the result of all the linear constraints applied to the extended witness. Given the prover's response the verifier checks if the response encodes values that sum up to 0. The idea here is that even if one of the linear relations do not hold, then the values encoded in the random linear combination will not sum up to 0 with very high probability.

4. **Testing quadratic constraints:** Quadratic constraints incorporate all the multiplication gates in C. The verifier tests these constraints analogously to the linear constraints. Specifically, the verifier checks if the prover's response encodes a vector of all zeros. This test utilizes the strong multiplicative property of the Reed-Solomon encoding [30].

5. **Column check:** Finally, the verifier checks if the responses provided by the prover in the three tests presented above are consistent with the code in the proof oracle. Since all the tests can be performed via row operations on the matrix, the verifier selects a random subset of the columns of the matrix and recomputes the results of the tests for these columns and checks if they are consistent with the responses.

Compiling the IOP system to a sublinear argument is achieved by replacing the proof oracle with the root hash of a Merkle hash tree with leaves as the elements of the code matrix and providing Merkle decommitments along with the elements (columns) revealed in the column check step [6, 25].

Next, we analyze the space complexity of the Ligero system, describe the obstacles to make it space-efficient and then explain our approach to overcome these obstacles.

1. The first step of the argument system involves the prover computing the code generated by encoding the witness where this codeword serves as the proof oracle. This is followed by computing the Merkle hash tree of the code. The size of the code is $O(|C|)$ and if we naively compute the Merkle tree it will require holding the entire code in memory. However, if the Interleaved Reed Solomon code can be computed one row at a time then the Merkle hash tree can be computed with space proportional to the length of the code (i.e. number of columns in the matrix) as the hash of the leaves can be iteratively aggregated using the Merkle-Damgard construction [17]. We remark that computing the code one row at a time is not straight forward as the

Ligero proof system actually requires the extended witness to be arranged in a specific structure. The verifier on the other hand can check the Merkle decommitments of the κ columns in space proportional to κ and $\mathsf{polylog}(T)$.

2. In the code test, the prover computes a random linear combination of the rows of the matrix. Once again, if we assume that the code matrix can be computed one row at a time, then the linear combination can also be computed in space proportional to the length of the code by maintaining a running aggregate.

3. The linear test is one of the main bottlenecks in terms of space complexity. As the wiring in the circuit C can be arbitrary the linear constraints can involve values encoded in arbitrary rows of the matrix. This means even if the code can be computed one row at a time, computing the response to the linear constraint could involve recomputing the entire code for each constraint to access different rows of the code and this blows up the running time of the prover beyond quasi-linear in the worst case. The issue of the wiring in the circuit C being arbitrary (as described in the previous step) poses a challenge to improving the verifier's space complexity as well. In addition to the same issues as discussed above, the verifier has more stringent space restrictions, and verifying the prover's response to the linear test in small space is non-trivial. We discuss our approach for the linear test below.

4. In the quadratic test, the verifier checks the correctness of all the multiplication gates. The prover prepares the extended witness in a specific way where the multiplication gates are batched and the wire values are aligned so that they can be tested for correctness as follows: the verifier provides randomness and the prover provides an aggregate computed via row operations which the verifier checks if it encodes the all 0's string. Making this space-efficient requires arranging each batch of multiplication gates in neighboring rows.

5. In the final step, the verifier queries the proof oracle on a subset of the columns and verifies if the responses provided by the prover for the code, linear and quadratic tests are consistent with the columns. In the Ligero system, all these tests are results of row operations on the encoded matrix. Hence the verifier can check the correctness by simply recomputing the row operations on the subset of columns opened by the verifier and checking against the prover's responses. If the tests can be computed by the prover in a space efficient manner, then the verifier can rely on a similar approach to recompute the responses for the columns in a space-efficient manner.

1.2.1   Our Approach

We want to design a space-efficient ZK-SNARK for RAM computations. First, we fix the RAM model of computation as a machine that has (multi-pass) uni-directional input tapes and a work tape with RAM access. Our first step is to rely on the transformation from [4,11] to transform the RAM computation into a (succinct) circuit C. We modify the compiler to generate directly a constraint system that can be consumed by the Ligero system. In slightly more detail, the Ligero constraint system is over a $m \times \ell$ matrix X that represents the "extended witness" and instantiated via a linear constraint (A, b) and quadratic constraint system specified by tuples of rows (i_l, i_r, i_o) on the matrix X. The linear constraint requires that $Ax = b$ where x is the flattening of the matrix X (namely concatenating the rows of X) and the quadratic constraint (i_l, i_r, i_o) requires that for every $j \in [\ell]$, $X_{i_l, j} \cdot X_{i_r, j} = X_{i_o, j}$.

By relying on the transformation of [4, 11], we will obtain a Ligero constraint system over a $\widetilde{O}(T/S) \times \widetilde{O}(S)$ matrix X where we can decompose X into $\widetilde{O}(T/S)$ blocks where a block, denoted by X_i, contains $\mathsf{polylog}(T)$ rows of X with the following properties:

1. First, a block can be stored in space $\widetilde{O}(S)$ (as opposed to storing X which requires $\widetilde{O}(T)$ space). The transformation will allow the prover to generate and encode X block-wise as needed by the Ligero proof system while using only $\widetilde{O}(S)$ space.
2. The linear and quadratic constraints over the extended witness X will be localized to a block or consecutive blocks i.e. these constraints only involve values within a block or consecutive blocks of X. We will show that this allows us to test constraints block-wise in a space efficient manner.

Next, we explain the main technical novelty of our approach - implementing the linear and quadratic tests.

Linear Test. In this step, the prover convinces the verifier that the extended witness X satisfies all the linear constraints. We observe from [4,11] that the linear constraints are "localized" to blocks of size $\widetilde{O}(S)$ and "uniform" i.e., the set of the constraints applied to each block are the same. The efficiency of the linear constraints relies on these two properties. In more detail, we express the linear constraints for each block as $Ay_i = b$ where A is a public matrix of size $\widetilde{O}(S) \times \widetilde{O}(S)$ extracted from the transformation, b is a public vector of size $\widetilde{O}(S)$ and y_i is $\widetilde{O}(S)$-sized flattened vector corresponding to block Y_i that is obtained by concatenating the rows of Y_i.

We briefly describe the linear test for "uniform" constraints. To verify these constraints, the witness is split into blocks y_i and the verifier verifies that $r^\mathsf{T}(Ay_i) = r^\mathsf{T}b$ for all blocks y_i, where r is a random challenge it provides of length $\widetilde{O}(S)$. We explain the rest of the test for a specific block. To apply batching, the output of the batched test is takes as the random linear combination of the individual tests. In such a test, the prover rearranges the vector $r^\mathsf{T}A$ as an $\widetilde{O}(1) \times \widetilde{O}(S)$ matrix and computes its Interleaved Reed Solomon encoding, denoted by R. Then, instead of sending $r^\mathsf{T}(Ay_i)$, the prover sends the vector $q = (\mathbf{1}_m)^\mathsf{T}(R \odot U_i)$ where U_i is an encoding of Y_i, $\mathbf{1}_m$ is the all ones length m vector and $\odot$ denotes pointwise product. By the multiplicative property of Reed-Solomon codes, it follows that checking whether $r^\mathsf{T}(Ay_i) = r^\mathsf{T}b$ is equivalent to checking whether the decoding of q satisfies that the sum of the decoded values equals $r^\mathsf{T}b$. Towards making this test efficient in terms of both time and space, the following three steps need to be computed efficiently.

1. The prover and the verifier need to compute $r^{\mathrm{T}}A$. Note that naively storing the entire matrix A requires space $\widetilde{O}(S^2)$. Instead, we observe the matrix A benefits from the following properties of the circuit (which is obtained from the RAM-to-Circuit reduction of [4,11]): (a) each wire of the circuit is involved in at most polylogarithmic linear and quadratic constraints and (b) all constraints involving a particular wire can be efficiently identified. This translates into the following properties for A: (a) A is a sparse matrix i.e., the number of non-zero elements in A is $\widetilde{O}(S)$ and (b) all the non-zero elements of a column can be efficiently computed in time $\widetilde{O}(1)$ and space $\widetilde{O}(1)$. To perform the matrix-vector multiplication, we just need to query the non-zero values for each column of A in time $\widetilde{O}(1)$ and then multiply each of these non-zero values with the appropriate randomness in r. The randomness associated with i^{th} row is set to s^i where s is a randomly generated seed. Hence, we can compute each element of $r^{\mathrm{T}}A$ in time $\widetilde{O}(1)$ and space $\widetilde{O}(1)$.

2. Next, both the prover and the verifier need to compute the encoding of $r^{\mathrm{T}}A$. The prover rearranges the $\widetilde{O}(S)$-length vector into a $\widetilde{O}(1) \times \widetilde{O}(S)$ matrix and then encodes each row using an RS encoding, denoted by R. The prover can do this by first interpolating each row i of the matrix to generate a polynomial $r_i(\cdot)$ and then evaluate $r_i(\cdot)$ at $\widetilde{O}(S)$ evaluation points; performing interpolation followed by evaluation (of size $\widetilde{O}(S)$) is done efficiently using iFFT followed by FFT and requires space $\widetilde{O}(S)$. The prover can perform these operations, but the verifier has much less space i.e., $\mathsf{poly}(\log T, \kappa)$. First, note that the verifier needs to compute only at $O(\kappa)$ columns of R (as opposed to the prover who needs to compute the entire codeword, which is of size $\widetilde{O}(S)$). However, this does not directly reduce the space to $\widetilde{O}(1)$ as interpolation followed by evaluation requires space $\widetilde{O}(S)$ to store the interpolated polynomials. By exploiting the structure of FFTs, we present an algorithm DEval that can implicitly evaluate the polynomial without storing all the coefficients at a particular point using $\widetilde{O}(1)$ space given an input of size $\widetilde{O}(S)$. This algorithm will allow the verifier to recompute the result of the linear test on the $\widetilde{O}(1)$ columns in $\widetilde{O}(1)$ space.

3. Lastly, the verifier needs to check if the prover's response in the linear test encodes values that sum up to $r^{\mathrm{T}}b$. Suppose $q(\cdot)$ is the polynomial associated with the prover's response, then the verifier needs to evaluate $q(\cdot)$ at ℓ points and check if they sum up to $r^{\mathrm{T}}b$ i.e., $\sum_{i \in [\ell]} q(\zeta_i) = r^{\mathrm{T}}b$ where $\{\zeta_i\}_{i \in [\ell]}$ are the interpolation points. It is non-trivial to ensure that both the time and space are optimal for this check as evidenced by the following two approaches where one is optimal in time but not in space and vice-versa.

    (a) If we use FFTs to evaluate the polynomial at ℓ points, then the check is optimal in time but not space i.e., this approach requires time $O(\ell \log \ell)$ and space $O(\ell)$.

    (b) Alternately, instead of storing all ℓ evaluations of $q(\cdot)$ and then adding them up, we can compute the running aggregate of the values encoded by $q(\cdot)$ while simultaneously evaluating the polynomial at all ℓ points. This approach updates the running partial aggregate as the terms of the polynomial are computed and just needs to store 1 field element. But the time to evaluate a t degree polynomial at ℓ points is at least $O(t\ell)$, which is $O(\ell^2)$ when $t = \ell$. Hence, this approach is optimal in terms of space but not time i.e., it requires space $O(1)$ and time $O(\ell^2)$ (if the degree of $q(\cdot)$ is ℓ).

We address this issue by setting the interpolation points to be the ℓth roots of unity. It turns out that the sum of the values encoded by $q(\cdot)$ is equal to $\ell(c_0 + c_\ell)$ i.e., $\sum_{i \in [\ell]} q(\zeta_i) = \ell(c_0 + c_\ell)$ where c_0 and c_ℓ are the coefficients of $q(\cdot)$. Our time and space-optimal approach is as follows. The prover sends only the coefficients c_0 and c_ℓ during the linear test. The verifier sums up the two coefficients and checks if it is equal to $r^\mathsf{T} b$ i.e., $c_0 + c_\ell = r^\mathsf{T} b$, which requires time $O(1)$ and space $O(1)$.

Quadratic Test. Similar to the linear constraints, the quadratic constraints are "localized" to a block i.e., the constraints involve only values within a block of X. Further, the quadratic constraints require the rows of X to be aligned in a specific way: the left, right, and output wire values of multiplication gates are aligned in corresponding rows of a block. During the test, The verifier provides a vector r' of length $\widetilde{O}(1)$ and tries to verify the following for all blocks $i \in [O(T/S)]$, $r'^\mathsf{T}(Y_i^{\text{left}} \odot Y_i^{\text{right}} - Y_i^{\text{out}}) = [0]_{1 \times \widetilde{O}(S)}$ where Y_i^{left}, Y_i^{right} and Y_i^{out} are submatrices of X is size $\widetilde{O}(1) \times \widetilde{O}(S)$ corresponding to left, right and output wire values respectively (and they are all aligned). Towards this, the prover computes the encoding of $r'^\mathsf{T}(Y_i^{\text{left}} \odot Y_i^{\text{right}} - Y_i^{\text{out}})$ for each block and then combines them by taking a random linear combination of such encodings.

Similar to the linear test, the verifier needs to additionally check if the prover's response encodes a vector of all zeros. A similar challenge as described in the linear test arises here as well. The verifier needs to evaluate the prover's response to the quadratic test, say $q(\cdot)$, at ℓ points and check if each of them is 0. Like the previous solution for linear test, we set the interpolation points to be the ℓth roots of unity. However, the solution for the previous step cannot be directly applied here as we need to check if each of the values is 0 (instead of the sum being 0). Instead, we observe that the polynomial $q(\cdot)$ can be expressed as a product of two polynomials $q'(\cdot)$ and $z(\cdot)$ such that $z(\cdot)$ evaluates to zero at all the interpolation points. We modify the quadratic test so that the prover sends $q'(\cdot)$ instead of $q(\cdot)$ and the verifier computes $q(\cdot)$ from $q'(\cdot)$ and $z(\cdot)$ where $z(\cdot)$ is a publicly known polynomial. This entirely avoids the need to check if $q(\cdot)$ encodes all 0 values.

IPCP to ZK-SNARK. We compile an IPCP to a ZKSNARK in two steps. First we compile an IPCP to a ZKIPCP and then transform ZKIPCP to a ZKSNARK.

In the first step, we need to ensure that the information revealed to the verifier is "zero-knowledge". Recall that information regarding the extended witness is revealed in each of the code, linear and quadratic tests and in the symbols (i.e. columns of the U matrix) queried by the verifier. The columns revealed can be protected by adding redundancy to the encoding. More precisely, we instantiate the Reed-Solomon code so that the columns of U matrix provide t-privacy as a secret sharing scheme where t is the number of symbols opened by the verifier. To make sure that the result of the tests leak no information, it suffices to mask the results by adding additional rows to the U matrix that blind the results of the tests. The IPCP protocol can be converted into ZKIPCP protocol without any additional overhead by: 1) adding blinding random codewords to encoded witness U and 2) adding randomness while generating U. This compilation only incurs a constant multiplicative overhead.

In the second step we rely on the compilation of Ben-Sasson et al. [6] (which in turn is based on [25]) using Merkle trees. We argue that this step affects the asymptotic computation or communication complexity only by a multiplicative factor proportional to $\mathsf{poly}(\kappa)$ where κ is computational security parameter.

Efficiency. To get the target space and time efficiency we will set the β parameter (length of a block) of the proof system to be $\widetilde{O}(S)$ and get a proof length of $\widetilde{O}((T/S) + S)$. The prover requires $\widetilde{O}(T)$-time and $\widetilde{O}(S)$-space, which is complexity-preserving. Further, the verifier is "succinct" and will require $\widetilde{O}(T/S + S)$-time and $\widetilde{O}(1)$-space to verify the proof.

Improving Proof Length. To improve the proof length, the protocol does not send the polynomials $q(\cdot)$ in the test. Instead, the polynomials generate a codeword which will be used as an oracle. The prover proves the degree of the polynomial using a low-degree testing protocol FRI [2] which requires polylogarithmic communication in the degree of polynomial, thereby reducing the proof length to $\widetilde{O}(T/S)$ and preserving the time and space complexities of both the prover and the verifier.

1.2.2   A Matching Lower Bound

We complement our positive result with a lower bound that demonstrates why getting a proof length better than $\widetilde{O}(T/S)$ will be hard using current techniques. As mentioned above, all techniques involve codes with constant distance in one form or another. We show that any code that makes polylogarithmic passes on an input message of length n and produces a code with constant distance must require space $\widetilde{O}(n)$. Interpreting the result in the context of proof systems, if we want to generate a code of a message of length T in quasilinear time, it will require space $\Omega(T)$. A slightly more refined implication is that with space S, encoding a T-length message in quasilinear time (in T), can yield a code of distance at most $S \cdot \mathsf{polylog}(T)/T$. Testing such codes typically requires queries inversely proportional to the distance i.e. $T/(S \cdot \mathsf{polylog}(T))$. Hence, any proof system that employs such a code and encodes a length T message, will need a query complexity of at least $T/(S \cdot \mathsf{polylog}(T))$, implying that the proof length will also be at least $T/(S \cdot \mathsf{polylog}(T))$.

The high-level idea of the lower bound is to prove that for any constant-distance code over a field $\mathbb{F}$, the encoding algorithm requires space $S > (n/(r\delta) - O(\log m)) \cdot \log |\mathbb{F}|$, where n is the message length, m is the codeword length, δ is the distance and r is the number of passes. We prove this in two steps.

First, consider an encoding algorithm that reads each block (i.e., contiguous portion) of a message and outputs a portion of the codeword. We show that there must be a message M that consists of a block of length $O(n/\delta)$ such that the number of elements output by the encoding algorithm corresponding to that block is $\delta m/2$.

Next, consider the set of all messages m' that agree with m everywhere except on that block (there are $|\mathbb{F}|^{O(n/\delta)}$ such messages). We show that there will be a subset of messages, say D, of size at least $|\mathbb{F}|^{O(n/\delta) - rS/\log |\mathbb{F}| - O(r \log m)}$ such that the encoding of any two messages will differ only in at most $\delta m/2$-elements where r is the number of passes made by the encoding algorithm on the input. If this set has at least two messages, then the encodings of these messages will differ in at most $\delta m/2$ locations, thereby violating the distance property of the codeword whose minimum distance is δm. To evade this contradiction, we require the size of D to be at most 1, i.e., $|\mathbb{F}|^{O(n/\delta) - rS/\log |\mathbb{F}| - O(r \log m)} \leq 1$ which implies that the space $S > (n/(r\delta) - O(\log m)) \cdot \log |\mathbb{F}|$.

1.3   A Comparison with Related Work

Related to the design of sub-linear zero-knowledge arguments, the work of Mohassel, Rosulek and Scafuro [29] constructs zero-knowledge arguments when modeling the NP relation via a RAM program, that are sublinear in a different sense. More precisely, they considered the scenario of a prover that commits to a large database of size M, and later wishes to prove several statements of the form $\exists w$ such that $\mathcal{R}_i(M, w) = 1$. After an initial setup with a computational cost of $O(M)$ only on the prover's side, they achieve computation and communication complexities for both parties that are proportional to $\widetilde{O}(T)$ where T is the running time of the RAM program implementing the relation and $\widetilde{O}$ hides a factor of $\mathsf{poly}(\log(T), \kappa)$.

Previously, the two works [9,10] also designed black-box constructions of ZK-SNARKs with polylogarithmic overhead in time and space. These works rely on the hardness of discrete logarithm and hidden order groups. Our protocol, on the other hand, relies on symmetric key operations and requires collision-resistant hash functions. The prover's time and space complexities of [9,10] match our complexity. This is the case for the verifier's space complexity as well. The verifier's running time in [9] is $\widetilde{O}(T)$ and $\widetilde{O}(n)$ in [10] where n is the input length. On the other hand, our verifier's complexity is $\widetilde{O}(T/S + S)$. Finally, the communication complexity of prior works is $\widetilde{O}(1)$ while we achieve $\widetilde{O}(T/S)$. We summarize these results in Table 1.

Table 1. The complexity analysis of black-box ZKSNARKs. T and S are the respective time and space complexities required by the RAM program to verify the NP relation. n is the input length and $\widetilde{O}(\cdot)$ ignores polynomial factors of $\log T$.

	$\mathcal{P}$ time	$\mathcal{P}$ space	$\mathcal{V}$ time	$\mathcal{V}$ space
[9]	$\widetilde{O}(T)$	$\widetilde{O}(S)$	$\widetilde{O}(T)$	$\widetilde{O}(1)$
[10]	$\widetilde{O}(T)$	$\widetilde{O}(S)$	$\widetilde{O}(n)$	$\widetilde{O}(1)$
Theorem 1	$\widetilde{O}(T)$	$\widetilde{O}(S)$	$\widetilde{O}(T/S + S)$	$\widetilde{O}(1)$

2 Preliminaries

Basic Notations. Let κ be the security parameter. We use lower-case letters such as x,y to represent vectors, and $x[i]$ denotes the ith element in vector x. We use capital letters such as X, Y to represent matrices. Also, $X[j]$ denotes the jth column and $X_{i,j}$ denote the element in i^{th} row and j^{th} column in matrix X. We use the notation $\widetilde{O}(.)$ to ignore polylog(.) terms. A matrix X is said to be *flattened* into a vector x (i.e. denoted by the lower-case letters of the corresponding matrix), if x is a rearrangement of the matrix X row-wise i.e., $x = (X_{1,1}, \ldots, X_{1,n}, \ldots, X_{m,1}, X_{m,n})$ where X is of size $m \times n$.

We also X_i or Y_i to denote matrices, especially when there many such matrices and i identifies a specific matrix in the set $\{X_i\}_{i \in [n]}$. Note that the flattened vector associated with X_i and Y_i are denoted by corresponding lower-case letters i.e. x_i and y_i respectively.

2.1 Circuit Notations

A arithmetic circuit C is defined over a field $\mathbb{F}$ and has input gates, output gates, intermediate gates, and directed wires between them. Each gate computes addition or multiplication over $\mathbb{F}$. We define the notion of a *transcript* for an arithmetic circuit C to be an assignment of values to the gates where the gates are ordered in a lexicographic order; each gate in circuit C will have a gate id $\mathsf{g_{id}}$ and will have two input wires and one output wire. Each wire will also have a wire id $\mathsf{w_{id}}$ and in case a wire value is an output wire of gate $\mathsf{g_{id}}$, then the wire id $\mathsf{w_{id}} = \mathsf{g_{id}}$. Each element in the transcript W is of the form $(\mathsf{g_{id}}, \mathsf{type}, \gamma)$ where $\mathsf{g_{id}}$ is the gate label, $\mathsf{type} \in \{\mathsf{inp}, \mathsf{add}, \mathsf{mult}, \mathsf{out}\}$ is the type of the gate and γ is the output wire value of gate $\mathsf{g_{id}}$.

2.2 Zero-Knowledge Arguments

A zero-knowledge argument system for an NP relationship $\mathcal{R}$ is a protocol between a computationally-bounded prover $\mathcal{P}$ and a verifier $\mathcal{V}$. At the end of the protocol, $\mathcal{V}$ is convinced by $\mathcal{P}$ that there exists a witness w such that $(x; w) \in \mathcal{R}$ for some input x, and learns nothing beyond that. We focus on arguments of knowledge which have the stronger property that if the prover convinces the verifier of the statement validity, then the prover must know w. Formally, consider the definition below, where we assume $\mathcal{R}$ is known to $\mathcal{P}$ and $\mathcal{V}$.

Definition 1. *Let $\mathcal{R}(x, w)$ be an NP relation corresponding to an NP language L. A tuple of algorithm $(\mathcal{P}, \mathcal{V})$ is an argument of knowledge for $\mathcal{R}$ if the following holds.*

- **Correctness.** *For every $(x, w) \in R$ and auxiliary input $z \in \{0, 1\}^*$, it holds:*

$$\langle \mathcal{P}(w), \mathcal{V}(z) \rangle(x) = 1$$

- **Soundness.** *For every $x \notin L$, every (unbounded) interactive machine $\mathcal{P}^*$, and every $w, z \in \{0, 1\}^*$ and a large enough security parameter λ,*

$$\Pr[\langle \mathcal{P}(w), \mathcal{V}(z) \rangle(x) = 1] \leq \mathsf{negl}(\lambda)$$

It is a zero-knowledge argument of knowledge it additionally satisfies:

- **Zero knowledge.** *There exists a PPT simulator $\mathcal{S}$ such that for any PPT algorithm $\mathcal{V}^*$, auxiliary input $z \in \{0, 1\}^*$, and $(x; w) \in \mathcal{R}$, it holds that*

$$\mathsf{View}(\langle \mathcal{P}(w), \mathcal{V}(z)^* \rangle(x)) \approx \mathcal{S}^{\mathcal{V}^*}(x, z)$$

Here $\mathcal{S}^{\mathcal{V}^*}$ denotes that the simulator $\mathcal{S}$ sees the randomness from a polynomial-size space of $\mathcal{V}^*$.

Succinct vs. Sublinear Arguments. We say an argument of knowledge is *succinct* if there exists a fixed polynomial $p(\cdot)$ such that the length of the proof is is bounded by $p(\lambda + \log |C|)$ where C is the circuit corresponding to the NP relation. Similarly, we say an argument of knowledge is *sublinear* if the proof length is $o_\lambda(|C|)$ where $o_\lambda(\cdot)$ hides multiplicative factors dependent on the security parameter λ.

2.3 Random-Access Machines (RAM)

A Random-Access Machines (RAM) comprises of a finite set of instructions that are executed sequentially on a finite set of registers and can make arbitrary memory accesses. We assume that each time step during the execution of a RAM program executes a single instruction or accesses the memory locations. We model the RAM as a Reduced-Instruction Set Computer (RISC) which more closely models programs compiled from high-level languages such as Java, C++. We adopt the formal notation for RAM from [4].

Definition 2 *(The RAM Model [4]). A random-access machine (RAM) is a tuple $M = (\mathsf{w}, k, \mathbb{A}, \mathcal{C}, \mathcal{T})$, where:*

- $\mathsf{w} \in \mathbb{N}$ *is the register size;*

- $k \in \mathbb{N}$ *is the number of registers;*
- $\mathcal{C} = (I_0, \ldots, I_{n-1})$ *is a set of instructions (or the code for the RAM program), where* $n \in \{1, \ldots 2^w\}$ *and each* I_i *is an instruction.*
- $\mathcal{J}$ *is a set of tapes which consists of a constant number of unidirectional input tapes with read-only access and single unidirectional output tape.*
- $\mathbb{W}$ *is a work tape with arbitrary read and write accesses.*

Consider a RAM program M that runs in time $T(n)$ and uses $S(n)$ memory cells on input x with n-bits. For simplicity, we use T and S instead of $T(n)$ and $S(n)$ as the input length can be easily inferred.

The RAM program M has arbitrary access to a work tape[1]. At any time step, the RAM program may read from or write into the cells (also referred to as memory cells) of the work tape using the load and store instructions respectively. We say a *RAM program uses space* S, if at most S memory cells of the tape were accessed during an execution of the M.

2.4 Succinct Matrix

We define succinct matrices which will be used in our zero-knowledge argument system.

Definition 3 (Succinct Matrix). *A succinct matrix A is a matrix of dimension $n_1 \times n_2$ with the following properties:*

- *There are $n_1 \cdot \mathsf{polylog}(n_1)$ non-zero values.*
- *There exists an algorithm getColumn(û) that takes input j and outputs a list L. The list L contains all non-zero elements of column j where each non-zero element is represented as a tuple (k, val) where k represents the row number and val represents the non-zero value. This algorithm runs in $\mathsf{polylog}(n_1)$.*

3 Lower Bound for Space-Efficient Encoding Schemes

In this section, we present our lower bound on space-efficient constant-distance codes. This lower bound provides evidence for why it is unlikely for current proof systems to be complexity preserving (in both time and space) when the underlying RAM machine uses space $S << T$ for non-trivial space.

3.1 Interpreting the Lower Bound in the Context of Proof Systems

As mentioned in the technical overview, all constructions of succinct non-interactive arguments based on symmetric-key primitives that are black-box in the underlying assumptions rely on constant-distance codes [1,3,5,25]. In slightly more detail, all constructions first rely transforming the circuit evaluation to an "execution" transcript that is proportional to the size of the circuit and then

---

[1] Generally, the RAM program has access to memory which we model as a work tape.

encoding the transcript via a constant-distance code. For a RAM machine, such a transformation typically results in a transcript of size T where T is the running time of the RAM computation. In this section, we will show that encoding a T-element message via a constant-distance code will require space $\Omega(T/r)$, where r is the number of passes taken by the algorithm on the input tape. In other words, current techniques for constructing a time-preserving ZK-SNARK, i.e. r is at most $\mathsf{polylog}(T)$, will require prover's space of $\Omega(T/r)$. In particular if the space of the underlying RAM machine is $S \ll T$, it is unlikely to get such a proof system that is complexity preserving (in time and space).

3.2   Warm Up: A Simple Lower Bound

As a warm up, we first present a lower bound where we assume a small restriction on the encoding algorithm and then prove a more general result. We begin with some notation that will help in our lower bounds.

Notation. We consider an encoding algorithm executed via a RAM machine with space S that encodes a message of length n. The encoding algorithm has unidirectional (i.e. linear) access to the input tape and can make multiple passes on the input. The machine also has a unidirectional output tape. Further, the encoding algorithm has RAM access to a work tape of size S bits (or equivalently $S/\log|\mathbb{F}|$ field elements). To keep track of the current position of the read head of the encoding algorithm on the input tape, we introduce the notion of *head*. Specifically, we use read head and write head to denote the heads in the input tape and output tapes, respectively (where the message to be encoded is read from the input tape and the codeword is written on to the output tape). Note that the contents of the work tape of the encoding algorithm differs depending on the position of the read head. It will be convenient to divide a msg into contiguous blocks of equal length. We will denote by $\mathsf{msg}[i]$ the ith block of msg. We denote by $\mathsf{c}_{\mathsf{msg}}$ the output of Enc on input msg. Let $\mathsf{c}_{\mathsf{msg}}[i, j]$ denote the part of the codeword output by the encoding algorithm when it reads the block $\mathsf{msg}[i]$ during the jth pass, i.e. when the read head moves from the left end to the right end of the block $\mathsf{msg}[i]$ in the jth pass. Let $\mathsf{c}_{\mathsf{msg}}[i]$ be the concatenation of $\{\mathsf{c}_{\mathsf{msg}}[i, 1], \ldots, \mathsf{c}_{\mathsf{msg}}[i, r]\}$. We will drop the subscript when the msg is understood from the context.

We present a high-level overview of the simplified version of the lower bound, which imposes certain restrictions on the encoding algorithm. Note that the encoding algorithm reads a certain portion of the message (referred to as a block), outputs a portion of the codeword (associated with this block) and then proceeds to the next message block. We make a simplifying assumption that the length of the codeword portion associated with any message block is independent of the contents of the message. This is formally stated in Assumption 1 below.

Assumption 1. *The position of the read head and write head at any step during the encoding is independent of the message.*

As a corollary we have the following: Suppose we divide the input message into $\lceil 2/\delta \rceil$ blocks of equal length. Given any two messages $\mathsf{msg}, \mathsf{msg}' \in \mathbb{F}^n$, the output of the encoding algorithm satisfies $|\mathsf{c}_{\mathsf{msg}}[i,j]| = |\mathsf{c}_{\mathsf{msg}'}[i,j]|$ for all blocks $i \in [2/\delta]$ and passes $j \in [r]$.

We begin with a proof overview. On a high-level the idea is to identify a set of messages whose encoding violate the minimum distance property. First, by a simple counting argument we can argue that there must be a message block t of length $O(n/2\delta)$ such that the total number of elements output by the encoding algorithm when the read head passes through block t (i.e. $\sum_j |c[t,j]|$) is at most $\delta m/2$. Observe that block t will have the same property for any message by our Assumption 1. Next, we will focus on messages that are identical everywhere except on block t; if we fix the remaining blocks then there are $|\mathbb{F}|^{\delta n/2}$ such messages as each block is of size $\delta n/2$. Out of these $|\mathbb{F}|^{\delta n/2}$ messages, we identify a subset of messages that result in identical work tapes after the encoding algorithm reads block t in each pass. These messages have property that the code can only differ in the portions output when reading block t, namely $c[t,j]$. We conclude by showing that there exist at least two messages in this set when $S \leq (\delta n/2r) \cdot \log |\mathbb{F}|$. Since the codewords corresponding to these messages only differ in at most $\delta m/2$ locations, but the minimum distance of the code is δm, we arrive at a contradiction.

Theorem 3. *Let $\mathcal{C}$ be a $[m, n, \delta m]$ code over $\mathbb{F}$ with message length n, codeword length m and minimum relative distance δ. Also, let $\mathsf{Enc}_{(T,S,r)} : \mathbb{F}^n \to \mathbb{F}^m$ be a Turing machine that on input $\mathsf{msg} \in \mathbb{F}^n$ outputs an encoding of msg in time T with a work tape of size S while making r passes on the message. Suppose Assumption 1 holds, then $S \geq (\delta n/2r) \cdot \log |\mathbb{F}|$.*

Proof. Assume for contradiction that there exists a $[m, n, \delta m]$ code $\mathcal{C}$ over $\mathbb{F}$ with an encoding algorithm $\mathsf{Enc}_{(T,S,r)}$. Consider an arbitrary message msg. Let's partition it into $2/\delta$ blocks each of length $\delta n/2$ elements.

Assumption 1 implies that the length of the output of the encoding algorithm associated with message block i, which is denoted by $|c[t]|$, is the same for all messages. Here, $c[i]$ is a concatenation of $\{c[i,1], \ldots, c[i,r]\}$ for some message msg. We drop the subscript for $|\mathsf{c}_{\mathsf{msg}}[t]|$ as the length is the same for all messages. Next, We show that there exists a message block t such that $c[t]$ is of length at most $\delta m/2$.

Lemma 1. *There exists a $t \in [2/\delta]$ such that $|c[t]| \leq \delta m/2$.*

Proof. Assume for contradiction, for every t, $|c[t]| > \delta m/2$. Then,

$$|c| = \sum_i |c[i]| > 2/\delta \times \delta m/2 > m$$

which is a contradiction.

Lemma 2. *Given message block $t \in [2/\delta]$ and pass $k \in [r]$, there exists a set of messages D_k of size at least $|\mathbb{F}|^{\frac{\delta n}{2} - kS/\log |\mathbb{F}|}$ such that for any two messages $\mathsf{msg}, \mathsf{msg}' \in \mathsf{D}_k$ the following holds:*

1. $\mathsf{msg}[i] = \mathsf{msg}'[i]$ *for all* $i \neq t$.
2. *At the end of the* k^{th} *pass,* $\mathsf{c_{msg}}$ *and* $\mathsf{c_{msg}'}$ *differ only at positions occupied by* $\mathsf{c}[t,1], \ldots, \mathsf{c}[t,k]$. *Furthermore, the contents of the work tape of the encoding algorithm at the end of the* k^{th} *pass for messages* msg *and* msg' *will be identical.*

Proof. Consider an arbitrary message msg, define D_0 to be the set of all messages that are identical to msg in every block $i \neq t$, but differ in block t. D_0 contains $|\mathbb{F}|^{\frac{\delta n}{2}}$ messages. We prove the claim via an induction on the number of passes.

Base Case: In the first pass, we show that there exists $D_1 \subseteq D_0$, such that the properties of the claim hold. By an averaging argument, there must exist a subset of D_0, say D_1, of size at least $|\mathbb{F}|^{\frac{\delta n}{2} - \frac{S}{\log |\mathbb{F}|}}$ with the following property: the contents of the work tapes are identical for any two messages in D_1 after the encoding algorithm finishes reading block t message during the first pass.

We now show that the codewords $\mathsf{c_{msg}}$ and $\mathsf{c_{msg}'}$ differ only in the codeword portions $\mathsf{c}[t,1]$ for any two messages $\mathsf{msg}, \mathsf{msg}' \in D_1$. Since all messages in D_0 are identical except for block t, the encoding will be identical before the codeword portion $\mathsf{c}[t,1]$. Next, since the contents of work tapes after reading block t are identical and the remaining part of the message (i.e., after message block t) are the same, the rest of the output until the encoding finishes the first pass will be the identical as well. Furthermore, the work tapes will be identical when the encoding finishes the first pass.

Induction: Suppose that there exists a set of messages D_k for which the conditions of the claim holds at the end of the kth pass. Then in the $(k+1)^{st}$ pass, the encoding algorithm starts with identical contents on the work tape for every message in D_k, so it will output the same elements until the encoding reaches block t. Applying another averaging argument, there must exists a subset $D_{k+1} \subseteq D_k$ of size at least $|\mathbb{F}|^{\frac{\delta n}{2} - \frac{kS}{\log |\mathbb{F}|}} / |\mathbb{F}|^{S / \log |\mathbb{F}|} = |\mathbb{F}|^{\frac{\delta n}{2} - \frac{(k+1)S}{\log |\mathbb{F}|}}$ such that the work tape will be identical when the encoding finishes reading block t in the $(k+1)^{st}$ pass. Similarly the contents of the work tapes and the output for these messages will also be identical for every two messages in D_{k+1} until the end of the $(k+1)^{st}$ pass. This completes the induction step.

Finally, we combine Lemmas 1 and 2 to prove Theorem 3 via contradiction. As per Lemma 1, there exists a message block t such that the encodings of messages differing only at this block have a distance of at most $\delta m/2$. If we instantiate Lemma 2 for block t, we get that there exists a set of messages D_r of size $|\mathbb{F}|^{\frac{\delta n}{2} - \frac{rS}{\log |\mathbb{F}|}}$ such that the encodings of any two messages in D_r differ in at most $\delta m/2$ locations. If we set $S < (\delta n/2r) \cdot \log |\mathbb{F}|$, then D_r will contain at least 2 messages whose encodings differ in at most $\delta m/2$ locations. This contradicts the distance requirements of the codeword $C_{\mathbb{F},n,m,\delta}$ whose minimum distance is at least δm.

3.3   Lower Bound for Multi-pass Space-Efficient Encoding Schemes

In this section, we extend the lower bound where we do not make Assumption 1. Without this assumption, for two different messages, the portion of the code affected by different blocks of the message could be different. The main idea to deal with the general case is to show that there exist sufficiently many messages for which Assumption 1 holds and then apply the preceding argument.

Theorem 4. *Let C be a $[m, n, \delta m]$ code over $\mathbb{F}$ with message length n, codeword length m and minimum relative distance δ. Also, let $\mathsf{Enc}_{(T,S,r)} : \mathbb{F}^n \to \mathbb{F}^m$ be a Turing machine that on input $\mathsf{msg} \in \mathbb{F}^n$ outputs an encoding of msg in time T with a work tape of size S while making r passes on the message. Then $S \geq (\delta n/4r - 2(\log_{|\mathbb{F}|} m) - 2/r) \cdot \log |\mathbb{F}|$.*

Proof. Assume for contradiction that there exists a code C and encoding algorithm Enc. We partition the message msg into $4/\delta$ blocks each of length $\delta n/4$. We first show that there exists a subset containing $|\mathbb{F}|^{\delta n/4-2}$ messages, say D, and an index t such that for each message msg in D, we have $|c_{\mathsf{msg}}[t]| \leq \delta m/2$. Note however, that since Assumption 1 does not hold, the corresponding code blocks for these messages might not be aligned.

Lemma 3. *There exists a set of messages D of size at least $|D| \geq |\mathbb{F}|^{\delta n/4-2}$ and $t \in [4/\delta]$ such that for any two $\mathsf{msg}, \mathsf{msg}' \in D$ the following holds:*

1. $\mathsf{msg}[i] = \mathsf{msg}'[i]$ for all $i \neq t$.
2. $|c_{\mathsf{msg}}[t]| \leq \delta m/2$.

Proof. Assume for contradiction that such a set D does not exist. Given a message msg, let $A_t[\mathsf{msg}]$ be the set of all possible messages that agree with msg on all blocks except block t. We know that the size of $A_t[\mathsf{msg}]$ is $|\mathbb{F}|^{\delta n/4}$. By our assumption, we have that for more than $|\mathbb{F}|^{\delta n/4} - |\mathbb{F}|^{\delta n/4-2}$ of the messages in $A_t[\mathsf{msg}]$, it holds that $c[t]$ is of length bigger than $\delta m/2$. We will now compute

$$\sum_{s \in \{0,1\}^{n-\delta n/4}} \sum_{t} \sum_{s' \in \{0,1\}^{\delta n/4}} |c_{Combine(s,s',t)}[t]|$$

where $Combine(a, b, i)$ denotes the string obtained by inserting b into string a at position $t \times \delta n/4$. Observe that the sum above, counts the sum total of the lengths of the encodings of every message, which should be equal to $m \times |\mathbb{F}|^n$. By our assumption, we can lower bound the sum as

$$|\mathbb{F}|^{n-\delta n/4} \times 4/\delta \times (|\mathbb{F}|^{\delta n/4} - |\mathbb{F}|^{\delta n/4-2}) \times \delta m/2 = 2 \times |\mathbb{F}|^n \times (1 - 1/|\mathbb{F}|^2) \times m$$
$$> |\mathbb{F}|^n \times m$$

where the last step holds for $|\mathbb{F}| \geq 2$. This is a contradiction.

Next, we show that there are sufficiently many messages in D and indices t, such that the message block t influences identical portions of the codeword. In other words, the assumption we made for the warm-up proof holds for a subset of the messages in D.

Lemma 4. *Given any index $t \in [4/\delta]$, set D of messages there exists a subset of messages $D' \subseteq D$ of size at least $|D|/m^{2r}$ such that for all messages $\mathsf{msg}', \mathsf{msg}''$ in D', the starting and ending positions of $c_{\mathsf{msg}'}[t, i]$ and $c_{\mathsf{msg}''}[t, i]$ w.r.t the code are identical for every $i \in [r]$.*

Proof. There are overall $2r$ positions considering the starting and ending points of $c_{\mathsf{msg}}[t, 1], \ldots, c_{\mathsf{msg}}[t, r]$ w.r.t the code. The number of possibilities for these $2r$ points is exactly $\binom{m}{2r}$ (because selection of $2r$ positions can be assigned as starting and ending positions uniquely to the code blocks). By an averaging argument there must be at least $\frac{|D|}{\binom{m}{2r}} \geq \frac{|D|}{m^{2r}}$ messages in D for which these $2r$ locations will be identical.

Combining Lemmas 3 and 4, we get that there exists a set B of size at least $|\mathbb{F}|^{\frac{\delta n}{4} - 2r \log_{|\mathbb{F}|}(m) - 2}$ and index t that satisfy the conditions in both the lemmas.

Lemma 5. *There exists a set of messages $D \subseteq B$ of size at least $|\mathbb{F}|^{\frac{\delta n}{4} - 2r(\log m) - \frac{rS}{\log |\mathbb{F}|} - 2}$ where the following properties hold for any messages $\mathsf{msg}, \mathsf{msg}' \in D$:*

1. $\mathsf{msg}[i] = \mathsf{msg}'[i]$ for all $i \neq t$.
2. At the end of the kth pass, c_{msg} and $c_{\mathsf{msg}'}$ differ only in the portions occupied by the blocks $c[t, 1], \ldots, c[t, k]$. Furthermore, the contents of the work tape of the encoding algorithm at the end of the kth pass will be identical.

Proof. Observe that all messages in B have the property that they are identical on all blocks except at block t. Moreover, the starting and ending positions w.r.t the code when the encoding algorithm reads block t are identical for all messages in B. We can now follow essentially the same argument as Claim 2 to prove this claim.

We conclude the proof of Theorem 4 by observing that if D has at least two messages we arrive at a contradiction because for every message in D, $c[t]$ is at most $\delta m/2$ and for any two messages the corresponding codes only differ in these locations. Thus, if $\frac{\delta n}{4} - 2r(\log_{|\mathbb{F}|} m) - \frac{rS}{\log |\mathbb{F}|} - 2 > 0$, we arrive at a contradiction.

4   Main Construction

In this section, we present a short overview of our space-efficient zero-knowledge argument system for RAM programs based on collision-resistant hash-functions. Please refer to the full version for a more detailed presentation.

The first main step in our construction is transforming a RAM program to the Ligero constraint system. This is summarized in the Lemma below.

Lemma 6. *Let M be an arbitrary (non-deterministic) Random Access Machine that on input strings (x, w) runs in time T and space S. Then, (M, x) can be transformed into the following system of constraints over a $m \times \ell$ matrix X:*

1. X *is a* $m \times \ell$ *matrix that is subdivided into sub-matrices or blocks* $X_1, \ldots, X_B$

   where each X_i *is a* $m' \times \ell$ *matrix,* $X = \begin{bmatrix} X_1 \\ X_2 \\ \vdots \\ X_B \end{bmatrix}$ *and* $B = O\left(\frac{T}{S}\right), m' =$

   $\mathsf{polylog}(T)$, $m = m' \cdot B$ *and* $\ell = S \cdot polylog(T)$. *We denote by* x_i *the "flattened" vector corresponding to matrix* X_i *(namely,* x_i *is the vector obtained by concatenating the rows of* X_i*).*

2. *(Intra-block Linear Constraints)* A *is of size* $(m' \cdot \ell) \times (m' \cdot \ell)$ *and* b *is a length* $(m' \cdot \ell)$*-vector and* $Ax_i = b$ *for all* $i \in [B]$.

3. *(Inter-block Linear Constraints)* A' *is a* $(2m' \cdot \ell) \times (2m' \cdot \ell)$ *matrix and* b' *is a length* $(2m' \cdot \ell)$*-vector and* $A' \begin{bmatrix} x_i \\ x_{i+1} \end{bmatrix} = b'$ *for all* $i \in [B-1]$.

4. *(Input-Consistency Constraint)* A'' *is a* $|x| \times (m' \cdot \ell)$ *matrix and* $A''x_1 = x$ *where* $|x|$ *is the size of* x.

5. *(Quadratic Constraints) For each* $i \in [B]$, $X_i^{left} \odot X_i^{right} = X_i^{out}$ *where* $\odot$

   denotes point-wise products and $X_i = \begin{bmatrix} X_i^{inp} \\ X_i^{left} \\ X_i^{right} \\ X_i^{out} \end{bmatrix}$ *where* X_i^{inp} *is* $m_{inp} \times \ell$

   matrix and $X_i^{left}, X_i^{right}, X_i^{out}$ *are* $m_{mult} \times \ell$ *matrices.*

Efficiency. *Furthermore, the matrices* A, A' *and* A'' *are succinct according to Definition 3 and an input-witness pair* (x, w) *that makes* M *accept can be mapped to an extended witness* X *by a RAM machine in* $T \cdot polylog(T)$ *and space* $S \cdot polylog(T)$.

Equivalency. *Any* X *that satisfies the system of constraints can be mapped to a* w *such that* M *accepts* (x, w).

The core of our construction is a space-efficient IPCP for the linear and quadratic tests. We will only focus on linear test in this version of the paper. For the full description of all the elements of our protocol, we refer the reader to the full version. A formal description of the linear test is given below.

Lemma 7. *Protocol 1 is an IOP/IPCP for testing linear constraints with the following properties:*

- **Completeness:** *If* $U \in L^m$ *is an encoding of a* $m \times \ell$ *matrix* X *such that, for every* $i \in [B]$, $Ay_i = b$ *where* y_i *is the flattened vector corresponding to* Y_i *and block* Y_i *is a* $m' \times \ell$ *submatrix of* X *starting at the* $I[i]^{th}$ *row of* X *and the* $\mathcal{P}$ *is honest, then* $\mathcal{V}$ *accepts with probability 1.*

Protocol 1 (Testing linear constraints over Interleaved RS Codes)
Input: L^m-codeword U, #blocks B, vectors $\{y_i\}_{i\in[B]}$ each of length $m'\ell$, indices $\{I[i]\}_{i\in[B]}$, matrix A of size $m_a \times m'\ell$, vector b of length m_a.
Oracle: A purported L^m-codeword U that should encode $m \times \ell$ matrix X such that, for every $i \in [B]$ we have $Ay_i = b$ where y_i is the flattened vector corresponding to Y_i and block Y_i is a $m' \times \ell$ submatrix of X starting at the $I[i]^{th}$ row of X.
Linear Test:

1. V picks two random seeds $s, s' \in \mathbb{F}$ and sends it to $\mathcal{P}$.
2. $\mathcal{P}$ sends $q(\cdot) = \sum_{i\in[B]} r'[i]q_i(\cdot)$ to V where $r = (1, s, s^2, \ldots, s^{m_a-1})$, $r' = (1, s', s'^2, \ldots, s'^{B-1}), r^T A = (r_{1,1}, \ldots r_{1,\ell}, \ldots, r_{m',1}, \ldots, r_{m',\ell})$ and $q_i(\cdot) = \sum_{k\in[m']} r_k(\cdot)p_{I[i]+k-1}(\cdot)$, and $r_i(\cdot)$ is the polynomial of degree $< \ell$ such that $r_i(\zeta_j) = r_{i,j}$ for all $j \in [\ell]$.
3. V queries a random subset $Q \subseteq [n]$ of size t to obtain the columns of U corresponding Q.
4. V accepts if
    (a) $q(\cdot)$ is of degree $< 2\ell - 1$.
    (b) $\sum_{k\in[\ell]} q(\zeta_k) = \sum_{i\in[B]} r'[i]r^T b$.
    (c) For every $i \in Q$,
        $\sum_{j\in[B], k\in[m']} r'[j] \cdot r_k(\eta_i)U_{k+I[j],i} = q(\eta_i)$.

Fig. 1. Protocol for linear test.

– **Soundness:** *Let e be a positive integer such that $e < d/2$ where d is minimal distance of Reed-Solomon code. Suppose that a badly formed matrix U^* is e-close to a codeword U that encodes a matrix X such that $\exists i \in [B]$, $Ay_i \neq b$ where y_i is the flattened vector corresponding to Y_i and block Y_i is a $m' \times \ell$ submatrix of X starting at the $I[i]^{th}$ row of X. Then for any malicious $\mathcal{P}^*$ strategy, V will reject except with probability $((e + 2\ell)/n)^t + (m_a + B)/|\mathbb{F}|$.*
– **Complexity:**
  $\mathcal{P}$ has X on its input tape and has a work tape of size $O(m'\ell)$. In this model, $\mathcal{P}$ makes a single pass on the input tape. We denote by $m\ell$ the length of X, the number of blocks as B and y_i is a flattened vector of a block within X of size $m' \times \ell$. Given that $\mathcal{P}$ is provided with a one-way linear access to X, matrix A is a public succinct matrix of dimension $m_a \times m'\ell$ as defined in Definition 3 then the following complexities are obtained:
  - *Prover's Time $= m'\ell\mathrm{poly}\log m_a + O(m'\ell B \log \ell)$.*
  - *Verifier's Time $= m'\ell\mathrm{poly}\log m_a + O(m'\ell\kappa + Bm'\kappa)$*
  - *Prover's Space $= O(m'\ell)$.*
  - *Verifier's Space $= O(\kappa m' + m_a)$.*
  - *Communication Complexity $= O(\ell)$.*
  - *Query Complexity $= O(\kappa)$.*

Our IPCP Protocol. Given a RAM program M, we construct a zero-knowledge argument system for $\mathsf{BH_{RAM}}(M)$ by composing the following two components.

1. A complexity-preserving reduction from $\mathsf{BH}_{\mathsf{RAM}}$ to extended witness X that satisfies the system of constraints defined in Lemma 6.
2. The protocols for testing interleaved linear codes, linear constraints and quadratic constraints require oracle access to L^m-codeword U that encodes the extended witness X. The prover computes the outputs of the tests by processing X block-by-block. The verifier has a "succinct" representation of the system of constraints imposed on X and can therefore check the outputs of the tests in a space-efficient manner.

We compose these two components as follows. At a high level, the prover generates the extended witness X block-by-block as described in the reduction from $\mathsf{BH}_{\mathsf{RAM}}$ to X. As and when a block is generated, the prover processes this block to compute "running partial outputs" for each of the three tests. The prover only needs to store a few blocks in memory at a time rather than the entire extended witness.

Theorem 5. *Fix parameters $m, m', m_{\mathsf{mult}}, n, \ell, B, t, e, d$ such that $e < d/3$ and $d = n - \ell + 1$. For every NP relation that can be verified by a time T and space S RAM machine M with input x has a public-coin IOP/IPCP with the following properties:*

1. *Completeness: If there exist an witness w such that $M(x, w)$ with time T and space S is accepted and $\mathcal{P}$ generated the oracle U honestly, then $\mathcal{V}$ accepts with probability 1.*
2. *Soundness: Let there exist no witness w such that $M(x, w)$ is accepted in time T and space S, then for every unbounded prover strategy $\mathcal{P}^*$, $\mathcal{V}$ will reject except with $(1 - e/n)^t + 4((e + 2\ell)/n)^t + (d + 3m'\ell + m_{mult} + |x| + 3B)/|\mathbb{F}|$.*
3. *Complexity: The complexities are in terms of the number of field operations performed or number of field elements over a field $\mathbb{F}$ below.*
   (a) The prover runs in time $T \cdot \mathsf{poly}(\log T, \kappa)$ and uses space $S \cdot \mathsf{poly}(\log T, \kappa)$.
   (b) The verifier runs in time $(T/S + S) \cdot \mathsf{poly}(\log T, \kappa)$ and uses space $\mathsf{poly}(\log T, \kappa)$.
   (c) The communication complexity is $S \cdot \mathsf{poly}(\log T, \kappa)$, query complexity of the verifier is $(T/S) \cdot \mathsf{poly}(\log T, \kappa)$ and number of rounds is a constant.

where κ is the statistical security parameter.

In the full version, we also show how to modify our IPCP to obtain zero-knowledge and then how to improve the communication to $\tilde{O}(T/S)$.

5   Space-Efficient Affine Code Testing for Interleaved Reed Solomon Codes

We begin by providing a high-level overview of our IPCP system. It follows the same blueprint of the Ligero system (described in the introduction). In a nutshell, our construction is a space-efficient variant of each phase of the Ligero blueprint. The main steps involved in our IPCP system are as follows.

1. **RAM to circuit reduction:** Given a RAM program M, we transform the RAM program to circuits by relying on the transformation of [4,11] where the resulting circuit C has a "succinct" representation.

2. **Preparing the proof oracle:** Next, the prover evaluates the circuit C on the private witness w to compute all wire values (input, intermediate and output) and arranges the values in a specific way in a $m \times \ell$ matrix X referred to as the extended witness. The prover then encodes the matrix using a Interleaved Reed Solomon (IRS) code to obtain a $m \times n$ matrix U, namely, each row of U is an encoding of a corresponding row in X using a Reed Solomon code; this is the proof oracle. The prover computes U in a row-by-row manner, which is space-efficient.

3. **Testing the encoding:** This step involves testing interleaved linear codes in a space efficient manner. This essentially follows as in the previous step as $r^{\mathrm{T}}U$ can be computed by recomputing U row-by-row and maintaining a running partial aggregate of $\sum_j r_j U_{j,\cdot}$.

4. **Testing linear constraints:** This step shows how the linear test can be performed in a space efficient manner. This is the non-trivial part of the construction as we need to utilize the succinct representation of C and the arrangement of the extended witness in U to compute the response in a space-efficient manner.

5. **Testing quadratic constraints:** This step relies on ideas from the previous two steps to obtain a space-efficient version of the quadratic test.

In this section, we focus on our space-efficient IPCP for the linear test (mentioned in step 4 above), which is one of the core aspects of our construction. We defer to the reader to the full version of our paper for the descriptions of the rest of the steps mentioned above.

This test checks if the linear constraints imposed by the addition gates and the circuit's structure are satisfied. The linear check is performed over blocks, where each block Y_i starts at the row $I[i]$ of the extended witness X and is of size $m' \times \ell$ for all $i \in B$. Precisely, given a public matrix A of size $(m' \cdot \ell) \times (m' \cdot \ell)$ and a vector b of size $(m' \cdot \ell)$, the linear constraints are $Ay_i = b$ for each $i \in [B]$ where y_i is the flattened vector of Y_i and is of size $(m' \cdot \ell)$. Note that linear constraints imposed on each block are the same, which are captured by same parameters A and b for all blocks.

Recall that the linear test in Ligero handles all the linear constraints over the extended witness X in a single shot (represented as a linear equation $A'X = b'$ for some public matrix A' and vector b'). Whereas we consider a variant of the linear test where the same set of linear constraints repeat over different sections (i.e., blocks) of the extended witness, which is represented as linear equations $Ay_i = b$ for all $i \in [B]$.

We first describe a simple algorithm for the new variant of linear test and later show how to further improve the verifier's time and space costs. At a high level, we apply Ligero's linear test on each block and then take a random linear combination of the outputs of the test for each block. At the prover's end, naively computing $r^{\mathrm{T}}A$ is expensive as A is a large matrix. By observing that the matrix

Table 2. Description of the parameters.

Parameter	Description
Y_i	Blocks associated with the linear constraints
y_i	Flattened vector corresponding to block Y_i
B	#Blocks associated with the linear test
m'	#Rows in each block Y_i
$I[i]$	Index of the first row of X included in Y_i
s	Seed 1 for randomness
s'	Seed 2 for randomness
r	Randomness vector 1
r'	Randomness vector 2
A	Linear constraint matrix
b	Linear constraint vector
m_a	#Linear constraint for each y_i
$r_{i,j}$	The value of the matrix at position (i,j) when parsing $r^T A$ into a matrix
$r_i(\cdot)$	i^{th} polynomial generated by encoding $r^T A$

A is sparse (more precisely, A is succinct), we reduce the time and space required significantly by efficiently computing the positions of the non-zero elements of A.

Roughly, the protocol for linear test proceeds as follows. The verifier provides two random seeds $s, s' \in \mathbb{F}$, from which the prover and verifier can generate random vectors r and r'. We require two randomness vectors where one is used as random linear combiners for rows within a block, while the other is used as random linear combiners across blocks. The prover computes the polynomial encoding $q_i(\cdot)$ of $(r^T A)y_i$ for each block Y_i and then computes the polynomial encoding $q(\cdot) = \sum_{i \in [B]} r'[i] \cdot q_i(\cdot)$ of all the blocks. Lastly, the verifier checks the consistency of $q(\cdot)$ with $\sum_{i \in [B]} r'[i] \cdot (r^T b)$ and U on t randomly chosen columns. Refer to Fig. 1 for a formal description of the protocol and Table 2 for a description of the parameters.

Algorithm DEval(v, R): On input (v, R), this algorithm outputs an evaluation vector $e = \{p(\eta_j)\}_{\eta_j \in R}$ where the polynomial $p(\cdot)$ is defined such that $p(\zeta_i) = v[i]$ for all $i \in [\ell]$, ζ_i are the interpolation points, η_j are the evaluation points and R is the set of query points. The input vector v is provided to the algorithm in an input tape where the algorithm individually reads and processes each element in vector v. The algorithm repeats until all the elements are read from the input tape. The input v is a vector of size ℓ which needs to be interpolated. We denote the set of interpolation points to be ζ and set of evaluation points to be η. Note that the set R needs to be a subset of η i.e. $R \subseteq \eta$.

We set the evaluation points and interpolation points to be related to the roots of unity. In more detail, let w be a primitive $2n^{th}$ root of unity where

$w^{2n} = 1$ but $w^m \neq 1$ for $0 < m < 2n$. We set the variable $f = n/\ell$, $\zeta = \{1, w^{2f}, w^{4f}, \ldots, w^{2f(\ell-1)}\}$ and $\eta = \{w, w^3, \ldots w^{2f(\ell-1)+1}\}$. Each individual interpolation point and evaluation point can be represented as $\zeta_i = w^{2(i-1)f}$ and $\eta_j = w^{2j-1}$ respectively. The algorithm is as follows:

1. Check if $R \subseteq \eta$. Abort if the check fails. If the check succeeds, initialize $e_j = 0$ for all j such that $\eta_j \in R$.
2. Upon receiving an element $v[k]$ from the input tape, update the running partial sum $e_j = e_j + \frac{1}{\ell} \frac{w^{(2j-1)\ell}-1}{w^{2k-1-2fk+2f}-1} v[k]$ for all j such that $\eta_j \in R$.
3. After processing each element from the vector v, output all $e_j's$ for all j such that $\eta_j \in R$.

Proof. **Correctness:** Define a vector c such that each element of c represents the coefficient of the polynomial $p(\cdot)$ and v is the vector which is being interpolated. We represent the relation between c and v as $v = Xc$ where X is a public matrix and the ith row of X can be represented as $X[i] = (\zeta_i^0, \zeta_i^1, \ldots \zeta_i^{\ell-1})$. Each element in X can be represented as $X[i, j] = \zeta_i^{j-1} = w^{2(i-1)(j-1)f}$. Another way to represent the same equation is $c = X^{-1}v$ where X^{-1} is the inverse of the matrix X i.e. $XX^{-1} = I$ and I is an identity matrix.

It now follows that $X^{-1}[i, j] = \frac{1}{\ell}w^{-2(i-1)(j-1)f}$. Lastly, to evaluate $p(\cdot)$ at η_j, we define a vector $w = (1, \eta_j, \ldots, \eta_j^{\ell-1})$ and represent $p(\eta_j)$ as $p(\eta_j) = w^T c = w^T X^{-1}v$. We calculate vector $w^T X^{-1}$ as:

$$w^T X^{-1}[k] = \sum_{l=1}^{\ell} w[l] \cdot X^{-1}[l, k]$$

$$= \sum_{l=1}^{\ell} \eta_j^{l-1} \cdot \frac{1}{\ell} w^{-2(l-1)(k-1)f}$$

$$= \frac{1}{\ell} \sum_{l=1}^{\ell} w^{(2j-1)(l-1)} \cdot w^{-2(l-1)(k-1)f}$$

$$= \frac{1}{\ell} \sum_{l=1}^{\ell} w^{(l-1)(2j-1-2kf+2f)}$$

$$= \frac{1}{\ell} \frac{w^{(2j-1)\ell} - 1}{w^{2j-1-2kf+2f} - 1}$$

$$p(\eta_j) = w^T X^{-1}v$$

$$= \sum_{k=1}^{\ell} w^T X^{-1}[k]v[k]$$

$$= \frac{1}{\ell} \sum_{k=1}^{\ell} \frac{w^{(2j-1)\ell} - 1}{w^{2j-1-2kf+2f} - 1} v[k]$$

The algorithm reads each element of the vector v sequentially from the input tape. Initialising $e_j = 0$ and after reading the element $v[k]$, the algorithm updates $e_j = e_j + \frac{w^{(2j-1)\ell}-1}{w^{2j-1-2k\ell+2\ell}-1}v[k]$. After processing the whole vector v, e_j will satisfy $e_j = p(\eta_j)$. Hence it shows the correctness of the algorithm.

Efficiency Analysis: For each element of v, the algorithm performs $O(1)$ operations per evaluation point. Thus, the overall computational cost is $O(t\ell)$ where t is the number of evaluations and ℓ is the size of v. The algorithm requires only $O(t)$ space to store only e_j's and the t evaluation points.

Lemma 8. *Protocol 1 is an IOP/IPCP for testing linear constraints with the following properties:*

- **Completeness:** *If $U \in L^m$ is an encoding of a $m \times \ell$ matrix X such that, for every $i \in [B]$, $Ay_i = b$ where y_i is the flattened vector corresponding to Y_i and block Y_i is a $m' \times \ell$ submatrix of X starting at the $I[i]^{th}$ row of X and the $\mathcal{P}$ is honest, then $\mathcal{V}$ accepts with probability 1.*
- **Soundness:** *Let e be a positive integer such that $e < d/2$ where d is minimal distance of Reed-Solomon code. Suppose that a badly formed matrix U^* is e-close to a codeword U that encodes a matrix X such that $\exists i \in [B]$, $Ay_i \neq b$ where y_i is the flattened vector corresponding to Y_i and block Y_i is a $m' \times \ell$ submatrix of X starting at the $I[i]^{th}$ row of X. Then for any malicious $\mathcal{P}^*$ strategy, $\mathcal{V}$ will reject except with probability $((e+2\ell)/n)^t + (m_a+B)/|\mathbb{F}|$.*
- **Complexity:**
  $\mathcal{P}$ has X on its input tape and has a work tape of size $O(m'\ell)$. In this model, $\mathcal{P}$ makes a single pass on the input tape. We denote by $m\ell$ the length of X, the number of blocks as B and y_i is a flattened vector of a block within X of size $m' \times \ell$. Given that $\mathcal{P}$ is provided with a one-way linear access to X, matrix A is a public succinct matrix of dimension $m_a \times m'\ell$ as defined in Definition 3 then the following complexities are obtained:
  - *Prover's Time $= O(m'\ell(poly\log m_a + B\log\ell))$.*
  - *Verifier's Time $= O(m'\ell(poly\log m_a + \kappa) + Bm'\kappa)$.*
  - *Prover's Space $= O(m'\ell)$.*
  - *Verifier's Space $= O(\kappa m' + m_a)$.*
  - *Communication Complexity $= O(\ell)$.*
  - *Query Complexity $= O(\kappa)$.*

Refer to the full version for the proof of completeness and soundness. Next, we discuss the time and space complexities for the prover and the verifier.

Prover's Time Complexity. Each column of A can be computed in time $O(poly\log m_a)$ and computing each element of $r^{\mathsf{T}}A$ requires the same complexity. As length of vector $r^{\mathsf{T}}A$ is $m'\ell$, computing $r^{\mathsf{T}}A$ needs $O(m'\ell poly\log m_a)$ time. The polynomials $r_i(\cdot)$ generated in Step 2 can be constructed using inverse-FFT in $O(m'\ell\log\ell)$ time. The intermediate proof polynomial $q_i(\cdot)$ is composed by multiplying m' pairs of polynomial, each multiplication costs $O(\ell\log\ell)$ using FFT. The proof polynomial $q(\cdot)$ requires $O(Bm'\ell\log\ell)$ time as it is generated by taking a random linear combination of all the intermediate proof polynomials. The prover's total time is $O(m'\ell(poly \log m_a + B \log \ell))$.

Before proceeding to the next analysis, we introduce a new lemma. This lemma allows the verifier to efficiently evaluate the sum of evaluation of a polynomial given the evaluation points are roots of unity.

Lemma 9. *Given a polynomial $p(\cdot)$ of degree t and H be the ℓth roots of unity, then $\sum_{a \in H} p(a) = \ell \sum_{i mod \ell = 0} c_i$.*

We refer the readers to the full version for the proof.

Verifier's Time Complexity. The verifier upon receiving the proof polynomial $q(\cdot)$, needs to execute two checks. The first check is to check whether $\sum_{j \in [\ell]} q(\zeta_j) = \sum_{i \in [B]} r'[i] r^T b$. To optimise the check, we leverage the structure of interpolation points ζ. We show that $\ell(c_0 + c_\ell) = \sum_{j \in [\ell]} q(\zeta_j)$ where c_0 and c_ℓ are the constant and ℓ^{th} coefficient of the polynomial $q(\cdot)$. To prove this, we directly use Lemma 9. This Lemma states that if a polynomial $p(\cdot)$ is evaluated at ℓ^{th} roots of unity, then the evaluation of the polynomial at all the roots of unity sums up to $\ell \sum_{i \mod \ell = 0} c_i$ where c_i is the ith coefficient of the polynomial $p(\cdot)$. Therefore, we can verify whether $\ell(c_0 + c_\ell) = \sum_{i \in [B]} r'[i] r^T b$. This requires $O(m_a + B)$ time. To verify the second check, the verifier needs to generate t evaluations of polynomial $r_i(\cdot)$ defined in Step 2. To compute it, the verifier first evaluates $r^T A$ element by element. For each vector $v = (r_{i,1}, \ldots, r_{i,\ell})$ which is computed element by element and stored in the input tape of algorithm DEval. The algorithm DEval outputs t evaluation $r_i(\cdot)$ where $r_i(\cdot)$ can be generated using v. Evaluating v requires $O(\ell poly \log m_a)$ time and $t = O(\kappa)$ evaluations is generated in $O(\ell \kappa)$. As there are total m' polynomials, all evaluations are completed in $O(m'\ell(poly \log m_a + \kappa))$ time. In addition, the verifier needs $O(\ell \kappa)$ for evaluating $q(\cdot)$ at $t = \kappa$ evaluations and require $O(Bm'\kappa)$ operations to verifying the consistency between $q(\cdot)$ and U. Therefore, the total time to verify this check is $O((Bm'+\ell)\kappa)$. The verifier's total time is $O(m'\ell(poly \log m_a + \kappa) + Bm'\kappa + m_a)$.

Prover's Space Complexity. Firstly, the prover computes $r^T A$ and the polynomials $r_i(\cdot)$ defined in Step 2 and stores them to be used for each $i \in [B]$ which requires $O(m'\ell)$ space in the work tape. To compute the polynomial $q(\cdot)$ in Step 2 in a space-efficient manner while making a single pass on input tape X, we implement Step 2 by maintaining a running partial aggregate. More precisely, the prover initialises the polynomial $agg(\cdot) = 0$. Next, the prover processes X row by row. It keeps track of the blocks Y_i that contain the current row. There can be at most m' blocks Y_i that contain X as there can be at most one block that starts from any row of X. Let min_i and max_i denote the first and last block indices which contain the ith row of X. The polynomial $agg(\cdot)$ is updated as follows:

$$agg(\cdot) = agg(\cdot) + p_i(\cdot) \sum_{l=min_i}^{max_i} r'[l] r_{i-I[l]}(\cdot) \tag{1}$$

After every row of X is processed, we set our proof polynomial as $q(\cdot) = agg(\cdot)$. The space required to generate the polynomial $q(\cdot)$ is the space for storing $p_i(\cdot)$,

$\mathsf{agg}(\cdot)$ and the product of two polynomials of degree $< \ell$. Since we can multiply polynomials via FFT, the space required is $O(\ell)$. Therefore, the overall space complexity of the prover in the interactive phase is dominated by storing the $r_i(\cdot)$ polynomials which is $O(m'\ell)$.

Verifier's Space Complexity. Upon receiving the proof polynomial $q(\cdot)$, the verifier performs the following three checks:

- The degree of q is at most $k + \ell - 1$. This can be done by simply counting the number of coefficients.
- The polynomial q satisfies $\sum_{j \in [\ell]} q(\zeta_j) = \sum_{i \in [B]} r'[i] r^{\mathsf{T}} b$. Following the optimization mentioned in the time complexity analysis, the verifier simply checks if $\ell \cdot (c_0 + c_\ell) = \sum_{i \in [B]} r'[i] r^{\mathsf{T}} b$ where c_0 and c_l are the constant and ℓ^{th} coefficient of the polynomial $q(\cdot)$. This requires $O(m_a)$ space to store b.
- Finally, the verifier needs to compute $t = O(\kappa)$ evaluations on polynomials $r_i(\cdot)$ generated in Step 2. As we described in the beginning of this section, the verifier will rely on the DEval algorithm is executed to generate these evaluations. The verifier needs $O(m'\kappa)$ space where m' is the number of polynomials. For each query $j \in Q$, the verifier initialises each variable $\mathsf{agg}_j = 0$. When the verifier processes the ith element (or i^{th} row of U) of each column of U queried, it computes public variables $\min_i$ and $\max_i$ just as the prover and each variable agg_j for all $j \in Q$ is updated as follows:

$$\mathsf{agg}_j = \mathsf{agg}_j + U_{i,j} \sum_{l=\min_i}^{\max_i} r'[l] r_{i-I[l]}(\eta_j) \tag{2}$$

As all $r_i(\eta_j)$ are already stored by the verifier, the verifier requires to store only the agg_j variable for each j. Overall the verifier's space is $O(m'\kappa + m_a)$.

Acknowledgements. We thank the anonymous TCC'22 reviewers for their helpful comments. The first author conducted research during her internship at JP Morgan. The second and third authors are supported by the BIU Center for Research in Applied Cryptography and Cyber Security in conjunction with the Israel National Cyber Bureau in the Prime Minister's Office and ISF grant No. 1316/18. The third and fourth authors are supported by DARPA under Contract No. HR001120C0087. Any opinions, findings and conclusions or recommendations expressed in this material are those of the author(s) and do not necessarily reflect the views of the United States Government or DARPA.

References

1. Ames, S., Hazay, C., Ishai, Y., Venkitasubramaniam, M.: Ligero: lightweight sublinear arguments without a trusted setup. In: CCS, pp. 2087–2104 (2017)
2. Ben-Sasson, E., Bentov, I., Horesh, Y., Riabzev, M.: Fast Reed-Solomon interactive oracle proofs of proximity. In: ICALP, pp. 14:1–14:17 (2018)

3. Ben-Sasson, E., Bentov, I., Horesh, Y., Riabzev, M.: Scalable zero knowledge with no trusted setup. In: Boldyreva, A., Micciancio, D. (eds.) CRYPTO 2019. LNCS, vol. 11694, pp. 701–732. Springer, Cham (2019). https://doi.org/10.1007/978-3-030-26954-8_23
4. Ben-Sasson, E., Chiesa, A., Genkin, D., Tromer, E.: Fast reductions from RAMs to delegatable succinct constraint satisfaction problems: extended abstract, In: ITCS, pp. 401–414 (2013)
5. Ben-Sasson, E., Chiesa, A., Riabzev, M., Spooner, N., Virza, M., Ward, N.P.: Aurora: transparent succinct arguments for R1CS. In: Ishai, Y., Rijmen, V. (eds.) EUROCRYPT 2019. LNCS, vol. 11476, pp. 103–128. Springer, Cham (2019). https://doi.org/10.1007/978-3-030-17653-2_4
6. Ben-Sasson, E., Chiesa, A., Spooner, N.: Interactive oracle proofs. In: Hirt, M., Smith, A. (eds.) TCC 2016. LNCS, vol. 9986, pp. 31–60. Springer, Heidelberg (2016). https://doi.org/10.1007/978-3-662-53644-5_2
7. Bhadauria, R., Fang, Z., Hazay, C., Venkitasubramaniam, M., Xie, T., Zhang, Y.: Ligero++: a new optimized sublinear IOP. In: CCS, pp. 2025–2038 (2020)
8. Bitansky, N., Chiesa, A.: Succinct arguments from multi-prover interactive proofs and their efficiency benefits. In: Safavi-Naini, R., Canetti, R. (eds.) CRYPTO 2012. LNCS, vol. 7417, pp. 255–272. Springer, Heidelberg (2012). https://doi.org/10.1007/978-3-642-32009-5_16
9. Block, A.R., Holmgren, J., Rosen, A., Rothblum, R.D., Soni, P.: Public-coin zero-knowledge arguments with (almost) minimal time and space overheads. In: Pass, R., Pietrzak, K. (eds.) TCC 2020. LNCS, vol. 12551, pp. 168–197. Springer, Cham (2020). https://doi.org/10.1007/978-3-030-64378-2_7
10. Block, A.R., Holmgren, J., Rosen, A., Rothblum, R.D., Soni, P.: Time- and space-efficient arguments from groups of unknown order. In: Malkin, T., Peikert, C. (eds.) CRYPTO 2021. LNCS, vol. 12828, pp. 123–152. Springer, Cham (2021). https://doi.org/10.1007/978-3-030-84259-8_5
11. Blumberg, A.J., Thaler, J., Vu, V., Walfish, M.: Verifiable computation using multiple provers. IACR Cryptology ePrint Archive, p. 846 (2014)
12. Bootle, J., Chiesa, A., Liu, S.: Zero-knowledge succinct arguments with a linear-time prover. IACR Cryptology ePrint Archive, p. 1527 (2020)
13. Bowe, S., Grigg, J., Hopwood, D.: Halo: Recursive proof composition without a trusted setup. IACR Cryptology ePrint Archive, p. 1021 (2019)
14. Bünz, B., Bootle, J., Boneh, D., Poelstra, A., Wuille, P., Maxwell, G.: Bulletproofs: short proofs for confidential transactions and more. In: Proceedings of 2018 IEEE Symposium on Security and Privacy, SP 2018, San Francisco, California, USA, 21–23 May 2018, pp. 315–334. IEEE Computer Society (2018)
15. Bünz, B., Chiesa, A., Mishra, P., Spooner, N.: Recursive proof composition from accumulation schemes. In: TCC, pp. 1–18 (2020)
16. Chiesa, A., Ojha, D., Spooner, N.: FRACTAL: post-quantum and transparent recursive proofs from holography. In: Canteaut, A., Ishai, Y. (eds.) EUROCRYPT 2020. LNCS, vol. 12105, pp. 769–793. Springer, Cham (2020). https://doi.org/10.1007/978-3-030-45721-1_27
17. Coron, J.-S., Dodis, Y., Malinaud, C., Puniya, P.: Merkle-Damgård revisited: how to construct a hash function. In: Shoup, V. (ed.) CRYPTO 2005. LNCS, vol. 3621, pp. 430–448. Springer, Heidelberg (2005). https://doi.org/10.1007/11535218_26
18. Ephraim, N., Freitag, C., Komargodski, I., Pass, R.: SPARKs: succinct parallelizable arguments of knowledge. In: Canteaut, A., Ishai, Y. (eds.) EUROCRYPT 2020. LNCS, vol. 12105, pp. 707–737. Springer, Cham (2020). https://doi.org/10.1007/978-3-030-45721-1_25

19. Fiat, A., Shamir, A.: How To prove yourself: practical solutions to identification and signature problems. In: Odlyzko, A.M. (ed.) CRYPTO 1986. LNCS, vol. 263, pp. 186–194. Springer, Heidelberg (1987). https://doi.org/10.1007/3-540-47721-7_12

20. Goldwasser, S., Micali, S., Rackoff, C.: The knowledge complexity of interactive proof-systems (extended abstract). In: STOC, pp. 291–304 (1985)

21. Hazay, C., Ishai, Y., Marcedone, A., Venkitasubramaniam, M.: LevioSA: lightweight secure arithmetic computation. In: CCS (2019)

22. Holmgren, J., Rothblum, R.: Delegating computations with (almost) minimal time and space overhead. In: Thorup, M. (ed.) 59th IEEE Annual Symposium on Foundations of Computer Science, FOCS 2018, Paris, France, 7–9 October 2018, pp. 124–135. IEEE Computer Society (2018). https://doi.org/10.1109/FOCS.2018.00021

23. Ishai, Y.: Zero-knowledge proofs from information-theoretic proof systems (2020). https://zkproof.org/2020/08/12/information-theoretic-proof-systems

24. Ishai, Y., Kushilevitz, E., Ostrovsky, R., Sahai, A.: Zero-knowledge from secure multiparty computation. In: STOC, pp. 21–30 (2007)

25. Kilian, J.: A note on efficient zero-knowledge proofs and arguments (extended abstract). In: Proceedings of the 24th Annual ACM Symposium on Theory of Computing, pp. 723–732 (1992)

26. Kothapalli, A., Masserova, E., Parno, B.: A direct construction for asymptotically optimal zkSNARKS. IACR Cryptology ePrint Archive, p. 1318 (2020)

27. Lee, J., Setty, S.T.V., Thaler, J., Wahby, R.S.: Linear-time zero-knowledge snarks for R1CS. IACR Cryptology ePrint Archive, p. 30 (2021)

28. Lindell, Y., Pinkas, B.: An efficient protocol for secure two-party computation in the presence of malicious adversaries. In: Naor, M. (ed.) EUROCRYPT 2007. LNCS, vol. 4515, pp. 52–78. Springer, Heidelberg (2007). https://doi.org/10.1007/978-3-540-72540-4_4

29. Mohassel, P., Rosulek, M., Scafuro, A.: Sublinear zero-knowledge arguments for RAM programs. In: Coron, J.-S., Nielsen, J.B. (eds.) EUROCRYPT 2017. LNCS, vol. 10210, pp. 501–531. Springer, Cham (2017). https://doi.org/10.1007/978-3-319-56620-7_18

30. Reed, I.S., Solomon, G.: Polynomial codes over certain finite fields. J. Soc. Ind. Appl. Math. 8(2), 300–304 (1960)

31. Reingold, O., Rothblum, G.N., Rothblum, R.D.: Constant-round interactive proofs for delegating computation. In: STOC, pp. 49–62 (2016)

32. Savage, J., Swamy, S.: Space-time trade-offs on the FFT algorithm. IEEE Trans. Inf. Theor. 24(5), 563–568 (1978). https://doi.org/10.1109/TIT.1978.1055938

33. Setty, S.: Spartan: efficient and general-purpose zkSNARKs without trusted setup. In: Micciancio, D., Ristenpart, T. (eds.) CRYPTO 2020. LNCS, vol. 12172, pp. 704–737. Springer, Cham (2020). https://doi.org/10.1007/978-3-030-56877-1_25

34. Setty, S.T.V., Lee, J.: Quarks: quadruple-efficient transparent zkSNARKs. IACR Cryptology ePrint Archive, p. 1275 (2020)

35. Thaler, J.: Proofs, arguments, and zero-knowledge (2021). https://people.cs.georgetown.edu/jthaler/ProofsArgsAndZK.html

36. Xie, T., Zhang, J., Zhang, Y., Papamanthou, C., Song, D.: Libra: succinct zero-knowledge proofs with optimal prover computation. In: Boldyreva, A., Micciancio, D. (eds.) CRYPTO 2019. LNCS, vol. 11694, pp. 733–764. Springer, Cham (2019). https://doi.org/10.1007/978-3-030-26954-8_24

37. Zhang, J., Xie, T., Zhang, Y., Song, D.: Transparent polynomial delegation and its applications to zero knowledge proof. In: S&P, pp. 859–876. IEEE (2020)

A Toolbox for Barriers on Interactive Oracle Proofs

Gal Arnon[1]([⊠]), Amey Bhangale[2], Alessandro Chiesa[3], and Eylon Yogev[4]

[1] Weizmann Institute, Rehovot, Israel
gal.arnon@weizmann.ac.il
[2] UC Riverside, Riverside, USA
amey.bhangale@ucr.edu
[3] EPFL, Lausanne, Switzerland
alessandro.chiesa@epfl.ch
[4] Bar-Ilan University, Ramat Gan, Israel
eylon.yogev@biu.ac.il

Abstract. Interactive oracle proofs (IOPs) are a proof system model that combines features of interactive proofs (IPs) and probabilistically checkable proofs (PCPs). IOPs have prominent applications in complexity theory and cryptography, most notably to constructing succinct arguments.

In this work, we study the limitations of IOPs, as well as their relation to those of PCPs. We present a versatile toolbox of IOP-to-IOP transformations containing tools for: (i) length and round reduction; (ii) improving completeness; and (iii) derandomization.

We use this toolbox to establish several barriers for IOPs:
- Low-error IOPs can be transformed into low-error PCPs. In other words, interaction can be used to construct low-error PCPs; alternatively, low-error IOPs are as hard to construct as low-error PCPs. This relates IOPs to PCPs in the regime of the sliding scale conjecture for inverse-polynomial soundness error.
- Limitations of quasilinear-size IOPs for 3SAT with small soundness error.
- Limitations of IOPs where query complexity is much smaller than round complexity.
- Limitations of binary-alphabet constant-query IOPs.

We believe that our toolbox will prove useful to establish additional barriers beyond our work.

Keywords: Probabilistically checkable proofs · Interactive oracle proofs · Lower bounds

G. Arnon—Supported in part by a grant from the Israel Science Foundation (no. 2686/20) and by the Simons Foundation Collaboration on the Theory of Algorithmic Fairness.

A. Chiesa—Supported in part by the Ethereum Foundation.

E. Yogev—Supported in part by the BIU Center for Research in Applied Cryptography and Cyber Security in conjunction with the Israel National Cyber Bureau in the Prime Minister's Office, and by the Alter Family Foundation.

E. Kiltz and V. Vaikuntanathan (Eds.): TCC 2022, LNCS 13747, pp. 447–466, 2022.
https://doi.org/10.1007/978-3-031-22318-1_16

1   Introduction

Probabilistic proof systems have enabled breakthroughs in complexity theory and cryptography in areas such as zero-knowledge, delegation of computation, hardness of approximation, and more.

A probabilistically checkable proof (PCP) [6,24] is a proof system in which a polynomial-time probabilistic verifier has query access to a proof string. The power of PCPs is often exemplified by the celebrated PCP theorem [4,5]: every language in NP can be decided, with constant soundness error, by probabilistically examining a constant number of bits in a polynomial-size proof. Decades of PCP research have achieved many other goals and applications.

Yet challenging open problems about PCPs remain. For example, the shortest PCPs known to date have quasi-linear length [13,20], and efforts to achieve linear length have not succeeded. As another example, it remains open to construct a PCP for NP with soundness error $1/n$, alphabet size $\text{poly}(n)$, query complexity $O(1)$, and randomness complexity $O(\log n)$. The existence of such "low-error" PCPs is known as the "sliding-scale conjecture".

Interactive Oracle Proofs. Due to the lack of progress on these and other open problems, researchers introduced an interactive variant of PCPs called *interactive oracle proofs* (IOP) [12,34]. A k-round IOP is a k-round IP where the verifier has PCP-like access to each prover message (the verifier may read a few symbols from any prover message).

A rich line of work constructs IOPs that provide significant efficiency improvements over known PCPs [8–11,14–17,28,31,35,36,38]. In particular, known IOPs achieve desirable properties such as linear proof length, fast provers, added properties such as zero-knowledge, and even good concrete efficiency. In turn, these IOPs have led to breakthroughs in the construction of highly-efficient cryptographic proofs, which have been widely deployed in real-world applications.

Another line of work shows that IOPs can also be used to prove hardness of approximation results for certain stochastic problems [2,3,19,22].

What is the Power of IOPs? Since IOPs were invented to bypass open problems of PCPs, it is crucial to understand the limitations of IOPs, and the relation to the limitations of PCPs.

What are the limitations of IOPs, and how do they compare to PCPs?

For example: What trade-offs are there between round complexity, query complexity, and soundness error in IOPs? How small can the soundness error of an IOP be if we require constant query complexity but allow increasing the alphabet size (as in a sliding-scale PCP)?

In this paper, we explore these and other questions.

1.1   Our Results

We show several results for IOPs in different regimes: (1) low-error IOPs imply low-error PCPs; (2) limitations of short IOPs; (3) limitations of high-round low-query IOPs; and (4) limitations of binary-alphabet constant-query IOPs. All these results follow from combining various tools from a new toolbox of transformations for IOPs. We discuss this toolbox in more detail in Sect. 2. We believe that our toolbox will prove useful to establish additional barriers beyond our work.

(1) Low-Error IOPs Imply Low-Error PCPs. The "sliding scale" conjecture [7] states that for every β with $1/\text{poly}(n) \leq \beta < 1$ there is a PCP system for NP that has perfect completeness, soundness error β, polynomial proof length over a $\text{poly}(1/\beta)$-size alphabet, constant query complexity, and logarithmic randomness complexity. A major open problem is constructing such PCPs when β is an inverse polynomial.

We show that (under a complexity assumption or using non-uniformity), a polylog-round IOP with inverse-polynomial soundness error and constant query complexity can be transformed into a sliding-scale PCP with inverse-polynomial soundness error.

Theorem 1 (informal). *Let R be a relation with a public-coin IOP with perfect completeness, soundness error $1/n$, round complexity $\text{polylog}(n)$, alphabet size $\text{poly}(n)$, proof length $\text{poly}(n)$, and query complexity $O(1)$. Then under a derandomization assumption[1] (or alternatively by using a non-uniform verifier) R has a PCP with perfect completeness, soundness error $1/n$, alphabet size $\text{poly}(n)$, proof length $\text{poly}(n)$, and query complexity $O(1)$.*

Our full theorem, described in the full version of this paper, allows for trade-offs between the parameters of the IOP and PCP.

Theorem 1 can be interpreted as a positive result or a negative result. The positive viewpoint is that efforts towards constructing sliding-scale PCPs can rely on interaction as an additional tool. The negative viewpoint is that constructing $\text{polylog}(n)$-round IOPs with sliding-scale parameters is as hard as constructing sliding-scale PCPs.

Our theorem does leave open the question of constructing $\text{poly}(n)$-round IOPs with constant query complexity and small soundness error.

(2) Limitations of Short IOPs. While the shortest PCPs known have quasi-linear proof length, constructing linear-size PCPs remains a major open problem. In contrast, interaction has enabled IOPs to achieve linear proof length (e.g., [10]). Yet, we do not have a good understanding of the relation between proof length and soundness error for IOPs. We show that, under the randomized exponential-time hypothesis (RETH),[2] short IOPs for 3SAT have high soundness error.

---

[1] There exists a function in E with circuit complexity $2^{\Omega(n)}$ for circuits with PSPACE gates.

[2] RETH states that there exists a constant $c > 0$ such that 3SAT $\notin \text{BPTIME}[2^{c \cdot n}]$.

Theorem 2 (informal). *Assume* RETH *and suppose that there exists a public-coin IOP for n-variate* 3SAT *with the following parameters: perfect completeness, soundness error β, round complexity* polylog(n), *alphabet size λ, (total) proof length* l, *and query complexity* q.

If $\left(\frac{l \cdot \log \lambda}{n}\right)^{\mathsf{q}} \leq n^{\text{polylog}(n)}$, then $\beta > \Omega\left(\frac{n}{l \cdot \log \lambda}\right)^{\mathsf{q}}$.

The theorem provides a barrier to improving some state-of-the-art PCPs. Dinur, Harsha, and Kindler [21] come close to a sliding-scale PCP in the inverse-polynomial regime: they construct a PCP for NP with perfect completeness, soundness error $1/\text{poly}(n)$, alphabet size $n^{1/\text{polyloglog}(n)}$, proof length poly$(n)$, and query complexity polyloglog(n). While IOPs have been useful in improving proof length over PCPs, Theorem 2 implies that IOPs are unlikely to help achieving nearly-linear proof length in the parameter regime of [21] (even when significantly increasing alphabet size).

Corollary 1. *Assuming* RETH, *there is no public-coin IOP for n-variate* 3SAT *with perfect completeness, soundness error $1/n$, round complexity* polylog(n), *alphabet size $n^{\text{polylog}(n)}$, proof length $n \cdot$polylog(n), and query complexity* polyloglog(n).

We leave open the question of whether IOPs in this parameter regime can be made to have linear proof length by using $O(n)$ rounds of interaction.

(3) Limitations of High-Round Low-Query IOPs. Goldreich, Vadhan, and Wigderson [27] show that IP[k] $\neq$ IP[o(k)] for every k, under reasonable complexity assumptions. In other words, IPs with k rounds cannot be "compressed" to have o(k) rounds. In contrast, Arnon, Chiesa, and Yogev [2] show that k-round IPs can be modified so that the verifier *reads* o(k) rounds. We show that reading o(k) rounds comes at the price of a large soundness error.

Theorem 3. *Let $L \in$ AM[k]\AM[k$'$] be a language for k$' <$ k and suppose that L has a public-coin IOP with perfect completeness, soundness error β, round complexity k, alphabet size $2^{\text{poly}(n)}$, proof length poly(n), and query complexity q $\leq$ k$'$. Then $\beta \geq \Omega\left(\frac{k'}{k}\right)^{\mathsf{q}} - n^{-c}$ for every constant $c > 0$.*

This provides a barrier to improving the parameters of IOPs in [2]. They show that any language in IP[$\log(n)$] has an IOP with perfect completeness, soundness error $1/\text{polylog}(n)$, round complexity polylog(n), alphabet size $2^{\text{poly}(n)}$, and query complexity $O(1)$. By Theorem 3 the soundness error $1/\text{polylog}(n)$ is tight unless IP[$\log(n)$] = IP[$O(1)$]. Moreover, since the soundness error of IOPs is closely related to the approximation factor for the value of stochastic constraint satisfaction problems (SCSP) (see [2]), our theorem additionally provides barriers to proving hardness of approximation results for SCSPs using IOPs.

(4) Limitations of Binary-Alphabet Constant-Query IOPs. PCPs with a binary alphabet and small query complexity cannot have good soundness. In more detail, assuming the randomized exponential-time hypothesis, any binary-alphabet PCP with perfect completeness, soundness error β, and query complexity q satisfies the following.

- If $q = 2$ then $\beta = 1$ (i.e., no such PCPs exist). This follows from the fact that we have linear time algorithms to check satisfiability of every binary-alphabet 2-ary constraint satisfaction problem.
- If $q = 3$ then $\beta > 5/8$. Zwick [39] gives a polynomial-time algorithm that, on input a satisfiable CSP with binary alphabet and arity 3, distinguishes whether the CSP is satisfiable or whether every assignment satisfies at most a 5/8 fraction of the constraints. This implies that, unless P = NP, every PCP for NP with binary alphabet, polynomial size, and query complexity 3 must have soundness error greater than $5/8$.[3] Håstad [30] shows that this lower bound on soundness error is essentially optimal: for every $\varepsilon > 0$, he constructs a PCP for NP with perfect completeness, soundness error $5/8 + \varepsilon$, binary alphabet, polynomial proof length, and query complexity 3.

We ask whether interaction can help in further reducing the soundness error in the constant-query regime. Our next result shows that this is unlikely if the number of rounds is not large.

Theorem 4. *Assume* RETH *and suppose that there exists a non-adaptive public-coin IOP for n-variate 3SAT with the following parameters: perfect completeness, soundness error β, round complexity k, alphabet size 2, proof length $2^{o(n)}$, query complexity q, verifier randomness r, and verifier running time $2^{o(n)}$.*

- *If $q = 2$ then $\beta > 1 - \varepsilon$ for every ε satisfying $k \cdot \log(r \cdot n/\varepsilon) = o(n)$.*
- *If $q = 3$ then $\beta > 5/8 - \varepsilon$ for every ε satisfying $k \cdot \log(r \cdot n/\varepsilon) = o(n)$.*

For example, assuming RETH, there is no public-coin IOP with perfect completeness, soundness error $\beta = 1 - 2^{-o(n)}$, round complexity $k = \text{polylog}(n)$, alphabet size 2, proof length $2^{o(n)}$, query complexity 2, and verifier randomness $r = 2^{o(n)}$.

The bound on the query complexity of PCPs can be extended to q queries for any $q = O(1)$ for which there is a polynomial-time algorithm that decides q-ary CSPs. Theorem 4 generalizes similarly to match the soundness error for PCPs. However, for $q > 3$, we do not know the exact optimal soundness error for PCPs with perfect completeness [29].

Constructing an IOP for 3SAT with polynomial round complexity, binary alphabet, constant query complexity, and small soundness error remains an open problem.

1.2 Related Work

Barriers on Probabilistic Proofs. We describe known limitations about PCPs, IPs, and IOPs.

- *PCPs.* If P $\neq$ NP then, for every $q = o(\log n)$ and $r = o(\log n)$, NP has no non-adaptive PCP with alphabet size $\lambda = O(1)$, query complexity q, and randomness complexity r. Indeed, the PCP-to-CLIQUE reduction in [23], given

---

[3] Assuming ETH, the proof length of the PCP can be $2^{o(n)}$.

an instance x for the language L of the PCP, produces, in polynomial time, a graph of size $\lambda^q \cdot 2^r \ll n$ whose maximum clique size is either large (if $x \in L$) or small (if $x \notin L$), where the gap between these sizes depends on the PCP's completeness and soundness errors. By iteratively applying that reduction a polynomial number of times, one can (in polynomial time) reduce x to a graph G of size $O(\log n)$, while preserving the large-or-small property of the maximum clique. Since the size of G is logarithmic, one can then determine in polynomial time whether the largest clique in G is large or small, and thereby decide membership for the original instance x.

Moreover, if $P \neq NP$ then NP does not have non-adaptive PCPs with alphabet size $\lambda = O(1)$, query complexity $q = O(1)$, and randomness complexity $r = O(\log n)$ with soundness error $\beta < \frac{\log \lambda}{\lambda^{q-1}}$. Indeed, such a non-adaptive PCP can be converted into a CSP of size $\text{poly}(n)$, and any efficient algorithm for approximating the CSP's number of satisfied constraints imposes a limitation on the soundness error β. For example, the bound $\frac{\log \lambda}{\lambda^{q-1}}$ follows from the approximation algorithm in [32]. Assuming ETH, these limitations can be extended to PCPs with super-polynomial proof length and super-constant alphabet size and query complexity. See the full version of this paper for a quantitative proof of how to combine PCPs with small soundness error for 3SAT and polynomial-time approximation algorithms for CSPs in order to decide 3SAT faster than is possible under ETH.

Notice that an adaptive PCP with alphabet size λ and query complexity q can be converted into a non-adaptive PCP with query complexity λ^q, which is constant when $\lambda = O(1)$ and $q = O(1)$. Hence the above discussion applies to adaptive PCPs in this regime as well.

– *IPs.* [26] show that public-coin IPs with bounded prover communication complexity can be decided in non-trivial (probabilistic) time. [27] strengthen these results for the case of private-coin IPs, showing that similar bounds on communication imply that the complement of the language can be decided in non-trivial non-deterministic time. Such results are limitations on IPs for languages believed to be hard, such as SAT.

– *IOPs.* In order to derive barriers for succinct arguments, [18] extend to IOPs the limitations of [26], showing barriers for IOPs with small soundness error relative to query complexity.

[33] show limitations for *succinct* IOPs for circuit SAT (CSAT), where the proof length is polynomial in the number n of circuit inputs. The results cover different parameters, depending on the "plausibility" of the complexity assumption used. For example (on the most probable end), suppose that the satisfiability of a circuit C cannot be decided by a $\text{poly}(n)$-space algorithm following $\text{poly}(|C|)$-time preprocessing. Then there is no succinct IOP for CSAT with constant round complexity and logarithmic query complexity.

IOP-to-IOP Transformations. Our toolbox (outlined in Sect. 2) contains IOP-to-IOP transformations that include round reduction, achieving perfect completeness, and derandomization.

- [2,3] provide IOP-to-IOP transformations for round reduction and achieving perfect completeness, but we cannot use them because those transformations do *not* preserve query complexity of the IOP (a key property for us).
- [33] show that any public-coin IOP can be transformed into one with less interaction randomness at the cost of introducing a "common reference string" (CRS) and satisfying only non-adaptive soundness. Their main goal is to achieve randomness complexity that depends (logarithmically) only on the prover-to-verifier communication complexity (but not the instance length) and on an error parameter over the choice of the CRS. They also show that the CRS can be replaced with non-uniform advice for the verifier at the cost of increasing the randomness complexity to also depend (logarithmically) on the instance length. Our derandomization lemma focuses on IOPs with a non-uniform verifier and allows choosing the target randomness complexity, rather than optimizing with regards to the prover-to-verifier communication complexity.
- [1] show how to derandomize *private-coin IPs* via non-uniform advice or PRGs. Our derandomization lemma applies to public-coin IOPs.

2   Techniques

We describe our tools for IOPs and sketch their proofs, and then show how they can be applied to achieve our main results. Further details on how these tools are constructed can be found in the full version of this paper. The tools are divided into three groups.

1. **Tools for length and round reduction:** Sect. 2.1 outlines transformations that decrease the length and round complexity of IOPs with low query complexity.
2. **Tools for improving completeness:** Section 2.2 outlines transformations that improve the completeness errors of IOPs.
3. **Tools for derandomization:** Section 2.3 outlines transformations that decrease the number of random bits used by the IOP verifier.

Following the presentation of our toolbox, in Sect. 2.4 we explain how we use the tools (in conjunction with additional arguments) to derive the theorems described in Sect. 1.1.

2.1   Tools for Length and Round Reduction

We describe how to decrease the length and round complexity of IOPs.

Lemma 1 (informal). *Let R be a relation with a public-coin IOP $(\mathbf{P}, \mathbf{V})$ with completeness error α, soundness error β, round complexity k, alphabet size λ, per-round proof length l, query complexity q, per-round verifier randomness r, and verifier running time vt.*

1. **Length reduction:** *Let ℓ be a parameter with $q \le \ell \le k \cdot l$. Then R has a public-coin IOP with completeness error $1 - (1 - \alpha) \cdot (\ell/(e \cdot k \cdot l))^q$, soundness error β, round complexity k, alphabet size λ,* **total proof length ℓ,** *query complexity q, per-round verifier randomness $r + \ell \cdot \log(k \cdot l)$, and verifier running time $\mathrm{poly}(vt, \ell)$.*
2. **Round reduction:** *Let k' be a parameter with $q \le k' \le k$. Then R has a public-coin IOP with completeness error $1 - (1 - \alpha) \cdot (k'/(e \cdot k))^q$, soundness error β,* **round complexity $k' + 1$,** *alphabet size λ, per-round proof length l, query complexity q, per-round verifier randomness $k \cdot (r + \log k)$, and verifier running time $\mathrm{poly}(vt)$.*
3. **Unrolling to PCP:** *R has a PCP with completeness error α, soundness error β, alphabet size λ, proof length $l \cdot 2^{O(k \cdot r)}$, query complexity q, randomness $k \cdot r$, and verifier running time $\mathrm{poly}(vt)$.*

Below we sketch the proofs of Items 1 and 2. Item 3 is folklore and follows by setting the PCP to equal the interaction tree of the IOP.

Length Reduction. The length of low-query IOPs can be reduced while incurring an increase in the completeness error. The intuition is that if the IOP has query complexity $q \ll k \cdot l$, then each symbol in the proof is read by the verifier with small probability. Hence, if the prover omits a random subset of the proof symbols, the verifier is unlikely to require these missing symbols.

Construction 1 (informal). The new prover $\mathbf{P}'$ receives as input an instance x and a witness w, while the verifier $\mathbf{V}'$ receives as input the instance x. They interact as follows.

1. $\mathbf{V}'$ *guesses the locations that $\mathbf{V}$ will query.* $\mathbf{V}'$ samples and sends a random set $I \subseteq [k \cdot l]$ of ℓ indices from among all the prover message symbols.
2. *The original IOP is simulated with prover messages omitted according to I.* For every $j \in [k]$:
   (a) $\mathbf{V}'$ sends $\rho_j \leftarrow \{0,1\}^r$.
   (b) $\mathbf{P}'$ computes $\pi_j := \mathbf{P}(x, w, \rho_1, \ldots, \rho_j)$ and sends π'_j equal to π_j with symbols outside of I omitted.
3. $\mathbf{V}'$ *simulates $\mathbf{V}$, and rejects if any queries are made outside of I.* $\mathbf{V}'$ simulates the decision stage of $\mathbf{V}$ given input x. Whenever an index $i \in I$ is queried, return the appropriate symbol from the prover messages. If an index $i \notin I$ is queried, then immediately reject. Output the same answer as $\mathbf{V}$.

The *total* proof length is ℓ since the prover $\mathbf{P}'$ sends only those symbols whose index is in I (which has size ℓ). The per-round verifier randomness at most $r + \ell \cdot \log(k \cdot l)$ because in the first round the verifier sends I (which can be described with $\ell \cdot \log(k \cdot l)$ random bits) and then it sends its first message of r bits. The rest of the complexity parameters follow straightforwardly from the construction.

Soundness follows from the fact that the changes made to the IOP can only increase the chance that the verifier rejects. We sketch the proof of completeness. Fix some $x \in L$. The locations read by $\mathbf{V}$ are independent of the set I. Therefore, the probability that $\mathbf{V}$ queries outside the set I is $\binom{k \cdot l - q}{l - q} / \binom{k \cdot l}{l} \geq (\ell/(e \cdot k \cdot l))^q$. Conditioned on $\mathbf{V}$ querying only inside I, $\mathbf{V}$ accepts with probability at least $1 - \alpha$. Hence the probability that the new verifier $\mathbf{V}'$ accepts is at least $(1 - \alpha) \cdot (\ell/(e \cdot k \cdot l))^q$.

Round Reduction. We sketch how the round-complexity of low-query IOPs can be reduced. The intuition behind this lemma is similar to that described for length reduction: if $q \ll k$, then the verifier is unlikely to need most of the rounds, so removing a random subset of the rounds does not harm completeness by much. Below we describe the transformation for IOP round reduction.

Construction 2 (informal). The new prover $\mathbf{P}'$ receives as input an instance x and a witness w, while the verifier $\mathbf{V}'$ receives as input the instance x. They interact as follows.

1. $\mathbf{V}'$ *guesses the rounds that* $\mathbf{V}$ *will query.* $\mathbf{V}'$ samples and sends a random set $I \subseteq [k]$ of k' indices. Denote $I := (i_1, \ldots, i_{k'})$ with $i_j < i_{j+1}$ and let $i_0 := 1$.
2. *The original IOP is simulated with rounds omitted according to* I. For every $j \in [k']$:
   (a) $\mathbf{V}'$ sends $\rho_{i_{(j-1)}+1}, \ldots, \rho_{i_j} \leftarrow \{0,1\}^r$.
   (b) $\mathbf{P}'$ computes and sends $\pi_j := \mathbf{P}(x, w, \rho_1, \ldots, \rho_{i_j})$.
3. $\mathbf{V}'$ *simulates* $\mathbf{V}$, *and rejects if any queries are made outside of* I. $\mathbf{V}'$ samples $\rho_{i_{k'}+1}, \ldots, \rho_k \leftarrow \{0,1\}^r$ simulates the decision stage of $\mathbf{V}$ given input x and verifier messages $\rho_1, \ldots, \rho_k$. Whenever an index in round $i \in I$ is queried, return the appropriate symbol in the prover messages. If a round $i \notin I$ is queried, then immediately reject. Output the same answer as $\mathbf{V}$.

A technical remark: as written above, the protocol is not public-coin because the verifier's first message I dictates the length of subsequent verifier messages. Nevertheless, the protocol can be made public-coin by padding verifier messages to $k \cdot r$ bits. The prover and verifier act as in the protocol description, ignoring the padding bits. The verifier additionally sends $k' \cdot \log k$ bits as the choice of the set I. Thus, the per-round randomness of the verifier is $k \cdot r + k' \cdot \log k \leq k \cdot (r + \log k)$.

2.2 Tools for Improving Completeness

A transformation for achieving perfect completeness for IPs is shown in [25]. Directly applying that transformation to IOPs increases the query complexity of the protocol significantly. We show a variant of the transformation in [25] that preserves query complexity up to a small additive constant.

Lemma 2 (informal). *Let* R *be a relation with a public-coin IOP* $(\mathbf{P}, \mathbf{V})$ *with completeness error* α, *soundness error* β, *round complexity* k, *alphabet size* λ, *per-round proof length* l, *query complexity* q, *per-round verifier randomness* r, *and verifier running time* vt.
    Then R *has a public-coin IOP with* **perfect completeness**, *soundness error* $O\left(\frac{\beta \cdot k \cdot r}{\log(1/\alpha)}\right)$, *round complexity* $k + 1$, *alphabet size* $\max\{\lambda, 2^{k \cdot r}\}$, *per-round proof length* $O\left(\frac{l \cdot k \cdot r}{\log(1/\alpha)}\right)$, *query complexity* $q + 2$, *per-round verifier randomness* r, *and verifier running time* poly(vt).

Remark 1. If only small completeness error is desired (rather than completeness error 0), then this can be achieved with similar query complexity but smaller overhead to the alphabet size. See the full version of this paper for more details.

Review: Perfect Completeness for IPs. Consider the set S of verifier random coins $\vec{\rho} = (\rho_1, \ldots, \rho_k)$ (over the entire protocol) where the honest prover has a strategy to make the verifier accept if it is sent these strings while interacting with the verifier. Given the matching prover messages, the verifier can efficiently check whether $\vec{\rho} \in S$. [25] shows that for large enough t there exist "shifts" $\vec{z}_1, \ldots, \vec{z}_t$ such that for *every* choice of verifier randomness $\vec{\rho}$ there exists j such that $(\vec{z}_j \oplus \vec{\rho}) \in S$. It follows that the honest prover needs only to send these shifts, and then run the protocol with the verifier, giving answers matching each shift. At the end of the protocol, the verifier accepts if and only if $\vee_{j=1}^{t}((\vec{z}_j \oplus \vec{\rho}) \overset{?}{\in} S) = 1$. The soundness error degrades by a multiplicative factor of t since a malicious prover only needs to convince the verifier in one execution.

Perfect Completeness for IOPs. The aforementioned verifier computes the "OR" of t expressions. We observe that, in order to prove the claim $\vee_{j=1}^{t}((\vec{z}_j \oplus \vec{\rho}) \overset{?}{\in} S) = 1$, it suffices for the prover to send the verifier a *single* index j where $(\vec{z}_j \oplus \vec{\rho}) \in S$, which is then checked by the verifier. The verifier only needs to check *a single execution* of the IOP, rather than t, and so the query complexity of the protocol is preserved up to reading the index j and shift $\vec{z}_j$.

Construction 3. Let $t := 2 \cdot \left(\frac{r \cdot k}{\log(1/\alpha)} \right)$. The new prover $\mathbf{P}'$ receives as input an instance $\mathbb{x}$ and a witness $\mathbb{w}$, while the verifier $\mathbf{V}'$ receives as input the instance $\mathbb{x}$. They interact as follows.

1. $\mathbf{P}'$ *sends t "shifts" for the verifier randomness.* $\mathbf{P}'$ sends

$$\vec{z}_1, \ldots, \vec{z}_t = (z_{1,1}, \ldots, z_{1,k}), \ldots, (z_{t,1}, \ldots z_{t,k}) \in \{0, 1\}^{r \cdot k} \, ,$$

   to the verifier such that for every $\vec{\rho}$ there exists j where $(\vec{z}_j \oplus \vec{\rho}) \in S$ (i.e., the original prover $\mathbf{P}$ has an accepting strategy for verifier randomness $(\vec{z}_j \oplus \vec{\rho})$).
2. *Original IOP is simulated, where for every verifier message, prover replies with a message for each shifted randomness.* For $i = 1, \ldots, k$:
   - $\mathbf{V}'$: Choose $\rho_i \leftarrow \{0, 1\}^r$ uniformly and send to the prover.
   - $\mathbf{P}'$: Send $\{\pi_{j,i}\}_{j \in [t]}$ where $\pi_{j,i} := \mathbf{P}(\mathbb{x}, \mathbb{w}, \rho_1 \oplus z_{j,1}, \ldots, \rho_i \oplus z_{j,i})$.
3. *Prover sends index j of shift where its messages succeed in convincing the verifier.* $\mathbf{P}'$: If there exists an index $j \in [t]$, such that $\mathbf{V}^{\pi_{j,1}, \ldots, \pi_{j,k}}(\mathbb{x}, \rho_1 \oplus z_{j,1}, \ldots, \rho_k \oplus z_{j,k}) = 1$, then send j to the verifier $\mathbf{V}'$ as a non-oracle message. Otherwise, send $\bot$.
4. $\mathbf{V}'$ *checks that $\mathbf{V}$ accepts the "shifted" j-th execution.* $\mathbf{V}'$: Receive j as a non-oracle message.

(a) If $j = \bot$, then reject.

(b) Otherwise, query $\vec{z}_j = (z_{j,1}, \ldots, z_{j,k})$ and check that

$$\mathbf{V}^{\pi_{j,1}, \ldots, \pi_{j,k}}\left(\mathbb{x}, \rho_1 \oplus z_{j,1}, \ldots, \rho_k \oplus z_{j,k}\right) = 1 \ ,$$

querying the appropriate proofs as required by $\mathbf{V}$.

2.3   Tools for Derandomization

We show how to derandomize public-coin IOPs based on non-uniform advice or based on pseudorandom generators (PRGs), while preserving the use of public-coins. Both transformations achieve logarithmic randomness complexity but slightly increase completeness and soundness error. Round complexity, proof length, and query complexity are preserved.

Lemma 3 (informal). *Let R be a relation with a public-coin IOP $(\mathbf{P}, \mathbf{V})$ with completeness error α, soundness error β, round complexity k, alphabet size λ, per-round proof length l, query complexity q, per-round verifier randomness r, and verifier running time vt.*

1. ***Derandomization using PRGs:*** *Suppose that there exists a PRG against polynomial-size PSPACE circuits with seed length ℓ, error ε and evaluation time $\mathsf{t}_{\mathsf{PRG}}$. Then R has a public-coin IOP with completeness error $1 - O((1 - \alpha) - \varepsilon \cdot \mathsf{k}^2)$, soundness error $O(\beta + \varepsilon \cdot \mathsf{k}^3)$, round complexity k, alphabet size λ, per-round proof length l, query complexity q, **per-round verifier randomness** ℓ, and verifier running time $\mathrm{poly}(\mathsf{vt}, \mathsf{t}_{\mathsf{PRG}})$.*
   (Such a PRG with seed length $\ell = O(\log |\mathbb{x}|)$, error $\varepsilon = 1/\mathrm{poly}(|\mathbb{x}|)$ and computation time $\mathsf{t}_{\mathsf{PRG}} = \mathrm{poly}(|\mathbb{x}|)$ exists if there exists a function in E with circuit complexity $2^{\Omega(n)}$ for circuits with PSPACE gates.)

2. ***Derandomization using non-uniformity:*** *Let $\varepsilon \in (0, 1)$ be a parameter. Then R has a public-coin IOP with completeness error $\alpha + \mathsf{k} \cdot \varepsilon$, soundness error $\beta + \mathsf{k} \cdot \varepsilon$, round complexity k, alphabet size λ, per-round proof length l, query complexity q, **per-round verifier randomness** $\Theta(\log ((\mathsf{r} \cdot \mathsf{k} + |\mathbb{x}|)/\varepsilon))$, and verifier running time $\mathrm{poly}(\mathsf{vt}, \mathsf{k}, \mathsf{l}, \mathsf{r}, 1/\varepsilon)$, where the verifier receives $\mathrm{poly}(|\mathbb{x}|, \mathsf{k}, \mathsf{r}, 1/\varepsilon)$ bits of non-uniform advice. Moreover, a random string constitutes good advice with probability $1 - 2^{-|\mathbb{x}|}$.*

We focus the overview below on Item 1. Item 2 can be shown in a similar manner.

Derandomization Using PRGs. We show that IOPs can be derandomized using a pseudo-random generator. In this transformation, the verifier samples seeds for the PRG rather than uniform random messages. Thus the verifier randomness per-round is as small as a seed of the PRG.

Construction 4 (informal).   On instance $\mathbb{x}$ and witness $\mathbb{w}$, the protocol $(\mathbf{P}', \mathbf{V}')$ proceeds as follows:

1. *Simulate original IOP where verifier messages are chosen using the PRG.* For $j = 1, \ldots, k$:
   (a) $\mathbf{V}'$: Sample and send a random $\rho_j \leftarrow \{0,1\}^\ell$.
   (b) $\mathbf{P}'$: Compute and send the prover message π_j that maximizes the probability that $\mathbf{V}$ accepts where all of the verifier messages are chosen using the PRG G.
2. $\mathbf{V}'$: Accept if and only if $\mathbf{V}^{\pi_1, \ldots, \pi_k}(\mathbf{x}, G(\rho_1), \ldots, G(\rho_k)) = 1$.

The verifier sends ℓ_{PRG} bits of randomness in each round, since it sends a seed for the PRG. The rest of the complexity parameters follow straightforwardly from the construction.

Interaction Trees. The *interaction tree* of a protocol on input $\mathbf{x}$, denoted $T_{\mathbf{x}}$ is the full tree of all possible transcripts corresponding to each choice of prover and verifier messages. The leaves are labelled as accepting or rejecting corresponding to whether the verifier accepts or rejects the full transcript represented by the leaf.

The *value* of an interaction tree $T_{\mathbf{x}}$, denoted by $\mathsf{val}(T_{\mathbf{x}})$, is the probability of reaching an accepting leaf from the root of the tree in a walk on the tree where verifier messages are chosen uniformly at random and prover messages are chosen so as to maximize the probability of reaching an accepting node. The notion of value extends to sub-trees as well, where the value is the probability of reaching an accepting leaf when beginning on the root of the sub-tree. Notice that $\mathsf{val}(T_{\mathbf{x}}) = \max_{\tilde{\mathbf{P}}} \{\Pr[\langle \tilde{\mathbf{P}}, \mathbf{V} \rangle(\mathbf{x}) = 1]\}$. Moreover, $\mathsf{val}(T_{\mathbf{x}})$ can be computed in space that is polynomial in $|\mathbf{x}|$, the round complexity, the proof length, and the verifier randomness of the IOP.

Completeness and Soundness. Completeness and soundness follow straightforwardly from Sect. 2.3, which says that the value of the interaction tree of the IOP does not change by much when the verifier messages are sampled via a PRG.

Claim. Let G be a PRG against circuits of size $\mathrm{poly}(|\mathbf{x}|)$ with PSPACE gates. Then for every instance $\mathbf{x}$:

$$O(\mathsf{val}(T) - \epsilon_{\mathsf{PRG}} \cdot k^2) \le \mathsf{val}(T_G) \le O(\mathsf{val}(T) + \epsilon_{\mathsf{PRG}} \cdot k^3) \ ,$$

where T is the interaction tree of the IOP and T_G is the interaction tree of $(\mathbf{P}', \mathbf{V}')$, which is identical to T except verifier randomness is always sampled using the PRG G.

We give a simplified sketch of the proof of the claim. Let $T^{(0)} := T_G$ and for $i = 1, \ldots, k$ let $T^{(i)}$ be the tree of an intermediate protocol where the messages $\rho_1, \ldots, \rho_i$ are chosen uniformly at random and $\rho_{i+1}, \ldots, \rho_k$ are chosen from the PRG. Notice that $T^{(k)} = T$.

We show that, under a simplifying assumption to be described later, there exist circuit families $\mathcal{C}^{(1)}, \ldots, \mathcal{C}^{(k)}$ each comprised of circuits of size $\mathrm{poly}(|\mathbf{x}|, k, \mathsf{l}, \mathsf{r})$ that have PSPACE gates, such that if G fools $\mathcal{C}^{(i)}$ then

$$|\mathsf{val}(T^{(i-1)}) - \mathsf{val}(T^{(i)})| \le \epsilon_{\mathsf{PRG}} \cdot \mathsf{k} \ .$$

Letting $\mathcal{C} := \cup_i \mathcal{C}_i$, we have that if G fools $\mathcal{C}$ (i.e., fools circuits of size $\max_{C \in \mathcal{C}} |C| = \mathsf{poly}(|\mathbf{x}|, \mathsf{k}, \mathsf{l}, \mathsf{r})$), then

$$|\mathsf{val}(T_\mathbf{x}) - \mathsf{val}(T_{\mathbf{x},\mathsf{G}})| \le \epsilon_{\mathsf{PRG}} \cdot \mathsf{k}^2 \ .$$

Fix some i. We show a family $\mathcal{C}^{(i)}$ such that if G fools $\mathcal{C}^{(i)}$ then $|\mathsf{val}(T^{(i-1)}) - \mathsf{val}(T^{(i)})| \le \epsilon_{\mathsf{PRG}} \cdot \mathsf{k}$. Consider a fixed node in $T^{(i)}$ corresponding to the transcript prefix $\mathsf{tr} = (\rho_1, m_1, \dots, \rho_{i-1}, m_{i-1})$ (which is empty if $i = 1$). For ρ_i let $T^{(i,\mathsf{tr})}(\rho_i)$ be the sub-tree of $T^{(i)}$ whose root corresponds to the transcript $(\mathsf{tr}\|\rho_i)$.
Define

$$S := \left\{ \left(1 + \frac{1}{3\mathsf{k}}\right)^{-1}, \dots, \left(1 + \frac{1}{3\mathsf{k}}\right)^{-O(\mathsf{k})}, 0 \right\} \ .$$

We make the simplifying assumption that $\mathsf{val}(T^{(i,\mathsf{tr})}(\rho_i)) \in S$ and $\mathsf{val}(T^{(i-1,\mathsf{tr})}(\rho_i)) \in S$ for every ρ_i. In the full proof of the claim we achieve this by discretizing the functions $\mathsf{val}(T^{(i,\mathsf{tr})}(\cdot))$ and $\mathsf{val}(T^{(i-1,\mathsf{tr})}(\cdot))$, which incurs additional errors. For simplicity, we ignore these errors in this overview.

For every transcript tr, let $\mathcal{C}^{(i,\mathsf{tr})} := \{C_p^{(i,\mathsf{tr})}\}_{p \in S}$ where each circuit $C_p^{(i,\mathsf{tr})}$, on input ρ_i, outputs 1 if and only if $\mathsf{val}(T^{(i,\mathsf{tr})}(\rho_i)) = p$. We observe that a careful implementation of $C_p^{(i,\mathsf{tr})}$ (computing the value of a tree can be done space proportional to its depth) has size at most $\mathsf{poly}(|\mathbf{x}|, \mathsf{k}, \mathsf{l}, \mathsf{r})$ using PSPACE gates. Thus, if G fools every circuit in the family $\mathcal{C}^{(i,\mathsf{tr})}$ we get that

$$\mathsf{val}(T^{(i-1,\mathsf{tr})}) = \sum_{p \in S} p \cdot \Pr_s[C_p^{(i,\mathsf{tr})}(\mathsf{G}(s)) = 1]$$

$$\le \sum_{p \in S} p \cdot \left(\Pr_{\rho_i}[C_p^{(i,\mathsf{tr})}(\rho_i) = 1] + \epsilon_{\mathsf{PRG}} \right)$$

$$= \mathsf{val}(T^{(i,\mathsf{tr})}) + \sum_{p \in S} p \cdot \epsilon_{\mathsf{PRG}}$$

$$\le \mathsf{val}(T^{(i,\mathsf{tr})}) + O(\epsilon_{\mathsf{PRG}} \cdot \mathsf{k}) \ ,$$

where $T^{(i-1,\mathsf{tr})}$ is the sub-tree of $T^{(i-1)}$ whose root corresponds to the transcript tr. The final inequality follows by the fact that $\sum_{p \in S} p = \sum_{i=1}^{O(\mathsf{k})} (1 + 1/3\mathsf{k})^{-i}$ is a geometric series bounded by $O(\mathsf{k})$.

We can similarly show that $\mathsf{val}(T^{(i-1,\mathsf{tr})}) \ge \mathsf{val}(T^{(i,\mathsf{tr})}) - O(\epsilon_{\mathsf{PRG}} \cdot \mathsf{k})$. Notice that $\mathsf{val}(T^{(i)}) = \mathbb{E}_{\mathsf{tr}}[\mathsf{val}(T^{(i,\mathsf{tr})})]$ and $\mathsf{val}(T^{(i-1)}) = \mathbb{E}_{\mathsf{tr}}[\mathsf{val}(T^{(i-1,\mathsf{tr})})]$ (where the expectation is over the verifier's random coins). Therefore, if the G fools the entire circuit family $\mathcal{C}^{(i)} := \cup_{\mathsf{tr}} \mathcal{C}^{(i,\mathsf{tr})}$ then we have

$$|\mathsf{val}(T^{(i-1)}) - \mathsf{val}(T^{(i)})| = |\mathbb{E}_{\mathsf{tr}}[\mathsf{val}(T^{(i-1,\mathsf{tr})})] - \mathbb{E}_{\mathsf{tr}}[\mathsf{val}(T^{(i,\mathsf{tr})})]|$$

$$\le \left| \mathbb{E}_{\mathsf{tr}} \left[\mathsf{val}(T^{(i,\mathsf{tr})}) + O(\epsilon_{\mathsf{PRG}} \cdot \mathsf{k}) \right] - \mathbb{E}_{\mathsf{tr}} \left[\mathsf{val}(T^{(i,\mathsf{tr})}) \right] \right|$$

$$= O(\epsilon_{\mathsf{PRG}} \cdot \mathsf{k}) \ .$$

2.4   Deriving Our Results Using the Tools

We use the toolbox developed in the previous sections to derive the theorems in Sect. 1.1. Each theorem is proved by applying a carefully chosen sequence of tools (along with other arguments). Figure 1 summarizes which tools are used to derive each theorem and the order of their use.

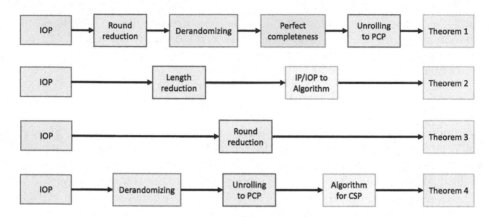

Fig. 1. Summary of how our tools are used to derive each theorem. The "IP/IOP to algorithm" and "Algorithm for CSP" boxes are due to prior work.

Low-Error IOPs to Low-Error PCPs. We sketch the proof of Theorem 1, which shows that low-error IOPs can be transformed into low-error PCPs. The proof is a sequence of transformations from our toolbox, whose goal is to transform the IOP into one that is efficient enough to be unrolled into a PCP via Item 3 of Lemma 1. This unrolling has an exponential dependency on the round complexity and on the verifier randomness complexity of the IOP, so we seek to decrease these without increasing the soundness error.

Decreasing the round complexity is done using the round-reduction transformation of Lemma 1, and decreasing the verifier randomness is done using either one of our derandomization lemmas (Lemma 3). Since both transformations degrade completeness, prior to applying the unrolling lemma (Item 3 of Lemma 1), we restore the IOP back to having perfect completeness using Lemma 2. Since the transformation for perfect completeness increases the soundness error, we counterbalance it by beginning the sequence of transformations with a small number of parallel repetitions.

In somewhat more detail, the sequence of transformations is as follows.

1. **Initial IOP.** We begin with an IOP with the following parameters: perfect completeness, soundness error $1/|\mathbb{x}|$, round complexity polylog($|\mathbb{x}|$), alphabet size poly($|\mathbb{x}|$), proof length poly($|\mathbb{x}|$), query complexity $O(1)$, and per-round randomness poly($|\mathbb{x}|$).

2. **Parallel repetition.** Repeat the protocol twice in parallel, and have the verifier accept if and only if both executions are accepted. This yields a public-coin IOP for R with: perfect completeness, **soundness error $1/|\mathbb{x}|^2$**, round complexity $\mathsf{k} = \mathrm{polylog}(|\mathbb{x}|)$, alphabet size $\mathrm{poly}(|\mathbb{x}|)$, query complexity $\mathsf{q} = O(1)$, and per-round randomness $\mathrm{poly}(|\mathbb{x}|)$.

3. **Round reduction.** Reduce the number of rounds of the IOP via Item 2 of Lemma 1 with $\ell := \mathsf{q}$ where $\mathsf{q} = O(1)$ is the query complexity of the IOP verifier. This transformation results in a public-coin IOP for R with: completeness error $1 - (\mathsf{q}/(e \cdot \mathsf{k}))^{\mathsf{q}} = 1 - 1/\mathrm{polylog}(|\mathbb{x}|)$, soundness error $1/|\mathbb{x}|^2$, **round complexity $O(1)$**, alphabet size $\mathrm{poly}(|\mathbb{x}|)$, query complexity $O(1)$, and per-round randomness $\mathrm{poly}(|\mathbb{x}|)$.

4. **Derandomization.** Derandomize the IOP verifier using either item of Lemma 3. This results in a public-coin IOP for R with: completeness error $1 - 1/\mathrm{polylog}(|\mathbb{x}|)$, soundness error $O(1/|\mathbb{x}|^2)$, round complexity $O(1)$, alphabet size $\mathrm{poly}(|\mathbb{x}|)$, query complexity $O(1)$, and **per-round randomness $O(\log |\mathbb{x}|)$**.

5. **Perfect completeness.** Improve the IOP to have perfect completeness using Lemma 2. The resulting IOP has the following parameters: **perfect completeness**, soundness error

$$O(1/|\mathbb{x}|^2) \cdot \left(\frac{\mathsf{q} \cdot O(\log |\mathbb{x}|)}{-\log(1 - 1/\mathrm{polylog}(|\mathbb{x}|))} \right) \leq 1/|\mathbb{x}| \ ,$$

round complexity $O(1)$, alphabet size $\mathrm{poly}(|\mathbb{x}|)$, query complexity $O(1)$, and randomness $O(\log |\mathbb{x}|)$.

6. **Unrolling to PCP.** Unroll the IOP with perfect completeness into a PCP via Item 3 of Lemma 1. This gives us our final PCP with parameters: perfect completeness, soundness error $1/|\mathbb{x}|$, alphabet size $\mathrm{poly}(|\mathbb{x}|)$, proof length $\mathrm{poly}(|\mathbb{x}|)$, query complexity $O(1)$, and randomness complexity $O(\log |\mathbb{x}|)$.

Limitations of Short IOPs. We sketch the proof of Theorem 2, which shows that short IOPs with small soundness contradict RETH, the hypothesis that 3SAT $\notin$ BPTIME$[2^{c \cdot n}]$ for a constant $c > 0$. First, we convert the IOP into a short IP, and then apply a transformation from [18] that converts short IPs into fast probabilistic algorithms. This leads to a fast algorithm for 3SAT, contradicting RETH.

Consider a public-coin IOP for n-variate 3SAT with parameters as in Theorem 2: perfect completeness, soundness error β, round complexity $\mathrm{polylog}(n)$, alphabet size λ, (total) proof length l, query complexity q, and verifier randomness $\mathrm{poly}(n)$. Suppose towards contradiction that $\mathsf{l} \geq n$ and $\left(\frac{\mathsf{l} \cdot \log \lambda}{n} \right)^{\mathsf{q}} \leq n^{\mathrm{polylog}(n)}$ and that $\beta = \frac{1}{2} \cdot \left(\frac{2 \cdot e \cdot \mathsf{l} \cdot \log \lambda}{c \cdot n} \right)^{-\mathsf{q}} \geq n^{-\mathrm{polylog}(n)}$.[4]

We apply the following transformations.

---

[4] It is sufficient to assume that $\beta = \frac{1}{2} \cdot \left(\frac{2 \cdot e \cdot \mathsf{l} \cdot \log \lambda}{c \cdot n} \right)^{-\mathsf{q}}$ to find contradiction in $\beta \leq \frac{1}{2} \cdot \left(\frac{2 \cdot e \cdot \mathsf{l} \cdot \log \lambda}{c \cdot n} \right)^{-\mathsf{q}}$ since we can always increase the soundness error without loss of generality.

1. **Length reduction.** Apply Item 1 of Lemma 1 with parameter $\ell := e \cdot l \cdot (2\beta)^{1/q}$. This results in an IOP with: completeness error $\alpha' := 1 - 2\beta$, soundness error β, round complexity $k' := \text{polylog}(n)$, alphabet size $\lambda' := \lambda$, and **proof length** $l' := e \cdot l \cdot (2\beta)^{1/q}$.

2. **IOP to algorithm.** Convert the IOP into an algorithm using a lemma from [18] that says that if a relation R has a public-coin IP with completeness error α', soundness error β', round complexity k', and prover-to-verifier communication length l' of symbols of size λ', then there is a probabilistic algorithm for deciding R in time $2^{O(d)+o(n)}$ for $d := l' \cdot \log \lambda' + k' \cdot \log \frac{k'}{1-\alpha'-\beta'}$. Notice that while the result from [18] applies to IPs rather than IOPs, one can straightforwardly convert an IOP into an IP by having the verifier read the prover's messages in their entirety.

Substituting the relevant parameters, we have that:

$$d = l' \cdot \log \lambda' + k' \cdot \log \frac{k'}{1 - \alpha' - \beta'}$$
$$= e \cdot l \cdot (2\beta)^{1/q} \cdot \log \lambda + k \cdot \log(k/\beta)$$
$$= c \cdot n/2 + \text{polylog}(n).$$

Thus, 3SAT is decidable in probabilistic time $2^{c \cdot n/2 + o(n)} < 2^{c \cdot n}$ in contradiction to RETH.

Limitations of High-Round Low-Query IOPs. We sketch the proof of Theorem 3, showing that relations not decidable in few rounds do not have small-query IOPs with good soundness error. As in the theorem statement, let $R \in \text{AM}[k] \backslash \text{AM}[k']$ be a relation for $k' < k$ and suppose that R has a k-round public-coin IOP $(\mathbf{P}, \mathbf{V})$ with perfect completeness, soundness error β, alphabet size $2^{\text{poly}(|x|)}$, proof length $\text{poly}(|x|)$, and query complexity $q \leq k'$.

By applying the round-reduction lemma (Item 2 of Lemma 1) to the k-round IOP $(\mathbf{P}, \mathbf{V})$ with parameter k', we get a k'-round IOP $(\mathbf{P}', \mathbf{V}')$ with completeness error $\alpha' := 1 - (k'/(e \cdot k))^q$ and soundness error β. Suppose towards contradiction that $\beta < (k'/(e \cdot k))^q - |x|^{-c}$ for some $c \in \mathbb{N}$. Then the (additive) gap between completeness and soundness error of $(\mathbf{P}', \mathbf{V}')$ is $1 - \alpha' - \beta > |x|^{-c}$.

Since the gap between completeness and soundness error of $(\mathbf{P}', \mathbf{V}')$ is inverse polynomial, it can be transformed into a k'-round public-coin IP $(\mathbf{P}''_{\text{IP}}, \mathbf{V}''_{\text{IP}})$ for R with completeness error $1/3$ and soundness error $1/3$. This is done by using the standard technique of taking $\text{poly}(|x|)$ parallel repetitions, computing the fraction of accepting transcripts, and accepting if the number of accepting transcripts is beyond some threshold that depends on α' and $|x|^{-c}$. The IP $(\mathbf{P}''_{\text{IP}}, \mathbf{V}''_{\text{IP}})$, then, contradicts the assumption that $R \notin \text{AM}[k']$.

Limitations of Binary-Alphabet Constant-Query IOPs. We sketch the proof of Theorem 4, showing that assuming RETH there are no binary-alphabet IOPs with 2 or 3 queries and small soundness error for 3SAT. We first discuss the following lemma which says that, assuming RETH, algorithms for solving constraint satisfaction problems (CSPs) cannot coexist with IOPs with a binary alphabet, constant query complexity, and small soundness error.

Lemma 4. (informal). *Assume RETH and suppose that both of the following exist.*

- *An IOP with perfect completeness, soundness error β, round complexity k, alphabet size 2, proof length $2^{o(n)}$, query complexity q, verifier randomness r, and verifier running time $2^{o(n)}$.*
- *A polynomial-time algorithm $\mathbf{A}$ for deciding whether a binary-alphabet CSP with arity q has value 1 or value at most γ.*

Then $\beta > \gamma - \varepsilon$ for every ε satisfying $k \cdot \log(r \cdot n/\varepsilon) = o(n)$.

The proof of the theorem is concluded by relying on known algorithms for solving CSPs with appropriate arities q and decision bounds γ.

- For $q = 2$, we rely on Schaefer's dichotomy theorem [37], which says that the satisfiability of a binary-alphabet CSP with arity 2 can be decided in polynomial time. In this case $\gamma = 1$.
- For $q = 3$, we rely on Zwick's algorithm [39], which decides in polynomial time whether a binary-alphabet CSP with arity 3 has value 1 or value smaller than $5/8$. In this case $\gamma = 5/8$.

Proof sketch of Lemma 4. Suppose towards contradiction that $\beta \leq \gamma - \varepsilon$ where ε satisfies $k \cdot \log(r \cdot n/\varepsilon) = o(n)$. The proof has two steps: (1) transform the IOP into a PCP for 3SAT that is "efficient-enough"; and (2) use the "efficient-enough" PCP and the algorithm $\mathbf{A}$ to decide 3SAT.

IOP to "Efficient-Enough" PCP. We apply these transformations from our toolbox.

1. **Derandomization using non-uniform advice.** Reduce the verifier randomness of the IOP using the non-uniform derandomization theorem (Lemma 3, Item 2) with error ε/k to get per-round randomness complexity of $O(\log(r \cdot n/\varepsilon))$ bits. The new IOP uses $\text{poly}(n, r, 1/\varepsilon)$ bits of non-uniform advice, where a random string is good advice with overwhelming probability. The resulting IOP has perfect completeness, **soundness error $\beta + \varepsilon \leq \gamma$**, round complexity k, alphabet size 2, proof length $2^{o(n)}$, query complexity q, **verifier randomness $O(\log(r \cdot n/\varepsilon))$**, and verifier running time $2^{o(n)} + \text{poly}(n, r, 1/\varepsilon) = 2^{o(n)}$.
2. **Unrolling to PCP.** Unroll the IOP into a PCP for 3SAT using Lemma 1, Item 3. This transformation preserves the number of advice bits, and also the fact that a random string is good advice with overwhelming probability. The resulting PCP has perfect completeness, soundness error γ, alphabet size 2, proof length $2^{O(k \cdot \log(k \cdot n/\varepsilon)) + o(n)} = 2^{o(n)}$, query complexity q, randomness complexity $O(\log(k \cdot n/\varepsilon)) = o(n)$, and verifier running time $2^{o(n)}$.

Solving 3SAT *Using the PCP and CSP Solvers.* We use the PCP and the algorithm $\mathbf{A}$ to design a probabilistic algorithm $\mathbf{A}'$ that decides whether a 3SAT formula ϕ over n variables is satisfiable in time $2^{o(n)}$. The algorithm $\mathbf{A}'$, on input the 3SAT formula ϕ, works as follows.

1. **Sample random advice.** Sample a random advice string z for the PCP resulting from the previous transformation.
2. **Transform formula to CSP.** Transform the 3SAT formula ϕ into a binary-alphabet CSP ψ with arity q. This is done using the standard method of translating a PCP into a CSP; each constraint in the CSP is indexed by a choice of verifier randomness ρ and described by the verifier circuit with the input formula ϕ, randomness ρ, and advice z hard-coded. The CSP ψ has size $\mathrm{poly}(2^{r'}, \mathsf{vt}') = 2^{o(n)}$ where $\mathsf{r}' = o(n)$ and $\mathsf{vt}' = 2^{o(n)}$ are the randomness complexity and verifier running time of the PCP. Additionally, assuming that z is good advice, we have that if $\phi \in$ 3SAT then the value of ψ is 1, and if $\phi \notin$ 3SAT, then the value of ϕ is at most γ.
3. **Solve CSP.** Run $\mathbf{A}(\psi)$ and say that ϕ is satisfiable if and only if $\mathbf{A}$ says that ψ's value is 1.

The algorithm $\mathbf{A}'$ decides 3SAT with high probability: with overwhelming probability the choice of advice z is good, and deciding whether the value of the CSP instance ψ is 1 or γ, as $\mathbf{A}$ does, is equivalent to deciding whether ϕ is satisfiable.

Moreover, the algorithm $\mathbf{A}'$ runs in probabilistic time $2^{o(n)}$: the advice sampled in the first step is polynomial; the second step can be done in time $\mathrm{poly}(2^{r'}, \mathsf{vt}') = 2^{o(n)}$ where $\mathsf{r}' = o(n)$ and $\mathsf{vt}' = 2^{o(n)}$ are the randomness complexity and verifier running time of the PCP; the final step takes $\mathrm{poly}(|\psi|) = 2^{o(n)}$, since $\mathbf{A}$ runs in polynomial time.

We obtained an algorithm for deciding 3SAT in probabilistic time $2^{o(n)}$, contradicting RETH. $\qquad\qquad\square$

References

1. Applebaum, B., Golombek, E.: On the randomness complexity of interactive proofs and statistical zero-knowledge proofs. In: Proceedings of the 2nd Conference on Information-Theoretic Cryptography, ITC 2021, pp. 4:1–4:23 (2021)
2. Arnon, G., Chiesa, A., Yogev, E.: Hardness of approximation for stochastic problems via interactive oracle proofs. In: Proceedings of the 37th Annual IEEE Conference on Computational Complexity, CCC 2022, pp. 24:1–24:16 (2022)
3. Arnon, G., Chiesa, A., Yogev, E.: A PCP theorem for interactive proofs. In: Proceedings of the 41st Annual International Conference on Theory and Application of Cryptographic Techniques, EUROCRYPT 2022, pp. 64–94 (2022)
4. Arora, S., Lund, C., Motwani, R., Sudan, M., Szegedy, M.: Proof verification and the hardness of approximation problems. J. ACM 45(3), 501–555 (1998). Preliminary version in FOCS '92
5. Arora, S., Safra, S.: Probabilistic checking of proofs: a new characterization of NP. J. ACM **45**(1), 70–122 (1998). Preliminary version in FOCS '92

6. Babai, L., Fortnow, L., Levin, L.A., Szegedy, M.: Checking computations in poly-logarithmic time. In: Proceedings of the 23rd Annual ACM Symposium on Theory of Computing, STOC 1991, pp. 21–32 (1991)
7. Bellare, M., Goldwasser, S., Lund, C., Russell, A.: Efficient probabilistically check-able proofs and applications to approximations. In: Proceedings of the 25th Annual ACM Symposium on Theory of Computing, STOC 1993, pp. 294–304 (1993)
8. Ben-Sasson, E., et al.: Computational integrity with a public random string from quasi-linear PCPs. In: Proceedings of the 36th Annual International Conference on Theory and Application of Cryptographic Techniques, EUROCRYPT 2017, pp. 551–579 (2017)
9. Ben-Sasson, E., Bentov, I., Horesh, Y., Riabzev, M.: Fast Reed-Solomon interactive oracle proofs of proximity. In: Proceedings of the 45th International Colloquium on Automata, Languages and Programming, ICALP 2018, pp. 14:1–14:17 (2018)
10. Ben-Sasson, E., Chiesa, A., Gabizon, A., Riabzev, M., Spooner, N.: Interactive oracle proofs with constant rate and query complexity. In: Proceedings of the 44th International Colloquium on Automata, Languages and Programming, ICALP 2017, pp. 40:1–40:15 (2017)
11. Ben-Sasson, E., Chiesa, A., Gabizon, A., Virza, M.: Quasilinear-size zero knowledge from linear-algebraic PCPs. In: Proceedings of the 13th Theory of Cryptography Conference, TCC 2016-A, pp. 33–64 (2016)
12. Ben-Sasson, E., Chiesa, A., Spooner, N.: Interactive oracle proofs. In: Proceedings of the 14th Theory of Cryptography Conference, TCC 2016-B, pp. 31–60 (2016)
13. Ben-Sasson, E., Sudan, M.: Short PCPs with polylog query complexity. SIAM J. Comput. **38**(2), 551–607 (2008). Preliminary version appeared in STOC '05
14. Bootle, J., Cerulli, A., Ghadafi, E., Groth, J., Hajiabadi, M., Jakobsen, S.K.: Linear-time zero-knowledge proofs for arithmetic circuit satisfiability. In: Proceed-ings of the 23rd International Conference on the Theory and Applications of Cryp-tology and Information Security, ASIACRYPT 2017, pp. 336–365 (2017)
15. Bootle, J., Chiesa, A., Groth, J.: Linear-time arguments with sublinear verification from tensor codes. In: Proceedings of the 18th Theory of Cryptography Conference, TCC 2020, pp. 19–46 (2020)
16. Bootle, J., Chiesa, A., Liu, S.: Zero-knowledge IOPs with linear-time prover and polylogarithmic-time verifier. In: Proceedings of the 41st Annual International Conference on Theory and Application of Cryptographic Techniques, EURO-CRYPT 2022, pp. 275–304 (2022)
17. Bordage, S., Nardi, J.: Interactive oracle proofs of proximity to algebraic geometry codes. In: Proceedings of the 37th Annual IEEE Conference on Computational Complexity, CCC 2022, pp. 30:1–30:45 (2022)
18. Chiesa, A., Yogev, E.: Barriers for succinct arguments in the random oracle model. In: Proceedings of the 18th Theory of Cryptography Conference, TCC 2020, pp. 47–76 (2020)
19. Condon, A., Feigenbaum, J., Lund, C., Shor, P.W.: Random debaters and the hardness of approximating stochastic functions. SIAM J. Comput. **26**(2), 369–400 (1997)
20. Dinur, I.: The PCP theorem by gap amplification. J. ACM **54**(3), 12 (2007)
21. Dinur, I., Harsha, P., Kindler, G.: Polynomially low error PCPs with polyloglog n queries via modular composition. In: Proceedings of the 47th Annual ACM Sym-posium on Theory of Computing, STOC 2015, pp. 267–276 (2015)
22. Drucker, A.: A PCP characterization of AM. In: Proceedings of the 38th Interna-tional Colloquium on Automata, Languages and Programming, ICALP 2011, pp. 581–592 (2011)

23. Feige, U., Goldwasser, S., Lovász, L., Safra, S., Szegedy, M.: Approximating clique is almost NP-complete (preliminary version). In: Proceedings of the 32nd Annual Symposium on Foundations of Computer Science, SFCS 1991, pp. 2–12 (1991)
24. Feige, U., Goldwasser, S., Lovász, L., Safra, S., Szegedy, M.: Interactive proofs and the hardness of approximating cliques. J. ACM **43**(2), 268–292 (1996). Preliminary version in FOCS '91
25. Fürer, M., Goldreich, O., Mansour, Y., Sipser, M., Zachos, S.: On completeness and soundness in interactive proof systems. Adv. Comput. Res. **5**, 429–442 (1989)
26. Goldreich, O., Håstad, J.: On the complexity of interactive proofs with bounded communication. Inf. Process. Lett. **67**(4), 205–214 (1998)
27. Goldreich, O., Vadhan, S., Wigderson, A.: On interactive proofs with a laconic prover. Comput. Complex. **11**(1/2), 1–53 (2002)
28. Golovnev, A., Lee, J., V., S.S.T., Thaler, J., Wahby, R.S.: Brakedown: linear-time and post-quantum snarks for R1CS. Cryptology ePrint Archive, Report 2021/1043 (2021)
29. Hast, G.: Beating a random assignment: approximating constraint satisfaction problems. Ph.D. thesis, KTH (2005)
30. Håstad, J.: On the NP-hardness of max-not-2. SIAM J. Comput. **43**(1), 179–193 (2014)
31. Lee, J., Setty, S.T.V., Thaler, J., Wahby, R.S.: Linear-time zero-knowledge snarks for R1CS. Cryptology ePrint Archive, Report 2021/30 (2021)
32. Manurangsi, P., Nakkiran, P., Trevisan, L.: Near-optimal NP-hardness of approximating MAX k-CSPR. Theory Comput. **18**(3), 1–29 (2022)
33. Nassar, S., Rothblum, R.D.: Succinct interactive oracle proofs: applications and limitations. In: Proceedings of the 42nd Annual International Cryptology Conference, CRYPTO 2022 (2022)
34. Reingold, O., Rothblum, R., Rothblum, G.: Constant-round interactive proofs for delegating computation. In: Proceedings of the 48th ACM Symposium on the Theory of Computing, STOC 2016, pp. 49–62 (2016)
35. Ron-Zewi, N., Rothblum, R.: Local proofs approaching the witness length. In: Proceedings of the 61st Annual IEEE Symposium on Foundations of Computer Science, FOCS 2020, pp. 846–857 (2020)
36. Ron-Zewi, N., Rothblum, R.D.: Proving as fast as computing: succinct arguments with constant prover overhead. In: Proceedings of the 54th ACM Symposium on the Theory of Computing, STOC 2022, pp. 1353–1363 (2022)
37. Schaefer, T.J.: The complexity of satisfiability problems. In: Proceedings of the 10th Annual ACM Symposium on Theory of Computing, STOC 1978, pp. 216–226 (1978)
38. Xie, T., Zhang, J., Zhang, Y., Papamanthou, C., Song, D.: Libra: succinct zero-knowledge proofs with optimal prover computation. In: Proceedings of the 39th Annual International Cryptology Conference, CRYPTO 1919, pp. 733–764 (2019)
39. Zwick, U.: Approximation algorithms for constraint satisfaction problems involving at most three variables per constraint. In: Proceedings of the 9th Annual Symposium on Discrete Algorithms, SODA 1998, pp. 201–210 (1998)

Scalable and Transparent Proofs over All Large Fields, via Elliptic Curves
(ECFFT Part II)

Eli Ben–Sasson[1] , Dan Carmon[1(✉)] , Swastik Kopparty[2] ,
and David Levit[1]

[1] StarkWare Industries Ltd., Netanya, Israel
{eli,dancar,david}@starkware.co
[2] University of Toronto, Toronto, Canada
swastik@cs.toronto.edu
https://starkware.co

Abstract. Concretely efficient interactive oracle proofs (IOPs) are of interest due to their applications to scaling blockchains, their minimal security assumptions, and their potential future-proof resistance to quantum attacks.

Scalable IOPs, in which prover time scales quasilinearly with the computation size and verifier time scales poly-logarithmically with it, have been known to exist thus far only over a set of finite fields of negligible density, namely, over "FFT-friendly" fields that contain a sub-group of size 2^k.

Our main result is to show that scalable IOPs can be constructed over *any* sufficiently large finite field, of size that is at least quadratic in the length of computation whose integrity is proved by the IOP. This result has practical applications as well, because it reduces the proving and verification complexity of cryptographic statements that are naturally stated over pre-defined finite fields which are not "FFT-friendly". Prior state-of-the-art scalable IOPs relied heavily on arithmetization via univariate polynomials and Reed–Solomon codes over FFT-friendly fields. To prove our main result and extend scalability to all large finite fields, we generalize the prior techniques and use new algebraic geometry codes evaluated on sub-groups of elliptic curves (elliptic curve codes). We also show a new arithmetization scheme that uses the rich and well-understood group structure of elliptic curves to reduce statements of computational integrity to other statements about the proximity of functions evaluated on the elliptic curve to the new family of elliptic curve codes.

1 Introduction

Arithmetization was first used to construct interactive proofs in the seminal work of Lund et al. [41] and shortly after played a key role in Shamir's proof of IP = PSPACE [47]. Ever since, this invaluable tool has dominated the construction of interactive proofs (IP), multiprover interactive proofs (MIP), zero knowledge proofs (ZK), probabilistically checkable proofs (PCP) and related protocols. Arithmetization reduces statements about computational integrity, like

> "I processed $T = 10,000$ valid Ethereum transactions, leading to new Ethereum state S"

to completely different statements, about low degree polynomials over a finite field $\mathbb{F}$, like

> "I know polynomials $A(X), B(X)$ over finite field $\mathbb{F}$ of degree at most T that satisfy a set of polynomial constraints".

The question studied in this paper is: Which finite fields $\mathbb{F}$ can be used to create transparent[1], scalable and concretely efficient proof systems? We start by surveying the existing state of the art in this area.

To Reach Polynomial Efficiency, Any Large Finite Field Suffices. Early uses of arithmetization, for example, in the seminal proofs of (i) MIP = NEXP [5], (ii) the poly-logarithmic verification of NP [4] and (iii) the PCP Theorem [2,3], all work with *any* sufficiently large finite field, of size at least poly(T), where T denotes the length of the (nondeterministic) computation whose integrity is being proved; in the case of the PCP Theorem, a field of size polylog(T) suffices. The communication complexity in all of these celebrated protocols is extremely efficient — at most poly-logarithmic in T. However, none of these early constructions were ever deployed in practice because their proofs, although of polynomial length in T, were of impractical size, and the arithmetic complexity of both prover and verifier were, concretely, prohibitively large.

Scalable Proof Systems Over FFT-Friendly Fields. The situation changed dramatically, in terms of both efficiency and field type, with the advent of *scalable* information theoretic proof systems. A proof system is called *scalable* when both (i) proving time[2] scales quasilinearly in T and, simultaneously (ii) verification time scales poly-logarithmically in T (and polynomially in the description of the computation whose integrity is proved); see [7, Definition 3.3] for an exact definition. Scalable PCP systems for any language in NEXP were presented by [13,18,20], improving proving time from $T^{O(1)}$ to $T \operatorname{polylog} T$. However, these constructions limited $\mathbb{F}$ to be *FFT-friendly* which means it must contain a subgroup of size 2^k, for integer k (the group can be multiplicative or additive)[3]. In

---

[1] A proof system is transparent when all verifier messages are public random coins; such systems are also called Arthur Merlin protocols.

[2] Unless mentioned otherwise, throughout the paper running time is measured in number of field operations, i.e., we assign unit cost to arithmetic operations over the finite field.

[3] More generally, scalable PCPs and IOPs can be constructed over any $\mathbb{F}$ which has a sub-group of size that is a product of small primes, but prover and verifier running time increase as the prime factors increase in number and size. For simplicity we stick to interpreting an FFT-friendly field as one containing a multiplicative subgroup of size 2^k.

spite of their improved efficiency, scalable PCPs are not used in practice because the exponents in the poly-log expressions for proving and verification time, and the amortized soundness error per PCP-query, are still, practically speaking, too large.

The last and final step needed to create concretely efficient proof systems for NEXP was taken within a relatively new computational model, the interactive oracle proof (IOP) model [16,45] that generalizes both IP and PCP. From a computational complexity point of view, IOP = MIP = PCP = NEXP (see [16]). Within this model, proving time was reduced to $O(\mathsf{T} \log \mathsf{T})$ and verification time to $O(\log \mathsf{T})$, with relatively small asymptotic constants [7]. The requirement that $\mathbb{F}$ be an FFT-friendly field remained.

To summarize, early IP, MIP and PCP constructions work over any sufficiently large finite field, but *scalable* PCPs and IOPs required FFT-friendly ones. This raises the question of whether FFT-friendliness is needed for scalability, and sets the ground for our main result.

1.1   Main Results

The language most naturally suited for creating scalable IOPs is that of arithmetic intermediate representations (AIR) [7,49]. Informally, an AIR instance of complexity m and length T is defined over a finite field $\mathbb{F}$ by a set of low-degree multivariate constraints, described by arithmetic circuits whose total sum (number of gates) is m, and by a cyclic group D of size T (see Definition 1). An AIR witness is a tuple of functions $f_1, \ldots, f_w : \mathsf{D} \to \mathbb{F}$ (see Definition 4), and the AIR instance is satisfied by it if the application of the polynomial constraints to the functions $f_1, \ldots, f_w$ and various cyclic shifts of them satisfy the polynomial constraints of the AIR instance (see Definition 5).

From a concrete complexity point of view, the language of AIRs is used to define computational integrity statements for scalable and transparent argument of knowledge (STARK) systems, directly for specific computations like hashing with ethSTARK [49], for domain specific languages like Winterfell, and for universal (Turing complete) virtual machines like Cairo [34]. In all these cases, the computations and virtual machines are specified by AIRs. Systems written over these machines, like StarkEx, have been used to process millions of transactions and billions of dollars on Ethereum, underscoring their practical relevance.

From an asymptotic complexity point of view, the language of satisfiable AIR instances is complete for NEXP. When restricting AIR to FFT-friendly fields, the ensuing sub-language (FFT-friendly-AIR) remains NEXP-complete. As mentioned earlier, prior to this work, it was known that the language of FFT-friendly-AIR has a *strictly* scalable and transparent IOP [7]. By strictly scalable we mean that (i) prover complexity is $\mathsf{T} \cdot (O(\log \mathsf{T}) + \mathsf{poly}(m))$ and, simultaneously, (ii) verifier complexity is $O(\log \mathsf{T}) + \mathsf{poly}(m)$, i.e., the exponents in all polylog expressions are 1.

The main result of this paper is to remove the FFT-friendly requirement about fields, leading to the following statement.

Theorem 1 (Main Theorem — Informal). *For any finite field $\mathbb{F}$ and $\mathsf{T} \leq \sqrt{|\mathbb{F}|}$, the satisfiability of AIR instances over $\mathbb{F}$ of size m and computation length at most T can be verified by a strictly scalable and transparent IOP of knowledge with advice[4]. In particular, there exist randomized procedures for proving and verification that require $\mathsf{T} \cdot (O(\log \mathsf{T}) + \mathrm{poly}(m))$ arithmetic operations over $\mathbb{F}$ for proving, and $\lambda \cdot (O(\log \mathsf{T}) + \mathrm{poly}(m))$ arithmetic operations over $\mathbb{F}$ for verification with knowledge soundness error at most $2^{-\lambda}$.*

We point out that our results apply to other NEXP complete languages for succinct IOPs, such as the succinct R1CS systems used in [15]; due to the concrete considerations mentioned above, as well as space limitations, we focus only on AIR.

Remark 1 (Zero Knowledge). The construction used in Theorem 1 can be augmented to achieve perfect zero knowledge, just like the FFT-friendly version of it (Theorem 3) can be augmented to an IOP with perfect zero knowledge [11]. We omit the addition of zero knowledge from this version due to space considerations.

Remark 2 (Post-quantum security). A number of works have shown that applying the Kilian-Micali and/or the BCS transformation from IOPs to noninteractive arguments are secure in the quantum random oracle model, and these generic transformations apply to all our results, rendering them post-quantum secure in this model [26–28].

Fast IOPs of Proximity for Reed–Solomon and Elliptic Curve codes. A major step, and bottleneck, in the construction of IOPs and PCPs is that of low-degree testing. This is the sub-protocol that is given oracle access to a function $f : \mathsf{D}' \to \mathbb{F}$ and is charged with distinguishing between the case that f is a low-degree polynomial, i.e., a Reed–Solomon (RS) codeword, and the case that f is far, in Hamming distance, from the RS code. Strictly scalable IOPs use the Fast RS IOPP (FRI) [6] protocol targeted for RS codes. For a function of blocklength $n = |\mathsf{D}'|$, the FRI protocol guarantees linear proving time ($O(n)$ arithmetic operations), strictly logarithmic verification time and query complexity ($O(\lambda \log n)$ arithmetic operations, to reduce the soundness error to $2^{-\lambda}$).

One of the main reasons that until now scalable IOPs were limited to FFT-friendly fields was the fact that the FRI protocol is tightly related to the FFT algorithm, and can be described as "randomly folding" an FFT. As part of our proof of Theorem 1 we also extend the FRI protocol from [6], and its analysis from [8], to hold over all fields, provided $|\mathbb{F}| \geq \Omega(n^2)$.

Theorem 2 (FRI over all fields, informal). *For any finite field $\mathbb{F}$ of size q, integer n a power of 2 satisfying $n \leq \sqrt{q}$, integer t and integer $\mathcal{R}$, the following holds.*

---

[4] The proving and verifying procedures depend on $O(\mathsf{T} \log q)$ bits of advice that depend only on $|\mathbb{F}|$ and T – furthermore, this advice can be generated by a randomized algorithm in time $O(\mathsf{T} \, \mathrm{polylog}(\mathsf{T} \cdot q))$ with high probability.

There exists a subset $D' \subseteq \mathbb{F}, |D'| = n$, *such that the family of RS codes of rate*[5] $\rho = 2^{-\mathcal{R}}$ *evaluated over* D' *has an IOP of proximity with:*

- $O(n)$ *proving complexity,*
- $O(t \cdot \log n)$ *verification complexity,*
- $t \cdot \log n$ *query complexity,*
- *the following soundness behavior: if f is δ-far in Hamming distance from the code, the probability that f is accepted by the protocol is at most*

$$\left(\max\left\{(1 - \delta), \sqrt{\rho}\right\} - o(1)\right)^t.$$

See Sect. 2.3 for more details and a formal statement of the result above.

We point out that we also obtain (and need, to prove Theorem 1) an IOPP for a more general family of codes – which comprises evaluations of functions over certain carefully selected points on an elliptic curve E; the points of evaluation are cosets of a cyclic group of size 2^k inside the elliptic curve group. We call this protocol an *elliptic curve* FRI, abbreviated EC-FRI, because the IOPP for this family of elliptic curve codes works by "decomposing" a function on the elliptic curve into a pair of RS codewords and applying Theorem 2 to this pair. See the online version [10] for details.

Applications to Concrete Scalability. We briefly argue why Theorem 1 is interesting from the point of view of concrete (rather than asymptotic) complexity, in applied cryptography settings. There are quite a few cryptographic primitives used in practice that are naturally defined over specific, and non-FFT-friendly, finite fields. Examples include the NIST Curve P-256 (used, e.g., on Apple smartphones) and the secp256k1 curve (used for Bitcoin signatures), both of which are prime, non-FFT-friendly, fields. Consider a prover attempting to prove she processed correctly a large batch of ECDSA signatures over either one of these primes, denoting it by p. Today, the prover would need to arithmetize her statement over some FFT-friendly field, and thus simulate the basic arithmetic operations of the (non-FFT friendly) field $\mathbb{F}_p$ over some other field $\mathbb{F}_q$, resulting in significant overhead. For example, the implementation of secp256k1 and NIST P-256 ECDSA in the Cairo programming language (which uses an IOP-based STARK over a 254-bit, FFT-friendly, prime field $\mathbb{F}_q$) requires roughly 128 arithmetic operations over $\mathbb{F}_q$ to simulate a single $\mathbb{F}_p$ multiplication (this implementation uses various optimizations, the naive bit-wise multiplication would be far costlier).

Using the construction of Theorem 1 one may do better. The statement for each of these curves could be constructed over the native prime field $\mathbb{F}_p$, meaning that each multiplication gate in the computation of the ECDSA "costs" only one constraint, and addition comes for free. When computing the tradeoff between

---

[5] The rate parameter, defined as the ratio between a code's dimension and its block-length, can be picked to be any constant $\rho < 1$, and affects the soundness error and proximity parameters; see [8] for state of the art soundness bounds as a function of rate.

using an FFT-friendly field $\mathbb{F}_q$ or our new construction over $\mathbb{F}_p$, one should carefully measure the difference resulting from the new construction (which, as explained later, involves elliptic curves rather than plain polynomials). We leave this interesting question for future work, but speculate that in most cases the new $\mathbb{F}_p$-native constructions will be far better, in terms of prover time, verifier time, and proof length, than arithmetization over a different, yet FFT-friendly, field.

Next we discuss the four parts in which FFT-friendliness was demanded in prior scalable systems, and then explain how we get rid of this requirement.

1.2   Why Do PCPs and IOPs Require FFT-friendliness?

The very first step taken by a scalable PCP/IOP prover, when writing a proof for the integrity of a computation of length T, is typically to view the execution trace of the computation as a series of functions $f_1, \ldots, f_w : \mathsf{D} \to \mathbb{F}$ for some evaluation domain $\mathsf{D} \subset \mathbb{F}, |\mathsf{D}| = \mathsf{T}$, and then compute the low degree extension of each f_i by first interpolating the polynomial $P_i(X), \deg(P_i) < \mathsf{T}$ that agrees with f_i, and then evaluating $P_1, \ldots, P_w$ on a larger domain $\mathsf{D}' \subset \mathbb{F}, |\mathsf{D}'| \gg |\mathsf{D}|$, leading to a new sequence $f_1', \ldots, f_w' : \mathsf{D}' \to \mathbb{F}$ that are submitted to the verifier as the very first part of the PCP/IOP. The four reasons D needs to be a cyclic group of size 2^k are explained next. If we wish to create scalable IOPs over all fields, including ones that do not contain such groups, we shall need to find other ways to achieve these properties.

- **Super-efficient Reed–Solomon encoding:** The main asymptotic bottleneck of scalable IOPs on the prover side is the computation of the low degree extensions of $f_1, \ldots, f_w$ from D to D'. When D is a subgroup of size 2^k and D' is a finite union of cosets of D, as used in all scalable PCP/IOP constructions, the classical FFT algorithm can be used to solve the encoding problem in time $O(w\mathsf{T}\log\mathsf{T})$; the asymptotic constants hidden by O-notation are rather small, which helps for concrete prover efficiency.
- **Codewords are invariant to cyclic shifts:** The algebraic constraints in AIRs over the trace involve elements from previous timesteps, which correspond to evaluations of $f_1', \ldots, f_w'$ at translated arguments. Thus we need work not only with the codewords $f_1', \ldots, f_w'$, but with words obtained by cyclic shifts of their values (where the cyclic order is determined by the indexing of the trace's elements by D). To control the degree of the evaluated constraints, it is necessary to know that these shifted words are also evaluations of polynomials of degree $< \mathsf{T}$, i.e. codewords. This is indeed the case when D is a cyclic group generated by g, D' is a finite union of its cosets, and the rows are indexed according to the cyclic order: shifting the values of $f_i'(x)$ by t yields the function $f_i'(\mathsf{g}^t x)$, which has the same degree as $f_i'(x)$ (each coset of D undergoes the same cyclic shift).
- **Polylogarithmic verification requires sparse domain polynomials:** To allow the verifier to check that the polynomial constraints arising out of the arithmetization reduction hold for each of the T steps of the computation,

as claimed by the prover, the verifier needs to evaluate the "vanishing polynomial" of D, denoted $Z_D(X)$, which is the degree-T monic polynomial whose roots are D, as well as polynomials that vanish on certain subsets $D_1, \ldots, D_s \subset D$, denoted $Z_{D_i}(X)$. To facilitate scalable (polylogarithmic) verification, the verifier needs to evaluate $Z_D(X), Z_{D_1}(X), \ldots, Z_{D_s}(X)$ all in time polylog T. When D is a multiplicative group of size T we have $Z_D(X) = X^T - 1$. This is a sparse polynomial that can be evaluated on any x_0 using $O(\log T)$ arithmetic operations. Likewise, when $D_1, \ldots, D_s$ are subgroups of D or, more generally, of "low-complexity" when expressed using subgroups (see Definition 3 for a definition of this term), then scalable (poly-logarithmic) verification is possible.

- **Low-degree testing:** Soundness of scalable PCPs/IOPs requires a protocol designed to verify that each of the functions $f'_1, \ldots, f'_w : D' \to \mathbb{F}$ submitted by the prover is an RS codeword (or is close to it in Hamming distance). All scalable protocols — from the quasilinear RS-PCP of Proximity (PCPP) of [20] to the linear Fast RS IOP of Proximity (IOPP) protocol of [6] (abbreviated as FRI) — rely on the FFT-friendly structure of the domain D' over which functions are evaluated. In more detail, the fact that a cyclic group of size 2^k has a cyclic group of size 2^{k-1} as a quotient group plays a vital role in the FRI protocol.

To summarize, there are four separate places in which FFT-friendliness is important in the construction of FRI-AIR STARK systems. RS encoding requires quasilinear running time over any finite field but the best asymptotic running time is obtained over multiplicative groups of order 2^k, i.e., within FFT-friendly fields. Expressing general constraints requires the RS codewords to be invariant to cyclic shifts, which occurs when the domain is itself a cyclic group. Scalable (poly-logarithmic) verification requires an evaluation domain that is represented by a sparse polynomial, and any multiplicative subgroup could be used. Finally, the low-degree testing protocol that lies at the heart of scalable PCP/IOP constructions requires an FFT-friendly domain.

1.3   Elliptic Curves Save the Day, Again

The virtues of elliptic curves in cryptography, computer science and mathematics are well established [40, 48, 50]. Here we make novel use of their properties — to create strictly scalable IOPs over any sufficiently large finite field, with the same asymptotic and concrete arithmetic complexity as obtained over FFT-friendly fields. A brief overview of some relevant standard facts and terms related to elliptic curves may be found in the online version [10].

Our starting point is our recent work [9], that showed how to use elliptic curve groups to enable an FFT-like computation over all finite fields, thus enabling fast low degree extensions. This essentially gives us (with some small modifications) the analogue of the first item from Sect. 1.2. Developing analogues of the remaining three items is completely new to this paper, and it requires us to dig deeper than [9] into the elliptic curve group structure and properties of Riemann–Roch spaces over elliptic curves.

Another contribution of this paper is a randomized near-linear time algorithm for doing all the (one-time) precomputation required for the ECFFT and the EC based IOP. Additionally, in this paper we also provide a more explicit description of the curves and maps that appear in the isogeny chain, which in turn give us more explicit formulas for the FFTs themselves. This allows for easy implementation and easy determination of running time with concrete constants. See the online version [10] for details.

Taking a 30,000-feet view, fix any finite field $\mathbb{F}$ of size q. The family of elliptic curves defined over $\mathbb{F}$ is a family of algebraic groups whose size range and structure are well understood. Size-wise, nearly any number in the Hasse–Weil bound $[q+1\pm 2\sqrt{q}]$ is the size of some elliptic curve over $\mathbb{F}$ (when q is prime then *every* number in that range is the size of an elliptic curve). The group structure of elliptic curves is somewhat more elaborate, but suffice to say that for any size 2^k, there will exist some elliptic curve that contains a *cyclic*[6] subgroup of size 2^k, permitted that 2^k is, roughly, at most $\sqrt{q}$.

Based on these observations, we shall replace the multiplicative subgroup of size 2^k (which may not exist inside $\mathbb{F}_q^*$) with a cyclic subgroup of size 2^k of points of some elliptic curve E defined over $\mathbb{F}_q$. Then, we shall use a novel arithmetization scheme that reduces computational problems to problems regarding "low-degree" functions defined over the points of the elliptic curve; formally, these functions will be members of a low-degree Riemann–Roch (RR) space. The choice of this Riemann–Roch space in a way that enables arithmetization is the crux of our IOP construction, and we discuss this next.

Arithmetization and Automorphisms. One property of polynomials (in the classical FFT-friendly field IOP setting) which is needed for efficient arithmetization is their invariance under certain linear transformations. In particular, if $G \subset \mathbb{F}_q$ is a multiplicative group generated by g, and $f : G \to \mathbb{F}_q$ is an evaluation of a polynomial of degree d, then $f(g \cdot x)$ is also a polynomial of degree d. In other words, the space of functions of degree at most d is invariant under the permutation that maps x to $g \cdot x$.

Now suppose we wish to arithmetize using a cyclic group H that is generated by a point h on an elliptic curve (i.e., H is a sub-group of the curve). A permutation that is natural in this context is given by $x \mapsto x + h$ (where x, h are points on the curve and $+$ is the curve's group operand). We need a space of functions that are invariant under this action, and this identifies a natural candidate space – the Riemann–Roch space of functions that is supported in a symmetric way on H, defined by the divisor $\sum_{z \in H}[z]$.

Another way of viewing this generalization is as follows. The space of polynomials of degree at most d in the projective space $\mathbb{P}^1$ is the Riemann–Roch

---

[6] The need for cyclic subgroups of size 2^k, as opposed to general subgroups of size 2^k, of elliptic curve groups is new to this paper in comparison to [9]. The cyclicity is essential for arithmetization.

space associated with the divisor $D = d \cdot [\infty]$ and D is invariant under the action $[x] \mapsto [g \cdot x]$. In the case of an elliptic curve group, $\infty \neq h + \infty$ so we cannot use D but rather need a different divisor, one that is invariant under the mapping induced by h. The natural divisor is $D' := \sum_{z \in H} [z]$ which is clearly invariant under the action of h because H is cyclic.

Key ingredients for the new IOPs, and the relationship to ECFFT Part I [9]. Let us now see the elliptic curve analogues of the four ingredients that go into IOPs in FFT-friendly fields. The first of these essentially comes from [9].

- **Super-efficient EC code encoding:** This essentially comes from [9]. Here we generalize the results slightly to extend low-degree functions evaluated over D to evaluations over a constant number of other cosets of D, in time $O(T \log T)$ and with small concrete asymptotic constants. See the online version [10] for details.
- **Invariance to cyclic shifts:** This is where the choice of the Riemann–Roch space is crucially used. It was specifically constructed to be invariant to translation of the argument by any element of the cyclic subgroup of size 2^k in E, similarly to the case of polynomials with bounded degree. Since D′ is a union of cosets of the cyclic subgroup, these translations correspond to cyclic permutations of each coset in D′.
- **Polylogarithmic evaluation of the "vanishing RR function" of D:** The verifier now needs to evaluate "low-degree" "vanishing RR functions" (the analogue of a vanishing polynomial in the Riemann–Roch space) $\hat{Z}_D(P)$ on an arbitrary point $P = (x_0, y_0)$ of E, where $\hat{Z}_D$ is the RR function that vanishes over D. It turns out that D can be constructed using a sequence of $k = \log T$ rational functions and this implies that $\hat{Z}_D(P)$ is computable using $O(\log T)$ arithmetic operations, as before. Likewise, for subsets $D_1, \ldots, D_s \subset D$ of "low complexity" (per Definition 3), the verifier can evaluate $\hat{Z}_{D_i}(P)$ as efficiently for subsets of elliptic curves as was the case with subsets of multiplicative groups.
- **Low-degree testing:** The FRI protocol can be described informally as "random folding of an FFT". Thus, once we have obtained a generalization of the FFT algorithm to codes defined over elliptic curve groups, we also generalize the FRI protocol to verify the proximity of functions to low-degree RR functions.

1.4 Related Work

Over the past decade we have experienced a Cambrian explosion in the field of concretely efficient proof systems, with and without zero knowledge. These systems are classified under various definitions including CS proofs [43], NIZKs and succinct NIZKs [33], SNARGs, SNARKs, STARKs, and more. Realizations in code include Pinocchio [44], C-SNARKs [14], PLONK [32], Halo [23], Fractal [28], Marlin [25], Ligero [1], Sonic [42], Bulletproofs [24] and more.

Nearly all of these systems involve arithmetization via polynomials (univariate and multivariate) over large fields, of size at least $\mathsf{poly}(\mathsf{T})$, and thus when efficiency (concrete and asymptotic) is of interest, FFT-friendliness is required, along with proving time that is quasi-linear (or worse). An interesting research question, not addressed here, is whether the techniques discussed in this paper are relevant to some of these works. It seems likely to conjecture that many of the works that are information theoretically secure, like the important lines of works based on "interactive proofs for muggles" [35] and "MPC in the head" [38] may be constructed with better efficiency over general large fields, using our results.

A class of concretely efficient and widely deployed ZK-SNARK systems is based on knowledge-of-exponent assumptions and bi-linear pairings, starting with the work of [44]. Several blockchain systems, including Zcash, Filecoin and Tornado cash use the popular and efficient Groth16 ZK-SNARK [37]. The use of bilinear pairings significantly limits the class of fields that can be arithmetized efficiently, requiring $\mathbb{F}$ to be a prime field with small embedding degree and ruling out fields that are of prime power size[7]. Other constructions that rely on number-theoretic assumptions but which do not require knowledge of exponent assumptions, nor bilinear pairings (e.g., BulletProofs and Halo), may be amenable to efficient constructions over non-FFT friendly, cryptographically large primes/curves (but it seems unlikely they can be amended to allow native arithmetization over fields of small characteristic).

An interesting and noteworthy recent line of works gives strictly linear proving time, thereby avoiding the need for FFTs [21,22,36,46] and large fields and offering strictly better asymptotic proving time than mentioned above. However, thus far this line of works has not produced scalable systems (per the definition above) and requires super-polylogarithmic verification time which should be performed either directly by the verifier or by a pre-processing entity trusted by it. In particular, our main results (Theorems 1 and 2) do not imply these works and vice versa.

Elliptic Curves and FFT. This work is a direct continuation of our previous paper on quasilinear time Elliptic Curve FFT [9] (cf. [31] for an earlier work on using elliptic curves to compute an FFT-like transform, as well as the discussion in [9] of that paper). Indeed, the sequence of isogenies used here is adapted from that work, and the EC-FRI protocol relies on our FFT-like interpolation and evaluation algorithms of that work. Although we made this paper self-contained, reading our previous work should help the reader with intuition (and notation) here. See Sect. 1.3 for a detailed discussion of what is new in this paper in comparison to [9].

Algebraic Geometry Codes and PCPs/IOPs. A line of works used algebraic geometry codes to obtain PCPs and IOPs with extremely efficient proof

---

[7] Arithmetization in the context of such SNARKs has as its output a system of R1CS constraints defined over an elliptic curve subgroup of prime order p that has small constant embedding degree.

length and query complexity over constant size fields [12,19]. Those works are incomparable to ours because the curves there are of much higher genus, and the end results are not related to our goal of constructing scalable proof systems over any finite field.

2 Main Results

Our main result below is a scalable and transparent IOP of knowledge (abbreviated as STIK) for the language of satisfiable AIR instances defined over *any* sufficiently large finite field. Thus, we start by defining this language (Definition 6). Then we state and discuss our main theorem (Theorem 4). We conclude with a statement of the auxiliary results on FRI and EC-FRI over any finite field.

2.1 The AIR Language and Relation

We recall the definition of an AIR instance from [7], using the more recent formulation in [49, Section 5], generalizing it slightly by using an abstract cyclic group instead of a multiplicative group[8] of a finite field. As shown in that paper, this language, even when restricted to FFT-friendly fields, is NEXP-complete. We start with the notion of an AIR instance.

Definition 1 (AIR Instance). *An Algebraic Intermediate Representation (AIR) instance is a tuple* $\mathsf{A} = (\mathbb{F}, \mathsf{w}, \mathsf{h}, \mathsf{d}, \mathsf{s}, \mathsf{H}_0, \mathsf{g}, \mathsf{I}, \mathsf{Cset})$ *where:*

- $\mathbb{F}$ *is a finite field*
- $\mathsf{w}, \mathsf{h}, \mathsf{d}, \mathsf{s}$ *are integers indicating the following sizes:*
  - w *is the number of columns in the trace*
  - h *denotes the logarithm of the size of the trace domain*
  - d *is the maximal degree of a constraint*
  - s *is the size of the set of constraints*
- H_0 *is a cyclic group of size* 2^{h}, *and* g *is a generator of it. We write* H_0 *multiplicatively, so that* $\mathsf{g}^j \cdot y$ *means applying* g^j *(the j-length cyclic shift) to* y. *We call* H_0 *the* trace domain.
- $\mathsf{I} \subseteq \{0, 1, \ldots, 2^{\mathsf{h}} - 1\} \times \{1, \ldots, \mathsf{w}\}$ *is a set of pairs known as the set of* mask indices. *Let* $\mathsf{Z} = \{\mathsf{Z}_{j,l} : (j, l) \in \mathsf{I}\}$ *be a set of formal variables, called the* mask variables, *indexed by elements of* I.
- $\mathsf{Cset} = \{\mathsf{C}_1, \ldots, \mathsf{C}_s\}$ *is a finite set of constraints, of size* s. *Each constraint is an ordered pair* $\mathsf{C}_\alpha = (\mathsf{Q}_\alpha, \mathsf{H}_\alpha)$ *where:*
  - $\mathsf{Q}_\alpha \in \mathbb{F}^{\leq \mathsf{d}}[\mathsf{Z}]$ *is a multivariate polynomial over the mask variables, of total degree at most* d, *called the* α-th constraint polynomial.
  - $\mathsf{H}_\alpha \subseteq \mathsf{H}_0$ *is a subset of the group, called the* α-th constraint enforcement domain.

---

[8] An AIR can also be defined using Hamiltonian paths in affine graphs, but restricting to cyclic groups suffices for NEXP-completeness, see [7].

The kind of result we will show is that the language of satisfiable AIRs over every field has an efficient IOPP. The efficiency will be in terms of the complexity of the constraints of the AIR, which we define next. Informally, the complexity of the AIR constraints depend on two things. The first is the circuit complexity of individual constraints, defined first (Definition 2). The second, less trivial, component, is the specification of the domain on which different constraints must be enforced (Definition 3).

Definition 2 (Complexity of Constraints of an AIR). *Given an AIR* $A = (\mathbb{F}, w, h, d, s, H_0, g, l, Cset)$, *we define the complexity of the constraints of* A, *denoted* $\|Cset\|$, *as:*

$$\|Cset\| := \sum_{\alpha=1}^{s} (\|Q_\alpha\| + \|H_\alpha\|),$$

where $\|Q_\alpha\|$ *is the arithmetic complexity of the circuit computing the polynomial* Q_α, *and* $\|H_\alpha\|$ *is the coset complexity of* H_α *(see definition below).*

As motivation for the following definition, consider a linear computation in which a constraint should be applied only to half of the timesteps. Informally, a constraint applied periodically, every other step (on even-numbered time steps) has lower complexity than a constraint that should be applied to a randomly selected set of time steps. We define the set of relevant time steps using polynomials and rational functions, and it turns out the the following measure is an upper bound on their complexity as arithmetic circuits.

Definition 3 (Coset Complexity). *For a subset S of a finite group H, we define the* coset complexity *of S, denoted $\|S\|$, to be the smallest value of*

$$\sum_i (\log_2(|J_i|) + 1),$$

over all ways of writing the indicator function 1_S of S as a signed sum of indicator functions:

$$1_S = \sum_i \epsilon_i \cdot 1_{J_i},$$

where each J_i is a coset of a subgroup of H and $\epsilon_i = \pm 1$.

Next, we recall the definition of an AIR witness.

Definition 4 (AIR witness and composition). *An AIR witness is a sequence of functions* $\mathbf{f} = (f_1, \ldots, f_w)$, *where each f_l is a function from H_0 to $\mathbb{F}$. The witness size is* $w \cdot |H_0|$.

Given an AIR constraint polynomial $Q \in \mathbb{F}[Z]$, the composition of Q and the witness $\mathbf{f}$ is the function

$$Q \circ \mathbf{f} : H_0 \to \mathbb{F},$$

where, for all $y \in H_0$:

$$(Q \circ \mathbf{f})(y) = Q\left(\left(f_l(g^j \cdot y) \right)_{j,l} \right).$$

(On the right hand side, we replaced the variable $Z_{j,l} \in Z$ that appears in $Q(Z)$ with $f_l(g^j \cdot y)$).

We now define which witnesses are said to satisfy an instance. As motivation, consider a typical way that an AIR can encode a computation. We could have a machine with w $\mathbb{F}_q$-registers, and ask that $f_l(g^j)$ represents the contents of the l-th register at time j. Then we use the constraints to (1) capture the transition rules between time step j and $j + 1$ for all j in the enforcement domain $[0, T]$, and (2) enforce boundary constraints on the values of the registers at time 0 and at time T.

Definition 5 (Satisfiability). *We say that the AIR witness $\mathbf{f} = (f_1, \ldots, f_w)$ satisfies the AIR instance $A = (\mathbb{F}, w, h, d, s, H_0, g, I, Cset)$ if and only if*

$$\forall \alpha \in [s] : \quad y \in H_\alpha \Rightarrow (Q_\alpha \circ \mathbf{f})(y) = 0.$$

In words, $\mathbf{f}$ satisfies A iff for every constraint $C_\alpha = (Q_\alpha, H_\alpha) \in Cset$ it holds that $Q_\alpha \circ \mathbf{f}$ vanishes on the α-th constraint enforcement domain H_α. We say that the AIR A is satisfiable if there exists an AIR witness $\mathbf{f}$ that satisfies it.

We now reach the main definition of this subsection, that of the language, and relation, corresponding to satisfiable AIRs over fields of quadratic size.

Definition 6 (AIR Language/Relation). *The AIR relation R_{AIR} is*

$$R_{AIR} = \{(A, \mathbf{f}) \mid A = (\mathbb{F}, w, h, d, s, H_0, g, I, Cset) \text{ is an AIR},$$
$$\mathbf{f} \text{ is a satisfying AIR witness for } A,$$
$$|\mathbb{F}| \geq \Omega(d^2 \cdot 2^{2h})\}.$$

The language of satisfiable AIRs is the projection of R_{AIR} onto its first coordinate,

$$L_{AIR} = \{A \mid \exists \mathbf{f} (A, \mathbf{f}) \in R_{AIR}\}.$$

Remark 3 (Field size). The definition above requires $|\mathbb{F}| > (d|H_0|)^2$. When this is not the case one may embed $\mathbb{F}$ in a finite extension field $\mathbb{K}$ which is sufficiently large, and apply our results to the AIR over $\mathbb{K}$. This increases the various complexity measures (proving time, verification time and query complexity) by a multiplicative factor of at most $M([\mathbb{K} : \mathbb{F}])$, where $M([\mathbb{K} : \mathbb{F}])$ denotes the complexity of $\mathbb{K}$-multiplication in terms of arithmetic operations over $\mathbb{F}$; notice that $M(k) \leq k^2$ for any $\mathbb{K}$ that is the degree k extension of $\mathbb{F}$. For instance, in the extremal case of the smallest possible field size, $\mathbb{F}_2$, any AIR per Definition 1 over $\mathbb{F}_2$, using an (abstract) group H_0 of size n, would lead to using $k = 2\log n + O(1)$, leading to total prover complexity of $O(n \log n \cdot M([\mathbb{F}_{2^{2\log n + O(1)}} : \mathbb{F}_2]) \leq O(n \log^3 n)$ measured in arithmetic operations over $\mathbb{F}_2$.

2.2   A Scalable and Transparent IOP for L_{AIR}

To state our main result we assume familiarity with the definition of an IOP, and briefly recall its main parameters [16,45].

An Interactive Oracle Proof (IOP) for a language L is an interactive proof system defined by a prover P and verifier V, in which the verifier need not read the prover's messages in full. Rather, the IOP model allows the verifier oracle access to the prover's messages. (The prover is assumed to read all verifier messages in entirety.) The main parameters of interest are:

- *query complexity* q is the total number of symbols queried by the verifier from the prover's messages
- *round complexity* k is the number of rounds of interaction between the two parties.
- *prover complexity* time_P and verifier complexity time_V, which, in this paper, will assume unit cost for arithmetic operations over the ambient field
- *proof length* I is the sum of lengths of oracles sent by the prover throughout the protocol.
- *soundness error* err is the probability of the verifier accepting a false statement.

Main Result. It was shown by [7] that the sub-language of L_{AIR} restricted to FFT-friendly fields has a scalable and transparent IOP of knowledge. Formally, let

$$L_{AIR,FFT} = \{A \in L_{AIR} \mid A = (\mathbb{F}, w, h, d, s, H_0, g, I, Cset) \text{ satisfies } 2^h \mid |\mathbb{F}| - 1\}.$$

The main theorem of [7] is:

Theorem 3 (STIK for $L_{AIR,FFT}$ – Prior state of art). *There is an IOP protocol for the language $L_{AIR,FFT}$ such that for $A = (\mathbb{F}, w, h, d, s, H_0, g, I, Cset)$ of witness size $n = w \cdot 2^h$ and parameter t we have:*

- **Completeness, Proving time and Proof size:** *There is a Prover algorithm that given f such that $(A, f) \in R_{AIR}$, makes the verifier accept with probability 1. Prover running time is*

$$O(n \cdot (\log n + \|Cset\|)),$$

and proof length I is $O(n)$.
- **Verifier runtime and query complexity:** *For all instances*

$$A = (\mathbb{F}, w, h, d, s, H_0, g, I, Cset),$$

the verifier runs in time $O(\|Cset\| + t \cdot h)$ and makes a total of of $q \leq t \log n$ queries
- **Knowledge soundness and soundness:** *There exists an efficient extractor running in time $\text{poly}(n)$ such that, given access to a Prover which satisfies the verifier with probability greater than 2^{-t}, outputs f such that $(A, f) \in R_{AIR}$. In particular, if $A \notin L_{AIR}$ then, for any Prover strategy, the verifier will reject with probability at least $1 - 2^{-t}$.*

Remark 4 (Soundness and knowledge soundness). Often in the analysis of interactive proofs, the soundness error parameter is smaller than the knowledge soundness parameter. In the theorem above we state the same parameter for both because the state-of-the-art soundness analysis in our case is actually efficient, and uses a witness extractor.

The first step of the above IOPP is to identify the cyclic group H_0 with a subgroup of the multiplicative group $\mathbb{F}_q^*$, and to view satisfying AIR witnesses $f_l : H_0 \to \mathbb{F}_q$ as the values of a low degree univariate polynomial $f_l(Y) \in \mathbb{F}_q[Y]$. This then makes the AIR a collection of constraints on the values of low-degree polynomials at certain points of the field $\mathbb{F}_q$, and brings the tools of algebra into play.

The FFT-friendliness is crucial for this approach — without it, there is no suitable multiplicative subgroup in $\mathbb{F}_q^*$ to identify the cyclic group H_0 with, and the above approach fails to get off the ground (see Sect. 1.2).

Our main result, given below, removes the FFT-friendliness restriction, and gives an IOPP for satisfiable AIRs over *all* finite fields with almost identical guarantees as Theorem 3. The key ingredient is to identify the cyclic group H_0 with a cyclic subgroup of an elliptic curve E over $\mathbb{F}$, and to view satisfying AIR witnesses $f_l : H_0 \to \mathbb{F}_q$ as the values of low degree rational functions f_l defined[9] on the curve E.

Theorem 4 (Scalable and Transparent IOPs of Knowledge over all large fields). *There is an IOP protocol for the language* L_{AIR} *with properties and parameters as stated in Theorem 3 above.*

The complexity parameters of the theorem, along with completeness, are argued along the lines of the proof of Theorem 3 (see [49, Section 5]). The most delicate part is the soundness analysis (as is always the case with IOP systems). The proof appears in the online version [10].

EC-STARKs. Assuming the existence of a family of collision resistant hash functions, and replacing the interactive oracles with Merkle commitment schemes a la [39], one obtains an interactive Scalable Transparent ARgument of Knowledge (STARK) as defined in [7]. Alternatively, working in the random oracle model and applying the BCS reduction [16], one obtains a noninteractive STARK (which is also, in particular, a transparent SNARK). Details of both reductions are identical to prior STARKs and discussed elsewhere (e.g., [16,29,30,39,43]). We point out that STARKs based on FFT-friendly fields (Theorem 3) are concretely practical, as evidenced by the StarkEx system which implements them to scale transactions on Ethereum. We conjecture that the new EC-based construction of Theorem 1 will have practical applications in certain settings (as discussed in Sect. 1.1).

---

[9] To be precise, we work with a suitable Riemann–Roch space.

2.3   IOPs of Proximity (IOPPs) for RS Codes over All Large Fields

In this section we state our auxiliary main result: FRI over all large finite fields. We start with a few necessary definitions.

We use Δ to denote relative Hamming distance between two vectors $u, v \in \mathbb{F}^n$, defined as $\Delta(u, v) = \frac{1}{n} |\{i \in [n] \mid u_i \neq v_i\}|$, and for a set $V \subset \mathbb{F}^n$ we let $\Delta(u, V) = \min \{\Delta(u, v) \mid v \in V\}$. The agreement of u, v and u, V is defined to be $\mathsf{agree}(u, v) = 1 - \Delta(u, v), \mathsf{agree}(u, V) = 1 - \Delta(u, V)$.

Definition 7 (IOP of Proximity (IOPP)). *Fix $V \subset \mathbb{F}^n$. An IOP system* (P, V) *is said to be an IOP of proximity (IOPP) for V with soundness error function* err : $[0, 1] \rightarrow [0, 1]$ *(and additional complexity parameters as defined for standard IOP systems above) if, assuming the verifier has oracle access to $v \in \mathbb{F}^n$, the following hold:*

- *There exists a prover* P *such that for $v \in V$,*

$$\Pr\left[\langle \mathsf{V}^v \leftrightarrow \mathsf{P}(v)\rangle = \mathsf{accept}\right] = 1$$

- *If $v \notin V$ (so $\Delta(v, V) > 0$) then for any prover* P* *we have*

$$\Pr\left[\langle \mathsf{V}^v \leftrightarrow \mathsf{P}(v)\rangle = \mathsf{accept}\right] \leq \mathsf{err}(\Delta(v, V))$$

Reed Solomon Codes. Let $\mathsf{RS}[\mathbb{F}_q, L, \rho]$ denote the Reed–Solomon code over field $\mathbb{F}_q$, evaluation domain L and rate ρ:

$$\mathsf{RS}[\mathbb{F}_q, L, \rho] = \{f : L \rightarrow \mathbb{F}_q : \deg(f) < \rho|L|\}. \tag{1}$$

Recall the previous state of the art with respect to IOPPs for Reed–Solomon codes. We call a finite field $\mathbb{F}$ *n-smooth* if it contains a sub-group (additive or multiplicative) of size $n = 2^k$ for integer k.

Theorem 5 (FRI over smooth fields [6,8]). *Let $\mathbb{F}$ be an n-smooth finite field. Then there is a subset $L \subseteq \mathbb{F}$ with size n such that for any rate parameter $\rho = 2^{-\mathcal{R}}$ ($\mathcal{R} \in \mathbb{N}$) and repetition parameter t, the Reed–Solomon code $\mathsf{RS}[\mathbb{F}, L, \rho]$ has an IOPP with:*

- *linear proving time* $\mathsf{time_P} = O(n)$ *and proof length* $\mathsf{I} < n$,
- *logarithmic query complexity* $\mathsf{q} = t \cdot \log(n) + O(1)$ *and verification time* $\mathsf{time_V} = O(t \log n)$
- *soundness error function* err, *where:*

$$\mathsf{err}(\delta) = O\left(\frac{n^2}{q}\right) + \left(\min(\delta, 1 - \sqrt{\rho}) - o(1)\right)^t.$$

Our second main result shows essentially the same bounds over any finite field, not just smooth ones.

Theorem 6 (FRI over all fields). *Let $\mathbb{F}$ be the finite field of size q, a prime power. Then for every $n \leq O(\sqrt{q})$ there exists a set $L \subseteq \mathbb{F}_q$ of size $\Theta(n)$ such that for any rate parameter $\rho = 2^{-\mathcal{R}}$ ($\mathcal{R} \in \mathbb{N}$) and repetition parameter t the Reed–Solomon code $\mathsf{RS}[\mathbb{F}, L, \rho]$ has an IOPP with the complexity measures as stated in Theorem 5.*

2.4   Fast IOPs of Proximity for Elliptic Curve Codes

We generalize Theorem 6 to certain algebraic geometry codes, evaluations of functions in a low-degree Riemann–Roch space over FFT-friendly subgroups of elliptic curves. To define the specific codes recall the definition of Algebraic Geometry (or Goppa) codes.

Definition 8 (Algebraic Geometry Codes). *Let X be a non-singular projective curve over a field $\mathbb{F}$, let $D = \{x_1, \ldots, x_n\}$ be a set of $\mathbb{F}$-rational points and G be a divisor with support disjoint from D. Let $\mathscr{L}(G)$ be the Riemann–Roch space defined by G. Then the algebraic geometry (AG) code (also known as a Goppa code) $C(D, G)$ is*

$$C(D, G) := \{f(x_1), \ldots, f(x_n) \mid f \in \mathscr{L}(G), x_i \in D\} \tag{2}$$

Our next result is the following.

Theorem 7 (Fast Elliptic Curve Code IOPP). *Let E be an elliptic curve over $\mathbb{F}$, let $G \subset E$ be a cyclic group of size 2^h and let D be a union of m nontrivial and disjoint cosets of G, such that $G \cap D = \emptyset$. Let $[G] := \sum_{P \in G}[P]$ be the divisor naturally associated with G Then, for any repetition parameter t and setting $\rho = 1/m$, the AG code $C(D, [G])$ has an IOPP with complexity parameters as in Theorem 5.*

3   Scalable IOPs for AIRs over Any Large Field

In this section we prove our main theorem – Theorem 4, relying on certain claims that are proved in later sections.

3.1   The ECFFT Infrastructure

The proof of Theorem 4 relies on delicately chosen elliptic curves, subgroups of those curves, Riemann–Roch spaces and AG codes, and special "degree-correction" functions on the curve. All of these are explained meticulously, and the required properties proven formally, in later sections. The goal of this section is to lay out, in a self-contained manner, all the results which are needed to derive our main results regarding IOPs and IOPs of proximity (in Sect. 3.2).

Due to space constraints, we briefly copy some the information from those sections so that we can describe our main IOP construction in the next section.

The EC Backbone. The backbone of all of the constructions in this paper is the chain of 2-isogenies whose existence was shown in [9, Theorem 4.9], which we quote here:

Theorem 8. *For any prime power $q \geq 7$ and any $1 < \mathsf{K} = 2^k \leq 2\sqrt{q}$, there exist elliptic curves $E_0, E_1, \ldots, E_k$ over $\mathbb{F}_q$ in extended Weierstrass form, a subgroup $G_0 \subseteq E_0$ of size K, 2-isogenies $\varphi_i : E_i \to E_{i+1}$ and rational functions $\psi_i : \mathbb{P}^1 \to \mathbb{P}^1$ of degree 2, such that the following diagram is commutative:*

$$
\begin{array}{ccccccc}
E_0 & \xrightarrow{\varphi_0} & E_1 & \xrightarrow{\varphi_1} & \cdots & \xrightarrow{\varphi_{k-1}} & E_k \\
\pi_0 \downarrow & & \pi_1 \downarrow & & & & \downarrow \pi_k \\
\mathbb{P}^1 & \xrightarrow{\psi_0} & \mathbb{P}^1 & \xrightarrow{\psi_1} & \cdots & \xrightarrow{\psi_{k-1}} & \mathbb{P}^1
\end{array}
\tag{3}
$$

where:

- *π_i are the projection maps to the x-coordinate of each curve;*
- *$|\varphi_{i-1} \circ \cdots \circ \varphi_0(G_0)| = \frac{1}{2^i}|G_0| = 2^{k-i}$.*
- *G_0 has a coset C such that $C \neq -C$ (as elements of the quotient group $E_0(\mathbb{F}_q)/G_0$).*

Note that this theorem is very abstract: It only establishes the existence of these curves and maps, but says almost nothing about the form of the equations defining E_i or of the isogenies φ_i and maps ψ_i, does not specify the structure of G_0, and does not show how to find such curves.

In this work we revisit this theorem, and strengthen and refine it for our needs. First, we show a realization of the above curve sequence using elliptic curves E_i of a simple form, and and obtain simple, explicit formulas for φ_i and ψ_i. Next, we show how to get the above sequence with G_0 being a *cyclic* group (isomorphic to $\mathbb{Z}/2^k\mathbb{Z}$) — this is crucial for doing efficient arithmetization of AIRs (which are defined in terms of cyclic groups). Finally, we give a probabilistic algorithm for finding such curves in nearly optimal $O(2^k \operatorname{polylog} q)$ time. The following statement summarizes these improvements to Theorem 8.

Theorem 9. *There exists a randomized algorithm* Find Curve, *that on input k and $q \geq \max\{7, 2^{2(k-1)}\}$, runs in time $O(2^k \log^2 q \log \log q)$, and with high probability finds elliptic curves E_i in Weierstrass form and maps φ_i, ψ_i as in Theorem 8, such that G_0 is a* **cyclic** *group of size 2^k and the maps φ_i, ψ_i are computable via $O(1)$ operations in $\mathbb{F}_q$.*

The upper bound on the algorithm's runtime can be improved by a $\tilde{O}(\log q)$ factor assuming the Riemann Hypothesis, and we believe that it should be even faster. See the online version [10] for details.

Function Spaces and Evaluation Domains. We are now ready to explicitly describe the setup we will need for our IOP for satisfiable AIRs. For analogues of the FFT and IFFT algorithms and the FRI protocol, we will need to identify some special functions and some special sets of evaluation points. These are captured below.

Proposition 1 (Setup). *For every q, k with $q \geq \Omega(2^{2k})$, there exists an elliptic curve $\mathsf{E}/\mathbb{F}_q$ such that $\mathsf{E}(\mathbb{F}_q)$ contains a cyclic group G of size 2^k.*

Fixing such a curve E, *we introduce some notation:*

- *For each $\ell \leq$ k, let $G^{\langle \ell \rangle}$ be the cyclic subgroup of G of size 2^ℓ.*
- *A basic subset S of $\mathsf{E}(\mathbb{F}_q)$ at scale ℓ is a set $S = C \cup (-C)$, where $C \subseteq \mathsf{E}(\mathbb{F}_q)$ is a coset of $G^{\langle \ell \rangle}$ with $C \neq -C$. Note that $|S| = 2|C| = 2^{\ell+1}$.*
- *An evaluation domain $\mathbf{S}$ of $\mathsf{E}(\mathbb{F}_q)$ at scale ℓ is a union of disjoint basic subsets of $\mathsf{E}(\mathbb{F}_q)$ at scale ℓ.*
- *Let $\mathcal{K}^{\langle \ell \rangle}$ be the $\mathbb{F}_q$-linear space $\mathscr{L}([G^{\langle \ell+1 \rangle}])$ of rational functions on E. By the Riemann–Roch theorem, we have $\dim(\mathcal{K}^{\langle \ell \rangle}) = 2^{\ell+1}$.*

We now set up similar notions on the projective line, obtained by projecting down to the x-coordinate via the map π. The curve E is assumed to be in Weierstrass form.

- *A basic subset T of $\mathbb{F}_q$ at scale ℓ is the projection $T = \pi(S)$ of a basic subset of $\mathsf{E}(\mathbb{F}_q)$ at scale ℓ. Note that $|T| = 2^\ell$.*
- *An evaluation domain of $\mathbb{F}_q$ at scale ℓ is a union of disjoint basic subsets of $\mathbb{F}_q$ at scale ℓ. Equivalently, it is a set of the form $\mathbf{T} = \pi(\mathbf{S})$, where $\mathbf{S}$ is an evaluation domain of $\mathsf{E}(\mathbb{F}_q)$.*
- *Let $\mathcal{M}^{\langle \ell \rangle}$ denote the space of polynomials in $\mathbb{F}_q[X]$ of degree at most $2^\ell - 1$. Note that $\dim(\mathcal{M}^{\langle \ell \rangle}) = 2^\ell$.*

The $\mathcal{K}^{\langle \ell \rangle}$ and $\mathcal{M}^{\langle \ell \rangle}$ spaces above are related through a certain univariate polynomial $\Omega^{\langle \ell \rangle}(X)$ of degree exactly $2^\ell - 1$ (see the online version [10] for an explicit description). This shows that every rational function $f(X, Y) \in \mathcal{K}^{\langle \ell \rangle}$ can be written uniquely in the following form:

$$f(X,Y) = \frac{1}{\Omega^{\langle \ell \rangle}(X)} \left(f_0(X) + \frac{Y}{X} f_1(X) \right), \tag{4}$$

where $f_0(X), f_1(X) \in \mathcal{M}^{\langle \ell \rangle}$. We will sometimes write this as:

$$f(Z) = \frac{1}{\Omega^{\langle \ell \rangle}(\pi(Z))} \left(f_0(\pi(Z)) + \zeta(Z) f_1(\pi(Z)) \right),$$

where $Z = (X, Y)$ is a pair of formal (related) variables representing a point on the curve, π is the projection from E onto the x-coordinate, and $\zeta((X, Y)) = \frac{Y}{X}$.

This representation will let us move between the space of rational functions $\mathcal{K}^{\langle \ell \rangle}$ and the space of polynomials $\mathcal{M}^{\langle \ell \rangle}$.

FFT and IFFT

The following theorems give the new FFT and IFFT transformations that we will need. The proofs of the following theorems appear in the online version [10].

The bases that appear in the theorems are defined there. Following the notation in [9], for a function f defined on an evaluation domain S, we denote by $\langle f \wr S \rangle$ the *evaluation table* of f on S. When f belongs in a linear space spanned by a basis β, we denote by $[f]_\beta$ the representation of f in the basis.

Theorem 10 (FFT *and* IFFT- Elliptic Curve Version). *For each ℓ, there is a basis $\kappa^{\langle \ell \rangle} = (\kappa_j^{\langle \ell \rangle})_{j=0}^{2^{\ell+1}-1}$ of $\mathcal{K}^{\langle \ell \rangle}$ such that for any basic set S at scale ℓ:*

- *there is a $O(\ell \cdot 2^{\ell})$ time algorithm FFT_S, that when given $[f]_{\kappa^{\langle \ell \rangle}}$ as input, computes $\langle f \wr S \rangle$.*
- *there is a $O(\ell \cdot 2^{\ell})$ time algorithm IFFT_S, that when given $\langle f \wr S \rangle$ as input for some $f \in \mathcal{K}^{\langle \ell \rangle}$, computes $[f]_{\kappa^{\langle \ell \rangle}}$. (In particular, $f \in \mathcal{K}^{\langle \ell \rangle}$ is uniquely specified by $\langle f \wr S \rangle$).*

Theorem 11 (FFT *and* IFFT- Univariate Polynomial Version). *For each ℓ, there is a basis $\mu^{\langle \ell \rangle} = (\mu_j^{\langle \ell \rangle})_{j=0}^{2^{\ell}-1}$ of $\mathcal{M}^{\langle \ell \rangle}$ such that for any basic subset T of $\mathbb{F}_q$ at scale ℓ:*

- *there is a $O(\ell \cdot 2^{\ell})$ time algorithm FFT_T, that when given $[g]_{\mu^{\langle \ell \rangle}}$ as input, computes $\langle g \wr T \rangle$.*
- *there is a $O(\ell \cdot 2^{\ell})$ time algorithm IFFT_T, that when given $\langle g \wr T \rangle$ as input for some $g \in \mathcal{M}^{\langle \ell \rangle}$, computes $[g]_{\mu^{\langle \ell \rangle}}$. (In particular, $g \in \mathcal{M}^{\langle \ell \rangle}$ is uniquely specified by $\langle g \wr T \rangle$).*

FRI Our key tool is the FRI protocol for testing proximity to univariate polynomials. Specifically, when the set of evaluation points $\mathbf{T}$ is an *evaluation domain* in $\mathbb{F}_q$, then the FFT infrastructure enables a version of the FRI protocol for $\mathsf{RS}[\mathbb{F}_q, \mathbf{T}, \rho]$, stated below. The proof appears in the online version [10].

Theorem 12 (Basic FRI). *Let $q, \mathsf{k}, \mathsf{E}$ and the setup be as above. Let $\ell \le \mathsf{k}$. Let $\mathcal{R}$ be a positive integer, and set $\rho = 2^{-\mathcal{R}}$. Let $\mathbf{T} \subseteq \mathbb{F}_q$ be an evaluation domain at scale ℓ with $|\mathbf{T}| = \frac{1}{\rho} 2^{\ell}$.*

Given a repetition parameter $t > 0$, there is an IOPP protocol (FRI) with prover P and verifier V for $\mathsf{RS}[\mathbb{F}_q, \mathbf{T}, \rho]$ with:

- **Completeness:** *There exists a prover P such that for any $f \in \mathsf{RS}[\mathbb{F}_q, \mathbf{T}, \rho]$ causes the verifier V to accept f with probability 1.*
- **Soundness:** *If f is δ far from $\mathsf{RS}[\mathbb{F}_q, \mathbf{T}, \rho]$ then for any prover P^*, we have*

$$\Pr\left[\langle \mathsf{V}(f) \leftrightarrow \mathsf{P}^*(f) \rangle = \mathsf{accept}\right] \le \left(1 - \min\left\{\Delta(f, \mathsf{RS}[\mathbb{F}_q, \mathbf{T}, \rho]), \sqrt{\rho}\right\} + o(1)\right)^t$$

- **Prover runtime:** *$O(|\mathbf{T}|)$ arithmetic operations over $\mathbb{F}_q$*
- **Verifier runtime:** *$O(t \log |\mathbf{T}|)$ arithmetic operations over $\mathbb{F}_q$*
- **Proof length:** *$O(|\mathbf{T}|)$ field elements in $\mathbb{F}_q$.*

From the proximity gap property of Reed–Solomon codes [8], this leads to a protocol for simultaneously checking a batch of functions evaluated on an evaluation domain in $\mathbb{F}_q$ are low-degree. The proof appears in the online version [10].

Theorem 13 (Batched FRI). *Let $q, \mathsf{k}, \mathsf{E}$ and the setup be as above. Let $\ell \le \mathsf{k}$. Let $\mathcal{R}$ be a positive integer, and set $\rho = 2^{-\mathcal{R}}$. Let $\mathbf{T} \subseteq \mathbb{F}_q$ be an evaluation domain at scale ℓ with $|\mathbf{T}| = \frac{1}{\rho} 2^{\ell}$.*

Let $d_1, \ldots, d_k$ be integers such that $d_i \le \rho|\mathbf{T}|$ for all i. Given a repetition parameter $t > 0$ and oracle access to functions

$$g_1, g_2, \ldots, g_k : \mathbf{T} \to \mathbb{F}_q,$$

there is an IOP protocol with the following behavior.

- **Completeness:** *If for all i, g_i is the evaluation of some polynomial in $\mathbb{F}_q[X]$ of degree $< d_i$, then there is a prover strategy to make the verifier accept with probability 1.*
- **Soundness:** *Suppose the protocol accepts with probability*

$$p \ge (\rho^{1/2} + \epsilon)^t + O\left(\frac{\rho^2|\mathbf{T}|^2}{\epsilon^7 q}\right).$$

Then there exist polynomials $G_1(X), \ldots, G_k(X) \in \mathbb{F}_q[X]$, with $\deg(G_i) < d_i$ and a set $V \subseteq \mathbf{T}$ such that:
1. *$|V| \ge (\rho^{1/2} + \epsilon)|\mathbf{T}|$,*
2. *$g_i(x) = G_i(x)$ for all $x \in V$, $i \in [k]$.*
- **Prover runtime:** *$O(k|\mathbf{T}|)$ arithmetic operations over $\mathbb{F}_q$*
- **Verifier runtime:** *$O(t(k + \log|\mathbf{T}|))$ arithmetic operations over $\mathbb{F}_q$*
- **Proof length:** *$O(|\mathbf{T}|)$ field elements in $\mathbb{F}_q$.*

Note: *The constants in $O(\cdot)$ in the last three items in both Theorems 12 and 13 are some explicit small constants that are each at most 10.*

Vanishing Detection. The final tool that we need is a way to check that some given rational function on E vanishes at a given set of points. See the online version [10] for details.

Theorem 14 (Vanishing detection). *Let $I \subseteq \mathsf{E}(\mathbb{F}_q)$ be a subset which is contained in a coset of $G^{\langle\ell\rangle}$.*

There is a well-defined rational function $\omega_I^{\langle\ell\rangle} \in \mathscr{L}([G^{\langle\ell+1\rangle} \setminus G^{\langle\ell\rangle}] - [G^{\langle\ell\rangle}] + [I])$ on E with the following properties:

- *For every $f \in \mathscr{L}(2[G^{\langle\ell\rangle}])$, we have:*

$$f \text{ vanishes on } I \Leftrightarrow \omega_I^{\langle\ell\rangle} \cdot f \in \mathscr{L}([G^{\langle\ell+1\rangle}]).$$

- *For almost every $P \in \mathsf{E}(\mathbb{F}_q)$, excluding at most three cosets of $G^{\langle\ell+1\rangle}$, $\omega_I^{\langle\ell\rangle}(P)$ can be computed using $O(\|I\| + \ell)$ $\mathbb{F}_q$-operations (where $\|I\|$ is the coset complexity of I).*

3.2   The IOP Protocol

In this section we describe an IOP for the satisfiable AIR language of Definition 6.

The crux of this protocol is for the prover to do a *"low-degree extension"* of a satisfying AIR-witness $\mathbf{f} = (f_1, \ldots, f_w)$, where each $f_l : H_0 \to \mathbb{F}_q$. This is not the standard univariate polynomial low-degree extension; instead it is an elliptic curve variant. Indeed, we first identify H_0 with a coset C of a cyclic subgroup of size 2^h of a suitable elliptic curve E over $\mathbb{F}_q$. Thus we may view each f_l as a function defined at some points of E. Next, we consider the Riemann–Roch space $\mathcal{K}^{\langle h \rangle}$ of E, and the prover finds elements $\widehat{f_l}$ of $\mathcal{K}^{\langle h \rangle}$ whose restrictions to C agree with the values taken on H_0 by the f_l's. Finally, the prover provides evaluations of these rational functions $\widehat{f_l}$'s at another set of points $D \subseteq E(\mathbb{F}_q)$. These extended evaluations are at the core of the prover's proof of satisfiability of an AIR.

To describe the IOP for L_{AIR} we need to fix some auxiliary parameters aux that will be used by it. For simplicity and ease of exposition, we will only describe the IOP for AIRs which have the constraint degree $d = 2$.

– The *rate parameter* $\rho = 2^{-\mathcal{R}}$ for some integer $\mathcal{R}$. In practical settings, ρ is typically fixed to a small constant such as $\frac{1}{16}$ (thus $\mathcal{R} = 4$), and it may help the reader to consider this setting on first reading.
– An elliptic curve E over $\mathbb{F}_q$ with a cyclic subgroup G of size 2^k, for $k = h+\mathcal{R}+5$. We then use the setup from Proposition 1 with respect to this curve.
– A choice of a coset C of $G^{\langle h \rangle}$ such that $C \neq -C$. We identify H_0 with C by first picking an arbitrary $Q_0 \in C$, an arbitrary generator g of $G^{\langle h \rangle}$, and identifying

$$g^j \leftrightarrow Q_0 + j \cdot g.$$

With this identification, the constraint enforcement domains $H_\alpha \subseteq H_0$ get identified with $U_\alpha \subseteq C$ using:

$$U_\alpha = \{Q_0 + j \cdot g \mid g^j \in H_\alpha\}.$$

Note that $C \cup (-C)$ is a basic set at scale h.
– An evaluation domain $\mathbf{S} \subseteq E(\mathbb{F}_q)$ at scale h of size $2^{k'} = d \cdot \frac{1}{\rho} \cdot 2^{h+1} = 2^{h+\mathcal{R}+1}$, which is disjoint from the trace domain H_0. Thus $\mathbf{S}$ is the union of $\frac{d}{\rho} = 2^{\mathcal{R}+1}$ basic sets at scale h.
– The projection $\mathbf{T} \subseteq \mathbb{F}_q$ of the evaluation domain $\mathbf{S}$ to the x-coordinate (recall the curve is in Weierstrass form) — this is an evaluation domain of $\mathbb{F}_q$ at scale h. Note that $|\mathbf{T}| = \frac{1}{\rho}2^{h+1} = 2^{h+\mathcal{R}+1}$.

Later in the protocol, we shall represent functions $f(x,y) : \mathbf{S} \to \mathbb{F}_q$ as a pair $f_0(x), f_1(x) : \mathbf{T} \to \mathbb{F}_q$ where $\mathbf{T}$ is the projection of $\mathbf{S}$ onto the x-coordinate, using the decomposition of (4), i.e., defining

$$f(x,y) := \frac{1}{\Omega^{\langle \ell \rangle}(x)} \left(f_0(x) + \frac{y}{x} \cdot f_1(x) \right),$$

where f is (or is supposed to be) an evaluation of a function in $\mathcal{K}^{\langle \ell \rangle}$.

We shall also use the following notation:

- For $f : \mathbf{T} \to \mathbb{F}_q$ and a function $u : A \to \mathbb{F}_q$, where $A \cap \mathbf{T} = \emptyset$, we define the *quotient* of f by u to be the function:

$$\text{Quotient}\,(f; u) : \mathbf{T} \to \mathbb{F}_q, \quad \text{Quotient}\,(f; u)\,(x) := \frac{f(x) - U(x)}{Z_A(x)},$$

where:
- $U(X) \in \mathbb{F}_q[X]$ is the unique polynomial of degree at most $|A| - 1$ with $U|_A = u$,
- $Z_A(X) = \prod_{a \in A}(X - a)$ is the vanishing polynomial of A.

Description of the Protocol. The protocol starts with an AIR instance $\mathsf{A} = (\mathbb{F}, \mathsf{w}, \mathsf{h}, \mathsf{d}, \mathsf{s}, \mathsf{H}_0, \mathsf{g}, \mathsf{I}, \mathsf{Cset})$ and auxiliary IOP parameters $\mathsf{aux} = (\mathsf{E}, G, C, \mathbf{S}, \mathsf{k}', t)$ given to both prover and verifier.

At the high level, the steps closely track the corresponding steps in the STARK protocol given in [49][10], with rational functions and points on the curve replacing univariate polynomials and points in $\mathbb{F}_q$.

At some points, we represent rational functions on the elliptic curve by pairs of univariate polynomials, and invoke results about univariate polynomials. A more natural and clean version could have been given if we had analogues of (i) the proximity gaps phenomenon [8], and (ii) the DEEP query and quotienting method [17], for AG codes on elliptic curves. We believe that this approach ought to work but have not pursued these here in the interest of the simplicity of relying on previous results for RS codes.

We now give the description of the IOP protocol.

1. **Execution trace oracle:** The prover first finds an AIR witness $\mathbf{f} = (\mathsf{f}_1, \ldots, \mathsf{f}_\mathsf{w})$ that satisfies the AIR instance A according to Definition 5. Next, the prover finds functions $\widehat{f}_1, \ldots, \widehat{f}_\mathsf{w} \in \mathcal{K}^{\langle \mathsf{h} \rangle}$ extending the f_l's. Specifically, $\widehat{f}_l$ is rational function $\widehat{f}_l(X, Y) \in \mathcal{K}^{\langle \mathsf{h} \rangle}$ such that $\widehat{f}_l\big|_C = \mathsf{f}_l|_{\mathsf{H}_0}$.

   Note that a function $\widehat{f}_l \in \mathcal{K}^{\langle \mathsf{h} \rangle}$ can be specified by giving its values on the entire basic set $C \cup (-C)$ (using the IFFT from Theorem 10); thus the prover has many valid choices for $\widehat{f}_l$, determined by the values of $\widehat{f}_l\big|_{-C}$.

   The prover then expresses each $\widehat{f}_l(X, Y)$ using a pair of univariate polynomials $\widehat{f}_{l,0}(X), \widehat{f}_{l,1}(X) \in \mathbb{F}_q[X]$ of degree $< 2^\mathsf{h}$, via the decomposition of (4), i.e.,

$$\widehat{f}_l(X, Y) := \frac{1}{\Omega^{\langle \mathsf{h} \rangle}(X)}\left(\widehat{f}_{l,0}(X) + \frac{Y}{X}\widehat{f}_{l,1}(X)\right).$$

   The prover then evaluates these 2w low-degree polynomials $\langle \widehat{f}_{l,0}, \widehat{f}_{l,1} \mid l \in [\mathsf{w}] \rangle$ at all the points of $\mathbf{T}$.

---

[10] Some optimizations from [49], which are important for practical considerations and could also be done here, are omitted for clarity.

> Prover sends $\langle \widehat{f}_{l,m} \wr \mathbf{T} \rangle$ for each $(l, m) \in [\mathsf{w}] \times \{0, 1\}$.

Note that these are evaluations of degree 2^{h} polynomials on a set $\mathbf{T}$ of size $\frac{1}{\rho} 2^{\mathsf{h}+1}$, so they are all supposed to be codewords of $\mathsf{RS}(\mathbb{F}_q, \mathbf{T}, \rho)$ (and even of $\mathsf{RS}(\mathbb{F}_q, \mathbf{T}, \rho/2)$).

2. **Constraint randomness:**

> Verifier samples uniform randomness $\mathbf{r} := (\mathsf{r}_1, \ldots, \mathsf{r}_s) \in \mathbb{F}_q^s$, one field element per constraint, and sends it to the prover.

We now explain the role of this step. These random field elements will be coefficients for taking a "random linear combination of the constraints" – and the prover will now try to convince the verifier that this random linear combination of the constraints is satisfied by the witness underlying the $\widehat{f}_{l,0}$'s and the $\widehat{f}_{l,1}$'s.

In more detail, constraint C_α asks that

$$Q_\alpha((f_l(\mathbf{g}^j \cdot t))_{l,j}) = 0,$$

for all $t \in \mathsf{H}_\alpha$.

If the $\widehat{f}_l \in \mathcal{K}^{\langle \mathsf{h} \rangle}$ are truly such that $\widehat{f}_l|_{\mathsf{H}_0} = f_l|_C$, then this is the same as:

$$Q_\alpha((\widehat{f}_l(P + j \cdot g))_{(l,j) \in \mathsf{I}}) = 0,$$

for all $P \in \mathsf{U}_\alpha \subset \mathsf{E}$.

Since $\widehat{f}_l \in \mathcal{K}^{\langle \mathsf{h} \rangle} = \mathcal{L}([G^{\langle \mathsf{h}+1 \rangle}])$ and Q_α has degree at most $\mathsf{d} = 2$, we get that the function $B_\alpha : \mathsf{E} \to \mathbb{F}_q$ defined by:

$$B_\alpha(P) := Q_\alpha((\widehat{f}_l(P + j \cdot g))_{(l,j) \in \mathsf{I}}) \quad \forall P \in \mathsf{E},$$

lies in $\mathcal{L}(2[G^{\langle \mathsf{h}+1 \rangle}])$. Note that the verifier can simulate oracle access to B_α at points in $\mathbf{S}$ using oracle access to evaluations of $\widehat{f}_l$ at points in $\mathbf{S}$, which themselves can be reconstituted from evaluations of $\widehat{f}_{l,0}$ and $\widehat{f}_{l,1}$ at points in $\mathbf{T}$.

Checking that B_α vanishes at all points in H_α is equivalent to checking that the rational function

$$\omega_\alpha \cdot B_\alpha$$

lies in $\mathcal{L}([G^{\langle \mathsf{h}+2 \rangle}]) = \mathcal{K}^{\langle \mathsf{h}+1 \rangle}$, where $\omega_\alpha := \omega_{\mathsf{H}_\alpha}$ is the degree adjustment function for U_α.

Now we can explain where the randomness $\mathbf{r}$ is used — it is to check all the above memberships of $\omega_\alpha \cdot B_\alpha$ in $\mathcal{K}^{\langle \mathsf{h}+1 \rangle}$ simultaneously. The prover will try to convince the verifier that the random linear combination:

$$\widehat{f}^{\mathbf{r}} = \sum_\alpha \mathsf{r}_\alpha \omega_\alpha B_\alpha \tag{5}$$

lies in $\mathcal{K}^{\langle \mathsf{h}+1 \rangle}$. This is what the prover does next.

3. **Constraint trace oracle:**
The Prover then represents the rational function $\widehat{f^r} \in \mathcal{K}^{\langle h+1 \rangle}$ as 2 univariate polynomials:

$$\widehat{f^r}(X, Y) = \frac{1}{\Omega^{\langle h+1 \rangle}(X)} \left(\widehat{f_0^r}(X) + \frac{Y}{X} \widehat{f_1^r}(X) \right),$$

where $\widehat{f_m^r} \in \mathcal{M}_{h+1}$ for $m \in \{0, 1\}$.
The prover then evaluates both univariate polynomials at the points of $\mathbf{T}$.

> Prover sends $\langle \widehat{f_0^r} \wr \mathbf{T} \rangle$, $\langle \widehat{f_1^r} \wr \mathbf{T} \rangle$.

Note that these are evaluations of univariate polynomials of degree $< 2^{h+1}$ at $2^{h+\mathcal{R}+1}$ points.

4. **DEEP query:**

> Verifier samples DEEP query $q = (x_0, y_0)$ uniformly at random from $E(\mathbb{F}_q) \setminus (\overline{C} \cup \mathbf{S})$, where $\overline{C} = G^{\langle h+2 \rangle} \cup (G^{\langle h+2 \rangle} + C) \cup (G^{\langle h+2 \rangle} - C)$ is a union of three cosets of $G^{\langle h+2 \rangle}$.

5. **DEEP answer:**

> Prover sends an answer sequence
>
> $$\mathsf{answer} = \langle\langle \alpha_{j,l,0}, \alpha_{j,l,1} : (j, l) \in \mathsf{I} \rangle, \langle \beta_0, \beta_1 \rangle\rangle \in \mathbb{F}_q^{\mathsf{I} \times \{0,1\}} \times \mathbb{F}_q^2.$$

The $\alpha_{j,l,m}$ are supposed to be the evaluations $\widehat{f_{l,m}}(q + jg)$, and β_m is supposed to be the evaluation $\widehat{f_m^r}(q)$. Following the DEEP philosophy [17], we can then incorporate these claimed evaluations of $\widehat{f_{l,m}}$ and $\widehat{f_m^r}$ by *quotienting*. This will be taken into account in the next step of the protocol.
But first, the verifier has to do a basic sanity check on the claimed evaluations. Letting

$$\alpha_{j,l} := \frac{1}{\Omega^{\langle h \rangle}(\pi(q + j \cdot g))} (\alpha_{j,l,0} + \zeta(q + j \cdot g) \cdot \alpha_{j,l,1})$$

$$\beta := \frac{1}{\Omega^{\langle h+1 \rangle}(\pi(q))} (\beta_0 + \zeta(q)\beta_1)$$

then supposedly $\alpha_{j,l} = \widehat{f_l}(q + j \cdot g)$ and $\beta = \widehat{f^r}(q)$.
We say the constraints Q_α are *validated* by answer if the following equality holds:

$$\sum_\alpha r_\alpha \omega_\alpha(q) Q_\alpha \big((\alpha_{j,l})_{(j,l) \in \mathsf{I}} \big) = \beta, \tag{6}$$

i.e., the answers are consistent with Eq. (5).

6. **FRI Protocol:** This step verifies the low-degreeness of various functions simultaneously. But first, we quotient out the functions $\widehat{f}_{l,m}$ and $\widehat{f}_m^r$ by their evaluations that the prover claimed in the previous step.
For $l \in [w]$, define $A_l \subseteq \mathbb{F}_q$ to be the set:

$$A_l = \{\pi(\mathsf{q} + j \cdot g) \mid (j,l) \in \mathsf{I}\}$$

Define $u_{l,m} : A_l \to \mathbb{F}_q$ to be:

$$u_{l,m}(\pi(\mathsf{q} + j \cdot g)) = \alpha_{j,l,m}.$$

For $l \in [w]$ and $m \in \{0,1\}$, define $\widehat{b}_{l,m} : \mathbf{T} \to \mathbb{F}_q$ by:

$$\widehat{b}_{l,m}(x) = \mathsf{Quotient}\left(\widehat{f}_{l,m}; u_{l,m}\right)(x),$$

and degree parameter $d_{l,m} = 2^h - 1 - |A_l|$.
For $m \in \{0,1\}$, define $u_m : \{\pi(\mathsf{q})\} \to \mathbb{F}_q$ by

$$u_m(\pi(\mathsf{q})) = \beta_m.$$

Now define $\widehat{b}_m^r : \mathbf{T} \to \mathbb{F}_q$ by:

$$\widehat{b}_m^r(x) = \mathsf{Quotient}\left(\widehat{f}_m^r; u_m\right)(x),$$

and degree parameter $d_m = 2^{h+1} - 2$.
Note that oracle access to these functions can be simulated by the verifier from oracle access to $\widehat{f}_{l,m}$ and $\widehat{f}_m^r$ on $\mathbf{T}$.

> Prover and Verifier now run the Batched FRI protocol from Theorem 13 on all the $\widehat{b}_{l,m}$ and the $\widehat{b}_m^r$ with degree parameters $d_{l,m}$ and d_m, and repetition parameter t.

Observe that all the degree parameters are smaller than $\rho|\mathbf{T}|$ – thus the soundness of this step is governed by ρ and t.

7. **Decision:**

> Verifier accepts iff (i) the constraints Q_α are validated by answer (i.e., equation (6) holds), and (ii) the FRI protocol accepts.

Due to space limitations of the conference version, full proofs are omitted. Full details appear in the online version [10].

References

1. Ames, S., Hazay, C., Ishai, Y., Venkitasubramaniam, M.: Ligero: lightweight sublinear arguments without a trusted setup. In: Proceedings of the 24th ACM Conference on Computer and Communications Security, pp. 2087–2104. CCS 2017 (2017)
2. Arora, S., Lund, C., Motwani, R., Sudan, M., Szegedy, M.: Proof verification and the hardness of approximation problems. J. ACM **45**(3), 501–555 (1998). Preliminary version in FOCS 1992
3. Arora, S., Safra, S.: Probabilistic checking of proofs: a new characterization of NP. J. ACM **45**(1), 70–122 (1998). Preliminary version in FOCS 1992
4. Babai, L., Fortnow, L., Levin, L.A., Szegedy, M.: Checking computations in polylogarithmic time. In: Proceedings of the 23rd Annual ACM Symposium on Theory of Computing, pp. 21–32. STOC 1991 (1991)
5. Babai, L., Fortnow, L., Lund, C.: Non-deterministic exponential time has two-prover interactive protocols. Comput. Complex. **1**, 3–40 (1991). Preliminary version appeared in FOCS 1990
6. Ben-Sasson, E., Bentov, I., Horesh, Y., Riabzev, M.: Fast reed-solomon interactive oracle proofs of proximity. In: Chatzigiannakis, I., Kaklamanis, C., Marx, D., Sannella, D. (eds.) ICALP. LIPIcs, vol. 107, pp. 1–17. Schloss Dagstuhl - Leibniz-Zentrum für Informatik (2018). https://www.dagstuhl.de/dagpub/978-3-95977-076-7
7. Ben-Sasson, E., Bentov, I., Horesh, Y., Riabzev, M.: Scalable zero knowledge with no trusted setup. In: Boldyreva, A., Micciancio, D. (eds.) CRYPTO 2019. LNCS, vol. 11694, pp. 701–732. Springer, Cham (2019). https://doi.org/10.1007/978-3-030-26954-8_23
8. Ben-Sasson, E., Carmon, D., Ishai, Y., Kopparty, S., Saraf, S.: Proximity gaps for reed-solomon codes. In: Irani, S. (ed.) 61st IEEE Annual Symposium on Foundations of Computer Science, FOCS 2020, Durham, NC, USA, 16–19 November 2020, pp. 900–909. IEEE (2020). https://doi.org/10.1109/FOCS46700.2020.00088
9. Ben-Sasson, E., Carmon, D., Kopparty, S., Levit, D.: Elliptic curve fast fourier transform (ECFFT) part I: fast polynomial algorithms over all finite fields. Electronic Colloquium on Computational Complexity, p. 103 (2021). https://eccc.weizmann.ac.il/report/2021/103
10. Ben-Sasson, E., Carmon, D., Kopparty, S., Levit, D.: Scalable and transparent proofs over all large fields, via elliptic curves (ECFFT Part II) (2022). https://eccc.weizmann.ac.il/report/2022/110
11. Ben-Sasson, E., Chiesa, A., Forbes, M.A., Gabizon, A., Riabzev, M., Spooner, N.: Zero knowledge protocols from succinct constraint detection. In: Kalai, Y., Reyzin, L. (eds.) TCC 2017. LNCS, vol. 10678, pp. 172–206. Springer, Cham (2017). https://doi.org/10.1007/978-3-319-70503-3_6
12. Ben-Sasson, E., Chiesa, A., Gabizon, A., Riabzev, M., Spooner, N.: Interactive oracle proofs with constant rate and query complexity. In: Chatzigiannakis, I., Indyk, P., Kuhn, F., Muscholl, A. (eds.) 44th International Colloquium on Automata, Languages, and Programming, ICALP 2017, 10–14 July 2017, Warsaw, Poland. LIPIcs, vol. 80, pp. 1–15. Schloss Dagstuhl - Leibniz-Zentrum für Informatik (2017). https://doi.org/10.4230/LIPIcs.ICALP.2017.40

13. Ben-Sasson, E., Chiesa, A., Genkin, D., Tromer, E.: On the concrete efficiency of probabilistically-checkable proofs. In: Boneh, D., Roughgarden, T., Feigenbaum, J. (eds.) Symposium on Theory of Computing Conference, STOC2013, Palo Alto, CA, USA, 1–4 June 2013, pp. 585–594. ACM (2013). https://doi.org/10.1145/2488608.2488681
14. Ben-Sasson, E., Chiesa, A., Genkin, D., Tromer, E., Virza, M.: SNARKs for C: verifying program executions succinctly and in zero knowledge. In: Proceedings of the 33rd Annual International Cryptology Conference, pp. 90–108. CRYPTO 2013 (2013)
15. Ben-Sasson, E., Chiesa, A., Goldberg, L., Gur, T., Riabzev, M., Spooner, N.: Linear-size constant-query IOPs for delegating computation. In: Proceedings of the 17th Theory of Cryptography Conference. TCC 2019 (2019)
16. Ben-Sasson, E., Chiesa, A., Spooner, N.: Interactive oracle proofs. In: Hirt, M., Smith, A. (eds.) TCC 2016. LNCS, vol. 9986, pp. 31–60. Springer, Heidelberg (2016). https://doi.org/10.1007/978-3-662-53644-5_2
17. Ben-Sasson, E., Goldberg, L., Kopparty, S., Saraf, S.: DEEP-FRI: sampling outside the box improves soundness. In: Vidick, T. (ed.) 11th Innovations in Theoretical Computer Science Conference, ITCS 2020, 12–14 January 2020, Seattle, Washington, USA. LIPIcs, vol. 151, pp. 1–32. Schloss Dagstuhl - Leibniz-Zentrum für Informatik (2020). https://doi.org/10.4230/LIPIcs.ITCS.2020.5
18. Ben-Sasson, E., Goldreich, O., Harsha, P., Sudan, M., Vadhan, S.: Short PCPs verifiable in polylogarithmic time. In: Proceedings of the 20th Annual IEEE Conference on Computational Complexity, pp. 120–134. CCC 2005 (2005)
19. Ben-Sasson, E., Kaplan, Y., Kopparty, S., Meir, O., Stichtenoth, H.: Constant rate pcps for circuit-sat with sublinear query complexity. J. ACM 63(4), 1–57 (2016). https://doi.org/10.1145/2901294
20. Ben-Sasson, E., Sudan, M.: Short PCPs with polylog query complexity. SIAM J. Comput. 38(2), 551–607 (2008)
21. Bootle, J., Cerulli, A., Ghadafi, E., Groth, J., Hajiabadi, M., Jakobsen, S.K.: Linear-time zero-knowledge proofs for arithmetic circuit satisfiability. In: Takagi, T., Peyrin, T. (eds.) ASIACRYPT 2017. LNCS, vol. 10626, pp. 336–365. Springer, Cham (2017). https://doi.org/10.1007/978-3-319-70700-6_12
22. Bootle, J., Chiesa, A., Groth, J.: Linear-time arguments with sublinear verification from tensor codes. In: Pass, R., Pietrzak, K. (eds.) TCC 2020. LNCS, vol. 12551, pp. 19–46. Springer, Cham (2020). https://doi.org/10.1007/978-3-030-64378-2_2
23. Bowe, S., Grigg, J., Hopwood, D.: Recursive proof composition without a trusted setup. Cryptology ePrint Archive, Report 2019/1021 (2019). https://ia.cr/2019/1021
24. Bünz, B., Bootle, J., Boneh, D., Poelstra, A., Wuille, P., Maxwell, G.: Bulletproofs: short proofs for confidential transactions and more. In: Proceedings of the 39th IEEE Symposium on Security and Privacy, pp. 315–334. S&P 2018 (2018)
25. Chiesa, A., Hu, Y., Maller, M., Mishra, P., Vesely, N., Ward, N.: Marlin: Preprocessing zkSNARKs with universal and updatable SRS. In: Proceedings of the 39th Annual International Conference on the Theory and Applications of Cryptographic Techniques, pp. 738–768. EUROCRYPT 2020 (2020)
26. Chiesa, A., Ma, F., Spooner, N., Zhandry, M.: Post-quantum succinct arguments. Electronic Colloquium on Computational Complexity, p. 38 (2021). https://eccc.weizmann.ac.il/report/2021/038
27. Chiesa, A., Manohar, P., Spooner, N.: Succinct arguments in the quantum random oracle model. In: Hofheinz, D., Rosen, A. (eds.) TCC 2019. LNCS, vol. 11892, pp. 1–29. Springer, Cham (2019). https://doi.org/10.1007/978-3-030-36033-7_1

28. Chiesa, A., Ojha, D., Spooner, N.: FRACTAL: post-quantum and transparent recursive proofs from holography. In: Canteaut, A., Ishai, Y. (eds.) EUROCRYPT 2020. LNCS, vol. 12105, pp. 769–793. Springer, Cham (2020). https://doi.org/10.1007/978-3-030-45721-1_27

29. Chiesa, A., Yogev, E.: Subquadratic SNARGs in the random oracle model. In: Malkin, T., Peikert, C. (eds.) CRYPTO 2021. LNCS, vol. 12825, pp. 711–741. Springer, Cham (2021). https://doi.org/10.1007/978-3-030-84242-0_25

30. Chiesa, A., Yogev, E.: Tight security bounds for Micali's SNARGs. In: Nissim, K., Waters, B. (eds.) TCC 2021. LNCS, vol. 13042, pp. 401–434. Springer, Cham (2021). https://doi.org/10.1007/978-3-030-90459-3_14

31. Chudnovsky, D.V., Chudnovsky, G.V.: Computational problems in arithmetic of linear differential equations. some diophantine applications. In: Chudnovsky, D.V., Chudnovsky, G.V., Cohn, H., Nathanson, M.B. (eds.) Number Theory. LNM, vol. 1383, pp. 12–49. Springer, Heidelberg (1989). https://doi.org/10.1007/BFb0083567

32. Gabizon, A., Williamson, Z.J., Ciobotaru, O.: Plonk: Permutations over Lagrange-bases for oecumenical noninteractive arguments of knowledge. Cryptology ePrint Archive, Report 2019/953 (2019). https://ia.cr/2019/953

33. Gennaro, R., Gentry, C., Parno, B., Raykova, M.: Quadratic span programs and succinct NIZKs without PCPs. In: Proceedings of the 32nd Annual International Conference on Theory and Application of Cryptographic Techniques, pp. 626–645. EUROCRYPT 2013 (2013)

34. Goldberg, L., Papini, S., Riabzev, M.: Cairo - a turing-complete stark-friendly CPU architecture. IACR Cryptol. ePrint Arch, p. 1063 (2021). https://eprint.iacr.org/2021/1063

35. Goldwasser, S., Kalai, Y.T., Rothblum, G.N.: Delegating computation: interactive proofs for muggles. In: Proceedings of the 40th Annual ACM Symposium on Theory of Computing, pp. 113–122. STOC 2008 (2008)

36. Golovnev, A., Lee, J., Setty, S., Thaler, J., Wahby, R.S.: Brakedown: Linear-time and post-quantum snarks for r1cs. Cryptology ePrint Archive, Report 2021/1043 (2021). https://ia.cr/2021/1043

37. Groth, J.: On the size of pairing-based non-interactive arguments. In: Fischlin, M., Coron, J.-S. (eds.) EUROCRYPT 2016. LNCS, vol. 9666, pp. 305–326. Springer, Heidelberg (2016). https://doi.org/10.1007/978-3-662-49896-5_11

38. Ishai, Y., Kushilevitz, E., Ostrovsky, R., Sahai, A.: Zero-knowledge from secure multiparty computation. In: Proceedings of the Thirty-Ninth Annual ACM Symposium on Theory of Computing, pp. 21–30. STOC 2007, Association for Computing Machinery, New York, NY, USA (2007).https://doi.org/10.1145/1250790.1250794

39. Kilian, J.: A note on efficient zero-knowledge proofs and arguments (extended abstract). In: Proceedings of the Twenty-Fourth Annual ACM Symposium on Theory of Computing, pp. 723–732. STOC 1992, Association for Computing Machinery, New York, NY, USA (1992). https://doi.org/10.1145/129712.129782

40. Koblitz, N.: Elliptic curve cryptosystems. Math. Comput. **48**, 203–209 (1987)

41. Lund, C., Fortnow, L., Karloff, H.J., Nisan, N.: Algebraic methods for interactive proof systems. J. ACM **39**(4), 859–868 (1992)

42. Maller, M., Bowe, S., Kohlweiss, M., Meiklejohn, S.: Sonic: zero-knowledge SNARKs from linear-size universal and updateable structured reference strings. Cryptology ePrint Archive, Report 2019/099 (2019)

43. Micali, S.: Computationally sound proofs. SIAM J. Comput. **30**(4), 1253–1298 (2000). https://doi.org/10.1137/S0097539795284959

44. Parno, B., Gentry, C., Howell, J., Raykova, M.: Pinocchio: nearly practical verifiable computation. In: Proceedings of the 34th IEEE Symposium on Security and Privacy, pp. 238–252. Oakland 2013 (2013)
45. Reingold, O., Rothblum, R., Rothblum, G.: Constant-round interactive proofs for delegating computation. In: Proceedings of the 48th ACM Symposium on the Theory of Computing, pp. 49–62. STOC 2016 (2016)
46. Ron-Zewi, N., Rothblum, R.: Proving as fast as computing: succinct arguments with constant prover overhead. Electronic Colloquium on Computational Complexity, pp. 180 (2021). https://eccc.weizmann.ac.il/report/2021/180
47. Shamir, A.: IP = PSPACE. J. ACM **39**(4), 869–877 (1992)
48. Silverman, J.H.: The Arithmetic of Elliptic Curves. GTM, vol. 106. Springer, New York (2009). https://doi.org/10.1007/978-0-387-09494-6
49. StarkWare: ethstark documentation. Cryptology ePrint Archive, Report 2021/582 (2021). https://eprint.iacr.org/2021/582
50. Washington, L.C.: Elliptic Curves: Number Theory and Cryptography, Second Edition. Chapman & Hall/CRC, 2 edn. (2008)

Doubly Efficient Interactive Proofs over Infinite and Non-commutative Rings

Eduardo Soria-Vazquez(✉)

Technology Innovation Institute, Abu Dhabi, UAE
eduardo.soria-vazquez@tii.ae

Abstract. We introduce the first proof system for layered arithmetic circuits over an arbitrary ring R that is (possibly) non-commutative and (possibly) infinite, while only requiring black-box access to its arithmetic and a subset $A \subseteq R$. Our construction only requires limited commutativity and regularity properties from A, similar to recent work on efficient information theoretic multi-party computation over non-commutative rings by Escudero and Soria-Vazquez (*CRYPTO 2021*), but furthermore covering infinite rings.

We achieve our results through a generalization of GKR-style interactive proofs (Goldwasser, Kalai and Rothblum, *Journal of the ACM*, 2015). When A is a subset of the center of R, generalizations of the sum-check protocol and other building blocks are not too problematic. The case when the elements of A only commute with each other, on the other hand, introduces a series of challenges. In order to overcome those, we need to introduce a new definition of polynomial ring over a non-commutative ring, the notion of *left* (and *right*) multi-linear extensions, modify the layer consistency equation and adapt the sum-check protocol.

Despite these changes, our results are compatible with recent developments such as linear time provers. Moreover, for certain rings our construction achieves provers that run in *sublinear* time in the circuit size. We obtain such result both for known cases, such as matrix and polynomial rings, as well as new ones, such as for some rings resulting from Clifford algebras. Besides efficiency improvements in computation and/or round complexity for several instantiations, the core conclusion of our results is that state of the art doubly efficient interactive proofs do not require much algebraic structure. This enables *exact* rather than *approximate* computation over infinite rings as well as "agile" proof systems, where the black-box choice of the underlying ring can be easily switched through the software life cycle.

1 Introduction

Interactive proofs (IPs) are a natural extension of the standard notion of a mathematical proof, where the *verifier* checking a proof is allowed to interrogate the *prover* who is providing it. They were introduced by Goldwasser, Micali and Rackoff [GMR89] in the 1980s and they soon made a huge impact in complexity

© The Author(s), under exclusive license to Springer Nature Switzerland AG 2022
E. Kiltz and V. Vaikuntanathan (Eds.): TCC 2022, LNCS 13747, pp. 497–525, 2022.
https://doi.org/10.1007/978-3-031-22318-1_18

theory. IPs have also been influential to practical proof systems, for which a lot of progress took place during the last decade. Usually, in those schemes, the prover tries to convince a verifier about the correctness of the evaluation of a circuit consisting of addition and multiplication gates. Moreover, the arithmetic of this circuit is often over a finite field, no matter how well represented under these constraints is the original computation whose correctness is being checked.

In 2008, Goldwasser, Kalai and Rothblum (GKR) presented the first *doubly-efficient* interactive proof [GKR15], where the prover is only required to perform a polynomial amount of work in the size of the (layered, over a finite field) arithmetic circuit and the verifier only needs to be quasi-linear in the same parameter. The prover's effort was later improved to quasi-linear [CMT12] and finally linear [XZZ+19] for the same family of circuits in 2019. Recently, the restriction to layered circuits was removed [ZLW+21] without affecting the linear complexity of the prover and only a slight increase in the verifier's work for non-layered circuits. In this work we are interested in a different kind of generalization of the GKR protocol. Namely, we set out to answer the following question:

> "Let C be a layered arithmetic circuit over a ring R. What algebraic properties does R need to satisfy in order to construct a doubly-efficient IP for C's correct evaluation, without emulating R's arithmetic?"

The most relevant part of our quest is that of avoiding the emulation of R's arithmetic, which we refer to as being *black-box* over R. We answer this question in a partial but constructive way by providing a doubly-efficient IP for rings R that are possibly *non-commutative* as well as *infinite*.

The *black-box* nature of our constructions has a theoretical interest, in the tradition of finding lower bounds and reducing assumptions. Namely, it helps us understand what are the *minimum* algebraic properties that need to be assumed for proof systems and their underlying techniques to go through, and how does this affect their complexity. Whereas this path has been more explored in the context of Multi-Party Computation (MPC, see e.g. [CFIK03, CDI+13, ACD+19, DLS20, ES21] just to name a few), it has been strangely overlooked in the context of proof and argument systems, with notable exceptions [AIK10, HR18, CCKP19, GNS21, BCFK21, BCS21]. The main take-away of our work is that, when it comes to GKR-style protocols and their complexity, the algebraic properties of the ring do not matter much as long as it contains a big enough *set* with "good enough" regular and commutative properties. Since infinite rings are allowed, this is a superset of the rings for which we know how to build efficient information-theoretic MPC in a black-box manner [ES21].

Besides the theoretical aspects of our work, we expect its generality to find applications in practice. Practically relevant infinite rings (such as the integers) and fields (such as rational or real numbers) as well as non-commutative rings (such as matrices and quaternions) did not fit previous systems. Their arithmetic had to be emulated (at best) or approximated (at worst) when compiled into circuits over either finite fields or finite commutative rings [CCKP19]. Avoiding this compilation step can bring improvements in several fronts. First of all, removing this stage simplifies the practitioners' work, who can now be *agile* with respect to the choice of rings that are more commonplace than finite fields. If, after deployment, they need to provide a new proof system with a different underlying arithmetic, they could simply change the underlying data type that represents the ring, rather than having to develop an ad-hoc compiler. Moreover, working natively over such data types (algebraic structures) allows them to easily use existing software libraries for those, since their arithmetic does not need to be compiled into circuits. This, in turn, results in circuits with significantly less gates, which can ultimately result in better concrete efficiency in terms of computation and round complexity. Finally, the soundness error of our black-box IP can also benefit from working over these rings. We encourage to read specific applications and instantiations in the full version [Sor22].

Related Work. In [AIK10] Applebaum, Ishai and Kushilevitz show how to construct a verifiable computation protocol out of message authentication codes (MACs) and randomized encodings (REs). For their construction to be a *proof* rather than an *argument* system, it would need to use information-theoretic MACs and statistically secure REs. It is a longstanding open problem whether such statistical REs could efficiently support layered arithmetic circuits over the non-commutative and infinite rings that we support, or even finite fields. In particular, such REs would imply efficient constant-round statistically secure multi-party computation protocols for such circuits, which in turn solves an open problem about locally decodable codes of quasi-polynomial parameters [IK04].

In 2013, Meir [Mei13] demonstrated how the **IP = PSPACE** result can be proven using error-correcting codes (ECCs) that are more general than low degree polynomials. Along the way, the sum-check protocol is generalized to work with tensor products of linear ECCs. While that work is also interested in reducing algebraic assumptions, the results and ECCs are defined over finite fields. Whereas Meir's goal is to provide a new proof for a complexity theory result, we want to expand the amount of rings that one can use in a black-box way for GKR-style protocols and we care about concrete efficiency.

1.1   Technical Overview

The GKR protocol [GKR15] is a doubly-efficient interactive proof for the evaluation of a layered arithmetic circuit, which consists of addition and multiplication gates of fan-in two. Parties move from the output (0-th layer) to the input layer (D-th layer) one layer at a time. Each gate in the i-th layer is supposed to take inputs from two wires in layer $i + 1$, and so the output wires of the i-th layer gates are checked to be consistent with the ones in the preceding layer. Let $V^{(i)} : \{0, 1\}^{s_i} \to \mathbb{F}$ be the function that maps the string x to the value of the x-th wire in layer i. Thus, layer i has (up to) 2^{s_i} wires. Furthermore, let $\mathsf{add}^{(i+1)} : \{0, 1\}^{s_i} \times \{0, 1\}^{s_{i+1}} \times \{0, 1\}^{s_{i+1}} \to \{0, 1\}$ be the function satisfying $\mathsf{add}^{(i+1)}(z, x, y) = 1$ if the z-th wire on layer i is the addition of the x-th and y-th wires in layer $i + 1$, otherwise $\mathsf{add}^{(i+1)}(z, x, y) = 0$. Define $\mathsf{mult}^{(i+1)}$ analogously. If we use $\hat{f} \in \mathbb{F}[\vec{X}]$ to denote a (low degree) multivariate polynomial such that for all $a \in \{0,1\}^s$, $\hat{f}(a) = f(a)$, we can express layer consistency as follows:

$$\hat{V}^{(i)}(\vec{Z}) = \sum_{x,y \in \{0,1\}^{s_{i+1}}} \left(\widehat{\texttt{mult}}^{(i+1)}(\vec{Z}, x, y) \cdot \left(\hat{V}^{(i+1)}(x) \cdot \hat{V}^{(i+1)}(y) \right) \right.$$

$$\left. + \widehat{\texttt{add}}^{(i+1)}(\vec{Z}, x, y) \cdot \left(\hat{V}^{(i+1)}(x) + \hat{V}^{(i+1)}(y) \right) \right). \quad (1)$$

The advantage of using the polynomial extensions $\hat{V}^{(i)}, \hat{V}^{(i+1)}, \widehat{\texttt{mult}}^{(i+1)}$ and $\widehat{\texttt{add}}^{(i+1)}$ is that the previous equation can be easily checked using the sum-check protocol [LFKN92]. Originally, as well as for most of its subsequent literature, the GKR protocol only worked for circuits over finite fields. Chen et al. [CCKP19] showed how to extend this result to finite commutative rings as long as the points used to define the polynomial extensions and the random challenges from the verifier belong to a set $A = \{a_1, \ldots, a_n\}$ where $\forall i \neq j, a_i - a_j$ is not a zero divisor. In our work, we denote such A a *regular difference* set.

As we realized, removing the finiteness assumption from [CCKP19] does not introduce any additional problems. Even if R is infinite, we only need a finite regular difference set A. On the other hand, when R is not commutative, we are presented with several issues. First, the definition of a polynomial ring with coefficients in R is not straightforward. One easily finds obstacles related to whether polynomial evaluation is a ring homomorphism (i.e., whether $f(a) + g(a) = (f + g)(a)$ and $f(a) \cdot g(a) = (f \cdot g)(a)$) or other crucial results, such as Euclidean division or bounding the number of roots of a polynomial. Nevertheless, if we restrict the regular difference set A to be contained in the center of the ring (i.e., $\forall r \in R, a \in A, a \cdot r = r \cdot a$), then Eq. (1) (and multi-linear extensions, the sum-check protocol, etc.) behave as expected. In this scenario, which we discuss in Sect. 4, we use the most common definition for polynomial over non-commutative rings (Definition 9, the same as in [ES21]).

The most challenging part of our work comes from relaxing the commutativity requirement on A, so that rather than $A \subset Z(R)$, we only ask that $\forall a_i, a_j \in A, a_i \cdot a_j = a_j \cdot a_i$. This was also the most difficult family of rings in [ES21], where Escudero and Soria-Vazquez showed how to build efficient information-theoretic MPC protocols with black-box access to such a ring[1]. Employing the same polynomial ring definition as in [ES21] fails in our context. This poses the question of whether there are inherently more *algebraic* limitations for doubly-efficient IPs than there are for information theoretic MPC, potentially ruling out these "less commutative" rings. Fortunately, we overcome most problems by putting forward a new polynomial ring definition (Definition 12) in Sect. 3, the notion of *sandwich* (and *toast*) polynomials (Sect. 3.1) and reworking many basic algebraic results related to these new polynomials. We show that there is no unique notion of multi-linear extension (MLE) in this setting, so we have to define both *left* and *right* MLEs. Equipped with these results, in Sect. 5 we show how to modify the layer consistency equation so that

---

[1] In fact, in [ES21] they only show how to work with *finite* rings in that family. An example interesting ring in this setting is $\mathcal{M}_{n \times n}(\mathbb{F}_2)$, which has $\mathbb{F}_{2^n}$ as a subfield.

it becomes a sandwich polynomial. We need to do this carefully, so that it is a toast polynomial on every indeterminate. Finally, we provide a new sum-check protocol for this layer consistency Eq. (Sect. 5.3), which we show how the prover can run in linear time in Sect. A.

2   Preliminaries

Notation. We use $[i, j]$, where $i < j$, to represent the set of positive integers $\{i, i + 1, \ldots, j\}$, and simply $[n]$ to represent $\{1, 2, \ldots, n\}$. Sometimes, we may use arrows to denote vectors, e.g. $\vec{b} = (b_1, \ldots, b_n)$. For a "sub-interval" of the elements of a vector, we might denote use $\vec{b}_{[i,j]} = (b_i, \ldots, b_j)$.

2.1   Interactive Proofs and the GKR Protocol

In order to capture more naturally our results, we present these definitions in terms of the prover $\mathcal{P}$ trying to convince a verifier $\mathcal{V}$ that the application of an arithmetic circuit C over a ring R on some input inp results on a specific output out, where inputs and outputs are elements of R.

Definition 1. *Let C be an arithmetic circuit over a ring R. A pair of interactive machines $\langle \mathcal{P}, \mathcal{V} \rangle$ is an ϵ-sound interactive proof (IP) for C if, on a claimed output out by $\mathcal{P}$:*

- *Completeness: For every inp s.t. $C(inp) = out$, it holds that $\Pr[\langle \mathcal{P}, \mathcal{V} \rangle(inp) = accept] = 1$.*
- *ϵ-Soundness: For any inp s.t. $C(inp) \neq out$, and any $\mathcal{P}^*$, it holds that $\Pr[\langle \mathcal{P}^*, \mathcal{V} \rangle(inp) = accept] \leq \epsilon$.*

We say that an interactive proof has the succinct property if the running time of $\mathcal{V}$ and the total communication between $\mathcal{P}$ and $\mathcal{V}$ is $\mathsf{poly}(|x|, \log(|C|))$.

The Sum-Check Protocol. Given an n-variate polynomial $f : \mathbb{F}^n \to \mathbb{F}$, the sum-check protocol [LFKN92] allows a verifier to outsource the computation of $\sum_{\vec{b} \in \{0,1\}^n} f(\vec{b})$ to a prover. If the verifier was to do this on their own, it would take them $O(2^n)$ time. Let d be an upper bound on the degree of each individual variable of f. The sum-check protocol is an n-round interactive proof for this task, where both the proof size and the verifier's work is $O(n \cdot d)$ and the soundness error is $\epsilon = n \cdot d \cdot |\mathbb{F}|^{-1}$. For a full description see either [LFKN92] or the full version of this work.

The GKR Protocol. The basics of how circuits and wire values are represented in the GKR protocol have been explained at the beginning of Sect. 1.1. Here we give a bit more details about how Eq. (1) is combined with the sum-check protocol and how to progress from the output to the input layer. $\mathcal{P}$ first sends the claimed output to $\mathcal{V}$, consisting of 2^{s_0} different values. $\mathcal{V}$ defines a multi-linear polynomial $\hat{V}^{(0)} : \mathbb{F}^{s_0} \to \mathbb{F}^{s_0}$ which extends $V^{(0)}$, samples a random $\gamma \in \mathbb{F}^{s_0}$ and sends it to $\mathcal{P}$. Both parties then evaluate $\hat{V}^{(0)}(\gamma)$ and run a sum-check protocol on Eq. (1) for $i = 0$ and evaluated at γ. Let $f_i(\vec{Z}, \vec{X}, \vec{Y})$ be the function such that Eq. (1) is $\hat{V}^{(i)}(\vec{Z}) = \sum_{x,y \in \{0,1\}^{s_{i+1}}} f_i(\vec{Z}, x, y)$. At the end of the protocol, $\mathcal{V}$ needs to compute $f_0(\gamma, \chi, \psi)$, where $\chi, \psi \in \mathbb{F}^{s_1}$ are two random values produced throughout the sum-check execution. Whereas $\mathcal{V}$ can evaluate $\widehat{\mathsf{add}}^{(1)}(\gamma, \chi, \psi)$ and $\widehat{\mathsf{mult}}^{(1)}(\gamma, \chi, \psi)$ on their own, it has to ask $\mathcal{P}$ for $\hat{V}^{(1)}(\chi), \hat{V}^{(1)}(\psi)$, since those evaluations require the knowledge of the wire values on layer 1. This way, a claim about the output layer has been reduced to two claims about layer one, $\hat{V}^{(1)}(\chi)$ and $\hat{V}^{(1)}(\psi)$. $\mathcal{V}$ and $\mathcal{P}$ could run one sum-check protocol for each of those claims using Eq. (1) for $i = 1$, but the number of sum-check executions would eventually become exponential in the depth of the circuit by following such a route. In order to avoid this, both claims are combined into a single claim. We provide a full description of the GKR protocol in the full version [Sor22]. Below, we state the complexity and soundness of its current most efficient version.

Theorem 1 ([XZZ+19]). *Let $C : \mathbb{F}^n \to \mathbb{F}^k$ be a depth-D layered arithmetic circuit. The GKR protocol is an interactive proof for C with soundness error $O(D \log |C|/|\mathbb{F}|)$. Its communication and round complexity is $O(D \log |C|)$. The prover complexity is $O(|C|)$ and the verifier complexity is $O(n+k+D \log |C|+T)$, where T is the optimal time to evaluate every $\widehat{\mathsf{add}}^{(i)}, \widehat{\mathsf{mult}}^{(i)}$ wiring predicate. For log-space uniform circuits, $T = \mathsf{poly} \log(|C|)$.*

2.2 Algebraic Background

We recap some basic notions in non-commutative algebra. Unless otherwise specified, whenever we talk about a ring R we mean a ring with identity $1 \neq 0$, for which we assume neither commutativity nor finiteness.

Definition 2. *Let R be a ring. An element $a \in R$ is a unit if there exists $b \in R$ such that $a \cdot b = b \cdot a = 1$. The set of all units is denoted by R^*.*

Definition 3. *An element $a \in R \setminus \{0\}$ is a left (resp. right) zero divisor if $\exists\, b \in R \setminus \{0\}$ such that $a \cdot b = 0$ (resp. $b \cdot a = 0$).*

Sets of elements whose pairwise differences are either regular or invertible will play a crucial role in our constructions.

Definition 4. *Let $A = \{a_1, \ldots, a_n\} \subset R$. We say that A is a regular difference set, or R.D. set for short, if $\forall i \neq j, a_i - a_j \in R$ is not a zero divisor. We define the regularity constant of R to be the maximum size of an R.D. set in R.*

Definition 5. *Let $A = \{a_1, \ldots, a_n\} \subset R$. We say that A is an exceptional set if $\forall i \neq j, a_i - a_j \in R^*$. We define the Lenstra constant of R to be the maximum size of an exceptional set in R.*

Besides "how regular" or "how invertible" are certain subsets of ring elements, we might also be interested in "how commutative" they are.

Definition 6. *The center of a ring R, denoted by $Z(R)$ consists of the elements $a \in Z(R)$ such that $\forall b \in R, a \cdot b = b \cdot a$.*

Definition 7 ([QBC13]). *Let $A = \{a_1, \ldots, a_n\} \subset R$. We say that A is a commutative set if $\forall a_i, a_j \in A, a_i \cdot a_j = a_j \cdot a_i$.*

Definition 8. *Let R be a ring and $A \subset R$. The centralizer of the set A in R is:*

$$C_R(A) = \{b \in R : b \cdot a = a \cdot b, \forall a \in A\}.$$

Lemma 1. *Let R be a ring and $A \subset R$ a commutative set. Then $C_R(A) \supseteq (A \cup Z(R))$. Furthermore, if $A \subseteq Z(R)$, then $C_R(A) = R$.*

3 Polynomials over Non-commutative Rings

There is no unique choice for how to define a polynomial ring with coefficients on a non-commutative ring R. Usually, as in [QBC13, ES21], univariate polynomials are defined in such a way that "the indeterminate commutes with coefficients", so as to *uniquely* express any polynomial $f \in R[X]_{\leq d}$ as $f(X) = \sum_{i=0}^{d} f_i X^i$, where $f_i \in R$. In the language of centralizers, this approach enforces $C_{R[X]}(\{X\}) = R[X]$. In the multivariate case, one can choose whether to define the ring so that indeterminates commute with each other or not. For rings where $A \subseteq Z(R)$, we will stick with the former case and refer to it as a *ring of non-commutative polynomials*. Due to space constraints, we defer the proofs of every statement in this section to the full version [Sor22].

Definition 9. *Let $(R, +, *)$ be a ring and let $\Sigma = \{X_1, \ldots, X_n\}$. Let Σ^* be the free commutative monoid generated by Σ, i.e. the monoid whose binary operation is the concatenation of finite strings and the letters of the alphabet Σ commute with each other. The ring of non-commutative polynomials $R[X_1, \ldots, X_n]$ is the monoid ring of Σ^* over R. Explicitly, $a \in R[X_1, \ldots, X_n]$ is of the form $a = \sum_{m \in \Sigma^*} a_m m$, where $a_m \in R$ and there is only a finite amount of $a_m \neq 0$. Addition and multiplication are defined as follows:*

- *Addition: $a + b = \sum_{m \in \Sigma^*} (a_m + b_m) m$*
- *Multiplication: $a \cdot b = \sum_{m_1, m_2 \in \Sigma^*} (a_{m_1} \cdot b_{m_2}) m_1 m_2$.*

Furthermore, for any set $S \subseteq R$, we define $S[X_1, \ldots, X_n]_{\leq d}$ to be the subset of polynomials in $R[X_1, \ldots, X_n]$ of degree at most d whose coefficients belong to S.

The previous definition has many advantages, but it requires to be careful about polynomial evaluation, which we next show to be a ring homomorphism if and only if the evaluation points belong to $Z(R)$. For example, consider polynomials $f(X) = f_0 + f_1 X$ and $g(X) = g_1 X + g_2 X^2$. We would have that $h(X) = f(X) \cdot g(X) = f_0 g_1 X + (f_0 g_2 + f_1 g_1) X^2 + f_1 g_2 X^3$. Unless α commutes with g_1 and g_2, this results in $h(\alpha) \neq f(\alpha) \cdot g(\alpha)$.

Lemma 2. *Let $A = \{\alpha_i\}_{i=1}^n \subset R$ be a commutative set and let $\alpha = (\alpha_1, \ldots, \alpha_n)$. Denote by $\mathrm{Ev}_\alpha : R[X_1, \ldots, X_n] \to R$ the map that takes a polynomial $f \in R[X_1, \ldots, X_n]$ to its evaluation[2] at α, by replacing each appearance of X_i with α_i and applying the product operation of R. Then:*

1. *$\forall f, g \in R[X_1, \ldots, X_n]$, $\mathrm{Ev}_\alpha(f) + \mathrm{Ev}_\alpha(g) = \mathrm{Ev}_\alpha(f + g)$.*
2. *$\mathrm{Ev}_\alpha(f) \cdot \mathrm{Ev}_\alpha(g) = \mathrm{Ev}_\alpha(f \cdot g)$ holds $\forall f, g \in R[X_1, \ldots, X_n]$ if and only if $A \subseteq Z(R)$.*

A different way to define the polynomial ring is by treating the indeterminate X as a formal, non-commuting symbol. Polynomial addition works as usual, whereas the product looks similar to string concatenation. In terms of centralizers, in this approach we enforce $C_{R[X]}(\{X\}) = \emptyset$. The advantage of this strategy is that polynomial evaluation at any $\alpha \in R$ becomes a ring homomorphism, in contrast with Definition 9, where that is only true if $\alpha \in Z(R)$ (Lemma 2). On the other hand, not being able to simplify polynomial expressions as in Definition 9 not only results in lengthier polynomials, but it also eliminates the possibility to prove many useful results about polynomials. We will refer to this construction as the *ring of totally non-commutative polynomials*.

Definition 10. *Let $(R, +, \odot)$ be a ring and let $\Sigma = R \cup \{X_1, \ldots, X_n\}$. Let $*$ denote the string concatenation operation. Let $\mathbf{M}$ be the monoid generated by Σ according to the non-commutative binary operation $\cdot : \mathbf{M} \times \mathbf{M} \to \mathbf{M}$, which we restrict to finite strings and where:*

$$r \cdot s = \begin{cases} r \odot s, & \text{if } r, s \in R \\ r * s, & \text{if } (r \in R \wedge s \in \{X_i\}_{i=1}^n) \vee (r \in \{X_i\}_{i=1}^n \wedge s \in R) \vee (r, s \in \{X_i\}_{i=1}^n) \end{cases} \tag{2}$$

The ring of totally non-commutative polynomials $R[\![X_1, \ldots, X_n]\!]$ consists of elements $a \in R[\![X_1, \ldots, X_n]\!]$ of the form $a = \sum_{m \in \mathbf{M}} a_m \cdot m$, where $a_m \in R$ and there is only a finite amount of $a_m \neq 0$. Addition (inherited from R) and multiplication (inherited from $\mathbf{M}$) are defined as follows:

- *Addition: $a + b = \sum_{m \in \mathbf{M}} (a_m + b_m) \cdot m$*
- *Multiplication: $a \cdot b = \sum_{m_1, m_2 \in \mathbf{M}} a_{m_1} \cdot m_1 \cdot b_{m_2} \cdot m_2$.*

Lemma 3. *$R[\![X_1, \ldots, X_n]\!]$ is a ring.*

Note 1. The only difference between $(\mathbf{M}, \cdot)$ in Definition 10 and the free monoid over Σ is that, in $\mathbf{M}$, strings containing sub-strings of the form $X_i * a * b * X_j$ do not exist, since in $\mathbf{M}$ those are "simplified" to $X_i * c * X_j$ where $c = a \odot b$.

Note 2. $R[\![X_1, \ldots, X_n]\!]$ allows for limited simplifications in polynomial expressions: Those inherited from the associative and distributive properties if we go from the "outside" to the "inside" of a monomial. E.g., it is true that $X r X^3 + X s X^3 = X(r + s)X^3$, but $\forall m_1 \neq m_2 \in \mathbf{M}$, we cannot simplify beyond $X r X^3 m_1 + X s X^3 m_2 = X(r X^3 m_1 + s X^3 m_2)$, since $m_1 \neq m_2$ "blocks" any simplification from the right end (besides any common factor at the right end of m_1, m_2).

---

[2] Throughout the text, we implicitly refer to $\mathrm{Ev}_\alpha(f)$ whenever we write either $f(\alpha)$ or $f(\alpha_1, \ldots, \alpha_n)$ and $f \in R[X_1, \ldots, X_n]$.

The rationale behind defining the ring of non-commutative polynomials as in Definition 9, as they do in e.g. [QBC13, ES21], is that in those works unique polynomial interpolation is the most crucial property. In our case, the most important requirement is that polynomial evaluation is a ring homomorphism, so that we can meaningfully apply a sumcheck protocol to the layer consistency Eq. (1). Unfortunately, the approach from Definition 10, where $C_{R[X]}(X) = \emptyset$, does not serve us either, since the layer consistency equation is *cubic*. As it will become clearer later on, when proving results about Euclidean division (Theorem 2) and Lemma 6, we cannot bound the number of roots of the product of three polynomials by simply following that route. Such bound is in turn necessary to establish the soundness error of our new interactive proofs.

Due to the above, we introduce a novel polynomial ring definition, somewhere between Definitions 9 and 10. We define the *polynomial ring with evaluation set A*, $R_A[X]$, by taking into account the specific set of points $A \subset R$ on which polynomials will be ever evaluated. Rather than constructing the ring so that $C_{R[X_1,\ldots,X_n]}(\{X_i\}_{i=1}^n) = R[X_1,\ldots,X_n]$ (as in Definition 9) or such that $C_{R[X_1,\ldots,X_n]}(\{X_i\}_{i=1}^n) = \emptyset$ (as in Definition 10), we will enforce $C_{R_A[X_1,\ldots,X_n]}(\{X_i\}_{i=1}^n) = C_R(A) \cup \{X_i\}_{i=1}^n$. Hence, in $R_A[X_1,\ldots,X_n]$, indeterminates commute with each other and "an indeterminate commutes with a coefficient $c \in R$ if and only if $c \in C_R(A)$". Formally, we construct $R_A[X_1,\ldots,X_n]$ by taking the quotient of the ring of totally non-commutative polynomials $R[\![X_1,\ldots,X_n]\!]$ with a "commutator ideal" I_A that enforces our precise commutativity requirements.

Definition 11. *Let $R[\![X_1,\ldots,X_n]\!]$ and let $A \subset R$. For $i,j = 1,\ldots n$, let $S_{i,j} = \{X_iX_j - X_jX_i\}$ and $S_i = \{X_ic - cX_i : c \in C_R(A)\}$. The two-sided ideal generated by $\bigcup_{i=1}^n \bigcup_{j=1}^{i-1} S_{i,j} \cup S_i$ is the* commutator ideal of A, *which we denote by I_A.*

For our specific goals, we will impose that the set A is commutative (see Definition 7). This is to ensure that $C_R(A) \supseteq (A \cup Z(R))$.

Definition 12. *Let $A \subset R$ be a commutative set and let I_A be the commutator ideal it defines. We define the* ring of polynomials with evaluation set A *to be $R_A[X_1,\ldots,X_n] = R[\![X_1,\ldots,X_n]\!]/I_A$. For any set $S \subseteq R$, we define $S_A[X_1,\ldots,X_n]$ to be the subset of polynomials in $R_A[X_1,\ldots,X_n]$ whose coefficients belong to S.*

Claim. Let $S \subseteq R$. Any $f \in S_A[X_1,\ldots,X_n]$ can be uniquely expressed as

$$f = \sum_{k=1}^{s} \Big(\prod_{\ell=1}^{m} \big(r_{k,\ell} \prod_{i=1}^{n} (X_i^{d_{i,\ell}}) \big) \Big),$$

where $r_{k,\ell} \in S \cup \{1\}, d_{i,\ell} \in \mathbb{Z}$ and m is the maximum length of any monomial in f. We consider X_i^0 to be the empty string, for any $i = 1,\ldots,n$.

By Lemma 1, when $A \subseteq Z(R)$ we have that $C_R(A) = R$, in which case the commutator ideal enforces $C_{R_A[X_1,\ldots,X_n]}(\{X_i\}_{i=1}^n) = R_A[X_1,\ldots,X_n]$. Intuitively, in this situation, the polynomial ring $R_A[X_1,\ldots,X_n]$ behaves *the same way* as $R[X_1,\ldots,X_n]$ in Definition 9: $R[X_1,\ldots,X_n]$ also satisfies that $C_{R[X_1,\ldots,X_n]}(\{X_i\}_{i=1}^n) = R[X_1,\ldots,X_n]$ and, when the evaluation points are in $A \subseteq Z(R)$, evaluating polynomials from $R[X_1,\ldots,X_n]$ is a ring homomorphism too (Lemma 2). In the full version [Sor22] we show in more detail how both definitions are interchangeable for our purposes when $A \subseteq Z(R)$.

For the sake of generality, we will state and prove our results using the more general ring $R_A[X_1,\ldots,X_n]$ from Definition 12. Nevertheless, when $A \subset Z(R)$, it is conceptually simpler to treat polynomials as elements from $R[X_1,\ldots,X_n]$ (Definition 9). For basic algebraic results that we will present in Sect. 3.1, such as Euclidean division or the number of roots of a polynomial, simplified statements and proofs for $R[X_1,\ldots,X_n]$ can be found in e.g. [ES21].

3.1 Sandwich Polynomials

In the previous block of results, we have seen that when $A \subset Z(R)$, the ring $R_A[X_1,\ldots,X_n]$ from Definition 12 behaves *the same way* as $R[X_1,\ldots,X_n]$ in Definition 9. It is when A is merely a commutative set –and hence $C_{R_A[X_1,\ldots,X_n]}(X_i) \supseteq (A \cup Z(R) \cup \{X_j\}_{j=1}^n)$– that our new Definition 12 will be necessary to enable our GKR-style protocol over a ring $R \supset A$.

Our protocols will be concerned with a particular *subset* of the polynomials in $R_A[X_1,\ldots,X_n]$, concretely the ones for which monomials have a single coefficient, possibly "surrounded" by indeterminates on both sides. We will refer to these as *sandwich polynomials*, metaphorically thinking of the indeterminates as bread and the coefficient as the content[3]. The goal of this subsection is to generalize the Schwartz-Zippel lemma to these polynomials, to the extent that it is possible.

Definition 13 (Sandwich polynomials). *Let A be a commutative subset of a ring R and let $R_A[X_1,\ldots,X_n]$ be the ring of polynomials with evaluation set A. Let $i = (i_1,\ldots,i_n)$, $j = (j_1,\ldots,j_n)$. We define the set of* sandwich polynomials *over R with left-degree at most d' and right-degree at most d to be:*

$$R_A[X_1,\ldots,X_n]_{\leq d',\leq d}$$
$$= \{f(X_1,\ldots,X_n) = \sum_{i\in[0,d']^n, j\in[0,d]^n} X_n^{i_n} \cdot \ldots \cdot X_1^{i_1} f_{i,j} X_1^{j_1} \cdot \ldots \cdot X_n^{j_n} \mid f_{i,j} \in R\}$$

The subset of polynomials with right-degree exactly d, $R_A[X_1,\ldots,X_n]_{\leq d',d} \subset R_A[X_1,\ldots,X_n]_{\leq d',\leq d}$, is given by further imposing that, for every X_k, the polynomial must have at least one monomial of right-degree d in X_k. Formally: $\forall k \in [n] \; \exists i \in [0,d']^n, j_1,\ldots,j_{k-1},j_{k+1},\ldots,j_n \in [0,d]$ such that

---

[3] The reader might find funny to think about multiplication as "stacking sandwiches" and addition as putting sandwiches next to each other. The commutativity of indeterminates with elements in $C_R(A)$, simplifications enabled by the distributive property and other results in this section provide some (metaphorical) food for thought!

$f_{i,(j_1,\ldots,j_{k-1},d,j_{k+1},\ldots,j_n)} \neq 0$. *The subset of polynomials with left-degree exactly d',* $R_A[X_1,\ldots,X_n]_{d',\leq d}$, *is defined analogously. Furthermore, for any set $S \subseteq R$, we define $S_A[X_1,\ldots,X_n]_{\leq d',\leq d}$ as the subset of polynomials in $R_A[X_1,\ldots,X_n]_{\leq d',\leq d}$ whose coefficients $f_{i,j}$ all belong to S. Polynomials of exact degrees are defined as in the previous paragraph.*

Definition 14 (Toast polynomials). *Let $\vec{X} = (X_1,\ldots,X_n)$. A sandwich polynomial f is a left (resp. right) toast polynomial if it is of right (resp. left) degree zero, i.e. $f \in R_A[\vec{X}]_{\leq d',0}$ (resp. $f \in R_A[\vec{X}]_{0,\leq d}$). If we do not want to specify the position of the indeterminate, we may simply refer to it as a toast polynomial.*

In the previous definitions, it is important to note that a polynomial in $R_A[X_1,\ldots,X_n]_{\leq d',\leq d}$ has at most $((d'+1)\cdot(d+1))^n$ monomials, i.e. for fixed powers $i \in [0,d']^n, j \in [0,d]^n$, an expression of the form $\sum_\ell X_n^{i_n}\cdot\ldots\cdot X_1^{i_1} f_{i,j}^{(\ell)} X_1^{j_1}\cdot\ldots\cdot X_n^{j_n}$ is simplified into $X_n^{i_n}\cdot\ldots\cdot X_1^{i_1} f_{i,j} X_1^{j_1}\cdot\ldots\cdot X_n^{j_n}$, where $f_{i,j} = \sum_\ell f_{i,j}^{(\ell)}$. Furthermore, when we talk about polynomials of *exact* right degree d or left degree d', we assume that all possible simplifications have taken place. In particular[4], for $f \in R_A[X]_{\leq d',d}$, we assume that $f_{i,d}$ is not simplified away with terms of the form $X^{i+k}f_{i+k,d-k}X^{d-k}$, where $k \in \{1,\ldots,d\}$, when $f_{i,d}, f_{i+k,d-k} \in C_R(A)$.

Lemma 4. *Let $\vec{X} = (X_1,\ldots,X_n)$. For $\ell = 1,\ldots m$, let $f^{(\ell)} \in R_A[\vec{X}]_{\leq d'_f,\leq d_f}$, $a^{(\ell)} \in C_R(A)[\vec{X}]_{\leq d'_a,\leq d_a}$ and $b^{(\ell)} \in C_R(A)[\vec{X}]_{\leq d'_b,\leq d_b}$. Let $g = \sum_{\ell=1}^m a^{(\ell)}f^{(\ell)}b^{(\ell)}$. Then $g \in R_A[\vec{X}]_{\leq(d'_a+d_a+d'_f),\leq(d'_b+d_b+d_f)}$.*

Lemma 5. *Let $f \in R_A[X_1,\ldots,X_n]_{\leq d',\leq d}$ and let $a_\ell \in A$. Then, $\forall \ell \in \{1,\ldots,n\}$:*

$$f(X_1,\ldots X_{\ell-1},a_\ell,X_{\ell+1},\ldots,X_n) \in R_A[X_1,\ldots X_{\ell-1},X_{\ell+1},\ldots,X_n]_{\leq d',\leq d}.$$

The advantage of sandwich polynomials is that they can be divided by monic polynomials in $S_A[X]$, where $S = C_R(A)$ (recall notation from Definition 12).

Theorem 2 (Euclidean division). *Let $f(X) \in R_A[X]_{d',d}$ be a non-zero sandwich polynomial and let $g(X) \in C_R(A)_A[X]_{0,m}$ be a monic polynomial[5]. There exist unique sandwich polynomials $q_\ell(X), r_\ell(X)$ (resp. $q_r(X), r_r(X)$) such that $f(X) = q_\ell(X)\cdot g(X) + r_\ell(X)$ (resp. $f(X) = g(X)\cdot q_r(X) + r_r(X)$), where $q_\ell(X) \in R_A[X]_{\leq d',\leq d-m}$ and $r_\ell(X) \in R_A[X]_{\leq d',\leq m-1}$ (resp. $q_r(X) \in R_A[X]_{\leq d-m,\leq d'}$, $r_r(X) \in R_A[X]_{\leq m-1,\leq d}$).*

Given the previous theorem, we can prove the following result about the maximum number of roots of toast polynomials on their evaluation set A, when A is not only commutative but also regular difference (Definition 4).

Lemma 6. *Let A be a commutative, regular difference set of R and let $f \in R_A[X]_{0,\leq d}$ (resp. $\tilde{f} \in R_A[X]_{\leq d,0}$) be a non-zero toast polynomial. Then f (resp. $\tilde{f}$) has at most d roots in A.*

---

[4] We give this example in the univariate case in order to avoid heavier notation.

[5] I.e. $g(X) = X^m + \sum_{\ell=0}^{m-1} g_\ell X^\ell$. Note that since $g_\ell \in C_R(A) \ \forall \ell \in [0,m-1]$, it is also true that $g(X) \in C_R(A)_A[X]_{m,0}$, that $g(X) \in C_R(A)_A[X]_{m-1,1}$, etc.

The proof of the previous is particularly useful to understand our need for *toast* polynomials. Whereas, given Theorem 2 and Lemma 6, one could hope to be able to bound the number of roots of any polynomial $f \in R_A[\mathtt{X}]_{\leq d', \leq d}$, we were unable to prove such a result. This is due to the fact that the Euclidean division of sandwich polynomials by a polynomial $g_i(\mathtt{X}) = (X - \alpha_i)$, where α_i is a root of f, provides us with a remainder that is of degree zero *only on the side from which $g_i(\mathtt{X})$ is dividing*. If α_1 is a root of f, by calling Theorem 2 so that $g_1(\mathtt{X})$ "divides on the right", we can prove that $f(\mathtt{X}) = f_1(\mathtt{X})(X - \alpha_1) + r_1(\mathtt{X})$, where $f_1 \in R_A[\mathtt{X}]_{\leq d', \leq d-1}, r_1 \in R_A[\mathtt{X}]_{\leq d', 0}$. If we divide $r_1(\mathtt{X})$ by $g_1(\mathtt{X})$ on the left, we get to $f(\mathtt{X}) = f_1(\mathtt{X})(\mathtt{X}-\alpha_1)+(\mathtt{X}-\alpha_1)f_2(\mathtt{X})$, where $f_2 \in R_A[\mathtt{X}]_{\leq d'-1, 0}$. The problem now is that, if $\alpha_2 \in A$ is another root, we find no way forward from the expression $0 = f(\alpha_2) = f_1(\alpha_2)(\alpha_2 - \alpha_1) + (\alpha_2 - \alpha_1)f_2(\alpha_2)$. Alternative strategies also beared no positive results. This important limitation will condition the generalization of almost every building block of our doubly-efficient IP over non-commutative rings when A is merely commutative, rather than $A \subseteq Z(R)$.

Lemma 7 generalizes the Schwartz-Zippel lemma to *toast* polynomials.

Lemma 7 (Schwartz-Zippel Lemma). *Let $A \subseteq R$ be a finite, commutative regular difference set. Let $\vec{\mathtt{X}} = (\mathtt{X}_1, \dots, \mathtt{X}_n)$ and let $f \in (R_A[\vec{\mathtt{X}}]_{\leq d, 0} \cup R_A[\vec{\mathtt{X}}]_{0, \leq d})$ be a non-zero toast polynomial. Then, $\Pr_{\vec{a} \leftarrow A^n}[f(\vec{a}) = 0] \leq n \cdot d \cdot |A|^{-1}$.*

Multi-linear extensions were introduced in [BFL91] and extensively used in [CMT12]. Here, we generalize their definition to toast polynomials (Definition 14).

Lemma 8. *Let A be a regular difference, commutative set s.t. $\{0, 1\} \subset A \subset R$. Given a function $V : \{0, 1\}^m \to R$, there exist unique multilinear polynomials $\hat{V}_L \in R_A[\mathtt{X}_1, \dots, \mathtt{X}_m]_{\leq 1, 0}$ and $\hat{V}_R \in R_A[\mathtt{X}_1, \dots, \mathtt{X}_m]_{0, \leq 1}$ extending V, i.e. $\hat{V}_L(a) = V(a) = \hat{V}_R(a)$ for all $a \in \{0, 1\}^m$. We call $\hat{V}_L$ (resp. $\hat{V}_R$) the left (resp. right) multilinear extension of V, which we will abbreviate by LMLE (resp. RMLE).*

When $A \subset Z(R)$, or when $V : \{0, 1\}^m \to C_R(A)$, it furthermore holds that $\hat{V}_L(\mathtt{X}_1, \dots, \mathtt{X}_m) = \hat{V}_R(\mathtt{X}_1, \dots, \mathtt{X}_m)$, in which case we will simply refer to the multilinear extension (MLE) of V and denote it by $\hat{V}(\mathtt{X}_1, \dots, \mathtt{X}_m)$.

4   Doubly-Efficient IP over Non-commutative Rings: Regular Difference Set Contained in $Z(R)$

In our first generalization, we assume that A is an R.D. set such that $A \subset Z(R)$. This greatly simplifies our protocol compared with the one we will present in Sect. 5, where we only assume that A is commutative.

As most building blocks work essentially as in the finite commutative ring case [CCKP19], we only give a high level overview of this simpler variant. Since $A \subset Z(R)$, all polynomials can be expressed as elements from $R[\mathtt{X}_1, \dots, \mathtt{X}_n]$ (the ring in Definition 9) rather than $R_A[\mathtt{X}_1, \dots, \mathtt{X}_n]$ (as we show in the full version). This simpler polynomial ring definition is good enough in this case, since polynomial evaluation at elements in A is a ring homomorphism (Lemma 2) and furthermore we can bound the number of roots of these polynomials in A. The latter has been proved in [QBC13, ES21], where they use exceptional rather than R.D. sets, but such assumption can be weakened for that result. Furthermore, we have unique MLEs rather than LMLEs and RMLEs (see Lemma 8) and both the layer consistency equation (Eq. (1)) and sum-check protocol generalize naturally.

The only state-of-the-art tool for doubly-efficient IPs that requires more care in this scenario is the linear time prover sum-check protocol from [XZZ+19]. This is a problem which we also encounter and solve in the harder case of Sect. 5. We refer the reader interested in the particularities of this case to the full version.

Theorem 3. *Let R be a ring and $A \subset Z(R)$ a regular difference set. Let $C : R^n \to R^k$ be a depth-D layered arithmetic circuit. There is an interactive proof for C with soundness error $O(D \log |C| / |A|)$. Its round complexity is $O(D \log |C|)$ and it communicates $O(D \log |C|)$ elements in R. The prover complexity is $O(|C|)$ and the verifier complexity is $O(n + k + D \log |C| + T)$, where T is the optimal time to evaluate every wiring predicate. For log-space uniform circuits, $T = \mathsf{poly} \log(|C|)$ and hence the IP is succinct.*

4.1 Improved Efficiency

The generality of our construction opens up possibilities for concrete efficiency improvements. One such example is the case when the ring R over which the circuit is defined can be seen as a free module of rank d over a ring S with a R.D. set $A \subseteq Z(S)$. Namely, as long as a product of elements in R takes more than d products in S, we have achieved our goal: Once the circuit has been evaluated, all operations the prover performs are the (sum of) evaluation of polynomials in $R[\mathsf{X}]$ at random elements from A. Polynomial evaluation is (the sum of) the product of elements of R with elements of S. Hence, if the ratio between the product of two elements in R and the product of an element of R with an element of S is bigger than the constants hidden in the $O(|C|)$ complexity of the prover, this results in a *sublinear* time prover! We are only aware of two previous examples in the literature where the prover is sublinear in the size of the circuit: Matrix multiplication [Fre79, Tha13] and Fast Fourier Transforms (FFT) [LXZ21].

In [LXZ21], the authors provide a sum-check protocol for FFTs where the prover only needs to do additional $O(d)$ work to produce a proof for a vector of size d. This is sublinear, since the FFT complexity is $O(d \log d)$. If FFTs are used for fast polynomial multiplication, we also obtain sublinear time provers by taking R to be the polynomial ring and S its coefficient ring. Multiplying two degree-d polynomials requires either $O(d^2)$ or $O(d \log d)$ operations in S (since in practice, for smaller values of d the former approach might be preferable). Multiplying such a polynomial with an element of S, on the other hand, requires exactly d operations in S, which is a gap of either $O(d)$ or $O(\log d)$ between both approaches. Thus, with our protocol we obtain a sublinear prover for polynomial multiplication *regardless* of whether FFT is actually employed in practice.

For a matrix ring $R = \mathcal{M}_{n \times n}(S)$, we have that R is a free module of rank n^2 over S. Since the best matrix multiplication algorithms we know require way more than n^2 operations, we once again obtain a sublinear prover by applying the observation at the beginning of this subsection. All in all, when taking every other complexity metric into account, Thaler's optimal MATMUL protocol [Tha13] is still preferable to our approach in terms of concrete efficiency. Nevertheless, we find interesting the extent to which our construction is versatile: We can obtain sublinear provers as simple, natural instantiations, rather than having to design a specific protocol. Furthermore, as far as we know, ours is only the third conceptually different method allowing for sublinear provers when dealing with matrix multiplication [Fre79, Tha13].

Even if they do not necessarily achieve sublinear time provers, many other rings R benefit from the improvement implied from being a rank-d module over a ring S. This is the case of many Clifford algebras, whose applications we discuss in the full version [Sor22]. For example, let $R = H(S)$ denote the quaternions with coefficients over a ring S. We have that $Z(R) = Z(S)$, and R is a free module of rank 4 over S. Multiplying two elements in R requires at least 7 multiplications in S for a commutative ring S (or at least 8 in the non-commutative case) [HL75]. Dual quaternions are of rank 8 over their coefficient ring S, whereas their product consists on three quaternion products. Hence, if S is commutative, the prover would roughly obtain a factor of $21/8 = 2.625$ improvement compared with running over [CCKP19] over S.

Theoretical Improvements. If we furthermore assumed that addition and multiplication of elements of the chosen non-commutative ring R can be performed at unit cost, we can obtain a series of theoretical results. Even though one could imagine to have specific hardware for that goal, these observations remain mostly theoretical, as they require to work with exponential size rings.

First of all, in [HY11] Hrubeš and Yehudayoff show that given a polynomial f (over a ring S) of degree d in n variables, there is a non-commutative extension ring R such that $S \subset Z(R)$ and f has a formula of size $O(dn)$ over R. On the other hand, if S is an algebraically closed field, no commutative extension ring R can reduce the formula or circuit complexity of f. These would all seem good news for us: Non-commutativity might be a requirement, the resulting formula is really small and furthermore R could potentially be a free module over S. Unfortunately, the dimension of this ring extension is roughly n^d.

In [SS10], Schott and Staples show how many **NP**-complete and ♯**P**-complete problems can be moved to class **P** if addition and multiplication in a Clifford algebra can be assumed to have unit cost. These include: Hamiltonian cycle problem, set covering problem, counting the edge-disjoint cycle decompositions of a finite graph, computing the permanent of an arbitrary matrix, computing the girth and circumference of a graph, and finding the longest path in a graph. Thus, in this model of computation, Theorem 3 provides us with a doubly-efficient IP for those languages[6]. Remember that, since for a language to have a doubly-efficient IP it has to belong to **BPP**, this was out of reach in the non-algebraic complexity world! Once again, the problem is that the algebra has an exponential dimension.

---

[6] In all precision, Theorem 3 only deals with layered arithmetic circuits, but our result can be generalized to general arithmetic circuits the same way as in [ZLW+21].

5   Doubly-Efficient IP over Non-commutative Rings: Commutative, Regular Difference Set

Our most general doubly-efficient IP supports rings that are possibly infinite and non-commutative, as long as they contain a commutative R.D. set A such that $A \subset R$. As a writing simplification, we will add the condition that[7] $\{0,1\} \subset A$. An example ring to which this section applies is $R = \mathcal{M}_{n \times n}(\mathbb{Z}/p^k\mathbb{Z})$ for a prime p. Since we can embed the Galois Ring $S = \mathsf{GR}(p^k, n)$ into R and S contains an exceptional set A of size p^n, we can pick that same A as our commutative, R.D. set [ES21]. On the other hand, we have that $Z(R) = \{a \cdot Id : a \in \mathbb{Z}/p^k\mathbb{Z}\}$, so the biggest regular difference set *contained* in $Z(R)$ is of size p. Hence, for small values of p, Sect. 4 might not be enough for soundness.

5.1   A New Layer Consistency Equation

Let us look at Eq. (1). The first problem when trying to generalize it to this setting, is that we cannot define MLEs of the $V_i : \{0,1\}^{s_i} \to R$ functions which map $b \in \{0,1\}^{s_i}$ to the b-th wire in the i-th layer. Instead, we need to content ourselves with either LMLEs or RMLEs for those functions (see Lemma 8). A natural impulse would be to settle for e.g. the LMLE $\hat{V}_L^{(i)}(\vec{Z})$ and express the consistency with layer $i+1$ as follows, where $\widehat{\mathsf{add}}^{(i+1)}(\vec{Z}, \vec{X}, \vec{Y}), \widehat{\mathsf{mult}}^{(i+1)}(\vec{Z}, \vec{X}, \vec{Y}) \in R_A[\vec{X}, \vec{Y}, \vec{Z}]_{\leq 1,0}$, $\hat{V}_L^{(i+1)}(\vec{X}) \in R_A[\vec{X}]_{\leq 1,0}$ and $\hat{V}_R^{(i+1)}(\vec{Y}) \in R_A[\vec{Y}]_{0,\leq 1}$:

$$\hat{V}_L^{(i)}(\vec{Z}) = \sum_{x,y \in \{0,1\}^{s_{i+1}}} \left(\widehat{\mathsf{mult}}^{(i+1)}(\vec{Z}, x, y) \cdot \left(\hat{V}_L^{(i+1)}(x) \cdot \hat{V}_R^{(i+1)}(y) \right) \right.$$
$$\left. + \widehat{\mathsf{add}}^{(i+1)}(\vec{Z}, x, y) \cdot \left(\hat{V}_L^{(i+1)}(x) + \hat{V}_R^{(i+1)}(y) \right) \right). \quad (3)$$

The right hand side is a *sandwich* polynomial in $R_A[\vec{X}, \vec{Y}, \vec{Z}]_{\leq 1, \leq 1}$, since the coefficients of the wiring predicates belong to $Z(R)$. Having such a sandwich is problematic when defining a sum-check protocol, which would progress through univariate polynomials in each indeterminate by partially evaluating the right hand side of Eq. (3). More specifically, the problem is with the Y_j indeterminates (for $j = 1, \ldots, s_{i+1}$), as the partial evaluations sent by the prover would be *sandwich* polynomials $R_A[Y_j]_{\leq 1, \leq 1}$. Since our Schwartz-Zippel lemma (Lemma 7) only copes with *toast* polynomials, this will not provide us with a sound protocol.

In order to have toast polynomials at every step of the sum-check protocol, we replace $\widehat{\mathsf{add}}^{(i+1)}(\vec{Z}, \vec{X}, \vec{Y}), \widehat{\mathsf{mult}}^{(i+1)}(\vec{Z}, \vec{X}, \vec{Y}) \in R_A[\vec{Z}, \vec{X}, \vec{Y}]_{\leq 1,0}$ in Eq. (3) with $\widehat{\mathsf{add}_L}^{(i+1)}(\vec{Z}, \vec{X}, \vec{W}), \widehat{\mathsf{mult}_L}^{(i+1)}(\vec{Z}, \vec{X}, \vec{W}) \in R_A[\vec{Z}, \vec{X}, \vec{W}]_{\leq 1,0}$, still evaluating $\vec{W}$ in y. This seemingly minor change requires to develop a new sum-check protocol which

---

[7] We can remove that simplification and work with polynomials in $R_{A \cup \{0,1\}}[\vec{U}, \vec{W}, \vec{X}, \vec{Y}]_{\leq 2, \leq 2}$ rather than $R_A[\vec{U}, \vec{W}, \vec{X}, \vec{Y}]_{\leq 2, \leq 2}$, since if A is a commutative set, so is $A \cup \{0,1\}$. For the purpose of clarity, we avoid that notation.

ensures that $\mathcal{P}$ evaluates $\vec{Y}$ and $\vec{W}$ at the same y. For the layer consistency equations featuring $\hat{V}_R^{(i)}(\vec{Z}) \in R_A[\vec{Z}]_{0,\leq 1}$, we will also do a change of variables, as we describe in Lemma 9. We display that information in Table 1.

Table 1. Polynomials involved in layer consistency equations. Note that MLEs such as $\widehat{\mathrm{add}}_L^{(i+1)}$ could be considered as either polynomials in $R_A[\vec{X}, \vec{W}, \vec{Z}]_{\leq 1,0}$ or $R_A[\vec{X}, \vec{W}, \vec{Z}]_{0,\leq 1}$.

Polynomial	$\widehat{\mathrm{add}}_L^{(i+1)}, \widehat{\mathrm{mult}}_L^{(i+1)}$	$\widehat{\mathrm{add}}_R^{(i+1)}, \widehat{\mathrm{mult}}_R^{(i+1)}$	$\hat{V}_L^{(i+1)}$	$\hat{V}_R^{(i+1)}$	$\hat{V}_L^{(i)}$	$\hat{V}_R^{(i)}$
(L/R)MLE	MLE	MLE	LMLE	RMLE	LMLE	RMLE
Ring	$R_A[\vec{X}, \vec{W}, \vec{Z}]_{\leq 1,0}$	$R_A[\vec{Y}, \vec{U}, \vec{Z}]_{\leq 1,0}$	$R_A[\vec{X}]_{\leq 1,0}$	$R_A[\vec{Y}]_{0,\leq 1}$	$R_A[\vec{Z}]_{\leq 1,0}$	$R_A[\vec{Z}]_{0,\leq 1}$

Lemma 9. *Let $\vec{Z} = (Z_1, \ldots, Z_{s_i})$. Toast multilinear polynomials $\hat{V}_L^{(i)} \in R_A[\vec{Z}]_{\leq 1,0}$ and $\hat{V}_R^{(i)} \in R_A[\vec{Z}]_{0,\leq 1}$ are equal to the following expressions:*

$$\hat{V}_L^{(i)}(\vec{Z}) = \sum_{x,y \in \{0,1\}^{s_{i+1}}} \left(\widehat{\mathrm{mult}}_L^{(i+1)}(\vec{Z}, x, y) \cdot \left(\hat{V}_L^{(i+1)}(x) \cdot \hat{V}_R^{(i+1)}(y) \right) \right.$$
$$\left. + \widehat{\mathrm{add}}_L^{(i+1)}(\vec{Z}, x, y) \cdot \left(\hat{V}_L^{(i+1)}(x) + \hat{V}_R^{(i+1)}(y) \right) \right). \quad (4)$$

$$\hat{V}_R^{(i)}(\vec{Z}) = \sum_{x,y \in \{0,1\}^{s_{i+1}}} \left(\left(\hat{V}_L^{(i+1)}(x) \cdot \hat{V}_R^{(i+1)}(y) \right) \cdot \widehat{\mathrm{mult}}_R^{(i+1)}(\vec{Z}, x, y) \right.$$
$$\left. + \left(\hat{V}_L^{(i+1)}(x) + \hat{V}_R^{(i+1)}(y) \right) \cdot \widehat{\mathrm{add}}_R^{(i+1)}(\vec{Z}, x, y) \right). \quad (5)$$

Where, in Eq. (4), $\widehat{\mathrm{add}}_L^{(i+1)}(\vec{Z}, \vec{X}, \vec{W}), \widehat{\mathrm{mult}}_L^{(i+1)}(\vec{Z}, \vec{X}, \vec{W}) \in R_A[\vec{X}, \vec{W}, \vec{Z}]_{\leq 1,0}$ and in Eq. (5), $\widehat{\mathrm{add}}_R^{(i+1)}(\vec{Z}, \vec{U}, \vec{Y}), \widehat{\mathrm{mult}}_R^{(i+1)}(\vec{Z}, \vec{U}, \vec{Y}) \in R_A[\vec{Y}, \vec{U}, \vec{Z}]_{\leq 1,0}$.

Proof. The term on each side of Eq. (4) (resp. Eq. (5)) is a multilinear polynomial in $R_A[\vec{Z}]_{\leq 1,0}$ (resp. $R_A[\vec{Z}]_{0,\leq 1}$), so by the uniqueness of LMLEs (resp. RMLEs), we are done if their evaluation at every $z \in \{0,1\}^{s_i}$ coincides. The latter follows from the definitions of $\widehat{\mathrm{add}}_L^{(i+1)}, \widehat{\mathrm{mult}}_L^{(i+1)}$ (resp. $\widehat{\mathrm{add}}_R^{(i+1)}, \widehat{\mathrm{mult}}_R^{(i+1)}$). ∎

Remark 1. An interesting detail about this construction, in which $A \not\subseteq Z(R)$, is that it is necessary for wiring predicates to be MLEs, rather than simply LMLEs or RMLEs. Otherwise, we would not obtain toast polynomials (in the X_i variables for Eq. (4), in Y_i variables for Eq. (5)) throughout the execution of the sumcheck protocol and we would be unable to apply Lemma 7 to determine soundness. Whereas for the standard addition and multiplication gates (since $\{0,1\} \subseteq Z(R) \subseteq C_R(A)$) we always obtain MLEs, if we use more complex wiring predicates which enable multiplication by hard-coded constants, those constants have to belong to $C_R(A)$.

5.2   2-to-1 Reduction

Our protocol starts with a simple layer consistency equation, which relates the output layer with layer 1 in the circuit according to the following equation:

$$\hat{V}_L^{(0)}(\gamma) = \sum_{x,y \in \{0,1\}^{s_1}} \left(\widehat{\mathtt{mult}}_L^{(1)}(\gamma, x, y) \cdot (\hat{V}_L^{(1)}(x) \cdot \hat{V}_R^{(1)}(y)) \right.$$
$$\left. + \widehat{\mathtt{add}}_L^{(1)}(\gamma, x, y) \cdot (\hat{V}_L^{(1)}(x) + \hat{V}_R^{(1)}(y)) \right). \tag{6}$$

At the conclusion of the sumcheck protocol which is run to verify Eq. (6), $\mathcal{V}$ needs to evaluate $\widehat{\mathtt{mult}}_L^{(1)}(\gamma, \vec{X}, \vec{W}) \cdot (\hat{V}_L^{(1)}(\vec{X}) \cdot \hat{V}_R^{(1)}(\vec{Y})) + \widehat{\mathtt{add}}_L^{(1)}(\gamma, \vec{X}, \vec{W}) \cdot (\hat{V}_L^{(1)}(\vec{X}) + \hat{V}_R^{(1)}(\vec{Y}))$ by replacing $\vec{X}, \vec{Y}, \vec{W}$ with respective random values $\chi^{(0)}, \psi^{(0)}, \omega^{(0)} \in A^{s_1}$. Since $\mathcal{V}$ cannot compute neither $\hat{V}_L^{(1)}(\chi^{(0)})$ nor $\hat{V}_R^{(1)}(\psi^{(0)})$ on their own, $\mathcal{P}$ will provide those values. These alleged evaluations have to satisfy their corresponding layer consistency equations, using LMLEs and RMLEs respectively. In order to avoid an exponential blow-up in the depth of the circuit, we perform a reduction from the two claimed values $\hat{V}_L^{(1)}(\chi^{(0)}), \hat{V}_R^{(1)}(\psi^{(0)})$ to a single one. We do so by sampling random values $\alpha^{(1)}, \beta^{(1)} \in A$ and combining their corresponding layer consistency equations as it is described next:

$$\alpha^{(i)} \hat{V}_L^{(i)}(\chi^{(i-1)}) + \beta^{(i)} \hat{V}_R^{(i)}(\psi^{(i-1)}) = \sum_{x,y \in \{0,1\}^{s_{i+1}}}$$
$$\left(\quad \alpha^{(i)} \cdot \widehat{\mathtt{mult}}_L^{(i+1)}(\chi^{(i-1)}, x, y) \cdot (\hat{V}_L^{(i+1)}(x) \cdot \hat{V}_R^{(i+1)}(y)) \right.$$
$$+ \beta^{(i)} \cdot (\hat{V}_L^{(i+1)}(x) \cdot \hat{V}_R^{(i+1)}(y)) \cdot \widehat{\mathtt{mult}}_R^{(i+1)}(\psi^{(i-1)}, x, y)$$
$$+ \alpha^{(i)} \cdot \widehat{\mathtt{add}}_L^{(i+1)}(\chi^{(i-1)}, x, y) \cdot (\hat{V}_L^{(i+1)}(x) + \hat{V}_R^{(i+1)}(y))$$
$$\left. + \beta^{(i)} \cdot (\hat{V}_L^{(i+1)}(x) + \hat{V}_R^{(i+1)}(y)) \cdot \widehat{\mathtt{add}}_R^{(i+1)}(\psi^{(i-1)}, x, y) \quad \right) \tag{7}$$

A justification for the soundness of the previous equation, as well as the two original layer consistency equations appears in the full version [Sor22], where we also provide a different approach using a 4-to-2 reduction, which reduces round complexity at the cost of increased communication.

5.3   Sum-Check for Non-commutative Layer Consistency

We provide the sum-check protocol for Eq. (7)[8]. The specific algorithm run by the prover and its complexity analysis appears in Appendix A. Remember that $A \supseteq H = \{0, 1\}$ is an R.D. commutative set.

---

[8] The simpler protocol for Eq. (6) can be found in the full version.

Sum-Check Protocol for Eq. (7): Let $\vec{x} = (x_1, \ldots, x_m)$, $\vec{y} = (y_1, \ldots, y_m)$. We provide a sum-check protocol for $\sum_{\vec{x}, \vec{y} \in H^m} f(\vec{x}, \vec{y}, \vec{x}, \vec{y}) = \beta$, where $f \in R_A[\vec{U}, \vec{W}, \vec{X}, \vec{Y}]_{\leq 2, \leq 2}$. If any of the checks throughout the protocol fails, $\mathcal{V}$ rejects.

1. In the first round, for $b \in \{0, 1\}$, $\mathcal{P}$ computes $g_{1,b} \in R_A[U_1]_{0, \leq 1}$, given by:

$$g_{1,b}(U_1) = \sum_{\substack{x_2, \ldots, x_m \in H \\ \vec{y} \in H^m}} f(U_1, x_2, \ldots, x_m, \vec{y}, b, x_2, \ldots, x_m, \vec{y}),$$

   and sends them to $\mathcal{V}$. Then $\mathcal{V}$ checks whether $g_{1,0}, g_{1,1} \in R_A[U_1]_{0, \leq 1}$ and $\sum_{b \in H} g_{1,b}(b) = \beta$. If true, $\mathcal{V}$ chooses a random $r_1 \in A$ and sends it to $\mathcal{P}$.
2. For rounds $2 \leq i \leq m$, define $\vec{x}_{(i,m]} = (x_{i+1}, \ldots, x_m)$ and $\vec{x}_{[1,i)} = (x_1, \ldots, x_{i-1})$. $\mathcal{P}$ sends the univariate toast polynomials $g_{i,0}, g_{i,1} \in R_A[U_i]_{0, \leq 1}$ given by:

$$g_{i,b}(U_i) = \sum_{\substack{\vec{x}_{[1,i)} \in H^{i-1}, \vec{x}_{(i,m]} \in H^{m-i} \\ \vec{y} \in H^m}} f(r_1, \ldots, r_{i-1}, U_i, \vec{x}_{(i,m]}, \vec{y}, \vec{x}_{[1,i)}, b, \vec{x}_{(i,m]}, \vec{y}),$$

   $\mathcal{V}$ checks whether $g_{i,b} \in R_A[U_i]_{0, \leq 1}$ and $\sum_{b \in H} g_{i,b}(b) - g_{i-1,b}(r_{i-1}) = 0$. If that is the case, $\mathcal{V}$ chooses a random element $r_i \in A$ and sends it to $\mathcal{P}$.
3. For rounds $m + 1 \leq i \leq 2m$, $\mathcal{P}$, define $j = i - m$, $\vec{r}_{[1,i)} = (r_1, \ldots, r_{i-1})$, $\vec{y}_{(j,m]} = (y_{j+1}, \ldots, y_m)$ and $\vec{y}_{[1,j)} = (y_1, \ldots, y_{j-1})$. $\mathcal{P}$ sends the univariate toast polynomials $g_{i,0}, g_{i,1} \in R_A[W_j]_{\leq 1, 0}$ given by:

$$g_{i,b}(W_j) = \sum_{\substack{\vec{y}_{[1,j)} \in H^{j-1}, \vec{y}_{(j,m]} \in H^{m-j} \\ \vec{x} \in H^m}} f(\vec{r}_{[1,i)}, W_j, \vec{y}_{(j,m]}, \vec{x}, \vec{y}_{[1,j)}, b, \vec{y}_{(j,m]}),$$

   $\mathcal{V}$ checks whether $g_{i,0}, g_{i,1} \in R_A[W_j]_{\leq 1, 0}$ and $\sum_{b \in H} g_{i,b}(b) - g_{i-1,b}(r_{i-1}) = 0$. If that is the case, $\mathcal{V}$ chooses a random element $r_i \in A$ and sends it to $\mathcal{P}$.
4. For round $i = 2m + 1$, define $\vec{r}_{[1,2m+1)} = (r_1, \ldots, r_{2m})$ and $\vec{x}_{(1,m]} = (x_2, \ldots, x_m)$. $\mathcal{P}$ sends the toast polynomial $g_{2m+1} \in R_A[X_1]_{\leq 2, 0}$:

$$g_{2m+1}(X_1) = \sum_{\vec{x}_{(1,m]} \in H^{m-1}, \vec{y} \in H^m} f(\vec{r}_{[1,2m+1)}, X_1, \vec{x}_{(1,m]}, \vec{y}),$$

   $\mathcal{V}$ checks whether $g_{2m+1} \in R_A[X_1]_{\leq 2, 0}$ and $\sum_{b \in H} g_{2m+1}(b) - g_{2m,b}(r_{2m}) = 0$. If so, $\mathcal{V}$ chooses a random element $r_{2m+1} \in A$ and sends it to $\mathcal{P}$.
5. For rounds $2m + 2 \leq i \leq 3m$, define $j = i - 2m$, $\vec{r}_{[1,i)} = (r_1, \ldots, r_{i-1})$ and $\vec{x}_{(j,m]} = (x_{j+1}, \ldots, x_m)$. $\mathcal{P}$ sends the toast polynomial $g_i \in R_A[X_j]_{\leq 2, 0}$:

$$g_i(X_j) = \sum_{\vec{x}_{(j,m]} \in H^{m-j}, \vec{y} \in H^m} f(\vec{r}_{[1,i)}, X_j, \vec{x}_{(j,m]}, \vec{y})$$

   $\mathcal{V}$ checks whether $g_i \in R_A[X_j]_{\leq 2, 0}$ and $\sum_{b \in H} g_i(b) = g_{i-1}(r_{i-1})$. If that is the case, $\mathcal{V}$ chooses a random element $r_i \in A$ and sends it to $\mathcal{P}$.

6. For rounds $3m + 1 \leq i \leq 4m$, define $j = i - 3m$, $\vec{r}_{[1,i)} = (r_1, \ldots, r_{i-1})$ and $\vec{y}_{(j,m]} = (y_{j+1}, \ldots, y_m)$. $\mathcal{P}$ sends the toast polynomial $g_i \in R_A[Y_j]_{0,\leq 2}$:

$$g_i(Y_j) = \sum_{\vec{y}_{(j,m]} \in H^{m-j}} f(\vec{r}_{[1,i)}, Y_j, \vec{y}_{(j,m]}),$$

$\mathcal{V}$ checks whether $g_i \in R_A[Y_j]_{0,\leq 2}$ and $\sum_{b \in H} g_i(b) = g_{i-1}(r_{i-1})$. If that is the case, $\mathcal{V}$ chooses a random element $r_i \in A$ and sends it to $\mathcal{P}$.

7. After the $4m$-th round, $\mathcal{V}$ checks whether $g_{4m}(r_{4m}) = f(r_1, \ldots, r_{4m})$ by querying[9] its oracles at $(r_1, \ldots, r_{4m})$.

Theorem 4. *Let A be a commutative R.D. set such that $\{0,1\} \subseteq A$. Let $f \in R_A[\vec{U}, \vec{W}, \vec{X}, \vec{Y}]_{\leq 2, \leq 2}$ be the multi-variate sandwich polynomial given by Eq. (7). The sum-check protocol is a public coin interactive proof with soundness error $\leq 8m \cdot |A|^{-1}$. The communication complexity is $14m$ elements in R.*

5.4   Putting Everything Together

Theorem 5. *Let R be a ring and $A \subset R$ a commutative, regular difference set such that $\{0,1\} \subset A$ Let $C : R^n \to R^k$ be a depth-D layered arithmetic circuit.*

Doubly-efficient interactive proof over a non-commutative ring

Input: Circuit input inp and claimed output out. **Output:** Accept or reject.

- Compute $\hat{V}_L^{(0)}(\mathbf{X})$ as the LMLE of out. $\mathcal{V}$ chooses a random $\gamma \in A^{s_0}$ and sends it to $\mathcal{P}$. Both parties compute $\hat{V}_L^{(0)}(\gamma)$.
- Run a sum-check protocol on Equation (6) as described in the full version. Let $\chi^{(0)}, \psi^{(0)}, \omega^{(0)}$ denote the challenge vectors corresponding to the $\vec{X}$, $\vec{Y}$ and $\vec{W}$ variables within that execution. $\mathcal{P}$ sends $\hat{V}_L^{(1)}(\chi^{(0)})$ and $\hat{V}_L^{(1)}(\psi^{(0)})$ to $\mathcal{V}$.
- $\mathcal{V}$ queries their oracles for $\widehat{\mathtt{mult}}_L^{(1)}(\gamma, \chi^{(0)}, \omega^{(0)})$ and $\widehat{\mathtt{add}}_L^{(1)}(\gamma, \chi^{(0)}, \omega^{(0)})$, so as to check that $\widehat{\mathtt{add}}_L^{(1)}(\gamma, \chi^{(0)}, \omega^{(0)}) \cdot (\hat{V}_L^{(1)}(\chi^{(0)}) + \hat{V}_R^{(1)}(\psi^{(0)})) + \widehat{\mathtt{mult}}_L^{(1)}(\gamma, \chi^{(0)}, \omega^{(0)}) \cdot (\hat{V}_L^{(1)}(\chi^{(0)}) \cdot \hat{V}_R^{(1)}(\psi^{(0)}))$ equals the last message of the sumcheck execution.
- For circuit layers $i = 1, \ldots, D - 1$, $\mathcal{V}$ samples $\alpha^{(i)}, \beta^{(i)} \in A$ and sends them to $\mathcal{P}$. They run a sumcheck protocol on Equation (7) as described in Figure 2 in Appendix A. Let $\chi^{(i)}, \psi^{(i)}$ denote the challenge vectors corresponding to the $\vec{X}$, and $\vec{Y}$ variables within that execution. At the end of the protocol, $\mathcal{P}$ sends $\hat{V}_L^{(i+1)}(\chi^{(i)})$ and $\hat{V}_R^{(i+1)}(\psi^{(i)})$ to $\mathcal{V}$, so that $\mathcal{V}$ can check the validity of the last message in the sumcheck execution. If the check passes, they proceed to the $(i+1)$-th layer, otherwise, $\mathcal{V}$ outputs reject and aborts.
- At the input layer D, $\mathcal{V}$ has received two claims $\hat{V}_L^{(D)}(\chi^{(D-1)})$ and $\hat{V}_R^{(D)}(\psi^{(D-1)})$. $\mathcal{V}$ queries the evaluation oracles of $\hat{V}_L^{(D)}$ and $\hat{V}_R^{(D)}$ at $\chi^{(D-1)}$ and $\psi^{(D-1)}$ respectively, and checks that they equal the sumcheck claims. If they do, $\mathcal{V}$ outputs accept, otherwise, $\mathcal{V}$ outputs reject.

Fig. 1. Doubly-efficient IP over a ring containing a commutative, regular difference set.

---

[9] As usual in the GKR protocol, some values are actually provided by $\mathcal{P}$, unless the input layer has been reached. This step is more detailed in Fig. 1.

Figure 1 is an interactive proof for C with soundness error $O(D \log |C|/|A|)$. Its round complexity is $O(D \log |C|)$ and it communicates $O(D \log |C|)$ elements in R. In terms of operations in R, the prover complexity is $O(|C|)$ and the verifier complexity is $O(n + k + D \log |C| + T)$, where T is the optimal time to evaluate every wiring predicate $(\widehat{\mathrm{add}}_L^{(i)}, \widehat{\mathrm{mult}}_L^{(i)}, \widehat{\mathrm{add}}_R^{(i)}, \widehat{\mathrm{mult}}_R^{(i)})$. For log-space uniform circuits, $T = \mathrm{poly} \log(|C|)$ and hence the IP is succinct.

A   Linear Time Prover for Eq. (7)

Multi-linear extensions were key for [CMT12] to improve the complexity of the Prover in [GKR15] from $\mathrm{poly}(|C|)$ to $O(|C| \log(|C|))$. In this section, we will show how to improve upon this to a complexity of $O(|C|)$, in a style similar to Libra [XZZ+19]. In order to achieve this, we will show how the Prover can

---

Algorithm
$\mathtt{Linear\_}\mathcal{P}\mathtt{\_Consistency}(T_f, T_{\widehat{\mathrm{mult}_L}}, T_{\widehat{\mathrm{add}_L}}, T_{\hat{V}_L}, T_{\widehat{\mathrm{mult}_R}}, T_{\widehat{\mathrm{add}_R}}, T_{\hat{V}_R}, \vec{\chi}, \vec{\psi}, \alpha, \beta, \vec{r})$

Input: $f \in R_A[\vec{U}, \vec{W}, \vec{X}, \vec{Y}]_{\leq 2, \leq 2}$ from Equation (7) and its initial lookup table T_f. Initial lookup tables of its constituent polynomials $T_{\widehat{\mathrm{mult}_L}}, T_{\widehat{\mathrm{add}_L}}, T_{\hat{V}_L}, T_{\widehat{\mathrm{mult}_R}}, T_{\widehat{\mathrm{add}_R}}, T_{\hat{V}_R}$. Challenge vector $\vec{r} = (r_1, \ldots, r_{4m}) \in A^{4m}$ and 2-to-1 reduction challenges $\alpha, \beta \in A$.
Output: Sum-check messages for the layer consistency Equation (7).

1. Run $\mathtt{Sumcheck\_\{U,W\}}(f, T_f, \vec{r}_{[1,2m]})$ as described in Figure 4.
2. Run $\mathtt{Setup\_X}(\widehat{\mathrm{mult}}_L, T_{\widehat{\mathrm{mult}_L}}, \widehat{\mathrm{add}}_L, T_{\widehat{\mathrm{add}_L}}, \widehat{\mathrm{mult}}_R, T_{\widehat{\mathrm{mult}_R}}, \widehat{\mathrm{add}}_R, T_{\widehat{\mathrm{add}_R}}, \vec{\chi}, \vec{\psi}, \vec{r}_{[1,2m]})$ as described in Figure 7 in order to obtain $\{T_{\widehat{\mathrm{mult}_L}}(x), T_{\widehat{\mathrm{add}_L}}(x), T_{\widehat{\mathrm{mult}_R}}(y), T_{\widehat{\mathrm{add}_R}}(y)\}$.
3. $\mathcal{F}_{\hat{V}_L} \leftarrow \mathtt{Function\_Evaluations}(\hat{V}_L, T_{\hat{V}_L}, r_{2m+1}, \ldots, r_{3m})$.
4. Run $\mathtt{Sumcheck\_X\_Left}(\widehat{\mathrm{mult}}_L, T_{\widehat{\mathrm{mult}_L}}, \widehat{\mathrm{add}}_L, T_{\widehat{\mathrm{add}_L}}, \mathcal{F}_{\hat{V}_L}, \hat{V}_R, T_{\hat{V}_R}, \vec{r}_{[2m+1,3m]})$ as described in Figure 8 in order to obtain $\{g_{2m+i}^{\mathrm{mult}_L}(\mathbf{X}_i), g_{2m+i}^{\mathrm{add}_L}(\mathbf{X}_i)\}_{i=1}^m$.
5. Run $\mathtt{Sumcheck\_X\_Right}(\widehat{\mathrm{mult}}_R, T_{\widehat{\mathrm{mult}_R}}, \widehat{\mathrm{add}}_R, T_{\widehat{\mathrm{add}_R}}, \mathcal{F}_{\hat{V}_L}, \hat{V}_R, T_{\hat{V}_R}, \vec{r}_{[2m+1,3m]})$ as described in Figure 9 in order to obtain $\{g_{2m+i}^{\mathrm{mult}_R}(\mathbf{X}_i), g_{2m+i}^{\mathrm{add}_R}(\mathbf{X}_i)\}_{i=1}^m$.
6. For $i \in [m]$, compute:

$$g_{2m+i}(\mathbf{X}_i) = \alpha \cdot \left(g_{2m+i}^{\mathrm{mult}_L}(\mathbf{X}_i) + g_{2m+i}^{\mathrm{add}_L}(\mathbf{X}_i) \right) + \beta \cdot \left(g_{2m+i}^{\mathrm{mult}_R}(\mathbf{X}_i) + g_{2m+i}^{\mathrm{add}_R}(\mathbf{X}_i) \right).$$

7. Run $\mathtt{Setup\_Y}(\widehat{\mathrm{mult}}_L, T_{\widehat{\mathrm{mult}_L}}, \widehat{\mathrm{add}}_L, T_{\widehat{\mathrm{add}_L}}, \vec{r}_{[2m+1,3m]})$ as described in Figure 10.
8. In order to obtain $\{g_{3m+i}(\mathbf{Y}_i)\}_{i=1}^m$, run $\mathtt{Sumcheck\_Y}(\widehat{\mathrm{mult}}_R, T_{\widehat{\mathrm{mult}_R}}, \widehat{\mathrm{add}}_R, T_{\widehat{\mathrm{add}_R}}, \hat{V}_R, T_{\hat{V}_R}, \hat{V}_L(\vec{r}_{[2m+1,3m]}), \alpha \cdot \widehat{\mathrm{mult}}_L(\vec{\chi}, \vec{r}_{[m+1,3m]}), \alpha \cdot \widehat{\mathrm{add}}_L(\vec{\chi}, \vec{r}_{[m+1,3m]}), \vec{r}_{[3m+1,4m]}, \beta)$ as described in Figure 11.

Fig. 2. Linear time prover for the sum-check protocol in Sect. 5.3.

Algorithm Function_Evaluations_{U,W}$(f, T_f, r_1, \ldots, r_{2m})$

Input: $f \in R_A[\vec{U}, \vec{W}, \vec{X}, \vec{Y}]_{\leq 2, \leq 2}$ from Equation (7), initial lookup table T_f, random challenges $\vec{r} = (r_1, \ldots, r_{2m}) \in A^{2m}$.
Output: Polynomials $f(r_1, \ldots, r_{i-1}, U_i, \vec{t}_{i,b}) \in R_A[U_i]_{0, \leq 1}$ for $i \in [1, m]$ and $\vec{t}_{i,b} \in H^{4m-i}$. Polynomials $f(r_1, \ldots, r_{i-1}, W_{i-m}, \vec{t}_{i,b}) \in R_A[W_{i-m}]_{\leq 1, 0}$ for $i \in [m+1, 2m]$ and $\vec{t}_{i,b} \in H^{4m-i}$.

- For $i \in [1, 2m]$ let $\vec{0}$ be the length-$(i-1)$ zero vector and $r_{[1,i)} = (r_1, \ldots, r_{i-1})$.
  - For $i \in [1, m]$: For $b \in H$, and for every $\vec{y} \in H^m$, $\vec{x}_{(i,m]} \in H^{m-i}$, $\vec{x}_{[1,i)} \in H^{i-1}$, define $\vec{t}_{i,b} = (\vec{x}_{(i,m]}, \vec{y}, \vec{x}_{[1,i)}, b, \vec{x}_{(i,m]}, \vec{y}) \in H^{4m-i}$ and do:

$$f(r_{[1,i)}, U_i, \vec{t}_{i,b}) \leftarrow T_f[\vec{0}, 1, \vec{t}_{i,b}] \cdot U_i + T_f[\vec{0}, 0, \vec{t}_{i,b}] \cdot (1 - U_i) \qquad (8)$$
$$T_f[\vec{0}, 0, \vec{t}_{i,b}] \leftarrow T_f[\vec{0}, 1, \vec{t}_{i,b}] \cdot r_i + T_f[\vec{0}, 0, \vec{t}_{i,b}] \cdot (1 - r_i)$$

  - For $i \in [m+1, 2m]$: For $b \in H$, and for every $\vec{x} \in H^m$, $\vec{y}_{(i-m,m]} \in H^{2m-i}$, $\vec{y}_{[1,i-m)} \in H^{i-m-1}$, define $\vec{t}_{i,b} = (\vec{y}_{(i-m,m]}, \vec{x}, \vec{y}_{[1,i-m)}, b, \vec{y}_{(i-m,m]}) \in H^{4m-i}$ and do:

$$f(r_{[1,i)}, W_{i-m}, \vec{t}_{i,b}) \leftarrow W_{i-m} \cdot T_f[\vec{0}, 1, \vec{t}_{i,b}] + (1 - W_{i-m}) \cdot T_f[\vec{0}, 0, \vec{t}_{i,b}] \qquad (9)$$
$$T_f[\vec{0}, 0, \vec{t}_{i,b}] \leftarrow r_i \cdot T_f[\vec{0}, 1, \vec{t}_{i,b}] + (1 - r_i) \cdot T_f[\vec{0}, 0, \vec{t}_{i,b}]$$

- Let $\mathcal{F}$ contain all polynomials in $R_A[U_i]_{0, \leq 1}$ (resp. $R_A[W_i]_{\leq 1, 0}$) defined at Equation (8) (resp. Equation (9)) throughout the execution.

Fig. 3. Evaluations of toast multi-linear polynomials prior to sum-check.

Algorithm Sumcheck_{U,W}$(f, T_f, r_1, \ldots, r_{2m})$

Input: $f \in R_A[\vec{U}, \vec{W}, \vec{X}, \vec{Y}]_{\leq 2, \leq 2}$ from Equation (7), initial lookup table T_f, random challenges $\vec{r} = (r_1, \ldots, r_{2m}) \in A^{2m}$.
Output: First $2m$ sumcheck messages for f.

- $\mathcal{F} \leftarrow$ Function_Evaluations_{U,W}$(f, T_f, r_1, \ldots, r_{2m})$
- For $i \in [1, m]$ and $b \in H$, define $\vec{t}_{i,b} = (\vec{x}_{(i,m]}, \vec{y}, \vec{x}_{[1,i)}, b, \vec{x}_{(i,m]}, \vec{y}) \in H^{4m-i}$ for every $\vec{y} \in H^m$, $\vec{x}_{(i,m]} \in H^{m-i}$, $\vec{x}_{[1,i)} \in H^{i-1}$. Compute and send:

$$g_{i,b}(U_i) = \sum_{\vec{t}_{i,b} \in H^{4m-i}} f(r_1, \ldots, r_{i-1}, U_i, \vec{t}_{i,b}).$$

- For $i \in [m+1, 2m]$ and $b \in H$, define $\vec{t}_{i,b} = (\vec{y}_{(i-m,m]}, \vec{x}, \vec{y}_{[1,i-m)}, b, \vec{y}_{(i-m,m]}) \in H^{4m-i}$ for every $\vec{x} \in H^m$, $\vec{y}_{(i-m,m]} \in H^{2m-i}$, $\vec{y}_{[1,i-m)} \in H^{i-m-1}$. Compute and send:

$$g_{i,b}(W_{i-m}) = \sum_{\vec{t}_{i,b} \in H^{4m-i}} f(r_1, \ldots, r_{i-1}, W_{i-m}, \vec{t}_{i,b}).$$

- Return $\{g_{i,b}(U_i)\}_{b \in H, i \in [1,m]}$, $\{g_{i,b}(W_{i-m})\}_{b \in H, i \in [m+1, 2m]}$.

Fig. 4. Sum-check polynomials for the block of $\vec{U}, \vec{W}$ variables.

execute the sum-check algorithm of Sect. 5.3 for Eq. (7). Recall that $\mathcal{P}$ has to sum the evaluations of $f \in R_A[\vec{U}, \vec{W}, \vec{X}, \vec{Y}]_{\leq 2, \leq 2}$ in the hypercube H^{4m}, where $H = \{0, 1\}$. Our following algorithms assume that $\mathcal{P}$ has an initial lookup table (LUT) T_f with these evaluations, as well as the same kind of lookup tables for its constituent (L/R)MLEs $T_{\widehat{\text{mult}_L}}, T_{\widehat{\text{add}_L}}, T_{\hat{V}_L}, T_{\widehat{\text{mult}_R}}, T_{\widehat{\text{add}_R}}, T_{\hat{V}_R}$. We also assume that $\mathcal{P}$ has received and stored the 2-to-1 reduction challenges $\alpha, \beta \in A$. For a simpler write-up, we write the different algorithms as if $\mathcal{P}$ already knew the challenge vector $\vec{r} = (r_1, \ldots, r_{4m}) \in A^{4m}$, even though they will receive the different r_i values as the progress through the execution of the sum-check protocol.

In constrast with [XZZ+19], we make the Prover provide the Verifier with explicit polynomials, rather than with their evaluations at (up to) three different points. We do this for the sake of generality[10], since interpolation requires exceptional rather than regular-difference sets, and the target ring (e.g. $\mathbb{Z}$) might not contain a commutative exceptional set of size three.

Algorithm Function_Evaluations(f,T_f,r_1,...,r_m)

Input: Lookup table T_f corresponding to either $f \in R_A[X_1, \ldots, X_m]_{\leq 1, 0}$ or $f \in R_A[Y_1, \ldots, Y_m]_{0, \leq 1}$, random challenges $\vec{r} = (r_1, \ldots, r_m) \in A^m$.
Output: Polynomials $f(r_1, \ldots, r_{i-1}, X_i, \vec{b}) \in R_A[X_i]$ (or $f(r_1, \ldots, r_{i-1}, Y_i, \vec{b}) \in R_A[Y_i]$) for $i \in [1, m]$ and $\vec{b} \in \{0, 1\}^{m-i}$.

- For $i = 1, \ldots, m$ let $\vec{0}$ be the length-$(i-1)$ zero vector and do:
  - For $\vec{b} = (b_{m-i}, \ldots, b_1) \in H^{m-i}$ do:
    * If $f \in R_A[Y_1, \ldots, Y_m]_{0, \leq 1}$, define:

$$f(r_1, \ldots, r_{i-1}, Y_i, \vec{b}) \leftarrow (T_f[\vec{0}, 1, \vec{b}] - T_f[\vec{0}, 0, \vec{b}]) \cdot Y_i + T_f[\vec{0}, 0, \vec{b}] \quad (10)$$
$$T_f[\vec{0}, 0, \vec{b}] \leftarrow (T_f[\vec{0}, 1, \vec{b}] - T_f[\vec{0}, 0, \vec{b}]) \cdot r_i + T_f[\vec{0}, 0, \vec{b}]$$

    * Else (i.e. if $f \in R_A[X_1, \ldots, X_m]_{\leq 1, 0}$), define:

$$f(r_1, \ldots, r_{i-1}, X_i, \vec{b}) \leftarrow X_i \cdot (T_f[\vec{0}, 1, \vec{b}] - T_f[\vec{0}, 0, \vec{b}]) + T_f[\vec{0}, 0, \vec{b}] \quad (11)$$
$$T_f[\vec{0}, 0, \vec{b}] \leftarrow r_i \cdot (T_f[\vec{0}, 1, \vec{b}] - T_f[\vec{0}, 0, \vec{b}]) + T_f[\vec{0}, 0, \vec{b}]$$

- Let $\mathcal{F}$ contain all polynomials in $R_A[X_i]_{\leq 1, 0}$ (resp. $R_A[Y_i]_{0, \leq 1}$) defined at Equation (11) (resp. Equation (10)) throughout the execution.

Fig. 5. Evaluations of toast multi-linear polynomials for sum-check.

---

[10] It would be easy to modify our algorithms to work by providing polynomial evaluations instead. In fact, the set $\{0, 1, \gamma\}$ is commutative and exceptional as long as γ and $\gamma - 1$ are invertible. If 2 is not a zero divisor, we can always pick $\gamma = 2$. Otherwise we may still find such γ easily (as e.g. in $\mathbb{F}_{2^d}$, $\mathsf{GR}(2^k, d)$, $\mathcal{M}_{n \times n}(\mathbb{Z}/2^k\mathbb{Z})$) or resort to ring extensions (e.g. embed $\mathbb{Z}/2^k\mathbb{Z}$ in $\mathsf{GR}(2^k, d)$ or $\mathbb{Z}$ in $\mathbb{R}$).

$\vec{U}, \vec{W}$ **Variables (Step 1).** This is the easiest phase, since we can directly reason about $f \in R_A[\vec{U}, \vec{W}, \vec{X}, \vec{Y}]_{\leq 2, \leq 2}$ from Eq. (7) and its LUT T_f. Sumcheck_$\{U, W\}$ (Fig. 4) provides with the polynomials for these first $2m$ messages. All terms in

---

Algorithm Precompute$(g_1, \ldots, g_\ell)$

Input: Random challenge $\vec{g} = (g_1, \ldots, g_\ell) \in A^\ell$.
Output: Lookup table $\{T_{\vec{g}}[\vec{b}]\}_{\vec{b} \in \{0,1\}^\ell}$ containing the evaluations of $I(\vec{g}, \vec{b}) = \prod_{i=1}^m \left(g_i \cdot b_i + (1 - g_i) \cdot (1 - b_i)\right)$.

- Set $T_{\vec{g}}[\vec{0}] \leftarrow (1 - g_1)$ and $T_{\vec{g}}[0, \ldots, 0, 1] \leftarrow g_1$.
- For $i = 1, \ldots, \ell - 1$, do:
  - For $(b_i, \ldots, b_1) \in \{0, 1\}^i$, do:
    * $T_{\vec{g}}[\vec{0}, 0, b_i, \ldots, b_1] \leftarrow T_{\vec{g}}[\vec{0}, b_i, \ldots, b_1] \cdot (1 - g_{i+1})$.
    * $T_{\vec{g}}[\vec{0}, 1, b_i, \ldots, b_1] \leftarrow T_{\vec{g}}[\vec{0}, b_i, \ldots, b_1] \cdot g_{i+1}$.

Fig. 6. Computing LUT for identity polynomial evaluated at a challenge.

Algorithm Setup_X$(f_1, T_{f_1}, f_2, T_{f_2}, f_3, T_{f_3}, f_4, T_{f_4}, \vec{\chi}, \vec{\psi}, \vec{r})$

Input: Multi-linear $f_1(z, x, y), f_2(z, x, y) \in R_A[\vec{X}, \vec{W}, \vec{Z}]_{\leq 1, 0}$, $f_3(z, x, y), f_4(z, x, y) \in R_A[\vec{Y}, \vec{U}, \vec{Z}]_{\leq 1, 0}$ and their initial look-up tables. Random challenges[a] $\vec{\chi}, \vec{\psi} \in A^m$, $\vec{r} \in A^{2m}$.
Output: Look-up tables T_{f_i} for the block of $\vec{X}$ variables.

- $T_{\vec{\chi}}[\vec{z}] \leftarrow$ Precompute$(\vec{\chi})$.
- $T_{\vec{\psi}}[\vec{z}] \leftarrow$ Precompute$(\vec{\psi})$.
- $T_{\vec{r}_{[1,m]}}[\vec{x}] \leftarrow$ Precompute$(\vec{r}_{[1,m]})$.
- $T_{\vec{r}_{[m+1,2m]}}[\vec{y}] \leftarrow$ Precompute$(\vec{r}_{[m+1,2m]})$.
- $\forall \vec{x}, \vec{y} \in \{0, 1\}^m$, set $T_{f_1}[\vec{x}] = T_{f_2}[\vec{x}] = T_{f_3}[\vec{y}] = T_{f_4}[\vec{y}] = 0$.
- For $i = 1, 2$ and for every $(\vec{z}, \vec{x}, \vec{y}) \in H^{3m}$ such that $f_i(\vec{z}, \vec{x}, \vec{y}) \neq 0$, do:

$$T_{f_i}[\vec{x}] \leftarrow T_{f_i}[\vec{x}] + T_{\vec{\chi}}[\vec{z}] \cdot T_{\vec{r}_{[m+1,2m]}}[\vec{y}] \cdot f_i(\vec{z}, \vec{x}, \vec{y}).$$

- For $i = 3, 4$ and for every $(\vec{z}, \vec{x}, \vec{y}) \in H^{3m}$ such that $f_i(\vec{z}, \vec{x}, \vec{y}) \neq 0$, do:

$$T_{f_i}[\vec{y}] \leftarrow T_{f_i}[\vec{y}] + f_i(\vec{z}, \vec{x}, \vec{y}) \cdot T_{\vec{\psi}}[\vec{z}] \cdot T_{\vec{r}_{[1,m]}}[\vec{x}].$$

- Return $T_{f_1}[x], T_{f_2}[x], T_{f_3}[y], T_{f_4}[y]$.

[a] For a shorter write-up, we describe this algorithm as if $\vec{z}, \vec{x}, \vec{y} \in \{0, 1\}^m$. In practice, since $\vec{z}$ comes from a different layer, it might have different length.

Fig. 7. Substituting $\vec{Z}, \vec{U}, \vec{W}$ in LUTs with their corresponding challenges.

Algorithm

Sumcheck_X_Left($\widehat{\text{mult}}_L, T_{\widehat{\text{mult}}_L}(\vec{x}), \widehat{\text{add}}_L, T_{\widehat{\text{add}}_L}(\vec{x}), \mathcal{F}_{\hat{V}_L}, \hat{V}_R, T_{\hat{V}_R}(\vec{y}), \vec{r}_{[2m+1,3m]}$)

Input: Parse $\vec{X} = (X_1, \ldots, X_m)$ and $\vec{Y} = (Y_1, \ldots, Y_m)$. Toast polynomials $\widehat{\text{mult}}_L(\vec{X}, \vec{r}_{[m+1,2m]}, \vec{X}), \widehat{\text{add}}_L(\vec{X}, \vec{r}_{[m+1,2m]}, \vec{X}), \hat{V}_L(\vec{X}) \in R_A[\vec{X}]_{\leq 1,0}$ and $\hat{V}_R(\vec{Y}) \in R_A[\vec{Y}]_{0,\leq 1}$, given by their lookup tables $T_{\widehat{\text{mult}}_L}(x), T_{\widehat{\text{add}}_L}(x), T_{\hat{V}_R}(y)$ containing all evaluations at H^m. Random challenges $\vec{r}_{[2m+1,3m]} \in A^m$ and table $\mathcal{F}_{\hat{V}_L} \leftarrow$ Function_Evaluations($\hat{V}_L, T_{\hat{V}_L}, r_{2m+1}, \ldots, r_{3m}$).

Output: $2m$ partial sumcheck messages, half for $\sum_{\vec{x},\vec{y} \in H^m} g_{2m+i}^{\text{mult}_L}(\vec{x}, \vec{y})$ and half for $\sum_{\vec{x},\vec{y} \in H^m} g_{2m+i}^{\text{add}_L}(\vec{x}, \vec{y})$. Each message is a polynomial in $R_A[X_i]_{\leq 2,0}$.

- $\mathcal{F}_{\widehat{\text{mult}}_L} \leftarrow$ Function_Evaluations($\widehat{\text{mult}}_L, T_{\widehat{\text{mult}}_L}, r_{2m+1}, \ldots, r_{3m}$).
- $\mathcal{F}_{\widehat{\text{add}}_L} \leftarrow$ Function_Evaluations($\widehat{\text{add}}_L, T_{\widehat{\text{add}}_L}, r_{2m+1}, \ldots, r_{3m}$).
- Compute $Y = \sum_{\vec{y} \in H^m} \hat{V}_R(\vec{y})$ from $T_{\hat{V}_R}(\vec{y})$ and store it for the next steps.
- For $i \in [m]$, compute as follows:

$$g_{2m+i}^{\text{mult}_L}(X_i) = \sum_{\vec{x} \in H^{m-i}} \widehat{\text{mult}}_L(\vec{r}_{[2m+1,2m+i-1]}, X_i, \vec{x}) \cdot \hat{V}_L(\vec{r}_{[2m+1,2m+i-1]}, X_i, \vec{x}) \cdot Y.$$

$$g_{2m+i}^{\text{add}_L}(X_i) = \sum_{\vec{x} \in H^{m-i}} \widehat{\text{add}}_L(\vec{r}_{[2m+1,2m+i-1]}, X_i, \vec{x}) \cdot \left(\hat{V}_L(\vec{r}_{[2m+1,2m+i-1]}, X_i, \vec{x}) + Y\right).$$

- Return each polynomial $\{g_{2m+1}^{\text{mult}_L}(X_1), g_{2m+1}^{\text{add}_L}(X_1), \ldots, g_{3m}^{\text{mult}_L}(X_m), g_{3m}^{\text{add}_L}(X_m)\}$.

Fig. 8. Sumcheck polynomials for $\vec{X}$ variables and "$\hat{V}_L^{(i)}$-side" of Eq. (7).

the sums of Fig. 4 can be found, in turn, in the lookup table $\mathcal{F}$ produced by Function_Evaluations_{U, W} (Fig. 3).

The algorithm in Fig. 3 follows from the simple observation that, because of linearity, any RMLE $f(\vec{r}, U_i, \vec{t}) \in R_A[U_i]_{0,\leq 1}$ satisfies that $f(\vec{r}, U_i, \vec{t}) = (f(\vec{r}, 1, \vec{t}) - f(\vec{r}, 0, \vec{t})) \cdot U_i + f(\vec{r}, 0, \vec{t})$. Notice that, whereas the initial lookup table T_f contains all the 2^{4m} evaluations of f from Eq. (7) in $H = \{0, 1\}$, modifications only occur on the first $2m$ indices, which are the ones related to variables U and W.

$\vec{X}$ **Variables (Steps 2–6).** In this phase, rather than reasoning about $f \in R_A[\vec{U}, \vec{W}, \vec{X}, \vec{Y}]_{\leq 2, \leq 2}$ from Eq. (7), we look at its constituent polynomials ($\widehat{\text{mult}}_L$, $\widehat{\text{add}}_L, \hat{V}_L, \widehat{\text{mult}}_R, \widehat{\text{add}}_R, \hat{V}_R$) separately. Dealing with non-commutative rings is the main reason for the different algorithms in these steps, compared with the simpler description in Libra [XZZ+19]. Whereas in Libra expressions of the

---

Algorithm

$\texttt{Sumcheck\_X\_Right}(\widehat{\texttt{mult}_\texttt{R}}, \boldsymbol{T}_{\widehat{\texttt{mult}_\texttt{R}}}(\vec{y}), \widehat{\texttt{add}_\texttt{R}}, \boldsymbol{T}_{\widehat{\texttt{add}_\texttt{R}}}(\vec{y}), \mathcal{F}_{\hat{V}_L}, \hat{V}_R, \boldsymbol{T}_{\hat{V}_R}(\vec{y}), \vec{r}_{[2m+1,3m]})$

Input: Parse $\vec{X} = (X_1, \ldots, X_m)$ and $\vec{Y} = (Y_1, \ldots, Y_m)$. Table $\mathcal{F}_{\hat{V}_L}$ with all evaluations of $\hat{V}_L(\vec{X}) \in R_A[\vec{X}]_{\leq 1,0}$ in H^m. Toast polynomials $\widehat{\texttt{mult}_\texttt{R}}(\psi, \vec{r}_{[1,m]}, \vec{Y}), \widehat{\texttt{add}_\texttt{R}}(\psi, \vec{r}_{[1,m]}, \vec{Y}), \hat{V}_R(\vec{Y}) \in R_A[\vec{Y}]_{0,\leq 1}$ given by their lookup tables $\boldsymbol{T}_{\widehat{\texttt{mult}_\texttt{R}}}(\vec{y}), \boldsymbol{T}_{\widehat{\texttt{add}_\texttt{R}}}(\vec{y}), \boldsymbol{T}_{\hat{V}_R}(\vec{y})$, containing all evaluations at H^m. Random challenges $\vec{r}_{[2m+1,3m]} \in A^m$ and table $\mathcal{F}_{\hat{V}_L} \leftarrow \texttt{Function\_Evaluations}(\hat{V}_L, \boldsymbol{T}_{\hat{V}_L}, r_{2m+1}, \ldots, r_{3m})$.

Output: $2m$ partial sumcheck messages, half for $\sum_{\vec{x},\vec{y} \in H^m} g^{\texttt{mult}_\texttt{R}}_{2m+i}(\vec{x}, \vec{y})$ and half for $\sum_{\vec{x},\vec{y} \in H^m} g^{\texttt{add}_\texttt{R}}_{2m+i}(\vec{x}, \vec{y})$. Each message is a polynomial in $R_A[X_i]_{\leq 1,0}$.

- For $i \in [m]$, compute $g^{\texttt{mult}_\texttt{R}}_{2m+i} \in R_A[X_i]_{\leq 1,0}$ as follows. Notice $\sum_{\vec{y} \in H^m} \hat{V}_R(\vec{y}) \cdot \widehat{\texttt{mult}_\texttt{R}}(\vec{y})$ can be computed once and in time $O(2^m)$ from $\boldsymbol{T}_{\hat{V}_R}(\vec{y})$ and $\boldsymbol{T}_{\widehat{\texttt{mult}_\texttt{R}}}(\vec{y})$ for all the steps.

$$g^{\texttt{mult}_\texttt{R}}_{2m+i}(X_i) = \sum_{\vec{x} \in H^{m-i}} \hat{V}_L(\vec{r}_{[2m+1,2m+i-1]}, X_i, \vec{x}) \cdot \left(\sum_{\vec{y} \in H^m} \hat{V}_R(\vec{y}) \cdot \widehat{\texttt{mult}_\texttt{R}}(\vec{y}) \right).$$

- For $i \in [m]$, compute $g^{\texttt{add}_\texttt{R}}_{2m+i} \in R_A[X_i]_{\leq 1,0}$ as follows. First, compute $\sum_{\vec{y} \in H^m} \widehat{\texttt{add}_\texttt{R}}(\vec{y})$. Next, compute $\sum_{\vec{y} \in H^m} \hat{V}_R(\vec{y}) \cdot \widehat{\texttt{add}_\texttt{R}}(\vec{y})$. Given those, the next expression can be computed in $O(2^{m-i})$ time.

$$g^{\texttt{add}_\texttt{R}}_{2m+i}(X_i) = \sum_{\vec{x} \in H^{m-i}} \sum_{\vec{y} \in H^m} \left(\hat{V}_L(\vec{r}_{[2m+1,2m+i-1]}, X_i, \vec{x}) + \hat{V}_R(\vec{y}) \right) \cdot \widehat{\texttt{add}_\texttt{R}}(\vec{y}).$$

- Return each polynomial $\{g^{\texttt{mult}_\texttt{R}}_{2m+1}(X_1), g^{\texttt{add}_\texttt{R}}_{2m+1}(X_1), \ldots, g^{\texttt{mult}_\texttt{R}}_{3m}(X_m), g^{\texttt{add}_\texttt{R}}_{3m}(X_m)\}$.

Fig. 9. Sumcheck polynomials for $\vec{X}$ variables and "$\hat{V}_R^{(i)}$-side" of Eq. (7).

form $\sum_{\vec{x},\vec{y} \in H^m} \texttt{wp}(\vec{g}, \vec{x}, \vec{y}) f_2(\vec{x}) f_3(\vec{y})$ are rewritten as $\sum_{\vec{x} \in H^m} f_2(\vec{x}) \cdot h_{\vec{g}}(\vec{x})$, where $h_{\vec{g}}(\vec{x}) = \sum_{\vec{y} \in H^m} \texttt{wp}(\vec{g}, \vec{x}, \vec{y}) f_3(\vec{y})$, we cannot assume this to be possible in our setting, since $f_2(\vec{x}) \in R$ might not commute with $\texttt{wp}(\vec{g}, \vec{x}, \vec{y})$.

Instead, we start by using the algorithm $\texttt{SetupX}$ (Fig. 7), which substitutes the $\vec{Z}, \vec{U}, \vec{W}$ variables in the LUTs of $\widehat{\texttt{mult}_\texttt{L}}, \widehat{\texttt{add}_\texttt{L}}, \widehat{\texttt{mult}_\texttt{R}}$ and $\widehat{\texttt{add}_\texttt{R}}$ with their corresponding challenges. Next, applying $\texttt{Function\_Evaluations}$ (Fig. 5) to the (updated) LUTs, we can produce LMLEs in the $\vec{X}$ variables for $\hat{V}_L$ (in Step 3) and $\widehat{\texttt{mult}_\texttt{L}}, \widehat{\texttt{add}_\texttt{L}}$ (which happens within $\texttt{Sumcheck\_X\_Left}$). Given two multilinear polynomials $f(X), g(X)$, we know that we can compute the sum-check pro-

---

Algorithm Setup_Y($\widehat{\text{mult}}_L, T_{\widehat{\text{mult}}_L}(\vec{x}), \widehat{\text{add}}_L, T_{\widehat{\text{add}}_L}(\vec{x}), \vec{r}_{[2m+1,3m]}$)

Input: $\widehat{\text{mult}}_L(\vec{\chi}, \vec{r}_{[m+1,2m]}, \vec{X}), \widehat{\text{add}}_L(\vec{\chi}, \vec{r}_{[m+1,2m]}, \vec{X}) \in R_A[\vec{X}]_{\leq 1,0}$ and their look-up tables after **Setup_X** (Figure 7). Random challenge $\vec{r}_{[2m+1,3m]} \in A^m$.
Output: Values $\widehat{\text{mult}}_L(\vec{g}, \vec{r}_{[m+1,2m]}, \vec{r}_{[2m+1,3m]})$ and $\widehat{\text{add}}_L(\vec{g}, \vec{r}_{[m+1,2m]}, \vec{r}_{[2m+1,3m]})$.

- $T_{\vec{r}_{[2m+1,3m]}}[\vec{x}] \leftarrow$ Precompute($\vec{r}_{[2m+1,3m]}$).
- Compute:

$$\widehat{\text{add}}_L(\vec{\chi}, \vec{r}_{[m+1,2m]}, \vec{r}_{[2m+1,3m]}) = \sum_{\vec{x} \in H} T_{\vec{r}_{[2m+1,3m]}}[\vec{x}] \cdot T_{\widehat{\text{add}}_L}[\vec{x}].$$

$$\widehat{\text{mult}}_L(\vec{\chi}, \vec{r}_{[m+1,2m]}, \vec{r}_{[2m+1,3m]}) = \sum_{\vec{x} \in H} T_{\vec{r}_{[2m+1,3m]}}[\vec{x}] \cdot T_{\widehat{\text{mult}}_L}[\vec{x}].$$

- Return $\widehat{\text{mult}}_L(\vec{g}, \vec{r}_{[m+1,2m]}, \vec{r}_{[2m+1,3m]})$ and $\widehat{\text{add}}_L(\vec{g}, \vec{r}_{[m+1,2m]}, \vec{r}_{[2m+1,3m]})$.

Fig. 10. Substituting $\vec{X}$ with $\vec{r}_{[2m+1,3m]} \in A^m$ in the LUTs of $\widehat{\text{mult}}_L, \widehat{\text{add}}_L$.

tocol on their product $f(X) \cdot g(X)$ in linear time [Tha13]. That is what we do in algorithms Sumcheck_X_Left (Fig. 8) and Sumcheck_X_Right (Fig. 9), where we compute, in linear time and without reordering its terms, the sum-check messages for $\sum_{\vec{x}, \vec{y} \in H^m} \text{wp}(\vec{g}, \vec{x}, \vec{y}) f_2(\vec{x}) f_3(\vec{y})$ corresponding to the $\vec{X}$ variables. The key observation for the latter two algorithms is that, for $i \in [m]$, $\vec{x} \in H^{m-i}$ and $\text{wp} \in \{\widehat{\text{add}}_L, \widehat{\text{mult}}_L, \widehat{\text{add}}_R, \widehat{\text{mult}}_R\}$, the set

$$\mathcal{N}_{\vec{x}}^i = \{\vec{y} \in H^m : \exists \vec{z} \in H^m, (x_1, \ldots, x_i) \in H^i \text{ s.t. } \text{wp}(\vec{z}, (x_1, \ldots, x_i), \vec{x}, \vec{y}) \neq 0\},$$

is s.t. $\sum_{\vec{x} \in H^{m-i}} |\mathcal{N}_{\vec{x}}^i| \in O(2^{m-i})$. We exploit the sparseness of our wiring predicates to keep an $O(2^m)$-time prover without reordering the terms of Eq. (7).

$\vec{Y}$ Variables (Steps 7–8). Setup_Y (Fig. 10) substitutes the $\vec{X}$ variables with $\vec{r}_{[2m+1,3m]} \in A^m$ in the LUTs of $\widehat{\text{mult}}_L, \widehat{\text{add}}_L$, so that $\mathcal{P}$ obtains values $\widehat{\text{add}}_L(\vec{g}, \vec{r}_{[m+1,2m]}, \vec{r}_{[2m+1,3m]})$ and $\widehat{\text{mult}}_L(\vec{g}, \vec{r}_{[m+1,2m]}, \vec{r}_{[2m+1,3m]})$. Applying Function_Evaluations (Fig. 5) to the LUT of $\hat{V}_R$ and the LUTs of $\widehat{\text{mult}}_R$ and $\widehat{\text{add}}_R$ (which were previously updated in SetupX, Fig. 7), we can produce the different RMLEs in the $\vec{Y}$ variables that are required for the execution of Sumcheck_Y (Fig. 11): For $i \in [m]$, $\vec{y} \in H^{m-i}$, polynomials $\hat{V}_R(\vec{r}_{[3m+1,3m+i-1]}, Y_i, \vec{y})$, $\widehat{\text{add}}_R(\vec{r}_{[3m+1,3m+i-1]}, Y_i, \vec{y})$ and $\widehat{\text{mult}}_R(\vec{r}_{[3m+1,3m+i-1]}, Y_i, \vec{y})$.

Algorithm Sumcheck_Y
$$(\widehat{\mathtt{mult}_\mathtt{R}}, \boldsymbol{T}_{\widehat{\mathtt{mult}_\mathtt{R}}}(y), \widehat{\mathtt{add}_\mathtt{R}}, \boldsymbol{T}_{\widehat{\mathtt{add}_\mathtt{R}}}(y), \hat{V}_R, \boldsymbol{T}_{\hat{V}_R}(y), \hat{V}_L(\vec{r}_{[2m+1,3m]}), m_L, a_L, \vec{s}, \beta)$$

Input: Toast polynomials $\widehat{\mathtt{mult}_\mathtt{R}}(\vec{\psi}, \vec{r}_{[1,m]}, \mathbf{\bar{Y}}), \widehat{\mathtt{add}_\mathtt{R}}(\vec{\psi}, \vec{r}_{[1,m]}, \mathbf{\bar{Y}}), \hat{V}_R(\mathbf{\bar{Y}}) \in R_A[\mathbf{\bar{Y}}]_{0,\leq 1}$ given by their lookup tables $\boldsymbol{T}_{\widehat{\mathtt{mult}_\mathtt{R}}}(\vec{y}), \boldsymbol{T}_{\widehat{\mathtt{add}_\mathtt{R}}}(\vec{y})$ (after the execution of Setup_X (Figure 7)) and $\boldsymbol{T}_{\hat{V}_R}(\vec{y})$. Values $m_L = \alpha \cdot \widehat{\mathtt{mult}_\mathtt{L}}(\vec{\chi}, \vec{r}_{[m+1,3m]})$ and $a_L = \alpha \cdot \widehat{\mathtt{add}_\mathtt{L}}(\vec{\chi}, \vec{r}_{[m+1,3m]})$. Random challenges $\vec{s} = \vec{r}_{[3m+1,4m]} \in A^m$.
Output: Last m sumcheck messages for Equation (7). Each message is a polynomial $g_{3m+i}(\mathbf{Y}_i) \in R_A[\mathbf{Y}_i]_{\leq 2,0}$.

- $\mathcal{F}_{\hat{V}_R} \leftarrow$ Function_Evaluations$(\hat{V}_R, \boldsymbol{T}_{\hat{V}_R}, s_1, \ldots, s_m)$.
- $\mathcal{F}_{\widehat{\mathtt{add}_\mathtt{R}}} \leftarrow$ Function_Evaluations$(\widehat{\mathtt{add}_\mathtt{R}}, \boldsymbol{T}_{\widehat{\mathtt{add}_\mathtt{R}}}, s_1, \ldots, s_m)$.
- $\mathcal{F}_{\widehat{\mathtt{mult}_\mathtt{R}}} \leftarrow$ Function_Evaluations$(\widehat{\mathtt{mult}_\mathtt{R}}, \boldsymbol{T}_{\widehat{\mathtt{mult}_\mathtt{R}}}, s_1, \ldots, s_m)$.
- For $i \in [m]$, compute $g_{3m+i}(\mathbf{Y}_i) = (g^L_{3m+i}(\mathbf{Y}_i) + g^R_{3m+i}(\mathbf{Y}_i)) \in R_A[\mathbf{Y}_i]_{0,\leq 2}$ as follows. Notice that given $\mathcal{F}_{\hat{V}_R}, \mathcal{F}_{\widehat{\mathtt{add}_\mathtt{R}}}, \mathcal{F}_{\widehat{\mathtt{mult}_\mathtt{R}}}$, computation takes $O(2^{m-i})$ time:

$$g^L_{3m+i}(\mathbf{Y}_i) = a_L \cdot \hat{V}_L(\vec{r}_{[2m+1,3m]}) + \sum_{\vec{y} \in H^{m-i}} \Big(a_L \cdot \hat{V}_R(\vec{s}_{[1,i-1]}, \mathbf{Y}_i, \vec{y})$$

$$+ m_L \cdot \hat{V}_L(\vec{r}_{[2m+1,3m]}) \cdot \hat{V}_R(\vec{s}_{[1,i-1]}, \mathbf{Y}_i, \vec{y}) \Big).$$

$$g^R_{3m+i}(\mathbf{Y}_i) = \beta \cdot \Big(\sum_{\vec{y} \in H^{m-i}} (\hat{V}_L(\vec{r}_{[2m+1,3m]}) + \hat{V}_R(\vec{s}_{[1,i-1]}, \mathbf{Y}_i, \vec{y})) \cdot \widehat{\mathtt{add}_\mathtt{R}}(\vec{s}_{[1,i-1]}, \mathbf{Y}_i, \vec{y})$$

$$+ \hat{V}_L(\vec{r}_{[2m+1,3m]}) \cdot \hat{V}_R(\vec{s}_{[1,i-1]}, \mathbf{Y}_i, \vec{y}) \cdot \widehat{\mathtt{mult}_\mathtt{R}}(\vec{s}_{[1,i-1]}, \mathbf{Y}_i, \vec{y}) \Big).$$

- Return each polynomial $\{g_{3m+1}(\mathbf{Y}_1), \ldots, g_{4m}(\mathbf{Y}_m)\}$.

Fig. 11. Sumcheck polynomials for the block of $\mathbf{\bar{Y}}$ variables

References

[ACD+19] Abspoel, M., Cramer, R., Damgård, I., Escudero, D., Yuan, C.: Efficient information-theoretic secure multiparty computation over $\mathbb{Z}/p^k\mathbb{Z}$ via galois rings. In: Hofheinz, D., Rosen, A. (eds.) TCC 2019, Part I. LNCS, vol. 11891, pp. 471–501. Springer, Cham (2019). https://doi.org/10.1007/978-3-030-36030-6_19

[AIK10] Applebaum, B., Ishai, Y., Kushilevitz, E.: From secrecy to soundness: efficient verification via secure computation. In: Abramsky, S., Gavoille, C., Kirchner, C., Meyer auf der Heide, F., Spirakis, P.G. (eds.) ICALP 2010, Part I. LNCS, vol. 6198, pp. 152–163. Springer, Heidelberg (2010). https://doi.org/10.1007/978-3-642-14165-2_14

[BCFK21] Bois, A., Cascudo, I., Fiore, D., Kim, D.: Flexible and efficient verifiable computation on encrypted data. In: Garay, J.A. (ed.) PKC 2021, Part II. LNCS, vol. 12711, pp. 528–558. Springer, Cham (2021). https://doi.org/10.1007/978-3-030-75248-4_19

[BCS21]   Bootle, J., Chiesa, A., Sotiraki, K.: Sumcheck arguments and their applications. In: Malkin, T., Peikert, C. (eds.) CRYPTO 2021, Part I. LNCS, vol. 12825, pp. 742–773. Springer, Cham (2021). https://doi.org/10.1007/978-3-030-84242-0_26

[BFL91]   Babai, L., Fortnow, L., Lund, C.: Non-deterministic exponential time has two-prover interactive protocols. Comput. Complex. 1(1), 3–40 (1991)

[CCKP19]   Chen, S., Cheon, J.H., Kim, D., Park, D.: Verifiable computing for approximate computation. Cryptology ePrint Archive, Report 2019/762 (2019). http://eprint.iacr.org/2019/762

[CDI+13]   Cohen, G., et al.: Efficient multiparty protocols via log-depth threshold formulae (extended abstract). In: Canetti, R., Garay, J.A. (eds.) CRYPTO 2013, Part II. LNCS, vol. 8043, pp. 185–202. Springer, Heidelberg (2013). https://doi.org/10.1007/978-3-642-40084-1_11

[CFIK03]   Cramer, R., Fehr, S., Ishai, Y., Kushilevitz, E.: Efficient multi-party computation over rings. In: Biham, E. (ed.) EUROCRYPT 2003. LNCS, vol. 2656, pp. 596–613. Springer, Heidelberg (2003). https://doi.org/10.1007/3-540-39200-9_37

[CMT12]   Cormode, G., Mitzenmacher, M., Thaler, J.: Practical verified computation with streaming interactive proofs. In: Goldwasser, S. (eds.) ITCS 2012, pp. 90–112. ACM, January 2012

[DLS20]   Dalskov, A., Lee, E., Soria-Vazquez, E.: Circuit amortization friendly encodingsand their application to statistically secure multiparty computation. In: Moriai, S., Wang, H. (eds.) ASIACRYPT 2020, Part III. LNCS, vol. 12493, pp. 213–243. Springer, Cham (2020). https://doi.org/10.1007/978-3-030-64840-4_8

[ES21]   Escudero, D., Soria-Vazquez, E.: Efficient information-theoretic multi-party computation over non-commutative rings. In: Malkin, T., Peikert, C. (eds.) CRYPTO 2021, Part II. LNCS, vol. 12826, pp. 335–364. Springer, Cham (2021). https://doi.org/10.1007/978-3-030-84245-1_12

[Fre79]   Freivalds, R.: Fast probabilistic algorithms. In: Bečvář, J. (ed.) MFCS 1979. LNCS, vol. 74, pp. 57–69. Springer, Heidelberg (1979). https://doi.org/10.1007/3-540-09526-8_5

[GKR15]   Goldwasser, S., Kalai, Y.T., Rothblum, G.N.: Delegating computation: interactive proofs for muggles. J. ACM (JACM) 62(4), 1–64 (2015)

[GMR89]   Goldwasser, S., Micali, S., Rackoff, C.: The knowledge complexity of interactive proof systems. SIAM J. Comput. 18(1), 186–208 (1989)

[GNS21]   Ganesh, C., Nitulescu, A., Soria-Vazquez, E.: Rinocchio: snarks for ring arithmetic. Cryptology ePrint Archive, Report 2021/322 (2021). http://eprint.iacr.org/2021/322

[HL75]   Howell, T.D., Lafon, J.-C.: The complexity of the quaternion product. Technical report, Cornell University (1975)

[HR18]   Holmgren, J., Rothblum, R.: Delegating computations with (almost) minimal time and space overhead. In: Thorup, M. (eds.) 59th FOCS, pp. 124–135. IEEE Computer Society Press, October 2018

[HY11]   Hrubeš, P., Yehudayoff, A.: Arithmetic complexity in ring extensions. Theory Comput. 7(1), 119–129 (2011)

[IK04]   Ishai, Y., Kushilevitz, E.: On the hardness of information-theoretic multi-party computation. In: Cachin, C., Camenisch, J.L. (eds.) EUROCRYPT 2004. LNCS, vol. 3027, pp. 439–455. Springer, Heidelberg (2004). https://doi.org/10.1007/978-3-540-24676-3_26

[LFKN92] Lund, C., Fortnow, L., Karloff, H., Nisan, N.: Algebraic methods for inter-active proof systems. J. ACM (JACM) **39**(4), 859–868 (1992)

[LXZ21] Liu, T., Xie, X., Zhang, Y.: zkCNN: zero knowledge proofs for convolutional neural network predictions and accuracy. In: Vigna, G., Shi, E. (eds.) ACM CCS 2021, pp. 2968–2985. ACM Press, November 2021

[Mei13] Meir, O.: IP = PSPACE using error-correcting codes. SIAM J. Comput. **42**(1), 380–403 (2013)

[QBC13] Quintin, G., Barbier, M., Chabot, C.: On generalized Reed-Solomon codes over commutative and noncommutative rings. IEEE Trans. Inf. Theory **59**(9), 5882–5897 (2013)

[Sor22] Soria-Vazquez, E.: Doubly efficient interactive proofs over infinite and non-commutative rings. Cryptology ePrint Archive, Paper 2022/587 (2022). http://eprint.iacr.org/2022/587

[SS10] Schott, R., Stacey Staples, G.: Reductions in computational complexity using Clifford algebras. Adv. Appl. Clifford Algebras **20**(1), 121–140 (2010)

[Tha13] Thaler, J.R.: Practical verified computation with streaming interactive proofs. Ph.D. thesis (2013)

[XZZ+19] Xie, T., Zhang, J., Zhang, Y., Papamanthou, C., Song, D.: Libra: succinct zero-knowledge proofs with optimal prover computation. In: Boldyreva, A., Micciancio, D. (eds.) CRYPTO 2019, Part III. LNCS, vol. 11694, pp. 733–764. Springer, Cham (2019). https://doi.org/10.1007/978-3-030-26954-8_24

[ZLW+21] Zhang, J., et al.: Doubly efficient interactive proofs for general arithmetic circuits with linear prover time. In: Proceedings of the 2021 ACM SIGSAC Conference on Computer and Communications Security, pp. 159–177 (2021)

Fully Succinct Batch Arguments for NP from Indistinguishability Obfuscation

Rachit Garg[1]([✉]), Kristin Sheridan[1], Brent Waters[1,2], and David J. Wu[1]

[1] University of Texas at Austin, Austin, TX, USA
{rachg96,kristin,bwaters,dwu4}@cs.utexas.edu
[2] NTT Research, Sunnyvale, CA, USA

Abstract. Non-interactive batch arguments for NP provide a way to amortize the cost of NP verification across multiple instances. In particular, they allow a prover to convince a verifier of multiple NP statements with communication that scales sublinearly in the number of instances.

In this work, we study *fully succinct* batch arguments for NP in the common reference string (CRS) model where the length of the proof scales not only sublinearly in the number of instances T, but also sublinearly with the size of the NP relation. Batch arguments with these properties are special cases of succinct non-interactive arguments (SNARGs); however, existing constructions of SNARGs either rely on idealized models or strong non-falsifiable assumptions. The one exception is the Sahai-Waters SNARG based on indistinguishability obfuscation. However, when applied to the setting of batch arguments, we must impose an *a priori* bound on the number of instances. Moreover, the size of the common reference string scales linearly with the number of instances.

In this work, we give a *direct* construction of a fully succinct batch argument for NP that supports an unbounded number of statements from indistinguishability obfuscation and one-way functions. Then, by additionally relying on a somewhere statistically-binding (SSB) hash function, we show how to extend our construction to obtain a fully succinct and *updatable* batch argument. In the updatable setting, a prover can take a proof π on T statements $(x_1, \ldots, x_T)$ and "update" it to obtain a proof π' on $(x_1, \ldots, x_T, x_{T+1})$. Notably, the update procedure only requires knowledge of a (short) proof for $(x_1, \ldots, x_T)$ along with a *single* witness w_{T+1} for the new instance x_{T+1}. Importantly, the update does *not* require knowledge of witnesses for $x_1, \ldots, x_T$.

1 Introduction

Non-interactive batch arguments (BARGs) provide a way to amortize the cost of NP verification across multiple instances. Specifically, in a batch argument, the prover has a collection of NP statements $x_1, \ldots, x_T$ and their goal is to convince the verifier that $x_i \in \mathcal{L}$ for all i, where $\mathcal{L}$ is the associated NP language. The trivial solution is to have the prover send over the associated NP witnesses

E. Kiltz and V. Vaikuntanathan (Eds.): TCC 2022, LNCS 13747, pp. 526–555, 2022.
https://doi.org/10.1007/978-3-031-22318-1_19

$w_1, \ldots, w_T$ and have the verifier check each one individually. The goal in a batch argument is to obtain *shorter* proofs—namely, proofs whose size scales *sublinearly* in T.

In this work, we operate in the common reference string (CRS) model where we assume that there is a one-time (trusted) sampling of a structured reference string. Within this model, we focus on the setting where where the proof is non-interactive (i.e., the proof consists of a single message from the prover to the verifier) and publicly-verifiable (i.e., verifying the proof only requires knowledge of the associated statements and the CRS). Finally, we require soundness to hold against computationally-bounded provers; namely, our goal is to construct batch *argument* systems. Recently, there has been a flurry of work constructing batch arguments for NP satisfying these requirements from standard lattice assumptions [CJJ21b, DGKV22], assumptions on groups with bilinear maps [WW22], and from a combination of subexponential hardness of the DDH assumption together with the QR assumption [CJJ21a].

This work: fully succinct batch arguments. The size of the proof in the aforementioned BARG constructions all scale linearly with the size of the NP relation. In other words, to check T statements for an NP relation that is computable by a circuit of size s, the proof sizes scale with $\mathsf{poly}(\lambda, s) \cdot o(T)$, where λ is the security parameter. In this work, we study the setting where the proof π scales *sublinearly* in *both* the number of instances T and the size s of the NP relation. More precisely, we require that $|\pi| = \mathsf{poly}(\lambda, \log s, \log T)$, and we refer to batch arguments satisfying this property to be "fully succinct." Our primary goal in this work is to *minimize* the communication cost (and in conjunction, the verifier cost) of batch NP verification.

We note that this level of succinctness is typically characteristic of succinct non-interactive arguments (SNARGs), and indeed any SNARG directly implies a fully succinct batch argument. However, existing constructions of SNARGs either rely on random oracles [Mic95, BBHR18, COS20, CHM+20, Set20], the generic group model [Gro16], or strong non-falsifiable assumptions [Gro10, BCCT12, DFH12, Lip13, PHGR13, GGPR13, BCI+13, BCPR14, BISW17, BCC+17, BISW18, ACL+22]. Indeed, Gentry and Wichs [GW11] showed that no construction of an (adaptively-sound) SNARG for NP can be proven secure via a black-box reduction to a falsifiable assumption [Nao03].

The only construction of (non-adaptively sound) SNARGs from falsifiable assumptions is the construction by Sahai and Waters based on indistinguishability obfuscation ($i\mathcal{O}$) [SW14] in conjunction with the recent breakthrough works of Jain et al. [JLS21, JLS22] that base indistinguishability obfuscation on falsifiable assumptions. However, the Sahai-Waters SNARG from $i\mathcal{O}$ imposes an *a priori* bound on the number of statements that can be proven, and in particular, the size of the CRS grows with the total length of the statement and witness (i.e., the CRS consists of an obfuscated program that reads in the statement and the witness and outputs a signature on the statements if the input is well-formed). When applied to the setting of batch verification, this limitation means that we need to impose an *a priori* bound of the number of instances that can be proved, and the size of the CRS necessarily scales with this bound. Our goal in this work is to construct a fully succinct batch argument for NP that supports an arbitrary number of instances from indistinguishability obfuscation and one-way functions (i.e., the same assumption as the construction of Sahai and Waters).

An approach using recursive composition. A natural approach to constructing a fully succinct batch argument that supports an arbitrary polynomial number of statements is to compose a SNARG with polylogarithmic verification cost (for a single statement) with a batch argument that supports an unbounded number of statements. Namely, to prove that $(x_1, \ldots, x_T)$ are true, the prover would proceed as follows:

1. First, for each statement $x_i \in \{0,1\}^\ell$, the prover constructs a SNARG proof π_i. If the SNARG has a polylogarithmic verification procedure, then the size of the SNARG verification circuit for checking (x_i, π_i) is bounded by $\mathsf{poly}(\lambda, \ell, \log s)$, where s is the size of the circuit for checking the underlying NP relation.

2. Next, the prover uses a batch argument to demonstrate that it knows $(\pi_1, \ldots, \pi_T)$ where π_i is an accepting SNARG proof on instance $x_i \in \{0,1\}^\ell$. This is a batch argument for checking T instances of the SNARG verification circuit, which has size $\mathsf{poly}(\lambda, \ell, \log s)$. If the size of the batch argument scales polylogarithmically with the number of instances, then the overall proof has size $\mathsf{poly}(\lambda, \ell, \log s, \log T)$.

Moreover, using a somewhere extractable commitment scheme [HW15, CJJ21b], it is possible to remove the dependence on the instance size ℓ.[1] This yields a fully succinct batch argument with proof size $\mathsf{poly}(\lambda, \log s, \log T)$. To argue (non-adaptive) soundness of this approach, we rely on soundness of the underlying SNARG and somewhere extractability of the underlying batch argument (i.e., a BARG where the CRS can be programmed to a specific (hidden) index i^* such that there exists an efficient extractor that takes any accepting proof π for a tuple $(x_1, \ldots, x_T)$ and outputs a valid witness w_{i^*} for instance x_{i^*}). We can now instantiate the SNARG with polylogarithmic verification cost using the Sahai-Waters construction based on $i\mathcal{O}$ and one-way functions, and the somewhere extractable BARG for an unbounded number of instances with the recent lattice-based scheme of Choudhuri et al. [CJJ21b]. This result provides a basic feasibility result for the existence of fully succinct batch arguments for NP. However, instantiating this compiler requires two sets of assumptions: $i\mathcal{O}$ and one-way functions for the underlying SNARG, and lattice-based assumptions for the BARG.

---

[1] One way to do this is to observe that the above approach already gives a fully succinct batch argument for index languages (i.e., a batch language where the $T \le 2^\lambda$ instances are defined to be $(x_1, x_2, \ldots, x_T) = (1, 2, \ldots, T)$). Then, we can apply the index BARG to BARG transformation from Choudhuri et al. [CJJ21b], which relies on somewhere extractable commitments.

This work. In this work, we provide a direct route for constructing fully succinct BARGs that support an unbounded number of statements from $i\mathcal{O}$ and one-way functions. Notably, combined with the breakthrough work of Jain, Lin, and Sahai [JLS22], this provides an instantiation of fully succinct BARGs *without* lattice assumptions (in contrast to the generic approach above). Using our construction, proving T statements for an NP relation of size s requires a proof of length $\mathsf{poly}(\lambda)$. This is *independent* of both the number of statements T and the size s of the associated NP relation. Like the scheme of Sahai and Waters, our construction satisfies *non-adaptive* soundness (and perfect zero-knowledge). We summarize this instantiation in the informal theorem below:

Theorem 1.1 (Fully Succinct BARG (Informal)). *Assuming the existence of indistinguishability obfuscation and one-way functions, there exists a fully succinct, non-adaptively sound batch argument for* NP. *The batch argument satisfies perfect zero knowledge.*

Updatable batch arguments. We also show how to extend our construction to obtain an *updatable* BARG through the use of somewhere statistically binding (SSB) hash functions [HW15, OPWW15]. In an updatable BARG, a prover is able to take an existing proof π_T on statements $(x_1, \ldots, x_T)$ along with a new statement x_{T+1} with associated NP witness w_{T+1} and update π to a new proof π' on instances $(x_1, \ldots, x_T, x_{T+1})$. Notably, the update algorithm does *not* require the prover to have a witness for any statement other than x_{T+1}. This is useful in settings where the full set of statements/witnesses are not fixed in advance (e.g., in a streaming setting). For example, a prover might want to compute a summary of all transactions that occur in a given day and then provide a proof that the summary reflects the complete set of transactions from the day. An updatable BARG would allow the prover to maintain just a single proof that authenticates all of the summary reports from different days, and moreover, the prover does *not* have to maintain the full list of transactions from earlier days to perform the update. We show how to obtain a fully succinct updatable BARG in Sect. 5, and we summarize this instantiation in the following theorem.

Theorem 1.2 (Updatable BARG (Informal)). *Assuming the existence of indistinguishability obfuscation scheme and somewhere statistical binding hash functions, there exists a fully succinct, non-adaptively sound updatable batch argument for* NP. *The batch argument satisfies perfect zero knowledge.*

1.1 Technical Overview

In this section, we provide an informal overview of the techniques that we use to construct fully succinct BARGs. Throughout this section, we consider the batch NP language of Boolean circuit satisfiability. Namely, the prover has a Boolean circuit C and a collection of instances $x_1, \ldots, x_T$, and its goal is to convince the verifier that there exist witnesses $w_1, \ldots, w_T$ such that $C(x_i, w_i) = 1$ for all $i \in [T]$.

The Sahai-Waters SNARG. As a warmup, we recall the Sahai-Waters [SW14] construction of SNARGs from $i\mathcal{O}$ for a single instance (i.e., the case where $T = 1$). In this construction, the common reference string (CRS) consists of two obfuscated programs: Prove and Verify. The Prove program takes in the circuit C, the statement x, and the witness w, and outputs a signature σ_x on x if $C(x, w) = 1$ and $\bot$ otherwise. The proof is simply the signature $\pi = \sigma_x$. The Verify program takes in the description of the circuit C, the statement x, and the proof $\pi = \sigma_x$ and checks whether σ_x is a valid signature on x or not. The signature in this case just corresponds to the evaluation of a pseudorandom function (PRF) on the input x. The key to the PRF is hard-coded in the obfuscated proving and verification programs. Security in turn, relies on the Sahai-Waters "punctured programming" technique.

Batch arguments for index languages. To construct fully succinct batch arguments, we start by considering the special case of an *index language* (similar to the starting point in the lattice-based construction of Choudhuri et al. [CJJ21b]). In a BARG for an index language, the statements are simply the indices $(1, 2, \ldots, T)$. The prover's goal is to convince the verifier that there exists w_i such that $C(i, w_i) = 1$ for all $i \in [T]$. We start by showing how to construct a fully succinct BARG for index languages with an unbounded number of instances (i.e., an index language for arbitrary polynomial T). Our construction proceeds *iteratively* as follows. Like the Sahai-Waters construction, the CRS in our scheme consists of the obfuscation of the following two programs:

- The proving program takes in a circuit C, an index i, a witness w_i for instance i and a proof π for the first $i-1$ statements. The program checks if $C(i, w_i) = 1$ and that the proof on the first $i - 1$ statements is valid. When $i = 1$, then we ignore the latter check. If both conditions are satisfied, the program outputs a signature on statement (C, i). Notably, the size of the prover program only scales with the size of the circuit and the bit-length of the number of instances (instead of linearly with the number of instances).

  Similar to the construction of Sahai and Waters, we define the "signature" on the statement (C, i) to be $\pi = \mathsf{F}(k, (C, i))$, where F is a puncturable PRF [BW13, KPTZ13, BGI14],[2] and k is a PRF key that is hard-coded in the proving program.
- To verify a proof on T statements (i.e., the instances $1, \ldots, T$), the verification program simply checks that the proof π is a valid signature on the pair (C, T). Based on how we defined the proving program above, this corresponds to checking that $\pi = \mathsf{F}(k, (C, T))$. Now, to argue soundness using the Sahai-Waters punctured programming paradigm, we modify this check and replace it with the check

---

[2] A puncturable PRF is a PRF where the holder of the master secret key can "puncture" the key on an input x^*. The resulting punctured key k' can be used to evaluate the PRF on all inputs except x^*. The value of the PRF at x^* remains pseudorandom (i.e., computationally indistinguishable from random) even given the punctured key k'. We provide the formal definition in Definition 2.2.

$$G(\pi) \stackrel{?}{=} G(F(k,(C,T))),$$

where G is a length-doubling pseudorandom generator. This will be critical for arguing soundness.

Soundness of the index BARG. To argue non-adaptive soundness of the above approach (i.e., the setting where the statement is chosen independently of the CRS), we apply the punctured programming techniques of Sahai and Waters [SW14]. Take any circuit C^* and suppose there is an index i^* where for all witnesses w, we have that $C^*(i^*, w) = 0$. Our soundness analysis proceeds in two steps:

- We first show that no efficient prover can compute an accepting proof π on instances $(1, \ldots, i^*)$ for circuit C^*.
- Then, we show how to "propagate" the inability to construct a valid proof on index i^* to all indices $i \geq i^*$. This in turn suffices to argue non-adaptive soundness for an arbitrary polynomial number of statements.

We now sketch the argument for the first step. In the following overview, suppose the output space of F is $\{0,1\}^\lambda$ and suppose that $G\colon \{0,1\}^\lambda \to \{0,1\}^{2\lambda}$ is length-doubling.

- The real CRS consists of obfuscations of the following proving and verification programs:

$\mathsf{Prove}(C, i, w_i, \pi)$:	$\mathsf{Verify}(C, i, \pi)$:
• If $C(i, w_i) = 0$, output $\perp$. • If $i = 1$, output $F(k,(C,i))$. • If $G(\pi) = G(F(k,(C, i-1)))$, output $F(k,(C,i))$. • Output $\perp$.	• If $G(\pi) = G(F(k,(C,i)))$, output 1 • Output 0.

- First, instead of embedding the real PRF key k in the proving and verification programs, we embed a punctured PRF key k' that is punctured on the input (C^*, i^*). Whenever the proving and verification program needs to evaluate F on the punctured point (C^*, i^*), we hard-code the value $z = F(k,(C^*, i^*))$:

$\mathsf{Prove}(C, i, w_i, \pi)$:	$\mathsf{Verify}(C, i, \pi)$:

• If $C(i, w_i) = 0$, output $\perp$.
• If $C = C^*$ and $i = i^*$, output $\perp$.
• If $i = 1$, output $F(k',(C,i))$.
• If $C = C^*$ and $i - 1 = i^*$:
    ∗ If $G(\pi) = G(z)$, output $F(k',(C,i))$.
    ∗ Otherwise, output $\perp$.
• If $G(\pi) = G(F(k',(C, i-1)))$, output $F(k',(C,i))$.
• Output $\perp$.
	• If $C = C^*$ and $i = i^*$, output 1 if $G(\pi) = G(z)$ and 0 otherwise.
	• If $G(\pi) = G(F(k',(C,i)))$, output 1.
	• Output 0.

Since the punctured PRF is functionality-preserving, on all inputs $(C,i) \neq (C^*, i^*)$, we have that $F(k,(C,i)) = F(k',(C,i))$. Since $z = F(k,(C^*,i^*))$, the input/output behavior of the verification program is unchanged. Next, $C(i^*, w) = 0$ for all w, so the input/output behavior of the proving program is also unchanged. Security of $i\mathcal{O}$ then ensures that the obfuscated proving and verification programs are computationally indistinguishable from those in the real scheme.

- Observe that both the proving and verification programs can be constructed given just the value of $G(z)$ *without* necessarily knowing z itself. We now replace the target value $G(z)$ with a uniform random string $t \xleftarrow{R} \{0,1\}^{2\lambda}$. This follows by (1) puncturing security of F which says that the value of $z = F(k, (C^*, i^*))$ is computationally indistinguishable from a uniform string $z \xleftarrow{R} \{0,1\}^\lambda$; and (2) by PRG security since the distribution of $G(z)$ where $z \xleftarrow{R} \{0,1\}^\lambda$ is computationally indistinguishable from sampling a uniform random string $t \xleftarrow{R} \{0,1\}^{2\lambda}$. With these modifications, the proving and verification programs behave as follows:

Prove(C, i, w_i, π):	Verify(C, i, π):

• If $C(i, w_i) = 0$, output $\perp$.
 • If $C = C^*$ and $i = i^*$, output $\perp$.
 • If $i = 1$, output $F(k', (C, i))$.
 • If $C = C^*$ and $i - 1 = i^*$:
  $*$ If $G(\pi) = t$, output $F(k', (C, i))$.
  $*$ Otherwise, output $\perp$.
 • If $G(\pi) = G(F(k', (C, i - 1)))$, output $F(k', (C, i))$.
 • Output $\perp$.
	• If $C = C^*$ and $i = i^*$, output 1 if $G(\pi) = t$ and 0 otherwise.
	 • If $G(\pi) = G(F(k', (C, i)))$, output 1.
	 • Output 0.

- Since t is uniform in $\{0,1\}^{2\lambda}$, the probability that t is even in the image of G is at most $2^{-\lambda}$. Thus, in this experiment, with probability $1 - 2^{-\lambda}$, there does not exist any accepting proof π for input (C^*, i^*). This means that we can now revert to using the PRF key k in both the proving and verification programs and simply reject all proofs on instance (C^*, i^*). In other words, we can replace the proving and verification programs with obfuscations of the following programs by appealing to the security of $i\mathcal{O}$:

Prove(C, i, w_i, π):	Verify(C, i, π):
• If $C(i, w_i) = 0$, output $\perp$. • If $C = C^*$ and $i = i^*$, output $\perp$. • If $i = 1$, output $F(k, (C, i))$. • If $C = C^*$ and $i - 1 = i^*$, output $\perp$. • If $G(\pi) = G(F(k, (C, i - 1)))$, output $F(k', (C, i))$. • Output $\perp$.	• If $C = C^*$ and $i = i^*$, output 0. • If $G(\pi) = G(F(k, (C, i)))$, output 1. • Output 0.

In this final experiment, there no longer exists an accepting proof π on instances $(1, \ldots, i^*)$ for circuit C^*. Next, we show how to extend this argument to *additionally* remove accepting proofs on the batch of instances $(1, \ldots, i^*, i^* + 1)$. We leverage a similar strategy as before:

- We replace the PRF key k with a punctured key k' that is punctured at $(C^*, i^* + 1)$ in both the proving and verification programs. Again, whenever the programs need to compute $F(k, (C^*, i^* + 1))$, we substitute a hard-coded value $z = F(k, (C^*, i^* + 1))$:

Prove(C, i, w_i, π):	Verify(C, i, π):
<ul><li>If $C(i, w_i) = 0$, output $\perp$.</li><li>If $C = C^*$ and $i^* \leq i \leq i^* + 1$, output $\perp$.</li><li>If $i = 1$, output $\mathsf{F}(k', (C, i))$.</li><li>If $C = C^*$ and $i - 1 = i^* + 1$:</li><ul><li>If $\mathsf{G}(\pi) = \mathsf{G}(z)$, output $\mathsf{F}(k', (C, i))$.</li><li>Otherwise, output $\perp$.</li></ul><li>If $\mathsf{G}(\pi) = \mathsf{G}(\mathsf{F}(k', (C, i - 1)))$, output $\mathsf{F}(k', (C, i))$.</li><li>Output $\perp$.</li></ul>	<ul><li>If $C = C^*$, and $i = i^*$, output 0.</li><li>If $C = C^*$, $i = i^* + 1$, output 1 if $\mathsf{G}(\pi) = \mathsf{G}(z)$ and 0 otherwise.</li><li>If $\mathsf{G}(\pi) = \mathsf{G}(\mathsf{F}(k', (C, i)))$, output 1.</li><li>Output 0.</li></ul>

Note that to simplify the notation, we merged the individual checks ($C = C'^*$ and $i = i^*$) and ($C = C^*$ and $i - 1 = i^*$) in the proving program into a single check that outputs $\perp$ if satisfied.

- Observe once again that the description of the proving and verification programs only depends on $\mathsf{G}(z)$ (and *not* z itself). By the same sequence of steps as above, we can appeal to puncturing security of F, pseudorandomness of G, and security of $i\mathcal{O}$ to show that the obfuscated proving and verification programs are computationally indistinguishable from the following programs:

Prove(C, i, w_i, π):	Verify(C, i, π):
<ul><li>If $C(i, w_i) = 0$, output $\perp$.</li><li>If $C = C^*$ and $i^* \leq i \leq i^* + 2$, output $\perp$.</li><li>If $i = 1$, output $\mathsf{F}(\bar{k}, (\bar{C}, i))$.</li><li>If $\mathsf{G}(\pi) = \mathsf{G}(\mathsf{F}(k, (C, i - 1)))$, output $\mathsf{F}(k, (C, i))$.</li><li>Output $\perp$.</li></ul>	<ul><li>If $C = C^*$ and $i^* \leq i \leq i^* + 1$, output 0.</li><li>If $\mathsf{G}(\pi) = \mathsf{G}(\mathsf{F}(k, (\bar{C}, i)))$, output 1.</li><li>Output 0.</li></ul>

We can repeat the above strategy any polynomial number of times. In particular, for any $T = \mathsf{poly}(\lambda)$, we can replace the obfuscated programs in the CRS with the following programs:

Prove(C, i, w_i, π):	Verify(C, i, π):
<ul><li>If $C(i, w_i) = 0$, output $\perp$.</li><li>If $C = C^*$ and $i^* \leq i \leq T + 1$, output $\perp$.</li><li>If $i = 1$, output $\mathsf{F}(\bar{k}, (\bar{C}, i))$.</li><li>If $\mathsf{G}(\pi) = \mathsf{G}(\mathsf{F}(k, (C, i - 1)))$, output $\mathsf{F}(k, (C, i))$.</li><li>Output $\perp$.</li></ul>	<ul><li>If $C = C^*$ and $i^* \leq i \leq T$, output 0.</li><li>If $\mathsf{G}(\pi) = \mathsf{G}(\mathsf{F}(k, (\bar{C}, i)))$, output 1.</li><li>Output 0.</li></ul>

By security of $i\mathcal{O}$, the puncturable PRF, and the PRG, this modified CRS is computationally indistinguishable from the real CRS. However, when the verification program is implemented as above, there are no accepting proofs on input (C^*, i) for any $i^* \leq i \leq T$. Moreover, the size of the obfuscated programs only depends on $\log T$ (and not T). As such, the scheme supports an arbitrary polynomial number of statements. We give the full analysis in Sect. 3.

Adaptive soundness and zero knowledge. Using standard complexity leveraging techniques, we show how to extend our BARG for index languages with non-adaptive soundness into one with adaptive soundness in the full version of this paper. We note that due to the reliance on complexity leveraging, the resulting BARGs we obtain are no longer fully succinct; the proof size now scales with the *size* of the NP relation, but critically, still sublinearly in the number of instances. We also note that much like the construction of Sahai and Waters, both our fully succinct non-adaptive BARG and our adaptive BARG satisfy perfect zero-knowledge.

From index languages to general NP *languages.* Next, we show how to bootstrap our fully succinct BARG for index languages to obtain a fully succinct BARG for NP that supports an arbitrary polynomial number of statements. In this setting, the prover has a Boolean circuit C and *arbitrary* instances $x_1, \ldots, x_T$; the prover's goal is to convince the verifier that for all $i \in [T]$, there exists w_i such that $C(x_i, w_i) = 1$.

The key difference between general NP languages and index languages is that the tuple of statements $(x_1, \ldots, x_T)$ no longer has a succinct description. This property was critical in our soundness analysis above. The soundness argument we described above works by embedding the instances $x_{i^*}, x_{i^*+1}, \ldots, x_T$ into the proving and verification programs (where x_{i^*} denotes a false instance) and have the programs always reject proofs on these statements (with respect to the target circuit C^*). For index languages, these instances just correspond to the interval $[i^* + 1, T]$, which can be described succinctly with $O(\log T)$ bits. When $x_{i^*}, x_{i^*+1}, \ldots, x_T$ are *arbitrary* instances, they do not have a short description, and we cannot embed these instances into the proving and verification programs without imposing an *a priori* bound on the number of instances.

Instead of modifying the above construction, we instead adopt the approach of Choudhuri et al. [CJJ21b] who previously showed how to generically upgrade any BARG for index languages to a BARG for NP by relying on somewhere extractable commitment schemes. If the underlying BARG for index languages supports an unbounded number of instances, then the transformed scheme also does. In our setting, we observe that if we only require (non-adaptive) soundness (as opposed to "somewhere extraction"), we can use a positional accumulator [KLW15] in place of the somewhere extractable commitment scheme. The advantage of basing the transformation on positional accumulators is that we can construct positional accumulators directly from indistinguishability obfuscation and one-way functions. Applied to the above index BARG construction (see also Sect. 3), we obtain a fully succinct batch argument for NP from the *same* set of assumptions. In contrast, if we invoke the compiler of Choudhuri et al., we would need to *additionally* assume the existence of a somewhere extractable commitment scheme which *cannot* be based solely on indistinguishability obfuscation together with one-way functions in a fully black-box way [AS15].

Very briefly, in the Choudhuri et al. approach, to construct a batch argument on the tuple $(C, x_1, \ldots, x_T)$, the prover first computes a succinct hash y of the statements $(x_1, \ldots, x_T)$. Using y, they define an index relation where instance i is satisfied if there exists an opening (x_i, π_i) to y at index i, and moreover, there exists a satisfying witness w_i where $C(x_i, w_i) = 1$. The proof then consists of the hash y and a proof for the index relation. In this work, we show that using a positional accumulator to instantiate the hash function suffices to obtain a BARG with non-adaptive soundness. We provide the full details in Sect. 4.

Updatable BARGs for NP . Our techniques also readily generalize to obtain an updatable batch argument (for general NP) from the same underlying set of assumptions. Recall that in an updatable BARG, a prover can take an existing proof π on a tuple $(C, x_1, \ldots, x_T)$ together with a new statement x_{T+1} and witness w_{T+1} and extend π to a new proof π' on the tuple $(C, x_1, \ldots, x_T, x_{T+1})$. One way to construct an updatable BARG is to recursive compose a succinct non-interactive argument of knowledge [BCCT13] or a rate-1 batch argument [DGKV22].[3] Here, we opt for a more direct approach based on the above techniques, which does not rely on recursive composition.

First, our index BARG construction described above is already updatable. However, if we apply the Choudhuri et al. [CJJ21b] transformation to obtain a BARG for NP, the resulting scheme is no longer updatable. This is because the transformation requires the prover to commit to the complete set of statements and then argue that the statement associated with each index is true (which in turn requires knowledge of all of the associated witnesses).

Instead, we take a different and more direct *tree-based* approach. For ease of exposition, suppose first that $T = 2^k$ for some integer k. Our construction will rely on a hash function H. Given a tuple of T statements $(x_1, \ldots, x_T)$, we construct a binary Merkle hash tree [Mer87] of depth k as follows: the leaves of the tree are labeled $x_1, \ldots, x_T$, and the value of each internal node v is the hash $H(v_1, v_2)$ of its two children v_1 and v_2. The output h of the hash tree is the value at the root node, and we denote this by writing $h = H_{\mathsf{Merkle}}(x_1, \ldots, x_T)$. A proof on the tuple of instances $(x_1, \ldots, x_T)$ is simply a signature on the root node $H_{\mathsf{Merkle}}(x_1, \ldots, x_T)$. Now, instead of providing an obfuscated program that takes a proof on index i and extends it into a proof on index $i + 1$, we define our obfuscated proving program to take in two signatures on hash values $h_1 = H_{\mathsf{Merkle}}(x_1, \ldots, x_T)$ and $h_2 = H_{\mathsf{Merkle}}(y_1, \ldots, y_T)$ and output a signature on the hash value $h = H(h_1, h_2) = H_{\mathsf{Merkle}}(x_1, \ldots, x_T, y_1, \ldots, y_T)$. This new "two-to-one" obfuscated program allows us to merge two proofs on T instances into a single proof on $2T$ instances. More generally, the (obfuscated) proving program in the CRS now supports the following operations:

- **Signing a single instance:** Given a circuit C, a statement x, and a witness w, output a signature on $(C, x, 1)$ if $C(x, w) = 1$ and $\perp$ otherwise. This can be viewed as a signature on a hash tree of depth 1.
- **Merge trees:** Given a circuit C, hashes h_1, h_2 associated with two trees of depth k, along with signatures σ_1, σ_2, check that σ_1 is a valid signature on (C, h_1, k), and σ_2 is a valid signature on (C, h_2, k). If both checks pass, output a signature on $(C, H(h_1, h_2), k+1)$. This is a signature on a hash tree of depth $k + 1$.

To construct a proof on instances $(x_1, \ldots, x_T)$ using witnesses $(w_1, \ldots, w_T)$ for *arbitrary* T, we now proceed as follows:

- Run the (obfuscated) proving algorithm on (C, x_1, w_1) to obtain a signature σ on $(C, x_1, 1)$. The initial proof π is simply the set $\{(1, x_1, \sigma)\}$.

---

[3] If the underlying BARG is not rate-1, then we can only compose a *bounded* number of times.

– Suppose $\pi = \{(i, h_i, \sigma_i)\}$ is a proof on the first $T-1$ statements. To update the proof π to a proof on the first T statements, first run the proving algorithm on (C, x_T, w_T) to obtain a signature σ on $(C, x_T, 1)$. Now, we apply the following merging procedure:

- Initialize $(k, h', \sigma') \leftarrow (1, x_T, \sigma)$ and $\pi' \leftarrow \pi$.
- While there exists $(i, h_i, \sigma_i) \in \pi'$ where $i = k$, run the (obfuscated) merge program on $(C, h_i, h', k, \sigma_i, \sigma')$ to obtain a signature σ'' on $(C, H(h_i, h'), k+1)$. Remove (i, h_i, σ_i) from π' and update $(k, h', \sigma') \leftarrow (k+1, H(h_i, h'), \sigma'')$.
- Add the tuple (k, h', σ'') to π' at the conclusion of the merging process.

Observe that the update procedure only requires knowledge of the new statement x_T, its witness w_T, and the proof on the previous statements π; it does *not* require knowledge of the witnesses to the previous statements. Moreover, observe that the number of hash-signature tuples in π is always bounded by $\log T$.

To verify a proof $\pi = \{(i, h_i, \sigma_i)\}$ with respect to a Boolean circuit C, the verifier checks that σ_i is a valid signature on (C, h_i, i) for all tuples in π, and moreover, that each of the intermediate hash values h_i are correctly computed from $(x_1, \ldots, x_T)$. Non-adaptive soundness of the above construction follows by a similar argument as that for our index BARG. Notably, we show that if an instance x_{i^*} is false, then the proving program will never output a signature on input $(C, x_{i^*}, 1)$. Using the same punctured programming technique sketched above, we can again "propagate" the inability to compute a signature on the leaf node i^* to argue that any efficient prover cannot compute a signature on any node that is an ancestor of x_{i^*} in the hash tree. Here, we will need to rely on the underlying hash function being somewhere statistically binding [HW15, OPWW15]. By a hybrid argument, we can eventually move to an experiment where there are no accepting proofs on tuples that contain x_{i^*}, and soundness follows. We provide the formal description in Sect. 5.

2   Preliminaries

Throughout this work, we write λ to denote the security parameter. We say a function f is negligible in the security parameter λ if $f = o(\lambda^{-c})$ for all $c \in \mathbb{N}$. We denote this by writing $f(\lambda) = \mathsf{negl}(\lambda)$. We write $\mathsf{poly}(\lambda)$ to denote a function that is bounded by a fixed polynomial in λ. We say an algorithm is PPT if it runs in probabilistic polynomial time in the length of its input. By default, we consider *non-uniform* adversaries (indexed by λ) where the algorithm may additionally take in an advice string (of $\mathsf{poly}(\lambda)$ length).

For a positive integer $n \in \mathbb{N}$, we write $[n]$ to denote the set $\{1, \ldots, n\}$ and $[0, n]$ to denote the set $\{0, \ldots, n\}$. For a finite set S, we write $x \xleftarrow{\mathsf{R}} S$ to denote that x is sampled uniformly at random from S. For a distribution $\mathcal{D}$, we write $x \leftarrow \mathcal{D}$ to denote that x is sampled from $\mathcal{D}$. We say an event E occurs with overwhelming probability if its complement occurs with negligible probability.

Some of our constructions in this work will rely on hardness against adversaries running in sub-exponential time or achieving sub-exponential advantage (i.e., success probability). To make this explicit, we formulate our security definitions in the language of (τ, ε)-security, where $\tau = \tau(\lambda)$ and $\varepsilon = \varepsilon(\lambda)$. Here, we say a primitive is (τ, ε)-secure if for all (non-uniform) polynomial time adversaries running in time $\tau(\lambda)$ and all sufficiently large λ, the adversary's advantage is bounded by $\varepsilon(\lambda)$. For ease of exposition, we will also write that a primitive is "secure" (without an explicit (τ, ε) characterization) if for *every* polynomial $\tau = \mathsf{poly}(\lambda)$, there exists a negligible function $\varepsilon(\lambda) = \mathsf{negl}(\lambda)$ such that the primitive is (τ, ε)-secure. We now review the main cryptographic primitives we use in this work.

Definition 2.1 (Indistinguishability Obfuscation [BGI+01]). *An indistinguishability obfuscator for a circuit class $\mathcal{C} = \{\mathcal{C}_\lambda\}_{\lambda \in \mathbb{N}}$ is a PPT algorithm $i\mathcal{O}(\cdot, \cdot)$ with the following properties:*

- **Correctness:** *For all security parameters $\lambda \in \mathbb{N}$, all circuits $C \in \mathcal{C}_\lambda$, and all inputs x,*
$$\Pr[C'(x) = C(x) : C' \leftarrow i\mathcal{O}(1^\lambda, C)] = 1.$$

- **Security:** *We say that $i\mathcal{O}$ is (τ, ε)-secure if for all adversaries $\mathcal{A}$ running in time at most $\tau(\lambda)$, there exists $\lambda_\mathcal{A} \in \mathbb{N}$, such that for all security parameters $\lambda > \lambda_\mathcal{A}$, all pairs of circuits $C_0, C_1 \in \mathcal{C}_\lambda$ where $C_0(x) = C_1(x)$ for all inputs x, we have,*
$$\mathsf{Adv}_\mathcal{A}^{i\mathcal{O}} := \left| \Pr[\mathcal{A}(i\mathcal{O}(1^\lambda, C_0)) = 1] - \Pr[\mathcal{A}(i\mathcal{O}(1^\lambda, C_1)) = 1] \right| \leq \varepsilon(\lambda).$$

Definition 2.2 (Puncturable PRF [BW13, KPTZ13, BGI14]). *A puncturable pseudorandom function family on key space $\mathcal{K} = \{\mathcal{K}_\lambda\}_{\lambda \in \mathbb{N}}$, domain $\mathcal{X} = \{\mathcal{X}_\lambda\}_{\lambda \in \mathbb{N}}$ and range $\mathcal{Y} = \{\mathcal{Y}_\lambda\}_{\lambda \in \mathbb{N}}$ consists of a tuple of PPT algorithms $\Pi_{\mathsf{PPRF}} = (\mathsf{KeyGen}, \mathsf{Eval}, \mathsf{Puncture})$ with the following properties:*

- $\mathsf{KeyGen}(1^\lambda) \to K$: *On input the security parameter λ, the key-generation algorithm outputs a key $K \in \mathcal{K}_\lambda$.*
- $\mathsf{Puncture}(K, S) \to K\{S\}$: *On input the PRF key $K \in \mathcal{K}_\lambda$ and a set $S \subseteq \mathcal{X}_\lambda$, the puncturing algorithm outputs a punctured key $K\{S\} \in \mathcal{K}_\lambda$.*
- $\mathsf{Eval}(K, x) \to y$: *On input a key $K \in \mathcal{K}_\lambda$ and an input $x \in \mathcal{X}_\lambda$, the evaluation algorithm outputs a value $y \in \mathcal{Y}_\lambda$.*

In addition, Π_{PPRF} should satisfy the following properties:

- **Functionality-Preserving:** *For every polynomial $s = s(\lambda)$, every security parameter $\lambda \in \mathbb{N}$, every subset $S \subseteq \mathcal{X}_\lambda$ of size at most s, and every $x \in \mathcal{X}_\lambda \setminus S$,*
$$\Pr[\mathsf{Eval}(K, x) = \mathsf{Eval}(K\{S\}, x) : K \leftarrow \mathsf{KeyGen}(1^\lambda), K\{S\} \leftarrow \mathsf{Puncture}(K, S)] = 1.$$

- **Punctured Pseudorandomness:** *For a bit $b \in \{0, 1\}$ and a security parameter λ, we define the (selective) punctured pseudorandomness game Π_{PPRF}, between an adversary $\mathcal{A}$ and a challenger as follows:*

- *At the beginning of the game, the adversary commits to a set $S \subseteq \mathcal{X}_\lambda$.*
- *The challenger then samples a key $K \leftarrow \mathsf{KeyGen}(1^\lambda)$, constructs the punctured key $K\{S\} \leftarrow \mathsf{Puncture}(K, S)$, and gives $K\{S\}$ to $\mathcal{A}$.*
- *If $b = 0$, the challenger gives the set $\{(x_i, \mathsf{Eval}(K, x_i))\}_{x_i \in S}$ to $\mathcal{A}$. If $b = 1$, the challenger gives the set $\{(x_i, y_i)\}_{x_i \in S}$ where each $y_i \xleftarrow{\mathrm{R}} \mathcal{Y}_\lambda$.*
- *At the end of the game, the adversary outputs a bit $b' \in \{0, 1\}$, which is the output of the experiment.*

We say that Π_{PPRF} satisfies (τ, ε)-punctured security if for all adversaries $\mathcal{A}$ running in time at most $\tau(\lambda)$, there exists $\lambda_\mathcal{A}$ such that for all security parameters $\lambda > \lambda_\mathcal{A}$,

$$|\Pr[b' = 1 : b = 0] - \Pr[b' = 1 : b = 1]| \leq \varepsilon(\lambda)$$

in the punctured pseudorandomness security game.

For ease of notation, we will often write $F(K, x)$ to represent $\mathsf{Eval}(K, x)$.

Definition 2.3 (Pseudorandom Generator). *A pseudorandom generator (PRG) on domain $\mathcal{X} = \{\mathcal{X}_\lambda\}_{\lambda \in \mathbb{N}}$ and range $\mathcal{Y} = \{\mathcal{Y}_\lambda\}_{\lambda \in \mathbb{N}}$ is a deterministic polynomial-time algorithm $\mathsf{PRG} \colon \mathcal{X} \to \mathcal{Y}$. We say that the PRG is (τ, ε)-secure if for all adversaries $\mathcal{A}$ running in time at most $\tau(\lambda)$, there exists $\lambda_\mathcal{A} \in \mathbb{N}$, such that for all security parameters $\lambda > \lambda_\mathcal{A}$, we have,*

$$\mathsf{Adv}_\mathcal{A}^{\mathsf{PRG}} := |\Pr[\mathcal{A}(\mathsf{PRG}(x)) = 1 : x \leftarrow \mathcal{X}_\lambda] - \Pr[\mathcal{A}(y) = 1 : y \leftarrow \mathcal{Y}_\lambda]| \leq \varepsilon(\lambda).$$

2.1 Batch Arguments for NP

We now introduce the notion of a non-interactive batch argument (BARG) for NP. We focus specifically on the language of Boolean circuit satisfiability.

Definition 2.4 (Circuit Satisfiability). *For a Boolean circuit $C \colon \{0, 1\}^\ell \times \{0, 1\}^m \to \{0, 1\}$, and a statement $x \in \{0, 1\}^n$, we define the language of Boolean circuit satisfiability $\mathcal{L}_{\mathsf{CSAT}}$ as follows:*

$$\mathcal{L}_{\mathsf{CSAT}} = \{(C, x) \mid \exists w \in \{0, 1\}^m : C(x, w) = 1\}.$$

Definition 2.5 (Batch Circuit Satisfiability). *For a Boolean circuit $C \colon \{0, 1\}^\ell \times \{0, 1\}^m \to \{0, 1\}$, positive integer $t \in \mathbb{N}$, and statements $x_1, \ldots, x_t \in \{0, 1\}^n$, we define the batch circuit satisfiability language as follows:*

$$\mathcal{L}_{\mathsf{BatchCSAT}, t} = \{(C, x_1, \ldots, x_t) \mid \forall i \in [t], \exists w_i \in \{0, 1\}^m : C(x_i, w_i) = 1\}.$$

Definition 2.6 (Batch Argument for NP). *A batch argument (BARG) for the language of Boolean circuit satisfiability consists of a tuple of PPT algorithms $\Pi_{\mathsf{BARG}} = (\mathsf{Gen}, \mathsf{P}, \mathsf{V})$ with the following properties:*

- $\mathsf{Gen}(1^\lambda, 1^\ell, 1^T, 1^s) \to \mathsf{crs}$: *On input the security parameter λ, a bound on the instance size ℓ, a bound on the number of statements T, and a bound on the circuit size s, the generator algorithm outputs a common reference string crs.*

- $\mathsf{P}(\mathsf{crs}, C, (x_1, \ldots, x_t), (w_1, \ldots, w_t)) \rightarrow \pi$: *On input the common reference string* crs, *a Boolean circuit* $C : \{0,1\}^\ell \times \{0,1\}^m \rightarrow \{0,1\}$, *a list of statements* $x_1, \ldots, x_t \in \{0,1\}^\ell$, *and a list of witnesses* $w_1, \ldots, w_t \in \{0,1\}^m$, *the prove algorithm outputs a proof* π.
- $\mathsf{V}(\mathsf{crs}, C, (x_1, \ldots, x_t), \pi) \rightarrow \{0,1\}$: *On input the common reference string* crs, *a Boolean circuit* $C : \{0,1\}^\ell \times \{0,1\}^m \rightarrow \{0,1\}$, *a list of statements* $x_1, \ldots, x_t \in \{0,1\}^\ell$, *and a proof* π, *the verification algorithm outputs a bit* $b \in \{0,1\}$.

Moreover, the BARG scheme should satisfy the following properties:

- **Completeness:** *For all security parameters* $\lambda \in \mathbb{N}$ *and bounds* $\ell \in \mathbb{N}$, $s \in \mathbb{N}$, $T \in \mathbb{N}$, $t \leq T$, *Boolean circuits* $C : \{0,1\}^\ell \times \{0,1\}^m \rightarrow \{0,1\}$ *of size at most* s, *all statements* $x_1, \ldots, x_t \in \{0,1\}^n$ *and all witnesses* $w_1, \ldots, w_t$ *where* $C(x_i, w_i) = 1$ *for all* $i \in [t]$, *it holds that*

$$\Pr\left[\mathsf{V}(\mathsf{crs}, C, (x_1, \ldots, x_t), \pi) = 1 : \begin{array}{l} \mathsf{crs} \leftarrow \mathsf{Gen}(1^\lambda, 1^\ell, 1^T, 1^s) \\ \pi \leftarrow \mathsf{P}(\mathsf{crs}, C, (x_1, \ldots, x_t), (w_1, \ldots, w_t)) \end{array}\right] = 1.$$

- **Succinctness:** *We require* Π_{BARG} *satisfy two notions of succinctness:*
  - *Succinct proof size: For all* $t \leq T$, *it holds that* $|\pi| = \mathsf{poly}(\lambda, \log t, s)$ *in the completeness experiment defined above. Moreover, we say the proof is* fully succinct *if* $|\pi| = \mathsf{poly}(\lambda, \log t, \log s)$.
  - *Succinct verification time: For all* $t \leq T$, *the running time of the verification algorithm* $\mathsf{V}(\mathsf{crs}, C, (x_1, \ldots, x_t), \pi)$ *is* $\mathsf{poly}(\lambda, t, \ell) + \mathsf{poly}(\lambda, \log t, s)$ *in the completeness experiment defined above.*
- **Soundness:** *We require two succinctness properties:*
  - **Non-adaptive soundness:** *For all polynomials* $T = T(\lambda), s = s(\lambda), \ell = \ell(\lambda), t = t(\lambda)$ *where* $t \leq T$, *and all PPT adversaries* $\mathcal{A}$, *there exists a negligible function* $\mathsf{negl}(\cdot)$ *such that for all* $\lambda \in \mathbb{N}$, *all circuit families* $C = \{C_\lambda\}_{\lambda \in \mathbb{N}}$ *where* $C_\lambda : \{0,1\}^{\ell(\lambda)} \times \{0,1\}^{m(\lambda)} \rightarrow \{0,1\}$ *is a Boolean circuit of size at most* $s(\lambda)$, *and all statements* $x_1, \ldots, x_t \in \{0,1\}^{\ell(\lambda)}$ *where* $(C_\lambda, (x_1, \ldots, x_t)) \notin \mathcal{L}_{\mathsf{BatchCSAT}, t}$,

$$\Pr\left[\mathsf{V}(\mathsf{crs}, C_\lambda, (x_1, \ldots, x_t), \pi) = 1 : \begin{array}{l} \mathsf{crs} \leftarrow \mathsf{Gen}(1^\lambda, 1^\ell, 1^T, 1^s); \\ \pi \leftarrow \mathcal{A}(1^\lambda, \mathsf{crs}, C_\lambda, (x_1, \ldots, x_t)) \end{array}\right] = \mathsf{negl}(\lambda).$$

  - **Adaptive soundness:** *For a security parameters* λ *and bounds* T, ℓ, s, *we define the adaptive soundness experiment between a challenger and an adversary* $\mathcal{A}$ *as follows:*
    * *The challenger samples* $\mathsf{crs} \leftarrow \mathsf{Gen}(1^\lambda, 1^\ell, 1^T, 1^s)$ *and sends* crs *to* $\mathcal{A}$.
    * *Algorithm* $\mathcal{A}$ *outputs a Boolean circuit* $C : \{0,1\}^\ell \times \{0,1\}^m \rightarrow \{0,1\}$ *of size at most* $s(\lambda)$, *statements* $x_1, \ldots, x_t \in \{0,1\}^{\ell(\lambda)}$, *and a proof* π. *Here, we require that* $t \leq T$.
    * *The experiment outputs* $b = 1$ *if* $\mathsf{V}(\mathsf{crs}, C, (x_1, \ldots, x_t), \pi) = 1$ *and* $(C, (x_1, \ldots, x_t)) \notin \mathcal{L}_{\mathsf{BatchCSAT}, T}$. *Otherwise it outputs* $b = 0$.

The scheme satisfies adaptive soundness if for every non-uniform polynomial time adversary $\mathcal{A}$, every polynomial $T = T(\lambda)$,$\ell = \ell(\lambda)$, and $s = s(\lambda)$, there exists a negligible function $\mathsf{negl}(\cdot)$ such that, $\Pr[b = 1] = \mathsf{negl}(\lambda)$ in the adaptive soundness experiment.

- **Perfect zero knowledge**: *The scheme satisfies perfect zero knowledge if there exists a PPT simulator $\mathcal{S}$ such that for all $\lambda \in \mathbb{N}$, all bounds $\ell \in \mathbb{N}$, $T \in \mathbb{N}$, $s \in \mathbb{N}$, all $t \leq T$, all tuples $(C, x_1, \ldots, x_t) \in \mathcal{L}_{\mathsf{BatchCSAT},t}$, and all witnesses $(w_1, \ldots, w_t)$ where $C(x_i, w_i) = 1$ for all $i \in [t]$, the following distributions are identically distributed:*
  - **Real distribution:** *Sample $\mathsf{crs} \leftarrow \mathsf{Gen}(1^\lambda, 1^\ell, 1^T, 1^s)$ and a proof $\pi \leftarrow \mathsf{P}(\mathsf{crs}, C, (x_1, \ldots, x_t), (w_1, \ldots, w_t))$. Output (crs, π).*
  - **Simulated distribution:** *Output $(\mathsf{crs}^*, \pi^*) \leftarrow \mathcal{S}(1^\lambda, 1^\ell, 1^T, 1^s, C, (x_1, \ldots, x_t))$.*

Definition 2.7 (BARGs for Unbounded Statements). *We say that a BARG scheme $\Pi_{\mathsf{BARG}} = (\mathsf{Gen}, \mathsf{P}, \mathsf{V})$ supports an unbounded polynomial of statements if the algorithm Gen in Definition 2.6 runs in time that is $\mathsf{poly}(\lambda, \ell, s, \log T)$, and correspondingly, output a CRS of size $\mathsf{poly}(\lambda, \ell, s, \log T)$. Notably, the dependence on the bound T is polylogarithmic. In this case, we implicitly set $T = 2^\lambda$ as the input to the Gen algorithm. Observe that in this case, the P and V algorithms can now take any arbitrary polynomial number $t = t(\lambda)$ of instances as input where $t \leq 2^\lambda$.*

Batch arguments for index languages. Similar to [CJJ21b], we also consider the special case of batch arguments for index languages. We recall the relevant definitions here.

Definition 2.8 (Batch Circuit Satisfiability for Index Languages). *For a positive integer $t \leq 2^\lambda$, we define the batch circuit satisfiability problem for index languages $\mathcal{L}_{\mathsf{BatchCSATindex},t} = \{(C, t) \mid \forall i \in [t], \exists w_i \in \{0,1\}^m : C(i, w_i) = 1\}$ where $C : \{0,1\}^\lambda \times \{0,1\}^m \rightarrow \{0,1\}$ is a Boolean circuit.[4]*

Definition 2.9 (Batch Arguments for Index Languages). *A BARG for index languages is a tuple of PPT algorithms $\Pi_{\mathsf{IndexBARG}} = (\mathsf{Gen}, \mathsf{P}, \mathsf{V})$ that satisfy Definition 2.7 for the index language $\mathcal{L}_{\mathsf{BatchCSATindex},t}$. Since we are considering index languages, the statements always consist of the indices $(1, \ldots, t)$. As such, we can modify the P and V algorithms in Definition 2.6 to take as input the single index t (of length λ bits) rather than the tuple of statements $(x_1, \ldots, x_t)$. Specifically, we modify the syntax as follows:*

- $\mathsf{P}(\mathsf{crs}, C, t, (w_1, \ldots, w_t)) \rightarrow \pi$: *The prove algorithm takes as input the common reference string crs, a Boolean circuit $C : \{0,1\}^\lambda \times \{0,1\}^m \rightarrow \{0,1\}$, the index $t \in \mathbb{N}$, and a list of witnesses $w_1, \ldots, w_t \in \{0,1\}^m$, and outputs a proof π.*

---

[4] Here, and throughout the exposition, we associate elements of the set $[2^\lambda]$ with their binary representation in $\{0,1\}^\lambda$, and the value 2^λ with the all-zeroes string 0^λ.

- $\mathsf{V}(\mathsf{crs}, C, t, \pi) \to \{0,1\}$: *The verification algorithm takes as input the common reference string* crs, *a Boolean circuit* $C : \{0,1\}^\lambda \times \{0,1\}^m \to \{0,1\}$, *the index* $t \in \mathbb{N}$, *and a proof* π, *and outputs a bit* $b \in \{0,1\}$.

The completeness and zero-knowledge properties are the same as those in Definition 2.6(adapted to the unbounded case where $T = 2^\lambda$). We define soundness analogously, but require that the adversary outputs the statement index t in unary. *Namely, the adversary is still restricted to choosing a polynomially-bounded number of instances $t = \mathsf{poly}(\lambda)$ even if the upper bound on t is $T = 2^\lambda$. For succinctness, we require the following stronger property on the verification time:*

- **Succinct verification time:** *For all $t \le 2^\lambda$, the verification algorithm $\mathsf{V}(\mathsf{crs}, C, t, \pi)$ runs in time $\mathsf{poly}(\lambda, s)$ in the completeness experiment.*

3   Non-Adaptive Batch Arguments for Index Languages

In this section, we show how to construct a batch argument for index languages that can support an arbitrary polynomial number of statements. We show how to obtain a construction with non-adaptive soundness. As described in Sect. 1.1, we include two obfuscated programs in the CRS to enable *sequential* proving and batch verification:

- The proving program takes as input a Boolean circuit $C: \{0,1\}^\lambda \times \{0,1\}^m \to \{0,1\}$, an instance number $i \in [2^\lambda]$, a witness $w \in \{0,1\}^m$ for instance i as well as a proof π for the first $i-1$ instances. The program validates the proof on the first $i-1$ instances and that $C(i, w) = 1$. If both checks pass, then the program outputs a proof for instance i. Otherwise, it outputs $\perp$.
- The verification program takes as input the circuit C, the *final* instance number $t \in [2^\lambda]$, and a proof π. It outputs a bit indicating whether the proof is valid or not. In this case, outputting 1 indicates that π is a valid proof on instances $(1, \dots, t)$.

Construction 3.1 (Batch Argument for Index Languages). Let λ be a security parameter and $s = s(\lambda)$ be a bound on the size of the Boolean circuit. We construct a BARG scheme that supports index languages with up to $T = 2^\lambda$ instances (i.e., which suffices to support an arbitrary polynomial number of instances) and circuits of size at most s. The instance indices will be taken from the set $[2^\lambda]$. For ease of notation, we use the set $[2^\lambda]$ and the set $\{0,1\}^\lambda$ interchangably in the following description. Our construction relies on the following primitives:

- Let PRF be a puncturable PRF with key space $\{0,1\}^\lambda$, domain $\{0,1\}^s \times \{0,1\}^\lambda$ and range $\{0,1\}^\lambda$.
- Let $i\mathcal{O}$ be an indistinguishability obfuscator.
- Let PRG be a pseudorandom generator with domain $\{0,1\}^\lambda$ and range $\{0,1\}^{2\lambda}$.

We define our batch argument $\Pi_{\mathsf{BARG}} = (\mathsf{Gen}, \mathsf{P}, \mathsf{V})$ for index languages as follows:

- $\mathsf{Gen}(1^\lambda, 1^s)$: On input the security parameter λ, and a bound on the circuit size s, the setup algorithm starts by sampling a PRF key $K \leftarrow \mathsf{PRF.Setup}(1^\lambda)$. The setup algorithm then defines the proving program $\mathsf{Prove}[K]$ and the verification program $\mathsf{Verify}[K]$ as follows:
  The setup algorithm constructs $\mathsf{ObfProve} \leftarrow i\mathcal{O}(1^\lambda, \mathsf{Prove}[K])$ and $\mathsf{ObfVerify} \leftarrow i\mathcal{O}(1^\lambda, \mathsf{Verify}[K])$. Note that both the proving circuit $\mathsf{Prove}[K]$ and $\mathsf{Verify}[K]$ are padded to the maximum size of any circuit that appears in the proof of Theorem 3.3. Finally, it outputs the common reference string $\mathsf{crs} = (\mathsf{ObfProve}, \mathsf{ObfVerify})$.
- $\mathsf{P}(\mathsf{crs}, C, (w_1, \ldots, w_t))$: On input $\mathsf{crs} = (\mathsf{ObfProve}, \mathsf{ObfVerify})$, a Boolean circuit $C \colon \{0,1\}^\lambda \times \{0,1\}^m \to \{0,1\}$, and a collection of witnesses $w_1, \ldots, w_t \in \{0,1\}^m$, the prover algorithm does the following:
  - Compute $\pi_1 \leftarrow \mathsf{ObfProve}(C, 1, w_1, \bot)$.
  - For $i = 2, \ldots, t$, compute $\pi_i \leftarrow \mathsf{ObfProve}(C, i, w_i, \pi_{i-1})$.
  - Output π_t.
- $\mathsf{V}(\mathsf{crs}, C, t, \pi)$: On input $\mathsf{crs} = (\mathsf{ObfProve}, \mathsf{ObfVerify})$, a Boolean circuit $C \colon \{0,1\}^\lambda \times \{0,1\}^m \to \{0,1\}$, the instance count $t \in [2^\lambda]$, and a proof $\pi \in \{0,1\}^\lambda$, the verification algorithm outputs $\mathsf{ObfVerify}(C, t, \pi)$.

Completeness and security analysis. We now state the completeness and security properties of Construction 3.1, but defer their proofs to the full version of this paper.

Theorem 3.2 (Completeness). *If $i\mathcal{O}$ is correct, then Construction 3.1 is complete.*

Theorem 3.3 (Soundness). *If PRF is functionality preserving and a secure puncturable PRF, PRG is a secure PRG, and $i\mathcal{O}$ is secure, then Construction 3.1 satisfies non-adaptive soundness.*

Theorem 3.4 (Succinctness). *Construction 3.1 is fully succinct.*

Theorem 3.5 (Zero Knowledge). *Construction 3.1 satisfies perfect zero knowledge.*

Constants: PRF key K
Input: Boolean circuit C of size at most s, instance number $i \in [2^\lambda]$, witness w_i, proof $\pi \in \{0,1\}^\lambda$

1. If $i = 1$ and $C(1, w_1) = 1$, output $\mathsf{PRF.Eval}(K, (C, 1))$.
2. Else if $\mathsf{PRG}(\pi) = \mathsf{PRG}(\mathsf{PRF.Eval}(K, (C, i-1)))$ and $C(i, w_i) = 1$, output $\mathsf{PRF.Eval}(K, (C, i))$.
3. Otherwise, output $\bot$.

Fig. 1. Program $\mathsf{Prove}[K]$

> **Constants:** PRF key K
> **Input:** Boolean circuit C of size at most s, instance count $t \in [2^\lambda]$, proof $\pi \in \{0,1\}^\lambda$
>
> 1. If $\mathsf{PRG}(\pi) = \mathsf{PRG}(\mathsf{PRF.Eval}(K,(C,t)))$, output 1.
> 2. Otherwise, output 0.

Fig. 2. Program $\mathsf{Verify}[K]$

4 Non-Adaptive BARGs for NP from BARGs for Index Languages

In this section, we describe an adaptation of the compiler of Choudhuri et al. [CJJ21b] for upgrading a batch argument for index language to a batch argument for NP. The transformation of Choudhuri et al. relied on somewhere extractable commitments, which can be based on standard lattice assumptions [HW15, CJJ21b] or pairing-based assumptions [WW22]. Here, we show that the same transformation is possible using the positional accumulators introduced by Koppula et al. [KLW15]. The advantage of basing the transformation on positional accumulators is that we can construct positional accumulators directly from indistinguishability obfuscation and one-way functions, so we can apply the transformation to Construction 3.1 from Sect. 3 to obtain a fully succinct batch argument for NP from the *same* set of assumptions. A drawback of using positional accumulators in place of somewhere extractable commitments is that our transformation can only provide *non-adaptive* soundness, whereas the Choudhuri et al. transformation satisfies the stronger notion of *semi-adaptive* somewhere extractability.

Positional accumulators. Like a somewhere statistically binding (SSB) hash function [HW15], a positional accumulator allows a user to compute a short "digest" or "hash" y of a long input $(x_1, \ldots, x_t)$. The scheme supports local openings where the user can open y to the value x_i at any index i with a *short* opening π_i. The security property is that the hash value y is statistically binding at a certain (hidden) index i^*. An important difference between positional accumulators and somewhere statistically binding hash functions is that positional accumulators are statistically binding for the hash y of a *specific* tuple of inputs $(x_1, \ldots, x_t)$ while SSB hash functions are binding for *all* hash values. We give the definition below. Our definition is a simplification of the corresponding definition of Koppula et al. [KLW15, §4] and we summarize the main differences in Remark 4.3.

Definition 4.1 (Positional Accumulators [KLW15, adapted]). *Let $\ell \in \mathbb{N}$ be an input length. A positional accumulator scheme for inputs of length ℓ is a tuple of PPT algorithms $\Pi_{\mathsf{PA}} = (\mathsf{Setup}, \mathsf{SetupEnforce}, \mathsf{Hash}, \mathsf{Open}, \mathsf{Verify})$ with the following properties:*

- Setup$(1^\lambda, 1^\ell) \rightarrow$ pp: *On input the security parameter λ and the input length ℓ, the setup algorithm outputs a set of public parameters* pp.
- SetupEnforce$(1^\lambda, 1^\ell, (x_1, \ldots, x_t), i^*) \rightarrow$ pp: *On input the security parameter λ, an input length ℓ, a tuple of inputs $x_1, \ldots, x_t \in \{0,1\}^\ell$, and an index $i^* \in [t]$, the enforcing setup algorithm outputs a set of public parameters* pp.
- Hash$($pp$, (x_1, \ldots, x_t)) \rightarrow y$: *On input the public parameters* pp, *a tuple of inputs $x_1 \in \{0,1\}^\ell, \ldots, x_t \in \{0,1\}^\ell$, the hash algorithm outputs a value y. This algorithm is deterministic.*
- Open$($pp$, (x_1, \ldots, x_t), i) \rightarrow \pi$: *On input the public parameters* pp, *a tuple of inputs $x_1 \in \{0,1\}^\ell, \ldots, x_t \in \{0,1\}^\ell$ and an index $i \in [t]$, the opening algorithm outputs an opening π.*
- Verify$($pp$, y, x, i, \pi) \rightarrow \{0,1\}$: *On input the public parameters* pp, *a hash value y, an input $x \in \{0,1\}^\ell$, an index $i \in \{0,1\}^\lambda$, and an opening π, the verification algorithm outputs a bit $\{0,1\}$.*

Moreover, the positional accumulator Π_{PA} should satisfy the following properties:

- **Correctness:** *For all security parameters $\lambda \in \mathbb{N}$ and input lengths $\ell \in \mathbb{N}$, all polynomials $t = t(\lambda)$, indices $i \in [t]$, and inputs $x_1, \ldots, x_t \in \{0,1\}^\ell$, it holds that*

$$\Pr\left[\mathsf{Verify}(\mathsf{pp}, y, x_i, i, \pi) = 1 : \begin{array}{l} \mathsf{pp} \leftarrow \mathsf{Setup}(1^\lambda, 1^\ell), \\ y \leftarrow \mathsf{Hash}(\mathsf{pp}, (x_1, \ldots, x_t)), \\ \pi \leftarrow \mathsf{Open}(\mathsf{pp}, (x_1, \ldots, x_t), i) \end{array}\right] = 1.$$

- **Succinctness:** *The length of the hash value y output by* Hash *and the length of the proof π output by* Open *in the completeness experiment satisfy $|y| = \mathsf{poly}(\lambda, \ell)$ and $|\pi| = \mathsf{poly}(\lambda, \ell)$.*
- **Setup indistinguishability:** *For a security parameter λ, a bit $b \in \{0,1\}$, and an adversary $\mathcal{A}$, we define the setup-indistinguishability experiment as follows:*
  - *Algorithm $\mathcal{A}$ starts by choosing inputs $x_1, \ldots, x_t \in \{0,1\}^\ell$, and an index $i \in [t]$.*
  - *If $b = 0$, the challenger samples* pp $\leftarrow$ Setup$(1^\lambda, 1^\ell)$. *Otherwise, if $b = 1$, the challenger samples* pp $\leftarrow$ SetupEnforce$(1^\lambda, 1^\ell, (x_1, \ldots, x_t), i)$. *It gives* pp *to $\mathcal{A}$.*
  - *Algorithm $\mathcal{A}$ outputs a bit $b' \in \{0,1\}$, which is the output of the experiment.*

  We say that Π_{PA} satisfies (τ, ε)-setup-indistinguishability if for all adversaries running in time $\tau = \tau(\lambda)$, there exists $\lambda_{\mathcal{A}} \in \mathbb{N}$ such that for all $\lambda > \lambda_{\mathcal{A}}$

  $$|\Pr[b' = 1 \mid b = 0] - \Pr[b' = 1 \mid b = 1]| \leq \varepsilon(\lambda).$$

  in the setup-indistinguishability experiment.
- **Enforcing:** *Fix a security parameter $\lambda \in \mathbb{N}$, block size $\ell \in \mathbb{N}$, a polynomial $t = t(\lambda)$, an index $i^* \in [t]$, and a set of inputs $x_1, \ldots, x_t$. We say that a set of public parameters* pp *are "enforcing" for a tuple $(x_1, \ldots, x_t, i^*)$ if there does not exist a pair (x, π) where $x \neq x_{i^*}$,* Verify$($pp$, y, x, i^*, \pi) = 1$, *and*

$y \leftarrow \mathsf{Hash}(\mathsf{pp}, (x_1, \ldots, x_t))$. *We say that the positional accumulator is enforcing if for every polynomial* $\ell = \ell(\lambda)$, $t = t(\lambda)$, *index* $i^* \in [t]$ *and inputs* $x_1, \ldots, x_t \in \{0,1\}^\ell$, *there exists a negligible function* $\mathsf{negl}(\cdot)$ *such that for all* $\lambda \in \mathbb{N}$,

$$\Pr[\mathsf{pp} \text{ is "enforcing" for } (x_1, \ldots, x_T, i^*) :$$
$$\mathsf{pp} \leftarrow \mathsf{SetupEnforce}(1^\lambda, 1^\ell, (x_1, \ldots, x_t), i^*)] \geq 1 - \mathsf{negl}(\lambda),$$

where the probability is taken over the random coins of $\mathsf{SetupEnforce}$.

Theorem 4.2 (Positional Accumulators [KLW15]). *Assuming the existence of an indistinguishability obfuscation scheme and one-way functions, there exists a positional accumulator for arbitrary polynomial input lengths* $\ell = \ell(\lambda)$.

Remark 4.3 (Comparison with [KLW15]). Definition 4.1 describes a simplified variant of the positional accumulator from Koppula et al. [KLW15, §4]. Specifically, we instantiate their construction with an (implicit) bound of $T = 2^\lambda$ for the number of values that can be accumulated. The positional accumulators from Koppula et al. also supports insertions (i.e., "writes") to the accumulator structure, whereas in our setting, all of the inputs are provided upfront (as an input to Hash).

Construction 4.4 (Batch Argument for NP Languages). Let λ be a security parameter and $s = s(\lambda)$ be a bound on the size of the Boolean circuit. We construct a BARG scheme that supports arbitrary NP languages with up to $T = 2^\lambda$ instances (i.e., which suffices to support an arbitrary polynomial number of instances) and Boolean circuits of size at most s. For ease of notation, we use the set $[2^\lambda]$ and the set $\{0,1\}^\lambda$ interchangably in the following description. Our construction relies on the following primitives:

- Let $\Pi_{\mathsf{PA}} = (\mathsf{PA.Setup}, \mathsf{PA.SetupEnforce}, \mathsf{PA.Hash}, \mathsf{PA.Open}, \mathsf{PA.Verify})$ be a positional accumulator for inputs of length ℓ.
- Let $\Pi_{\mathsf{IndexBARG}} = (\mathsf{IndexBARG.Gen}, \mathsf{IndexBARG.P}, \mathsf{IndexBARG.V})$ be a BARG for index languages (that supports up to $T = 2^\lambda$ instances).[5]

We define our batch argument $\Pi_{\mathsf{BARG}} = (\mathsf{Gen}, \mathsf{P}, \mathsf{V})$ for batch circuit satisfiability languages as follows:

- $\mathsf{Gen}(1^\lambda, 1^\ell, 1^s)$: On input the security parameter λ, the statement length ℓ, and a bound on the circuit size s, sample $\mathsf{pp} \leftarrow \mathsf{PA.Setup}(1^\lambda, 1^\ell)$. Let s' be a bound on the size of the following circuit:
  Then, sample $\mathsf{IndexBARG.crs} \leftarrow \mathsf{IndexBARG.Gen}(1^\lambda, 1^{s'})$. Output the common reference string $\mathsf{crs} = (\mathsf{pp}, \mathsf{IndexBARG.crs})$.

---

[5] Our transformation also applies in the setting where the number of instances is bounded and the transformed scheme inherits the same bound. For simplicity of exposition, we just describe the transformation for the unbounded case.

Constants: Public parameters pp for Π_{PA}, a hash value h (for Π_{PA}), and a Boolean circuit C of size at most s
Inputs: Index $i \in \{0,1\}^\lambda$, a tuple (x, σ, w) where $x \in \{0,1\}^\ell$

1. If $C(x, w) = 0$, output 0.
2. If PA.Verify(pp, h, x, i, σ) = 0, output 0.
3. Otherwise, output 1.

Fig. 3. The Boolean circuit $C'[\mathsf{pp}, h, C]$ for an index relation

- P(crs, $C, (x_1, \ldots, x_t), (w_1, \ldots, w_t)$): On input the common reference string crs $=$ (pp, IndexBARG.crs), a Boolean circuit $C \colon \{0,1\}^\ell \times \{0,1\}^m \to \{0,1\}$, statements $x_1, \ldots, x_t \in \{0,1\}^\ell$, and witnesses $w_1, \ldots, w_t \in \{0,1\}^m$, compute $h \leftarrow$ PA.Hash(pp, $(x_1, \ldots, x_t)$). Then, for each $i \in [t]$, let $\sigma_i \leftarrow$ PA.Open(pp, $(x_1, \ldots, x_t), i$) and let $w_i' = (x_i, \sigma_i, w_i)$. Output $\pi \leftarrow$ IndexBARG.P(IndexBARG.crs, $C'[\mathsf{pp}, h, C], t, (w_1', \ldots, w_t')$), where $C'[\mathsf{pp}, h, C]$ is the circuit for the index relation from Fig. 3.
- V(crs, $C, (x_1, \ldots, x_t), \pi$): On input the common reference string crs $=$ (pp, IndexBARG.crs), the Boolean circuit $C \colon \{0,1\}^\ell \times \{0,1\}^m \to \{0,1\}$, instances $x_1, \ldots, x_t \in \{0,1\}^\ell$, and a proof π, the verification algorithm computes $h \leftarrow$ PA.Hash(pp, $(x_1, \ldots, x_t)$) and outputs IndexBARG.V(IndexBARG.crs, $C'[\mathsf{pp}, h, C], t, \pi$), where $C'[\mathsf{pp}, h, C]$ is the circuit for the index relation from Fig. 3.

Completeness and security analysis. We now state the completeness and security properties of Construction 4.4, but defer their formal analysis to the full version of this paper.

Theorem 4.5 (Completeness). *If $\Pi_{\mathsf{IndexBARG}}$ is complete and Π_{PA} is correct, then Construction 4.4 is complete.*

Theorem 4.6 (Soundness). *Suppose $\Pi_{\mathsf{IndexBARG}}$ satisfies non-adaptive soundness, Π_{PA} satisfies setup-indistinguishability and is enforcing. Then, Construction 4.4 satisfies non-adaptive soundness.*

Theorem 4.7 (Succinctness). *If $\Pi_{\mathsf{IndexBARG}}$ is succinct (resp., fully succinct), Π_{PA} is efficient, then Construction 4.4 is succinct (resp., fully succinct).*

Theorem 4.8 (Zero Knowledge). *If $\Pi_{\mathsf{IndexBARG}}$ is perfect zero-knowledge, then Construction 4.4 is perfect zero-knowledge.*

Remark 4.9 (Weaker Notions of Zero Knowledge). If $\Pi_{\mathsf{IndexBARG}}$ satisfies computational (resp., statistical) zero-knowledge, then Construction 4.4 satisfies computational (resp., statistical) zero-knowledge. In other words, Construction 4.4 preserves the zero-knowledge property on the underlying index BARG.

5   Updatable Batch Argument for NP

We say that a BARG scheme is *updatable* if it supports an *a priori* unbounded number of statements (see Definition 2.7) and the prover algorithm is updatable. Formally, we replace the prover algorithm P in the BARG with an UpdateP algorithm. The UpdateP algorithm takes in statements $(x_1, \ldots, x_t)$, a proof π_t on these t statements, a new statement x_{t+1}, along with an associated witness w_{t+1}, and outputs an "updated" proof π_{t+1} on the new set of statements $(x_1, \ldots, x_{t+1})$. The updated proof should continue to satisfy the same succinctness requirements as before. We give the formal definition below:

Definition 5.1 (Updatable BARGs). *An updatable batch argument (BARG) for the language of Boolean circuit satisfiability consists of a tuple of PPT algorithms $\Pi_{\mathsf{BARG}} = (\mathsf{Gen}, \mathsf{UpdateP}, \mathsf{V})$ with the following properties:*

– $\mathsf{Gen}(1^\lambda, 1^\ell, 1^s) \to \mathsf{crs}$: *On input the security parameter $\lambda \in \mathbb{N}$, a bound on the instance size $\ell \in \mathbb{N}$, and a bound on the maximum circuit size $s \in \mathbb{N}$, the generator algorithm outputs a common reference string crs.*

– $\mathsf{UpdateP}(\mathsf{crs}, C, (x_1, \ldots, x_t), \pi_t, x_{t+1}, w_{t+1}) \to \pi_{t+1}$: *On input the common reference string crs, a Boolean circuit $C \colon \{0,1\}^\ell \times \{0,1\}^m \to \{0,1\}$, a list of statements $x_1, \ldots, x_t \in \{0,1\}^\ell$, a proof π_t, a new statement $x_{t+1} \in \{0,1\}^\ell$ and witness $w_{t+1} \in \{0,1\}^m$, the update algorithm outputs an updated proof π_{t+1}. Note that the list of statements $(x_1, \ldots, x_t)$ is allowed to be empty. We will write $\perp$ to denote an empty list of statements.*

– $\mathsf{V}(\mathsf{crs}, C, (x_1, \ldots, x_t), \pi) \to b$: *On input the common reference string crs, a Boolean circuit $C \colon \{0,1\}^\ell \times \{0,1\}^m \to \{0,1\}$, a list of statements $x_1, \ldots, x_t \in \{0,1\}^\ell$, and a proof π, the verification algorithm outputs a bit $b \in \{0,1\}$.*

An updatable BARG scheme should satisfy the following properties:

– **Completeness:** *For every security parameter $\lambda \in \mathbb{N}$ and bounds $t \in \mathbb{N}$, $\ell \in \mathbb{N}$, and $s \in \mathbb{N}$, Boolean circuits $C \colon \{0,1\}^\ell \times \{0,1\}^m \to \{0,1\}$ of size at most s, any collection of statements $x_1, \ldots, x_t \in \{0,1\}^\ell$ and associated witnesses $w_1, \ldots, w_t \in \{0,1\}^m$ where $C(x_i, w_i) = 1$ for all $i \in [t]$, we have that*

$$\Pr\left[\forall i \in [t] : \mathsf{V}(\mathsf{crs}, C, (x_1, \ldots, x_i), \pi_i) = 1 : \begin{array}{c} \mathsf{crs} \leftarrow \mathsf{Gen}(1^\lambda, 1^\ell, 1^s), \pi_0 \leftarrow \perp, \\ \pi_i \leftarrow \mathsf{UpdateP}(\mathsf{crs}, C, (x_1, \ldots, x_{i-1}), \pi_{i-1}, x_i, w_i) \\ \text{for all } i \in [t] \end{array} \right] = 1.$$

– **Succinctness:** *Similar to Definition 2.6, we require two succinctness properties:*
  - *Succinct proof size: There exists a universal polynomial $\mathsf{poly}(\cdot, \cdot, \cdot)$, such that for every $i \in [t]$, $|\pi_i| = \mathsf{poly}(\lambda, \log i, s)$ in the completeness experiment above.*
  - *Succinct verification time: There exists a universal polynomial $\mathsf{poly}(\cdot, \cdot, \cdot)$ such that for all $i \in [t]$, the verification algorithm $\mathsf{V}(\mathsf{crs}, C, (x_1, \ldots, x_i), \pi_i)$ runs in time $\mathsf{poly}(\lambda, i, \ell) + \mathsf{poly}(\lambda, \log i, s)$ in the completeness experiment above.*

– **Soundness:** *The soundness definition is defined exactly as in Definition 2.6.*

– **Perfect zero knowledge:** *The zero-knowledge definition is defined exactly as in Definition 2.6.*

5.1   Updatable BARGs for NP from Indistinguishability Obfuscation

We now give a direct construction of an updatable batch argument for NP languages from indistinguishability obfuscation together with somewhere statistically binding (SSB) hash functions [HW15]. We start with a construction that provides non-adaptive soundness. We then show to use complexity leveraging to obtain a construction with adaptive soundness.

Two-to-one somewhere statistically binding hash functions. Our construction will rely on a two-to-one somewhere statistically binding (SSB) hash function [OPWW15]. Informally, a two-to-one SSB hash function hashes two input blocks to an output whose size is comparable to the size of a single block. We recall the definition below:

Definition 5.2 (Two-to-One Somewhere Statistically Binding Hash Function [OPWW15]). *Let λ be a security parameter. A two-to-one somewhere statistically binding (SSB) hash function with block size $\ell_{\mathsf{blk}} = \ell_{\mathsf{blk}}(\lambda)$ and output size $\ell_{\mathsf{out}} = \ell_{\mathsf{out}}(\lambda, \ell_{\mathsf{blk}})$ is a tuple of efficient algorithms $\Pi_{\mathsf{SSB}} = (\mathsf{Gen}, \mathsf{GenTD}, \mathsf{LocalHash})$ with the following properties:*

- $\mathsf{Gen}(1^\lambda, 1^{\ell_{\mathsf{blk}}}) \to \mathsf{hk}$: *On input the security parameter λ and the block size ℓ_{blk}, the generator algorithm outputs a hash key hk.*
- $\mathsf{GenTD}(1^\lambda, 1^{\ell_{\mathsf{blk}}}, i^*) \to \mathsf{hk}$: *On input a security parameter λ, a block size ℓ_{blk}, and an index $i^* \in \{0, 1\}$, the trapdoor generator algorithm outputs a hash key hk.*
- $\mathsf{LocalHash}(\mathsf{hk}, x_0, x_1) \to y$: *On input a hash key hk and two inputs $x_0, x_1 \in \{0, 1\}^{\ell_{\mathsf{blk}}}$, the hash algorithm outputs a hash $y \in \{0, 1\}^{\ell_{\mathsf{out}}}$.*

Moreover, Π_{SSB} should satisfy the following requirements:

- **Succinctness:** *The output length ℓ_{out} satisfies $\ell_{\mathsf{out}}(\lambda, \ell_{\mathsf{blk}}) = \ell_{\mathsf{blk}} \cdot (1 + 1/\Omega(\lambda)) + \mathsf{poly}(\lambda)$.*
- **Index hiding:** *For a security parameter λ, a bit $b \in \{0, 1\}$, and an adversary $\mathcal{A}$, we define the index-hiding experiment as follows:*
  - *Algorithm $\mathcal{A}$ starts by choosing a block size ℓ_{blk}, and an index $i \in \{0, 1\}$.*
  - *If $b = 0$, the challenger samples $\mathsf{hk}_0 \leftarrow \mathsf{Gen}(1^\lambda, 1^{\ell_{\mathsf{blk}}})$. Otherwise, if $b = 1$, the challenger samples $\mathsf{hk}_1 \leftarrow \mathsf{GenTD}(1^\lambda, 1^{\ell_{\mathsf{blk}}}, i)$. It gives hk_b to $\mathcal{A}$.*
  - *Algorithm $\mathcal{A}$ outputs a bit $b' \in \{0, 1\}$, which is the output of the experiment.*
  We say that Π_{SSB} satisfies (τ, ε)-index-hiding, if for all adversaries running in time $\tau = \tau(\lambda)$, there exists $\lambda_{\mathcal{A}} \in \mathbb{N}$ such that for all $\lambda > \lambda_{\mathcal{A}}$, $|\Pr[b' = 1 \mid b = 0] - \Pr[b' = 1 \mid b = 1]| \le \varepsilon(\lambda)$ in the index-hiding experiment.
- **Somewhere statistically binding:** *Let $\lambda \in \mathbb{N}$ be a security parameter and $\ell \in \mathbb{N}$ be an input length. We say a hash key hk is "statistically binding" at index $i \in \{0, 1\}$, if there does not exist two inputs (x_0, x_1) and (x_0^*, x_1^*) such that $x_i^* \ne x_i$ and $\mathsf{Hash}(\mathsf{hk}, (x_0, x_1)) = \mathsf{Hash}(\mathsf{hk}, (x_0^*, x_1^*))$. We then say that the hash function is somewhere statistically binding if for all polynomials $\ell_{\mathsf{blk}} = \ell_{\mathsf{blk}}(\lambda)$, there exists a negligible function $\mathsf{negl}(\cdot)$ such that for all indices $i^* \in \{0, 1\}$ and all $\lambda \in \mathbb{N}$,*

$$\Pr[\mathsf{hk} \text{ is statistically binding at index } i : \mathsf{hk} \leftarrow \mathsf{GenTD}(1^\lambda, 1^{\ell_{\mathsf{blk}}}, i)] \ge 1 - \mathsf{negl}(\lambda).$$

Theorem 5.3 (Somewhere   Statistically-Binding   Hash   Functions [OPWW15]). *Under standard number-theoretic assumptions (e.g., DDH, DCR, LWE, or ϕ-Hiding), there exists a two-to-one somewhere statistically binding hash function for arbitrary polynomial block size $\ell_{\mathsf{blk}} = \ell_{\mathsf{blk}}(\lambda)$.*

Notation. Our updatable BARG construction uses a tree-based construction. Before describing the construction, we introduce some notation. First, for an integer $t < 2^d$, we write $\mathsf{bin}_d(t) \in \{0,1\}^d$ to denote the d-bit binary representation of t. For two strings $\mathsf{ind} \in \{0,1\}^*$, $\mathsf{ind}' \in \{0,1\}^*$, let $\mathsf{pad}(\mathsf{ind})$ and $\mathsf{pad}(\mathsf{ind}')$ be the respective strings padded with zeros to the length $\max\{|\mathsf{ind}|, |\mathsf{ind}'|\}$. We say $\mathsf{ind} \le \mathsf{ind}'$ if $\mathsf{pad}(\mathsf{ind})$ comes before $\mathsf{pad}(\mathsf{ind}')$ lexicographically. For strings $s_1, s_2 \in \{0,1\}^*$, we write $s_1\|s_2$ to denote their concatenation. We say that a string $x \in \{0,1\}^*$ is a prefix of a string $y \in \{0,1\}^*$ if there exists a string $z \in \{0,1\}^*$ such that $y = x\|z$.

Binary trees. A binary tree Γ of height d consists of nodes where each node is indexed by a binary string of length at most d. We now define a recursive labeling scheme for the nodes of the tree; subsequently, we will refer to nodes by their labels.

– **Root node:** The root node is labeled with the empty string ε.
– **Child nodes:** The left child of node ind has label $\mathsf{ind}\|0$ and the right child has label $\mathsf{ind}\|1$. We also say that node $\mathsf{ind}\|0$ is the "left sibling" of the node $\mathsf{ind}\|1$.

We define the *level* of a node ind by $\mathsf{level}(\mathsf{ind}) = d - |\mathsf{ind}|$. In particular, the root node is at level d while the leaf nodes are at level 0. We write $\{0,1\}^{\le d}$ to denote the set of node labels associated in the binary tree (i.e., the set of all binary strings of length at most d). Finally, we can also associate each node in the binary tree with a value; formally, for a binary tree Γ we write $\mathsf{val}(\mathsf{ind})$ to denote the value associated with the node ind. When we write $(\Gamma, \mathsf{val}(\cdot))$, we imply our binary tree has been initialized with the corresponding value function. Finally, we define the notion of a "path" and a "frontier" of a node in a binary tree Γ:

– **Path of a node:** We define the path associated with a node $\mathsf{ind} \in \{0,1\}^{\le d}$ as
$$\mathsf{path}(\mathsf{ind}) = \{\mathsf{ind}' \mid \mathsf{ind}' \in \{0,1\}^{\le d} \text{ and } \mathsf{ind}' \text{ is a prefix of } \mathsf{ind}\}.$$

Namely, $\mathsf{path}(\mathsf{ind})$ consists of the nodes along the path from the root to ind.
– **Frontier of a node:** For any $\mathsf{ind} \in \{0,1\}^{\le d}$, we define
$$\mathsf{frontier}(\mathsf{ind}) = \{\mathsf{ind}\} \cup \{\mathsf{ind}' \in \{0,1\}^{\le d} \mid \mathsf{ind}' \text{ is a left sibling of a node in } \mathsf{path}(\mathsf{ind})\}.$$

Construction 5.4 (Non-Adaptive Updatable Batch Argument for NP). Let λ be a security parameter, $\ell = \ell(\lambda)$ be the statement size, and $s = s(\lambda)$ be a bound on the size of the Boolean circuit. We construct an updatable BARG

Constants: PRF key K, hash keys $\mathsf{hk} = (\mathsf{hk}_1, \ldots, \mathsf{hk}_d)$
Input: Boolean circuit $C\colon \{0,1\}^\ell \times \{0,1\}^m \to \{0,1\}$ of size at most s, node values $h_1, h_2 \in \{0,1\}^{\le \ell_{\max}}$, index $\mathsf{ind} \in \{0,1\}^{\le d}$, and proofs $\pi_1, \pi_2 \in \{0,1\}^{\le \max(m,\lambda)}$

1. If $\mathsf{ind} \in \{0,1\}^d$ (i.e., a leaf in the binary tree),
   (a) Parse h_1 as a statement $x_1 \in \{0,1\}^\ell$ and π_1 as a witness $w_1 \in \{0,1\}^m$.
   (b) If $C(x_1, w_1) \ne 1$, output $\perp$. Otherwise, output $\mathsf{PRF.Eval}(K, (C, x_1, \mathsf{ind}))$.
2. Otherwise, if $\mathsf{ind} \in \{0,1\}^{<d}$ (i.e., an internal node in the binary tree),
   (a) Let $d' = \mathsf{level}(\mathsf{ind})$ and compute $h \leftarrow \mathsf{SSB.LocalHash}(\mathsf{hk}_{d'}, h_1, h_2)$.
   (b) Check the following conditions:
     - $\mathsf{PRG}(\pi_1) = \mathsf{PRG}(\mathsf{PRF.Eval}(K, (C, h_1, \mathsf{ind}\|0)))$;
     - $\mathsf{PRG}(\pi_2) = \mathsf{PRG}(\mathsf{PRF.Eval}(K, (C, h_2, \mathsf{ind}\|1)))$.

     If either check fails, output $\perp$. Otherwise, output $\mathsf{PRF.Eval}(K, (C, h, \mathsf{ind}))$.

Fig. 4. Program $\mathsf{Prove}[K, \mathsf{hk}]$

scheme that supports NP languages with up to $T = 2^\lambda$ instances of length ℓ and circuit size at most s. Note that setting $T = 2^\lambda$ means the construction support an arbitrary polynomial number of instances. Our construction relies on the following primitives:

- Let $\Pi_{\mathsf{SSB}} = (\mathsf{SSB.Gen}, \mathsf{SSB.GenTD}, \mathsf{SSB.LocalHash})$ be a two-to-one somewhere statistically binding hash function with output length $\ell_{\mathsf{out}} = \ell_{\mathsf{out}}(\lambda, \ell_{\mathsf{blk}})$, where ℓ_{blk} denotes the block length. Our construction will consider a binary tree of depth $d = \lambda$, and we define a sequence of block lengths $\ell_0, \ldots, \ell_d$ where $\ell_0 = \ell$ and for $j \in [d]$, let $\ell_j = \ell_{\mathsf{out}}(\lambda, \ell_{j-1})$.[6] Let $\ell_{\max} = \max(\ell_0, \ldots, \ell_j)$.
- Let $\Pi_{\mathsf{PRF}} = (\mathsf{PRF.Setup}, \mathsf{PRF.Puncture}, \mathsf{PRF.Eval})$ be a puncturable PRF with key space $\{0,1\}^\lambda$, domain $\{0,1\}^{\le s} \times \{0,1\}^{\le \ell_{\max}} \times \{0,1\}^d$ and range $\{0,1\}^\lambda$.
- Let $i\mathcal{O}$ be an indistinguishability obfuscator for general circuits.
- Let PRG be a pseudorandom generator with domain $\{0,1\}^\lambda$ and range $\{0,1\}^{2\lambda}$.

We define our updatable batch argument $\Pi_{\mathsf{BARG}} = (\mathsf{Gen}, \mathsf{UpdateP}, \mathsf{Verify})$ for NP languages as follows:

- $\mathsf{Gen}(1^\lambda, 1^\ell, 1^s)$: On input the security parameter λ, the statement size ℓ, and a bound on the circuit size s, the setup algorithm starts by sampling a PRF key $K \leftarrow \mathsf{PRF.Setup}(1^\lambda)$. For $j \in [d]$, sample $\mathsf{hk}_j \leftarrow \mathsf{SSB.Gen}(1^\lambda, 1^{\ell_{j-1}})$, Let $\mathsf{hk} \leftarrow (\mathsf{hk}_1, \ldots, \mathsf{hk}_d)$ and define the proving program $\mathsf{Prove}[K, \mathsf{hk}]$ and the

---

[6] Formally, our hash function will take inputs in $\{0,1\}^{\ell_{j-1}} \cup \{\perp\}$. For ease of exposition, we drop the special input symbol $\perp$ in our block length description.

Constants: PRF key K
Input: Boolean circuit C of size at most s, node value $h \in \{0,1\}^{\le \ell_{\max}}$, index ind $\in \{0,1\}^{\le d}$, a proof $\pi \in \{0,1\}^{\lambda}$

1. Output 1 if $\mathsf{PRG}(\pi) = \mathsf{PRG}(\mathsf{PRF.Eval}(K,(C,h,\mathsf{ind})))$ and 0 otherwise.

Fig. 5. Program Verify$[K]$

verification program Verify$[K]$ as follows:
The setup algorithm obfuscates the above programs to obtain ObfProve $\leftarrow i\mathcal{O}(1^{\lambda}, \mathsf{Prove}[K, \mathsf{hk}])$ and ObfVerify $\leftarrow i\mathcal{O}(1^{\lambda}, \mathsf{Verify}[K])$. Note that both the proving circuit Prove$[K, \mathsf{hk}]$ and Verify$[K]$ are padded to the maximum size of any circuit that appears in the proof of Theorem 5.6. Finally, it outputs the common reference string crs = (ObfProve, ObfVerify, hk).

– UpdateP(crs, $C, (x_1, \dots, x_t), \pi_t, x_{t+1}, w_{t+1}$): On input a common reference string crs = (ObfProve, ObfVerify, hk), a Boolean circuit $C: \{0,1\}^{\ell} \times \{0,1\}^m \to \{0,1\}$, a set of statements $x_1, \dots, x_t, x_{t+1} \in \{0,1\}^{\ell}$, a proof $\pi_t = \{(\mathsf{ind}, \pi_{\mathsf{ind}})\}_{\mathsf{ind} \in \mathcal{I}}$ on the first t statements where $\mathcal{I} \subset \{0,1\}^{\le d}$, and a witness $w_{t+1} \in \{0,1\}^m$, the update algorithm proceeds as follows:

1. If $t = 0$, let $\mathsf{ind}^{(1)} = \mathsf{bin}_d(0) = 0^d$. Let $\pi \leftarrow \mathsf{ObfProve}(C, x_1, \bot, \mathsf{ind}^{(1)}, w_1, \bot)$ and output $\{(\mathsf{ind}^{(1)}, \pi)\}$.

2. Otherwise, if $t \ne 0$, the update algorithm computes $\mathsf{ind}^{(t)} = \mathsf{bin}_d(t-1)$ and checks that $\mathsf{frontier}(\mathsf{ind}^{(t)}) = \mathcal{I}$. If the check fails, then the update algorithm outputs $\bot$.

3. Next, the update algorithm constructs a binary tree $(\Gamma_{\mathsf{hash}}, \mathsf{val}_{\mathsf{hash}}) \leftarrow \mathsf{Hash}[\mathsf{hk}](x_1, \dots, x_t)$ of depth d whose values correspond to the statements $(x_1, \dots, x_t)$ and their hashes. Specifically, we define the Hash$[\mathsf{hk}]$ function as follows:
   Essentially, Hash$[\mathsf{hk}]$ computes a Merkle tree on the statements $(x_1, \dots, x_t)$.

4. The update algorithm then defines a binary tree Γ_{proof} of depth d with the following value function $\mathsf{val}_{\mathsf{proof}}$:
   - For each index ind $\in \mathcal{I}$, let $\mathsf{val}_{\mathsf{proof}}(\mathsf{ind}) = \pi_{\mathsf{ind}}$.
   - Let $\mathsf{ind}^{(t+1)} = \mathsf{bin}_d(t)$. Let $\mathsf{val}_{\mathsf{proof}}(\mathsf{ind}^{(t+1)}) = \mathsf{ObfProve}(C, x_{t+1}, \bot, \mathsf{ind}^{(t+1)}, w_{t+1}, \bot)$.
   - For all other nodes ind $\notin \mathcal{I}$, let $\mathsf{val}_{\mathsf{proof}}(\mathsf{ind}) = \bot$.
   The invariant will be that the nodes ind associated with the frontier of leaf node t (with index $\mathsf{bin}_d(t-1)$) are associated with a proof π_{ind}.

5. Let ind' be the longest common prefix to $\mathsf{ind}^{(t)}$ and $\mathsf{ind}^{(t+1)}$. Write $\mathsf{ind}^{(t)} = b_1 \cdots b_d$ and ind' $= b_1 \cdots b_{\rho}$, where $\rho = |\mathsf{ind}'|$ denotes the length of the common prefix. If $\rho < d - 1$, then we apply the following procedure for $k = d-1, \dots, \rho+1$ to merge proofs:

- Let ind $= b_1 \cdots b_K$ and compute

$$\mathsf{val}_{\mathsf{proof}}(\mathsf{ind}) \leftarrow \mathsf{ObfProve}\left(C, h_1, h_2, \mathsf{ind}, \mathsf{val}_{\mathsf{proof}}(\mathsf{ind}\|0), \mathsf{val}_{\mathsf{proof}}(\mathsf{ind}\|1)\right),$$

where $h_1 \leftarrow \mathsf{val}_{\mathsf{hash}}(\mathsf{ind}\|0)$ and $h_2 \leftarrow \mathsf{val}_{\mathsf{hash}}(\mathsf{ind}\|1)$.
6. Output the updated proof, $\pi_{t+1} = \{(\mathsf{ind}, \mathsf{val}_{\mathsf{proof}}(\mathsf{ind}))\}_{\mathsf{ind}\in\mathsf{frontier}(\mathsf{ind}^{(t+1)})}$.
- $\mathsf{V}(\mathsf{crs}, C, (x_1, \ldots, x_t), \pi)$: On input $\mathsf{crs} = (\mathsf{ObfProve}, \mathsf{ObfVerify}, \mathsf{hk})$, a Boolean circuit $C\colon \{0,1\}^\ell \times \{0,1\}^m \to \{0,1\}$, statements $x_1, \ldots, x_t \in \{0,1\}^\ell$ and a proof $\pi = \{(\mathsf{ind}, \pi_{\mathsf{ind}})\}_{\mathsf{ind}\in\mathcal{I}}$, the verification algorithm proceeds as follows:
  1. The algorithm constructs a binary tree $(\Gamma_{\mathsf{hash}}, \mathsf{val}_{\mathsf{hash}}) \leftarrow \mathsf{Hash}[\mathsf{hk}](x_1, \ldots, x_t)$ (defined in Fig. 6) of depth d whose values correspond to the statements $(x_1, \ldots, x_t)$ and their hashes.
  2. Let $\mathsf{ind}^{(t)} = \mathsf{bin}_d(t-1)$. If $\mathcal{I} \neq \mathsf{frontier}(\mathsf{ind}^{(t)})$, output $\bot$.
  3. Finally, the verification algorithm checks that $\mathsf{ObfVerify}(C, \mathsf{val}_{\mathsf{hash}}(\mathsf{ind}), \mathsf{ind}, \pi_{\mathsf{ind}}) = 1$ for all $\mathsf{ind} \in \mathsf{frontier}(\mathsf{ind}^{(t)})$. If any checks fail, output 0. Otherwise output 1.

Completeness and security analysis. We now state the completeness and security properties of Construction 5.4, but defer their proofs to the full version of this paper.

Theorem 5.5 (Completeness). *If $i\mathcal{O}$ is correct, then Construction 5.4 is complete.*

Theorem 5.6 (Soundness). *If Π_{PRF} is correct and a secure puncturable PRF, PRG is a secure PRG, Π_{SSB} is a secure statistically binding two-to-one SSB hash and $i\mathcal{O}$ is secure, then Construction 5.4 satisfies non-adaptive soundness.*

Theorem 5.7 (Succinctness). *If Π_{SSB} is succinct, then, Construction 5.4 is fully succinct.*

Theorem 5.8 (Zero-knowledge). *Construction 5.4 satisfies perfect zero-knowledge.*

Combining Theorems 5.5 to 5.8, we obtain the following corollary:

Corollary 5.9 (Non-Adaptive Updatable BARGs). *Assuming the existence of a secure indistinguishability obfuscation scheme and of somewhere extractable hash functions, there exists an updatable batch argument for NP.*

Acknowledgments. We thank the anonymous TCC reviewers for helpful feedback on this work. B. Waters is supported by NSF CNS-1908611, a Simons Investigator award, and the Packard Foundation Fellowship. D. J. Wu is supported by NSF CNS-2151131, CNS-2140975, a Microsoft Research Faculty Fellowship, and a Google Research Scholar award.

Constants: Hash key $\mathsf{hk} = (\mathsf{hk}_1, \ldots, \mathsf{hk}_d)$
Input: Statements $x_1, \ldots, x_t \in \{0, 1\}^\ell$

On input a collection of statements $(x_1, \ldots, x_t)$, the hash algorithm constructs a binary tree Γ_{hash} of depth d with a value function $\mathsf{val}_{\mathsf{hash}}$ defined recursively as follows:

- **Leaf nodes:** For a leaf node $\mathsf{ind} \in \{0, 1\}^d$, let $i \in [0, 2^d - 1]$ be its associated value (when viewed as an integer). Then, associate the value $\mathsf{val}_{\mathsf{hash}}(\mathsf{ind})$ as follows:

$$\mathsf{val}_{\mathsf{hash}}(\mathsf{ind}) = \begin{cases} x_{i+1} & i + 1 \leq t \\ \bot & \text{otherwise.} \end{cases}$$

- **Internal nodes:** For an internal node $\mathsf{ind} \in \{0, 1\}^{<d}$, we define its value as follows:
  * For all indices where $\mathsf{ind} > \mathsf{bin}_d(t - 1)$, define $\mathsf{val}_{\mathsf{hash}}(\mathsf{ind}) \leftarrow \bot$.
  * If $\mathsf{ind} \leq \mathsf{bin}_d(t - 1)$, define $\mathsf{val}_{\mathsf{hash}}(\mathsf{ind})$ to be the hash of its children $\mathsf{ind}\|0$ and $\mathsf{ind}\|1$ computed using $\mathsf{hk}_{d'}$, where $d' = \mathsf{level}(\mathsf{ind})$. Namely,

$$\mathsf{val}_{\mathsf{hash}}(\mathsf{ind}) \leftarrow \mathsf{SSB.LocalHash}\big(\mathsf{hk}_{d'}, \mathsf{val}_{\mathsf{hash}}(\mathsf{ind}\|0), \mathsf{val}_{\mathsf{hash}}(\mathsf{ind}\|1)\big).$$

We assume that $\mathsf{val}_{\mathsf{hash}}$ is efficiently encoded such that on any input $\mathsf{ind} \in \{0, 1\}^{\leq d}$, where $\mathsf{ind} > \mathsf{bin}_d(t-1)$, $\mathsf{val}_{\mathsf{hash}}$ outputs $\bot$ and initialized on nodes $\leq \mathsf{bin}_d(t - 1)$ and thus initialized on $\leq 2t$ nodes.
Output $(\Gamma_{\mathsf{hash}}, \mathsf{val}_{\mathsf{hash}})$.

Fig. 6. The function $\mathsf{Hash}[\mathsf{hk}](x_1, \ldots, x_t)$

References

[ACL+22] Albrecht, M.R., Cini, V., Lai, R.W.F., Malavolta, G., Thyagarajan, S.: Lattice-based SNARKs: publicly verifiable, preprocessing, and recursively composable. In: CRYPTO (2022)

[AS15] Asharov, G., Segev, G.: Limits on the power of indistinguishability obfuscation and functional encryption. In: FOCS, pp. 191–209 (2015)

[BBHR18] Eli, B.-S., Bentov, I., Horesh, Y., Riabzev, M.: Scalable, transparent, and post-quantum secure computational integrity. IACR Cryptol. ePrint Arch. (2018)

[BCC+17] Bitansky, N., et al.: The Hunting of the SNARK. J. Cryptology **30**(4), 989–1066 (2016). https://doi.org/10.1007/s00145-016-9241-9

[BCCT12] Bitansky, N., Canetti, R., Chiesa, A., Tromer, E.: From extractable collision resistance to succinct non-interactive arguments of knowledge, and back again. In: ITCS (2012)

[BCCT13] Bitansky, N., Canetti, R., Chiesa, A., Tromer, E.: Recursive composition and bootstrapping for SNARKS and proof-carrying data. In: STOC, pp. 111–120 (2013)

[BCI+13] Bitansky, N., Canetti, R., Ishai, Y., Ostrovsky, R., Paneth, O.: Succinct non-interactive arguments via linear interactive proofs. In: TCC (2013)

[BCPR14] Bitansky, N., Canetti, R., Paneth, O., Rosen, A.: On the existence of extractable one-way functions. In: STOC (2014)

[BGI+01] Barak, B., et al.: On the (im)possibility of obfuscating programs. In: CRYPTO, pp. 1–18 (2001)

[BGI14] Boyle, E., Goldwasser, S., Ivan, I.: Functional signatures and pseudorandom functions. In: PKC, pp. 501–519 (2014)

[BISW17] Boneh, D., Ishai, Y., Sahai, A., Wu, D.J.: Lattice-based SNARGs and their application to more efficient obfuscation. In: EUROCRYPT (2017)

[BISW18] Boneh, D., Ishai, Y., Sahai, A., Wu, D.J.: Quasi-optimal snargs via linear multi-prover interactive proofs. In: EUROCRYPT, pp. 222–255 (2018)

[BW13] Boneh, D., Waters, B.: Constrained pseudorandom functions and their applications. In: ASIACRYPT, pp. 280–300 (2013)

[CHM+20] Chiesa, A., Hu, Y., Maller, M., Mishra, P., Vesely, N., Ward, N.P.: Marlin: Preprocessing zkSNARKs with universal and updatable SRS. In: EUROCRYPT (2020)

[CJJ21a] Choudhuri, A.R., Jain, A., Jin, Z.: Non-interactive batch arguments for NP from standard assumptions. In: CRYPTO, pp. 394–423 (2021)

[CJJ21b] Choudhuri, A.R., Jain, A., Jin, Z.: Snargs for $\mathcal{P}$ from LWE. In: FOCS, pp. 68–79 (2021)

[COS20] Chiesa, A., Ojha, D., Spooner, N.: Post-quantum and transparent recursive proofs from holography. In: EUROCRYPT, Fractal (2020)

[DFH12] Damgård, I., Faust, S., Hazay, C.: Secure two-party computation with low communication. In: TCC (2012)

[DGKV22] Devadas, L., Goyal, R., Kalai, Y., Vaikuntanathan, V.: Rate-1 non-interactive arguments for batch-NP and applications. IACR Cryptol. ePrint Arch. (2022)

[GGPR13] Gennaro, R., Gentry, C., Parno, B., Raykova, M.: Quadratic span programs and succinct NIZKs without PCPs. In: EUROCRYPT (2013)

[Gro10] Groth, J.: Short pairing-based non-interactive zero-knowledge arguments. In: ASIACRYPT (2010)

[Gro16] Groth, J.: On the size of pairing-based non-interactive arguments. In: EUROCRYPT (2016)

[GW11] Gentry, C., Wichs, D.: Separating succinct non-interactive arguments from all falsifiable assumptions. In: STOC, pp. 99–108 (2011)

[HW15] Hubácek, P., Wichs, D.: On the communication complexity of secure function evaluation with long output. In: ITCS, pp. 163–172 (2015)

[JLS21] Jain, A., Lin, H., Sahai, A.: Indistinguishability obfuscation from well-founded assumptions. In: STOC, pp. 60–73 (2021)

[JLS22] Jain, A., Lin, H., Sahai, A.: Indistinguishability obfuscation from LPN over f_p, dlin, and prgs in nc̃0. In: EUROCRYPT (2022)

[KLW15] Koppula, V., Lewko, A.B., Waters, B.: Indistinguishability obfuscation for turing machines with unbounded memory. In: STOC, pp. 419–428 (2015)

[KPTZ13] Kiayias, A., Papadopoulos, S., Triandopoulos, S., Zacharias, T.: Delegatable pseudorandom functions and applications. In: ACM CCS, pp. 669–684 (2013)

[Lip13] Lipmaa, H.: Succinct non-interactive zero knowledge arguments from span programs and linear error-correcting codes. In: ASIACRYPT (2013)

[Mer87] Merkle, R.C.: A digital signature based on a conventional encryption function. In: CRYPTO, pp. 369–378 (1987)

[Mic95] Micali, S.: Computationally-sound proofs. In: Proceedings of the Annual European Summer Meeting of the Association of Symbolic Logic (1995)

[Nao03] Naor, M.: On cryptographic assumptions and challenges. In: CRYPTO (2003)

[OPWW15] Okamoto, T., Pietrzak, K., Waters, B., Wichs, D.: New realizations of somewhere statistically binding hashing and positional accumulators. In: ASIACRYPT, pp. 121–145 (2015)

[PHGR13] Parno, B., Howell, J., Gentry, C., Raykova, M.: Nearly practical verifiable computation. In: IEEE Symposium on Security and Privacy, Pinocchio (2013)

[Set20] Setty, S.T.V.: Spartan: efficient and general-purpose zkSNARKs without trusted setup. In: CRYPTO (2020)

[SW14] Sahai, A., Waters, B.: How to use indistinguishability obfuscation: deniable encryption, and more. In: STOC (2014)

[WW22] Waters, B., Wu, D.J.: Batch arguments for NP and more from standard bilinear group assumptions. In: CRYPTO (2022)

Identity-Based Encryption and Functional Encryption

Lower Bounds for the Number of Decryption Updates in Registration-Based Encryption

Mohammad Mahmoody[1], Wei Qi[1(✉)], and Ahmadreza Rahimi[2]

[1] University of Virginia, Charlottesville, VA, USA
{mohammad,wq4sr}@virginia.edu
[2] Max Planck Institute for Security and Privacy, Bochum, Germany
ahmadreza.rahimi@mpi-sp.org

Abstract. Registration-based encryption (Garg, Hajiabadi, Mahmoody, Rahimi, TCC'18) aims to offer what identity-based encryption offers without the key-escrow problem, which refers to the ability of the private-key generator to obtain parties' decryption keys at wish. In RBE, parties generate their own secret and public keys and register their public keys to the *key curator* (KC) who updates a *compact* public parameter after each registration. The updated public parameter can then be used to securely encrypt messages to registered identities.

A major drawback of RBE, compared with IBE, is that in order to decrypt, parties might need to periodically request so-called *decryption updates* from the KC. Current RBE schemes require $\Omega(\log n)$ number of updates after n registrations, while the public parameter is of length $\text{poly}(\log n)$. Clearly, it would be highly desirable to have RBEs with only, say, a constant number of updates. This leads to the following natural question: *are so many (logarithmic) updates necessary for RBE schemes, or can we decrease the frequency of updates significantly?*

In this paper, we prove an almost tight lower bound for the number of updates in RBE schemes, as long as the times that parties receive updates only depend on the registration time of the parties, which is a natural property that holds for all known RBE constructions. More generally, we prove a trade-off between the number of updates in RBEs and the length of the public parameter for any scheme with fixed update times. Indeed, we prove that for any such RBE scheme, if there are $n \geq \binom{k+d}{d+1}$ identities that receive at most d updates, the public parameter needs to be of length $\Omega(k)$. As a corollary, we find that RBE systems with fixed update times and public parameters of length $\text{poly}(\log n)$, require $\Omega(\log n / \log\log n)$ decryption updates, which is optimal up to a $O(\log\log n)$ factor.

1 Introduction

Identity-based encryption (IBE) [Sha84, BF01] is a powerful encryption primitive that allows a large group of identities to have a single public parameter pp in

M. Mahmoody—Supported by NSF grants CCF-1910681 and CNS1936799.
W. Qi—Supported by NSF grants CNS1936799.

E. Kiltz and V. Vaikuntanathan (Eds.): TCC 2022, LNCS 13747, pp. 559–587, 2022.
https://doi.org/10.1007/978-3-031-22318-1_20

such a way that encryption to any identity id is possible solely based on the public parameter and id. The main weakness of IBE is the so-called key-escrow problem [Rog15, BF01, ARP03]. In particular, IBE schemes need a master secret key msk that is needed to generate personalized *decryption keys* dk_{id} for each identity id, so that id can decrypt messages that are encrypted for them. This means the holder of msk, called the "private-key generator" (PKG) can decrypt all the messages, even the ones that are encrypted to parties who have not even requested their decryption keys yet!

To address the key escrow problem with IBE, Garg et al. [GHMR18] introduced a new primitive called Registration-based encryption (RBE). RBE is indeed a hybrid of IBE and the more basic primitive of public-key encryption. In RBE, every identity generates their own pair of public and secret keys (pk_{id}, sk_{id}). Then, if a party id decides to "register" (i.e. join the system), they can send a request to a central party who manages the keys and is called the *key curator* (KC). KC runs a deterministic and fully transparent algorithm and updates two pieces of information: an auxiliary information aux_n as well as a *compact* public parameter pp_n, where n shows how many people have registered in the system so far. The public parameter pp_n could be used like a public parameter of IBE to encrypt messages to any of the n identities who have registered so far. The auxiliary information aux_n will be used to facilitate the next registration (and another operation called update, which is discussed below). A key advantage of RBE over IBE is that parties own their secret keys. However, they might sometimes need extra help from the KC to decrypt ciphertexts that are encrypted to them, but perhaps using public parameters that are generated after the recipient identity is registered in the system. However, these "decryption updates" shall be needed rarely to make RBE useful.

Number of Updates vs. Compactness of Public-Parameters. If one puts no bound on the length of the public parameter pp_n, then a simple concatenation of all the public keys of the registered parties $pp_n = \{pk_1, \ldots, pk_n\}$ can be used to trivially achieve RBE. Here the parties simply pick the public key of the receiver to encrypt their messages to them. This trivial scheme does not need any decryption updates! Hence, RBE is only meaningfully useful, if $|pp_n| = o(n)$ grows sublinearly. In [GHMR18], it was suggested to keep $|pp_n| = \text{poly}(\kappa, \log n)$ as the default level of compactness for the public parameter and keep the number of needed decryption updates to be $O(\log n)$. The work of [GHMR18] also constructed such schemes based on indistinguishability obfuscation [BGI+01, GGH+13, JLS21] and somewhere-statistically binding hashing schemes [HW15].

At a very high level, the public parameter pp_n in [GHMR18] is the root of a Merkle tree that hashes all the public parameters of the registered identities, and so it can also be viewed as a commitment to all those public keys. This makes the job of the KC very similar to that of accumulators [BdM94, BP97, CL02]. The ciphertexts in [GHMR18] are obfuscations of programs that anticipate an "opening" into the identity's public key and output encryption of the message under such public keys. Therefore, to decrypt a message an identity id_i would need to know the "decommitment" (opening) to its public key pk_i with respect to the commitment message pp_n. When the identities register, the Merkle tree grows and decommitment needs to be updated as well. Therefore, when more parties register, the previously registered parties need to request decryption updates to keep their decommitments up to date. This approach led to $\Theta(\log n)$ number of updates. The work of Garg et al. [GHM+19] further improved the assumptions needed for constructing RBE to more standard ones (such as CDH or LWE) by, roughly speaking, substituting the obfuscation part with the powerful garbling techniques of [DG17]. Furthermore, Goyal and Vusirikala [GV20] added efficient verifiability mechanisms for membership and non-membership of identities.

All the RBE schemes so far have the same asymptotic efficiency barriers built into them: they all use the same level of $\text{poly}(\kappa, \log n)$ compactness for the public parameter and require $\Theta(\log n)$ number of updates to guarantee successful decryption. In this work, we revisit these bounds and ask the following question.

How many decryption updates are needed in RBEs with public parameters of length $\text{poly}(\kappa, \log n)$? More generally, what is the trade-off between the number of updates and the length of the public parameter?

Our main result provides an answer to the question above by proving an almost tight lower bound for the number of updates of any RBE schemes in which the update times are fixed. We say an RBE scheme has fixed update times if for every $i \leq j$, it is known ahead of any actual registrations whether or not id_i (i.e., the ith registered identity) needs a decryption update after the registration of id_j.[1] Interestingly, all known constructions of RBE [GHMR18, GHM+19, GV20] have fixed update times, and it is indeed unclear whether the times for the updates can be tied to the public keys and (and the CRS) in a meaningful way.[2] See Remark 1.3 for more discussions on how fixed updates arise in the current constructions naturally, and why they are a useful property to have on their own. More generally, we prove a *trade-off* between the number of updates that are needed and the size of the public parameter.

Theorem 1.1 (Main Result). *Let Π be any RBE scheme in which only d decryption updates are needed for each identity when we limit the scheme to only n identities. Further, suppose the times of the updates are only a function of the time when a party registers and the total number of parties so far, and that the length of the public parameter $|pp_n|$ is non-decreasing in n.[3] Then,*

$$\binom{|pp_n| + d}{d + 1} \geq n.$$

---

[1] More formally, there is an "update graph" G that is fixed and tells us if id_i needs an update after id_j registers or not.

[2] By "meaningful", here we mean that the novel scheme cannot be trivially turned into one with fixed update patterns, as it is not hard to come up with contrived schemes whose update times depend on the public keys.

[3] Notice that, one can always make $|pp_n|$ non-decreasing using simple padding (with zeros) that prevents pp_n from shrinking when n grows.

In particular, for constant number of updates $d = O(1)$, one needs public param-eters of length $|\mathsf{pp}_n| \geq \Omega(n^{1/(d+1)})$, and for public parameters of length at most $|\mathsf{pp}_n| \leq \mathrm{poly}(\log n)$ one needs at least $d \geq \Omega(\log n/\log\log n)$ many updates.

See Theorem 4.1 and Corollary 1 for more details.

Our result leaves it open to either extend our lower bound to RBE schemes with *dynamic* update times that depend on the public keys or to invent new RBE schemes with dynamic update times that bypass our lower bound. In addition, it remains open to close the rather small gap of $1/\log\log n$ factor between our lower bound and the upper bounds of previously constructed RBE schemes.

1.1   Technical overview

We prove Theorem 1.1 by giving an explicit polynomial-time attack on any RBE scheme that does not satisfy the stated trade-off between the public parameters' length and the number of updates. Below, we fix n to be the number of the parties who register in the system. For simplicity, we work with registered identities $\{\mathsf{id}_1 = 1, \mathsf{id}_2 = 2, \ldots\}$ who register in this exact order.

Good Identity Tuples for the Attack. At a very high level, we show that for any RBE scheme with n parties, d update at fixed times (independently of the keys), and compact public parameter $\binom{|\mathsf{pp}_n|+d}{d+1} < n$, there exists a tuple $(i, k) \in [n]^2, i \leq k$ that is "good for the attacker" in the following sense. If one encrypts a message m for $\mathsf{id}_i = i$ using pp_k (i.e., the public parameter right after id_k registers), then the adversary can successfully decrypt the ciphertext back into m, even though it does not have the real secret key of id_i. Note that we prove this, despite the fact that the public parameter pp_k could still be "linked" with the public and secret keys of id_i (through the algorithm used by the KC). Yet, we prove that if compared to the number of updates the public parameter is not long enough, there is always a tuple (i, k) that is good for the attacker to succeed.

Before proving the existence of good tuples and explaining how the adversary actually uses them in its attack, we first outline the ideas that we develop to achieve our goals. At a high level, we use two types of ideas as follows.

- *Information theoretic* ideas will rely on the length of the public parameter.
- *Combinatorial* tools will rely on the number of decryption updates.

In the following, we explain both of these ideas and how they play their role in our attack and its analysis. In order to do that, we first go over the simplest form of RBE schemes, in which *no updates* are allowed. This allows us to explain information theoretic ideas more clearly. We then extend the attack and its analysis to RBE schemes that allow *one* updates. Even this simple case will be instructive to show the challenges that arise and the new (combinatorial) tools that become necessary to overcome these challenges. The full poofs for the general case can be found in Sect. 4. For simplicity of the presentation, we ignore the existence of a CRS, but our proofs extend to having CRS as well.

Breaking RBEs with No Updates: Information Theoretic Tools. Suppose an RBE scheme has *no updates*. This is not entirely impossible, as one can always concatenate the public keys and store them as one giant public parameter that grows linearly with the number of parties n. But is this linear dependence on n necessary? Here we observe, using basic information theoretic tools, that this is indeed the case. First, we define a notation for keys as random variables.

Notation. We use $\mathsf{KEY}_i = (\mathsf{PK}_i, \mathsf{SK}_i)$ to denote the public/secret keys of id_i, as random variables. We also use PP_k to denote pp_k as a random variable.

Bounding the Mutual Information. If $|\mathsf{pp}_n| \leq \ell$, then the (Shannon) entropy of PP_n can be at most ℓ bits.[4] Therefore, the mutual information $I(\mathsf{KEY}_{1,\ldots,n}; \mathsf{PP}_n)$ between PP_n and concatenation of all the keys $\mathsf{KEY}_{1,\ldots,n} = (\mathsf{KEY}_1, \ldots, \mathsf{KEY}_n)$ is also bounded by ℓ.[5] Since the keys are generated *independently* for different identities, the average mutual information between PP_n and KEY_i of a random party i is bounded $\mathbb{E}_{i \leftarrow [n]}[I(\mathsf{KEY}_i; \mathsf{PP}_n)] \leq \ell/n$. Therefore, there exists $i \in [n]$, such that $I(\mathsf{KEY}_i; \mathsf{PP}_n) \leq \ell/n$. Such pair $(i, k = n)$ will be *good* for the attacker.

From Bounded Mutual Information to Independence. If $I(\mathsf{KEY}_i; \mathsf{PP}_n) \leq \ell/n = \varepsilon$ is sufficiently small (e.g., due to the small length of the public parameter), we can use the Pinsker's inequality (see Lemma B.5) to conclude that the two distributions below are $O(\sqrt{\varepsilon})$-statistically close

$$(\mathsf{KEY}_i, \mathsf{PP}_n) \approx_{O(\sqrt{\varepsilon})} (\mathsf{KEY}_i \otimes \mathsf{PP}_n),$$

where in the left side $(\mathsf{KEY}_i, \mathsf{PP}_n)$ is the *jointly* sampled pair of PP_n and keys KEY_i for id_i, while in the right side the $\otimes$ notation indicates that KEY_i and PP_n are sampled from their corresponding true marginal distribution, but they are sampled *independently* of each other.

From Independence to Successful Attacks. The argument above shows that due to the (almost) independence of the keys KEY_i of id_i and PP_n, if the adversary simply picks a fresh pair of fake keys $(\mathsf{PK}'_i, \mathsf{SK}'_i) = \mathsf{KEY}'_i$ for id_i and uses SK'_i to decrypt the messages encrypted for id_i, it will succeed with probability $\rho - O(\sqrt{\varepsilon})$, where ρ is the completeness of the scheme. The reason is that using the correct keys would succeed with probability ρ, and switching to fake keys will affect this probability by at most $O(\sqrt{\varepsilon})$.

The attack above on the simple RBE schemes with no updates crucially uses the fact that no decryption updates are received by the parties at any time during the course of the system. In fact, the information theoretic argument above completely breaks down even if the registered parties receive just *one* update right after they register! To see why suppose u_i is the single decryption update received by id_i at some point after they register. Then, decrypting messages that are encrypted to id_i might require both sk_i and the update u_i to succeed. Therefore, we cannot simply rely on $(\mathsf{KEY}_i, \mathsf{PP}_n) \approx_{O(\sqrt{\varepsilon})} (\mathsf{KEY}_i \otimes \mathsf{PP}_n)$, and e.g., stronger conditions that also involve u_i might be necessary.

---

[4] See Definition 2.5 for the definition of entropy.
[5] See Definition B.1 for the definition of mutual information.

Breaking RBEs with Single Immediate Updates. For the simpler case that the update u_i is generated *right* after the registration of id_i, we can still use the ideas for the no-update setting and slightly more powerful information theoretic tools. First, note that the adversary needs to generate some form of (fake) u_i' to run the decryption. A natural way to do it is to generate this fake update u_i' *using the fake keys* KEY_i' that it has generated for the vulnerable party id_i (where (i, n) is a good pair as explained above). A key point is that this update u_i' cannot be generated using KEY_i' alone, and it also needs to use as input the publicly available *auxiliary information* that is stored at the key curator. This public information is a function of (the CRS and) the registered public keys. Hence, u_i is a function of KEY_i' and the previously registered public keys.

The above subtle point shows that the approximate independence of KEY_i and PP_n is no longer sufficient for the attack's success, and we need to *also condition* on the previously registered (public keys). Fortunately, this is not a problem, as we can start from a stronger condition that still can be proven based on the length of the public parameter: $\mathbb{E}_{i \leftarrow [n]}[I(KEY_i; PP_n | KEY_1, \ldots, KEY_{i-1})] \leq \ell/n$. (Note that we are now conditioning on the previous keys). Therefore, there exists $i \in [n]$, such that $I(KEY_i; PP_n | KEY_1, \ldots, KEY_{i-1}) \leq \ell/n$. Therefore, we can again use a variant of Pinsker's inequality and show that $(KEY_i, PP_n) \approx_{O(\sqrt{\varepsilon})} (KEY_i \otimes PP_n)$, holds even conditioned on the previously registered keys. Such i will again make the pair $(i, k = n)$ a *good pair* for the attack.

Breaking RBEs with Single Updates Arriving at Arbitrary Times. When updates can arrive at arbitrary times, the simple information theoretic arguments above break down, as we cannot simply use the fake keys of the party id_i to generate its needed decryption update. This means that we might need to go a few steps further in time and even fake the keys of the parties $id_{i+1}, \ldots$ to be able to generate a useful update. But this will increase the length of the random variables that we fake and that kills the small mutual information with the public parameter. At a high level, we will *group* the identities in such a way that different groups can be seen as "large identity" groups that can collectively generate the needed update for the first identity in that group.

More formally, to attack RBEs with single updates that can arrive at any moment after registration of id_i, we define the notion of a good *triple* $i \leq j \leq k$ (for the attack) such that when the triple (i, j, k) is good, according to our definition, then the pair (i, k) would be good (for the attacker) as described above; namely, id_i will become vulnerable to attacks after the kth registration. The number j with $i \leq j \leq k$ denotes *how* this attack will be done. In particular, we call (i, j, k) a good triple if it has both of the following two properties.

1. *Being useful in relation with updates.* We require that id_i will not receive *any* updates during the registrations of $id_{j+1}, \ldots, id_k$. This means that, if we only use the updates generated for id_i till the registration of id_j, id_i can still decrypt messages that are encrypted till the registration of id_k.

2. *Being useful in relation with key independence.* We require that the concatenation of the keys of the identities $(\mathsf{KEY}_i, \mathsf{KEY}_{i+1}, \ldots, \mathsf{KEY}_j)$, as one big random variable, is almost independent of PP_k, and this holds when we condition on the first $i - 1$ pair of keys $(\mathsf{KEY}_1, \ldots, \mathsf{KEY}_{i-1})$.

If the above two conditions hold for a triple (i, j, k), then one can still use an almost identical attack to that of the simpler cases above on the target identity i as follows. The adversary simply asks a message to be encrypted to id_i using pp_k. Then, it *re-samples* fake keys $\{\mathsf{KEY}_i, \ldots, \mathsf{KEY}_j\}$ for *all* parties $\{\mathsf{id}_i, \ldots, \mathsf{id}_j\}$. It then registers all these fake keys in its head starting from the auxiliary information aux_{i-1} of the KC for the moment right before the registration of id_i. During these fake registrations, the adversary looks for any potential (fake) decryption updates that might be generated for id_i. The adversary uses all of these fake updates and the fake secret key $\mathsf{sk}'_i \leftarrow \mathsf{SK}'_i$ for id_i and tries to decrypt the challenge ciphertext. Therefore, all we need to do is to prove good triples exist. Below, we sketch why good triples exist by relying on the fact that the public parameter is small enough compared to the number of updates. For this, we would need to introduce some useful graph theoretical notions.

DAGs of Decryption Update Times. Let G be the following directed acyclic graph (DAG) on nodes $[n]$ in regard to an RBE scheme Π. Connect i to j, if id_i receives a decryption update right after id_j registers. Note that the number of updates d translates into an upper bound on the *out-degree* of the nodes in G. We refer to G as the *update graph* of the RBE scheme Π.

Skipping Sequences in DAGs. We now identify a special type of sub-graphs of DAGs like G that can help an adversary break an RBE scheme whose graph of update times is G. Let G be a DAG modeling the update times of our RBE scheme as explained above over the vertices (identities) $[n]$. We call a sequence $\mathcal{S} = \{u_1 < u_2 < \cdots < u_\ell\} \subseteq [n]$ a *skipping sequence* if for every $t \le \ell - 1$ and every edge $(u_t, v) \in G$ (denoting that the u_tth identity id_{u_t} gets an update when the vth identity id_v registers), it holds that $v \notin \{u_{t+1}, u_{t+1} + 1, \ldots, u_\ell\}$. In other words, identity id_{u_t} will either get updates before time $\mathsf{id}_{u_{t+1}}$ registers, or after time id_{u_ℓ}, but not in between.[6] Intuitively, the sequence $\{u_1 < u_2 < \cdots < u_\ell\}$ allows us to group the identities into ℓ groups such that each group internally generate the update needed for their first member.

Skipping Sequences Imply Good Triples. Here we show that if a skipping sequence in the update graph G is long enough, it implies the existence of a good triple (i, j, k). To see why, let $\mathcal{S} = \{u_1 < u_2 < \cdots < u_\ell\} \subseteq [n]$ be a skipping sequence.

- For all $t \in [k]$, $(i = u_t, j = u_{t+1} - 1, k = u_\ell)$ satisfies the first property that a good triple needs. This is directly implied by the non-existence of update edges going from u_i to any of the vertices $u_{t+1}, u_{t+1} + 1, \ldots, u_\ell$, as guaranteed by the definition of skipping sequences.

---

[6] See Definition 3.1 for a formal definition.

– Partition the set of (pairs of) keys of the registered identities into bigger random variables as follows. Put the keys KEY_u of identity id_u in group $\mathcal{K}_t$ if $u_t \leq u < u_{t+1}$. This partitions the set of all keys of parties corresponding to the vertices $\{u_1, \ldots u_\ell\}$ into $\ell - 1$ groups. Using the chain rule for mutual information, we can again conclude that at least for *one* of these groups $\mathcal{K}_t$, it holds that the keys in the group $\mathcal{K}_t$ (jointly) have at most $|\mathsf{pp}_k|/\ell$ mutual information with PP_k, when we condition on the keys of all the parties who registered prior to id_{u_t}. Therefore, we can again apply Pinsker's inequality and prove that the triple $(i = u_t, j = u_{t+1} - 1, k = u_\ell)$ also satisfies the second property needed for a triple to be good.

DAGs of Bounded Out-Degrees Contain Long Skipping Sequences. It remains to show that any DAG with a "small" out degree contains a "large" skipping sequence. Here we explain the proof for the simple case of out-degrees equal to 1. The idea, however, can be extended to arbitrary (bounded) out-degrees (see Theorem 3.2). We call a finite graph G a *forward* DAG if the vertices of G are $[n]$ and all the edges are of the form (i, j) for $i \leq j$. We use $\deg^+(u)$ to denote the out-degree of u, which is the number of nodes like v where (u, v) is an edge in G.

Claim 1.2 (Long Skipping Sequence in Forward DAGs of Out-Degree at Most 1). Let $G = (\mathcal{V}_G = [n], \mathcal{E}_G)$ be a forward DAG of size $n = \binom{k+1}{2}$ for $k \in \mathbb{N}$, and that $\deg^+(G) \leq 1$. Then, there exists a skipping sequence in G of size k.

In the following, we prove this claim. Since $n = \binom{k+1}{2} = \sum_{i=1}^{k} i$, we divide the n vertices into k *groups* $\{\mathcal{G}_i\}_{i \in [k]}$ such that when we read the vertices in the order $1, \ldots, n$, the members of the group $\mathcal{G}_i$ are immediately after the vertices of group $\mathcal{G}_{i-1}$ and the ith group $\mathcal{G}_i$ has $(k + 1 - i)$ vertices.

We say an edge (u, v) *lies in* a group $\mathcal{G}_i$ if both $u, v \in \mathcal{G}_i$. We say a group $\mathcal{G}_i$ is *green* if there exists at least one vertex in $\mathcal{G}_i$ whose out-going edge lies in $\mathcal{G}_i$ and we call any such vertex a *representative* of $\mathcal{G}_i$. Otherwise, group $\mathcal{G}_i$ is *red*.

Now we do as follows to find a skipping sequence of the size we want:

1. If all k groups are green, then we select exactly one representative r_i from each group $\mathcal{G}_i$ and construct sequence $\mathcal{S} = \{r_1 < r_2 < \cdots < r_k\}$. By construction, for $i < k$ the out-going edge (r_i, v) must lie in $\mathcal{G}_i$, which implies that $v < r_{i+1}$. Thus, $\mathcal{S}$ is a skipping sequence.
2. If red groups exist, let $\mathcal{G}_j$ be the red group with smallest j. We then construct the sequence $\mathcal{S} = \{r_1 < r_2 < \cdots < r_{j-1}\} \cup \mathcal{G}_j$ of size k.

Where Did We Rely on the Fixed Update Times? In the proof sketched above, we partition the keys into groups based on the skipping sequence $\mathcal{S}$ that comes out of the update graph G. We then argued that, because this sequence is long enough, the mutual information between pp_k and one of the groups of keys *defined by* $\mathcal{S}$ is small. If we allow the graph G itself to be correlated with the public parameter pp_k, the graph itself can carry information. Alternatively, one might try to first *sample* and fix the graph G based on the execution of the system. After all, it will again be a low-out-degree graph and it *will* be guaranteed to have a long skipping sequence $\mathcal{S} = \{u_1 < \cdots < u_\ell\}$. However, if we pick a triple $(u_t, u_{t+1} - 1, u_\ell)$ as a candidate good triple, even an adversary who has the *real* keys for the identities corresponding to $\{u_t, \ldots, u_{t+1} - 1\}$ might fail to decrypt the challenge ciphertext! That is because when we change the keys, the update times might change and now identity u_t might need an update *after* time u_{t+1}.

Remark 1.3 (How to Interpret the Assumption of Fixed Update Times). As mentioned before, all known constructions of RBE have fixed update times. Here we sketch the reason. Despite their differences, the RBE schemes so far consist of two components: a data structure that serves as a commitment/accumulator for identity-key pairs, and a "crypto" component that either employs IO or garbling to achieve a form of "delayed encryption". The first component in known constructions of RBE always consists of "subsets" whose *sizes* determine the update times, while these sizes only depend on the number of identities registered so far. Moreover, fixed update times seems like a meaningful feature on its own to have for an RBE scheme, as it allows the parties in an RBE system to know when they will need updates solely based on their registration time and the total number of registered parties (without the need for failing in decryption to realize that their credentials are outdated). In fact, if the RBE system is designed in a (natural) way that KC itself takes on the role of pushing the updates then having fixed update times would be even more natural, as the KC actually does *not* have parties' secret keys to even try any decryption. As it remains open to potentially bypass our lower bound by leveraging on dynamic update times that depend on the registered keys, we point out a success story that might have some resemblance. Indeed, in the context of memory-hard functions, in which a DAG is also built on top of the input data, provable barriers against memory-hard functions have been overcome using data-*dependent* ones [BH22].

1.2   Related Work

Here we review some further related work.

In addition to the works [GHMR18, GHM+19, GV20] that studied the feasibility and asymptotic efficiency of RBE, Cong, Eldefrawy, and Smart [CES21] studied the non-asymptotic practicality of implementing RBE schemes by estimating the concrete communication and computation costs of RBE and further optimizing it using alternative tools instead of Merkle trees.

Prior to RBE, other approaches have been pursued to address the key-escrow problem with IBE. One approach proposed by [BF01] was to make the PKG *decentralized* and run by multiple parties. Goyal [Goy07, GLSW08] proposed an after-the-fact approach of making PKG "accountable", by hoping to catch an irresponsible PKG in case of misuse. The works of [CCV04, Cho09, WQT18] aimed at (a related goal of) making it harder for the PKG to find out the receiver identity by hiding it in a large set of identities. Chow [Cho09] also studied ways to allow the users to interactively obtain secret keys without revealing their identities, and Emura et al. [EKW19] further formalized this approach.

The work of [ARP03] pursued another approach to mix IBE and public-key encryption by constructing "Certificateless" Public Key Cryptography. However, we shall clarify that, since the key-escrow is inherent to IBE, none of these approaches (including RBE) can really eliminate the key-escrow problem of IBE.

2   Definitions and Preliminaries

2.1   Registration-Based Encryption

In this subsection, we first define the syntax of RBE. We then present new definitions of security and completeness for RBEs that are used in our lower bounds. Standard definitions can be found in Sect. A. Our security notion is weaker than (and implied by) the standard RBE security definition; in our definition, the adversary does not get any secret keys. Using this definition makes a lower bound stronger. Our completeness is stronger than (and implies) the standard completeness definition of RBEs; in our definition, the update times are fixed. It remains open to extend our lower bounds to the standard completeness definition of RBE or to find a new construction that bypasses our lower bound.

Definition 2.1 (Syntax of Registration-Based Encryption). *Five PPT algorithms* (Gen, Reg, Enc, Upd, Dec) *form a* registration-based encryption *(RBE for short) if they work together as follows.*

- **Generating CRS.** *A common random string* crs *of length* $\mathrm{poly}(\kappa)$ *is publicly sampled at the beginning, for the security parameter* κ.
- **Key Generation.** $\mathsf{Gen}(1^\kappa) \to (\mathsf{pk}, \mathsf{sk})$: *The randomized algorithm* Gen *outputs a pair of public and secret keys* (pk, sk). *The key generation algorithm is run by any honest party locally who wants to register itself into the system.*
- **Registration.** $\mathsf{Reg}^{[\mathsf{aux}]}(\mathsf{crs}, \mathsf{pp}, \mathsf{id}, \mathsf{pk}) \to \mathsf{pp}'$: *The deterministic algorithm* Reg *takes as input the CRS* crs, *current public parameter* pp, *a registering identity* id *and a public key* pk *(supposedly for the identity* id*), and it outputs* pp' *as the updated public parameters. The* Reg *algorithm uses* read *and* write *access to auxiliary information* aux *which will be updated into* aux' *during the process of registration and helps with the efficiency of the registration and updates (below). The system is initialized with* pp, aux = $\perp$.
- **Encryption.** $\mathsf{Enc}(\mathsf{crs}, \mathsf{pp}, \mathsf{id}, \mathsf{m}) \to \mathsf{ct}$: *The randomized algorithm* Enc *takes as input the CRS* crs, *a public parameter* pp, *a recipient identity* id, *and a plaintext message* m, *and it outputs a ciphertext* ct.
- **Update.** $\mathsf{Upd}^{\mathsf{aux}}(\mathsf{pp}, \mathsf{id}, \mathsf{pk}) \to \mathsf{u}$: *The deterministic algorithm* Upd *takes as input the current public parameter* pp, *an identity* id, *and a public key* pk. *It has* read only *oracle access to* aux *and generates an update information* u *that can help* id *to decrypt its messages.*
- **Decryption.** $\mathsf{Dec}(\mathsf{sk}, \mathsf{u}, \mathsf{ct}) \to \mathsf{m}$: *The deterministic decryption algorithm* Dec *takes as input a secret key* sk, *an update information* u, *and a ciphertext* ct, *and it outputs a message* m $\in \{0,1\}^*$ *or in* $\{\perp, \mathsf{GetUpd}\}$. *The symbol* $\perp$ *indicates a syntax error while* GetUpd *indicates that more recent update information (than* u*) might be needed for decryption.*

The Reg *and* Upd *algorithms are performed by the party called* key curator, *which we call KC for short, and* aux *can be seen as the state held by the KC.*

See Definitions A.1 and A.2 for the standard definitions of completeness and security of RBEs. Below we present new definitions that are relevant to us.

We now introduce a generalization of the security of RBE called k-corruption security. In the original security definition of RBE (see Definition A.2), the adversary samples secret keys of all non-target identities. Here we only allow it to sample the keys of up to k non-target identities. In the extreme case where $k = n - 1$ (, meaning all but the target identity is corrupted,) the definition matches Definition A.2. In the extreme case where $k = 0$, the adversary is essentially an observer who is curious to decrypt messages sent to parties.

Definition 2.2 (k-Corruption Security for RBE). *Let k be a positive integer. For any interactive PPT adversary $\mathcal{A}$, consider the following game* $\mathsf{Sec}_{\mathcal{A}}^{k\text{-}c}(\kappa)$ *between $\mathcal{A}$ and a challenger $\mathcal{C}$.*

1. **Initialization.** $\mathcal{C}$ *sets* pp $= \perp$, aux $= \perp$, *(the set of non-corrupted identities)* $\mathcal{D}_{\mathsf{nc}} = \emptyset$, *(the set of corrupted identities)* $\mathcal{D}_{\mathsf{c}} = \emptyset$, id$^* = \perp$, crs $\leftarrow U_{\mathsf{poly}(\kappa)}$ *and sends the sampled* crs *to $\mathcal{A}$.*
2. *Till $\mathcal{A}$ continues (which is at most* $\mathsf{poly}(\kappa)$ *steps), proceed as follows. At every iteration, $\mathcal{A}$ chooses exactly one of the actions below to perform.*
   (a) **Registering a corrupted (non-target) identity.** *This step is allowed only if $|\mathcal{D}_{\mathsf{c}}| < k$. $\mathcal{A}$ sends some* id $\notin \mathcal{D}_{\mathsf{nc}} \cup \mathcal{D}_{\mathsf{c}}$ *and* pk *to $\mathcal{C}$. $\mathcal{C}$ registers* (id, pk) *by letting* pp $:= \mathsf{Reg}^{[\mathsf{aux}]}(\mathsf{crs}, \mathsf{pp}, \mathsf{id}, \mathsf{pk})$ *and* $\mathcal{D}_{\mathsf{c}} := \mathcal{D}_{\mathsf{c}} \cup \{\mathsf{id}\}$.
   (b) **Registering an uncorrupted (potentially target) identity.** *$\mathcal{A}$ sends an* id $\notin \mathcal{D}_{\mathsf{nc}} \cup \mathcal{D}_{\mathsf{c}}$ *to $\mathcal{C}$. $\mathcal{C}$ samples* (pk, sk) $\leftarrow \mathsf{Gen}(1^\kappa)$, *runs* pp $:=$ $\mathsf{Reg}^{[\mathsf{aux}]}(\mathsf{crs}, \mathsf{pp}, \mathsf{id}, \mathsf{pk})$, $\mathcal{D}_{\mathsf{nc}} := \mathcal{D}_{\mathsf{nc}} \cup \{\mathsf{id}\}$, *and sends* pk *to $\mathcal{A}$.*
3. **Encrypting for a target identity.** *$\mathcal{A}$ first sends some* id$^* \notin \mathcal{D}_{\mathsf{c}}$ *to $\mathcal{C}$. (If* id$^* \in \mathcal{D}_{\mathsf{nc}}$, *then the adversary is targeting one of the registered uncorrupted identities, otherwise it is targeting a non-registered identity). Next $\mathcal{A}$ sends messages m_0, m_1 of equal lengths $|m_0| = |m_1|$ to the adversary. Then, $\mathcal{C}$ generates* ct $\leftarrow \mathsf{Enc}(\mathsf{crs}, \mathsf{pp}, \mathsf{id}^*, m_b)$, *where $b \leftarrow \{0, 1\}$ is a random bit, and sends* ct *to $\mathcal{A}$. The adversary $\mathcal{A}$ outputs a bit b' and wins if $b = b'$.*

We call the scheme k-corruption secure, if for all PPT $\mathcal{A}$, it holds that

$$P[\mathcal{A} \text{ wins } \mathsf{Sec}_{\mathcal{A}}^{k\text{-}c}(\kappa)] < \frac{1}{2} + \mathsf{negl}(\kappa).$$

We now formally define RBE schemes with *fixed* update times. In such schemes, when a person registers at time i, they already know the indices $j > i$ such that they would need an update when the jth identity registers. More formally, we use the following game which is similar to the game of Definition A.1, with the difference that the updates are generated as soon as they are required by an "updates graph" (DAG) G.

Definition 2.3 (Forward DAGs). *Let* $G = (\mathcal{V}_G, \mathcal{E}_G)$ *be a directed acyclic graph (DAG) with vertices* $\mathcal{V}_G = [n]$ *(in case of being finite) or* $\mathcal{V}_G = \mathbb{N}$ *(in case of being infinite). We write* $(i,j) \in G$ *if* $(i,j) \in \mathcal{E}_G$ *(i.e., there is an edge from i to j in G). We call G a forward DAG, if for all* $(i,j) \in G$, *we have* $i \leq j$.

The definition below captures the property that by making the updates according to the graph G, namely, by giving the update to person i whenever person j registers and $(i,j) \in G$, then there will be no need for further updates. The definition is written for the setting where an "adversary" targets a specific identity (and aims to make the updates *insufficient* for it). However, the definition implies that even if there is more than one identity with honestly generated keys, their updates would never be necessary outside what graph G instructs.

Definition 2.4 (Completeness of RBE with a Fixed Update Times). *Let G be an infinite forward DAG. For an RBE scheme and any interactive computationally unbounded adversary $\mathcal{A}$ that still has a limited* $\text{poly}(\kappa)$ *round complexity, consider the game* $\text{UpdTimes}_{\mathcal{A}}^{G}(\kappa)$ *between $\mathcal{A}$ and a challenger $\mathcal{C}$ as follows.*

1. **Initialization.** *$\mathcal{C}$ sets* $\text{pp} = \bot$, $\text{aux} = \bot$, $\text{u} = \bot$, $\mathcal{D} = \emptyset$, $\mathcal{S} = \emptyset$, $t = 0$, *and* $\text{crs} \leftarrow U_{\text{poly}(\kappa)}$, *and sends the sampled* crs *to $\mathcal{A}$.*
2. *Till $\mathcal{A}$ continues (which is at most* $\text{poly}(\kappa)$ *steps), proceed as follows. At every iteration, $\mathcal{A}$ chooses exactly one of the actions below to perform.*
   (a) **Registering identities.** *$\mathcal{A}$ performs exactly one out of Step 2(a)i and Step 2(a)ii below, but regardless of this choice, $\mathcal{C}$ will continue to send the updates as described next.*
      (i) **Registering a corrupted non-target identity.** *$\mathcal{A}$ sends some* $\text{id} \notin \mathcal{D}$ *and* pk *to $\mathcal{C}$. $\mathcal{C}$ registers* (id, pk) *by letting* $\text{pp} := \text{Reg}^{[\text{aux}]}(\text{crs}, \text{pp}, \text{id}, \text{pk})$ *and* $\mathcal{D} := \mathcal{D} \cup \{\text{id}\}$.
      (ii) **Registering the target uncorrupted identity.** *This step is allowed only if* $\text{id}^* = \bot$. *In that case, $\mathcal{A}$ sends some* $\text{id}^* \notin \mathcal{D}$ *to $\mathcal{C}$. $\mathcal{C}$ then samples* $(\text{pk}^*, \text{sk}^*) \leftarrow \text{Gen}(1^\kappa)$, *runs* $\text{pp} := \text{Reg}^{[\text{aux}]}(\text{crs}, \text{pp}, \text{id}^*, \text{pk}^*)$, $\mathcal{D} := \mathcal{D} \cup \{\text{id}^*\}$, *and sends* pk^* *to $\mathcal{A}$.*
      Immediately updating the target identity, if required by G. This step is allowed only if $\text{id}^* \neq \bot$ *(otherwise this step is skipped). Suppose* id^* *was the ith registered identity, and let the identity registered in either of Step 2(a)i Step or 2(a)ii be the jth identity.*[7] *If* $(i,j) \in G$ *(i.e., there is an edge from i to j), then we update the decryption information* $\text{u} = \text{Upd}^{\text{aux}}(\text{pp}, \text{id}^*)$ *for the target identity.*[8]
   (b) **Encrypting for the target identity.** *This step is allowed only if* $\text{id}^* \neq \bot$. *In that case, $\mathcal{C}$ sets* $t = t + 1$. *$\mathcal{A}$ sends* $\text{m}_t \in \{0,1\}^*$ *to $\mathcal{C}$ who then sets* $\text{m}'_t := \text{m}_t$ *and sends back a corresponding ciphertext* $\text{ct}_t \leftarrow \text{Enc}(\text{crs}, \text{pp}, \text{id}^*, \text{m}_t)$ *to $\mathcal{A}$.*
   (c) **Decryption for the target identity.** *$\mathcal{A}$ sends* $j \in [t]$ *to $\mathcal{C}$ who lets* $\text{m}'_j = \text{Dec}(\text{sk}^*, \text{u}, \text{ct}_j)$.

---

[7] Note that this registered identity itself could be id^*.
[8] This update might not be really necessary, but we still run them as instructed.

The adversary $\mathcal{A}$ wins above, if there is some $j \in [t]$ for which $\mathsf{m}'_j \neq \mathsf{m}_j$. This particularly holds, e.g., if $m'_j = \mathsf{GetUpd}$. We say that G is an update graph for the RBE scheme, if $\mathsf{P}[\mathcal{A}\ wins] = \mathrm{negl}(\kappa)$. In this case, we also say that the completeness holds with fixed update graph G.

2.2   Information-Theoretic Notation and the Twig Lemma

Notation. We use capital letters to refer to random variables and usually use lowercase letters of the same type to refer to samples from those random variables. $x \leftarrow X$ refers to sampling x from the random variable X. For jointly distributed random variables X, Y, by XY or (X, Y) we refer to their joint samples, and by $X \otimes Y$, we refer to sampling X, Y from their marginals independently. For jointly distributed XY and $y \in Y$, by $X|_y$ we refer to the random variable X conditioned on the sampled y. By $X|_Y$ we emphasize that X is sampled jointly with (and conditioned on) Y, even though $X|Y$ only refers to a sample from X. Using this notation $(X|_Y)Y$ means the same thing as XY. For distributed X, Y, Z, by $(X|_Z \otimes Y|_Z)Z$ we refer to sampling $z \leftarrow Z$ first, and then sampling $X|_z, Y|_z$ independently from their marginals. By $X \equiv Y$ we mean that X, Y are identically distributed. We write $\approx_\varepsilon$ to denote ε-closeness in statistical distance. By $\mathrm{Supp}(X)$ we mean the support set of the random variable (or probability distribution) X. When we use X as set, we refer to its support set. So, $X \cup Y$ means $\mathrm{Supp}(X) \cup \mathrm{Supp}(Y)$. We let $\mathsf{P}_X[x] = \mathsf{P}[X = x]$. log means logarithm in base 2 and ln means logarithm in base e.

Definition 2.5 (Shannon Entropy).   *The Shannon Entropy of a random variable X is defined as $H(X) = \sum_{x \in X} -\mathsf{P}_X[x] \log \mathsf{P}_X[x]$. The conditional Shannon entropy $H(X|Y)$ is defined as $\mathbb{E}_{y \leftarrow Y}[H(X|_y)]$. The entropy chain rule states that $H(XY) = H(X) + H(Y|X) = H(Y) + H(X|Y)$.*

Definition 2.6 (Statistical Distance). *Let X and Y be two random variables. We define the statistical distance between these two distributions as:*

$$\mathrm{SD}(X, Y) = \sum_{z \in X \cup Y} \frac{|\mathsf{P}_X[z] - \mathsf{P}_Y[z]|}{2}$$

We prove the following lemma in Sect. B.

Lemma 2.7 (The Twig Lemma). *Let $X_0, \ldots, X_\ell, Y$ be jointly distributed random variables. Then,*

$$\mathop{\mathbb{E}}_{i \leftarrow [\ell]}[\mathrm{SD}(X_0 \ldots X_i Y, X_0 \ldots X_{i-1} X'_i Y)] \leq \sqrt{\frac{H(Y) \ln 2}{2\ell}}$$

in which $Y X_i \ldots X_0$ are sampled jointly, while $Y X'_i X_{i-1}, \ldots, X_0$ is sampled by first sampling $x_0 \ldots, x_{i-1} y \leftarrow X_0 \ldots X_{i-1} Y$ and then sampling X'_i from

$X_i|_{x_1...x_{i-1}}$ by ignoring the sampled y.[9] In particular, if the length of the samples from Y are at most d, there exists $i \in [\ell]$ such that

$$\mathrm{SD}(X_0 \ldots X_i Y, X_0 \ldots X_{i-1} X_i' Y) \leq \sqrt{\frac{d \ln 2}{2\ell}}.$$

3   Skipping Sequences in DAGs

In this section, we formally study skipping sequences in DAGs and prove that they emerge when the out degrees are small. In Sect. C, we prove that the bounds of this section are tight. This means that our approach of using skipping sequences cannot improve our lower bound of $\log n / \log\log n$ updates in RBEs. This leaves open to close the gap between our lower bound and the upper bound of $\log n$ updates for future work.

Intuition for Skipping Sequence. Intuitively, we want to find a sequence of identities whose updates are relatively independent from the next identity in the sequence. Namely, every identity (except the last one) should receive all her updates before the next identity in the sequence joins. Looking forward, we will attack an RBE scheme immediately after the last identity of the sequence joins, so it is irrelevant whether the identities will potentially receive another update after the last one joins. This intuition is formalized by the following definition.

Definition 3.1 (Skipping Sequence). *Let G be a forward DAG (see Definition 2.3). We call $\mathcal{S} = \{u_1 < u_2 < \cdots < u_k\} \subseteq \mathcal{V}_G$ a skipping sequence if for every $i \leq k - 1$ and every edge $(u_i, v) \in G$, it holds that: either $v < u_{i+1}$ or $v > u_k$ (i.e., $v \notin \{u_{i+1}, u_{i+1} + 1, \ldots, u_k\}$).*

See Fig. 1 for examples.

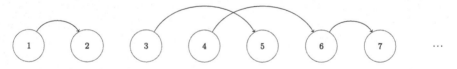

Fig. 1. Example of a forward DAG G with $\deg^+(G) = 1$. $\{1, 3, 6\}$ and $\{1, 3, 4\}$ are skipping sequences. $\{1, 3, 4, 6\}$ is not a skipping sequence, because vertex 3 has an outgoing edge to vertex 5 which is smaller than vertex 6 but larger than vertex 4.

We let $\deg^+(u) = |\{v \mid (u, v) \in G\}|$ be the *out-degree* of u and $\deg^+(G) = \max\{\deg^+(u) \mid u \in [n]\}$ to be the maximum out-degree in G.

Our main result in this subsection is the following theorem.

Theorem 3.2 (Skipping Sequences from Bounded Out-Degrees). *Let G be a forward DAG with at least $\binom{k+d}{d+1}$ vertices (for $k, d \in \mathbb{N}$) and that $\deg^+(G) \leq d$. Then, there exists a skipping sequence in G of size at least k.*

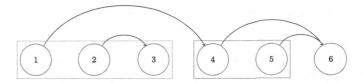

Fig. 2. Above is a forward DAG $G = ([6], \mathcal{E}_G)$ with out-degree $\deg^+(G) = 1$. Group $\mathcal{G}_1$ consists of vertices $\{1, 2, 3\}$ and it is a green group because the only out-going edge from vertex 2 is $(2, 3)$ and vertex 3 also belongs to $\mathcal{G}_1$. Namely, edge $(2,3)$ lies in $\mathcal{G}_1$. Vertex 2 is a representative of $\mathcal{G}_1$. Group $\mathcal{G}_2$ consists of vertices $\{4, 5\}$ and it is a red group because no edge lies in it. (Color figure online)

In Theorem C.1 we prove that the bound of Theorem 3.2 is tight.

Proof (of Theorem 3.2). We prove Theorem 3.2 by induction. Without loss of generality, we assume that G has exactly $n = \binom{k+d}{d+1}$ vertices. We use induction on the out-degree d. We first prove the base case for out-degree $d = 0$. In that case, all the k vertices of a forward DAG G with out-degree $\deg^+(G) = 0$ form a skipping sequence since none of the vertices has an out-going edge.

Assume the claim is true for forward DAGs of out-degree $d-1$. We now prove that the claim is true for forward DAGs of out-degree d. To this end, consider an arbitrary forward DAG $G = (\mathcal{V}_G, \mathcal{E}_G)$ where $|\mathcal{V}_G| = n = \binom{k+d}{d+1}$ and $\deg^+(G) \leq d$. From the hockey-stick identity we know

$$n = \binom{k+d}{d+1} = \sum_{i=1}^{k} \binom{i+d-1}{d}.$$

We divide the n vertices into k groups $\{\mathcal{G}_i\}_{i \in [k]}$ such that when we read the vertices $1, \ldots, n$, the members of the group $\mathcal{G}_i$ are exactly those after the vertices of group $\mathcal{G}_{i-1}$ and the i-th group $\mathcal{G}_i$ has $\binom{k+d-i}{d}$ vertices.

We say an edge (u, v) *lies in* a group $\mathcal{G}_i$ if both $u, v \in \mathcal{G}_i$. We say a group $\mathcal{G}_i$ is *green* if there exists at least one vertex in $\mathcal{G}_i$ all of whose outgoing edges lie in $\mathcal{G}_i$ and we call any such vertex a *representative* of $\mathcal{G}_i$. Otherwise, group $\mathcal{G}_i$ is *red* (Fig. 2).

1. If all k groups are green, then we select exactly one representative r_i from each group $\mathcal{G}_i$ for $i \in [k]$ and construct a sequence $\mathcal{S} = \{r_1 < r_2 < \cdots < r_k\}$. In that case, we know that for $i \in [k-1]$ all out-going edges of r_i lie in $\mathcal{G}_i$. Therefore, $\mathcal{S}$ is a skipping sequence.
2. If there is at least one red group, let $\mathcal{G}_j$ be the red group with the smallest j. By the induction hypothesis, there is a skipping sequence $\mathcal{S}'$ of size $k+1-j$ in group $\mathcal{G}_j$ since it contains $\binom{k+d-j}{d}$ vertices all of which have at most $d-1$ outgoing edges that lie in the group. We then construct our desired skipping sequence as $\mathcal{S} = \{r_1 < r_2 < \cdots < r_{j-1}\} \cup \mathcal{S}'$ of size k.

$\square$

---

[9] Using our notation, that means $YX_i'X_{i-1}, \ldots, X_0 \equiv (Y|_z \otimes X_i|_z)Z$ for $Z = X_{i-1}, \ldots, X_0$.

4   Breaking RBEs with Few Updates

In this section, we present a trade-off between the length of the public parameter of RBEs with fixed update times and the number of such updates. At a high level, we design an attack against any RBE scheme with fixed update times assuming that the number of updates is "sufficiently small" compared to the public parameter. The key technical result of this section is Theorem 4.1 below. After stating Theorem 4.1, we first derive some corollaries about the number of updates. We then define a notion of "good tuple" (i, j, k) that can serve as a *useful advice* for breaking an RBE scheme. We then show how to break RBE schemes given a good tuple. Then, we prove Theorem 4.1 by showing that good tuples exist and how to find successful attacks without being given a good tuple.

Theorem 4.1 (Main Result). *Let Π be an RBE scheme with a fixed update graph G (see Definition 2.4) and at most d updates for n registered identities; namely, $\deg^+(G) \leq d$ when we limit the graph G to the first n nodes/identities. Suppose the scheme has completeness probability ρ. If $n \geq \binom{\ell+d}{d+1}$ and $|\mathsf{pp}_i| \leq \alpha$ for all the first n registrations, then there is a 0-corruption (see Definition 2.2) $\mathrm{poly}(\kappa)$-time adversary who breaks Π with probability $\rho - \sqrt{\alpha \ln 2/(2\ell)} - \delta$ (i.e., advantage $\rho - 1/2 - \sqrt{\alpha \ln 2/(2\ell)} - \delta$) for arbitrarily small $\delta = 1/\mathrm{poly}(\kappa)$.*

Before proving Theorem 4.1, we derive a corollary for the extreme cases of constant number of (e.g., one) updates, and poly-logarithmic public parameters.

Corollary 1 *Let Π be an RBE scheme with a fixed update graph G and secure against 0-corruption. Let $\alpha_n = \max_{i \in [n]} |\mathsf{pp}_i|$ be the maximum length of the public parameter when n identities register.*

1. *If $\deg^+(G) \leq d$ for a constant d, then $\alpha_n \geq \Omega(n^{1/(d+1)})$.*
2. *If $\deg^+(G) \leq c \log n/\log\log n$ for a constant c, then $|\alpha_n| \geq \Omega(\log^{1/c} n)$.*
3. *If $|\alpha_n| \leq \mathrm{poly}(\kappa, \log n)$ for security parameter n, then $\deg^+(G)$ cannot be $o(\log n/\log\log n)$. (I.e., there will be a constant c and an infinite sequence of n for which $\deg^+(G) \geq c \cdot \log n/\log\log n$.)*

Proof (of Corollary 1 using Theorem 4.1). First observe that by Theorem 4.1, if the scheme is complete $\rho > 0.99$, it holds that when $n = \binom{\ell+d}{d+1}$, then $\alpha_n \geq \ell/10$, as otherwise the scheme will not be secure.

1. If $\deg^+(G) \leq d = O(1)$: In this case, since we have $n = \binom{\ell+d}{d+1} = \Theta(\ell^{d+1})$, therefore we get $\alpha_n \geq \Omega(\ell) \geq \Omega(n^{1/(d+1)})$.
2. If $\deg^+(G) \leq d = c \log n/\log\log n$: Using the well-known upper bound on the binomial coefficients we get $n \leq \left(\frac{(\ell+d)e}{d+1}\right)^{d+1}$. Taking logarithm, this implies

$$\log n \leq (c \cdot (\log n/\log\log n) + 1) \cdot (\log(e\ell + ed) - \log(d+1)).$$

It can be observed already that $\ell = \Omega(\log n)$ (for constant c), as otherwise, the right hand side will be $o(\log n)$. Therefore, it holds that $d = o(\ell)$. Therefore, we can simplify the above to the following for sufficiently large n

$$\log n \leq \left(c \cdot \frac{\log n}{\log\log n} + 1 \right) \cdot \log((e + o(1))\ell) < \left(c \cdot \frac{\log n}{\log\log n} + 1 \right) \cdot \log(3\ell),$$

which implies that $\log\log n \leq c \log(3\ell)$, and so $\alpha_n \geq \Omega(\ell) \geq \Omega(\log^{1/c} n)$.

3. We use the previous item. Suppose $\alpha_n = O(\log^s n)$ for (fixed κ and) constant s, while $\deg^+(G) = o(\log n / \log\log n)$. Then, pick any (sufficiently small) constant c such that $1/c > s$. In this case, we still have $\deg^+(G) \leq c \cdot \log n / \log\log n$, and $\alpha_n \geq \Omega(\log^{1/c} n)$, contradicting $\alpha_n = O(\log^s n)$.

$\square$

Proof of Theorem 4.1. In the rest of this section, we prove Theorem 4.1 in three steps. We first define a notion of *good* tuple (i, j, k) and prove that good tuples exist. We then show that the attack can be launched successfully *if* a good tuple is given as advice. These two steps already show the existence of an efficient *nonuniform* attack. Finally, we show how to make the attack uniform by, roughly speaking, finding a good-enough advice efficiently.

4.1 Defining Good Tuples and Proving Their Existence

We now define the notion of good tuples and prove that they actually exist under certain conditions. These tuples later are shown to be useful, as advice to an adversary, to break RBE schemes.

Definition 4.2 (Good Tuples for Forward DAGs). *Let G be a forward DAG with vertices $[n]$. For $i, j, k \in [n]$ where $i \leq j \leq k$, we say the tuple (i, j, k) is a* good tuple *for G, if the following holds:*

$$\nexists j' \in V \text{ such that } j < j' \leq k \wedge (i, j') \in G.$$

In other words, the ith registered identity will not need any updates starting from the $(j+1)$th registration till right after the kth registration.

Notation. We use the notation defined in Sect. 1.1 and use sans serif font for the random variables denoting the keys and public parameters. Using the same style, we also use CRS to refer to the CRS as a random variable.

Definition 4.3 (Good Tuples for RBE Schemes). *Let Π be any RBE scheme, and fix the first n identities to be $\{1, \dots, n\}$. For $i, j, k \in [n]$ where $i \leq j \leq k$ we say the tuple (i, j, k) is $(1 - \varepsilon)$-good for Π if the following two distributions are ε-close in statistical distance:*

$$(\mathsf{CRS}, \mathsf{KEY}_1 \dots \mathsf{KEY}_j, \mathsf{PP}_k), \text{ and}$$

$$(\mathsf{CRS}, \mathsf{KEY}_1 \dots \mathsf{KEY}_{i-1}, \mathsf{KEY}'_i \dots \mathsf{KEY}'_j, \mathsf{PP}_k)$$

*where in the first distribution all components are sampled jointly from an honest
execution of the registration experiment in which the parties $[n]$ are registered in
that order, while in the second distribution $\mathsf{KEY}'_i \ldots \mathsf{KEY}'_j$ are sampled independently of the other components.*[10]

Definition 4.4 (Good Tuples). *For an RBE scheme Π with fixed updates
graph G and $\varepsilon < 1$, we simply call (i, j, k) a $(1 - \varepsilon)$-good tuple, if it is both good
for G and $(1 - \varepsilon)$-good for Π.*

In the next subsection, we will show that *if* a good tuple is given to the
attacker, it can successfully break RBEs. But to obtain such attacks, we need
to at least prove that good tuples *exist* to begin with. That is exactly what the
next lemma does.

Lemma 4.5 *Let Π be an RBE scheme with a fixed update graph G. Suppose
$\deg^+(G) \leq d$ when limited to the first n identities, $\alpha \geq \max_{i \in [n]} |\mathsf{pp}_i|$, and
$n \geq \binom{\ell+d}{d+1}$. Then, there exists an $(1 - \varepsilon)$-good tuple (i, j, k) for $\varepsilon = \sqrt{\frac{\alpha \ln 2}{2\ell}}$.*

Proof (of Lemma 4.5). From Theorem 3.2 we know that there is a skipping
sequence $\{s_1 < s_2 < \cdots < s_\ell\}$ in G. Below, we show that there exists $t \in [\ell]$
such that $(s_t, s_{t+1} - 1, s_\ell)$ is both good for G and $(1 - \varepsilon)$-good for Π. For $t = \ell$,
we define $s_{\ell+1} = s_\ell + 1$ for simplicity so that the selected tuple is well defined,
and it will be (s_ℓ, s_ℓ, s_ℓ). We now show that *every* such tuple is good for G, and
that at least one of them is $(1 - \varepsilon)$-good for Π.

Good for G. By definition of skipping sequences, for all $t \in [\ell]$, any outgoing
edge (s_t, v) will either satisfy $v < s_{t+1}$ or $v > s_\ell$. (This also holds for $t = \ell$, as
this condition becomes always true in that case). Therefore $(s_t, s_{t+1} - 1, s_\ell)$ is
good for G for all $t \in [\ell]$.

Good for Π. For $i \in [\ell - 1]$, define the random variable

$$X_0 = (\mathsf{CRS}, \mathsf{KEY}_1, \ldots, \mathsf{KEY}_{s_1-1}),$$

$$X_i = (\mathsf{KEY}_{s_i}, \mathsf{KEY}_{s_i+1}, \ldots, \mathsf{KEY}_{s_{i+1}-1}),$$

$$X_\ell = \mathsf{KEY}_{s_\ell}, \quad Y = \mathsf{pp}_{s_\ell}.$$

Now, by the branching lemma (Lemma 2.7),

$$\mathop{\mathbb{E}}_{t \leftarrow [\ell]}[\mathsf{SD}(X_0 \ldots X_t Y, X_0 \ldots X_{t-1} X'_t Y)] \leq \sqrt{\frac{H(Y) \ln 2}{2\ell}} \leq \sqrt{\frac{\alpha \ln 2}{2\ell}}$$

in which X'_t is sampled independently of Y. As a result, one can fix $t \in [\ell]$ in the
expectation above so that the inequality still holds. In our setting, this means
$(s_t, s_{t+1} - 1, s_\ell)$ is $(1 - \varepsilon)$-good for Π where $\varepsilon = \sqrt{\frac{\alpha \ln 2}{2\ell}}$. $\square$

---

[10] Alternatively, one can pretend that there has been *true* values of $\mathsf{KEY}_i \ldots \mathsf{KEY}_j$
that were sampled jointly with $\mathsf{CRS}, \mathsf{KEY}_1 \ldots \mathsf{KEY}_{i-1}, \mathsf{PP}_k$ and were thrown out to
be replaced with fresh samples at the end.

4.2   Non-Uniform Attacks Using Good Tuples as Advice

We now present an attack that takes a tuple (i, j, k) that is guaranteed to be $(1 - \varepsilon)$-good. (Namely, it is both good for G and $(1 - \varepsilon)$-good for Π, where $\varepsilon = \sqrt{\frac{\alpha \ln 2}{2\ell}}$). Looking ahead, we will later prove that a simple modification of the attack will succeed even without the given advice.

Construction 4.6 (Attacking RBE with Advice). *Let Π be an RBE scheme with update graph G. Suppose (i, j, k) is given as advice. The adversary $\mathcal{A}(i, j, k)$ proceeds as the following.*

1. *Identities: The adversary registers identities $1, \ldots, k$, while none are corrupted. Therefore, the adversary can reconstruct all the intermediate auxiliary information and the public parameters, including pp_k.[11]*
2. *Target identity: the adversary announces i to be the target identity.*
3. *The adversary simply picks messages $m_0 = 0, m_1 = 1$, one of which will be encrypted to identity i under the public parameter pp_k.*
4. *To guess which message was decrypted, the adversary does as follows.*
   (a) Re-sample fake keys $\mathsf{sk}'_i, \mathsf{pk}'_i, \ldots, \mathsf{pk}'_j$ for identities $i, i + 1, \ldots, j$.
   (b) Use $\mathsf{pk}'_i, \ldots, \mathsf{pk}'_j$ to re-register all the identities $i, \ldots, j$ starting from the auxiliary information aux_{i-1} that refers to the auxiliary information of the system for the moment before identity i registers. As mentioned above, aux_{i-1} is known to adversary, as it is a deterministic (efficiently computable) function of $\mathsf{crs}, \mathsf{pk}_1, \ldots, \mathsf{pk}_{i-1}$.
   (c) Let u' be the fake update that is generated for the identity i, while (fake) registering identities $i, \ldots, j$.
   (d) Use sk'_i and u' and try to decrypt the challenge as $m' \leftarrow \mathsf{Dec}(\mathsf{sk}'_i, \mathsf{u}', \mathsf{ct})$.
   (e) If $m' \in \{0, 1\}$, then simply output m'.

The claim below is sufficient for proving Theorem 4.1, as explained above.

Claim 4.7. The adversary of Construction 4.6, once given an $(1 - \varepsilon)$-good tuple (i, j, k) where $\varepsilon = \sqrt{\frac{\alpha \ln 2}{2\ell}}$, it succeeds in winning the security game of Definition 2.2 with probability $\rho - \varepsilon$.

Proof (of Claim 4.7). We will consider two worlds Real, Ideal.

1. Real: HERE the adversary $\mathcal{A}$ behaves as described in attack 4.6.
2. Ideal: This is the world where the adversary is *given* the real keys (including the decryption key of the target identity).

Claim 4.7 directly follows from the following two Claims 4.8 and 4.9.

Claim 4.8. The adversary in Ideal wins with probability $\geq \rho$, where ρ is the completeness probability of the scheme.

---

[11] Note that the public keys and the CRS will still be given to the adversary.

Proof. Claim 4.8 directly follows from the ρ-completeness of the RBE scheme and the fact that the given advice (i, j, k) is good for G. In particular, the fact that (i, j, k) is good for G implies that the ith identity will not receive any updates between the jth registration till end of kth registration. Therefore, all the updates received before the jth registration would be enough for decrypting a ciphertext that is encrypted using the kth public parameter. $\qquad\square$

Claim 4.9. Let p_R be the probability that the adversary successfully decrypts $m' = m_b$ in the world Real, and let P_I be the corresponding probability in the Ideal world. Then, $|p_R - p_I| \leq \varepsilon$.

Proof. Claim 4.9 directly follows from the fact that the given advice (i, j, k) is $(1 - \varepsilon)$-good for Π. The key idea is that even though there are going to be updates generated for the ith person till the encryption happens after the kth registration, these updates are all functions of the keys of the first j parties. More formally, Since (i, j, k) is $(1 - \varepsilon)$-good for Π, the following two random variables $\mathsf{D}_I, \mathsf{D}_R$ stay ε-close, in which R_E is the randomness for encryption and $\mathsf{M} \leftarrow \{0, 1\}$ is the random challenge bit to be encrypted:

$$\mathsf{D}_I \equiv (\mathsf{CRS}, \mathsf{KEY}_1 \ldots \mathsf{KEY}_j, \mathsf{PP}_k, \mathsf{R}_E, \mathsf{M}),$$

$$\mathsf{D}_R \equiv (\mathsf{CRS}, \mathsf{KEY}_1 \ldots \mathsf{KEY}_{i-1}, \mathsf{KEY}'_i \ldots \mathsf{KEY}'_j, \mathsf{PP}_k, \mathsf{R}_E, \mathsf{M})$$

Now, observe that actions of the adversary in the Real and Ideal followed by encryption of the challenge bit $b \leftarrow \mathsf{M}$ and decrypting it only differs based on whether we use D_I or D_R. In particular, all the updates generated for the ith identity generated after jth registration and before $(k + 1)$st registration are deterministic functions of the first k keys and the CRS (as KC is a deterministic algorithm). By the data-processing inequality, the probability of successfully decrypting back $b \leftarrow \mathsf{M}$ in the security game will not change by more than ε across the experiments Real and Ideal. This finishes the proof of Claim 4.9. $\qquad\square$

This finishes the proof of Claim 4.7. $\qquad\square$

4.3 Efficient Uniform Attack Without Advice

Finally, we prove Theorem 4.1 using the results from the above subsections.

Proof (of Theorem 4.1). If one could *test* whether a given (i, j, k) is a good tuple, there would be no need to have one explicitly given as in Construction 4.6, because the adversary could enumerate all $(i \leq j \leq k) \in [n]^3$ cases. Unfortunately, we do not know how to test being $(1 - \varepsilon)$-good for Π, even if we could test being good for G (e.g., due to knowing G explicitly). However, we can do as follows.

- **Defining good tuples for attack.** For fixed parameters (including ε) define (i, j, k) to be δ-*good* for attack, if by using (i, j, k) in Construction 4.6, the adversary wins the attack with probability at least $\rho - \varepsilon - \delta$. When $\delta = 0$, simply call (i, j, k) good for the attack.

- **There are tuples that are good for the attack.** Due to Claim 4.7, we already know that there exist tuples that are both good for G and $(1 - \varepsilon)$-good for the RBE scheme. Therefore, by Claim 4.7, there exists at least one tuple that is good for the attack.
- **Finding tuples that are good for the attack.** Finally, we observe that, even though one might not be able to directly test whether a given (i, j, k) is good for G or Π, one can indeed find a tuple (i, j, k) that is guaranteed to be δ-good for the attack in time $\mathrm{poly}(\kappa/\delta)$. All the adversary does is to go over all $(i \leq j \leq k) \in [n]^3$ tuples, run the attack enough *in its head* for $q = \kappa/\delta$ times to approximate its probability of success within $\pm\delta$ with probability $1 - \mathrm{negl}(\kappa)$. Finally, the adversary simply uses the tuple (i, j, k) that leads to the maximum (estimated) probability of success. Since we already know that there is at least one tuple that is good for the attack, the adversary can always find a δ-good one this way.

Putting this together, the adversary first finds a $(\delta/2)$-good tuple for the attack with probability $1 - \mathrm{negl}(\kappa)$, and then plugs it into Construction 4.6 and runs the attack against the challenger. The overall probability of adversary's success, this way, will be at least $\rho - \varepsilon - \delta/2 - \mathrm{negl}(\kappa) \geq \rho - \varepsilon - \delta$. □

4.4 Extensions

In this subsection, we show some extensions to our main result Theorem 4.1.

Allowing Update Times to Depend on Identities. We first observe that the lower bound of Theorem 4.1 holds even if the update graph G of the scheme can depend on the registered identities and the CRS (but not on the keys).

It is easier to see that the update graph G can depend on the name of the registered identities, as the adversary simply picks the identities to be $\mathrm{id}_i = i$ and fixes them throughout the attack.

Allowing dependence on the CRS is slightly more subtle. In summary, this dependence is allowed, because the CRS is sampled and fixed *before* the keys are sampled. In more detail, the main observation is that for *every* crs ← CRS, the following hold.

1. The update graph G_{crs} is fixed (with bounded out-degree). Therefore, there will be a skipping sequence in G_{crs}, as proved in Theorem 3.2.
2. Definition 4.3 of $(1 - \varepsilon)$-good can be adapted for any fixed crs.
3. Therefore, Lemma 4.5 can be stated and proved (using the same exact proof) for the fixed crs, showing that a good tuple exists conditioned on crs.
4. Tuples that are good conditioned on the fixed crs can be used exactly as before to break the RBE scheme.

Allowing Frequent Updates for Some Identities. Theorem 4.1 is stated for schemes in which *all* parties receive up to d updates. However, a closer look at the proof reveals that all we need is a fixed update graph[12] such that there are at least $n \geq \binom{\ell+d}{d+1}$ identities who receive at most d updates and that $|\mathsf{pp}_i| \leq \alpha$ for all the first i registrations. The conclusion of Theorem 4.1 holds as stated.

To see why the above mentioned extension holds, all we have to show is that any update graph G with $n \geq \binom{\ell+d}{d+1}$ vertices of out-degree at most d has a tuple that is $(1-\varepsilon)$-good. In order to show such tuples exist, all we have to do is to show that sufficiently large skipping sequences exist in DAGs with sufficiently many nodes with bounded out-degrees. Although we can prove such a result by adapting the proof of Theorem 3.2, we prove this extension through a black-box use of Theorem Theorem 3.2.

Theorem 4.10 (Skipping Sequences from Sufficiently Many Nodes of Bounded Out-Degrees). *Let G be a forward DAG and there exists $\mathcal{S} \subseteq \mathcal{V}_G$ such that: $|\mathcal{S}| = \binom{k+d}{d+1}$ (for $k, d \in \mathbb{N}$) and $\deg^+(u) \leq d$ for all $u \in \mathcal{S}$. Then, there exists a skipping sequence in G of size at least k.*

Proof Let $\mathcal{S} = \{v_1 < v_2 \cdots < v_n\}$. Construct a DAG $G_\mathcal{S}$ as follows. $G_\mathcal{S}$ has n vertices. For the convenience of presentation, we keep the labels of the vertices of $G_\mathcal{S}$ as $\{v_1 < v_2 \cdots < v_n\}$ and do not rename them to $[n]$. For any edge $(v_i, v) \in G$, let $j \in [n]$ be the largest number such that $v_j \leq v$ (note that j always exits and it could be the same as i), and then add the edge (v_i, v_j) to $G_\mathcal{S}$.

Observe that the out-degrees $G_\mathcal{S}$ remain at most d. That is because we do not add any outgoing edges to any vertex (although we do add incoming edges to some). Therefore, by Theorem 3.2, there is a skipping sequence $\mathcal{U} = \{u_1 < \cdots < u_k\}$ in the graph $G_\mathcal{S}$. We claim that the same sequence $\mathcal{U}$ is also skipping in G. Below, we prove this by contradiction.

Suppose $\mathcal{U}$ is *not* skipping in G. This means that there is $t \in [k-1]$ and an edge $(u_t, v) \in G$ such that $u_{t+1} \leq v \leq u_k$. By the definition of $G_\mathcal{S}$, the edge $(u_t, v) \in G$ will generate an edge $(u_t, v_j) \in G_\mathcal{S}$ for $u_{t+1} \leq v_j \leq u_k$, which contradicts the assumption that $\mathcal{U}$ is a skipping sequence in $G_\mathcal{S}$. □

Putting all the extensions above together, we obtain the following theorem.

Theorem 4.11 (Extension of the Main Result). *Let Π be an RBE scheme with completeness probability ρ whose update graph G is fixed for any fixed sequence $\mathsf{id}_1, \mathsf{id}_2, \ldots$ of identities and fixed CRS crs. Moreover, suppose the update graph for the fixed crs and the fixed set of n identities has at least $\binom{\ell+d}{d+1}$ identities who receive at most d updates, and that $|\mathsf{pp}_i| \leq \alpha$ for all the n registrations. Then there is a 0-corruption $\mathrm{poly}(\kappa)$-time adversary who breaks Π with probability $\rho - \sqrt{\alpha \ln 2/(2\ell)} - \delta$ for arbitrarily small $\delta = 1/\mathrm{poly}(\kappa)$.*

Handling Schemes with an Amortized Bound on the Number of Updates. The extension above allows us to use an amortized (i.e., average-case) upper bound on the number of updates as well. For example, if the expected number of updates is d among n registered parties, then by an averaging argument, for at least $n/2$

---

[12] As discussed before, this graph can depend on the identities and/or the CRS.

of the parties, the number of received updates is at most $2d$. As a result, if the public parameter remains at most α bits and $n \geq 2 \cdot \binom{\ell+2d}{2d+1}$, then the adversary can break the RBE scheme with probability $\rho - \sqrt{\alpha \ln 2 / (2\ell)} - \delta$.

Acknowledgements. We thank Sanjam Garg, Mohammad Hajiabadi, and Saeed Mahloujifar for useful discussions. We also thank the anonymous reviewers of TCC 2022 for useful suggestions, including the extension of the main result allowing some identities to receive frequent updates.

Appendix

A   Completeness and Security of RBE Schemes

Definition A.1 (Completeness, Compactness, and Efficiency of RBE).
Consider the following game $\mathsf{Comp}_{\mathcal{A}}(\kappa)$ *between a challenger* $\mathcal{C}$ *and an interactive computationally unbounded adversary* $\mathcal{A}$ *who is yet limited to* $\mathrm{poly}(\kappa)$ *rounds of interaction.*

1. ***Initialization.*** $\mathcal{C}$ *sets* $\mathsf{pp} = \bot$, $\mathsf{aux} = \bot$, $\mathsf{u} = \bot$, $\mathcal{D} = \emptyset$, $\mathsf{id}^* = \bot$, $t = 0$, *and* $\mathsf{crs} \leftarrow U_{\mathrm{poly}(\kappa)}$, *and sends the sampled* crs *to* $\mathcal{A}$.
2. *Till* $\mathcal{A}$ *continues (which is at most* $\mathrm{poly}(\kappa)$ *steps), proceed as follows. At every iteration,* $\mathcal{A}$ *chooses exactly one of the actions below to perform.*
   (a) ***Registering a corrupted (non-target) identity.*** $\mathcal{A}$ *sends some* $\mathsf{id} \notin \mathcal{D}$ *and* pk *to* $\mathcal{C}$. $\mathcal{C}$ *registers* $(\mathsf{id}, \mathsf{pk})$ *by letting* $\mathsf{pp} := \mathsf{Reg}^{[\mathsf{aux}]}(\mathsf{crs}, \mathsf{pp}, \mathsf{id}, \mathsf{pk})$ *and* $\mathcal{D} := \mathcal{D} \cup \{\mathsf{id}\}$.
   (b) ***Registering the (uncorrupted) target identity.*** *This step is allowed only if* $\mathsf{id}^* = \bot$. *In that case,* $\mathcal{A}$ *sends some* $\mathsf{id}^* \notin \mathcal{D}$ *to* $\mathcal{C}$. $\mathcal{C}$ *then samples* $(\mathsf{pk}^*, \mathsf{sk}^*) \leftarrow \mathsf{Gen}(1^\kappa)$, *updates* $\mathsf{pp} := \mathsf{Reg}^{[\mathsf{aux}]}(\mathsf{crs}, \mathsf{pp}, \mathsf{id}^*, \mathsf{pk}^*)$ *and* $\mathcal{D} := \mathcal{D} \cup \{\mathsf{id}^*\}$, *and sends* pk^* *to* $\mathcal{A}$.
   (c) ***Encrypting for the target identity.*** *This step is allowed only if* $\mathsf{id}^* \neq \bot$. *In that case,* $\mathcal{C}$ *sets* $t = t + 1$. $\mathcal{A}$ *sends* $\mathsf{m}_t \in \{0,1\}^*$ *to* $\mathcal{C}$ *who then sets* $\mathsf{m}'_t := \mathsf{m}_t$ *and sends back a corresponding ciphertext* $\mathsf{ct}_t \leftarrow \mathsf{Enc}(\mathsf{crs}, \mathsf{pp}, \mathsf{id}^*, \mathsf{m}_t)$ *to* $\mathcal{A}$.
   (d) ***Decryption for the target identity.*** $\mathcal{A}$ *sends a* $j \in [t]$ *to* $\mathcal{C}$. $\mathcal{C}$ *then lets* $\mathsf{m}'_j = \mathsf{Dec}(\mathsf{sk}^*, \mathsf{u}, \mathsf{ct}_j)$. *If* $\mathsf{m}'_j = \mathsf{GetUpd}$, $\mathcal{C}$ *gets* $\mathsf{u} = \mathsf{Upd}^{\mathsf{aux}}(\mathsf{pp}, \mathsf{id}^*)$ *and then* $\mathsf{m}'_j = \mathsf{Dec}(\mathsf{sk}^*, \mathsf{u}, \mathsf{ct}_j)$.

Let $n = |\mathcal{D}|$ *be the number of identities registered when the adversary ends the game. We require the following properties to hold for such* $\mathcal{A}$ *(as specified above) in the game* $\mathsf{Comp}_{\mathcal{A}}(\kappa)$.

- ***Completeness.*** *The adversary* $\mathcal{A}$ *wins, if there is some* $j \in [t]$ *for which* $\mathsf{m}'_j \neq \mathsf{m}_j$. *We require that* $\mathsf{P}[\mathcal{A} \text{ wins } \mathsf{Comp}_{\mathcal{A}}(\kappa)] = \mathrm{negl}(\kappa)$.[13]

---

[13] For perfectly complete schemes we require this probability to be zero.

- *Compactness and efficiency.* For the following three properties, here we state the default requirements for standard RBE; however, in this work, we also consider the relaxed version of RBE in which these quantities could be other parameters that are still sublinear in n (e.g., $\mathrm{poly}(\kappa) \cdot \sqrt{n}$) for compactness and runtime efficiency. For number of updates, we also allow any sublinear function of n to be a feasible number for RBE.
  - *Compactness.* $|\mathsf{pp}|, |\mathsf{u}| \leq \mathrm{poly}(\kappa, \log(n))$.
  - *Efficiency of runtime of registration and update.* The running time of each invocation of Reg and Upd is at most $\mathrm{poly}(\kappa, \log(n))$.
  - *Efficiency of the number of updates.* The total number of invocations of Upd for identity id^* in Step 2(d) of the game $\mathsf{Comp}_{\mathcal{A}}(\kappa)$ is at most $O(\log(n))$.

Definition A.2 (Security of RBE). *For any interactive PPT adversary $\mathcal{A}$, consider the following game $\mathsf{Sec}_{\mathcal{A}}(\kappa)$ between $\mathcal{A}$ and a challenger $\mathcal{C}$.*

1. *Initialization.* $\mathcal{C}$ sets $\mathsf{pp} = \bot$, $\mathsf{aux} = \bot$, $\mathcal{D} = \emptyset$, $\mathsf{id}^* = \bot$, $\mathsf{crs} \leftarrow U_{\mathrm{poly}(\kappa)}$ and sends the sampled crs to $\mathcal{A}$.
2. *Till $\mathcal{A}$ continues (which is at most $\mathrm{poly}(\kappa)$ steps), proceed as follows. At every iteration, $\mathcal{A}$ chooses exactly one of the actions below to perform.*
   (a) *Registering non-target identity.* $\mathcal{A}$ sends some $\mathsf{id} \notin \mathcal{D}$ and pk to $\mathcal{C}$. $\mathcal{C}$ registers $(\mathsf{id}, \mathsf{pk})$ by $\mathsf{pp} := \mathsf{Reg}^{[\mathsf{aux}]}(\mathsf{crs}, \mathsf{pp}, \mathsf{id}, \mathsf{pk})$ and $\mathcal{D} := \mathcal{D} \cup \{\mathsf{id}\}$.
   (b) *Registering the target identity.* This step can be run only if $\mathsf{id}^* = \bot$. $\mathcal{A}$ sends some $\mathsf{id}^* \notin \mathcal{D}$ to $\mathcal{C}$. $\mathcal{C}$ then samples $(\mathsf{pk}^*, \mathsf{sk}^*) \leftarrow \mathsf{Gen}(1^\kappa)$, updates $\mathsf{pp} := \mathsf{Reg}^{[\mathsf{aux}]}(\mathsf{crs}, \mathsf{pp}, \mathsf{id}^*, \mathsf{pk}^*)$, $\mathcal{D} := \mathcal{D} \cup \{\mathsf{id}^*\}$, and sends pk^* to $\mathcal{A}$.
3. *Encrypting for the target identity.* If $\mathsf{id}^* = \bot$, then $\mathcal{A}$ first sends some $\mathsf{id}^* \notin \mathcal{D}$ to $\mathcal{C}$ (this is for modeling encryptions for non-registered target identities.) Next $\mathcal{A}$ sends two messages m_0, m_1 of the same length to $\mathcal{C}$. Next, $\mathcal{C}$ generates $\mathsf{ct} \leftarrow \mathsf{Enc}(\mathsf{crs}, \mathsf{pp}, \mathsf{id}^*, m_b)$, where $b \leftarrow \{0, 1\}$ is a random bit, and sends ct to $\mathcal{A}$.[14]
4. *The adversary $\mathcal{A}$ outputs a bit b' and wins the game if $b = b'$.*

An RBE scheme is secure if for all PPT $\mathcal{A}$, $\mathsf{P}[\mathcal{A} \text{ wins } \mathsf{Sec}_{\mathcal{A}}(\kappa)] < \frac{1}{2} + \mathrm{negl}(\kappa)$.

B   Information-Theoretic Notions and Lemmas

Definition B.1 (Mutual Information). *The mutual information of two discrete random variables X, Y is defined as*

$$I(X; Y) = H(X) + H(Y) - H(XY) = H(X) - H(X|Y) = H(Y) - H(Y|X).$$

The conditional mutual information $I(X; Y|Z)$ is defined as $\mathbb{E}_{z \leftarrow Z}[I(X|_z; Y|_z)]$. The chain rule for mutual information states that $I(X; YZ) = I(X; Y) + I(X; Z|Y)$.

---

[14] In the original paper of [GHMR18], the scheme's security was defined for bit encryption. Even though secure bit-encryption schemes can be extended for full-fledged schemes by independently encrypting every bit, here we write the definition directly for the resulting scheme.

Definition B.2 (Kullback-Leibler Divergence). *For any two random variables X and Y where $X \subseteq Y$, the he Kullback-Leibler (KL) divergence (in base 2) is defined as*

$$D_{\mathrm{KL}}(X \parallel Y) = \sum_{x \in X} \mathsf{P}_X[x] \cdot \log \frac{\mathsf{P}_X[x]}{\mathsf{P}_Y[x]}.$$

Lemma B.3 (Conditional Mutual Information vs. KL Div). *For any three jointly distributed random variables X, Y, Z the following holds:*

$$I(X; Y|Z) = D_{\mathrm{KL}}(XYZ \parallel (X|_Z \otimes Y|_Z)Z).$$

In particular, when Z does not exist, we have $I(X; Y) = D_{\mathrm{KL}}(XY \parallel X \otimes Y)$.

We give a proof for completeness.

Proof By definition, we know

$$I(X; Y|Z) = \mathop{\mathbb{E}}_{z \leftarrow Z}[I(X|_z; Y|_z)] = \sum_{z \in Z} \mathsf{P}_Z[z] I(X|_z; Y|_z).$$

Now, if we call $P = X|_z$ and $Q = Y|_z$, then $I(X|_z; Y|_z) = I(P; Q)$ is equal to:

$$= H(P) + H(Q) - H(PQ)$$

$$= -\sum_{x \in P} \mathsf{P}_P[x] \log \mathsf{P}_P[x] - \sum_{y \in Q} \mathsf{P}_Q[y] \log \mathsf{P}_Q[y] + \sum_{x \in P} \sum_{y \in Q} \mathsf{P}_{PQ}[x, y] \log \mathsf{P}_{PQ}[x, y]$$

$$= -\sum_{x \in P} \sum_{y \in Q} \mathsf{P}_{PQ}[x, y] \log \mathsf{P}_P[x] - \sum_{y \in Q} \sum_{x \in P} \mathsf{P}_{PQ}[x, y] \log \mathsf{P}_Q[y]$$

$$\qquad + \sum_{x \in P} \sum_{y \in Q} \mathsf{P}_{PQ}[x, y] \log \mathsf{P}_{PQ}[x, y]$$

$$= \sum_{x \in P} \sum_{y \in Q} \mathsf{P}_{PQ}[x, y] \log \frac{\mathsf{P}_{PQ}[x, y]}{\mathsf{P}_P[x] \cdot \mathsf{P}_Q[y]}.$$

Therefore, we get

$$I(X; Y|Z) = \sum_{z \in Z} \left(\mathsf{P}_Z[z] \sum_{x \in X} \sum_{y \in Y} \mathsf{P}_{XY|z}[x, y] \log \frac{\mathsf{P}_{XY|z}[x, y]}{\mathsf{P}_{X|z}[x] \cdot \mathsf{P}_{Y|z}[y]} \right)$$

$$= \sum_{z \in Z} \sum_{x \in X} \sum_{y \in Y} \mathsf{P}_{XYZ}[x, y, z] \log \frac{\mathsf{P}_{XY|z}[x, y]}{\mathsf{P}_{X|z}[x] \cdot \mathsf{P}_{Y|z}[y]}$$

$$= \sum_{z \in Z} \sum_{x \in X} \sum_{y \in Y} \mathsf{P}_{XYZ}[x, y, z] \log \frac{\mathsf{P}_{XY|z}[x, y] \cdot \mathsf{P}_Z[z]}{\mathsf{P}_{X|z}[x] \cdot \mathsf{P}_{Y|z}[y] \cdot \mathsf{P}_Z[z]}$$

$$= \sum_{z \in Z} \sum_{x \in X} \sum_{y \in Y} \mathsf{P}_{XYZ}[x, y, z] \log \frac{\mathsf{P}_{XYZ}[x, y, z]}{\mathsf{P}_{X|z}[x] \cdot \mathsf{P}_{Y|z}[y] \cdot \mathsf{P}_Z[z]}$$

$$= D_{\mathrm{KL}}(XYZ \parallel (X|_Z \otimes Y|_Z)Z).$$

$\square$

Theorem B.4 (Pinsker's Inequality). *For random variables X, Y we have*

$$SD(X, Y) \leq \sqrt{\frac{D_{KL}(X \parallel Y) \cdot \ln 2}{2}}$$

The following lemma follows from Lemma B.3 and Pinsker's inequality.

Lemma B.5. *For random variables X, Y, Z, it holds that*

$$SD(XYZ, (X|_Z \otimes Y|_Z)Z) \leq \sqrt{\frac{I(X; Y|Z) \cdot \ln 2}{2}}.$$

In particular, when Z does not exist, we have $SD(XY, X \otimes Y) \leq \sqrt{\frac{I(X;Y) \cdot \ln 2}{2}}$.

We finally prove the twig lemma (i.e., Lemma 2.7).

Proof (of Lemma 2.7). Let $I(Y; X_0 \ldots X_\ell) = \alpha$ and $\alpha_i = I(Y; X_i | X_{i-1} \ldots X_0)$. Firstly, we have $\alpha = H(Y) - H(Y|X_0 \ldots X_\ell) \leq H(Y)$. By repeated applications of the chain rule of mutual information,

$$H(Y) \geq \alpha = I(Y; X_0) + \sum_{i \in [\ell]} I(Y; X_i | X_0 \ldots X_{i-1}) \geq \ell \cdot \mathop{\mathbb{E}}_{i \in [\ell]}[\alpha_i].$$

For each $i \in [\ell]$, we get $\alpha_i = D_{KL}(YX_i \ldots, X_0 \parallel YX'_i X_{i-1} \ldots X_0)$ by letting $X = X_i, Z = X_0 \ldots X_{i-1}$ in Lemma B.3. By applying Pinsker's inequality through Lemma B.5 we now get

$$SD(YX_i \ldots, X_0, YX'_i X_{i-1} \ldots X_0) \leq \sqrt{\frac{\alpha_i \ln 2}{2}}.$$

To conclude, we get

$$\mathop{\mathbb{E}}_{i \leftarrow [\ell]} \left[\sqrt{\frac{\alpha_i \ln 2}{2}} \right] \leq \sqrt{\frac{\mathbb{E}_{i \leftarrow [\ell]}[\alpha_i \ln 2]}{2}} \leq \sqrt{\frac{(\alpha/\ell) \ln 2}{2}} \leq \sqrt{\frac{H(Y) \ln 2}{2\ell}}.$$

The first inequality is due to the concavity of $\sqrt{\cdot}$, and Jensen's inequality.

C   Theorem 3.2 is Optimal

In this section, we show that the bound in Theorem 3.2 is tight. Namely, we prove the following theorem.

Theorem C.1 (Optimality of Theorem 3.2). *For all $n = \binom{k+d}{d+1} - 1$ where integers $k \geq 1, d \geq 0$, there exists a forward DAG $G_{k,d}$ of n vertices and $\deg^+(G_{k,d}) \leq d$ that does not have any skipping sequence of size k.*

We will use induction on d to prove Theorem C.1.

Construction C.2 (Construction of Optimal DAG of Out-Degree d**)**
Let $k \geq 1, d \geq 0$ be integer. We construct a graph $G_{k,d}$ recursively as follows (Fig. 3).

1. *If $d = 0$, $G_{k,0}$ has $k - 1$ vertices and no edges.*[15]
2. *If $d \geq 1$, do the following.*
   (a) *For $i \in [k - 1]$ let $\mathcal{G}_i$ be a copy of $G_{k-i+1,d-1}$ followed by a new vertex u_i at the end. Moreover, in addition to the edges in $G_{k-i+1,d-1}$, for all $v \in \mathcal{G}_i$ (including $v = u_i$) add the edge (v, u_i) to $\mathcal{G}_i$.*
   (b) *Divide the vertices of $G_{k,d}$ into $k - 1$ groups, such that the i-th group is a copy of $\mathcal{G}_i$ that comes right after $\mathcal{G}_{i-1}$.*

To prove Theorem C.1, it suffices to prove the following lemma.

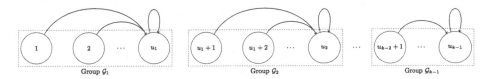

Fig. 3. Illustration of the construction of the optimal forward DAG $G_{k,d} = (\mathcal{V}_{G_{k,d}}, \mathcal{E}_{G_{k,d}})$ where $\mathcal{V}_{G_{k,d}} = [\binom{k+d}{d+1} - 1]$. Group $\mathcal{G}_1$ has $\binom{k+d-1}{d}$ vertices and each vertex of $\mathcal{G}_1$ has an out-going edge to vertex u_1 which is the last vertex of $\mathcal{G}_1$. Group $\mathcal{G}_{k-1}$ has $\binom{d+1}{d}$ vertices and each vertex of $\mathcal{G}_{k-1}$ has an out-going edge to vertex u_{k-1}.

Lemma C.3. *Graph $G_{k,d}$ of Construction C.2 has $n = \binom{k+d}{d+1} - 1$ vertices, degree d and all of its skipping sequences are of size at most $k - 1$.*

Note that by Theorem C.1 we already know that if $k \geq 1$, then $G_{k,d}$ has a skipping sequence of size $\geq k - 1$; so by proving Lemma C.3 we actually conclude that its maximum size of skipping sequences will be exactly $k - 1$.

Proof (of Lemma C.3). The proof is by induction. For $d = 0$, the proof is trivial.

Now suppose $d \geq 1$. The number vertices of $G_{k,d}$ by induction and the hockey-stick identity will be

$$\sum_{i\in[k-1]} |\mathcal{V}_{G_{k-i+1,d-1}}| + 1 = \sum_{i\in[k-1]} \binom{k+d-i}{d} = \binom{k+d}{d+1} - \binom{d}{d}.$$

Let $\mathcal{S}$ be any skipping sequence in $G_{k,d}$. Let $j \in [k-1]$ be the largest integer such that there is a vertex from $\mathcal{G}_j$ in $\mathcal{S}$. We first show that there can be at most one vertex from each of the previous $j - 1$ groups $\{\mathcal{G}_i\}_{i\in[j-1]}$ in $\mathcal{S}$. Assume that there are two vertices $u < v$ such that $u, v \in \mathcal{S} \cap \mathcal{G}_i$. Let $x \in \mathcal{G}_j \cap \mathcal{S}$. Then,

---

[15] For $k = 1$, this graph is the empty graph that has no vertices.

$v < u < x$ will all be in $\mathcal{S}$, while v has an outgoing edge to u_i (the last vertex in $\mathcal{G}_i$) with $u \leq u_i < x$, but this contradicts the definition of skipping sequences.

Let $\mathcal{S} = \mathcal{S}_1 \cup \mathcal{S}_2$, where $\mathcal{S}_1 = \mathcal{S} \cap (\cup_{i<j}\mathcal{G}_i)$ and $\mathcal{S}_2 = \mathcal{S} \cap \mathcal{G}_j$. We already know that $|\mathcal{S}_1| \leq j - 1$. It is sufficient to show that $|\mathcal{S}_2| \leq k - j$. Firstly, note that if u_j (i.e., the last node in $\mathcal{G}_j$) belongs to $\mathcal{S}$, then no other vertex in $\mathcal{G}_j$ can belong to $\mathcal{S}$, as otherwise, it will contradict the definition of skipping sequences. Secondly, note that if $\mathcal{S}$ is a skipping sequence, then its restriction $\mathcal{S}_2 = \mathcal{S} \cap \mathcal{G}_j$ shall be skipping as well. Therefore, by induction $|\mathcal{S}_2| \leq \max\{1, k - j\} = k - j$, and so $|\mathcal{S}| = |\mathcal{S}_1| + |\mathcal{S}_2| \leq j - 1 + k - j = k - 1$. $\qquad\square$

References

ARP03. Al-Riyami, S.S., Paterson, K.G.: Certificateless public key cryptography. In: Laih, C.-S. (ed.) ASIACRYPT 2003. LNCS, vol. 2894, pp. 452–473. Springer, Heidelberg (2003). https://doi.org/10.1007/978-3-540-40061-5_29

BdM94. Benaloh, J., de Mare, M.: One-way accumulators: a decentralized alternative to digital signatures. In: Helleseth, T. (ed.) EUROCRYPT 1993. LNCS, vol. 765, pp. 274–285. Springer, Heidelberg (1994). https://doi.org/10.1007/3-540-48285-7_24

BF01. Boneh, D., Franklin, M.: Identity-based encryption from the weil pairing. In: Kilian, J. (ed.) CRYPTO 2001. LNCS, vol. 2139, pp. 213–229. Springer, Heidelberg (2001). https://doi.org/10.1007/3-540-44647-8_13

BGI+01. Barak, B., et al.: On the (Im)possibility of obfuscating programs. In: Kilian, J. (ed.) CRYPTO 2001. LNCS, vol. 2139, pp. 1–18. Springer, Heidelberg (2001). https://doi.org/10.1007/3-540-44647-8_1

BH22. Blocki, J., Holman, B.: Sustained space and cumulative complexity tradeoffs for data-dependent memory-hard functions. Cryptology ePrint Archive, Paper 2022/832 (2022). eprint.iacr.org/2022/832

BP97. Barić, N., Pfitzmann, B.: Collision-free accumulators and fail-stop signature schemes without trees. In: Fumy, W. (ed.) EUROCRYPT 1997. LNCS, vol. 1233, pp. 480–494. Springer, Heidelberg (1997). https://doi.org/10.1007/3-540-69053-0_33

CCV04. Cheng, Z., Comley, R., Vasiu, L.: Remove key escrow from the identity-based encryption system. In: Levy, J.-J., Mayr, E.W., Mitchell, J.C. (eds.) TCS 2004. IIFIP, vol. 155, pp. 37–50. Springer, Boston, MA (2004). https://doi.org/10.1007/1-4020-8141-3_6

CES21. Cong, K., Eldefrawy, K., Smart, N.P.: Optimizing registration based encryption. In: Paterson, M.B. (ed.) IMACC 2021. LNCS, vol. 13129, pp. 129–157. Springer, Cham (2021). https://doi.org/10.1007/978-3-030-92641-0_7

Cho09. Chow, S.S.M.: Removing escrow from identity-based encryption. In: Jarecki, S., Tsudik, G. (eds.) PKC 2009. LNCS, vol. 5443, pp. 256–276. Springer, Heidelberg (2009). https://doi.org/10.1007/978-3-642-00468-1_15

CL02. Camenisch, J., Lysyanskaya, A.: Dynamic accumulators and application to efficient revocation of anonymous credentials. In: Yung, M. (ed.) CRYPTO 2002. LNCS, vol. 2442, pp. 61–76. Springer, Heidelberg (2002). https://doi.org/10.1007/3-540-45708-9_5

DG17.   Döttling, N., Garg, S.: Identity-based encryption from the diffie-hellman assumption. In: Katz, J., Shacham, H. (eds.) CRYPTO 2017. LNCS, vol. 10401, pp. 537–569. Springer, Cham (2017). https://doi.org/10.1007/978-3-319-63688-7_18

EKW19. Emura, K., Katsumata, S., Watanabe, Y.: Identity-based encryption with security against the KGC: a formal model and its instantiation from lattices. In: Sako, K., Schneider, S., Ryan, P.Y.A. (eds.) ESORICS 2019. LNCS, vol. 11736, pp. 113–133. Springer, Cham (2019). https://doi.org/10.1007/978-3-030-29962-0_6

GGH+13. Garg, S., Gentry, C., Halevi, S., Raykova, M., Sahai, A., Waters, B.: Candidate indistinguishability obfuscation and functional encryption for all circuits. In: 54th Annual Symposium on Foundations of Computer Science, 26–29 Oct 2013, pp. 40–49. IEEE Computer Society Press, Berkeley, CA, USA (2013)

GHM+19. Garg, S., Hajiabadi, M., Mahmoody, M., Rahimi, A., Sekar, S.: Registration-based encryption from standard assumptions. In: Lin, D., Sako, K. (eds.) PKC 2019. LNCS, vol. 11443, pp. 63–93. Springer, Cham (2019). https://doi.org/10.1007/978-3-030-17259-6_3

GHMR18. Garg, S., Hajiabadi, M., Mahmoody, M., Rahimi, A.: Registration-based encryption: removing private-key generator from IBE. In: Beimel, A., Dziembowski, S. (eds.) TCC 2018. LNCS, vol. 11239, pp. 689–718. Springer, Cham (2018). https://doi.org/10.1007/978-3-030-03807-6_25

GLSW08. Goyal, V., Lu, S., Sahai, A., Waters, B.: Black-box accountable authority identity-based encryption. In: Proceedings of the 15th ACM Conference on Computer and Communications Security, pp. 427–436. ACM (2008)

Goy07. Goyal, V.: Reducing trust in the PKG in identity based cryptosystems. In: Menezes, A. (ed.) CRYPTO 2007. LNCS, vol. 4622, pp. 430–447. Springer, Heidelberg (2007). https://doi.org/10.1007/978-3-540-74143-5_24

GV20.   Goyal, R., Vusirikala, S.: Verifiable registration-based encryption. In: Micciancio, D., Ristenpart, T. (eds.) CRYPTO 2020. LNCS, vol. 12170, pp. 621–651. Springer, Cham (2020). https://doi.org/10.1007/978-3-030-56784-2_21

HW15.   Hubacek, P., Wichs, D.: On the communication complexity of secure function evaluation with long output. In: Roughgarden, T. (ed.) ITCS 2015: 6th Conference on Innovations in Theoretical Computer Science, 11–13 Jan 2015, pp. 163–172. Association for Computing Machinery, Rehovot, Israel (2015)

JLS21. Jain, A., Lin, H., Sahai, A.: Indistinguishability obfuscation from well-founded assumptions. In: Proceedings of the 53rd Annual ACM SIGACT Symposium on Theory of Computing, pp. 60–73 (2021)

Rog15. Rogaway, P.: The moral character of cryptographic work. Cryptology ePrint Archive, Report 2015/1162 (2015). eprint.iacr.org/2015/1162

Sha84. Shamir, A.: Identity-based cryptosystems and signature schemes. In: Blakley, G.R., Chaum, D. (eds.) CRYPTO 1984. LNCS, vol. 196, pp. 47–53. Springer, Heidelberg (1985). https://doi.org/10.1007/3-540-39568-7_5

WQT18. Wei, Q., Qi, F., Tang, Z.: Remove key escrow from the BF and Gentry identity-based encryption with non-interactive key generation. Telecommunication Systems, pp. 1–10 (2018)

IBE with Incompressible Master Secret and Small Identity Secrets

Nico Döttling[1], Sanjam Garg[2,3], Sruthi Sekar[2(✉)], and Mingyuan Wang[2]

[1] Helmholtz Center for Information Security (CISPA), Saarbrücken, Germany
[2] University of California, Berkeley, Berkeley, USA
{sanjamg,sruthi,mingyuan}@berkeley.edu
[3] NTT Research, Palo Alto, USA

Abstract. Side-stepping the protection provided by cryptography, exfiltration attacks are becoming a considerable real-world threat. With the goal of mitigating the exfiltration of cryptographic keys, big-key cryptosystems have been developed over the past few years. These systems come with very large secret keys which are thus hard to exfiltrate. Typically, in such systems, the setup time must be large as it generates the large secret key. However, subsequently, the encryption and decryption operations, that must be performed repeatedly, are required to be efficient. Specifically, the encryption uses only a small public key and the decryption only accesses small ciphertext-dependent parts of the full secret key. Nonetheless, these schemes require decryption to have access to the entire secret key. Thus, using such big-key cryptosystems necessitate that users carry around large secret-keys on their devices, which can be a hassle and in some cases might also render exfiltration easy.

With the goal of removing this problem, in this work, we initiate the study of big-key identity-based encryption (bk-IBE). In such a system, the master secret-key is allowed to be large but we require that the identity-based secret keys are short. This allows users to use the identity-based short keys as the ephemeral secret keys that can be more easily carried around and allow for decrypting ciphertexts matching a particular identity, e.g. messages that were encrypted on a particular date. In particular:

- We build a new definitional framework for bk-IBE capturing a range of applications. In the case when the exfiltration is small our definition promises stronger security—namely, an adversary can break semantic security for only a few identities, proportional to the amount of leakage it gets. In contrast, in the catastrophic case where a large fraction of the master secret key has been ex-filtrated, we can still resort to a guarantee that the ciphertexts generated for a randomly chosen identity (or, an identity with enough entropy) remain protected. We demonstrate how this framework captures the best possible security guarantees.
- We show the first construction of such a bk-IBE offering strong security properties. Our construction is based on standard assumptions on groups with bilinear pairings and brings together techniques from seemingly different contexts such as leakage resilient cryptography, reusable two-round MPC, and laconic oblivious transfer. We expect our techniques to be of independent interest.

E. Kiltz and V. Vaikuntanathan (Eds.): TCC 2022, LNCS 13747, pp. 588–617, 2022.
https://doi.org/10.1007/978-3-031-22318-1_21

1   Introduction

Compromises of deployed cryptographic schemes by means of cryptanalysis are becoming increasingly rare. Instead, real-world adversaries try to circumvent the protection offered by cryptography via side-channel attacks. The most high-value targets for such side-channel attacks are cryptographic secret keys, which, if somehow exfiltrated, give the adversary unrestrained access to its victim's confidential communication. For advanced notions of public-key encryption such as identity-based encryption (IBE), exfiltration of the long-term master secret key is the single biggest risk coming with the adoption of such a system. This risk can be somewhat mitigated by distributing the master secret across several servers [BF01, Goy07, KG10, Cha12], but this comes with an additional overhead of maintaining multiple servers with shares of the master key.

Big-Key Cryptography in Bounded-Retrieval Model. The pervasiveness of side-channel attacks has motivated the development of cryptosystems that remain secure even when the adversary may have the ability to leak secrets of honest parties. One line of defense against such attacks, is to develop cryptosystems that have very large secret keys, or what is called *big-key* cryptography (see e.g., [Dzi06a, DLW06, CDD+07, ADW09, ADN+10, BKR16, MW20]). Big-key cryptosystems are developed with huge secret keys with the intent of making it hard to exfiltrate or leak on such keys. Furthermore, leakage of large amounts of data from a device can often be easier to detect and mitigate, or the bandwidth of any residual side-channels of such a device can be bounded conservatively[1]. Such cryptosystems aim to provide appropriate security even when a large amount of *arbitrary* leakage occurs on the big secret key. Prior works have focused on constructing various big-key primitives in the bounded-retrieval model, including symmetric-key encryption [BKR16], public-key encryption [ADN+10, MW20] and authenticated key agreement [Dzi06b, CDD+07, ADW09].

In the symmetric key setting [BKR16], the big-key setup involves a procedure to bound the adversary's probability of predicting an optimal length sub-key of the original exfiltrated big key, and using this to design an encapsulation mechanism that can extract a random key (such a key encapsulation mechanism directly gives an encryption scheme). Here, the encapsulation and decapsulation procedures only make local access to the big-key, thus ensuring efficiency. The key technique leveraged here is a primitive called "reusable locally-computable computational extractors" [Dzi06b, CDD+07, BKR16].

On the other hand, in the public-key setting, only the secret key is big and prone to exfiltration, while the public key is still short. The efficiency goals are that the encryption and decryption running times do not grow with the size of the big secret key. This naturally leads to the decryption procedure only making a few local ciphertext-dependent access to the big secret key. The security goal in this setting is typically to achieve semantic security, even when the adversary

---

[1] *Screaming Channels* [CPM+18] are one such example, which optimistically transfers at most 1 bit per second.

can obtain arbitrary leakage on the big secret key. The security is only required for fresh ciphertexts that are generated after the leakage by the adversary. In contrast, no meaningful security can be offered for the old ciphertexts based on which the leakage can be performed, e.g., the adversary might obtain leakage corresponding to a few bits of the plaintext for a given ciphertext.

The use of big-keys in a big-key public-key encryption scheme limits their usability and principal practicality. In particular, a user does not a priori know what parts of a secret key it will need to decrypt a ciphertext on a particular device. Thus, the user must carry around the entire large secret keys on all her devices. This poses two challenges: (1) including large secret keys on a number of devices can be a significant burden, e.g., wastage of limited storage space on a mobile device; and (2) the replication of a large secret key across multiple devices makes the user once again more susceptible to leakage based attacks, e.g., the loss of a mobile device could leak the entire big key.

1.1 Leakage-Resilient Identity-Based Encryption: Our Approach and Challenges

Motivated by these concerns, in this work, we will focus on the notion of identity-based encryption (IBE) as a natural proxy for encryption schemes that allow the delegation of decryption tokens. Recall that in an IBE scheme [BF01] a setup algorithm generates a pair $(\mathsf{mpk}, \mathsf{msk})$ of master public and master secret keys. The identity key generation algorithm takes the master secret key msk and an identity string id and outputs an identity secret key $\mathsf{sk}_{\mathsf{id}}$. To encrypt a message m, the encryption algorithm takes a master public key mpk and an identity string id and produces a ciphertext c. Finally, the decryption algorithm takes an identity secret key $\mathsf{sk}_{\mathsf{id}}$ and a ciphertext c and returns a message m. In terms of correctness, we require that if $\mathsf{sk}_{\mathsf{id}}$ is a user secret key corresponding to an identity id and a ciphertext c was encrypted to this same identity, then decrypting c with $\mathsf{sk}_{\mathsf{id}}$ returns the message that was encrypted.

Mapping our goal of designing a system with large long-term secrets but succinct public keys, ephemeral keys, and ciphertexts to the notion of IBE, we obtain the requirement that all system parameters except the master secret key should be succinct. We refer to this notion as big-key identity-based encryption (or bk-IBE for short).

Defining Security. In terms of security, the standard security notion for IBE requires that a ciphertext c^* encrypted to an identity id^* should remain secure, even if that adversary has access to any (polynomial number of) other secret keys $\mathsf{sk}_{\mathsf{id}}$ for $\mathsf{id} \neq \mathsf{id}^*$. Depending on whether the adversary has to specify the challenge identity id^* at the start of the experiment or is allowed to choose it adaptively depending on the master public key and some identity secret keys, we refer to selective or full security, respectively.

Now, when we consider (selective or full) security under leakage, the adversary additionally gets a leakage, $L(\mathsf{msk})$, on the master secret key. In the bounded retrieval model [Dzi06a, DLW06], we only limit the number of bits that the function L outputs, but otherwise allow L to perform any (efficient) computation on msk, i.e., L may try to somehow compress L first before producing its output. However, how does this notion of leakage resilience go along with our goal of making all system parameters small *except* the master secret key?

A moment of reflection points to the following dilemma, even in the setting of selective security: if the bit-length of the leakage function's output is allowed to be larger than the bit-length of an identity secret key, then the leakage function may just compute the key generation algorithm for the challenge identity id^* on msk and output the identity secret key sk_{id^*} thus obtained. This makes the adversary's task of breaking the security of the challenge ciphertext c^* essentially trivial: the leakage sk_{id^*} allows to recover the challenge message via the legitimate decryption algorithm!

For this reason, all prior works which studied the notion of leakage resilient IBE thus restricted themselves to a setting where the identity secret keys are large, and the master secret key is either large or permits no leakage [ADN+10, CDRW10, LRW11, HLWW13, CZLC16, NY19]. This brings us to the following question:

How can we meaningfully reconcile our design goal of short public parameters, identity secret keys, and ciphertexts with security against large amounts of master secret key leakage?

1.2 A New Security Notion and Construction for bk-IBE

From the above discussion, it is clear that we have to depart from the standard security notion of IBE. One way of relaxing the IBE security to circumvent the problem of exfiltration of the challenge identity key, described above, could consist of choosing the challenge identity at random or from a distribution of sufficiently high entropy, *after the adversary has obtained his leakage.*

While this indeed leads to a meaningful notion sufficient for certain use cases, the requirement of the challenge identity to be *entropic* puts restrictions on most of the use cases we envision. As an example, if the identities correspond to calendar dates, then choosing the challenge identity from a high entropy distribution would imply that the point in time corresponding to the challenge message necessarily needs to be highly uncertain—something that may not always be true.

However, we do expect exfiltration of a large portion of the already pretty big master secret key to be hard, particularly while also avoiding detection. Note that detection of leakage allows for alternative remedies such as revoking old keys and replacing them with new ones. Thus, a natural way to think of the leakage obtained by the adversary is as a *budget* of information about the master secret key, which we expect to be relatively smaller than the size of the master secret key. Of course, in a catastrophic event, a large fraction of the master secret key may be leaked, in which case, we would like to revert to the weaker entropic security guarantees.

The main intuition behind our new definition is as follows: the adversary may spend his exfiltration budget arbitrarily, and yet, he should not obtain more information than what he could get via a *trivial exfiltration attack*– leaking the identity secret keys of a number of challenge identities. Further, as mentioned above, catastrophic leakage of a large fraction of the master secret key still preserves entropic security.

In light of this, our security definition aims to capture how many identities the adversary could break. In particular, suppose the adversary obtains an ℓ-bit leakage from the master secret key. We define our big-key IBE to be secure if the adversary cannot break the security of $\geq \ell + 1$ number of identities. This is nearly-optimal as the adversary could launch the trivial attack by leaking $\Theta(\ell/\lambda)$ identity secret keys[2] in the entirety and, hence, breaking $\Theta(\ell/\lambda)$ identities.

Observe that this security notion is sufficiently strong for our applications. For instance, if the identities are the calendar dates, our security guarantees that an adversary leaking ℓ bits cannot break the security for more than ℓ days. Moreover, a random identity with sufficiently high entropy will also be secure since an adversary can break at most polynomially many identities.

Our Construction. Given this new security definition, we construct the first bk-IBE that achieves selective security based on the hardness of standard assumptions on groups with bilinear pairing. Our construction builds on seemingly very different tools such as leakage-resilient encryption scheme [HLWW13], reusable two-round MPC [BL20], and laconic OT [CDG+17].

Potential Extensions to ABE/HIBE. In the context of IBE, it is usual to also consider stronger encryption systems such as attribute-based encryption and hierarchical identity-based encryption, which typically offer a single small secret key that can be used to decrypt large families of ciphertexts. This is at odds with the goals of this paper, where we aim to not have a single short key that can decrypt large families of circuits, as such a key could end up getting leaked.

1.3   Technical Outline

bk-PKE via random selection. We will start by discussing the existing paradigms to construct bk-PKE and the challenges that arise when trying to adapt these techniques to the bk-IBE setting. One of the core ideas in the construction of bk-PKE [ADN+10, MW20] is *random selection*. For the sake of simplicity, let us drop the requirement of a short public key for a moment. Then there is a natural idea to construct bk-PKE via the following approach, as detailed in [ADN+10]. Let (KeyGen, Enc, Dec) be any public key encryption scheme, and consider the following transformed scheme $(KEYGEN, ENC, DEC)$. The $KEYGEN$ algorithm produces a pair of public key $PK = (\mathsf{pk}_1, \ldots, \mathsf{pk}_\ell)$ and a secret key $SK = (\mathsf{sk}_1, \ldots, \mathsf{sk}_\ell)$ for a *largeness parameter* ℓ, where each key-pair $(\mathsf{pk}_i, \mathsf{sk}_i)$ has been independently generated. The encryption algorithm

---

[2] Without loss of generality, we define the length of the identity secret keys to be the security parameter.

ENC takes the public key PK and a message m and selects a random subset $I = \{i_1, \ldots, i_\lambda\} \subseteq [\ell]$ of size (say) λ. Next, it computes a λ-out-of-λ secret sharing of $s_1, \ldots, s_\lambda$ of m (e.g. via additive secret sharing), computes ciphertexts $c_1 = \mathsf{Enc}(\mathsf{pk}_{i_1}, s_1), \ldots, c_\lambda = \mathsf{Enc}(\mathsf{pk}_{i_\lambda}, s_\lambda)$ and outputs the ciphertext $C = (I, c_1, \ldots, c_\lambda)$. To decrypt such a ciphertext C, the decryption algorithm DEC retrieves the secret keys sk_i (for $i \in I$) from SK, decrypts the c_i and reconstructs the message m.

Note first, that the ciphertext C is small (i.e., of size $\mathsf{poly}(\lambda, \log(\ell))$) and that both the encryption algorithm ENC and the decryption algorithm DEC are *local*, in the sense that ENC only accesses PK in λ location and DEC accesses SK in λ locations respectively.

Somewhat oversimplified, security is argued as follows, making critical use of the random selection of the set I: Given any leakage $L(SK)$ of size sufficiently smaller than ℓ bits, many of the individual secret keys $\mathsf{sk}_1, \ldots, \mathsf{sk}_\ell$ will be information-theoretically hidden from the adversary. As the set I is chosen randomly *after* the leak $L(SK)$ has been computed, with very high probability over the choice of I, there is an index $i \in I$ for which $L(SK)$ contains essentially no information about sk_i. Thus, one can argue that the ciphertext component c_i hides the share s_i, and therefore the message m is hidden.

Returning to the issue of large public keys, compressing the public key PK while keeping the secret key SK incompressible was, in fact, the main technical challenge in the original construction of [ADN+10]. This was achieved via the notion of *identity-based hash-proof-systems*.

With more recently developed tools, namely laconic oblivious transfer, hash functions with encryption or registration-based encryption [CDG+17, DG17b], [DGHM18, DGGM19, GHMR18, GHM+19, MW20], there is a significant shortcut to compress the public key PK. Instead of providing the public key PK in its entirety, only a short hash $H(PK)$ of PK is provided. This hash $H(PK)$ then allows the encrypter to *delegate* the computation of the ciphertexts $c_1, \ldots, c_\lambda$ to the decrypter in a secure way. As a matter of fact, looking ahead, our construction will rely on the same tools to compress the master public keys.

Challenges for Extending to bk-IBE. To adapt this high level idea to the IBE setting, one encounters several bottlenecks, which we highlight below.

Firstly, recall that in the case of bk-PKE, the random selection of the set I, containing the indices of secret keys that will be accessed by the decryption, needs to be crucially made at the encryption time. This leads to a critical problem in the bk-IBE setting: since our target is to keep the identity secret keys (decryption keys) short, this information pertaining to selection of the identity keys must be fixed independent of the random coins of the encryption.

Secondly, one might think the above issue is no longer relevant if the challenge identity is picked randomly. For example, suppose every identity id implicitly defines some subset S_{id}, and its identity secret-key corresponds to $\{\mathsf{sk}_i : i \in S_{\mathsf{id}}\}$. Then, one might hope a similar argument will prove the security of a randomly-selected identity. However, recall that the adversary is given unbounded access to $KEYGEN$ in IBE schemes, through which he could potentially learn all the

sk_i's, thus breaking the security. This challenge posed by an unbounded access to $KEYGEN$ queries does not exist in the bk-PKE schemes.

Thus, one might wonder if we could handle the $KEYGEN$ queries by starting with a leakage-resilient IBE scheme and amplifying the leakage tolerance on the master secret key through the above parallel repetition idea. For such an amplification, we must start with an IBE scheme that tolerates some bounded leakage, say m-bits, on the master secret key, and the only known prior scheme allowing that is [LRW11] (other schemes only tolerate bounded leakage on large identity secret keys, and not on the master key itself). The new scheme is obtained by generating ℓ independent instances of this underlying IBE scheme. Now, every identity id is associated with a subset $S_{\mathsf{id}} \subseteq [\ell]$ and its identity secret key is the identity secret keys for all the instances $i \in S_{\mathsf{id}}$. It is plausible to conjecture that a random identity is secure in this new scheme tolerating (approximately) $m \cdot \ell$-bit leakage. However, the only known techniques of proving such leakage amplification (using parallel repetition) are based on information-theoretic arguments [ADW09, ADN+10, BK12, HLWW13]. In particular, the security proof requires that the ciphertext is indistinguishable from some simulated ciphertext, which contains information-theoretic entropy in the adversary's view.[3] However, no known leakage-resilience IBE supports such a proof structure (as no entropy is left, given all the unbounded identity queries), and hence the parallel repetition does not give an amplification. In fact, there are works (e.g., [LW10, JP11]) which show that in general, parallel repetition of a leakage-resilient encryption scheme *does not* amplify the leakage-resilience.

Our work precisely circumvents the problems listed above, and builds a leakage-resilient IBE scheme from scratch, such that it supports such an information-theoretic argument. In particular, we show that there is a way to simulate the entire view of the adversary including all the secret key queries such that (1) the adversary cannot distinguish the simulated view from the real view and (2) in this simulated view, the challenge ciphertext retains information-theoretic entropy, given the leakage. The key primitive that helps us achieve this is a *big-key pseudo-entropy function*.

Our Ideas. We construct our bk-IBE scheme by anchoring the leakage resilience properties from the corresponding properties of a simpler primitive, namely a big-key pseudo-entropy function. A pseudo-entropy function (PEF) [BHK11] has the property that its output at certain inputs are still *unpredictable*, even if the distinguisher has obtained leakage about the PEF key (in addition to the output of the PEF elsewhere). While ideally we would want to rely on pseudo-random functions (PRFs), they cannot even tolerate a single bit of leakage.

In this work, we will focus on the selective security notion, both for IBE and for PEFs. A pseudo-entropy function PEF is selectively secure for t inputs against ℓ bits of leakage, if for any inputs $x_1, \ldots, x_t$ it holds that

---

[3] Given such a proof structure, parallel repetition amplifies the total entropy of the simulated ciphertexts and, hence, naturally amplifies the leakage-resilience of the system as well.

$PEF(K, x_1), \ldots, PEF(K, x_t)$ is unpredictable given $L(K)$, where $L(\cdot)$ is an ℓ-bit leakage function. For our construction, we will need a *locally computable* PEF, i.e., $PEF(K, x)$ will access the key K only in a few locations.[4]

Leakage Resilient Public-Key Encryption. Our big-key IBE scheme is conceptually built on the *weak hash proof system* framework of Hazay et al. [HLWW13]. This work constructs a leakage resilient key-encapsulation mechanism from any (non-leakage resilient) public key encryption scheme. The main ideas of their construction can roughly be summarized as follows. The public key PK of their scheme consists of $2n$ pairs $(\mathsf{pk}_{1,0}, \mathsf{pk}_{1,1}), \ldots, (\mathsf{pk}_{n,0}, \mathsf{pk}_{n,1})$ of public keys for an underlying public key encryption scheme. The secret key SK on the other hand, contains a random vector $b = (b_1, \ldots, b_n)$ and only contains one secret key sk_{i,b_i} for every index i. Key encapsulation proceeds as follows: To encapsulate a randomly chosen key $k = (k_1, \ldots, k_n) \leftarrow \{0,1\}^n$, compute ciphertexts $c_{i,0}$ and $c_{i,1}$ (for $i = 1, \ldots, n$), where $c_{i,0}$ encrypts k_i under $\mathsf{pk}_{i,0}$ and $c_{i,1}$ encrypts k_i under $\mathsf{pk}_{i,1}$. To decapsulate such a ciphertext, compute $k_i = \mathsf{Dec}(\mathsf{sk}_{i,b_i}, c_{i,b_i})$ for each index i.

Leakage resilience of this encapsulation mechanism is established as follows: Let $c = ((c_{1,0}, c_{1,1}), \ldots, (c_{1,n}, c_{1,n}))$ be a challenge ciphertext. In the real CPA experiment, both $c_{i,0}$ and $c_{i,1}$ encrypt the same bit k_i for all i. Since for each i the secret key corresponding to $pk_{i,1-b_i}$ is *not part* of the secret key SK, by relying on the IND-CPA security of the underlying encryption scheme we can switch each $c_{i,1-b_i}$ to encrypt $1 - k_i$ instead of k_i. Note that even an adversary in possession of SK would not notice this switch. Now, since the b_i are chosen uniformly at random, the encapsulated key depends on the entropy of b (which is part of the secret key). Specifically, decapsulating such a malformed ciphertext produces a key $k' = k \oplus b$. But this means that unless the adversary knows the vector b entirely, k' has entropy from the adversary's view. In other words, as long as the adversary's leakage is sufficiently shorter than n, the key encapsulated in such a malformed ciphertext will be unpredictable from the adversary's point of view. Establishing a uniform key follows via standard randomness extraction techniques in a post-processing step.

Towards Identity-Based Encryption. Alas, this idea does not translate directly to the setting of identity-based encryption. For each identity secret key $\mathsf{sk}_{\mathsf{id}}$ we would need to argue that some part of $\mathsf{sk}_{\mathsf{id}}$, similar to the vector b above, must retain entropy in the adversary's view, even given leakage about the *master secret key* msk. However, since msk is a compact representation of *all* identity secret keys, msk will be used to compute both $\mathsf{sk}_{\mathsf{id},i,0}$ and $\mathsf{sk}_{\mathsf{id},i,1}$ (to stay with the above notation). In other words, msk cannot just *forget* half of the secret keys for each identity.

---

[4] For technical reasons, we need that the locations in which K is queried do not depend on K itself. For this reason, our actual PEF construction relies on an additional common reference string.

Anchoring Leakage resilience in PEFs. Our approach is to adapt the [HLWW13] technique so as to push the entire entropy of the master secret key into the key K of a pseudo-entropy function. Furthermore, we will not rely on pairs of public keys $\mathsf{pk}_{i,0}, \mathsf{pk}_{i,1}$ as the construction of [HLWW13], but instead rely on a special type of witness encryption scheme [BL20] which allows us to use information relating to the PEF key K to decrypt. Looking ahead, for each identity id the role of the random vector b in the construction of [HLWW13] will be played by a function value $PEF(K, \mathsf{id})$. We first describe a version of our construction with non-succinct public parameters and later show how these can be compressed into succinct public parameters via a laconic OT-based non-interactive secure computation (NISC) [CDG+17, DG17b, DG17a]. The master secret key msk of our scheme is simply the key K for a leakage resilient local big-key PEF. Assume that $K = (K_1, \ldots, K_n)$, where the K_i are "short" blocks of size $\mathsf{poly}(\lambda)$ (independent of the leakage bound ℓ).

The public parameters pp consist of commitments to the blocks K_i of K, as well as a common reference string crs for a special NIZK proof system. Both the commitment scheme and the NIZK proof system need to be compatible with the special witness encryption scheme of [BL20].

Identity secret keys in our scheme are generated as follows. First, the KeyGen algorithm computes $s_\mathsf{id} = PEF(K, \mathsf{id})$. Since PEF is local, this will only access a small number of the blocks K_i. Further recall that the indices of these blocks do not depend on K itself. The KeyGen algorithm now computes NIZK proofs Π_i, for each $i = 1, \cdots, \lambda$, corresponding to the statements $x_i =$ "the i-th bit of $PEF(K, \mathsf{id})$ is $s_{\mathsf{id},i}$" (where K relates to the commitments in the public parameters pp). We stress that since $PEF(K, \mathsf{id})$ only accesses a small number of blocks of K, both the statements x_i and the proofs Π_i are succinct, i.e. independent of ℓ. The identity secret key sk_id now consists of s_id, the statements x_i and the NIZK proofs Π_i.

We will now describe the encapsulation and decapsulation algorithms. For an identity id, we encapsulate a random key $u = (u_1, \ldots, u_\lambda) \leftarrow \{0,1\}^\lambda$ as follows: for each index i we compute two ciphertexts $c_{i,0}$ and $c_{i,1}$ using the special witness encryption scheme, both encrypting u_i. The statement under which we encrypt $c_{i,0}$ is $x_{i,0} =$ "the i-th bit of $PEF(K, \mathsf{id})$ is 0", whereas the corresponding statement for $c_{i,1}$ is $x_{i,1} =$ "the i-th bit of $PEF(K, \mathsf{id})$ is 1". The ciphertext C consists of $(c_{1,0}, c_{1,1}), \ldots, (c_{\lambda,0}, c_{\lambda,1})$. To decapsulate such a ciphertext C using an identity secret key sk_id, for each $i \in \{1, \ldots, \lambda\}$ we decrypt $c_{i,s_{\mathsf{id},i}}$ using Π_i as a witness. Correctness follows routinely from the correctness of the components.

Security. We will establish security roughly following the blueprint of [HLWW13]. Specifically, assume we have challenge identities $\mathsf{id}_1, \ldots, \mathsf{id}_t$ and challenge ciphertexts $C_1, \ldots, C_t$. Our first step of modification relies on the fact that, for each pair of ciphertexts $c_{i,0}, c_{i,1}$, one of the statements $x_{i,0}$ or $x_{i,1}$ must be false. Consequently, by the security of the witness encryption scheme we can flip one of the encrypted bits, effectively pushing entropy from $s_\mathsf{id} = PEF(K, \mathsf{id})$ into the corresponding challenge ciphertext.

In the second step, we use the simulation property of the NIZK to remove the dependence of the proofs Π_i's (in the identity secret keys) on the PEF key K. Likewise, we can replace the commitments in the public parameters with fake commitments, which are generated independently of the PEF key K.

Now observe that, the only part of the identity secret key that still depends on the key K is $PEF(K, \text{id})$. To handle this, our PEF comes with a puncture mode, where, given a set of challenge identities $\text{id}_1, \ldots, \text{id}_t$, the PEF samples a punctured key $K^\odot$, such that: (A) it satisfies correctness for all non-challenge identities, i.e., $PEF(K, \text{id}) = PEF(K^\odot, \text{id})$ for all $\text{id} \notin \{\in \text{id}_1, \ldots, \text{id}_t\}$. This ensures that we can answer all KeyGen queries using $K^\odot$; (B) the PEF outputs $(PEF(K, \text{id}_1), \ldots, PEF(K, \text{id}_t))$ contain "high-enough" entropy, given $K^\odot$. This property ensures that the challenge ciphertexts are unpredictable, given the adversary's view (which now does not depend on K, but only on $K^\odot$).

Finally, we reduce the selective security to the security of the underlying PEF. The above arguments help us to push all the entropy of the $PEF(K, \text{id}_i)$ to the corresponding challenge ciphertexts. Hence, we now invoke the selective leakage resilience of the PEF to information-theoretically show that for some identity id_i the adversary cannot have a non-trivial advantage in distinguishing the corresponding challenge ciphertext.

1.4 Future Directions

Our work leaves open several exciting problems. We discuss a few of them below.

As in IBE schemes, there are two flavors of security one could imagine, namely, selective and adaptive/full security. In this work, we achieve selective security, where the adversary must select the challenge set, $\mathcal{J}$, of $\ell + 1$ identities before the setup of the system, and succeeds only if she breaks all the identities in $\mathcal{J}$. In contrast, full security allows the adversary to adaptively pick this set, i.e., she succeeds as long as she breaks the security of all the identities in any set $\mathcal{J}$ of size $\ell + 1$. We leave the problem of building a fully secure big-key IBE as a fascinating open problem.

Secondly, having initiated the study of big-key IBE, the next natural step towards making it truly practical would be to build it with only black-box use of the underlying primitives. Another practically useful feature to add to our big-key IBE would be to incorporate the updatability of the keys.

The third interesting problem that we leave open stems from the recent technique [MW20] of making the secret keys "catalytic", i.e., the large secret key is no longer needed to be a completely random string (which the user doesn't utilize elsewhere), but is generated as a (randomized) encoding of some public data (e.g., music library) that cannot be compressed further by the adversary. Extending the study of such public-key encryption schemes with catalytic keys to our big-key IBE setup would be another exciting problem to explore.

Finally, we note that typically, in IBE security definitions, the adversary is given access to a KeyGen oracle, which outputs identity secret keys. The only restriction is that the adversary cannot query the challenge identity id^*. In our security definition, we do not allow the adversary to query KeyGen on any identity in the set of challenge identities $\mathcal{J}$ accordingly. While such a restriction seems natural, one may wonder whether it is necessary. Consider a relaxation of this assumption where the adversary is allowed to make KeyGen queries with keys in the set $\mathcal{J}$ of challenge identities, which are subsequently removed from $\mathcal{J}$. We claim that any scheme with a deterministic KeyGen algorithm (as is the case for most IBE constructions) would be immediately insecure. The reason is that the leakage function L may leak a succinct *parity information* about the keys of the challenge identities, e.g. $\mathsf{leak} = \bigoplus_{\mathsf{id} \in \mathcal{J}} \mathsf{sk}_{\mathsf{id}}$. Given this leakage leak, the adversary could query the KeyGen oracle on all but one of the identities in $\mathcal{J}$, say id^*, and then reconstruct $\mathsf{sk}_{\mathsf{id}^*}$ via $\mathsf{sk}_{\mathsf{id}^*} = \mathsf{leak} \oplus \bigoplus_{\mathsf{id} \in \mathcal{J} \setminus \{\mathsf{id}^*\}} \mathsf{sk}_{\mathsf{id}}$. As the question of achieving such a stronger security notion by relying on additional randomization of the KeyGen procedure seems quite challenging and is beyond the scope of this work, we leave it open for future work.

2   Preliminaries

Notations. We use λ to denote the security parameter. $\mathsf{negl}(\cdot)$ denotes a negligible function. For $n \in \mathbb{Z}$, $[n]$ denotes the set $[n] = \{1, \cdots, n\}$. For a distribution X, we use $x \leftarrow X$ to denote the process of sampling x from X. For a set $\mathcal{X}$, we use $x \leftarrow \mathcal{X}$ to denote sampling x from $\mathcal{X}$ uniformly at random. We also use $U_{\mathcal{X}}$ for the uniform distribution over $\mathcal{X}$. We define statistical difference as $\Delta(X; Y) = 1/2 \sum_a |\Pr[X = a] - \Pr[Y = a]|$, and say that X and Y are statistically close if their statistical difference is bounded by a negligible function of the security parameter. We say that X and Y are computationally indistinguishable if for any PPT adversary D, $|\Pr[D(X) = 1] - \Pr[D(Y) = 1]| \leq \mathsf{negl}(\lambda)$.

2.1   Min-Entropy

Let X be a random variable supported on a finite set $\mathcal{X}$ and let $Z \in \mathcal{Z}$ be another random variable (possibly correlated with X). The min-entropy of X is defined as $H_\infty(X) = -\log(\max_x \Pr[X = x])$. The *average conditional min-entropy* [DORS08] of X given Z is defined by

$$\tilde{H}_\infty(X|Z) = -\log\left(\mathsf{E}_{z \sim Z} \left[\max_{x \in \mathcal{X}} \Pr[X = x | Z = z] \right] \right).$$

We use the following weak chain rule about average conditional min-entropy.

Lemma 1 (Weak Min-Entropy Chain Rule [DORS08]). *Let $X \in \mathcal{X}$ and $Z \in \mathcal{Z}$ be random variables. Then it holds that*

$$\tilde{H}_\infty(X|Z) \geq H_\infty(X) - \log(|\mathcal{Z}|).$$

Additionally, for any $\delta > 0$, with probability at least $1 - \delta$ over $z \leftarrow Z$, we have

$$H_\infty(X|Z = z) \geq \tilde{H}_\infty(X|Z) - \log(1/\delta).$$

Further, our proof requires the following min-entropy splitting lemma, the proof of which, essentially follows from recursively invoking [DFR+07, Lemma 4.2].

Lemma 2 (Min-Entropy Splitting Lemma). *Let $X_1, \ldots, X_\kappa$ be a sequence of random variables such that $H_\infty(X_1, \ldots, X_\kappa) \geq \alpha$. There exists a random variable C over $[\kappa]$ s.t.*

$$H_\infty(X_C | C) \geq \alpha/\kappa - \log \kappa.$$

Our construction also relies on a randomness extractor, which we recall below.

Definition 1 (Randomness Extractor). *A function* $\mathsf{Ext} \colon \{0,1\}^n \times \{0,1\}^d \to \{0,1\}^m$ *is called a* (k, ε)*-strong randomness extractor if, for all distributions X over $\{0,1\}^n$ such that $H_\infty(X) \geq k$, we have*

$$\Delta\Big(\big(s, \mathsf{Ext}(X,s)\big) \,;\, \big(U_{\{0,1\}^d}, U_{\{0,1\}^m}\big) \Big) \leq \varepsilon,$$

where the seed s is chosen uniformly at random from $\{0,1\}^d$.

3   Puncturable Local Pseudo-Entropy Functions

In this section, we will provide definitions and construction of local pseudo-entropy functions. Our target security notion is selective security, i.e., before receiving leakage and getting access to the function, the adversary has to announce his challenge inputs.

Definition 2. *Given a parameter ℓ, a puncturable local pseudo-entropy function is specified by a pair of PPT algorithms* $(\mathsf{Gen}, \mathsf{PEF})$ *with the following syntax.*

- $\mathsf{Gen}(1^\lambda, \ell)$: *Outputs a pair* (CRS, K), *where* CRS *is a common reference string of size* $\mathsf{poly}(\lambda)$, *and* $K = (K_1, \ldots, K_n)$ *is a key consisting of $K_i \in \{0,1\}^{\mathsf{poly}(\lambda)}$.[5]*
- $\mathsf{PEF}(\mathsf{CRS}, K, x)$: *Takes as input* CRS *and x and gets RAM access to K, and outputs a* $Y \in \{0,1\}^{\mathsf{poly}(\lambda)}$.

We also require the existence of $(\mathsf{Gen}_2, \mathsf{PEF}_2)$ *with the following syntax.*

- $\mathsf{Gen}_2(1^\lambda, \ell, x_1, \ldots, x_\kappa)$: *Outputs a tuple* $(\mathsf{CRS}, K, K^\odot)$.
- $\mathsf{PEF}_2(\mathsf{CRS}, K^\odot, x)$: *Takes as input* CRS, $K^\odot$, x, *and outputs a Y.*

We require the following properties to hold.

- *Locality:* $\mathsf{PEF}(\mathsf{CRS}, K, \cdot)$ *makes at most* $\mathsf{poly}(\lambda)$ *(independent of ℓ) RAM access to $K = (K_1, \ldots, K_n)$.*
- *Mode-Indistinguishability: Fix* $x_1, \ldots, x_\kappa \in \{0,1\}^\lambda$ *and let* $(\mathsf{CRS}', K', K^\odot) \leftarrow \mathsf{Gen}_2(1^\lambda, \ell, x_1, \ldots, x_\kappa)$. *Then* (CRS', K') *is computationally indistinguishable from* $(\mathsf{CRS}, K) \leftarrow \mathsf{Gen}(1^\lambda, \ell)$.

---

[5] The length of CRS and every K_i do not depend on ℓ, but n shall depend on ℓ.

- *Punctured correctness: Fix $x_1, \ldots, x_\kappa \in \{0,1\}^\lambda$ and let $(\mathsf{CRS}, K, K^\odot) \leftarrow$ $\mathsf{Gen}_2(1^\lambda, \ell, x_1, \ldots, x_\kappa)$. Then it holds for all $x \notin \{x_1, \ldots, x_\kappa\}$ that $\mathsf{PEF}(\mathsf{CRS}, K, x) = \mathsf{PEF}_2(\mathsf{CRS}, K^\odot, x)$, except with negligible probability over the coins of Gen_2.*
- *k-Selective β-Pseudo-Entropy Security: Fix $x_1, \ldots, x_\kappa \in \{0,1\}^\lambda$ and let $(\mathsf{CRS}, K, K^\odot) \leftarrow \mathsf{Gen}_2(1^\lambda, \ell, x_1, \ldots, x_\kappa)$. Then it holds that*

$$\tilde{H}_\infty\Big(\mathsf{PEF}(\mathsf{CRS}, K, x_1), \ldots, \mathsf{PEF}(\mathsf{CRS}, K, x_\kappa) \,\Big|\, \mathsf{CRS}, K^\odot\Big) \geq \beta.$$

Observe that, by the punctured correctness, one could use $K^\odot$ to correctly evaluate PEF at all inputs $x \notin \{x_1, \ldots, x_\kappa\}$. Therefore, this property implicitly states that, even if the adversary obtains $\mathsf{PEF}(x)$ at all inputs $x \notin \{x_1, \ldots, x_\kappa\}$, $\mathsf{PEF}(\mathsf{CRS}, K, x_1), \ldots, \mathsf{PEF}(\mathsf{CRS}, K, x_\kappa)$ is still (information - theoretically) unpredictable.

The notion of pseudo-entropy functions is first proposed by Braverman, Hassidim, and Kalai [BHK11]. Their definition supports puncturing at one input and does not require locality. Let us recall their result.[6]

Theorem 1 (**[BHK11] Thm. 4.1**). *Let $\delta > 0$ be an arbitrary constant. Under the decisional Diffie Hellman assumption, there exists a family of 1-selective $\gamma = (1 - \delta)\alpha$-pseudo-entropy functions, where α is the length of the secret key.*

In other words, [BHK11] constructed a PEF such that, after puncturing at one input x, $\mathsf{PEF}(\mathsf{CRS}, K, x)$ preserves almost the entire entropy of the key K.

Remark 1. We make a few remarks about our definition.

- **Leakage-resilience.** The leakage-resilience of the PEF simply follows from the min-entropy chain rule (Lemma 1). That is, given an m-bit leakage $L(K)$ of the key K, the entropy guarantee in the definition

$$\tilde{H}_\infty\Big(\mathsf{PEF}(\mathsf{CRS}, K, x_1), \ldots, \mathsf{PEF}(\mathsf{CRS}, K, x_\kappa) \,\Big|\, \mathsf{CRS}, K^\odot\Big) \geq \gamma$$

implies

$$\tilde{H}_\infty\Big(\mathsf{PEF}(\mathsf{CRS}, K, x_1), \ldots, \mathsf{PEF}(\mathsf{CRS}, K, x_\kappa) \,\Big|\, \mathsf{CRS}, K^\odot, L(K)\Big) \geq \gamma - m.$$

Braverman et. al. [BHK11] choose to incorporate the leakage resilience in their definition. Here, our definition simply states the min-entropy guarantee, and we shall handle the leakage within corresponding proofs directly.

---

[6] Their work predates the first mention of punctured PRFs [BGI14]. While they do not use puncturing formalism, they implicitly define a punctured generation and evaluation algorithm in their proof.

– **Parameters Setting.** Looking ahead, we shall use our PEF to construct our big-key IBE scheme. The big-key scheme first specifies a leakage parameter ℓ that it aims to achieve, which, in turn, determines the number κ of inputs our PEF needs to puncture in order to obtain sufficiently high (e.g., $\geq \ell$) min-entropy guarantee. Finally, the number of inputs to be punctured determines the number n of blocks we need to have in the key $K = (K_1, \ldots, K_n)$.

– **CRS.** We note that our definition includes a CRS. Intuitively, the locations in K that one needs to access in order to evaluate $\mathsf{PEF}(\mathsf{CRS}, K, x)$ must be fixed and public, given the CRS and x. As it will become clear in our big-key IBE construction, this ensures that the encryption algorithm is also local (i.e., independent of ℓ). We shall elaborate more on this later.

Finally, we note that the construction of [BHK11] does not have a CRS. Hence, we omit the CRS when we use their PEF as a building block.

Finally, the following simple Lemma about random bipartite graphs shall be useful to us, whose proof follows by a simple probabilistic argument.

Lemma 3 *Let $N, M > 0$ be integers with $N \leq (1 - \varepsilon)M$ for a constant $\varepsilon > 0$ and $d > 0$ be an integer. Let $L = [N]$ and $R = [M]$. Let $\Gamma \subseteq L \times R$ be a random graph which is chosen as follows: For every vertex $v \in L$ the neighborhood $\Gamma(v)$ is sampled by choosing $w_1, \ldots, w_d \leftarrow R$ uniformly at random and setting $\Gamma(v) = \{w_1, \ldots, w_d\}$. Let MATCH be the event that every vertex $v \in L$ can be matched with a unique vertext $w \in R$, i.e. for each $v \in L$ there exists a $W(v) \in \Gamma(v)$ such that for $v \neq v'$ it holds that $W(v) \neq W(v')$. Then we have*

$$\Pr[\mathsf{MATCH}] \geq 1 - N \cdot (1 - \varepsilon)^d \geq 1 - N \cdot e^{-\varepsilon \cdot d}.$$

Furthermore, one can efficiently find this matching except with probability $N \cdot (1 - \varepsilon)^d$.[7]

We omit the proof due to space constraint and refer the reader to the full version.

3.1   Our Construction

We will now provide our construction of a local pseudo-entropy function. Our construction will start from the PEF construction of [BHK11] which is not local, and amplify this to a PEF which can be evaluated by a local algorithm.

Let $(\mathsf{Gen}', \mathsf{PEF}')$ be the family of pseudo-entropy functions (without local evaluation) from Theorem 1, and let PRF be a pseudorandom function which takes as input an $x \in \{0,1\}^\lambda$ and outputs a sequence of elements $(i_1, \ldots, i_d) \in [\ell]^d$.

$\mathsf{Gen}(1^\lambda, \ell)$: For $i = 1, \ldots, n$, compute $K_i \leftarrow \mathsf{Gen}'(1^\lambda)$ and choose $K^* \leftarrow \{0,1\}^\lambda$.
     Output $\mathsf{CRS} = K^*$ and $K = (K_1, \ldots, K_n)$.
$\mathsf{PEF}(\mathsf{CRS}, K, x)$:
     – Parse $\mathsf{CRS} = K^*$

---

[7] Note that the failure probability is negligible for $N = \mathsf{poly}(\lambda)$ and $\varepsilon \cdot d \geq \omega(\log(\lambda))$.

- Compute $(i_1, \ldots, i_d) \leftarrow \mathsf{PRF}(K^*, x)$
- Retrieve $K_{i_1}, \ldots, K_{i_d}$ via oracle access to K
- Compute and output $Y \leftarrow (\mathsf{PEF}'(K_{i_1}, x), \ldots, \mathsf{PEF}'(K_{i_d}, x))$

First note that PEF is local, as it only accesses K at $d = \mathsf{poly}(\lambda)$ locations $i_1, \ldots, i_d$. Moreover, the location it accesses is fixed by CRS and x.

Selective Security. We will first provide the punctured key generation and evaluation algorithms. Let $\mathsf{Gen}'_2(1^\lambda, \cdot)$ and $\mathsf{PEF}'_2(1^\lambda, \cdot)$ be the punctured key generation and evaluation algorithms for $(\mathsf{Gen}', \mathsf{PEF}')$.

- $\mathsf{Gen}_2(1^\lambda, \ell, x_1, \ldots, x_\kappa)$: Generate the key PRF key $K^* \leftarrow \{0,1\}^\lambda$ and set CRS $= K^*$. Let **MATCH** be the event that for every index $i \in [\kappa]$ that there is an index j_i such that j_i appears in the list generated by $\mathsf{PRF}(K^*, x_i)$, but j_i appears in no other list generated by $\mathsf{PRF}(K^*, x_{i'})$ for $i' \neq i$. If the event holds, compute such a matching. For each $i = 1, \ldots, \kappa$, compute $(K_{j_i}, K_{j_i}^\odot) \leftarrow \mathsf{Gen}'_2(1^\lambda, x_i)$. For all remaining indices $i \in [n] \setminus \{j_1, \ldots, j_\kappa\}$, compute K_i via $K_i \leftarrow \mathsf{Gen}'(1^\lambda)$ and set $K_i^\odot = K_i$. Set $K = (K_1, \ldots, K_n)$, $K^\odot = (K_1^\odot, \ldots, K_n^\odot)$ and output $(\mathsf{CRS}, K, K^\odot)$.
- $\mathsf{PEF}_2(\mathsf{CRS}, K^\odot, x)$:
  - Parse CRS $= K^*$
  - Compute $(i_1, \ldots, i_d) \leftarrow \mathsf{PRF}(K^*, x)$
  - Compute and output $Y \leftarrow (\mathsf{PEF}'(K_{i_1}^\odot, x), \ldots, \mathsf{PEF}'(K_{i_d}^\odot, x))$.

Theorem 2. *Let $\delta > 0$ be a constant, let $\kappa = (1 - \delta)n$ and let $\gamma = \mathsf{poly}(\lambda)$. Assume that $(\mathsf{Gen}', \mathsf{PEF}')$ is a family of 1-selective γ-pseudo-entropy functions and PRF is a pseudo-random function. Then $(\mathsf{Gen}, \mathsf{PEF})$ has punctured correctness, and satisfies the mode-indistinguishability and κ-selective $(\kappa \cdot \gamma)$-pseudo-entropy properties.*

Remark 2. We stress that $\kappa \cdot \gamma$ can get arbitrary close to the entropy of the PEF key K. Observe that the key $K = (K_1, \ldots, K_n)$ supports puncturing κ inputs, which is nearly n since $\kappa = (1 - \delta)n$. Additionally, for every input x_i, the γ entropy of $\mathsf{PEF}(\mathsf{crs}, K, x_i)$ is nearly the entire entropy of some block K_{j_i} (by Theorem 1). Overall, the entropy of $(\mathsf{PEF}(\mathsf{crs}, K, x_1), \ldots, \mathsf{PEF}(\mathsf{crs}, K, x_\kappa))$ is nearly the entire entropy of the key K. In other words, for an adversary who may leak almost the entire key K, $(\mathsf{PEF}(\mathsf{crs}, K, x_1), \ldots, \mathsf{PEF}(\mathsf{crs}, K, x_\kappa))$ still contains unpredictability.

Due to space constraint, we omit the proof and refer the reader to the full version.

4 Big-Key Identity-Based Key Encapsulation Mechanism

In this section, we define and build a big-key identity-based key encapsulation mechanism (IB-KEM). This construction of IB-KEM will have a large public parameter. Afterward, one can generically transform it into an IBE scheme with a short public parameter by using Non-interactive Secure Computation (NISC) from [CDG+17]. We refer the reader to the full version for this transformation.

4.1 Definition

Syntactically, a big-key identity-based key encapsulation mechanism consists of the following efficient algorithms. All algorithms (except for Setup) implicitly take the public parameter pp as input. We omit it to avoid cluttering.

- $(\mathsf{pp}, \mathsf{msk}) \leftarrow \mathsf{Setup}(1^\lambda)$: This algorithm takes the security parameter as input, and samples the public parameter pp and a master secret-key msk.
- $\mathsf{sk_{id}} \leftarrow \mathsf{KeyGen}(\mathsf{msk}, \mathsf{id})$: This algorithm takes the master secret-key msk and the identity id as inputs, and samples an identity secret-key $\mathsf{sk_{id}}$. In particular, KeyGen has RAM access to msk.[8]
- $(\mathsf{ct}, u) \leftarrow \mathsf{Encap}(\mathsf{id})$: This algorithm takes the identity id as input, and samples a ciphertext ct and its associated encapsulated key u.
- $u = \mathsf{Dec}(\mathsf{id}, \mathsf{ct}, \mathsf{sk_{id}})$: This algorithm takes the identity id, the ciphertext ct, and the identity secret-key $\mathsf{sk_{id}}$ as inputs, and output a decapsulated key u.

Definition 3 (Selective Secure IB-KEM). *We say that an IB-KEM (Setup, KeyGen, Encap, Dec) is selectively secure under bounded leakage if it satisfies the following correctness, efficiency and security properties.*

- *Correctness. For any identity* id, *it holds that*

$$\Pr\left[\begin{array}{l} (\mathsf{pp}, \mathsf{msk}) \leftarrow \mathsf{Setup}(1^\lambda), \ (\mathsf{ct}, u) \leftarrow \mathsf{Encap}(\mathsf{id}) \\ \mathsf{sk_{id}} \leftarrow \mathsf{KeyGen}(\mathsf{msk}, \mathsf{id}), \ u' = \mathsf{Dec}(\mathsf{id}, \mathsf{ct}, \mathsf{sk_{id}}) \end{array} : u = u'\right] = 1.$$

- *Efficiency. The running time of* KeyGen, Encap, *and* Dec *are independent of the leakage parameter* ℓ. *This implicitly mandates that the identity secret-key* $\mathsf{sk_{id}}$ *is succinct (i.e., its length is independent of* ℓ). *Additionally, the length of the public parameter* pp *is also required to be succinct.*[9]
- *Selective Security under Bounded Leakage. Fix an* $\ell > 0$. *We say that an IB-KEM (Setup, KeyGen, Encap, Dec) is selectively secure, if for all PPT adversaries* $\mathcal{A} = (\mathcal{A}_1, \mathcal{A}_2, \mathcal{A}_3)$, *for all non-negligible* ε, *it holds that*

$$\Pr_{(\mathsf{msk}, \mathsf{pp}, \mathcal{J}, \mathsf{state}, \mathsf{leak})}\left[\forall \ \mathsf{id} \in \mathcal{J}, \mathsf{Adv}^{\mathsf{id}}(\mathsf{msk}, \mathsf{pp}, \mathsf{state}, \mathsf{leak}) \geq \varepsilon\right] = \mathsf{negl}(\lambda),$$

where $(\mathsf{msk}, \mathsf{pp}, \mathcal{J}, \mathsf{state}, \mathsf{leak})$ *are sampled from the Phase I of* $\mathrm{IND}^{\mathsf{blsKEM}}(1^\lambda)$ *(refer to Fig. 1) and the random variable* $\mathsf{Adv}^{\mathsf{id}}(\mathsf{msk}, \mathsf{pp}, \mathsf{state}, \mathsf{leak})$ *is defined as follows.*

$$\mathsf{Adv}^{\mathsf{id}}(\mathsf{msk}, \mathsf{pp}, \mathsf{state}, \mathsf{leak}) = \left|\Pr[\mathsf{Exp}^{\mathsf{id}}(\mathsf{msk}, \mathsf{pp}, \mathsf{state}, \mathsf{leak}) = 1] - \frac{1}{2}\right|$$

Here, the random variable $\mathsf{Exp}^{\mathsf{id}}(\mathsf{msk}, \mathsf{pp}, \mathsf{state}, \mathsf{leak})$ *is as defined in Phase II, and* $\mathcal{A}_3$ *is not allowed to query the* KeyGen *on* $\mathcal{J}$.

---

[8] The length of the master secret-key msk depends on the leakage parameter, ℓ, and hence is long. However, the running time of KeyGen will be independent of ℓ. That is, it will only read a few bits of msk to create the short identity secret-key.

[9] The running time of Setup and the length of the master secret-key msk, however, will inevitably depend on the leakage parameter ℓ.

$\mathsf{IND}^{\mathsf{blsKEM}}(1^\lambda):$

- **Phase I.** *The system is set up as follows.*
  1. *Let* $(\mathcal{J}, \mathsf{state}) \leftarrow \mathcal{A}_1(1^\lambda)$, *where* $\mathcal{J}$ *is a set of identities of size* $\ell + 1$.
  2. $(\mathsf{msk}, \mathsf{pp}) \leftarrow \mathsf{Setup}(1^\lambda)$.
  3. $f \leftarrow \mathcal{A}_2(\mathsf{state}, \mathsf{pp})$, *where the output length of* f *is (at most)* ℓ. *Let* $\mathsf{leak} := f(\mathsf{msk})$.
- **Phase II.** *For any* $\mathsf{id} \in \mathcal{J}$, *we define a security game* $\mathsf{Exp}^{\mathsf{id}}(\mathsf{msk}, \mathsf{pp}, \mathsf{state}, \mathsf{leak})$ *as follows*
  1. $(\mathsf{ct}, u) \leftarrow \mathsf{Encap}(\mathsf{id})$.
  2. *Let* u' *be an independent random string.*
  3. *Sample* $b \leftarrow \{0, 1\}$.
  4. *If* $b = 0$, *let* $b' = \mathcal{A}_3^{\mathsf{KeyGen}(\mathsf{msk}, \cdot)}(\mathsf{state}, \mathsf{leak}, \mathsf{pp}, \mathsf{id}, \mathsf{ct}, u)$;
  5. *If* $b = 1$, *let* $b' = \mathcal{A}_3^{\mathsf{KeyGen}(\mathsf{msk}, \cdot)}(\mathsf{state}, \mathsf{leak}, \mathsf{pp}, \mathsf{id}, \mathsf{ct}, u')$;
  6. *Output 1 if* $b = b'$; *otherwise, output 0.*

Fig. 1. Selective security experiment for IB-KEMs

Remark 3. Note that, in the above definition, the adversary $\mathcal{A}_2$ does not get access to the KeyGen oracle. This is not restrictive since the leakage function f gets access to the entire secret key msk. Hence, any leakage function f with access to KeyGen oracle can be transformed into a leakage function f' that does not have access to KeyGen oracle.

4.2 Witness Encryption for NIZK of Commitment Scheme

As a crucial building block for our IBE scheme, we shall use a witness encryption scheme for NIZK of commitment scheme. This was recently introduced and constructed by Benhamouda and Lin [BL20]. Let us start with the definition.

Definition 4 (*[BL20]*)**.** *A witness encryption for NIZK of commitment scheme that supports a circuit class* $\mathcal{G}$ *consists of the following efficient algorithms.*

- **CRS Setup:** $\mathsf{crs} \leftarrow \mathsf{Setup}(1^\lambda)$ *on input the security parameter* λ, *generates a CRS* crs.
- **Commitment:** $c \leftarrow \mathsf{Com}(\mathsf{crs}, x; r)$ *on input the CRS* crs *and a message* x, *generates a commitment* c. *The decommitment is the message* x *and the private randomness* r.
- **Language** $\mathcal{L}$: *A language* $\mathcal{L}$ *is defined by the CRS* crs *as follows. A statement* $\mathsf{st} = (c, G, y)$, *where* c *is a commitment and* $G \in \mathcal{G}$ *is a circuit, is in the language* $\mathcal{L}$ *with witness* (x, r) *if it holds that (1)* $c = \mathsf{Com}(\mathsf{crs}, x; r)$; *(2)* $G(x) = y$.
- **NIZK Proof:** $\pi \leftarrow \mathsf{Prove}(\mathsf{crs}, c, G, (x, r))$ *on input the CRS* crs, *a commitment* c, *a circuit* $G \in \mathcal{G}$, *and a decommitment* (x, r), *generates a proof* π *proving the statement* $(c, G, G(x)) \in \mathcal{L}$ *with witness* (x, r).

- **Witness Encryption:** $\mathsf{ct} \leftarrow \mathsf{WEnc}(\mathsf{crs}, \mathsf{msg}, (c, G, y))$ on input the CRS crs, a message msg, and a statement (c, G, y), generates a ciphertext ct.
- **Witness Decryption:** $\mathsf{msg} = \mathsf{WDec}(\mathsf{crs}, \mathsf{ct}, (c, G, y), \pi)$ on input the CRS crs, a ciphertext ct, a statement (c, G, y), and a NIZK proof π, computes a message msg.
- **Simulated CRS:** $(\mathsf{crs}, \tau) \leftarrow \mathsf{SimSetup}(1^\lambda)$ on input the security parameter λ, generates a simulation CRS crs and its associated trapdoor τ.
- **Simulated Commitment:** $(c, \mathsf{aux}) \leftarrow \mathsf{SimCom}(\mathsf{crs})$, on input the CRS crs, generates a simulated commitment c with its auxiliary information aux.
- **Simulated Decommit:** $r = \mathsf{SimDecom}(\mathsf{crs}, \tau, c, \mathsf{aux}, x)$, on input the simulated CRS crs and its associated trapdoor τ, the simulated commitment c and its associated auxilliary information aux, and any message x, generates a decommitment r such that (x, r) is a valid decommitment of c with crs.
- **Simulated Proof:** $\pi \leftarrow \mathsf{SimProve}((\mathsf{crs}, \tau, \mathsf{aux}), (c, G, G(x)))$ on input the simulated CRS crs, its associated trapdoor τ, the auxiliary information aux for the commitment c, and finally a statement $(c, G, G(x))$, generates a simulated proof π proving the statement $(c, G, G(x))$.

This set of algorithms satisfy the following guarantees.

- **Perfect Correctness.** For all input x, circuit $G \in \mathcal{G}$, and message msg, we have

$$\Pr\left[\begin{array}{c} \mathsf{crs} \leftarrow \mathsf{Setup}(1^\lambda), \ c = \mathsf{Com}(\mathsf{crs}, x; r) \\ \mathsf{ct} \leftarrow \mathsf{WEnc}(\mathsf{crs}, \mathsf{msg}, (c, G, G(x))) \\ \pi \leftarrow \mathsf{Prove}(\mathsf{crs}, c, G, (x, r)) \\ \mathsf{msg}' = \mathsf{WDec}(\mathsf{crs}, \mathsf{ct}, (c, G, G(x)), \pi) \end{array} : \mathsf{msg} = \mathsf{msg}'\right] = 1.$$

- **Perfect binding using honest CRS.** For an honest CRS, the commitment is perfectly binding. That is, there do not exist (x, r) and (x', r') such that

$$\mathsf{Com}(\mathsf{crs}, x; r) = \mathsf{Com}(\mathsf{crs}, x'; r'),$$

where $\mathsf{crs} \leftarrow \mathsf{Setup}(1^\lambda)$.
- **(Perfect) Semantic Security.** Let msg and msg' be any two messages. For all circuit G, input x, and $y \neq G(x)$, it holds that

$$\mathsf{WEnc}(\mathsf{crs}, \mathsf{msg}, (c, G, y)) \equiv \mathsf{WEnc}(\mathsf{crs}, \mathsf{msg}', (c, G, y)),$$

where $\mathsf{crs} \leftarrow \mathsf{Setup}(1^\lambda)$ and $c \leftarrow \mathsf{Com}(\mathsf{crs}, x)$. That is, when the CRS crs and commitment c are sampled honestly, then the witness encryption satisfies perfect semantic security.

– **Zero-knowledge.**[10] *For any PPT adversary* $(\mathcal{A}_1, \mathcal{A}_2)$, *it holds that*

$$\left| \Pr \left[\begin{array}{l} \mathsf{crs} \leftarrow \mathsf{Setup}(1^\lambda) \\ (\mathsf{state}, x) \leftarrow \mathcal{A}_1(\mathsf{crs}) \; : \; \mathcal{A}_2^{\mathcal{O}_1(\cdot)}(\mathsf{state}, c, (x, r)) = 1 \\ c = \mathsf{Com}(\mathsf{crs}, x; r) \end{array} \right] - \right.$$

$$\left. \Pr \left[\begin{array}{l} (\mathsf{crs}, \tau) \leftarrow \mathsf{SimSetup}(1^\lambda) \\ (\mathsf{state}, x) \leftarrow \mathcal{A}_1(\mathsf{crs}) \\ (c, \mathsf{aux}) = \mathsf{SimCom}(\mathsf{crs}) \\ r = \mathsf{SimDecom}(\mathsf{crs}, \tau, c, \mathsf{aux}, x) \end{array} \; : \; \mathcal{A}_2^{\mathcal{O}_2(\cdot)}(\mathsf{state}, c, (x, r)) = 1 \right] \right| = \mathsf{negl}(\lambda),$$

where $\mathcal{O}_1(G) := \mathsf{Prove}(\mathsf{crs}, c, G, (x, r))$ *and* $\mathcal{O}_2(G) := \mathsf{SimProve}((\mathsf{crs}, \tau, \mathsf{aux}), (c, G, G(x)))$. *That is, the adversary could choose the message* x, *and is given its commitment* c *with the decommitment* (x, r). *Still, given oracle access to the proof of* $(c, G, G(x))$, *where the adversary chooses the circuit* G *arbitrarily, it cannot distinguish the simulated proof from the honest proof.*

Observe that these properties implicitly guarantee additional properties. For example, the zero-knowledge property implies that the honest CRS and the simulated CRS are computationally indistinguishable. Since our construction does not explicitly use those properties, we do not state them explicitly here. We will refer the readers to [BL20] for details.

Instantiation. We will use a witness encryption for NIZK of commitment scheme that supports all polynomial-size circuits, recently constructed by [BL20] under pairing assumptions.

Locality. The construction of Benhamouda and Lin [BL20] satisfies the following local property. To commit to a message $x = (x_1, \ldots, x_N)$, Com actually commits to every x_i independently. That is, $\mathsf{Com}(\mathsf{CRS}, x; r) = (\mathsf{Com}'(\mathsf{CRS}, x_1; r_1), \ldots, \mathsf{Com}'(\mathsf{CRS}, x_N; r_N))$, where Com' is some subroutine that commits a single group element. Moreover, suppose G is a circuit that only depends on m coordinates from x. Given RAM access to the commitment $c = (c_1, \ldots, c_N)$,

---

[10] Our definition is slightly different from the zero-knowledge definition in [BL20]. In particular, in our definition, the adversary is additionally given the decommitment r. Nonetheless, the construction of [BL20] satisfies our definition since the zero-knowledge property holds for any circuit that the adversary queries. For example, the adversary may query a circuit G defined to be $G(x) = x_1$, where $x = (x_1, \ldots, x_N)$. In this case, the construction of [BL20] simply sends the decommitment of x_1 as the proof. Therefore, without loss of generality, we may assume that the adversary also has the decommitment information.

where $c_i = \mathsf{Com}'(\mathsf{CRS}, x_i; r_i)$, the running times of both generating the NIZK proof π of the statement $(c, G, G(x))$ and the witness encryption/decryption with $\left((c, G, G(x)), \pi\right)$ depend only on the locality m. In particular, if G depends only on $x_{i_1}, \ldots, x_{i_m}$, then the statement $\mathsf{st} = (c, G, G(x))$ can be expressed succinctly as $\mathsf{st}' = \left((c_{i_1}, \ldots, c_{i_m}), G, G(x_{i_1}, \ldots, x_{i_m})\right)$ and the witness $(x_{i_1}, r_{i_1}, \ldots, x_{i_m}, r_{i_m})$ is succinct as well.

In summary, if the circuit G only depends on m coordinates of its input x, then the encryption/decryption and NIZK proof process all enjoy locality m.

4.3   Construction of Big-Key IB-KEM

Construction Overview. Our construction employs witness encryption for NIZK of commitment scheme and a puncturable local pseudo-entropy function.

- **Setup.** Let $\ell > 0$ be a fixed parameter (which we will use for the leakage bound later). To set up a public parameter and a master public-key, we shall first sample a CRS $\mathsf{crs_{pef}}$, a key k for the PEF, and also a CRS crs for the witness encryption for NIZK of commitment scheme. The $(\mathsf{crs_{pef}}, \mathsf{crs})$ and the commitment c of the secret-key k shall be the public parameter. The master secret-key shall be the secret-key k and the necessary decommitment information $(r_1, \ldots, r_N)$.
- **Identity Secret-key.** The identity secret-key $\mathsf{sk_{id}}$ consists of two parts. The first part is the evaluation of the PEF, i.e., $\mathsf{PEF}(\mathsf{crs_{pef}}, k, \mathsf{id}) = (y_1, \ldots, y_\lambda)$. Second, for every index $i \in [\lambda]$, we generate a proof π_i proving the statement that c is a commitment of the key k such that $\mathsf{PEF}(\mathsf{crs_{pef}}, k, \mathsf{id})_i = y_i$. Therefore, the identity secret-key $\mathsf{sk_{id}}$ is $\{y_i, \pi_i\}_{i=1}^\lambda$.
- **Encapsulation.** To sample a ciphertext encapsulating a key, we shall use the witness encryption. In particular, we sample a random string $v = (v_1, \ldots, v_\lambda)$. For every index $i \in [\lambda]$, we encrypt v_i twice as[11]

$$\mathsf{ct}_0^i := \mathsf{WEnc}\left(\mathsf{crs}, v_i, \left(c, (\mathsf{id}, i), 0\right)\right) \text{ and } \mathsf{ct}_1^i := \mathsf{WEnc}\left(\mathsf{crs}, v_i, \left(c, (\mathsf{id}, i), 1\right)\right).$$

That is, we encrypt v_i using two different statements. The 0-statement is that c is a commitment of k such that $\mathsf{PEF}(\mathsf{crs_{pef}}, k, \mathsf{id})_i = 0$ and the 1-statement is that c is a commitment of k such that $\mathsf{PEF}(\mathsf{crs_{pef}}, k, \mathsf{id})_i = 1$.[12] Finally, we ask the encryptor to sample an additional seed s, and we shall apply the seeded extractor $\mathsf{Ext}(\cdot, s)$ on the string v. That is, the ciphertext is $\left(\{\mathsf{ct}_0^i, \mathsf{ct}_1^i\}_{i=1}^\lambda, s\right)$ and the encapsulated key is $u = \mathsf{Ext}(v, s)$.

---

[11] We write (id, i) for a circuit. Refer to the figure for the definition of (id, i).

[12] Note that only one of the statements will be in $\mathcal{L}$ by the perfect binding property.

Building Blocks:

1. $(\mathsf{Setup}', \mathsf{Com}, \mathsf{Prove}, \mathsf{WEnc}, \mathsf{WDec}, \mathsf{SimSetup}', \mathsf{SimCom}, \mathsf{SimDecom}, \mathsf{SimProve})$
   be a witness encryption for NIZK of commitments (Definition 4).
2. $(\mathsf{Gen}, \mathsf{PEF})$ be a puncturable local pseudo-entropy function (Definition 2),
   where given a $\mathsf{crs_{pef}}$ and key k generated by Gen, $\mathsf{PEF}(\mathsf{crs_{pef}}, k, \cdot) \colon \{0,1\}^\lambda \to$
   $\{0,1\}^\lambda$ accesses at most $m(\lambda)$ locations of the key k (locality). Fix the pa-
   rameter $\ell > 0$, taken as input by Gen.
3. Let $\mathsf{Ext} \colon \{0,1\}^\lambda \times \{0,1\}^\mu \to \{0,1\}^{\lambda'}$ be a seeded randomness extractor.

Notation for circuits:

– For a fixed $\mathsf{crs_{pef}}$, for brevity, we abuse notation and write (id, i) for a
  circuit $G \colon \{0,1\}^N \to \{0,1\}$ defined as

$$G(x) := \mathsf{PEF}(\mathsf{crs_{pef}}, x, \mathsf{id})_i.$$

  That is, given the input x, $G(x)$ outputs the ith bit of the output PEF
  with key x and input id.

The Construction:

– $\mathsf{Setup}(1^\lambda)$: Let $(\mathsf{crs_{pef}}, k) \leftarrow \mathsf{Gen}(1^\lambda, \ell)$. $\mathsf{crs} \leftarrow \mathsf{Setup}'(1^\lambda)$. Let $k := (k_1, \ldots,$
  $k_N)$. For $i \in [N]$, sample r_i at random. For all $i \in [\lambda]$, let $c_i = \mathsf{Com}(\mathsf{crs}, k_i; r_i)$.
  Return $\mathsf{msk} := \{k_i, r_i\}_{i=1}^N$ and $\mathsf{pp} := (\mathsf{crs_{pef}}, \mathsf{crs}, c_1, \ldots, c_N)$
– $\mathsf{KeyGen}(\mathsf{msk}, \mathsf{id})$: Given the input id, let $t_1, t_2, \ldots, t_m$ be the indices of the
  key k that $\mathsf{PEF}(\mathsf{crs_{pef}}, \cdot, \mathsf{id})$ depends on. Let $y_i = \mathsf{PEF}(\mathsf{crs_{pef}}, k, \mathsf{id})_i$. Let
  statement $\mathsf{st}_i := \Big((c_{t_1}, \ldots, c_{t_m}), (\mathsf{id}, i), y_i \Big) \in \mathcal{L}$. Define and return

$$\mathsf{sk_{id}} := \left\{ y_i, \mathsf{Prove}\Big(\mathsf{crs}, \mathsf{st}_i, \{k_{t_j}, r_{t_j}\}_{j=1}^m \Big) \right\}_{i=1}^\lambda.$$

– $\mathsf{Encap}(\mathsf{id})$: For all $i \in [\lambda]$, sample $v_i \leftarrow \{0,1\}$. Let $v := (v_1, v_2, \ldots, v_\lambda)$.
  Let $s \leftarrow \{0,1\}^\mu$. For all $i \in [\lambda]$, define

$$\mathsf{ct}_0^i := \mathsf{WEnc}\left(\mathsf{crs}, v_i, \Big((c_{t_1}, \ldots, c_{t_m}), (\mathsf{id}, i), 0\Big)\right);$$

$$\mathsf{ct}_1^i := \mathsf{WEnc}\left(\mathsf{crs}, v_i, \Big((c_{t_1}, \ldots, c_{t_m}), (\mathsf{id}, i), 1\Big)\right).$$

  Let $\mathsf{ct} := \Big(\{\mathsf{ct}_0^i, \mathsf{ct}_1^i\}_{i=1}^\lambda, s\Big)$ and $u := \mathsf{Ext}(v, s)$. Return (ct, u).
– $\mathsf{Dec}\Big(\mathsf{id}, \mathsf{ct} = \Big(\{\mathsf{ct}_0^i, \mathsf{ct}_1^i\}_{i=1}^\lambda, s\Big), \mathsf{sk_{id}} = \{y_i, \pi_i\}_{i=1}^\lambda\Big)$: For all $i \in [\lambda]$, define

$$v_i := \mathsf{WDec}\Big(\mathsf{crs}, \mathsf{ct}_{y_i}^i, \mathsf{st}_i, \pi_i\Big).$$

  Let $v := (v_1, \ldots, v_n)$ and $u := \mathsf{Ext}(v, s)$. Return u.

Fig. 2. Our Big-key IB-KEM

Auxiliary Algorithms for the Security Proof:

- $\mathsf{SimSetup}(1^\lambda)$: $(\mathsf{crs}_{\mathsf{pef}}, k) \leftarrow \mathsf{Gen}(1^\lambda, \ell)$, $(\mathsf{crs}, \tau) \leftarrow \mathsf{SimSetup}'(1^\lambda)$. Let $(c_i, \mathsf{aux}_i) = \mathsf{SimCom}(\mathsf{crs})$, $k := (k_1, \ldots, k_N)$ and $r_i = \mathsf{SimDecom}(\mathsf{crs}, \tau, c_i, \mathsf{aux}_i, k_i)$. Return $\mathsf{msk} := \{k_i, r_i\}_{i=1}^N$ and $\mathsf{pp} := (\mathsf{crs}_{\mathsf{pef}}, \mathsf{crs}, c_1, \ldots, c_n)$.

- $\mathsf{SimKeyGen}(\mathsf{msk}, \mathsf{id})$: Let $(t_1, \ldots, t_m)$, $(y_1, \ldots, y_\lambda)$, and $(\mathsf{st}_1, \ldots, \mathsf{st}_\lambda)$ be as defined in KeyGen. Define and return

$$\mathsf{sk}_{\mathsf{id}} := \left\{ y_i, \mathsf{SimProve}\left((\mathsf{crs}, \tau, \{\mathsf{aux}_{t_j}\}_{j=1}^m), \mathsf{st}_i\right)\right\}_{i=1}^\lambda.$$

- $\mathsf{Encap}^*(\mathsf{id})$: For all $i \in [\lambda]$, sample $v_i \leftarrow \{0, 1\}$. Sample $s \leftarrow \{0, 1\}^\mu$. Define

$$\mathsf{ct}_0^i := \mathsf{WEnc}\left(\mathsf{crs}, v_i, \left((c_{t_1}, \ldots, c_{t_m}), (\mathsf{id}, i), 0\right)\right)$$

$$\mathsf{ct}_1^i := \mathsf{WEnc}\left(\mathsf{crs}, v_i + 1, \left((c_{t_1}, \ldots, c_{t_m}), (\mathsf{id}, i), 1\right)\right)$$

Let $\mathsf{ct} := \left(\{\mathsf{ct}_0^i, \mathsf{ct}_1^i\}_{i=1}^\lambda, s\right)$. Return ct.
Observe that Encap^* does not output an associated key u. In particular, the decryption of $\mathsf{ct} \leftarrow \mathsf{Encap}^*$ will be $\mathsf{Ext}((v_1 + y_1, \ldots, v_\lambda + y_\lambda), s)$.

Fig. 2. (*continued*)

Remark 4 (Need for a $\mathsf{crs}_{\mathsf{pef}}$). Note that the Encap algorithm above requires the knowledge of the exact m locations of k that were accessed by the PEF. This information is fixed and public, given the $\mathsf{crs}_{\mathsf{pef}}$ and the input id. Thus having a $\mathsf{crs}_{\mathsf{pef}}$ is essential to ensure that the Encap algorithm remains efficient and local (i.e., independent of ℓ). This explains why our PEF construction has a CRS.

We will prove the selective security of the above construction, assuming the selective security of the underlying PEF, along with the security guarantees of the witness encryption scheme. We formally state the theorem below.

Theorem 3. *Assuming that the pseudo-entropy function PEF satisfies the selective security (Definition 2) and assuming the security of the witness encryption for NIZK of the commitment scheme (Definition 4), the IB-KEM construction from Fig. 2 is a big-key identity-based key encapsulation mechanism that satisfies the selective security under bounded leakage (Definition 3). In particular, we can instantiate the underlying schemes to get a leakage rate (i.e., $\frac{\ell}{|\mathsf{msk}|}$, where ℓ is the size of the leakage allowed on msk) of $1/3$.*

The correctness of our construction follows from the correctness of the witness encryption scheme. The efficiency property follows from the locality of both the PEF, and the witness encryption for the NIZK of commitment scheme. We now give a full proof of the selective security under bounded leakage.

4.4 Proof of Selective Security Under Bounded Leakage

Proof Overview. Our security proof mainly consists of the following steps.

- **Switch to invalid ciphertext.** We first define another encapsulation algorithm Encap* that generates an invalid ciphertext ct. ct is invalid in that the two ciphertexts ct_i^0 and ct_i^1 encrypt two different messages. Our first step is to switch from a valid ciphertext using Encap to an invalid ciphertext using Encap*. Since only one of the two statements (i.e., $(c, (id, i), 0)$ and $(c, (id, i), 1)$) is in the language, by the semantic security of the witness encryption scheme, the two hybrids are indistinguishable.

- **Switch to the simulation mode.** Next, we define two auxiliary algorithms SimSetup and SimKeyGen. In these two algorithms, instead of generates the CRS and proof honestly, we switch to the simulation mode. That is, the CRS and commitments are generated with trapdoors such that they are equivocal. Then, all the proofs in the identity secret-key are given by the simulated proof. By the zero-knowledge property of the witness encryption for NIZK of commitment scheme, these two hybrids are indistinguishable.

- **Switch to the punctured mode.** In this step, we shall sample the key of the PEF using the punctured mode. By invoking the mode-indistinguishability of the PEF, the two hybrids are indistinguishable. Note that the key k sampled in the punctured mode comes with a punctured key $k^\odot$, where the identities $\{id \in \mathcal{J}\}$ are the punctured places. This allows us to sample identity secret-keys for all identities but those from the challenge set $\mathcal{J}$. Crucially, this implies that the entire view of the adversary can be simulated using only $k^\odot$, *without* k.

- **Invoke the security of PEF and the randomness extractor Ext.** Finally, we argue that the adversary cannot distinguish the key encapsulated inside the (invalid) ciphertext from a random string. We reduce this to the security of the PEF. Intuitively, the output of the PEF at $\mathcal{J}$, i.e., $\{PEF(crs, k, id) : id \in \mathcal{J}\}$, guarantees sufficiently high entropy even conditioned on the adversary's view (which only depends on $k^\odot$), and hence we can use the extractor security.

Proof. Now, we will prove that our scheme from Fig. 2 satisfies the selective security under a bounded leakage from the master secret key, i.e., we show that for any adversary $\mathcal{A} = (\mathcal{A}_1, \mathcal{A}_2, \mathcal{A}_3)$, trying to break the selective security game $IND^{blsKEM}(1^\lambda)$ (refer to Fig. 1) under ℓ-leakage, and for all non-negligible ε, it holds that:

$$\Pr_{(msk, pp, \mathcal{J}, state, leak)} \left[\forall\, id \in \mathcal{J}, Adv^{id}(msk, pp, state, leak) \geq \varepsilon \right] = negl(\lambda),$$

where $(msk, pp, \mathcal{J}, state, leak)$ are sampled from the Phase I of $IND^{blsKEM}(1^\lambda)$ and the random variable $Adv^{id}(msk, pp, state, leak)$ is defined as follows.

$$Adv^{id}(msk, pp, state, leak) = \left| \Pr[Exp^{id}(msk, pp, state, leak) = 1] - \frac{1}{2} \right|$$

Here, the random variable $Exp^{id}(msk, pp, state, leak)$ is as defined in Phase II of $IND^{blsKEM}(1^\lambda)$, and $\mathcal{A}_3$ is not allowed to query the KeyGen on $\mathcal{J}$.

We prove this using a sequence of indistinguishable hybrids described below.

Hybrid 0: This hybrid is the real distribution $\mathsf{IND}^{\mathsf{blsKEM}}(1^\lambda)$ (recall that $\mathcal{A}_3$ is not allowed to query KeyGen on the challenge identities $\mathcal{J}$), defined as:

- **Phase I.** The system is set up as follows.
    1. Let $(\mathcal{J}, \mathsf{state}) \leftarrow \mathcal{A}_1(1^\lambda)$, where $\mathcal{J}$ is a set of identities such that $|\mathcal{J}| = \ell + 1$.
    2. $(\mathsf{msk}, \mathsf{pp}) \leftarrow \mathsf{Setup}(1^\lambda)$.
    3. $f \leftarrow \mathcal{A}_2(\mathsf{state}, \mathsf{pp})$, where the output length of f is (at most) ℓ. Let $\mathsf{leak} := f(\mathsf{msk})$.
- **Phase II.** For any $\mathsf{id} \in \mathcal{J}$, we define a security game $\mathsf{Exp}^{\mathsf{id}}(\mathsf{msk}, \mathsf{pp}, \mathsf{state}, \mathsf{leak})$ as follows
    1. $(\mathsf{ct}, u) \leftarrow \mathsf{Encap}(\mathsf{id})$.
    2. Let u' be an independent random string.
    3. Sample $b \leftarrow \{0, 1\}$.
    4. If $b = 0$, let $b' = \mathcal{A}_3^{\mathsf{KeyGen}(\mathsf{msk}, \cdot)}(\mathsf{state}, \mathsf{leak}, \mathsf{pp}, \mathsf{id}, \mathsf{ct}, u)$;
    5. If $b = 1$, let $b' = \mathcal{A}_3^{\mathsf{KeyGen}(\mathsf{msk}, \cdot)}(\mathsf{state}, \mathsf{leak}, \mathsf{pp}, \mathsf{id}, \mathsf{ct}, u')$;
    6. Output 1 if $b = b'$; otherwise, output 0.

Hybrid 1: This hybrid is identical to Hybrid 0, except that for each $\mathsf{id} \in \mathcal{J}$, instead of using Encap to generate the challenge ciphertext and the key, we use Encap^* to sample the invalid ciphertext and give its decryption to the adversary when the choice bit b is 0.

- **Phase I.** The system is set up as follows.
    1. Let $(\mathcal{J}, \mathsf{state}) \leftarrow \mathcal{A}_1(1^\lambda)$, where $\mathcal{J}$ is a set of identities such that $|\mathcal{J}| = \ell + 1$.
    2. $(\mathsf{msk}, \mathsf{pp}) \leftarrow \mathsf{Setup}(1^\lambda)$.
    3. $f \leftarrow \mathcal{A}_2(\mathsf{state}, \mathsf{pp})$, where the output length of f is (at most) ℓ. Let $\mathsf{leak} := f(\mathsf{msk})$.
- **Phase II.** For any $\mathsf{id} \in \mathcal{J}$, we define a security game $\mathsf{Exp}^{\mathsf{id}}(\mathsf{msk}, \mathsf{pp}, \mathsf{state}, \mathsf{leak})$ as follows
    1. $\mathsf{ct} \leftarrow \mathsf{Encap}^*(\mathsf{id})$.
    2. Let u' be an independent random string.
    3. Sample $b \leftarrow \{0, 1\}$.
    4. If $b = 0$, let $b' = \mathcal{A}_3^{\mathsf{KeyGen}(\mathsf{msk}, \cdot)}(\mathsf{state}, \mathsf{leak}, \mathsf{pp}, \mathsf{id}, \mathsf{ct}, \mathsf{Dec}(\mathsf{id}, \mathsf{ct}, \mathsf{sk}_{\mathsf{id}}))$;
    5. If $b = 1$, let $b' = \mathcal{A}_3^{\mathsf{KeyGen}(\mathsf{msk}, \cdot)}(\mathsf{state}, \mathsf{leak}, \mathsf{pp}, \mathsf{id}, \mathsf{ct}, u')$;
    6. Output 1 if $b = b'$; otherwise, output 0.

Claim 1. *Hybrid 0 and Hybrid 1 are identically distributed.*

This claim follows from the (perfect) semantics security of the WE scheme. We omit the proof and refer the reader to the full version.

Hybrid 2: This hybrid is identical to Hybrid 1, except that we use the subroutines SimSetup and SimKeyGen instead of using Setup and KeyGen. This switches the actual NIZK proofs with the simulated ones.

- **Phase I.** The system is set up as follows.
    1. Let $(\mathcal{J}, \text{state}) \leftarrow \mathcal{A}_1(1^\lambda)$, where $\mathcal{J}$ is a set of identities such that $|\mathcal{J}| = \ell + 1$.
    2. $(\text{msk}, \text{pp}) \leftarrow \text{SimSetup}(1^\lambda)$.
    3. $f \leftarrow \mathcal{A}_2(\text{state}, \text{pp})$, where the output length of f is (at most) ℓ. Let $\text{leak} := f(\text{msk})$.
- **Phase II.** For any $\text{id} \in \mathcal{J}$, we define a security game $\text{Exp}^{\text{id}}(\text{msk}, \text{pp}, \text{state}, \text{leak})$ as follows
    1. $\text{ct} \leftarrow \text{Encap}^*(\text{id})$.
    2. Let u' be an independent random string.
    3. Sample $b \leftarrow \{0, 1\}$.
    4. If $b = 0$, let $b' = \mathcal{A}_3^{\text{SimKeyGen}(\text{msk},\cdot)}(\text{state}, \text{leak}, \text{pp}, \text{id}, \text{ct}, \text{Dec}(\text{id}, \text{ct}, \text{sk}_{\text{id}}))$;
    5. If $b = 1$, let $b' = \mathcal{A}_3^{\text{SimKeyGen}(\text{msk},\cdot)}(\text{state}, \text{leak}, \text{pp}, \text{id}, \text{ct}, u')$;
    6. Output 1 if $b = b'$; otherwise, output 0.

Claim 2. *Hybrid 1 and Hybrid 2 are computationally indistinguishable.*

This claims follows from the zero-knowledge property of the NIZK scheme. We omit the full proof and refer the reader to the full version.

Hybrid 3: This hybrid is identical to Hybrid 2, except that we will switch to using the punctured key of the PEF (punctured at the points $\text{id} \in \mathcal{J}$) for answering all the SimKeyGen queries.

- **Phase I.** The system is set up as follows.
    1. Let $(\mathcal{J}, \text{state}) \leftarrow \mathcal{A}_1(1^\lambda)$, where $\mathcal{J}$ is a set of identities such that $|\mathcal{J}| = \ell + 1$.
    2. $(\text{msk}, \text{pp}) \leftarrow \text{SimSetup}^\odot(1^\lambda)$. Here, $\text{SimSetup}^\odot$ first generates $(\text{crs}_{\text{pef}}, k, k^\odot) \leftarrow \text{Gen}_2(1^\lambda, N, \mathcal{J})$ and uses k in msk and pp, generated as in SimSetup.
    3. $f \leftarrow \mathcal{A}_2(\text{state}, \text{pp})$, where the output length of f is (at most) ℓ. Let $\text{leak} := f(\text{msk})$.
- **Phase II.** For any $\text{id} \in \mathcal{J}$, we define a security game $\text{Exp}^{\text{id}}(\text{msk}, \text{pp}, \text{state}, \text{leak})$ as follows
    1. $\text{ct} \leftarrow \text{Encap}^*(\text{id})$.
    2. Let u' be an independent random string.
    3. Sample $b \leftarrow \{0, 1\}$.
    4. If $b = 0$, let $b' = \mathcal{A}_3^{\text{SimKeyGen}^\odot(\text{msk},\cdot)}(\text{state}, \text{leak}, \text{pp}, \text{id}, \text{ct}, \text{Dec}(\text{id}, \text{ct}, \text{sk}_{\text{id}}))$;
    5. If $b = 1$, let $b' = \mathcal{A}_3^{\text{SimKeyGen}^\odot(\text{msk},\cdot)}(\text{state}, \text{leak}, \text{pp}, \text{id}, \text{ct}, u')$;
       Here, $\text{SimKeyGen}^\odot$ works exactly like SimKeyGen, except that it uses $\text{PEF}_2(\text{crs}_{\text{pef}}, k^\odot, .)$ for the PEF evaluations.
    6. Output 1 if $b = b'$; otherwise, output 0.

Claim 3. *Hybrid 2 and Hybrid 3 are computationally indistinguishable.*

Proof. We use the mode indistinguishability of the PEF to prove the claim. Particularly, if Hybrid 2 and Hybrid 3 were computationally distinguishable, we can build an adversary $\mathcal{B}$ breaking the mode indistinguishability of the PEF.

$\mathcal{B}$ sends the challenge inputs $\mathcal{J}$ and receives the $(\mathsf{crs}_{\mathsf{pef}}, k)$ from the mode indistinguishability challenger, which either corresponds to the actual key generation or the punctured mode. Having this, $\mathcal{B}$ can simulate the entire hybrids, while using k to answer the $\mathsf{SimKeyGen}$ or $\mathsf{SimKeyGen}^{\odot}$. Since the queries do not contain the punctured points $\mathcal{J}$, by the punctured correctness, the $\mathsf{SimKeyGen}^{\odot}$ responses will be same as the PEF evaluations on k. Depending on whether the challenger returns the actual PEF key or the one in the punctured mode, $\mathcal{B}$ simulates Hybrid 2 or Hybrid 3. Thus, if the two hybrids are distinguishable, $\mathcal{B}$ can break the mode indistinguishability of PEF. This completes the proof.

Observe that, in the case $b = 0$, in Hybrid 3, $\mathsf{Dec}(\mathsf{id}, \mathsf{ct}, \mathsf{sk}_{\mathsf{id}}) = \mathsf{Ext}((v_1 + y_1, v_2 + y_2, \ldots, v_\lambda + y_\lambda), s)$, where $(y_1, \cdots, y_\lambda) = \mathsf{PEF}(\mathsf{crs}_{\mathsf{pef}}, k, \mathsf{id})$, the PEF output on the original key k. We will use this in completing the proof below.

Proving Selective Security: To finish proving the selective security, we need to show that for all non-negligible ε, it holds that:

$$\Pr_{(\mathsf{msk}, \mathsf{pp}, \mathcal{J}, \mathsf{state}, \mathsf{leak})} \left[\forall \, \mathsf{id} \in \mathcal{J}, \mathsf{Adv}^{\mathsf{id}}(\mathsf{msk}, \mathsf{pp}, \mathsf{state}, \mathsf{leak}) \geq \varepsilon \right] = \mathsf{negl}(\lambda), \quad (1)$$

where $(\mathsf{msk}, \mathsf{pp}, \mathcal{J}, \mathsf{state}, \mathsf{leak})$ are sampled from the Phase I of Hybrid 3 and the random variable $\mathsf{Adv}^{\mathsf{id}}(\mathsf{msk}, \mathsf{pp}, \mathsf{state}, \mathsf{leak})$ is defined as follows.

$$\mathsf{Adv}^{\mathsf{id}}(\mathsf{msk}, \mathsf{pp}, \mathsf{state}, \mathsf{leak}) = \left| \Pr[\mathsf{Exp}^{\mathsf{id}}(\mathsf{msk}, \mathsf{pp}, \mathsf{state}, \mathsf{leak}) = 1] - \frac{1}{2} \right|.$$

Here, the random variable $\mathsf{Exp}^{\mathsf{id}}(\mathsf{msk}, \mathsf{pp}, \mathsf{state}, \mathsf{leak})$ is as defined in Phase II of Hybrid 3. By the $|\mathcal{J}|$-selective, $\gamma \cdot |\mathcal{J}|$-pseudo-entropy security of the PEF (Theorem 2), we have that

$$\tilde{H}_\infty \left(\{ \mathsf{PEF}(\mathsf{crs}_{\mathsf{pef}}, k, \mathsf{id}) : \mathsf{id} \in \mathcal{J} \} \, \middle| \, \mathsf{crs}_{\mathsf{pef}}, k^{\odot} \right) \geq \gamma \cdot |\mathcal{J}|.$$

Here, note that the leakage $f(\mathsf{msk})$ in Hybrid 4, takes as input k and $(r_1, \cdots, r_N)$, and depends on pp, which in turn depends on $\mathsf{crs}_{\mathsf{pef}}$. Hence, we can define the following function g on the PEF key k, by hardwiring the values $(\mathsf{crs}_{\mathsf{pef}}, \tau, \{c_i, \mathsf{aux}_i\}_{i=1}^{\lambda})$:

$$g(k_1, k_2, \ldots, k_N) := \left\{ \begin{array}{c} \forall i, \ r_i = \mathsf{SimDecom}(\mathsf{crs}, \tau, c_i, \mathsf{aux}_i, k_i) \\ \mathsf{Output} \ f((k_1, r_1), \ldots, (k_N, r_N)) \end{array} \right\}.$$

Thus, $f(\mathsf{msk}) = g(k)$, in Hybrid 4. Now, by Lemma 1, in the presence of this ℓ-bit leakage on msk we get that

$$\tilde{H}_\infty \left(\{ \mathsf{PEF}(\mathsf{crs}_{\mathsf{pef}}, k, \mathsf{id}) : \mathsf{id} \in \mathcal{J} \} \, \middle| \, \mathsf{crs}_{\mathsf{pef}}, k^{\odot}, f(\mathsf{msk}) \right) \geq \gamma \cdot |\mathcal{J}| - \ell.$$

Now, by Lemma 1, with overwhelming probability over the fixing of $\mathsf{crs}_{\mathsf{pef}}, k^{\odot}, f(\mathsf{msk})$, we have

$$H_{\infty}\Big(\{\mathsf{PEF}(\mathsf{crs}_{\mathsf{pef}}, k, \mathsf{id}) : \mathsf{id} \in \mathcal{J}\}\Big) \geq \Theta(\gamma \cdot |\mathcal{J}| - \ell).$$

Next, by Lemma 2, there exists a distribution I over the identities $\mathcal{J}$ such that

$$\tilde{H}_{\infty}(\mathsf{PEF}(\mathsf{crs}_{\mathsf{pef}}, k, I)|I) \geq \frac{\Theta(\gamma \cdot |\mathcal{J}| - \ell)}{|\mathcal{J}|} - \log|\mathcal{J}| = \Theta(\gamma) \quad (\text{Recall } |\mathcal{J}| = \ell + 1.)$$

In other words, with high probability (in particular, over the observed leakage and I), there exists an $\mathsf{id}^* \in \mathcal{J}$ such that the min-entropy of $\mathsf{PEF}(\mathsf{crs}_{\mathsf{pef}}, k, \mathsf{id}^*)$ is $\geq t_{ext}$, where we set $t_{ext} = \Theta(\gamma)$. Now, by the definition of randomness extractor, we can send $\mathcal{A}_3$ a uniform string u' irrespective of the choice of b in Hybrid 4, making the output of $\mathsf{Exp}^{\mathsf{id}^*}$ uniformly random (as b' would be uncorrelated to b).

The extractor security can be applied in $\mathsf{Exp}^{\mathsf{id}^*}$, because:

- The source $\mathsf{PEF}(\mathsf{crs}_{\mathsf{pef}}, k, \mathsf{id}^*)$ has high entropy, given $\mathsf{crs}_{\mathsf{pef}}, k^{\odot}$ and $f(\mathsf{msk})$.
- The view of the adversary in this game is $\mathsf{state}, \mathsf{leak}, \mathsf{pp}, \mathsf{id}^*, \mathsf{ct} = \Big(\{\mathsf{ct}_0^i, \mathsf{ct}_1^i\}_{i=1}^{\lambda}, s\Big)$, where the seed s is uniformly random and independent from everything else in the hybrid.
- $(v_1, v_2, \ldots, v_{\lambda})$ is independent of $(\mathsf{crs}_{\mathsf{pef}}, f(\mathsf{msk}), \mathsf{id}^*, k^{\odot})$, but is correlated with ct and, hence, the adversary's view.

Thus, given the adversary's view in $\mathsf{Exp}^{\mathsf{id}^*}$, it cannot distinguish

$$\mathsf{Ext}\Big((v_1 + y_1, \ldots, v_{\lambda} + y_{\lambda}), s\Big),$$

which is what $\mathcal{A}_3$ gets in Hybrid 3 when $b = 0$, from uniform since $(y_1, \ldots, y_{\lambda})$ is sampled from a high min-entropy distribution that is independent of $(v_1, \ldots, v_{\lambda})$.

Hence, in Hybrid 3, with high probability, there exists $\mathsf{id}^* \in \mathcal{J}$ such that $\mathsf{Exp}^{\mathsf{id}}(\mathsf{msk}, \mathsf{pp}, \mathsf{state}, \mathsf{leak})$ in Phase II, outputs 1 with probability $1/2 + \mathsf{negl}(\lambda)$ (where $\mathsf{negl}(\lambda)$ comes from the extractor security error), which implies that the security as needed in Equation 1 holds.

The Claims 1, 2, and 3 and the above argument complete the security proof.

Instantiation and Parameters. We can instantiate our construction with the PEF from Theorem 2, the witness encryption for NIZK of commitment scheme from [BL20] (see Sect. 4.2) and any randomness extractor (e.g., left-over hash from [HILL99]). We allow a leakage of ℓ bits from our msk. Now, our msk consists of the PEF key k and additionally the randomness r_i's used in the commitment scheme. The witness encryption from [BL20] uses 2 random group elements to commit to a single group element (i.e., the ratio of k_i (being committed) to length of randomness r_i is $1/2$). Since the PEF gives a leakage rate of 1 (Remark 2), our big-key IB-KEM allows a leakage rate of $1/3$.

Acknowledgement. This research is supported in part by DARPA under Agreement No. HR00112020026, AFOSR Award FA9550-19-1-0200, NSF CNS Award 1936826, and research grants by the Sloan Foundation, and Visa Inc. Any opinions, findings and conclusions or recommendations expressed in this material are those of the author(s) and do not necessarily reflect the views of the United States Government or DARPA.

Nico Döttling: Funded by the European Union. Views and opinions expressed are however those of the author(s) only and do not necessarily reflect those of the European Union or the European Research Council. Neither the European Union nor the granting authority can be held responsible for them. (ERC-2021-STG 101041207 LACONIC)

References

[ADN+10] Alwen, J., Dodis, Y., Naor, M., Segev, G., Walfish, S., Wichs, D.: Public-key encryption in the bounded-retrieval model. In: Gilbert, H. (ed.) EURO-CRYPT 2010. LNCS, vol. 6110, pp. 113–134. Springer, Heidelberg (2010). https://doi.org/10.1007/978-3-642-13190-5_6

[ADW09] Alwen, J., Dodis, Y., Wichs, D.: Leakage-resilient public-key cryptography in the bounded-retrieval model. In: Halevi, S. (ed.) CRYPTO 2009. LNCS, vol. 5677, pp. 36–54. Springer, Heidelberg (2009). https://doi.org/10.1007/978-3-642-03356-8_3

[BF01] Boneh, D., Franklin, M.: Identity-based encryption from the Weil pairing. In: Kilian, J. (ed.) CRYPTO 2001. LNCS, vol. 2139, pp. 213–229. Springer, Heidelberg (2001). https://doi.org/10.1007/3-540-44647-8_13

[BGI14] Boyle, E., Goldwasser, S., Ivan, I.: Functional signatures and pseudorandom functions. In: Krawczyk, H. (ed.) PKC 2014. LNCS, vol. 8383, pp. 501–519. Springer, Heidelberg (2014). https://doi.org/10.1007/978-3-642-54631-0_29

[BHK11] Braverman, M., Hassidim, A., Kalai, Y.T.: Leaky pseudo-entropy functions. In: Chazelle, B. (ed.) ICS 2011, pp. 353–366. Tsinghua University Press, January 2011

[BK12] Brakerski, Z., Kalai, Y.T.: A parallel repetition theorem for leakage resilience. In: Cramer, R. (ed.) TCC 2012. LNCS, vol. 7194, pp. 248–265. Springer, Heidelberg (2012). https://doi.org/10.1007/978-3-642-28914-9_14

[BKR16] Bellare, M., Kane, D., Rogaway, P.: Big-key symmetric encryption: resisting key exfiltration. In: Robshaw, M., Katz, J. (eds.) CRYPTO 2016. LNCS, vol. 9814, pp. 373–402. Springer, Heidelberg (2016). https://doi.org/10.1007/978-3-662-53018-4_14

[BL20] Benhamouda, F., Lin, H.: Mr NISC: multiparty reusable non-interactive secure computation. In: Pass, R., Pietrzak, K. (eds.) TCC 2020. LNCS, vol. 12551, pp. 349–378. Springer, Cham (2020). https://doi.org/10.1007/978-3-030-64378-2_13

[CDD+07] Cash, D., Ding, Y.Z., Dodis, Y., Lee, W., Lipton, R., Walfish, S.: Intrusion-resilient key exchange in the bounded retrieval model. In: Vadhan, S.P. (ed.) TCC 2007. LNCS, vol. 4392, pp. 479–498. Springer, Heidelberg (2007). https://doi.org/10.1007/978-3-540-70936-7_26

[CDG+17] Cho, C., Döttling, N., Garg, S., Gupta, D., Miao, P., Polychroniadou, A.: Laconic oblivious transfer and its applications. In: Katz, J., Shacham, H. (eds.) CRYPTO 2017. LNCS, vol. 10402, pp. 33–65. Springer, Cham (2017). https://doi.org/10.1007/978-3-319-63715-0_2

[CDRW10] Chow, S.S.M., Dodis, Y., Rouselakis, Y., Waters, B.: Practical leakage-resilient identity-based encryption from simple assumptions. In: Al-Shaer, E., Keromytis, A.D., Shmatikov, V. (eds.) ACM CCS 2010, pp. 152–161. ACM Press, October 2010. https://doi.org/10.1145/1866307.1866325

[Cha12] Chan, A.C.-F.: Distributed private key generation for identity based cryptosystems in ad hoc networks. IEEE Wirel. Commun. Lett. 1(1), 46–48 (2012). https://doi.org/10.1109/WCL.2012.120211.110130

[CPM+18] Camurati, G., Poeplau, S., Muench, M., Hayes, T., Francillon, A.: Screaming channels: when electromagnetic side channels meet radio transceivers. In: Lie, D., Mannan, M., Backes, M., Wang, X.F. (eds.) ACM CCS 2018, pp. 163–177. ACM Press, October 2018. https://doi.org/10.1145/3243734.3243802

[CZLC16] Chen, Yu., Zhang, Z., Lin, D., Cao, Z.: Generalized (identity-based) hash proof system and its applications. Secur. Commun. Netw. 9(12), 1698–1716 (2016)

[DFR+07] Damgård, I.B., Fehr, S., Renner, R., Salvail, L., Schaffner, C.: A tight high-order entropic quantum uncertainty relation with applications. In: Menezes, A. (ed.) CRYPTO 2007. LNCS, vol. 4622, pp. 360–378. Springer, Heidelberg (2007). https://doi.org/10.1007/978-3-540-74143-5_20

[DG17a] Döttling, N., Garg, S.: From selective IBE to full IBE and selective HIBE. In: Kalai, Y., Reyzin, L. (eds.) TCC 2017. LNCS, vol. 10677, pp. 372–408. Springer, Cham (2017). https://doi.org/10.1007/978-3-319-70500-2_13

[DG17b] Döttling, N., Garg, S.: Identity-based encryption from the Diffie-Hellman assumption. In: Katz, J., Shacham, H. (eds.) CRYPTO 2017. LNCS, vol. 10401, pp. 537–569. Springer, Cham (2017). https://doi.org/10.1007/978-3-319-63688-7_18

[DGGM19] Döttling, N., Garg, S., Goyal, V., Malavolta, G.: Laconic conditional disclosure of secrets and applications. In: Zuckerman, D. (ed.) 60th FOCS, pp. 661–685. IEEE Computer Society Press, November 2019. https://doi.org/10.1109/FOCS.2019.00046

[DGHM18] Döttling, N., Garg, S., Hajiabadi, M., Masny, D.: New constructions of identity-based and key-dependent message secure encryption schemes. In: Abdalla, M., Dahab, R. (eds.) PKC 2018. LNCS, vol. 10769, pp. 3–31. Springer, Cham (2018). https://doi.org/10.1007/978-3-319-76578-5_1

[DLW06] Di Crescenzo, G., Lipton, R., Walfish, S.: Perfectly secure password protocols in the bounded retrieval model. In: Halevi, S., Rabin, T. (eds.) TCC 2006. LNCS, vol. 3876, pp. 225–244. Springer, Heidelberg (2006). https://doi.org/10.1007/11681878_12

[DORS08] Dodis, Y., Ostrovsky, R., Reyzin, L., Smith, A.D.: Fuzzy extractors: how to generate strong keys from biometrics and other noisy data. SIAM J. Comput. 38(1), 97–139 (2008)

[Dzi06a] Dziembowski, S.: Intrusion-resilience via the bounded-storage model. In: Halevi, S., Rabin, T. (eds.) TCC 2006. LNCS, vol. 3876, pp. 207–224. Springer, Heidelberg (2006). https://doi.org/10.1007/11681878_11

[Dzi06b] Dziembowski, S.: On forward-secure storage. In: Dwork, C. (ed.) CRYPTO 2006. LNCS, vol. 4117, pp. 251–270. Springer, Heidelberg (2006). https://doi.org/10.1007/11818175_15

[GHM+19] Garg, S., Hajiabadi, M., Mahmoody, M., Rahimi, A., Sekar, S.: Registration-based encryption from standard assumptions. In: Lin, D., Sako, K. (eds.) PKC 2019. LNCS, vol. 11443, pp. 63–93. Springer, Cham (2019). https://doi.org/10.1007/978-3-030-17259-6_3

[GHMR18] Garg, S., Hajiabadi, M., Mahmoody, M., Rahimi, A.: Registration-based encryption: removing private-key generator from IBE. In: Beimel, A., Dziembowski, S. (eds.) TCC 2018. LNCS, vol. 11239, pp. 689–718. Springer, Cham (2018). https://doi.org/10.1007/978-3-030-03807-6_25

[Goy07] Goyal, V.: Reducing trust in the PKG in identity based cryptosystems. In: Menezes, A. (ed.) CRYPTO 2007. LNCS, vol. 4622, pp. 430–447. Springer, Heidelberg (2007). https://doi.org/10.1007/978-3-540-74143-5_24

[HILL99] Håstad, J., Impagliazzo, R., Levin, L.A., Luby, M.: A pseudorandom generator from any one-way function. SIAM J. Comput. **28**(4), 1364–1396 (1999)

[HLWW13] Hazay, C., López-Alt, A., Wee, H., Wichs, D.: Leakage-resilient cryptography from minimal assumptions. In: Johansson, T., Nguyen, P.Q. (eds.) EUROCRYPT 2013. LNCS, vol. 7881, pp. 160–176. Springer, Heidelberg (2013). https://doi.org/10.1007/978-3-642-38348-9_10

[JP11] Jain, A., Pietrzak, K.: Parallel repetition for leakage resilience amplification revisited. In: Ishai, Y. (ed.) TCC 2011. LNCS, vol. 6597, pp. 58–69. Springer, Heidelberg (2011). https://doi.org/10.1007/978-3-642-19571-6_5

[KG10] Kate, A., Goldberg, I.: Distributed private-key generators for identity-based cryptography. In: Garay, J.A., De Prisco, R. (eds.) SCN 2010. LNCS, vol. 6280, pp. 436–453. Springer, Heidelberg (2010). https://doi.org/10.1007/978-3-642-15317-4_27

[LRW11] Lewko, A., Rouselakis, Y., Waters, B.: Achieving leakage resilience through dual system encryption. In: Ishai, Y. (ed.) TCC 2011. LNCS, vol. 6597, pp. 70–88. Springer, Heidelberg (2011). https://doi.org/10.1007/978-3-642-19571-6_6

[LW10] Lewko, A.B., Waters, On the insecurity of parallel repetition for leakage resilience. In: 51st FOCS, pp. 521–530. IEEE Computer Society Press, October 2010. https://doi.org/10.1109/FOCS.2010.57

[MW20] Moran, T., Wichs, D.: Incompressible Encodings. In: Micciancio, D., Ristenpart, T. (eds.) CRYPTO 2020. LNCS, vol. 12170, pp. 494–523. Springer, Cham (2020). https://doi.org/10.1007/978-3-030-56784-2_17

[NY19] Nishimaki, R., Yamakawa, T.: Leakage-resilient identity-based encryption in bounded retrieval model with nearly optimal leakage-ratio. In: Lin, D., Sako, K. (eds.) PKC 2019. LNCS, vol. 11442, pp. 466–495. Springer, Cham (2019). https://doi.org/10.1007/978-3-030-17253-4_16

Bounded Functional Encryption for Turing Machines: Adaptive Security from General Assumptions

Shweta Agrawal[1], Fuyuki Kitagawa[2], Anuja Modi[1(✉)], Ryo Nishimaki[2], Shota Yamada[3], and Takashi Yamakawa[2]

[1] IIT Madras, Chennai, India
shweta.a@cse.iitm.ac.in, anujamodi97@gmail.com
[2] NTT Social Informatics Laboratories, Tokyo, Japan
{fuyuki.kitagawa.yh,ryo.nishimaki.zk,
takashi.yamakawa.ga}@hco.ntt.co.jp
[3] AIST, Tokyo, Japan
yamada-shota@aist.go.jp

Abstract. The recent work of Agrawal et al. [Crypto '21] and Goyal et al. [Eurocrypt '22] concurrently introduced the notion of dynamic bounded collusion security for functional encryption (FE) and showed a construction satisfying the notion from identity based encryption (IBE). Agrawal et al. [Crypto '21] further extended it to FE for Turing machines in non-adaptive simulation setting from the sub-exponential learining with errors assumption (LWE). Concurrently, the work of Goyal et al. [Asiacrypt '21] constructed attribute based encryption (ABE) for Turing machines achieving adaptive indistinguishability based security against bounded (static) collusions from IBE, in the random oracle model. In this work, we significantly improve the state of art for dynamic bounded collusion FE and ABE for Turing machines by achieving *adaptive* simulation style security from a broad class of assumptions, in the standard model. In more detail, we obtain the following results:

1. We construct an adaptively secure (AD-SIM) FE for Turing machines, supporting dynamic bounded collusion, from sub-exponential LWE. This improves the result of Agrawal et al. which achieved only non-adaptive (NA-SIM) security in the dynamic bounded collusion model.

2. Towards achieving the above goal, we construct a *ciphertext policy* FE scheme (CPFE) for circuits of *unbounded* size and depth, which achieves AD-SIM security in the dynamic bounded collusion model from IBE and *laconic oblivious transfer* (LOT). Both IBE and LOT can be instantiated from a large number of mild assumptions such as the computational Diffie-Hellman assumption, the factoring assumption, and polynomial LWE. This improves the construction of Agrawal et al. which could only achieve NA-SIM security for CPFE supporting circuits of unbounded depth from IBE.

3. We construct an AD-SIM secure FE for Turing machines, supporting dynamic bounded collusions, from LOT, ABE for NC[1] (or NC) and private information retrieval (PIR) schemes which satisfy certain properties. This significantly expands the class of assumptions on which AD-SIM secure FE for Turing machines can be based. In particular, it leads to new constructions of FE for

E. Kiltz and V. Vaikuntanathan (Eds.): TCC 2022, LNCS 13747, pp. 618–647, 2022.
https://doi.org/10.1007/978-3-031-22318-1_22

Turing machines including one based on polynomial LWE and one based on the combination of the bilinear decisional Diffie-Hellman assumption and the decisional Diffie-Hellman assumption on some specific groups. In contrast the only prior construction by Agrawal et al. achieved only NA-SIM security and relied on *sub-exponential* LWE.

To achieve the above result, we define the notion of CPFE for read only RAM programs and succinct FE for LOT, which may be of independent interest.

4. We also construct an *ABE* scheme for Turing machines which achieves AD-IND security in the *standard model* supporting dynamic bounded collusions. Our scheme is based on IBE and LOT. Previously, the only known candidate that achieved AD-IND security from IBE by Goyal et al. relied on the random oracle model.

Keywords: Turing machines · Functional encryption · Attribute based encryption

1   Introduction

Functional encryption (FE) [15,38] is a powerful generalization of public key encryption, which goes beyond the traditional "all or nothing" access to encrypted data. In FE, a secret key is associated with a function f, a ciphertext is associated with an input $\mathbf{x}$ and decryption allows to recover $f(\mathbf{x})$. Security intuitively requires that the ciphertext and secret keys do not reveal anything other than the output of the computation. This can be formalized by positing the existence of a simulator which can simulate ciphertexts and secret keys given only the functions f_i and their outputs on the messages $\mathbf{x}_j$, namely $f_i(\mathbf{x}_j)$ for all secret keys sk_{f_i} and ciphertexts $\mathsf{ct}_{\mathbf{x}_j}$ seen by the adversary in the real world. This "simulation style" notion of security, commonly referred to as SIM security, is ruled out by lower bounds in a general security game [2,15]. However, it can still be achieved in the *bounded* collusion model [30], which restricts the adversary to only request an a-priori bounded number of keys and challenge ciphertexts.

There has been intensive research in the community on FE in the last two decades, studying the feasibility for general classes of functions, from diverse assumptions, satisfying different notions of security. An exciting line of research has focused on FE for uniform models of computation supporting *unbounded* input lengths, such as Deterministic or Non-deterministic Finite Automata, Turing machines and Random Access machines [4,7,8,11,28,34], in contrast to non-uniform models such as circuits. While circuits are expressive, they suffer from two major drawbacks in the context of FE. First, they force the input length to be fixed, a constraint that is inflexible and wasteful in most applications. Second, they necessitate the worst-case running time of the function on every input. By overcoming these limitations, FE schemes can fit demands of real world applications more seamlessly.

In this work, we study FE for Turing machines (henceforth TMFE) in the *bounded collusion* model, namely a security model which restricts the adversary to only request a bounded number of keys. Introduced by Gorbunov et al. [30], this model has been popular since i) it is sufficient for multiple interesting real world scenarios, ii) it can support SIM style security, and iii) it can enable constructions from weaker assumptions or for more general functionalities. In the context of TMFE, the very recent work of Agrawal et al. [5] provided the first construction of bounded TMFE from the (sub-exponential) Learning With Errors assumption (LWE).[1] Furthermore, this work achieved the notion of *dynamic* bounded collusion, where the collusion bound Q does not have to be declared during setup and may be chosen by the encryptor differently for each ciphertext, based on the sensitivity of the encrypted data. Thus, in their construction, the encryptor can choose an input x of unbounded length, a collusion bound Q and a time bound t, the key generator can choose a machine M of unbounded length and the decryptor runs M on x for t steps and outputs the result.

The work of Agrawal et al. [5] takes an important step forward in our understanding of bounded TMFE by providing the first feasibility result in a flexible dynamic model. However, it still leaves several important questions unanswered. For instance, the security notion achieved by TMFE is *non-adaptive* (denoted by NA-SIM) [15] where the adversary must send all the secret key requests before seeing the challenge ciphertext. Moreover, this limitation appears as a byproduct of the security notion achieved by the ingredient sub-schemes used for the construction (more on this below). Additionally, [5] relies on the heavy machinery of *succinct* single key FE for circuits [29], where succinctness means that the ciphertext size does not depend on the size of circuits supported (but may depend on output length and depth). Succinct FE is known to be constructible only from sub-exponential LWE[2] which necessitates the same assumption to underlie TMFE. This seems unnecessarily restrictive – in contrast, for the circuit model, bounded FE can be constructed from the much milder and more general assumption of public key encryption (PKE) [12,30]. This raises the question of whether a strong primitive like succinct FE is really necessary to support the Turing machine model. As detailed below, succinct FE is a crucial tool in the construction, on whose properties the design relies heavily, and it is not clear whether this requirement can be weakened.

For the more limited primitive of *Attribute Based Encryption* (ABE), the recent work of [34] does provide a construction supporting Turing machines in the bounded collusion model (albeit without the dynamic property discussed above), assuming only the primitive of identity based encryption (IBE). Recall that ABE is a restricted class of FE in which the ciphertext is associated with both an input x and a message m and secret key is associated with a machine M. Decryption yields m given a secret key sk_M such that $M(x) = 1$. Since IBE is a much weaker primitive than succinct FE and can be constructed from several weak assumptions such as the computational Diffie-Hellman assumption (CDH), the factoring assumption (Factoring), LWE and such others, this state of affairs is more satisfying. However, ABE is significantly weaker than FE since it does not hide the data on which the computation actually occurs, and is also an "all or nothing" primitive. Moreover, while their construction achieves strong adaptive security (denoted by AD-IND hereon), their construction relies on the random oracle model, unlike [5] which is NA-SIM in the standard model.

---

[1] Here, sub-exponential (resp., polynomial) LWE refers to the assumption that assumes the distinguishing advantage of the adversary for the decision version of LWE is sub-exponentially (resp., negligibly) small. The modulus to error ratio, which is another important parameter in LWE, will be referred to as approximation factor in this paper.

[2] Aside from obfustopia primitives such as compact FE [9,13].

1.1   Our Results

In this work, we significantly improve the state of the art for dynamic bounded collusion TMFE by achieving adaptive simulation style security from a broad class of assumptions. In more detail, we obtain the following results:

1. We construct an adaptively secure (AD-SIM) TMFE, supporting dynamic bounded collusion, from sub-exponential LWE. This improves the result of [5] which achieved only NA-SIM security in the dynamic bounded collusion model.
2. Towards achieving the above goal, we construct a *ciphertext policy* FE[3] scheme (CPFE) for circuits of *unbounded* size and depth, which achieves AD-SIM security in the dynamic bounded collusion model from IBE and *laconic oblivious transfer* (LOT). Both IBE and LOT can be instantiated from a large number of mild assumptions such as CDH, Factoring or polynomial LWE. This improves the construction of [5] which could only achieve NA-SIM security for CPFE supporting circuits of unbounded depth from IBE.
3. We construct an AD-SIM secure TMFE, supporting dynamic bounded collusions, from LOT, ABE for NC^1 (or NC) and private information retrieval (PIR) schemes which satisfy certain properties. This significantly expands the class of assumptions on which AD-SIM secure TMFE can be based since ABE for NC^1 can be constructed from pairing based assumptions like the bilinear decisional Diffie-Hellman assumption (DBDH) [35] as well as *polynomial* LWE with slightly super-polynomial approximation factors[4] [14,31], LOT can be based on CDH, Factoring and polynomial LWE [16,20,21], and PIR with the required properties can also be based on LWE [17], the decisional Diffie-Hellman assumption (DDH), or the quadratic residuosity assumption (QR) [22]. This leads to new constructions of TMFE as follows:
   - one based on the polynomial hardness of LWE with quasi-polynomial approximation factors,
   - one based on the combination of DBDH and DDH on some specific groups.
   - one based on the combination of DBDH and QR.
   If we instantiate PIR with LWE, we need ABE for NC and LWE with quasi-polynomial approximation factors [32] since the answer function of PIR from LWE [17,27] is in NC. See Sect. 5 for the detail. In contrast the only prior construction by [5] achieved only NA-SIM security and relied on *sub-exponential* LWE. When instantiated with LWE, we observe that the above construction improves the first construction we described. However, we still present the first construction because it is much simpler.
4. We also construct an ABE scheme for Turing machines which achieves AD-IND security in the *standard model* supporting dynamic bounded collusions. Our scheme is based on IBE and LOT. Previously, the only known candidate that achieved AD-IND security from IBE relied on the random oracle model [34].

---

[3] A secret key and a ciphertext are associated with an input x and a function f, respectively unlike the standard FE.

[4] That is, $O(\lambda^{\omega(1)})$.

Table 1. Comparison for bounded collusion-resistant FE for uniform models of computation

FE	Class	Security	Model	Assumption
[7]	TM	1-key NA-SIM	Static	$(\mathsf{sub\text{-}exp}, \mathsf{sub\text{-}exp})\text{-}\mathsf{LWE}^a$
[6] (SKFE)	NFA	Sel-SIM	Static	$(\mathsf{sub\text{-}exp}, \mathsf{sub\text{-}exp})\text{-}\mathsf{LWE}^a$
[5]	NL	AD-SIM	Dynamic	$(\mathsf{sub\text{-}exp}, \mathsf{sub\text{-}exp})\text{-}\mathsf{LWE}^a$
[5]	TM	NA-SIM	Dynamic	$(\mathsf{sub\text{-}exp}, \mathsf{sub\text{-}exp})\text{-}\mathsf{LWE}^a$
Ours §4	TM	AD-SIM	Dynamic	$(\mathsf{sub\text{-}exp}, \mathsf{sub\text{-}exp})\text{-}\mathsf{LWE}^a$
Ours §5	TM	AD-SIM	Dynamic	$(\mathsf{poly}, \mathsf{quasi\text{-}poly})\text{-}\mathsf{LWE}^a$
Ours §5	TM	AD-SIM	Dynamic	DDH^b & DBDH
Ours §5	TM	AD-SIM	Dynamic	QR & DBDH

a For $\mathsf{adv} \in \{\mathsf{poly}, \mathsf{sub\text{-}exp}\}$ and $\mathsf{apprx} \in \{\mathsf{quasi\text{-}poly}, \mathsf{sub\text{-}exp}\}$, $(\mathsf{adv}, \mathsf{apprx})\text{-}\mathsf{LWE}$ means that {polynomial, sub-exponential} hardness of LWE with {quasi-polynomial, sub-exponential} approxiation factors, respectively.

b DDH over the multiplicative sub-group of $\mathbb{Z}_q$ where q is a prime.

1.2 Other Related Work

A *key policy* FE[5] (KPFE) for Turing machines supporting only a *single* key request was provided by Agrawal and Singh [7] based on sub-exponential LWE. Agrawal, Maitra and Yamada [6] provided a construction of KPFE for non-deterministic finite automata (NFA) which is secure against bounded collusions of arbitrary size. However, this construction is in the symmetric key setting. These constructions do not support the dynamic collusion setting. The first works to (concurrently) introduce and support the notion of dynamic bounded collusion are [5,23]. Both works obtain simulation secure KPFE schemes for circuits with dynamic collusion resistance. [5] additionally obtain succinct CPFE/KPFE schemes for circuits with dynamic collusion property, and also to support Turing machines and NL with different security trade-offs. We provide a comparison for bounded collusion-resistant FE for uniform models of computation in Table 1. All the results in the table are about FE whose encryption time depends on the running-time of computation. There are FE schemes whose encryption time does not depend the running-time of computation [4,11,28,36]. However, such constructions are based on strong assumptions such as extractable witness encryption [28] and compact FE [4,11,36]. We also omit works based on indistinguishability obfuscation. The focus of the present work is on weak assumptions.

1.3 Our Techniques

In this section, we provide an overview of our techniques. Our final construction is obtained by going through number of steps. We refer to Fig. 1 for the overview.

---

[5] This is the same as the standard FE. We use this term to distinguish from CPFE.

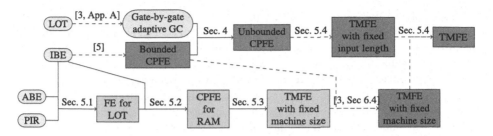

Fig. 1. Illustration of our construction path. Each rectangle represents FE and rounded rectangles represents other primitives. "Bounded CPFE" (resp., "Unbounded CPFE") means CPFE for bounded (resp., unbounded) size circuits. The red (resp., blue) rectangles represent FE with AD-SIM security under bounded dynamic collusion (resp., NA-SIM security under single key collusion). The dashed lines indicate known implications or implications that can be shown by adapting previous techniques relatively easily. The solid lines indicate implications that require new ideas and are shown by us. We do not include (selectively secure) garbled circuits, secret key encryption, and PRF in the figure in order to simplify the presentation. (Color figure online)

Recap of TMFE **by [5]:** To begin, we recap some of the ideas used in the construction of TMFE provided by [5]. At a high level, their approach is to separate the cases where the length of the input x and running time bound 1^t is larger than the machine size $|M|$ and one where the opposite is true, i.e. $|(x, 1^t)| \leq |M|$ and $|(x, 1^t)| > |M|$. They observe that running these restricted schemes in parallel allows supporting either case, where the one sub-scheme is used to decrypt a ciphertext if $|(x, 1^t)| \leq |M|$ and the second is used otherwise. We note that such a compiler was first developed by [6] in the symmetric key setting and [5] uses ideas from [33] to upgrade it to the public key setting.

To construct the restricted sub-schemes, [5] uses KPFE for the case $|(x, 1^t)| \leq |M|$ and CPFE for $|(x, 1^t)| > |M|$. For concreteness, let us consider the case $|(x, 1^t)| \leq |M|$. Now, using the "delayed encryption" technique of [33] (whose details are not relevant for our purpose), one may assume that there exists an infinite sequence of KPFE instances and the i-th instance supports circuits with input length i. To encrypt a message x with respect to the time bound 1^t, they use the $|(x, 1^t)|$-th instance of KPFE. To generate the secret key for a Turing machine M, they encode M into a set of circuits $C_{i,M}$ for $i = 1, \ldots, |M|$, where $C_{i,M}$ is a circuit that takes as input a string $(x, 1^t)$ of length i, and then runs the machine M for t steps on this input to generate the output. Secret keys for $C_{i,M}$ are generated using the i-th instance of KPFE for all of $i \in [|M|]$. A crucial detail here is that M can be of unbounded size, because each KPFE instance supports unbounded size circuits. Now, decryption is possible when $|(x, 1^t)| \leq |M|$ by using the $|(x, 1^t)|$-th instance. To construct the KPFE scheme, the authors enhance constructions of "succinct KPFE" from the literature [1,29], which can be constructed from (sub-exponential) LWE. The resultant scheme satisfies AD-SIM security against (dynamic) bounded collusions.

To handle the opposite case, namely $|(x, 1^t)| > |M|$, the authors follow the "dual" of the above procedure, using a CPFE scheme in place of KPFE, which supports circuits of unbounded depth (hence size). In more detail, to encrypt a message $(x, 1^t)$, they construct a circuit $\{U_{i,x,t}\}_{i \in [|(x,1^t)|]}$, where $U_{i,x,t}$ is a circuit that takes as input a string M of length i, interprets it as a description of a Turing machine, runs it on input x for t steps and outputs the result. They encrypt the circuit $U_{i,x,t}$ using the i-th instance of CPFE for all of $i \in [|(x, 1^t)|]$. Note that it is necessary that the CPFE scheme support circuits of unbounded *depth* and not just size, since the circuit must run Turing machine for t steps, where t may be arbitrarily large. The authors use IBE to instantiate such a CPFE. However, they can only achieve NA-SIM, where the adversary must make all its key requests before obtaining the challenge ciphertext. This limitation is inherited by the resultant TMFE scheme even though KPFE satisfies AD-SIM security as discussed above.

TMFE with AD-SIM Security: As discussed above, the missing piece in constructing TMFE with AD-SIM security from LWE is an instantiation of CPFE supporting unbounded depth circuits with AD-SIM security. We now show how to design this by carefully combining (in a non black-box way) two ingredients – i) an AD-SIM secure CPFE for circuits of *bounded* depth, size and output, denoted by BCPFE, which was constructed in [5] using IBE, and ii) adaptively secure garbled circuits (GC) based on LOT [24]. Our construction makes crucial use of the structural properties of the LOT based adaptive GC constructed by Garg and Srinivasan [24]. We describe this next.

Adaptively Secure Garbled Vircuits via LOT: Garg and Srinivasan [24] provided a construction of adaptively secure GC with near optimal online rate by leveraging the power of LOT. Recall that LOT [18] is a protocol between two parties: sender and a receiver. The receiver holds a large database $D \in \{0, 1\}^N$ and sends a short digest d (of length λ) of the database to the sender. The sender has as input a location $L \in [N]$ and two messages (m_0, m_1). It computes a read-ciphertext c using its private inputs and the received digest d by running in time $\text{poly}(\log N, |m_0|, |m_1|, \lambda)$ and sends c to the receiver. The receiver recovers the message $m_{D[L]}$ from the ciphertext c and the security requirement is that the message $m_{1-D[L]}$ remains hidden. Updatable LOT additionally allows updates to the database.

The main idea in [24] is to "linearize" the garbled circuit, namely to ensure that the simulation of a garbled gate g depends only on simulating one additional gate. With this linearization in place, they designed a careful sequence of hybrids based on a pebbling strategy where the number of changes required in each intermediate hybrid is $O(\log(|C|))$. In more detail, their construction views the circuit C to be garbled as a sequence of step circuits along with a database D, where the ith step circuit implements the ith gate in the circuit. The database D is initialized with the input x and updated to represent the state of the computation as the computation progresses. Thus, at step i, the database contains the output of every gate $g < i$ in the execution of C on x. The ith step circuit reads contents from two pre-determined locations in the database, corresponding to the input wires, and writes a bit, corresponding to the output of the gate, to location i. Thus, they reduce garbling of the circuit to garbling each step circuit along with the database D.

Coming back to our goal of CPFE for unbounded depth circuits, a starting point idea is to use a sequence of bounded size schemes BCPFE to encode a sequence of low depth step circuits described above. Intuitively, we leverage the decomposability of the adaptive GC construction so that a BCPFE scheme can generate each garbled version of the step circuit, using randomness that is derived jointly from the encryptor and key generator via a pseudorandom function (PRF). Specifically, the key generator provides BCPFE keys for input x, along with a PRF input tag, and the encryptor provides BCPFE ciphertexts for the GC step circuits along with a PRF seed. Put together, BCPFE decrypts to provide the inner decomposable GC (generated using jointly computed PRF output), which may then be evaluated to recover $C(x)$. A crucial detail swept under the rug here is how the sequence of GCs interacts with the database which captures the state of the computation. In particular, as the computation proceeds, the database must be updated, and these updates must be taken into account while proceeding with the remainder of the evaluation. This detail is handled via the *updatable* property of our LOT similarly to [24]. In the interest of brevity, we do not describe it here, and refer the reader to Sect. 3 for details.

Assuming the sequence of BCPFE schemes can produce the garbled step circuits and garbled database, we still run into another problem in the security proof – the number of BCPFE ciphertexts is as large as the size of the circuit being encrypted while on the other hand, there is an information-theoretic barrier that the key size of an AD-SIM secure CPFE should grow with the number of challenge ciphertexts [15]. This would bring us right back to where we started as we want to handle unbounded depth circuits and the key generator cannot even know this depth, so we cannot create enough space in the key to support this embedding. Our key observation to overcome this hurdle is that we do not need to simulate all the ciphertexts simultaneously. In particular, by relying on the pebbling-based simulation strategy used in [24], we can upper bound the number of ciphertexts in "simulation mode" by a fixed polynomial in each hybrid in the proof. This allows us to embed a simulated GC into the BCPFE secret key which is of fixed size, thereby allowing the post challenge queries required for AD-SIM security. To formalize this idea, we introduce an abstraction which we call "gate-by-gate garbling" (see Sect. 3), which is similar to locally simulatable garbling introduced by Ananth and Lombardi [10]. For more details, please see Sects. 3 and 4.

TMFE *Without Succinct* KPFE *for Circuits:* We now describe our construction of TMFE *without* using succinct KPFE for circuits. The high level template for the final construction is the same as discussed earlier, namely, to construct two sub-schemes that handle the cases $|(x, 1^t)| \leq |M|$ and $|(x, 1^t)| > |M|$ separately. Previously, we showed how to construct CPFE with AD-SIM security, for unbounded depth circuits from IBE and LOT, and used this to handle the case $|(x, 1^t)| > |M|$. The counterpart $|(x, 1^t)| \leq |M|$ was handled using KPFE for circuits of unbounded size, which was constructed in [5] by upgrading the succinct, single key KPFE of Goldwasser et al. [29] from (sub-exponential) LWE. Our goal is to construct FE that can handle the case of $|(x, 1^t)| \leq |M|$ and satisfies AD-SIM security *without* relying on succinct KPFE.

To begin, observe that the generalized bundling technique discussed above lets us focus on the case where $|x, 1^t|$ is fixed, but $|M|$ is unbounded. Moreover, it suffices to restrict ourselves to 1-NA-SIM security, since 1-NA-SIM implies AD-SIM for FE with bounded message length (please see Section [3, Sect. 6.4]). In [5], the authors use succinct KPFE to instantiate this scheme by taking advantage of the fact that the size of the circuit associated with the secret key in the succinct KPFE is unbounded. Thus, we can embed a machine M of unbounded size into the secret key. Then we can run the Turing machine inside the circuit for $|M|$ steps, which exceeds t (since we have $t < |M|$) and thus finishes the computation.

Our starting point observation is that since $|(x, 1^t)| \leq |M|$, where $|(x, 1^t)|$ is fixed and $|M|$ is unbounded, we can think of M as a large database, x as a short input and t as bounded running time, which naturally suggest the random access machines (RAM) model of computation. Intuitively, if $|M|$ is massive but $|x|$ and t are small, then running M on x requires only a bounded number of lookups in the transition table and a bounded number of steps, regardless of the size of M. Motivated by this observation, we cast M as a large database and construct a program P which has $(x, 1^t)$ hardwired in it, and executes $M(x)$ via RAM access to M. It is important to note that even if the program does not have M as an input, RAM access to M suffices, because the transition only depends on the description of the current state and the bit that is pointed to by the header. To capture this notion in the setting of FE, we introduce a new primitive, which we call CPFE for (read only) RAM programs. Here, the encryptor encrypts the program $P_{(x,1^t)}$ above, the key generator provides a key for database M and decryption executes $P_{(x,1^t)}$ on M, which is equal to $M(x)$. Crucially, the running time of encryption is required to be independent of $|D|$.

To construct a CPFE for read only RAM, we build upon ideas that were developed in the context of garbled RAM constructions [37]. In these constructions, a garbled RAM program consists of t garbled copies of an augmented "step circuit" which takes as input the current CPU state, the last read bit and outputs an updated state and the next read location. Copy i of the CPU step circuit is garbled so that the labels for the output wires corresponding to the output state match the labels of the input wires corresponding to the input state in the next copy $i + 1$ of the circuit. The obvious question in this context is how to incorporate data from memory into the computation – clearly, decomposing the computation necessitates some mechanism in which the sequence of garbled circuits communicate with the outside memory[6]. To enable this, previous works have used IBE and oblivious RAM (ORAM) [25, 37]. At a very high level, IBE is used to choose the correct label of the GC as follows – the garbled memory can consist of IBE secret keys for identity (i, b) where i is the given location and b is the bit stored in it, while the garbled circuits can output IBE ciphertexts whose messages are the labels of the next circuit, under identities (i, b). On the other hand, ORAM hides the position read.

However, an immediate hurdle is that ORAM necessitates two parties (client and server) to agree on a secret key. Translated into our setting, this would require that the encryptor and key generator share some secret information – but this is not possible as we are in the public key setting. To overcome this barrier, we introduce the notion of FE for LOT, denoted by LOTFE (Sect. 5.1). In LOTFE, the encryptor has two messages (μ_0, μ_1) and a database location i. The key generator has a database D as input. Decryption allows to recover $\mu_{D[i]}$ and security hides both $\mu_{1-D[i]}$ as well as the

---

[6] The careful reader may note the similarity with the adaptive garbled circuit construction by [24] discussed above.

position i. This corresponds to hiding the "other label" as well as the position that was read, in the garbled RAM approach.

It remains to construct LOTFE. Observe that LOTFE must still satisfy the desired succinctness properties, in that a secret key should encode unbounded size data and the running time of the encryption algorithm should be independent of this size. However, by reducing the requisite functionality to something simple like LOT, we earn several benefits over using succinct KPFE. In particular, since we only need to support the table lookup functionality, we can replace the fully homomorphic encryption (FHE) which was used in the succinct KPFE construction [29] with the much weaker *private information retrieval* (PIR). Due to this, we can replace ABE for circuits that is used in the construction of [29] by the much weaker ABE for NC^1 (or NC), which in turn can be constructed by a wider variety of assumptions. We discuss this in more detail below.

Let us briefly recall the main ideas used to construct succinct KPFE. The construction of [29] carefully stitches together ABE for circuits, FHE and GC as follows. At a very high level, FHE is used to encrypt the input x, and this ciphertext $\hat{x}$ is then used as the attribute string for ABE. To encode the circuit f, we construct an ABE secret key for a closely related circuit f', which is used to restrict computation on the FHE ciphertext embedded in the ABE encodings. During decryption, we can check if $f'(\hat{x}) = 1$ and recover the message if so. Intuitively, $f'(\hat{x})$ will represent the bits of an FHE encryption of $f(x)$, denoted by $\widehat{f(x)}$ and provide a message $\mathsf{lbl}_{i,0}$ if the ith bit of $\widehat{f(x)}$ is 0 and $\mathsf{lbl}_{i,1}$ if the ith bit of $\widehat{f(x)}$ is 1. These labels are then used as inputs to the GC which encodes the FHE decryption circuit, so that the decryptor can recover $f(x)$ as desired. Note that the usage of GC implies that the construction can only support a single function key, since otherwise the adversary can recover labels for multiple inputs, violating GC security.

Following a similar template, we can construct 1-NA-SIM secure LOTFE using ABE for NC^1 (or NC), PIR and GC. We encrypt labels under attributes corresponding to the PIR query and provide a key for the PIR answer function to recover the labels corresponding to the PIR answer. These are subsequently fed into the garbled circuit to recover the answer in the clear. We need that the PIR answer function is in NC^1 so that it fits ABE for NC^1. Towards this, we show that PIR from QR or DDH has its answer function in NC^1 and thus can be combined with ABE for NC^1. If we instantiate PIR with an FHE-based scheme [17,27], the answer function is in NC and we need ABE for NC, which can be instantiated with LWE with quasi-polynomial approximation factors. Our LOTFE not only allows to use various assumptions other than LWE, which was not possible before, but also allows us to remove the complexity leveraging required for the LWE based construction described before, while achieving AD-SIM secure TMFE at the end[7]. We need Sel-IND secure ABE as a building block to achieve 1-NA-SIM secure LOTFE.

The reason why Sel-IND security suffices for our case is that the reduction algorithm can guess the target attribute the adversary chooses only with polynomial guess. Although there are exponentially many possible PIR queries, the reduction algorithm

---

[7] We observe that the above construction when instantiated with LWE improves the first construction we described. However, we still present the first construction because it is much simpler.

only has to guess an input that is encoded inside PIR.query. This is because the randomness used for computing the query is not controlled by the adversary, but by the reduction algorithm. Since there are only polynomial number of possible inputs to PIR query function, the guessing can be done only with polynomial security loss. Please see Sect. 5 for the complete description.

ABE for TM from LOT *and* IBE: Lastly, we construct ABE for Turing machines supporting AD-SIM security with dynamic bounded collusions. Our construction relies on LOT and IBE. In contrast to the construction of [34], we do not rely on the random oracle and moreover, we support dynamic bounded collusions.

As before, we consider two cases, namely $|(x, 1^t)| \leq |M|$ and the opposite $|(x, 1^t)| > |M|$. Observe that for the case of longer input, the LOT based CPFE construction discussed above suffices since it implies TMFE where $|(x, 1^t)| > |M|$ with dynamic bounded collusions as discussed above. Therefore we focus on the case of shorter input. For this, our starting point is the *single* key, NA-IND secure (non-adaptively indistinguishable) ABE for TM constructed by the recent work of Goyal et al. [34], which relies on IBE. We upgrade this to adaptively (AD-SIM) secure ABE for TM supporting dynamic bounded collusions of arbitrary size, when $|(x, 1^t)| \leq |M|$, as follows. To begin, we observe that single key NA-IND security in fact implies single key NA-SIM security in the context of ABE (see [3, Remark 2.5] for an argument). Then, we combine the above single key NA-SIM ABE for Turing machines, denoted by 1-TMABE and AD-SIM secure BCPFE (for bounded circuits) with bounded dynamic collusion similarly to [5, Sect. 4].

In more detail, the master public key and master secret key of the final ABE scheme are those of BCPFE. To encrypt message m under attribute $(x, 1^t)$ for a collusion bound 1^Q, the encryptor first constructs a circuit 1-TMABE.Enc$(\cdot, x, 1^t, m)$, which is an encryption algorithm of the single-key abe for TM scheme, that takes as input a master public key and outputs an encryption of the attribute $(x, 1^t)$ and message m under the key. The encryptor then encrypts the circuit using the BCPFE scheme with respect to the bound 1^Q. To generate a secret key for a Turing machine M, the key generator freshly generates a master key pair of 1-TMABE, namely (1-TMABE.mpk, 1-TMABE.msk). It then generates a BCPFE secret key BCPFE.sk corresponding to the string 1-TMABE.mpk and an ABE secret key 1-TMABE.sk$_M$ for the machine M. The final secret key is (BCPFE.sk, 1-TMABE.sk$_M$). Decryption is done by first decrypting the BCPFE ciphertext using the BCPFE secret key to recover 1-TMABE.Enc(1-TMABE.mpk, $x, 1^t, m$) and then using the secret key 1-TMABE.sk$_M$ to perform ABE decryption and recover the message m if $M(x) = 1$ within t steps. Security follows from the individual security of the two underlying schemes and yields an AD-SIM secure ABE for TM for an a-priori bounded $|(x, 1^t)|$ with bounded dynamic collusion.

To remove the restriction on $|(x, 1^t)|$, we use the "generalized bundling" trick of [5, Sect. 6.2.2], for the case of $|(x, 1^t)| < |M|$. Thus, we obtain AD-SIM ABE for TM where $|(x, 1^t)| < |M|$ with dynamic bounded collusions. Finally, we combine AD-SIM ABE for TM with $|(x, 1^t)| > |M|$ and one with $|(x, 1^t)| \leq |M|$ as described above. The transformation yields AD-SIM secure ABE for TM with dynamic bounded collusions, which readily implies AD-IND security. Please see [3, Sec 6] for further details.

2 Preliminaries

Here, we define functional encryption (FE) with dynamic bounded collusion, which is introduced by [5,23]. The notion is stronger than conventional bounded collusion FE [12,30] in that the collusion bound can be determined by an encryptor dynamically, rather than being determined when the system is setup. We note that some of the definitions here are taken verbatim from [5]. We refer to [3, Sect. 2] for additional preliminaries.

2.1 Functional Encryption

Let $R : \mathcal{X} \times \mathcal{Y} \to \{0, 1\}^*$ be a two-input function where $\mathcal{X}$ and $\mathcal{Y}$ denote "message space" and "key attribute space", respectively. Ideally, we would like to have an FE scheme that handles the relation R directly, where we can encrypt any message $x \in \mathcal{X}$ and can generate a secret key for any key attribute $y \in \mathcal{Y}$. However, in many cases, we are only able to construct a scheme that poses restrictions on the message space and key attribute space. To capture such restrictions, we introduce a parameter prm and consider subsets of the domains $\mathcal{X}_{\mathsf{prm}} \subseteq \mathcal{X}$ and $\mathcal{Y}_{\mathsf{prm}} \subseteq \mathcal{Y}$ specified by it and the function R_{prm} defined by restricting the function R on $\mathcal{X}_{\mathsf{prm}} \times \mathcal{Y}_{\mathsf{prm}}$. An FE scheme for $\{R_{\mathsf{prm}} : \mathcal{X}_{\mathsf{prm}} \times \mathcal{Y}_{\mathsf{prm}} \to \{0, 1\}^*\}_{\mathsf{prm}}$ is defined by the following PPT algorithms:

$\mathsf{Setup}(1^\lambda, \mathsf{prm}) \to (\mathsf{mpk}, \mathsf{msk})$: The setup algorithm takes as input the security parameter λ in unary and a parameter prm that restricts the domain and range of the function and outputs the master public key mpk and a master secret key msk.

$\mathsf{Encrypt}(\mathsf{mpk}, x, 1^Q) \to \mathsf{ct}$: The encryption algorithm takes as input a master public key mpk, a message $x \in \mathcal{X}_{\mathsf{prm}}$, and a bound on the collusion Q in unary. It outputs a ciphertext ct.

$\mathsf{KeyGen}(\mathsf{msk}, y) \to \mathsf{sk}$: The key generation algorithm takes as input the master secret key msk, and a key attribute $y \in \mathcal{Y}_{\mathsf{prm}}$. It outputs a secret key sk. We assume that y is included in sk.

$\mathsf{Dec}(\mathsf{ct}, \mathsf{sk}, 1^Q) \to m$ or $\perp$: The decryption algorithm takes as input a ciphertext ct, a secret key sk, and a bound Q associated with the ciphertext. It outputs the message m or $\perp$ which represents that the ciphertext is not in a valid form.

Remark 1. We also consider single collusion FE, which is a special case where Q is always fixed to be $Q = 1$. In such a case, we drop 1^Q from the input to the algorithms for simplicity of the notation.

Definition 1 (Correctness). *An FE scheme* $\mathsf{FE} = (\mathsf{Setup}, \mathsf{KeyGen}, \mathsf{Enc}, \mathsf{Dec})$ *is correct if for all* prm, $x \in \mathcal{X}_{\mathsf{prm}}$, $y \in \mathcal{Y}_{\mathsf{prm}}$, *and* $Q \in \mathbb{N}$,

$$\Pr\left[\begin{array}{c} (\mathsf{mpk}, \mathsf{msk}) \leftarrow \mathsf{Setup}(1^\lambda, \mathsf{prm}) : \\ \mathsf{Dec}\big(\mathsf{Enc}(\mathsf{mpk}, x, 1^Q), \mathsf{KeyGen}(\mathsf{msk}, y), 1^Q\big) \neq R(x, y) \end{array}\right] = \mathrm{negl}(\lambda)$$

where probability is taken over the random coins of Setup, KeyGen *and* Enc.

We define simulation-based security notions for FE in the following.

Definition 2 (AD-SIM Security for FE with Dynamic Bounded Collusion). *Let* FE $=$ (Setup, KeyGen, Enc, Dec) *be a (public key) FE scheme with dynamic bounded collusion for the function family* $\{R_{\mathsf{prm}} : \mathcal{X}_{\mathsf{prm}} \times \mathcal{Y}_{\mathsf{prm}} \to \{0,1\}^*\}_{\mathsf{prm}}$. *For every stateful PPT adversary* A *and a stateful PPT simulator* Sim $=$ (SimEnc, SimKG), *we consider the experiments in Fig. 2.*

$\mathsf{Exp}^{\mathsf{real}}_{\mathsf{FE,A}}\left(1^\lambda\right)$	$\mathsf{Exp}^{\mathsf{ideal}}_{\mathsf{FE,Sim}}\left(1^\lambda\right)$
1. prm $\leftarrow$ A(1^λ)	1. prm $\leftarrow$ A(1^λ)
2. (mpk, msk) $\leftarrow$ Setup$(1^\lambda, \mathsf{prm})$	2. (mpk, msk) $\leftarrow$ Setup$(1^\lambda, \mathsf{prm})$
3. $(x, 1^Q) \leftarrow$ A$^{\mathsf{KeyGen(msk,\cdot)}}$(mpk)	3. $(x, 1^Q) \leftarrow$ A$^{\mathsf{KeyGen(msk,\cdot)}}$(mpk)
	$-$ Let $(y^{(1)}, \dots, y^{(Q_1)})$ be A's oracle queries.
	$-$ Let $\mathsf{sk}^{(q)}$ be the oracle reply to $y^{(q)}$.
	$-$ Let $\mathcal{V}:=\{(z^{(q)}:=R(x, y^{(q)}), y^{(q)}, \mathsf{sk}^{(q)})\}_{q \in [Q_1]}$.
4. ct $\leftarrow$ Enc(mpk, $x, 1^Q$)	4. (ct, st) $\leftarrow$ SimEnc(mpk, $\mathcal{V}, 1^{|x|}, 1^Q$)
5. $b \leftarrow$ A$^{\mathcal{O}(\mathsf{msk,\cdot})}$(mpk, ct)	5. $b \leftarrow$ A$^{\mathcal{O}'(\mathsf{st,msk,\cdot})}$(mpk, ct)
6. Output b	6. Output b

Fig. 2. AD-SIM security for FE

We emphasize that the adversary A *is stateful, even though we do not explicitly include the internal state of it into the output above for the simplicity of the notation. On the other hand, the above explicitly denotes the internal state of the simulator* Sim *by* st. *In the experiments:*

- *The oracle* $\mathcal{O}(\mathsf{msk}, \cdot) = $ KeyGen$(\mathsf{msk}, \cdot)$ *with* $1 \leq Q_1 \leq Q$, *and*
- *The oracle* $\mathcal{O}'(\mathsf{st}, \mathsf{msk}, \cdot)$ *takes as input the q-th key query* $y^{(q)}$ *for* $q \in [Q_1+1, Q_1+Q_2]$ *and returns* SimKG$(\mathsf{st}, \mathsf{msk}, R(x, y^{(q)}), y^{(q)})$, *where* $Q_1 + Q_2 \leq Q$

The FE scheme FE *is then said to be simulation secure for one message against adaptive adversaries (AD-SIM-secure, for short) if there is a* PPT *simulator* Sim *such that for every* PPT *adversary* A, *the following holds:*

$$\left|\Pr[\mathsf{Exp}^{\mathsf{real}}_{\mathsf{FE,A}}\left(1^\lambda\right) = 1] - \Pr[\mathsf{Exp}^{\mathsf{ideal}}_{\mathsf{FE,Sim}}\left(1^\lambda\right) = 1]\right| = \mathsf{negl}(\lambda). \tag{2.1}$$

Remark 2 (Non-adaptive security). We can consider a variant of the above security definition where the adversary is not allowed to make a secret key query after the ciphertext ct is given (i.e., $Q_1 = Q$). We call the notion non-adaptive simulation security (NA-SIM). In particular, when we consider single collusion FE, the notion is called 1-NA-SIM. We refer to [3, Sect. 2.4] for the formal definitions.

Special Classes of FE. We define various kinds of FE by specifying the relation.

CPFE for Circuits. To define CPFE for circuits, we set $\mathcal{X}$ to be the set of all circuits and $\mathcal{Y} = \{0,1\}^*$ and define $R(C, x) = C(x)$ if the length of the string x and the input length of C match and otherwise $R(C, x) = \perp$. In this paper, we will consider the circuit class $\mathcal{C}_{\mathsf{inp}}$ that consists of circuits with input length $\mathsf{inp} := \mathsf{inp}(\lambda)$. To do so, we set $\mathsf{prm} = 1^{\mathsf{inp}}$, $\mathcal{X}_{\mathsf{prm}} = \mathcal{C}_{\mathsf{inp}}$, and $\mathcal{Y}_{\mathsf{prm}} = \{0,1\}^{\mathsf{inp}}$.

Remark 3. In the definition of CPFE for circuits, even though the input length of the circuits in $\mathcal{C}_{\mathsf{inp}}$ is bounded, the size of the circuits is unbounded.

FE for Turing Machines. To define FE for Turing machines, we set $\mathcal{X} = \{0,1\}^*$, $\mathcal{Y}$ to be set of all Turing machine, and define $R : \mathcal{X} \times \mathcal{Y} \to \{0,1\}$ as

$$R((x, 1^t), M) = \begin{cases} 1 & \text{if } M \text{ accepts } x \text{ in } t \text{ steps} \\ 0 & \text{otherwise.} \end{cases}$$

3 Gate-by-Gate Garbling with Pebbling-Based Simulation

We define a notion of *gate-by-gate garbling* and its *pebbling-based simulation*. This is an abstraction of the backbone of the adaptive garbling by Garg and Srinivasan [24].

First, we define a syntax of a standard garbling scheme.[8] A garbling scheme for a circuit class $\mathcal{C}$ cosists of PPT algorithms $\mathsf{GC} = (\mathsf{GCkt}, \mathsf{GInp}, \mathsf{GEval})$ with the following syntax:

$\mathsf{GCkt}(1^\lambda, C) \to (\widetilde{C}, \mathsf{st})$: The circuit garbling algorithm takes as input the unary representation of the security parameter λ and a circuit $C \in \mathcal{C}$ and outputs a garbled circuit $\widetilde{C}$ and state information st.

$\mathsf{GInp}(\mathsf{st}, x) \to \widetilde{x}$: The input garbling algorithm takes as input the state information st and an input x and outputs a garbled input $\widetilde{x}$.

$\mathsf{GEval}(\widetilde{C}, \widetilde{x}) \to y$: The evaluation algorithm takes as input the garbled circuit $\widetilde{C}$ and garbled input $\widetilde{x}$ and outputs an output y.

Definition 3 (Correctness). *A garbling scheme* $\mathsf{GC} = (\mathsf{GCkt}, \mathsf{GInp}, \mathsf{GEval})$ *is correct if for all circuits* $C \in \mathcal{C}$ *and its input* x,

$$\Pr[(\widetilde{C}, \mathsf{st}) \leftarrow \mathsf{GCkt}(1^\lambda, C), \widetilde{x} \leftarrow \mathsf{GInp}(\mathsf{st}, x) : \mathsf{GEval}(\widetilde{C}, \widetilde{x}) = C(x)] = 1.$$

In addition to the security notion for a standard garbling scheme in [3, Definition 2.8], we introduce a new security notion specific to gate-by-gate garbling, which we call *pebbling-based security*. For defining gate-by-gate garbling, we prepare some notations about circuits.

---

[8] Note that the syntax defined here is more general than that of Yao's garbling defined in [3, Definition 2.8].

Notations. For a circuit C, we denote by Gates the set of all gates of C. We use inp and out to mean the input-length and output-length of C, respectively. A unique index from 1 to N is assigned to each bit of input and gate where N is the sum of the input-length and the number of gates of C. In particular, each bit of input is assigned by indices from 1 to inp, each intermediate gate is assigned by indices from inp $+ 1$ to $N -$ out, and each output gate is assigned by indices from $N -$ out $+ 1$ to N. We assume that a circuit has fan-in 2 and unbounded fan-out without loss of generality. A gate $\mathsf{G} \in$ Gates is represented as $(g_\mathsf{G}, i_\mathsf{G}, A_\mathsf{G}, B_\mathsf{G})$ where $g_\mathsf{G} : \{0,1\} \times \{0,1\} \to \{0,1\}$ is a function corresponding to G, i_G is the index of G, and A_G and B_G are indices of the input bits or gates whose values are passed to G as input. We assume $A_\mathsf{G} < i_\mathsf{G}$ and $B_\mathsf{G} < i_\mathsf{G}$ without loss of generality. We call $(i_\mathsf{G}, A_\mathsf{G}, B_\mathsf{G})$ the *topology* of G and denote it by top(G). We call the set of topology of all gates the topology of C and denote it by top(C).

Intuitively, gate-by-gate garbling is a garbling scheme whose circuit garbling algorithm can be decomposed into gate garbling algorithms for each gate, whose efficiency is independent of the size of the circuit. The formal definition is given below:

Definition 4 (Gate-by-Gate Garbling:). *A garbling scheme* GC $=$ (GCkt, GInp, GEval) *for a circuit class* C *is said to be gate-by-gate garbling with* $N_{\mathsf{rand}} = N_{\mathsf{rand}}(\mathsf{top}(C))$ *randomness slots and randomness length* ℓ *if* GCkt *can be decomposed into PPT sub-algorithms* (GSetup, GGate) *as follows:*

GCkt($1^\lambda, C$): *The circuit garbling algorithm proceeds as follows:*
1. *Run* GSetup(1^λ, top(C)) *to generate a public parameter* pp.
2. *For* $i \in [N_{\mathsf{rand}}]$, *generate a randomness* $\mathsf{R}_i \leftarrow \{0,1\}^\ell$ *for* $\ell = \mathsf{poly}(\lambda)$ *that does not depend on* C.
3. *For* $\mathsf{G} \in$ Gates, *run* GGate(pp, G, $\{\mathsf{R}_i\}_{i \in S(\mathsf{G})}$) *to generate a garbled gate* $\widetilde{\mathsf{G}}$. *Here,* $S(\mathsf{G}) \subseteq [N_{\mathsf{rand}}]$ *is a subset of size* $O(1)$ *that is efficiently computable from* G *and* top(C).
4. *Output a garbled circuit* $\widetilde{C} := \left(\mathsf{pp}, \{\widetilde{\mathsf{G}}\}_{\mathsf{G} \in \mathsf{Gates}}\right)$ *and the state information* st $:=$ (pp, $\{\mathsf{R}_i\}_{i \in S_{\mathsf{st}}}$) *where* $S_{\mathsf{st}} \subseteq [N_{\mathsf{rand}}]$ *is a subset of size* $O(\mathsf{inp} + \mathsf{out})$ *that is efficiently computable from* top(C).

We require GC *to satisfy the following requirements.*

1. GGate(pp, G, $\{\mathsf{R}_i\}_{i \in S(\mathsf{G})}$) *runs in time* $\mathsf{poly}(\lambda)$ *independently of the size of* C *where* pp $\leftarrow$ GSetup(1^λ, top(C)) *and* $\mathsf{R}_i \leftarrow \{0,1\}^\ell$ *for* $i \in [N_{\mathsf{rand}}]$.
2. GInp(st, x) *is deterministic and runs in time* $\mathsf{poly}(\lambda, \mathsf{inp}, \mathsf{out})$ *independently of the size of* C *where* pp $\leftarrow$ GSetup(1^λ, top(C)), $\mathsf{R}_i \leftarrow \{0,1\}^\ell$ *for* $i \in [N_{\mathsf{rand}}]$, *and* st $:=$ (pp, $\{\mathsf{R}_i\}_{i \in S_{\mathsf{st}}}$).

We require gate-by-gate garbling to satisfy (M, T)-*pebbling-based security* for some parameters M and T, which intuitively requires the following: There are three modes of gate garbling algorithms, the white mode, black mode, and gray mode. The white mode gate garbling algorithm is identical to the real gate garbling algorithm. The black mode gate garbling algorithm is a "simulation" algorithm that simulates a garbled gate without knowing the functionality of the gate. The gray mode garbling algorithm is an "input-dependent simulation" algorithm that simulates a garbled gate by using both the circuit C and its input x that are being garbled. We call a sequence of modes of each gate of C a configuration of C. There is a configuration-based input-garbling algorithm that simulates a garbled input by using C and a configuration as additional inputs. When the configuration is all-white, it corresponds to the real input garbling algorithm, and when the configuration is all-black, it corresponds to a legitimate "simulation" algorithm that only uses $C(x)$ instead of C and x. The security requires that there is a sequence of configurations of length T that starts from the all-white configuration, which corresponds to the real garbling algorithm, to the all-black configuration, which corresponds to the simulation algorithm, such that:

1. the number of gates in the gray mode in any intermediate configuration is at most M, and
2. garbled circuits and garbled inputs generated in neighboring configurations are computationally indistinguishable even if the distinguisher can specify all the randomness needed for generating garbled gates whose modes are black or white in both of those configurations.

We give the formal definition of pebbling-based security in [3, Sect. 3.1].

Instantiation. Our definition of gate-by-gate garbling with pebbling-based simulation security captures the backbone of the proof technique of adaptive garbling in [24]. The following lemma is implicit in their work. The lemma is proven in [3, Appendix A] for completeness.

Lemma 1 (Implicit in [24]). *If there exists LOT, which exists assuming either of* CDH, Factoring, *or* LWE, *there exists a gate-by-gate garbling for all polynomial-size circuits that satisfies* (M, T)-*pebbling-based simulation security for* $M = O(\log \text{size})$ *and* $T = \text{poly}(\text{size})$ *where* size *is the size of a circuit being garbled.*

4   AD-SIM CPFE with Dynamic Bounded Collusion

In this section, we construct an AD-SIM secure CPFE scheme CPFE for unbounded polynomial-size circuits with dynamic bounded collusion. CPFE supports the function class $\mathcal{C}_{\text{inp,out}}$ for any polynomials $\text{inp} = \text{inp}(\lambda)$ and $\text{out} = \text{out}(\lambda)$ where $\mathcal{C}_{\text{inp,out}}$ is the class of circuits with input-length inp and output-length out.

Ingredients. We now describe the underlying building blocks used to obtain CPFE:

1. A gate-by-gate garbling scheme $\mathsf{GC} = (\mathsf{GCkt}, \mathsf{GInp}, \mathsf{GEval})$ for $\mathcal{C}_{\text{inp,out}}$ with N_{rand} randomness slots and randomness length ℓ that satisfies (M, T)-pebbling-based simulation security for $M = \text{poly}(\lambda)$ and $T = \text{poly}(\lambda)$. By Lemma 1, such a scheme exists under the existence of laconic OT, which in turn exists under either of CDH, Factoring, or LWE. We denote by $\mathcal{R}$ the randomness space of GGate.
2. A PRF $\mathsf{PRF} = (\mathsf{PRF.Setup}, \mathsf{PRF.Eval})$ from $\{0, 1\}^{\text{inp}}$ to $\{0, 1\}^{\ell}$.
3. A PRF $\mathsf{PRF'} = (\mathsf{PRF'.Setup}, \mathsf{PRF'.Eval})$ from $\{0, 1\}^{\text{inp}}$ to $\mathcal{R}$.

Circuit GarbleCirc

Input: A string $x \in \{0,1\}^{\mathsf{inp}}$ and a key-tag $r \in \{0,1\}^{\lambda}$

Hardwired value: a public parameter pp, gate G, set $S(\mathsf{G})$, tuple of PRF keys $\{\mathsf{K}_i\}_{i \in S(\mathsf{G})}$, and PRF key K'_G.

1. Compute $\mathsf{R}_i \leftarrow \mathsf{PRF.Eval}(\mathsf{K}_i, r)$ for $i \in S(\mathsf{G})$ and $\mathsf{R}'_\mathsf{G} \leftarrow \mathsf{PRF'.Eval}(\mathsf{K}'_\mathsf{G}, r)$.
2. Output $\widetilde{\mathsf{G}} := \mathsf{GGate}(\mathsf{pp}, \mathsf{G}, \{\mathsf{R}_i\}_{i \in S(\mathsf{G})}; \mathsf{R}'_\mathsf{G})$.

Fig. 3. The description of GarbleCirc

4. An M-CT AD-SIM secure CPFE scheme with dynamic bounded collusion denoted by BCPFE $=$ (BCPFE.Setup, BCPFE.Enc, BCPFE.KeyGen, BCPFE.Dec) for bounded polynomial-size circuits. Here, M-CT AD-SIM security roughly means security against adversaries that see M challenge ciphertexts. Due to a technical reason, however, our notion of M-CT AD-SIM security is slightly different from the standard one e.g., [30, Appendix A]. Our definition is given in [3, Sec 4.1.2]. We construct a CPFE scheme for bounded polynomial-size circuits that satisfies this security notion from IBE in [3, Appendix B.1].
   We require BCPFE to support a circuit class $\mathcal{C}_{\mathsf{BCPFE.inp},\mathsf{BCPFE.out},\mathsf{BCPFE.size}}$ consisting of circuits with input length BCPFE.inp, output length BCPFE.out, and size at most BCPFE.size, where BCPFE.inp $:=$ inp $+ \lambda$ and BCPFE.out and BCPFE.size are output-length and the maximum size of the circuit GarbleCirc defined in Fig. 3, respectively. By the efficiency requirements of GC (Definition 4), BCPFE.out $= \mathrm{poly}(\lambda, \mathsf{inp})$ and BCPFE.size $= \mathrm{poly}(\lambda, \mathsf{inp})$ independently of the size of the circuit C being encrypted.
5. A (single-ciphertext) AD-SIM-secure CPFE scheme with dynamic bounded collusion denoted by BCPFE' $=$ (BCPFE'.Setup, BCPFE'.Enc, BCPFE'.KeyGen, BCPFE'.Dec) for bounded polynomial-size circuits. We require BCPFE' to support a circuit class $\mathcal{C}_{\mathsf{BCPFE'.inp},\mathsf{BCPFE'.out},\mathsf{BCPFE'.size}}$ consisting of circuits with input length BCPFE'.inp, output length BCPFE'.out, and size at most BCPFE'.size, where BCPFE'.inp $:=$ inp $+ \lambda$ and BCPFE'.out and BCPFE'.size are the output length and the maximum size of the circuit GarbleInp defined in Fig. 4, respectively. By the efficiency requirements of GC (Definition 4), BCPFE'.out $= \mathrm{poly}(\lambda, \mathsf{inp})$ and BCPFE'.size $= \mathrm{poly}(\lambda, \mathsf{inp})$ independently of the size of the circuit C being encrypted.

Construction. In the construction, for a circuit C, we define the universal circuit U_C such that $U_C(x) = C(x)$. We define U_C in such a way that the topology of U_C does not reveal anything beyond the size of C.[9] The description of CPFE is given below.

Setup(1^λ, prm): On input the security parameter λ and the parameter prm, do the following:
   1. Run (BCPFE.mpk, BCPFE.msk) $\leftarrow$ BCPFE.Setup(1^λ, BCPFE.prm).
   2. Run (BCPFE'.mpk, BCPFE'.msk) $\leftarrow$ BCPFE'.Setup(1^λ, BCPFE'.prm).

---

[9] We explain how to construct such U_C in [3, Sect. 2.1].

Circuit GarbleInp

Input: A string $x \in \{0,1\}^{\mathsf{inp}}$ and a key-tag $r \in \{0,1\}^{\lambda}$
Hardwired value: a public parameter pp and a tuple of PRF keys $\{\mathsf{K}_i\}_{i \in S_{\mathsf{st}}}$.

1. Compute $\mathsf{R}_i \leftarrow \mathsf{PRF.Eval}(\mathsf{K}_i, r)$ for $i \in S_{\mathsf{st}}$.
2. Set $\mathsf{st} := (\mathsf{pp}, \{\mathsf{R}_i\}_{i \in S_{\mathsf{st}}})$.
3. Output $\widetilde{x} := \mathsf{GInp}(\mathsf{st}, x)$.

Fig. 4. The description of GarbleInp

3. Output $(\mathsf{mpk}, \mathsf{msk}) := ((\mathsf{BCPFE.mpk}, \mathsf{BCPFE}'.\mathsf{mpk}), (\mathsf{BCPFE.msk}, \mathsf{BCPFE}'.$
   $\mathsf{msk}))$.

$\mathsf{Enc}(\mathsf{mpk}, C, 1^Q)$: On input the master public key $\mathsf{mpk} = (\mathsf{BCPFE.mpk}, \mathsf{BCPFE}'.$
$\mathsf{mpk})$, a circuit $C \in \mathcal{C}_{\mathsf{inp,out}}$, and the query bound $1 \leq Q \leq 2^{\lambda}$ in unary form,
do the following:

1. Compute the universal circuit U_C. In the following, we write Gates to mean the set of gates of U_C rather than C.
2. Run $\mathsf{pp} \leftarrow \mathsf{GSetup}(1^{\lambda}, \mathsf{top}(U_C))$.
3. For $i \in [N_{\mathsf{rand}}]$, generate $\mathsf{K}_i \leftarrow \mathsf{PRF.Setup}(1^{\lambda})$
4. For $G \in$ Gates generate $\mathsf{K}'_G \leftarrow \mathsf{PRF}'.\mathsf{Setup}(1^{\lambda})$.
5. For $G \in$ Gates, run

$$\mathsf{BCPFE.ct}_G \leftarrow \mathsf{BCPFE.Enc}(\mathsf{BCPFE.mpk}, \mathsf{GarbleCirc}[\mathsf{pp}, G, S(G), \{\mathsf{K}_i\}_{i \in S(G)}, \mathsf{K}'_G], 1^Q)$$

   where $\mathsf{GarbleCirc}[\mathsf{pp}, G, S(G), \{\mathsf{K}_i\}_{i \in S(G)}, \mathsf{K}'_G]$ is the circuit as defined in Fig. 3.
6. Run $\mathsf{BCPFE}'.\mathsf{ct} \leftarrow \mathsf{BCPFE}'.\mathsf{Enc}(\mathsf{BCPFE}'.\mathsf{mpk}, \mathsf{GarbleInp}[\mathsf{pp}, \{\mathsf{K}_i\}_{i \in S_{\mathsf{st}}}])$ where $\mathsf{GarbleInp}[\mathsf{pp}, \{\mathsf{K}_i\}_{i \in S_{\mathsf{st}}}]$ is the circuit as defined in Fig. 4.
7. Output $\mathsf{ct} := (\{\mathsf{BCPFE.ct}_G\}_{G \in \mathsf{Gates}}, \mathsf{BCPFE}'.\mathsf{ct})$.

$\mathsf{KeyGen}(\mathsf{msk}, x)$: On input the master secret key $\mathsf{msk} = (\mathsf{BCPFE.msk}, \mathsf{BCPFE}'.\mathsf{msk})$
and an input $x \in \{0,1\}^{\mathsf{inp}}$, do the following:

1. Generate $r \leftarrow \{0,1\}^{\lambda}$.
2. Run $\mathsf{BCPFE.sk} \leftarrow \mathsf{BCPFE.KeyGen}(\mathsf{BCPFE.msk}, (x,r))$.
3. Run $\mathsf{BCPFE}'.\mathsf{sk} \leftarrow \mathsf{BCPFE}'.\mathsf{KeyGen}(\mathsf{BCPFE}'.\mathsf{msk}, (x,r))$.
4. Output $\mathsf{sk} := (r, \mathsf{BCPFE.sk}, \mathsf{BCPFE}'.\mathsf{sk})$.

$\mathsf{Dec}(\mathsf{ct}, \mathsf{sk}, 1^Q)$: On input a ciphertext $\mathsf{ct} = (\{\mathsf{BCPFE.ct}_G\}_{G \in \mathsf{Gates}}, \mathsf{BCPFE}'.\mathsf{ct})$ and a
secret key $\mathsf{sk} = (r, \mathsf{BCPFE.sk}, \mathsf{BCPFE}'.\mathsf{sk})$, do the following:

1. For $G \in$ Gates, run $\widetilde{G} \leftarrow \mathsf{BCPFE.Dec}(\mathsf{BCPFE.ct}_G, \mathsf{BCPFE.sk}, 1^Q)$
2. Run $\widetilde{x} \leftarrow \mathsf{BCPFE}'.\mathsf{Dec}(\mathsf{BCPFE}'.\mathsf{ct}, \mathsf{BCPFE}'.\mathsf{sk}, 1^Q)$.
3. Set $\widetilde{U_C} := (\mathsf{pp}, \{\widetilde{G}\}_{G \in \mathsf{Gates}})$.
4. Compute and output $\mathsf{GEval}(\widetilde{U_C}, \widetilde{x})$.

Correctness. Let $\mathsf{ct} = (\{\mathsf{BCPFE.ct}_G\}_{G \in \mathsf{Gates}}, \mathsf{BCPFE}'.\mathsf{ct})$ be an honestly generated ciphertext for a circuit C and $\mathsf{sk} = (r, \mathsf{BCPFE.sk}, \mathsf{BCPFE}'.\mathsf{sk})$ be an honestly generated secret key for an input x. By the correctness of BCPFE, for each

$G \in$ Gates, if we generate $\widetilde{G} \leftarrow$ BCPFE.Dec(BCPFE.ct$_G$, BCPFE.sk, 1^Q), then we have $\widetilde{G} =$ GGate(pp, G, $\{R_i\}_{i \in S(G)}$; R'_G) where $R_i \leftarrow$ PRF.Eval(K_i, r) for $i \in S(G)$ and $R'_G \leftarrow$ PRF'.Eval(K'_G, r). Similarly, by the correctness of BCPFE', if we generate $\widetilde{x} \leftarrow$ BCPFE'.Dec(BCPFE'.ct, BCPFE'.sk, 1^Q), then we have $\widetilde{x} =$ GInp(st, x) where $R_i \leftarrow$ PRF.Eval(K_i, r) for $i \in S_{st}$ and st := (pp, $\{R_i\}_{i \in S_{st}}$). Then, by the (perfect) correctnes of GC, GEval($\widetilde{U_C}, \widetilde{x}$) = $U_C(x) = C(x)$ where $\widetilde{U_C}$:= (pp, $\{\widetilde{G}\}_{G \in \text{Gates}}$).

Security. The following theorem asserts the security of CPFE. The proof appears in [3, Sec 4.2].

Theorem 1. *If* GC *satisfies* (M, T)-*pebbling-based simulation security for* $M = \text{poly}(\lambda)$ *and* $T = \text{poly}(\lambda)$, BCPFE *is* M-*CT* AD-SIM-*secure against dynamic bounded collusion,* BCPFE' *is* AD-SIM-*secure against dynamic bounded collusion, and* PRF *and* PRF' *are secure pseudorandom functions, then* CPFE *is* AD-SIM-*secure against dynamic bounded collusion.*

FE for Turing Machines. Agrawal et al. [5] (implicitly) showed that one can construct FE for TM with AD-SIM security against dynamic bounded collusion based on CPFE for unbounded polynomial-size circuits with AD-SIM security against dynamic bounded collusion additionally assuming sub-exponential LWE. Since (even polynomial) LWE implies LOT and IBE, by combining their result and Theorem 1, we obtain the following theorem:

Theorem 2. *Assuming sub-exponential* LWE, *we have FE for TM with* AD-SIM *security against dynamic bounded collusion.*

This improves one of the main results of [5] that constructed a similar scheme with NA-SIM security based on the same assumption. Since this is further improved in regard to assumptions in Sect. 5, we omit the details.

5   TMFE Without Succinct FE

In this section, we propose an alternative route to construct FE for Turing machine that does not use succinct FE. We refer to Sect. 1 for the overview.

5.1   FE for Laconic OT Functionality

Here, we define FE for LOT functionality by specifying the relation $R_{\text{LOTFE}} : \mathcal{X}_{\text{LOTFE}} \times \mathcal{Y}_{\text{LOTFE}} \rightarrow \{0, 1\}^*$.

FE for Laconic OT Functionality. To define FE for LOT functionality, we set prm = $\bot$, $\mathcal{X}_{\text{LOTFE}} = \mathbb{N} \times \mathbb{N} \times \{0, 1\}^* \times \{0, 1\}^*$, and $\mathcal{Y}_{\text{LOTFE}} = \{0, 1\}^*$. An element in $\mathcal{X}_{\text{LOTFE}}$ is represented by (N, i, μ_0, μ_1) with $N \in \mathbb{N}$, $i \in [N]$, and $\mu_0, \mu_1 \in \{0, 1\}^*$ with $|\mu_0| = |\mu_1|$. We assume that both i and N are represented in binary form. We then define

$$R_{\text{LOTFE}}((N, i, \mu_0, \mu_1), D) = \begin{cases} (N, \mu_{D[i]}) & \text{if } |D| = N \\ (N, 1^{|\mu_0|}) & \text{otherwise} \end{cases},$$

where $|D|$ is the length of D as a binary string and $D[i]$ is the i-th bit of D.

Remark 4 (Succinctness). We note that the encryption algorithm should run in fixed polynomial time in λ that is independent from N, since N is input to the encryption algorithm in binary form. This in particular implies that the running time of the encryption algorithm is independent from the size of the database D supported by the scheme. This property can be seen as an analogue of the efficiency requirements for the succinctness of FE [29] or laconic OT [18].

Remark 5. We also note that the above FE has similar functinality to that of LOT [18]. However, the important difference is that we intend to hide the index i while they do not. This security requirement is captured by the definition of R_{LOTFE} above, where i is not part of the output.

Ingredients. We now describe the underlying building blocks used for our construction of FE for LOT functionality. We need the following ingredients.

1. PIR scheme $\mathsf{PIR} = (\mathsf{PIR.query}, \mathsf{PIR.Answer}, \mathsf{PIR.Reconstruct})$ that satisfies the efficiency requirements in [3, Definition 2.9]. In particular, we require that $\mathsf{PIR.Query}$ and $\mathsf{PIR.Reconstruct}$ run in fixed polynomial time for any $N \leq 2^{\log^2 \lambda}$ (even for super-polynomial N). This implies that the lengths of $\mathsf{PIR.query}$, $\mathsf{PIR.answer}$, and $\mathsf{PIR.st}$ are bounded by a fixed polynomial in the security parameter that is independent of N. We use the uniform upper bound $\ell_{\mathsf{PIR}} = \mathrm{poly}(\lambda)$ for them and assume that they are represented by binary strings of length ℓ_{PIR}. Additionally, we require that the function $\mathsf{PIR.Answer}$ has shallow circuit implementations. As we show in [3, Appendix C], we have the following instantiations:
   (a) PIR constructions from (the polynomial hardness of) LWE [17, 27] has implementation of the answer function in NC.
   (b) For PIR constructions from DDH/QR [22], we have implementations of the answer function in NC^1. For DDH based construction, we have to use the multiplicative sub-group of $\mathbb{Z}_q$ for prime q.
2. 1-Sel-IND
   secure ABE scheme $\mathsf{ABE} = (\mathsf{ABE.Setup}, \mathsf{ABE.KeyGen}, \mathsf{ABE.Enc}, \mathsf{ABE.Dec})$ for circuits that can evaluate the answer function of PIR in the above. We consider two types of instantiations:
   (a) We can use general ABE for circuit [14, 31]. If the answer function of PIR is implemented in NC, we can base the security of the scheme on polynomial hardness of LWE with quasi-polynomial approximation factors (i.e., $O(\lambda^{\mathrm{poly}(\log \lambda)})$).
   (b) We can use ABE for NC^1 circuits. In more details, we need the scheme to support circuit with fixed input length and any depth d, where we allow the key generation algorithm and the decryption algorithms to run in time $\mathrm{poly}(\lambda, 2^d)$. This effectively limits the class of the circuits to be NC^1. We can instantiate such an ABE from (the polynomial hardness of) LWE with super-polynomial approximation factor [32] (i.e., $O(\lambda^{\omega(1)})$) or various assumptions on pairing groups including DBDH or CBDH (the computational bilinear Diffie-Hellman assumption) [35].
3. Selectively secure garbled circuit $\mathsf{GC} = (\mathsf{GC.Garble}, \mathsf{GC.Sim})$. We can instantiate it from any one-way function [39].

Circuit $C[N, \text{PIR.st}, \mu_0, \mu_1]$

Hardwired constants: The integer N, The PIR secret state PIR.st, the messages μ_0, μ_1.
Input: String $X \in \{0,1\}^{\ell_{\text{PIR}}}$

    1. Parse $X \to \text{PIR.answer}$.
    2. Run PIR.Reconstruct(PIR.st, PIR.answer, N) $\to b$.
    3. Output μ_b.

Fig. 5. Circuit $C[N, \text{PIR.st}, \mu_0, \mu_1]$

4. IBE scheme IBE = (IBE.Setup, IBE.KeyGen, IBE.Enc, IBE.Dec) with AD-IND security. Since IBE with AD-IND security is implied by IBE with Sel-IND [19] and the latter is trivially implied by the ABE for NC^1 circuit, this does not add a new assumption.

We assume that all the ingredients above have perfect correctness for simplicity. We consider correctness error only for PIR, because DDH based instantiation does not have perfect correctness.

Construction. Here, we describe our scheme LOTFE = (Setup, KeyGen, Enc, Dec). The construction is similar to that of succinct FE by [29] where FHE is replaced by PIR. In the construction, we assume that $N, |D| \leq 2^{\log^2 \lambda}$. This is sufficient for dealing with unbounded size D, because $2^{\log^2 \lambda} = \lambda^{\log \lambda}$ is super-polynomial.

Setup(1^λ): On input the security parameter λ, do the following:
    1. Run (IBE.mpk, IBE.msk) $\leftarrow$ IBE.Setup(1^λ).
    2. Run (ABE.mpk, ABE.msk) $\leftarrow$ ABE.Setup(1^λ, prm), where prm:=$1^{\ell_{\text{PIR}}+2\lambda}$. This means that the ABE supports circuit with input length $\ell_{\text{PIR}} + 2\lambda$.
    3. Output mpk:=(ABE.mpk, IBE.mpk) and msk:=(ABE.msk, IBE.msk).
Enc(mpk, (N, i, μ_0, μ_1)): On input the master public key mpk = (ABE.mpk, IBE.mpk) and the message (N, i, μ_0, μ_1), do the following:
    1. Run (PIR.query, PIR.st) $\leftarrow$ PIR.Query($1^\lambda, i, N$).
    2. Pick $\text{lab}_{k,b} \leftarrow \{0,1\}^\lambda$ for $k \in [\ell_{\text{PIR}}]$, $b \in \{0,1\}$.
    3. For $k \in [\ell_{\text{PIR}}]$, $b \in \{0,1\}$, compute

$$\text{ABE.ct}_{k,b} \leftarrow \text{ABE.Enc}(\text{ABE.mpk}, (\text{PIR.query}, k, b), \text{lab}_{k,b}).$$

    4. Construct circuit $C[N, \text{PIR.st}, \mu_0, \mu_1]$ as Fig. 5.
    5. Run $\widetilde{C} \leftarrow \text{GC.Garble}\left(1^\lambda, C[N, \text{PIR.st}, \mu_0, \mu_1]\right)$.
    6. Set msg:=$\left(\widetilde{C}, \text{PIR.query}, \{\text{ABE.ct}_{k,b}\}_{k\in[\ell_{\text{PIR}}], b\in\{0,1\}}\right)$.
    7. Run IBE.ct $\leftarrow$ IBE.Enc(IBE.mpk, N, msg).
    8. Output ct:=$(N, 1^{|\mu_0|}, \text{IBE.ct})$.
KeyGen(msk, D): On input the master secret key msk = (ABE.msk, IBE.msk), an input $D \in \{0,1\}^*$ with $|D| \leq 2^{\log^2 \lambda}$, do the following:
    1. Construct the circuit $F[D]$ as Fig. 6.

Circuit $F[D]$

Hardwired constants: The data $D \in \{0,1\}^{|D|}$.
Input: String $X \in \{0,1\}^{\ell_{\mathsf{PIR}}+\lambda+1}$

1. Parse the input as $X \to (\mathsf{PIR.query}, k, b)$ where $\mathsf{PIR.query} \in \{0,1\}^{\ell_{\mathsf{PIR}}}$, $k \in \{0,1\}^{\lambda}$, and $b \in \{0,1\}$.
2. If $k \notin [\ell_{\mathsf{PIR}}]$, output 0, where k is interpreted as an integer.
3. Run $\mathsf{PIR.Answer}(\mathsf{PIR.query}, D, 1^{|D|}) \to \mathsf{PIR.answer}$.
4. Compute $b' = \mathsf{PIR.answer}_k \oplus b \oplus 1$, where $\mathsf{PIR.answer}_k$ is the k-th bit of $\mathsf{PIR.answer}$.
5. Output b'.

Fig. 6. Circuit $F[D]$

2. Run
$$\mathsf{ABE.sk} \leftarrow \mathsf{ABE.KeyGen}(\mathsf{ABE.msk}, F[D]).$$

3. Run $\mathsf{IBE.sk} \leftarrow \mathsf{IBE.KeyGen}(\mathsf{IBE.msk}, |D|)$.
4. Output $\mathsf{sk} := (D, \mathsf{ABE.sk}, \mathsf{IBE.sk})$.

$\mathsf{Dec}(\mathsf{ct}, \mathsf{sk})$: On input a ciphertext $\mathsf{ct} = (N, 1^{|\mu_0|}, \mathsf{IBE.ct})$, a secret key $\mathsf{sk} = (D, \mathsf{ABE.sk}, \mathsf{IBE.sk})$, do the following:

1. If $|D| \neq N$, output $(N, 1^{|\mu_0|})$.
2. Run $\mathsf{msg} \leftarrow \mathsf{IBE.Dec}(\mathsf{IBE.sk}, \mathsf{IBE.ct})$.
3. Parse $\mathsf{msg} \to (\widetilde{C}, \mathsf{PIR.query}, \{\mathsf{ABE.ct}_{k,b}\}_{k \in [n], b \in \{0,1\}})$.
4. Run $\mathsf{PIR.answer} \leftarrow \mathsf{PIR.Answer}(\mathsf{PIR.query}, D, 1^N)$.
5. Run $\mathsf{lab}_k \leftarrow \mathsf{ABE.Dec}(\mathsf{ABE.sk}, \mathsf{ABE.ct}_{k, \mathsf{PIR.answer}_k})$ for $k \in [\ell_{\mathsf{PIR}}]$.
6. Compute $\mu := \mathsf{GC.Eval}(\widetilde{C}, \{\mathsf{lab}_k\}_k)$.
7. Output (N, μ).

Efficiency. We discuss the efficiency of the scheme. It is not hard to see that Setup and Enc run in polynomial time in its input length. We note that Enc runs in polynomial time in λ and $|\mu|$ even for super-polynomial N as large as $2^{\log^2 \lambda}$ by the efficiency property of PIR.Query and PIR.Reconstruct. For evaluating the efficiency of KeyGen, we consider two settings based on how we instantiate ABE and PIR. The first case is the combination of ABE for circuits and any PIR, whereas the second case is ABE for NC^1 circuits and PIR with answer function in NC^1. We focus on the latter case since the former case is much simpler. Evaluating the efficiency of KeyGen in this case is a bit subtle, because ABE.KeyGen used inside the algorithm runs in exponential time in the depth of the input circuit. In order to bound the running time of the algorithm, we evaluate the depth of $F[D]$ by going over all the computation steps inside the circuit. We observe that only the second and the third steps out of the five steps are non-trivial. The second step can be implemented by a circuit of depth $O(\log \ell_{\mathsf{PIR}}) = O(\log \lambda)$ by checking $k \stackrel{?}{=} i$ for all $i \in [\ell_{\mathsf{PIR}}]$ in parallel and taking OR of all the outcomes. The third step can be implemented by a circuit of depth $O(\log |D|)$ by our assumption on PIR.

Overall, the depth of the circuit $F[D]$ can be upper bounded by $O(\log \lambda + \log |D|)$ and thus the key generation algorithm runs in time

$$2^{O(\log \lambda + \log |D|)} = \text{poly}(\lambda, |D|)$$

as desired. We finally observe that the decryption algorithm runs in time polynomial in the length of ct and sk, which are bounded by $\text{poly}(\lambda, |D|)$ by the efficiency of the encryption and key generation algorithms. Therefore, the decryption algorithm runs in time $\text{poly}(\lambda, |D|)$ as well.

Correctness. We focus on the case of $|D| = N$, since otherwise it is trivial. By the correctness of IBE, msg is correctly recovered in the first step of the decryption. Furthermore, since $F[D](\text{PIR.query}, k, \text{PIR.answer}_k) = \text{PIR.answer}_k \oplus \text{PIR.answer}_k \oplus 1 = 1$, we observe that lab_k recovered in the 5-th step of the decryption equals to $\text{lab}_{k, \text{PIR.answer}_k}$ by the correctness of ABE. Finally, by the correctness of GC and PIR, μ recovered in the 6-th step of the decryption equals to $C[N, \text{PIR.st}, \mu_0, \mu_1](\text{PIR.answer}) = \mu_{D[i]}$ with overwhelming probability as desired.

Security. The following theorem addresses the security of LOTFE, whose proof is similar to that of succinct FE by [29]. However, we need somewhat more careful analysis in order to base the security of the scheme on Sel-IND security of the underlying ABE rather than on AD-IND security. The reason why Sel-IND security suffices for our case is that the reduction algorithm can guess the target attribute the adversary chooses only with polynomial security loss. In more detail, we change ABE ciphertexts encrypting $\text{lab}_{k, 1-\text{PIR.answer}_k}$ for attribute $(\text{PIR.query}, k, 1 - \text{PIR.answer}_k)$ to be that encrypting $\text{lab}_{k, \text{PIR.answer}_k}$ in the security proof. A naive way of guessing the attribute $(\text{PIR.query}, k, 1 - \text{PIR.answer}_k)$ ends up with exponential security loss, since there are exponentially many possible PIR.query. However, the reduction algorithm only has to guess (N, i) that is encoded inside PIR.query, because the randomness used for computing the query is not controlled by the adversary, but by the reduction algorithm. Since there are only polynomial number of possible $(N, i, k, 1 - \text{PIR.answer}_k)$, the guessing can be done only with polynomial security loss.

Theorem 3. *If* IBE *is* AD-IND *secure,* ABE *is* Sel-IND *secure,* GC *is selectively secure, and* PIR *is private, then the above FE is* 1-NA-SIM *secure.*

The proof of Theorem 3 appears in [3, Sec 5.1].

5.2   CPFE for Read only RAM

Here, we define CPFE for read only RAM by specifying the relation R_{CPRAMFE} : $\mathcal{X}_{\text{CPRAMFE}} \times \mathcal{Y}_{\text{CPRAMFE}} \rightarrow \{0, 1\}^*$.

CPFE for Read only RAM Computation. To define CPFE for read only RAM, we set $\mathcal{Y}_{\text{CPRAMFE}} = \{0, 1\}^*$ and $\mathcal{X}_{\text{CPRAMFE}}$ to be a set of read only RAM programs of the form $P = \{P^\tau\}_{\tau \in [t]}$. We define $R_{\text{CPRAMFE}}(P, D) \in \{0, 1\}^*$ to be the output obtained by executing P with the RAM access to the data D. In our case, we consider RAM programs with some specific structure. To define this, we introduce the parameter prm =

$1^{\ell_{st}}$ and the set of RAM programs $\mathcal{P}_{T,\text{size}}$. We then constrain the domain as $\mathcal{X}_{\text{prm}} = \mathcal{P}_{T,\text{size}}$ and $\mathcal{Y}_{\text{prm}} = \{0,1\}^*$. A RAM program in $\mathcal{P}_{T,\text{size}}$ is of the form $P = \{P^\tau\}_\tau$ where the step circuit P^τ is of the form $P^\tau : \{0,1\}^{\ell_{st}} \to \{0,1\}^{\ell_{st}-1} \times \{0,1\}^{\log^2 \lambda}$. For $D \in \{0,1\}^N$ and $P = \{P^\tau\}_{\tau \in [t]}$, we define $(\text{st}^\tau, L^\tau) \in \{0,1\}^{\ell_{st}-1} \times \{0,1\}^{\log^2 \lambda}$ for $\tau \in [2, t]$ by induction as

$$(\text{st}^\tau, L^\tau) := P^{\tau-1}(\text{st}^{\tau-1}, D[L^{\tau-1}]) \quad \text{where} \quad (\text{st}^1, D[L^1]) := (0^{\ell_{st}-1}, 0). \tag{5.1}$$

Here, st^τ and $L^\tau \in \{0,1\}^{\log^2 \lambda}$ output by $P^{\tau-1}$ represent the state information and the position L^τ to be read from the data D respectively. The state st^τ and the read bit $D[L^\tau]$, which is the L^τ-th bit of D, is then input to the next step circuit P^τ. In the above computation, the initial state st^1 and the initial read bit $D[L^1]$ are defined to be zero strings. Note that the position to be read is assumed to be represented by a binary string of $\{0,1\}^{\log^2 \lambda}$, which is interpreted as an integer in $[0, 2^{\log^2 \lambda}]$. Since $2^{\log^2 \lambda} = \lambda^{\log \lambda}$ is super-polynomial, this is sufficient for pointing a position in any unbounded size data. The output obtained by running P with the RAM access to the data D is denoted by P^D and is defined to be $P^D := \text{st}^{t+1}$.

Remark 6 (Succinctness). Similarly to the case of LOTFE, the running time of the encryption algorithm is independent from the size of the database D supported by the scheme. This property can be seen as an analogue of the efficiency requirements for the succinctness of FE [29] or laconic OT [18].

Remark 7 (Efficiency). We note that we do not require the decryption time to be independent of the size of the database D, while the encryption time is required to be so. This is in contrast to ABE/FE for RAM efficiency in the literature [8, 26], where the decryption time is also required to be sublinear in the size of the database. However, our weaker definition suffices for our purpose of constructing FE for TM.

Ingredients. We now describe the underlying building blocks used for our construction of CPFE for read only RAM.

1. FE with laconic OT functionality LOTFE = (LOTFE.Setup, LOTFE.KeyGen, LOTFE.Enc, LOTFE.Dec) with 1-NA-SIM security. This can be instantiated by the scheme in Sect. 5.1. For simplicity, we assume that the encryption algorithm of LOTFE only requires randomness of λ bits. This can be achieved by using the randomness as a PRF key to derive longer pseudorandom string for example.
2. IBE scheme IBE = (IBE.Setup, IBE.KeyGen, IBE.Enc, IBE.Dec) with AD-IND security. Since the construction of LOTFE in Sect. 5.1 already uses IBE, this does not add new assumption.
3. Selectively secure garbled circuit GC = (GC.Garble, GC.Sim). We can instantiate it from any one-way function [39].

Construction. Here, we describe our scheme CPRAMFE = (Setup, KeyGen, Enc, Dec). The construction is inspired by the garbled RAM construction by [25], which in turn is based on [37], where a sequence of garbled circuits read the memory stored

---

Circuit SC$[\tau, P^\tau, \mathsf{LOTFE.mpk}, \mathsf{R}^\tau, \{\mathsf{lab}_{k,b}^{\tau+1}\}_{k,b}]$

Hardwired constants: The step number τ, the step circuit P^τ, the master public key $\mathsf{LOTFE.mpk}$, randomness R^τ, and the set of labels $\{\mathsf{lab}_{k,b}^{\tau+1}\}_{k\in[n], b\in\{0,1\}}$.

Input: String $X \in \{0,1\}^n$.

1. Parse the input as $X \to (N, \mathsf{st}, \mathsf{rData})$, where $N \in \{0,1\}^{\log^2 \lambda}$, $\mathsf{st} \in \{0,1\}^{\ell_{\mathsf{st}}-1}$, and $\mathsf{rData} \in \{0,1\}$.
2. Run $P^\tau(\mathsf{st}, \mathsf{rData}) = (\mathsf{st}', L)$.
3. Run $\mathsf{LOTFE.Enc}\,(\mathsf{LOTFE.mpk}, (N, L, \mathsf{lab}_{n,0}^{\tau+1}, \mathsf{lab}_{n,1}^{\tau+1}); \mathsf{R}^\tau) \to \mathsf{LOTFE.ct}$.
4. Set $Y := (N, \mathsf{st}')$.
5. Output $\begin{cases} \left(\left\{ \mathsf{lab}_{k,Y_k}^{\tau+1} \right\}_{k\in[n-1]}, \mathsf{LOTFE.ct} \right) & \text{if } \tau \neq t \\ \mathsf{st}' & \text{if } \tau = t \end{cases}$

Fig. 7. Circuit $\mathsf{SC}^\tau = \mathsf{SC}[\tau, P^\tau, \mathsf{LOTFE.mpk}, \mathsf{R}^\tau, \{\mathsf{lab}_{k,b}^{\tau+1}\}_{k,b}]$

outside of the circuits via RAM access. Whereas they use the combination of IBE and ORAM to enable the oblivious access to the memory, we use LOTFE for this purpose instead. This change is crucial for us because ORAM is a secret key primitive and is not compatible with our setting of public key FE.

$\mathsf{Setup}(1^\lambda, \mathsf{prm})$: On input the security parameter λ, the parameter $\mathsf{prm} = 1^{\ell_{\mathsf{st}}}$, do the following:

1. Run $(\mathsf{IBE.mpk}, \mathsf{IBE.msk}) \leftarrow \mathsf{IBE.Setup}(1^\lambda)$.
2. Run $(\mathsf{LOTFE.mpk}, \mathsf{LOTFE.msk}) \leftarrow \mathsf{LOTFE.Setup}(1^\lambda)$.
3. Output $\mathsf{mpk} := (\mathsf{LOTFE.mpk}, \mathsf{IBE.mpk})$ and $\mathsf{msk} := (\mathsf{LOTFE.msk}, \mathsf{IBE.msk})$.

$\mathsf{Enc}(\mathsf{mpk}, P)$: On input the master public key $\mathsf{mpk} = (\mathsf{LOTFE.mpk}, \mathsf{IBE.mpk})$, a read only RAM program $P = \{P_\tau\}_{\tau\in[t]} \in \mathcal{P}_{\ell_{\mathsf{st}}}$, do the following:

1. Set $n := \log^2 \lambda + \ell_{\mathsf{st}}$.
2. Pick $\mathsf{lab}_{k,b}^\tau \leftarrow \{0,1\}^\lambda$ for $\tau \in [t]$, $k \in [n]$, and $b \in \{0,1\}$.
3. Pick $\mathsf{R}^\tau \leftarrow \{0,1\}^\lambda$ for $\tau \in [t]$.
4. Construct circuit $\mathsf{SC}^\tau := \mathsf{SC}[\tau, P^\tau, \mathsf{LOTFE.mpk}, \mathsf{R}^\tau, \{\mathsf{lab}_{k,b}^{\tau+1}\}_{k,b}]$ for $\tau \in [t]$ as Fig. 7, where we define $\mathsf{lab}_{k,b}^{t+1} = \bot$ for $k \in [n]$, $b \in \{0,1\}$.
5. For all $\tau \in [t]$, run

$$\widetilde{\mathsf{SC}}^\tau \leftarrow \mathsf{GC.Garble}\left(1^\lambda, \mathsf{SC}^\tau, \{\mathsf{lab}_{k,b}^\tau\}_{k,b}\right).$$

6. For all $k \in [n]$, $b \in \{0,1\}$, run

$$\mathsf{IBE.ct}_{k,b} \leftarrow \mathsf{IBE.Enc}(\mathsf{IBE.mpk}, (k, b), \mathsf{lab}_{k,b}^1).$$

7. Output $\mathsf{ct} := \left(\{\widetilde{\mathsf{SC}}^\tau\}_{\tau\in[t]}, \{\mathsf{IBE.ct}_{k,b}\}_{k\in[n], b\in\{0,1\}} \right)$.

$\mathsf{KeyGen}(\mathsf{msk}, D)$: On input the master secret key $\mathsf{msk} = \mathsf{LOTFE.msk}$, an input $D \in \{0,1\}^N$, where $N \leq 2^{\log^2 \lambda}$, do the following:

1. Run
$$\mathsf{LOTFE.sk} \leftarrow \mathsf{LOTFE.KeyGen}(\mathsf{LOTFE.msk}, D).$$

2. Set $X = N \| 0^{n - \log^2 \lambda}$, where N is represented as a string in $\{0, 1\}^{\log^2 \lambda}$.
3. For all $k \in [n]$, run
$$\mathsf{IBE.sk}_{k, X_k} \leftarrow \mathsf{IBE.KeyGen}(\mathsf{IBE.msk}, (k, X_k)).$$

4. Output $\mathsf{sk} := \big(D, \mathsf{LOTFE.sk}, \{\mathsf{IBE.sk}_{k, X_k}\}_{k \in [n]} \big)$.

$\mathsf{Dec}(\mathsf{ct}, \mathsf{sk})$: On input a ciphertext $\mathsf{ct} = (\{\widetilde{\mathsf{SC}}^\tau\}_\tau, \{\mathsf{IBE.ct}_{k, b}\}_{k, b})$ and a secret key $\mathsf{sk} = (D, \mathsf{LOTFE.sk}, \{\mathsf{IBE.sk}_{k, X_k}\}_k)$, do the following:

1. Run Set $X := N \| 0^{n - \log^2 \lambda}$.
2. Run $\underline{\mathsf{lab}_k^1} := \mathsf{IBE.Dec}(\mathsf{IBE.sk}_{k, X_k}, \mathsf{IBE.ct}_{k, X_k})$ for $k \in [n]$.
3. Set $\overline{\mathsf{label}} := \{\mathsf{lab}_k^1\}_{k \in [n]}$.
4. For $\tau = 1, \ldots, t$
    (a) Compute $\mathsf{gout} := \mathsf{GC.Eval}(\widetilde{\mathsf{SC}}^\tau, \overline{\mathsf{label}})$.
    (b) If $\tau = t$, set $y := \mathsf{gout}$ and break out of the loop.
    (c) Parse $\mathsf{gout} \to \big(\{\mathsf{lab}_k\}_{k \in [n-1]}, \mathsf{LOTFE.ct}\big)$.
    (d) Compute $(N, \mathsf{lab}_n) := \mathsf{LOTFE.Dec}(\mathsf{LOTFE.sk}, \mathsf{LOTFE.ct})$.
    (e) Set $\overline{\mathsf{label}} := \{\mathsf{lab}_k\}_{k \in [n]}$.
5. Output y.

Correctness and Security. The correctness of CPRAMFE is shown in [3, Sec 5.2]. We prove that CPRAMFE is 1-NA-SIM secure in [3, Sec 5.2].

Efficiency. By the efficiency of LOTFE and IBE, it is easy to see that Setup and KeyGen run in time $\mathrm{poly}(\lambda)$ and $\mathrm{poly}(\lambda, |D|)$, respectively. We can also see that $|\widetilde{\mathsf{SC}}^\tau| = \mathrm{poly}(\lambda, |P^\tau|)$ and thus the running time of Enc can be bounded by $\mathrm{poly}(\lambda, |P|)$. Finally, Dec runs in polynomial time in its input length by the efficiency of the underlying primitives and thus run in time $\mathrm{poly}(\lambda, |P|, |D|)$.

5.3 FE for Turing Machines with Fixed Input Length

Here, we show that CPRAMFE we constructed in Sect. 5.2 can easily be converted into FE for TM. The resulting construction can handle TM of unbounded size, but it is only 1-NA-SIM secure and can only handle the case where the length of $(x, 1^t)$ is bounded. These limitations will be removed in the next subsection.

RAM Programs Reading Multi-bit at once. To simplify the description, we assume that each step of RAM computation reads a block consisting of $B(\lambda) = \mathrm{poly}(\lambda)$ bits at once instead of reading a single bit. Correspondingly, we assume that the database contains B bits of data at a single location. This is without loss of generality because a RAM program that reads single bit at once can be converted into that reads B bits at once by making the length of step circuits B times longer and increasing the size of each step circuit so that it can keep B bits inside it.

Representing Turing Machine Computation as RAM Computation. In order to represent the computation executed by a Turing machine as a computation by RAM program, we introduce the following mappings:

$$P_{(x,1^t)}^{\tau}$$

Hardwired constants: The step number τ, the input x to the TM, and the running time t.
Input: $(\mathsf{st}, \mathsf{rData}) \in \{0,1\}^{t+2\lambda} \times \{0,1\}^B$.

1. Parse the input as $\mathsf{st} \to (i, W, q)$, where $i, q \in \{0,1\}^\lambda$ and $W \in \{0,1\}^t$ and $\mathsf{rData} \to ((q_0', b_0', \Delta i_0), (q_1', b_1', \Delta i_1), \mathsf{pre}_0, \mathsf{pre}_1)$.
2. If $\tau = 1$, replace W with $W = x \| 0^{t-n}$.
3. Set $i' := i + \Delta i_{W[i]}$, $q' = q'_{W[i]}$, $\mathsf{pre}' = \mathsf{pre}_{W[i]}$, and $W'[j] = \begin{cases} W[j] & \text{if } j \neq i \\ b'_{W[i]} & \text{if } j = i \end{cases}$

    for $j \in [t]$.
4. Set $(\mathsf{st}', L) = ((i', W', q'), q')$.
5. Output $\begin{cases} (\mathsf{st}', L) & \text{if } \tau \neq t \\ \mathsf{pre}' & \text{if } \tau = t \end{cases}$

Fig. 8. Circuit $P_{(x,1^t)}^{\tau}$

f : This mapping takes as input $(x \in \{0,1\}^n, 1^t)$ and then convert it into a read only RAM program $P_{(x,1^t)} = \{P_{(x,1^t)}^{\tau}\}_{\tau \in [t]}$ defined as in Fig. 8. Here, we set $B(\lambda) = 3\lambda$. In the circuit, q, q_0', and q_1' are represented by strings in $\{0,1\}^\lambda$. In particular, this means that the circuit can handle any size of Turing machines because we can assume $q \leq Q < 2^\lambda$ without loss of generality.

g : This mapping takes as input description of a Turing machine $M = (Q, \delta, F)$ and outputs a database D_M that contains Q blocks each consisting of B bits. At its q-th block, D_M contains

$$D_M[q] := (\delta(q, 0), \delta(q, 1), \mathsf{pre}_0, \mathsf{pre}_1),$$

where $\mathsf{pre}_c \in \{0,1\}$ for $c \in \{0,1\}$ indicates whether q_c' defined by $\delta(q, c) = (q_c', b_c', \Delta i_c)$ is in the set of accepting states F or not. Since $\delta(q, b) \in [Q] \times \{0,1\} \times \{0, \pm 1\}$ and $Q < 2^\lambda$, each block can be represented by a binary string of length at most $B(\lambda) = 3\lambda$.

We observe that the output of $P_{(x,1^t)}^{D_M}$ is the same as that obtained by running the Turing machine M on input x for t steps. This is because each step circuit $P_{(x,1^t)}^{\tau}$ of $P_{(x,1^t)}$ is designed to emulate τ-th step of the computation done by the machine. This means that by applying the above mappings, we can convert CPRAMFE into an FE scheme for Turing machine with fixed input length. It is easy to see that the security and correctness of the scheme are preserved. In particular, the resulting scheme inherits the 1-NA-SIM security. We also observe that the size of the program $P = \{P_{(x,1^t)}^{\tau}\}_\tau$ is bounded by a fixed polynomial in $|(x, 1^t)|$.

5.4   Getting the Full-Fledged Construction

Here, we remove the restrictions from the consturction in Sect. 5.3 and obtain full-fledged FE scheme for TM.

Removing the Non-adaptive and Single Key Restriction. In the first step, we apply the conversion in [3, Sect. 6.4], which is essentially the same as the conversion given by Agrawal et. al [5, Sect. 4], to the scheme to upgrade the security. The resulting scheme is AD-SIM secure against bounded dynamic collusion. We refer to [3, Sect. 6.4] for the details.

Removing the Fixed Input Length Restriction. Our goal in the second step is constructing an FE scheme for $R^{\leq} : \mathcal{A} \times \mathcal{B} \to \mathcal{M} \cup \{\bot\}$, where $\mathcal{A} = \{0, 1\}^*$, $\mathcal{B}$ is the set of all Turing machines, and

$$R^{\leq}((x, 1^t), M) = \begin{cases} 1 & \text{(if } M \text{ accepts } x \text{ in } t \text{ steps)} \wedge (|(x, 1^t)| \leq |M|) \\ 0 & \text{otherwise.} \end{cases}$$

This step is done in essentially the same manner as [5, Sect. 6.2.2] using [3, Theorem 2.1]. We observe that the FE scheme that we obtained above can be seen as an FE scheme for $\mathsf{prm} = 1^i$, $R_i : \mathcal{X}_i \times \mathcal{Y}_i \to \{0, 1\}$ where $\mathcal{X}_i = \{0, 1\}^i$ and $\mathcal{Y}_i$ is the set of all Turing machines, and

$$R_i((x, 1^t), M) = \begin{cases} 1 & \text{(if } M \text{ accepts } x \text{ in } t \text{ steps)} \\ 0 & \text{otherwise.} \end{cases}$$

That is, $|(x, 1^t)|$ is a-priori bounded by i. We set $\mathcal{S}, \mathcal{T}, f$, and g as

$$\mathcal{S}(i) = i, \quad \mathcal{T}(i) = \{1, \ldots, i\}, \quad f(x, 1^t) = (x, 1^t), \quad g(M) = \{M\}_{i \in [|M|]}.$$

Here, we crucially rely on $|(x, 1^t)| \leq |M|$.

Recall that

$$R^{\mathsf{bndl}}(x, y) = \{R_i(f(x)_i, g(y)_i)\}_{i \in \mathcal{S}(|x|) \cap \mathcal{T}(|y|)}, \tag{5.2}$$

where $f(x)_i \in \mathcal{X}_i$, and $g(y)_i \in \mathcal{Y}_i$ are the i-th entries of $f(x)$ and $g(x)$, respectively.

It is easy to see that R^{bndl} is equivalent to $R^{\leq}$ except for the case $|(x, 1^t)| > |M|$. In this case, the decryption outputs an empty set $\emptyset$. However, the output should be 0 in FE for $R^>$. This issue can be easily fixed as observed by Agrawal et al. [5, Sect. 6.2.2]. Namely, we modify the decryption algorithm so that it outputs 0 if the decryption result is $\emptyset$. We note that the resulting scheme inherits AD-SIM security, which is guaranteed by [3, Theorem 2.1].

Removing the Shorter Input Length Restriction. In the above construction, there is a restriction that the decryption is possible only when $|(x, 1^t)| \leq |M|$. To remove the restriction, we first construct an AD-SIM secure FE scheme for TM such that the decryption is possible only when $|(x, 1^t)| > |M|$. Such a scheme can be obtained by applying the conversion by Agrawal et al. [5, Sects. 6.1 and 6.2.1] to AD-SIM secure CPFE with dynamic bounded collusion for $\mathcal{C}_{\mathsf{inp,out}}$ obtained in Sect. 4. We then combine these two schemes to obtain the full-fledged scheme without the restriction by applying the conversion by Agrawal et al. [5, Sect. 6.2.3]. Then, we obtain AD-SIM secure FE for TM. Based on the discussion above, we obtain the following theorem:

Theorem 4. *Assuming IBE with* AD-IND *security, ABE for circuits with circuit class C with* Sel-IND *security, updatable LOT (as per [3, Definition A.1]), and PIR (as per [3, Definition 2.9] whose answer function is in C, we have FE for TM with* AD-SIM *security against dynamic bounded collusion.*

Acknowledgements. This work of Shweta Agrawal is partly supported by the DST "Swarnajayanti" fellowship, the Indian National Blockchain Project, and the CCD Center of Excellence. Shota Yamada is partially supported by JST AIP Acceleration Research JPMJCR22U5 and JSPS KAKENHI Grant Number 19H01109.

References

1. Agrawal, S.: Stronger security for reusable garbled circuits, new definitions and attacks. In: CRYPTO (2017)
2. Agrawal, S., Gorbunov, S., Vaikuntanathan, V., Wee, H.: Functional encryption: new perspectives and lower bounds. In: CRYPTO (2013)
3. Agrawal, S., Kitagawa, F., Modi, A., Nishimaki, R., Yamada, S., Yamakawa, T.: Bounded functional encryption for Turing machines: adaptive security from general assumptions. Cryptology ePrint Archive, Paper 2022/316 (2022)
4. Agrawal, S., Maitra, M.: FE and IO for Turing machines from minimal assumptions. In: TCC (2018)
5. Agrawal, S., Maitra, M., Vempati, N.S., Yamada, S.: Functional encryption for Turing machines with dynamic bounded collusion from LWE. In: CRYPTO (2021)
6. Agrawal, S., Maitra, M., Yamada, S.: Attribute based encryption (and more) for nondeterministic finite automata from LWE. In: CRYPTO (2019)
7. Agrawal, S., Singh, I.P.: Reusable garbled deterministic finite automata from learning with errors. In: ICALP (2017)
8. Ananth, P., Fan, X., Shi, E.: Towards attribute-based encryption for RAMs from LWE: sublinear decryption, and more. In: ASIACRYPT (2019)
9. Ananth, P., Jain, A.: Indistinguishability obfuscation from compact functional encryption. In: CRYPTO (2015)
10. Ananth, P., Lombardi, A.: Succinct garbling schemes from functional encryption through a local simulation paradigm. In: TCC (2018)
11. Ananth, P., Sahai, A.: Functional encryption for Turing machines. In: TCC (2016)
12. Ananth, P., Vaikuntanathan, V.: Optimal bounded-collusion secure functional encryption. In: TCC (2019)
13. Bitansky, N., Vaikuntanathan, V.: Indistinguishability obfuscation from functional encryption. J. ACM **65**(6), 39:1–39:37 (2018)
14. Boneh, D., et al.: Fully key-homomorphic encryption, arithmetic circuit ABE and compact garbled circuits. In: EUROCRYPT (2014)
15. Boneh, D., Sahai, A., Waters, B.: Functional encryption: Definitions and challenges. In: TCC (2011)
16. Brakerski, Z., Lombardi, A., Segev, G., Vaikuntanathan, V.: Anonymous IBE, leakage resilience and circular security from new assumptions. In: EUROCRYPT (2018)
17. Brakerski, Z., Vaikuntanathan, V.: Efficient fully homomorphic encryption from (standard) LWE. In: FOCS (2011)
18. Cho, C., Döttling, N., Garg, S., Gupta, D., Miao, P., Polychroniadou, A.: Laconic oblivious transfer and its applications. In: CRYPTO (2017)
19. Döttling, N., Garg, S.: From selective IBE to full IBE and selective HIBE. In: TCC (2017)

20. Döttling, N., Garg, S.: Identity-based encryption from the Diffie-Hellman assumption. In: CRYPTO (2017)
21. Döttling, N., Garg, S., Hajiabadi, M., Masny, D.: New constructions of identity-based and key-dependent message secure encryption schemes. In: PKC (2018)
22. Döttling, N., Garg, S., Ishai, Y., Malavolta, G., Mour, T., Ostrovsky, R.: Trapdoor hash functions and their applications. In: CRYPTO (2019)
23. Garg, R., Goyal, R., Lu, G., Waters, B.: Dynamic collusion bounded functional encryption from identity-based encryption. In Eprint 2021/847 (2021), to appear in Eurocrypt 2022
24. Garg, S., Srinivasan, A.: Adaptively secure garbling with near optimal online complexity. In: EUROCRYPT (2018)
25. Gentry, C., Halevi, S., Raykova, M., Wichs, D.: Garbled RAM revisited, part I. In: EUROCRYPT (2014)
26. Gentry, C., Halevi, S., Raykova, M., Wichs, D.: Outsourcing private RAM computation. In: FOCS (2014)
27. Gentry, C., Sahai, A., Waters, B.: Homomorphic encryption from learning with errors: conceptually-simpler, asymptotically-faster, attribute-based. In: CRYPTO (2013)
28. Goldwasser, S., Tauman Kalai, Y., Popa, R., Vaikuntanathan, V., Zeldovich, N.: How to run Turing machines on encrypted data. In: CRYPTO (2013)
29. Goldwasser, S., Tauman Kalai, Y., Popa, R., Vaikuntanathan, V., Zeldovich, N.: Reusable garbled circuits and succinct functional encryption. In: STOC (2013)
30. Gorbunov, S., Vaikuntanathan, V., Wee, H.: Functional encryption with bounded collusions from multiparty computation. In: CRYPTO (2012)
31. Gorbunov, S., Vaikuntanathan, V., Wee, H.: Attribute based encryption for circuits. In: STOC (2013)
32. Gorbunov, S., Vinayagamurthy, D.: Riding on asymmetry: Efficient ABE for branching programs. In: ASIACRYPT (2015)
33. Goyal, R., Koppula, V., Waters, B.: Semi-adaptive security and bundling functionalities made generic and easy. In: TCC (2016)
34. Goyal, R., Syed, R., Waters, B.: Bounded collusion ABE for TMs from IBE. In: ASIACRYPT (2021)
35. Goyal, V., Pandey, O., Sahai, A., Waters, B.: Attribute-based encryption for fine-grained access control of encrypted data. In: CCS (2006)
36. Kitagawa, F., Nishimaki, R., Tanaka, K., Yamakawa, T.: Adaptively secure and succinct functional encryption: improving security and efficiency, simultaneously. In: CRYPTO (2019)
37. Lu, S., Ostrovsky, R.: How to garble RAM programs. In: EUROCRYPT (2014)
38. Sahai, A., Waters, B.: Fuzzy identity-based encryption. In: EUROCRYPT (2005)
39. Yao, A.C.: How to generate and exchange secrets (extended abstract). In: FOCS (1986)

Attribute-Based Encryption
and Functional Encryption

Multi-authority ABE from Lattices Without Random Oracles

Brent Waters[1,2], Hoeteck Wee[2,3], and David J. Wu[1(✉)]

[1] University of Texas at Austin, Austin, TX, USA
dwu4@cs.utexas.edu
[2] NTT Research, Sunnyvale, CA, USA
[3] CNRS, ENS, PSL, Paris, France

Abstract. Attribute-based encryption (ABE) extends public-key encryption to enable fine-grained control to encrypted data. However, this comes at the cost of needing a central *trusted* authority to issue decryption keys. A multi-authority ABE (MA-ABE) scheme decentralizes ABE and allows anyone to serve as an authority. Existing constructions of MA-ABE only achieve security in the random oracle model.

In this work, we develop new techniques for constructing MA-ABE for the class of subset policies (which captures policies such as conjunctions and DNF formulas) whose security can be based in the plain model *without* random oracles. We achieve this by relying on the recently-proposed "evasive" learning with errors (LWE) assumption by Wee (EUROCRYPT 2022) and Tsabury (CRYPTO 2022).

Along the way, we also provide a modular view of the MA-ABE scheme for DNF formulas by Datta et al. (EUROCRYPT 2021) in the random oracle model. We formalize this via a general version of a related-trapdoor LWE assumption by Brakerski and Vaikuntanathan (ITCS 2022), which can in turn be reduced to the plain LWE assumption. As a corollary, we also obtain an MA-ABE scheme for subset policies from *plain* LWE with a *polynomial* modulus-to-noise ratio in the random oracle model. This improves upon the Datta et al. construction which relied on LWE with a *sub-exponential* modulus-to-noise ratio. Moreover, we are optimistic that the generalized related-trapdoor LWE assumption will also be useful for analyzing the security of other lattice-based constructions.

1 Introduction

Attribute-based encryption (ABE) [SW05, GPSW06] extends classic public-key encryption to support fine-grained access control on encrypted data. For instance, in a ciphertext-policy ABE (CP-ABE) scheme, each ciphertext ct is associated with a policy f together with a message μ while decryption keys sk are associated with an attribute x. Decryption successfully recovers the message μ when x satisfies f. Security requires that an adversary who only possesses secret keys for a collection of attributes $x_1, \ldots, x_n$ that do not satisfy f does not learn anything about the message. In this work, we are interested in systems that are secure against *unbounded* collusions: that is, security holds against an adversary that has any arbitrary (polynomial) number of non-satisfying attributes.

© The Author(s), under exclusive license to Springer Nature Switzerland AG 2022
E. Kiltz and V. Vaikuntanathan (Eds.): TCC 2022, LNCS 13747, pp. 651–679, 2022.
https://doi.org/10.1007/978-3-031-22318-1_23

Multi-authority ABE. In a traditional ABE scheme, there exists a central trusted authority that generates and issues decryption keys. The central authority has the ability to decrypt *all* ciphertexts encrypted using the system. To mitigate the reliance on a single central trusted authority, a line of works [Cha07,LCLS08, MKE08,CC09] have introduced and studied the notion of a "multi-authority" ABE (MA-ABE) scheme where *anyone* can become an authority. In an MA-ABE scheme, each authority controls different attributes and can *independently* issue secret keys corresponding to the set of attributes under their control. Policies in an MA-ABE system are formulated with respect to the attributes of one or more authorities. To decrypt, a user combines the secret keys for attributes from a set of authorities that satisfy the policy. Security is still required to hold against users who possess an arbitrary number of unauthorized secret keys, with an additional challenge that some subset of the authorities (associated with the ciphertext policy) could now be corrupted and colluding with the adversary.

Earlier constructions of MA-ABE had various limitations in terms of functionality or security (or both). The first construction that achieved the first fully decentralized MA-ABE scheme was by Lewko and Waters [LW11]. Unlike previous schemes, the Lewko-Waters scheme allows any user to become an authority, and moreover, the only coordination needed among users and authorities is a one-time sampling of a set of global parameters. The Lewko-Waters construction supports any access policy computable by an NC^1 circuit (i.e., a Boolean formula) and security relies on assumptions on groups with bilinear maps and in the random oracle model. Subsequently, a number of works have realized new constructions for NC^1 policies based on bilinear maps [RW15,DKW21b], and recently, Datta et al. [DKW21a] showed how to construct an MA-ABE scheme for access policies computable by DNF formulas (of *a priori* bounded size) from the learning with errors (LWE) assumption [DKW21a]. All of these constructions rely on the random oracle model. This motivates the following question:

Can we construct a multi-authority ABE scheme without random oracles?

1.1 Our Contributions

In this work, we show how to leverage the recently-introduced evasive LWE assumption [Wee22, Tsa22] to obtain an MA-ABE scheme for subset policies *without* random oracles. Subset policies capture DNF policies as in [DKW21a].[1] Moreover, our MA-ABE construction supports subset policies and DNFs of arbitrary polynomial size which improves upon the previous lattice-based construction in the random oracle model [DKW21a]. We summarize this result in the following informal theorem and provide the full details in Sect. 6:

---

[1] As noted in [DKW21a, Remark 6.1], the MA-ABE scheme therein requires a *monotone* secret-sharing scheme where reconstruction has small coefficients and the joint distribution of the unauthorized shares are uniformly random; such a scheme is only known for subset policies and DNFs.

Theorem 1.1. (Informal). *Assuming polynomial hardness of LWE and of evasive LWE (both with a sub-exponential modulus-to-noise ratio), there exists a statically-secure multi-authority ABE for subset policies (of arbitrary polynomial size).*

Understanding the Evasive LWE Assumption. While the evasive LWE assumption is much less well-understood compared to the plain LWE assumption, our construction provides a new avenue towards realizing MA-ABE *without* random oracles. In particular, putting assumptions aside, our construction constitutes the first heuristic MA-ABE without random oracles. In all previous constructions of multi-authority ABE, the random oracle was used to hash a global user identifier (denoted gid) to obtain common randomness that is used to bind different keys to a single user. For the particular case of [DKW21a], the random oracle was used to hash an identifier to obtain a discrete Gaussian sample. Our candidate replaces the random oracle with a subset product of public low-norm matrices. To prove security of the resulting scheme, we rely on the fact that under LWE, multiplying a secret key by a subset product of (public) low-norm matrices yields a pseudorandom function [BLMR13] in addition to the evasive LWE assumption.

A Modular Approach in the Random Oracle Model. The starting point of our construction is the MA-ABE construction for (bounded-size) DNF policies by Datta et al. [DKW21a]. Along the way to our construction without random oracles (Theorem 1.1), we provide a more modular description of the Datta et al. scheme. Specifically, we extract a new trapdoor sampling lemma that is implicitly used in their construction. This lemma can be viewed as a generalization of the related trapdoor LWE lemma from the recent work of Brakerski and Vaikuntanathan [BV22], and may prove useful for constructing other primitives from the *standard* LWE assumption. We provide an overview of our generalized related-trapdoor lemma in Sect. 2 and provide the full details in Sect. 4.

Using our generalized related-trapdoor LWE lemma, we in turn provide a more modular description of the MA-ABE scheme of Datta et al. [DKW21a], and moreover, base hardness on the plain LWE assumption with a *polynomial* modulus-to-noise ratio in the random oracle model. Previously, Datta et al. relied on noise smudging for trapdoor sampling in their security analysis[2], and consequently, could only reduce security to LWE with a *sub-exponential* modulus-to-noise ratio. We summarize these results in the following (informal) theorem and provide the full details in Sect. 5:

Theorem 1.2. (Informal). *Let λ be a security parameter. Assuming polynomial hardness of LWE with a polynomial modulus-to-noise ratio, there exists a statically-secure multi-authority ABE scheme for subset policies of a priori bounded length $L = L(\lambda)$ in the random oracle model. The size of the ciphertext is quasi-linear in the bound L.*

---

[2] See the descriptions of Hybrid 5 and the analysis of Lemmas 5.5 and 6.5 in [DKW21a], where noise smuging is used for simulating secret keys.

Like previous lattice-based MA-ABE constructions in the random oracle model [DKW21a], the global public parameters in Theorem 1.2 imposes an *a priori* bound L on the size of the policies that can be associated with ciphertexts, and moreover, the ciphertext size increases as a function of L. We note that our construction based on the stronger evasive LWE assumption (Theorem 1.1) supports policies of arbitrary polynomial size in the plain model.

1.2 Additional Related Work

Kim [Kim19] and Wang et al. [WFL19] also studied constructions of multi-authority ABE (for bounded-depth circuits and Boolean formulas, respectively) from lattice-based assumptions. However, both schemes operate in a model where there is a single central authority that generates the public keys and secret keys for each of the authorities in the system. Relying on a central trusted party runs against the original goal of *decentralizing* trust. Moreover, these constructions only ensure security against bounded collusions. In this work, we focus exclusively on the fully decentralized setting introduced by Lewko and Waters [LW11] that neither requires a centralized setup nor assumes an a priori bound on the number of authorities or corruptions.

Recently, Tsabury [Tsa22] and Vaikuntanathan et al. [VWW22] showed how to build witness encryption from a *stronger* variant of the evasive LWE assumption with private-coin auxiliary input and sub-exponential hardness. In contrast, our multi-authority ABE construction in the standard model relies on evasive LWE with *public-coin* auxiliary input and polynomial hardness with a sub-exponential modulus-to-noise ratio; this was also the case for the optimal broadcast encryption scheme by Wee [Wee22]. While vanilla witness encryption implies single-authority ABE [GGSW13], we currently do not know how to construct multi-authority ABE from *vanilla* witness encryption.

2 Technical Overview

In this section, we provide a technical overview of our lattice-based MA-ABE constructions. Throughout this work, we focus exclusively on *subset policies* (which suffices for supporting DNF formulas). In an ABE scheme for subset policies, ciphertexts are associated with a set A and secret keys are associated with a set B. Decryption succeeds if $A \subseteq B$.

Lattice Preliminaries. The learning with errors (LWE) assumption [Reg05] says that the distribution $(\mathbf{A}, \mathbf{s}^{\mathsf{T}}\mathbf{A} + \mathbf{e}^{\mathsf{T}})$ is computationally indistinguishable from $(\mathbf{A}, \mathbf{u}^{\mathsf{T}})$ where $\mathbf{A} \xleftarrow{\scriptscriptstyle R} \mathbb{Z}_q^{n \times m}$, $\mathbf{s} \xleftarrow{\scriptscriptstyle R} \mathbb{Z}_q^n$, $\mathbf{e} \leftarrow D_{\mathbb{Z},\chi}^m$, and $\mathbf{u} \xleftarrow{\scriptscriptstyle R} \mathbb{Z}_q^m$, where n, m, q, χ are lattice parameters and $D_{\mathbb{Z},\chi}$ is the discrete Gaussian distribution with parameter χ. To simplify the presentation in the technical overview, we will use *curly underlines* in place of (small) noise terms. Namely, instead of writing $\mathbf{s}^{\mathsf{T}}\mathbf{A} + \mathbf{e}^{\mathsf{T}}$, we simply write $\underset{\sim}{\mathbf{s}^{\mathsf{T}}}\mathbf{A}$.

For a matrix $\mathbf{A} \in \mathbb{Z}_q^{n \times m}$ and a target vector $\mathbf{y} \in \mathbb{Z}_q^n$, we write $\mathbf{A}_\chi^{-1}(\mathbf{y})$ to denote a random variable $\mathbf{x} \in \mathbb{Z}_q^m$ whose distribution is a discrete Gaussian distribution $D_{\mathbb{Z},\chi}^m$ conditioned on $\mathbf{A}\mathbf{x} = \mathbf{y}$. For ease of notation, we will drop the subscript χ in this technical overview. A sequence of works [Ajt96, GPV08, ABB10b, ABB10a, CHKP10, MP12] (see also Sect. 3.2) have shown how to sample a matrix $\mathbf{A} \in \mathbb{Z}_q^{n \times m}$ together with a trapdoor $\mathsf{td}_\mathbf{A}$ to enable efficient sampling from the distribution $\mathbf{A}^{-1}(\mathbf{y})$ for any target $\mathbf{y} \in \mathbb{Z}_q^n$.

In the following description, we write $\mathbf{I}_n \in \mathbb{Z}_q^{n \times n}$ to denote the n-by-n identity matrix and $\mathbf{G} = \mathbf{I}_n \otimes \mathbf{g}^\mathsf{T} \in \mathbb{Z}_q^{n \times m}$, where $\mathbf{g}^\mathsf{T} = [1 \mid 2 \mid \cdots \mid 2^{\lfloor \log q \rfloor}]$, to denote the standard gadget matrix [MP12].

2.1 Starting Point: Single-Authority CP-ABE for Subset Policies

We start by describing a simple CP-ABE for subset policies that lies at the core of our MA-ABE scheme. In the following, let $[L]$ be the universe of attributes. Each ciphertext is associated with a subset $A \subseteq [L]$ and each secret key is associated with a subset $B \subseteq [L]$; decryption succeeds as long as $A \subseteq B$.

- The master public key consists of $(\mathbf{A}_1, \mathbf{B}_1, \mathbf{p}_1), \ldots, (\mathbf{A}_L, \mathbf{B}_L, \mathbf{p}_L) \xleftarrow{\text{R}} \mathbb{Z}_q^{n \times m} \times \mathbb{Z}_q^{n \times m(2L-1)} \times \mathbb{Z}_q^n$.
- The master secret key consist of the trapdoors $\mathsf{td}_{\mathbf{A}_1}, \ldots, \mathsf{td}_{\mathbf{A}_L}$ for $\mathbf{A}_1, \ldots, \mathbf{A}_L$, respectively.
- An encryption of a message bit $\mu \in \{0, 1\}$ with respect to a set $X \subseteq [L]$ is a tuple

$$\mathsf{ct} = \left(\underset{\sim}{\{\mathbf{s}^\mathsf{T} \mathbf{A}_i\}_{i \in X}} \, , \, \mathbf{s}^\mathsf{T} \underbrace{\sum_{i \in X} \mathbf{B}_i}_{} \, , \, \mathbf{s}^\mathsf{T} \underbrace{\sum_{i \in X} \mathbf{p}_i}_{} + \mu \cdot \lfloor q/2 \rfloor \right),$$

  where $\mathbf{s} \xleftarrow{\text{R}} \mathbb{Z}_q^n$.
- A secret key for a set $Y \subseteq [L]$ consists of a tuple

$$\mathsf{sk} = \left(\left\{ \mathbf{A}_i^{-1}(\mathbf{p}_i + \mathbf{B}_i \mathbf{r}) \right\}_{i \in Y} \, , \, \mathbf{r} \right),$$

  where $\mathbf{r} \leftarrow D_{\mathbb{Z},\chi}^{m(2L-1)}$ is sampled from a discrete Gaussian distribution.

Decryption uses the fact that

$$-\underbrace{\left(\mathbf{s}^\mathsf{T} \sum_{i \in X} \mathbf{B}_i \right)}_{} \cdot \mathbf{r} + \sum_{i \in X} \underset{\sim}{\mathbf{s}^\mathsf{T} \mathbf{A}_i} \cdot \mathbf{A}_i^{-1}(\mathbf{p}_i + \mathbf{B}_i \mathbf{r}) \approx -\mathbf{s}^\mathsf{T} \sum_{i \in X} \mathbf{B}_i \mathbf{r} + \mathbf{s}^\mathsf{T} \sum_{i \in X} (\mathbf{p}_i + \mathbf{B}_i \mathbf{r}) = \mathbf{s}^\mathsf{T} \sum_{i \in X} \mathbf{p}_i,$$

since $\mathbf{r}$ and $\mathbf{A}^{-1}(\cdot)$ are small. Looking ahead to our multi-authority construction, observe that key generation can be carried out in a decentralized manner: given a "public" Gaussian vector $\mathbf{r}$, computing the secret-key components $\mathbf{A}_i^{-1}(\mathbf{p}_i + \mathbf{B}_i \mathbf{r})$ associated with index i only requires knowledge of $\mathbf{B}_i, \mathbf{p}_i$ and the trapdoor for $\mathbf{A}_i$, which are all *specific* to attribute i (and could be independently generated by the ith authority).

Selective Security. To argue that this CP-ABE scheme is selectively secure[3], we proceed as follows:

1. First, we show how to sample a secret key for a set $Y \subseteq [L]$ given a trap-door for $\mathbf{B}_Y$, where $\mathbf{B}_Y \in \mathbb{Z}_q^{n|Y| \times m(2L-1)}$ is the matrix formed by vertically concatenating $\mathbf{B}_i$ for all $i \in Y$.
2. Next, we show that under the LWE assumption, $\mathbf{s}^\mathsf{T} \underset{\sim}{\sum_{i \in X}} \mathbf{B}_i$ is pseudorandom

   even given an oracle for $\mathbf{B}_Y^{-1}(\cdot)$ for arbitrary $Y \subseteq [L]$ of the adversary's choos-ing, provided that for each Y, it is the case that $X \not\subseteq Y$. Here, $X \subseteq [L]$ is the set associated with the challenge ciphertext. Technically, we additionally require that $\mathbf{s}^\mathsf{T} \underset{\sim}{\mathbf{A}_i}$ and $\mathbf{s}^\mathsf{T} \underset{\sim}{\sum_{i \in X} \mathbf{p}_i}$ are also pseudorandom, but these com-

   ponents are easily handled by the standard LWE assumption. For ease of exposition, we do not focus on these additional components in this overview and refer instead to Sects. 4 and 5 for the full description.

For the second step, we prove a more general statement which generalizes the related-trapdoor LWE lemma previously introduced by Brakerski and Vaikun-tanathan [BV22] in the context of constructing compact CP-ABE for circuits.

Generalized Related-Trapdoor LWE. Our generalized related-trapdoor LWE assumption asserts that for any non-zero vector $\mathbf{u} \in \{0,1\}^L$, the vector $\mathbf{s}^\mathsf{T} \underset{\sim}{(\mathbf{u}^\mathsf{T} \otimes \mathbf{I}_n) \mathbf{B}}$ is pseudorandom given an oracle for the function $(\mathbf{M}, \mathbf{t}) \mapsto$

$((\mathbf{M} \otimes \mathbf{I}_n) \mathbf{B})^{-1}(\mathbf{t})$, as long as the matrix $\bar{\mathbf{M}} = \begin{bmatrix} \mathbf{M} \\ \mathbf{u}^\mathsf{T} \end{bmatrix} \in \mathbb{Z}_q^{(k+1) \times L}$ is full rank (and $k < L$).[4] To show that the standard LWE assumption implies the gener-alized related-trapdoor LWE assumption, we take an LWE matrix $\hat{\mathbf{A}}$ and the vector $\mathbf{u} \in \{0,1\}^L$, and we set the matrix $\mathbf{B}$ to be

$$\mathbf{B} = \left[\hat{\mathbf{A}} \mid \hat{\mathbf{A}}\mathbf{R} + \mathbf{U}^\perp \otimes \mathbf{G} \right]$$

where $\mathbf{R}$ is a (random) low-norm matrix and $\mathbf{U}^\perp \in \{0,1\}^{L \times (L-1)}$ is a full-rank basis for the kernel of $\mathbf{u}^\mathsf{T}$. By design, $(\mathbf{u} \otimes \mathbf{I}_n)\mathbf{B} = [(\mathbf{u} \otimes \mathbf{I}_n)\hat{\mathbf{A}} \mid (\mathbf{u} \otimes \mathbf{I}_n)\hat{\mathbf{A}}\mathbf{R}]$ which means we do *not* know a trapdoor for $(\mathbf{u} \otimes \mathbf{I}_n)\mathbf{B}$. On the other hand,

$$(\mathbf{M} \otimes \mathbf{I}_n)\mathbf{B} \underbrace{\begin{bmatrix} -\mathbf{R} \\ \mathbf{I}_{\hat{m}(L-1)} \end{bmatrix}}_{\tilde{\mathbf{R}}} = (\mathbf{M} \otimes \mathbf{I}_n)(\mathbf{U}^\perp \otimes \mathbf{G}) = \mathbf{M}\mathbf{U}^\perp \otimes \mathbf{G}.$$

When $\bar{\mathbf{M}} = \begin{bmatrix} \mathbf{M} \\ \mathbf{u}^\mathsf{T} \end{bmatrix}$ is full rank, then $\mathbf{M}\mathbf{U}^\perp$ is also full rank. Since $\tilde{\mathbf{R}}$ is low-norm, it is a trapdoor for $(\mathbf{M} \otimes \mathbf{I}_n)\mathbf{B}$ (see [MP12] and Corollary 3.12).

---

[3] In the selective security game, the adversary starts by committing to the set X associated with the challenge ciphertext. The reduction algorithm is then allowed to program X into the public parameters of the scheme.

[4] Some restriction on $\mathbf{M}$ is also necessary. For instance, it is easy to distinguish $\mathbf{s}^\mathsf{T} \underset{\sim}{(\mathbf{u} \otimes \mathbf{I}_n) \mathbf{B}}$ if $\mathbf{M} = \mathbf{u}^\mathsf{T}$, or more generally, if $\mathbf{u}_0^\mathsf{T}\mathbf{M} = \mathbf{u}$ for some $\mathbf{u}_0 \in \{0,1\}^k$.

Returning to the proof of selective security for the above CP-ABE scheme, observe that showing $\mathbf{s}^\top \sum_{i \in X} \mathbf{B}_i$ given an oracle for $\mathbf{B}_Y^{-1}(\cdot)$ directly maps to an instance of the related-trapdoor LWE assumption:

- Let $\mathbf{B} \in \mathbb{Z}_q^{nL \times m(2L-1)}$ be the matrix obtained by vertically stacking $\mathbf{B}_1, \ldots, \mathbf{B}_L \in \mathbb{Z}_q^{n \times m(2L-1)}$.
- The vector $\mathbf{u} \in \{0, 1\}^L$ is the indicator vector for the challenge set X. Namely, $u_i = 1$ if $i \in X$ and 0 otherwise. Then, $(\mathbf{u} \otimes \mathbf{I}_n)\mathbf{B} = \sum_{i \in X} \mathbf{B}_i$.
- The oracle $\mathbf{B}_Y^{-1}(\cdot)$ can be simulated by querying the related-trapdoor oracle on matrix $\mathbf{M}_Y \in \mathbb{Z}_q^{|Y| \times L}$ formed by taking the rows of $\mathbf{I}_L$ corresponding to the indices in Y. In this case $(\mathbf{M} \otimes \mathbf{I}_n)\mathbf{B} = \mathbf{B}_Y$ defined previously. Moreover, by construction of $\mathbf{M}_Y$, whenever $X \nsubseteq Y$, we have that $\mathbf{u}^\top$ is *not* in the row-span of $\mathbf{M}_Y$.

Finally, we remark here that the original version of the related-trapdoor LWE assumption formulated by Brakerski and Vaikuntanathan [BV22] considered the special case where the matrix $\mathbf{M}$ is a row vector with a specific structure.[5] Our formulation considers a general matrix $\mathbf{M}$ which is useful for constructing an ABE scheme with a *distributed* setup. We also note that this type of trapdoor sampling was also implicit in the CP-ABE construction of Datta et al. [DKW21a]; however, they critically relied on noise flooding to simulate the analog of the $((\mathbf{M} \otimes \mathbf{I}_n)\mathbf{B})^{-1}(\cdot)$ oracle. As a result, the security of their scheme relied on LWE with a super-polynomial modulus-to-noise ratio in the random oracle model. In this work, we both provide a modular description of the core trapdoor sampling lemma (Sect. 4) and then show how to leverage it to obtain a multi-authority ABE for subset policies using LWE with a polynomial modulus-to-noise ratio in the random oracle model (Sect. 5). We are optimistic that our generalized version of the related trapdoor LWE assumption will also be useful for analyzing the security of other lattice-based constructions.

2.2   MA-ABE for Subset Policies in the Random Oracle Model

First, we observe that our core CP-ABE scheme naturally extends to yield a MA-ABE scheme for subset policies in the random oracle model. We make the following modifications to the base scheme:

- The authority associated with attribute i samples $\mathbf{A}_i, \mathbf{B}_i, \mathbf{p}_i$ along with a trapdoor $\mathsf{td}_{\mathbf{A}_i}$ for $\mathbf{A}_i$.
- To generate a key for a user with identifier gid, we derive $\mathbf{r}$ *deterministically* from $\mathsf{H}(\mathsf{gid})$ and output $\mathbf{A}^{-1}(\mathbf{p}_i + \mathbf{B}_i \mathbf{r})$.

Security of the core CP-ABE implies that the ensuing MA-ABE scheme remains secure as long as no authority is corrupted. On the other hand, it is easy to see

---

[5] Concretely, $\mathbf{u}^\top = [1 \mid \mathbf{x}^\top]$ and $\mathbf{M} = [1 \mid \mathbf{y}^\top]$ for some $\mathbf{x}, \mathbf{y} \in \{0, 1\}^{L-1}$. The adversary is restricted to queries $\mathbf{y} \neq \mathbf{x}$, which is implied by our requirement that $\bar{\mathbf{M}}$ has full rank.

that the scheme is insecure if we allow authority corruptions, since we can use an authority's trapdoor to recover the LWE secret $\mathbf{s}$ from $\underset{\sim}{\mathbf{s}^\mathsf{T} \mathbf{A}_i}$.

Security with Authority Corruptions. To defend against corrupted authorities, we modify the ciphertext structure. Instead of having a single LWE secret $\mathbf{s}$ that is shared across *authorities*, we instead sample a fresh $\mathbf{s}_i$ for each attribute $i \in X$. That is, the ciphertext is now given by:

$$\mathsf{ct} = \left(\left\{ \underset{\sim}{\mathbf{s}_i^\mathsf{T} \mathbf{A}_i} \right\}_{i \in X}, \underbrace{\sum_{i \in X} \mathbf{s}_i^\mathsf{T} \mathbf{B}_i}_{}, \underbrace{\sum_{i \in X} \mathbf{s}_i^\mathsf{T} \mathbf{p}_i + \mu \cdot \lfloor q/2 \rceil}_{} \right)$$

Key generation proceeds as before. Decryption still follows from a similar relation as before:

$$-\underbrace{\left(\sum_{i \in X} \mathbf{s}_i^\mathsf{T} \mathbf{B}_i \right)}_{} \cdot \mathbf{r} + \sum_{i \in X} \underset{\sim}{\mathbf{s}_i^\mathsf{T} \mathbf{A}_i} \cdot \mathbf{A}_i^{-1} (\mathbf{p}_i + \mathbf{B}_i \mathbf{r}) = \sum_{i \in X} \mathbf{s}_i^\mathsf{T} \mathbf{p}_i.$$

Static Security with Authority Corruptions. We now argue that the resulting MA-ABE scheme is statically secure.[6] Let $\mathcal{C}$ denote the set of authorities that are corrupted. The adversary gets to choose the public keys and secret keys for authorities in $\mathcal{C}$. In the multi-authority setting, a secret-key query consists of a pair (Y, gid) where Y is a set of *honest* authorities (i.e., $Y \cap \mathcal{C} = \varnothing$) and gid is the user identifier. Let X be the set of authorities associated with the challenge ciphertext. The admissibility criterion is that $X \not\subseteq Y \cup \mathcal{C}$.

The proof of security proceeds similarly to that of our core CP-ABE, except we replace the challenge set X with the set $X \setminus \mathcal{C}$. Since $Y \cap \mathcal{C} = \varnothing$, the MA-ABE admissibility criterion $X \not\subseteq Y \cup \mathcal{C}$ is equivalent to $X \setminus \mathcal{C} \not\subseteq Y$, which coincides with the criterion from our CP-ABE analysis. In particular, the security reduction can basically *ignore* the ciphertext components associated with corrupted authorities (since the ciphertext component of each authority is associated with *independent* LWE secrets $\mathbf{s}_i$) and just focus on the attributes controlled by the honest authorities. The general argument again relies on our (generalized) related-trapdoor LWE assumption:

1. First, we show how to sample a secret key for Y given a trapdoor for $\mathbf{B}_Y$ (where $\mathbf{B}_Y \in \mathbb{Z}_q^{n|Y| \times m(2L-1)}$ is again the matrix formed by vertically stacking the matrices $\mathbf{B}_i$ associated with the authorities $i \in Y$.
2. As in the analysis of the CP-ABE scheme, we use the oracle in the related-trapdoor LWE assumption to compute $\mathbf{B}_Y^{-1}(\cdot)$ in the proof. Arguing the correctness of this step additionally requires the ability to "program" the random

---

[6] In the static security model [RW15], we require the adversary to commit to the set of corrupted authorities, the secret-key queries, and the challenge ciphertext query at the beginning of the security game. Previous lattice-based MA-ABE constructions were also analyzed in the static security model [DKW21a].

oracle. This is because in the real scheme, the secret keys are sampled by computing $\mathbf{r} \leftarrow \mathsf{H}(\mathsf{gid})$ and then sampling $\mathbf{u}_i \leftarrow \mathbf{A}_i(\mathbf{p}_i + \mathbf{B}_i \mathbf{r})$ for each $i \in X$. The reduction algorithm will instead sample $\mathbf{u}_i \leftarrow D_{\mathbb{Z},\chi}^m$ itself and then obtain $\mathbf{r} \in \mathbb{Z}_q^{m(2L-1)}$ using its oracle $\mathbf{B}_Y^{-1}(\cdot)$. In the random oracle model, the reduction then programs $\mathsf{H}(\mathsf{gid})$ to $\mathbf{r}$. We refer to Sect. 5 for more details.

3. Finally, to simulate the challenge ciphertext, the reduction algorithm samples a random $\mathbf{s}_i \xleftarrow{\text{R}} \mathbb{Z}_q^n$ for each corrupted authority $i \in \mathcal{C}$. For the honest authorities $i \in X \setminus \mathcal{C}$, the reduction sets the secret key to be $\hat{\mathbf{s}}_i$ and programs $\mathbf{s}_i := \mathbf{s} + \hat{\mathbf{s}}_i$, where $\mathbf{s}$ is the secret in the related-trapdoor

We provide the formal analysis in Sect. 5. This construction yields a MA-ABE scheme for subset policies from the related-trapdoor LWE assumption in the random oracle model. The related-trapdoor LWE assumption we rely on here reduces to the standard LWE assumption with a polynomial modulus-to-noise ratio. This yields Theorem 1.2.

2.3 Removing Random Oracles via Evasive LWE

To obtain an MA-ABE construction *without* random oracles, we describe a way to *concretely* implement the hash function H in our basic construction above. Our specific instantiation relies on computing a subset product of low-norm matrices. Specifically, let $\mathbf{D}_0, \mathbf{D}_1 \in \mathbb{Z}_q^{m \times m}$ be low-norm matrices. These are fixed public matrices that will be included as part of the global parameters. For an input $x \in \{0, 1\}^\ell$, we define $\mathsf{H}(x) := \left(\prod_{i \in [\ell]} \mathbf{D}_{x_i}\right)\boldsymbol{\eta} \in \mathbb{Z}_q^m$, where $\boldsymbol{\eta} \in \mathbb{Z}_q^m$ is the first canonical basis vector. Previously, Boneh et al. [BLMR13] showed that for any sequence of $x_1, \ldots, x_k \in \{0, 1\}^\ell$ the values $\left\{\underset{\sim}{\mathbf{s}^\mathsf{T}\mathsf{H}(x_i)}\right\}_{i \in [k]}$ are pseudorandom. While we do not know how to prove security of the MA-ABE construction instantiated with this subset-product hash function using the plain learning with errors assumption, we show how to do so using the recently-introduced evasive LWE assumption by Wee [Wee22] and Tsabury [Tsa22].

Evasive LWE. We start by describing a variant of the evasive LWE assumption introduced by Wee [Wee22] and refer to Sect. 3.2 for the formal description. Let $\mathbf{P}_1, \ldots, \mathbf{P}_\ell$ be drawn from some efficiently-sampleable distribution of matrices. Roughly speaking, the evasive LWE assumption says that if the distribution $\{\mathbf{A}_i , \underset{\sim}{\mathbf{s}^\mathsf{T}\mathbf{P}_i}\}_{i \in [\ell]}$ is pseudorandom, then the distributions

$$\{\mathbf{A}_i , \underset{\sim}{\mathbf{s}^\mathsf{T}\mathbf{A}_i} , \mathbf{A}_i^{-1}(\mathbf{P}_i)\}_{i \in [\ell]} \quad \text{and} \quad \{\mathbf{A}_i , \mathbf{u}_i^\mathsf{T} , \mathbf{A}_i^{-1}(\mathbf{P}_i)\}_{i \in [\ell]}$$

are computationally indistinguishable. Intuitively, the evasive LWE assumption says that the presence of $\mathbf{A}_i^{-1}(\mathbf{P}_i)$ does *not* help break LWE so long as $\underset{\sim}{\mathbf{s}^\mathsf{T}\mathbf{P}_i}$ is pseudorandom. Indeed, if the distinguisher multiplied $\underset{\sim}{\mathbf{s}^\mathsf{T}\mathbf{A}}$ with $\mathbf{A}^{-1}(\mathbf{P})$, then it roughly obtains $\underset{\sim}{\mathbf{s}^\mathsf{T}\mathbf{P}}$, which is pseudorandom by assumption.

In the context of our MA-ABE scheme, the matrices $\mathbf{A}_1, \ldots, \mathbf{A}_\ell$ will be associated with the public keys for the honest authorities, and the columns of $\mathbf{P}_i$ will consists of $\mathbf{p}_i + \mathbf{B}_i \mathbf{r}_{\mathsf{gid}}$ for the user identifiers gid that appear in the adversary's secret-key queries. By setting $\mathbf{P}_i$ properly (see Sect. 6), the reduction algorithm can in turn answer the secret-key queries *without* switching to using a trapdoor for $\mathbf{B}_Y$ to answer key queries. We highlight the key differences in reduction strategies here:

- Previously (Sect. 2.2), the reduction sampled $\mathbf{u}_i$ itself and used the trapdoor for $\mathbf{B}_Y$ to sample $\mathbf{r} = \mathsf{H}(\mathsf{gid})$. This was necessary because the reduction did not (and cannot) possess a trapdoor for each $\mathbf{A}_i$ to sample $\mathbf{u}_i$ as in the real scheme. If the reduction did possess such a trapdoor for every i that appears in the challenge ciphertext, then it could trivially break security itself. Then, to ensure consistency of the sampled key with respect to the outputs of H, this requires the reduction to *program* the outputs of H. Hence, we model H as a random oracle in this case.
- In contrast, when we use evasive LWE, the reduction computes $\mathbf{r} = \mathsf{H}(\mathsf{gid})$ normally and then directly constructs $\mathbf{u}_i$ using the terms provided in the evasive LWE challenge. These terms can be simulated *without* knowledge of a trapdoor for $\mathbf{A}_i$. Observe that this strategy only relies on the ability to compute $\mathsf{H}(\cdot)$, *not* the ability to program its outputs. In general, the evasive LWE assumptions allows us to reduce the task of proving security to that of reasoning about the pseudorandomness of LWE samples with respect to correlated public matrices. In the latter distribution, there are no Gaussian samples, and no need to implement any kind of trapdoor sampling.

When we use evasive LWE, the computation of $\mathbf{s}^\mathsf{T} \mathbf{P}$ essentially translates to computing $\mathbf{s}^\mathsf{T} \mathsf{H}(\mathsf{gid})$, which is pseudorandom by the Boneh et al. [BLMR13] analysis.

We refer to Sect. 6 for the formal description.

While the evasive LWE assumption is much less well understood compared to the classic LWE assumption, proving security under evasive LWE at the minimum indicates that replacing the random oracle with a subset-product hash function is a sound *heuristic* for constructing an MA-ABE scheme in the plain model. It is an interesting challenge to try and prove the security of our construction from the plain LWE assumption; such a proof would provide the first construction of MA-ABE from standard assumptions in the plain model. Alternatively, it is also interesting to further cryptanalyze the evasive LWE assumption.

3 Preliminaries

We write λ to denote the security parameter. For a positive integer $n \in \mathbb{N}$, we write $[n]$ to denote the set $\{1, \ldots, n\}$. For a positive integer $q \in \mathbb{N}$, we write $\mathbb{Z}_q$ to denote the integers modulo q. We use bold uppercase letters to denote matrices (e.g., $\mathbf{A}, \mathbf{B}$) and bold lowercase letters to denote vectors (e.g., $\mathbf{u}, \mathbf{v}$).

We use non-boldface letters to refer to their components: $\mathbf{v} = (v_1, \ldots, v_n)$. For matrices $\mathbf{A}_1, \ldots, \mathbf{A}_\ell \in \mathbb{Z}_q^{n \times m}$, we write $\mathrm{diag}(\mathbf{A}_1, \ldots, \mathbf{A}_\ell) \in \mathbb{Z}_q^{n\ell \times m\ell}$ to denote the block diagonal matrix with blocks $\mathbf{A}_1, \ldots, \mathbf{A}_\ell$ along the main diagonal (and 0s elsewhere).

We write $\mathsf{poly}(\lambda)$ to denote a function that is $O(\lambda^c)$ for some $c \in \mathbb{N}$ and $\mathsf{negl}(\lambda)$ to denote a function that is $o(\lambda^{-c})$ for all $c \in \mathbb{N}$. An algorithm is efficient if it runs in probabilistic polynomial time in its input length. We say that two families of distributions $\mathcal{D}_1 = \{\mathcal{D}_{1,\lambda}\}_{\lambda \in \mathbb{N}}$ and $\mathcal{D}_2 = \{\mathcal{D}_{2,\lambda}\}_{\lambda \in \mathbb{N}}$ are computationally indistinguishable if no efficient algorithm can distinguish them with non-negligible probability. We denote this by writing $\mathcal{D}_1 \overset{c}{\approx} \mathcal{D}_2$. We say they are statistically indistinguishable if the statistical distance $\Delta(\mathcal{D}_1, \mathcal{D}_2)$ is bounded by a negligible function in λ and denote this by writing $\mathcal{D}_1 \overset{s}{\approx} \mathcal{D}_2$. We say a distribution $\mathcal{D}$ is B-bounded if $\Pr[\|x\| \le B : x \leftarrow \mathcal{D}] = 1$.

3.1 Multi-authority Attribute-Based Encryption

In this section, we introduce the syntax of a multi-authority ABE scheme [LW11]. We start with the definition of a monotone access structure [Bei96].

Definition 3.1. (Access Structure [Bei96]). *Let S be a set and let 2^S denote the power set of S (i.e., the set of all subsets of S). An access structure on S is a set $\mathbb{A} \subseteq 2^S \setminus \varnothing$ of non-empty subsets of S. We refer to the elements of $\mathbb{A}$ as the* authorized *sets and those not in $\mathbb{A}$ as the* unauthorized *sets. We say an access structure is* monotone *if for all sets $B, C \in 2^S$, if $B \in \mathbb{A}$ and $B \subseteq C$, then $C \in \mathbb{A}$.*

Definition 3.2. (Multi-Authority ABE [LW11, RW15, adapted]). *Let λ be a security parameter, $\mathcal{M}$ be a message space, $\mathcal{AU} = \{\mathcal{AU}_\lambda\}_{\lambda \in \mathbb{N}}$ be the universe of authority identifiers, and $\mathcal{GID} = \{\mathcal{GID}_\lambda\}_{\lambda \in \mathbb{N}}$ be the universe of global identifiers for users. To simplify the exposition, we follow the convention in [RW15, DKW21a] and assume that each authority controls a single attribute; this definition generalizes naturally to the setting where each authority controls an arbitrary polynomial number of attributes (see [RW15]). A multi-authority attribute-based encryption scheme for a class of policies $\mathcal{P} = \{\mathcal{P}_\lambda\}_{\lambda \in \mathbb{N}}$ (each described by a monotone access structure on a subset of $\mathcal{AU}$) consists of a tuple of efficient algorithms $\Pi_{\mathsf{MA-ABE}} = (\mathsf{GlobalSetup}, \mathsf{AuthSetup}, \mathsf{KeyGen}, \mathsf{Encrypt}, \mathsf{Decrypt})$ with the following properties:*

- $\mathsf{GlobalSetup}(1^\lambda) \to \mathsf{gp}$: *On input the security parameter λ, the global setup algorithm outputs the global parameters gp.*
- $\mathsf{AuthSetup}(\mathsf{gp}, \mathsf{aid}) \to (\mathsf{pk}_{\mathsf{aid}}, \mathsf{msk}_{\mathsf{aid}})$: *On input the global parameters gp and an authority identifier $\mathsf{aid} \in \mathcal{AU}$, the authority setup algorithm outputs a public key $\mathsf{pk}_{\mathsf{aid}}$ and a master secret key $\mathsf{msk}_{\mathsf{aid}}$.*
- $\mathsf{KeyGen}(\mathsf{gp}, \mathsf{msk}, \mathsf{gid}) \to \mathsf{sk}$: *On input the global parameters gp, the authority's master secret key msk, and the user identifier $\mathsf{gid} \in \mathcal{GID}$, the key-generation algorithm outputs a decryption key sk.*

- Encrypt($\mathsf{gp}, \mathbb{A}, \{\mathsf{pk}_{\mathsf{aid}}\}_{\mathsf{aid} \in A}, \mu$) → ct: *On input the global parameters* gp*, an access structure* $\mathbb{A} \in \mathcal{P}$ *on a set of authorities* $A \subseteq \mathcal{AU}$*, the set of public keys* $\mathsf{pk}_{\mathsf{aid}}$ *associated with each authority* $\mathsf{aid} \in A$*, and a message* $\mu \in \mathcal{M}$*, the encryption algorithm outputs a ciphertext* ct*.*
- Decrypt($\mathsf{gp}, \{\mathsf{sk}_{\mathsf{aid}}\}_{\mathsf{aid} \in A}, \mathsf{ct}$) → μ: *On input the global parameters* gp*, a collection of secret keys* $\mathsf{sk}_{\mathsf{aid}}$ *issued by a set of authorities* $\mathsf{aid} \in A$*, and a ciphertext* ct*, the decryption algorithm outputs a message* $\mu \in \mathcal{M} \cup \{\perp\}$*.*

Moreover, $\Pi_{\mathsf{MA\text{-}ABE}}$ *should satisfy the following properties:*

- **Correctness:** *The exists a negligible function* $\mathsf{negl}(\cdot)$ *such that for every* $\lambda \in \mathbb{N}$*, every message* $\mu \in \mathcal{M}$*, every identifier* $\mathsf{gid} \in \mathcal{GID}_\lambda$*, every set of authorities* $A \subseteq \mathcal{AU}_\lambda$*, every access structure* $\mathbb{A} \in \mathcal{P}_\lambda$ *on* A*, and every subset of authorized authorities* $B \in \mathbb{A}$*,*

$$\Pr \left[\mu' = \mu : \begin{array}{l} \mathsf{gp} \leftarrow \mathsf{GlobalSetup}(1^\lambda); \\ \forall \mathsf{aid} \in A : (\mathsf{pk}_{\mathsf{aid}}, \mathsf{msk}_{\mathsf{aid}}) \leftarrow \mathsf{AuthSetup}(\mathsf{gp}, \mathsf{aid}); \\ \forall \mathsf{aid} \in B : \mathsf{sk}_{\mathsf{gid},\mathsf{aid}} \leftarrow \mathsf{KeyGen}(\mathsf{gp}, \mathsf{msk}_{\mathsf{aid}}, \mathsf{gid}); \\ \mathsf{ct} \leftarrow \mathsf{Encrypt}(\mathsf{gp}, \mathbb{A}, \{\mathsf{pk}_{\mathsf{aid}}\}_{\mathsf{aid} \in A}, \mu); \\ \mu' \leftarrow \mathsf{Decrypt}(\mathsf{gp}, \{\mathsf{sk}_{\mathsf{gid},\mathsf{aid}}\}_{\mathsf{aid} \in B}, \mathsf{ct}) \end{array} \right] = 1 - \mathsf{negl}(\lambda).$$

- **Static security:** *For a security parameter* $\lambda \in \mathbb{N}$*, an adversary* $\mathcal{A}$*, and a bit* $b \in \{0, 1\}$*, we define the static security game for an multi-authority ABE scheme as follows:*
  - **Setup:** *The challenger starts by sampling* $\mathsf{gp} \leftarrow \mathsf{GlobalSetup}(1^\lambda)$ *and gives* gp *to* $\mathcal{A}$*.*
  - **Attacker queries.** *The adversary* $\mathcal{A}$ *now specifies the following:*
    * *A set* $\mathcal{C} \subseteq \mathcal{AU}_\lambda$ *of corrupt authorities together with a public key* $\mathsf{pk}_{\mathsf{aid}}$ *for each corrupt authority* $\mathsf{aid} \in \mathcal{C}$*.*
    * *A set* $\mathcal{N} \subseteq \mathcal{AU}_\lambda$ *of non-corrupt authorities, where* $\mathcal{N} \cap \mathcal{C} = \varnothing$*.*
    * *A set* $\mathcal{Q} = \{(\mathsf{gid}, A)\}$ *of secret key queries where each query consists of a global identifier* $\mathsf{gid} \in \mathcal{GID}_\lambda$ *and a subset of non-corrupt authorities* $A \subset \mathcal{N}$*.*
    * *A pair of challenge messages* $\mu_0, \mu_1 \in \mathcal{M}$*, a set of authorities* $A^* \subseteq \mathcal{C} \cup \mathcal{N}$*, and an access structure* $\mathbb{A} \in \mathcal{P}_\lambda$ *on* A^**.*
  - **Challenge.** *The challenger then samples* $(\mathsf{pk}_{\mathsf{aid}}, \mathsf{msk}_{\mathsf{aid}}) \leftarrow \mathsf{AuthSetup}(\mathsf{gp}, \mathsf{aid})$ *for each authority* $\mathsf{aid} \in \mathcal{N}$*. It responds to the adversary with the following:*
    * *The public keys* $\mathsf{pk}_{\mathsf{aid}}$ *for the non-corrupted authority* $\mathsf{aid} \in \mathcal{N}$*.*
    * *For each secret-key query* (gid, A)*, the secret keys* $\mathsf{sk}_{\mathsf{gid},\mathsf{aid}} \leftarrow \mathsf{KeyGen}(\mathsf{gp}, \mathsf{msk}_{\mathsf{aid}}, \mathsf{gid})$ *for each* $\mathsf{aid} \in A$*.*
    * *The challenge ciphertext* $\mathsf{ct}_b \leftarrow \mathsf{Encrypt}(\mathsf{gp}, \mathbb{A}, \{\mathsf{pk}_{\mathsf{aid}}\}_{\mathsf{aid} \in A^*}, \mu_b)$*.*
  - **Output phase:** *Finally, algorithm* $\mathcal{A}$ *outputs a bit* $b' \in \{0, 1\}$*, which is the output of the experiment.*

We say an adversary $\mathcal{A}$ *is admissible for the above security game if* $A^* \cap \mathcal{C} \notin \mathbb{A}$ *and moreover, for every secret key query* (gid, A)*, it holds that* $(A \cup \mathcal{C}) \cap A^* \notin \mathbb{A}$*. Finally, we say* $\Pi_{\mathsf{MA\text{-}ABE}}$ *satisfies static security if for all efficient and* *admissible adversaries* $\mathcal{A}$, *there exists a negligible function* $\mathsf{negl}(\cdot)$ *such that for all* $\lambda \in \mathbb{N}$, $|\Pr[b' = 1|b = 0] - \Pr[b' = 1|b = 1]| = \mathsf{negl}(\lambda)$ *in the above security game.*

Remark 3.3 (Static Security in the Random Oracle Model). Following [RW15, DKW21a], we also extend Definition 3.2 to the random oracle model [BR93]. In this setting, we assume that a global hash function H (modeled as a random oracle) is published as part of the global public parameters and accessible to all of the parties in the system. When extending static security to the random oracle model, we require that the adversary submits its random oracle queries as part of its initial query in the static security game. The challenger then includes the responses to the random oracle queries as part of the challenge. We also allow the adversary to further query the random oracle during the challenge phase of the game.

Remark 3.4 (Security Notions). The static security requirement in Definition 3.2 requires that the adversary commits to *all* of its queries upfront. A stronger notion of security is adaptive security under static corruptions [LW11] which requires the adversary pre-commit to the set of corrupted authorities, but thereafter, the adversary can adaptively make secret-key queries both before and after making its challenge ciphertext query. We can also consider intermediate notions where the adversary needs to commit to the policy associated with the challenge ciphertext, but can then issue secret key queries adaptively (i.e., the analog of "selective security" in single-authority ABE). Achieving stronger notions of security (beyond static security) for multi-authority ABE from lattice-based assumptions is an interesting open problem.

Multi-authority ABE for Subset Policies. Our focus in this work is on constructing multi-authority ABE for the class of subset policies. Here, the ciphertext is associated with a set of authorities A and decryption succeeds whenever a user possesses keys from a set of authorities B where $A \subseteq B$. We define this more formally below.

Definition 3.5 (Multi-Authority ABE for Subset Policies). *Let* λ *be a security parameter and* $\mathcal{AU} = \{\mathcal{AU}_\lambda\}_{\lambda \in \mathbb{N}}$ *be the universe of authority identifiers. We define the class of subset policies* $\mathcal{P} = \{\mathcal{P}_\lambda\}_{\lambda \in \mathbb{N}}$ *to be the set*

$$\mathcal{P}_\lambda = \{\mathbb{A} : \mathbb{A} = \{B : A \subseteq B\} \text{ where } A \subseteq \mathcal{AU}_\lambda\}.$$

Notably, an access structure $\mathbb{A}$ *for a subset policy is fully determined by the set* $A \subseteq \mathcal{AU}_\lambda$. *Thus, when describing an MA-ABE scheme* $\Pi_{\mathsf{MA\text{-}ABE}} = (\mathsf{GlobalSetup}, \mathsf{AuthSetup}, \mathsf{KeyGen}, \mathsf{Encrypt}, \mathsf{Decrypt})$ *for the class of subset policies, we omit the specification of* $\mathbb{A}$ *in the encryption algorithm and have the encryption algorithm only take as input the public keys associated with the authorities in* A. *More precisely, we modify the syntax of the encryption algorithm as follows:*

- $\mathsf{Encrypt}(\mathsf{gp}, \{\mathsf{pk}_{\mathsf{aid}}\}_{\mathsf{aid} \in A}, \mu) \to \mathsf{ct}$: *On input the global parameters* gp, *the set of public keys* $\mathsf{pk}_{\mathsf{aid}}$ *associated with each authority* $\mathsf{aid} \in A$, *and a message* $\mu \in \mathcal{M}$, *the encryption algorithm outputs a ciphertext* ct.

Remark 3.6 (Multi-Authority ABE for DNFs). A multi-authority ABE scheme for subset policies directly implies a multi-authority ABE scheme for access structures that can be decided by a polynomial-size conjunction or a DNF formula. First, we define the notion of an access structure decidable by a Boolean formula. Let $\mathbb{A}$ be an access structure on a set $A = \{a_1, \ldots, a_n\}$. For a subset $B \subseteq A$, we define indicator bits $b_1, \ldots, b_n$ where $b_i = 1$ if $a_i \in B$ and 0 otherwise. We say that $\mathbb{A}$ can be computed by a Boolean formula φ if there exists a Boolean formula $\varphi \colon \{0,1\}^n \to \{0,1\}$ such that $B \in \mathbb{A}$ if and only if $\varphi(b_1, \ldots, b_n) = 1$. It is straightforward to use an MA-ABE scheme for subset policies to construct MA-ABE schemes for policies computable by either a conjunction or a DNF:

- **Conjunction:** Let $\mathbb{A}$ be an access structure on A that is computable by a conjunction on variables $b_{i_1}, \ldots, b_{i_d}$. This is equivalent to a subset policy for the set $\{a_{i_1}, \ldots, a_{i_d}\}$.
- **DNF formulas:** Let $\mathbb{A}$ be an access structure on A that is computable by a DNF $\varphi \colon \{0,1\}^n \to \{0,1\}$. By construction, we can write $\varphi(x_1, \ldots, x_n) = \bigvee_{i \in [t]} \varphi_i(x_1, \ldots, x_n)$, where each φ_i is a conjunction. In this case, decryption succeeds as long as at least one of the φ_i is satisfied. In this case, we simply concatenate t ciphertexts together, where the ith ciphertext is an encryption to the ith conjunction φ_i. Correctness follows by construction while security follows by a standard hybrid argument.

Remark 3.7 (Multi-Authority ABE for k-CNFs). In the single-authority setting, ABE for subset policies implies an ABE scheme for k-CNF formulas for constant $k \in \mathbb{N}$ [Tsa19, GLW21]. However, this generic approach does not easily translate to the multi-authority setting. Here, a k-CNF formula $\varphi \colon \{0,1\}^n \to \{0,1\}$ can be written as $\varphi(x_1, \ldots, x_n) = \bigwedge_{i \in [t]} \varphi_i(x_1, \ldots, x_n)$, where each clause $\varphi_i(x_1, \ldots, x_n)$ is a disjunction on up to k variables. To support k-CNF formulas $\varphi \colon \{0,1\}^n \to \{0,1\}$ on a set $A = \{a_1, \ldots, a_n\}$, the approach is to first define a universe U of size $|U| = O(kn^k)$, where each element $u \in U$ is associated with a distinct subset of $S_u \subseteq A$ of size $|S_u| \leq k$. A secret key for a_i consists of secret keys for all $u \in U$ where $a_i \in S_u$. A k-CNF policy $\varphi(x_1, \ldots, x_n) = \bigwedge_{i \in [t]} \varphi_i(x_1, \ldots, x_n)$ where each clause φ_i depends on a set $T_i \subseteq A$ of at most k variables corresponds to a subset policy for the set $\{u_{T_1}, \ldots, u_{T_t}\}$.

In the multi-authority setting, different authorities own the different attributes $a_1, \ldots, a_n$. To implement k-CNF policies as subset policies via the above transformation, we require a multi-authority ABE scheme that supports subset policies where the basic attributes are *combinations* of attributes from *different* authorities. This conflicts with the requirement that authorities be independent in the multi-authority setting. It is an interesting question to construct a multi-authority ABE scheme capable of supporting k-CNF formulas from one that supports subset policies.

3.2 Lattice Preliminaries

Throughout this work, we always use the ℓ_∞ norm for vectors and matrices. Specifically, for a vector $\mathbf{u}$, we write $\|\mathbf{u}\| := \max_i |x_i|$, and for a matrix $\mathbf{A}$, we write $\|\mathbf{A}\| = \max_{i,j} |A_{i,j}|$. For a dimension $k \in \mathbb{N}$, we write $\mathbf{I}_k \in \mathbb{Z}_q^{k \times k}$ to denote the k-by-k identity matrix.

Discrete Gaussians. We write $D_{\mathbb{Z},\chi}$ to denote the (centered) discrete Gaussian distribution over $\mathbb{Z}$ with parameter $\chi \in \mathbb{R}^+$. For a matrix $\mathbf{A} \in \mathbb{Z}_q^{n \times t}$, and a vector $\mathbf{v} \in \mathbb{Z}_q^n$, we write $\mathbf{A}_\chi^{-1}(\mathbf{v})$ to denote a random variable $\mathbf{x} \leftarrow D_{\mathbb{Z},\chi}^m$ conditioned on $\mathbf{A}\mathbf{x} = \mathbf{v} \bmod q$. We extend $\mathbf{A}_s^{-1}$ to matrices by applying $\mathbf{A}_s^{-1}$ to each column of the input. Throughout this work, we will use the following standard tail bound on Gaussian distributions:

Fact 3.8 (Gaussian Tail Bound). Let λ be a security parameter and $s = s(\lambda)$ be a Gaussian width parameter. Then, for all polynomials $n = n(\lambda)$, there exists a negligible function $\mathsf{negl}(\lambda)$ such that for all $\lambda \in \mathbb{N}$,

$$\Pr\left[\|\mathbf{v}\| > \sqrt{\lambda}s : \mathbf{v} \leftarrow D_{\mathbb{Z},s}^n\right] = \mathsf{negl}(\lambda).$$

Assumption 3.9 (Learning with Errors [Reg05]). Let λ be a security parameter and let $n = n(\lambda)$, $m = m(\lambda)$, $q = q(\lambda)$, $\chi = \chi(\lambda)$ be integers. Then, the decisional learning with errors assumption $\mathsf{LWE}_{n,m,q,\chi}$ states that for $\mathbf{A} \xleftarrow{\text{R}} \mathbb{Z}_q^{n \times m}$, $\mathbf{s} \xleftarrow{\text{R}} \mathbb{Z}_q^n$, $\mathbf{e} \leftarrow D_{\mathbb{Z},\chi}^m$, and $\mathbf{u} \xleftarrow{\text{R}} \mathbb{Z}_q^m$,

$$(\mathbf{A}, \mathbf{s}^\mathsf{T}\mathbf{A} + \mathbf{e}^\mathsf{T}) \overset{c}{\approx} (\mathbf{A}, \mathbf{u}).$$

The Gadget Matrix. We recall the definition of the gadget matrix [MP12]. For positive integers $n, q \in \mathbb{N}$, let $\mathbf{G}_n = \mathbf{I}_n \otimes \mathbf{g}^\mathsf{T} \in \mathbb{Z}_q^{n \times m}$ be the gadget matrix where $\mathbf{g}^\mathsf{T} = [1, 2, \ldots, 2^{\log q - 1}]$ and $m = n \lceil \log q \rceil$. The inverse function $\mathbf{G}_n^{-1} \colon \mathbb{Z}_q^{n \times t} \to \mathbb{Z}_q^{m \times t}$ expands each entry $x \in \mathbb{Z}_q$ into a column of size $\lceil \log q \rceil$ consisting of the bits in the binary representation of x. By construction, for every matrix $\mathbf{A} \in \mathbb{Z}_q^{n \times t}$, it follows that $\mathbf{G}_n \cdot \mathbf{G}_n^{-1}(\mathbf{A}) = \mathbf{A} \bmod q$. When the lattice dimension n is clear, we will omit the subscript and simply write $\mathbf{G}$ and $\mathbf{G}^{-1}(\cdot)$ to denote $\mathbf{G}_n$ and $\mathbf{G}_n^{-1}(\cdot)$.

Lattice Trapdoors. In this work, we use the gadget trapdoors introduced by Micciancio and Peikert [MP12]. Our description below follows many of the notational conventions from [BTVW17].

Theorem 3.10 (Lattice   **Trapdoors** [Ajt96, GPV08, ABB10b, ABB10a, CHKP10, MP12]).** *Let n, m, q be lattice parameters. Then there exist efficient algorithms* (TrapGen, SamplePre) *with the following syntax:*

- TrapGen$(1^n, q, m) \to (\mathbf{A}, \mathsf{td}_\mathbf{A})$: *On input the lattice dimension n, the modulus q, the number of samples m, the trapdoor-generation algorithm outputs a matrix $\mathbf{A} \in \mathbb{Z}_q^{n \times m}$ together with a trapdoor $\mathsf{td}_\mathbf{A}$.*

- SamplePre$(\mathbf{A}, \mathrm{td}_{\mathbf{A}}, \mathbf{v}, s) \to \mathbf{u}$: *On input a matrix* $\mathbf{A}$, *a trapdoor* $\mathrm{td}_{\mathbf{A}}$, *a target vector* $\mathbf{v}$, *and a Gaussian width parameter* s, *the preimage-sampling algorithm outputs a vector* $\mathbf{u}$.

Moreover, there exists a polynomial $m_0 = m_0(n,q) = O(n \log q)$ *such that for all* $m \geq m_0$, *the above algorithms satisfy the following properties:*

- **Trapdoor distribution:** *The matrix* $\mathbf{A}$ *output by* TrapGen$(1^n, q, m)$ *is statistically close to uniform. Specifically, if* $(\mathbf{A}, \mathrm{td}_{\mathbf{A}}) \leftarrow$ TrapGen$(1^n, q, m)$ *and* $\mathbf{A}' \xleftarrow{R} \mathbb{Z}_q^{n \times m}$, *then* $\Delta(\mathbf{A}, \mathbf{A}') \leq 2^{-n}$.
- **Trapdoor quality:** *The trapdoor* $\mathrm{td}_{\mathbf{A}}$ *output by* TrapGen$(1^n, q, m)$ *is a* τ-*trapdoor where* $\tau = O(\sqrt{n \log q \log n})$. *We refer to the parameter* τ *as the quality of the trapdoor.*
- **Preimage sampling:** *Suppose* $\mathrm{td}_{\mathbf{A}}$ *is a* τ-*trapdoor for* $\mathbf{A}$. *Then, for all* $s \geq \tau \cdot \omega(\sqrt{\log n})$ *and all target vectors* $\mathbf{v} \in \mathbb{Z}_q^n$, *the statistical distance between the following distributions is at most* 2^{-n}:

$$\{\mathbf{u} \leftarrow \mathsf{SamplePre}(\mathbf{A}, \mathrm{td}_{\mathbf{A}}, \mathbf{v}, s)\} \quad \text{and} \quad \{\mathbf{u} \leftarrow \mathbf{A}_s^{-1}(\mathbf{v})\}.$$

Gadget Trapdoors. In this work, we will work with the gadget trapdoors introduced by Micciancio and Peikert [MP12]. We recall the key properties of gadget trapdoors from [MP12] and then state a direct corollary that we will use in this work (Corollary 3.12).

Theorem 3.11 (Gadget Trapdoors [MP12]). *The gadget matrix* $\mathbf{G} \in \mathbb{Z}_q^{n \times m}$ *has a public* τ-*trapdoor* $\mathrm{td}_{\mathbf{G}}$ *where* $\tau = O(1)$. *In addition, if* $\mathbf{AR} = \mathbf{HG}$ *where* $\mathbf{A} \in \mathbb{Z}_q^{n \times m'}$, $\mathbf{R} \in \mathbb{Z}_q^{m' \times m}$, $m = n \lceil \log q \rceil$, *and* $\mathbf{H} \in \mathbb{Z}_q^{n \times n}$ *is invertible, then* $\mathrm{td}_{\mathbf{A}} = (\mathbf{R}, \mathbf{H})$ *can be used as a* τ-*trapdoor (by extending* SamplePre *from Theorem 3.10 accordingly) for* $\mathbf{A}$ *where* $\tau = s_1(\mathbf{R})$ *and* $s_1(\mathbf{R}) \leq \sqrt{mm'}\|\mathbf{R}\|$ *denotes the largest singular value of* $\mathbf{R}$.

Corollary 3.12 (Gadget Trapdoors). *Let* $\mathbf{H} \in \mathbb{Z}_q^{k \times t}$ *be a full rank matrix where* $k \leq t$ (i.e., $\mathbf{H}$ *has full row rank). Suppose* $\mathbf{AR} = \mathbf{H} \otimes \mathbf{G}$. *Let* $\mathbf{A} \in \mathbb{Z}_q^{kn \times m'}$ *and* $\mathbf{R} \in \mathbb{Z}_q^{m' \times mt}$ *with* $m = n \lceil \log q \rceil$. *Then,* $\mathrm{td}_{\mathbf{A}} = (\mathbf{R}, \mathbf{H})$ *can be used as a* τ-*trapdoor for* $\mathbf{A}$ *where* $\tau \leq \sqrt{kmm'} \cdot mt\|\mathbf{R}\|$.

Proof We can write $\mathbf{H} \otimes \mathbf{G} = (\mathbf{H} \otimes \mathbf{I}_n)(\mathbf{I}_t \otimes \mathbf{G}) = (\mathbf{H} \otimes \mathbf{I}_n)\mathbf{G}_{nt}$. Since $\mathbf{H}$ is full rank (with $k \leq t$), there exists a matrix $\mathbf{H}^* \in \mathbb{Z}_q^{t \times k}$ such that $\mathbf{HH}^* = \mathbf{I}_k$. Correspondingly, $(\mathbf{H} \otimes \mathbf{I}_n)(\mathbf{H}^* \otimes \mathbf{I}_n) = \mathbf{I}_{kn}$. Let $\bar{\mathbf{R}} = \mathbf{R}\mathbf{G}_{nt}^{-1}((\mathbf{H}^* \otimes \mathbf{I}_n)\mathbf{G}_{kn}) \in \mathbb{Z}_q^{m' \times km}$. Now, we can write

$$\mathbf{A}\bar{\mathbf{R}} = \mathbf{AR}\mathbf{G}_{nt}^{-1}((\mathbf{H}^* \otimes \mathbf{I}_n)\mathbf{G}_{kn}) = (\mathbf{H} \otimes \mathbf{I}_n)\mathbf{G}_{nt}\mathbf{G}_{nt}^{-1}((\mathbf{H}^* \otimes \mathbf{I}_n)\mathbf{G}_{kn}) = \mathbf{G}_{kn},$$

and so $\bar{\mathbf{R}}$ is a trapdoor for $\mathbf{A}$ (Theorem 3.11). Moreover, $\|\bar{\mathbf{R}}\| \leq mt\|\mathbf{R}\|$, and the claim follows.

Preimage Sampling. We will also use the following property of discrete Gaussian distributions which follows from [GPV08]:

Lemma 3.13 (Preimage Sampling [GPV08, adapted]). *Let n, m, q be lattice parameters. There exists polynomials $m_0(n, q) = O(n \log q)$ and $\chi_0(n, q) = \sqrt{n \log q} \cdot \omega(\sqrt{\log n})$ such that for all $m \geq m_0(n, q)$ and $\chi \geq \chi_0(n, q)$, the statistical distance between the following distributions is $\mathsf{negl}(n)$:*

$$\{(\mathbf{A}, \mathbf{x}, \mathbf{A}\mathbf{x}) : \mathbf{A} \xleftarrow{\mathrm{R}} \mathbb{Z}_q^{n \times m}, \mathbf{x} \leftarrow D_{\mathbb{Z}, \chi}^m\} \text{ and } \{(\mathbf{A}, \mathbf{x}, \mathbf{y}) : \mathbf{A} \xleftarrow{\mathrm{R}} \mathbb{Z}_q^{n \times m}, \mathbf{y} \xleftarrow{\mathrm{R}} \mathbb{Z}_q^n, \mathbf{x} \leftarrow \mathbf{A}_\chi^{-1}(\mathbf{y})\}.$$

Lemma 3.14 (Leftover Hash Lemma [ABB10a]). *Let n, m, q be lattice parameters where $q > 2$ is prime. There exists a polynomial $m_0(n, q) = O(n \log q)$ such that for all $m \geq m_0(n, q)$, all vectors $\mathbf{e} \in \mathbb{Z}_q^m$, and all polynomials $k = k(n)$, the statistical distance between the following distributions is $\mathsf{negl}(n)$:*

$$\{(\mathbf{A}, \mathbf{A}\mathbf{R}, \mathbf{e}^\mathsf{T}\mathbf{R}) : \mathbf{A} \xleftarrow{\mathrm{R}} \mathbb{Z}_q^{n \times m}, \mathbf{R} \xleftarrow{\mathrm{R}} \{-1, 1\}^{m \times k}\}$$

$$and$$

$$\{(\mathbf{A}, \mathbf{B}, \mathbf{e}^\mathsf{T}\mathbf{R}) : \mathbf{A} \xleftarrow{\mathrm{R}} \mathbb{Z}_q^{n \times m}, \mathbf{B} \xleftarrow{\mathrm{R}} \mathbb{Z}_q^{n \times k}, \mathbf{R} \xleftarrow{\mathrm{R}} \{-1, 1\}^{m \times k}\}. \quad (3.1)$$

Smudging Lemma. We will also use the following standard smudging lemma (see [BDE+18] for a proof):

Lemma 3.15 (Smudging Lemma). *Let λ be a security parameter. Take any $e \in \mathbb{Z}$ where $|e| \leq B$. Suppose $\chi \geq B \cdot \lambda^{\omega(1)}$. Then, the statistical distance between the distributions $\{z : z \leftarrow D_{\mathbb{Z}, \chi}\}$ and $\{z + e : z \leftarrow D_{\mathbb{Z}, \chi}\}$ is $\mathsf{negl}(\lambda)$.*

The Evasive LWE Assumption. We now state a variant of the evasive LWE assumption introduced by Wee [Wee22] and Tsabury [Tsa22]. We compare our formulation with the original version by Wee in Remark 3.18.

Assumption 3.16 (Evasive LWE). Let λ be a security parameter, and let $n = n(\lambda), m = m(\lambda), q = q(\lambda), \chi = \chi(\lambda), s = s(\lambda)$ with $s \geq O(\sqrt{m \log q})$. Let Samp be an algorithm that takes the security parameter 1^λ as input and outputs a matrix $\mathbf{B} \in \mathbb{Z}_q^{n\ell \times m'}$, a set of ℓ target matrices $\mathbf{P}_1 \in \mathbb{Z}_q^{n \times N_1}, \ldots, \mathbf{P}_\ell \in \mathbb{Z}_q^{n \times N_\ell}$, and auxiliary information $\mathsf{aux} \in \{0, 1\}^*$. Then, for adversaries $\mathcal{A}_0$ and $\mathcal{A}_1$, we define advantage functions

$$\mathsf{Adv}_{\mathcal{A}_0}^{(\mathrm{PRE})}(\lambda) := |\Pr[\mathcal{A}_0(\{(\mathbf{A}_i, \mathbf{s}_i^\mathsf{T}\mathbf{A}_i + \mathbf{e}_{1,i}^\mathsf{T})\}_{i \in [\ell]}, \mathbf{B}, \mathbf{s}^\mathsf{T}\mathbf{B} + \mathbf{e}_2^\mathsf{T}, \{\mathbf{s}_i^\mathsf{T}\mathbf{P}_i + \mathbf{e}_{3,i}^\mathsf{T}\}_{i \in [\ell]}, \mathsf{aux}) = 1]$$
$$- \Pr[\mathcal{A}_0(\{(\mathbf{A}_i, \mathbf{u}_{1,i}^\mathsf{T})\}_{i \in [\ell]}, \mathbf{B}, \mathbf{u}_2^\mathsf{T}, \{\mathbf{u}_{3,i}^\mathsf{T}\}_{i \in [\ell]}, \mathsf{aux}) = 1]|$$

$$\mathsf{Adv}_{\mathcal{A}_1}^{(\mathrm{POST})}(\lambda) := |\Pr[\mathcal{A}_1(\{(\mathbf{A}_i, \mathbf{s}_i^\mathsf{T}\mathbf{A}_i + \mathbf{e}_{1,i}^\mathsf{T})\}_{i \in [\ell]}, \mathbf{B}, \mathbf{s}^\mathsf{T}\mathbf{B} + \mathbf{e}_2^\mathsf{T}, \{\mathbf{K}_i\}_{i \in [\ell]}, \mathsf{aux}) = 1]$$
$$- \Pr[\mathcal{A}_1(\{(\mathbf{A}_i, \mathbf{u}_{1,i}^\mathsf{T})\}_{i \in [\ell]}, \mathbf{B}, \mathbf{u}_2^\mathsf{T}, \{\mathbf{K}_i\}_{i \in [\ell]}, \mathsf{aux}) = 1]|,$$

where

$$(\mathbf{B}, \mathbf{P}_1, \ldots, \mathbf{P}_\ell, \mathsf{aux}) \leftarrow \mathsf{Samp}(1^\lambda),$$
$$\mathbf{A}_1, \ldots, \mathbf{A}_\ell \xleftarrow{\mathrm{R}} \mathbb{Z}_q^{n \times m},$$
$$\mathbf{s}_1, \ldots, \mathbf{s}_\ell \xleftarrow{\mathrm{R}} \mathbb{Z}_q^n, \mathbf{s}^\mathsf{T} \leftarrow [\mathbf{s}_1^\mathsf{T} \mid \cdots \mid \mathbf{s}_\ell^\mathsf{T}] \in \mathbb{Z}_q^{n\ell},$$
$$\mathbf{u}_{1,i} \xleftarrow{\mathrm{R}} \mathbb{Z}_q^m, \mathbf{e}_{1,i} \leftarrow D_{\mathbb{Z}, \chi}^m \; \forall i \in [\ell],$$
$$\mathbf{u}_2 \xleftarrow{\mathrm{R}} \mathbb{Z}_q^{m'}, \mathbf{e}_2 \leftarrow D_{\mathbb{Z}, \chi}^{m'},$$
$$\mathbf{u}_{3,i} \xleftarrow{\mathrm{R}} \mathbb{Z}_q^{N_i}, \mathbf{e}_{3,i} \leftarrow D_{\mathbb{Z}, \chi}^{N_i} \; \forall i \in [\ell],$$
$$\mathbf{K}_i \leftarrow (\mathbf{A}_i)_s^{-1}(\mathbf{P}_i) \; \forall i \in [\ell].$$

We say that the evasive LWE assumption holds if for every efficient sampler Samp and every efficient adversary $\mathcal{A}_1$, there exists an efficient algorithm $\mathcal{A}_0$, polynomial $\mathsf{poly}(\cdot)$, and negligible function $\mathsf{negl}(\cdot)$ such that for all $\lambda \in \mathbb{N}$,

$$\mathsf{Adv}_{\mathcal{A}_0}^{(\mathrm{PRE})}(\lambda) \geq \mathsf{Adv}_{\mathcal{A}_1}^{(\mathrm{POST})}(\lambda)/\mathsf{poly}(\lambda) - \mathsf{negl}(\lambda).$$

Remark 3.17 (Auxiliary Input Distribution). As in [Wee22], we only require that the assumption holds for samplers where aux additionally contains all of the coin tosses used by Samp (i.e., *public-coin* samplers). This avoids obfuscation-based counter-examples where aux contains an obfuscation of a program related to a trapdoor for matrix $\mathbf{B}$ or $\mathbf{P}_i$. This is a *weaker* assumption compared to the evasive LWE assumptions needed to realize witness encryption (which rely on security of evasive LWE to hold for private-coin samplers) [Tsa22, VWW22].

Remark 3.18 (Comparison with [Wee22]). The original formulation of the evasive LWE assumption by Wee [Wee22] corresponds to the special case where $\ell = 1$ (i.e., there is just a single matrix $\mathbf{A}_1$ and single target $\mathbf{P}_1$). When constructing multi-authority ABE, we rely on multiple *independent* matrices $\mathbf{A}_1, \ldots, \mathbf{A}_\ell$ (one associated with each authority). It is an interesting question to reduce Definition 3.16 to the simpler setting of $\ell = 1$. We note that the justification given in [Wee22] for evasive LWE are equally applicable to this setting.

4   Generalized Related-Trapdoor LWE Assumption

In this section, we introduce a generalized variant of the related-trapdoor robust LWE assumption of Brakerski and Vaikuntanathan [BV22] and then show that its hardness can be based on the standard LWE assumption (Theorem 4.2). As described in Sect. 2, the generalized related-trapdoor LWE assumption essentially asserts that given a vector $\mathbf{u} \in \{0,1\}^L$, an LWE sample with respect to $(\mathbf{u} \otimes \mathbf{I}_n)\mathbf{B}$ is pseudorandom (where $\mathbf{B} \in \mathbb{Z}_q^{n \times mL}$) given an oracle that takes as input $(\mathbf{M}, \mathbf{t})$ and outputs $(\mathbf{M} \otimes \mathbf{I}_n)\mathbf{B})^{-1}(\mathbf{t})$ whenever $\bar{\mathbf{M}} = \left[\begin{smallmatrix} \mathbf{M} \\ \mathbf{u}^\mathsf{T} \end{smallmatrix}\right] \in \mathbb{Z}_q^{(k+1) \times L}$ is full rank. The original formulation of the related trapdoor assumption in [BV22] (for the setting of *single-authority* ciphertext-policy ABE) considered the special case where the matrix $\mathbf{M} \in \mathbb{Z}_q^{1 \times L}$ is a row vector. Here, we consider the case where $\mathbf{M}$ can be an arbitrary matrix. This generalization will be useful for distributing the setup in an ABE scheme to obtain a multi-authority ABE (see Sect. 5).

A similar approach is also implicit in the ciphertext-policy ABE scheme by Datta et al. [DKW21a]. Their approach relied on noise smudging to simulate the preimage-sampling oracle, and as such, security relied on a super-polynomial modulus. In this work, we abstract out the core technique through the related-trapdoor LWE assumption and then show a direct reduction to LWE without relying on noise smudging. This allows us to base security on LWE with a *polynomial* modulus.

Assumption 4.1 (Generalized Related-Trapdoor LWE). Let $\lambda \in \mathbb{N}$ be a security parameter, and $n = n(\lambda)$, $m = m(\lambda)$, $\hat{m} = \hat{m}(\lambda)$, and $\chi = \chi(\lambda)$ be lattice parameters. Let $q = q(\lambda)$ be a prime modulus. Let $L = L(\lambda)$ be a length parameter. For a bit $b \in \{0,1\}$, we define the related-trapdoor LWE game between a challenger and an adversary $\mathcal{A}$:

1. The adversary $\mathcal{A}$ starts by choosing a non-zero vector $\mathbf{u} \in \{0,1\}^L$.
2. The challenger samples matrices $\mathbf{A} \xleftarrow{\text{R}} \mathbb{Z}_q^{n \times m}$ and $\mathbf{B} \xleftarrow{\text{R}} \mathbb{Z}_q^{nL \times \hat{m}(2L-1)}$ and constructs the challenge as follows:
   - If $b = 0$, the challenger samples $\mathbf{s} \xleftarrow{\text{R}} \mathbb{Z}_q^n$, $\mathbf{R} \xleftarrow{\text{R}} \{-1,1\}^{\hat{m}L \times \hat{m}(L-1)}$, $\mathbf{e} \leftarrow D_{\mathbb{Z},\chi}^m$, $\hat{\mathbf{e}}_0 \leftarrow D_{\mathbb{Z},\chi}^{\hat{m}L}$, $\hat{\mathbf{e}}^\mathsf{T} \leftarrow \hat{\mathbf{e}}_0^\mathsf{T}[\mathbf{I}_{\hat{m}L} \mid \mathbf{R}] \in \mathbb{Z}_q^{\hat{m}(2L-1)}$, and gives $\big(\mathbf{A},\, \mathbf{B},\, \mathbf{s}^\mathsf{T}\mathbf{A} + \mathbf{e}^\mathsf{T},\, \mathbf{s}^\mathsf{T}(\mathbf{u}^\mathsf{T} \otimes \mathbf{I}_n)\mathbf{B} + \hat{\mathbf{e}}^\mathsf{T}\big)$ to $\mathcal{A}$.
   - If $b = 1$, the challenger samples $\mathbf{v} \xleftarrow{\text{R}} \mathbb{Z}_q^m$, $\hat{\mathbf{v}} \xleftarrow{\text{R}} \mathbb{Z}_q^{\hat{m}(2L-1)}$ and gives $(\mathbf{A}, \mathbf{B}, \mathbf{v}^\mathsf{T}, \hat{\mathbf{v}}^\mathsf{T})$ to $\mathcal{A}$.
3. Adversary $\mathcal{A}$ can now make queries of the form $(\mathbf{M}, \mathbf{t})$ where $\mathbf{M} \in \mathbb{Z}_q^{k \times L}$ where $k < L$ and $\mathbf{t} \in \mathbb{Z}_q^{kn}$.
   - Define the matrix $\bar{\mathbf{M}} = \begin{bmatrix} \mathbf{M} \\ \mathbf{u}^\mathsf{T} \end{bmatrix}$. If $\bar{\mathbf{M}}$ is not full rank (over $\mathbb{Z}_q$), the challenger replies with $\perp$.
   - If $\mathbf{t}$ is not in the column span of $(\mathbf{M} \otimes \mathbf{I}_n)\mathbf{B}$, then the challenger also replies with $\perp$.
   - Otherwise, it samples and replies with $\mathbf{y} \leftarrow ((\mathbf{M} \otimes \mathbf{I}_n)\mathbf{B})_\chi^{-1}(\mathbf{t})$. Namely, $\mathbf{y} \in \mathbb{Z}_q^{m(2L-1)}$ is sampled from the distribution $D_{\mathbb{Z},\chi}^{m(2L-1)}$ conditioned on $(\mathbf{M} \otimes \mathbf{I}_n)\mathbf{B}\mathbf{y} = \mathbf{t}$.
4. At the end of the game, algorithm $\mathcal{A}$ outputs a bit $b' \in \{0,1\}$, which is also the output of the experiment.

We say that the $\mathsf{RTLWE}_{n,m,\hat{m},q,\chi,L}$ assumption holds if for all efficient adversaries $\mathcal{A}$, there exists a negligible function $\mathsf{negl}(\cdot)$ such that for all $\lambda \in \mathbb{N}$, $|\Pr[b' = 1 \mid b = 0] - \Pr[b' = 1 \mid b = 1]| = \mathsf{negl}(\lambda)$ in the above security game.

The generalized related-trapdoor LWE assumption reduces to the vanilla LWE assumption. We state the formal theorem below and refer to the full version of this paper [WWW22] for a proof.

Theorem 4.2 (Generalized Related-Trapdoor LWE). *Let λ be a security parameter, and let $n = n(\lambda)$, $q = q(\lambda)$, $m = m(\lambda)$, $\hat{m} = \hat{m}(\lambda)$, and $\chi = \chi(\lambda)$ be lattice parameters. Suppose that $q > 2$ is a prime and $\chi > 2\hat{m}^2 L^2 \cdot \omega(\sqrt{\log n})$. Then, there exists a fixed polynomial $m_0(n, q) = O(n \log q)$ such that for all $\hat{m} > m_0(n, q)$ and under the $\mathsf{LWE}_{n,m+\hat{m}L,q,\chi}$ assumption, the $\mathsf{RTLWE}_{n,m,\hat{m},q,\chi,L}$ assumption holds.*

5 Multi-Authority ABE from LWE in the Random Oracle Model

In this section, we describe our construction of multi-authority ABE for the family of subset policies in the random oracle model. Our construction follows a similar structure as the multi-authority ABE scheme of Datta et al. [DKW21a] except we provide a direct reduction to the (generalized) related trapdoor LWE problem (Sect. 4). Notably, this allows us to base security on polynomial hardness of the plain LWE assumption with a *polynomial* modulus. The previous construction of Datta et al. relied on LWE with a *super-polynomial* modulus-to-noise ratio.

Construction 5.1 (Multi-Authority ABE in the Random Oracle Model). Let λ be a security parameter, and $n = n(\lambda)$, $m = m(\lambda)$, $q = q(\lambda)$, and $\chi = \chi(\lambda)$ be lattice parameters. Let $L = L(\lambda)$ be a bound on the number of attributes associated with a ciphertext. Let $\mathcal{GID} = \{0,1\}^\lambda$ be the set of user identifiers and $\mathcal{AU} = \{0,1\}^\lambda$ be the set of authority identifiers. The construction will rely on a hash function $\mathsf{H} \colon \mathcal{GID} \to \mathbb{Z}_q^{m(2L-1)}$, which will be modeled as a random oracle as follows:

– For ease of exposition in the following description, we will start by assuming that the outputs of the random oracle H are distributed according to a *discrete Gaussian distribution*. Specifically, on every input $\mathsf{gid} \in \mathcal{GID}$, the output $\mathsf{H}(\mathsf{gid})$ is a sample from the distribution $D_{\mathbb{Z},\chi}^{m(2L-1)}$. In Sect. 5.1 and Remark 5.7, we show that using inversion sampling, we can implement H using a *standard* random oracle $\mathsf{H}' \colon \mathcal{GID} \to \{0,1\}^{\lambda m(2L-1)}$, where the outputs of $\mathsf{H}'(\mathsf{gid})$ are distributed uniformly over $\{0,1\}^{\lambda m(2L-1)}$ as usual.

We construct a multi-authority ABE scheme for subset policies with message space $\mathcal{M} = \{0,1\}$ as follows:

– GlobalSetup(1^λ): Output the global parameters $\mathsf{gp} = (\lambda, n, m, q, \chi, L, \mathsf{H})$.
– AuthSetup($\mathsf{gp}, \mathsf{aid}$): On input the global parameters gp and an authority identifier $\mathsf{aid} \in \mathcal{AU}$, sample $(\mathbf{A}_\mathsf{aid}, \mathsf{td}_\mathsf{aid}) \leftarrow \mathsf{TrapGen}(1^n, q, m)$, $\mathbf{p}_\mathsf{aid} \xleftarrow{\text{R}} \mathbb{Z}_q^n$, and $\mathbf{B}_\mathsf{aid} \xleftarrow{\text{R}} \mathbb{Z}_q^{n \times m(2L-1)}$. Output the authority public key $\mathsf{pk}_\mathsf{aid} \leftarrow (\mathbf{A}_\mathsf{aid}, \mathbf{B}_\mathsf{aid}, \mathbf{p}_\mathsf{aid})$ and the authority secret key $\mathsf{msk}_\mathsf{aid} = \mathsf{td}_\mathsf{aid}$.
– KeyGen($\mathsf{gp}, \mathsf{msk}, \mathsf{pk}, \mathsf{gid}$): On input the global parameters $\mathsf{gp} = (\lambda, n, m, q, \chi, L, \mathsf{H})$, the master secret key $\mathsf{msk} = \mathsf{td}$, the public key $\mathsf{pk} = (\mathbf{A}, \mathbf{B}, \mathbf{p})$, and the user identifier gid, the key-generation algorithm computes $\mathbf{r} \leftarrow \mathsf{H}(\mathsf{gid}) \in \mathbb{Z}_q^{m(2L-1)}$ and uses td to sample $\mathbf{u} \leftarrow \mathbf{A}_\chi^{-1}(\mathbf{p} + \mathbf{Br})$. It outputs $\mathsf{sk}_{\mathsf{aid},\mathsf{gid}} = \mathbf{u}$.
– Encrypt($\mathsf{gp}, \{\mathsf{pk}_\mathsf{aid}\}_{\mathsf{aid} \in A}, \mu$): On input the global parameters $\mathsf{gp} = (\lambda, n, m, q, \chi, L, \mathsf{H})$, a set of of public keys $\mathsf{pk}_\mathsf{aid} = (\mathbf{A}_\mathsf{aid}, \mathbf{B}_\mathsf{aid}, \mathbf{p}_\mathsf{aid})$ associated with a set of authorities A, and the message $\mu \in \{0,1\}$, the encryption algorithm samples $\mathbf{s}_\mathsf{aid} \xleftarrow{\text{R}} \mathbb{Z}_q^n$, $\mathbf{e}_{1,\mathsf{aid}} \leftarrow D_{\mathbb{Z},\chi}^m$, $\mathbf{R} \xleftarrow{\text{R}} \{0,1\}^{mL \times m(L-1)}$, $\hat{\mathbf{e}}_2 \leftarrow D_{\mathbb{Z},\chi}^{mL}$, and $\mathbf{e}_2^\mathsf{T} \leftarrow \hat{\mathbf{e}}_2^\mathsf{T}[\mathbf{I}_{mL} \mid \mathbf{R}]$, and $e_3 \leftarrow D_{\mathbb{Z},\chi}$ for each $\mathsf{aid} \in A$. It outputs the ciphertext

$$\mathsf{ct} = \left(\left\{ \mathbf{s}_\mathsf{aid}^\mathsf{T} \mathbf{A}_\mathsf{aid} + \mathbf{e}_{1,\mathsf{aid}}^\mathsf{T} \right\}_{\mathsf{aid} \in A} , \ \sum_{\mathsf{aid} \in A} \mathbf{s}_\mathsf{aid}^\mathsf{T} \mathbf{B}_\mathsf{aid} + \mathbf{e}_2^\mathsf{T} , \ \sum_{\mathsf{aid} \in A} \mathbf{s}_\mathsf{aid}^\mathsf{T} \mathbf{p}_\mathsf{aid} + e_3 + \mu \cdot \lfloor q/2 \rceil \right).$$

– Decrypt($\mathsf{gp}, \{\mathsf{sk}_{\mathsf{aid},\mathsf{gid}}\}_{\mathsf{aid} \in A}, \mathsf{ct}, \mathsf{gid}$): On input the global parameters $\mathsf{gp} = (\lambda, n, m, q, \chi, L, \mathsf{H})$, a set of secret keys $\mathsf{sk}_{\mathsf{aid},\mathsf{gid}} = \mathbf{u}_{\mathsf{aid},\mathsf{gid}}$ associated with authorities $\mathsf{aid} \in A$ and user identifier gid, and a ciphertext $\mathsf{ct} = (\{\mathbf{c}_{1,\mathsf{aid}}^\top\}_{\mathsf{aid} \in A}, \mathbf{c}_2^\top, c_3)$, the decryption algorithm computes $\mathbf{r} \leftarrow \mathsf{H}(\mathsf{gid})$ and outputs

$$\left\lfloor \frac{2}{q} \cdot \left(c_3 + \mathbf{c}_2^\top \mathbf{r} - \sum_{\mathsf{aid} \in A} \mathbf{c}_{1,\mathsf{aid}}^\top \mathbf{u}_{\mathsf{aid},\mathsf{gid}} \bmod q \right) \right\rceil .$$

We now state the correctness and security theorems for Construction 5.1, but defer their formal proofs to the full version of this paper [WWW22].

Theorem 5.2 (Correctness). *Suppose the conditions of Theorem 3.10 and Lemma 3.13 hold (i.e., $m \geq m_0(n, q) = O(n \log q)$ and $\chi > \chi_0(n, q) = \sqrt{n \log q} \cdot \omega(\sqrt{\log n})$). Then, there exists a polynomial $q_0 = O(\lambda \chi^2 m^2 L^2)$ such that for all $q > q_0$, Construction 5.1 is correct.*

Theorem 5.3 (Static Security). *Suppose the conditions of Theorem 3.10 and Lemma 3.13 hold (i.e., $m \geq m_0(n, q) = O(n \log q)$ and $\chi > \chi_0(n, q) = \sqrt{n \log q} \cdot \omega(\sqrt{\log n})$). Then, under the $\mathsf{RTLWE}_{n, Lm+1, m, q, \chi, L}$ assumption and modeling $\mathsf{H} \colon \mathcal{GID} \to \mathbb{Z}_q^{m(2L-1)}$ as a random oracle (with outputs distributed according to $D_{\mathbb{Z},\chi}^{m(2L-1)}$), Construction 5.1 is statically secure.*

Parameter Setting. Let λ be a security parameter. We can now instantiate Construction 5.1 as follows:

- We set the lattice dimension $n = \lambda$.
- To rely on Theorem 5.3, we rely on the $\mathsf{RTLWE}_{n, Lm+1, m, q, \chi, L}$ assumption. By Theorem 4.2, this reduces to $\mathsf{LWE}_{n, 2Lm+1, q, \chi}$ if we set $m = O(n \log q)$, $q > 2$ to a prime, and $\chi = O(m^2 L^2 \log n)$.
- For correctness (Theorem 5.2), we additionally require $q = O(\lambda \chi^2 m^2 L^2)$.

In particular, this means we can choose m, q, χ to be polynomials in λ, and thus, base hardness on LWE with a *polynomial* modulus-to-noise ratio. We summarize the instantiation below:

Corollary 5.4 (Multi-Authority ABE for Subset Policies in the Random Oracle Model). *Let λ be a security parameter. Assuming polynomial hardness of LWE with a polynomial modulus-to-noise ratio, there exists a statically-secure multi-authority ABE scheme for subset policies of a priori bounded length $L = L(\lambda)$ in the random oracle model. The size of the ciphertext scales quasi-linearly with the bound L.*

5.1   Instantiating Using a Random Oracle with Uniform Outputs

As described, Construction 5.1 and Corollary 5.4 relies on a random oracle $\mathsf{H} \colon \mathcal{GID} \to \mathbb{Z}_q^{m(2L-1)}$ whose output distribution is the discrete Gaussian distribution $D_{\mathbb{Z},\chi}^{m(2L-1)}$. Since $\chi = \mathsf{poly}(\lambda)$ in our setting, we describe a simple way to instantiate H using a random oracle $\mathsf{H}' \colon \mathcal{GID} \to \{0,1\}^{\lambda m(2L-1)}$ whose output distribution is the uniform distribution via inversion sampling. The function

H' coincides with the usual way we model the output distribution of a random oracle [BR93].

Previously, Brakerski et al. [BCTW16] sketched an alternative approach for instantiating a random oracle outputting samples from a discrete Gaussian distribution by adapting the rejection sampler of Lyubashevsky and Wichs [LW15]. Datta et al. [DKW21a] rely on noise smudging in their setting (which would in turn necessitate using a super-polynomial modulus-to-noise ratio). In our setting where we have a distribution with polynomial-size support, we describe a simple alternative based on inversion sampling. This is a simple approach used in concrete implementations of lattice-based cryptography [BCD+16].

Lemma 5.5 (Inversion Sampling). *Let λ be a security parameter, $t = t(\lambda)$ be an input length, and D be a discrete B-bounded distribution with an efficiently-computable cumulative distribution function. Then, there exists a pair of efficient algorithms* (Project, SampleR) *with the following properties:*

- Project$(x) \to y$: *On input an input $x \in \{0,1\}^t$, the projection algorithm outputs a sample $y \in [-B, B]$. The projection algorithm is* deterministic.
- SampleR$(y) \to x$: *On input a value $y \in [-B, B]$, the reverse sampling algorithm outputs an $x \in \{0,1\}^t$.*

In addition, the following properties hold:

- **Correctness:** *For all $y \in [-B, B]$, $\Pr[\mathsf{Project}(\mathsf{SampleR}(y)) = y] = 1$.*
- **Reverse-sampleability:** *For all $t > \log B + \omega(\log \lambda)$, the following two distributions are statistically indistinguishable:*

$$\{(x, \mathsf{Project}(x)) : x \xleftarrow{R} (\{0,1\}^t)\} \quad and \quad \{(\mathsf{SampleR}(y), y) : y \leftarrow D\}.$$

Proof. We take (Project, SampleR) to be the standard inversion sampling algorithm. Let $f \colon [-B-1, B] \to [0,1]$ be the cumulative distribution function for D, and let $T = 2^t - 1$. We construct the two algorithms as follows:

- Project(x): On input $x \in \{0,1\}^t$, let $X \in [0, T]$ be the integer whose binary representation is x. Output $y \in [-B, B]$ where $T \cdot f(y-1) < X \leq T \cdot f(y)$.
- SampleR(y): On input $y \in [-B, B]$, let $x_0 \leftarrow T \cdot f(y-1)$ and $x_1 \leftarrow T \cdot f(y)$. Output the binary representation of the element $x \xleftarrow{R} (x_0, x_1] \cap \mathbb{Z}$.

Since the cumulative distribution function f is efficiently-computable and the Project algorithm can be computed with $\mathsf{polylog}(B)$ calls to f (e.g., using binary search), the Project algorithm is efficiently-computable. The SampleR algorithm only requires making two calls to f and is likewise efficient. Next, correctness of the algorithm follows by construction. Finally, for the reverse-sampleability property, take any $Y \in [-B, B]$. Then,

$$\Pr[\mathsf{Project}(x) = Y : x \xleftarrow{R} \{0,1\}^t] = \frac{\lfloor T \cdot f(Y) \rfloor - \lceil T \cdot f(Y-1) \rceil}{T} = f(Y) - f(Y-1) + e$$

$$= \Pr[y = Y : y \leftarrow D] + e$$

where $|e| \leq 2/T$. Thus, the statistical distance between $\{\mathsf{Project}(x) : x \xleftarrow{R} \{0,1\}^t\}$ and D is at most $2(2B+1)/T = \mathsf{negl}(\lambda)$. Finally, on input $y \in [-B, B]$, SampleR(y) outputs a uniform $x \xleftarrow{R} \{0,1\}^t$ conditioned on Project$(x) = y$.

Remark 5.6 (Extending to Product Distributions). We can extend (Project, SampleR) to sample from a product distribution D^n in the natural way. The projection algorithm takes as input a vector of bit-strings $\mathbf{x} \in (\{0,1\}^t)^n$ and applies the projection operator component-wise. The reverse sampling algorithm is defined analogously. Correctness and reverse-sampleability then follow via a standard hybrid argument.

Remark 5.7 (Implementing the Random Oracle in Corollary 5.4). We can now implement the random oracle $\mathsf{H} \colon \mathcal{GID} \to \mathbb{Z}_q^{m(2L-1)}$ in Corollary 5.4 (whose outputs are distributed according to $D_{\mathbb{Z},\chi}^{m(2L-1)}$) with a random oracle $\mathsf{H}' \colon \mathcal{GID} \to \{0,1\}^{\lambda m(2L-1)}$ whose outputs are uniform as follows:

- Let $\tilde{D}_{\mathbb{Z},\chi}$ be the discrete Gaussian distribution $D_{\mathbb{Z},\chi}$ truncated to the interval $[-\sqrt{\lambda}\chi, \sqrt{\lambda}\chi]$. Namely, to sample $\tilde{x} \leftarrow \tilde{D}_{\mathbb{Z},\chi}$, we first sample $x \leftarrow D_{\mathbb{Z},\chi}$ and output x if $x \in [-\sqrt{\lambda}\chi, \sqrt{\lambda}\chi]$ and output 0 otherwise. By Fact 3.8, $\tilde{D}_{\mathbb{Z},\chi}$ is statistically indistinguishable from $D_{\mathbb{Z},\chi}$. In addition, $\tilde{D}_{\mathbb{Z},\chi}$ is B-bounded for $B = \sqrt{\lambda}\chi$.
- Let (Project, SampleR) be the inversion sampling algorithm from Lemma 5.5 and Remark 5.6 for the product distribution $\tilde{D}_{\mathbb{Z},\chi}^{m(2L-1)}$. We now define

$$\mathsf{H}(\mathsf{gid}) := \mathsf{Project}(\mathsf{H}'(\mathsf{gid})).$$

Since $\chi = \chi(\lambda)$ is polynomially-bounded, the cumulative distribution function of $\tilde{D}_{\mathbb{Z},\chi}$ is efficiently-computable. Then, by Lemma 5.5 and Remark 5.6, for all polynomial-size collections of distinct inputs $\mathsf{gid}_1, \ldots, \mathsf{gid}_\ell \in \mathcal{GID}$, the joint distributions of

$$\{\mathsf{H}(\mathsf{gid}_i)\}_{i \in [\ell]} \quad \text{and} \quad \left\{\mathbf{r}_i \leftarrow D_{\mathbb{Z},\chi}^{m(2L-1)}\right\}_{i \in [\ell]}$$

are statistically indistinguishable.
- Finally, the proof of Theorem 5.3 critically relies on the ability to *program* the outputs of the random oracle in the reduction. Here, we rely on the SampleR algorithm. Namely, to program $\mathsf{H}(\mathsf{gid})$ to a vector $\mathbf{r}_{\mathsf{gid}} \leftarrow D_{\mathbb{Z},\chi}^{m(2L-1)}$, the reduction algorithm would sample $x_{\mathsf{gid}} \leftarrow \mathsf{SampleR}(\mathbf{r}_{\mathsf{gid}})$ and program $\mathsf{H}'(\mathsf{gid})$ to x_{gid}. This induces the correct distribution by Lemma 5.5 and Remark 5.6.

6 Multi-authority ABE Without Random Oracles

We now give our construction of a multi-authority ABE scheme without random oracles. Specifically, we instantiate the hash function from Construction 5.1 with a subset-product construction (i.e., the lattice-based PRF from Theorem 6.1) and then prove security under the evasive LWE assumption (Assumption 3.16) and lattice-based PRFs [BPR12, BLMR13].

Lattice-Based PRFs. Our analysis will rely on an *unrounded* lattice-based PRF. We state the theorem and provide a proof sketch below, and refer readers to [BPR12, Theorem 5.2] for a more formal exposition. Our presentation here is adapted from the work of Chen et al. [CVW18, Lemma 7.4] who use a similar theorem for analyzing the security of their private constrained PRF construction. We state the theorem here and refer to [BPR12, BLMR13, CVW18] for the proof.

Theorem 6.1 (Lattice-Based PRFs [BPR12, BLMR13]). *Let λ be a security parameter and let $n = n(\lambda)$, $q = q(\lambda)$, $\chi = \chi(\lambda)$, $k = k(\lambda)$ be integers. Let $\chi_{\mathsf{smudge}} = \chi_{\mathsf{smudge}}(\lambda)$ be a noise parameter that will used for noise smudging. Let $\boldsymbol{\eta} \in \mathbb{Z}_q^k$ be the first elementary basis vector (i.e., $\eta_1 = 1$ and $\eta_i = 0$ for all $i \neq 1$). For a bit $b \in \{0, 1\}$, an input length $\tau = \tau(\lambda)$, and an adversary $\mathcal{A}$, define the following pseudorandomness game between a challenger and $\mathcal{A}$:*

1. *The challenger begins by sampling $(\mathbf{D}_0, \mathbf{D}_1) \xleftarrow{\text{R}} D_{\mathbb{Z}, \chi}^{k \times k}$ and a secret key $\mathbf{s} \xleftarrow{\text{R}} \mathbb{Z}_q^k$. It gives $\mathbf{D}_0$ and $\mathbf{D}_1$ to $\mathcal{A}$.*
2. *Algorithm $\mathcal{A}$ can now adaptively submit queries $x \in \{0, 1\}^\tau$ to the challenger. If $b = 0$, the challenger samples $e_x \xleftarrow{\text{R}} D_{\mathbb{Z}, \chi_{\mathsf{smudge}}}$ and outputs*

$$f_{\mathbf{D}_0, \mathbf{D}_1, \mathbf{s}}(x) := \mathbf{s}^\top \left(\prod_{i \in [\tau]} \mathbf{D}_{x_i} \right) \boldsymbol{\eta} + e_x \in \mathbb{Z}_q. \tag{6.1}$$

Otherwise, if $b = 1$, the challenger replies with $y \xleftarrow{\text{R}} \mathbb{Z}_q$.
3. *After $\mathcal{A}$ is done making queries, it outputs a bit $b' \in \{0, 1\}$, which is the output of the experiment.*

An adversary $\mathcal{A}$ is admissible if all of the queries it submits are distinct. Then, for all polynomials $\tau = \tau(\lambda)$, $q = q(\lambda)$, parameters $k \geq 6n \log q$, $\chi = \Omega(\sqrt{n \log q})$, $\chi_{\mathsf{smudge}} > \lambda^{\tau + \omega(1)} \cdot (k\chi)^\tau$, and assuming the $\mathsf{LWE}_{n, m, q, \chi}$ assumption for some $m = \mathsf{poly}(k, \tau, Q)$, for all efficient and admissible adversaries $\mathcal{A}$ making up to Q queries, there exists a negligible function $\mathsf{negl}(\cdot)$ such that for all $\lambda \in \mathbb{N}$, $|\Pr[b' = 1 : b = 0] - \Pr[b' = 1 : b = 1]| = \mathsf{negl}(\lambda)$.

MA-ABE for Subset Policies Without Random Oracles. We now give the full construction of our MA-ABE scheme without random oracles. As described in Sect. 2, our construction essentially instantiates the random oracle in Construction 5.1 with a subset-product of low-norm matrices (which can be used as the basis for constructing a PRF according to Theorem 6.1). Arguing security in turn relies on the evasive LWE assumption (Assumption 3.16). Using the evasive LWE assumption to argue security has the extra benefit of allowing support for policies of arbitrary (polynomial) length (recall that Construction 5.1 as well as the previous lattice-based construction of Datta et al. [DKW21a] required imposing an *a priori* bound on the policy length, and the size of the ciphertext in turn grew with the maximum length).

Construction 6.2 (Multi-Authority ABE without Random Oracles).
Let λ be a security parameter, and $n = n(\lambda)$, $m = m(\lambda)$, $q = q(\lambda)$, and $\chi = \chi(\lambda)$ be lattice parameters. Let $\chi_{\mathsf{PRF}} = \chi_{\mathsf{PRF}}(\lambda)$ be a Gaussian width parameter used to define the hash function. Let $\tau = \tau(\lambda)$ be the bit-length of identities and let $\mathcal{GID} = \{0,1\}^\tau$ be the set of user identifiers. Let $\mathcal{AU} = \{0,1\}^\lambda$ be the set of authorities. We construct an MA-ABE scheme for subset policies (Definition 3.5) with message space $\mathcal{M} = \{0,1\}$ as follows:

- GlobalSetup(1^λ): Sample $\mathbf{D}_0, \mathbf{D}_1 \leftarrow D_{\mathbb{Z},\chi_{\mathsf{PRF}}}^{m \times m}$. Define the hash function $\mathsf{H}\colon \{0,1\}^\tau \to \mathbb{Z}_q^m$ by the function $\mathsf{H}(x) := \left(\prod_{i \in [\tau]} \mathbf{D}_{x_i}\right)\boldsymbol{\eta}$ where $\boldsymbol{\eta} \in \mathbb{Z}_q^m$ is the first canonical basis vector (i.e., $\eta_1 = 1$ and $\eta_i = 0$ for all $i \neq 1$). Output
$$\mathsf{gp} = (\lambda, n, m, q, \chi, \chi_{\mathsf{PRF}}, \tau, \mathbf{D}_0, \mathbf{D}_1).$$

  For ease of exposition, whenever we write $\mathsf{H}(\cdot)$ in the following, we refer to the hash function defined by the matrices $\mathbf{D}_0, \mathbf{D}_1$ in the global parameters.

- AuthSetup($\mathsf{gp}, \mathsf{aid}$): On input the global parameters $\mathsf{gp} = (\lambda, n, m, q, \chi, \chi_{\mathsf{PRF}}, \tau, \mathbf{D}_0, \mathbf{D}_1)$ and an authority identifier $\mathsf{aid} \in \mathcal{AU}$, sample $(\mathbf{A}_{\mathsf{aid}}, \mathsf{td}_{\mathsf{aid}}) \leftarrow \mathsf{TrapGen}(1^n, q, m)$, $\mathbf{p}_{\mathsf{aid}} \xleftarrow{R} \mathbb{Z}_q^n$, and $\mathbf{B}_{\mathsf{aid}} \xleftarrow{R} \mathbb{Z}_q^{n \times m}$. Output the authority public key $\mathsf{pk}_{\mathsf{aid}} \leftarrow (\mathbf{A}_{\mathsf{aid}}, \mathbf{B}_{\mathsf{aid}}, \mathbf{p}_{\mathsf{aid}})$ and the authority secret key $\mathsf{msk}_{\mathsf{aid}} = \mathsf{td}_{\mathsf{aid}}$.

- KeyGen($\mathsf{gp}, \mathsf{msk}, \mathsf{pk}, \mathsf{gid}$): On input the global parameters $\mathsf{gp} = (\lambda, n, m, q, \chi, \chi_{\mathsf{PRF}}, \tau, \mathbf{D}_0, \mathbf{D}_1)$, the master secret key $\mathsf{msk} = \mathsf{td}$, the public key $\mathsf{pk} = (\mathbf{A}, \mathbf{B}, \mathbf{p})$, the user identifier $\mathsf{gid} \in \{0,1\}^\tau$, the key-generation algorithm computes $\mathbf{r} \leftarrow \mathsf{H}(\mathsf{gid}) \in \mathbb{Z}_q^m$ and uses td to sample $\mathbf{u} \leftarrow \mathbf{A}_\chi^{-1}(\mathbf{p} + \mathbf{B}\mathbf{r})$. It outputs $\mathsf{sk}_{\mathsf{aid},\mathsf{gid}} = \mathbf{u}$.

- Encrypt($\mathsf{gp}, \{\mathsf{pk}_{\mathsf{aid}}\}_{\mathsf{aid} \in A}, \mu$): On input the global parameters $\mathsf{gp} = (\lambda, n, m, q, \chi, \chi_{\mathsf{PRF}}, \tau, \mathbf{D}_0, \mathbf{D}_1)$, a set of of public keys $\mathsf{pk}_{\mathsf{aid}} = (\mathbf{A}_{\mathsf{aid}}, \mathbf{B}_{\mathsf{aid}}, \mathbf{p}_{\mathsf{aid}})$ associated with a set of authorities A, and the message $\mu \in \{0,1\}$, the encryption algorithm samples $\mathbf{s}_{\mathsf{aid}} \xleftarrow{R} \mathbb{Z}_q^n$, $\mathbf{e}_{1,\mathsf{aid}} \leftarrow D_{\mathbb{Z},\chi}^m$, $\mathbf{e}_2 \leftarrow D_{\mathbb{Z},\chi}^m$, and $e_3 \leftarrow D_{\mathbb{Z},\chi}$ for each $\mathsf{aid} \in A$. It outputs the ciphertext
$$\mathsf{ct} = \left(\left\{\mathbf{s}_{\mathsf{aid}}^\mathsf{T}\mathbf{A}_{\mathsf{aid}} + \mathbf{e}_{1,\mathsf{aid}}^\mathsf{T}\right\}_{\mathsf{aid} \in A}, \sum_{\mathsf{aid} \in A}\mathbf{s}_{\mathsf{aid}}^\mathsf{T}\mathbf{B}_{\mathsf{aid}} + \mathbf{e}_2^\mathsf{T}, \sum_{\mathsf{aid} \in A}\mathbf{s}_{\mathsf{aid}}^\mathsf{T}\mathbf{p}_{\mathsf{aid}} + e_3 + \mu \cdot \lfloor q/2 \rceil\right).$$

- Decrypt($\mathsf{gp}, \{\mathsf{sk}_{\mathsf{aid},\mathsf{gid}}\}_{\mathsf{aid} \in A}, \mathsf{ct}, \mathsf{gid}$): On input the global parameters $\mathsf{gp} = (\lambda, n, m, q, \chi, \chi_{\mathsf{PRF}}, \tau, \mathbf{D}_0, \mathbf{D}_1)$, a set of secret keys $\mathsf{sk}_{\mathsf{aid},\mathsf{gid}} = \mathbf{u}_{\mathsf{aid},\mathsf{gid}}$ associated with authorities $\mathsf{aid} \in A$ and user identifier gid, a ciphertext $\mathsf{ct} = \left(\{\mathbf{c}_{1,\mathsf{aid}}^\mathsf{T}\}_{\mathsf{aid} \in A}, \mathbf{c}_2, c_3\right)$, the decryption algorithm computes $\mathbf{r} \leftarrow \mathsf{H}(\mathsf{gid})$ and outputs
$$\left\lfloor \frac{2}{q} \cdot \left(c_3 + \mathbf{c}_2^\mathsf{T}\mathbf{r} - \sum_{\mathsf{aid} \in A}\mathbf{c}_{1,\mathsf{aid}}^\mathsf{T}\mathbf{u}_{\mathsf{aid},\mathsf{gid}} \bmod q\right)\right\rceil.$$

Correctness and Security Analysis. We now state the correctness and security properties of Construction 6.2, but due to space limitations, defer their proofs to the full version of this paper [WWW22].

Theorem 6.3 (Correctness). *Let $L = L(\lambda)$ be a bound on the number of attributes associated with a ciphertext. Suppose the conditions of Theorem 3.10 and 3.13 hold (i.e., $m \geq m_0(n, q) = O(n \log q)$ and $\chi > \chi_0(n, q) = \sqrt{n \log q} \cdot \omega(\sqrt{\log n})$). Then, there exists $q_0 = O\left(Lm\lambda\chi^2 + (\sqrt{\lambda}m\chi_{\mathsf{PRF}})^{\tau+1}\chi \right)$ such that for all $m > m_0$, $q > q_0$, and $\chi > \chi_0$, Construction 6.2 is correct.*

Theorem 6.4 (Static Security). *There exists a polynomial $m_0(n, q) = O(n \log q)$ such that under the following conditions and assumptions, Construction 6.2 is statically secure:*

- *The number of samples m satisfies $m \geq m_0$.*
- *Let $\chi_{\mathsf{smudge}} = \chi_{\mathsf{smudge}}(\lambda)$ be a smudging parameter where $\chi_{\mathsf{smudge}} > \lambda^{\tau+\omega(1)}(m\chi_{\mathsf{PRF}})^{\tau+1}$.*
- *The noise parameter χ satisfies $\chi > \lambda^{\omega(1)}\ell\chi_{\mathsf{smudge}}$.*
- *The $\mathsf{LWE}_{n,m',q,\chi_{\mathsf{PRF}}}$ assumption holds where $m' = \mathsf{poly}(m, \tau, Q)$ and Q is a bound on the number of secret-key queries the adversary makes.*
- *The evasive LWE assumption with parameters $n, m, q, \chi, s = \chi$ holds (in particular, the preimages $\mathbf{K} \leftarrow \mathbf{A}^{-1}(\mathbf{P})$ are distributed according to a discrete Gaussian with parameter $s = \chi$).*

Parameter setting. Let λ be a security parameter. We now instantiate Construction 6.2 as follows:

- Let the lattice dimension be $n = \lambda^{1/\varepsilon}$ for some constant $\varepsilon > 0$.
- We can set the length of the identities gid to be $\tau = \lambda$.
- For security (Theorem 6.4), we require that $\chi_{\mathsf{smudge}} > \lambda^{\lambda+\omega(1)}(m\chi_{\mathsf{PRF}})^{\lambda+1}$ and $\chi > \lambda^{\omega(1)}\ell\chi_{\mathsf{smudge}}$. Each of $\ell = \ell(\lambda), m = m(\lambda), \chi_{\mathsf{PRF}} = \chi_{\mathsf{PRF}}(\lambda)$ are polynomially-bounded. Thus, we can set $\chi = 2^{\tilde{O}(n^\varepsilon)}$ to satisfy these requirements, where $\tilde{O}(\cdot)$ suppresses constant and logarithmic factors.
- To support arbitrary polynomial-size ciphertext policies, we set the bound $L = 2^\lambda$ in Theorem 6.3. To ensure correctness, we can set $m = O(n \log q)$ and $q = O(2^\lambda m\lambda\chi^2 + (\lambda m\chi_{\mathsf{PRF}})^{\lambda+1}\chi)$. Setting $q = 2^{\tilde{O}(n^\varepsilon)}$ suffices to satisfy these requirements.

This yields the following corollary:

Corollary 6.5 (Multi-Authority ABE for Subset Policies from Evasive LWE). *Assuming polynomial hardness of LWE and of the evasive LWE assumption (both with a sub-exponential modulus-to-noise ratio), there exists a statically-secure multi-authority ABE for subset policies (of arbitrary polynomial size).*

Acknowledgments. We thanks the TCC reviewers for helpful suggestions. B. Waters is supported by NSF CNS-1908611, a Simons Investigator award, and the Packard Foundation Fellowship. D. J. Wu is supported by NSF CNS-2151131, CNS-2140975, a Microsoft Research Faculty Fellowship, and a Google Research Scholar award.

References

[ABB10a] Agrawal, S., Boneh, D., Boyen, X.: Efficient lattice (H)IBE in the standard model. In: Gilbert, H. (ed.) EUROCRYPT 2010. LNCS, vol. 6110, pp. 553–572. Springer, Heidelberg (2010). https://doi.org/10.1007/978-3-642-13190-5_28

[ABB10b] Agrawal, S., Boneh, D., Boyen, X.: Lattice basis delegation in fixed dimension and shorter-ciphertext hierarchical IBE. In: Rabin, T. (ed.) CRYPTO 2010. LNCS, vol. 6223, pp. 98–115. Springer, Heidelberg (2010). https://doi.org/10.1007/978-3-642-14623-7_6

[Ajt96] Ajtai, M.: Generating hard instances of lattice problems (extended abstract). In: STOC, pp. 99–108 (1996)

[BCD+16] Bos, J.W., et al.: Frodo: take off the ring! practical, quantum-secure key exchange from LWE. In: ACM CCS, pp. 1006–1018 (2016)

[BCTW16] Brakerski, Z., Cash, D., Tsabary, R., Wee, H.: Targeted homomorphic attribute-based encryption. In: Hirt, M., Smith, A. (eds.) TCC 2016. LNCS, vol. 9986, pp. 330–360. Springer, Heidelberg (2016). https://doi.org/10.1007/978-3-662-53644-5_13

[BDE+18] Bootle, J., Delaplace, C., Espitau, T., Fouque, P.-A., Tibouchi, M.: LWE without modular reduction and improved side-channel attacks against BLISS. In: Peyrin, T., Galbraith, S. (eds.) ASIACRYPT 2018. LNCS, vol. 11272, pp. 494–524. Springer, Cham (2018). https://doi.org/10.1007/978-3-030-03326-2_17

[Bei96] Beimel, A.: Secure schemes for secret sharing and key distribution. Ph.D. thesis, Technion (1996)

[BLMR13] Boneh, D., Lewi, K., Montgomery, H., Raghunathan, A.: Key homomorphic PRFs and their applications. In: Canetti, R., Garay, J.A. (eds.) CRYPTO 2013. LNCS, vol. 8042, pp. 410–428. Springer, Heidelberg (2013). https://doi.org/10.1007/978-3-642-40041-4_23

[BPR12] Banerjee, A., Peikert, C., Rosen, A.: Pseudorandom functions and lattices. In: Pointcheval, D., Johansson, T. (eds.) EUROCRYPT 2012. LNCS, vol. 7237, pp. 719–737. Springer, Heidelberg (2012). https://doi.org/10.1007/978-3-642-29011-4_42

[BR93] Bellare, M., Rogaway, P.: Random oracles are practical: a paradigm for designing efficient protocols. In: ACM CCS, pp. 62–73 (1993)

[BTVW17] Brakerski, Z., Tsabary, R., Vaikuntanathan, V., Wee, H.: Private constrained PRFs (and more) from LWE. In: Kalai, Y., Reyzin, L. (eds.) TCC 2017. LNCS, vol. 10677, pp. 264–302. Springer, Cham (2017). https://doi.org/10.1007/978-3-319-70500-2_10

[BV22] Brakerski, Z., Vaikuntanathan, V.: Lattice-inspired broadcast encryption and succinct ciphertext-policy ABE. In: ITCS, pp. 28:1–28:20 (2022)

[CC09] Chase, M., Chow, S.S.M.: Improving privacy and security in multi-authority attribute-based encryption. In: ACM CCS, pp. 121–130 (2009)

[Cha07] Chase, M.: Multi-authority attribute based encryption. In: Vadhan, S.P. (ed.) TCC 2007. LNCS, vol. 4392, pp. 515–534. Springer, Heidelberg (2007). https://doi.org/10.1007/978-3-540-70936-7_28

[CHKP10] Cash, D., Hofheinz, D., Kiltz, E., Peikert, C.: Bonsai trees, or how to delegate a lattice basis. In: Gilbert, H. (ed.) EUROCRYPT 2010. LNCS, vol. 6110, pp. 523–552. Springer, Heidelberg (2010). https://doi.org/10.1007/978-3-642-13190-5_27

[CVW18] Chen, Y., Vaikuntanathan, V., Wee, H.: GGH15 beyond permutation branching programs: proofs, attacks, and candidates. In: Shacham, H., Boldyreva, A. (eds.) CRYPTO 2018. LNCS, vol. 10992, pp. 577–607. Springer, Cham (2018). https://doi.org/10.1007/978-3-319-96881-0_20

[DKW21a] Datta, P., Komargodski, I., Waters, B.: Decentralized multi-authority ABE for DNFs from LWE. In: Canteaut, A., Standaert, F.-X. (eds.) EUROCRYPT 2021. LNCS, vol. 12696, pp. 177–209. Springer, Cham (2021). https://doi.org/10.1007/978-3-030-77870-5_7

[DKW21b] Datta, P., Komargodski, I., Waters, B.: Decentralized multi-authority ABE for nc^1 from computational-bdh. IACR Cryptol. ePrint Arch. 1325 (2021)

[GGSW13] Garg, S., Gentry, C., Sahai, A., Waters, B.: Witness encryption and its applications. In: STOC, pp. 467–476 (2013)

[GLW21] Goyal, R., Liu, J., Waters, B.: Adaptive security via deletion in attribute-based encryption: solutions from search assumptions in bilinear groups. In: Tibouchi, M., Wang, H. (eds.) ASIACRYPT 2021. LNCS, vol. 13093, pp. 311–341. Springer, Cham (2021). https://doi.org/10.1007/978-3-030-92068-5_11

[GPSW06] Goyal, V., Pandey, O., Sahai, A., Waters, B.: Attribute-based encryption for fine-grained access control of encrypted data. In: ACM CCS, pp. 89–98 (2006)

[GPV08] Gentry, C., Peikert, C., Vaikuntanathan, V.: Trapdoors for hard lattices and new cryptographic constructions. In: STOC, pp. 197–206 (2008)

[Kim19] Kim, S.: Multi-authority attribute-based encryption from LWE in the OT model. IACR Cryptol. ePrint Arch. 280 (2019)

[LCLS08] Lin, H., Cao, Z., Liang, X., Shao, J.: Secure threshold multi authority attribute based encryption without a central authority. In: Chowdhury, D.R., Rijmen, V., Das, A. (eds.) INDOCRYPT 2008. LNCS, vol. 5365, pp. 426–436. Springer, Heidelberg (2008). https://doi.org/10.1007/978-3-540-89754-5_33

[LW11] Lewko, A., Waters, B.: Decentralizing attribute-based encryption. In: Paterson, K.G. (ed.) EUROCRYPT 2011. LNCS, vol. 6632, pp. 568–588. Springer, Heidelberg (2011). https://doi.org/10.1007/978-3-642-20465-4_31

[LW15] Lyubashevsky, V., Wichs, D.: Simple lattice trapdoor sampling from a broad class of distributions. In: Katz, J. (ed.) PKC 2015. LNCS, vol. 9020, pp. 716–730. Springer, Heidelberg (2015). https://doi.org/10.1007/978-3-662-46447-2_32

[MKE08] Müller, S., Katzenbeisser, S., Eckert, C.: Distributed attribute-based encryption. In: Lee, P.J., Cheon, J.H. (eds.) ICISC 2008. LNCS, vol. 5461, pp. 20–36. Springer, Heidelberg (2009). https://doi.org/10.1007/978-3-642-00730-9_2

[MP12] Micciancio, D., Peikert, C.: Trapdoors for lattices: simpler, tighter, faster, smaller. In: Pointcheval, D., Johansson, T. (eds.) EUROCRYPT 2012. LNCS, vol. 7237, pp. 700–718. Springer, Heidelberg (2012). https://doi.org/10.1007/978-3-642-29011-4_41

[Reg05] Regev, O.: On lattices, learning with errors, random linear codes, and cryptography. In: STOC, pp. 84–93 (2005)

[RW15] Rouselakis, Y., Waters, B.: Efficient statically-secure large-universe multi-authority attribute-based encryption. In: Böhme, R., Okamoto, T. (eds.) FC 2015. LNCS, vol. 8975, pp. 315–332. Springer, Heidelberg (2015). https://doi.org/10.1007/978-3-662-47854-7_19

[SW05] Sahai, A., Waters, B.: Fuzzy identity-based encryption. In: Cramer, R. (ed.) EUROCRYPT 2005. LNCS, vol. 3494, pp. 457–473. Springer, Heidelberg (2005). https://doi.org/10.1007/11426639_27

[Tsa19] Tsabary, R.: Fully secure attribute-based encryption for t-CNF from LWE. In: Boldyreva, A., Micciancio, D. (eds.) CRYPTO 2019. LNCS, vol. 11692, pp. 62–85. Springer, Cham (2019). https://doi.org/10.1007/978-3-030-26948-7_3

[Tsa22] Tsabary, R.: Candidate witness encryption from lattice techniques. In: Dodis, Y., Shrimpton, T. (eds.) CRYPTO 2022. LNCS, vol. 13507, pp. 535–559. Springer, Cham (2022). https://doi.org/10.1007/978-3-031-15802-5_19

[VWW22] Vaikuntanathan, V., Wee, H., Wichs, D.: Witness encryption and null-IO from evasive LWE. In: ASIACRYPT (2022)

[Wee22] Wee, H.: Optimal broadcast encryption and CP-ABE from evasive lattice assumptions. In: Dunkelman, O., Dziembowski, S. (eds.) EUROCRYPT 2022. LNCS, vol. 13276, pp. 217–241. Springer, Cham (2022). https://doi.org/10.1007/978-3-031-07085-3_8

[WFL19] Wang, Z., Fan, X., Liu, F.-H.: FE for inner products and its application to decentralized ABE. In: Lin, D., Sako, K. (eds.) PKC 2019. LNCS, vol. 11443, pp. 97–127. Springer, Cham (2019). https://doi.org/10.1007/978-3-030-17259-6_4

[WWW22] Waters, B., Wee, H., Wu, D.J.: Multi-authority ABE from lattices without random oracles. IACR Cryptol. ePrint Arch. (2022)

ABE for Circuits with Constant-Size Secret Keys and Adaptive Security

Hanjun Li$^{(\boxtimes)}$, Huijia Lin$^{(\boxtimes)}$, and Ji Luo$^{(\boxtimes)}$

Paul G. Allen School of Computer Science & Engineering,
University of Washington, Seattle, USA
{hanjul,rachel,luoji}@cs.washington.edu

Abstract. An important theme in the research on attribute-based encryption (ABE) is minimizing the sizes of secret keys and ciphertexts. In this work, we present two new ABE schemes with *constant-size* secret keys, i.e., the key size is independent of the sizes of policies or attributes and dependent only on the security parameter λ.

- We construct the first key-policy ABE scheme for circuits with constant-size secret keys, $|\mathsf{sk}_f| = \mathrm{poly}(\lambda)$, which concretely consist of only three group elements. The previous state-of-the-art scheme by [Boneh et al., Eurocrypt '14] has key size polynomial in the maximum depth d of the policy circuits, $|\mathsf{sk}_f| = \mathrm{poly}(d, \lambda)$. Our new scheme removes this dependency of key size on d while keeping the ciphertext size the same, which grows linearly in the attribute length and polynomially in the maximal depth, $|\mathsf{ct}_\mathbf{x}| = |\mathbf{x}| \mathrm{poly}(d, \lambda)$.
- We present the first ciphertext-policy ABE scheme for Boolean formulæ that simultaneously has constant-size keys and succinct ciphertexts of size independent of the policy formulæ, namely, $|\mathsf{sk}_f| = \mathrm{poly}(\lambda)$ and $|\mathsf{ct}_\mathbf{x}| = \mathrm{poly}(|\mathbf{x}|, \lambda)$. Concretely, each secret key consists of only two group elements. Previous ciphertext-policy ABE schemes either have succinct ciphertexts but non-constant-size keys [Agrawal–Yamada, Eurocrypt '20, Agrawal–Wichs–Yamada, TCC '20], or constant-size keys but large ciphertexts that grow with the policy size as well as the attribute length. Our second construction is the first ABE scheme achieving *double succinctness*, where both keys and ciphertexts are smaller than the corresponding attributes and policies tied to them.

Our constructions feature new ways of combining lattices with pairing groups for building ABE and are proven selectively secure based on LWE and in the generic (pairing) group model. We further show that when replacing the LWE assumption with its adaptive variant introduced in [Quach–Wee–Wichs FOCS '18], the constructions become adaptively secure.

1 Introduction

Attribute-based encryption (ABE) [24,37] is a novel generalization of public-key encryption for enforcing fine-grained access control. In this work, we focus on

© The Author(s), under exclusive license to Springer Nature Switzerland AG 2022
E. Kiltz and V. Vaikuntanathan (Eds.): TCC 2022, LNCS 13747, pp. 680–710, 2022.
https://doi.org/10.1007/978-3-031-22318-1_24

improving the efficiency of ABE schemes, especially on minimizing the sizes of secret keys while keeping ciphertexts small. In key-policy (KP) ABE, a secret key sk_f is tied to a policy f and a ciphertext $\mathsf{ct}_\mathbf{x}$ encrypting a message μ is tied to an attribute $\mathbf{x}$, so that a secret key is only "authorized" to decrypt a ciphertext if the associated attribute $\mathbf{x}$ satisfies the policy f. At first glance, since a secret key specifies the associated policy f, it appears that the size of the secret key would have to depend at least *linearly* on the (description) size of f. Similarly, a ciphertext would have to grow *linearly* with the length of the associated attribute $\mathbf{x}$. Secret keys and ciphertexts with linear dependency of their sizes on the policies and attributes they are tied to are said to be *compact*, and most ABE schemes are indeed compact.

However, upon closer examination, as ABE does not guarantee privacy of the policies nor the attributes, it is possible to give a description of the policy f in the clear in the secret key, and the *non-trivial* part of the secret key may be smaller than the policy. In this case, the right measure of efficiency should be the size of the non-trivial part (i.e., the overhead), which we now view as *the* secret key. We can now aim for secret keys of size smaller than that of the policy — i.e., $|\mathsf{sk}_f| = o(|f|)$ — referred to as *succinct* keys, or even keys of size independent of that of the policy — i.e., $|\mathsf{sk}_f| = O(1)$ — referred to as *constant-size* keys.[1] Similarly, *succinct* ciphertexts have size smaller than the length of the attributes, $|\mathsf{ct}_\mathbf{x}| = o(|\mathbf{x}|)$, and *constant-size* ciphertexts satisfy $|\mathsf{ct}_\mathbf{x}| = O(1)$. We further examine the efficiency of ciphertext-policy (CP) ABE [10], which enables instead the ciphertexts ct_f to specify the policies, so that only secret keys $\mathsf{sk}_\mathbf{x}$ with attributes satisfying the policies can decrypt them. Naturally, succinct keys and ciphertexts have size $|\mathsf{sk}_\mathbf{x}| = o(|\mathbf{x}|)$ and $|\mathsf{ct}_f| = o(|f|)$, and constant size means the same as in KP-ABE.

How close can we get to the *ideal efficiency* of having both constant-size keys and ciphertexts? Despite tremendous effort, the state-of-the-art is still far from the ideal. Current ABE schemes with either succinct keys or succinct ciphertexts can be broadly classified as follows (see Figs. 1 and 2):

- The work of [11] built KP-ABE based on LWE for polynomial-size circuits with succinct keys $|\mathsf{sk}_f| = \mathrm{poly}(d)$ and ciphertexts of size $|\mathsf{ct}_\mathbf{x}| = |\mathbf{x}|\,\mathrm{poly}(d)$, where d is the depth of the circuit.
- Several works [5–7,32,38,42,43] constructed KP-ABE and CP-ABE for low-depth computations with *either* constant-size secret keys *or* constant-size ciphertexts from pairing, i.e., *either* $|\mathsf{sk}| = O(1)$ *or* $|\mathsf{ct}| = O(1)$, at the cost of the other component being much larger, of size $\Omega(|f| \cdot |\mathbf{x}|)$.
- The recent works of [3,4] constructed CP-ABE for Boolean formulae with succinct ciphertexts $|\mathsf{ct}_f| = \Theta(|\mathbf{x}|)$ and compact keys $|\mathsf{sk}_\mathbf{x}| = \Theta(|\mathbf{x}|)$. These schemes are based on LWE and strong assumptions on pairing groups — either the generic (pairing) group model [4] or knowledge assumptions [3].

In this work, we set out to improve the state-of-the-art towards the direction of ideal efficiency. We observe that though there are ABE schemes for low-depth

---

[1] We always ignore polynomial factors in the security parameter.

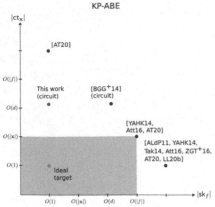

Fig. 1. Efficiency comparison for KP-ABE schemes. The pink region highlights succinctness for $|ct_x|$ and $|sk_f|$. This work and [BGG+14] are KP-ABE schemes for circuits, while the rest of the schemes are for low-depth computation (Color figure online).

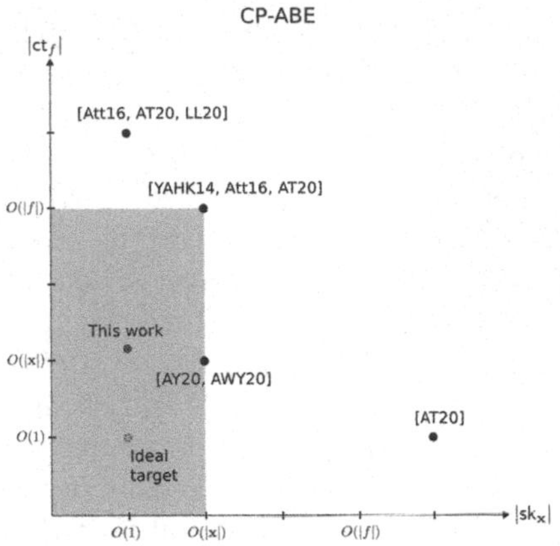

Fig. 2. Efficiency comparison for CP-ABE schemes. The pink region highlights succinctness for $|ct_f|$ and $|sk_x|$. All the included schemes are CP-ABE for low-depth computation (Color figure online).

computations with constant-size keys, we do not have such ABE for general circuits. We ask:

Can we construct ABE for circuits with constant-size keys?

Furthermore, all of the above schemes either have succinct keys or succinct ciphertexts, but never both at the same time. If we were to eventually achieve ideal efficiency, we would have to first overcome the intermediate barrier of simultaneously having succinct keys and ciphertexts — we refer to this as *double succinctness*. We thus ask:

Can we construct ABE for expressive policies with
both *succinct keys* and *succinct ciphertexts?*

We note that the above questions are unanswered even when assuming the strong primitive of indistinguishability obfuscation (iO). Several works [17,18,27] constructed ABE for circuits (or even functional encryption for circuits) using indistinguishability obfuscation or related primitives. However, they all have large secret keys of size poly($|f|$). The only work that manages to obtain ABE for RAM with constant-size keys [20] rely on a strong primitive called extractable witness encryption, which however lacks provably secure instantiation.

Our Results. We address both questions. For the former, we construct the first KP-ABE scheme for circuits with constant-size keys while keeping the ciphertext size the same as in [11]. Concretely, each secret key consists of only 3 group elements. For the latter, we present the first CP-ABE scheme for Boolean formulae achieving double succinctness — it has constant-size keys and succinct ciphertexts. Concretely, each secret key consists of only 2 group elements. Both constructions rely on LWE and the generic (pairing) group model, similar to [4].

Theorem (KP-ABE). *Assuming LWE, in the generic (pairing) group model, there is a KP-ABE for circuits (Construction 2) that achieves selective security and has key size* $|\mathsf{sk}_C| = \mathrm{poly}(\lambda)$ *(concretely, containing 3 group elements) and ciphertext size* $|\mathsf{ct}_\mathbf{x}| = |\mathbf{x}|\,\mathrm{poly}(\lambda, d)$*, where* d *is the maximum depth of the policy circuits.*

Theorem (CP-ABE). *Assuming LWE, in the generic (pairing) group model, there is a CP-ABE for Boolean formulae [31] that achieves very selective security, and has constant-size keys* $|\mathsf{sk}_\mathbf{x}| = \mathrm{poly}(\lambda)$ *(concretely, containing 2 group elements) and ciphertexts of size* $|\mathsf{ct}_f| = |\mathbf{x}|^2\,\mathrm{poly}(\lambda)$ *independent of the formula size* $|f|$.

Additional Contribution — Adaptive Security. The standard security property of ABE is collusion resistance, which stipulates that no information of the message μ encrypted in a ciphertext should be revealed even when multiple secret keys are issued, as long as none of the keys alone is authorized to decrypt the ciphertext. Adaptive security requires collusion resistance to hold even when attributes and policies tied to the challenge ciphertext and the secret keys are chosen adaptively by the adversary. The weaker selective security restricts the adversary to commit to the attribute (in KP-ABE) or the policy (in CP-ABE) associated with the challenge ciphertext before seeing any parameters of the system, and very selective security further requires all attributes and policies in both the challenge ciphertext and the secret keys to be chosen statically.

Adaptive security guards against more powerful adversaries than selective security. It is known that the latter can be generically lifted to the former via complexity leveraging, at the cost of subexponential hardness assumptions. However, complexity leveraging is undesirable not only because it requires subexponential hardness, but also because it requires scaling the security parameter to be polynomial in the length of the information to be guessed, $\lambda = \mathrm{poly}(|x|)$ in KP-ABE or $\lambda = \mathrm{poly}(|f|)$ in CP-ABE. As a result, complexity leveraging is not a viable solution when aiming for constant-size keys, as key size $\mathrm{poly}(\lambda)$ would already depends on $|x|$ or $|f|$.

Instead, we show that in our constructions of KP- and CP-ABE, if assume adaptive LWE instead of plain LWE, then they achieve *adaptive security* and our reduction only incurs a polynomial amount of security loss. The adaptive LWE assumption [36] postulates that LWE samples of the form $\{\mathbf{s}^\mathsf{T}(\mathbf{A}_i - \mathbf{x}[i]\mathbf{G}) + \mathbf{e}_i^\mathsf{T}\}_i$ are pseudorandom, even if the adversary adaptively chooses $\mathbf{x}$ depending on the random matrices $\{\mathbf{A}_i\}_i$.

Theorem (adaptive security). *Assuming the polynomial hardness of adaptive LWE (instead of LWE), in the generic (pairing) group model, the KP-ABE scheme (Construction 2) and the CP-ABE scheme [31] are adaptively secure.*

In the literature, the ABE schemes for circuits based on lattices [11,21] achieve only selective security (without complexity leveraging). Adapting it to have adaptive security has remained a technical barrier, except for very limited classes of policies such as 3-CNF [39]. Alternatively, there are schemes based on indistinguishability obfuscation or functional encryption for all circuits that are adaptively secure [27,40], but requiring stronger assumptions. Our technique can be viewed as making the lattice-based schemes adaptively secure when combined with pairing. Note that this is not trivial, for instance, the recent CP-ABE schemes in [3,4] that combine [11] with pairing groups inherit the selective security of the former (even if assuming adaptive LWE).

Organization. In Sect. 2, we present an overview of our techniques. In Sect. 3, we introduce preliminaries. In Sect. 4, we define nearly linear secret sharing schemes and non-annihilability, and construct such a scheme for bounded-depth circuits based on the adaptive LWE assumption. In Sect. 5, we present our adaptively secure KP-ABE for bounded-depth circuits. Due to space constraints, we refer the readers to the full version [31] for our doubly succinct CP-ABE as well as the secret sharing scheme and our new analysis of IPFE of [1] for that.

2   Technical Overview

High-Level Ideas. Let's focus on our KP-ABE scheme for circuits first. The first known construction of KP-ABE for circuits from LWE [22] has keys of size $|f|\operatorname{poly}(d,\lambda)$. The scheme of [11] reduces the key size to $\operatorname{poly}(d,\lambda)$. Both schemes achieve only selective security because they rely on the *lattice trapdoor simulation techniques*. Consider the BGG$^+$ scheme. Its ciphertext encodes the attributes $\mathbf{x}$ and message μ as follows.

$$\text{BGG}: \quad \mathbf{s}^\mathsf{T}\mathbf{A}+\mathbf{e}^\mathsf{T}, \quad \mathbf{s}^\mathsf{T}\big(\overbrace{(\mathbf{A}_1||\cdots||\mathbf{A}_\ell)}^{\mathbf{B}} - \mathbf{x}\otimes\mathbf{G}\big)+(\mathbf{e}')^\mathsf{T}, \quad \mathbf{s}^\mathsf{T}\mathbf{v}+e''+\mu\lfloor q/2\rceil.$$

One can homomorphically evaluate any circuit f on the attribute encoding to obtain $\mathbf{s}^\mathsf{T}(\mathbf{B}_f - f(x)\mathbf{G})+\mathbf{e}_f^\mathsf{T}$. To decrypt, the secret key sk_f simply is a *short* vector $\mathbf{r}_{\mathbf{A},f}$ satisfying $(\mathbf{A}||\mathbf{B}_f)\mathbf{r}_{\mathbf{A},f} = \mathbf{v}$, which can be sampled using a trapdoor $\mathbf{T}_\mathbf{A}$ for $\mathbf{A}$. This approach however has two drawbacks:

- Difficulty towards Constant-Size Keys. The short vector $\mathbf{r}_{\mathbf{A},f}$ contained in the secret key sk_f has size $\operatorname{poly}(d,\lambda)$. This is because it has dimension $m = n\log q$ for $\log q = \operatorname{poly}(d,\lambda)$ and entries of magnitude exponential in d.
- Difficulty towards Adaptive Security. The security proof relies on the ability to simulate trapdoors for these matrices $\mathbf{A}||\mathbf{B}_f$ corresponding to secret keys that are *unauthorized* to decrypt the challenge ciphertext with attribute $\mathbf{x}^*$, that is $f(\mathbf{x}^*) = 1$. However, to do so, current technique plants $\mathbf{x}^*$ in the public matrices $\mathbf{A}_i$'s (contained in mpk), leading to selective security. Note that even with the stronger adaptive LWE assumption, it is unclear how to simulate these trapdoors in another way.

Towards constant-size keys and adaptive security, our construction circumvents the use of lattice trapdoors all together. At a high level, we turn attention to a much weaker lattice primitive called attribute-based laconic function evaluation (AB-LFE) [36], and lifts it to a KP-ABE scheme for circuits using pairing. AB-LFE is an interactive protocol where a receiver sends a digest of a function, which is exactly the matrix $\mathbf{B}_f$ in BGG. The sender then encodes the attribute $\mathbf{x}$ and message μ as follows.

$$\text{AB-LFE}: \quad \mathbf{s}^\top\big((\mathbf{A}_1||\cdots||\mathbf{A}_\ell) - \mathbf{x} \otimes \mathbf{G}\big) + (\mathbf{e}')^\top, \quad \mathbf{s}^\top\mathbf{B}_f\mathbf{r} + e'' + \mu\lfloor q/2\rceil.$$

where $\mathbf{r} = \mathbf{G}^{-1}(\mathbf{a})$ is the bit decomposition of a random vector $\mathbf{a}$. Security guarantees that the encoding reveals only the output $f(\mathbf{x})$. At a first glance, the LFE encoding appears the same as BGG, but the novelty is in details. Since the LFE encoding depends on $\mathbf{B}_f$ (and hence f), it can be generated without using lattice trapdoors — the short vector $\mathbf{r}$ sampled first, and $\mathbf{B}_f\mathbf{r}$ computed next. When $f(x) = 1$, the hiding of μ follows directly from the pseudorandomness of LWE samples $\mathbf{s}^\top((\mathbf{A}_1||\cdots||\mathbf{A}_\ell)-\mathbf{x}\otimes\mathbf{G}))+\mathbf{e}'$ and $\mathbf{s}^\top\mathbf{a}+e'''$. When $\mathbf{x}$ is adaptively chosen, security follows naturally from adaptive LWE.

However, AB-LFE is able to avoid lattice trapdoor only because it is significantly weaker than ABE, or even 1-key ABE: *1)* its message encoding depends on $\mathbf{B}_f$ (unknown at ABE encryption time), and *2)* it is only secure for a single function. Our next challenge is lifting AB-LFE back to full ABE, for which we use pairing.

More specifically, we first modify the AB-LFE scheme of [36] to obtain a *nearly linear secret sharing scheme* for circuits. It contains two parts.

$$\text{Our LSS encoding}: \quad L_\mathbf{x} = \mathbf{s}^\top\big((\mathbf{A}_1||\cdots||\mathbf{A}_\ell) - \mathbf{x} \otimes \mathbf{G}\big) + (\mathbf{e}')^\top \bmod q,$$
$$L_f = \mathbf{s}^\top\text{Round}(\mathbf{B}_f\mathbf{r}) + e'' + \mu\lfloor p/2\rceil \bmod p.$$

Note that we round $\mathbf{B}_f\mathbf{r}$ from modulus q of $\text{poly}(d)$ length to p of $\text{poly}(\lambda)$ length so that the component L_f in the secret sharing that depends on f and μ has *constant size*, which is the key towards constant-size ABE keys. To solve the problem that L_f requires knowledge of $\mathbf{B}_f$ unknown at encryption time, we use a pairing-based inner-product functional encryption (IPFE) to compute L_f in the exponent, by viewing it as inner product $L_f = \langle\mathbf{s}^\top||\mu\lfloor p/2\rceil, \text{Round}(\mathbf{B}_f\mathbf{r})||1\rangle$, where the two vectors are known respectively at ABE encryption and key generation time. To overcome that AB-LFE only guarantees security for a single L_f. We follow the idea of [3,4] to compute $\delta_f \cdot L_f$ in the exponent instead, where δ_f is an independent and random scalar chosen at key generation time. In GGM, the presence of δ_f prevents adversaries from meaningfully "combining" information from multiple L_f for different f.

Comparison with [3,4]. Our way of combining lattice-based LSS with pairing-based IPFE differs from that of [3,4], in order to address unique technical difficulties. To start with, they use an LSS scheme based on the BGG ABE and inherits the selective security. Second, our KP-ABE scheme reveals part of the secret h $L_\mathbf{x}$ *in the clear* (in ciphertext), and only compute L_f in the exponent, whereas [3,4] computes the entire LSS in the exponent. This is because the decryptor needs to perform the non-linear rounding operation on the result of homomorphic evaluation on $L_{\mathbf{x}}$, in order to obtain $\mathsf{Round}(\mathbf{s}^\mathsf{T}(\mathbf{B}_f - f(x)\mathbf{G})\mathbf{r} + \mathbf{e}_f^\mathsf{T})$ for decryption. Keeping $L_{\mathbf{x}}$ in the clear allows rounding, but renders security harder to prove.

Furthermore, the security proof of AB-LFE relies on noise flooding — their technique can only show that $L_f + \tilde{e}$ is secure for a super-polynomially large $\tilde{e}$. But noise flooding is incompatible with computing L_f in the exponent, since we must keep noises polynomially small in order for decryption to be efficient (which performs discrete logarithm). Without noise flooding, we cannot prove that unauthorized shares are pseudorandom as in [36]. Nevertheless, we show that unauthorized shares are "entropic", captured by a new notion called *non-annihilability*, and that the "entropic" L_f computed in the exponent still hides the message μ. The proof of non-annihilability combines techniques from AB-LFE and leakage simulation [16,25]. The work of [3,4] does not encounter issues with super-polynomial noises.

We add a note on our doubly succinct CP-ABE for Boolean formulae. It is closer to the CP-ABE scheme of [3,4]. However, to obtain constant-size keys, we rely on an IPFE scheme with strong (selective) simulation security — it enables simultaneously simulating a polynomial number k of ciphertexts, by programming k inner products for every secret key, while keeping the secret key *constant-size* (independent of k). Such strong simulation is impossible in the standard model following an incompressibility argument. We show that this is possible in GGM, in particular, the IPFE scheme of [1] satisfies it. IPFE with such strong simulation may find other applications.

Next, we explain our ideas in more details.

Combining LSS with IPFE. An IPFE scheme enables generating keys $\mathsf{isk}(\mathbf{v}_j)$ and ciphertexts $\mathsf{ict}(\mathbf{u}_i)$ associated with vectors $\mathbf{v}_j, \mathbf{u}_i \in \mathbb{Z}_p^N$ such that decryption reveals only their inner products $\langle \mathbf{u}_i, \mathbf{v}_j \rangle$ and hides all other information about $\mathbf{u}_i$ encrypted in the ciphertexts (whereas $\mathbf{v}_j$ associated with the keys are public). It can be based on a variety of assumptions such as MDDH, LWE, or DCR [1,2].

A *nearly* linear secret sharing scheme enables generating shares $L_f, L_0, \{L_i^b\}$ associated with a policy f and some secret μ, such that for any input $\mathbf{x} \in \{0,1\}^\ell$, its corresponding subset of shares $L^{\mathbf{x}} = (L_0, \{L_i^{\mathbf{x}[i]}\})$, together with L_f can be used to *approximately* reconstruct the secret μ if and only if $f(\mathbf{x}) = 0$:

$$(L_f, L_0, \{L_i^b\}_{i\in[\ell],b\in\{0,1\}}) \leftarrow \mathsf{Share}(f, \mu; \mathbf{r})$$
$$f(x) = 0 \implies \mu \approx \mathsf{Recon}(f, \mathbf{x}, L_f, L^{\mathbf{x}}).$$

Near linearity means that Recon is linear in the shares $L_f, L^{\mathbf{x}}$ and that its output is close to the secret μ.

How can we combine these two primitives to construct a KP-ABE? We require $L_0, \{L_i^b\}$ to be independent of f and μ, and L_f to be linear in μ and the randomness $\mathbf{r}$ of Share. The first requirement allows us to simply put $L^{\mathbf{x}}$ in the ciphertext. The second requirement allows us to encode $\mu, \mathbf{r}$ into ict's and the coefficients (of L_f as a function of $\mu, \mathbf{r}$) into isk's, so that their inner product is exactly L_f. For convenience, we write $[\![x]\!]_i$ for g_i^x and use additive notation for the groups. The idea is as follows:

$$
\left.
\begin{array}{ll}
\mathsf{kp.sk}_f : & [\![\delta]\!]_2, \quad \mathsf{isk}(\text{coefficients of } \delta L_f) \\
\mathsf{kp.ct}_\mathbf{x} : & L^\mathbf{x}, \quad \mathsf{ict}(\mu, \mathbf{r})
\end{array}
\right\} \quad [\![\delta L_f]\!]_\mathrm{T} \text{ and } L^\mathbf{x}. \tag{1}
$$

If $f(\mathbf{x}) = 0$, the linear reconstruction can be carried out in the exponents to approximately obtain $[\![\delta\mu]\!]_\mathrm{T}$. Decryption enumerates all possible errors to recover μ exactly. We stress again that different from [3,4], we keep $L_\mathbf{x}$ in the clear (in the ciphertext), instead of computing the entire secret sharing $L_\mathbf{x}, L_f$ in the exponent, which is important for achieving constant-size keys, but makes proving security more difficult.

We construct a secret sharing scheme that features L_f of *constant size*, which translates to KP-ABE with constant-size secret keys.

Combining secret sharing and IPFE to construct CP-ABE is similar. We can encode $L_0, \{L_i^b\}$ in ict's, and a "selection" vector according to $\mathbf{x}$ in isk's, so that their inner products are exactly $L^\mathbf{x}$:

$$
\left.
\begin{array}{ll}
\mathsf{cp.sk}_\mathbf{x} : & [\![\delta]\!]_2, \quad \mathsf{isk}(\delta \cdot \text{selection vector for } \mathbf{x}) \\
\mathsf{cp.ct}_f : & [\![L_f]\!]_1, \quad \mathsf{ict}(L_0, \{L_i^b\}).
\end{array}
\right\} \quad [\![\delta L_f]\!]_\mathrm{T} \text{ and } [\![\delta L^\mathbf{x}]\!]_\mathrm{T}.
$$
$$\tag{2}$$

We use an IPFE scheme with secret keys of constant size, independent of the vector dimension or the number of ciphertexts, and a secret sharing scheme whose $L_f, L^\mathbf{x}$ grows only with the input length $|\mathbf{x}|$. This translates to CP-ABE with double succinctness.

Lattice-Based Nearly Linear Secret Sharing. The BGG^+ ABE scheme introduces an important homomorphic evaluation procedure: Given public matrices $\mathbf{B} = (\mathbf{A}_1 || \cdots || \mathbf{A}_{|\mathbf{x}|})$, and the following encoding of an input $\mathbf{x}$, one can homomorphically evaluate any circuit f on the encodings to obtain an encoding of the output.

$$
\mathbf{c}^\top = \mathbf{s}^\top(\mathbf{B} - (1, \mathbf{x}) \otimes \mathbf{G}) + \mathbf{e}_2^\top,
$$
$$
\mathsf{EvalCX}(\mathbf{c}_2, f, \mathbf{x}) = \mathbf{c}_f^\top = \mathbf{s}^\top(\mathbf{B}_f - f(\mathbf{x})\mathbf{G}) + \mathbf{e}_f^\top, \text{ where } \mathsf{EvalC}(\mathbf{B}, f) = \mathbf{B}_f. \tag{3}
$$

As discussed before, the BGG^+ ABE scheme uses lattice trapdoor simulation technique, which we try to avoid in order to get constant-size key and adaptive security.

We hence turn to using the weaker primitive of AB-LFE scheme introduced by [36]. It is a two-party protocol between a sender and a receiver who share the LWE public matrix $\mathbf{B}$ as the common reference string. The receiver first computes a digest $\mathbf{B}_f = \mathsf{EvalC}(\mathbf{B}, f)$ for a function f and sends it to the sender.

Upon receiving the digest, the sender masks a message μ by an LWE sample $c_0 = \mathbf{s}^\mathsf{T}\mathbf{v}_f + e + \mu\lfloor q/2\rceil$, where $\mathbf{r} = \mathbf{G}^{-1}(\mathbf{a})$ and $\mathbf{v}_f = \mathbf{B}_f\mathbf{r}$ are analogues of $\mathbf{r}_{\mathbf{A},f}$ and $\mathbf{v}$ in BGG$^+$. It also encodes an attribute $\mathbf{x}$ into LWE samples $\mathbf{c}_1$ as described below.

<table>
<tr><td>

AB-LFE.crs : $\mathbf{B}$

AB-LFE.digest : $\mathbf{B}_f = \mathsf{EvalC}(\mathbf{B}, f)$

</td><td>

AB-LFE.ct$_{f,\mathbf{x}}(\mu)$:

$\mathbf{a} \xleftarrow{\$} \mathbb{Z}_q^n$

$c_0 = \mathbf{s}^\mathsf{T}\underbrace{\mathbf{B}_f\mathbf{G}^{-1}(\mathbf{a})}_{\mathbf{v}_f} + \mu\lfloor q/2\rceil + e$

$\mathbf{c}_1^\mathsf{T} = \mathbf{s}^\mathsf{T}(\mathbf{B} - (1, \mathbf{x}) \otimes \mathbf{G}) + \mathbf{e}_1^\mathsf{T}$

</td></tr>
</table>

To decrypt, first run $\mathsf{EvalCX}(\mathbf{c}_1, f, \mathbf{x})$ to obtain $\mathbf{c}_f = \mathbf{s}^\mathsf{T}(\mathbf{B}_f - f(\mathbf{x})\mathbf{G}) + \mathbf{e}_f^\mathsf{T}$. If $f(\mathbf{x}) = 0$, the decryptor can compute $c_0 - \mathbf{c}_f^\mathsf{T}\mathbf{r} = \mu\lfloor q/2\rceil + (e - \mathbf{e}_f^\mathsf{T}\mathbf{r})$ and round it to recover μ.

Observe that the above scheme can be viewed as a nearly linear secret sharing scheme, where the shares chosen by $\mathbf{x}$ are exactly $\mathbf{L}^{\mathbf{x}} = \mathbf{c}_1$ and the shares dependent on f and μ is $L_f = c_0$. At the moment, the bit-length of L_f is $\Theta(\log q)$. Since the noise growth during the homomorphic evaluation is exponential to the depth of the computation, q is a poly(d, λ)-bit modulus in order to accommodate for the noise growth. We next turn to reducing the size of L_f to a constant independent of d.

Rounding to Make L_f Constant-Size. Since the encrypted message is only a single bit, we can afford to lose a lot of precision in the above decryption process. In particular, the scheme is still correct if we round down the digest $\mathbf{B}_f$ to a much smaller, depth-independent, modulus $p \ll q$, and change c_0 to use the rounded digest (while keeping $\mathbf{c}_1^\mathsf{T}$ unchanged):

$$c_0' = \mathbf{s}^\mathsf{T}\lfloor\mathbf{B}_f\mathbf{G}^{-1}(\mathbf{a})\rceil_p + \mu\lfloor p/2\rceil + e \qquad \text{over } \mathbb{Z}_p.$$

During decryption, one now computes, over $\mathbb{Z}_p$,

$$c_0' - \lfloor\mathbf{c}_f^\mathsf{T}\mathbf{G}^{-1}(\mathbf{a})\rceil_p = c_0' - \lfloor\mathbf{s}^\mathsf{T}\mathbf{B}_f\mathbf{G}^{-1}(\mathbf{a}) + f(\mathbf{x})\mathbf{s}^\mathsf{T}\mathbf{a} + \mathbf{e}_f^\mathsf{T}\mathbf{G}^{-1}(\mathbf{a})\rceil_p$$

$$= c_0' - \left(\mathbf{s}^\mathsf{T}\lfloor\mathbf{B}_f\mathbf{G}^{-1}(\mathbf{a})\rceil_p + f(\mathbf{x})\lfloor\mathbf{s}^\mathsf{T}\mathbf{a}\rceil_p + \underbrace{\lfloor\mathbf{e}_f^\mathsf{T}\mathbf{G}^{-1}(\mathbf{a})\rceil_p}_{e_f'} + e_s\right)$$

$$= \mu\lfloor p/2\rceil - f(\mathbf{x})\lfloor\mathbf{s}^\mathsf{T}\mathbf{a}\rceil_p + (e - e_f' - e_s), \qquad (4)$$

where the rounding error e_s is of magnitude $|e_s| = \Theta(\|\mathbf{s}\|_1)$. As long as the error terms are much smaller than $p/2$, when $f(\mathbf{x}) = 0$, one can still recover μ. We can now recast the above rounded AB-LFE scheme into a secret sharing scheme with L_f of bit-length $\Theta(\log p)$, independent of depth d. (Only the larger modulus q will, and thus $\mathbf{e}_f$ itself can, grow with d.)

$$\begin{aligned}
\mathsf{SS.pp}: \quad &\mathbf{a}, \mathbf{B} &&\mod q; \\
L_f: \quad &c_0' = \mathbf{s}^\mathsf{T}\lfloor\mathbf{B}_f\mathbf{G}^{-1}(\mathbf{a})\rceil_p + \mu\lfloor p/2\rceil + e &&\mod p \ll q; \\
\mathbf{L}^{\mathbf{x}}: \quad &\mathbf{c}_1^\mathsf{T} = \mathbf{s}^\mathsf{T}(\mathbf{B} - (1, \mathbf{x}) \otimes \mathbf{G}) + \mathbf{e}_1^\mathsf{T} &&\mod q.
\end{aligned}$$

As shown in Eq. (1), to obtain KP-ABE, we will use a pairing-based IPFE to compute L_f in the exponent. Specifically, the IPFE secret key isk encodes $(\lfloor \mathbf{B}_f \mathbf{G}^{-1}(\mathbf{a}) \rceil_p, \lfloor p/2 \rceil)$, and the IPFE ciphertext ict encodes $(\mathbf{s}^\mathsf{T}, \mu)$. Together, they decrypt to exactly $[\![L_f]\!]_\mathsf{T}$. Since both vectors live in $\mathbb{Z}_p$, the KP-ABE key, consisting of only isk, is of size independent of d. Our secret sharing scheme is summarized below. It turns out that arguing security is actually tricky and requires additional modification.

Our Secret Sharing Scheme for KP-ABE

$\mathsf{Setup}(1^\lambda) : \mathsf{pp} = \mathsf{LFE.pp} = (\mathbf{a}, \mathbf{B}) = (\mathbf{a}, \mathbf{A}_0, \mathbf{A}_1, \ldots, \mathbf{A}_\ell)$.

$\mathsf{ShareX}(\mathsf{pp}) :$ Compute LWE samples

$$\mathbf{L}_0 = \mathbf{s}^\mathsf{T} \mathbf{A}_0 + \mathbf{e}_0, \quad \mathbf{L}_i^b = \mathbf{s}^\mathsf{T}(\mathbf{A}_i - b\mathbf{G}) + \mathbf{e}_i^\mathsf{T}.$$

Output $(\mathbf{L}_0, \{\mathbf{L}_i^b\}, \mathbf{s})$.

$\mathsf{ShareF}(\mathsf{pp}, f, \mu, \mathbf{s}) :$ Compute $\mathbf{B}_f = \mathsf{EvalC}(\mathbf{B}, f)$.

Output $L_f = \mathbf{s}^\mathsf{T} \lfloor \mathbf{B}_f \mathbf{G}^{-1}(\mathbf{a}) \rceil_p + \mu \lfloor p/2 \rceil$.

$\forall \mathbf{x} \in \{0,1\}^\ell : \mathbf{L}^\mathbf{x} = (\mathbf{L}_0, \mathbf{L}_1^{\mathbf{x}[1]}, \ldots, \mathbf{L}_\ell^{\mathbf{x}[\ell]})$

$\mathsf{Recon}(\mathsf{pp}, f, L_f, \mathbf{x}, \mathbf{L}^\mathbf{x}) :$ If $f(\mathbf{x}) = 1$, output $\bot$.

Otherwise, compute $\mathbf{c}_f = \mathsf{EvalCX}(\mathbf{L}^\mathbf{x}, f, \mathbf{x})$, and

recover μ from $L_f - \lfloor \mathbf{c}_f^\mathsf{T} \mathbf{G}^{-1}(\mathbf{a}) \rceil_p \approx \mu \lfloor p/2 \rceil$.

Non-Annihilability by Leakage Simulation. However, using AB-LFE creates a further complication, as its security relies on flooding the e'_f, e_s terms (which may contain information of $\mathbf{s}$ and $\mathbf{x}$) with e, in order to prove pseudorandomness of L_f. By Eqs. (3, 4), when $f(\mathbf{x}) = 1$ we have

$$L_f = \lfloor \mathsf{EvalCX}(\mathbf{L}^\mathbf{x}, f, \mathbf{x})^\mathsf{T} \mathbf{G}^{-1}(\mathbf{a}) \rceil_p$$
$$- \lfloor \mathbf{s}^\mathsf{T} \mathbf{a} + e_a \rceil_p + \mu \lfloor p/2 \rceil + (e - e'_f - e_s). \tag{5}$$

Observe that in the above, for later convenience, an additional polynomial LWE noise e_a is introduced in the term $\lfloor \mathbf{s}^\mathsf{T} \mathbf{a} + e_a \rceil_p$ (which by rounding simply equals to $\lfloor \mathbf{s}^\mathsf{T} \mathbf{a} \rceil_p$).

At this point, in order to show that L_f is pseudorandom, given that $\mathbf{x}$ is selected before Setup, one could program the public matrices as $\mathbf{A}_i = \mathbf{A}'_i + x_i \mathbf{G}$ according to $\mathbf{x}$, where $\mathbf{B}' = (\mathbf{A}'_0, .., \mathbf{A}'_\ell)$ are sampled at random. And one would hope to apply LWE to argue that

$$\mathbf{L}_\mathbf{x} = \mathbf{s}^\mathsf{T}(\mathbf{B} + (1, \mathbf{x}) \otimes \mathbf{G}) + \mathbf{e}_1^\mathsf{T} = \mathbf{s}^\mathsf{T} \mathbf{B}' + \mathbf{e}_1^\mathsf{T},$$

and $(\mathbf{s}^\mathsf{T} \mathbf{a} + e_a)$ are jointly pseudorandom. However, the noise terms e'_f and e_s may leak information about $\mathbf{e}_2$ and $\mathbf{s}$.

The solution in [36] is noise flooding. By setting e to be super-polynomially larger than $(e'_f + e_s)$, we have $e - e'_f - e_s \approx_s e$. By LWE, we can now switch $\mathbf{L}^\times$ and $(\mathbf{s}^\mathsf{T}\mathbf{a} + e_a)$ to random and conclude that L_f is pseudorandom.

However, the unique challenge here is that L_f is going to be computed in the exponent of the pairing group, and decryption only recovers $(\mu\lfloor p/2\rceil + e)$ in the exponent. When e is super-polynomial, we can no longer extract μ out of the exponent. Our solution is avoiding flooding altogether and remove the noise e from L_f. As such, we cannot prove pseudorandomness of L_f, but only a weaker security notion that we call non-annihilability (for L_f). This notion captures that L_f is still entropic.

Non-Annihilability. Non-annihilability requires that no adversary, after seeing $\mathbf{L}^\times$ (but not L_f) can come up with an affine function γ such that $\gamma(L_f) = 0$. As we will see, this security notion, combined with GGM, suffices for our proof.

Towards proving non-annihilability, we want to show that L_f is highly entropic (even without e). Our idea is to view the noises e'_f, e_s as leakage of the randomness that generates $\mathbf{L}^\times$ and $(\mathbf{s}^\mathsf{T}\mathbf{a} + e_a)$ as well as the other information, and simulate e'_f, e_s using leakage simulation [16,25]. Crucially, because e'_f, e_s have polynomial range, the simulation can run in polynomial time. More precisely, the leakage simulation lemma of [16] states that for any joint distribution $(X, Z) \sim \mathcal{D}$ (Z viewed as leakage of randomness for generating X), adversary size bound s, and error bound ϵ, there is a simulator h simulating Z as $h(X)$ such that (X, Z) and $(X, h(X))$ are (s, ϵ)-indistinguishable. Furthermore, the running time of h is $O(s\epsilon^{-2}2^{|Z|})$. Suppose for contradiction that there is an adversary $\mathcal{A}$ of size $s = \text{poly}(\lambda)$ winning the non-annihilability game with probability $2\epsilon \geq 1/\text{poly}(\lambda)$. Consider the joint distribution $\mathcal{D}$ of running the game with $\mathcal{A}$, defined in the first line below:

$$\mathcal{D} \to \{X = (\mathsf{pp}, \mathbf{x}, \mathbf{L}^\times, f, \mu, \gamma, \psi = \mathbf{s}^\mathsf{T}\mathbf{a} + e_a), \qquad Z = e'_f + e_s\}$$

$$\overset{s,\epsilon}{\approx} \text{Hybrid 1} \to \{X = (\mathsf{pp}, \mathbf{x}, \mathbf{L}^\times, f, \mu, \gamma, \psi = \mathbf{s}^\mathsf{T}\mathbf{a} + e_a), \qquad Z = h(X)\}$$

$$\approx \text{Hybrid 2} \to \{X = (\mathsf{pp}, \mathbf{x}, \mathbf{L}^\times \text{ random}, f, \mu, \gamma, \psi \text{ random}), \quad Z = h(X)\}.$$

Using (X, Z), one can emulate L_f as (cf. Eq. (5) with e removed and $(e'_f + e_s)$ replaced by Z)

$$L_f = \lfloor \mathsf{EvalCX}(\mathbf{L}^\times, f, \mathbf{x})\mathbf{G}^{-1}(\mathbf{a})\rceil_p - \lfloor\psi\rceil_p + \mu\lfloor p/2\rceil - Z.$$

Since $Z = e'_f + e_s$, and s, ϵ^{-1} are all polynomially bounded, we can simulate Z by $h(X)$ in polynomial time (Hybrid 1). Now, we can apply LWE to switch $\mathbf{L}^\times$, $\psi = \mathbf{s}^\mathsf{T}\mathbf{a} + e_a$ to random (Hybrid 2). At this point, it seems that L_f is just pseudorandom by the pseudorandomness of ψ. However, there is a subtle issue: $Z = h(X)$ depends on ψ contained in X, and hence $(\lfloor\psi\rceil_p - Z)$ may not be pseudorandom, and neither may be L_f. Despite this dependency, thanks again to $(e'_f + e_s)$, thus $h(X)$, being polynomially bounded, $(-\lfloor\psi\rceil_p + h(X))$ still has almost full entropy (up to a logarithmic loss). Therefore, the probability that L_f is annihilated by an affine function γ chosen by $\mathcal{A}$ before ψ is randomly sampled is negligible. This gives a contradiction and concludes the proof of non-annihilability.

Multi-Key Security of KP-ABE in GGM. Our KP-ABE scheme combines an IPFE scheme with the secret sharing scheme described above. As described before, in our KP-ABE scheme, we only compute the L_f part of secret sharing using IPFE, and leave the $\mathbf{L}^{\mathbf{x}}$ part in the clear so that rounding can be performed. To achieve multi-key security, we further employ the idea from [3,4] to "isolate" each ABE secret key in GGM by multiplying it with a fresh random element δ.

$$\left.\begin{array}{ll} \text{kp.sk}: & [\![\delta]\!]_2, \quad \text{isk}([\![\delta(\lfloor \mathbf{B}_f \mathbf{G}^{-1}(\mathbf{a})\rceil_p, \lfloor p/2 \rfloor)]\!]_2) \\ \text{kp.ct}: & \mathbf{L}^{\mathbf{x}}, \qquad\qquad\qquad \text{ict}([\![(\mathbf{s},\mu)]\!]_1) \end{array}\right\} \text{decrypt to } [\![\delta L_f]\!]_{\mathrm{T}}.$$

The decryption algorithm first computes IPFE decryption to recover $[\![\delta L_f]\!]_{\mathrm{T}}$. It then computes (homomorphically in the exponent of g_{T})

$$[\![\delta L_f]\!]_{\mathrm{T}} - [\![\delta]\!]_{\mathrm{T}} \lfloor \mathbf{c}_f^{\mathsf{T}} \mathbf{G}^{-1}(\mathbf{a})\rceil_p = [\![\delta(\mu\lfloor p/2 \rfloor - (e_f' + e_s))]\!]_{\mathrm{T}}.$$

Since the noise $(e_f' + e_s)$ has a polynomial range, the decryption algorithm enumerates all its possible values to recover μ.

Multi-key security, at a high level, relies on the fact that in GGM, an adversary can only learn information about $[\![\delta L_f]\!]_{\mathrm{T}}$ by submitting zero-test queries of affine functions. When the adversary attacks multiple keys, it essentially submits zero-test queries over the terms $\{\delta_j L_{f_j}\}$. Let $\gamma(\{\delta_j L_{f_j}\})$ be any zero-test query submitted by $\mathcal{A}$, we can view it as a degree-1 polynomial over δ_j's:

$$\gamma(\{\delta_j L_{f_j}\}) = \sum_j \gamma_j(L_{f_j})\delta_j + \gamma_0,$$

where $\gamma_j(L_{f_j})$ is the coefficient of δ_j. Since each δ_j is sampled independently at random, by Schwartz–Zippel, with all but negligible probability, γ evaluates to zero only if all γ_j's evaluate to zero. In other words, the adversary is effectively constrained to annihilate each L_{f_j} individually. By the non-annihilability for L_f, if γ_j is not the zero function, it evaluates to non-zero with overwhelming probability. Hence the adversary learns no information of each L_{f_j} and the message μ encoded in them.

Our KP-ABE Scheme

$\mathsf{Setup}(1^\lambda):$ Output $\mathsf{mpk} = \mathsf{impk}$ for IPFE, pp for secret sharing and $\mathsf{msk} = \mathsf{imsk}$ for IPFE.

$\mathsf{KeyGen}(\mathsf{msk}, C):$ Sample $\delta \xleftarrow{\$} \mathbb{Z}_p$ and compute $\mathbf{B}_f = \mathsf{EvalC}(\mathbf{B}, f)$.

Output $\mathsf{sk} = ([\![\delta]\!]_2, \mathsf{isk}([\![\delta(\lfloor \mathbf{B}_f \mathbf{G}^{-1}(\mathbf{a})\rceil_p, \lfloor p/2 \rceil)]\!]_2)).$

$\mathsf{Enc}(\mathsf{mpk}, \mathbf{x}, \mu):$ Compute $(\mathbf{L}_0, \{\mathbf{L}_i^b\}, \mathbf{s}) \xleftarrow{\$} \mathsf{ShareX}(\mathsf{pp}).$

Output $\mathsf{ct} = (\mathbf{L}^{\mathbf{x}}, \mathsf{ict}([\![\mathbf{s}, \mu]\!]_1)).$

$\mathsf{Dec}(\mathsf{mpk}, \mathsf{sk}, C, \mathsf{ct}, \mathbf{x}):$ Run IPFE decryption to recover $[\![\delta L_f]\!]_{\mathrm{T}}.$

Compute $\mathbf{c}_f = \mathsf{EvalCX}(\mathbf{L}^{\mathbf{x}}, f, \mathbf{x})$ and find μ from

$$[\![\delta L_f]\!]_{\mathrm{T}} - [\![\delta]\!]_{\mathrm{T}} \lfloor \mathbf{c}_f^{\mathsf{T}} \mathbf{G}^{-1}(\mathbf{a})\rceil_p = [\![\delta(\mu\lfloor p/2 \rceil - e_s - e_f')]\!]_{\mathrm{T}}.$$

Summary of Our KP-ABE. Combining the above secret sharing scheme with an IPFE scheme, we obtain a KP-ABE scheme for bounded-depth circuits as summarized above.

We note that our KP-ABE scheme achieves the same asymptotic ciphertext compactness as the BGG$^+$ scheme. Let d be an upper bound on the depth of the policy f, then $|\mathsf{ct}| = \mathrm{poly}(\lambda, d)|\mathbf{x}|$. The secret keys of our scheme contains only $O(1)$ group elements, in fact only *three* using the IPFE scheme of [2] in a group of order p. We set $\log p = \mathrm{poly}(\lambda)$ and hence obtain constant size keys.

Security Sketch for KP-ABE. Finally, for completeness, we add a security sketch that puts the previous ideas together. We emphasize that we only use GGM in the last argument, when we need to isolate the share L_{f_j} for each f.

The selective security game of ABE (summarized in H_0 below) at a high level is as follows: The adversary $\mathcal{A}$ first decides a challenge attribute $\mathbf{x}^*$ before receiving a master public key mpk and a ciphertext ct^* from the challenger $\mathcal{C}$. It is then allowed to repeatedly query secret keys sk_j for functions f_j. The adversary wins if every queried function f_j satisfies $f_j(\mathbf{x}^*) \neq 0$, and if it guesses the encrypted bit μ correctly.

$$H_0 \qquad\qquad\qquad H_1$$

$$\mathcal{C} \xleftarrow{\quad\mathbf{x}^*\quad} \mathcal{A} \qquad\qquad \mathcal{C} \xleftarrow{\quad\mathbf{x}^*\quad} \mathcal{A}$$
$$\mathcal{C} \xrightarrow{\mathsf{mpk},\, \mathsf{ct}^* = \mathbf{L}^{\mathbf{x}^*},\, \mathsf{ict}([\![\mathbf{s},\mu]\!]_1)} \mathcal{A} \qquad \mathcal{C} \xrightarrow{\mathsf{mpk},\, \mathsf{ct}^* = \mathbf{L}^{\mathbf{x}^*},\, \widetilde{\mathsf{ict}}(\bot)} \mathcal{A}$$

$$\xleftarrow{\qquad f_j \qquad} \qquad\qquad \xleftarrow{\qquad f_j \qquad}$$

$$\left.\begin{array}{c}\mathsf{sk}_j = ([\![\delta_j]\!]_2,\\ \mathsf{isk}([\![\delta_j(\lfloor \mathbf{B}_f\mathbf{G}^{-1}(\mathbf{a})\rceil_p, \lfloor p/2\rceil)]\!]_2))\end{array}\right\} \text{repeat} \qquad \left.\begin{array}{c}\mathsf{sk}_j = ([\![\delta_j]\!]_2,\\ \widetilde{\mathsf{isk}}([\![\delta_j L_{f_j}]\!]_2))\end{array}\right\} \text{repeat}$$

$$\xRightarrow{\text{IPFE}}$$

Note that we can generate the IPFE ciphertext $\mathsf{ict}([\![\mathbf{s},\mu]\!]_1)$ before any IPFE secret keys $\mathsf{isk}([\![\delta(\lfloor \mathbf{B}_{f_j}\mathbf{G}^{-1}(\mathbf{a})\rceil_p, \lfloor p/2\rceil)]\!]_2)$. Relying on the selective simulation security of IPFE, we can (as summarized in H_1 above) replace $\mathsf{ict}([\![\mathbf{s},\mu]\!]_1)$ with a simulated ciphertext $\widetilde{\mathsf{ict}}(\bot)$, and each $\mathsf{isk}([\![\delta_j(\lfloor \mathbf{B}_{f_j}\mathbf{G}^{-1}(\mathbf{a})\rceil_p, \lfloor p/2\rceil)]\!]_2)$ with a simulated secret key $\widetilde{\mathsf{isk}}([\![\delta_j L_{f_j}]\!]_2)$ using their inner products.

In GGM, we can now argue that $\mathcal{A}$ only learns information about μ through zero-test queries over $\{\delta_j L_{f_j}\}$. As argued before, by the non-annihilability of L_f, the adversary learns no information of μ.

Building Doubly Succinct CP-ABE. To build a CP-ABE scheme we need a different secret sharing construction, because the previous rounding solution does not work anymore. As described in Eq. (2), in the CP case, we use IPFE to compute $\mathbf{L}^{\mathbf{x}}$ in the exponent, hence cannot perform rounding on it. Without rounding, the $\mathbf{e}_f$ term, as a result of EvalCX, in Eq. (4) becomes super-polynomial. This again makes the ABE decryption inefficient.

Fortunately, for Boolean formulae, the work of [23] develops specialized homomorphic evaluation procedures $\mathsf{EvalF}, \mathsf{EvalFX}$ that ensure the evaluation noise $\mathbf{e}_f$

has a polynomial range. Therefore, our secret sharing scheme for CP removes the rounding and replaces EvalC, EvalCX by EvalF, EvalFX. We summarize our modified secret sharing scheme below (Setup, ShareX are kept the same).

Modified Secret Sharing Scheme for CP-ABE

ShareF$'$(pp, $f, \mu, \mathbf{s}$) : Compute $\mathbf{B}_f = $ EvalF($\mathbf{B}, f$).

Output $L_f = \mathbf{s}^\top \mathbf{B}_f \mathbf{G}^{-1}(\mathbf{a}) + \mu \lfloor p/2 \rceil + e$.

Recon$'$(pp, $f, L_f, \mathbf{x}, \mathbf{L}^{\mathbf{x}}$) : If $f(\mathbf{x}) = 1$, output $\perp$.

Otherwise, compute $\mathbf{c}_f = $ EvalFX($\mathbf{L}^{\mathbf{x}}, f, \mathbf{x}$),

and find μ from $L_f - \mathbf{c}_f^\top \mathbf{G}^{-1}(\mathbf{a}) = \mu \lfloor p/2 \rceil + (e - e_f')$.

As noted before, in our CP-ABE scheme we use IPFE to compute $\mathbf{L}^{\mathbf{x}}$. To achieve double succinctness, we carefully implement a pair of functions Sel, Encode using an IPFE with constant-size isk's, such that Sel($[\![\mathbf{x}]\!]_2$) and Encode($[\![\mathbf{L}_0, \{\mathbf{L}_i^b\}]\!]_1$) decrypts exactly to $[\![\mathbf{L}^{\mathbf{x}}]\!]_T$. We obtain a CP-ABE scheme for Boolean formulae as summarized below.

Our CP-ABE Scheme

Setup(1^λ) : Output mpk = impk for IPFE and pp for secret sharing, and msk = imsk for IPFE.

KeyGen(msk, $\mathbf{x}$) : Sample $\delta \xleftarrow{\$} \mathbb{Z}_p$.

Output sk = ($[\![\delta]\!]_2$, Sel($[\![\delta\mathbf{x}]\!]_2$)).

Enc(mpk, f, μ) : Compute $(\mathbf{L}_0, \{\mathbf{L}_i^b\}, \mathbf{s}) \xleftarrow{\$} $ ShareX(pp)

and $L_f \xleftarrow{\$} $ ShareF$'$(pp, $f, \mu, \mathbf{s}$).

Output ct = ($[\![L_f]\!]_1$, Encode($[\![\mathbf{L}_0, \{\mathbf{L}_i^b\}]\!]_1$)).

Dec(mpk, sk, $\mathbf{x}$, ct, f) : Run IPFE decryption to recover $[\![\delta\mathbf{L}^{\mathbf{x}}]\!]_T$.

Compute $[\![\delta\mathbf{c}_f]\!]_T = $ EvalFX($[\![\delta\mathbf{L}^{\mathbf{x}}]\!]_T, f, \mathbf{x}$),

and find μ from

$[\![L_f]\!]_1 [\![\delta]\!]_2 - [\![\delta\mathbf{c}_f^\top]\!]_T \mathbf{G}^{-1}(\mathbf{a}) = [\![\delta(\mu\lfloor p/2 \rceil + (e - e_f'))]\!]_T$.

We now describe the Sel, Encode functions. Let $\ell = |\mathbf{x}|$ denote the length of $\mathbf{x}$. The Sel algorithm first computes the "selection vector" for $\mathbf{x}$ as

$$\mathbf{v} = (1, 1 - \mathbf{x}[1], \mathbf{x}[1], \ldots, 1 - \mathbf{x}[i], \mathbf{x}[i], \ldots),$$

and then computes an IPFE secret key $\mathsf{isk}(\llbracket \mathbf{v} \rrbracket_2)$. The Encode algorithm places input shares in the matrix

$$
\begin{pmatrix}
\mathbf{L}_0 & 0 & 0 & \cdots & 0 & 0 & \cdots & 0 & 0 \\
0 & \mathbf{L}_1^0 & \mathbf{L}_1^1 & \cdots & 0 & 0 & \cdots & 0 & 0 \\
0 & \vdots & \vdots & \ddots & \vdots & \vdots & \ddots & \vdots & \vdots \\
0 & 0 & 0 & \cdots & \mathbf{L}_i^0 & \mathbf{L}_i^1 & \cdots & 0 & 0 \\
0 & \vdots & \vdots & \ddots & \vdots & \vdots & \ddots & \vdots & \vdots \\
0 & 0 & 0 & \cdots & 0 & 0 & \cdots & \mathbf{L}_\ell^0 & \mathbf{L}_\ell^1
\end{pmatrix}
$$

and computes one IPFE ciphertext for each row $\mathbf{u}_l$ of the matrix. Our CP-ABE has both succinct keys and ciphertexts: $|\mathsf{sk}| = O(1)$ and $|\mathsf{ct}| = \mathrm{poly}(\lambda)|\mathbf{x}|^2$.

Simulation Security for IPFE in GGM. Similar to the security proof for KP-ABE, our security proof for CP-ABE requires selective simulation security of IPFE.

$$
\begin{array}{ll}
\mathsf{Sel}: & \mathsf{isk}(\llbracket \mathbf{v} \rrbracket_2) \\
\mathsf{Encode}: \forall l & \mathsf{ict}(\llbracket \mathbf{u}_l \rrbracket_1)
\end{array}
\quad \overset{c}{\approx} \quad
\begin{array}{l}
\widetilde{\mathsf{isk}}(\llbracket \mathbf{L}^{\mathbf{x}} \rrbracket_2) \\
\widetilde{\mathsf{ict}}(\bot)
\end{array}
$$

Note that above we need to simulate *multiple* IPFE ciphertexts and program all their decryption outcome $\mathbf{L}^{\mathbf{x}}$ in each secret key. This is possible using existing IPFE schemes [2,32], but at the cost of having the secret key size proportional to the number $k = |\mathbf{L}^{\mathbf{x}}|$ of ciphertexts to be simulated. However, we aim for constant-size secret keys (independent of k). Unfortunately, in the standard model, it is impossible to achieve simulation security for k ciphertexts if the secret key is shorter than k bits by an incompressibility argument [12]. We show that simulation security for unbounded polynomially many ciphertexts can nevertheless be achieved with constant-size secret keys in the GGM. In particular, the IPFE scheme of [1], whose secret key contains a single group element, satisfies it. Roughly speaking, in the GGM, an adversary only learns information about values in the exponent through zero-test queries over the pairings of keys and ciphertexts, which the simulator can answer by translating them into zero-test queries over the inner products. As a side note, we can in fact prove *adaptive* simulation security for the [1] IPFE scheme, though our ABE scheme only relies on *selective* simulation security.

Achieving Adaptive Security. Examining the security sketch for KP-ABE, we observe that in our construction, the $\mathsf{ict}(\llbracket \mathbf{s}, \mu \rrbracket_1)$ component of ciphertext ct^* doesn't depend on the challenge attribute $\mathbf{x}^*$. This means that even in the adaptive KP-ABE game, where $\mathbf{x}^*$ is decided after some key queries, the $\mathsf{ict}(\llbracket \mathbf{s}, \mu \rrbracket_1)$ component of ct^* can be fixed at the beginning of the game, before any key queries. Therefore, we can still rely on selective simulation security of IPFE for the first proof step.

However, when we next need to invoke non-annihilability for L_f, we run into a problem: the security for L_f only holds when $\mathbf{x}^*$ is chosen before the LWE public matrix $\mathbf{B}$ is revealed in the public parameter pp of the secret sharing. To achieve adaptive security, what we need is adaptive non-annihilability property, which allows $\mathbf{x}^*$ to be chosen adaptively dependent on pp. We show that this is implied by the *adaptive* LWE assumption formulated in [36].

In summary, we obtain adaptively secure KP-ABE for circuits and CP-ABE for Boolean formulae both with constant-size keys from GGM and Adaptive LWE.

3 Preliminaries

Let λ be the security parameter, which runs through $\mathbb{N}$. Except in the definitions, we suppress λ for brevity. We write $[a..b]$ for the set $\{a, a+1, \ldots, b\}$ and $[n]$ for $[1..n]$. Vectors and matrices are written in boldface, and are always indexed using $[\cdot]$, i.e., $\mathbf{A}[i, j]$ is the (i, j)-entry of $\mathbf{A}$. The infinity norm of a vector and its induced operator norm of a matrix are denoted by $\|\cdot\|_\infty$. We will use the following lemma for various proofs:

Lemma 1 (Schwartz–Zippel). *Let $P(\mathbf{z})$ be a non-zero polynomial with Z indeterminates of degree at most d over $\mathbb{Z}_p$, then $\Pr\big[\mathbf{z} \xleftarrow{\$} \mathbb{Z}_p^Z : P(\mathbf{z}) = 0\big] \leq d/p$.*

3.1 Attribute-Based Encryption

Definition 1 (ABE [24]). *Let $\mathcal{P} = \{\mathcal{P}_\lambda\}_{\lambda \in \mathbb{N}}$ be a sequence of predicate families with $\mathcal{P}_\lambda = \{P : X_P \times Y_P \to \{0, 1\}\}$. An attribute-based encryption scheme for $\mathcal{P}$ consists of 4 efficient algorithms:*

- Setup$(1^\lambda, P)$ *takes as input the security parameter 1^λ and a predicate $P \in \mathcal{P}_\lambda$, and outputs a pair of master public/secret keys (mpk, msk).*
- KeyGen(msk, y) *takes as input the master secret key msk and some $y \in Y_P$, and outputs a secret key sk.*
- Enc(mpk, x, μ) *takes as input the master public key mpk, some $x \in X_P$, and a message $\mu \in \{0, 1\}$, and it outputs a ciphertext ct.*
- Dec$(\mathsf{mpk}, \mathsf{sk}, y, \mathsf{ct}, x)$ *takes as input the master public key mpk, a secret key sk, its associated y, a ciphertext ct, and its associated x, and is supposed to recover the message if $P(x, y) = 1$.*

The scheme is required to be correct, *i.e., for all $\lambda \in \mathbb{N}$, $P \in \mathcal{P}_\lambda$, $x \in X_P$, $y \in Y_P$, $\mu \in \{0, 1\}$ such that $P(x, y) = 1$, it holds that*

$$\Pr\left[\begin{array}{c} (\mathsf{mpk}, \mathsf{msk}) \xleftarrow{\$} \mathsf{Setup}(1^\lambda, P) \\ \mathsf{sk} \xleftarrow{\$} \mathsf{KeyGen}(\mathsf{msk}, y) : \mathsf{Dec}(\mathsf{mpk}, \mathsf{sk}, y, \mathsf{ct}, x) = \mu \\ \mathsf{ct} \xleftarrow{\$} \mathsf{Enc}(\mathsf{mpk}, x, \mu) \end{array}\right] = 1.$$

In KP-ABE, each $y \in Y_P$ describes a function from X_P to $\{0, 1\}$, each $x \in X_P$ is an input (bit-string) to the functions, and $P(x, y)$ evaluates y on x. When we want to emphasize x (resp. y) is a bit-string (resp. circuit), we write $\mathbf{x}$ (resp. C) instead.

Security. Due to space constraints, we refer the readers to [4, 29, 31] for the definitions of *adaptive, selective,* and *very selective* security for ABE.

Computation Model. We will consider KP-ABE for bounded-depth circuits for any polynomial bound. Our CP-ABE for NC^1 can be found in the full version [31].

Definition 2 (KP-ABE for circuits). *A KP-ABE for (bounded-depth) circuits is ABE for* $\mathcal{P}^{\mathsf{Ckt}}$.[2]

$$X^{\mathsf{Ckt}}_{\lambda,\ell,d} = \{0,1\}^\ell, \quad Y^{\mathsf{Ckt}}_{\lambda,\ell,d} = \{\text{Boolean circuit } C : \{0,1\}^\ell \to \{0,1\} \text{ of depth } d\},$$

$$P^{\mathsf{Ckt}}_{\lambda,\ell,d}(\mathbf{x},C) = \neg C(\mathbf{x}), \quad \mathcal{P}^{\mathsf{Ckt}}_\lambda = \{P^{\mathsf{Ckt}}_{\lambda,\ell,d} | \ell, d \in \mathbb{N}, d \leq D_\lambda\}, \quad \mathcal{P}^{\mathsf{Ckt}} = \{\mathcal{P}^{\mathsf{Ckt}}_\lambda\}_{\lambda \in \mathbb{N}}.$$

Here, D_λ *is a super-polynomial function (specified by the constructions). As an input to* Setup, *the predicate* $P^{\mathsf{Ckt}}_{\lambda,\ell,d}$ *is represented by* $(1^\ell, 1^d)$.

Note that since Setup takes the unary representation of ℓ, d, which will be polynomial in λ, as input, they are bounded by *that* polynomial once the system is set up. However, d can be up to D_λ, which is super-polynomial in λ, so one can set up the system for any polynomial depth, i.e., our KP-ABE for circuits supports bounded-depth circuits for arbitrary polynomial depth bound.

Compactness and Succinctness. Since KeyGen, Enc run in polynomial time, the lengths of key and ciphertext could grow polynomially in $|y|, |x|$, respectively. Moreover, the input length is an argument passed into Setup, so both keys and ciphertexts could have polynomial size dependency on it. We are interested in ABE schemes with short keys and ciphertexts:

Definition 3 (ABE efficiency). *A KP-ABE for circuits (of depth at most d) has*

- succinct keys *if* $|\mathsf{sk}| = \mathrm{poly}(\lambda, d)$ *is independent of* $|C|, |\mathbf{x}|$;
- compact ciphertexts *if* $|\mathsf{ct}| = |\mathbf{x}| \, \mathrm{poly}(\lambda, d)$ *is independent of* $|C|$.

We remark that an ideally succinct component should be of length $\mathrm{poly}(\lambda)$. Nevertheless, our version defined above is still meaningful as the circuit size can be much larger than its depth.

3.2   Lattice Tools

Homomorphic Evaluation. We use the following abstraction of homomorphic evaluation for ABE over lattices, developed in a series of works [11, 19, 23] with the syntax in [13, 14]. The actual algorithm we use is a slightly changed version of that for ABE for circuits in [11]. In our version, instead of using $\mathbf{G}$ as the

---

[2] When working with lattices, it is more convenient to indicate authorization of decryption by zero, thus the negation of $C(\mathbf{x})$.

gadget matrix, we consider $\mathbf{QG}$ for any invertible $\mathbf{Q}$. Note that $\mathbf{G}^{-1}(\mathbf{Q}^{-1} \times \cdot)$ is a right inverse of $\mathbf{QG}$ with binary output. We replace any invocation of $\mathbf{G}^{-1}(\cdot)$ in the original algorithms by $\mathbf{G}^{-1}(\mathbf{Q}^{-1} \times \cdot)$ to obtain the following:

Lemma 2 (homomorphic evaluation for circuits, adapted from [11]). *EvalC and EvalCX are two efficient deterministic algorithms. Let n, ℓ, q be positive integers, $m = n\lceil \log_2 q \rceil$, $\mathbf{G}$ the gadget matrix, $\mathbf{B}$ a matrix over $\mathbb{Z}_q$ of shape $n \times (\ell + 1)m$, $\mathbf{Q}$ an invertible matrix over $\mathbb{Z}_q$ of shape $n \times n$, $\mathbf{x}$ an ℓ-bit string (row vector), and C a circuit of depth d with input length ℓ. The algorithms work as follows:*

- *EvalC$(\mathbf{B}, \mathbf{Q}, C)$ outputs $\mathbf{H}_C \in \mathbb{Z}^{(\ell+1)m \times m}$;*
- *EvalCX$(\mathbf{B}, \mathbf{Q}, C, \mathbf{x})$ outputs $\widehat{\mathbf{H}}_{C,\mathbf{x}} \in \mathbb{Z}^{(\ell+1)m \times m}$.*

The outputs satisfy

$$\|\mathbf{H}_C^\mathsf{T}\|_\infty, \|\widehat{\mathbf{H}}_{C,\mathbf{x}}^\mathsf{T}\|_\infty \leq (m+1)^d, \quad (\mathbf{B} - (1, \mathbf{x}) \otimes \mathbf{QG})\widehat{\mathbf{H}}_{C,\mathbf{x}} = \mathbf{B}\mathbf{H}_C - C(\mathbf{x})\mathbf{QG}.$$

Gadget Matrix [33]. Let n, q be positive integers and $m = n\lceil \log_2 q \rceil$. The gadget matrix is $\mathbf{G} = \mathbf{g}^\mathsf{T} \otimes \mathbf{I}_n$, where $\mathbf{g}^\mathsf{T} = (2^0, 2^1, \dots, 2^{\lceil \log_2 q \rceil - 1})$. There exists an efficiently computable function $\mathbf{G}^{-1} : \mathbb{Z}_q^n \to \{0, 1\}^m$ such that $\mathbf{G} \cdot \mathbf{G}^{-1}(\mathbf{u}) = \mathbf{u}$ for all $\mathbf{u} \in \mathbb{Z}_q^n$.

Assumption. We rely on the following assumption, a small-secret version of adaptive learning with errors (LWE), which itself is a natural variant of LWE first proposed in [36]:

Definition 4 (small-secret adaptive LWE). *We suppress the security parameter λ and all the parameters are dependent on λ. Let n be the dimension, q the modulus, χ the error distribution, $m = n\lceil \log_2 q \rceil$, and $\mathbf{G}$ the gadget matrix. The small-secret adaptive LWE assumption sALWE$_{n,q,\chi}$ statesthat $\mathsf{Exp}^0_{\mathsf{sALWE}} \approx \mathsf{Exp}^1_{\mathsf{sALWE}}$, where $\mathsf{Exp}^b_{\mathsf{sALWE}}(1^n, q, \chi)$ with adversary $\mathcal{A}$ proceeds as follows:*

- **Setup.** *The challenger launches $\mathcal{A}$ and receives $(1^\ell, 1^{m'})$ from it. The challenger samples $\mathbf{A} \xleftarrow{\$} \mathbb{Z}_q^{n \times m'}$, $\mathbf{B} \xleftarrow{\$} \mathbb{Z}_q^{n \times (\ell+1)m}$, and a uniformly random invertible $\mathbf{Q} \in \mathbb{Z}_q^{n \times n}$. It sends $\mathbf{A}, \mathbf{B}, \mathbf{Q}$ to $\mathcal{A}$.*
- **Challenge.** *$\mathcal{A}$ submits $\mathbf{x} \in \{0, 1\}^\ell$. Depending on b,*

  if $b = 0$: $\quad \boxed{\mathbf{s} \xleftarrow{\$} \chi^n}, \quad \mathbf{e} \xleftarrow{\$} \chi^{m'}, \quad \mathbf{f} \xleftarrow{\$} \chi^{(\ell+1)m},$
  $$\mathbf{c}^\mathsf{T} = \mathbf{s}^\mathsf{T}\mathbf{A} + \mathbf{e}^\mathsf{T}, \qquad \mathbf{d}^\mathsf{T} = \mathbf{s}^\mathsf{T}(\mathbf{B} - (1, \mathbf{x}) \otimes \mathbf{QG}) + \mathbf{f}^\mathsf{T};$$

  if $b = 1$: $\quad \mathbf{c}^\mathsf{T} \xleftarrow{\$} \mathbb{Z}_q^{m'}, \qquad \mathbf{d}^\mathsf{T} \xleftarrow{\$} \mathbb{Z}_q^{(\ell+1)m}.$

  The challenger sends $\mathbf{c}, \mathbf{d}$ to $\mathcal{A}$.
- **Guess** *$\mathcal{A}$ outputs a bit, which is the outcome of the experiment.*

Lemma 3 (small-secret adaptive LWE). *The small-secret adaptive LWE assumption holds if the adaptive LWE assumption [36] holds for the same parameters.*

The proof of Lemma 3 can be found in the full version [31].

Parameter Settings. We rely on the hardness of small-secret LWE with subexponential modulus-to-noise ratio. For some $0 < \delta < \frac{1}{2}$, the small-secret LWE assumption is assumed to be hard when the dimension is $n = \text{poly}(\lambda)$, the *prime* modulus is $q = O(2^{n^\delta})$, and the error distribution χ is the discrete Gaussian over $\mathbb{Z}$ of width $\overline{B}/\lambda$ truncated within $[-\overline{B}..\overline{B}]$ for $\overline{B} = \text{poly}(\lambda)$.[3] Hereafter we default to these parameters.

3.3 Pairing Groups and Generic Asymmetric Pairing Group Model

We construct our ABE using pairing groups and prove its security in the generic pairing group model.

Pairing Groups. Throughout the paper, we use a sequence of pairing groups

$$\mathcal{G} = \{(p_\lambda, G_{\lambda,1}, G_{\lambda,2}, G_{\lambda,\mathrm{T}}, g_{\lambda,1}, g_{\lambda,2}, g_{\lambda,\mathrm{T}}, e_\lambda)\}_{\lambda \in \mathbb{N}},$$

where $G_{\lambda,1}$ (resp. $G_{\lambda,2}, G_{\lambda,\mathrm{T}}$) is a cyclic group generated by $g_{\lambda,1}$ (resp. $g_{\lambda,2}, g_{\lambda,\mathrm{T}}$) of prime order $p_\lambda = 2^{\lambda^{\Theta(1)}}$ and $e_\lambda : G_{\lambda,1} \times G_{\lambda,2} \to G_{\lambda,\mathrm{T}}$ is the pairing operation, satisfying $e_\lambda(g_{\lambda,1}^a, g_{\lambda,2}^b) = g_{\lambda,\mathrm{T}}^{ab}$ for all integers a, b. We require the group operations as well as the pairing operation to be efficiently computable.

For a fixed security parameter λ, we denote $g_{\lambda,i}^x$ by $[\![x]\!]_i$ for $i \in \{1, 2, \mathrm{T}\}$. The notation extends to matrices, $[\![\mathbf{A}]\!]_i = g_{\lambda,i}^{\mathbf{A}}$, where exponentiation is done component-wise. With these notations, the group operations are written additively and the pairing operation multiplicatively. For example, $[\![\mathbf{A}]\!]_1 - \mathbf{B}[\![\mathbf{C}]\!]_1\mathbf{D} = [\![\mathbf{A} - \mathbf{BCD}]\!]_1$ and $[\![\mathbf{X}]\!]_2[\![\mathbf{Y}]\!]_1 = [\![\mathbf{XY}]\!]_\mathrm{T}$.

Generic Asymmetric Pairing Group. The security of our ABE scheme holds in the generic asymmetric pairing group model (GGM), where the pairing groups can only be accessed via (non-unique) handles representing group elements and oracles for operating the handles. Due to space constraints, we refer the readers to the full version [31] for the formal definition of the version we use in this work.

3.4 Inner-Product Functional Encryption

Inner-product functional encryption schemes enable generating keys and ciphertexts tied to vectors. Decryption reveals the inner product and nothing more about the plaintext vector. In this work, we consider IPFE schemes based on pairing, where keys and ciphertexts are encoded in the two source groups and decryption recovers inner products encoded in the target group.

Definition 5 (group-based IPFE). *Let $\mathcal{G}$ be a sequence of pairing groups of order $\{p_\lambda\}_{\lambda \in \mathbb{N}}$. An inner-product functional encryption (IPFE) scheme based on $\mathcal{G}$ consists of 4 efficient algorithms:*

---

[3] This truncation only introduces an exponentially small statistical error.

- Setup$(1^\lambda, 1^N)$ *takes as input the security parameter* 1^λ *and the vector dimension* 1^N. *It outputs a pair of master public/secret keys* (impk, imsk).
- KeyGen(imsk, $[\![\mathbf{v}]\!]_2$) *takes as input the master secret key and a vector (encoded in* G_2), *and outputs a secret key* isk.
- Enc(impk, $[\![\mathbf{u}]\!]_1$) *takes as input the master public key and a vector (encoded in* G_1), *and outputs a ciphertext* ict.
- Dec(isk, $[\![\mathbf{v}]\!]_2$, ict) *takes a secret key, the vector in the secret key, and a ciphertext as input, and is supposed to compute the inner product encoded in* G_T.

The scheme is required to be correct, *meaning that for all* $\lambda, N \in \mathbb{N}, \mathbf{u}, \mathbf{v} \in \mathbb{Z}_{p_\lambda}^N$,

$$
\Pr \left[
\begin{array}{c}
(\mathsf{impk}, \mathsf{imsk}) \xleftarrow{\$} \mathsf{Setup}(1^\lambda, 1^N) \\
\mathsf{isk} \xleftarrow{\$} \mathsf{KeyGen}(\mathsf{imsk}, [\![\mathbf{v}]\!]_2) : \mathsf{Dec}(\mathsf{isk}, [\![\mathbf{v}]\!]_2, \mathsf{ict}) = [\![\mathbf{u}^\mathsf{T}\mathbf{v}]\!]_\mathrm{T} \\
\mathsf{ict} \xleftarrow{\$} \mathsf{Enc}(\mathsf{impk}, [\![\mathbf{u}]\!]_1)
\end{array}
\right] = 1.
$$

Definition 6 (key-succinct IPFE). *An IPFE scheme (Definition 5) is* (key-)succinct *if the length of* isk *is a fixed polynomial in* λ, *independent of* N.

Security. Our basic security notion is selective simulation:

Definition 7 (selective simulation [32,41]). *A simulator for an IPFE scheme (Definition 5) consists of 3 efficient algorithms:*

- $\widetilde{\mathsf{Setup}}(1^\lambda, 1^N)$ *takes the same input as* Setup, *and outputs simulated keys* $(\widetilde{\mathsf{impk}}, \widetilde{\mathsf{imsk}})$.
- $\widetilde{\mathsf{KeyGen}}(\widetilde{\mathsf{imsk}}, [\![\mathbf{v}]\!]_2, [\![z_i]\!]_2)$ *takes as input the simulated master secret key, a vector encoded in* G_2, *and an inner product encoded in* G_2. *It outputs a simulated key* $\widetilde{\mathsf{isk}}$.
- $\widetilde{\mathsf{Enc}}(\widetilde{\mathsf{imsk}})$ *takes as input the simulated master secret key. It outputs a simulated ciphertext* $\widetilde{\mathsf{ict}}$.

The IPFE scheme is selectively simulation-secure *if there exists a simulator such that* $\mathsf{Exp}_{\mathrm{real}} \approx \mathsf{Exp}_{\mathrm{sim}}$, *where* $\mathsf{Exp}_{\mathrm{real}}(1^\lambda)$ *or* $\mathsf{Exp}_{\mathrm{sim}}(1^\lambda)$ *with* $\mathcal{A}$ *proceeds as follows:*

- **Challenge.** The challenger launches $\mathcal{A}(1^\lambda)$ and receives from it the vector dimension 1^N and the challenge vector $\mathbf{u} \in \mathbb{Z}_p^N$.
- **Setup.** The challenger runs

$$
\begin{array}{lll}
\text{in } \mathsf{Exp}_{\mathrm{real}}: & (\mathsf{impk}, \mathsf{imsk}) \xleftarrow{\$} \mathsf{Setup}(1^\lambda, 1^N), & \mathsf{ict} \xleftarrow{\$} \mathsf{Enc}(\mathsf{impk}, [\![\mathbf{u}]\!]_1); \\
\text{in } \mathsf{Exp}_{\mathrm{sim}}: & (\mathsf{impk}, \widetilde{\mathsf{imsk}}) \xleftarrow{\$} \widetilde{\mathsf{Setup}}(1^\lambda, 1^N), & \mathsf{ict} \xleftarrow{\$} \widetilde{\mathsf{Enc}}(\widetilde{\mathsf{imsk}});
\end{array}
$$

and sends impk, ict to $\mathcal{A}$.

– **Query.** The following is repeated for arbitrarily many rounds determined by $\mathcal{A}$: In each round, $\mathcal{A}$ submits a vector $[\![\mathbf{v}_j]\!]_2$ encoded in G_2. Upon receiving the query, the challenger runs

$$\text{in } \mathsf{Exp}_{\mathrm{real}}: \qquad \mathsf{isk}_j \xleftarrow{\$} \mathsf{KeyGen}(\mathsf{imsk}, [\![\mathbf{v}_j]\!]_2);$$

$$\text{in } \mathsf{Exp}_{\mathrm{sim}}: \qquad \mathsf{isk}_j \xleftarrow{\$} \widetilde{\mathsf{KeyGen}}(\widetilde{\mathsf{imsk}}, [\![\mathbf{v}_j]\!]_2, \mathbf{u}^{\mathsf{T}}[\![\mathbf{v}_j]\!]_2);$$

and sends isk_j to $\mathcal{A}$.

– **Guess** $\mathcal{A}$ outputs a bit b, which is the output of the experiment.

Lemma 4 ([2,41]). *Assuming the MDDH assumption (true in GGM), there exists a succinct selectively simulation-secure IPFE scheme. Its components have sizes*

$$|\mathsf{impk}| = k(k+1+N)|G_1|, \qquad |\mathsf{imsk}| = (k+1)N\log_2 p,$$
$$|\mathsf{isk}| = (k+1)|G_2|, \qquad |\mathsf{ict}| = (k+1+N)|G_1|,$$

where p is the modulus, k is the MDDH parameter (can be 1 in GGM), N is the dimension, and $|G_i|$ is the bit-length of an element in G_i.

4   Computational Secret Sharing with Adaptive Security

Secret sharing schemes have been used extensively to construct ABE schemes. The seminal work of [24] and a long line of follow-up works ([5,28–30,35] to name a few) used *linear* secret sharing schemes to construct ABE schemes in pairing groups. Policies with polynomial-sized shares and information-theoretic security are in NC [8,9,15,26,34].

The works of [3,4] introduced the notion of *nearly linear* secret sharing with *computational* security. The relaxations enabled greater expressiveness and better efficiency. Assuming LWE, such a scheme exists for all polynomial-sized circuits [3,4,11,23] and the shares are *succinct*, i.e., they only grow with the circuit depth, but not the circuit size. However, the scheme is only *selectively* secure. Furthermore, due to technical reasons, when combined with pairing to obtain ABE, it only applies to Boolean formulae (equivalent to 5-PBP).

This work follows the blueprint of [3,4] for the notions of secret sharing schemes, but departs from them in three important aspects. First, we consider a different security notion, *adaptive non-annihilability*, which is incomparable[4] to selective pseudorandomness considered in [3,4] and enables us to prove adaptive security of ABE. Second, we further relax the linearity requirement so that it could apply to KP-ABE for polynomial-sized circuits. Third, we refine the syntax to separate encodings of input and function.

---

[4] It is stronger in that it is adaptive, but weaker in that the shares are not necessarily pseudorandom.

Definition 8 (secret sharing). *Let* $\mathcal{F} = \{\mathcal{F}_{\lambda,\ell,\mathsf{param}}\}_{\lambda,\ell\in\mathbb{N},\mathsf{param}}$ *be an ensemble of Boolean function families such that for all* $\lambda, \ell \in \mathbb{N}$ *and* param, *every* $f \in \mathcal{F}_{\lambda,\ell,\mathsf{param}}$ *is a function mapping* $\{0,1\}^\ell$ *to* $\{0,1\}$. *A secret sharing scheme for* $\mathcal{F}$ *consists of 4 efficient algorithms:*

- $\mathsf{Setup}(1^\lambda, 1^\ell, \mathsf{param})$ *takes the security parameter* 1^λ, *the input length* 1^ℓ, *and additional parameters* param *as input. It outputs some public parameter* pp.
- $\mathsf{ShareX}(\mathsf{pp})$ *takes the public parameter* pp *as input. It outputs* $1 + 2\ell$ *shares*, $L_0, \{L_i^b\}_{i\in[\ell]}^{b\in\{0,1\}}$, *and some shared randomness* r. *For* $x \in \{0,1\}^\ell$, *we denote by* L^x *the set of shares* $L_0, \{L_i^{x[i]}\}_{i\in[\ell]}$.
- $\mathsf{ShareF}(\mathsf{pp}, f, \mu, r)$ *takes the public parameter* pp, *a function* $f \in \mathcal{F}_{\lambda,\ell,\mathsf{param}}$, *a secret* $\mu \in \{0,1\}$, *and the shared randomness* r *(output by* ShareX*) as input. It outputs a share* L_f.
- $\mathsf{Recon}(\mathsf{pp}, f, \mathbf{x}, L_f, L^x)$ *takes the public parameter* pp, *the Boolean function* $f \in \mathcal{F}_{\lambda,\ell,\mathsf{param}}$, *the input* $\mathbf{x} \in \{0,1\}^\ell$ *to* f, *and the shares* L_f, L^x *as input. It is supposed to recover the secret* μ *if* $f(\mathbf{x}) = 0$. [5]

The scheme is required to be correct, *i.e., for all* $\lambda, \ell \in \mathbb{N}$, param, $\mathbf{x} \in \{0,1\}^\ell$, $f \in \mathcal{F}_{\lambda,\ell,\mathsf{param}}$, $\mu \in \{0,1\}$ *such that* $f(\mathbf{x}) = 0$, *it holds that*

$$\Pr\left[\begin{array}{l} \mathsf{pp} \xleftarrow{\$} \mathsf{Setup}(1^\lambda, 1^\ell, \mathsf{param}) \\ (L_0, \{L_i^b\}_{i\in[\ell]}^{b\in\{0,1\}}, r) \xleftarrow{\$} \mathsf{ShareX}(\mathsf{pp}) \\ L_f \xleftarrow{\$} \mathsf{ShareF}(\mathsf{pp}, f, \mu, r) \end{array} : \mathsf{Recon}(\mathsf{pp}, f, \mathbf{x}, L_f, L^x) = \mu\right] = 1.$$

Definition 9 (succinct shares). *A secret sharing scheme is* succinct *if the size of each share output by* $\mathsf{ShareX}, \mathsf{ShareF}$ *is a fixed polynomial in* λ, *independent of the length of* $\mathbf{x}$ *or the description size of* f, *i.e.,* $|L_f|, |L_0|, |L_i^b|$ *are all* $\mathrm{poly}(\lambda, |\mathsf{param}|)$, *where* $i \in [\ell]$, $b \in \{0,1\}$.[6]

While correctness (Definition 8) and succinctness (Definition 9) are defined similarly to that of [3], our linearity and security notions are different.

4.1 Secret Sharing for Bounded-Depth Circuits from Adaptive LWE

In our KP-ABE construction, we need a secret sharing scheme with two linearity properties. The first is a relaxation of the nearly linear reconstruction requirement in [3]. requirement on reconstruction. Our relaxed version (Definition 10) only stipulates it to be linear in $\mathbf{L}_f$ (and possibly non-linear in L^x).

Definition 10 (weakly nearly linear reconstruction). *A secret sharing scheme (Definition 8) is* weakly nearly linear *if it satisfies the following requirements:*

- *Let* $\{p_\lambda\}_{\lambda\in\mathbb{N}}$ *be a sequence of prime numbers.* $\mathbf{L}_f = L_f$ *is a vector over* $\mathbb{Z}_{p_\lambda}$.

---

[5] We use $f(\mathbf{x}) = 0$ to express authorization.

[6] There are $2|\mathbf{x}| + 2$ shares, so the total share size is linear in the length of $\mathbf{x}$.

– *There is an efficient coefficient-finding algorithm* $\mathsf{FindCoef}(\mathsf{pp}, f, \mathbf{x}, L^{\mathbf{x}})$, *taking as input the public parameter* pp, *a Boolean function* $f \in \mathcal{F}_{\lambda,\ell,\mathsf{param}}$, *an input* $\mathbf{x} \in \{0,1\}^{\ell}$ *to* f, *and the shares* $L^{\mathbf{x}}$. *It outputs an affine function* γ *and a noise bound* 1^B. *For all* $\lambda, \ell \in \mathbb{N}, \mathsf{param}, \mathbf{x} \in \{0,1\}^{\ell}, f \in \mathcal{F}_{\lambda,\ell,\mathsf{param}}, \mu \in \{0,1\}$ *such that* $f(\mathbf{x}) = 0$, *it holds that*

$$
\Pr\left[
\begin{array}{l}
\mathsf{pp} \xleftarrow{\$} \mathsf{Setup}(1^{\lambda}, 1^{\ell}, \mathsf{param}) \\
(L_0, \{L_i^b\}_{i \in [\ell]}^{b \in \{0,1\}}, r) \xleftarrow{\$} \mathsf{ShareX}(\mathsf{pp}) \\
\mathbf{L}_f \leftarrow \mathsf{ShareF}(\mathsf{pp}, f, \mu, r) \\
(\gamma, 1^B) \xleftarrow{\$} \mathsf{FindCoef}(\mathsf{pp}, f, \mathbf{x}, L^{\mathbf{x}})
\end{array}
:
\begin{array}{l}
4B + 1 < p_{\lambda} \text{ and} \\
\exists e \in [-B..B] \text{s.t.} \\
\gamma(\mathbf{L}_f) = \mu \lfloor p/2 \rfloor + e
\end{array}
\right] = 1.
$$

The second is an additional linearity requirement on ShareF.

Definition 11 (linear function sharing). *Let* $\{p_{\lambda}\}_{\lambda \in \mathbb{N}}$ *be a sequence of primes. A secret sharing scheme (Definition 8) has* linear function sharing *if* $\mathbf{r} = r$ *is a vector over* $\mathbb{Z}_{p_{\lambda}}$ *and* $\mathsf{ShareF}(\mathsf{pp}, f, \mu, \mathbf{r})$ *is deterministic and linear in* $(\mu, \mathbf{r})$.

A (weakly) nearly linear scheme is by definition correct. Given $\mathsf{FindCoef}$, we let Recon call $\mathsf{FindCoef}$ to obtain γ, B and output the unique $\mu \in \{0,1\}$ satisfying $\gamma(\mathbf{L}_f) - \mu \lfloor p/2 \rfloor \in [-B..B]$. The constructed Recon is efficient and correct. Since Recon is implied by $\mathsf{FindCoef}$, we will only specify $\mathsf{FindCoef}$ and omit Recon when constructing (weakly) nearly linear secret sharing schemes.

Security. We consider a new security notion called *non-annihilability*. Unlike [3], which fixes the choice of policy f before Setup is run, we allow the adversary to adaptively choose f after seeing the public parameters pp and the input shares $L^{\mathbf{x}}$. Another difference is that instead of requiring all shares $(L_f, L^{\mathbf{x}})$ to look random, we only require that efficient adversaries cannot find a non-trivial affine function (potentially dependent on $L^{\mathbf{x}}$) that evaluates to zero on $\mathbf{L}_f$. This notion suffices for the security proofs of our KP-ABE scheme.

Definition 12 (non-annihilability for $\mathbf{L}_f$). *Let* $\{p_{\lambda}\}_{\lambda \in \mathbb{N}}$ *be a sequence of prime numbers. A secret sharing scheme (Definition 8) is* adaptively non-annihilable *for* $\mathbf{L}_f$ *if the output* $\mathbf{L}_f$ *of* ShareF *is a vector over* $\mathbb{Z}_{p_{\lambda}}$ *and all efficient adversary wins* $\mathsf{Exp}_{\mathsf{ANN-f}}$ *with negligible probability, where in* $\mathsf{Exp}_{\mathsf{ANN-f}}^{\mathcal{A}}(1^{\lambda})$, *the adversary* $\mathcal{A}$ *interacts with the challenger as follows:*

– **Setup.** *The challenger launches* $\mathcal{A}(1^{\lambda})$ *and receives from it the input length* 1^{ℓ} *and the additional parameter* param. *The challenger sets up the system by running* $\mathsf{pp} \xleftarrow{\$} \mathsf{Setup}(1^{\lambda}, 1^{\ell}, \mathsf{param})$, *and sends* pp *to* $\mathcal{A}$.
– **Share.** $\mathcal{A}$ *first submits an input* $\mathbf{x} \in \{0,1\}^{\ell}$. *Upon receiving it, the challenger creates the input shares by running* $(L_0, \{L_i^b\}_{i \in [\ell]}^{b \in \{0,1\}}, r) \xleftarrow{\$} \mathsf{ShareX}(\mathsf{pp})$ *and sends* $L^{\mathbf{x}}$ *to* $\mathcal{A}$.
– **Challenge.** $\mathcal{A}$ *outputs a Boolean function* $f \in \mathcal{F}_{\lambda,\ell}$, *a message bit* $\mu \in \{0,1\}$, *and an affine function* γ. *Upon receiving them, the challenger runs*

$\mathbf{L}_f \xleftarrow{\$} \mathsf{ShareF}(\mathsf{pp}, f, \mu, r)$ *and determines the outcome of the experiment.* $\mathcal{A}$ *wins if i)* $f(\mathbf{x}) = 1$; *ii)* γ *is not the zero function; and iii)* $\gamma(\mathbf{L}_f) = 0$. *Otherwise,* $\mathcal{A}$ *loses.*

Furthermore, a secret sharing scheme is selectively non-annihilable *if it satisfies the above conditions, with the change that the adversary must choose the input* **x** *before receiving* pp.

We now construct a succinct secret sharing scheme, satisfying the above linearity and adaptive annihilability for bounded-depth circuits from small-secret adaptive LWE. Our construction is based on the attribute-based laconic function evaluation scheme [11,36].

Construction 1 (secret sharing for circuits). Let n be the LWE dimension, $p = 2^{\omega(\log \lambda)}$ a fixed prime modulus, (the LWE parameters will be chosen during Setup). We construct a weakly nearly linear and succinct secret sharing scheme, with linear function sharing, for the family of bounded-depth circuits (see Definition 2):

$$\mathsf{Ckt}_{\lambda,\ell,d} = \big\{ \text{Boolean circuit } C : \{0,1\}^\ell \to \{0,1\} \text{ of depth at most } d \big\},$$

where $d \leq \frac{p^{\delta/4} - \log_2 p}{(1+\delta^{-1})\Theta(1)}$. Let $(\mathsf{EvalC}, \mathsf{EvalCX})$ be the algorithms in Lemma 2.

- $\mathsf{Setup}(1^\lambda, 1^\ell, 1^d)$ takes the input length ℓ in unary as input. It sets

$$n = \overline{B} = \big((d+1)(\delta^{-1}+1) + \log_2 p + \mathrm{O}(d)\big)^{2/\delta}, \quad q = 2^{n^\delta}, \quad m = n\lceil \log_2 q \rceil,$$

and picks χ to be $\overline{B}$-bounded. It next samples and sets

$$\mathbf{a} \xleftarrow{\$} \mathbb{Z}_q^n, \quad \mathbf{A}_0, \mathbf{A}_1, \ldots, \mathbf{A}_\ell \xleftarrow{\$} \mathbb{Z}_q^{n \times m}, \quad \mathbf{B} = (\mathbf{A}_0, \mathbf{A}_1, \ldots, \mathbf{A}_\ell).$$

It finally samples a random invertible matrix $\mathbf{Q} \in \mathbb{Z}_q^{n \times n}$, and outputs $\mathsf{pp} = (n, q, m, \overline{B}, \chi, \mathbf{a}, \mathbf{B}, \mathbf{Q})$.

Note: *Recall that δ is a constant depending on the underlying adaptive LWE assumption. The choice of $n, \overline{B}, q$ are subject to the requirement of the underlying adaptive LWE assumption as well as correctness and efficiency of the scheme. They satisfy $q/\overline{B} \geq (m+1)^{d+1}$ and $4((n+1)\overline{B}+3)+1 < p$.*

- $\mathsf{ShareX}(\mathsf{pp})$ takes the public parameter pp as input. It samples and sets

$$\mathbf{s} \xleftarrow{\$} \chi^n, \quad \mathbf{e}_0, \mathbf{e}_1, \ldots, \mathbf{e}_\ell \xleftarrow{\$} \chi^m,$$

$$\mathbf{L}_0 = \mathbf{s}^\mathsf{T}(\mathbf{A}_0 - \mathbf{Q}\mathbf{G}) + \mathbf{e}_0^\mathsf{T}, \quad \{\mathbf{L}_i^b = \mathbf{s}^\mathsf{T}(\mathbf{A}_i - b\mathbf{Q}\mathbf{G}) + \mathbf{e}_i^\mathsf{T}\}_{i \in [\ell]}^{b \in \{0,1\}},$$

and outputs $(\mathbf{L}_0, \{\mathbf{L}_i^b\}_{i \in [\ell]}^{b \in \{0,1\}}, \mathbf{s})$.

- $\mathsf{ShareF}(\mathsf{pp}, f, \mu, \mathbf{s})$ takes as input the public parameter pp, some $f \in \mathsf{Ckt}_{\lambda,\ell,d}$, a secret bit $\mu \in \{0,1\}$, and the shared randomness **s**. It runs $\mathbf{H}_f \leftarrow \mathsf{EvalC}(\mathbf{B}, \mathbf{Q}, f)$, and sets and outputs

$$\mathbf{L}_f = \mathbf{s}^\mathsf{T}\lfloor \mathbf{B}\mathbf{H}_f\mathbf{G}^{-1}(\mathbf{a})\rceil_p + \mu\lfloor p/2\rceil, \quad \text{where } \lfloor x\rceil_p = \lfloor px/q\rceil.$$

Note: *The scheme indeed has linear function sharing (Definition 11) because* ShareF *is a deterministic linear function over* $\mu, \mathbf{s}$ *with coefficients* $\lfloor p/2 \rfloor$, $\lfloor \mathbf{BH}_f \mathbf{G}^{-1}(\mathbf{a}) \rfloor_p$. *The scheme is also succinct as* $\mathbf{L}_f$ *contains 1 element in* $\mathbb{Z}_p$, *and each share output by* ShareX *contains m elements in* $\mathbb{Z}_q$. *Note that m is a fixed polynomial in* λ, d *and is independent of the description size of* f *and the input length* ℓ.

- FindCoef$(\mathsf{pp}, f, \mathbf{x}, \mathbf{L}^{\mathbf{x}})$ takes as input the public parameter pp, some $\mathbf{x} \in \{0,1\}^\ell$, some $f \in \mathsf{Ckt}_{\lambda,\ell,d}$, and the shares $\mathbf{L}^{\mathbf{x}}$. If $f(\mathbf{x}) = 1$, it outputs $\perp$ and terminates. Otherwise, it runs $\widehat{\mathbf{H}}_{f,\mathbf{x}} \leftarrow \mathsf{EvalCX}(\mathbf{B}, \mathbf{Q}, f, \mathbf{x})$, and defines

$$\gamma(\mathbf{L}_f) = \mathbf{L}_f - \lfloor \mathbf{L}^{\mathbf{x}} \widehat{\mathbf{H}}_{f,\mathbf{x}} \mathbf{G}^{-1}(\mathbf{a}) \rfloor_p, \quad B = (n+1)\overline{B} + 3,$$

The algorithm outputs $(\gamma, 1^B)$.

Note: *The procedure is indeed efficient since* $n, \overline{B}$ *are polynomials in* λ, d. *We show that* FindCoef *is correct, i.e., if* $f(\mathbf{x}) = 0$, *then* $4B + 1 \leq p$ *and* $\gamma(\mathbf{L}_f) = \mu \lfloor p/2 \rfloor + e$ *for some* $e \in [-B, B]$. *First, by the choice of* $n, \overline{B}$,

$$4B + 1 = 4((n+1)\overline{B} + 3) + 1 \leq p.$$

Next, by construction we have

$$
\begin{aligned}
\gamma(\mathbf{L}_f) &= \mathbf{L}_f - \lfloor \mathbf{L}^{\mathbf{x}} \widehat{\mathbf{H}}_{f,\mathbf{x}} \mathbf{G}^{-1}(\mathbf{a}) \rfloor_p \\
&= \underbrace{\mathbf{s}^{\mathsf{T}} \lfloor \mathbf{BH}_f \mathbf{G}^{-1}(\mathbf{a}) \rfloor_p + \mu \lfloor p/2 \rfloor}_{\mathbf{L}_f} \\
&\quad - \lfloor \big(\underbrace{\mathbf{s}^{\mathsf{T}}(\mathbf{B} - (1,\mathbf{x}) \otimes \mathbf{QG}) + (\mathbf{e}_0^{\mathsf{T}}, \mathbf{e}_1^{\mathsf{T}}, \ldots, \mathbf{e}_\ell^{\mathsf{T}})}_{\mathbf{L}^{\mathbf{x}}}\big) \widehat{\mathbf{H}}_{f,\mathbf{x}} \mathbf{G}^{-1}(\mathbf{a}) \rfloor_p
\end{aligned}
$$

(Lemma 2) $= \mathbf{s}^{\mathsf{T}} \lfloor \mathbf{BH}_f \mathbf{G}^{-1}(\mathbf{a}) \rfloor_p + \mu \lfloor p/2 \rfloor$

$$- \lfloor \mathbf{s}^{\mathsf{T}}(\mathbf{BH}_f - \underbrace{f(\mathbf{x})}_{=0} \mathbf{QG})\mathbf{G}^{-1}(\mathbf{a}) + \underbrace{(\mathbf{e}_0^{\mathsf{T}}, \mathbf{e}_1^{\mathsf{T}}, \ldots, \mathbf{e}_\ell^{\mathsf{T}})\widehat{\mathbf{H}}_{f,\mathbf{x}}\mathbf{G}^{-1}(\mathbf{a})}_{=e_f} \rfloor_p$$

$$= \mathbf{s}^{\mathsf{T}} \lfloor \mathbf{BH}_f \mathbf{G}^{-1}(\mathbf{a}) \rfloor_p + \mu \lfloor p/2 \rfloor - \lfloor \mathbf{s}^{\mathsf{T}} \mathbf{BH}_f \mathbf{G}^{-1}(\mathbf{a}) + e_f \rfloor_p$$

Since $\mathbf{G}^{-1}(\mathbf{a}) \in \{0,1\}^m$, *by the definition of* EvalCX *(Lemma 2), we have*

$$|e_f| \leq m \cdot \|\widehat{\mathbf{H}}_{f,\mathbf{x}}^{\mathsf{T}}\|_\infty \cdot \|(\mathbf{e}_0^{\mathsf{T}}, \mathbf{e}_1^{\mathsf{T}}, \ldots, \mathbf{e}_\ell^{\mathsf{T}})^{\mathsf{T}}\|_\infty \leq (m+1)^{(d+1)}\overline{B}$$

Note that we can break a rounded sum into a sum of individually rounded terms, at the expense of some rounding errors:

$$\lfloor \mathbf{s}^{\mathsf{T}} \mathbf{BH}_f \mathbf{G}^{-1}(\mathbf{a}) + e_f \rfloor = \lfloor \mathbf{s}^{\mathsf{T}} \mathbf{BH}_f \mathbf{G}^{-1}(\mathbf{a}) \rfloor_p + \lfloor e_f \rfloor_p + \epsilon, \text{ where } |\epsilon| \leq 3,$$

$$\lfloor \mathbf{s}^{\mathsf{T}} \mathbf{BH}_f \mathbf{G}^{-1}(\mathbf{a}) \rfloor_p = \mathbf{s}^{\mathsf{T}} \lfloor \mathbf{BH}_f \mathbf{G}^{-1}(\mathbf{a}) \rfloor_p + e_s, \text{ where } |e_s| \leq n \cdot \|\mathbf{s}\|_\infty \leq n\overline{B}.$$

Finally, we have

$$
\begin{aligned}
\gamma(\mathbf{L}_f) &= \mu \lfloor p/2 \rfloor + \mathbf{s}^{\mathsf{T}} \lfloor \mathbf{BH}_f \mathbf{G}^{-1}(\mathbf{a}) \rfloor_p - \lfloor \mathbf{s}^{\mathsf{T}} \mathbf{BH}_f \mathbf{G}^{-1}(\mathbf{a}) + e_f \rfloor_p \\
&= \mu \lfloor p/2 \rfloor + \mathbf{s}^{\mathsf{T}} \lfloor \mathbf{BH}_f \mathbf{G}^{-1}(\mathbf{a}) \rfloor_p - \lfloor \mathbf{s}^{\mathsf{T}} \mathbf{BH}_f \mathbf{G}^{-1}(\mathbf{a}) \rfloor_p - \lfloor e_f \rfloor_p - \epsilon \\
&= \mu \lfloor p/2 \rfloor \underbrace{- e_s - \lfloor e_f \rfloor_p - \epsilon}_{=e}.
\end{aligned}
$$

By the definition of e_f, e_s, ϵ, and the setting of q, we have

$$|e| \leq |e_s| + |\lfloor e_f \rceil_p| + |\epsilon| \leq \left\lceil \frac{(m+1)^{(d+1)}}{q/p} \overline{B} \right\rceil + n\overline{B} + 3 \leq B.$$

Efficiency. In the above construction, the public parameters pp mainly consists of three matrices $\mathbf{a} \in \mathbb{Z}_q^n, \mathbf{B} \in \mathbb{Z}_q^{n \times (m\ell)}, \mathbf{Q} \in \mathbb{Z}_q^{n \times n}$, where $n = \mathrm{poly}(\lambda, d), q = 2^{n^\delta}$, and $m = n\lceil \log q \rceil = \mathrm{poly}(\lambda, d)$. Therefore, the bit length of pp is $|\mathsf{pp}| = \mathrm{poly}(\lambda, d) \cdot \ell$. The shares $\mathbf{L}_0$ and $\{\mathbf{L}_i^b\}$ are $2\ell + 1$ vectors in $\mathbb{Z}_q^m$. Therefore $|\mathbf{L}_0| = |\mathbf{L}_i^b| = \mathrm{poly}(\lambda, d)$. Finally, $\mathbf{L}_f$ is a single element in $\mathbb{Z}_p$, where $p = 2^{\omega(\log \lambda)}$. Therefore, $|\mathbf{L}_f| = \mathrm{poly}(\lambda)$.

We next state non-annihilability security for $\mathbf{L}_f$ of the scheme. The proof can be found in the full version [31].

Proposition 5. *Assuming the small-secret adaptive LWE assumption, Construction 1 is non-annihilable for $\mathbf{L}_f$.*

5 KP-ABE for Bounded-Depth Circuits

In this section, we combine a succinct and weakly nearly linear secret sharing scheme that has linear function sharing, with a succinct and selectively simulation-secure IPFE scheme to obtain a compact and adaptively secure KP-ABE scheme.

Construction 2 (KP-ABE). All variables x_λ are indexed by λ. For simplicity of notations, we suppress λ in subscripts. Our construction uses the following two ingredients:

– A group based IPFE scheme (IPFE.Setup, IPFE.KeyGen, IPFE.Enc, IPFE.Dec) with modulus p given by Lemma 4.
– A secret sharing scheme (SS.Setup, SS.ShareX, SS.ShareF, SS.FindCoef) for bounded-depth circuits as in Construction 1. Recall that the scheme has three properties. First, the shares are succinct: $\mathbf{L}_0$ and $\mathbf{L}_i^b$ are vectors in $\mathbb{Z}_q$ of length $m = \mathrm{poly}(\lambda, d)$, and $\mathbf{L}_C$ is a single element in $\mathbb{Z}_p$. Second, the scheme has weakly nearly linear reconstruction: the algorithm SS.FindCoef outputs an affine function γ over $\mathbf{L}_C$ that approximately evaluates to $\mu \lfloor p/2 \rfloor$. Third, the scheme has linear function sharing: $\mathsf{SS.ShareF}_{\mathsf{SS.pp}, C}(\cdot, \cdot)$ is a deterministic linear function over $\mathbb{Z}_p$.

Our KP-ABE for circuits (see Definition 2) works as follows:

– Setup$(1^\lambda, P)$ takes as input the security parameter λ in unary, and a predicate $P \in \mathsf{Ckt}$. Let ℓ, d be the attribute length and depth for P. The algorithm runs and sets

$$\mathsf{SS.pp} \xleftarrow{\$} \mathsf{SS.Setup}(1^\lambda, 1^\ell, 1^d),$$
$$(\mathsf{impk}, \mathsf{imsk}) \xleftarrow{\$} \mathsf{IPFE.Setup}(1^\lambda, 1^N) \text{ for dimension } N = n + 1,$$
$$\mathsf{mpk} = (\mathsf{SS.pp}, \mathsf{impk}), \quad \mathsf{msk} = \mathsf{imsk}.$$

It outputs mpk, msk.

- KeyGen(msk, C) takes as input the master secret key msk and a policy $C \in \mathsf{Ckt}_{\ell,d}$. Since the secret sharing scheme has linear function sharing (Definition 11), the $\mathsf{SS.ShareF}_{\mathsf{SS.pp},C}(\cdot, \cdot)$ function is a deterministic linear function with coefficients $\mathbf{c} = (c_\mu, \mathbf{c_r})$. The KeyGen algorithm samples $\delta \xleftarrow{\$} \mathbb{Z}_p \backslash \{0\}$, runs

$$\mathsf{isk} \xleftarrow{\$} \mathsf{IPFE.KeyGen}(\mathsf{imsk}, [\![\delta\mathbf{c}]\!]_2),$$

and outputs $\mathsf{sk} = ([\![\delta]\!]_2, \mathsf{isk})$ as the secret key for C.

- Enc(mpk, $\mathbf{x}, \mu$) takes as input the master public key mpk, an attribute $\mathbf{x} \in \{0,1\}^\ell$, and a message $\mu \in \{0,1\}$. The algorithm runs

$$\left(\mathbf{L}_0, \{\mathbf{L}_i^b\}_{i\in[\ell]}^{b\in\{0,1\}}, \mathbf{r}\right) \xleftarrow{\$} \mathsf{SS.ShareX}(\mathsf{SS.pp}), \quad \mathsf{ict} \xleftarrow{\$} \mathsf{IPFEEnc}(\mathsf{impk}, [\![(\mu, \mathbf{r})]\!]_1),$$

and outputs $\mathsf{ct} = (\mathbf{L}^\mathbf{x}, \mathsf{ict})$.

- Dec(mpk, sk, C, ct, $\mathbf{x}$) takes as input the master public key mpk, a secret key sk, its associated policy C, a ciphertext ct, and its associated attribute $\mathbf{x}$. If $P(\mathbf{x}, C) = 0$, the algorithm outputs $\bot$ and terminates. Otherwise, it parses $\mathsf{sk} = ([\![\delta]\!]_2, \mathsf{isk})$, and computes the coefficients $\mathbf{c} = (c_\mu, \mathbf{c_r})$ for $\mathsf{ShareF}_{\mathsf{SS.pp},C}(\cdot, \cdot)$ as in KeyGen. The algorithm next parses ct into $\mathbf{L}^\mathbf{x}$, ict, and runs

$$\Lambda_C \xleftarrow{\$} \mathsf{IPFE.Dec}(\mathsf{isk}, [\![\delta]\!]_2\mathbf{c}, \mathsf{ict}), \quad (\gamma, 1^B) \xleftarrow{\$} \mathsf{SS.FindCoef}(\mathsf{SS.pp}, C, \mathbf{x}, \mathbf{L}^\mathbf{x}).$$

The algorithm applies the affine function γ homomorphically in the exponent of G_T to compute $\gamma(\Lambda_C)$. It then finds and outputs the unique $\mu' \in \{0,1\}$ (as the decrypted message) such that $\gamma(\Lambda_C) = [\![\mu'\lfloor p/2 \rfloor + e]\!]_1[\![\delta]\!]_2$, for some $e \in [-B..B]$, by enumerating over all possible e. Note: *We show that the scheme is correct. By the correctness of IPFE and by linear function sharing of the secret sharing scheme, we have*

$$\Lambda_C = [\![\delta(c_\mu \cdot \mu + \mathbf{c_r} \cdot \mathbf{r})]\!]_\mathsf{T} = [\![\delta\mathsf{SS.ShareF}_{\mathsf{SS.pp},C}(\mu, \mathbf{r})]\!]_\mathsf{T} = [\![\delta\mathbf{L}_C]\!]_\mathsf{T}.$$

Therefore, $\gamma(\Lambda_C) = [\![\delta\gamma(\mathbf{L}_C)]\!]_\mathsf{T} = [\![\gamma(\mathbf{L}_C)]\!]_1[\![\delta]\!]_2$. By the correctness of the weakly nearly linear secret sharing scheme, the decryption algorithm outputs the correct bit $\mu' = \mu$.

Efficiency. By Lemma 4, for MDDH dimension $k = \mathsf{poly}(\lambda)$ and input vector length $N = n + 1$, the IPFE components have bit lengths $|\mathsf{impk}|, |\mathsf{imsk}|, |\mathsf{ict}| = \mathsf{poly}(\lambda, d), |\mathsf{isk}| = \mathsf{poly}(\lambda)$. Also recall that the secret sharing components have bit lengths $|\mathsf{SS.pp}| = \mathsf{poly}(\lambda, d) \cdot \ell, |\mathbf{L}_0| = |\mathbf{L}_i^b| = \mathsf{poly}(\lambda, d), |\mathbf{L}_C| = \mathsf{poly}(\lambda)$. In the above construction,

- the master public key consists of SS.pp and impk, hence has bit length $|\mathsf{mpk}| = |\mathsf{SS.pp}| + |\mathsf{impk}| = \mathsf{poly}(\lambda, d) \cdot \ell$.

- The master secret key consists of imsk, hence has bit length
  $|\mathsf{msk}| = |\mathsf{imsk}| = \mathrm{poly}(\lambda, d)$.
- A secret key consists of a single isk, and $[\![\delta]\!]_2$ in G_2, hence has bit length
  $|\mathsf{sk}| = |\mathsf{isk}| + |G_2| = \mathrm{poly}(\lambda)$.
- A ciphertext consists of a single ict, and $\ell + 1$ shares, hence has bit length
  $|\mathsf{ct}| = |\mathsf{ict}| + (\ell + 1)|\mathbf{L}_0| = \mathrm{poly}(\lambda, d) \cdot \ell$.

We now state adaptive IND-CPA security of the scheme. The proof can be found in the full version [31].

Proposition 6. *Suppose in Construction 2, the IPFE scheme is selectively simulation-secure, and the secret sharing scheme is non-annihilable for $\mathbf{L}_f$. Then the constructed KP-ABE scheme is adaptively IND-CPA in GGM.*

Acknowledgement. The authors were supported by NSF grants CNS-1528178, CNS-1929901, CNS-1936825 (CAREER), CNS-2026774, a Hellman Fellowship, a JP Morgan AI Research Award, the Defense Advanced Research Projects Agency (DARPA) and Army Research Office (ARO) under Contract No. W911NF-15-C-0236, and a subcontract No. 2017-002 through Galois. The views expressed are those of the authors and do not reflect the official policy or position of the Department of Defense, the National Science Foundation, or the U.S. Government. The authors thank the anonymous reviewers for their valuable comments

References

1. Abdalla, M., Bourse, F., De Caro, A., Pointcheval, D.: Simple functional encryption schemes for inner products. In: Katz, J. (ed.) PKC 2015. LNCS, vol. 9020, pp. 733–751. Springer, Heidelberg (2015). https://doi.org/10.1007/978-3-662-46447-2_33
2. Agrawal, S., Libert, B., Stehlé, D.: Fully secure functional encryption for inner products, from standard assumptions. In: Robshaw, M., Katz, J. (eds.) CRYPTO 2016. LNCS, vol. 9816, pp. 333–362. Springer, Heidelberg (2016). https://doi.org/10.1007/978-3-662-53015-3_12
3. Agrawal, S., Wichs, D., Yamada, S.: Optimal broadcast encryption from LWE and pairings in the standard model. In: Pass, R., Pietrzak, K. (eds.) TCC 2020. LNCS, vol. 12550, pp. 149–178. Springer, Cham (2020). https://doi.org/10.1007/978-3-030-64375-1_6
4. Agrawal, S., Yamada, S.: Optimal broadcast encryption from pairings and LWE. In: Canteaut, A., Ishai, Y. (eds.) EUROCRYPT 2020. LNCS, vol. 12105, pp. 13–43. Springer, Cham (2020). https://doi.org/10.1007/978-3-030-45721-1_2
5. Attrapadung, N.: Dual system encryption framework in prime-order groups via computational pair encodings. In: Cheon, J.H., Takagi, T. (eds.) ASIACRYPT 2016. LNCS, vol. 10032, pp. 591–623. Springer, Heidelberg (2016). https://doi.org/10.1007/978-3-662-53890-6_20
6. Attrapadung, N., Libert, B., de Panafieu, E.: Expressive key-policy attribute-based encryption with constant-size ciphertexts. In: Catalano, D., Fazio, N., Gennaro, R., Nicolosi, A. (eds.) PKC 2011. LNCS, vol. 6571, pp. 90–108. Springer, Heidelberg (2011). https://doi.org/10.1007/978-3-642-19379-8_6

7. Attrapadung, N., Tomida, J.: Unbounded dynamic predicate compositions in ABE from standard assumptions. In: Moriai, S., Wang, H. (eds.) ASIACRYPT 2020. LNCS, vol. 12493, pp. 405–436. Springer, Cham (2020). https://doi.org/10.1007/978-3-030-64840-4_14

8. Beimel, A.: Secure schemes for secret sharing and key distribution. Ph.D. thesis, Technion-Israel Institute of Technology (1996)

9. Berkowitz, S.J.: On computing the determinant in small parallel time using a small number of processors. Inf. Process. Lett. **18**(3), 147–150 (1984). https://doi.org/10.1016/0020-0190(84)90018-8

10. Bethencourt, J., Sahai, A., Waters, B.: Ciphertext-policy attribute-based encryption. In: 2007 IEEE Symposium on Security and Privacy, pp. 321–334. IEEE Computer Society Press (2007). https://doi.org/10.1109/SP.2007.11

11. Boneh, D., et al.: Fully key-homomorphic encryption, arithmetic circuit ABE and compact garbled circuits. In: Nguyen, P.Q., Oswald, E. (eds.) EUROCRYPT 2014. LNCS, vol. 8441, pp. 533–556. Springer, Heidelberg (2014). https://doi.org/10.1007/978-3-642-55220-5_30

12. Boneh, D., Sahai, A., Waters, B.: Functional encryption: definitions and challenges. In: Ishai, Y. (ed.) TCC 2011. LNCS, vol. 6597, pp. 253–273. Springer, Heidelberg (2011). https://doi.org/10.1007/978-3-642-19571-6_16

13. Brakerski, Z., Tsabary, R., Vaikuntanathan, V., Wee, H.: Private constrained PRFs (and more) from LWE. In: Kalai, Y., Reyzin, L. (eds.) TCC 2017. LNCS, vol. 10677, pp. 264–302. Springer, Cham (2017). https://doi.org/10.1007/978-3-319-70500-2_10

14. Brakerski, Z., Vaikuntanathan, V.: Constrained key-homomorphic PRFs from standard lattice assumptions. In: Dodis, Y., Nielsen, J.B. (eds.) TCC 2015. LNCS, vol. 9015, pp. 1–30. Springer, Heidelberg (2015). https://doi.org/10.1007/978-3-662-46497-7_1

15. Buntrock, G., Damm, C., Hertrampf, U., Meinel, C.: Structure and importance of logspace-MOD class. Math. Syst. Theory **25**(3), 223–237 (1992). https://doi.org/10.1007/BF01374526

16. Chen, Y.-H., Chung, K.-M., Liao, J.-J.: On the complexity of simulating auxiliary input. In: Nielsen, J.B., Rijmen, V. (eds.) EUROCRYPT 2018. LNCS, vol. 10822, pp. 371–390. Springer, Cham (2018). https://doi.org/10.1007/978-3-319-78372-7_12

17. Garg, S., Gentry, C., Halevi, S., Raykova, M., Sahai, A., Waters, B.: Candidate indistinguishability obfuscation and functional encryption for all circuits. In: 54th FOCS, pp. 40–49. IEEE Computer Society Press (2013). https://doi.org/10.1109/FOCS.2013.13

18. Garg, S., Gentry, C., Sahai, A., Waters, B.: Witness encryption and its applications. In: Boneh, D., Roughgarden, T., Feigenbaum, J. (eds.) 45th ACM STOC, pp. 467–476. ACM Press (2013). https://doi.org/10.1145/2488608.2488667

19. Gentry, C., Sahai, A., Waters, B.: Homomorphic encryption from learning with errors: conceptually-simpler, asymptotically-faster, attribute-based. In: Canetti, R., Garay, J.A. (eds.) CRYPTO 2013. LNCS, vol. 8042, pp. 75–92. Springer, Heidelberg (2013). https://doi.org/10.1007/978-3-642-40041-4_5

20. Goldwasser, S., Kalai, Y.T., Popa, R.A., Vaikuntanathan, V., Zeldovich, N.: How to run turing machines on encrypted data. In: Canetti, R., Garay, J.A. (eds.) CRYPTO 2013. LNCS, vol. 8043, pp. 536–553. Springer, Heidelberg (2013). https://doi.org/10.1007/978-3-642-40084-1_30

21. Gorbunov, S., Vaikuntanathan, V., Wee, H.: Functional encryption with bounded collusions via multi-party computation. In: Safavi-Naini, R., Canetti, R. (eds.) CRYPTO 2012. LNCS, vol. 7417, pp. 162–179. Springer, Heidelberg (2012). https://doi.org/10.1007/978-3-642-32009-5_11

22. Gorbunov, S., Vaikuntanathan, V., Wee, H.: Attribute-based encryption for circuits. In: Boneh, D., Roughgarden, T., Feigenbaum, J. (eds.) 45th ACM STOC, pp. 545–554. ACM Press (2013). https://doi.org/10.1145/2488608.2488677

23. Gorbunov, S., Vinayagamurthy, D.: Riding on asymmetry: efficient ABE for branching programs. In: Iwata, T., Cheon, J.H. (eds.) ASIACRYPT 2015. LNCS, vol. 9452, pp. 550–574. Springer, Heidelberg (2015). https://doi.org/10.1007/978-3-662-48797-6_23

24. Goyal, V., Pandey, O., Sahai, A., Waters, B.: Attribute-based encryption for fine-grained access control of encrypted data. In: Juels, A., Wright, R.N., De Capitani di Vimercati, S. (eds.) ACM CCS 2006, pp. 89–98. ACM Press (2006). https://doi.org/10.1145/1180405.1180418. available as Cryptology ePrint Archive Report 2006/309

25. Jetchev, D., Pietrzak, K.: How to fake auxiliary input. In: Lindell, Y. (ed.) TCC 2014. LNCS, vol. 8349, pp. 566–590. Springer, Heidelberg (2014). https://doi.org/10.1007/978-3-642-54242-8_24

26. Karchmer, M., Wigderson, A.: On span programs. In: Proceedings of Structures in Complexity Theory, pp. 102–111 (1993)

27. Kitagawa, F., Nishimaki, R., Tanaka, K., Yamakawa, T.: Adaptively secure and succinct functional encryption: improving security and efficiency, simultaneously. In: Boldyreva, A., Micciancio, D. (eds.) CRYPTO 2019. LNCS, vol. 11694, pp. 521–551. Springer, Cham (2019). https://doi.org/10.1007/978-3-030-26954-8_17

28. Kowalczyk, L., Wee, H.: Compact adaptively secure abe for NC^1 from k-Lin. In: Ishai, Y., Rijmen, V. (eds.) EUROCRYPT 2019. LNCS, vol. 11476, pp. 3–33. Springer, Cham (2019). https://doi.org/10.1007/978-3-030-17653-2_1

29. Lewko, A., Okamoto, T., Sahai, A., Takashima, K., Waters, B.: Fully secure functional encryption: attribute-based encryption and (hierarchical) inner product encryption. In: Gilbert, H. (ed.) EUROCRYPT 2010. LNCS, vol. 6110, pp. 62–91. Springer, Heidelberg (2010). https://doi.org/10.1007/978-3-642-13190-5_4

30. Lewko, A., Waters, B.: New proof methods for attribute-based encryption: achieving full security through selective techniques. In: Safavi-Naini, R., Canetti, R. (eds.) CRYPTO 2012. LNCS, vol. 7417, pp. 180–198. Springer, Heidelberg (2012). https://doi.org/10.1007/978-3-642-32009-5_12

31. Li, H., Lin, H., Luo, J.: ABE for circuits with constant-size secret keys and adaptive security. Cryptology ePrint Archive, Report 2022/659 (2022). https://eprint.iacr.org/2022/659

32. Lin, H., Luo, J.: Succinct and adaptively secure ABE for ABP from k-Lin. In: Moriai, S., Wang, H. (eds.) ASIACRYPT 2020. LNCS, vol. 12493, pp. 437–466. Springer, Cham (2020). https://doi.org/10.1007/978-3-030-64840-4_15

33. Micciancio, D., Peikert, C.: Trapdoors for lattices: simpler, tighter, faster, smaller. In: Pointcheval, D., Johansson, T. (eds.) EUROCRYPT 2012. LNCS, vol. 7237, pp. 700–718. Springer, Heidelberg (2012). https://doi.org/10.1007/978-3-642-29011-4_41

34. Mulmuley, K.: A fast parallel algorithm to compute the rank of a matrix over an arbitrary field. Combinatorica $7(1)$, 101–104 (1987). https://doi.org/10.1007/BF02579205

35. Okamoto, T., Takashima, K.: Fully secure functional encryption with general relations from the decisional linear assumption. In: Rabin, T. (ed.) CRYPTO 2010. LNCS, vol. 6223, pp. 191–208. Springer, Heidelberg (2010). https://doi.org/10.1007/978-3-642-14623-7_11

36. Quach, W., Wee, H., Wichs, D.: Laconic function evaluation and applications. In: Thorup, M. (ed.) 59th FOCS, pp. 859–870. IEEE Computer Society Press (Oct 2018). https://doi.org/10.1109/FOCS.2018.00086

37. Sahai, A., Waters, B.: Fuzzy identity-based encryption. In: Cramer, R. (ed.) EUROCRYPT 2005. LNCS, vol. 3494, pp. 457–473. Springer, Heidelberg (2005). https://doi.org/10.1007/11426639_27

38. Takashima, K.: Expressive attribute-based encryption with constant-size ciphertexts from the decisional linear assumption. In: Abdalla, M., De Prisco, R. (eds.) SCN 2014. LNCS, vol. 8642, pp. 298–317. Springer, Cham (2014). https://doi.org/10.1007/978-3-319-10879-7_17

39. Tsabary, R.: Fully secure attribute-based encryption for t-CNF from LWE. In: Boldyreva, A., Micciancio, D. (eds.) CRYPTO 2019. LNCS, vol. 11692, pp. 62–85. Springer, Cham (2019). https://doi.org/10.1007/978-3-030-26948-7_3

40. Waters, B.: A punctured programming approach to adaptively secure functional encryption. In: Gennaro, R., Robshaw, M. (eds.) CRYPTO 2015. LNCS, vol. 9216, pp. 678–697. Springer, Heidelberg (2015). https://doi.org/10.1007/978-3-662-48000-7_33

41. Wee, H.: Attribute-hiding predicate encryption in bilinear groups, revisited. In: Kalai, Y., Reyzin, L. (eds.) TCC 2017. LNCS, vol. 10677, pp. 206–233. Springer, Cham (2017). https://doi.org/10.1007/978-3-319-70500-2_8

42. Yamada, S., Attrapadung, N., Hanaoka, G., Kunihiro, N.: A framework and compact constructions for non-monotonic attribute-based encryption. In: Krawczyk, H. (ed.) PKC 2014. LNCS, vol. 8383, pp. 275–292. Springer, Heidelberg (2014). https://doi.org/10.1007/978-3-642-54631-0_16

43. Zhang, K., et al.: Practical and efficient attribute-based encryption with constant-size ciphertexts in outsourced verifiable computation. In: Chen, X., Wang, X., Huang, X. (eds.) ASIACCS 16, pp. 269–279. ACM Press (2016)

Multi-Input Quadratic Functional Encryption: Stronger Security, Broader Functionality

Shweta Agrawal[1], Rishab Goyal[2], and Junichi Tomida[3](✉) iD

[1] IIT Madras, Chennai, India
shweta.a@cse.iitm.ac.in
[2] UW-Madison, Madison, USA
rishab@cs.wisc.edu
[3] NTT Social Informatics Laboratories,Tokyo, Japan
tomida.junichi@gmail.com

Abstract. Multi-input functional encryption, MIFE, is a powerful generalization of functional encryption that allows computation on encrypted data coming from multiple different data sources. In a recent work, Agrawal, Goyal, and Tomida (CRYPTO 2021) constructed MIFE for the class of quadratic functions. This was the first MIFE construction from bilinear maps that went beyond inner product computation. We advance the state-of-the-art in MIFE, and propose new constructions with *stronger security* and *broader functionality*.

- *Stronger Security:* In the typical formulation of MIFE security, an attacker is allowed to either corrupt *all or none* of the users who can encrypt the data. In this work, we study MIFE security in a stronger and more natural model where we allow an attacker to corrupt any subset of the users, instead of only permitting all-or-nothing corruption. We formalize the model by providing each user a unique encryption key, and letting the attacker corrupt all non-trivial subsets of the encryption keys, while still maintaining the MIFE security for ciphertexts generated using honest keys. We construct a secure MIFE system for quadratic functions in this fine-grained corruption model from bilinear maps. Our construction departs significantly from the existing MIFE schemes as we need to tackle a more general class of attackers.
- *Broader Functionality:* The notion of multi-client functional encryption, MCFE, is a useful extension of MIFE. In MCFE, each encryptor can additionally tag each ciphertext with appropriate metadata such that ciphertexts with only matching metadata can be decrypted together. In more detail, each ciphertext is now annotated with a unique *label* such that ciphertexts encrypted for different slots can now only be combined together during decryption as long as the associated labels are an exact match for all individual ciphertexts. In this work, we upgrade our MIFE scheme to also support *ciphertext labelling*. While the functionality of our scheme matches that of MCFE for quadratic functions, our security guarantee falls short of

the general corruption model studied for MCFE. In our model, all
encryptors share a secret key, therefore this yields a secret-key version of quadratic MCFE, which we denote by SK-MCFE. We leave
the problem of proving security in the general corruption model as
an important open problem.

1   Introduction

Functional encryption (FE) [18,19,31] is a generalization of public key encryption that enables fine grained control over access to encrypted data. In FE, the
secret key is associated with a function f, the ciphertext is associated with an
input $\mathbf{x}$ from the domain of f, and decryption enables recovery of $f(\mathbf{x})$ and
nothing else. Importantly, no information about $\mathbf{x}$ is revealed beyond what is
revealed by $\{f_i(\mathbf{x})\}_i$ for any set of secret decryption keys corresponding to functions $\{f_i\}_i$ in possession of the adversary. This *collusion resistance* property
of FE makes it very suitable for computing on encrypted data – a ciphertext
encrypting the genomic data of hundreds of individuals can now be decrypted
using function keys corresponding to various statistical functionalities studying correlations between genomic sequences and disease, while guaranteeing privacy of individual genomic sequences. Motivated by several important applications, including the construction of the powerful notion of *indistinguishability
obfuscation* (iO) [12,16], FE has received an enormous amount of attention in
the community, with scores of elegant constructions from diverse assumptions,
achieving various useful functionalities and satisfying assorted notions of security [3,6,14,15,20,24,25,34].

Multi-Input Functional Encryption. Functional encryption was first generalized to support aggregated computation over multiple input sources by the
celebrated work of Goldwasser et al. [26]. The premise of multi-input FE, denoted
by MIFE, is that in many natural applications of FE it is essential to support
generalized functionalities where arity is greater than one. For instance, in the
above example of genome wide association studies, the ciphertext must encrypt
genomic data of multiple individuals for it to be useful for the statistical studies in question, but this suggests that this data must be encrypted all at once
by a single entity, which is an unreasonable assumption in practice. Genomic
data is highly sensitive information and it is much more meaningful to allow
every individual to encrypt their own data locally and generalize the construction to support functions of large arity that can process several ciphertexts at a
time. This constraint is organically captured by MIFE, where n independent
encryptors may individually generate ciphertexts for vectors $\{\mathbf{x}_i^j\}_{i\in[n],j\in[\mathsf{poly}]}$
and a secret key for function f allows to compute $f(\mathbf{x}_1^{j_1}, \mathbf{x}_2^{j_2}, \dots, \mathbf{x}_n^{j_n})$ for any
$j_1, \dots, j_n \in [\mathsf{poly}]$.

Since its inception, MIFE received substantial attention which quickly bifur-
cated into two parallel branches – (i) the first builds on top of powerful primitives
such as iO or *compact* single-input FE for general models of computation, like

circuits or Turing machines and uses these to construct MIFE for circuits or Turing machines [11,12,16], (ii) the second focuses on efficient direct constructions for restricted functionalities from simple assumptions such as pairings or learning with errors [1,2,4,5,9,21,23,29,32]. In this work, we continue development of the second branch by making advances to the recently proposed construction of MIFE for quadratic functions by Agrawal, Goyal, and Tomida [9].

Modelling Security. Given the tension between functionality and security, where functionality seeks to reveal partial information about the input, while security seeks to protect privacy of the input, the question of modelling security in functional encryption has turned out to be subtle, and has been examined in multiple works [7,8,18,30]. For the setting of *unbounded* collusion, namely where the adversary can obtain any polynomial number of function keys, in the security game, the *indistinguishability* based definition of security has emerged as the gold standard (due to impossibilities that plague the alternative simulation-based security [7,8,18]). In the single-input setting, both symmetric and public key FE have been studied and are relevant for different applications. In the multi-input setting, it was observed by Goldwasser et al. [26] that the symmetric key setting, where the encryptor requires a secret key to compute a ciphertext, is much more relevant for applications. This is to prevent the primitive from becoming meaningless due to excessive leakage occurring by virtue of functionality. In more detail, let us consider a two input scheme where a given first slot ciphertext hides a challenge bit b. Now, in the public key setting, an adversary can compute an unbounded encryptions for slot 2 herself and match these with the challenge ciphertext of slot 1 to learn a potentially unbounded amount of information. This unrestricted information leakage can be prevented by requiring the encryption algorithm to require a secret key.

However, in the symmetric key multi-input setting, an additional subtlety emerges related to the uniqueness of each user's encryption key. For instance, if we consider the application of encrypting genomic data discussed above, it quickly becomes apparent that having all users share the same encryption key is problematic – if the genomic data is encrypted and stored in a central repository, then any malicious insider, who has contributed data and is hence in possession of the master encryption key, can download and decrypt data belonging to any other user! As data is supposed to span hundreds of users, the master encryption key will become widely distributed and the privacy of honest user data can very quickly and easily get compromised. Hence, it is crucial for security that encryption keys be unique to users, and the adversary gaining control of a particular user's key does not compromise the security of other users' data.

Multi-Input FE for Quadratic Functions. Recently, Agrawal, Goyal, and Tomida (AGT) [9] provided the first construction of multi-input functional encryption for quadratic functions. In more detail, they construct an n-input MIFE scheme for the function class $\mathcal{F}_{m,n}$, which is defined as follows. Each function $f \in \mathcal{F}_{m,n}$ is represented by a vector $\mathbf{c} \in \mathbb{Z}^{(mn)^2}$. For inputs $\mathbf{x}_1, \ldots, \mathbf{x}_n \in \mathbb{Z}^m$, f is defined as $f(\mathbf{x}_1, \ldots, \mathbf{x}_n) = \langle \mathbf{c}, \mathbf{x} \otimes \mathbf{x} \rangle$ where $\mathbf{x} = (\mathbf{x}_1 || \cdots || \mathbf{x}_n)$ and $\otimes$ denotes the Kronecker product. In their quadratic MIFE scheme for $\mathcal{F}_{m,n}$, a user can encrypt $\mathbf{x}_i \in \mathbb{Z}^m$ to CT_i for slot $i \in [n]$, a key generator can compute a secret key SK for $\mathbf{c} \in \mathbb{Z}^{(mn)^2}$, and decryption of $\mathsf{CT}_1, \ldots, \mathsf{CT}_n$ with SK reveals only $\langle \mathbf{c}, \mathbf{x} \otimes \mathbf{x} \rangle$ and nothing else.

However, while this result makes exciting progress in the domain of direct constructions for MIFE by providing the first candidate supporting quadratic functions, it suffers from the severe drawback that all the encryptors must share the same master key for encryption. As described above, this limits the applicability of the construction for many meaningful practical applications, e.g. when the system is susceptible to insider attacks. Moreover, having a single master key for all users creates a single point of failure which makes the system vulnerable to not only attack but also inadvertent leakage/misuse. Decentralizing trust is an overarching goal in cryptography, and this motivates to design a scheme where users have unique encryption keys and the adversarial model is strong enough to capture corruption of some subset of these.

Multi-Client Functional Encryption. A generalization of multi-input functional encryption is the notion of multi-client functional encryption (MCFE) where the ciphertext is additionally associated with a label. In more detail, encryptor i now encrypts not only the input $\mathbf{x}_i$ but also a public label ℓ_i to obtain $\mathsf{CT}(i, \mathbf{x}_i, \ell_i)$. A functional key SK_f for any n-ary function f can be used to decrypt $\{\mathsf{CT}(i, \mathbf{x}_i, \ell_i)\}_{i \in [n]}$ if and only if all the labels match, i.e. $\ell_i = \ell$ for all $i \in [n]$. Note that setting all labels to a single value (say "TRUE") recovers the notion of MIFE, which allows unrestricted combinations of ciphertexts across slots. The more expressive MCFE provides additional control over allowable combinations of ciphertexts, which is very useful for several applications – for instance, in the example of computing on encrypted genomic data discussed above, being able to filter records based on some label such as *ethnicity* = *African* may help to substantially reduce the number of inputs that participate in the study, making the process more efficient.

We emphasize that regardless of the security model (all-or-nothing or fine-grained), the motivation of labelling functionality is to better control the decryption pattern to reduce the information that a decrypter can learn. In the plain n input MIFE setting, where Q ciphertexts per slot are available, the decrypter can potentially compute Q^n function values, which reveal a large amount of information about the underlying plaintexts. However, using Q distinct labels to label every ciphertext in each slot, we can reduce the number of function values revealed to as little as Q. Thus, the labelling functionality is quite useful for controlling the amount of information that a decrypter learns.

It is worth noting that for an MIFE construction supporting general circuits, MCFE can easily be captured by adding an additional check in the function key to verify that all the labels are equal, but for restricted function classes like linear or quadratic functions, MCFE is more powerful than MIFE. In the arena of direct constructions from simple assumptions, the notion of MCFE has been studied for the case of linear functions [1,2,21,26,29] but not for quadratic functions, to the best of our knowledge.

Our Results. We advance the state-of-the-art in MIFE, and propose new constructions with *stronger security* and *broader functionality*.

- *Stronger Security:* Typically, in the MIFE security game, an attacker is allowed to either corrupt *all or none*[1] of the users who can encrypt the data. Here we study MIFE security in a "fine-grained" corruption model where an attacker can corrupt even *non-trivial* subset of the users, *instead of only the trivial subsets*.

  We formalize such a fine-grained corruption model by providing each user a unique encryption key, and letting the attacker corrupt any subset of the encryption keys. We require that, even after corruption of any non-trivial subset of encryption keys, the scheme still satisfies the MIFE-style security for all ciphertexts generated using honest encryption keys. We give a construction for a MIFE system whose security can be proven in this fine-grained corruption model, instead of the standard *all-or-nothing* corruption model. Our construction departs significantly from the existing AGT quadratic MIFE scheme [9] as we need to tackle a more general class of attackers.

  We observe that while several inner product MIFE schemes already have stronger security in the context of MCFE [1,10,22], achieving it in quadratic MIFE is much more difficult. Intuitively, a decrypter in a quadratic MIFE system is allowed to learn a function value on cross terms derived from different slots, and achieving this without heavy machinery such as obfuscation seems to require the encryption keys to be correlated with each other (this is also the case for the AGT scheme). Due to the correlation, the corruption of even a single encryption key affects the security of ciphertexts for all the other slots. This is in contrast to inner product MIFE, which is basically obtained by running independent single-input inner product FE instances in parallel.

- *Broader Functionality:* In MCFE, each encryptor can specify a special label, to tag each ciphertext with appropriate metadata, such that ciphertexts with only exactly matching metadata/labels can be decrypted together. Here we upgrade our MIFE scheme to additionally support *ciphertext labelling*. While the functionality of our upgraded MIFE scheme matches that of MCFE for quadratic functions, our security guarantee falls short of the general corruption model studied for MCFE. In our model, all encryptors share a secret key, therefore this yields a secret-key version of quadratic MCFE, which we denote by SK-MCFE. We leave the problem of proving security in the general corruption model as an important open problem.

1.1 Technical Overview

The starting point for both of our MIFE and SK-MCFE schemes for quadratic functions is the recent AGT scheme [9]. The AGT construction necessitates that

---

[1] An MIFE scheme where corruption of all encrypting users is allowed is more commonly regarded as public-key MIFE, while disallowing corruption of any encrypting user is regarded as secret-key MIFE.

all encryptors share the same master secret key, thus throughout the sequel we will refer to it as the "SK-MIFE" scheme.

A Simplified Overview of the AGT SK-MIFE Scheme. The AGT scheme uses three building blocks – (i) SK-FE for inner product (IPFE), (ii) SK-FE for *predicate* inner product (pIPFE), and (iii) SK-MIFE for *mixed-group* inner product. The mixed-group property of (iii) is necessary for a technical reason in the security proof, but for now we can consider it as SK-MIFE for inner product (IP-MIFE). And, for security, all of the underlying schemes are required to satisfy the corresponding function-hiding security property. Concretely, the required MIFE schemes are summarized in Table 1.[2]

Table 1. Description of input and function classes for IPFE, pIPFE, IP-MIFE.

Scheme type	No. of inputs	Input class(es)	Function class	Description of functions
IPFE	1	$\mathcal{X} = \mathbb{Z}_p^m$	$\mathcal{F} = \mathbb{Z}_p^m$	$f_{\mathbf{y}}(\mathbf{x}) = \langle \mathbf{x}, \mathbf{y} \rangle$
pIPFE	1	$\mathcal{X} = \mathbb{Z}_p^{m_1} \times \mathbb{Z}_p^{m_2}$	$\mathcal{F} = \mathbb{Z}_p^{m_1} \times \mathbb{Z}_p^{m_2}$	$f_{\mathbf{y}_1, \mathbf{y}_2}(\mathbf{x}_1, \mathbf{x}_2) = \begin{cases} \langle \mathbf{x}_2, \mathbf{y}_2 \rangle & \text{if } \langle \mathbf{x}_1, \mathbf{y}_1 \rangle = 0, \\ \perp & \text{otherwise.} \end{cases}$
IP-MIFE	n	$\mathcal{X}_1 = \cdots \mathcal{X}_n = \mathbb{Z}_p^m$	$\mathcal{F} = \mathbb{Z}_p^{mn}$	$f_{\mathbf{y}}(\mathbf{x}_1, \ldots, \mathbf{x}_n) = \langle (\mathbf{x}_1 || \cdots || \mathbf{x}_n), \mathbf{y} \rangle$

Notation. We denote IPFE ciphertexts of $\mathbf{v}$ by $\mathsf{iCT}[\mathbf{v}]$, pIPFE ciphertexts of $(\mathbf{v}_1, \mathbf{v}_2)$ by $\mathsf{pCT}[(\mathbf{v}_1, \mathbf{v}_2)]$ and IP-MIFE ciphertexts of $\mathbf{v}$ for slot i by $\mathsf{miCT}_i[\mathbf{v}]$ under some master secret keys iMSK, pMSK, miMSK, respectively. Similarly we denote IPFE secret keys of $\mathbf{v}$ by $\mathsf{iSK}[\mathbf{v}]$, pIPFE secret keys of $(\mathbf{v}_1, \mathbf{v}_2)$ by $\mathsf{pSK}[(\mathbf{v}_1, \mathbf{v}_2)]$ and IP-MIFE secret keys for $\mathbf{v}$ by $\mathsf{miSK}[\mathbf{v}]$ under the same master secret keys iMSK, pMSK, miMSK, respectively.

AGT Scheme Description. Let us start by recalling the structure of ciphertexts and secret keys in the AGT SK-MIFE scheme. At a high level, an AGT ciphertext CT_i of $\mathbf{x} \in \mathbb{Z}^m$ and SK for $\mathbf{c} \in \mathbb{Z}_p^{(mn)^2}$ are of the following form:

$$\mathsf{CT}_i = \left(\left\{ \mathsf{pCT}[(\mathbf{h}, \mathbf{b}_j)], \; \mathsf{pSK}[(\widetilde{\mathbf{h}}, \widetilde{\mathbf{b}}_j)] \right\}_{j \in [m]}, \; \mathsf{iCT}[\mathbf{d}], \; \mathsf{iSK}[\widetilde{\mathbf{d}}], \; \mathsf{miCT}_i[\mathbf{f}] \right) \quad (1)$$

$$\mathsf{SK} = \left(\left\{ \sigma_{i,k} \right\}_{i,k \in [n]}, \; \mathsf{miSK}[\widetilde{\mathbf{f}}] \right) \quad (2)$$

for some $\mathbb{Z}_p$ vectors $\mathbf{b}_j, \widetilde{\mathbf{b}}_j, \mathbf{d}, \widetilde{\mathbf{d}}, \mathbf{f}, \widetilde{\mathbf{f}}, \mathbf{h}, \widetilde{\mathbf{h}}$ and $\mathbb{Z}_p$ elements $\sigma_{i,k}$.

Now a message vector $\mathbf{x}$ is encoded in the vectors $\mathbf{b}_j, \widetilde{\mathbf{b}}_j$, and the remaining vectors in the ciphertext are only added to either tie together separate components of different AGT ciphertexts, or randomize a portion of a single AGT ciphertext. We refer the reader to [9] for a more detailed overview, but for our purposes, it is enough to understand how the decryption algorithm works.

---

[2] Formally, the inner product functionalities defined need to involve group elements as it is necessary for the proof. However, for simplicity of the overview, we use directly define them over $\mathbb{Z}_p$.

Consider a sequence of n AGT ciphertexts $\mathsf{CT}_1, \ldots, \mathsf{CT}_n$ and a corresponding secret key SK. The decryptor first runs the decryption algorithm for the pIPFE scheme for all possible input combinations. That is, for all $i, k \in [n]$ and $j, \ell \in [m]$, it computes

$$z_{i,j,k,\ell} = \mathsf{pDec}(\mathsf{pCT}[(\mathbf{h}_i, \mathbf{b}_{i,j})], \mathsf{pSK}[(\widetilde{\mathbf{h}}_k, \widetilde{\mathbf{b}}_{k,\ell})]). \tag{3}$$

As it turns out, the underlying encoding procedure used in AGT ensures that each such term is of the form $z_{i,j,k,\ell} = \mathbf{x}_i[j]\mathbf{x}_k[\ell] + u_{i,j,k,\ell}$, where $u_{i,j,k,\ell}$ is a pseudorandom masking term such that $\sum \mathbf{c}[(i, j, k, \ell)]u_{i,j,k,\ell} = \langle \mathbf{c}, \mathbf{u} \rangle$ can be computed by combining the remaining portions of the ciphertexts and secret key. That is, the decryptor first computes

$$\sum \mathbf{c}[(i, j, k, \ell)]z_{i,j,k,\ell} = \sum \mathbf{c}[(i, j, k, \ell)]\mathbf{x}_i[j]\mathbf{x}_k[\ell] + \sum \mathbf{c}[(i, j, k, \ell)]u_{i,j,k,\ell}$$

where $\sum \mathbf{c}[(i, j, k, \ell)]\mathbf{x}_i[j]\mathbf{x}_k[\ell]$ is the desired output, and then it computes $\sum \mathbf{c}[(i, j, k, \ell)]u_{i,j,k,\ell} = \langle \mathbf{c}, \mathbf{u} \rangle$ by combining the $(\mathsf{iCT}[\mathbf{d}], \mathsf{iSK}[\widetilde{\mathbf{d}}], \mathsf{miCT}_i[\mathbf{f}])$ portion of each ciphertext amongst themselves and also with the secret key $(\{\sigma_{i,k}\}_{i,k\in[n]}, \mathsf{miSK}[\widetilde{\mathbf{f}}])$.

Achieving Strong Fine-Grained Security. Recall that in the stronger fine-grained corruption model, each encryptor has a unique encryption key, and the adversary is allowed to corrupt any subset of encryption keys in the security game. Throughout the sequel, we refer to such a scheme as plain MIFE in contrast to SK-MIFE.

Before describing our main ideas, we highlight the reason as to why AGT is not already secure in this stronger corruption model. Observe that each component of the AGT ciphertext CT_i is generated under the same master secret key of the corresponding scheme over all slots. In other words, it is essential that all encryption keys include the same IPFE, pIPFE, and IP-MIFE master secret keys. As it turns out, this is one of the main barriers to proving the SK-MIFE construction of AGT to be strongly secure. This is because the scheme ends up being completely insecure if encryption keys for any slot are revealed! Basically, revealing only the underlying pIPFE master secret key allows one to completely decrypt any ciphertexts of the AGT scheme.

While this seems like a major technical barrier at first, we observe that there is a very elegant way to get around this problem by relying on the underlying homomorphic properties satisfied by the SK-MIFE scheme. Although, the AGT SK-MIFE construction can not be used as is since the usage of the pIPFE scheme prevents any useful type of ciphertext homomorphism, we are able to simplify the underlying SK-MIFE construction that not only avoids the usage of pIPFE completely, but also leads to an interesting homomorphism property that we show is very useful in upgrading any weakly secure SK-MIFE into a strongly secure MIFE scheme.

The Special Property. Let us start by describing the special homomorphism property P that we crucially rely on. It states that there exists an *explicit* and *efficient* algorithm $\widetilde{\mathsf{Enc}}$, and a sequence of *public* elementary messages $e_{i,1}, \ldots, e_{i,d} \in \mathcal{X}_i$ ($\forall i \in [n]$) such that – for every slot $i \in [n]$ and message $x_i \in \mathcal{X}_i$, the following two distributions are statistically indistinguishable:

$$\left\{ (\mathsf{PP}, \{\mathsf{CT}_{i,j}\}_{j \in [d]}, \mathsf{CT}_i) : \mathsf{CT}_i \leftarrow \mathsf{Enc}(\mathsf{MSK}, i, x_i) \right\},$$

$$\left\{ (\mathsf{PP}, \{\mathsf{CT}_{i,j}\}_{j \in [d]}, \mathsf{CT}_i) : \mathsf{CT}_i \leftarrow \widetilde{\mathsf{Enc}}(\{\mathsf{CT}_{i,j}\}_j, x_i) \right\}$$

where $(\mathsf{PP}, \mathsf{MSK}) \leftarrow \mathsf{Setup}(1^\lambda)$ and $\mathsf{CT}_{i,j} \leftarrow \mathsf{Enc}(\mathsf{MSK}, i, e_{i,j})$ for $j \in [d]$.

Property P to MIFE. Assuming there exists an SK-MIFE scheme satisfying property P, our main observation is that there exists a generic compiler to upgrade it to a MIFE for the same function class in which an attacker can corrupt any arbitrary set of encryption keys. That is, consider any SK-MIFE scheme $(\mathsf{Setup}', \mathsf{Enc}', \mathsf{KeyGen}', \mathsf{Dec}')$ for some function class $\mathcal{F}$ satisfying property P, our compiler upgrades it to an MIFE scheme $(\mathsf{Setup}, \mathsf{Enc}, \mathsf{KeyGen}', \mathsf{Dec}')$ for $\mathcal{F}$ as follows:

$\mathsf{Setup}(1^\lambda, 1^n)$: It computes $\mathsf{PP}, \mathsf{MSK} \leftarrow \mathsf{Setup}'(1^\lambda)$ and $\mathsf{CT}_{i,j} \leftarrow \mathsf{Enc}'(\mathsf{MSK}, i, e_{i,j})$ for all $i \in [n], j \in [d]$, and sets $\mathsf{EK}_i = \{\mathsf{CT}_{i,j}\}_j$ for all $i \in [n]$. Then, it outputs the parameters as $\mathsf{PP}, \{\mathsf{EK}_i\}_i, \mathsf{MSK}$.

$\mathsf{Enc}(\mathsf{EK}_i, x)$: It computes $\mathsf{CT}_i \leftarrow \widetilde{\mathsf{Enc}}(\{\mathsf{CT}_{i,j}\}_j, x)$ and outputs CT_i.

The correctness follows directly from the correctness of the underlying SK-MIFE scheme and the statistical closeness of the output distributions between Enc and $\widetilde{\mathsf{Enc}}$. And, the proof of security also follows via a hybrid argument. The main idea is to first switch how each challenge ciphertext is generated. That is, instead of computing it as $\widetilde{\mathsf{Enc}}(\{\mathsf{CT}_{i,j}\}_j, x^\beta)$, the challenger computes it directly as $\mathsf{Enc}(\mathsf{MSK}, i, x^\beta)$ (where $\beta \in \{0, 1\}$ and x^0, x^1 are the challenge messages). Note that this readily follows from the statistical closeness, and thus, by relying on the regular security of the underlying SK-MIFE scheme, we can prove the stronger security for our MIFE scheme. This is because the reduction algorithm can simulate a corrupted encryption key $\mathsf{EK}_i = \{\mathsf{CT}_{i,j}\}_{j \in [d]}$ by querying its own oracle on the elementary messages $e_{i,1}, \ldots, e_{i,d}$. For more details, we refer the reader to the main body.

Building SK-MIFE with Property P. In order to obtain our final result, we need to instantiate the above generic compiler with an SK-MIFE scheme for quadratic functions with property P. As mentioned earlier, our core idea in this part is to rely on the homomorphic structure of the AGT SK-MIFE scheme. Recall that a ciphertext in the AGT scheme consists of bilinear source group elements. Thus, we can define a group operation over the AGT ciphertexts by element-wise multiplication of group elements (and we use addition for the group operation in what follows). Let $\mathsf{CT}_i[\mathbf{x}]$ be a slot-i encryption of $\mathbf{x}$ in the AGT scheme. Our observation is that if for any $a_1, a_2 \in \mathbb{Z}_p$, we have

$$a_1 \mathsf{CT}_i[\mathbf{x}_1] + a_2 \mathsf{CT}_i[\mathbf{x}_2] = \mathsf{CT}_i[a_1 \mathbf{x}_1 + a_2 \mathbf{x}_2], \tag{4}$$

then we can achieve P by simply setting the elementary messages to be $\mathbf{e}_1, \ldots, \underbrace{\mathbf{e}_n}$, where $\mathbf{e}_j$ is the one-hot vector with the j-th element being one, and defining $\overline{\mathsf{Enc}}$ using the appropriate group operations. Unfortunately, this is not the case!

Insufficiency of AGT. To better understand the reason for failure, we need to open up the encryption abstractions used in AGT to their underlying bilinear form. Informally, an AGT ciphertext CT_i for $\mathbf{x} \in \mathbb{Z}_p^m$ looks like $\mathsf{CT}_i = ([\mathbf{vM}_i]_1, [\mathbf{wN}_i]_2)$. Here $[\cdot]_1, [\cdot]_2$ denote element-wise group exponentiation in bilinear groups G_1, G_2, and $\mathbf{M}_i, \mathbf{N}_i$ are common matrices shared among all ciphertexts for slot i. Also, each element of $\mathbf{v}, \mathbf{w}$ depends on $\mathbf{x}$ and the random tape used in encryption. Concretely, each element of $\mathbf{v}, \mathbf{w}$ is one of the following four types — (i) 1; (ii) $\mathbf{x}[j]$ for some $j \in [m]$; (iii) a fresh random $\mathbb{Z}_p$ element; or (iv) an element of the tuple $(b, c, b\ell, c\ell)$ where b, c, ℓ are fresh random $\mathbb{Z}_p$ elements.

From the viewpoint of well-formedness of a homomorphically operated ciphertext, it is not hard to see that the elements (ii) and (iii) will stay consistent with the homomorphism Eq. (4), while the elements (i) and (iv) will no longer be well-formed after the group operations. This is because, after the homomorphic addition as Eq. (4), the element (i) becomes $a_1 + a_2$, while the element (iv) become an elements of the tuple $(a_1 b_1 + a_2 b_2, a_1 c_1 + a_2 c_2, a_1 b_1 \ell_1 + a_2 b_2 \ell_2, a_1 c_1 \ell_1 + a_2 c_2 \ell_2)$. While an element (i) can still be well-formed as long as $a_1 + a_2 = 1$, an element (iv) will never be well-formed (unless $\ell_1 = \ell_2$, which occurs with only negligible probability).

Stripping Away pIPFE from AGT. Diving a bit further into the structure and semantics of the AGT SK-MIFE scheme, we find out that the elements (iv) are derived from the pIPFE scheme. So, a natural thought is if we can remove the pIPFE scheme from AGT, then we can eliminate the elements (iv) thereby solving the above problem. However, the usage of the pIPFE scheme in the AGT template was crucial as replacing it with a (non-predicate) IPFE scheme enabled a mix-and-match attack wherein an attacker can illegally combine portions of two different ciphertexts for the *same slot*. Concretely, for two ciphertexts $\mathsf{CT}_i^1, \mathsf{CT}_i^2$ in the same slot, pIPFE prevents decryptor from computing $\mathsf{pDec}(\mathsf{pCT}_{i,j}^1, \mathsf{pCT}_{i,\ell}^2)$ in the decryption process as in Eq. (3) (meaning that $\langle \mathbf{h}^1, \widetilde{\mathbf{h}^2} \rangle \neq 0$ if $\mathbf{h}^1$ and $\widetilde{\mathbf{h}^2}$ are vectors derived from two different ciphertexts for the same slot i).

Although this seems to be a major bottleneck at first, we make an important observation that if each encryptor computes and encrypts all possible quadratic terms between its own message vector at the time of encryption, then a decryptor does not need to generate the quadratic terms derived from the same slot via the pIPFE decryption. Therefore, the mix-and-match problem can be rather easily solved by replacing pIPFE with a plain (non-predicate) IPFE scheme. And, since this new encryption method only increases the length of the underlying encrypted vector from m to m^2, thus it is still efficient. We refer to Definition 2.6 and 2.7 for more details.

Final Rerandomization Trick. While it seems that we are done at this point, unfortunately this is still not sufficient. And, the reason is the fact that even after removing elements (iv), we cannot achieve the property P by using $\mathbf{e}_1, \ldots, \mathbf{e}_n$ as the public elementary messages from two reasons. First, $\sum_j \mathbf{x}[j]$ is not necessarily 1, and thus elements (i) may not be 1 after the homomorphic addition. Second, elements (iii) depend on $\mathbf{x}$ and the random tape used to generate the ciphertexts of $\mathbf{e}_i$, and thus not independently random after the homomorphic addition. The second reason can be visualized as the resulting ciphertext containing far less entropy than a freshly sampled ciphertext.

However, we solve these issues by the following rerandomization trick. Our idea is to additionally include a large sequence of $\mathbf{0}$ vectors to the list of elementary messages, and sample a fresh sequence of random elements which will be used to homomorphically add each encryption of $\mathbf{0}$ to the underlying homomorphically computed ciphertext such that the resulting ciphertext has sufficient entropy. That is, for a sufficiently large D, we define $\widetilde{\mathsf{Enc}}$ as follows: $\widetilde{\mathsf{Enc}}\left((\{\mathsf{CT}_i[\mathbf{e}_j]\}_{j\in[m]}, \{\mathsf{CT}_{i,j}[\mathbf{0}]\}_{j\in[D]}), \mathbf{x} \right)$ computes $\mathsf{CT}_i[\mathbf{x}]$ as

$$\mathsf{CT}_i[\mathbf{x}] = \mathsf{CT}_{i,1}[\mathbf{0}] + \sum_{j\in[m]} \mathbf{x}_i[j](\mathsf{CT}_i[\mathbf{e}_j] - \mathsf{CT}_{i,1}[\mathbf{0}]) + \sum_{j\in[\frac{D-1}{2}]} \gamma_j(\mathsf{CT}_{i,2j}[\mathbf{0}] - \mathsf{CT}_{i,2j+1}[\mathbf{0}]),$$

where $\gamma_1, \ldots, \gamma_{(D-1)/2} \leftarrow \mathbb{Z}_p$.

This solves the second problem as now the elements (iii) are distributed randomly if D is sufficiently large due to the fresh entropy introduced by $\gamma_1, \ldots, \gamma_{(D-1)/2}$. And, since we have $\sum_{j\in[m]}(\mathbf{x}_i[j] - \mathbf{x}_i[j]) + \sum_{j\in[(D-1)/2]}(\gamma_j - \gamma_j) = 0$, thus element (i) is also equal to 1 in $\mathsf{CT}_i[\mathbf{x}]$. Hence, the above rerandomization trick combined with the pIPFE removal strategy gives us our SK-MIFE scheme for quadratic functions with property P, which in turn gives us our quadratic MIFE scheme secure in the stronger fine-grained corruption model.

Supporting the Ciphertext Labelling Functionality. Finally, we provide a rather simple yet incredibly useful mechanism to annotate labels with SK-MIFE ciphertexts. This adds the feature of multi-client style encryption to the quadratic SK-MIFE scheme. To this end, we look back at the existing techniques to achieve desired labelling for IP-MIFE schemes (that is, the ideas used to obtain IP-MCFE, or in other words, MCFE for inner product), but find that all techniques are rather specific to inner product. The prior works basically use the following blueprint [1,10,21,22]. The MCFE schemes use a (single-input) IPFE scheme as a building block, and a ciphertext of the MCFE for the i-th slot message $\mathbf{x}_i$ with a label lab is simply a ciphertext of the IPFE scheme for some vector $\widetilde{\mathbf{x}}_i$ related to $\mathbf{x}_i$ and lab. A secret key of the MCFE scheme for $\mathbf{c} = (\mathbf{c}_1 || \ldots || \mathbf{c}_n)$ contains IPFE secret keys for some vector $\widetilde{\mathbf{c}}_i$ related to $\mathbf{c}$ for $i \in [n]$, and decryption for slot-i reveals

$$\langle \widetilde{\mathbf{x}}_i, \widetilde{\mathbf{c}}_i \rangle = \langle \mathbf{x}_i, \mathbf{c}_i \rangle + u_i$$

where u_i is a masking term such that $\sum_{i\in[n]} u_i$ is equal to 0 (or a computable value by the decryptor) only when $\widetilde{\mathbf{x}}_i$ is associated with the same label for all i. Hence, the decryptor can learn only $\sum_i \langle \mathbf{x}_i, \mathbf{c}_i \rangle$ as desired. However, the structure of the only known MIFE scheme for quadratic functions by AGT, as observed, is quite different from this blueprint, and thus we need a new approach.

Our starting point is again the AGT MIFE scheme where recall the ciphertext has the form as described in Eq. (1). A natural first thought is to try to replace all the three underlying IPFE, pIPFE, and IP-MIFE schemes with their labelled counterparts. After a quick glance, it appears that this would be a viable strategy since if we could annotate each component in the AGT ciphertext with a label, then the entire AGT ciphertext will be labelled as well.

As we elaborated during the description of our MIFE construction, the application of pIPFE in the AGT template can be replaced with any IPFE scheme (ignoring the quadratic increase in the overall ciphertext size). Concretely, we showed that the ciphertext CT of the modified AGT scheme can be written as

$$\mathsf{CT}_i = \left(\left\{ \mathsf{iCT}^{(1)}[\mathbf{b}_j], \mathsf{iSK}^{(1)}[\widetilde{\mathbf{b}}_j] \right\}_{j \in [m]}, \ \mathsf{iCT}^{(2)}[\mathbf{d}], \ \mathsf{iSK}^{(2)}[\widetilde{\mathbf{d}}], \ \mathsf{miCT}_i[\mathbf{f}] \right),$$

where $(\mathsf{iCT}^{(1)}, \mathsf{iSK}^{(1)})$ and $(\mathsf{iCT}^{(2)}, \mathsf{iSK}^{(2)})$ are generated by two separate master secret keys $\mathsf{iMSK}^{(1)}$ and $\mathsf{iMSK}^{(2)}$, respectively. Thus, it seems like if we can annotate both, the IPFE and the IP-MIFE, components of the modified AGT scheme with the same label, then the resulting quadratic MIFE scheme will also support ciphertext labelling functionality.

Now to annotate the IP-MIFE component of the ciphertext, we need a labelled version of the SK-MIFE scheme for *mixed-group* inner products with *function-hiding security* as a counterpart. Although such a scheme for inner product is not already known, we were able to construct a new scheme with the desired properties by combining ideas from the SK-MIFE scheme for mixed-group inner product in [9] and the MCFE scheme for inner product in [10]. We refer the reader to Sect. 3 for the exact details.

Finally, to get the desired result, we simply need a mechanism to annotate the IPFE component of the AGT ciphertexts with labels such that ciphertexts with different labels can no longer be combined. Our idea is to simply keep a PRF key K as part of the overall system master key, and use the PRF key K to sample a *label-dependent* IPFE key at the time of encryption. That is, the setup no longer samples the IPFE keys used during the encryption, but instead the encryptor first samples the IPFE keys using $\mathsf{PRF}(K, \mathsf{lab})$ as the randomness where lab is the specified label, and then uses those keys to compute the appropriate ciphertext components. Clearly, ciphertexts encrypted w.r.t. different labels can no longer be combined since the underlying ciphertext components are now incompatible (as they are sampled using independent IPFE keys). And, basically by iterating the hybrid sequence of the SK-MIFE scheme for quadratic functions in [9] *per queried label*, we can also prove security in the secret-key MCFE setting.

Open Problems. We conclude the introduction by discussing some open problems. To the best of our knowledge, this is the first work proposing a technique to convert SK-MIFE to MIFE with stronger security. Since our technique is applicable to all SK-MIFE schemes with property P, exploring other classes of MIFE to which our technique is applicable is an interesting open problem. We observe that this conversion does seem applicable to group-based SK-MIFE schemes for inner product in [4, 5] since they enjoy a nice homomorphic property. However,

MIFE schemes for inner product with the stronger security are already known so this does not yield a new result. Nevertheless it does give a new pathway to obtaining these results since known MCFE schemes for inner product are constructed without going through SK-MIFE.

The second open question is the construction of a (public-key) MCFE scheme for quadratic functions. Interestingly, while the above ideas are sufficient for SK-MCFE for quadratic functions, we were unable to prove security in the public-key setting. First, in the above abstraction, the usage of PRFs to annotate the IPFE portion of the modified AGT ciphertext requires the encryption key for each slot to contain the secret PRF key K. Thus, corruption of even one encryption key completely breaks down the scheme. An approach is to sample a separate PRF key for each pair of encryption slots, however, even that does not seem to suffice as corrupting even a single secret key for a particular encryption slot seems to provide an attacker a mechanism to maul the labels from honest ciphertexts, thereby breaking security. Other natural approaches run into similar roadblocks. We leave the question full fledged MCFE as an exciting open problem.

We remark that the approach of providing generic compilers to "upgrade" security notions of primitives can be very useful in enabling new constructions since it simplifies the minimum building block that must be instantiated. For the case of restricted functionalities like linear [1] or quadratic functions (this), such compilers have required the underlying scheme to satisfy "nice" algebraic properties. Can this requirement be removed? Given current techniques, it seems difficult to remove such requirements without relying on strong tools like obfuscation. However, exploring this question more fully is a promising line of research.

Finally, it is evidently a fascinating question whether we can "lift" the degree of the underlying function class beyond 2 without relying on strong tools like compact functional encryption or obfuscation. Currently, we have results from single assumptions in the arena of degree ≤ 2 [1,2,4,5,9,21,23,29,32] and results from combinations of assumptions for classes like NC_1 and beyond [27,28] even in the single input setting. While compact functional encryption can be generalized to the multi-input setting [13,17], can we have constructions of MIFE and MCFE for bigger classes of functions without relying on obfustopia primitives?

2   Preliminaries

Notation. We begin by defining the notation that we will use throughout the paper. We use bold letters to denote vectors and the notation $[a, b]$ to denote the set of integers $\{k \in \mathbb{N} \mid a \leq k \leq b\}$. We use $[n]$ to denote the set $[1, n]$. For vector $\mathbf{v}$, $\mathbf{v}[i]$ denotes the i-th element of $\mathbf{v}$. For $(i_n, \ldots, i_1) \in [N_n] \times \cdots \times [N_1] \subset \mathbb{N}^n$, we sometimes identify $(i_n, \ldots, i_1)$ as $\sum_{j \in [2,n]} \left((i_j - 1) \prod_{\ell \in [j-1]} N_\ell \right) + i_1$, which is an element in $[N_1 N_2 \cdots N_n]$. This identification is used to introduce an order in the elements in $[N_1] \times \cdots \times [N_n]$. For a matrix $\mathbf{A} = (a_{j,\ell})_{j,\ell}$ over $\mathbb{Z}_p$, $[\mathbf{A}]_i$ denotes a matrix over G_i whose (j, ℓ)-th entry is $g_i^{a_{j,\ell}}$, and we use this notation for vectors and scalars similarly. Throughout the paper, we use λ to denote the security parameter.

We will use a pseudorandom function (PRF) and standard cryptographic bilinear groups where the matrix decisional Diffie-Hellman (MDDH) assumption holds.

2.1   Multi-Input Functional Encryption

Syntax. Let n be the number of encryption slots, and $\mathcal{F} = \{\mathcal{F}_n\}_{n \in \mathbb{N}}$ be a function family such that, for all $f \in \mathcal{F}_n$, $f : \mathcal{X}_1 \times \cdots \times \mathcal{X}_n \to \mathcal{Y}$. Here $\mathcal{X}_i$ and $\mathcal{Y}$ be the input and output spaces (respectively). A multi-input functional encryption (MIFE)[3] scheme for function family $\mathcal{F}$ consists of following algorithms.

Setup($1^\lambda, 1^n$) $\to$ (PP, $\{\mathsf{EK}_i\}_i$, MSK). It takes a security parameter 1^λ, number of slots 1^n, and outputs public parameters PP, n encryption keys $\{\mathsf{EK}_i\}_{i \in [n]}$, a master secret key MSK. (The remaining algorithms implicitly take PP as input.)

Enc(EK_i, x) $\to$ CT_i. It takes the i-th encryption key EK_i and an input $x \in \mathcal{X}_i$, and outputs a ciphertext CT_i.

KeyGen(MSK, f) $\to$ SK. It takes the master key MSK and a function $f \in \mathcal{F}$ as inputs, and outputs a decryption key SK.

Dec($\mathsf{CT}_1, \ldots, \mathsf{CT}_n$, SK) $\to$ y. It takes n ciphertexts $\mathsf{CT}_1, \ldots, \mathsf{CT}_n$ and decryption key SK, and outputs a decryption value $y \in \mathcal{Y}$ or a special abort symbol $\bot$.

Correctness. An MIFE scheme for function family $\mathcal{F}$ is correct if for all $\lambda, n \in \mathbb{N}$, $(x_1, \ldots, x_n) \in \mathcal{X}_1 \times \cdots \times \mathcal{X}_n$, $f \in \mathcal{F}_n$, we have

$$
\Pr \left[y = f(x_1, \ldots, x_n) : \begin{array}{l} (\mathsf{PP}, \{\mathsf{EK}_i\}_i, \mathsf{MSK}) \leftarrow \mathsf{Setup}(1^\lambda, 1^n) \\ \{\mathsf{CT}_i \leftarrow \mathsf{Enc}(i, \mathsf{EK}_i, x_i)\}_i \\ \mathsf{SK} \leftarrow \mathsf{KeyGen}(\mathsf{MSK}, f) \\ y = \mathsf{Dec}(\mathsf{CT}_1, \ldots, \mathsf{CT}_n, \mathsf{SK}) \end{array} \right] = 1.
$$

Definition 2.1. *For security, we define two indistinguishability-based security definitions: message-hiding security and function-hiding security. An MIFE scheme is sel-XX-YY-IND-secure (XX $\in$ {pos, any}, YY $\in$ {mh, fh})[4] if for any stateful admissible PPT adversary $\mathcal{A}$, there exists a negligible function $\mathsf{negl}(n)(\cdot)$ such that for all $\lambda, n \in \mathbb{N}$, the following probability is negligibly close to 1/2 in λ:*

---

[3] When $n = 1$, we call MIFE just functional encryption (FE).

[4] "sel" stands for "selective" meaning that the adversary has to select the challenge elements at the beginning of the security game. The opposite notion is "adaptive". "pos" stands for "positive". In MCFE, a user can decrypt ciphertexts only when it has ciphertexts for all slots with the same label, and a portion of them is useless for decryption. "pos" prohibits the adversary from querying the oracle on such useless challenge elements. "mh" and "fh" stand for "message-hiding" and "function-hiding", respectively.

$$\Pr\left[\mathcal{A}(\{\mathsf{EK}_i\}_{i \in \mathcal{CS}}, \{\mathsf{CT}_\mu\}_\mu, \{\mathsf{SK}_\nu\}_\nu) = \beta : \begin{array}{l} \beta \leftarrow \{0,1\} \\ \mathsf{PP}, \{\mathsf{EK}_i\}_{i \in [n]}, \mathsf{MSK} \leftarrow \mathsf{Setup}(1^\lambda, 1^n) \\ (\mathcal{CS}, \mathcal{MS}, \mathcal{FS}) \leftarrow \mathcal{A}(1^\lambda, \mathsf{PP}) \ s.t. \\ \mathcal{CS} \subseteq [n] \\ \mathcal{MS} = \{i^\mu, x^{\mu,0}, x^{\mu,1}\}_{\mu \in [q_c]} \\ \mathcal{FS} = \{f^{\nu,0}, f^{\nu,1}\}_{\nu \in [q_k]} \\ \{\mathsf{CT}_\mu \leftarrow \mathsf{Enc}(i^\mu, \mathsf{EK}_{i^\mu}, x^{\mu,\beta})\}_\mu \\ \{\mathsf{SK}_\nu \leftarrow \mathsf{KeyGen}(\mathsf{MSK}, f^{\nu,\beta})\}_\nu \end{array}\right]$$

where the adversary $\mathcal{A}$ is said to be admissible if and only if:

1. $f^0(x_1^0, \ldots, x_n^0) = f^1(x_1^1, \ldots, x_n^1)$ for all sequences $(x_1^0, \ldots, x_n^0, x_1^1, \ldots, x_n^1,$ $f^0, f^1)$ such that:
   - For all $i \in [n]$, $[(i, x_i^0, x_i^1) \in \mathcal{MS}]$ or $[i \in \mathcal{CS}$ and $x_i^0 = x_i^1]$,
   - $(f^0, f^1) \in \mathcal{FS}$.
2. When $XX = pos$, $q_c[i] > 0$ for all $i \in [n]$, where $q_c[i]$ denotes the number of elements of the form $(i, *, *)$ in $\mathcal{MS}$.
3. When $YY = mh$, $f^{\nu,0} = f^{\nu,1}$ for all $\nu \in [q_k]$.

MIFE security in secret-key setting. We say an MIFE scheme is secret-key MIFE (SK-MIFE) scheme if all the n encryption keys EK_i are basically the master secret key MSK. The security of an SK-MIFE scheme is defined the same way as an MIFE scheme except that the adversary has to set $\mathcal{CS} = \emptyset$.

2.2   Multi-Client Functional Encryption

A multi-client functional encryption (MCFE) scheme is an extension of MIFE where each ciphertext is now annotated with a unique label such that ciphertexts encrypted for different slots can now only be combined together during decryption as long as the associated labels match for all individual ciphertext pieces. We first define its syntax where we highlight in terms of changes, how MCFE compares with MIFE.

Syntax. An MCFE system is associated with a label space $\mathcal{L}$, in addition to the number of encryption slots n and function class $\mathcal{F}$ as in MIFE. A multi-client functional encryption scheme for function family $\mathcal{F}$ consists of following algorithms.

$\mathsf{Setup}, \mathsf{KeyGen}, \mathsf{Dec}$ have the same syntax as in MIFE.
$\mathsf{Enc}(\mathsf{EK}_i, \mathsf{lab}, x) \to \mathsf{CT}$. The encryption algorithm takes the i-th encryption key EK_i, a label lab, and an input $x \in \mathcal{X}_i$, and outputs a ciphertext CT_i.

Correctness. An MCFE scheme for function family $\mathcal{F}$ is correct if for all $\lambda, n \in \mathbb{N}$, $(x_1, \ldots, x_n) \in \mathcal{X}_1 \times \cdots \times \mathcal{X}_n$, $f \in \mathcal{F}$, and label $\mathsf{lab} \in \mathcal{L}$, we have

$$\Pr\left[y = f(x_1, \ldots, x_n) : \begin{array}{l} (\mathsf{PP}, \{\mathsf{EK}_i\}_i, \mathsf{MSK}) \leftarrow \mathsf{Setup}(1^\lambda, 1^n) \\ \{\mathsf{CT}_i \leftarrow \mathsf{Enc}(i, \mathsf{EK}_i, \mathsf{lab}, x_i)\}_i \\ \mathsf{SK} \leftarrow \mathsf{KeyGen}(\mathsf{MSK}, f) \\ y = \mathsf{Dec}(\mathsf{CT}_1, \ldots, \mathsf{CT}_n, \mathsf{SK}) \end{array}\right] = 1.$$

That is, if all the ciphertexts are encrypted for the same label, then the decryption works as in MIFE.

MCFE Security in Secret-key Setting. In this work we are mostly interested in the secret-key setting. The intuition behind security for secret-key MCFE is similar to that for secret-key MIFE, with the difference that the admissibility constraint for ciphertexts is defined for each label individually. Below we define it formally.

Definition 2.2. *An SK-MCFE scheme is sel-XX-YY-IND-secure (XX $\in$ {pos, any}], YY $\in$ {mh, fh}) if for any stateful admissible PPT adversary $\mathcal{A}$, there exists a negligible function $\mathsf{negl}(n)(\cdot)$ such that for all $\lambda, n \in \mathbb{N}$, the following probability is negligibly close to $1/2$ in λ:*

$$\Pr \left[\mathcal{A}(\{\mathsf{CT}_\mu\}_\mu, \{\mathsf{SK}_\nu\}_\nu) = \beta : \begin{array}{l} (\mathsf{PP}, \mathsf{MSK}) \leftarrow \mathsf{Setup}(1^\lambda, 1^n), \beta \leftarrow \{0, 1\} \\ (\mathcal{MS}, \mathcal{FS}) \leftarrow \mathcal{A}(1^\lambda, \mathsf{PP}) \ s.t. \\ \mathcal{MS} = \{i^\mu, \mathsf{lab}^\mu, x^{\mu,0}, x^{\mu,1}\}_{\mu \in [q_c]} \\ \mathcal{FS} = \{f^{\nu,0}, f^{\nu,1}\}_{\nu \in [q_k]} \\ \{\mathsf{CT}_\mu \leftarrow \mathsf{Enc}(\mathsf{MSK}, i^\mu, \mathsf{lab}^\mu, x^{\mu,\beta})\}_\mu \\ \{\mathsf{SK}_\nu \leftarrow \mathsf{KeyGen}(\mathsf{MSK}, f^{\nu,\beta})\}_\nu \end{array} \right]$$

where the adversary $\mathcal{A}$ is said to be admissible if and only if:

1. $f^0(x_1^0, \ldots, x_n^0) = f^1(x_1^1, \ldots, x_n^1)$ *for all sequences* $(x_1^0, \ldots, x_n^0, x_1^1, \ldots, x_n^1, f^0, f^1, \mathsf{lab})$ *such that:*
   - *For all* $i \in [n]$, $(i, \mathsf{lab}, x_i^0, x_i^1) \in \mathcal{MS}$,
   - $(f^0, f^1) \in \mathcal{FS}$.
2. *When* $XX = pos$, *for any label* lab *queried by the adversary,* $q_c[i, \mathsf{lab}] > 0$ *for all* $i \in [n]$, *where* $q_c[i, \mathsf{lab}]$ *denotes the number of elements of the form* $(i, \mathsf{lab}, *, *)$ *in* $\mathcal{MS}$.
3. *When* $YY = mh$, $f^{\nu,0} = f^{\nu,1}$ *for all* $\nu \in [q_k]$.

Remark 2.3. In this paper, we only consider pos-security since a sel-pos-YY-secure MIFE/MCFE scheme can be generically transformed into a sel-any-YY-secure MIFE/MCFE scheme [1,2,5,23].

2.3 Functionalities

In this section, we define basic function classes for MIFE/SK-MCFE that is used in this paper.

Definition 2.4 (Inner Product over Bilinear Groups). *Let* $\mathbb{G} = (p, G_1, G_2, G_T, g_1, g_2, e)$ *be bilinear groups. A function family* $\mathcal{F}^{\mathsf{IP}}_{m,n,\mathbb{G}}$ *for inner products over bilinear groups consists of functions* $f : (G_1^m)^n \to G_T$. *Each* $f \in \mathcal{F}^{\mathsf{IP}}_{m,n,\mathbb{G}}$ *is specified by* $[(\mathbf{y}_1, \ldots, \mathbf{y}_n)]_2$ *where* $\mathbf{y}_i \in \mathbb{Z}_p^m$ *and defined as* $f([\mathbf{x}_1]_1, \ldots, [\mathbf{x}_n]_1) = [\sum_{i \in [n]} \langle \mathbf{x}_i, \mathbf{y}_i \rangle]_T$. *We call MIFE/SK-MCFE for* $\mathcal{F}^{\mathsf{IP}}_{m,n,\mathbb{G}}$ *MIFE/SK-MCFE for inner product. Especially, we sometimes call FE for* $\mathcal{F}^{\mathsf{IP}}_{m,1,\mathbb{G}}$ *inner product functional encryption (IPFE).*

Note that constructions of IPFE and SK-MCFE for inner product with function-hiding (sel-any-fh) security are already known [10,33].

Definition 2.5 (Mixed-Group Inner Products). Let $\mathbb{G} = (p, G_1, G_2, G_T, g_1, g_2, e)$ be bilinear groups. A function family $\mathcal{F}^{\mathsf{MG}}_{m_1, m_2, n, \mathbb{G}}$ for mixed-group inner products consists of functions $f : (G_1^{m_1} \times G_2^{m_2})^n \to G_T$. Each $f \in \mathcal{F}^{\mathsf{MG}}_{m_1, m_2, n, \mathbb{G}}$ is specified by $([\mathbf{y}_{1,1}]_2, [\mathbf{y}_{1,2}]_1, \ldots, [\mathbf{y}_{n,1}]_2, [\mathbf{y}_{n,2}]_1)$ where $\mathbf{y}_{i,1} \in \mathbb{Z}_p^{m_1}$ and $\mathbf{y}_{i,2} \in \mathbb{Z}_p^{m_2}$ and defined as $f(([\mathbf{x}_{1,1}]_1, [\mathbf{x}_{1,2}]_2), \ldots, ([\mathbf{x}_{n,1}]_1, [\mathbf{x}_{n,2}]_2)) = [\langle \mathbf{x}, \mathbf{y} \rangle]_T$ where $\mathbf{x} = (\mathbf{x}_{1,1}, \mathbf{x}_{1,2}, \ldots, \mathbf{x}_{n,1}, \mathbf{x}_{n,2})$ and $\mathbf{y} = (\mathbf{y}_{1,1}, \mathbf{y}_{1,2}, \ldots, \mathbf{y}_{n,1}, \mathbf{y}_{n,2})$. We call MIFE/SK-MCFE for $\mathcal{F}^{\mathsf{MG}}_{m_1, m_2, n, \mathbb{G}}$ MIFE/SK-MCFE for mixed-group inner product.

Definition 2.6 (Bounded-Norm Quadratic functions over $\mathbb{Z}$). A function family $\mathcal{F}^{\mathsf{QF}}_{m, n, X, C}$ for bounded-norm multi-input quadratic functions consist of functions $f : (\mathcal{X}^m)^n \to \mathbb{Z}$ where $\mathcal{X} = \{i \in \mathbb{Z} \mid |i| \leq X\}$. Each $f \in \mathcal{F}^{\mathsf{QF}}_{m, n, X, C}$ is specified by $\mathbf{c} \in \mathbb{Z}^{(mn)^2}$ s.t. $||\mathbf{c}||_\infty \leq C$ and $\mathbf{c}[(i, j, k, \ell)] = 0$ if $i \geq k$. Then, f specified by $\mathbf{c}$ is defined as $f(\mathbf{x}_1, \ldots, \mathbf{x}_n) = \sum_{i, k \in [n], j, \ell \in [m]} \mathbf{c}[(i, j, k, \ell)] \mathbf{x}_i[j] \mathbf{x}_k[\ell]$. We call MIFE/SK-MCFE for $\mathcal{F}^{\mathsf{QF}}_{m, n, X, C}$ MIFE/SK-MCFE for quadratic functions.

Remark 2.7. The original definition of quadratic functions in [9] provides that $\mathbf{c}$ is a vector s.t. $\mathbf{c}[(i, j, k, \ell)] = 0$ if $(i, j) > (k, \ell)$ instead of $i \geq k$. Actually, the functionality in Definition 2.6 implies the original functionality by defining $g(\mathbf{x}_1, \ldots, \mathbf{x}_n) = f(\mathbf{x}'_1, \ldots, \mathbf{x}'_n)$ where $\mathbf{x}'_i = (\mathbf{x}_i \otimes \mathbf{x}_i, \mathbf{x}_i, 1)$ and $f \in \mathcal{F}^{\mathsf{QF}}_{m, n, X, C}$.

Formally, our contribution in this paper is the constructions of MIFE and SK-MCFE for quadratic functions from pairings. Note that only an SK-MIFE scheme for quadratic functions based on pairings [9] is know prior to our work.

3   SK-MCFE for Mixed-Group Inner Product

In this section, we provide our construction for function-hiding SK-MCFE for mixed-group inner-product (Definition 2.5), which is used as a building block of our MIFE and SK-MCFE schemes for quadratic functions. The construction is similar to the function-hiding SK-MIFE for mixed-group inner-product in [9] by Agrawal, Goyal, and Tomida (AGT). Recall that the AGT SK-MIFE for mixed-group inner-product is obtained by combining a function-hiding SK-MIFE for inner-product and a function-hiding SK-FE for inner product. Our SK-MCFE for mixed-group inner-product is obtained by replacing a function-hiding SK-MIFE for inner-product in the AGT scheme with a function-hiding SK-MCFE for inner-product. Note that a function-hiding SK-MCFE for inner product can be obtained from a function-hiding MCFE scheme for inner product in [10] since SK-MCFE is the special case of MCFE. Additionally, while the MCFE scheme in [10] uses a hash function modeled as a random oracle in encryption, we can replace it with a PRF in the secret-key setting. The function-hiding SK-MCFE scheme for inner product without a random oracle is presented in Fig. 2.

Formally, we construct a function-hiding SK-MCFE scheme for $\mathcal{F}^{\mathsf{MG}}_{m_1, m_2, n, \mathbb{G}}$ with label space $\mathcal{L}$ from a function-hiding SK-MCFE scheme for $\mathcal{F}^{\mathsf{IP}}_{m, n, \mathbb{G}}$ with the same label space $\mathcal{L}$ and a function-hiding FE scheme for $\mathcal{F}^{\mathsf{IP}}_{m, 1, \mathbb{G}}$ in a generic way.

Let icFE = (icSetup, icEnc, icKeyGen, icDec) be a function-hiding SK-MCFE for $\mathcal{F}_{m,n,\mathbb{G}}^{\mathsf{IP}}$, and iFE = (iSetup, iEnc, iKeyGen, iDec) be a function-hiding IPFE scheme (SK-FE for $\mathcal{F}_{m,1,\mathbb{G}}^{\mathsf{IP}}$). Then, our function-hiding SK-MCFE for mixed-group inner product $\mathcal{F}_{m_1,m_2,n,\mathbb{G}}^{\mathsf{MG}}$ is constructed as shown in Fig. 1.

$\mathsf{Setup}(1^\lambda, 1^n)$: It generates master secret keys of icFE and iFE as follows:

$\mathsf{icPP}, \mathsf{icMSK} \leftarrow \mathsf{icSetup}(1^\lambda, 1^n)$, $(\mathsf{iPP}_1, \mathsf{iMSK}_1), \ldots, (\mathsf{iPP}_n, \mathsf{iMSK}_n) \leftarrow \mathsf{iSetup}(1^\lambda)$

where the vector lengths of icFE and iFE are set as $m_1 + m_2 + k + 1$ and $m_2 + k + 1$, respectively. Note that $k \geq 2$ is the parameter of the bilateral MDDH assumption.

Then it outputs PP, MSK as follows:

$\mathsf{PP} = (\mathsf{icPP}, \mathsf{iPP}_1, \ldots, \mathsf{iPP}_n)$, $\mathsf{MSK} = (\mathsf{icMSK}, \mathsf{iMSK}_1, \ldots, \mathsf{iMSK}_n)$.

$\mathsf{Enc}(\mathsf{MSK}, i, \mathsf{lab}, ([\mathbf{x}_{i,1}]_1, [\mathbf{x}_{i,2}]_2))$: It output CT_i as follows:

$\mathbf{z} \leftarrow \mathbb{Z}_p^k$, $\widetilde{\mathbf{x}}_{i,1} = (\mathbf{x}_{i,1}, 0^{m_2}, \mathbf{z}, 0) \in \mathbb{Z}_p^{m_1+m_2+k+1}$, $\widetilde{\mathbf{x}}_{i,2} = (\mathbf{x}_{i,2}, -\mathbf{z}, 0) \in \mathbb{Z}_p^{m_2+k+1}$

$\mathsf{icCT}_i \leftarrow \mathsf{icEnc}(\mathsf{icMSK}, i, \mathsf{lab}, [\widetilde{\mathbf{x}}_{i,1}]_1)$, $\mathsf{iSK}_i \leftarrow \mathsf{iKeyGen}(\mathsf{iMSK}_i, [\widetilde{\mathbf{x}}_{i,2}]_2)$, $\mathsf{CT}_i = (\mathsf{icCT}_i, \mathsf{iSK}_i)$

$\mathsf{KeyGen}(\mathsf{MSK}, \{[\mathbf{y}_{i,1}]_2, [\mathbf{y}_{i,2}]_1\}_{i \in [n]})$: It output SK as follows:

$\mathbf{a} \leftarrow \mathbb{Z}_p^k$, $\widetilde{\mathbf{y}}_{i,1} = (\mathbf{y}_{i,1}, 0^{m_2}, \mathbf{a}, 0) \in \mathbb{Z}_p^{m_1+m_2+k+1}$, $\widetilde{\mathbf{y}}_{i,2} = (\mathbf{y}_{i,2}, \mathbf{a}, 0) \in \mathbb{Z}_p^{m_2+k+1}$, $\widetilde{\mathbf{y}} = (\widetilde{\mathbf{y}}_{1,1}, \ldots, \widetilde{\mathbf{y}}_{n,1})$

$\mathsf{icSK} \leftarrow \mathsf{icKeyGen}(\mathsf{icMSK}, [\widetilde{\mathbf{y}}]_2)$, $\mathsf{iCT}_i \leftarrow \mathsf{iEnc}(\mathsf{iMSK}_i, [\widetilde{\mathbf{y}}_{i,2}]_1)$, $\mathsf{SK} = (\mathsf{icSK}, \{\mathsf{iCT}_i\}_{i \in [n]})$

$\mathsf{Dec}(\mathsf{CT}_1, \ldots, \mathsf{CT}_n, \mathsf{SK})$: It output z as follows:

Outputs $\mathsf{icDec}(\mathsf{icCT}_1, \ldots, \mathsf{icCT}_n, \mathsf{icSK}) \prod_{i \in [n]} \mathsf{iDec}(\mathsf{iCT}_i, \mathsf{iSK}_i)$

Fig. 1. Our mixed-group IP-MIFE scheme.

Due to the limit of the space, we present the correctness and the security proof in the full version.

4   SK-MCFE for Quadratic Functions

As explained in the technical overview, i) our MIFE scheme for quadratic functions can be generically obtained from the modified AGT SK-MIFE scheme for quadratic functions, which does not use a SK-FE scheme for *predicate* inner product; ii) the modified SK-MIFE scheme can be seen as the special case of our SK-MCFE scheme, where the label space consists of one element. Considering the above two facts, we first present our SK-MCFE scheme for quadratic functions to save the effort of presenting the security proof of the modified SK-MIFE scheme in the construction of our MIFE scheme.

4.1   Construction

Let mgFE = (mgSetup, mgEnc, mgKeyGen, mgDec) be an SK-MCFE scheme for mixed-group inner product (Sect. 3) with label space $\mathcal{L}$, and iFE = (iSetup, iEnc, iKeyGen, iDec) be a function-hiding IPFE scheme. Also, let PRF = $\{\mathsf{PRF}_\lambda\}_{\lambda \in \mathbb{N}}$ be a PRF family where $\mathsf{PRF}_\lambda : \{0,1\}^\lambda \times \mathcal{L} \to \{0,1\}^\lambda$ and $\mathbb{G}$ be bilinear groups. Below we provide an SK-MCFE scheme for function class $\mathcal{F}_{m,n,X,C}^{\mathsf{QF}}$

with the same label space $\mathcal{L}$. Similarly to [9], we can construct our SK-MCFE scheme from MDDH_k, while it makes the construction and security proof far more complicated as we can see in [9]. Thus, we present the construction based on MDDH_1 for better readability in this paper.

$\mathsf{Setup}(1^\lambda, 1^n)$ samples a random PRF key $K \leftarrow \{0,1\}^\lambda$ and the master keys for the underlying IPFE and SK-MCFE scheme as $(\mathsf{iPP}^{(2)}, \mathsf{iMSK}^{(2)}) \leftarrow \mathsf{iSetup}(1^\lambda)$, $(\mathsf{mgPP}, \mathsf{mgMSK}) \leftarrow \mathsf{mgSetup}(1^\lambda, 1^n)$ where the vector length of iFE is set as 2, and the vector length of mgFE is set as $m^2 n + 2$ and 1. Note that $\mathsf{iPP}^{(2)} = \mathsf{mgPP} = \mathbb{G}$. It also samples a sequence of randomization terms as:

$$\forall\, i, k \in [n], j, \ell \in [m], \qquad w_{(i,j,k,\ell)} \leftarrow \mathbb{Z}_p$$
$$\forall\, i \in [n], j \in [m], \qquad u_{i,j}, \widetilde{u}_{i,j}, v_{i,j}, \widetilde{v}_{i,j} \leftarrow \mathbb{Z}_p$$

It outputs the public parameters and master key as

$$\mathsf{PP} = \mathbb{G}, \quad \mathsf{MSK} = \left(K, \mathsf{iMSK}^{(2)}, \mathsf{mgMSK}, \{w_{(i,j,k,\ell)}\}_{i,j,k,\ell}, \{u_{i,j}, \widetilde{u}_{i,j}, v_{i,j}, \widetilde{v}_{i,j}\}_{i,j} \right).$$

$\mathsf{Enc}(\mathsf{MSK}, i, \mathsf{lab}, \mathbf{x})$ parses MSK as above, and using the PRF key K, it samples a IPFE master key of vector length $mn + 3m + 4$ as $(\mathsf{iPP}^{(1)}, \mathsf{iMSK}^{(1)}) \leftarrow \mathsf{iSetup}(1^\lambda; \mathsf{PRF}(K, \mathsf{lab}))$. Here we assume (w.l.o.g.) that the MIFE setup algorithm takes λ bits as random coins. It then samples random elements $s, \widetilde{s}, r, t \leftarrow \mathbb{Z}_p$. And, it sets vectors $\mathbf{b}_j, \widetilde{\mathbf{b}}_j$ for $j \in [m]$ as follows:

$$\mathbf{b}_j = (\mathbf{x}[j], 0, s\mathbf{e}_{(i,j)}, ru_{i,j}, v_{i,j}, \mathbf{0}_{3m}), \quad \widetilde{\mathbf{b}}_j = (\mathbf{x}[j], 0, \widetilde{s}\mathbf{w}_{(*,*,i,j)}, \widetilde{u}_{i,j}, t\widetilde{v}_{i,j}, \mathbf{0}_{3m}).$$

where $\mathbf{e}_{(i,j)}$ is the mn-dimensional one-hot vector with the (i,j)-th element being 1, and vector $\mathbf{w}_{(*,*,i,j)} \in \mathbb{Z}_p^{mn}$ is defined as follows:

$$\forall\, j \in [m], \quad \mathbf{w}_{(*,*,i,j)} = (w_{(1,1,i,j)}, w_{(1,2,i,j)}, \ldots, w_{(n,m,i,j)})$$

The encryptor encodes the vectors $\mathbf{b}_j, \widetilde{\mathbf{b}}_j$ under MIFE as follows:

$$\forall\, j \in [m], \quad \mathsf{iCT}_j \leftarrow \mathsf{iEnc}(\mathsf{iMSK}^{(1)}, [\mathbf{b}_j]_1), \quad \mathsf{iSK}_j \leftarrow \mathsf{iKeyGen}(\mathsf{iMSK}^{(1)}, [\widetilde{\mathbf{b}}_j]_2).$$

It also encodes the random elements $s, \widetilde{s}$ as follows:

$$\mathsf{iCT} \leftarrow \mathsf{iEnc}(\mathsf{iMSK}^{(2)}, [(s, 0)]_1), \quad \mathsf{iSK} \leftarrow \mathsf{iKeyGen}(\mathsf{iMSK}^{(2)}, [(\widetilde{s}, 0)]_2).$$

Lastly, it sets $\mathbf{f} = (r, t, \mathbf{0}_{m^2 n})$, $h = 0$, and encrypts elements $\mathbf{f}, h$ as

$$\mathsf{mgCT} \leftarrow \mathsf{mgEnc}(\mathsf{mgMSK}, i, \mathsf{lab}, ([\mathbf{f}]_1, [h]_2)).$$

And the resulting ciphertext is set as below:

$$\mathsf{CT} = (\{\mathsf{iCT}_j\}_j, \{\mathsf{iSK}_j\}_j, \mathsf{iCT}, \mathsf{iSK}, \mathsf{mgCT}).$$

KeyGen(MSK, $\mathbf{c}$) parses MSK as above, and the key vector $\mathbf{c}$ lies in the space $\mathbb{Z}^{(mn)^2}$. Let the vector $\widetilde{\mathbf{f}}_i \in \mathbb{Z}_p^{(2+m^2n)}$ be the following vector: for all $i \in [n]$,

$$\widetilde{\mathbf{f}}_i[1] = \sum_{j,\ell \in [m], k \in [n]} \mathbf{c}[(i,j,k,\ell)]u_{i,j}\widetilde{u}_{k,\ell}, \quad \widetilde{\mathbf{f}}_i[2] = \sum_{j,\ell \in [m], k \in [n]} \mathbf{c}[(k,\ell,i,j)]v_{k,\ell}\widetilde{v}_{i,j}$$

and $\widetilde{\mathbf{f}}_i$ is zeros at all other places. It also sets $\widetilde{h}_i = 0$ for all $i \in [n]$. The key generator samples a SK-MCFE secret key corresponding to vectors $\{\widetilde{\mathbf{f}}_i, \widetilde{h}_i\}_i$ as mgSK $\leftarrow$ mgKeyGen(mgMSK, $\{[\widetilde{\mathbf{f}}_i]_2, [\widetilde{h}_i]_1\}_{i \in [n]}$), and partial derandomization terms:

$$\forall\, i,k \in [n], \quad \sigma_{i,k} = \sum_{j,\ell \in [m]} \mathbf{c}[(i,j,k,\ell)]w_{(i,j,k,\ell)}$$

And, it outputs the secret key as

$$\mathsf{SK} = (\mathbf{c}, \mathsf{mgSK}, \{\sigma_{i,k}\}_{i,k})\,.$$

Dec($\mathsf{CT}_1, \ldots, \mathsf{CT}_n, \mathsf{SK}$) parses the ciphertexts and secret key as:

$$\mathsf{CT}_i = (\{\mathsf{iCT}_{i,j}\}_{i,j}, \{\mathsf{iSK}_{i,j}\}_{i,j}, \mathsf{iCT}_i, \mathsf{iSK}_i, \mathsf{mgCT}_i), \quad \mathsf{SK} = (\mathbf{c}, \mathsf{mgSK}, \{\sigma_{i,k}\}_{i,k})\,.$$

It runs the MIFE decryption algorithm as:

$$[z_1]_T = \prod_{\substack{i,k \in [n] \\ j,\ell \in [m]}} \mathsf{iDec}(\mathsf{iCT}_{i,j}, \mathsf{iSK}_{k,\ell})^{\mathbf{c}[(i,j,k,\ell)]}, \quad [z_2]_T = \prod_{i,k \in [n]} \mathsf{iDec}(\mathsf{iCT}_i, \mathsf{iSK}_k)^{\sigma_{i,k}}$$

It also runs the SK-MCFE decryption algorithm as:

$$[z_3]_T = \mathsf{mgDec}(\mathsf{mgCT}_1, \ldots, \mathsf{mgCT}_n, \mathsf{mgSK})$$

Finally it outputs z where $[z]_T = [z_1 - z_2 - z_3]_T$ by searching for z within the range of $z \leq |m^2 n^2 C X^2|$.

Correctness. Let $s_i, \widetilde{s}_i, r_i, t_i$ for $i \in [n]$ be random elements used to generate CT_i. Due to the correctness of iFE, mgFE, in decryption, we have

$$z_1 = \sum_{i,k \in [n], j,\ell \in [m]} \mathbf{c}[(i,j,k,\ell)](\mathbf{x}_i[j]\mathbf{x}_k[\ell] + s_i\widetilde{s}_k w_{(i,j,k,\ell)} + r_i u_{i,j}\widetilde{u}_{k,\ell} + t_k v_{i,j}\widetilde{v}_{k,\ell})$$

$$z_2 = \sum_{i,k \in [n], j,\ell \in [m]} \mathbf{c}[(i,j,k,\ell)]s_i\widetilde{s}_k w_{(i,j,k,\ell)}$$

$$z_3 = \sum_{i,k \in [n], j,\ell \in [m]} \mathbf{c}[(i,j,k,\ell)](r_i u_{i,j}\widetilde{u}_{k,\ell} + t_k v_{i,j}\widetilde{v}_{k,\ell}).$$

Therefore, we have $z = \sum_{i,k \in [n], j,\ell \in [m]} \mathbf{c}[(i,j,k,\ell)]\mathbf{x}_i[j]\mathbf{x}_k[\ell]$.

4.2 Security

For security, we have the following theorem.

Theorem 4.1. *If* iFE *and* mgFE *are sel-pos-fh-IND-secure, and the* $MDDH_1$ *assumption holds in* $\mathbb{G}$, *then the proposed SK-MCFE for quadratic functions is sel-pos-mh-IND-secure.*

Due to the limit of the space, we present the security proof in the full version.

5 MIFE for Quadratic Functions

In this section, we provide our construction for MIFE for quadratic functions.

5.1 Homomorphism in Underlying Schemes

For the construction of our MIFE for quadratic functions, we use the same building blocks as SK-MCFE for quadratic functions Sect. 4, namely, a function-hiding SK-MCFE scheme mgFE for mixed-group inner product and a function-hiding IPFE scheme iFE. Additionally, we require them to have homomorphism for the construction of MIFE for quadratic functions. Precisely iFE needs to have homomorphism for both encryption and key generation while mgFE needs to have homomorphism for only encryption.

Homomorphism of iFE. We use function-hiding IPFE in [33] for iFE with homomorphism. In their construction from $MDDH_1$, the setup algorithm chooses a bilinear group $\mathbb{G}$ and a random matrix $\mathbf{B}$ in $\mathbb{Z}_p^{(m+3)\times(m+3)}$, and sets $\mathsf{PP} = \mathbb{G}, \mathsf{MSK} = (\mathbf{B}, \mathbf{B}^*)$ where $\mathbf{B}^* = (\mathbf{B}^{-1})^\top$. Encryption of $[\mathbf{x}]_1 \in G_1^m$ chooses $r \leftarrow \mathbb{Z}_p$ and outputs $\mathsf{iCT} = [(\mathbf{x}, r, 0, 0)\mathbf{B}]_1$. Similarly, key generation of $[\mathbf{y}]_2 \in G_2^m$ chooses $s \leftarrow \mathbb{Z}_p$ and outputs $\mathsf{iSK} = [(\mathbf{y}, 0, s, 0)\mathbf{B}^*]_2$. Thus, the random-tape space of iEnc and iKeyGen can be seen as $\mathbb{Z}_p$ and, for all $\mathbf{x}_1, \mathbf{x}_2, \mathbf{y}_1, \mathbf{y}_2 \in \mathbb{Z}_p^m, a_1, a_2, r_1, r_2, s_1, s_2 \in \mathbb{Z}_p$ we have the following homomorphism of $\mathbb{Z}_p$-module with respect to encryption and key generation:

$$a_1\mathsf{iEnc}(\mathsf{iMSK}, [\mathbf{x}_1]_1; r_1) + a_2\mathsf{iEnc}(\mathsf{iMSK}, [\mathbf{x}_2]_1; r_2)$$
$$= \mathsf{iEnc}(\mathsf{iMSK}, [a_1\mathbf{x}_1 + a_2\mathbf{x}_2]_1; a_1r_1 + a_2r_2)$$
$$a_1\mathsf{iKeyGen}(\mathsf{iMSK}, [\mathbf{y}_1]_2; s_1) + a_2\mathsf{iKeyGen}(\mathsf{iMSK}, [\mathbf{y}_2]_2; s_2)$$
$$= \mathsf{iKeyGen}(\mathsf{iMSK}, [a_1\mathbf{y}_1 + a_2\mathbf{y}_2]_2; a_1s_1 + a_2s_2)$$

We can confirm this as follows:

$$a_1[(\mathbf{x}_1, r_1, 0, 0)\mathbf{B}]_1 + a_2[(\mathbf{x}_2, r_2, 0, 0)\mathbf{B}]_1 = [(a_1\mathbf{x}_1 + a_2\mathbf{x}_2, a_1r_1 + a_2r_2, 0, 0)\mathbf{B}]_1$$
$$a_1[(\mathbf{y}_1, 0, s_1, 0)\mathbf{B}^*]_2 + a_2[(\mathbf{y}_2, 0, s_2, 0)\mathbf{B}^*]_2 = [(a_1\mathbf{y}_1 + a_2\mathbf{y}_2, 0, a_1s_1 + a_2s_2, 0)\mathbf{B}^*]_2.$$

Homomorphism of mgFE. As shown in Sect. 3, our SK-MCFE scheme mgFE for mixed-group inner product uses a function-hiding SK-MCFE scheme icFE for inner product and function-hiding FE scheme iFE for inner product as a building block. For a function-hiding SK-MCFE scheme for inner product, we use a slightly modified function-hiding MCFE scheme for inner product proposed in [10], which is described in Fig. 2. The modification lies in the way of generating t in encryption, which is generated via a random oracle in the MCFE scheme in [10], but PRF suffices in the secret-key setting. Since an icFE ciphertext consists of a iFE ciphertext, a mgFE ciphertext of $([\mathbf{x}_1]_1, [\mathbf{x}_2]_2) \in G_1^{m_1} \times G_2^{m_2}$ can be generated as

$$r_1, r_2 \leftarrow \mathbb{Z}_p, \quad \mathbf{z} \leftarrow \mathbb{Z}_p^k, \quad t = \mathsf{PRF}(K, \mathsf{lab})$$

$$\mathsf{iEnc}(\mathsf{iMSK}^{(1)}, ([(\mathbf{x}_1, 0^{m_2}, \mathbf{z}, 0, 0^{m_1 + m_2 + k + 1}, t, 0)]_1); r_1)$$

$$\mathsf{iKeyGen}(\mathsf{iMSK}^{(2)}, ([(\mathbf{x}_2, -\mathbf{z}, 0,)]_2); r_2)$$

for some master secret keys $\mathsf{iMSK}^{(1)}, \mathsf{iMSK}^{(2)}$ and PRF key K. Thus, the random-tape space of mgEnc can be set as $\mathbb{Z}_p^{k+2}$, and by using the homomorphism of iFE, we can obtain the following homomorphism of ciphertexts in mgFE. For all $N \in \mathbb{N}$, $i \in [n]$, $\mathsf{lab} \in \mathcal{L}$, $a_1, \ldots, a_N \in \mathbb{Z}_p$ s.t. $\sum_{j \in [N]} a_j = 1$, $\mathbf{x}_{1,1}, \ldots, \mathbf{x}_{N,1} \in \mathbb{Z}_p^{m_1}$, $\mathbf{x}_{1,2}, \ldots, \mathbf{x}_{N,2} \in \mathbb{Z}_p^{m_2}$, $\mathbf{r}_1, \ldots, \mathbf{r}_N \subset \mathbb{Z}_p^{k+2}$, we have

$$\sum_{j \in [N]} a_j \mathsf{mgEnc}(\mathsf{mgMSK}, i, \mathsf{lab}, ([\mathbf{x}_{j,1}]_1, [\mathbf{x}_{j,2}]_2); \mathbf{r}_j)$$

$$= \mathsf{mgEnc}(\mathsf{mgMSK}, i, \mathsf{lab}, ([\sum_{j \in [N]} a_j \mathbf{x}_{j,1}]_1, [\sum_{j \in [N]} a_j \mathbf{x}_{j,2}]_2); \sum_{j \in [N]} a_j \mathbf{r}_j)$$

5.2   Construction

Let $\mathsf{mgFE} = (\mathsf{mgSetup}, \mathsf{mgEnc}, \mathsf{mgKeyGen}, \mathsf{mgDec})$ be an SK-MCFE scheme for mixed-group inner product (Sect. 3) with label space $\mathcal{L}$, and $\mathsf{iFE} = (\mathsf{iSetup}, \mathsf{iEnc}, \mathsf{iKeyGen}, \mathsf{iDec})$ be a function-hiding IPFE scheme. Also, let $\mathsf{PRF} = \{\mathsf{PRF}_\lambda\}_{\lambda \in \mathbb{N}}$ be a PRF family where $\mathsf{PRF}_\lambda : \{0,1\}^\lambda \times \mathcal{L} \to \{0,1\}^\lambda$. Let lab_0 be a fixed label in $\mathcal{L}$ and $D = 4m + 2k + 17$ where k is the parameter for the bilateral MDDH assumption used for mgFE. Below we provide an MIFE scheme for function class $\mathcal{F}_{m,n,X,C}^{\mathsf{QF}}$. Note that MstEnc is a subroutine algorithm used in Setup, which corresponds to $\widetilde{\mathsf{Enc}}$ of property P in the technical overview.

Setup($1^\lambda, 1^n$): Let $\mathsf{PRF} = \{\mathsf{PRF}_\lambda\}_{\lambda \in \mathbb{N}}$ be a PRF family where $\mathsf{PRF}_\lambda : \{0,1\}^\lambda \times \mathcal{L} \to \mathbb{Z}_p$. On input the security parameter 1^λ and the number of slots 1^n, the setup algorithm outputs (PK, MSK) as follows.

$$\{\mathsf{iPP}_i, \mathsf{iMSK}_i \leftarrow \mathsf{iSetup}(1^\lambda)\}_{i \in [n]}, \quad K \leftarrow \{0,1\}^\kappa$$
$$\mathsf{PP} = \{\mathsf{PP}_i\}_{i \in [n]}, \quad \mathsf{MSK} = (K, \{\mathsf{MSK}_i\}_{i \in [n]}).$$

Enc(MSK, i, lab, $[\mathbf{x}_i]_1$): The encryption algorithm takes as input user MSK, user index $i \in [n]$, an input vector $[\mathbf{x}_i]_1$, a label lab and outputs CT_i as follows.

$$t = \mathsf{PRF}(K, \mathsf{lab}), \quad \widehat{\mathbf{x}}_i = (\mathbf{x}_i, 0^m, t, 0), \quad \mathsf{CT}_i = \mathsf{iCT}_i \leftarrow \mathsf{iEnc}(\mathsf{iMSK}_i, [\widehat{\mathbf{x}}_i]_1).$$

KeyGen(MSK, $\{[\mathbf{y}_i]_2\}_{i \in [n]}$): The key generation algorithm takes as input the master secret key MSK, and vectors $\{[\mathbf{y}_i]_2\}_{i \in [n]}$ and outputs SK as follows. It randomly chooses $r_i \in \mathbb{Z}_p$ so that $\sum_{i \in [n]} r_i = 0$ and compute

$$\widehat{\mathbf{y}}_i = (\mathbf{y}_i, 0^m, r_i, 0), \quad \mathsf{iSK}_i \leftarrow \mathsf{iKeyGen}(\mathsf{iMSK}_i, [\widehat{\mathbf{y}}_i]_2), \quad \mathsf{SK} = \{\mathsf{iSK}_i\}_{i \in [n]}.$$

Dec(SK, $\mathsf{CT}_1, ..., \mathsf{CT}_n$): The decryption algorithm takes as input the secret key SK, ciphertexts $\mathsf{CT}_1, \ldots, \mathsf{CT}_n$ and outputs d as follows.

$$[d]_T = \prod_{i \in [n]} \mathsf{iDec}(\mathsf{iSK}_i, \mathsf{iCT}_i).$$

Fig. 2. Function-Hiding SK-MCFE for inner product

Setup($1^\lambda, 1^n$) samples a random PRF key $K \leftarrow \{0,1\}^\lambda$ and the master keys for the underlying IPFE and SK-MCFE scheme as $(\mathsf{iPP}^{(2)}, \mathsf{iMSK}^{(2)}) \leftarrow \mathsf{iSetup}(1^\lambda)$, $(\mathsf{mgPP}, \mathsf{mgMSK}) \leftarrow \mathsf{mgSetup}(1^\lambda, 1^n)$ where the vector length of iFE is set as 2, and the vector length of mgFE is set as $m^2n + 2$ and 1. Note that $\mathsf{iPP}^{(2)} = \mathsf{mgPP} = \mathbb{G}$. It also samples a sequence of randomization terms as:

$$\forall i, k \in [n], j, \ell \in [m], \qquad w_{(i,j,k,\ell)} \leftarrow \mathbb{Z}_p$$
$$\forall i \in [n], j \in [m], \qquad u_{i,j}, \widetilde{u}_{i,j}, v_{i,j}, \widetilde{v}_{i,j} \leftarrow \mathbb{Z}_p$$

It sets the public parameters and master key as

$$\mathsf{PP} = \mathbb{G}, \quad \mathsf{MSK} = \left(K, \mathsf{iMSK}^{(2)}, \mathsf{mgMSK}, \{w_{(i,j,k,\ell)}\}_{i,j,k,\ell}, \{u_{i,j}, \widetilde{u}_{i,j}, v_{i,j}, \widetilde{v}_{i,j}\}_{i,j} \right).$$

It runs MstEnc described below to generate master ciphertexts, which forms encryption keys, as

$$\forall i \in [n], j \in [m], \quad \mathsf{MCT}_{1,i,j} \leftarrow \mathsf{MstEnc}(\mathsf{MSK}, i, \mathbf{e}_j)$$
$$\forall i \in [n], j \in [D], \quad \mathsf{MCT}_{0,i,j} \leftarrow \mathsf{MstEnc}(\mathsf{MSK}, i, \mathbf{0}_m).$$

Finally it output encryption keys together with the public key and master secret key as

$$\forall\, i \in [n], \quad \mathsf{EK}_i = (\{\mathsf{MCT}_{1,i,j}\}_{j\in[n]}, \{\mathsf{MCT}_{0,i,j}\}_{j\in[D]}).$$

$\mathsf{MstEnc}(\mathsf{MSK}, i, \mathbf{x})$ parses MSK as above, and using the PRF key K, it samples a IPFE master key of vector length $mn + 3m + 4$ as:

$$(\mathsf{iPP}^{(1)}, \mathsf{iMSK}^{(1)}) \leftarrow \mathsf{iSetup}(1^\lambda; \mathsf{PRF}(K, \mathsf{lab}_0))$$

It then samples random elements $s, \widetilde{s}, r, t \leftarrow \mathbb{Z}_p$. And, it sets vectors $\mathbf{b}_j, \widetilde{\mathbf{b}}_j$ for $j \in [m]$ as follows:

$$\mathbf{b}_j = (\mathbf{x}[j], 0, s\mathbf{e}_{(i,j)}, ru_{i,j}, v_{i,j}, \mathbf{0}_{3m}), \quad \widetilde{\mathbf{b}}_j = (\mathbf{x}[j], 0, \widetilde{s}\mathbf{w}_{(*,*,i,j)}, \widetilde{u}_{i,j}, t\widetilde{v}_{i,j}, \mathbf{0}_{3m}).$$

where where $\mathbf{e}_{(i,j)}$ is the mn-dimensional one-hot vector with the (i,j)-th element being 1, and vector $\mathbf{w}_{(*,*,i,j)} \in \mathbb{Z}_p^{mn}$ is defined as follows:

$$\forall\, j \in [m], \quad \mathbf{w}_{(*,*,i,j)} = (w_{(1,1,i,j)}, w_{(1,2,i,j)}, \ldots, w_{(n,m,i,j)})$$

The encryptor encodes the vectors $\mathbf{b}_j, \widetilde{\mathbf{b}}_j$ under MIFE as follows:

$$\forall\, j \in [m], \quad \mathsf{iCT}_j \leftarrow \mathsf{iEnc}(\mathsf{iMSK}^{(1)}, [\mathbf{b}_j]_1), \quad \mathsf{iSK}_j \leftarrow \mathsf{iKeyGen}(\mathsf{iMSK}^{(1)}, [\widetilde{\mathbf{b}}_j]_2).$$

It also encodes the random elements $s, \widetilde{s}$ as follows:

$$\mathsf{iCT} \leftarrow \mathsf{iEnc}(\mathsf{iMSK}^{(2)}, [(s, 0)]_1), \quad \mathsf{iSK} \leftarrow \mathsf{iKeyGen}(\mathsf{iMSK}^{(2)}, [(\widetilde{s}, 0)]_2).$$

Lastly, it sets $\mathbf{f} = (r, t, \mathbf{0}_{m^2 n})$, $h = 0$, and encrypts elements $\mathbf{f}, h$ with respect to label lab_0 as

$$\mathsf{mgCT} \leftarrow \mathsf{mgEnc}(\mathsf{mgMSK}, i, \mathsf{lab}_0, ([\mathbf{f}]_1, [h]_2)).$$

The resulting ciphertext is set as $\mathsf{MCT} = (\{\mathsf{iCT}_j\}_j, \{\mathsf{iSK}_j\}_j, \mathsf{iCT}, \mathsf{iSK}, \mathsf{mgCT})$. $\mathsf{Enc}(\mathsf{EK}_i, \mathbf{x})$ parses EK_i as above. It then samples random elements $\gamma_1, \ldots, \gamma_{(D-1)/2} \leftarrow \mathbb{Z}_p$. And, it encrypts $\mathbf{x}$ to CT by homomorphic addition of master ciphertexts as follows:

$$\mathsf{CT} = \sum_{j\in[m]} \mathbf{x}[j]\mathsf{MCT}_{1,i,j} - \left(\sum_{j\in[m]} \mathbf{x}[j] - 1\right) \mathsf{MCT}_{0,i,1}$$
$$+ \sum_{j\in[(D-1)/2]} \gamma_j(\mathsf{MCT}_{0,i,2j} - \mathsf{MCT}_{0,i,2j+1})$$

where the above is the component-wise homomorphic addition with respect to ciphertexts of iFE and mgFE. Then, it outputs CT.

KeyGen(MSK, **c**) parses MSK as above, and the key vector **c** lies in the space $\mathbb{Z}_p^{(mn)^2}$. Let the vector $\widetilde{\mathbf{f}}_i \in \mathbb{Z}_p^{(2+m^2n)}$ be the following vector: for all $i \in [n]$

$$\widetilde{\mathbf{f}}_i[1] = \sum_{j,\ell \in [m], k \in [n]} \mathbf{c}[(i,j,k,\ell)] u_{i,j} \widetilde{u}_{k,\ell}, \quad \widetilde{\mathbf{f}}_i[2] = \sum_{j,\ell \in [m], k \in [n]} \mathbf{c}[(k,\ell,i,j)] v_{k,\ell} \widetilde{v}_{i,j}$$

and $\widetilde{\mathbf{f}}_i$ is zeros at all other places. It also sets $\widetilde{h}_i = 0$ for all $i \in [n]$. The key generator samples a SK-MCFE secret key corresponding to vectors $\{\widetilde{\mathbf{f}}_i, \widetilde{h}_i\}_i$ as mgSK $\leftarrow$ mgKeyGen(mgMSK, $\{[\widetilde{\mathbf{f}}_i]_2, [\widetilde{h}_i]_1\}_{i \in [n]}$), and partial derandomization terms:

$$\forall\, i,k \in [n], \quad \sigma_{i,k} = \sum_{j,\ell \in [m]} \mathbf{c}[(i,j,k,\ell)] w_{(i,j,k,\ell)}$$

And, it outputs the secret key as $\mathsf{SK} = (\mathbf{c}, \mathsf{mgSK}, \{\sigma_{i,k}\}_{i,k})$.
Dec($\mathsf{CT}_1, \ldots, \mathsf{CT}_n, \mathsf{SK}$) parses the ciphertexts and secret key as:

$$\mathsf{CT}_i = (\{\mathsf{iCT}_{i,j}\}_{i,j}, \{\mathsf{iSK}_{i,j}\}_{i,j}, \mathsf{iCT}_i, \mathsf{iSK}_i, \mathsf{mgCT}_i),$$
$$\mathsf{SK} = (\mathbf{c}, \mathsf{mgSK}, \{\sigma_{i,k}\}_{i,k}).$$

It runs the MIFE decryption algorithm as:

$$[z_1]_T = \prod_{\substack{i,k \in [n], \\ j,\ell \in [m]}} \mathsf{iDec}(\mathsf{iCT}_{i,j}, \mathsf{iSK}_{k,\ell})^{\mathbf{c}[(i,j,k,\ell)]}, \quad [z_2]_T = \prod_{i,k \in [n]} \mathsf{iDec}(\mathsf{iCT}_i, \mathsf{iSK}_k)^{\sigma_{i,k}}$$

It also runs the SK-MCFE decryption algorithm as:

$$[z_3]_T = \mathsf{mgDec}(\mathsf{mgCT}_1, \ldots, \mathsf{mgCT}_n, \mathsf{mgSK})$$

Finally it outputs z where $[z]_T = [z_1 - z_2 - z_3]_T$ by searching for z within the range of $z \leq |m^2 n^2 C X^2|$.

Correctness. Let $s_{b,i,j}, \widetilde{s}_{b,i,j}, r_{b,i,j}, t_{b,i,j}$ for $b \in \{0,1\}, i \in [n], j \in [D]$ be random elements used to generate $\mathsf{MCT}_{b,i,j}$ in EK_i. Thanks to the homomorphism of iFE and mgFE, Enc($\mathsf{EK}_i, \mathbf{x}$) outputs $\mathsf{CT}_i = (\{\mathsf{iCT}_{i,j}\}_j, \{\mathsf{iSK}_{i,j}\}_j, \mathsf{iCT}_i, \mathsf{iSK}_i, \mathsf{mgCT}_i)$, which are encryption of

$$[\mathbf{b}]_1 = [(\mathbf{x}_i[j], 0, s_i \mathbf{e}_{(i,j)}, r_i u_{i,j}, v_{i,j}, \mathbf{0}_{3m})]_1$$
$$[\widetilde{\mathbf{b}}]_2 = [(\mathbf{x}_i[j], 0, \widetilde{s}_i \mathbf{w}_{(*,*,i,j)}, \widetilde{u}_{i,j}, t_i \widetilde{v}_{i,j}, \mathbf{0}_{3m})]_2 \tag{5}$$
$$[(s_i, 0)]_1, \quad [(\widetilde{s}_i, 0)]_2, \quad ([\mathbf{f}]_1, [h]_2) = ([(r_i, t_i, \mathbf{0}_{m^2 n})]_1, [0]_2) \quad \text{for label } \mathsf{lab}_0$$

respectively, where

$$s_i = \sum_{j \in [m]} \mathbf{x}_i[j] s_{1,i,j} - \left(\sum_{j \in [m]} \mathbf{x}_i[j] - 1 \right) s_{0,i,1} + \sum_{j \in [(D-1)/2]} \gamma_j (s_{0,i,2j} - s_{0,i,2j+1})$$

$$\widetilde{s}_i = \sum_{j \in [m]} \mathbf{x}_i[j] \widetilde{s}_{1,i,j} - \left(\sum_{j \in [m]} \mathbf{x}_i[j] - 1 \right) \widetilde{s}_{0,i,1} + \sum_{j \in [(D-1)/2]} \gamma_j (\widetilde{s}_{0,i,2j} - \widetilde{s}_{0,i,2j+1})$$

$$r_i = \sum_{j \in [m]} \mathbf{x}_i[j] r_{1,i,j} - \left(\sum_{j \in [m]} \mathbf{x}_i[j] - 1 \right) r_{0,i,1} + \sum_{j \in [(D-1)/2]} \gamma_j (r_{0,i,2j} - r_{0,i,2j+1})$$

$$t_i = \sum_{j \in [m]} \mathbf{x}_i[j] t_{1,i,j} - \left(\sum_{j \in [m]} \mathbf{x}_i[j] - 1 \right) t_{0,i,1} + \sum_{j \in [(D-1)/2]} \gamma_j (t_{0,i,2j} - t_{0,i,2j+1}).$$

$$(6)$$

Hence, similarly to the correctness of our SK-MCFE for quadratic functions (Sect. 4), in decryption, we have

$$z_1 = \sum_{i,k \in [n], j, \ell \in [m]} \mathbf{c}[(i,j,k,\ell)] (\mathbf{x}_i[j] \mathbf{x}_k[\ell] + s_i \widetilde{s}_k w_{(i,j,k,\ell)} + r_i u_{i,j} \widetilde{u}_{k,\ell} + t_k v_{i,j} \widetilde{v}_{k,\ell})$$

$$z_2 = \sum_{i,k \in [n], j, \ell \in [m]} \mathbf{c}[(i,j,k,\ell)] s_i \widetilde{s}_k w_{(i,j,k,\ell)}$$

$$z_3 = \sum_{i,k \in [n], j, \ell \in [m]} \mathbf{c}[(i,j,k,\ell)] (r_i u_{i,j} \widetilde{u}_{k,\ell} + t_k v_{i,j} \widetilde{v}_{k,\ell}).$$

Since $\mathbf{c}[(i,j,k,\ell)] = 0$ for $i \geq k$, we have $z = \sum_{i,k \in [n], j, \ell \in [m]} \mathbf{c}[(i,j,k,\ell)] \mathbf{x}_i[j] \mathbf{x}_k[\ell]$.

5.3   Security

For security, we have the following theorem. Let qcFE be SK-MCFE scheme for quadratic functions in Sect. 4.

Theorem 5.1. *If* qcFE *are sel-pos-mh-IND-secure, then the proposed MIFE for quadratic functions is sel-pos-mh-IND-secure.*

Proof. Wlog, in the pos setting, we can denote challenge messages by $\{i, \mathbf{x}_i^{\mu,0}, \mathbf{x}_i^{\mu,1}\}_{i \in [n], \mu \in [q_c]}$ for some q_c instead of $\{i^\mu, \mathbf{x}_{i^\mu}^{\mu,0}, \mathbf{x}_{i^\mu}^{\mu,1}\}_{\mu \in [q'_c]}$. For notational convenience, we use the former notation in this proof. We prove Theorem 5.1 via a series of hybrids $\mathsf{H}_1^\beta, \mathsf{H}_f^\beta$. We show that $\mathsf{H}_0^\beta \approx_c \mathsf{H}_1^\beta \approx_c \mathsf{H}_f^\beta$, where H_0^β is the original security game for MIFE defined in Definition 2.1. Each hybrid is defined as described in Fig. 3, where the reply for the ciphertext query is computed by MstEnc instead of Enc. We denote the probability that $\mathcal{A}$ outputs β in hybrid H^β by $\mathsf{P}(\mathcal{A}, \mathsf{H}^\beta)$ in what follows.

Theorem 5.1 directly follows from Lemma 5.2 and Lemma 5.3 since $\mathcal{A}$ does not obtain the information on β in H_f^β. $\qquad\square$

$$\boxed{\begin{array}{l} \mathsf{H}_0^\beta, \ \mathsf{H}_1^\beta\ , \ \mathsf{H}_f^\beta \\ \hline \beta \leftarrow \{0,1\}, \ \mathsf{PP}, \{\mathsf{EK}_i\}_{i \in [n]}, \mathsf{MSK} \leftarrow \mathsf{Setup}(1^\lambda) \\ (\mathcal{CS}, \{i, \mathbf{x}_i^{\mu,0}, \mathbf{x}_i^{\mu,1}\}_{i \in [n], \mu \in [q_c]}, \{\mathbf{c}^\nu\}_{\nu \in [q_k]}) \leftarrow \mathcal{A}(\mathsf{PP}) \\ \{\mathsf{CT}_i^\mu \leftarrow \mathsf{Enc}(\mathsf{EK}_i, \mathbf{x}_i^{\mu,\beta})\}_{i,\mu} \\ \{\mathsf{CT}_i^\mu \leftarrow \mathsf{MstEnc}(\mathsf{MSK}, i, \mathbf{x}_i^{\mu,\beta})\}_{i,\mu} \\ \{\mathsf{CT}_i^\mu \leftarrow \mathsf{MstEnc}(\mathsf{MSK}, i, \mathbf{x}_i^{\mu,0})\}_{i,\mu} \\ \{\mathsf{SK}^\nu \leftarrow \mathsf{KeyGen}(\mathsf{MSK}, \mathbf{c}^\nu)\}_\nu \\ \beta' \leftarrow \mathcal{A}(\{\mathsf{EK}_i\}_{i \in \mathcal{CS}}, \{\mathsf{CT}_i^\mu\}_{i,\mu}, \{\mathsf{SK}^\nu\}_\nu) \end{array}}$$

Fig. 3. Description of hybrids

Lemma 5.2. *For all PPT adversaries $\mathcal{A}$, we have $|\mathsf{P}(\mathcal{A}, \mathsf{H}_0^\beta) - \mathsf{P}(\mathcal{A}, \mathsf{H}_1^\beta)| \leq 2^{-\Omega(\lambda)}$.*

Proof. The difference between H_0^β and H_1^β lies in the way of generating challenge ciphertexts. That is, the challenge ciphertexts are generated by Enc in H_0^β while they are generated by MstEnc in H_1^β. Recall that the random elements used in MstEnc are $s, \widetilde{s}, r, t \in \mathbb{Z}_p$ and the random tapes used to generate $(\{\mathsf{iCT}_\ell\}_{\ell \in [m]}, \{\mathsf{iSK}_{\ell \in [m]}\}_\ell, \mathsf{iCT}, \mathsf{iSK}, \mathsf{mgCT})$. Since $\mathsf{iEnc}, \mathsf{iKeyGen}$ can use a random element in $\mathbb{Z}_p$, and mgEnc can use a random element in $\mathbb{Z}_p^{k+2}$ as a random tape, we can use a random element in $\mathbb{Z}_p^{2m+k+8}$ as a random tape of MstEnc. Due to the homomorphism of iFE and mgFE, for all $N \in \mathbb{N}$, $i \in [n]$, $a_1, \ldots, a_N \in \mathbb{Z}_p$ s.t. $\sum_{j \in [N]} a_j = 1$, $\mathbf{x}_1, \ldots, \mathbf{x}_N \in \mathbb{Z}_p^m$, $\mathbf{r}_1, \ldots, \mathbf{r}_N \in \mathbb{Z}_p^{2m+k+8}$, we have the following homomorphism of MstEnc:

$$\sum_{j \in [N]} a_j \mathsf{MstEnc}(\mathsf{MSK}, i, \mathbf{x}; \mathbf{r}_j) = \mathsf{MstEnc}(\mathsf{MSK}, i, \sum_{j \in [N]} a_j \mathbf{x}_j; \sum_{j \in [N]} a_j \mathbf{r}_j).$$

Parse $\mathsf{EK}_i = (\{\mathsf{MCT}_{1,i,j}\}_{i \in [n], j \in [m]}, \{\mathsf{MCT}_{0,i,j}\}_{i \in [n], j \in [D]})$ and let $\mathbf{r}_{b,i,j} \in \mathbb{Z}_p^{2m+k+8}$ be the random tape used to generate $\mathsf{MCT}_{b,i,j}$ for $b \in \{0,1\}$, $i \in [n]$, $j \in [D]$. In other words,

$$\mathsf{MCT}_{b,i,j} = \begin{cases} \mathsf{MstEnc}(\mathsf{MSK}, i, \mathbf{e}_j); \mathbf{r}_{b,i,j}) & b = 1 \\ \mathsf{MstEnc}(\mathsf{MSK}, i, \mathbf{0}_m); \mathbf{r}_{b,i,j}) & b = 0 \end{cases}$$

From the homomorphism of MstEnc and the fact that Enc can use $\gamma = (\gamma_1, \ldots, \gamma_{(D-1)/2}) \in \mathbb{Z}_p^{(D-1)/2}$ for a random tape, we have

$$\mathsf{Enc}(\mathsf{EK}_i, \mathbf{x} : \gamma) = \mathsf{MstEnc}(\mathsf{MSK}, i, \sum_{j \in [m]} \mathbf{x}[j]\mathbf{e}_j; \mathbf{r})$$

where

$$\mathbf{r} = \sum_{j \in [m]} \mathbf{x}_i[j]\mathbf{r}_{1,i,j} - \left(\sum_{j \in [m]} \mathbf{x}_i[j] - 1 \right) \mathbf{r}_{0,i,1} + \sum_{j \in [(D-1)/2]} \gamma_j(\mathbf{r}_{0,i,2j} - \mathbf{r}_{0,i,2j+1}).$$

(7)

Here, we use the equality: $\sum_{j \in [m]} \mathbf{x}_i[j] - \left(\sum_{j \in [m]} \mathbf{x}_i[j] - 1 \right) + \sum_{j \in [(D-1)/2]} (\gamma_j - \gamma_j) = 1$. Hence, to prove the lemma, it suffices to show that the following distributions are statistically close for all $i \in [n]$:

$$\left\{ (\mathbf{r}, \{\mathbf{r}_{1,i,j}\}_{j \in [m]}, \{\mathbf{r}_{0,i,j}\}_{j \in [D]}) : \begin{array}{l} \forall (b,i,j), \mathbf{r}_{b,i,j} \leftarrow \mathbb{Z}_p^{2m+k+8}, \ \gamma \leftarrow \mathbb{Z}_p^{(D-1)/2} \\ \mathbf{r} \text{ is defined as Eq. (7)} \end{array} \right\}$$

and

$$\left\{ (\mathbf{r}, \{\mathbf{r}_{1,i,j}\}_{j \in [m]}, \{\mathbf{r}_{0,i,j}\}_{j \in [D]}) : \forall (b,i,j), \mathbf{r}_{b,i,j} \leftarrow \mathbb{Z}_p, \ \mathbf{r} \leftarrow \mathbb{Z}_p^{2m+k+8} \right\}$$

This can be shown as follows. For all $j \in [(D - 1)/2]$, $\widetilde{\mathbf{r}}_j = \mathbf{r}_{0,i,2j} - \mathbf{r}_{0,i,2j+1}$ is uniformly distributed in $\mathbb{Z}_p^{2m+k+8}$, and thus $\widetilde{\mathbf{r}}_1, \ldots, \widetilde{\mathbf{r}}_{(D-1)/2}$ span $\mathbb{Z}_p^{2m+k+8}$ with overwhelming probability if $(D - 1)/2 \geq 2m + k + 8$. Hence, $\sum_{j \in [(D-1)/2]} \gamma_j(\mathbf{r}_{0,i,2j} - \mathbf{r}_{0,i,2j+1}) = \sum_{j \in [(D-1)/2]} \gamma_j \widetilde{\mathbf{r}}_j$ is randomly distributed even given $(\{\mathbf{r}_{1,i,j}\}_{j \in [m]}, \{\mathbf{r}_{0,i,j}\}_{j \in [D]})$. This concludes the proof.

Lemma 5.3. *For all PPT adversaries $\mathcal{A}$, there exists a PPT adversary $\mathcal{B}$ against qcFE in Sect. 4 such that $|\mathsf{P}(\mathcal{A}, \mathsf{H}_1^\beta) - \mathsf{P}(\mathcal{A}, \mathsf{H}_f^\beta)| \leq \mathsf{Adv}_{\mathcal{B}}^{\mathsf{qcFE}}(\lambda)$.*

Proof. The difference of these hybrids is whether CT_i^μ is encryption of $\mathbf{x}_i^{\mu,\beta}$ or $\mathbf{x}_i^{\mu,0}$. We can construct $\mathcal{B}$ as follows.

1. $\mathcal{B}$ is given qcPP and gives it to $\mathcal{A}$.
2. $\mathcal{A}$ outputs $(\mathcal{CS}, \{i, \mathbf{x}_i^{\mu,0}, \mathbf{x}_i^{\mu,1}\}_{i \in [n], \mu \in [q_c]}, \mathcal{FS} = \{\mathbf{c}^\nu\}_{\nu \in [q_k]})$, and $\mathcal{B}$ chooses $\beta \leftarrow \{0,1\}$ and queries its own oracle on $\mathcal{MS}, \mathcal{FS}$ where

$$\mathcal{MS} = \left(\begin{array}{l} \{i, \mathsf{lab}_0, \mathbf{e}_j, \mathbf{e}_j\}_{i \in \mathcal{CS}, j \in [m]}, \{(i, \mathsf{lab}_0, \mathbf{0}_m, \mathbf{0}_m) \times D\}_{i \in \mathcal{CS}} \\ \{i, \mathsf{lab}_0, \mathbf{x}_i^{\mu,\beta}, \mathbf{x}_i^{\mu,0}\}_{i \in [n], \mu \in [q_c]} \end{array} \right).$$

3. $\mathcal{B}$ is given

$$\left(\{\mathsf{cCT}_{1,i,j}\}_{i \in \mathcal{CS}, j \in [m]}, \{\mathsf{cCT}_{0,i,j}\}_{i \in \mathcal{CS}, j \in [D]}, \{\mathsf{cCT}_i^\mu\}_{i \in [n], \mu \in [q_c]}, \{\mathsf{cSK}^\nu\}_{\nu \in [q_k]} \right)$$

where $\mathsf{cCT}_{1,i,j}, \mathsf{cCT}_{0,i,j}, \mathsf{cCT}_i^\mu$ are ciphertexts of qcFE for $(i, \mathsf{lab}_0, \mathbf{e}_j)$, $(i, \mathsf{lab}_0, \mathbf{0}_m), (i, \mathsf{lab}_0, \mathbf{x}_i^{\mu,\beta/0})$, respectively, and gives it to $\mathcal{A}$ by setting $\mathsf{EK}_i = (\{\mathsf{cCT}_{1,i,j}\}_{j \in [m]}, \{\mathsf{cCT}_{0,i,j}\}_{j \in [D]})$.
4. $\mathcal{A}$ outputs β', and $\mathcal{B}$ outputs β' as it is.

We can confirm the above simulation of $\mathcal{B}$ is valid from the three observations. First, $\mathcal{B}$'s query satisfies the game condition (recall that the adversary can query any pair of the same messages for corrupted slot). Second, $\mathsf{qcPP} = \mathsf{iPP}^{(1)} = \mathbb{G}$ where qcPP is the public parameter of qcFE. Third, $\mathsf{MstEnc}(\mathsf{MSK}, \cdot, \cdot)$ and $\mathsf{qcEnc}(\mathsf{cMSK}, \cdot, \mathsf{lab}_0, \cdot)$ (the encryption algorithm of qcFE) are the exactly the same.

References

1. Abdalla, M., Benhamouda, F., Gay, R.: From single-input to multi-client inner-product functional encryption. In: Galbraith, S.D., Moriai, S. (eds.) ASIACRYPT 2019, Part III. LNCS, vol. 11923, pp. 552–582. Springer, Heidelberg (2019)
2. Abdalla, M., Benhamouda, F., Kohlweiss, M., Waldner, H.: Decentralizing inner-product functional encryption. In: Lin, D., Sako, K. (eds.) PKC 2019, Part II. LNCS, vol. 11443, pp. 128–157. Springer, Heidelberg (2019)
3. Abdalla, M., Bourse, F., De Caro, A., Pointcheval, D.: Simple functional encryption schemes for inner products. In: Katz, J. (ed.) PKC 2015. LNCS, vol. 9020, pp. 733–751. Springer, Heidelberg (2015)
4. Abdalla, M., Catalano, D., Fiore, D., Gay, R., Ursu, B.: Multi-input functional encryption for inner products: function-hiding realizations and constructions without pairings. In: Shacham, H., Boldyreva, A. (eds.) CRYPTO 2018, Part I. LNCS, vol. 10991, pp. 597–627. Springer, Heidelberg (2018)
5. Abdalla, M., Gay, R., Raykova, M., Wee, H.: Multi-input inner-product functional encryption from pairings. In: Coron, J.S., Nielsen, J.B. (eds.) EUROCRYPT 2017, Part I. LNCS, vol. 10210, pp. 601–626. Springer, Heidelberg (2017)
6. Abdalla, M., Gong, J., Wee, H.: Functional encryption for attribute-weighted sums from k-Lin. In: Micciancio, D., Ristenpart, T. (eds.) CRYPTO 2020, Part I. LNCS, vol. 12170, pp. 685–716. Springer, Heidelberg (2020)
7. Agrawal, S., Koppula, V., Waters, B.: Impossibility of simulation secure functional encryption even with random oracles. In: Beimel, A., Dziembowski, S. (eds.) TCC 2018. LNCS, vol. 11239, pp. 659–688. Springer, Cham (2018). https://doi.org/10.1007/978-3-030-03807-6_24
8. Agrawal, S., Gorbunov, S., Vaikuntanathan, V., Wee, H.: Functional encryption: new perspectives and lower bounds. In: Canetti, R., Garay, J.A. (eds.) CRYPTO 2013, Part II. LNCS, vol. 8043, pp. 500–518. Springer, Heidelberg (2013)
9. Agrawal, S., Goyal, R., Tomida, J.: Multi-input quadratic functional encryption from pairings. In: Malkin, T., Peikert, C. (eds.) CRYPTO 2021, Part IV. LNCS, vol. 12828, pp. 208–238. Springer, Heidelberg, Virtual Event (2021)
10. Agrawal, S., Goyal, R., Tomida, J.: Multi-party functional encryption. In: Nissim, K., Waters, B. (eds.) TCC 2021. LNCS, vol. 13043, pp. 224–255. Springer, Cham (2021). https://doi.org/10.1007/978-3-030-90453-1_8
11. Agrawal, S., Maitra, M.: FE and iO for turing machines from minimal assumptions. In: Beimel, A., Dziembowski, S. (eds.) TCC 2018, Part II. LNCS, vol. 11240, pp. 473–512. Springer, Heidelberg (2018)
12. Ananth, P., Jain, A.: Indistinguishability obfuscation from compact functional encryption. In: Gennaro, R., Robshaw, M.J.B. (eds.) Part I. LNCS, vol. 9215, pp. 308–326. Springer, Heidelberg (2015)
13. Ananth, P., Jain, A.: Indistinguishability obfuscation from compact functional encryption. In: Gennaro, R., Robshaw, M. (eds.) CRYPTO 2015. LNCS, vol. 9215, pp. 308–326. Springer, Heidelberg (2015). https://doi.org/10.1007/978-3-662-47989-6_15
14. Baltico, C.E.Z., Catalano, D., Fiore, D., Gay, R.: Practical functional encryption for quadratic functions with applications to predicate encryption. In: Katz, J., Shacham, H. (eds.) CRYPTO 2017. LNCS, vol. 10401, pp. 67–98. Springer, Heidelberg (2017)
15. Bishop, A., Jain, A., Kowalczyk, L.: Function-hiding inner product encryption. In: Iwata, T., Cheon, J.H. (eds.) ASIACRYPT 2015. LNCS, vol. 9452, pp. 470–491. Springer, Heidelberg (2015)

16. Bitansky, N., Vaikuntanathan, V.: Indistinguishability obfuscation from functional encryption. In: Guruswami, V. (ed.) 56th FOCS, pp. 171–190. IEEE Computer Society Press (2015)
17. Bitansky, N., Vaikuntanathan, V.: Indistinguishability obfuscation from functional encryption. In: IEEE 56th Annual Symposium on Foundations of Computer Science, FOCS 2015, Berkeley, CA, USA, 17–20 October, 2015, pp. 171–190 (2015)
18. Boneh, D., Sahai, A., Waters, B.: Functional encryption: definitions and challenges. In: Ishai, Y. (ed.) TCC 2011. LNCS, vol. 6597, pp. 253–273. Springer, Heidelberg (2011)
19. Boneh, D., Waters, B.: Conjunctive, subset, and range queries on encrypted data. In: Vadhan, S.P. (ed.) TCC 2007. LNCS, vol. 4392, pp. 535–554. Springer, Heidelberg (2007). https://doi.org/10.1007/978-3-540-70936-7_29
20. Brakerski, Z., Segev, G.: Function-private functional encryption in the private-key setting. In: Dodis, Y., Nielsen, J.B. (eds.) TCC 2015, Part II. LNCS, vol. 9015, pp. 306–324. Springer, Heidelberg (Mar 2015)
21. Chotard, J., Dufour Sans, E., Gay, R., Phan, D.H., Pointcheval, D.: Decentralized multi-client functional encryption for inner product. In: Peyrin, T., Galbraith, S. (eds.) ASIACRYPT 2018, Part II. LNCS, vol. 11273, pp. 703–732. Springer, Heidelberg (2018)
22. Chotard, J., Dufour Sans, E., Gay, R., Phan, D.H., Pointcheval, D.: Multi-client functional encryption with repetition for inner product. Cryptology ePrint Archive, Report 2018/1021 (2018). https://eprint.iacr.org/2018/1021
23. Datta, P., Okamoto, T., Tomida, J.: Full-hiding (unbounded) multi-input inner product functional encryption from the k-Linear assumption. In: Abdalla, M., Dahab, R. (eds.) PKC 2018. LNCS, vol. 10770, pp. 245–277. Springer, Heidelberg (2018)
24. Garg, S., Gentry, C., Halevi, S., Raykova, M., Sahai, A., Waters, B.: Candidate indistinguishability obfuscation and functional encryption for all circuits. In: 54th FOCS, pp. 40–49. IEEE Computer Society Press (2013)
25. Garg, S., Gentry, C., Halevi, S., Zhandry, M.: Functional encryption without obfuscation. In: Kushilevitz, E., Malkin, T. (eds.) TCC 2016. LNCS, vol. 9563, pp. 480–511. Springer, Heidelberg (2016)
26. Goldwasser, S., et al.: Multi-input functional encryption. In: Nguyen, P.Q., Oswald, E. (eds.) EUROCRYPT 2014. LNCS, vol. 8441, pp. 578–602. Springer, Heidelberg (2014)
27. Jain, A., Lin, H., Sahai, A.: Indistinguishability obfuscation from well-founded assumptions. In: Proceedings of the 53rd Annual ACM SIGACT Symposium on Theory of Computing, pp. 60–73 (2021)
28. Jain, A., Lin, H., Sahai, A.: Indistinguishability obfuscation from LPN over f_p, dlin, and prgs in nc^0. In: Dunkelman, O., Dziembowski, S. (eds.) Advances in Cryptology EUROCRYPT 2022. Lecture Notes in Computer Science, vol. 13275, pp. 670–690. Springer, Cham (2022). https://doi.org/10.1007/978-3-031-06944-4_23
29. Libert, B., Titiu, R.: Multi-client functional encryption for linear functions in the standard model from LWE. In: Galbraith, S.D., Moriai, S. (eds.) ASIACRYPT 2019, Part III. LNCS, vol. 11923, pp. 520–551. Springer, Heidelberg (2019)
30. O'Neill, A.: Definitional issues in functional encryption. Cryptology ePrint Archive, Report 2010/556 (2010). https://eprint.iacr.org/2010/556
31. Sahai, A., Waters, B.: Fuzzy identity-based encryption. In: Cramer, R. (ed.) EUROCRYPT 2005. LNCS, vol. 3494, pp. 457–473. Springer, Heidelberg (2005). https://doi.org/10.1007/11426639_27

32. Tomida, J.: Tightly secure inner product functional encryption: multi-input and function-hiding constructions. In: Galbraith, S.D., Moriai, S. (eds.) ASIACRYPT 2019. LNCS, vol. 11923, pp. 459–488. Springer, Heidelberg (2019)
33. Tomida, J., Abe, M., Okamoto, T.: Efficient inner product functional encryption with full-hiding security. IEICE Trans. Fundam. Electron. Commun. Comput. Sci. **103**-A(1), 33–40 (2020)
34. Tomida, J., Takashima, K.: Unbounded inner product functional encryption from bilinear maps. In: Peyrin, T., Galbraith, S. (eds.) ASIACRYPT 2018. LNCS, vol. 11273, pp. 609–639. Springer, Heidelberg (2018)

Author Index

Printed in the United States
by Baker & Taylor Publisher Services